T0305266

Risk Management and Shareholders' Value in Banking

For other titles in the Wiley Finance Series
please see www.wiley.com/finance

Risk Management and Shareholders' Value in Banking

From Risk Measurement Models to Capital Allocation Policies

Andrea Resti and Andrea Sironi

John Wiley & Sons, Ltd

Copyright © 2007   John Wiley & Sons Ltd, The Atrium, Southern Gate, Chichester,
West Sussex PO19 8SQ, England

Telephone (+44) 1243 779777

Email (for orders and customer service enquiries): cs-books@wiley.co.uk
Visit our Home Page on www.wileyeurope.com or www.wiley.com

All Rights Reserved. No part of this publication may be reproduced, stored in a retrieval system or
transmitted in any form or by any means, electronic, mechanical, photocopying, recording, scanning or
otherwise, except under the terms of the Copyright, Designs and Patents Act 1988 or under the terms of a
licence issued by the Copyright Licensing Agency Ltd, 90 Tottenham Court Road, London W1T 4LP, UK,
without the permission in writing of the Publisher. Requests to the Publisher should be addressed to
the Permissions Department, John Wiley & Sons Ltd, The Atrium, Southern Gate, Chichester,
West Sussex PO19 8SQ, England, or emailed to permreq@wiley.co.uk, or faxed to (+44) 1243 770620.

Designations used by companies to distinguish their products are often claimed as trademarks. All brand
names and product names used in this book are trade names, service marks, trademarks or registered
trademarks of their respective owners. The Publisher is not associated with any product or vendor mentioned
in this book.

This publication is designed to provide accurate and authoritative information in regard to the subject matter
covered. It is sold on the understanding that the Publisher is not engaged in rendering professional services. If
professional advice or other expert assistance is required, the services of a competent professional should be
sought.

Other Wiley Editorial Offices

John Wiley & Sons Inc., 111 River Street, Hoboken, NJ 07030, USA

Jossey-Bass, 989 Market Street, San Francisco, CA 94103-1741, USA

Wiley-VCH Verlag GmbH, Boschstr. 12, D-69469 Weinheim, Germany

John Wiley & Sons Australia Ltd, 42 McDougall Street, Milton, Queensland 4064, Australia

John Wiley & Sons (Asia) Pte Ltd, 2 Clementi Loop #02-01, Jin Xing Distripark, Singapore 129809

John Wiley & Sons Canada Ltd, 6045 Freemont Blvd, Mississauga, Ontario, L5R 4J3, Canada

Wiley also publishes its books in a variety of electronic formats. Some content that appears
in print may not be available in electronic books.

Library of Congress Cataloging-in-Publication Data

Sironi, Andrea.
  Risk management and shareholders' value in banking : from risk measurement models to capital allocation
policies / Andrea Sironi and Andrea Resti.
        p. cm.
  Includes bibliographical references and index.
  ISBN 978-0-470-02978-7 (cloth : alk. paper)
1. Asset-liability management. 2. Bank management. 3. Banks and banking – Valuation.
4. Financial institutions – Valuation. 5. Risk management. I. Resti, Andrea. II. Title.
  HG1615.25.S57 2007
  332.1068'1 – dc22

                                                                                2006102019

British Library Cataloguing in Publication Data

A catalogue record for this book is available from the British Library

ISBN 978-0-0470-02978-7 (HB)

Typeset in 10/12pt Times by Laserwords Private Limited, Chennai, India
Printed and bound in Great Britain by Antony Rowe Ltd, Chippenham, Wiltshire
This book is printed on acid-free paper responsibly manufactured from sustainable forestry
in which at least two trees are planted for each one used for paper production.

To our parents

Contents

Foreword

Risk Management and Shareholders' Value in Banking is quite simply the best written and most comprehensive modern book that combines all of the major risk areas that impact bank performance. The authors, Andrea Resti and Andrea Sironi of Bocconi University in Milan are well known internationally for their commitment to and knowledge of risk management and its application to financial institutions. Personally, I have observed their maturation into world class researchers, teachers and consultants since I first met Sironi in 1992 (when he was a visiting scholar at the NYU Salomon Center) and Resti (when, a few years later, he was on the same program as I at the Italian Financial Institution Deposit Insurance Organization (FITD)). This book is both rigorous and easily understandable and will be attractive to scholars and practitioners alike.

It is interesting to note that the authors' knowledge of risk management paralleled the transformation of the Italian Banking System from a relatively parochial and unsophisticated system, based on relationship banking and cultural norms, to one that rivals the most sophisticated in the world today based on modern value at risk (VaR) principles. In a sense, the authors and their surroundings grew-up together.

Perhaps the major motivations to the modern treatment of risk management in banking were the regulatory efforts of the BIS in the mid-to-late 1990's – first with respect to market risk in 1995 and then dealing with credit risk, and to a lesser extent operational risk, in 1999 with the presentation of the initial version of Basel II. These three elements of risk management in banking form the core of the book's focus. But, perhaps the greatest contribution of the book is the discussion of the interactions of these elements and how they should impact capital allocation decisions of financial institutions. As such, the book attempts to fit its subject matter into a modern corporation finance framework – namely the maximization of shareholder wealth.

Not surprisingly, my favorite part of the book is the treatment of credit risk and my favorite chapter is the one on "Portfolio Models" within the discussion of "Credit Risk" (Chapter 14 in Part III of the book). As an introduction to these sophisticated, yet controversial models, the authors distinguish between expected and unexpected loss – both in their relationships to estimation procedures and to their relevance to equity valuation, i.e., the concept of economic capital in the case of unexpected loss. While there are many structures discussed to tackle the portfolio problem, it is ironic that despite its importance, the Basel Committee, in its Basel II guidelines, does not permit banks to adjust their regulatory capital based on this seemingly intuitively logical concept. Perhaps the major conceptual reason is that the metric for measuring correlations between credit risks of different assets in the portfolio is still approached by different theories and measures. Is it the co-movement of firm's equity values which presumably subsumes both macro and industry factors as well as individual factors, or is it the default risk correlation as measured by the bimodal or continuous credit migration result at the appropriate horizon. Or, is it simply the result of a simulation of all of these factors.

While the use of market equity values is simply impossible in many countries and for the vast majority of non-publicly traded companies worldwide, perhaps the major impediment is the difficulty in back-testing these models (as the authors point out) and the fact that banks simply do not make decisions on individual investments based on portfolio guidelines (except in the most general way and by exception, e.g., industry or geographical limits). In any event, the portfolio management of the banks' credit policies remains a fertile area for research.

It is understandable, yet still a bit frustrating, that the operations risk area only receives minor treatment in this book (two chapters). The paradox is that we simply do not know a great deal about this area, at least not in a modern, measurable and modelable way, yet operational problems, particularly human decisions or failures, are probably the leading causes of bank failure crises, and will continue to be.

In summary, I really enjoyed this book and I believe it is the most comprehensive and instructive risk management book available today.

Edward I. Altman
Max L. Heine Professor of Finance
NYU Stern School of Business

Motivation and Scope of this Book: A Quick Guided Tour

Banks operating in the main developed countries have been exposed, since the Seventies, to four significant drivers of change, mutually interconnected and mutually reinforcing.

The first one is a stronger integration among national financial markets (such as stock markets and markets for interest rates and FX rates) which made it easier, for economic shocks, to spread across national boundaries. Such an increased integration has made some financial institutions more prone to crises, sometimes even to default, as their management proved unable to improve their response times by implementing adequate systems for risk measurement and control.

A second trend of change is "disintermediation", which saw savers moving from bank deposits to more profitable investment opportunities, and non-financial companies turning directly to the capital markets to raise new debt and equity capital. This caused banks to shift their focus from the traditional business of deposits and loans to new forms of financial intermediation, where new risks had to be faced and understood. Such a shift, as well as a number of changes in the regulatory framework, has undoubtedly blurred the traditional boundaries between banks and other classes of financial institutions. As a result, different types of financial intermediaries may now be investing in similar assets, exposing themselves to similar risk sources.

A third, significant trend is the supervisors' growing interest in capital adequacy schemes, that is, in supervisory practices that aim at verifying that each bank's capital be enough to absorb risks, in order to ensure the stability of the whole financial system. Capital-adequacy schemes have by now almost totally replaced traditional supervisory approaches based on direct controls on markets and intermediaries (e.g., limiting the banks' geographic and functional scope of operation) and require banks to develop a thorough and comprehensive understanding of the risks they are facing.

Finally, the liberalisation of international capital flows has led to sharper competition among institutions based in different countries to attract business and investments, as well as to an increase in the average cost of equity capital, as the latter has become a key factor in bank management. This increasing shareholders' awareness has been accompanied and favoured, at least in continental Europe, by a wave of bank privatisations which, while being sometimes dictated by public budget constraints, have brought in a new class of shareholders, more aware about the returns on their investments, and thereby increased managerial efficiency. This has made the banking business more similar to other forms of entrepreneurship, where a key management goal is the creation of adequate shareholders' returns. Old, protected national markets, where bank management could pursue size targets and other "private" objectives, has given way to a more competitive, international market arena, where equity capital must be suitably rewarded, that is, where shareholders' value must be created.

The four above-mentioned drivers look closely interwoven, both in their causes and consequences. Higher financial integration, disintermediation and the convergence among different financial intermediation models, capital adequacy-based regulatory schemes and an increased mobility/awareness in bank equity investors: all these facts have strongly emphasised the relevance of risk and the ability of bank managers to create value for their shareholders..

Accordingly, the top management of banks – just like the management of any other company – needs to increase profitability in order to meet the expectations of their share-holders, which are now much more skilled and careful in measuring their investment's performance.

Bank management may therefore get caught in a sort of "targets' dilemma": increasing capital profitability requires to rise profits, which in turn calls for new businesses and new risks to be embraced. However such an expansion, due to both economic and regulatory reasons, needs to be supported by more capital, which in turn calls for higher profitability.

In the short term, such a dilemma may be solved by increasing per-dollar profits through slashing operating expenses and raising operational efficiency. In the long term, however, it requires that the risk-adjusted profitability of the bank's different businesses be carefully assessed and optimised.

Such a strategy hinges on three key tools.

The first one is an effective risk measurement and management system: the bank must be able to identify, measure, control and above all price all the risks taken aboard, more or less consciously, in and off its balance sheet. This is crucial not only to the bank's profitability, but also to its solvency and future survival, as bank crises always arise from an inappropriate identification, measurement, pricing or control of risks.

The second key tool is an effective capital allocation process, through which share-holders' capital is allotted to the different risk-taking units within the bank, according to the amount of risks that each of them is allowed to generate, and consequently must reward. Note that, according to this approach, bank capital plays a pivotal role not just in the supervisors' eyes (as a cushion protecting creditors and ensuring systemic stability), but also from the managers' perspective: indeed capital, being a scarce and expensive resource, needs to be optimally allocated across all the bank's business units to maximise its rate of return. Ideally, this should be achieved by developing, inside the bank, a sort of "internal capital market" where business units compete for capital (to increase their risk-taking capacity), by committing themselves to higher return targets.

The third key tool, directly linked to the other two, is organisation: a set of processes, measures, mechanisms that help the different units of the bank to share the same value-creation framework. This means that the rules for risk measurement, management and capital allocation must be clear, transparent, as well as totally shared and understood by the bank's managers, as well as by its board of directors. An efficient organisa-tion is indeed a necessary condition for the whole value creation strategy to deliver the expected results.

This book presents an integrated scheme for risk measurement, capital management and value creation that is consistent with the strategy outlined above, as well as with the four drivers surveyed at the outset of this preface. Moving from the definition of the measurement criteria for the main risk types to which a bank is exposed, we aim at defining the criteria for an effective capital allocation process and the management rules that should support a corporate policy aimed at maximizing shareholders' value creation.

This will be based on three logical steps: in the first step (Parts I–IV), individual risks are defined and measured. This makes it possible to assess the amount of capital absorbed by the risks generated by the different business units within a bank. Also, this enables the bank to price its products correctly (where it is free to set their price), or at least to estimate their risk-adjusted profitability (where the price is fixed by the market). Note that, while risk can be defined, in very general terms, as an unexpected change in the value of the bank or of its profits, different classes of risk exist which refer to different uncertainty sources ("risk factors"); therefore, different models and approaches will be needed, in order to get a comprehensive picture of the risks to which the bank is exposed.

In the second step (Part V), external regulatory constraints, in the form of minimum capital requirements, must be analyzed, in order to take into account their implications for the overall risk and capital management process.

The third step (Part VI) requires: (i) setting the total amount of capital that the bank needs to hold, based on the risks it is facing; (ii) fine-tuning its composition taking profit of hybrid instruments such as subordinated debt; (iii) estimating the "fair" return that shareholders are likely to expect on equity capital; (iv) finally, comparing actual profits to the "fair" cost of capital in order to assess the value creation capacity of the bank.

More specifically, the six parts of this book will cover the following topics (see also Figure 1).

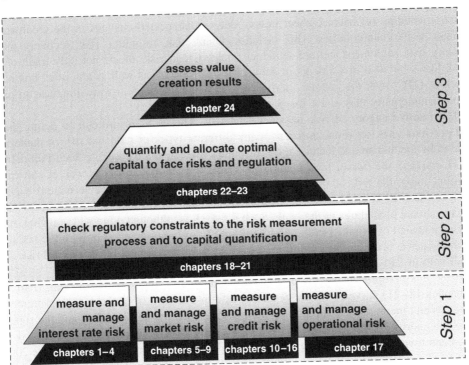

Figure 1   Plan of the book

Parts I–IV will deal with the main classes of risks that affect a bank's profitability and solvency. The first one is interest rate risk (Part I, Chapters 1–4), arising from the different maturity structure of the banks' traditional assets and liabilities (the so-called "banking book"). The models and approaches developed by academics and practitioners to tackle this type of risk have evolved significantly and can now be used to gain an accurate and comprehensive assessment of the effects that unexpected changes in the level of market interest rates produce on the net value of the bank, as well as on its profits.

The second category of risks (Part II, Chapters 5–9) revolves around market risk, that is, the risk of a decrease in the value of the bank's net investments, due to unexpected changes in market prices (such as FX rates, stock and commodities prices). Unlike the models for interest rate risk discussed in Part I, which are applied across the whole spectrum of the bank's assets and liabilities, the measurement and management of market risk usually focuses on a limited portion of the bank's balance sheet, that is, the set of investments (including short positions and derivatives) aimed at producing trading profits in the short-term, and therefore called "trading book". Note that the factors creating market risk also include the price of traded bills and bonds, which in turn depends on the level of interest rates; therefore, interest rate risk, when producing changes in the value of the bank's trading book, can also be considered part of market risk. Similarly, if a secondary market for corporate bonds exists, where credit spreads are priced, reflecting the issuer's creditworthiness, then the risk of an increase in market spreads, although it pertains to credit risk and therefore, which is addressed specifically in Part III, can also be seen as a specific type of market risk.

The third risk class faced by a bank (Part III, Chapters 10–16), and probably the most significant one, is credit risk, that is, the risk of changes in the fair value of the bank's assets (including off-balance sheet items), due to unexpected changes in the creditworthiness of its counterparties. This includes default risk, migration risk, recovery risk, country risk, settlement and pre-settlement risks. Credit risk affects not only traditional bank loans, but also investments in debt securities (bonds), as well as any other contract (such as OTC–over the counter–derivatives) in which the inability/unwillingness to pay of the counterparty may cause losses to the bank.

The fourth category of risk is operational risk. This is more difficult to define than the previous ones, as it encompasses many different types of risk: the risk of damages caused by the human and technological resources used by the bank (e.g., due to infidelity or IT crashes); the risk of losses caused by errors (e.g. human errors as well as software malfunctions); the risk of fraud and electronic theft; the risk of adverse natural events or robberies; all risks due to the inadequacy of the procedures, control systems and organizational procedures of the bank. Such a risk class, although quite wide-ranging, has been somewhat overlooked in the past and started receiving attention only in the last ten years. Issues concerning the definition, measurement, management of operational risk are dealt with in Part IV (Chapter 17).

After this comprehensive discussion of the main risk types facing a bank, Part V (Chapters 18–21) surveys the exogenous constraints arising from the risk-measurement schemes and the minimum capital requirements imposed by the regulation and the supervisory authorities. Special emphasis is given to the Basel Capital Accord approved in 1988 and revised subsequently in 1996 and 2004. The logic and implications of the 2004 update of the Accord will be discussed carefully in Chapters 20 and 21, showing how the new rules, while imposing a regulatory constraint on banks, also provide them with a robust conceptual scheme through which their risks (especially credit and operational risk) can be understood, measured and managed.

Part VI of the book relates to capital management and value creation. Chapter 22 will show how the optimal amount of capital for a bank can be quantified, taking into account both economic capital (that is, the capital required to cover risks discussed in Parts I–IV) and regulatory capital (that is, the minimal capital imposed by the Basel rules). Chapter 23 will discuss techniques for allocating capital to the different business units inside the bank (such as the credit department, the asset management unit, the treasury and so on), taking into account the benefits of diversification, and how risk-adjusted performance measures can be computed, to assess the true level of profitability of the different units. Finally, Chapter 24, after showing how to estimate the "fair" level of profits that the bank's shareholders can reasonably expect, will focus on tools (such as Raroc and Eva) that enable the top management to estimate the value margins created (or destroyed) by the bank, both in the short run and in a medium-term perspective.

Although some of the models and algorithms described in Parts I–IV (as well as the regulatory schemes presented in Part V) may sometimes look rather technical in nature, the reader should keep in mind that a proper understanding of these techniques is required, in order to fully assess the correctness and reliability of the value-creation metrics discussed in the last Part of the book. In a word, risk management and regulation are too serious to be left totally to. . .risk managers and regulators. A full and critical awareness of these instruments, as well as a constant and sharp commitment to their enterprise-wide implementation, is required directly from the bank's top management, in order for the value-creation paradigm to be deployed safely and consistently.

In order to help the reader understand the more technical concepts presented in the book, many numerical examples and exercises are included in each chapter. Most of them (indicated by a symbol like the one on the right) are replicated and solved in the excel files found on the book's website (www.wiley.com/go/rmsv/). Answers to end-of-chapter questions, errata and other materials may also be found on this companion site.

Finally, we would like to thank our wives for their patience and kind support during the months spent on this book. We will also be grateful to all readers that will provide us with comments and advice on this first edition.

Part I
Interest Rate Risk

INTRODUCTION TO PART I

One of the primary functions of the financial system is to transform maturities: in most cases, banks finance their investments in loans or bonds by issuing liabilities whose average maturity is shorter than that of those same investments. The resulting imbalance between maturities of assets and liabilities implies interest rate risk-taking.

To see why, let's take a 10-year fixed rate mortgage of 100,000 euros at 6%. To finance this investment the bank issues a 1-year certificate of deposit of the same amount with a 2% fixed rate. The net interest income (NII) of this operation is 4% of the total amount: 4,000 euros.

Assume that during the year market interest rates (both on assets and liabilities) rise by one percentage point. When the certificate of deposit matures, the bank will be obliged to refinance the mortgage by issuing a new CD at a higher rate (3%), though it's still getting a 6% return on its investment. So, the NII would shrink from 4,000 to 3,000 euros (that is, from 4% to 3% of the investment).

When the maturity on an asset is longer than that of a liability, the bank is exposed to *refinancing risk* (namely, the risk that the cost associated with financing an interest-earning position rises, resulting in a lower interest margin).

The opposite is true if the maturity of an asset is shorter than that of a liability. For example, think of a 1-year loan to an industrial firm at a fixed rate of 5%, financed by issuing 10-year bonds at a 4% fixed rate. If market interest rates fell, the bank would have to reinvest the funds from the bonds in assets with a lower yield once the loan had matured. As a result, we would see a reduction in the interest margin. When there are assets with a shorter maturity than liabilities, the bank is exposed to *reinvestment risk*.

Therefore, interest rate risk in its broadest sense can be defined as the risk that changes in market interest rates impact the profitability and economic value of a bank. Note that this risk does not derive solely from the circumstances described above (i.e. possible changes in flows of interest income and expenses, and in the market value of assets and liabilities brought about by an imbalance between their maturities). An indirect effect can also occur, which is linked to the impact that rate changes can have on volumes negotiated by a bank.

So, for example, a rise in interest rates not only triggers an upsurge in interest earned and paid by the bank, along with a slump in the market value of fixed-rate assets and liabilities.[1] Usually such a change also causes a decline in demand liabilities and call loans. In effect, when market rates go up, account holders usually find it more convenient to transfer their funds to more profitable types of investment. At the same time, the bank's debtors (be they firms or individuals) tend to cut down on the use of credit lines due to the higher cost of these services. This last phenomenon does not depend on the imbalance between the average maturities of assets and liabilities, but rather on the elasticity of demand for deposits and loans to rate changes. This problem does not affect only on-demand items, but also term loans with options for early repayment, or conversion from fixed to floating (which allow customers to act at their own discretion, making interest rate risk estimation even more complex).

To estimate this risk in the most comprehensive possible way, we need to take into account all the factors described above. In the upcoming three chapters, we'll discuss

---

[1] The relationship between market rates and market value of fixed-rate assets and liabilities is detailed in Chapter 3.

risk-measurement methods developed by banks. Though they have been considerably fine-tuned in the past 20 years, these methods often focus on just a few of these factors, namely on those deriving from the maturity structure of assets and liabilities.

Sometimes interest rate risk is only measured on the *trading book*, i.e. the overall set of securities and financial contracts that the bank buys for trading on the secondary market with the aim of making capital gains.[2]

Nonetheless, interest rate risk pertains to *all positions* in the bank's assets and liabilities portfolio (namely, the *banking book*). To measure this risk we have to consider all interest-earning and interest-bearing financial instruments and contracts on both sides of the balance sheet, as well as any derivatives whose value depends on market interest rates.

Guidelines on how to go about estimating interest rate risk on the banking book were drawn up by the Basel Committee (an advisory body whose members are representatives of banking supervisory authorities from major industrialized countries) in January 1997. These 12 fundamental principles[3] are intended as a tool for facilitating the work of authorities for banking supervision from individual nations who are responsible for evaluating the adequacy and effectiveness of interest rate risk management systems developed by banks under their supervision. The 12 principles address the role of boards of directors and senior management; policies and procedures for managing interest rate risk; systems for measuring and monitoring risk, and for internal controls; and information to be provided to supervisory bodies on a periodic basis. These standards, therefore, are not simply methodological instructions, but go further to provide recommendations on organizational issues. This approach reflects the authorities' desire to leave risk measurement to a bank's managers and focus simply on providing suggestions (based on a "moral-suasion" approach), so that risk measurement is complemented by an effective and well-organized system of risk management.

These principles, which have served as an important standard for banks the world over, were reviewed and increased to 15 in July 2004.[4] The addition of three new principles was closely linked to the finalization of a new accord on capital adequacy requirements for banks, which is known as Basel II.[5] This agreement (approved by the Basel Committee in June 2004) does not call for a specific capital requirement for interest rate risk arising from the banking book. Rather, it focuses on transparency, and gives supervisory bodies in member countries the right to request extra capital from banks exposed to high interest rate risks. Consequently, Principle 14, introduced in 2004, requires that banks report results from their internal measurement systems to national supervisory bodies.[6]

The 15 principles laid down in 2004 are listed in the box on page 11. Briefly, the most crucial and ground-breaking points are the following:

First of all, a significant emphasis is given to the involvement of senior management (Principle 2). Although this might appear obvious, it still represents a critical issue for many banks, where risk measurement systems were introduced independently by the

---

[2] In this case, interest rate risk represents a specific kind of market risk, i.e. the risk that a financial portfolio is hit by unexpected losses due to trends in one or more market variables (such as share prices, exchange rates, or interest rates). Part II addresses market risk.

[3] See Basel Committee on Banking Supervision (1997).

[4] Basel Committee on Banking Supervision (2004b)

[5] See Chapter 20 for further information.

[6] More specifically, banks have to estimate their potential decrease in their value, if a "standard shock" were to occur to interest rates. This standard shock might be, for example, a parallel shift in the rate curve of 200 basis points (or else, a change that is consistent with shocks witnessed in the five previous years).

budget and control department, the finance department or the research department, without any direct involvement by senior management. According to the Basel Committee, instead, top managers should participate in the definition of objectives, criteria, and procedures of the risk management system.

A second crucial point (Principle 3) is that risk management is to be assigned to an independent unit (separated, e.g., from the Finance or Treasury department). Such a risk management unit must support senior management from a technical point of view and its duties and responsibilities must include the definition of criteria for measuring risk, the validation of risk measures provided by individual business units in the bank, and the updating of parameter estimates needed to feed the system. The risk management unit has to be independent, in order to be perceived as authoritative and credible.

Third, Principle 4 highlights the importance of measuring and managing interest rate risk at a consolidated level. By doing so, the Basel Committee acknowledges that interest rate risk can be adequately appraised and managed only by taking into account the bank as a whole, instead of focusing on individual areas.

Lastly, the risk measurement system should be integrated into the day-to-day management of the bank. Accordingly, any criteria developed for measuring interest rate risk have to be used in practice, as a means to steer corporate policy, and must not simply be seen as a purely theoretical tool used only by risk managers.

Interest rate risk on the banking book: Principles of the Basel Committee

Board and senior management oversight of interest rate risk

1: In order to carry out its responsibilities, the board of directors in a bank should approve strategies and policies with respect to interest rate risk management and ensure that senior management takes the steps necessary to monitor and control these risks consistent with the approved strategies and policies. The board of directors should be informed regularly of the interest rate risk exposure of the bank in order to assess the monitoring and controlling of such risk against the board's guidance on the levels of risk that are acceptable to the bank.

2: Senior management must ensure that the structure of the bank's business and the level of interest rate risk it assumes are effectively managed, that appropriate policies and procedures are established to control and limit these risks, and that resources are available for evaluating and controlling interest rate risk.

3: Banks should clearly define the individuals and/or committees responsible for managing interest rate risk and should ensure that there is adequate separation of duties in key elements of the risk management process to avoid potential conflicts of interest. Banks should have risk measurement, monitoring, and control functions with clearly defined duties that are sufficiently independent from position-taking functions of the bank and which report risk exposures directly to senior management and the board of directors. Larger or more complex banks should have a designated independent unit responsible for the design and administration of the bank's interest rate risk measurement, monitoring, and control functions.

Adequate risk management policies and procedures

4: It is essential that banks' interest rate risk policies and procedures are clearly defined and consistent with the nature and complexity of their activities. These policies should be applied on a consolidated basis and, as appropriate, at the level of individual affiliates, especially when recognising legal distinctions and possible obstacles to cash movements among affiliates.

5: It is important that banks identify the risks inherent in new products and activities and ensure these are subject to adequate procedures and controls before being introduced or undertaken. Major hedging or risk management initiatives should be approved in advance by the board or its appropriate delegated committee.

Risk measurement, monitoring, and control functions

6: It is essential that banks have interest rate risk measurement systems that capture all material sources of interest rate risk and that assess the effect of interest rate changes in ways that are consistent with the scope of their activities. The assumptions underlying the system should be clearly understood by risk managers and bank management.

7: Banks must establish and enforce operating limits and other practices that maintain exposures within levels consistent with their internal policies.

8: Banks should measure their vulnerability to loss under stressful market conditions - including the breakdown of key assumptions – and consider those results when establishing and reviewing their policies and limits for interest rate risk.

9: Banks must have adequate information systems for measuring, monitoring, controlling, and reporting interest rate exposures. Reports must be provided on a timely basis to the bank's board of directors, senior management and, where appropriate, individual business line managers.

Internal controls

10: Banks must have an adequate system of internal controls over their interest rate risk management process. A fundamental component of the internal control system involves regular independent reviews and evaluations of the effectiveness of the system and, where necessary, ensuring that appropriate revisions or enhancements to internal controls are made. The results of such reviews should be available to the relevant supervisory authorities.

Information for supervisory authorities

11: Supervisory authorities should obtain from banks sufficient and timely information with which to evaluate their level of interest rate risk. This information should take appropriate account of the range of maturities and currencies in each bank's portfolio, including off-balance sheet items, as well as other relevant factors, such as the distinction between trading and non-trading activities.

Capital adequacy

12: Banks must hold capital commensurate with the level of interest rate risk they undertake.

Disclosure of interest rate risk

13: Banks should release to the public information on the level of interest rate risk and their policies for its management.

Supervisory treatment of interest rate risk in the banking book

14: Supervisory authorities must assess whether the internal measurement systems of banks adequately capture the interest rate risk in their banking book. If a bank's internal measurement system does not adequately capture the interest rate risk, the bank must bring the system to the required standard. To facilitate supervisors' monitoring of interest rate risk exposures across institutions, banks must provide the results of their internal measurement systems, expressed in terms of the threat to economic value, using a standardised interest rate shock.

15: If supervisors determine that a bank is not holding capital commensurate with the level of interest rate risk in the banking book, they should consider remedial action, requiring the bank either to reduce its risk or hold a specific additional amount of capital, or a combination of both.

These guidelines set by the Basel Committee have prompted a significant evolution in systems used by banks for managing interest rate risk, which have gradually become more accurate and comprehensive.

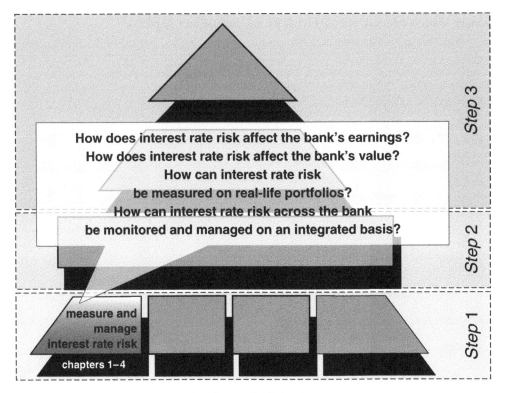

Figure I.1   Key questions answered by Part I of this Book

The aim of Part I (see Figure I.1) is to illustrate this evolution by means of several examples. Specifically, the next chapter reviews the characteristics, strengths and weaknesses of one of the most popular approaches: the *repricing gap* model. We'll see how this model centres on the effect of changes in market rates on a bank's net interest income (that is, on its profit and loss account). Also, the limitations of this model will be discussed, that prevent it from providing a really complete picture of a bank's exposure to unexpected changes in interest rates.

In an attempt to overcome these limitations, *duration gap* models were developed, which are discussed in Chapter 2. This type of techniques shifts the focus from a bank's current earnings to its net worth, thus including medium-to-long term effects that repricing gap would basically overlook. However, they are usually based on the assumption that interest rates are subject to uniform changes across maturities, that is, to parallel shifts in the yield curve.

To overcome such an unrealistic hypothesis, interest risk measurement evolved towards cash-flow mapping techniques, which aim to measure and manage the effects of different changes in rates, associated with different maturities. These models, among which cash-flow *clumping* is one of the most widely known, are examined in Chapter 3.

The techniques presented in Chapters 1–3 can only be applied if the bank manages the maturity structure of its assets and liabilities on an integrated basis. This means that different financial contracts (e.g., loans, bonds and deposits) originated by each branch must be combined into a bank-wide, up-to-date picture. This can be done through a system of internal transfer rates (ITRs), which enable banks to aggregate interest rate risks originated by various business units and make it possible for bank managers to manage interest rate risk effectively: ITRs are covered in Chapter 4.

1

The Repricing Gap Model

1.1 INTRODUCTION

Among the models for measuring and managing interest rate risk, the *repricing gap* is certainly the best known and most widely used. It is based on a relatively simple and intuitive consideration: a bank's exposure to interest rate risk derives from the fact that interest-earning assets and interest-bearing liabilities show differing sensitivities to changes in market rates.

The repricing gap model can be considered an income-based model, in the sense that the target variable used to calculate the effect of possible changes in market rates is, in fact, an income variable: the net interest income (NII – the difference between interest income and interest expenses). For this reason this model falls into the category of "earnings approaches" to measuring interest rate risk. Income-based models contrast with equity-based methods, the most common of which is the *duration gap* model (discussed in the following chapter). These latter models adopt the market value of the bank's equity as the target variable of possible immunization policies against interest rate risk.

After analyzing the concept of *gap*, this chapter introduces *maturity-adjusted gaps*, and explores the distinction between marginal and cumulative gaps, highlighting the difference in meaning and various applications of the two risk measurements. The discussion then turns to the main limitations of the repricing gap model along with some possible solutions. Particular attention is given to the standardized gap concept and its applications.

1.2 THE GAP CONCEPT

The gap is a concise measure of interest risk that links changes in market interest rates to changes in NII. *Interest rate risk* is identified by possible unexpected changes in this variable. The gap (G) over a given time period t (*gapping period*) is defined as the difference between the amount of rate-sensitive assets (SA) and rate-sensitive liabilities (SL):

$$G_t = SA_t - SL_t = \sum_j sa_{t,j} - \sum_j sl_{t,j} \tag{1.1}$$

The term "sensitive" in this case indicates assets and liabilities that mature (or are subject to repricing) during period t. So, for example, to calculate the 6-month gap, one must take into account all fixed-rate assets and liabilities that mature in the next 6 months, as well as the variable-rate assets and liabilities to be repriced in the next 6 months. The gap, then, is a quantity expressed in monetary terms. Figure 1.1 provides a graphic representation of this concept.

By examining its link to the *NII*, we can fully grasp the usefulness of the gap concept. To do so, consider that *NII* is the difference between interest income (*II*) and interest expenses (*IE*). These, in turn, can be computed as the product of total financial assets (*FA*) and the average interest rate on assets (r_A) and total financial liabilities (*FL*) and average interest rate on liabilities (r_L) respectively. Using *NSA* and *NSL* as financial assets and

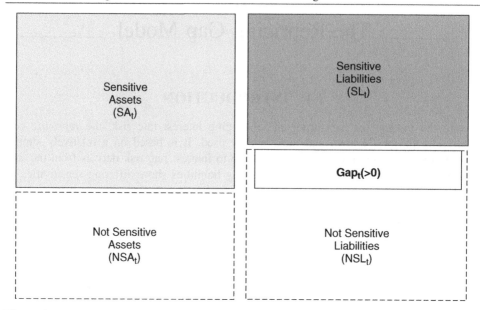

Figure 1 The repricing gap concept

liabilities which are not sensitive to interest rate fluctuations, and omitting t (which is considered given) for brevity's sake, we can represent the *NII* as follows:

$$NII = II - IE = r_A \cdot FA - r_L \cdot FL = r_A \cdot (SA + NSA) - r_L \cdot (SL + NSL) \qquad (1.2)$$

from which:

$$\Delta NII = \Delta r_A \cdot SA - \Delta r_L \cdot SL \qquad (1.3)$$

Equation (1.3) is based on the simple consideration that changes in market interest rates affect only rate-sensitive assets and liabilities. If, lastly, we assume that the change in rates is the same both for interest income and for interest expenses

$$\Delta r_A = \Delta r_L = \Delta r \qquad (1.4)$$

the result is:

$$\Delta NII = \Delta r \cdot (SA - SL) = \Delta r \cdot \left(\sum_j sa_j - \sum_j sl_j \right) = \Delta r \cdot G \qquad (1.5)$$

Equation (1.5) shows that the change in NII is a function of the gap and interest rate change. In other words, the gap represents the variable that links changes in NII to changes in market interest rates. More specifically, (1.5) shows that a rise in interest rates triggers an increase in the *NII* if the gap is positive. This is due to the fact that the quantity of rate-sensitive assets which will be renegotiated, resulting in an increase in interest income, exceeds rate-sensitive liabilities. Consequently, interest income grows faster than interest expenses, resulting in an increase of *NII*. Vice versa, if the gap is negative, a rise in interest rates leads to a lower *NII*.

Table 1.1 reports the possible combinations of the effects of interest rate changes on a bank's *NII*, depending on whether the gap is positive or negative and the direction of the interest rate change.

Table 1.1 Gaps, rate changes, and effects on *NII*

Gap \ Δr	G > 0 positive net reinvestment	G < 0 positive net refinancing
> 0 higher rates	$\Delta NII > 0$	$\Delta NII < 0$
< 0 lower rates	$\Delta NII < 0$	$\Delta NII > 0$

The table also helps us understand the guidelines that may be inferred from gap analysis. When market rates are expected to increase, it is in the bank's best interest to reduce the value of a possible negative gap or increase the size of a possible positive gap and vice versa. Assuming that one-year rate-sensitive assets and liabilities are 50 and 70 million euros respectively, and that the bank expects a rise in interest rates over the coming year of 50 basis points (0.5 %),[1] the expected change in the *NII* would then be:

$$E(\Delta NII) = G \cdot E(\Delta r) = (-20,000,000) \cdot (+0.5\%) = -100,000 \qquad (1.6)$$

In a similar situation, the bank would be well-advised to cut back on its rate-sensitive assets, or as an alternative, add to its rate-sensitive liabilities. On the other hand, where there are no expectations about the future evolution of market rates, an immunization policy for safeguarding NII should be based on zero gap.

Some very common indicators in interest rate risk management can be derived from the gap concept. The first is obtained by comparing the gap to the bank's net worth. This allows one to ascertain the impact that a change in market interest rates would have on

---

[1] Expectations on the evolution of interest rates must be mapped out by bank management, which has various tools at its disposal in order to do so. The simplest one is the forward yield curve presented in Appendix 1B.

the NII/net worth ratio. This frequently-used ratio is an indicator of return on asset and liability management (ALM) – that is, traditional credit intermediation:

$$\Delta \left(\frac{NII}{NW} \right) = \frac{G}{NW} \cdot \Delta r \qquad (1.7)$$

Applying (1.7) to a bank with a positive gap of 800 million euros and net worth of 400 million euros, for example, would give the following:

$$\Delta \left(\frac{NII}{NW} \right) = \frac{800}{400} \cdot \Delta r = 2 \cdot \Delta r$$

If market interest rates drop by 50 basis points (0.5 %), the bank would suffer a reduction in its earnings from ALM of 1 %.

In the same way, drawing a comparison between the gap and the total interest-earning assets (IEA), we come up with a measure of rate sensitivity of another profit ratio commonly used in bank management: the ratio of NII to interest-earning assets. In analytical terms:

$$\Delta \left(\frac{NII}{IEA} \right) = \frac{G}{IEA} \cdot \Delta r \qquad (1.8)$$

A third indicator often used to make comparisons over time (evolution of a bank's exposure to interest rate risk) and in space (with respect to other banks) is the ratio of rate-sensitive assets to rate-sensitive liabilities, which is also called the *gap ratio*. Analytically:

$$Gap\,Ratio = \frac{SA}{SL} \qquad (1.9)$$

Unlike the absolute gap, which is expressed in currency units, the gap ratio has the advantage of being unaffected by the size of the bank. This makes it particularly suitable as an indicator to compare different sized banks.

1.3   THE MATURITY-ADJUSTED GAP

The discussion above is based on the simple assumption that any changes in market rates translate into changes in interest on rate-sensitive assets and liabilities *instantaneously*, that is, affecting the entire gapping period. In fact, only in this way does the change in the annual NII correspond exactly to the product of the gap and the change in market rates.

In the case of the bank summarized in Table 1.2, for example, the "basic" gap computed as in (1.1), relative to a t of one year, appears to be zero (the sum of rate-sensitive assets, 500 million euros, looks identical to the total of rate-sensitive liabilities). However, over the following 12 months rate-sensitive assets will mature or be repriced at intervals which are not identical to rate-sensitive liabilities. This can give rise to interest rate risk that a rudimentary version of the repricing gap may not be able to identify.

One way of considering the problem (another way is described in the next section) hinges on the *maturity-adjusted gap*. This concept is based on the observation that when there is a change in the interest rate associated with rate-sensitive assets and liabilities,

Table 1.2 A simplified balance sheet

Assets	€ m	Liabilities	€ m
1-month interest-earning interbank deposits	200	1-month interest-bearing interbank deposits	60
3m gov't securities	30	Variable-rate CDs (next repricing in 3 months)	200
5yr variable-rate securities (next repricing in 6 months)	120	Variable-rate bonds (next repricing in 6 months)	80
5m consumer credit	80	1yr fixed-rate CDs	160
20yr variable-rate mortgages (next repricing in 1 year)	70	5yr fixed-rate bonds	180
5yr treasury bonds	170	10yr fixed-rate bonds	120
10yr fixed-rate mortgages	200	20yr subordinated securities	80
30yr treasury bonds	130	Equity	120
Total	1000	Totals	1000

this change is only felt from the date of maturity/repricing of each instrument to the end of the gapping period (usually a year). For example, in the case of the first item in Table 1.2, (interbank deposits with one-month maturity), the new rate would become effective only after 30 days (that is, at the point in time indicated by p in Figure 1.2) and would continue to impact the bank's profit and loss account for only 11 months of the following year.

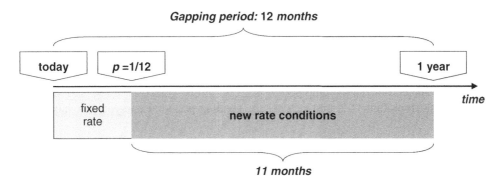

Figure 1.2   An example of repricing without immediate effect

More generally, in the case of any rate-sensitive asset j that yields an interest rate r_j, the interest income accrued in the following year would be:

$$ii_j = sa_j \cdot r_j \cdot p_j + sa_j \cdot (r_j + \Delta r_j) \cdot (1 - p_j) \qquad (1.10)$$

where p_j indicates the period, expressed as a fraction of the year, from today until the maturity or repricing date of the jth asset. The interest income associated with a generic rate-sensitive asset is therefore divided into two components: (i) a known component, represented by the first addendum of (1.10), and (ii) an unknown component, linked to future conditions of interest rates, represented by the second addendum of (1.10). Thus, the change in interest income is determined exclusively by the second component:

$$\Delta ii_j = sa_j \cdot (1 - p_j) \cdot \Delta r_j \tag{1.11}$$

If we wish to express the overall change of interest income associated with all the n rate-sensitive assets of the bank, we get:

$$\Delta II = \sum_{j=1}^{n} sa_j \cdot \Delta r_j \cdot (1 - p_j) \tag{1.12}$$

Similarly, the change in interest expenses generated by the kth rate-sensitive liability can be expressed as follows:

$$\Delta ie_k = sl_k \cdot \Delta r_k \cdot (1 - p_k) \tag{1.13}$$

Furthermore, the overall change of interest expenses associated with all the m rate-sensitive liabilities of the bank comes out as:

$$\Delta IE = \sum_{k=1}^{m} sl_k \cdot \Delta r_k \cdot (1 - r_k) \tag{1.14}$$

Assuming a uniform change in the interest rates of assets and liabilities ($\Delta r_j = \Delta r_k = \Delta r$ $\forall j, \forall k$), the estimated change in the bank's NII simplifies to:

$$\Delta NII = \Delta II - \Delta IE = \left(\sum_j sa_j \cdot (1 - p_j) - \sum_j sl_j \cdot (1 - p_j) \right) \cdot \Delta r \equiv G^{MA} \cdot \Delta i \tag{1.15}$$

where G^{MA} stands for the maturity-adjusted gap, i.e. the difference between rate-sensitive assets and liabilities, each weighted for the time period from the date of maturity or repricing to the end of the gapping period, here set at one year.[2]

Using data from Table 1.2, and keeping the gapping period at one-year, we have:

$$\Delta II = \sum_j ir_j = \sum_j sa_j \cdot (1 - p_j) \cdot \Delta r = 312.5 \cdot \Delta r$$

$$\Delta IE = \sum_k ip_k = \sum_k sl_k \cdot (1 - p_k) \cdot \Delta r = 245 \cdot \Delta r$$

and finally

$$\Delta NII = G^{MA} \cdot \Delta r = (312.5 - 245) \cdot \Delta r = 67.5 \cdot \Delta r$$

---

[2] As Saita (2007) points out, by using (1.15), on the basis of the maximum possible interest rate variation (Δi_{wc}, 'worst case') it is also possible to calculate a measure of "NII at risk", i.e. the maximum possible decrease of the NII: $IMaR = G^{MA} \cdot \Delta i_{wc}$. This is somewhat similar to "Earnings at Risk" (see Chapter 23), although the latter refers to overall profits, not just to net interest income

Therefore, where the "basic" gap is seemingly zero, the maturity-adjusted gap is nearly 70 million euros. A drop in the market rates of 1% would therefore cause the bank to earn 675,000 euros less. The reason for this is that in the following 12 months more assets are repriced earlier than liabilities.

1.4   MARGINAL AND CUMULATIVE GAPS

To take into account the actual maturity profile of assets and liabilities within the gapping period, an alternative to the maturity-adjusted gap is the one based on marginal and cumulative gaps.

It is important to note that there is no such thing as an "absolute" gap. Instead, different gaps exist for different gapping periods. In this sense, then, we can refer to a 1-month gap, a 3-month gap, a 6-month gap, a 1-year gap and so on.[3]

An accurate interpretation of a bank's exposure to market rate changes therefore requires us to analyze several gaps relative to various maturities. In doing so, a distinction must be drawn between:

- *cumulative gaps* (G_{t1}, G_{t2}, G_{t3}), defined as the difference between assets and liabilities that call for renegotiation of interest rates *by* a set future date ($t1, t2 > t1, t3 > t2$, etc.)
- *period or marginal gaps* ($G'_{t1}, G'_{t2}, G'_{t3}$), defined as the difference between assets and liabilities that renegotiate rates *in* a specific period of time in the future (e.g. from 0 to $t1$, from $t1$ to $t2$, etc.)

Note that the cumulative gap relating to a given time period t is nothing more than the sum of all marginal gaps at t and previous time periods. Consequently, marginal gaps can also be calculated as the difference between adjacent cumulative gaps. For example:

$$G_{t2} = G'_{t1} + G'_{t2}$$

$$G'_{t2} == G_{t2} - G_{t1}$$

Table 1.3 provides figures for marginal and cumulative gaps computed from data in Table 1.2. Note that, setting the gapping period to the final maturity date of all assets and liabilities in the balance sheet (30 years), the cumulative gap ends up coinciding with the value of the bank's equity (that is, the difference between total assets and liabilities).

As we have seen in the previous section, the one-year cumulative gap suggests that the bank is fully covered from interest risk, that is, the *NII* is not sensitive to changes in market rates. We know, however, that this is misleading. In fact, the marginal gaps reported in Table 1.3 indicate that the bank holds a long position (assets exceed liabilities) in the first month and in the period from 3 to 6 months, which is set off by a short position from 1 to 3 months and from 6 to 12 months.

---

[3] For a bank whose non-financial assets (e.g. buildings and real estate assets) are covered precisely by its equity (so there is a perfect balance between interest-earning assets and interest-bearing liabilities), the gap calculated as the difference between all rate-sensitive assets and liabilities on an infinite time period ($t = \infty$) would realistically be zero. Extending this horizon indefinitely, in fact, all financial assets and liabilities prove sensitive to interest rate changes. Therefore, if financial assets and liabilities coincide, the gap calculated as the difference between the two is zero.

Table 1.3 marginal and cumulative gaps

Period	RATE-SENSITIVE ASSETS	RATE-SENSITIVE LIABILITIES	MARGINAL GAP G'_t	CUMULATIVE GAP G_t
0–1 months	200	60	140	140
1–3 months	30	200	−170	−30
3–6 months	200	80	120	90
6–12 months	70	160	−90	0
1–5 years	170	180	−10	−10
5–10 years	200	120	80	70
10–30 years	130	80	50	120
Total	1000	880	–	–

We see now how marginal gaps can be used to estimate the real exposure of the bank to future interest rate changes. To do so, for each time period indicated in Table 1.3 we calculate an average maturity (t_j*), which is simply the date halfway between the start date $(t_j - 1)$ and the end date (t_j) of the period:

$$t_j^* \equiv \frac{t_j + t_{j-1}}{2}$$

For example, for the second marginal gap (running from 1 to 3 months) the value of $t*_2$ equals 2 months, or 2/12.

Using $t*_j$ to estimate the repricing date for all rate-sensitive assets and liabilities that fall in the marginal gap G'_{tj}, it is now possible to write a simplified version of (1.15) which does not require the knowledge of the actual repricing date of each rate-sensitive asset or liability, but only information on the value of various marginal gaps:

$$\Delta NII \cong \Delta r \cdot \sum_{j|t_j \leqslant 1} G'_{t_j}(1 - t_j^*) = \Delta r \cdot G_1^W \tag{1.16}$$

G_1^W represents the *one-year weighted cumulative gap*. This is an indicator (also called *NII duration*) of the sensitivity of the *NII* to changes in market rates, computed as the sum of marginal gaps, each one weighted by the average time left until the end of the gapping period (one year).

For the portfolio in Table 1.2, G_1^W is 45 million euros (see Table 1.4 for details on the calculation). As we can see, this number is different (and less precise) from the maturity-adjusted gap obtained in the preceding section (67.5). However, its calculation did not require to specify the repricing dates of the bank's single assets and liabilities (which can actually be much more numerous than those in the simplified example in Table 1.2). What is more, the "signal" this indicator transmits is similar to the one given by the maturity-adjusted gap. When rates fall by one percentage point, the bank risks a reduction in NII of approximately 450,000 euros.

Table 1.4 Example of a weighted cumulative gap calculation

Period	G'_t	t_j	$t*_j$	$1 - t*_j$	$G'_t \times (1 - t*_j)$
up to 1 month	140	1/12	1/24	23/24	134.2
up to 3 months	−170	3/12	2/12	10/12	−141.7
up to 6 months	120	6/12	9/24	15/24	75.0
up to 12 months	−90	1	9/12	3/12	−22.5
Total	0				45.0

Besides speeding up calculations by substituting the maturity-adjusted gap with the weighted cumulative gap, marginal gaps are well-suited to an additional application: they allow banks to forecast the impact on NII of several *infra-annual changes in interest rates*.

To understand how, consider the evolution of interest rates indicated in Table 1.5. Note that variation runs parallel in both rates (a decrease in rates during the first month, an increase during the second and third months, etc.), leaving the size of the spread unchanged. Moreover, changes in these rates with respect to the conditions at the starting point (in t_0) always have the opposite sign $(+/-)$ than the marginal gap relative to the same period (as is also clear from Figure 1.3).

Table 1.5 Marginal gaps and interest rate changes

Period	INTEREST RATE ON ASSETS	INTEREST RATE ON LIABILITIES	Δi RELATIVE TO t_0 (BASIS POINTS)	G'_t. (€ MLN)	EFFECT ON NII
t_0	6.0 %	3 %			
1 month	5.5 %	2.5 %	−50	140	⇩
3 months	6.3 %	3.3 %	+30	−170	⇩
6 months	5.6 %	2.6 %	−40	120	⇩
12 months	6.6 %	3.6 %	+60	−90	⇩
Total					⇩

In this situation, the bank's *NII* is bound to fall monotonically. In each sub-period, in fact, changes in market rates are such that they adversely affect renegotiation conditions for assets and liabilities nearing maturity. At the end of the first month, for example, the bank will have more assets to reinvest than liabilities to refinance ($G'_{1/12}$ is positive at 140). Consequently, the *NII* will suffer due to the reduction in market rates. In three months' time, on the other hand, there will be more debt to refinance than investments to renew ($G'_{3/12} = -170$), so that a rise in returns will translate once again into a lower *NII*.

The example illustrates that in order to actually quantify the effects of several infra-annual market changes on the bank's *NII*, we must consider the different time periods when the effects of these variations will be felt. Therefore, marginal gaps provide a way

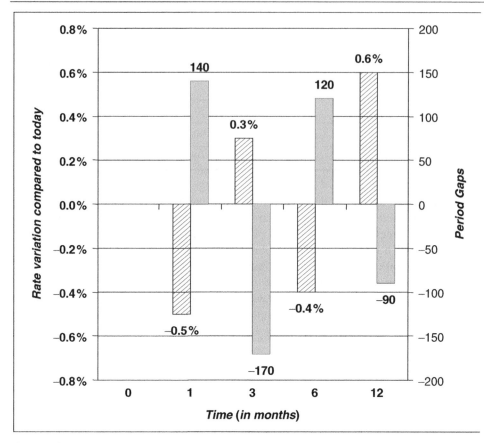

Figure 1.3   Marginal gaps and possible rate variations

to analyze the impact of a possible *time path of market rates* on margins, rather than a simple isolated change.

Summing up, there are two primary reasons why non zero marginal gaps can generate a change in *NII* even when there is a zero cumulative gap:

(1) a *single change* of market rates has different effects on the *NII* generated by rate-sensitive assets and rate-sensitive liabilities that form the basis of single period gaps (the case of weighted cumulative gap not equal to zero[4], see formula 1.16);
(2) the possibility that within this timeframe *several changes of market rates* come into play with opposite signs $(+/-)$ than the marginal gaps (the case of marginal gaps not equal to zero, see Table 1.5 and Figure 1.3).[5]

---

[4] Note that where there are infra-annual marginal gaps that are all equal to zero, even the weighted cumulative gap calculated with (1.16) would be zero. It would be then logical to conclude that the bank is immunized against possible market rate changes.
[5] We can see that in theory situations could arise in which the infra-annual marginal gaps not equal to zero bring about a cumulative marginal gap of zero. It is possible then that case number 2 may occur (losses when there are several infra-annual changes) but not number 1 (losses when there is only one rate change).

At this point, it is clear that an immunization policy to safeguard NII against market rate changes (in other words, the complete immunization of interest risk following a repricing gap logic) requires that marginal gaps of every individual period be zero. However, even quarterly or monthly gaps could be disaggregated into shorter ones, just like the one-year has been decomposed into shorter-term gaps in Table 1.5. Hence, a perfect hedging from interest risk would imply that all marginal gaps, even for very short time periods, be equal to zero.

A bank should therefore equate all daily marginal gaps to zero (that is, the maturity of all assets and liabilities should be perfectly matched, with every asset facing a liability of equal value and duration). Given a bank's role in transforming maturities, such a requirement would be completely unrealistic.

Moreover, although many banks have information on marginal gaps relating to very short sub-periods, still they prefer to manage and hedge only a small set of gaps relative to certain standard periods (say: 0–1 month, 1–3 months, 3–6 months, 6–12 months, 1–3 years, 3–5 years, 5–10 years, 10–30 years, over 30 years). As we will see further on, the reason for this standardization (beyond the need for simplification) is mainly related to the presence of some hedging instruments that are available only for some standard maturities.

1.5 THE LIMITATIONS OF THE REPRICING GAP MODEL

Measuring interest risk with the repricing gap technique, as common as this practice is among banks, involves several problems.

1. *The assumption of uniform changes of interest rates of assets and liabilities and of rates for different maturities*

   The gap model gives an indication of the impact that changes in market interest rates have on the bank's *NII* in a situation where the change of interest rates on assets is equal to the one of liabilities. In practice, some assets or liabilities negotiated by the bank are likely to readjust more noticeably than others. In other words, the different assets and liabilities negotiated by the bank can have differing degrees of sensitivity to relative interest rates. This, in turn, can be caused by the different bargaining power the bank may enjoy with various segments of its clientele. Generally speaking, therefore, the degree of sensitivity of interest rates of assets and liabilities to changes in market rates is not necessarily constant across-the-board. In addition to this, the repricing gap model assumes that rates of different maturities within the same gapping period are subject to the same changes. This is clearly another unrealistic assumption.

2. *Treatment of demand loans and deposits*

   One of the major problems associated with measuring repricing gaps (and interest risk as a whole) arises from on-demand assets and liabilities, i.e. those instruments that do not have a fixed maturity date. Examples are current account deposits or credit lines. Following the logic used to this point, these items would be assigned a very short (even daily) repricing period. In fact, where there is a rise in market rates, an account holder could in principle ask immediately for a higher interest rate (and if this request is denied, transfer her funds to another bank). In the same way, when a drop in market rates occurs, customers might immediately ask for a rate reduction on their financing (and again, if this request is not granted, they may pay back their loans and turn to another bank). In practice, empirical analysis demonstrates that interest rates relative to on-demand instruments do not immediately respond to market rate changes. Various factors account for this delay, such as: (a) transaction costs that retail customers or companies must inevitably sustain to transfer their financial dealings to another bank, (b) the fact that the terms a bank might agree to for a loyal business customer often result from a credit standing assessment based on a long-term relationship (so the company in question would not easily obtain the same conditions by going to a new bank), (c) the fact that some companies' creditworthiness would not allow them to easily get a credit line from another bank. We can also see that, in addition to being sticky, returns from on-demand instruments also tend to adjust asymmetrically. In other words, adjustments happen more quickly for changes that give the bank an immediate economic advantage (e.g. increases in interest income, decreases in interest expenses). This stickiness and lack of symmetry can be stronger or weaker for customers with different bargaining power. For example, one can expect decreases in market rates to take longer to reflect on interest rates paid on retail customers' deposits. On the other hand, rate drops would be quicker to impact interest rates applied to deposits for large businesses.

3. *The effects of interest rate changes on the amount of intermediated funds are disregarded*

The gap model focuses on the effects that changes in market interest rates produce on the bank's *NII*, i.e. on interest income and expenses. The attention is concentrated on flows only, without any consideration of possible effects on stocks, that is, on the value of assets and liabilities of the bank. However, a reduction in market interest rates could, for example, prompt the customer to pay off fixed-rate financing and to increase demand for new financing. In the same way, an increase in market rates would encourage depositors to look for more profitable forms of savings than deposits in current accounts, and as a result the bank's on-demand liabilities would shrink.

4. *The effects of rate changes on market values are disregarded.*

A further problem of the repricing gap model is that the impact of interest rate changes on the market value of assets and liabilities is not taken into account. Indeed, an increase in interest rates has effects which are not limited exclusively to income flows associated with interest-earning assets or interest-bearing liabilities – the market value of these instruments is also modified. So, for example, a rise in market rates leads to a decrease in the market value of a fixed-rate bond or mortgage. These effects are, for all practical purposes, ignored by the repricing gap.

Each of these problems is addressed in the following section, and solutions are described whenever possible.

1.6 SOME POSSIBLE SOLUTIONS

1.6.1 Non-uniform rate changes: the standardized gap

One way to overcome the first problem mentioned above (different sensitivity of interest rates on assets and liabilities to changes in market rates) is based on an attempt to estimate this sensitivity and to use these sensitivities when calculating the gap. More specifically, the method of analysis is based on three different phases:

√ Identifying a reference rate, such as the 3-month interbank rate (Euribor 3m).
√ Estimating the sensitivity of various interest rates of assets and liabilities with respect to changes in the reference rate.
√ Calculating an "adjusted gap" that can be used to estimate the actual change that the bank's *NII* would undergo when there is a change in the market reference rate.

At this point, let us assume that an estimation has been made[6] of the sensitivity of interest rates of assets and liabilities with respect to changes in the 3 month interbank rate, and that the results obtained are those reported in Table 1.6. This table shows the case of a short-term bank which, besides its equity, only holds assets and liabilities sensitive to a one-year gapping period. For these instruments, the relative Euribor sensitivity coefficients are also included in the table (indicated by β_j and γ_k respectively for assets and liabilities).

Table 1.6 Example of a simplified balance sheet structure

Assets	€ m	β	Liabilities	€ m	γ
On-demand credit lines	460	0.95	Clients' deposits	380	0.8
Interbank 1 m deposits	80	1.1	1m interbank deposits	140	1.1
3 month gov't. securities	60	1.05	Variable-rate CDs (next repricing in 3m)	120	0.95
5yr variable-rate consumer credit (repricing in 6m)	120	0.9	10yr variable-rate bonds (*euribor* + 50 bp, repricing in 6m)	160	1
10yr variable-rate mortgages (Euribor+100 basis points, repricing in 1yr)	280	1	1yr fixed-rate CDs	80	0.9
			Equity	120	
Total / average	1000	0.98	Total / average	1000	0.91

On the basis of the data in the table, it is possible to calculate a gap that takes into account the different sensitivity of assets and liabilities rates to changes in the reference market rate by simply multiplying each one by the relative sensitivity coefficient.

In fact, if on-demand loans show a rate-sensitivity coefficient of 0.95, this means that when there is a change of one percentage point of the three-month Euribor rate the relative interest rate varies on average by 0.95% (see Figure 1.4). It follows that interest rates

---

[6] This can be done, e.g., by ordinary least squares (OLS). Readers who are not familiar with OLS and other simple statistical estimation techniques will find a comprehensive presentation, e.g., in Mood et al. (1974) or Greene (2003).

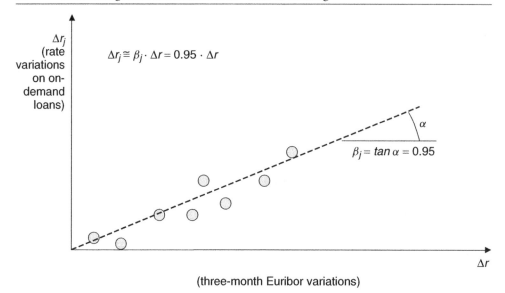

Figure 1.4   example of an estimate of the beta of a rate-sensitive asset

on these loans also undergo a similar change. Since this is true for all rate-sensitive n assets and m liabilities, we can rewrite the change in *NII* following changes in the three-month Euribor as:

$$\Delta NII = \sum_{j=1}^{n} sa_j \cdot \Delta r_j - \sum_{k=1}^{m} sl_k \cdot \Delta r_k \cong \sum_{j=1}^{n} sa_j \cdot \beta_j \cdot \Delta r - \sum_{k=1}^{m} sl_k \cdot \gamma_k \cdot \Delta r =$$

$$= \left(\sum_{j=1}^{n} sa_j \cdot \beta_j - \sum_{k=1}^{m} sl_k \cdot \gamma_k \right) \cdot \Delta r \equiv G^s \cdot \Delta r \qquad (1.17)$$

The quantity in parenthesis is called the standardized gap:

$$G^s = \sum_{j=1}^{n} sa_j \cdot \beta_j - \sum_{k=1}^{m} sl_k \cdot \gamma_k \qquad (1.18)$$

and represents the repricing gap adjusted for the different degrees of sensitivity of assets and liabilities to market rate changes.

Applying (1.18) to the example in the table we come up with a standardized one-year gap of 172 (See Table 1.7 for details on the calculation). This value is greater than the gap we would have gotten without taking into consideration the different rate-sensitivities of assets and liabilities (120). This is due to the fact that rate-sensitive assets, beyond being larger than liabilities, are also more sensitive to Euribor changes (the average weighted value of β, in the last line of Table 1.6, exceeds the average weighted value of γ by 7 percentage points.)

Table 1.7 Details of the standardized gap calculation

Assets	as_j	β_j	$as_j \times \beta_j$
On-demand credit lines	460	95 %	437
1m interbank deposits	80	110 %	88
3m government securities	60	105 %	63
5yr variable-rate consumer credit (repricing in 6m)	120	90 %	108
10yr variable-rate mortgages (Euribor + 100 basis points, repricing in 1 yr)	280	100 %	280
Total assets			976
Liabilities	ps_k	γ_k	$ps_k \times \gamma_k$
Customers' deposits	380	80 %	304
1m interbank deposits	140	110 %	154
Variable-rate CDs (next repricing in 3m)	120	95 %	114
10yr variable-rate bonds (Euribor + 50 bp, repricing in 6m)	160	100 %	160
1yr fixed-rate CDs	80	90 %	72
Total liabilities			804
Assets / liabilities imbalance (gap)			*172*

Given the positive value of the standardized gap, formula (1.18) suggests that in the event of a rise in market rates, the bank will experience an increase in its net interest income. The size of this increase is obviously greater than that estimated with the simple repricing gap. The same is true when market interest rates fall (the bank's *NII* undergoes a greater decrease than that estimated with a non-standardized gap.)

1.6.2   Changes in rates of on-demand instruments

The standardized gap method can be fine-tuned even further to deal with on-demand instruments which have no automatic indexing mechanism.[7]

First of all, for each of these instruments we need to estimate the structure of average delays in rate adjustments with respect to the point in time when a market rate change occurs. This can be done by means of a statistical analysis of past data, as shown in Table 1.8, which gives an example relating to customers' deposits. Here the overall sensitivity coefficient (γ_k) to the 3-month Euribor rate is 80 %, which tells us that for a change of one percentage point of the Euribor, the average return on demand deposits

---

[7] If in fact such a mechanism were present, as is often the case for current account deposits with standard conditions granted to customers belonging to particular groups with high bargaining power (employees of the same company, members of an association, etc.) or for opening a credit line on an account for companies with a high credit standing, the relative instruments would be treated as if they had a maturity date equal to the indexing delay.

only varies by 80 basis points.[8] Moreover, of these 80 basis points only 10 appear within a month of the Euribor variation, while for the next 50, 12 and 8 there is a delay of 3, 6, and 12 months respectively. In this case, not only in calculating the standardized gap, the bank's demand deposits (380 million euros in the example in Table 1.6) are multiplied by γ_k and counted only for 304 (380·0.80) million. This amount is allocated to the various marginal gaps on the basis of delays which were found in past repricing. This means that 38 million (380·0.10) will be placed in the one-month maturity bracket, while 190 million (380·0.50) will be positioned in the three-month bracket and so on (see the right hand column in Table 1.8.)

Table 1.8 Example of progressive repricing of demand deposits

Timeframe	Percentage of variation absorbed	Funding allocated in different time periods (millions of €)
On-demand	0 %	0.0
1 month	10 %	38.0
3 month	50 %	190.0
6 month	12 %	45.6
1 year	8 %	30.4
Total	80 %	304.0

In the previous section we mentioned the fact that on-demand loans and deposits adjust to changes in benchmark rates asymmetrically (that is, banks are quicker at reducing rates on deposits and increasing rates on earning assets). If this is so, Table 1.8 should be split into two versions, measuring the progressive repricing of demand deposits when Euribor rates rise or fall. This implies that the of earnings on on-demand instruments to different marginal gaps (last column in the table) will be done differently if we want to predict the effects of positive, rather than negative, interest rate changes on NII. Following this logic (which applies to all on-demand instruments, both interest-earning and interest-bearing) leads us to calculate two different repricing gaps the bank can use to measure the sensitivity of *NII* to increases and decreases of market rates.

1.6.3 Price and quantity interaction

In principle, the coefficients β and γ used in the calculation of the standardized gap could be modified to take into account the elasticity of quantities relative to prices: if, for example, given a 1 % change of benchmark rates, a given rate-sensitive asset undergoes a rate change of β, but at the same time records- a volume change of x%, a modified β equal to $\beta' = \beta·(1 + x\%)$ would be enough to capture the effect on expected interest income flows both of unit yields as well as intermediate quantities. The γ coefficients of

---

[8] This reduced rate-sensitivity comes from the fact that the public does not hold current accounts for investment purposes only, but also for liquidity purposes. For this reason, the return on deposits is not particularly sensitive to changes in market rates.

rate-sensitive liabilities could likewise be modified. The change of the *NII* estimated in this way would then be adjusted to make allowances for the value of funds bought or sold on the interbank market as a result of possible imbalances between new volumes of assets and liabilities.

In practice, this type of correction would prove extremely arbitrary, since demand for bank assets and liabilities does not react only to interest rates, but also to a number of other factors (state of the economic cycle, preference for liquidity, returns on alternative investments). In addition, this would distance the model from its original significance, making its conclusions less readable and less transparent. For this reason, in calculating the interest rate risk on the balance sheet of a bank, the effect associated with the interaction of prices and quantities is usually ignored.

1.6.4 Effects on the value of assets and liabilities

As mentioned above, a change in market rates can cause changes in the value of assets and liabilities that go beyond the immediate effects on the *NII*. The repricing gap, being an income-based method anchored to a target variable taken from the profit and loss account, is intrinsically unsuitable for measuring such changes. To do so, we have to take on a different perspective and adopt an equity method, such as the duration gap presented in the next chapter.

SELECTED QUESTIONS AND EXERCISES

1. What is a "sensitive asset" in the repricing gap model?
   (A) An asset maturing within one year (or renegotiating its rate within one year);
   (B) An asset updating its rate immediately when market rates change;
   (C) It depends on the time horizon adopted by the model;
   (D) An asset the value of which is sensitive to changes in market interest rates.

2. The assets of a bank consist of € 500 of floating-rate securities, repriced quarterly (and repriced for the last time 3 months ago), and of € 1,500 of fixed-rate, newly issued two-year securities; its liabilities consist of € 1,000 of demand deposits and of € 400 of three-year certificates of deposit, issued 2,5 years ago.
   Given a gapping period of one year, and assuming that the four items mentioned above have a sensitivity ("beta") to market rates (e.g, to three-month interbank rates) of 100 %, 20 %, 30 % and 110 % respectively, state which of the following statements is correct:
   (A) The gap is negative, the standardized gap is positive;
   (B) The gap is positive, the standardized gap is negative;
   (C) The gap is negative, the standardized gap is negative;
   (D) The gap is positive, the standardized gap is positive.

3. Bank Omega has a maturity structure of its own assets and liabilities like the one shown in the Table below. Calculate:
   (A) Cumulated gaps relative to different maturities;
   (B) Marginal (periodic) gaps relative to the following maturities: (i) 0–1 month, (ii) 1–6 months, (iii) 6 months–1 year, (iv) 1–2 years, (v) 2–5 years, (vi) 5–10 years, (vii) beyond 10 years;

(C) The change experienced by the bank's net interest income next year if lending and borrowing rates increase, for all maturities, by 50 basis points, assuming that the rate repricing will occur exactly in the middle of each time band (e.g., after 15 days for the band between 0 and 1 month, 3.5 months for the band 1−6 months, etc.).

Sensitive assets and liabilities for Bank Omega (data in million euros)

	1 month	6 months	1 year	2 years	5 years	10 years	Beyond10 years
Total sensitive assets	5	15	20	40	55	85	100
Total sensitive liabilities	15	40	60	80	90	95	100

4. The interest risk management scheme followed by Bank Lambda requires it to keep all marginal (periodic) gaps at zero, for any maturity band. The Chief Financial Officer states that, accordingly, the bank's net interest income is immune for any possible change in market rates. Which of the following events could prove him wrong?
   (I) a change in interest rates not uniform for lending and borrowing rates;
   (II) a change in long term rates which affects the market value of items such as fixed-rate mortgages and bonds;
   (III) the fact that borrowing rates are stickier than lending rates;
   (IV) a change in long term rates greater than the one experienced by short-term rates.

   (A) I and III;
   (B) I, III and IV;
   (C) I, II and III;
   (D) All of the above.

5. Using the data in the Table below (and assuming, for simplicity, a 360-day year made of twelve 30-day months):
   (i) compute the one-year repricing gap and use it to estimate the impact, on the bank's net interest income, of a 0.5 % increase in market rates;
   (ii) compute the one-year maturity-adjusted gap and use it to estimate the effect, on the bank's net interest income, of a 0.5 % increase in market rates;
   (iii) compute the one-year standardised maturity-adjusted gap and use it to estimate the effect, on the bank's net interest income, of a 0.5 % increase in market rates;
   (iv) compare the differences among the results under (i), (ii) and (iii) and provide an explanation.

Assets	Amount	Days to maturity/ repricing	β
Demand loans	1000	0	90 %
Floating rate securities	600	90	100 %
Fixed-rate instalment loans	800	270	80 %
Fixed-rate mortgages	1200	720	100 %
Liabilities	Amount	Days to maturity/ repricing	γ
Demand deposits	2000	0	60 %
Fixed-rate certificates of deposit	600	180	90 %
Floating-rate bonds	1000	360	100 %

6. Which of the following represents an advantage of the zero-coupon rates curve relative to the yield curve?
   (A) The possibility to take into account the market expectations implied in the interest rates curve
   (B) The possibility of assuming non parallel shifts of the interest rates curve;
   (C) The possibility of associating each cash flow with its actual return;
   (D) The possibility of achieving a more accurate pricing of stocks.

Appendix 1A
The Term Structure of Interest Rates

1A.1 FOREWORD

The term structure of interest rates is usually represented by means of a curve (yield curve) indicating market rates for different maturities. This is usually based on rates paid on Treasury bonds, where default risk can be considered negligible (especially if the issuer is a sovereign state belonging to the G-10 and having a high credit rating); different rates (like those on interbank deposits, up to one year, and interest rate swaps, for longer maturities) may also be used. However, the rates must refer to securities that are homogeneous in all main characteristics (such as default risk, the size of any coupons, etc.) except their time-to-maturity. When based on zero-coupon securities, the yield curve is usually called *zero-coupon curve*.

The yield curve may take different shapes: it can be upward sloping (if short-term rates are lower than long-term ones), downward sloping, flat or hump-shaped see Figure B.4) when rates first increase (decrease) and then decrease (increase) as maturities rise further.

Four main theories try to explain the shape of the yield curve: (i) the theory of expectations, originally due to Fischer,[9] back in 1930; (ii) the theory of the preference for liquidity, proposed by Hicks[10] in 1946; (iii) the theory of the preferred habitat, due to Modigliani and Sutch in 1966 and (iv) the theory of market segmentation. Generally speaking, all these theories acknowledge the role of market expectations in shaping forward rates, hence the slope of the yield curve. They differ in that they may or may not assign a role to other factors, such as liquidity premiums, institutional factors preventing the free flow of funds across maturities, and so on.

1A.2 THE THEORY OF UNBIASED EXPECTATIONS

Based on the expectations theory, the shape of the yield curve depends only on market expectations on the future level of short-term rates. According to this theory, long term rates are simply the product of current short term rates and of the short term rates expected in the future. Hence if, for example, the one-year rate is lower than the two-year rate, this is due to the fact that the market expects one-year rates to increase in the future.

More formally, investors are supposed to be equally well off either investing over long maturities or rolling over a series of short term investments. Formally:

$$(1 + r_T)^T = \prod_{j=0}^{T-1} \left[1 + E(_j r_1) \right] \tag{1A.1}$$

where r_T is the rate on a T-year investment and $E(_j r_1)$ denotes the expected rate on a one-year investment starting at time j.

---

[9] Fischer (1965).
[10] Hicks (1946).

Long-term rates like r_T therefore depend on expected future short-term rates:

$$r_T = \left\{ \prod_{j=0}^{T-1} \left[1 + E(_j r_1) \right] \right\}^{1/T} - 1 \tag{1A.2}$$

Suppose, e.g., that the one-year return on Treasury bills is 3%, while the expected one-year returns for the following four years are $E(_1 r_1) = 3.5\%$, $E(_2 r_1) = 4\%$, $E(_3 r_1) = 4.5\%$ and $E(_4 r_1) = 5\%$.

According to the expectations theory, the spot five-year rate would be

$$r_5 = \left\{ \prod_{j=0}^{4} \left[1 + E(_j r_1) \right] \right\}^{1/5} - 1 =$$

$$= \sqrt[5]{(1 + 3\%) \cdot (1 + 3.5\%) \cdot (1 + 4\%) \cdot (1 + 4.5\%) \cdot (1 + 5\%)} - 1 = 4.00\%$$

Similarly, rates for shorter maturities could be found as:

$$r_4 = \sqrt[4]{(1 + 3\%)(1 + 3.5\%)(1 + 4\%)(1 + 4.5\%)} - 1 = 3.75\%$$

$$r_3 = \sqrt[3]{(1 + 3\%)(1 + 3.5\%)(1 + 4\%)} - 1 = 3.50\%$$

$$r_2 = \sqrt{(1 + 3\%)(1 + 3.5\%)} - 1 = 3.25\%$$

These results are shown in Figure A.1:

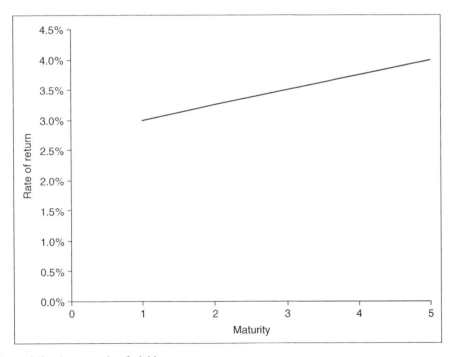

Figure A.1   An example of yield curve

According to the expectations theory, an upward-sloped yield curve denotes expectations of an increase in short term interest rates. The opposite is true when the curve is downward-sloped.

The expectations theory is based on a very demanding hypothesis: that investors are risk neutral and decide how to invest based on their expectations. To appreciate the implications in this hypothesis, consider the fair two-year spot rate found in the example above (3.25 %, following from a current one-year rate of 3 % and an expected one-year rate, after one year, of 3.5 %). Now, suppose that the actual two-year rate is 3.2 %, that is, lower than this equilibrium value. To get the higher rate (3.25 %), a rational investor would invest for the first year at 3 %, then roll over its investment at a rate that, based on his/her expectations, should be 3.5 %. However, this strategy is not risk-free, since the rate for the second year (3.5 %) is not certain, but only represents an expectation; it could turn out to be lower than expected, driving the average return on the two-year strategy well below the expected 3.25 %. Hence, a risk-averse investor could abandon this strategy and accept a risk-free 2-year investment offering 3.2 %. In this case, long-term rates would differ from the equilibrium values dictated by market expectations.

1A.3 THE LIQUIDITY PREFERENCE THEORY

Empirical evidence shows that the yield curve is usually positively sloped. If market expectations were the only driver of the curve, this would imply that short-term rates are always expected to increase. Hence, some other factor must be invoked, besides market expectation, to explain this upward slope.

The liquidity preference theory states that investors tend to prefer investments that, all other things being equal, have a shorter maturity and therefore are more liquid. This is mainly due to the fact that, when underwriting a long-term investment, investors commit their money over a longer horizon and "lock" a rate of return that cannot be subsequently modified. Hence, investors are willing to invest over longer maturities only if they get compensated through higher returns.

Due to such liquidity premiums, the curve might be upward sloped even if expectations on future short-term rates were steady. More formally, indicating by $_jL_1$ the liquidity premium required by investors to face the opportunity cost linked to the uncertainty surrounding the level of future one-year rates at time j, we get:

$$r_T = \left\{ \prod_{j=0}^{T-1} \left[1 + E(_jr_1) + {}_jL_1 \right] \right\}^{1/T} - 1 \qquad (1A.3)$$

As the uncertainty in the level of future short-term rates increases with time, we have that $_1L_1 < _2L_1 < \ldots < _{T-1}L_1$. This causes the curve to be positively sloped even when expectations on short rates are steady.

1A.4 THE THEORY OF PREFERRED HABITATS

The theory of preferred habitats assumes that different classes of investors are characterised by different investment horizons. Accordingly, families and individuals tend to prefer short maturities, whereas institutional investors like insurance companies funding life insurance policies and pension funds tend to have a longer investment horizon.

Therefore, different maturity brackets or "habitats" exist, where different investors can be found. Investors are reluctant to pursue arbitrage strategies that would involve leaving their preferred habitat and tend to do so only if the gains implied by such strategies are large enough to compensate them.

While the liquidity preference theory dictates that rates increase with maturities, the preferred habitat hypothesis may also be compatible with a market where long-term rates are lower. This would simply imply that, due to demand and supply conditions, issuers of short-term securities have to offer a premium to lure long-term-minded investors out of their preferred habitat, and that such a premium is higher than any liquidity premium associated with longer maturities.

1A.5   THE MARKET SEGMENTATION HYPOTHESIS

This is the only approach that does not include expectations on future rates as a driver of the current yield curve. In fact, this theory states that maturity brackets represent separate markets, where rates of return are determined independently, based on supply and demand conditions, as well as on some macroeconomic variables. Namely, while monetary variables tend to affect rates on short term maturities, long-term rates are mainly driven by the state of the real economy. Similar to the preferred habitats theory, the segmented market hypothesis acknowledges the fact that different types of investors operate in different maturity segments.

Appendix 1B
Forward Rates

Consider an investor wishing to invest 10,000 euros for two years. She may either buy a one-year Treasury bill (paying a yield of 3.5 %) or a two-year Treasury bond (offering a return of 3.8 %). What alternative would be more attractive? The answer clearly depends on the future value of the one-year rates. In fact, while the two-year bond offers a given return for the whole investment period, the one-year T-bill creates a reinvestment risk for the second year.

Now, suppose that it is possible, today, to lock the rate on a one-year investment starting in one year. Such a rate, fixed today but referred to a future investment, is called a *forward rate* (as opposed to "spot rates", that is, rates for "normal" investments starting immediately).

The two investment strategies would be equivalent only if they gave rise to the same per-euro outcome at the end of the second year:

$$(1 + r_2)^2 = (1 + r_1)(1 + {_1}r_1) \tag{1B.1}$$

where ${_j}r_t$ denotes the forward rate on a t-year investment starting at time j. Note that all rates in equation 1B.1 are assumed to be known with certainty. In fact, the forward rate ${_1}r_1$, while related to an investment taking place in the future, is agreed upon today and cannot be changed subsequently.

From (1B.1) it follows that the "fair" forward rate can be computed as

$${_1}r_1 = \frac{(1 + r_2)^2}{(1 + r_1)} - 1 \tag{1B.2}$$

More generally:

$${_j}r_t = \frac{(1 + r_{t+j})^{t+j}}{(1 + r_j)^j} - 1 \tag{1B.3}$$

Applying equation (1B.3) to our example, we get a forward rate of:

$${_1}r_1 = \frac{(1 + 3.8\%)^2}{1 + 3.5\%} - 1 \cong 4.10\%$$

Note that this forward rate is higher than the two spot rates. This is logical: forward rates can be seen as estimates of the expected future rates and the fact that r_2 is greater than r_1 suggests that future rates are expected to rise.

Note that any value for the forward rate above or below the one dictated by equations 1B.2 and 1B.3 would immediately give rise to arbitrage strategies. Suppose, e.g., that the forward rate in our example be lower than 4.10 % (for instance, 4 %). In this case, an investor could invest, say, 1,000 euros in the two-year bond (yielding 3.8 % per year) while financing herself with two one-year loans at 3.5 % and 4 %, respectively. The final value of the bond would be $1,000 \cdot (1 + 3.8\%)^2 \cong 1,077$ euros, while the final value of the loan would be $1,000 \cdot (1 + 3.5\%) \cdot (1 + 4\%) \cong 1,076$ euros. Hence, a risk-less profit of one euro profit could be achieved. Such arbitrage schemes would of course increase the demand for two-year investments, as well as the demand for one-year loans (both spot and forward). The rates on the former would then decrease, while the cost of one-year loans would rise, until any arbitrage opportunities have disappeared, and market rates are consistent with equations 1B.2 and 1B.3.

Based on (1B.3), forward rates can be computed, starting from spot rates, for any future time window. Suppose, e.g., that the three-year spot rate is 4.5 %. Then, the one-year forward rate for investments taking place after two years ($_2r_1$) can be found as:

$$_2r_1 = \frac{(1 + 4.05\,\%)^3}{(1 + 3.8\,\%)^2} - 1 = 4.552\,\%$$

Once again, as the three-year rate exceeds the two-year one, the forward rate is higher than both of them. Generally speaking, when the yield curve is positively sloped, forward rates stay above spot rates; the opposite occurs when spot rates decrease with maturities. Again, this is quite logical if we follow the expectations theory and if forward rates can be interpreted as an estimate of expected spot rates in the future. In fact, if forward rates are above spot rates, then short-term rates are expected to increase, and this must be reflected in higher long-term rates (see Figure 1B.1, panel I). If, on the other hand, lower forward rates signal an expected reduction in future short-term rates, spot rates will decrease as maturities increase, accounting for these expectations (Figure 1B.1, panel II). Finally, if forward rates were to be equal to spot rates with the same maturity, this would signal that rates are expected to stay constant, and the spot curve would be flat (Figure 1B.1, panel III).

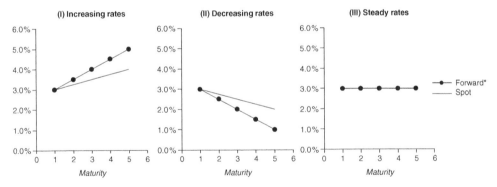

Figure A.1   Spot and forward curves

Note that in this appendix we used annual compounding, as this is the most widely used approach for banks and financial markets. When using continuously-compound rates, the relationship between spot and forward rates becomes even more straightforward. In fact, (1B.1) becomes

$$e^{2r_2} = e^{r_1}e^{_1r_1} = e^{r_1 + _1r_1} \tag{1B.4}$$

and equations (1B.2) and (1B.3) simplify to:

$$_1r_1 = 2r_2 - r_1 \tag{1B.5}$$

$$_jr_t = (j + t)r_{j+t} - jr_j \tag{1B.6}$$

2

The Duration Gap Model

2.1 INTRODUCTION

One of the problems with the repricing gap model examined in the previous chapter, and also the most significant one from a management standpoint, is that it doesn't take into account the effects that changes in market rates have on the market values of a bank's assets and liabilities. This problem is tackled and overcome by the *duration gap* model. This model uses the bank's equity at market value as the target variable to measure the impact of changes in market rates and, consequently, to establish risk management policies. As opposed to the repricing gap model, which uses an income-based flow variable (*NII, net interest income*), the duration gap model adopts an equity-based target variable.

The advantages of the duration gap compared to the traditional repricing gap model have become increasingly clear, given that financial intermediaries are more and more often using *mark-to-market* to evaluate their assets and liabilities. This in turn is the result of a growing weight of trading activities and securitization transactions. Pressure from supervisory authorities also contributes to the success of the duration gap model.

After briefly covering the logic behind a mark-to-market accounting system, this chapter focuses on the concept of a financial instrument's duration and application of this concept to a bank's assets and liabilities. This is followed by an analysis of the duration gap concept and its use as a tool to measure and manage interest rate risk. The chapter ends with a review of the assumptions underlying the duration gap model and its limitations.

2.2 TOWARDS MARK-TO-MARKET ACCOUNTING

Consider the simplified balance sheet for Alfa Bank on 31 December 2006 illustrated in Table 2.1. For simplicity's sake assume that both the mortgage and certificates of deposit have just been issued and call for a one-time repayment of capital at maturity.

Table 2.1 Alfa Bank Balance Sheet – 31 December 2006

Assets	€M	Liabilities	€M
10yr 5 % fixed-rate mortgage	100	2yr 3 % fixed-rate CDs	90
		Equity	10
Total	100	Total	100

If no interest rate changes occur during 2007 then Alfa Bank would earn an *NII* of:

$$NII_{2007} = II_{2007} - IPE_{2007} = (5\% \cdot 100) - (3\% \cdot 90) = 5 - 2.7 = 2.3$$

where *IIR* and *IEP* denote interest income and interest expenses

Return on equity (ROE) would therefore be 23 %[1]. The new balance sheet at the end of 2004 would be as shown in Table 2.2.[2] Similarly, for the following year it would be as indicated in Table 2.3.

Table 2.2 Alfa Bank Balance Sheet – 31 December 2007

Assets	€M	Liabilities	€M
Cash	2.3	2yr 3 % fixed-rate CDs	90
10yr 5 % fixed-rate mortgage	100	Net Profit (Loss) for the period	2.3
		Equity	10
Total	102.3	Total	102.3

Table 2.3 Alfa Bank Balance Sheet – 31 December 2008

Assets	€M	Liabilities	€M
Cash	4.6	3 % fixed-rate CDs	90
5 % fixed-rate mortgage	100	Net Profit (Loss) for the period	2.3
		Equity	12.3
Total	104.6	Total	104.6

Assume at this point that effective from January 2007 the Central Bank had opted for a restrictive monetary policy and market interest rates rose by one percentage point. In such a scenario Alfa Bank's *NII* for 2007 would remain unchanged from the calculation reported above. In fact, as both the assets (mortgage) and liabilities (CDs) are at a fixed rate the *NII* would still be 2.3 million euros. The same is true for the following year, 2008. As both the mortgage and certificates of deposit have a maturity at or beyond 31 December 2008, they continue to generate the same interest income and expenses. Similarly, Alfa Bank's balance sheet for the two years ending 31 December 2007 and 31 December 2008 would still be the same as indicated in Tables 2.2 and 2.3 respectively.

However, in 2009 Alfa Bank would be forced to refinance the 10-year loan by raising new funds at the new market conditions. Assume for simplicity that at maturity the bank were able renew the certificates of deposit with new CDs for the same amount but at a one-point higher interest rate (4 %). The *NII* for 2009 would then be:

$$NII_{2009} = II_{2009} - IE_{2009} = (5 \% \cdot 100) - (4 \% \cdot 90) = 5 - 3.6 = 1.4$$

---

[1] Note that we are using Return on Equity (based on fair-value measure of the bank's capital) as a performance indicator since this is an easily-understood and widespread ratio. However, as will be shown in Part VI, ratios based on actual capital may not adequately reflect the riskiness of the bank's assets, and may therefore be replaced with indicators, like Raroc (risk-adjusted return on capital) based on capital at risk, that is, by ratios where the bank's profits are not divided by its value, but rather by the value of the risks it is facing.

[2] To simplify matters it is assumed that every year the *NII* increases cash on hand and doesn't generate interest. Tax effects have also been ignored.

The reduction in *NII* would also be reflected in a similar decrease in ROE for 2009 equal to:

$$ROE_{2009} = \frac{1.4}{14.6} = 9.59\%$$

Note how, by applying the logic underlying the repricing gap model, a change in market rates at the beginning of 2007 is only reflected two years later, namely in 2009, in Alfa Bank's final profitability, with a reduction in the relevant *NII*.

Rather than using traditional accounting methods, let us now assume the Alfa Bank's assets and liabilities are evaluated at the relevant market value. As we know an increase in interest rates leads to a reduction in the market value of fixed-rate financial assets and liabilities. More specifically, consider the impact the one percentage point rise in interest rates in 2007 would have on the market value of the fixed-rate mortgage in our example. At the end of 2007 the latter would have a residual life of 9 years. Considering that new mortgages would be disbursed at the new 6% interest rate, the value of the mortgage paying 5% interest would be:

$$MV_{5\%-Mortgage} = \sum_{t=1}^{9} \frac{5}{(1+6\%)^t} + \frac{100}{(1+6\%)^9} = 93.2$$

An increase in interest rates would therefore produce a 6.8 million euro reduction in the value of the mortgage. There would also be a reduction (although a lower one, given their shorter maturity) in the value of the certificates of deposit.

At the end of 2007 the value would, in fact, be:

$$MV_{3\%-CD} = \frac{92.7}{(1+4\%)} = 89.13$$

In this case the rate increase leads to a reduction of 0.87 million euros.

If we now dispense with the traditional accounting method and restate Alfa Bank's balance sheet at year-end 2007 at market values, the result is as shown in Table 2.4.

Table 2.4 Alfa Bank mark-to-market Balance Sheet – 31 December 2007

Assets	€M	Liabilities	€M
Cash	2.3	3% fixed-rate CDs	89.13
5% fixed-rate mortgage	93.20	Net Profit (Loss) for the period	(3.63)
		Equity	10
Total	95.5	Total	95.5

Note how the Alfa Bank's equity, including profit/loss for the period, drops to 6.37 instead of increasing from 10 to 12.3 million euros (as in the balance sheet in Table 2.2). The effect of a one percentage point increase in rates in 2007 can now be seen in the same year in which it took place. From an economic standpoint, based on a mark-to-market approach, the profit/loss for the year is calculated as the sum of *NII* and the change in the market value of the bank's equity (ΔMV_B, the latter expressed as the difference between the change in market value of assets and liabilities):

$$E_{2007} = NII + \Delta MV_B = NII + \Delta MV_A - \Delta MV_L \qquad (2.1)$$

Applying equation (2.1) to the example would give us:

$$E_{2007} = (5 - 2.7) + [(93.2 - 100) - (89.13 - 90)] = -3.63$$

The 3.63 million euro loss is therefore the result of a net reduction of 5.93 (given by the balance between the change in value for assets and liabilities) and *NII* amounting to 2.3.

For the following year (2008) we assume there is no further change in market interest rates. Bearing in mind that the mortgage will have 8 years to run at the end of the year, its residual value will be:

$$MV_{5\%-Mortgage} = \sum_{t=1}^{8} \frac{5}{(1+6\%)^t} + \frac{100}{(1+6\%)^8} = 93.79$$

Vice versa, the market value of the certificates of deposit, which mature at the end of this year, will once again be 90. Apart from interest due, this amount is what Alfa Bank will have to reimburse to depositors and refinance to cover its assets. Consequently the mark-to-market balance sheet situation at the end of 2008 will be as shown in Table 2.5.

Table 2.5 Alfa Bank mark-to-market Balance Sheet – 31 December 2008

Assets	€M	Liabilities	€M
Cash on hand [3]	4.6	3 % fixed-rate CDs	90
5 % fixed-rate mortgage	93.79	Net Profit (Loss) for the period	2.02
		Equity	6.37
Total	98.39	Total	98.39

Once again the net profit for the period is the difference between *NII* and the change in market value of the bank's equity:

$$E_{2008} = NII + \Delta MV_B = (5 - 2.7) + [(93.79 - 93.2) - (90 - 89.13)] = 2.02$$

Returning to 2007, when the change in market rates took place, we can estimate what increase in interest rates would have made Alfa Bank "technically insolvent" (i.e. its equity at market value would have been zero). In fact, with an interest rate change of 2.19 % the market value of the mortgage would have been:

$$MV_{5\%-Mortgage} = \sum_{t=1}^{9} \frac{5}{(1+7.19\%)^t} + \frac{100}{(1+7.19\%)^9} = 85.82$$

---

[3] The increase in cash from 2.3 to 4.6 million euros represents the balance between interest income (5) and expense (2.7).

whereas the market value of the CDs would have been:

$$MV_{3\%-CD} = \frac{92.7}{(1 + 5.19\%)} = 88.12$$

At year-end 2007 Alfa Bank's mark-to-market balance sheet would have been as shown in Table 2.6 below.

Table 2.6 Alfa Bank mark-to-market Balance Sheet – 31 December 2007

Assets	€M	Liabilities	€M
Cash	2.3	3% fixed-rate CDs	88.12
5% fixed-rate mortgage	85.82	Net Profit (Loss) for the period	(10)
		Equity	10
Total	88.12	Total	88.12

As we can see, the bank's equity (including losses) is now zero as a result of the rise in market interest rates, given that the loss for the year is exactly 10 (the sum of *NII* of 2.3 and the change in net asset and liability values, equal to −12.3).

2.3   THE DURATION OF FINANCIAL INSTRUMENTS

2.3.1   Duration as a weighted average of maturities

The duration of a financial instrument is calculated by taking the average of cash-flow maturities associated with it, where every maturity is weighted according to the ratio between the present value of the cash-flow for a given maturity and the price (or total market value) of the financial instrument. Calculated this way, duration represents a risk indicator that takes into account both the instrument's residual life (given the same interest flows, assets with a higher residual life are more sensitive to changes in interest rates) and the amount of intermediate flows (given the same residual life, assets with lower coupons are more sensitive to changes in market rates). This *Macauley duration*, named after one of the first economists to propose this concept, can be stated analytically as follows:

$$D = \sum_{t=1}^{T} t \cdot \frac{\frac{CF_t}{(1+r)^t}}{P} \qquad (2.2)$$

where:

D = duration
t = maturity of individual cash flows expressed in years
CF_t = t-th cash flow
r = effective yield to maturity requested by the market for maturity T
P = price or market value of the instrument concerned
T = maturity of the asset, namely, of the final cash flow

The following example will clarify the utility and possible applications of the duration concept. Assume it is 1 January 2007, and consider a bond carrying an annual coupon of 6% that has a residual life of four years (maturity 31 December 2010). If the effective yield to maturity requested by the market is 6%, the market price for this bond will be the sum of the present value of the individual cash flows discounted by 6%, as illustrated in Table 2.7.

Table 2.7 Cash flow structure for a 4-year bond with annual coupon of 6%

Date	31/12/07	31/12/08	31/12/09	31/12/10
Flow	6	6	6	106
Present value	5.660	5.340	5.037	83.963
Nominal price				100.00

Given that this bond pays an annual coupon (6%) exactly equal to the yield requested by the market, its price is equal to the redemption value (100), namely, the bond is quoted at par. To calculate the duration of this bond all we need to do is to apply a weighting at every maturity equal to the ratio between the present value of the cash-flow maturing at a given time and the price of the bond, as shown in Table 2.8.

Table 2.8 Calculation of the duration of a 4-year bond with an annual coupon of 6%

Maturity (years) (1)	1	2	3	4	Total
Cash flow (2)	6	6	6	106	
Present value (3)	5.660	5.340	5.037	83.962	100.00
Present value / Price (4)	0.0566	0.0534	0.05037	0.83962	1.00
(1) x (4) = (5)	0.0566	0.1068	0.1511	3.3585	
Duration = ($\sum$ (5))					**3.6730**

As the maturities are expressed in years and the duration is an average of these, we can say that the bond has a duration of 3.67 years. If instead the bond had been a zero-coupon bond, then its duration would have been equal to its residual life (4 years). Indeed, if there had been no intermediate cash-flows, the average of the maturities would have been equal to that of the only cash flow involved. However, when there are intermediate cash-flows, the bond's duration no longer coincides with its residual life but instead becomes lower as the number and amount of intermediate cash-flows increases.

2.3.2 Duration as an indicator of sensitivity to interest rates changes

Duration is an indicator of a bond's risk because it allows to measure how sensitive the price of that bond is to changes in the market yield rate. Using the link between the price of a bond (P) and the yield to maturity requested by the market (r) as a starting point:

$$P = \sum_{t=1}^{T} \frac{CF_t}{(1+r)^t} \tag{2.3}$$

we can come up with the following analytical relationship by deriving with respect to the yield rate:

$$\frac{dP}{dr} = \frac{-1 \cdot CF_1}{(1+r)^2} + \frac{-2 \cdot CF_2}{(1+r)^3} + \cdots + \frac{-T \cdot FC_T}{(1+i)^{T+1}} \tag{2.4}$$

From (2.4) it follows that:

$$\frac{dP}{dr} = -\frac{1}{(1+r)} \left[\frac{CF_1}{(1+r)} + \frac{2 \cdot CF_2}{(1+r)^2} + \cdots + \frac{T \cdot CF_n}{(1+r)^T} \right] \tag{2.5}$$

Dividing both sides by P gives us:

$$\frac{dP}{dr}\frac{1}{P} = -\frac{1}{1+r} \sum_{t=1}^{T} t \cdot \frac{\frac{CF_t}{(1+r)^t}}{P} = -\frac{D}{1+r} \tag{2.6}$$

and consequently:

$$\frac{dP}{P} = -\frac{D}{1+r} \cdot dr \tag{2.7}$$

The expression $\frac{D}{1+r}$ is called modified duration; it enables us to quantify the percentage change in price that would result from an extremely small change in market yield. If finite changes in the yield rate (Δr) are considered, (2.7) instead provides an approximate (but still indicative) estimate of the consequent percentage change in price:

$$\frac{\Delta P}{P} \cong -\frac{D}{1+r} \cdot \Delta r \tag{2.8}$$

To get a better grasp of this concept, imagine we want to estimate the price change for the bond shown in Table 2.8 in the event the market yield rate were to increase from 6 % to 7 %. In other words, we want to know what the price reduction would be for this bond if the market requested a one percentage point higher effective yield. By applying (2.8) we get:

$$\frac{\Delta P}{100} \cong -\frac{3.67}{1+6\%} \cdot 1\% = -3.46\%$$

which means we can make an estimate of the bond's new price after the hypothetical rate change:

$$P + \Delta P = 100 - 3.46 = 96.54$$

If market rates were to increase by one percentage point the bond price would immediately drop by around 3.46 % from 100 to 96.54. If the rate change were negative the bond price would rise by the same percentage to 103.46. A bond's percentage price change as a result of a percentage change in its yield to maturity is roughly the same as the bond's modified duration. This indicator therefore represents a bond's sensitivity to a change in market rates. If a bond has a shorter residual life and/or higher coupons, the same market rate change (up or down) would lead to a smaller price change (respectively, lower or higher) because both its duration and modified duration are shorter.

2.3.3 The properties of duration

As already mentioned, the calculation of duration is based on the weighted average of maturities and is therefore expressed in time, generally in years. So, for example, a duration of 3.5 indicates a period of 3 years and 6 months.

Furthermore, we have seen that duration of a fixed-rate financial instrument is greater: (i) the longer the residual life of the instrument concerned, all other factors being equal; (ii) the lower the coupons, given the same residual life. Indeed, bonds with a greater duration are those with a longer residual life and lower coupon. Equation (2.2) also shows that in the case of a zero-coupon bond the duration is exactly the same as the residual life of the bond itself.

Another key characteristic has to do with duration for portfolios containing a number of bonds. One could easily show that the duration of a portfolio is nothing more than the average of the durations of the individual bonds which make up that portfolio, each one weighted for its market value. If we know the duration and market value of a bank's individual assets we can calculate the duration of its total assets; by the same token we can also establish the duration of its liabilities.

2.4 ESTIMATING THE DURATION GAP

The Alfa Bank example in Section 2.2 analyzes the impact of rate changes on the market values of assets, liabilities and, consequently, the bank's equity. But since this kind of analysis is made after the interest rate shock has occurred, it cannot provide any useful indications for those who are responsible for managing interest rate risk and coming up with policies that can immunize the bank against it.

The *duration gap* concept can be used to compensate for this shortcoming. As noted above, the duration of a financial instrument is an indicator that synthesizes the sensitivity of its market value to changes in interest rates. It therefore allows us to estimate the market values of a bank's assets and liabilities when interest rates change. Analytically, using MD to stand for modified duration, we have:

$$\frac{\Delta MV_A}{MV_A} \cong -\frac{D_A}{(1+r_A)} \cdot \Delta r_A = -MD_A \cdot \Delta r_A \tag{2.9}$$

$$\frac{\Delta MV_L}{MV_L} \cong -\frac{D_L}{(1+r_L)} \cdot \Delta r_L = -MD_L \cdot \Delta r_L \tag{2.10}$$

from which:

$$\Delta MV_A \cong -MV_A \cdot MD_A \cdot \Delta r_A \tag{2.11}$$

$$\Delta MV_L \cong -MV_L \cdot MD_L \cdot \Delta r_L \tag{2.12}$$

where D_A and D_L represent the average weighted durations of the bank's assets and liabilities, MD_A and MD_L, the respective modified durations and r_A and r_P, the average asset and liability yield rates.

By combining (2.11) and (2.12) we can estimate the change in the market value of the bank's equity:

$$\Delta MV_B = \Delta MV_A - \Delta MV_P \cong (-MV_A \cdot MD_A \cdot \Delta r_A) - (-MV_L \cdot MD_L \cdot \Delta r_L) \tag{2.13}$$

Assuming that changes in asset and liability yield rates are the same ($\Delta r_A = \Delta r_L = \Delta r$) this gives:

$$\Delta MV_B \cong -(MV_A \cdot MD_A - MV_L \cdot MD_L) \cdot \Delta r \tag{2.14}$$

Dividing both sides of equation (2.14) by the asset market value we get:

$$\frac{\Delta MV_B}{MV_A} \cong -\left(MD_A - \frac{MV_L}{MV_A} \cdot MD_L\right) \cdot \Delta r \tag{2.15}$$

and

$$\Delta MV_B \cong -(MD_A - L \cdot MD_L) \cdot \Delta MV_A \cdot \Delta r = -DG \cdot MV_A \cdot \Delta r \tag{2.16}$$

where L represents an indicator of the bank's financial leverage, expressed by the ratio between the market value of the liabilities and the one of the assets $\left(\dfrac{MV_L}{MV_A}\right)$ and DG (see below) is the duration gap.

Equation (2.16) shows that the change in the market value of a bank's equity following a change in interest rates is a direct function of three factors:

(i) the intermediation activity undertaken by the bank, measured by the market value of its total assets;
(ii) the size of the interest rate change;
(iii) the difference between the modified duration of the assets and liabilities adjusted by the bank's financial leverage ("leverage-adjusted duration gap"), which from now on will be referred to simply as the duration gap (DG). Analytically: $DG = MD_A - L \cdot MD_L$.

Equation (2.16) also highlights the main conditions for immunizing the market value of equity from changes in interest rates. If the initial net value is zero ($MV_B = MV_A - MV_L = 0$), the market value of the bank's equity will be immunized against interest rate changes when the sensitivity of assets and liabilities is equal ($MD_A = MD_L$). If, instead (and this is usually the case), the value of assets is greater than the one of liabilities ($MV_A > MV_L$; $MV_B > 0$), we need a zero duration gap to guarantee immunization ($DG = 0$). If this is the case, then $MD_A = L \cdot MD_L$ and therefore the modified duration of the assets must be lower than the one of liabilities. The fact that liabilities show a greater sensitivity to market rate changes is a guarantee that their absolute value (initially lower than the assets' one) varies in the same way, leaving the market value of equity unchanged.

A zero duration gap immunizes the bank from market rate changes, in the sense that these changes in theory have no effect on the market value of its equity. If, on the other hand, DG is not zero, equation (2.16) still allows us to calculate the expected change of the market value of the bank's equity, given a change in market rates.

Now we can apply (2.16) to the Alfa Bank example in order to estimate the impact of a market rate change on market value. To do so, let's say we find ourselves on 31 December 2007, moments before the effects of the Central Bank's decision to increase rates are to be reflected into new market values for Alfa Bank's balance sheet. Let's calculate the modified duration of the bank's assets and liabilities, namely, the 10-year mortgage and the 2-year CDs. In analytical terms we have:

$$D_A = D_{5\%-Mortgage} = \sum_{t=1}^{9} \frac{t \cdot \dfrac{CF_t}{(1+r_A)^t}}{MV_A} = \sum_{t=1}^{8} t \cdot \frac{\dfrac{5}{(1+5\%)^t}}{100} + 9 \cdot \frac{\dfrac{105}{(1+5\%)^9}}{100} = 7.46$$

from which:

$$MD_A = \frac{D_A}{(1+r_A)} = \frac{7.46}{1+5\%} = 7.11$$

Similarly (bearing in mind that on 31 December 2007 the CDs have one year to run to maturity and that the only flow forecast is reimbursement of the capital sum), this means:

$$D_L = D_{3\%-CD} = \sum_{t=1}^{1} \frac{t \cdot \dfrac{CF_t}{(1+r_L)^t}}{MV_L} = 1$$

from which:

$$MD_L = \frac{D_L}{(1+r_L)} = \frac{1}{1+3\%} = 0.97$$

Using the data above we can now estimate Alfa Bank's duration gap:

$$DG = (MD_A - L \cdot MD_L) = (7.11 - 0.90 \cdot 0.97) = 6.23$$

and we can estimate how the bank's market value equity would change to reflect a 1% increase in market rates:

$$\Delta MV_B \cong -DG \cdot MV_A \cdot \Delta r = -6.23 \cdot 100 \cdot 1\% = -6.23$$

The result indicates that following a one percentage point increase in market rates the Alfa Bank's market value would immediately decrease by 6.23 million euros, more than 60% of its initial value.

Note that the result is different from the 5.93 million euro decrease calculated in Section 2.2, when the 10-year mortgage and 2-year CDs were revalued the day after the rate increase. This difference (albeit quite negligible) can be explained by the fact that when we use duration to estimate the effect of finite changes in market rates on the value of a financial asset we're making an approximation that is subject to error (as explained in Section 3.2).

2.5 PROBLEMS OF THE DURATION GAP MODEL

Despite its strong points, the duration gap model has often been criticized because it is difficult to apply to real risk management problems. These criticisms can be classified in one of four main categories:

I – The first concerns the dynamic nature of interest risk immunization policies based on the duration gap model. If in fact a bank manages to eliminate its duration gap by means of appropriate balance sheet restructuring policies or through the use of interest rate derivatives, the effectiveness of this immunization strategy will last a very short time. This is due to several factors:

(a) The change in the duration of the bank's assets and liabilities can diverge over time, so modifying the bank's duration gap. If a market rate change occurs immediately after introducing the immunization policy, the bank's equity could possibly remain unchanged. But if, on the other hand, the market rate change takes place one month later, it is likely that as time passes the duration gap will migrate away from zero, as well as the change in the bank's market value.[4]

(b) Interest rate changes in turn modify the duration of assets and liabilities, so modifying the bank's duration gap. From this standpoint immunization policies based on this measure are not very "manageable" as they have to be adjusted every time there is a change in market interest rates.

II – A second problem of the duration gap model concerns the costs associated with immunization policies. Indeed, these policies require to modify the duration, and therefore the maturity, of the bank's assets and liabilities. These are apparently based on balance sheet restructuring policies and may lead to significant costs or foregoing profitable opportunities to place or gather funds. In reality these policies can be implemented through interest rate derivatives, such as interest rate swaps, options or futures. The instruments most widely used for this purpose are contracts traded over the counter (OTC), such as forward rate agreements (FRA), interest rate swaps (IRS) and interest rate options (cap, floor and collar).

III – A third problem of the duration gap model is that it estimates the impact of interest rate changes on the market values of the bank's assets and liabilities with a certain margin of error. Generally speaking, duration is based on a linear approximation of the function linking a financial instrument's market value to its yield to maturity. Since this function is actually convex, duration leads to a larger estimation error the stronger the change in market rates. This problem can easily be overcome by measuring the degree of convexity of this function. This way the duration gap can be integrated by a convexity gap in order to obtain a more precise measure. More specifically, by using the convexity gap we can

---

[4] To clarify the problem, here is a very simplified example: a bank has assets consisting of a mortgage with a market value of 100 million euros and a modified duration of 5 years, and liabilities comprising a zero-coupon bond with a market value of 90 million euros and modified duration of 5.55 years. The bank's duration gap is zero: $DG = (5 - 5.55 \cdot 90/100) = 0$. As time goes by, however, the duration of the asset decreases at a slower rate than the liabilities' one. This is because a zero-coupon financial instrument decreases in line with its residual life, while the duration of a coupon paying financial instrument, being lower than the residual life, decreases at a slower rate. This leads to a positive duration gap and the bank, which was initially immunized against market rate changes, becomes progressively exposed to the risk of an increase in interest rates.

estimate the change in market value of the bank's equity more accurately, while also taking into account the curvature of the relationship. Analytically:

$$\Delta MV_B \cong -(MV_A \cdot MD_A - MV_L \cdot MD_L) \cdot \Delta r$$

$$+ (MV_A \cdot MC_A - MV_L \cdot MC_L) \cdot \frac{(\Delta r)^2}{2} \qquad (2.17)$$

where MC_A and MC_P respectively represent the modified convexity of the bank's assets and liabilities.[5] We can derive the following from equation (2.17):

$$\Delta MV_B \cong -DG \cdot MV_A \cdot \Delta r + CG \cdot MV_A \cdot \frac{(\Delta r)^2}{2} \qquad (2.18)$$

where CG indicates the convexity gap, which reflects the degree of dispersion of the bank's asset and liability cash flows around their own durations, and can be calculated as follows:

$$CG = MC_A - L \cdot MC_L \qquad (2.19)$$

IV – Finally, as we saw with the repricing gap, the duration gap too is based on the assumption of uniform changes in interest rates of assets and liabilities. In reality a change in market rates (for instance, the 3-month interbank rate) can give rise to different changes in the interest rates of a bank's assets and liabilities. This phenomenon, also known as basis risk, can be taken into account by using an estimate of the varying degree of sensitivity of interest rates of assets and liabilities to changes in a given benchmark rate.

Using β_A and β_L to indicate the average degree of sensitivity of asset and liability rates to a change in this benchmark rate $\left(\beta_A = \frac{dr_A}{dr}; \beta_L = \frac{dr_L}{dr} \right)$, the market value sensitivity of the bank's equity to changes in this benchmark rate (Δr) can be restated as follows:

$$\Delta MV_B \cong -BDG \cdot MV_A \cdot \Delta r \qquad (2.20)$$

where BDG indicates the bank's *beta duration gap*, defined as:

$$BDG = MD_A\beta_A - MD_L \cdot \beta_L \cdot L \qquad (2.21)$$

Equation (2.21) indicates the impact of a change in the market benchmark rate (for instance, the 3-month interbank rate) on the market value of the bank's equity. This in turn depends mainly on three main factors:

√ the average modified duration of assets and liabilities;
√ the average degree of sensitivity of interest rates of assets and liabilities to changes in the market benchmark rate, measured by the relevant beta coefficient;
√ the ratio between liability value and asset value (indicating financial leverage).

---

[5] A security's convexity is calculated as $C = \sum_{t=1}^{T} (t + t^2) \frac{\frac{CF_t}{(1+r)^t}}{P}$; the modified convexity is expressed as $\frac{C}{(1+r)^2}$. The convexity of a portfolio (therefore, also a bank's assets or liabilities) is the average, weighted by market value, of the convexities of the individual securities it contains. More details are provided in Appendix 2A.

SELECTED QUESTIONS AND EXERCISES

1. Which of the following does not represent a limitation of the repricing gap model which is overcome by the duration gap model?

   (A) Not taking into account the impact of interest rates changes on the market value of non sensitive assets and liabilities.
   (B) Delay in recognizing the impact of interest rates changes on the economic results of the bank.
   (C) Not taking into account the impact on profit and loss that will emerge after the gapping period.
   (D) Not taking into account the consequences of interest rate changes on current account deposits.

2. Consider a bullet bond with a face value of 1,000 euros, paying a 3% bi-annual coupon, due to expire in 3 years and 2 months. Assuming market rates are flat at 4% (annually compounded) compute the bond's current value and modified duration; based on the duration, estimate the impact of a 2% decrease in market rates on the value of the bond. Finally, consider a different bond, with the same maturity, a face value of 1,100 euros and a bi-annual coupon of 1.5%. Again, compute current value and modified duration. State why, in your opinion, the two bonds' present values are similar while the modified duration is different. Tell whether the effect on the second bond of a 2% increase in market rates would be stronger or weaker than for the first one, and why.

3. A bank's assets have a market value of 100 million euro and a modified duration of 5.5 years. Its liabilities have a market value of 94 million euro and a modified duration of 2.3 years. Calculate the bank's duration gap and estimate which would be the impact of a 75 basis points interest rate increase on the bank's equity (market value).

4. Which of the following statements is NOT correct?

   (A) The convexity gap makes it possible to improve the precision of an interest-rate risk measure based on duration gap.
   (B) The convexity gap is a second-order effect.
   (C) The convexity gap is an adjustment needed because the relationship between the interest rate and the value of a bond portfolio is linear.
   (D) The convexity gap is the second derivative of the value function with respect to the interest rate, divided by a constant which expresses the bond portfolio's current value.

5. Using the data in the table below

   (I) compute the bank's net equity value;
   (II) compute the bank's duration gap;
   (III) compute the bank's convexity gap;
   (IV) based on the duration gap only, estimate the impact of a 50 basis points increase in the yield curve on the bank's net value;
   (V) based on both duration and convexity gap together, estimate the impact of a 50 basis points increase in the yield curve on the bank's net value;

(VI) comment briefly on the results.

Assets	Value	Modified duration	Modified convexity
Open credit lines	1000	0	0
Floating rate securities	600	0.25	0.1
Fixed rate loans	800	3.00	8.50
Fixed rate mortgages	1200	8.50	45
Liabilities	Value	Modified duration	Modified convexity
Checking accounts	1200	0	0
Fixed rate CDs	600	0.5	0.3
Fixed rate bonds	1000	3	6.7

Appendix 2A
The Limits of Duration

2A.1 ASSUMING PARALLEL SHIFTS ACROSS MATURITIES

In this chapter, when computing the value of an asset and its duration, we have relied on two key assumptions:

- all cash flows CF_t, related to different maturities, could be discounted with a single rate r; one simple interpretation for this is that the zero coupon curve had to be flat at r (that is, with $r_t = r$ for any t);
- changes in rates, Δr, had to be the same across all maturities. In other words, no twists could occur, implying different changes for different maturities.

Those two assumptions clearly limit the validity of results based on duration when the rate curve is not flat, and/or when movements in rates are not parallel shifts.

However, the first assumption is not as demanding as it might seem. Indeed if, rather than using annual compounding as in this chapter, one were to use continuously-compounded (that is, exponential) interest, the present value of an asset could be written as follows:

$$P = \sum_t CF_t e^{-r_t t}$$

and its duration would be:

$$D = \frac{1}{P} \sum_t t CF_t e^{-r_t t}$$

(note that we are now using maturity-specific discount rates, so the assumption of a flat curve is no more required).

If all rates experience an arbitrarily small parallel shift, moving from r_t to $r_t + q$, the percent change in the value of the asset will be

$$\frac{dP/P}{dq} = \frac{1}{P} \sum_t -t CF_t e^{-r_t t} = -D$$

which, for a finite shift of magnitude Δq, would lead to

$$\frac{\Delta P}{P} \cong -D \Delta q$$

Hence, approximations based on duration could still be used, provided that the change in interest rates be the same (Δq) across all maturities.

This shows that, even turning to a more sophisticated computation scheme, like continuously-compounded interest, the second assumption stated above (parallel shifts) *cannot* be removed.

However, if a bank has estimated of the sensitivities of the different r_ts to a benchmark rate r, it can use the "beta duration gap" model discussed in this chapter to circumvent this limitation, or at least to minimize its practical consequences.

2A.2   ASSUMING A LINEAR RELATIONSHIP BETWEEN YIELD AND PRICE

Another limit of the duration is that it approximates the change in the market value of a security, following from a change in its yield, based on a linear approximation.

Consider, e.g., the bond shown in Table 2.7 of this chapter, paying a 6 % coupon and therefore quoting at par ($P = 100$) when market rates are at 6 %. Based on duration, we estimated that a 1 % increase in market yields (from 6 % to 7 %) would cause a decrease of 3.46 % in its price. However, this is just an approximation of the true value.

In fact, if one computes the new market value of the security, by discounting all cash flows with the new market rate (7 %), the following value would be found:

$$P|_{r=7\%} = \sum_{t=1}^{3} \frac{6}{(1.07)^t} + \frac{106}{(1.07)^4} \cong 96.53$$

The actual decrease in price would therefore be of $100 - 96, 61 = 3, 39$. This is 3.39 % of the original price. Similarly, if market rates were to experience a decrease to 5 %, the new price of the bond would be

$$P|_{r=5\%} = \sum_{t=1}^{3} \frac{6}{(1.05)^t} + \frac{106}{(1.05)^4} \cong 103.47$$

with a price increase of 3.47 %.

Figure 2A.1 shows the reason of such differences. As can be seen, the true price/yield relationship is convex: approximating it with a linear function leads to errors, which become larger as the change in yields increases.

2A.3   CONVEXITY

To improve the quality of this approximation, one can use an index of convexity that helps to make the estimated price change closer to the actual one. Such an index is (unsurprisingly) called *convexity*.

Consider the Taylor expansion of the true function, $P(r)$, linking bond price and market rates. This would be:

$$P(r_0 + \Delta r) = P(r_0) + \sum_{j=1}^{\infty} P^{(j)}(r_0) \frac{(\Delta r)^j}{j!} \qquad (2A.1)$$

where r_0 denotes the current level of interest rates and $P(j)(r_0)$ denotes the j-th order derivative of $P(.)$, evaluated at $r = r_0$.

Using duration only is equivalent to stopping (2A.1) at the first-order derivative:

$$P(r_0 + \Delta r) \cong P(r_0) + P'(r_0)\Delta r = P(r_0) - P(r_0) \cdot MD \cdot \Delta r \qquad (2A.2)$$

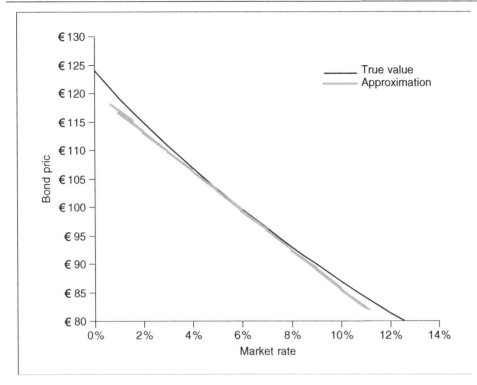

Figure 2A.1 Price of a bond as a function of market rate, r

To improve precision, we could instead stop the Taylor approximation at the second-order derivative, getting:

$$P(r_0 + \Delta r) \cong P(r_0) + P'(r_0)\Delta r + P''(r_0)\frac{(\Delta r)^2}{2}$$

$$= P(r_0) - P(r_0) \cdot MD \cdot \Delta r + P''(r_0)\frac{(\Delta r)^2}{2} \qquad (2A.3)$$

that is

$$\frac{\Delta P}{P(r_0)} \cong -MD \cdot \Delta r + \frac{P''(r_0)}{P(r_0)} \cdot \frac{(\Delta r)^2}{2} \qquad (2A.4)$$

Recalling equation (2.5), the second-order derivative can be computed as

$$P''(r_0) = \frac{d}{dr}\sum_{t=1}^{T} -t \cdot CF_t(1+r)^{-t-1} = \sum_{t=1}^{T} -t(-t-1)CF_t(1+r)^{-t-2}$$

$$= \frac{1}{(1+r)^2}\sum_{t=1}^{T}(t^2+t)\frac{CF_t}{(1+r)^t} \qquad (2A.5)$$

and dividing both quantities by P, one gets:

$$\frac{P''(r_0)}{P} = \frac{1}{(1+r)^2} \sum_{t=1}^{T} (t^2 + t) \frac{CF_t/(1+r)^t}{P} \qquad (2A.6)$$

The right-hand side in equation (2A.6) is called *modified convexity* (MC)[6]. Plugging it back into equation (2A.4), we get:

$$\frac{\Delta P}{P(r_0)} \cong -DM \cdot \Delta r + MC \cdot \frac{(\Delta r)^2}{2} \qquad (2A.7)$$

Equation (2A.7) highlights two effects: the first, and largest, one depends on duration and is inversely related to the shift in market rates; the second (and less important) one is due to convexity and is always positive (regardless of the sign of the shift in rates).

Table 2A.1 reports the computations already shown in Table 2.8 in this chapter, plus some further results leading to the modified convexity of the bond.

Table 2A.1 Duration and convexity of a 4-year bullet bond with 6% coupon

Maturity (years) (1)	1	2	3	4	Total
Cash flow (2)	6	6	6	106	
Present value (3)	5.660	5.340	5.037	83.962	100.00
Present value/Price (4)	0.0566	0.0534	0.05037	0.83962	1.00
$(1) \times (4) = (5)$	0.0566	0.1068	0.1511	3.3585	
Duration $= (\sum (5))$					3.6730
$(t + t^2)$ (6)	2.00	6.00	12.00	20.00	
$(4) \times (6) = (7)$	0.1132	0.3204	0.6045	16.7924	
Convexity $(8) = \sum (7)$					17.8305
Modified convexity $((8)/(1+r)^2)$					15.8691

We can now use (2A.7) to estimate the impact of a 1% increase (from 6% to 7%) in market rates. This leads to a percentage change in the bond price of

$$\frac{\Delta P}{P(r_0)} \cong -3.673 \cdot 1\% + 15.8691 \cdot \frac{(1\%)^2}{2} \cong -3.39\%$$

---

[6] "Pure" convexity, C, can be obtained by multiplying MC by $(1+r)^2$, getting $C = \sum_{t=1}^{T} (t^2 + t) \frac{CF_t/(1+r)^t}{P}$.

which is virtually identical to the actual price change computed in §A.2. Conversely, if rates were to decrease to 5 %, equation (2A.7) would lead to the following price change

$$\frac{\Delta P}{P(r_0)} \cong +3.673 \cdot 1\% + 15.8691 \cdot \frac{(1\%)^2}{2} \cong +3.54\%$$

again, almost undistinguishable from the true price change seen in the previous paragraph.

Table 2A.2 shows actual and estimated price changes (computed both with and without convexity) for a wide range of market rates. Three interesting results emerge:

– as highlighted by Figure 2A.1, the error made by using duration alone increases with the shift in market rates;
– convexity always improves the precision of the approximated price change;

Table 2A.2 Actual and estimated price changes for a 4-year bullet bond with 6 % coupon

Market rate	Change in market rate	True value	Approximated values	
			Duration only (equation 2A.8)	Duration and convexity (equation 2A.7)
0 %	−6 %	€24,00	€20.79	€23.65
1 %	−5 %	€19.51	€17.33	€19.31
2 %	−4 %	€15.23	€13.86	€15.13
3 %	−3 %	€11.15	€10.40	€11.11
4 %	−2 %	€7.26	€6.93	€7.25
5 %	−1 %	€3.55	€3.47	€3.54
6 %	0 %	€0.00	€0.00	€0.00
7 %	1 %	– €3.39	– €3.47	– €3.39
8 %	2 %	– €6.62	– €6.93	– €6.61
9 %	3 %	– €9.72	– €10.40	– €9.68
10 %	4 %	– €12.68	– €13.86	– €12.59
11 %	5 %	– €15.51	– €17.33	– €15.34
12 %	6 %	– €18.22	– €20.79	– €17.93
13 %	7 %	– €20.82	– €24.26	– €20.37
14 %	8 %	– €23.31	– €27.72	– €22.64
15 %	9 %	– €25.69	– €31.19	– €24.76
16 %	10 %	– €27.98	– €34.65	– €26.72

– yet, even including convexity, estimated price changes slightly differ from actual ones, and the error increases with the shift in market rates.

The latter results follows from the fact that the degree of convexity of P(r) is not constant (like in 2A.7), but rather changes with r. By keeping convexity constant at a value of 17.83, we therefore make an error, which is more and more considerable as we move away from the point on the rate/price curve where convexity has been measured.

2A.4   CONVEXITY: PROPERTIES AND ECONOMIC MEANING

From a theoretical point of view, if duration indicates the slope of the price/rate relationship, convexity shows the change in that slope, that is, the bending of the price/return curve. Generally speaking, that curve is convex for all fixed rate coupon paying securities. The higher that convexity, the larger the error made by estimating price changes based on duration only.

   When rate movements consist of parallel shifts, like in our examples, a high convexity looks as a desirable feature: in fact (see again Figure 2A.1), when market rates decrease, a high convexity produces a sharper increase in the bond price. Conversely, when market rates go down, the decrease in price is less marked for bonds having a high convexity.

   While having discussed the geometric meaning of convexity, we still need to provide an economic interpretation for it. Financially speaking, convexity measures how dispersed individual cash flows are around the bond's duration. Zero-coupon bonds (having just one final cash-flow) therefore have a lower convexity than bullet bonds, where coupons are also present. Moreover, bonds with a longer time to maturity have, all other things being equal, a higher convexity (see Table 2A.3 for an example).

Table 2A.3 An example of factors affecting convexity

	Convexity and time-to-maturity		Convexity and coupon, for a given duration	
	Bond A	Bond B	Bond A	Bond C
Time to maturity (years)	6	18	6	5
Yield	8 %	8 %	8 %	8 %
Annual coupon	8 %	8 %	8 %	0 %
Duration (D)	5	10,12	5	5
Convexity	32.7	151.7	32.7	30

2A.5   CONVEXITY GAP

Using convexity, we can improve our estimate of a bank's sensitivity to market rates.

   In this chapter, we saw that the change in the market value of a bank's equity following from a parallel shift in market rates could be estimated as follows:

$$\Delta MV_B \cong -DG \cdot MV_A \cdot \Delta r$$

where DG is the duration gap.

Based on (2A.7), we are now in a position to improve this estimate, by including a convexity measure:

$$\Delta MV_B = -DG \cdot MV_A \cdot \Delta r + \frac{CG}{2} \cdot MV_A \cdot (\Delta r)^2 \qquad (2A.8)$$

where CG stands for "convexity gap", a function of the modified convexity of assets and liabilities[7] that can be computed as follows:

$$CG = MC_A - L \cdot MC_L \qquad (2A.9)$$

Based on (2A.8), a bank may calibrate the duration gap and the convexity gap to immunize its value from shifts in market rates. Note however that, like all the duration-based results presented in this chapter, (2A.8) does not hold when changes in market rates differ across maturities.

---

[7] Just like the (modified) duration, the (modified) convexity of a portfolio of assets/liabilities can be computed straightforwardly, simply as the average of the (modified) convexities of individual assets/liabilities, each one weighted by its market value.

3
Models Based on Cash-Flow Mapping

3.1 INTRODUCTION

One of the main limitations of the models for measuring and managing risk discussed in the previous chapter is that they assume a uniform change in interest rates with different maturities. In practice, rates on different maturities often vary to differing degrees (and as a result the yield curves show asymmetrical shifts). In such cases, the models analyzed previously can lead to estimation error and ill-defined management policies.

In this chapter we present a family of techniques based on cash-flow mapping which overcomes this limit by allowing for different interest rate changes for various maturities. Unlike the duration gap, based on *yield to maturity* and *yield curve*, cash-flow mapping models work on the basis of *zero-coupon* or *term-structure* rate curves. These schemes also make use of techniques to "map" the individual cash flows that make up a bank's assets and liabilities, associating each to a small number of nodes, or maturities, of the term structure.

After a brief discussion of the problems related to the models reviewed previously, this chapter investigates the common aims of various cash-flow mapping techniques. The focus then turns to two methodologies: one based on discrete intervals, and the other called clumping. A real life application of the first is presented: the interest risk monitoring system introduced in 1993 by the Basel Committee (a variation based on the concept of modified residual life). The second is explained in detail, and a numerical example is also given. J.P. Morgan's version of clumping, based on the so-called "price volatility" concept, is also briefly described. This approach was adopted in the well-known RiskMetrics model[1] and has therefore become very popular in the past few years.

3.2 THE OBJECTIVES OF CASH-FLOW MAPPING AND TERM STRUCTURE

As mentioned before, the duration gap model is limited by its basic premise: that uniform rate changes occur on different maturities. Reality is obviously different: if, for example, a bank's assets consist solely of two fixed-rate mortgages, which mature at 5 and 10 years respectively, the change in relative interest rates may differ (e.g. $+1\%$ and -0.6%). If we only use one value (e.g., an average change), this would not reflect the real situation. In fact, when two rate changes move in opposite directions not even the standardized version of the duration gap would be of much use.

Actually, Each of the two mortgages could be thought of as a set of cash flows with different maturities; in other words as a portfolio of *zero-coupon bonds*, each linked to a different market rate (which may vary to differing degrees). So, for example, if the 10-year mortgage was set up with quarterly payments, it could be treated like a set of 40 zero-coupon bonds with different maturities. Each of these cash-flows should be evaluated on the basis of its specific yield. Following this line of reasoning, assuming one standard

---
[1] For more information on RiskMetrics, see Part II.

change in the interest rate of the mortgage is like assuming that each of these 40 different rates undergoes the same change.

To compensate for this shortcoming and arrive at an estimate of the impact that different rate changes on various maturities would have on the market value of a bank's equity, we need two things:

√ a yield curve that allows us to match a specific interest rate to each cash flow that makes up an asset or liability;
√ a method that enables us to identify a limited number of maturities at which the individual cash flows can be mapped to and for which different rate changes can be estimated.

A solution to the first point is to build a *term structure* or *zero-coupon rate curve*, based on yields related to financial instruments that have no intermediate cash flows prior to maturity, i.e. zero-coupon bonds. With a bond's market price as a starting point, this curve can be estimated by using various techniques. One of the most common is "bootstrapping" which begins with market prices for short-term bonds and, through an iterative process, extrapolates zero-coupon rates for longer maturities.

The second point can be briefly addressed as follows. Let's go back to the 10-year mortgage made up of 40 zero-coupon cash flows: if we drew up a zero-coupon rate curve, we could then match each of these cash flows with a specific maturity on the curve and therefore with a specific rate. However, this would involve estimating and monitoring 40 different points on the curve. If we did so with all the bank's assets and liabilities, we would likely end up with thousands of cash flows, related to hundreds of different maturities and rates on the zero-coupon curve.

Hence, if we wanted to estimate the impact of a rate change on the market value of a bank's equity, we would have to monitor rates associated with each and every maturity and to calculate hundreds of different changes in zero-coupon yields. Clearly, starting with a simplified solution like the duration gap model based on a single standard rate change for various maturities, we would end up at the opposite extreme, with far too many rate changes. This would make interest rate risk extremely complicated to measure and effectively impossible to manage.

A compromise between these two extremes must therefore be found, which is why cash-flow mapping techniques were introduced. The best known of such techniques are based on the use of discrete intervals (described in Section 3.4, which also presents the so-called "modified residual life" method) as well as on a methodology called clumping (covered in Section 3.5). Both serve to channel all cash flows, which actually correspond to a number of dates (p) too high to ensure reliable monitoring, into a number of standard dates ($q < p$), which we call "nodes" or "vertices" of the curve.

Before detailing the techniques mentioned above, we briefly discuss how to choose the q nodes of the term structure where the bank's actual cash flows are mapped.

3.3   CHOOSING THE VERTICES OF THE TERM STRUCTURE

To estimate the number and position of the vertices on the zero-coupon curve that a bank would use for risk management, three key factors must be taken into consideration:

(a) Changes in short-term interest rates are usually greater and more frequent than changes in long-term rates.
(b) Consequently, volatility in interest rates usually decreases as maturities increase. Volatility also gravitates toward a constant level due to the effect of the *mean reversion phenomenon*.[2]
(c) A bank's cash flows are more concentrated in the short term.

All this means we would be well advised to have more nodes in the short term and make sure that no single node absorbs an excessive amount of cash flows.

Moreover, nodes should be selected with an eye to the feasibility of implementing hedging policies, in particular in futures markets. The fact that bond futures are usually available for a fixed set of maturities, such as 5, 10, and 30 years, suggests that nodes should be chosen which coincide with these maturities.[3]

Furthermore, banks should be flexible when selecting vertices, taking into account the characteristics of national markets. On the UK market we find a number of exchange-listed bonds with maturities ranging up to 30 years with only a few gaps; in Germany and Italy, on the other hand, 10-year maturities are most common on bond issues, with a few 30-year exceptions. In the US, instead, despite the very large number of bonds traded in the market, there is a wide gap from 9 to 17 years where traditional bonds are rare or nonexistent.[4]

3.4 TECHNIQUES BASED ON DISCRETE INTERVALS

3.4.1 The duration intervals method

A first, and quite intuitive, way to streamline a bank's portfolio into a small number of nodes would be based on the residual life of each position. Assets/liabilities with comparable maturities could be grouped together in discrete intervals, and the midpoint value for every interval would then become a node in the bank's term structure. Yet this approach disregards the fact that the degree of risk in a fixed-rate asset/liability does not depend exclusively on its residual life, but also on the number and weight of any intermediate cash flows.

In fact, in Chapter 2 we saw that to gauge a position's vulnerability to interest rate risk, the most accurate method to use is modified duration. So, assets and liabilities should be grouped in discrete intervals according to this measure. For instance, all assets/liabilities with a modified duration between 0 and 6 months can be mapped together to the term structure node associated with a three-month maturity; those falling between 6 and 18 months are matched with a one-year maturity peak and so on. Of course, this is an approximation (as a 5-month position and one with a few weeks of residual life are treated in the same way). However, as such it is consistent with the aim, shared by all cash-flow mapping techniques, to simplify the term structure of a bank's assets and liabilities.

---

[2] The *mean reversion* phenomenon refers to the fact that when there are high interest rates, downward changes are more likely than upward changes, and vice versa – when rates are low the direction of change is more likely to be up than down.

[3] The solutions adopted in practice are often very different. For example, the *RiskMetrics*™ method provides for 15 nodes, where Barra recommends 7 vertices.

[4] Here, instead, we find *callable bonds*, which the issuer can withdraw from the market before they mature.

The problem with this kind of approach is that while residual life is recorded and saved in the bank's files, the duration of individual positions might not be. This is all the more true for traditional customer services, operations which normally are not subject to mark-to-market.

3.4.2 The modified residual life method

We can use intervals based on residual life without neglecting the effect of intermediate cash flows by adopting the modified residual life method, which is actually used by the Basel Committee on Banking Supervision (see Section 3.4.3).

Figure 3.1 shows the relationship between residual life and modified duration of bonds with different coupons. Lower coupons give us an almost straight line; the higher the coupon the more pronounced the curve.

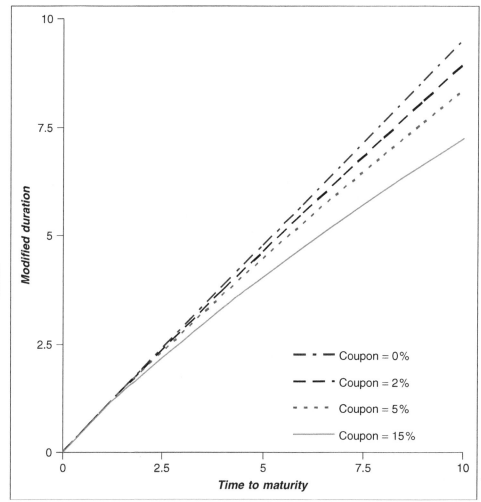

Figure 3.1 Relationship between residual life and modified duration for different coupon levels

Now, for simplicity's sake, let's look at just two of these curves: the first plots the relationship between residual life and modified duration of a fairly low coupon (Figure 3.2, left-hand panel); the second illustrates the case with a higher coupon (right hand panel). On the vertical axis of both figures, let's chart a set of intervals in terms of modified duration (e.g. 0–1 year, 1–2 years, 2–4 years, and so on). The midpoint values of these intervals (e.g. 6 months, 18 months, 3 years) will be the q nodes of the bank's zero-coupon curve.

By using the two curves, we can transform these classes of modified duration into an identical number of intervals plotted on the horizontal axes, i.e. with respect to residual life. Note that the x-axis is segmented differently in the two figures because different coupons alter the relationship between modified duration and residual life.

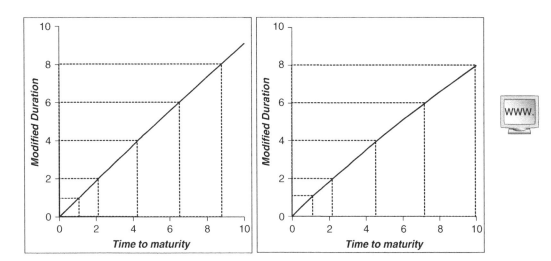

Figure 3.2   Modified duration intervals derived from residual life for a low coupon (left panel) and high coupon (right panel) bond

The graphs in Figure 3.2 enable us to sort a bank's positions, according to duration, using only information on life to maturity and coupon. For example, an asset with a residual life of 9 years and 3 months and a low coupon (left-hand panel) will fall in the 8–10 year modified duration bracket (so we'll use the term structure node that corresponds to a 9–year duration). If the same asset had a higher coupon, by convention it would be mapped to the 6–8 year duration bracket (which is associated with the term-structure node with a 7-year maturity). The criteria used to gather exposures into a finite number of nodes, therefore, are the positions' residual life and the presence of a high or low coupon. This is why this method is usually referred to as the "modified residual life".

3.4.3   The Basel Committee Method

The technique illustrated in the previous section (duration intervals based on modified residual life) was adopted by the Basel Committee for Banking Supervision in January 1996.

The method defined by the Committee (introduced when bank capital requirements were extended to market risk[5]) calls on banks to calculate an indicator that synthesizes their interest rate risk. The aim is to single out banks with "excessive" exposure, as compared to the industry average. To build such an indicator, each bank divides up its assets, liabilities and off-balance sheet items in 13 different maturity brackets (see Table 3.1). Maturities (or renegotiation dates) are taken into account along with high coupons, when applicable. The cash-flow mapping of positions on the 13 nodes of the term structure is done according to modified residual life. Note, for example, that items with high coupons and 5- to 7-year residual lives are grouped together with positions with low (or no) coupons and residual lives of 4.3 to 5.7 years (in both cases, in fact, we assume a modified duration of 4.65 years).

Table 3.1 Factors for calculating the Basel Committee Indicator

Residual Life Bracket (i)		Average modified duration (MD_i)	Change in Yield (Δr_i)	Risk Coefficient $(MD_i \cdot \Delta r_i)$
Coupon < 3%	Coupon ≥ 3%			
Up to 1 month	Up to 1 month	0.00	1.00%	0.00%
1–3 months	1–3 months	0.20	1.00%	0.20%
3–6 months	3–6 months	0.40	1.00%	0.40%
6–12 months	6–12 months	0.70	1.00%	0.70%
1.0–1.9 years	1–2 years	1.40	0.90%	1.25%
1.9–2.8 years	2–3 years	2.20	0.80%	1.75%
2.8–3.6 years	3–4 years	3.00	0.75%	2.25%
3.6–4.3 years	4–5 years	3.65	0.75%	2.75%
4.3–5.7 years	5–7 years	4.65	0.70%	3.25%
5.7–73 years	7–10 years	5.80	0.65%	3.75%
7.3–9.3 years	10–15 years	7.50	0.60%	4.50%
9.3–10.6 years	15–20 years	8.75	0.60%	5.25%
10.6–12 years	Over 20 years	10.00	0.60%	6.00%
12–20 years	–	13.50	0.60%	8.00%
Over 20 years	–	21.00	0.60%	12.50%

Now, it is interesting to see how the Committee's method provides us with a quick and dirty way to calculate an index that synthesizes risk after linking all the bank's positions to a small number of nodes. Once again, as illustrated in Table 3.1, the net position of

---

[5] See Chapter 19.

every i^{th} bracket (NP_i) is weighted on the basis of the average modified duration of the relative interval (MD_i) and for a possible rate change Δr_i (note that this change is less pronounced for medium to long term maturities, acknowledging that in empirical terms rates associated with longer maturities are less volatile[6]). The result is a simplified estimate of possible changes in the net value of assets and liabilities slotted into each interval, calculated along the lines of formulae (2.11) and (2.12) in Chapter 2:

$$\Delta NP_i \cong -NP_i \cdot MD_i \cdot \Delta r_i \qquad (3.1)$$

using the book value of the net position (NP_i) instead of its market value.[7]

Clearly, whether changes in value estimated on various intervals are positive or negative depends on the sign of the net position: if it is positive (negative) an increase in rates will bring about a loss (profit) and vice versa.

The Committee's methodology does not allow banks to fully offset positive and negative ΔNP_i (implementing a system of brackets and zones like the one used to measure the generic risk of debt instruments[8]). In other words, after making a few minimal compensations, the different ΔNP_is have to be added together in absolute terms to come up with an estimate of possible losses across the entire balance sheet of the bank. The intent of the Committee in prohibiting a perfect offset between long and short positions is to acknowledge the fact that shifts in the terms structure don't always occur symmetrically (which is the underlying theme of this chapter). In fact, an increase in short-term rates may coincide with a drop in long-term rates. More generally, non-parallel shifts of the term structure may occur.

Note that this ability to allow for different changes (and volatilities) in rates of different maturities is possible through the use of cash-flow mapping, which allows us to group together all the bank's assets and liabilities in a collection of nodes on the rate curve.

Note too that the methodology reviewed in this section was introduced mainly for regulatory purposes (rather than for internal management): the estimate of the bank's potential losses (in domestic and foreign currency) obtained by summing the absolute ΔNP_i (with limited compensations) is compared to the amount of regulatory capital of the bank, and the ratio between the two can be used as an indicator of capital adequacy against interest rate risk.

The approach outlined in this section brings up various methodological problems, clearly acknowledged by the Committee itself. The most important are listed below:

√ the fact that the calculation is based on the book value (as opposed to the market value, which would be more accurate) of assets and liabilities;

√ the presence of instruments which, due to their amortization schedule, are not paid off at a single maturity date (making the relationship between duration and residual life very different from that implied in Table 3.1);

√ the presence of instruments without a fixed renegotiation date, such as loans indexed to the prime rate or deposits pegged to the official repo rate;

---

[6] See Section 3.3

[7] In measuring interest risk exposure, therefore, the Basel Committee favoured an indicator based on modified duration of assets and liabilities. In other words, this involves an approach aimed at evaluating the impact of changes in interest rates on a bank's equity (duration gap) rather than net interest income (repricing gap).

[8] See Chapter 19.

√ the presence of instruments without a fixed maturity (on-demand deposits, prepayable mortgage loans, fixed assets, equity, etc.);
√ the lack of adequate methods for including derivatives used by banks as hedging tools;
√ the somewhat arbitrary choice of compensation limits between net positions corresponding to different maturity brackets, i.e. on different segments of the yield curve;
√ the decision to allow compensation between positions associated with different currencies (that is, with different yield curves where fluctuations are not perfectly correlated).

To address these problems, the Basel Committee simply sketched out some possible solutions, leaving bank supervisors in individual countries ample leeway in adopting definitive solutions. This decision was prompted on one hand by the fact that the risk indicator serves as a simple monitoring mechanism which provides for no explicit capital requirement, and on the other by the inevitable disparity in contract profiles (hence risk) of instruments negotiated in different countries.

3.5 CLUMPING

3.5.1 Structure of the methodology

Clumping, also known as cash bucketing, "translates" actual cash flows of an asset/liability into a set of virtual or conventional cash flows linked to maturities that coincide with one or more nodes on the term structure. More specifically, unless it matures exactly where a node on the curve is, every real cash flow is broken down into two virtual cash flows with maturities that correspond to the vertex before and the one after the real maturity.

In creating these virtual cash flows, one has to leave the characteristics of the individual original assets/liabilities basically unchanged; the same must be true when the bank's overall portfolio of assets and liabilities is dealt with.

Namely, when a real cash flow with maturity t is broken down into two virtual flows with maturities fixed within preset vertices, n and $n+1$ (with $n < t < n+1$), the new cash flows must guarantee:

(a) identical market values – the sum of market values of the two virtual cash flows has to equal the market value of the real cash flow;
(b) identical risk (expressed in terms of modified duration[9]) – the weighted average risk of the two virtual cash flows has to be equal to the risk of the real cash flow.

In analytical terms:

$$\begin{cases} MV_t = \dfrac{FV_t}{(1+r_t)^t} = MV_n + MV_{n+1} = \dfrac{FV_n}{(1+r_n)^n} + \dfrac{FV_{n+1}}{(1+r_{n+1})^{n+1}} \\ MD_t = MD_n \dfrac{MV_n}{MV_n + MV_{n+1}} + MD_{n+1} \dfrac{MV_{n+1}}{MV_n + MV_{n+1}} \\ \quad = MD_n \dfrac{MV_n}{MV_t} + MD_{n+1} \dfrac{VV_{n+1}}{MV_t} \end{cases} \quad (3.2)$$

[9] The methodology described here is based on the modified duration criterion (MD) as a measure of interest rate risk. The price volatility method, instead, is based on the equivalence of the volatility in the market value of the cash flows. This second method is discussed in Section 3.5.3.

where

✓ r_i is the zero coupon rate of maturity i (with $i = t, n$ or $n+1$);
✓ MV_i is the market value of the cash flow that matures at i;
✓ FV_i is the face value of the cash flow that matures at i;
✓ MD_i is the modified duration of the cash flow that matures at i.

The first condition allows us to keep the real value of the portfolio constant, even after having changed the maturities. The second ensures that the change in market value of the two virtual cash flows, in the event of a given change in the zero-coupon rates at the different maturities (t, n, and $n+1$), will be equivalent to that experienced by the real cash flow. The market values that satisfy both conditions and solve system (3.2) are:

$$\begin{cases} MV_n = MV_t \dfrac{(MD_t - MD_{n+1})}{(MD_n - MD_{n+1})} \\[4mm] MV_{n+1} = MV_t \dfrac{(MD_n - MD_t)}{(MD_n - MD_{n+1})} \end{cases} \qquad (3.3)$$

As a result, face values of the virtual cash flows are:

$$\begin{cases} FV_n = MV_t \dfrac{(MD_t - MD_{n+1})}{(MD_n - MD_{n+1})}(1 + r_{n+1})^n = FV_t \dfrac{(MD_t - MD_{n+1})}{(MD_n - MD_{n+1})} \dfrac{(1 + r_{n+1})^n}{(1 + r_t)^t} \\[4mm] FV_{n+1} = MV_t \dfrac{(MD_n - MD_t)}{(MD_n - MD_{n+1})}(1 + r_n)^{n+1} = FV_t \dfrac{(MD_n - MD_t)}{(MD_n - MD_{n+1})} \dfrac{(1 + r_n)^{n+1}}{(1 + r_t)^t} \end{cases}$$
$$(3.4)$$

3.5.2   An example

Now, let's assume we want to map a real cash flow with a face value of 50,000 euros which matures at 3 years and 3 months: in other words, we have to allocate it to the two nearest adjacent nodes on the interest rate curve. First, we need to know the term structure adopted by the bank, that is, the maturities the bank has chosen to include into its zero-coupon rate curve. These maturities, along with relative rates, are listed in Table 3.2.

The zero-coupon rate associated with the 3.25 years maturity is not listed in the table. However, by using linear interpolation of the 3-year and 4-year rates, it turns out to be 3.55 %.[10]

In order to use system (3.3) and break down the 3.25-year cash flow into two virtual cash flows with maturities at 3 and 4 years respectively, we first calculate the market value and modified duration of the real cash flow:

$$MV_t = \frac{FV_t}{(1 + r_t)^t} = \frac{50,000}{(1.0355)^{3.25}} = 44,640.82$$

$$MD_t = \frac{D_t}{(1 + r_t)} = \frac{3.25}{(1.0355)} = 3.139$$

---

[10] Analytically: $r_{3.25} = r_3 + (r_4 - r_3)\dfrac{(3.25 - 3)}{(4 - 3)} = 3.5\% + (3.7\% - 3.5\%)\dfrac{0.25}{1} = 3.55\%$

Table 3.2 Nodes of the zero-coupon curve

Maturity (years)	Zero-coupon rate
1 month	2.80 %
2 months	2.85 %
3 months	2.90 %
6 months	3.00 %
9 months	3.10 %
12 months	3.15 %
18 months	3.25 %
2 years	3.35 %
3 years	3.50 %
4 years	3.70 %
5 years	3.80 %
7 years	3.90 %
10 years	4.00 %
15 years	4.10 %
30 years	4.25 %

Next, we find the modified duration of the two virtual cash flows with maturities in the two adjacent nodes on the curve, 3 and 4 years:

$$MD_n = \frac{D_n}{(1 + r_n)} = \frac{3}{(1.035)} = 2.899$$

$$MD_{n+1} = \frac{D_{n+1}}{(1 + r_{n+1})} = \frac{4}{(1.037)} = 3.857$$

Now we have all the data we need to calculate the market value of two virtual cash flows using system (3.3):

$$\begin{cases} MV_n = 44,640.82 \cdot \dfrac{(3.139 - 3.857)}{(2.899 - 3.857)} = 33,464.45 \\ MV_{n+1} = 44,640.82 \cdot \dfrac{(2.899 - 3.139)}{(2.899 - 3.857)} = 11,176.37 \end{cases}$$

Note that the sum of the market values of the two virtual cash flows exactly match the market value of the real cash flow (condition (a) from the previous section). Moreover, the market value of the cash flow on the 3-year maturity node is greater than the one on the 4-year node. Since the maturity of the real cash flow is closer to the first virtual cash flow than the second, this result is fully consistent with condition (b) from the previous section (the weighted average modified duration of the two virtual cash flows must be equal to the modified duration of the real cash flow.)

Finally, on the basis of market values, we can come up with the face values of the two virtual cash flows:

$$\begin{cases} FV_3 = MV_3 \cdot (1 + 3.5\,\%)^3 = 37,102.63 \\ FV_4 = MV_4 \cdot (1 + 3.7\,\%)^4 = 12,924.56 \end{cases}$$

Another option would have been to use system (3.4) directly:

$$\begin{cases} FV_3 = FV_{3.25} \dfrac{(MD_{3.25} - MD_4)}{(MD_3 - MD_4)} \dfrac{(1+r_3)^3}{(1+r_{3.25})^{3.25}} \\ FV_4 = FV_t \dfrac{(MD_3 - MD_{3.25})}{(MD_3 - MD_4)} \dfrac{(1+r_4)^4}{(1+r_{3.25})^{3.25}} \end{cases}$$

obtaining the same results.

Table 3.3 summarizes the initial data and the results of the various calculations we have made. The data in bold are all we need to know to begin with.

Table 3.3 The clumping model – example of mapping

	T	VN	VM	R	D	DM
Real flow	**3.25**	**50,000.00**	44,640.82	**3.55 %**	**3.25**	3.139
Virtual 3-year flow	**3.00**	37,102.63	33,464.45	**3.50 %**	3	2.899
Virtual 4-year flow	**4.00**	12,924.56	11,176.37	**3.70 %**	4	3.857

3.5.3 Clumping on the basis of price volatility

Another form of clumping, a variation of the method based on identical modified duration, centres on the equivalence between price volatility of the initial flow and the total price volatility of the two new virtual positions. This is calculated by taking into account also the correlations existing between volatilities associated with price changes for different maturities[11].

$$\sigma_t^2 = \alpha^2 \sigma_n^2 + (1-\alpha)^2 \sigma_{n+1}^2 + 2 \cdot \alpha(1-\alpha)\sigma_n \sigma_{n+1} \rho_{n,n+1} \qquad (3.5)$$

where:

---

[11] This alternative method is consistent with the underlying logic of VaR models, which are discussed later in this book. In fact, the price volatility technique has been adopted by the authors of the most renowned VaR model for market risk: RiskMetrics™. This variation aims at addressing the fact that "standard" clumping (as presented in Section 5.2) treats as equally risky (only because they have the same modified duration) a position centered on just one maturity (the original cash flow) and a portfolio spread over two maturities (the two virtual cash flows). For further information, see J.P. Morgan (1996). The price volatility criterion outlined in the text has recently been refined by its authors (cf. Mina & Xiao, 2001)

- α indicates the relationship between the market value of the cash flow associated with maturity n and the market value of the original cash flow (VM_n/VM_t);
- σ_t, σ_n and σ_{n+1} represent the volatility of price changes in zero-coupon bonds maturing at time t, n and $n+1$;
- $\rho_{n,n+1}$ stands for the correlation coefficient between price changes of zero-coupon bonds with maturity n and $n+1$.

Since this is a quadratic equation, we get two solutions for α. This means that in order to break down the original cash flow, we need to assume that the original position and the two new virtual positions have the same sign (that is, we must set the condition that $0 \leq \alpha \leq 1$).

3.6   CONCLUDING COMMENTS

This chapter has addressed cash-flow mapping techniques. Specifically, after presenting the purpose of these techniques and providing certain criteria for choosing nodes on the term structure, we examined two methodologies: those based on discrete intervals (with special attention to the criterion of modified residual life, used in the Basel Committee's indicator for interest rate risk) and those based on clumping.

Clumping gives more precise results, but requires an in-depth knowledge of all cash flows that make up an asset or liability. Instead, with the residual life criterion (adjusted for a high coupon, when applicable) we only need to know the final maturity of each position and the type of coupon associated with it. This, too, explains why, while clumping is usually applied to a small portion of the balance sheet (e.g. a bond portfolio held for trading purposes), techniques based on discrete intervals are often adopted when we want to arrive at a rough estimation of interest rate risk for the entire bank.

Though each of these methodologies involve varying degrees of complexity, both allow us to associate cash flows expected by a bank on its assets and liabilities (normally linked to a very high number p of future maturities) to a set of $q < p$ nodes on the zero-coupon rate curve.

Once this is done we can:

√ estimate the effects on a bank's mark-to-market balance sheet of different rate changes associated with various maturities;

√ establish policies for managing interest rate risk with the aim of exploiting forecasted rate changes at different maturities;

√ implement hedging policies to immunize the bank's mark-to-market balance sheet against changes in market rates.

We can also grasp the usefulness of cash-flow mapping by considering the fact that the nodes on the curve to which real positions are mapped generally coincide with standard maturities for which hedging instruments are available, such as forward rate agreements (FRA), interest rate swaps (IRS) and futures. Accordingly, once a bank's portfolio has been translated into a small number of virtual positions corresponding to the nodes of the curve, the above-mentioned derivatives can be used to develop policies for hedging and interest risk management in general.

SELECTED QUESTIONS AND EXERCISES

1. A bank holds a zero-coupon T-Bill with a time to maturity of 22 months and a face value of one million euros. The bank wants to map this position to two given nodes in its zero-rate curve, with a maturity of 18 and 24 months, respectively. The zero coupon returns associated with those two maturities are 4.2 % and 4.5 %. Find the face values of the two virtual cash flows associated with the two nodes, based on a clumping technique that leaves both the market value and the modified duration of the portfolio unchanged.

2. Cash flow bucketing (clumping) for a bond involves ...

   (A) ... each individual bond cash flow gets transformed into an equivalent cash flow with a maturity equal to that of one of the knots.
   (B) ... the different bond cash flows get converted into one unique cash flow.
   (C) ... only those cash flows with maturities equal to the ones of the curve knots are kept while the ones with different maturity get eliminated through compensation ("cash-flow netting").
   (D) ... each individual bond cash flow gets transformed into one or more equivalent cash flows which are associated to one or more knots of the term structure.

3. Which of the following are likely to be bound together according to a cash-flow mapping method based on modified residual life, like the one used by the Basel Committee?

   (A) Zero-coupon bonds with residual life between 6 and 8 years and bullet bonds with a residual life between 7 and 9.5 years;
   (B) All bonds having an annualized coupon 3 % and below;
   (C) Zero-coupon bonds with residual life between 7 and 9.5 years and bullet bonds with a residual life between 6 and 8 years;
   (D) All bonds having an annualized coupon of more the 3 %.

4. Bank X adopts a zero-coupon rate curve (term structure) with nodes at one month, three months, six months, one year, two years. The bank holds a security paying a coupon of 6 million euros in eight months and another cash flow (coupon plus principal) of 106 million euros in one year and eight months.

   Using a clumping technique based on the correspondence between present values and modified durations, and assuming that the present term structure is flat at 5 % for all maturities between one month and two years, indicate what flows the bank must assign to the three-month, six-month, one-year and two-year nodes.

5. Based on the following market prices and using the bootstrapping method, compute the yearly-compounded zero-coupon rate for a maturity of 2.5 years.

Prices of Treasury Bonds

Security	Maturity	Price
6-month T-bill, zero coupon	0.5	98
12-month T-bill, zero coupon	1	96
18-month T-bill, zero coupon	1.5	94
24-month T-bill, zero coupon	2	92
30-month T-bond with a 2 % coupon every 6 months	2.5	99

Appendix 3A
Estimating the Zero-Coupon Curve

The simplest way of describing the term structure of interest rates is the *zero-coupon curve*. This curve shows, for different maturities, the rates of return offered by zero-coupon investments paying no intermediate cash flows.

However, listed zero coupon bonds are unlikely to span the whole maturity spectrum for which the curve must be estimated. For medium-to-long maturities, the market may rather offer "bullet" bonds, like US Treasury notes and Treasury bonds, paying coupons before their final maturity.

There are several approaches to the problem of estimating a zero-coupon curve based on the prices of coupon-bearing securities. In this Appendix we present the *bootstrapping* method, a simple and widely-used approach.

Bootstrapping extracts zero-coupon rates from the prices of coupon-bearing bonds *after accounting for the value of intermediate payments*. To see how, consider the following example.

The market for Government bonds is quoting two zero-coupon bonds: a 6-month T-bill traded at 98 cents a euro, and a 12-month T-bill traded at 96 cents. Also, quotes are available for a Treasury note with life to maturity of 18 months, paying two bi-annual coupons of 1% each, and for a Treasury note maturing in 2 years, also paying 1%, bi-annual coupons. These data are summarised in Table 3A.1.

Table 3A.1 Examples of listed bonds and their prices

Maturity (t, years)	Type of security	Price per 100 euros of face value	Bi-annual coupon (euros)
0.5	Treasury bill	98.00	0
1	Treasury bill	96.00	0
1.5	Treasury note	95.70	1
2	Treasury note	94.30	1

Based on these data, we can compute zero coupon rates for all four maturities. As far as T-bills are concerned, we simply get the (annually compound) rates as:

$$r_t = \left(\frac{100}{P}\right)^{\frac{1}{t}} - 1 \qquad (3A.1)$$

which leads to a 6-month rate of

$$r_{0.5} = \left(\frac{100}{98}\right)^{\frac{1}{0,5}} - 1 \cong 4.12\%$$

and to a one-year rate of

$$r_1 = \left(\frac{100}{96}\right)^1 - 1 \cong 4.17\%$$

Let us now turn to the Treasury note maturing in 18 months. It will pay three cash flows, as indicated in Table 3A.2. As far as the first two are concerned, we can compute their present value using $r_{0.5}$ and r_1: the results (0.98 and 0.96 euros, respectively) are shown in the Table. We also know that the present value assigned by the market to all three cash flows paid by this bond is 95.7 euros, since this is the price of the bond as a whole. We can therefore compute, as a difference, the price assigned by the market to the third cash flow alone, that is:

$$95.70 - 0.98 - 0.96 \cong 93.76$$

Table 3A.2 Cash-flows associated with the T-note maturing in 18 months

Time	Cash flows	Zero-coupon rate	Discounted cash flow
0.5	1	4.12%	0.98
1	1	4.17%	0.96
1.5	101	**4.39%**	93.76
Total			95.70

Plugging this price as P into (A.1), we get the 18-month zero-coupon rate:

$$r_{1.5} = \left(\frac{100}{93.76}\right)^{1.5} - 1 \cong 4.39\%$$

The same procedure can be repeated for the last bond (see Table 3A.3). Again, we first use $r_{0.5}$, r_1 and the newly-found $r_{1.5}$ to compute the present value of the intermediate payments. Those values (0.98, 0.96 and 0.9376 euros) are then deducted from the market

Table 3A.3 Cash-flows associated with the T-note maturing in 24 months

Time	Cash flows	Zero-coupon rate	Discounted cash flow
0.5	1	4.12%	0.98
1	1	4.17%	0.96
1.5	1	4.39%	0.94
2	101	**4.59%**	91.42
Total			94.30

price of the bond (94.3 euros), to find the present value (91.4224 euros) of the final payment. Substituting this value for P in (3A.1), we get

$$r_2 = \left(\frac{100}{91.4224}\right)^2 - 1 \cong 4.59\,\%$$

Figure 3A.1 shows our zero-coupon curve; by considering more bond prices, it could easily be extended to longer maturities. Note that the zero coupon rates extracted from bullet bonds are *not* their yields to maturity[12]. In fact, while yields to maturity account for the value of all flows paid by an investment, zero coupon rates only consider the value of the last cash flow, once the market value of intermediate coupons has been stripped away.

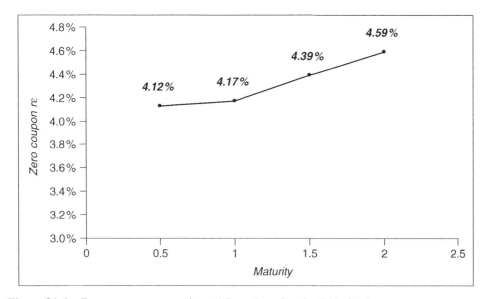

Figure 3A.1   Zero coupon curve estimated from the prices in Table 3A.1

Let us now turn to a more complex and realistic example, where a zero coupon curve will be estimated based on interbank rates like those in Table 3A.4.

The Table reports bid rates, ask rates and their averages for a number of different maturities. In the following, we will focus on the average rates (last column) to derive the associated zero-coupon curve.

The data in the Table refer to either interbank deposits or interest rate swaps. These are investments paying annual coupons at the rates shown in the Table; because of these periodic payments, the rates in the Table are not zero-coupon rates. Such rates have to be worked out based on the procedure seen above.

The one-year rate (3.49 %) is given in the Table. The two-year rate is derived by imposing that:

$$100 = \frac{3.66}{(1 + 3.49\,\%)} + \frac{103.66}{(1 + r_2)^2}.$$

---

[12] For example, the yield to maturity of the 2-year Treasury note can be shown to be about 5.09 % (in fact, by discounting *all* future cash flows paid by the bond at a rate of 5.09 % we get the bond's market price, that is 94.3). This is different from the zero-coupon rate r_2 (4.59 %).

Table 3A.4 Rates on interbank deposits (1 year) and interest rate swaps (longer maturities)

Years	Bid	Ask	Average
1	3.44 %	3.54 %	3.49 %
2	3.63 %	3.68 %	3.66 %
3	3.73 %	3.78 %	3.76 %
4	3.81 %	3.86 %	3.84 %
5	3.90 %	3.95 %	3.93 %
6	3.97 %	4.02 %	4.00 %
7	4.04 %	4.09 %	4.07 %
8	4.09 %	4.14 %	4.12 %
9	4.14 %	4.19 %	4.17 %
10	4.19 %	4.24 %	4.22 %

If by v_t we indicate the present value of one euro paid at the end of the t-th year (that is, the t-year discount factor), the equation can be rewritten as follows:

$$100 = 3.66v_1 + 103.66v_2$$

From $r_1 = 3,49$ follows that $v_1 = (1+3,49)^{-1} \cong 0.966$. Hence:

$$v_2 = \frac{100 - 0.966 \cdot 3.66}{103.66} \cong 0.9306$$

and

$$r_2 = \sqrt{\frac{1}{v_2} - 1} \cong 3.658\,\%.$$

We can now compute the 3-year zero-coupon rate, based on the following equation:

$$100 = \frac{3.76}{(1 + 3.49\,\%)} + \frac{3.76}{(1 + 3.66\,\%)^2} + \frac{103.76}{(1 + r_3)^3}$$

that is:

$$100 = 3.76v_1 + 3.76v_2 + 103.76v_3$$

Solving for v_3 gets

$$v_3 = \frac{100 - 0.966 \cdot 3.76 - 0.9306 \cdot 3.76}{103.76} = 0.895$$

and

$$r_3 = \sqrt[3]{\frac{1}{v_3}} - 1 \cong 3.76\,\%.$$

Repeating these computations for all remaining maturities, the whole zero-coupon curve can be derived (see Table 3A.5 and Figure 3A.2). More precisely, each discount factor v_t

Table 3A.5 Yield curve and zero-coupon curve

years	Yield curve	zero-coupon curve
1	3.49 %	3.49 %
2	3.66 %	3.66 %
3	3.76 %	3.76 %
4	3.84 %	3.84 %
5	3.93 %	3.94 %
6	4.00 %	4.02 %
7	4.07 %	4.09 %
8	4.12 %	4.15 %
9	4.17 %	4.21 %
10	4.22 %	4.27 %

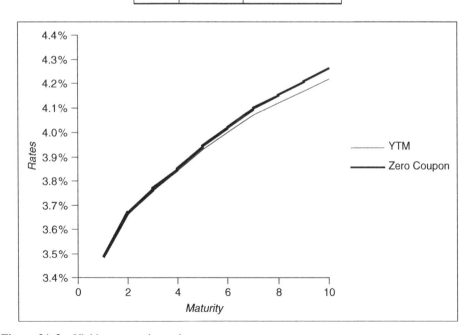

Figure 3A.2 Yields to maturity and zero-coupon rates

associated with the zero-coupon rate r_t can be found as:

$$v_t = \frac{1 - \left[y_t \sum_{i=1}^{t-1} v_i \right]}{1 + y_t} \tag{3A.2}$$

where y_t is the rate on a t-year swap, as shown in Table 3A.4:

Generally speaking, when the yield curve is sloped upwards, the zero-coupon curve lies above it (just like the forward rate curve does with spot rates, see Appendix 1B). If the former is flat, the latter will also be flat and the two curves will be the same. Figure 3A.3 shows three different possible configurations for the yield curve and the zero-coupon curve.

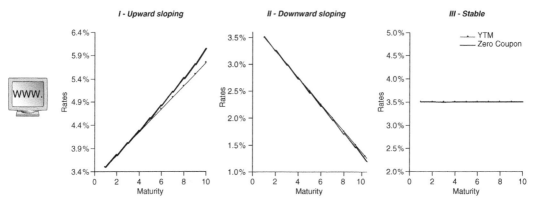

Figure 3A.3   Different configurations for the Yield Curve and the Zero-Coupon Curve

4

Internal Transfer Rates

4.1 INTRODUCTION

A proper interest rate risk (i.e, gap risk) management system requires banks to set up a system of internal interest transfer rates (ITR). This comprises a series of virtual trans-actions within the bank in order to centralize all the decisions on the bank's exposures to changes in market rates. Such changes include parallel shifts of the zero-coupon rate curve as well as changes in the relative level of rates for different maturities (changes in the slope of the curve also known as twists).

In greater detail, the main aims of an ITR system are:

√ to transfer interest rate risk from the various units of the bank that generate it (for instance, branches that accept deposits and grant loans) to a central unit. This would normally be the treasury Department (referred to as treasury throughout this chapter), which can correctly evaluate and manage this risk and, when necessary, apply hedging policies;

√ to evaluate the actual profitability of this activity by assigning interest rate risk man-agement to a single centralized unit;

√ to relieve the various operating units from the need to care about the funding of their loans (or, conversely, the investment of deposits raised from customers);

√ to provide a more accurate assessment of the contribution each operating unit gives to the bank's overall profitability.

After showing briefly – by means of a simplified example – how an ITR system can achieve the above aims, this chapter outlines the main problems associated with intro-ducing these systems. Specifically, we first focus on the difference between a single ITR and a multiple ITRs system (highlighting how this alternative involves the choice between systems based on gross or net flows). Examples are then given of how ITRs are established for major lending transactions, with a special emphasis on loans issued at non-market rates (i.e., rates fixed by some industry association or supervisory authority) and on lending transactions involving embedded options. The chapter ends with a review of the ideal features for an ITR system.

4.2 BUILDING AN ITR SYSTEM: A SIMPLIFIED EXAMPLE

Let's take the case of a bank branch that has issued a 1-year certificate of deposit at a rate of 3% for one million euros, and has granted a 3-year loan at a fixed rate of 6%, again for one million euros. We'll assume that market rates are those indicated in Figure 4.1 and increase with maturities.

The 1-year and 3-year rates are 4% and 5% respectively. The fact that the branch has managed to negotiate a lower 1-year deposit rate (3%) and a higher 3-year loan rate (6%) reflects both the services the branch offers to its customers (and the relative costs) and the credit risk run by the branch in granting a business loan.

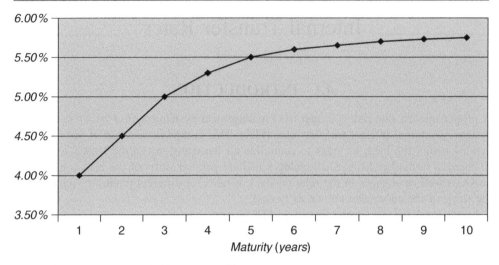

Figure 4.1 Market rates of different maturities

However, in addition to a credit risk, this branch also has an exposure to interest rate risk. Indeed, if market rates were to experience an increase during the first year, the branch would have to raise funds at more costly conditions once the certificate of deposit has expired. However, this would not involve a corresponding increase in the rate of interest earned.

To relieve branches from such risks, banks implement ITR systems. Under such a system, the branch in our example would grant a virtual 1-year loan to treasury and simultaneously enter a virtual 3-year deposit with treasury. The internal transfer rates (ITRs) applied to the two deals are the market rates for the relevant maturities (in this case 4% and 5%, as indicated in Figure 4.1).

Figure 4.2 shows a summary of these two virtual (that is, internal) deals and their impact on the financial results of the branch and the treasury.

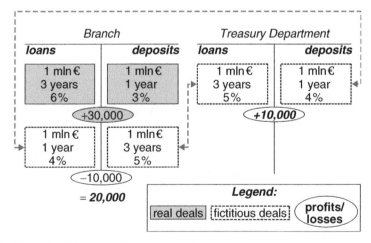

Figure 4.2 Example of how an ITR system works

Clearly, those two deals originated by the ITR system result in a drop in branch profits from 30,000 to 20,000 euros. The difference is allocated to treasury to cover the management of interest rate risk (10,000 euros, i.e. 1 % of the negotiated funds). Note that this amount is positive because the difference between the ITRs applied to the virtual deals is positive (4 % and 5 %). Normally, though, owing to mismatching of maturities, the sign (+ or −) and amount of this margin depends on the slope of the interest rate curve.

If the treasury decided to hedge the interest rate risk it would have to raise 3-year funds on the market at a rate of 5 % and simultaneously invest funds for one year at 4 %, again on the market. The effect of these two transactions would be to eliminate the interest rate risk, although it would also mean forgoing any profit from risk management. Alternatively, the treasury could decide not to hedge the risk and so earn the positive margin between interest income and expenses, but it would also be exposed to losses if market rates increased.[1]

We should keep in mind that, whatever the policy adopted by the treasury and the future evolution of interest rates, the branch has a guaranteed positive profit of 20,000 euros, or 2 % on negotiated funds. In turn this result can be broken down into two components:

(i) a positive margin of 1 % on the deposit (4 % − 3 %), guaranteed for one year, to cover the associated costs;
(ii) a positive margin of 1 % on lending (6 % − 5 %), guaranteed for three years, to cover the associated costs and risks.

4.3 SINGLE AND MULTIPLE ITRS

The example we'll review next concerns a multiple rates ITR system: this means that virtual transactions with treasury take place at different rates depending on maturity. In the past, however, many banks used single-rate ITR systems in which transactions between branches and the treasury took place at one single interest rate, independent of their maturity.

Although a single ITR is easier to manage, it can be criticized from several standpoints. First, it implies that many transactions between branches and the treasury take place at an arbitrary rate, different from the market one. This is the case of long-term deposits and loans if the bank adopts a short-term money market rate (e.g. three months) as the single ITR.

Second, as we will see shortly, single ITR systems only handle net flows. This means that each operating unit merely transfers to the treasury the net balance between deposits and loans (incoming and outgoing flows), yet each unit is still responsible for managing part of its own interest rate risk.[2] This means that a branch's financial results are affected

---

[1] In this case the positive slope of the curve would guarantee that the treasury had a positive margin. If the rate curve had a negative slope, the margin allocated to treasury would be negative. In this case, however, it could still hedge to eliminate both the interest rate risk and the negative margin. A negative slope for the curve also implies that the market expect interest rates to fall, so if the treasury decided not to hedge the risk it would still benefit from a reduction in interest rates if the forecast embedded in the curve were correct (a drop in rates would initially reduce its deposit costs and only two years later its earnings from lending).
[2] Net flow ITR systems assume that, given the reduced scale, individual operating units are able to manage the majority of problems associated with coordinating asset and liability positions typically handled by the bank as a whole. Such systems are used by some banks for their foreign branches.

by the evolution of market interest rates. Furthermore, since under such a system the bank's exposure to interest rate risk differs from the sum of the exposures of individual operating units, this means that the true financial impact of interest rate risk cannot be measured properly. On the contrary, in a gross flow system all incoming and outgoing cash flows generated by a bank's operating unit are reflected in virtual transactions with the treasury, which means that each branch's balance sheet is perfectly balanced by maturities, and only treasury will have an imbalance.

To clarify the difference between single and multiple ITRs, Table 4.1 shows an example of a bank with only two branches, A and B (each with an imbalance between deposits and loans). The table shows deposits and loans for the two branches and the bank as a whole, with the relevant maturity and interest rate conditions negotiated with customers. For simplicity's sake, let's assume the bank finances all of its loans (200,000 euros) from third-party liabilities and therefore doesn't have any equity capital. The interest rate curve remains that of the previous example (see Figure 4.1).

Table 4.1 An example with two branches

	Amount	Maturity	Rate
Branch A			
Deposits	50,000	1 year	3%
Loans	150,000	3 years	6%
NII with customers	7,500		
Branch B			
Deposits	150,000	1 year	3%
Loans	50,000	3 years	6%
NII with customers	−1,500		
Bank			
Deposits	200,000	1 year	3%
Loans	200,000	3 years	6%
NII with customers	6,000		

Table 4.2 shows the results for a multiple ITR system using the same data as above. In this case all deposit and loan flows are transferred to treasury using different transfer rates depending on their maturity. Both branches show the same result (2,000 euros) and will not be impacted by future changes in market rates. Interest rate risk is, in fact, transferred entirely to the treasury, which can then decide whether or not to hedge risks on a centralized basis. If it decided to accept the interest rate risk associated with the mismatching between deposit and loan maturities (one and three years respectively) it would make a profit of 2,000 euros.

Table 4.2 Multiple ITRs

	Amount	Maturity	Rate
Branch A			
NII with customers	7,500		
Loans to treasury	50,000	1 year	4.00 %
Deposits from treasury	150,000	3 years	5.00 %
NII with treasury	−5,500		
Total NII	2,000		
Branch B			
NII with customers	−1,500		
Loans to treasury	150,000	1 year	4.00 %
Deposits from treasury	50,000	3 years	5.00 %
NII with treasury	3,500		
Total NII	2,000		
Treasury			
Deposits from branches	200,000	3 years	5.00 %
Loans to branches	200,000	1 year	4.00 %
NII with branches	2,000		
Bank			
Deposits	200,000	1 year	3 %
Loans	200,000	3 years	6 %
NII with customers	6,000		

Table 4.3, instead, shows how things would work under a single-ITR system, arbitrarily based on a 2-year market rate (4.5 %). Note that each branch simultaneously makes deposits or loans to treasury for 50,000 euros (i.e. the lower amount, deposits or loans). As these two transactions take place at the same rate, they end up canceling each other out and the bank's ITR system actually operates on a net flow basis. In other words, Branch A receives a virtual loan equal to its deposit deficit (100,000 euros) at the single ITR of 4.5 % (regardless of the maturities associated to its assets and liabilities with customers). Similarly, Branch B makes a virtual deposit with treasury equal to its deposit excess (100,000 euros) at the single, standard ITR of 4.5 %.

Working with net balances only (Table 4.3b) in fact leads to the same financial results as in Table 4.3 for the branches, treasury and bank as a whole.

Table 4.3 Single ITR with gross flows

	Amount	Maturity	Rate
Branch A			
NII with customers	7,500		
Loans to treasury	50,000	2 years	4.5%
Deposits from treasury	150,000	2 years	4.5%
NII with treasury	−4,500		
Total NII	3,000		
Branch B			
NII with customers	−1,500		
Loans to treasury	150,000	2 years	4.5%
Deposits from treasury	50,000	2 years	4.5%
NII with treasury	4,500		
Total NII	3,000		
Treasury			
Deposits from branches	200,000	2 years	4.5%
Loans to branches	200,000	2 years	4.5%
NII with branches	0		
Bank			
Deposits	200,000	1 year	3%
Loans	200,000	3 years	6%
NII with customers	6,000		

Note that the single ITR system, being based on net flows, means that a maturity-consistent transfer rate cannot be assigned to all assets and liabilities with customers. Moreover, total interest rate risk is not transferred to treasury, so branches are not fully hedged from it.[3] In fact in the above example only branches are exposed to interest rate risk, whereas the treasury takes no risk and therefore doesn't make a profit.

Moreover, as mentioned above, a problem arises because of the arbitrary nature of a single ITR: the rate set for internal transactions between the treasury and branches ends up having an unjustified impact on their financial results.

To see why this occurs, let's recalculate the data in Table 4.3b using the 1-year interest rate of 4% for the internal transactions. The results, found in the first three columns

[3] Readers may want to compute the 1-year repricing gap and duration gap for Branches A and B in the two cases (Table 4.2 and Table 4.3 or 4.3b) and check if such risk measures, which take a value of zero in the first case, show non-zero values when a single IRT system based on net flows is adopted.

Table 4.3b Single ITR with net flows

	Amount	Maturity	Rate
Branch A			
NII with customers	7,500		
Deposits with treasury	100,000	2 years	4.5 %
NII with treasury	−4,500		
Total NII	3,000		
Branch B			
NII with customers	−1,500		
Loans to treasury	100,000	2 years	4.5 %
NII with treasury	4,500		
Total NII	3,000		
Treasury			
Deposits from branches	100,000	2 years	4.5 %
Loans to branches	100,000	2 years	4.5 %
NII with branches	0		
Bank			
Deposits	200,000	1 year	3 %
Loans	200,000	3 years	6 %
NII with customers	6,000		

of Table 4.4,[4] show a higher interest margin for Branch A, which has a funding deficit (3,500 euros) compared with Branch B which instead has excess funds (2,500). Clearly, however, in this case Branch A has financed all of its 3-year loan activity with 1-year deposits (150,000 euros). As a result, it's exposed to the risk of an increase in market rates. Vice versa, since Branch B used part of its 3-year deposits (50,000 euros) to issue loans with a 1-year maturity, it's exposed to a drop in market rates, though to a lesser extent than Branch A. So the branches' different financial results can be explained, on the one hand, by a different degree of risk exposure (greater for Branch A), and on the other, by the positive slope of the rate curve which forecasts a rising trend.

If, instead, the single ITR established by treasury were the 4-year rate (5 %) then results for the two branches, shown in the next three columns of the table, would be the opposite: Branch A would show a lower net interest income (2,500 euros) and would have less exposure to risk.

---

[4] As Tables 4.3 and 4.3b are equivalent, the simplest one, Table 4.3b, is used to develop Table 4.4.

Table 4.4 Effects of different ITRs on branch profits

	ITR = 1-year rate (4%)			ITR = 3-year rate (5%)		
	Amount	Maturity	Rate	Amount	Maturity	Rate
Branch A						
NII with customers	7,500			7,500		
Deposits from treasury	100,000	1 year	4.00%	100,000	3 years	5.00%
NII with treasury	−4,000			−5,000		
Total NII	3,500			2,500		
Branch B						
NII with customers	−1,500			−1,500		
Loans to treasury	100,000	1 year	4.00%	100,000	3 years	5.00%
NII with treasury	4,000			5,000		
Total NII	2,500			3,500		
Treasury						
Deposits from branches	100,000	1 year	4.00%	100,000	3 years	5.00%
Loans to branches	100,000	1 year	4.00%	100,000	3 years	5.00%
NII with branches	0			0		
Bank						
Deposits	200,000	1 year	3%	200,000	1 year	3%
Loans	200,000	3 years	6%	200,000	3 years	6%
NII with customers	6,000			6,000		

4.4 SETTING INTERNAL INTEREST TRANSFER RATES

We will now examine the problem of setting an ITR for certain specific transactions with customers.

4.4.1 ITRs for fixed-rate transactions

The ITR for fixed-rate transactions is established at the time a transaction takes place and remains constant until its maturity. So if a branch grants a 10-year mortgage at 5% it receives internal financing from treasury at the 10-year rate negotiated on the market at that time, which will remain fixed for the entire duration of the mortgage. If, for instance, the rate is 4%, the branch 'blocks' an interest margin of 1 percentage point that covers the costs of arranging the mortgage and the relevant credit risk. Figure 4.3 illustrates this mechanism.

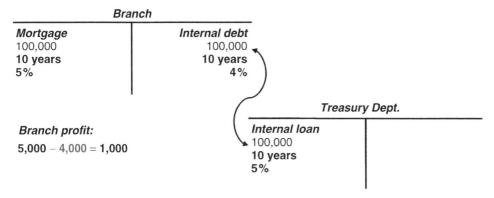

Figure 4.3   ITR for a fixed-rate transaction

4.4.2   ITRs for floating-rate transactions

In the case of indexed transactions the ITR is a floating interest rate. For instance, if a branch grants a 10-year mortgage at Euribor + 1.5 %, it receives internal financing from the treasury with the same maturity at the Euribor rate. In this way the branch 'freezes' an interest margin of 150 basis points and is covered for the risk of a drop in market rates. Figure 4.4 illustrates this mechanism.

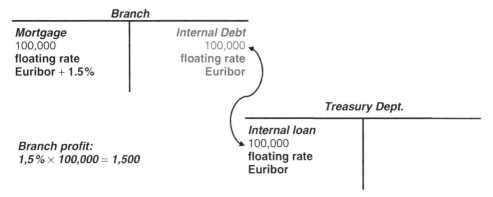

Figure 4.4   ITR for a floating-rate transaction

When the indexing parameter is a market rate (for instance, an interbank rate such as Libor or Euribor), the mechanism for setting the ITR is simple. In fact, funding can easily be obtained at that rate on the market and the treasury has no problem hedging the risk associated with the virtual floating-rate financing. It simply sets up mirror transactions on the market (in this example, by contracting a 10-year financing at the Euribor rate) or by using a derivative (in this example, by selling a 10-year interest-rate swap, through which it periodically receives a fixed rate against Euribor).

4.4.3   ITRs for transactions indexed at "non-market" rates

The situation becomes more complex in the case of 'non-market' floating rates. These are transactions indexed to non-market rates (that is, rates fixed by some supervisory body) such as the Repo rate (the rate for security repurchase agreements established by the European Central Bank, ECB) or benchmark rates published periodically by certain banking associations. As opposed to rates set by supply and demand on the market (as in the case of Libor or Euribor rates), these rates are decided at an administrative level.

This gives rise to two problems: (a) no financial instruments are available on the market to hedge the risk associated with changes in these rates; (b) if hedging is achieved using market instruments there is a basis risk, namely, the risk of sudden and unexpected changes in the spread between the market and non-market rate.

Take the example of a branch that has granted a loan indexed to the ECB Repo rate. Two options can be considered when setting the ITR:

(1) Libor rate.
(2) Repo rate plus a fixed spread.

The first option doesn't transfer the entire interest rate risk to the treasury. In fact, even though the Repo and Libor rates tend to be close and move similarly over time, the difference between the two (the so-called 'basis') can change and have an unexpected impact on a branch's profitability (see Figure 4.5 for an example covering the time period from June 2000 to June 2003). If the aim of a transfer rate is to leave a branch responsible for credit risk only, then any change in its profitability should derive exclusively from this type of risk.

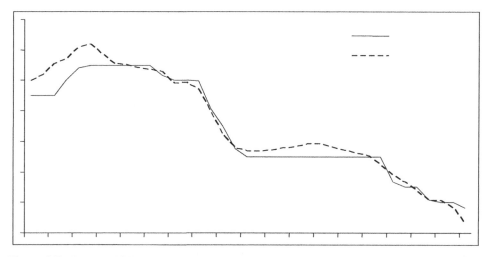

Figure 4.5 Repo and Libor rates

The second option ensures that the basis risk is transferred to the treasury, leaving the branch responsible for managing credit risk only. From this standpoint, it is preferable to the first one. However, even the treasury may find it difficult to measure basis risk; furthermore, the lack of financial instruments to hedge this risk makes it difficult to manage. Arguably, transferring this type of risk to the treasury could be considered pointless, given that no guaranteed tools are available to govern it.

Both options, therefore, have positive and negative aspects, which makes it impossible to claim that one is clearly better than the other. In any event the important thing is that rates applied in transactions between branches and the treasury create a valid system of incentives to remunerate the party taking basis risk. The costs of such a risk, while difficult to define, should always be transferred to the final customer. An example of how this can be achieved is given in Figure 4.6.

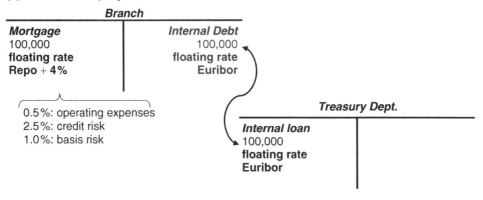

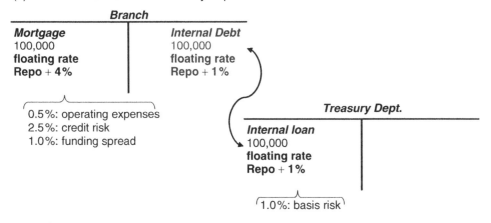

Figure 4.6 ITR for transactions at non-market rates

The chart shows two possible options. In the upper section, the branch finances an indexed loan at the Repo rate and this transaction is covered by funds provided from the treasury at Euribor. In addition to the Repo rate, the spread applied to the customer must be sufficient to cover the branch for the risk of a future reduction in the difference between the loan rate and the funding rate. Alternatively, in the lower section, the treasury finances the branch by means of an internal transaction indexed to the Repo rate, and the branch is released from any basis risk. In this case, the treasury charges the branch with an adequate extra spread, which impacts the latter's profit and loss account and compensates the treasury for the basis risk.

4.5   ITRs FOR TRANSACTIONS WITH EMBEDDED OPTIONS

Very often financial transactions negotiated with banks incorporate embedded options. For instance, a mortgage can include options for early repayment or conversion from a fixed to a floating rate. In those cases, it is as if the bank had not only granted a fixed-rate mortgage, but sold the debtor an option as well (actually, a call option on the residual debt). Similarly, if the bank grants a floating-rate mortgage with a cap rate of 6 %, it is as if the debtor had been granted a floating-rate mortgage with an option to exchange the floating market rate into a fixed rate of 6 %.

In such cases an effective transfer of interest rate risk from the bank's operating units to the bank's treasury requires an ITR system that can quantify and remunerate such options. The more frequent cases are illustrated below, together with the relevant valuation methods and transfer mechanisms.

4.5.1   Option to convert from fixed to floating rate

If, in a deposit or loan transaction, the bank gives the counterparty the right to convert the fixed rate into a floating rate (or vice versa), it is as if it were selling a *swaption*. This is a contract giving the buyer the option (though not the obligation) to perform an interest rate swap transaction with the bank (conversion from a fixed to a floating interest rate or vice versa). The conditions of this operation are established at the outset (fixed rate, duration, notional capital). In other words, a swaption is a call option allowing the purchase of an interest rate swap contract (with no obligation). Let's review the following two examples.

Example 1 – The branch grants a 3-year loan at a fixed rate of 7 %. After the first year the contract allows the debtor to convert the fixed rate into a floating rate (more precisely, the debtor can change from 7 % to the Libor rate plus a spread (s) established at the outset, for instance, 2 %). In practice, in the event of conversion it's as if the customer had kept the fixed-rate debt and in addition set up an interest rate swap to receive 7 % from the bank, paying Libor $+s$ (see Table 4.5). This is equivalent to the branch granting a swaption (although not explicitly), allowing the customer to operate an interest rate swap, although without the obligation to do so.

Table 4.6 Example of a loan converted from fixed to floating

Date	Interest on the loan	Interest Rate Swap flows (from when the swaption is exercised)		Final net flows
+1 year	−7 %	(not available)		−7 %
+2 years	−7 %	+7 %	−(Libor+s)	−(Libor+s)
+3 years	−7 %	+7 %	−(Libor+s)	−(Libor+s)

In such a case the branch buys an option identical to the one it is selling to the customer and pays a price to the treasury for this internal deal. The treasury, in turn, decides whether to retain the risk of being called to execute the interest rate swap with the branch, or to buy an equivalent swaption on the market, paying a price equal to the premium received from the branch.

The transaction is summarized in Figure 4.7. In the example, the market value of the swaption granted to the customer is 1,000 euros. The rate applied to the customer (7 %) represents the sum of the cost of 3-year funds (5 %) plus the premium requested by the branch to cover its credit risk, operating costs, and fees associated with buying the swaption from the treasury.

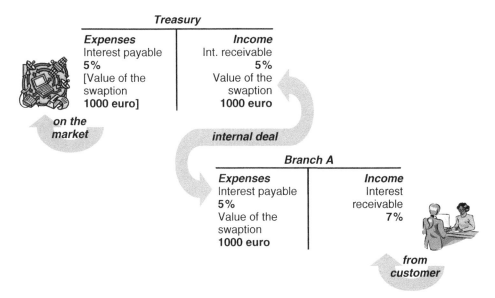

Figure 4.7   ITR for a fixed rate loan convertible to floating rate

Example 2 – A branch grants a 5-year loan at Libor $+s$, where s represents the spread. The contract gives the debtor an option to convert from a floating to a fixed rate after three years. This embedded option is valued at two million euros.

Again in this case the branch will set up two internal contracts with the treasury: a loan and a swaption. The former provides for the payment of the Libor rate whereas the latter is subject to a payment of two million euros, which will be charged to the branch's profit and loss account. As in the previous case, the spread with the customer will clearly have to cover: (a) the credit risk of the transaction; (b) the branch's operating costs; (c) the costs of the swaption negotiated with the treasury. In other words, the embedded option cannot be given for free to the debtor but must be reflected in the loan spread. This means that its market value will have to be calculated (which in turn will normally depend on the level and the volatility of market rates). The treasury will assist the branch in converting this 'absolute' price of the option (in euros) to an annual percentage spread to be applied to the customer.

4.5.2   Floating rate loan subject to a cap

When a bank finances a customer at a floating rate and at the same time fixes a cap M for this rate, it's like selling the customer an *interest rate cap* (that is, the debtor will never have to pay a higher rate than M). In turn, the cap represents a contract encompassing a number of options, each of which allows the customer to exchange a future payment at floating rate (the first year, second year, third year payment, and so on) for a fixed interest payment at the rate of M. The value of the cap, therefore, is the sum of the value of the individual options (which in turn depends on their maturity, the level and volatility of market rates, and so on).

Once again, the option the branch is (implicitly) giving must be paid for by the debtor, either up front when the contract is signed or by installments (in which case it would be incorporated in the interest rate). Furthermore, the cap that the branch sells to the customer must be virtually repurchased from the treasury, to free the branch from any interest rate risk.

4.5.3 Floating rate loan subject to a floor

When the bank issues a floating-rate loan, in order to reduce the spread s required from the customer it can agree to a minimum value m for the loan rate (i.e. it asks for a guarantee from the debtor that the rate will never be lower than m). In this case it's as if the bank were buying an interest rate floor[5] from the customer (see Figure 4.8). If we assume that the value of this option (paid by installments and expressed as a percentage of the loan principal) is equal to x, then the spread paid by the customer in addition to the Libor rate will be $s - x$, namely, lower than the spread s (including operating and credit risk costs) that would have applied had there not been a floor rate.

In order for all of the bank's interest rate risk to be centralized, the floor must be virtually sold by the branch to the treasury, which can then decide whether or not to sell it on the market (see Figure 4.8).

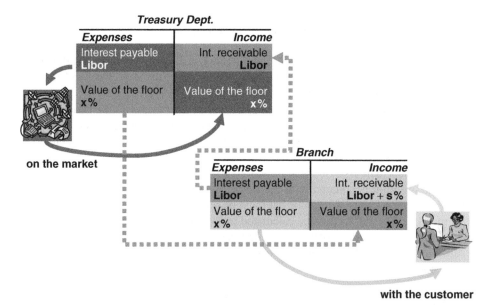

Figure 4.8   ITR for a floating-rate loan with a floor

---

[5] Just like a cap, a floor involves a contract with a number of options, each of which allows the swap of a future floating-rate payment (for the first year, second year, and so on) with a fixed interest payment at a rate of m. Note that in this case the bank itself has the option to make this swap, although it is not committed to do so.

Note that if in the future the Libor rate dropped below m, the customer would have to pay the branch $m + s$. Having sold a floor to the treasury, the branch, in turn, would have to give up the (positive) difference between m and the Libor rate to the treasury. By means of this transfer mechanism the effects of exercising the option would be shifted, quite rightly, to the unit (the treasury) responsible for managing interest rate risk.

4.5.4   Floating rate loan subject to both a floor and a cap

When the bank finances a customer at a floating rate and fixes both a cap rate M and a floor rate m, it is simultaneously selling a cap and buying a floor from the customer. This, then, is a combination of the cases discussed in the previous sections. The debtor must pay a premium for the cap purchase and receive a premium from the bank for sale of the floor.

The level of the two premiums (and the sign of the net balance between them) clearly depends on the value of M and m compared with current market rates. Let's assume that, given the market situation and the agreed floor and cap, the cap premium is 0.8 % of the principal and the floor premium is 0.6 %. In this case the debtor will pay a net premium of:

$$P_{Cap} - P_{Floor} = 0.8\% - 0.6\% = 0.2\%$$

This premium represents the value of an *interest rate collar*, that is, a contract derived from the combination of the cap and floor for the same loan. It can be paid immediately when the contract is stipulated or by installments (included in the interest rate). The collar sold by the branch to the customer must then be virtually repurchased by the treasury.

If, in the future, the Libor rate dropped below the floor rate m, the debtor would still have to pay m. The branch, having previously sold the floor to the treasury, would have to pay the difference between m and the market rate to the treasury. If, instead, the Libor rate were greater than the cap rate M, the customer would only pay M, but the branch would obtain the (positive) difference between the market rate and M from the treasury (which had previously sold it a cap).

In this manner the effects of the two embedded options on interest rates would be shifted, quite rightly, entirely to the unit responsible for managing interest rate risk.

4.5.5   Option for early repayment

Sometimes banks give customers an option to repay the debt before maturity. In this case it's as if the bank had granted a call (a purchase option) on the previously contracted debt. So a value must be assigned to this option and the branch must ensure this value is included in the rate paid by the customer; also, the branch must in turn purchase an identical option from the treasury.

Let's consider the following example: a bank grants a loan at a fixed rate (8 %) and simultaneously grants the customer a right of early repayment of the loan. The bank, furthermore, asks the counterparty to pay for this option in advance (for the sake of simplicity, let's assume this is a one-off payment of 500 euros).

Before this early repayment option is possibly exercised, (real) transfers between the branch and the customer and (virtual) transfers between the branch and the treasury will take place, as indicated in Figure 4.9.

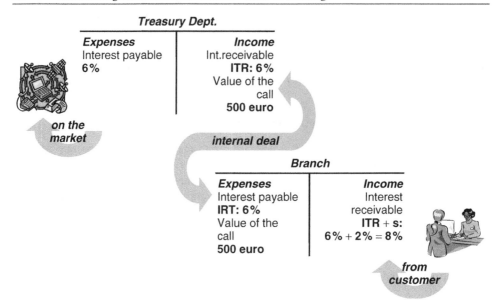

Figure 4.9   ITR for a loan with an early repayment option

Now, let's imagine that the market rate falls to 5 %. The debtor will have an incentive to exercise the early repayment option in order to refinance the loan at a lower cost (5 % plus a spread of 2 %). The branch will exercise the virtual option purchased from the treasury too. After the two options have been exercised the situation will be as illustrated in Figure 4.10.

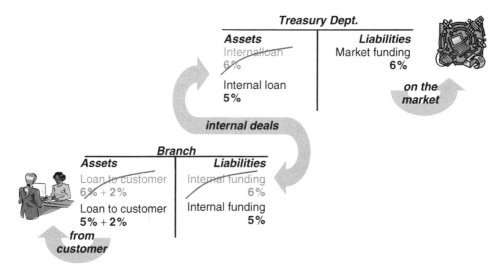

Figure 4.10   Effects of exercising the early repayment option

The treasury bears the interest rate risk since it has to issue a loan at 5 % while continuing to pay 6 % on its funding. But one has to recall that, to bear such a risk, it had received an amount corresponding to the value of the option (500 euros) and it could have hedged the effects of early repayment by buying an option on the market (at a cost of 500 euros) identical to that virtually sold to the branch.

Note that, quite often, bank branches don't explicitly make customers pay the cost of this kind of prepayment option; instead they prefer to include the cost in the spread s applied to the loan. Furthermore, they apply a penalty if loans are repaid in advance, which acts as a deterrent to exercising the option and covers operating costs associated with paying off the loan (and the need to reinvest the capital loaned before the agreed maturity).

4.6   Summary: the ideal features of an ITR system

In this chapter we have described the ideal features of an internal interest transfer rate system. These can be summarized as follows:

(1) The system should ensure that changes in branch profitability are due only to credit risk.[6]

(2) Specifically, the system must protect the branches from the risk of changes in interest rates.

(3) The system must protect the branches from the risks associated with embedded options.

(4) The system must allow for different interest rates according to maturity (multiple ITRs).

(5) The system must operate on the basis of gross flows.

(6) The sum of the profits of the individual operating units (including the treasury) must be equal to the bank's overall profit.

(7) The ITR system must be arbitrage-free, inasmuch as the operating units must not be able to carry out arbitrage[7] against the treasury.

(8) As a general rule, ITRs must be market rates that the treasury can negotiate effectively in the market; an exception could possibly be allowed for non-market rate transactions (for instance, loans issued at Repo rate), if one wants to isolate branches from basis risk (which is centralized and managed by the treasury).

This last condition is necessary if the treasury is to be able to implement hedging policies and transfer risk to the market. The need to use actual market rates involves two additional conditions, normally present in the ITR systems adopted by major banks (to simplify matters these were not taken into account in the examples given in this chapter).

(9) There must be different ITRs for deposit and loan transactions. More specifically, ITRs for the virtual financing of loan transactions must be 'ask' rates and those for virtual deposits, 'bid' rates. These are the rates at which the treasury can effectively negotiate transactions to hedge interest rate risk and that the bank's branches would be able to obtain if they were to enter the market directly.

---

[6] Other factors affecting branch profitability are changes in outstanding volumes, service income and operating costs. However, if one focuses on financial risks, credit risk and market risk are the main drivers of profit volatility for bank branches.

[7] For arbitrage we mean a financial transaction (or a set of related transactions) that enable a profit to be made without risk, by taking advantage of inconsistencies between the prices existing in a market (in this case, in the internal market in which funds are exchanged between branches and the treasury).

(10) Lastly, it's best to assign specific ITRs to each of the existing individual cash flows originating from an asset or liability. That is, every individual deposit/loan transaction must be 'broken down' into a number of zero-coupon transactions corresponding to the cash flows deriving from it (using a logic similar, to some extent, to *coupon stripping*); a specific transfer rate should then be applied to each cash flow.

SELECTED QUESTIONS AND EXERCISES

1. Branch A of a bank only has fixed-rate deposits, with a maturity of one year, for 100 million euros; branch B has only fixed-rate loans, for the same amount, with a maturity of three years. Market rates, on the 1 and 3 year maturity respectively, currently are 5% and 4%. Consider the following statements:

   I. One cannot use market rates as ITRs, as they would lead to a negative margin for the Treasury Unit;
   II. 3- and 4-years ITRs must be set exactly at 5% and 4%;
   III. The Treasury Unit can both cover interest rate risk and meanwhile have a positive net income;
   IV. The Treasury Unit can cover interest rate risk, but doing so it brings its net income down to zero.

   Which one(s) is (are) correct?

   (A) All four.
   (B) II and IV.
   (C) I and III
   (D) II and III.

2. Consider the following statements: "internal transfer rate systems based on flat rates (uniform rates for all maturities)...:

   (i) ...are wrong because internal trades take place at non-market rates";
   (ii) ...are correct because internal trades involve no credit risk, so there is no need for maturity-dependent risk-premiums";
   (iii) ...are wrong because they are equivalent to a system where only net balances are transferred between the branches and the Treasury department";
   (iv) ...are wrong because part of the interest rate risk remains with the branches".

   Which of them would you agree with?

   (A) Only (ii);
   (B) Both (i) and (iv);
   (C) All but (ii);
   (D) Both (iii) and (iv).

3. A bank has two branches, A and B. Branch A has 100 million euros of one-year term deposits, at a fixed rate of 1.5%, and 40 million euros of three-year fixed-rate loans at 5%. Branch B has 100 million euros of three-year fixed rate loans at 5%, and 6-month deposits for 80 million euros, at 1%. Market yields for 6-month, 1-year and 3-years funds are 2%, 3%, 4% respectively. The overnight market rate is 1%.

Compute the (maturity adjusted) one-year repricing gap and the expected annual profits of both branches (assuming that short term items can be rolled over at the same rate), under the following alternative assumptions:

   (a) each branch funds (or invests) its net balance (between assets and liabilities with customers) on the market for overnight funds;
   (b) each branch funds (or invests) its net balance (between assets and liabilities) through virtual one-year deals with the Treasury;
   (c) the bank has a system of ITRs based on gross cash flows and market rates.

Finally, suppose you are the manager of branch B and that your salary depends on the profits and losses experienced by your branch. Which solution, among (a), (b) and (c) would you like best if you were expecting rates to stay stable? How could your choice be criticised?

4. A branch issues a 10-year floating-rate loan at Libor + 1 %. The borrower may convert it to a fixed rate loan after five years; also, he may payback the entire debt after eight years. If the bank is using a complete and correct system of internal transfer rates the branch should

   (A) buy from the treasury a five-year swaption and an eight-year call option on the residual debt;
   (B) buy from the Treasury a five-year swaption and sell the Treasury an eight-year call option on the residual debt;
   (C) sell the Treasury a five-year swaption and an eight-year put option on the residual debt;
   (D) buy from the Treasury a five-year swaption and an eight-year put option on the residual debt.

5. A bank is issuing a floating-rate loan, with a collar limiting rates between 5 % and 12 %. Suppose s is spread on the loan and p is the spread on a comparable loan (same borrower, same collateral, same maturity, etc.) with no collar. Which of the following statements is correct?

   (A) $s > p$, because the borrower is actually buying an option from the bank;
   (B) $s < p$, because the borrower is actually selling the bank an option;
   (C) $s = p$, because the bank is both selling and buying an option;
   (D) the relationship between s and p depends on the level of market interest rates.

Appendix 4A
Derivative Contracts on Interest Rates

4A.1 FORWARD RATE AGREEMENTS (FRAS)

A FRA(t, T) is a forward contract on interest rates, whereby an interest rate is fixed, regarding a future period of time ("FRA period"), limited by two future dates, t and T. FRAs are widely used as tools for managing interest rate risk on short maturities. The buyer of a FRA "locks" a funding rate on a future loan: e.g., by buying a FRA(1,4) he/she sets the interest to be paid on a quarterly loan starting in one month. This kind of contract is also known as a "one against four months" FRA.

The key elements of a FRA are the following:

- the capital on which interest is computed ("notional", N);
- the trade date (on which the contract is agreed);
- the effective date (t), on which the future loan starts;
- the termination date (T) of the loan;
- the fixed rate (FRA rate, r_f);
- the market rate (floating rate, r_m) against which the FRA will be marked to market.

The FRA involves the payment of an interest rate differential, that is, of the difference between the FRA rate and the market rate (on the effective date, t), multiplied by the notional of the contract. For a FRA (1,4), e.g., if on the effective date (one month after the trade date) the three-month market rate happens to be higher (lower) than the FRA rate, then the seller (buyer) of the FRA will have to pay the buyer (seller) the difference between the two rates, times the notional.

More precisely, the payment (or cash flow, CF) from the seller to the buyer is given by:

$$CF = \frac{[r_m(t) - r_f] \cdot N \cdot (T - t)}{1 + r_m(T - t)} \qquad (4A.1)$$

(where T and t are expressed in years)

If this cash flow were negative (that is, if the market rate in t were below the FRA rate) the payment would flow from the buyer to the seller. In fact, the FRA (being a forward contract, not an option) will always be binding for both parties involved.

Note that, in (4A.1), since the payment is made in advance (that is, at time t, not on the termination date), the interest rate differential must be discounted, using the market rate r_m, over the FRA period ($T - t$).

Consider the following example. On June 19, a FRA(1,4) is traded with a notional of 1 million euros, a FRA rate of 3% and 3-month Euribor as a market (benchmark) rate. On July 19, the 3-month Euribor is 3.5%; this means that the seller of the FRA will have to pay the buyer the following amount:

$$CF = \frac{(3.5\% - 3.0\%) \cdot 1,000,000 \cdot \dfrac{3}{12}}{\left(1 + 3.5\% \cdot \dfrac{3}{12}\right)} = 1,239.16 \text{ euros}$$

4A.2   INTEREST RATE SWAPS (IRS)

An interest rate swap (IRS) is a contract whereby two parties agree to trade, periodically, two flows of payments computed by applying two different rates to the same notional capital.

In *plain vanilla swaps* (the most common type of contract), one party undertakes to make payments at a fixed rate, while receiving payments at a floating rate (based on some benchmark market rate).

In *basis swaps*, both payments are variable but depend on two different benchmark rates (e.g., one party pays interest at the 3-month Euribor rate, while the other one pays interest at the rate offered by 3-month T-bills).

The key elements of an IRS contract are the following:

– the capital on which interest is computed ("notional", N). Note that the notional only serves as reference for interest computation, and is never actually traded by the two parties;
– the trade date (on which the contract is agreed);
– the effective date (t), on which the actual swap starts;
– the termination date (T) of the swap;
– the duration $(T - t)$, also called the *tenor* of the contract;
– the m dates at which payments will take place (e.g, every six months between t and T);
– the fixed rate (swap rate, r_s);
– the market rate (floating rate, r_m) against which the swap rate will be traded.

An IRS can be used for several reasons:

– to transform a fixed-rate liability into a floating-rate one, or vice versa (liability swap);
– to transform a fixed-rate asset into a floating-rate one, or vice versa (asset swap);
– to hedge risks due to maturity mismatching between assets and liabilities;
– to reduce funding costs;
– to speculate on the future evolution of interest rates.

The i-th periodic payment on an IRS (to be computed on each of the m payment dates) is given by:

$$CF_i = [r_s - r_m(i)] \cdot N \cdot \frac{T - t}{m} \tag{4A.2}$$

where $r_m(i)$ is the market rate at time i and $(T - t)/m$ is the time between two payments (e.g., if the contract entails four payments over two years, $(T - t)/m$ will be equal to six months).

If this cash flow is positive, then the party who has agreed to pay the fixed rate, and receive the floating one, will make a net payment to the other one. The payment will flow in the opposite direction if the amount in (4A.2) is negative.

Consider, as an example, a 3-year IRS, with a notional N of 1 million euros, swap rate (r_s) of 6% and variable rate given by 6-month Euribor. Suppose the evolution of Euribor between t and T is the one shown in Table 4A.1 (column 2): the same Table shows the cash flows due between the parties of the swap (columns 3–4) and the net

Table 4A.1 Cash flows generated by an IRS contract

Maturities	Euribor	Variable-rate cash flows (euros)	Fixed-rate cash flows (euros)	Net flows (euros) for the party paying variable and receiving fixed
6 months	3.50 %	17,500	20,000	−2,500
12 months	3.80 %	19,000	20,000	−1,000
18 months	4.00 %	20,000	20,000	−
24 months	4.20 %	21,000	20,000	1,000
30 months	4.40 %	22,000	20,000	2,000
36 months	4.50 %	22,500	20,000	2,500

cash flows for the party paying variable and receiving fixed (column 5; negative values denote outflows).

4A.3   INTEREST RATE CAPS

An interest rate cap is an option (or rather, a portfolio of m options) which, against payment of a premium, gives the buyer the right to receive from the seller, throughout the duration of the contract, the difference between a floating and a fixed rate, times a notional, if such difference is positive. The fixed rate is called *cap rate*, or *strike rate*. No payment takes place if the floating rate is lower than the cap rate.

The buyer of the cap hedges the risk of a rise in floating rates, which would lead to an increase in his/her funding costs, without missing the benefits (in terms of lower interest charges) of a possible decrease. In other words, the cap sets a maximum ceiling (but no minimum floor) to the cost of his/her debt, which will be given by the cap rate, plus the cost of the premium (expressed on an annual basis).

The key elements of a cap contract are the following:

– the capital on which interest is computed ("notional", N);
– the trade date (on which the contract is agreed);
– the effective date (t), on which the option starts;
– the termination date (T) of the option;
– the duration ($T - t$) of the contract;
– the m dates at which the option could be used (e.g, every six months between t and T);
– the cap rate (r_c);
– the market rate (floating rate, r_m) against which the cap rate could be traded;
– the premium (option price), to be settled upfront or (less frequently) through periodic payments.

The cash flow from the cap seller to the cap buyer, at time i, will be:

$$CF_i = Max\left[0, [r_m(i) - r_c] \cdot N \cdot \frac{T - t}{m}\right] \qquad (4A.3)$$

Note that, as the cap is an option, no payment takes place at time i if the difference $r_m - r_c$ is negative.

Consider the following example. On October 1, 2007, an interest rate cap is traded, on 6-month Euribor (r_m), with $r_c = 4\%$, $N = 1$ million euros, duration $(T - t)$ of four years, bi-annual payments and a premium of 0.25 % per annum, to be paid periodically, every six months.

Table 4A.2 shows a possible evolution for the Euribor, as well as the payments (from the cap seller to the buyer) that would follow from this evolution.

Table 4A.2 An example of cash flows generated by an interest rate cap

Date (i)	Euribor r_m (i)	Cap Rate (r_c)	r_m (i)−r_c	$CF_i(€)$	Periodic premium (€)	Net flows (€)
1/04/2008	3.00 %	4.00 %	−1.00 %	0	1,250	−1,250
1/10/2008	3.20 %	4.00 %	−0.80 %	0	1,250	−1,250
1/04/2009	3.50 %	4.00 %	−0.50 %	0	1,250	−1,250
1/10/2009	4.00 %	4.00 %	0.00 %	0	1,250	−1,250
1/04/2010	4.25 %	4.00 %	0.25 %	1,250	1,250	0
1/10/2010	4.50 %	4.00 %	0.50 %	2,500	1,250	1,250
1/04/2011	4.75 %	4.00 %	0.75 %	3,750	1,250	2,500
1/10/2011	5.00 %	4.00 %	1.00 %	5,000	1,250	3,750

4A.4   INTEREST RATE FLOORS

An interest rate floor is an option (or rather, a portfolio of options) which, against payment of a premium, gives the buyer the right to receive from the seller, throughout the duration of the contract, the difference between a fixed and a variable rate, times a notional, if such difference is positive. The fixed rate is called *floor-rate*, or *strike-rate*. No payment takes place if the floating rate is higher than the floor rate.

The buyer of the floor hedges the risk of a fall in floating rates, which would lead to a decrease in the interest income on his/her investments, without missing the benefits (in terms of higher interest income) of a possible increase in rates. In other words, the floor sets a minimum limit (but no maximum ceiling) to the return on his/her investments, which will be given by the floor rate, minus the cost of the premium (expressed on an annual basis).

The key elements of a floor contract are the same as for a cap. The only difference is that the fixed rate specified by the contract is now called a floor rate (r_f).

The cash flow from the floor seller to the floor buyer, at time i, will be:

$$CF_i = Max \left[0, [r_f - r_m(i)] \cdot N \cdot \frac{T - t}{m} \right] \qquad (4A.4)$$

Note that, as the floor is an option, no payment is made if the difference $r_f - r_m$ is negative at time i.

Consider the following example. On October 1, 2007, an interest rate floor is traded, on 6-month Euribor (r_m), with $r_f = 2\%$, $N = 1$ million euros, duration $(T - t)$ of four years, bi-annual payments and a premium of 0.25 % per annum, to be paid periodically, every six months.

Table 4A.3 shows a possible evolution for the Euribor, as well as the payments (from the floor seller to the buyer) that would follow from this evolution.

Table 4A.3 An example of cash flows generated by an interest rate cap

Date (i)	Floor Rate (r_f)	Euribor R_m (i)	$r_f - r_m$ (i)	CF_i (€)	Periodic premium (€)	Net flows (€)
1/04/2008	2.00 %	3.00 %	−1.00 %	0	1,250	−1,250
1/10/2008	2.00 %	2.75 %	−0.75 %	0	1,250	−1,250
1/04/2009	2.00 %	2.50 %	−0.50 %	0	1,250	−1,250
1/10/2009	2.00 %	2.20 %	−0.20 %	0	1,250	−1,250
1/04/2010	2.00 %	2.00 %	0.00 %	0	1,250	−1,250
1/10/2010	2.00 %	1.70 %	0.30 %	1,500	1,250	250
1/04/2011	2.00 %	1.50 %	0.50 %	2,500	1,250	1,250
1/10/2011	2.00 %	1.25 %	0.75 %	3,750	1,250	2,500

4A.5   INTEREST RATE COLLARS

An interest rate collar is simply a combination of a cap and a floor having different strike rates (namely, having $r_f < r_c$). Namely, buying a collar is equivalent to buying a cap and selling a floor; conversely, selling a collar involves selling a cap and buying a floor.

The collar makes it possible to constrain the variable rate within a predetermined range ("putting a collar" to it), comprised between r_f and r_c.

The key elements of a collar are fundamentally the same as for a cap or a floor. The only difference is that the contract now specifies both the cap (r_c) and the floor rate (r_f).

The possible cash flow from the collar seller to the collar buyer at time i, if any, will be:

$$CF_i = Max \left[0, [r_m(i) - r_c] \cdot N \cdot \frac{T - t}{m} \right]$$

while the possible cash flow from the buyer to the seller is:

$$CF_i = Max \left[0, [r_f - r_m(i)] \cdot N \cdot \frac{T - t}{m} \right]$$

Note that those two equations are the same as (4A.3) and (4A.4) seen above. This is consistent with the fact that a collar, as mentioned before, is simply a combination of a long cap and a short floor.

The cash flow equations indicate that the collar buyer cashes the difference between the market rate and the cap rate when the former exceeds the latter; on the other hand, he/she has to pay the difference between the floor rate and the market rate, if the latter drops below the former. A collar can therefore be used to hedge a floating-rate liability, ensuring that the net rate paid by its issuer (including the cash flows on the collar) will always be between r_f and r_c; this means that the risk of a rate increase above r_c will be hedged but, also, that the benefits of a fall in rates below r_f will be forgone.

This marks an important difference with caps, where the benefits from a decrease in rates remain entirely with the buyer; however, being a combination of a long cap and a short floor, a collar has a significantly lower cost than a cap. In fact, the premium on a collar is the difference between the premium on the cap (paid) and that on the floor (received); depending on the actual values of r_c and r_f, as well as on the current value of market rates, this premium could even be negative.

Finally, consider the following example. On 1 October 2007, a bank raises 1 million euros issuing a 4-year bond indexed to the 6-month Euribor rate. To hedge against rate increases, while limiting the cost of the hedge, the bank buys the following collar:

- notional (N) of one million euros;
- floor rate: 3%: cap rate: 4%;
- duration: 4 years;
- benchmark rate: 6-month Euribor;
- premium: 0% per annum.

Table 4A.5 shows the cash flows associated with the collar. Note that, as market rates rise above r_c (driving up the interest expenses associated with the bond), the bank gets compensated by a positive cash flow on the collar. However, when market rates fall, part of the savings due to lower interest charges on the bond are offset by the payments due on the collar.

Table 4A.5 An example of cash flows associated with an interest rate collar

Time (i)	r_f	r_c	Euribor ($r_m(i)$)	$r_m - r_c$	$r_f - r_m$	CF_i	Periodic premium	Net flow
1/04/2008	3.00%	4.00%	3.50%	−0.50%	−0.50%	0	0	0
1/10/2008	3.00%	4.00%	3.00%	−1.00%	0.00%	0	0	0
1/04/2009	3.00%	4.00%	2.50%	−1.50%	0.50%	−2,500	0	−2,500
1/10/2009	3.00%	4.00%	2.75%	−1.25%	0.25%	−1,250	0	−1,250
1/04/2010	3.00%	4.00%	3.25%	−0.75%	−0.25%	0	0	0
1/10/2010	3.00%	4.00%	4.00%	0.00%	−1.00%	0	0	0
1/04/2011	3.00%	4.00%	4.25%	0.25%	−1.25%	1,250	0	1,250
1/10/2011	3.00%	4.00%	4.50%	0.50%	−1.50%	2,500	0	2,500

Part II
Market Risks

INTRODUCTION TO PART II

1 MARKET RISK: DEFINITION AND TYPES

The need to measure and control the risks taken by a bank adequately is felt particularly in the investment and securities trading business, which is exposed to asset prices volatility. As a matter of fact, for institutions taking speculative positions in currencies, bonds or stocks, there is a concrete possibility that the losses associated with an individual position will – over a short lapse of time – wipe out the profits realized in the course of months.

This type of risk is generally classified under the term "market risk" , or "price risk" . More precisely, market risk means the risk of changes in the market value of an instrument or portfolio of financial instruments, connected with unexpected changes in market conditions (stock prices, interest rates, exchange rates, and volatility of these variables); it therefore includes risks on currency, bond and stock positions, as well as on all other financial assets and liabilities traded by a bank. Market risks are generally only identified (by regulatory authorities, as well) as the risks inherent in the trading portfolio – meaning the set of positions taken for a short or very short time horizon with the intent to benefit from changes in market prices;[1] in reality, however, they concern all financial assets/liabilities held by a bank, including those purchased for investment purposes, and intended to be kept in the financial statements for a long period of time.

It is clear that market risks can take on different connotations depending on the type of price to which reference is made. As a general rule, five main market risk categories can be identified:[2]

√ *Exchange rate risk*: When the market value of a position is sensitive to changes in exchange rates (this is the case of foreign currency denominated financial assets and liabilities and derivative contracts whose value depends on the exchange rate[3]).
√ *Interest-rate risk*: When the market value of a position is sensitive to changes in interest rates (bonds, forward rate agreements, interest rate futures, interest rate swaps, caps, floors, collars, etc.).

---

[1] This distinction between trading portfolio and other assets/liabilities ("banking book"), however artificial, meets the classification used by the European Directive (93/6/EEC) and the January 1996 proposals by the Basel Committee, both concerning extension of capital ratios to market risks.

[2] A second market risk taxonomy, which is particularly important when derivatives trading is considered, is grounded on the type of exposure (Group of Thirty, 1993).

√ *Absolute price/rate risk, or delta risk*: It represents the exposure to changes in the market value of a position or portfolio as a consequence of a given change in the underlying asset price.
√ *Convexity risk, or gamma risk*: It represents the risk emerging when the relation between the market value of a position and/or portfolio and the underlying asset price/rate is not linear.
√ *Volatility risk, or vega risk:* This risk is typically associated with option contracts, and represents the exposure to changes in the expected underlying asset price volatility.
√ *Time decay risk, or theta risk*: It is typically associated with option contracts, and represents the loss of market value of a position and/or portfolio connected with the passing of time.
√ *Base or correlation risk*: It represents the exposure to differences in the changes in the price of a position and/or portfolio and those relating to the hedging instruments used.
√ *Discount rate risk, or rho risk:* It represents the exposure to changes in the value of a position or portfolio connected with a change in the interest rate used to discount back future cash flows.

[3] For instance: cash and forward purchases and sales, currency swaps, currency futures, currency options, stocks, bonds and others.

√ *Equity risk*: When the market value of a position is sensitive to equity market performance (stocks, stock-index futures, stock options, etc.).

√ *Commodity risk*: When the market value of a position is sensitive to changes in commodity prices (cash and forward purchases/sales of commodities, commodity swaps, commodity futures, commodity options, etc.).

√ *Volatility risk*: When the market value of a position is sensitive to changes in the volatility of any of the variables considered above (this is typically the case of options).

Note that one of the categories in list above is interest rate risk, that is, the same risk type that was already discussed in Part I. However, two differences must be borne in mind:

- when assessing interest rate risk as a subcategory of market risk, the focus is usually kept on financial instruments for which a secondary market exists. This implies that the risk horizon of the bank is limited to a few days, the time needed to sell risk positions on the market and terminate risk.
- accordingly, while the approaches discussed in Part I are applied across the whole spectrum of the bank's assets and liabilities, the measurement and management of interest rate risk as subcategory of market risk usually centers on a limited portion of the bank's balance sheet. This is called the "trading book" and only includes marketable investments (including short positions and derivatives) aimed at producing trading profits in the short-term.

Market risks have been gaining in importance on international financial markets over the last decade as a result of three main phenomena.

The first one is connected with the securitization process, which has resulted in illiquid assets (loans, mortgages) being progressively replaced by assets having a liquid secondary market, and therefore a price. This process has promoted the spread of mark-to-market measurement criteria for assets held by financial institutions.

The second phenomenon is the progressive growth of the financial derivatives market, whose main risk profile for financial intermediaries is exactly the change in the relevant market value caused by changes in underlying asset prices and/or their volatility conditions.

The third phenomenon is related to more widespread adoption of new accounting standards (such as IFRS 39), which provide for the market value (and no longer the historical purchase cost) of a wide range of financial assets and liabilities to be entered into the financial statements. These standards, which result in immediately highlighting the profits and losses connected with short-term changes in market conditions, have contributed to make market risk effects more visible, accentuating their importance.

This growing focus on market risks has not concerned exclusively financial institutions and the academic world, but has also extended to regulatory authorities. As a matter of fact, in January 1996, the Basel Committee on Banking Supervision put forward some proposals to extend capital requirements to market risks. A similar recommendation came from the EU Directive concerning capital adequacy of investment companies and banks (93/6/EEC). These proposals were then implemented by regulatory authorities in the major economically developed countries.

2   TRADITIONAL APPROACHES TO MARKET RISK MEASUREMENT

The traditional approach to market risk measurement and management was generally based on the nominal values of individual positions. Risk exposure was considered to be directly proportional to the nominal value of the financial instruments held, and any limitations imposed upon the individual business units' risk-taking capacity were also expressed in terms of nominal value of positions.

This approach is appreciable because of its simplicity, relatively low cost, and little need for information and updates (since the nominal value of an asset remains constant); however, it is characterized by numerous limitations. In particular, three of them can be identified:

(1) the nominal value of a position does not reflect its market value. So, for instance, a position comprising 100 shares in company A having a nominal value of 10 Euros each is considered to be equivalent to a position comprising 10 shares in company B having a nominal value of 100 Euros each (the nominal value is 1,000 Euros for both). However, shares A might be worth 5 Euros on the market, whereas shares B might have a market value of 200 Euros: in this case, the market value of the second position would be four times as high as the first one's; their nominal value would not capture this difference, or the differences arising from future price changes. Moreover, nominal value does not make it possible to distinguish between long positions (which generate profits in case of a rise in market price) and short positions (which generate profits in case of a drop in the price).
(2) Nominal values cannot capture the different degree of sensitivity of different securities to changes in market factors. Take, as an example, a position in one-year T-bills and another one, having the same nominal value, in ten-year Treasury bonds: the market value of the latter is evidently much more sensitive to changes in market interest rates than is the case for the former.
(3) Nominal value does not consider the volatility and correlation conditions of market prices/rates. As a matter of fact, positions which are sensitive to market factors characterised by higher volatility – their nominal value being equal – are riskier (just think, for example, of stocks, whose value depends on a more volatile market than, for instance, is the case for bonds). Moreover, portfolios comprising positions which are sensitive to highly correlated market factors are characterized by a higher risk – their nominal value being equal. Similarly, increased market volatility and/or correlations are not reflected in an increased portfolio risk, if this is measured based on its simple nominal value.

The inadequacy of the nominal value method has emerged in a significant manner as a result of the major international financial institutions' growing involvement in options trading. As a matter of fact, options have particularly volatile market values; moreover, this volatility is significantly different according to whether the underlying asset price is close or not to the strike price (i.e., according to whether the option is at the money, in the money or out of the money[4]). The use of a risk measure (for instance, in order to

---

[4] See Appendix 5B.

impose position limits to traders) expressed in terms of nominal value of the underlying asset was therefore particularly inadequate.

Such problems have led to the use of specific risk measures for the different types of positions: duration and basis point value for bonds, beta[5] for stocks, delta, gamma, vega and rho coefficients for options.[6]

So, for instance, the position limit imposed to a bond market trader was (and often still is) expressed in terms of basis point value (also referred to as "delta value 01", or simply "dv01"): this measure indicates the expected reduction in a bond's value as a result of an increase in market interest rates by one basis point (0.01 %). It takes account of the positions' market value and risk sensitivity (as a matter of fact, it is calculated based on the position's market value and modified duration, and namely as dv01 = P·MD·0.01 %[7]): in this way, the above-mentioned problems 1 and 2 are solved.

Please consider, for instance, the two bond positions illustrated in Table 1. It is noticed that – notwithstanding their equivalent nominal values – the two positions show a significant difference in their respective dv01, as a result of different durations, i.e., different sensitivities to interest rate changes, and different market values.

Table 1 Nominal Value and Basis Point Value of Two Bond Positions

Bond	5-year Treasury bond	10-year Treasury bond
Nominal value (€)	100	100
Market price (€)	100	90
Modified duration (MD–years)	3.5	7
Nominal value of the position (€ mln)	10	10
Market value (P) of the position (€ mln)	10	9
Basis point value – dv01 (€)	3,500	6,300

The use of sensitivity measures, however, still has several limitations:

(1) Positions of different type are quantified by different measures. This use of different "languages" prevents the risks taken in different trading areas (stocks, options, bonds) from being compared and aggregated. This hinders both horizontal communication among different categories of traders, and vertical communication to the bank's senior management, who would like to have a measure of the overall risk taken by the institution.

(2) Even within the same category of positions, sensitivity measures are not additive, and therefore cannot be aggregated. So, for instance, the delta of an option cannot be added to the gamma of this same option. Similarly, the duration or dv01 of a

[5] See Appendix 5A for a review of the estimation methods and economic significance of a stock's beta coefficient.
[6] See Appendix 5B for a review of option sensitivity coefficients.
[7] Symbols have the same meaning as in Chapter 2. Compared to duration, dv01 has the advantage of being expressed in monetary terms, and of reflecting the market value P of the financial instrument.

Euro-denominated bond cannot be added to those of a dollar-denominated bond. As a matter of fact, in the former case, the risk factor is represented by the changes in the Euro yield curve, whereas, in the latter case, it is represented by the changes in the dollar curve. The first example shows that it is not possible to aggregate different risk measures (delta and gamma) connected with the same position; the second one shows that it is not possible to add similar risk measures connected with different positions (Euros and dollars).

(3) The third limitation of the nominal value method – i.e., non-consideration of the different degree of volatility and correlation of risk factors – is not solved. In this connection, please consider the example shown in Table 2. As can be noted, the example is similar to the one in Table 1 above, with the only difference that the value of the position in five-year T-bonds is higher. It follows that, in this case, the two bond positions have the same dv01.

Table 2 Market Value, Basis Point Value and Volatility

Bond	5-year Treasury bonds	10-year Treasury bonds
Nominal value (€)	100	100
Market price (€)	100	90
Modified duration (MD–years)	3.5	7
Nominal value of the position (€ mln)	18	10
Market value (P) of the position (€ mln)	18	9
Basis point value – dv01 (€)	6,300	6,300
Yield to maturity (YTM) volatility	3%	2%

Although the two positions have equivalent sensitivity to market rate changes in monetary terms, they have a different degree of risk, because the relevant market factor (yield to maturity) is characterized by a different degree of volatility (last row in the Table). As a matter of fact, in this case, the yield to maturity of the five-year bond is more volatile (i.e., subject to broader and more frequent changes) than that of the ten-year bond.[8]

3   MODERN APPROACHES AND VALUE AT RISK (VAR)

The attempt to overcome the above-mentioned problems led some financial institutions to develop models which would make it possible to quantify, compare and aggregate the risk connected with different positions and portfolios. These models, which were originally introduced by the major US commercial banks in the first half of the eighties and then spread among the majority of financial institutions of economically developed countries,

---

[8] If instead of considering two securities we considered two portfolios, the differences in the degree of correlation among the changes in the market values of the individual positions comprising them might be added to volatility differences.

are generally referred to as "value at risk" (VaR) models, from the name of the risk measure which is usually generated by these models.[9]

One of the first institutions to develop a VaR model, and the first one to make it public, was the US commercial bank J.P. Morgan, which authored the *RiskMetrics*[TM] model.[10] At the end of the eighties, the then Chairman of the bank, Mr Dennis Weatherstone, requested that – every day at 4.15 p.m.[11] – he should receive a summary piece of information, encapsulated in a single monetary value, concerning the whole bank's market risks in the main market segments (equity, bond, currencies, derivatives, commodities, emerging markets, etc.) and the different geographical areas where the bank did business. In response to this need, the bank's risk managers introduced VaR,[12] a measure of the maximum loss that a position or portfolio of positions can suffer, given a certain confidence level, over a predetermined time horizon. In other words, VaR models tend to answer the following basic question: "*What is the maximum loss which could be suffered over a certain time horizon, so that there is a very low probability – for instance 1 % – that the actual loss will exceed this amount?*"

In this sense, the risk definition adopted by VaR models is characterized by three key elements:

- It indicates the maximum potential loss that a position or portfolio can suffer, but
- with a certain confidence level (lower than 100 %) and
- limited to a certain time horizon.

VaR is therefore a probabilistic measure, and takes different values at different confidence levels. If $prob(E)$ indicates the probability of event E, c the confidence level, and L the loss over the selected time horizon, the following is obtained:[13]

$$prob(L > VaR) = 1 - c \qquad (1)$$

Please note that the definition of VaR recognizes the possibility of excess losses (with a probability of $1 - c$); if this event occurs, however, no information about the extent of losses is provided by VaR.

VaR can be calculated for different financial instruments and portfolios, making their relevant risks comparable. For this reason, as will be better explained in the following chapters, it is used for three basic requirements: to compare the different investment options for a financial institution's risk capital; to compare return on capital employed; and, finally, to correctly "price" individual transactions based upon their relevant degree of risk.

"Value at risk" models can be used to generate additional risk measures other than VaR, such as standard deviation of changes in portfolio value, and expected shortfall. In fact,

---

[9] A synonym for VaR is CaR ("capital at risk"). As will be seen in the following chapters, other risk measures which can be calculated with these models are standard deviation and expected shortfall.

[10] The *RiskMetrics*[TM] model was made public by *J.P. Morgan* in 1995 (Morgan, 1995). In 1998, the team of researchers who had authored the model set up an independent company, partly controlled by *J.P. Morgan* itself, which took on the same name as the model.

[11] From this request, the name of the *RiskMetrics*[TM] model's application software, called "4.15" (*"four-fifteen"*), was derived.

[12] VaR models were originally introduced by some US institutions (*Citibank*, *J.P.Morgan*, *Chase Manhattan* and *Bankers Trust*) and called alternatively "dollars at risk", "value at risk", or "earnings at risk". Here, it was preferred to use the most widespread term, i.e., value at risk (VaR).

[13] Note that, in case the distribution of losses is discrete, the definition in the text must be generalised as follows: VaR is the smallest value v, such that the probability that losses will exceed v is no more than 1-c. Formally: VaR − min {v|pr(L > v) < 1-c}.

such models do not consist in a single methodology, but rather in a family of techniques whose purpose is to achieve the following three objectives (cf. Figure 1):

(1) to define the risk factors (e.g., exchange rates, interest rates, stock prices, commodities'prices) which can affect the bank's portfolio value, and to represent their possible future trend (by assigning them a probability distribution);
(2) to construct the probability distribution of the bank's possible future portfolio values (or, equivalently, of the losses compared to the current value) associated with each of the possible values taken by risk factors; this second step involves mapping the value of the individual financial instruments in the bank's portfolio to the values taken by risk factors;
(3) to summarise the probability distribution of the bank's possible future portfolio values in one or more risk measures (of which VaR is certainly the most widespread one); to make the selected risk measure understandable to the top management, for instance by breaking it down into more detailed risk measures.

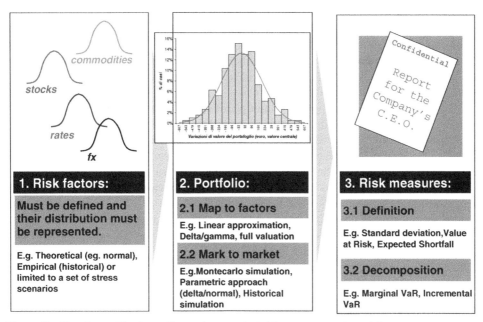

Figure 1   The three objectives of a modern market risk measurement model

Within this "family" of working hypotheses, calculation methodologies, risk measures, the easiest (and traditionally most widespread) approach is the so-called variance-covariance approach (also referred to as analytical or parametric method). It is characterized by the following elements:

– it assumes that the possible changes in value of all market factors (or, alternatively, of the returns of the assets in the portfolio) follow a normal distribution;
– the information on the possible future values of market factors and their correlations is therefore entirely summarised in a variance-covariance matrix;

- so, the possible losses on the bank's portfolio depend on this matrix and on the sensitivity (which is usually approximated by a linear function with constant coefficients) of the individual positions in the portfolio to changes in market factors;
- VaR is obtained as a multiple of the standard deviation of future losses.

The variance-covariance approach is undoubtedly the most widespread one within the framework of risk management systems, if nothing else because the *RiskMetrics*™ database, on which numerous financial institutions rely to develop their own in-house models, follows this methodological approach.

Another very popular approach is the one based on simulation techniques. It differs from the variance-covariance approach because

- the possible changes in the value of market factors are not necessarily distributed according to a normal distribution: as a matter of fact, a different distribution can be used, for instance, based upon the changes which were empirically detected from the historical data for the past few months or years, or considering only a limited number of "extreme" scenarios (stress tests);[14]
- the impact of the possible future values of market factors on the bank's possible losses is quantified through full valuation, i.e., recalculating the value of each asset or liability as a function of new market conditions. So, no recourse is made to linear sensitivity coefficients, but rather all the positions in the bank's portfolio are revalued using appropriate pricing models. It is therefore a more accurate approach, which, however, is also more computationally intensive.
- VaR cannot be estimated simply as a multiple of standard deviation, but must be looked for by analysing the entire distribution of future losses, and identifying their maximum value after excluding a percentage of cases equal to 1-c, starting from the worst ones.

The purpose of this part of the volume (see Figure 2) is to illustrate the features, applications, merits and limitations of the major market risk measurement and management models, making use of numerical examples and real data.

More specifically, in Chapter 5 the focus will be on the variance-covariance approach (also known as parametric, or analytical approach), discussing its theoretical underpinnings, practical implementation and limitations.

The accuracy of the results of a Value at Risk model depend crucially on the ability to produce a consistent and up-to-date estimate of market volatility, as well as of the correlation among different risk factors. Chapter 6 is devoted to a set of techniques that may help making such an estimation process both reliable and flexible.

Chapter 7 will be devoted to the simulation approach, which represents the main alternative to the parametric methods discussed in Chapter 5. Its operation, working hypotheses, and limitations will be analyzed. The simulation approach includes several VaR estimation methods, such as historical simulation or Monte Carlo simulations; a further VaR measurement methodology, known as the hybrid approach and combining some advantages of the parametric and historical simulation approaches, will also be reviewed. The chapter ends with a discussion of stress tests, that is, a special type of simulations that can be used to assess the model's (and the bank's) reaction to extreme market scenarios.

---

[14] As will be better clarified below, three different market risk measurement methods are therefore referable to the simulation approach: historical simulations, Monte Carlo simulations, and stress tests.

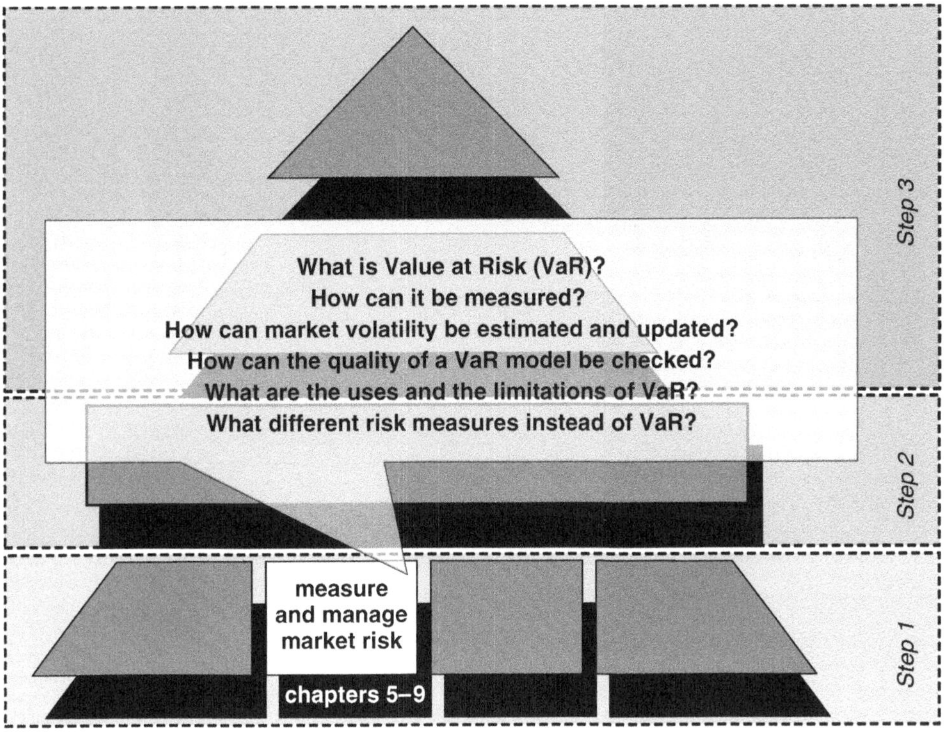
What is Value at Risk (VaR)?
How can it be measured?
How can market volatility be estimated and updated?
How can the quality of a VaR model be checked?
What are the uses and the limitations of VaR?
What different risk measures instead of VaR?
measure and manage market risk
chapters 5–9
Step 3
Step 2
Step 1

Figure 2 Key questions answered by Part II of this Book

Chapter 8 will be devoted to an analysis of the alternative techniques used to evaluate the quality of a VaR model. In particular, after illustrating the results generated by alternative VaR models on a simplified stock portfolio, the focus will be on backtesting techniques. The final section of the chapter will analyze the decisions taken by the Basel Committee concerning backtesting, highlighting their merits and limitations.

Finally, Chapter 9 will examine the main applications and limitations of VaR market risk models. The analysis will focus on two major real problems of VaR measures – non-subadditivity and non-consideration of the size of excess losses – and on an alternative risk measure – expected shortfall, or extreme VaR – which makes it possible to overcome these limitations.

The Variance-Covariance Approach

5.1 INTRODUCTION

Among the different possible approaches to market risk measurement, the variance-covariance approach – also referred to as parametric approach – is undoubtedly the one which is most widespread among financial institutions. There are diverse and interrelated reasons for its spread:

– First of all, this approach presents a key advantage over the simulation approaches which will be analyzed in the next chapter, i.e., simplicity. This simplicity concerns not so much its conceptual profile, but its calculation intensiveness and therefore use of support information systems.
– Moreover, the variance-covariance approach is the original version of VaR models, i.e., the one which was developed first and which rapidly spread among Anglo-Saxon banks.
– Finally, the choice of the variance-covariance approach is encouraged by the presence of a database (*RiskMetrics*™, originally developed by the US commercial bank J.P. Morgan) which is based upon this approach, and is used by a large number of products developed by the software industry.

Notwithstanding these advantages, the variance-covariance approach has several disadvantages, mainly related to the theoretical hypotheses underlying the whole methodology. As will be pointed out below, these hypotheses concern in particular two aspects:

√ the market factors' returns distribution;
√ the sensitivity of portfolio positions to changes in market factors.

5.2 VaR DERIVATION ASSUMING NORMAL RETURN DISTRIBUTION

5.2.1 A simplified example

Consider Table 5.1, which shows the daily log returns of a stock market index for a period of 100 days. Returns are calculated as

$$R_t = \ln \left(\frac{S_t}{S_{t-1}} \right) \approx \frac{\Delta S_t}{S_{t-1}} \tag{5.1}$$

where S_t is the value of the index at day t.

Based upon these data, mean and standard deviation can be estimated, and are 0.03 % and 1.65 %, respectively (the last section of the table also shows the skewness and kurtosis of the return distribution). It can be noted that the daily return is higher than the standard deviation on several days (23 out of 100): assuming a long position on the stock market, which is therefore exposed to declines in the index, losses in excess of the standard

Table 5.1 Daily Fluctuations in MIB 30 (Milan Stock Exchange Index) – 1/06/1998–16/10/1998

Date	Rt $Ln(P_t/P_{t-1})$	Date	Rt $Ln(P_t/P_{t-1})$	Date	Rt $Ln(P_t/P_{t-1})$	Date	Rt $Ln(P_t/P_{t-1})$
1-Jun-98	0.01 %	6-Jul-98	0.47 %	10-Aug-98	−0.58 %	14-Sep-98	2.03 %
2-Jun-98	0.21 %	7-Jul-98	−0.23 %	11-Aug-98	−1.32 %	15-Sep-98	0.77 %
3-Jun-98	−0.96 %	8-Jul-98	1.01 %	12-Aug-98	1.42 %	16-Sep-98	0.75 %
4-Jun-98	1.11 %	9-Jul-98	−0.67 %	13-Aug-98	−0.86 %	17-Sep-98	−2.58 %
5-Jun-98	1.72 %	10-Jul-98	0.50 %	14-Aug-98	−1.14 %	18-Sep-98	0.12 %
8-Jun-98	0.17 %	13-Jul-98	0.07 %	17-Aug-98	1.95 %	21-Sep-98	0.37 %
9-Jun-98	0.24 %	14-Jul-98	1.06 %	18-Aug-98	1.60 %	22-Sep-98	0.56 %
10-Jun-98	−0.55 %	15-Jul-98	−0.24 %	19-Aug-98	−0.29 %	23-Sep-98	3.48 %
11-Jun-98	−1.60 %	16-Jul-98	0.78 %	20-Aug-98	−0.59 %	24-Sep-98	−2.22 %
12-Jun-98	0.39 %	17-Jul-98	0.23 %	21-Aug-98	−0.95 %	25-Sep-98	0.19 %
15-Jun-98	−2.01 %	20-Jul-98	−0.22 %	24-Aug-98	0.64 %	28-Sep-98	0.38 %
16-Jun-98	0.98 %	21-Jul-98	−1.62 %	25-Aug-98	0.43 %	29-Sep-98	0.03 %
17-Jun-98	1.78 %	22-Jul-98	−0.09 %	26-Aug-98	−0.80 %	30-Sep-98	−3.10 %
18-Jun-98	−0.07 %	23-Jul-98	−2.11 %	27-Aug-98	−3.91 %	1-ott-98	−3.06 %
19-Jun-98	−0.52 %	24-Jul-98	0.09 %	28-Aug-98	−1.49 %	2-ott-98	1.63 %
22-Jun-98	0.24 %	27-Jul-98	0.57 %	31-Aug-98	−7.04 %	5-ott-98	−1.41 %
23-Jun-98	1.46 %	28-Jul-98	−1.50 %	1-Sep-98	3.79 %	6-ott-98	−0.40 %
24-Jun-98	1.19 %	29-Jul-98	−0.45 %	2-Sep-98	−0.38 %	7-ott-98	−1.42 %
25-Jun-98	−0.32 %	30-Jul-98	1.56 %	3-Sep-98	−0.83 %	8-ott-98	−1.16 %
26-Jun-98	0.35 %	31-Jul-98	−1.97 %	4-Sep-98	−0.86 %	9-ott-98	2.57 %
29-Jun-98	0.47 %	3-Aug-98	−0.74 %	7-Sep-98	2.51 %	12-ott-98	1.34 %
30-Jun-98	−0.41 %	4-Aug-98	−3.69 %	8-Sep-98	2.45 %	13-ott-98	−0.29 %
1-Jul-98	1.29 %	5-Aug-98	0.86 %	9-Sep-98	−1.70 %	14-ott-98	1.07 %
2-Jul-98	−0.19 %	6-Aug-98	0.76 %	10-Sep-98	−2.62 %	15-ott-98	4.09 %
3-Jul-98	0.47 %	7-Aug-98	−0.02 %	11-Sep-98	2.90 %	16-ott-98	0.85 %
Mean				−0.03 %			
Standard deviation				1.65 %			
Skewness				−0.69			
Kurtosis				2.87			
Number of days on which ASS(Rt) > Std. Dev.				23			
Number of days on which Rt < -(Std. Dev..)				12			
Max				4.09 %			
Min				−7.04 %			

deviation would have been sustained on as many as 12 out of 100 days. On a particular day – 31 August 1998 – the loss would even have been 4 times higher than the standard deviation.

Figure 5.1 represents – through a bar chart – the probability distribution of the log returns shown in the table. As can be seen, it is not incorrect to assume that the data in question come from a normal distribution: the variance-covariance approach is grounded precisely on this hypothesis (or – which is the same – on the hypothesis that prices are distributed according to a log-normal).

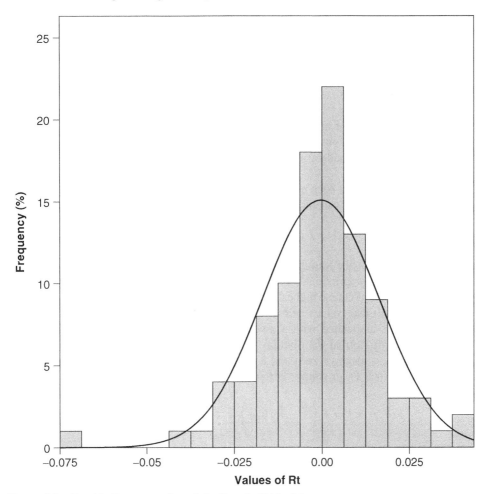

Figure 5.1   Graphic Representation of the Data in Table 5.1

The normal distribution is widely used to describe random movements, and is characterized by two parameters only: mean and standard deviation. In analytical terms, it is represented as follows:

$$f(x) = \frac{1}{\sqrt{2\pi}\sigma} e^{-\left(\frac{x-\mu}{2\sigma}\right)^2}$$
(5.2)

where $f(x)$ is the density function, μ the mean, and σ the standard deviation.

The integral between $-\infty$ and u of an $f(x)$ whose mean is equal to μ and standard deviation is equal to σ is referred to as cumulative density function, and is usually indicated by $F(u;\mu,\sigma)$:

$$F(u;\mu,\sigma) \equiv \int_{-\infty}^{u} f(x)\,dx = \int_{-\infty}^{u} \frac{1}{\sqrt{2\pi}\sigma} e^{-\left(\frac{x-\mu}{2\sigma}\right)^2} dx$$

It proves to be very useful to calculate the probability associated with a given range of values taken by R_t (and, more in general, by a stochastic variable such as the change in a share price, interest rate, exchange rate, etc.). For instance, if one wished to calculate the probability that the value of R_t is lower than $+1.62\,\%$, i.e., than the mean μ $(-0.03\,\%)$ plus one time the standard deviation $(1.65\,\%)$, it would be sufficient to calculate the following:[1]

$$F(u;\mu,\sigma) = F(1.62\,\%; -0.03\,\%, 1.65\,\%) = 84.12\,\%$$

So, there is a probability of approximately $84\,\%$ that the value of R_t will not exceed its mean value by more than one standard deviation.[2] Symmetrically, it can be concluded that the variable under consideration will stay below this threshold in the remaining $16\,\%$ of cases.

If a higher threshold had been considered – for instance, $\mu + 2\sigma$ (i.e., $+3.27\,\%$) – the cumulative density function would have taken the following value:

$$F(u;\mu,\sigma) = F(3.27\,\%; -0.03\,\%, 1.65\,\%) = 97.72\,\%$$

So, the probability that the variable will not exceed its mean value by more than two standard deviations is approximately $98\,\%$ (as the threshold is higher than the previous one, the probability is of course higher). Similarly to what was noted above, the probability that the variable will take values below the threshold is approximately $2\,\%$.

The probabilities associated with a given threshold can also be calculated by having recourse to *standard* normal distribution (i.e., that particular normal distribution which is characterized by a mean of zero and a standard deviation of one) and its cumulative density function $F(\alpha;0.1)$, or simply $F^*(\alpha)$:

$$F(u;\mu,\sigma) = F\left(\frac{u-\mu}{\sigma};0,1\right) = F*\left(\frac{u-\mu}{\sigma}\right) = F*(\alpha) \qquad (5.3)$$

In order to use the standard normal cumulative density function, it is therefore necessary to replace u with

$$\alpha = \frac{u-\mu}{\sigma}$$

In the first example above, we would get

$$\alpha = \frac{1.62\,\% - (-0.03\,\%)}{1.65\,\%} = 1$$

---

[1] This can be done, for instance, with an Excel spreadsheet, using the NORM.DISTRIB $(1.62\,\%;-0.03\,\%;$ $1.65\,\%;1)$ function.
[2] The value $1.62\,\%$ is therefore close to the 84th percentile of the probability distribution of R_t.

and obtain

$$F * (\alpha) = F * (1) = 84.12 \%$$

Conversely, in the second example, we have

$$\alpha = \frac{3.27 \% - (-0.03 \%)}{1.65 \%} = 2$$

and

$$F * (\alpha) = F * (2) = 97.72 \%$$

Using the standard normal cumulative density function is advantageous because this no longer depends on μ and σ, but only on α. A precise link between different values of α and the corresponding probability levels can therefore be established, and remains valid regardless of the values taken by the mean and standard deviation of the variable considered. An example is provided in Table 5.2.

Table 5.2 Probability Levels Corresponding to the Different Values of α

Probability Level	$\alpha = \dfrac{x - \mu}{\sigma}$
99.99 %	3.719
99.98 %	3.500
99.97 %	3.432
99.87 %	3.000
99.90 %	3.090
99.50 %	2.576
99.38 %	2.500
99.00 %	2.326
98.00 %	2.054
97.72 %	2.000
97.50 %	1.960
97.00 %	1.881
96.00 %	1.751
95.00 %	1.645
93.32 %	1.500
84.13 %	1.000

The assumption of a normal distribution of returns therefore allows to convert a selected probability level into an appropriate scaling factor α (to which a threshold u – represented by the mean plus α times the standard deviation – corresponds).[3] So, for instance, Table 5.2 tells us that, if the distribution of R_t is normal, the probability of obtaining a return below the mean, increased by three times the standard deviation, is 99.87%; consequently, the probability of obtaining a return *above* this threshold is approximately 0.13%; moreover, as the normal distribution is symmetrical and mean-centred, the probability of obtaining returns *below* the mean *minus* three times the standard deviation will still be 0.13%.

At this point, it must be specified that, even if the whole range of possible returns is considered, if the purpose is to determine potential losses, and therefore value at risk, every position is *de facto* exposed exclusively to half of the events contained in the probability distribution. As a matter of fact, long positions are only exposed to the risk of *lower* than expected returns (and therefore only take the left-hand side of the distribution into account), whereas short positions are only exposed to the risk of *higher* than expected returns (so they concentrate in the right-hand side of the distribution).

As a consequence, if our bank holds a long position in the stockmarket index, we will select the value of α in such a way as to isolate the left tail of the distribution in Figure 5.1. For example, we could select $\alpha = -1.65$, so as to isolate 5% of lower returns.[4]

The value

$$u \quad = \mu + \alpha \cdot \sigma = -0.03\% - 1.65 \cdot 1.65\% \cong -2.69\% \tag{5.4}$$

would then be the threshold which should not be exceeded in 5% of cases. It would therefore be the probable maximum loss, over a span of time of one day (as a matter of fact, R_t are daily returns), at 95% confidence level. In other words, it would be the 95 per cent VaR of our long stock position (expressed in terms of percentage loss: in order to know the absolute loss, it would be sufficient to multiply it by the market value, MV, of the stock portfolio owned by the bank).

The variance-covariance approach is often used assuming that market factor returns have a zero *mean*. This simplifying assumption is acceptable, as trading positions generally have a short-term time horizon; in fact, with reference to daily time horizons, empirical studies show that the best prediction of the future return is not the historical mean return, but rather a value of zero. In fact, as the mean return which occurred over a certain period of time in the past cannot be considered to be indicative of the expected return, it is more reasonable to rely on estimates of the latter which are unrelated to historical data (for instance, imposing that it should be equal to the risk-free rate of return, or to zero, if very short time horizons are considered).[5]

If an expected return μ of zero is assumed, (5.4) will become:

$$u \quad = \alpha \cdot \sigma \tag{5.4b}$$

---

[3] The possibility of associating confidence intervals with multiples of standard deviation is not an exclusive result of the normal distribution. For every random, discrete or continuous variable with mean μ and standard deviation σ, the Chebishev inequality applies, according to which: $P\{|x - \mu| \geqslant \alpha\sigma\} \leqslant \dfrac{1}{\alpha^2}$. Of course, the intervals obtained by assuming normality are more informative than those deriving from the Chebishev inequality.

[4] From Table 5.2 we notice that F*(+1.65)= 95%; from the symmetry of the normal, it follows that F*(−1.65)= 5%

[5] Just think of the case in which the stock exchange index recorded a negative daily mean return over the historical period of time considered: it would make no sense to use this negative datum as an estimate of the expected return for the future! It would be relatively more sensible – especially if a short-term investment horizon is adopted – to assume that the best estimate of this expected return is a value of zero.

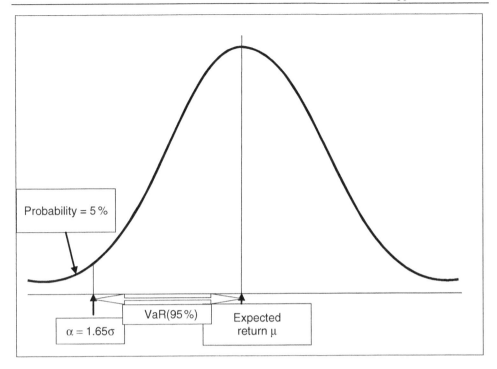

Probability = 5 %

VaR(95 %)

Expected
return μ

$\alpha = 1.65\sigma$

Figure 5.2 Variance-Covariance VaR Derivation

which, multiplied by the market value (MV) of the portfolio at risk, will result in:

$$VaR = MV \cdot \alpha \cdot \sigma \qquad (5.5)$$

So, in this first simplified example, we have obtained the VaR of a position as the product of three elements:

(i) its market value (MV);
(ii) the relevant market factor's estimated return volatility (σ);
(iii) a scaling factor α which – given the hypothesis of a normal distribution of market factor returns – allows to obtain a risk measure corresponding to the desired confidence level (for instance $\alpha = 2$ for a 97.7 % confidence level).

Note that the product of the terms α and σ represents a potential unfavourable change in the market factor (in our case, the stock exchange index return) obtained by making reference to the 5th percentile of the distribution of R_t.

5.2.2 Confidence level selection

As noted above, the greater is the confidence interval, the higher are α and – other things equal – value at risk. By selecting a high α, a financial institution obtains a greater degree of protection, in the sense that the probability of occurrence of excess losses is reduced.

If the bank has an amount of shareholders' equity that is equal to VaR, the protection will also be extended to its creditors and clients, as they will know that there are internal resources to meet losses covering a high proportion of possible scenarios.

The critical variable in confidence interval selection is therefore the individual financial institution's degree of risk aversion. I.e.,: more risk-averse institutions will be driven to select a higher multiple of volatility, so as to obtain a greater degree of protection. This choice will inevitably lead them to reject numerous risk-taking opportunities, because these will generate an excessive VaR compared to the expected return associated therewith; their portfolio will therefore be less risky and, assuming efficient capital markets, this lower risk will correspond to a lower cost of equity capital, i.e., a lower risk premium demanded by shareholders.[6]

An interesting method to determine the confidence interval was originally proposed by Bank of America,[7] and then adopted by the majority of large international banks and recognised by the supervisory authorities themselves.[8] It is inspired by an observation by Robert Merton and André Perold:[9] They noticed that one of the distinctive features of financial institutions, compared to non-finance companies, is the fact that the former's clients are often their main creditors, as well. This is true, for instance, for depositors or for their trading counterparties. For this reason, clients set particular value on a bank's credit rating, and therefore creditworthiness. In this sense, the possibility for a bank to continue to carry on its business (for instance, trading derivative instruments or participating in a securities underwriting syndicate) and to generate the relevant profits is closely related to retention of its creditworthiness, i.e., its rating.

Following this logic, Bank of America decided to hold an amount of equity capital – quantified through a VaR model – which would be sufficient to preserve its AA3 rating. As (based upon the statistics compiled by rating agencies) this rating corresponded to a mean annual default probability of of 0.03 %, a confidence level of 99.97 % was selected.[10] Assuming a normal distribution of returns, this level corresponds to a multiple of standard deviation of 3.43. Table 5.3, based on Moody's data, shows the confidence levels implied in the one-year default probabilities for the different rating classes.

This relation between confidence level and rating tends to result in banks characterized by a better rating needing more equity capital – other conditions being equal – and therefore being characterised by a higher tier 1 ratio. Figure 5.3, which was developed based upon the data in Table 5.4, shows that this relation actually reflects the reality of the major European banking groups.[11]

---

[6] It is interesting to note that the confidence interval selection is neutral in terms of the *capital allocation* process among the different risk-taking units (i.e., in terms of investment *selection*). Indeed, if the same confidence interval is adopted to evaluate capital absorption in all of a financial institution's risk-taking units, the selection of a higher or lower multiple will not result in any allocative distortion. In this sense, the volatility is multiplied by a simple scaling factor which increases or decreases all risks by the same order of magnitude. Vice versa, this choice becomes important – as noted above – when determining the total volume of risk taken, and, consequently, when determining the cost of equity capital.

[7] See Zaik, Walter, Kelling and James (1996).

[8] In this connection, see Federal Reserve (1998).

[9] Merton and Perold (1993).

[10] Please note that this confidence level determination logic is subject to the adoption of a yearly time horizon, similar to the one along which the default probabilities corresponding to different rating classes are generally estimated. Of course, this horizon is very different from the daily horizon which is typically used to estimate VaR connected with market risks.

[11] See Chapter 18 for a review of the meaning of "Tier 1 ratio".

Table 5.3 Rating Classes and Confidence Levels

Moody's Rating Class	1-Year Probability of Insolvency	Confidence Level
Aaa	0.001 %	99.999 %
Aa1	0.01 %	99.99 %
Aa2	0.02 %	99.98 %
Aa3	0.03 %	99.97 %
A1	0.05 %	99.95 %
A2	0.06 %	99.94 %
A3	0.09 %	99.91 %
Baa1	0.13 %	99.87 %
Baa2	0.16 %	99.84 %
Baa3	0.70 %	99.30 %
Ba1	1.25 %	98.75 %
Ba2	1.79 %	98.21 %
Ba3	3.96 %	96.04 %
B1	6.14 %	93.86 %
B2	8.31 %	91.69 %
B3	15.08 %	84.92 %

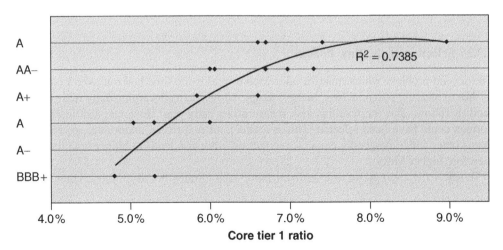

Figure 5.3   Tier 1 Ratio and Rating in Major European Banking Groups

Table 5.4 Tier 1 Ratio and S&P Rating of Some Large European Banking Groups

	Tier 1 Ratio	S&P Rating
UBS	9.00 %	AA
Lloyds TSB	7.40 %	AA
Abbey National	6.70 %	AA
Societé Generale	6.60 %	AA
Deutsche Bank	7.30 %	AA−
BNP Paribas	7.00 %	AA−
Unicredito	6.10 %	AA−
BBVA	6.00 %	AA−
San Paolo IMI	6.60 %	A+
Credit Suisse Group	5.80 %	A+
Credit Lyonnais	6.00 %	A
Commerzbank	6.00 %	A
Banca Intesa	5.30 %	A
Monte dei Paschi	5.00 %	A
Santander	5.00 %	A
Capitalia (*)	5.30 %	BBB+
BNL	4.80 %	BBB+

(*) Based on Fitch's rating.

5.2.3 Selection of the time horizon

The second problem which must be addressed concerns the time horizon over which one wishes to measure potential loss. In the example above, data concerning daily returns were used. It follows that the resulting risk measure is a daily one. However, a different time horizon could have been selected. This is a choice of non-trivial importance, considering that – other conditions being equal – a longer time horizon leads to higher volatility, and therefore higher VaRs.

To select the appropriate time horizon, three factors must be taken into account.

(1) The most important factor is an objective one (i.e., unrelated to the bank's subjective preferences): the degree of liquidity of the individual position's market. Indeed, VaR represents a maximum loss only if the position which generated the losses can be disposed of – within the risk horizon – before it can cause any further capital losses. Therefore, the time interval within which a position can on average be unwound needs to be taken into account. For currency positions, for example, the high liquidity of

the foreign exchange market makes it possible to select a very short time interval – not longer than one day. Vice versa, the time horizon for a position in an
unlisted company's stock should be longer.
(2) A second factor (which is closely connected with the previous one) concerns the size
of the position. As a matter of fact, the selection of a certain time horizon implies the
assumption that this horizon will allow to unwind an outstanding position in case it
is generating losses. The possibility of selling an investment, however, also depends
on its size. For instance, if a certain equity position is higher than the average daily
trading volume, the time required to unwind it is likely to be longer than the time
required by a smaller position.
(3) A third factor, conversely, is a subjective one, in the sense that it originates directly
from the individual trader's and/or financial institution's intent. It is the individual
position's holding period. In this sense, a trading position taken with a very short-
term speculative view should be evaluated with a shorter time horizon than the one
used for a position in the same financial instrument which is considered to be an
investment, and therefore taken with a longer holding period.

Estimating volatility for long time intervals often involves problems due to the lack
of available data and their limited significance if they are used to predict the future.
For instance, if a one-year time horizon is adopted and future annual volatility is to be
predicted, theoretically, the annual returns which occurred in the past should be used, and
their volatility should be estimated. In order for the estimate to be significant, however,
the sample must be sufficiently large, i.e., there must be a sufficiently large number of
annual returns (20, 30 observations). For several market variables (just think, for example,
of the prices of recently listed securities), this can make it difficult to find the necessary
data; moreover, the data relating to periods which are very distant in time might hardly
be useful to estimate the future trend of risk factors.

A possible solution to these problems involves deriving an estimate of volatility for
longer periods from daily volatility. Indeed, if daily returns r are assumed to be represented
by independent and identically distributed random variables, with a mean of $\bar{r}$ and a
variance of σ_r^2, then the return for a period of T days, $R_T = \sum_{t=1}^{T} R_t$, is also normally
distributed, with a mean of $T \cdot \bar{r}$ and a variance of $T \cdot \sigma_r^2$.[12] Standard deviation σ_T for
the period T can therefore be obtained from the daily one σ_D as:

$$\sigma_T = \sigma_D \sqrt{T} \tag{5.6}$$

A particular case of use of (5.6) is the transformation of daily volatility into decadal
volatility by multiplying the former by the square root of ten. This transformation is
allowed and, at the same time, required by the Basel Committee, which subordinates the
possibility of using an internal model to determine the capital requirements in view of
market risks to the adoption of holding periods of at least ten working days (two weeks).[13]

Another example may concern the estimate of monthly volatility: assuming that a month
comprises on average 22 trading days, this can be obtained from daily volatility as:

$$\sigma_T = \sigma_D \sqrt{22}$$

[12] The variable obtained as the sum of n independent random variables – $x_1, x_2, x_3 \ldots x_n$ – all characterized
by the same normal distribution with mean μ and variance σ^2 is also distributed according to a normal, with
mean $n\mu$ and variance $n\sigma^2$.
[13] See Chapter 19.

Once standard deviation has been "scaled", VaR over a risk horizon of T days can be expressed as a multiple of the "new" standard deviation at T days.[14]

It is important to stress that equation (5.7) is subject to the hypothesis that the T daily returns are independent, and therefore requires them to be serially uncorrelated. This hypothesis amounts to assuming that the change in market factors (stock prices, interest rates, exchange rates, etc.) which occurred on day t is independent of the one for day $t-1$, and does not in any way affect the one for day $t+1$. Several empirical studies have shown that, in reality, changes in market factors are often characterised by a serial correlation phenomenon. This is particularly true during periods of market strain, i.e., when particular shocks occur.[15] So, for example, when a generalised stock market crash occurs, as was the case in the period between April 2000 and July 2000, negative returns are often followed by other negative returns. There can be different reasons underlying this serial auto-correlation of market factor returns:

√ the fact that prices are the result of transactions, and therefore reflect the bid-offer spread: it may happen that there is a fluctuation between bid and offer prices, with the consequence that negative serial correlation is recorded, without the equilibrium price undergoing any changes;
√ discontinuity in trading of some instruments, which may cause the effects of a significant piece of information to manifest themselves not on continuous basis, but rather according to a leaping process, thus resulting in positive serial correlation;
√ the structural factors of some markets (low thickness or liquidity), which influence how information is reflected in prices.

Table 5.5 shows, by way of example, the results of a simple indirect empirical test of (5.6). Estimated daily, weekly and monthly standard deviations for the returns of five stock indexes in the two-year period from 1995 to 1996 are reported. For each of these indexes, the estimated weekly and monthly standard deviations obtained from actual weekly (100 observations) and monthly (24 observations) return data are compared with those obtained from transforming the daily standard deviation by applying (5.6). It is noted that the transformation based upon the square root of the number of days contained in the period considered offers acceptable results when one moves from daily to weekly volatility. Vice versa, in case of a shift from daily to monthly volatility, the error is amplified and, moreover, has a different sign, depending on the variable considered.

5.3 SENSITIVITY OF PORTFOLIO POSITIONS TO MARKET FACTORS

5.3.1 A more general example

The example of Table 5.1 above represents a simplified case. In fact, as our risk factor coincided with the portfolio return, its values (including the percentile used to construct VaR) resulted *pari passu* in percentage changes in the value of the bank's stock portfolio.

---

[14] If market value sensitivity to changes in market factors is assumed to be linear, (5.6) can also be used to transform a daily VaR measure (daily earnings at risk, or *DEAR,* using the definition adopted by RiskMetrics™) into a VaR measure for a longer period of T days: $VaR_T = VaR_D\sqrt{T} = DEAR\sqrt{T}$.
[15] Diebold et al. (1997) illustrate the problems which may originate from the use of (5.6).

Table 5.5 A Test of the Hypothesis of Serial Independence of Returns
(1/1/1995–31/12/1996)

	Daily Volatility	Weekly Volatility	Monthly Volatility
		MIB 30	
ACTUAL	1.02 %	2.64 %	6.01 %
ESTIMATED	–	2.28 %	4.78 %
ERROR	–	0.37 %	1.24 %
		S&P 500	
ACTUAL	0.63 %	1.40 %	2.40 %
ESTIMATED	–	1.40 %	2.94 %
ERROR	–	0.00 %	−0.54 %
		CAC 40	
ACTUAL	0.96 %	2.07 %	4.00 %
ESTIMATED	–	2.14 %	4.49 %
ERROR	–	−0.07 %	−0.50 %
		Nikkei	
ACTUAL	1.23 %	2.68 %	6.30 %
ESTIMATED	–	2.75 %	5.76 %
ERROR	–	−0.07 %	0.54 %
		FTSE 100	
ACTUAL	0.61 %	1.52 %	5.16 %
ESTIMATED	–	1.35 %	2.84 %
ERROR	–	0.16 %	2.31 %

In other words, the sensitivity of changes in the value of the stock position to the market factor R_t was unitary.

In more general terms, the variance-covariance approach provides that this sensitivity may not be unitary. This prompts us to rewrite (5.5) as

$$VaR = MV \cdot \delta \cdot \alpha \cdot \sigma \tag{5.7}$$

which contains – besides already known variables – a coefficient (δ) that is representative of the sensitivity of the position's market value to changes in the market factor.[16]

An example will help us understand the role of δ.

---

[16] More precisely, the delta represents the change which the position's market value would suffer as a result of a unitary change in the relevant market factor. More details will be provided below in this chapter.

Suppose we want to measure the VaR of a position in 10-year Treasury bonds whose nominal value is 1 million euros and whose price is 105.

Imagine we want to obtain a risk measure with a 99% confidence level (so, $\alpha = 2.326$) and – based upon historical data – we have estimated a standard deviation of daily changes in the yield to maturity of 10-year T-bonds of 15 basis points. The product of these two quantities is approx. 35 basis points, i.e., +0.35%: the potential unfavourable change in the market factor (here: the yield to maturity of 10-year T-bonds) on which we want to focus is therefore an increase in the yield (Δr) by 35 basis points.

As you may remember from Chapter 2, an increase in market rates is transmitted to the value of a position in T-bonds through modified duration. As a matter of fact, the change in the market value of bonds is given by:

$$\Delta MV \cong -MV \cdot MD \cdot \Delta r$$

If Δr is replaced by the product of α and σ, and the loss in absolute value is considered, the following will be obtained:

$$VaR = MV \cdot MD \cdot \alpha \cdot \sigma$$

By comparing this formula with (5.7), it is realized that, in this case, the sensitivity coefficient δ is given by modified duration. Let us imagine that this is 7 years: VaR of the position in T-bonds will then be equal to:

$$VaR = 1,050,000 \cdot 7 \cdot 0.15\% \cdot 2.326 = 25,644.15$$

Note that this risk measure (unlike the basis point value which was reviewed in the introduction to this part of the volume) reflects not only the degree of sensitivity of the price of securities to changes in interest rates, but also the volatility of these changes. So, the different degree of sensitivity of the different types of financial instruments and the different degree of volatility of the different market factors are both taken into adequate consideration by VaR measures.

5.3.2 Portfolio VaR

When one wants to shift from an individual position to a portfolio of multiple positions, not only the volatilities of individual returns, but also their covariances need to be taken into account – similarly to what happens in the portfolio model originally developed by Markowitz. Estimating the VaR of a portfolio P of positions which are sensitive to N different market factors ($VaR_{P,N}$) therefore requires an additional input, i.e., the correlation coefficients among market factor returns.

If, for the sake of simplicity, we imagine that every i-th position is affected by a different, i-th market factor, the percentage change in its value will be given by

$$\Delta MV\,\%_i \quad = \delta_i \cdot R_i, \tag{5.8}$$

where, as usual, δ_i is the sensitivity of the position's market value to changes in the relevant market factor, and R_i is the possible log change in the market factor over the selected risk horizon (for instance: one day).[17]

The volatility of this percentage change in value (which is a linear transformation of R_i) will be given by

$$\sigma_{\Delta MV_i} = \delta_i \sigma_i \tag{5.9}$$

where σ_i indicates the volatility of R_i.

The variance of $\Delta MV\%_i$ will simply be the square of the previous expression:

$$\sigma_{\Delta MV_i}^2 = \delta_i^2 \sigma_i^2 \tag{5.10}$$

or also

$$\sigma_{\Delta MV_i}^2 = \sigma_{\Delta MV_i, \Delta MV_i}^2 = \rho_{i,i} \delta_i^2 \sigma_i^2 \tag{5.11}$$

considering that $\rho_{i,i}$ (a variable's auto-correlation coefficient) is one, by definition.

Conversely, the covariance between the percentage changes in the value of position i and of another position j will, as usual, be

$$\sigma_{\Delta MV_i, \Delta MV_j}^2 = \rho_{i,j} \sigma_{\Delta MV_i} \sigma_{\Delta MV_j} \tag{5.12}$$

which, in this case, in view of (5.9), can be rewritten as:

$$\sigma_{\Delta MV_i, \Delta MV_j}^2 = \rho_{i,j} \delta_i \sigma_i \delta_j \sigma_j \tag{5.13}$$

Finally, let us consider the expression of the overall change in value of a portfolio comprising N different positions. It will be simply given by a combination of the different positions' percentage changes in value, each multiplied by the value (MV_i) of the position itself::

$$\Delta MV_P = \sum_{i=1}^{N} MV_i \cdot \Delta MV_i \tag{5.14}$$

As MV_i are known and ΔMV_i are uncertain, the variance of ΔMV_P will be given – as is the case in models à la Markowitz – by:

$$\sigma_{\Delta MV_P}^2 = \sum_{i=1}^{N} \sum_{j=1}^{N} MV_i \cdot MV_j \cdot \sigma_{\Delta MV_i, \Delta MV_j}^2 \tag{5.15}$$

which, considering (5.11) and (5.13), becomes

$$\sigma_{\Delta MV_P}^2 = \sum_{i=1}^{N} \sum_{j=1}^{N} MV_i MV_j \rho_{i,j} \delta_i \sigma_i \delta_j \sigma_j \tag{5.16}$$

---

[17] For the sake of simplicity, we will disregard subscript "t".

If the square root of this expression is taken, the expression of the standard deviation of the changes in value of portfolio P will eventually be obtained.

$$\sigma_{\Delta MV_P} = \sqrt{\sum_{i=1}^{N}\sum_{j=1}^{N} MV_i MV_j \rho_{i,j}\delta_i\sigma_i\delta_j\sigma_j} \qquad (5.17)$$

At this point, we need to highlight that, since risk factors are assumed to be normally distributed, then the change in the portfolio's value (equation 5.14) is also distributed according to a normal, as it represents a linear combination of normal variables.

The VaR associated with a confidence level c can therefore be found by multiplying $\sigma_{\Delta MV_P}$ by an appropriate α (selected, as was seen in §5.2, so that $F^*(\alpha) = 1 - c$).
Hence:

$$VaR_P = \alpha \cdot \sigma_{\Delta MV_P}$$

Using (5.17) and a little algebra, it is then shown that the portfolio's VaR

$$VaR_P = \alpha \cdot \sigma_{\Delta MV_P} = \sqrt{\sum_{i=1}^{N}\sum_{j=1}^{N} \alpha^2\, MV_i MV_j \rho_{i,j}\delta_i\sigma_i\delta_j\sigma_j} =$$

$$= \sqrt{\sum_{i=1}^{N}\sum_{j=1}^{N} (MV_i\delta_i\alpha\sigma_i)(MV_j\delta_j\alpha\sigma_j)\rho_{i,j}} = \sqrt{\sum_{i=1}^{N}\sum_{j=1}^{N} VaR_i VaR_j \rho_{i,j}} \qquad (5.18)$$

is given by a function which contains all the VaRs of the individual portfolio positions and the correlation coefficients among the relevant risk factors. Note that, if all risk factors were perfectly correlated, the following would be obtained

$$VaR_P = \sqrt{\sum_{i=1}^{N}\sum_{j=1}^{N} VaR_i VaR_j \cdot 1} = \sum_{i=1}^{N} VaR_i$$

and the overall value at risk would coincide with the sum of individual VaRs. As, however, $\rho_{i,j} \leq 1$, the following will be obtained:

$$VaR_P \leqslant \sum_{i=1}^{N} VaR_i$$

VaR calculated using the parametric approach is therefore a subadditive risk measure, in the sense that, when multiple positions are combined, the total risk – measured through VaR – can only be lower, and never higher, than the sum of individual positions' risks. So, this risk measure correctly implements the risk diversification principle.

Now, let us apply (5.18) with an example. Assume we want to estimate the value at risk connected with two currency positions, a long one in US dollars and a short one in Japanese yens, with market values of 50 and 10 million euros, respectively. In addition, assume that the daily volatility of log returns of the two exchange rates, EUR/USD and EUR/YEN, is 2 % and 3 %, respectively, and that the correlation coefficient between these returns is 0.6.

The daily value at risk of the dollar exposure, measured with a 99.5 % confidence level (which corresponds to an α of 2.576), is given by:

$$VaR = MV \cdot \delta \cdot \alpha \cdot \sigma$$

$$VaR_{USD} = MV \cdot \delta \cdot \alpha \cdot \sigma = 50 \cdot 1 \cdot 2.576 \cdot 2\% \cong 2.576$$

million euros, while the VaR of the yen exposure is:

$$VaR_{YEN} = -10 \cdot 2.576 \cdot 3\% \cong -0.773$$

where the negative sign was used to remind the reader that – since this is a short position – the loss (773,000 euros) occurs when there is *an increase*, and not a decrease, in the Euro/Yen exchange rate.

Finally, the entire portfolio's VaR will be given by:

$$VaR_P = \sqrt{2.576^2 + (-0.773)^2 + 2 \cdot 2.576 \cdot (-0.773) \cdot 0.6} \cong 2.2$$

million euros. Note that the signs of the two positions (long or short) must explicitly be taken into account in estimating the portfolio's VaR. Indeed, the fact that the two positions have opposite signs makes VaR equivalent to the one which would be obtained in the case of two positions having equivalent signs and a negative correlation coefficient.

When we move from the case of two positions to the one of an actual portfolio comprising several positions which are sensitive to different market factors, it becomes easier to have recourse to matricial algebra. Consider a portfolio comprising N positions, characterized by values at risk of VaR_1, VaR_2, ... VaR_N, respectively. The values at risk for the individual positions can be expressed in vector form as:[18]

$$\mathbf{v} = \begin{bmatrix} VaR_1 \\ VaR_2 \\ \cdots \\ VaR_N \end{bmatrix} \tag{5.19}$$

Similarly, the correlation coefficients among market factor returns can be expressed combined in the following matrix:

$$\mathbf{C} = \begin{bmatrix} 1 & \rho_{1,2} & \cdots & \rho_{1,N} \\ \rho_{2,1} & 1 & \cdots & \rho_{2,N} \\ \cdots & \cdots & \cdots & \cdots \\ \rho_{N,1} & \cdots & \cdots & 1 \end{bmatrix} \tag{5.20}$$

[18] Within the vector, values at risk must be shown with the appropriate algebraic signs of the original positions, as was done in the example of the short position in yen.

and (5.18) can simply be rewritten as:

$$VaR_P = \sqrt{\mathbf{v'} \cdot \mathbf{C} \cdot \mathbf{v}} \qquad (5.21)$$

where $\mathbf{v'}$ indicates the transpose of $\mathbf{v}$.[19]

5.3.3 Delta-normal and asset-normal approaches

Note that, up to this point, we have used correlation coefficients and volatilities of market factor returns. As a matter of fact, we assumed a normal distribution with reference to the (log)[20] changes in these factors (interest rates, exchange rates, etc.). This hypothesis, on the contrary, did *not* concern the (log) changes in the unit prices of the securities in the portfolio.

To understand the difference, let us think about the case of T-bonds which was reviewed in section 5.3.1: we assumed that (for instance, daily) changes *in its market risk factor* (long-term interest rate) were distributed according to a normal. Conversely, no hypothesis was made with regard to the distribution followed by changes *in the bond price*.

Since reference was made to the distribution of rates, and not prices, we had to include into the VaR formula (equation 5.7) a coefficient δ (which, in the case of fixed-rate securities, coincided – as was seen – with modified duration), whose function was to link the value of the security to the value of the relevant risk factor (interest rate).

This approach is called delta-normal. It proceeds from the distribution of market factors (or better, of their relevant changes), and "links" it to the distribution of changes in the portfolio positions' prices through linear sensitivity coefficients; in this way, the probability distribution of the changes in the portfolio positions' prices is also normal, and VaR can be calculated using an appropriate multiple of the standard deviation. The same is true for changes in the portfolio value, which – as was seen – are a linear combination of normal variables (and so are also characterized by a normal distribution).

Alternatively, we could have proceeded from the probability distribution of the prices of the assets in the portfolio, and could have assumed the latter to be log-normal (i.e., the relevant log changes to be normal). This approach, which is followed by Risk-Metrics™ is called asset-normal. In the example of the bond, the changes in the price of the bond on the secondary market – and not the changes in its relevant yield to maturity – would have been distributed according to a normal; so, there would have been no need for any delta coefficient to compute VaR, because the percentage changes in the bond price would have been directly and immediately reflected in the changes in the value of the entire portfolio position, and therefore in possible future losses. So, compared to the delta-normal approach, the asset-normal approach has the advantage of simplifying the analysis when calculating a portfolio's VaR, because, *de facto*, it just considers the positions' returns, without introducing the problem of the relation between market factors and position values.

---

[19] It is evident that, in order for VaR calculation to be correct, it is necessary to have a good and reliable estimate of the standard deviations of risk factors, as well as of the correlations collected in matrix C. See Chapter 6 for some techniques which can be used to estimate them.

[20] Log changes ($\log S_t - \log S_{t-1}$, or, $\log(S_t/S_{t-1})$) are usually employed, because they appropriately approximate percentage changes (see paragraph 5.1). An exception is given by interest rates, for which it may be easier to use absolute changes $S_t - S_{t-1}$ (difference between today's and yesterday's levels of the rate) – as was done in the example in section 5.3.1.

Sometimes, in the delta-normal approach, δ is equal to one: in these cases, there is no difference between the delta-normal and the asset-normal approach. We saw an example of this in section 5.3.2, considering currency positions: for this type of investments, the position's return and the return of the relevant market factor (exchange rate) coincide (if the EUR/USD rate increases by 20%, the value in euros of an investment in dollars will also increase by the same percentage). In other cases, however, the two differ. Take as an example the case of a zero-coupon bond: the market factor return (changes in the zero-coupon rate) does not coincide with the position's return (changes in the price of the zero-coupon bond).

Just as, when measuring an individual position's value at risk, the asset-normal approach is based upon the volatility of the position's (log) return, likewise, the calculation of the VaR of a portfolio comprising multiple positions must be based upon the correlation matrix among these returns. So, this approach provides that the same equation as illustrated above – (5.18 or 5.21) – will be applied, replacing correlation coefficients among market factor returns with correlation coefficients among the returns of the individual positions.

5.4   MAPPING OF RISK POSITIONS

So far, each individual position has been assumed to be sensitive to one market factor only. In reality, however, it often happens that positions' market values are a function of multiple market factors. Take as an example the case of a German bank purchasing a US ten-year Treasury bond. The latter has a value in euros which depends on two main market factors: (i) the EUR/USD exchange rate, and (ii) the level of dollar interest rates.[21]

In general, VaR estimation within the variance-covariance approach provides for individual positions to be first broken down – following appropriate mapping techniques[22] – into elementary components. The latter must be such that their value will depend on changes in a *single* market factor. The risk of the entire position can then be determined based upon the risks connected with the individual elementary components, aggregated based upon the correlations among the relevant market factor returns.

In this paragraph we will show the mapping techniques that are used for some widespread financial instruments in banks' portfolios.

5.4.1   Mapping of foreign currency bonds

Let us start with the just mentioned example: the case of a German bank investing a given amount (let's say 100 million euros) in a US dollar bond whose modified duration is 7 years.

In this case, as was said, the bank is exposed to both an exchange rate risk (risk factor: EUR/USD exchange rate, in short FX) and a dollar interest-rate risk (risk factor: dollar

---

[21] If one wanted to be more precise, it could be argued that the security's market value depends on 21 different market factors: the exchange rate, and the 20 zero-coupon rates of yield to maturity of the security's cash flows. Here we will just consider the bond's equilibrium yield to maturity, which summarises the entire rate structure, as the risk factor.

[22] This mapping is conceptually similar to the one illustrated with reference to interest-rate risk, when discussing the clumping technique (Chapter 3).

interest rate, in short r, if we adopt a delta-normal approach[23]). The possible losses are therefore roughly the same as for a bank with:

(1) a spot (cash) position in dollars of one million euros;
(2) an exchange rate risk-free position in US bonds (exposed to the interest-rate risk only).

So, let us calculate the two positions' VaRs (using a 99.5 % confidence level, corresponding to an α of 2.572). For the first one, assuming that the volatility of changes in the EUR/USD exchange rate is 2 %, the following is obtained:

$$VaR_1 = MV \cdot \delta \cdot \alpha \cdot \sigma = 100 \cdot 1 \cdot 2.576 \cdot 2\% \cong 5.152$$

For the second one, assuming that the dollar interest rate has a volatility of 1 %, the following is obtained:

$$VaR_2 = -MV \cdot MD \cdot \alpha \cdot \sigma = -100 \cdot 7 \cdot 2.576 \cdot 1\% = -18.031$$

(where we left the negative sign just to remind us that losses occur when the relevant risk factor – i.e., interest rate – increases).

In order to find this "portfolio"'s VaR based upon (5.18), we also need to know the correlation coefficient between the two risk factors (percentage changes in the exchange rate and changes in the interest rate); let us imagine that this correlation is positive and equal to 30 % (so, we are assuming that, when US bond rates rise, the dollar on average appreciates over the Euro).

(5.18) leads us to estimate the following VaR:

$$VaR_P = \sqrt{5.152^2 + (-18.031)^2 + 2 \cdot 5.152(-18.031) \cdot 0.3} \cong 17.202$$

Holding the foreign currency denominated bond therefore involves a VaR of approximately three million euros. Note that this is lower than that of a USD-denominated position in bonds with no FX risk (approx. 18 million euros) because, when dollar interest rates increase, causing the bank's investment to depreciate, the dollar is likely to appreciate with respect to the Euro, raising the bond's value and partly offsetting the effect of rising interest rates.

It is also possible to provide a more rigorous explanation of the equivalence between the investment in a foreign currency bond and the two elementary components (spot investment in dollars, exchange rate risk-free dollar bond) we used. In order to do so, it is useful to remind that the market value of a position of this kind is a function of two variables: FX (the EUR/USD exchange rate) and r (the interest rate on dollar bonds):

$$VM = f(FX, r)$$

---

[23] The risk factor would be the *price* of dollar bonds if we adopted an asset-normal approach.

Changes in the position's value can therefore be linearly approximated by a first-degree Taylor series expansion:

$$dMV \cong f'_{FX} dFX + f'_r \, dr = f'_{FX} FX \frac{dFX}{FX} + f'_r \, dr \qquad (5.22)$$

Now we note that:

- $f'_{FX} = \dfrac{MV}{FX}$: the sensitivity of a currency position to percentage changes in the exchange rate is given by the position's countervalue expressed in a foreign currency (market value in domestic currency divided by the exchange rate);

- $f'_r \equiv \dfrac{dMV}{dr} = -MV \cdot MD$: the sensitivity of a bond position to changes in the interest rate is given by the market value, with changed sign, multiplied by its modified duration.

Considering these two points, (5.22) becomes:

$$dMV \cong \frac{MV}{FX} FX \frac{dFX}{FX} - MV \cdot MD \cdot dr = MV \frac{dFX}{FX} - MV \cdot MD \cdot dr \qquad (5.23)$$

from which it is inferred that the change in value on a foreign currency bond can be broken down into two components, which correspond:

- to the change in value on a cash foreign currency position;
- to the change in value on a foreign bond position held by a foreign investor (i.e., exchange rate risk-free),

respectively.

So, these are the two elementary components into which the bank's position needs to be broken down.

5.4.2 Mapping of forward currency positions

Forward purchase or sale of foreign currencies is equivalent to the simultaneous taking of three different positions (elementary components) which are sensitive to three different market factors: the spot exchange rate and the interest rates of the two currencies involved in the forward transaction.

To better understand this breakdown, let us consider an example. Let us assume that a French bank has purchased 1 million dollars at 6 months. This position can be broken down into three different virtual positions:

(1) a 6-month Euro-denominated debt, such as to generate – in 6 month's time – a cash outflow equal to the forward countervalue of 1 million dollars.
(2) an investment in dollars, such as to produce – in 6 month's time – a principal of 1 million dollars.
(3) a spot dollar purchase (whereby we pay euros and receive dollars), such as to cancel the flows generated by the transactions as per (1) and (2) today.

As Figure 5.4 clearly shows, the sum of these three elementary components produces a – cash flow – result which is perfectly equivalent to the one associated to the forward purchase transaction.

Mapping the original transaction therefore requires determining the value of the three virtual positions and combining them considering the correlations among risk factors.

To complete the example, assume that market data are as shown in Table 5.6.[24]

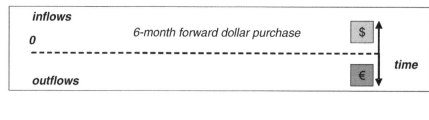

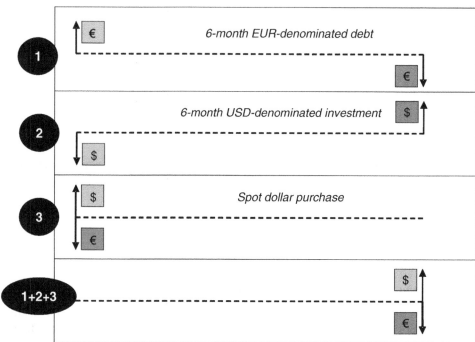

Figure 5.4   Mapping of a 6-Month Forward Dollar Purchase

Incidentally, it can be seen that the 6-month forward interest rate quoted by the market corresponds to the value which can be obtained based upon "covered interest rate parity".[25]

$$F_t = S \cdot \frac{1 + r_d \cdot t}{1 + r_f \cdot t}$$
(5.24)

---

[24] For the sake of simplicity, bid-offer differentials are disregarded. In compliance with market conventions, simple compounding of interest rates is used.

[25] Covered interest rate parity is an equilibrium parity based upon an arbitrage logic. This means that, if it were not complied with, it would be possible to make arbitrage transactions and thus obtain a risk-free profit.

Table 5.6 Exchange and Interest Rates

EUR/USD spot exchange rate (S)	1.2
6-month EUR interest rate (r_d)	3.50 %
6-month USD interest rate (r_f)	2.00 %
6-month EUR/USD exchange rate (F_t)	1.209

where F_t indicates the forward exchange rate for maturity t, S the spot exchange rate, r_d the domestic interest rate, and r_f the foreign currency interest rate. If (5.12) is applied to the example under consideration, the following will be obtained:

$$F_{6m} = 1.2 \cdot \frac{1 + 0.035 \cdot 0.5}{1 + 0.02 \cdot 0.5} = 1.209$$

At this point, the value of the three elementary components into which the forward dollar purchase can be broken down has to be calculated.

(1) First of all, the 6-month dollar investment transaction must be such as to generate, in 6 months time, a principal and interest of 1 million dollars: only in this case can a dollar cash inflow equal to the one obtained from the forward purchase be obtained. This investment will therefore be equal to the present value of 1 million dollars, calculated using the 6-month dollar interest rate:

$$MV_1 = \frac{1,000,000}{(1 + 0.02 \cdot 0.5)} = \$ 990,099$$

(2) In the second place, a Euro-denominated debt such as to purchase a dollar amount equal to VM_1 (990,099 dollars) is needed. Analytically:

$$MV_2 = MV_1 \cdot S = 990,099 \cdot 1.2 = 1,188,119$$

(3) This same amount is also the dollar amount which needs to be purchased spot against euros:

$$MV_3 = MV_2 \cdot = 1,188,119$$

A 6-month forward purchase of 1 million dollars against euros can therefore be broken down into three virtual positions:

(1) 6-month investment of 990,099 dollars;
(2) 6-month debt amounting to 1,188,119 euros;
(3) spot purchase of 990,099 dollars.

Table 5.7 Volatility and Correlations – Market Factors for a Forward Position

Market factor	Volatility	EUR/USD	i_{EUR6m}	i_{USD6m}
			Correlation with	
EUR/USD spot exchange rate	3 %	1	−0.2	+0.4
6-month EUR interest rate (i_{EUR6m})	1.5 %	−0.2	1	+0.6
6-month USD interest rate (i_{USD6m})	1.2 %	+0.4	0.6	1

Using the volatility data for the three market factors (see Table 5.7), it is now possible to estimate the VaR connected with the individual elementary components (for the individual steps, see also Table 5.8):

$$VaR_1 = 990,099 \cdot 1.2\% \cdot 2.326 \cdot 0.490 = 13,549$$

$$VaR_2 = 1,188,119 \cdot 1.5\% \cdot 2.326 \cdot 0.483 = 20,029$$

$$VaR_3 = 990,099 \cdot 3\% \cdot 2.326 = 69,099$$

Note that the first and the last values are in USD, and must be converted into euros at the spot rate (getting 16,259 and 82,919 respectively).

Considering the correlations among risk factors (Table 5.7), the VaR of the original forward position (seen as a "portfolio" of three elementary components) can now be estimated as follows:

$$VaR_P = \sqrt{\begin{array}{c} VaR_1^2 + VaR_2^2 + VaR_3^2 + 2 \cdot VaR_1 VaR_2 \rho_{1,2} + \\ +2 \cdot VaR_1 VaR_3 \rho_{1,3} + 2 \cdot VaR_2 VaR_3 \rho_{2,3} \end{array}} =$$

$$= \sqrt{\begin{array}{c} 16,259^2 + 20,029^2 + 82,919^2 + 2 \cdot (-16,259) \cdot 20,029 \cdot 0.6 + \\ +2 \cdot (-16,259) \cdot 82,919 \cdot 0.4 + 2 \cdot 20,029 \cdot 82,919 \cdot (-0.2) \end{array}} = 73,536$$

Note that the VaR of the virtual position represented by the USD investment is shown with a negative sign. This is due to the fact that this position's market value is inversely related to changes in the relevant market factor (an increase in the dollar interest rate would result in a reduction in this position's market value).

Table 5.8 Virtual Positions' VaRs – Mapping of a Forward Position

Position	MV	σ	α	i	Duration	DM	VaR
USD investment	990,099	1.20 %	2.326	2.00 %	0.5	0.490	13,549
EUR-denominated debt	1,188,119	1.50 %	2.326	3.50 %	0.5	0.483	20,029
Spot USD purchase	990,099	3.00 %	2.326	–	–	–	69,099

5.4.3   Mapping of forward rate agreements

A forward rate agreement (FRA) is an agreement locking in the interest rate on an investment (or on a debt) running for a pre-determined period ("FRA period"), from a certain future date (see Appendix 4A).

A FRA is a notional contract. Therefore, there is no actual exchange of principal at the expiry date; rather, the value of the contract (based on the difference between the pre-determined rate and the current spot rates) is usually settled in cash at the start of the FRA period.

However, for pricing purposes, a FRA can be seen as an investment/debt taking place in the future. For example, a three-month 1 million Euro FRA effective in 3 month's time can be seen as an agreement binding a party to pay – in three month's time – a sum of 1 million euros to the other party, which undertakes to return it, three months later, increased by interest at the forward rate agreed upon.[26]

Such an agreement could, for instance, have been underwritten on 1 August 2000, specifying a forward rate of 5.136 %.[27] The investment would therefore run from 1 November, and would terminate on 1 February 2001 with the delivery of a final principal and interest equal to

$$1,000,000 * (1 + 0.05136 * 92/365) = 1,012,964 \text{ euros.}$$

Figure 5.5 shows that this transaction is equivalent to the following two spot transactions (which represent the elementary components into which the forward transaction is to be broken down):

1. a 3-month debt with final principal and interest of one million euros;
2. 6-month investment of the principal obtained from the transaction as per 1.

In more general terms, if the FRA runs from time m and terminates at time f, it can be "mapped" into two elementary components, i.e.:

1. a debt from today to f, whose principal and interest correspond to the notional amount of the FRA;
2. an investment from today to m, whose principal and interest correspond to the FRA's notional amount and interest.

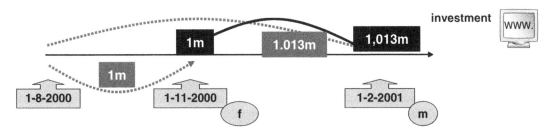

Figure 5.5   Mapping of a Forward Rate Agreement

---

[26] Under this type of contract the seller of the FRA would indeed have the obligation to pay the buyer the difference – if positive – between the 3 months interest rate prevailing in the market after three months and the agreed rate (the FRA contractual interest rate). On the other side, the buyer of the contract would be obliged to pay the seller this same difference if negative. See Appendix 4A for more details.

[27] Following a convention which is widespread on the markets for these instruments, we use simple compounding.

Assuming that 3- and 6-month spot rates are 5% and 5.10%[28] respectively, the two elementary components will be equal to those indicated in Table 5.9. The algebraic sum of their flows (last column in the Table) will obviously coincide with the FRA's flows: this shows that our mapping logic is correct.

Table 5.9 Mapping of a Forward Rate Position

			1. Debt	2. Investment	1 + 2 = FRA
		rate	5.000%	5.10%	
		duration (days)	92	184	92
Cash flows	Today	01/08/2000	+987,554	−987,554	0
	F	01/11/2000	−1,000,000		−1,000,000
	M	01/02/2001		+1,012,946	1,012,946

If we want to calculate the FRA's VaR, VaR_1 and VaR_2 (the VaRs of the two 3- and 6-month 987,554 Euro fictitious spot positions) need to be calculated and combined according to (5.18). This in turn would require to estimate the historical correlation between the changes in the 3-month spot rate (first risk factor) and the changes in the six-month spot rate (second risk factor).

5.4.4 Mapping of stock positions

The estimation of the risk connected with equity positions poses an opposite problem to what happens for forward currency positions. Unlike a forward purchase or sale, whose value is sensitive to multiple market factors, a stock position has a market value which is sensitive to one factor only: the stock price. In this case, the problem is related to the fact that, if every single stock price were considered as a risk factor, in the case of a trading portfolio comprising many different stocks (also belonging to different worldwide stock exchange markets), a very large number of market factors whose volatilities and correlations should be estimated would be obtained. In this case, therefore, the problem is not to break each individual position down into multiple virtual positions which are sensitive to different market factors, but rather to aggregate multiple positions based upon their common sensitivity to a single market factor.

The criterion which is generally adopted for this purpose involves relating an individual stock position to a virtual position towards the relevant stock exchange market, based upon an appropriate sensitivity coefficient. In this way, stock positions are related to a limited number of fictitious positions towards the relevant stock exchange indexes (this number is equal to the number of stock exchange markets on which the bank is active). For this

---

[28] The values in the example are not random. As a matter of fact, the three-month FRA market rate, effective in three month's time (in symbols $_3r_3$) is a function of spot rates. More precisely, in order for no arbitrages to arise, it must be such that $1 + r_6\frac{6}{12} = \left(1 + r_3\frac{3}{12}\right)\left(1 + {}_3r_3\frac{3}{12}\right)$. It is easy to see that the values in the example meet this condition.

purpose, the individual i-th position is "mapped" to the relevant j-th stock market based upon its beta coefficient:[29]

$$MV_i^* = MV_i \cdot \beta_{i,j} \qquad (5.25)$$

where MV^*_i indicates the market value of the virtual position in the stock exchange index associated with the market value MV_i of the actual position in the i-th security. By aggregating all stocks listed on market j, the bank's overall virtual position in the relevant stock exchange index is obtained

$$MV_j = \sum_{i \in j} MV_i^* = \sum_{i \in j} MV_i \cdot \beta_{i,j} \qquad (5.26)$$

This way, the *VaR* for the position in the i-th stock can be estimated based upon the volatility of the return of the stock exchange market index on which it is traded.
The overall VaR for the j-th stock market would be given by:

$$VaR_j = MV_j \cdot \alpha \cdot \sigma_j = \left(\sum_{i \in j} MV_i \cdot \beta_{i,j} \right) \cdot \alpha \cdot \sigma_j \qquad (5.27)$$

Where σ_j is the standard deviation of (log) changes in the market's stock exchange index, and δ was omitted, as it is unitary.
To clarify the advantages and potential problems of this mapping methodology, consider the three stock positions shown in Table 5.10. For each stock, the actual position and the corresponding virtual position in the stock exchange index – based upon the relevant beta coefficient – are shown. Moreover, volatility and correlation data for the individual stocks are reported.

Table 5.10 An Example of Mapping of Stock Positions

	Stock A	Stock B	Stock C	Index	Portfolio
Market Value (€ m)	10	15	20	–	45
Beta	1,4	1,2	0,8	–	1.067
Virtual position in the index (€ m)	14	18	16	–	48
Volatility	15.0 %	12.0 %	10.0 %	7 %	–
Correlation with A	1	0.5	0.8		
Correlation with B	0.5	1	0		
Correlation with C	0.8	0	1		

Using the data from the Table, and selecting an appropriate confidence level (for instance 99 %, which is associated with $\alpha = 2.326$), we can compute VaR in two ways:

---

[29] The beta coefficient of a stock i is the sensitivity of the stock's return to the return of the market (j) on which it is listed. In this connection, see Appendix 5A to this chapter.

- either by using mapping, i.e., considering the virtual positions in the index and the latter's volatility;
- or without having recourse to mapping, i.e., considering the actual positions and using three risk factors, corresponding to the returns of stocks A, B, C.

If mapping is used, the VaR of the portfolio comprising the three stocks – based upon (5.27) – will be:

$$VaR_P^* = \left(\sum_{i \in j} MV_i \cdot \beta_{i,j} \right) \cdot \alpha \cdot \sigma_j = 48 \cdot 2.326 \cdot 0.07 = 7.817$$

million euros.

Alternatively, the portfolio's VaR can be estimated using the volatility and correlation data of the individual stocks, and applying 5.19. The following will then be obtained:

$$VaR_P = \sqrt{ \begin{array}{c} VaR_A^2 + VaR_B^2 + VaR_C^2 \\ +2VaR_A VaR_B \rho_{A,B} + 2VaR_A VaR_C \rho_{A,C} + 2VaR_B VaR_C \rho_{B,C} \end{array} } = 9.589$$

(for a breakdown of individual VaRs and a summary of results, see Table 5.11).

The VaR obtained by applying the mapping methodology described above (€7,817,000) is lower than the one based upon volatility of returns of individual stocks and the relevant correlations (€9,589,000). Such a result is easily explained: indeed, the mapping procedure is based on the assumption that the return volatility of each individual stock can be entirely explained by the return volatility of the stock market on which this stock is traded.

Table 5.11 VaR of a Stock Portfolio

	Individual stocks			Portfolio	
	Stock A	Stock B	Stock C	Mapping	Volatility & Correlations
VaR (99 %)	3.490	4.187	4.653	7.817	9.589

This amounts to assuming that:

√ a stock's risk is given by systematic risk only, i.e., the return volatility component which cannot be eliminated through an adequate portfolio diversification policy; the specific risk, i.e. the volatility component which can be eliminated through an adequate diversification policy, is therefore disregarded;

√ in turn, a stock's systematic risk can be adequately captured by beta, i.e., through a single-factor model such as the CAPM.

The mapping procedure therefore leads to risk estimation errors in the event that:

√ the trading portfolio comprises a limited number of stocks or has a high degree of concentration onto a limited number of stocks; as a matter of fact, in this case, the stocks' specific risk is likely not to be eliminated by diversification;

√ a stock's systematic risk is more correctly captured by a multi-factor model (such as the Arbitrage Pricing Theory).

In particular, if the first condition occurs, the mapping procedure based upon the beta coefficient is likely to lead to risk underestimation. This is the case of the example which was presented above (comprising three stocks only). For this reason, numerous financial institutions prefer to avoid mapping, and base the calculation of their stock portfolios' VaRs on volatility and correlation data concerning the returns of individual stocks.

5.4.5   Mapping of bonds

So far, we have assumed that the risk of a bond can be modelled using a single risk factor, which we have called from time to time "yield to maturity", "market rate of return", etc.

In fact, the duration-based formula used to estimate a bond's price change driven by a change in the market rate requires the use of the bond's specific yield to maturity. This in turn depends on the security's maturity and the structure of its coupons; it follows that different bonds have different yields to maturity.

A bank holding many bonds in its portfolio should therefore use a very large number of risk factors. Moreover, the yield to maturity associated with a given security is hard to monitor over time, because the characteristics of the bond itself (in particular, its residual maturity) change over time. So, as we go back in time, the historical series of the yield to maturity of a specific bond which has now a 5 years residual maturity contain data which are valid for a 6-, 7-, 8-year maturity bond, and so on.

For all these reasons, banks prefer not to use yields to maturity, but zero-coupon rates related to a pre-determined set of maturities, which is the term structure (see. Chapter 3), as risk factors.

This implies that a Treasury bond must be broken down into its elementary cash flows (coupons plus redemption value), and that each of these elementary flows must in turn be translated (according to the clumping techniques shown in Chapter 3) into "fictitious" cash flows associated with the nodes of the term structure.

The changes in the zero-coupon rates associated with the corresponding nodes in the curve and the relevant volatilities are subsequently applied, as risk factors, to the fictitious flows generated by these mapping procedures. The resulting individual risk measures can then be aggregated based upon the correlation among the changes in the rates for the relevant maturities.

5.5   SUMMARY OF THE VARIANCE-COVARIANCE APPROACH AND MAIN LIMITATIONS

At this point, it may be useful to review the main choices which are typical of the variance/covariance approach, as we have presented it in this chapter. To this end, let us go back to the Figure appearing in the introduction to this part of the volume, in order to stress once again that:

– the parametric approach assumes that (log) changes in risk factors are distributed according to a normal distribution with a variance of zero and stable volatility over time; in the asset-normal approach, this assumption is applied directly to (log) price changes;
– changes in positions' values are derived from those in risk factors through linear coefficients (delta); in the presence of particular positions (for instance, foreign currency

bonds, forward exchange rates, FRAs), not the original position, but a set of elementary components derived through mapping techniques are used;
– changes in the value of a portfolio of positions and/or elementary components are obtained in a parametric manner using the risk factor changes correlation matrix;
– VaR – of both individual positions and of a portfolio – is obtained in a parametric manner by multiplying the standard deviation by a scaling factor α which depends on the selected confidence level.

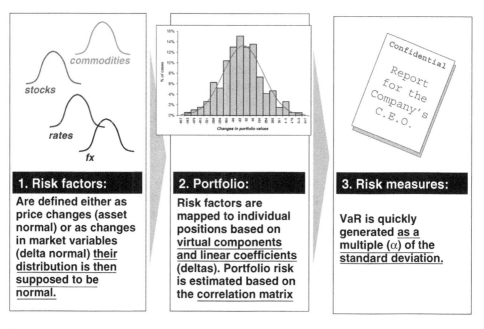

Figure 5.6   Main Characteristics of the Parametric Approach

These hypotheses give rise to four main limitations:

$\sqrt{}$ normal distribution of market factor returns;
$\sqrt{}$ stable distribution of market factor returns (and therefore, of the variance/covariance matrix, as well),
$\sqrt{}$ and serial independence of the same returns;
$\sqrt{}$ linear payoff profiles for the risk position.

Let us analyze these limitations in more detail, showing the main correctives developed in the literature.

5.5.1 The normal distribution hypothesis

The normal return distribution hypothesis has been the target of the following criticisms:

$\sqrt{}$ Empirical distributions of financial assets returns generally have fatter tails than are typical of a normal distribution. The probability of occurrence of price changes that are far from the mean value is therefore higher than the one implied in a normal distribution.[30] This characteristic is called *leptokurtosis*.

✓ Price changes, and consequently financial assets returns, are generally distributed in a not perfectly symmetrical manner, in the sense that more observations can be found at the left-hand extreme (values considerably below the mean) than at the right-hand extreme (values considerably above the mean) of the distribution. This phenomenon (which can also be found in Figure 5.1) is called "negative skewness".

✓ One last point concerns the distribution of interest rates, and, in particular, of money-market rates. As these are directly affected by the effects of monetary policy, they clearly follow a discretionary and non-random path. So, their changes generally do not follow a normal distribution, precisely because the monetary policy is not managed at random.

Fat tails are perhaps the most serious problem among the above-mentioned ones. This phenomenon suggests that particularly high losses occur more frequently than implied in a normal distribution. So, the probability of incurring losses in excess of the parametric VaR calculated, for instance, with a 99 per cent confidence level is in reality higher than 1%.

Fortunately, even if the distribution of individual market factor returns were not normal, the returns of a diversified portfolio whose value depends on multiple independent market factors would be likely to be distributed according to a normal anyway;[31] however, it must be mentioned that market factors are not, in general, independent, indeed, they tend to move in a correlated manner precisely in the event of heavy losses due to catastrophic events.

The problems described above prompted academics and practitioners to search for alternative solutions to the normal distribution hypothesis. A first solution to the problem of leptokurtosis is to replace the normal distribution with other distributions, such as the Student t, which is characterized by fatter tails than the normal distribution (and therefore more adequately reflects the probability associated with extreme market factor movements). This solution – besides being a better market approximation[32] – has the advantage of considering the variance-covariance matrix itself as a random variable about which only limited information is available.[33]

The Student's t-distribution is entirely defined by the mean, μ, and variance, σ^2, of the market factor return, and by an additional parameter called "degrees of freedom", v, which controls the degree of leptokurtosis (i.e., the thickness of the tails). The lower the degrees of freedom, the thicker the tails. As v increases, Student's t-distribution converges towards a normal distribution with a mean of μ 956/and a variance of σ^2.

---

[30] For an example, see Figure 5.1. For a review of the problem of "fat tails" accompanied by interesting empirical evidence, see Chew (1994), pp. 63–70, and Duffie and Pan (1997).

[31] This result is explained by the central limit theorem, according to which the sum of independent and identically distributed (i.i.d.) random variables has an asymptotically normal distribution. In particular, given n i.i.d. variables $X_1, X_2, \ldots, X_n$, with $E(X_i) = \mu$ $Var(X_i) = \sigma^2$ and, then: $Z = \dfrac{\sum_{i=1}^{n} X_i - n\mu}{\sigma \sqrt{n}}$ converges in probability to $N(0,1)$.

[32] Student's t-distribution has a leptokurtic pattern. See Blattberg and Gonedes (1974); Rogalski and Vinso (1978).

[33] For a close examination of the application of Student's t-distribution to VaR and an empirical comparison of the two return distribution hypotheses, see T. Wilson (1993).

Table 5.12 shows the multiple of the standard deviation associated with different confidence levels using a standard normal distribution and various Students' t-distributions (which, like the standard normal one, take a mean of zero and a unitary standard deviation here) characterised by different degrees of freedom. As can be seen, mean and standard deviation being equal, a Student's t-distribution generates higher VaR estimates than the ones generated using the normal distribution assumption. The lower the degrees of freedom - i.e., the thicker the distribution tails – the truer this is.

Table 5.12 Comparison of Normal and Student's t-Distributions – Multiples of the Standard Deviation Corresponding to Different Confidence Levels

Confidence level	Standardised normal distribution	Multiple of the standard deviation						
		Student's t with v degrees of freedom						
		$v = 10$	$v = 9$	$v = 8$	$v = 7$	$v = 6$	$v = 5$	$v = 4$
99.99 %	3.72	6.21	6.59	7.12	7.89	9.08	11.18	15.53
99.50 %	2.58	3.58	3.69	3.83	4.03	4.32	4.77	5.60
99.00 %	2.33	3.17	3.25	3.36	3.50	3.71	4.03	4.60
98.00 %	2.05	2.76	2.82	2.90	3.00	3.14	3.36	3.75
97.50 %	1.96	2.63	2.69	2.75	2.84	2.97	3.16	3.50
95.00 %	1.64	2.23	2.26	2.31	2.36	2.45	2.57	2.78
90.00 %	1.28	1.81	1.83	1.86	1.89	1.94	2.02	2.13

A second solution to the problem of fat tails is to use a mixture of normals, characterized by the same mean but different variances, as a representative model of the trend of financial variables. This hypothesis is particularly suitable to capture the exceptional or extreme events which a single normal distribution would not capture adequately, i.e., to solve the problem of fat tails.

For instance, it is possible to use two normal distributions, both with a mean of zero – the first one with unitary variance (standard normal), the second one with a much higher variance.[34] To obtain the mixture of normals distribution, each of the two distributions is assigned a probability, *de facto* attributing market factor returns a different probability of being extracted from either distribution. The resulting probability density function is as follows:

$$PDF = p_1 \cdot N(0, \sigma_1) + p_2 \cdot N(0, \sigma_2) \tag{5.28}$$

where p_1 and p_2 represent the probabilities (whose sum is one) that a certain return will be extracted from the first or second distribution. By assigning the second distribution a much greater variance ($\sigma_2 > \sigma_1$) and a much lower probability ($p_2 < p_1$) than for the first one, the result of a mixed distribution which adequately considers extreme events characterized by a low probability of occurrence will be obtained. As a matter of fact, the mixture of normals distribution finds its empirical justification in the observation that

---

[34] See J.P. Morgan (1996), pp. 7–25.

the volatility of financial variables is influenced by two types of factors: structural and cyclical factors. The former are bound to permanently affect the volatility level. In the case of stocks, they may be, for example, changes in the company's financial structure, or events involving the stock market structure and operation. Vice versa, cyclical factors more rarely influence the volatility level: still with reference to stocks, they might be detachments of dividends or particular days of the month.

5.5.2 Serial independence and stability of the variance-covariance matrix

The variance-covariance approach assumes that market factor returns are characterized by a normal and stable distribution, with constant means, variances and covariances. To justify this hypothesis, the market factor trend is assumed (as is the case for the best-known option pricing models[35]) to be appropriately represented by a geometric Brownian motion such as the one described by the following stochastic differential equation:[36]

$$dS_t = \mu S_t \, dt + \sigma S_t dW_t \qquad (5.29)$$

Here, dS_t is the instantaneous change in the market factor, μ is its expected annual rate of change, σ is volatility, dt indicates an infinitesimal change in time, and dW_t is a Wiener process,, i.e. a normal random variable with a mean of zero and a variance of dt.[37] In practice, (5.29) assumes the return of the asset under consideration to be represented by a known or deterministic component, referred to as "drift" effect (μ), and an unknown component, or "noise", which is "extracted" from a normal distribution. It also assumes the "surprises" arising from the noise component which occur at different time intervals (today, tomorrow, the day after tomorrow, etc.) to be independent, and to follow a constant distribution (*independent and identically distributed – i.i.d.*).

In other words, (5.29) assumes that:

√ the risk factor considered (S) follows a random walk which is consistent with the hypothesis of weak market efficiency (Markov process), but characterized by an expected return (drift) other than zero, equal to μ; the returns for different time intervals are independent (serial independence hypothesis) and normally distributed;

√ volatility σ is "noise" in what would otherwise be a process guided solely by the expected change μ;

√ the return of the financial asset is characterized by a constant variance, which is proportional to time only $(\sigma^2 dt)$.

In practice, market factor returns follow a normal distribution, with constant variance, and the returns for successive intervals are uncorrelated. Far from finding empirical confirmation, these hypotheses are often disproved by the actual behaviour of financial variables:

---

[35] See. Hull (1993), pp. 190–198.

[36] The geometric Brownian motion adequately describes the trend of the price of such financial assets as stocks. It is conversely inadequate to describe the pattern of interest rates. As a matter of fact, since the latter are characterised by mean reversion, i.e., by the tendency to revert to a mean long-term equilibrium value, the drift component (μ) cannot be considered to be constant.

[37] A Wiener process is a particular type of Markov stochastic process which, besides involving independence between two price changes concerning distinct time intervals (efficiency in weak form), has a variance which is proportional to the time interval considered. More in detail, this process is given by the following formula: $dz = \varepsilon \sqrt{dt}$, where ε is random extraction from a standardized normal distribution. See. Hull (1993), pp.192–193.

- variance varies over time, so much that it justified the development of econometric estimation models to forecast volatility, and, in particular, GARCH models, which will be discussed in the next chapter;
- serial independence of returns is very rarely tested: evidence thereof was obtained previously (see Table 5.5 above) by showing the errors made, on real data, by the rule used to estimate volatility at T days ($\sigma_T = \sigma_d \sqrt{T}$) as a function of daily volatility σ_d; as a matter of fact, these errors are attributable to the serial independence assumption implied in the rule, which is therefore not realistic.

5.5.3   The linear payoff hypothesis and the delta/gamma approach

The hypothesis of a linear relation between changes in the relevant market factor(s) and changes in the market value of the position/portfolio also represents a weakness of the parametric approach. This assumption is indeed incompatible with the behavior of some significant types of financial instruments. A typical case concerns bonds, whose market value varies *non-linearly* as yields to maturity change. Indeed, in this case the linearity assumption means disregarding the convexity (and all higher-order moments) of the function linking a bond's price to the relevant yield to maturity; in other words, this hypothesis amounts to considering the duration of securities to be constant as yields to maturity change.[38] Another important case concerns option positions, whose value depends on the underlying asset price according to a non-linear relation; it follows that, if an option position is translated into an equivalent position in the underlying asset by relying upon the delta coefficient only, this coefficient is bound to change continuously as a function of the underlying asset price.

A first solution to the problem of non-linear payoff based on an approximation of the function linking the individual positions' market values to the risk factors' values, by using a second-degree or "curving" term. Technically, this amounts to stopping the Taylor function series approximation at the second instead of first order. In the case of bonds, this amounts to considering not only duration, but also convexity; in the case of option positions, it amounts to considering – besides the delta coefficient – also the "gamma" coefficient. For this reason, it is no longer called a delta-normal approach, but a "delta-gamma" approach.

Analytically, the first-order approximation

$$\Delta MV \cong \frac{dMV}{dR} \cdot \Delta R = \delta \cdot \Delta R$$

where ΔMV indicates the change in the position's market value, and ΔR the change in the risk factor (for instance, the price of the asset underlying an option, or a bond's yield to maturity), is replaced by the following second-order development:

$$\Delta MV \cong \frac{dMV}{dR} \cdot \Delta R + \frac{1}{2} \frac{d^2 MV}{dR^2} \cdot (\Delta R)^2 = \delta \cdot \Delta R + \frac{\gamma}{2} \cdot (\Delta R)^2 \qquad (5.30)$$

where γ is the second derivative of the position's value with respect to the risk factor. At this point, it is as if the position's market value were a linear function (with δ and

---

[38] See Appendix 2A.

$\gamma/2$ coefficients) of two distinct risk factors, ΔR and its square. Knowing their volatility, and following the logic underlying the model, it thus becomes possible to obtain a VaR measure based upon a more accurate approximation of the relation between the position's value and the risk factor's value.

The greater the estimated shock in the market factor (i.e., the greater the position's holding period[39]), and the greater the degree of "curvature" of the position, the greater the increase in accuracy achieved through delta/gamma approximation. So, for instance, the improvement is particularly marked for options with a high gamma coefficient (such as at-the-money options which are close to maturity).

The main problem with this approach lies in its effects on the form of the distribution of changes in the position's value. In the case of a delta approximation, as the changes in the position's value are linear functions of the changes in market factors, and the latter are distributed according to a normal, changes in the portfolio's value are also normally distributed. Conversely, in the case of delta-gamma approximation, the distribution of changes in the position's value is derived from the combination of a normally distributed variable (ΔR) and a variable (ΔR^2) which is clearly not normal (just think that, as it is a square, it cannot take negative values). In particular, if ΔR is normal, then ΔR^2 is distributed according to a Chi-square with one degree of freedom, and therefore ΔMV, a linear combination of a normal and a Chi-square, is not distributed like a normal. It follows that the delta-gamma approach outlined above may lead to biased VaR estimates.[40]

Consider, for instance, the case of a call option whose value C depends on the price S of the underlying asset. By adopting the delta/gamma approach, the following is obtained:

$$\Delta C \approx \partial \Delta S + \frac{\gamma}{2} \Delta S^2 \qquad (5.31)$$

It is evident that ΔS and ΔS^2 cannot be both characterized by a normal distribution, so ΔC cannot be normally distributed.

Besides this first problem, one also has to take into account that the second order development, while improving the quality of the approximation, also leads to an estimate which is subject to error anyway. The latter is higher precisely when changes in risk factors (such as the ones generating extreme loss values like VaR) are high. In practice, the second-order coefficient is considered exactly at the values at which it is characterized by a considerable margin of error.

A third limitation concerns especially options, for which the estimation of the effects of changes in market factors (underlying asset price, volatility of the latter, and risk-free short-term interest rate) is typically based upon delta, gamma, vega and rho coefficients.

---

[39] Although apparently simple, the delta-gamma approach turns out to be quite complex if, when calculating the individual positions' VaR, the market value volatility (for instance, in the case of a bond, volatility of the value of the cash flows comprising it) – as is the case in the asset-normal approach followed by *RiskMetrics*™ – is used rather than the risk factor volatility (still in the case of a bond, the volatility of its yield to maturity) – as is the case in the delta-normal approach. If the starting point is represented by the risk factor volatility, then the distribution remains normal, as was originally assumed, regardless of whether the standard deviation is multiplied by the first derivative only or, conversely, an adjustment based upon the second derivative is also used. Vice versa, if the starting point is market value volatility, the distribution of the latter may not be normal if, instead of just considering the linear approximation given by the first-order coefficient, an adjustment based upon the second-order coefficient is also used.

[40] This problem was addressed by Wilson (1996), who proposed an alternative approach requiring no explicit assumption concerning the functional form of the distribution, and by Jamshidian and Zhu (1997).

While these coefficients prove to be empirically effective in estimating changes in an option's market value in the presence of changes in any market variables, a joint use of the same coefficients produces less effective results in the presence of joint shocks of multiple market factors.[41]

A fourth limitation concerns specific cases, in which the payoff is not only non-linear, but also non-derivable and non-monotonic. For this purpose, consider Figure 5.7, which shows the payoff at maturity for a straddle, i.e., an option trading strategy based upon an expectation of increased volatility, which is composed of the simultaneous purchase of two options – a call and a put – with the same strike price. The payoff of the strategy at maturity has a characteristic V shape, with the vertex at the strike price.

Let us imagine that the current value of the risk factor (the price of the underlying asset) is equal to the value indicated by "A" in the Figure. In this case, the delta-gamma method coincides with a linear approximation, considering that the second derivative is zero, and so is gamma. This linear approximation of the payoff, however, can lead to patently incorrect results: indeed, it is quite clear that the highest losses that the portfolio can suffer do not correspond to extreme market factor movements.

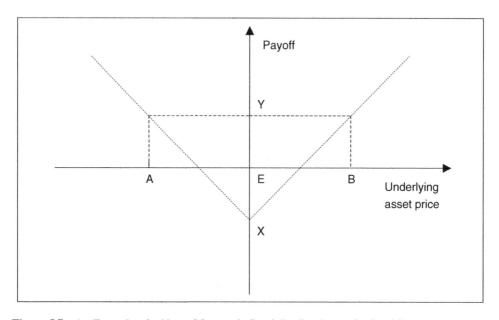

Figure 5.7   An Example of a Non - Monotonic Portfolio: Purchase of a Straddle

As shown by the chart, the highest loss will occur if, at maturity, the underlying asset has a value which is equal to the strike price, indicated by letter E. A price increase of up to E would result in a loss equal to the distance between points Y and X. However, a twofold change in the underlying asset market price, from A to B, would not involve twice as high a loss as the previous one for the straddle holder, but a P&L of zero. Indeed, the payoff at maturity corresponding to market price B is exactly equal to the initial one

---

[41] See Appendix 5B for more clarifications about the meaning of the different coefficients and the mentioned problem.

(Y). It follows that, if one wanted to be more cautious, and considering a higher multiple α of the standard deviation, the VaR would end up being dramatically overestimated. With respect to a bias of this type, the delta/gamma method leads to no improvement, as the payoff is linear at times and the second derivative, if any, is zero.

The delta/gamma approach is not the only possible solution to the problems of a non-linear relation between the position's value and risk factors' values. An alternative approach involves recalculating the position's value (and therefore the portfolio's value) based upon a pricing model and the new possible market conditions, rather than just approximating the possible change in value (loss) resulting from the change in risk factors. This approach is referred to as "full valuation", and is typically used by non-parametric VaR models, which will be covered in Chapter 7.

In conclusion, it is important to mention that, notwithstanding the limitations discussed in this section, the variance-covariance approach has some major merits. The first one concerns computational efficiency: indeed this approach, thanks to the use of linear sensitivity coefficients and the normal distribution hypothesis, allows to compute VaR for a bank's entire portfolio in a very short time. Secondly, as it is not based upon full valuation, but on the use of simple sensitivity coefficients, this approach does not require a pricing model for each individual instrument in the bank's portfolio. Finally, thanks to the central limit theorem, the methodology underlying the variance-covariance approach can also be applied if risk factors are not normally distributed, provided that they are sufficiently numerous and relatively independent.

SELECTED QUESTIONS AND EXERCISES

1. An investment bank holds a zero-coupon bond with a residual maturity of 5 years, a yield-to-maturity of 7 % and a market value of € 1 million. The historical average of daily changes in the yield is 0 %, and its volatility is 15 basis points. Find: (i) the modified duration; (ii) the price volatility; (iii) the daily VaR with a confidence level of 95 %, computed based on the parametric (delta-normal) approach.

2. A trader in a French bank has just bought Japanese yen, against euro, in a 6-month forward deal. Which of the following alternatives correctly maps his/her position?
   (A) Buy euro against yen spot, go short (make a debt) on yen for 6 months, go long (make an investment) on euro for 6 months.
   (B) Buy yen against euro spot, go short (make a debt) on yen for 6 months, go long (make an investment) on euro for 6 months.
   (C) Buy yen against euro spot, go short on euro for 6 months, go long on yen for 6 months.
   (D) Buy euro against yen spot, go short on euro for 6 months, go long on euro for 6 months.
3. Using the parametric approach, find the VaR of the following portfolio: (i) assuming zero correlations; (ii) assuming perfect correlations; (iii) using the correlations shown in the Table.

Asset	VaR	$\rho(S,C)$	$\rho(S,B)$	$\rho(C,B)$
Stocks (S)	50,000	0,5	0	−0,2
Currencies (C)	20,000			
Bonds (B)	80,000			

4. Which of the following problems may cause the VaR of a stock position, estimated using the volatility of the stock market index, to underestimate the actual risk?

    (A) Systematic risk is overlooked.
    (B) Specific risk is overlooked.
    (C) Unexpected market-wide shocks are overlooked.
    (D) Changes in portfolio composition are overlooked

5. The daily VaR of a bank's trading book is 10 million euros. Find the 10-day VaR and show why, and based on what hypotheses, the 10-day VaR is less than 10 times the daily VaR.

6. Using the data shown in the following table, find the parametric VaR, with a confidence level of 99 %, of a portfolio made of three stocks (A, B and C), using the following three approaches: (1) using volatilities and correlations of the returns on the individual stocks; (2) using the volatility of the rate of return of the portfolio as a whole (portfolio-normal approach) (3) using the volatility of the stock market index and the betas of the individual stocks (CAPM). Then, comment the results and explain why some VaR measures are higher or lower than others.

	Stock A	Stock B	Stock C	Portfolio	Market index
Market value (€ million)	15	15	20	50	–
Beta	1.4	1.2	0.8	1.1	1
Volatility	15 %	12 %	10 %	9 %	7 %
Correlation with A	1	0,5	0,8	–	–
Correlation with B	0,5	1	0	–	–
Correlation with C	0,8	0	1	–	–

7. In a parametric VaR model, the sensitivity coefficient of a long position on Treasury bonds (expressing the sensitivity of the position's value to changes in the underlying risk factor) is:

    (A) positive if we use an asset normal approach;
    (B) negative if we use an asset normal approach;
    (C) equal to convexity, if we use a delta normal approach;

(D) it is not possible to measure VaR with a parametric approach for Treasury bonds: this approach only works with well diversifies equity portfolios.

8. A bank finds that VaR estimated with the asset normal approach is lower than VaR estimated with the delta normal approach. Consider the following possible explanations.

(I) Because the position has a sensitivity equal to one, as for a currency position.

(II) Because the position has a linear sensitivity, as for a stock.

(III) Because the position has a non-linear sensitivity, as for a bond, which is being overestimated by its delta (the duration).

Which explanation(s) is/are correct?

(A) Only I.

(B) Only II.

(C) Only III.

(D) Only II and III.

9. An Italian bank has entered a three-months forward purchase of one million Swiss francs against euros. Using the market data on exchange rates and interest rates (simple interest rates) reported in the following Table, find the virtual positions – and their respective amounts – into which this forward purchase can be mapped.

Spot FX rate EURO/SWF	0.75
3-month EURO rate	4.25 %
3-month SWF rate	3.75 %

10. Consider the following statements. In a VaR model for market risk, the hypothesis that risk factor returns are distributed according to a Student t with less than 10 degrees of freedom, rather than according to a normal...

(I) ... is useless, because such a distribution is, actually, quite close to the normal;

(II) ... could prove useful when the empirical distribution shows extreme values that are less frequent than indicated by a normal with the same mean and variance;

(III) ... could prove useful, to have a distribution more similar to the empirical one, but also very complex, because a linear combination of Student t is not, itself, a Student t;

(IV) ... could prove useful, but requires a Monte Carlo simulation.

Which statements are correct?

(A) II and IV;

(B) III and IV;

(C) I;

(D) All but I.

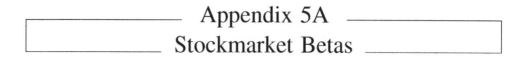

Appendix 5A
Stockmarket Betas

5A.1 INTRODUCTION

The beta coefficient of a stock is an indicator of its degree of systematic risk, i.e., of the portion of the stock's return volatility, which can be explained by the dependence of its returns on those of the market as a whole. As a matter of fact, a security's return variability can be divided into two components: specific or idiosyncratic risk, which can be eliminated through an adequate portfolio diversification policy; and generic or systematic risk, which depends on factors that are common to other securities, as well, and therefore cannot be eliminated. A stock's systematic risk therefore reflects the covariance of its return with the market index return. In this sense, therefore, beta expresses the sensitivity of a security's return to the mean market return.

5A.2 THE CAPITAL ASSET PRICING MODEL

The beta coefficient was originally introduced by Sharpe (1963), and subsequently developed within the framework of the Capital Asset Pricing Model (CAPM), a model aimed at determining the equilibrium return, and therefore price, of risky assets. The CAPM is an equilibrium asset pricing model. In other words: it was developed to show what the equilibrium price of risky assets should be.

The CAPM, which was developed at the same time by Sharpe (1964), Lintner (1965) and Mossin (1966), proceeds from Markowitz's portfolio theory and adopts the same hypotheses (rational investors, perfect markets and normal distribution of securities' returns). If these assumptions are true, then every financial asset should offer an expected return which is consistent with its degree of systematic risk, i.e., with that portion of risk which cannot be eliminated through diversification. In other words, a risky financial asset return must reflect the contribution which it gives to the variance of the market portfolio return, i.e., of the set of assets which may be held by investors. Analytically, this contribution can be measured by the ratio between the covariance of the individual security's rate of return and the market portfolio's return ($\sigma_{i,M}$) and the variance of the market portfolio's return (σ_M^2):

$$\beta_i = \frac{\sigma_{i,M}}{\sigma_M^2} \qquad (5A.1)$$

So, in order for an individual security to be in equilibrium, its expected return must be a function of its beta. More precisely, it must be:

$$E(R_i) = R_f + \beta_i[E(R_M) - R_f] \qquad (5A.2)$$

I.e.: the expected return of share i is equal to the risk-free rate (R_f) plus the product of two elements:

(i) the degree of systematic (or non-diversifiable) risk of the security itself, measured by beta,

(ii) the risk premium which the stock market as a whole "pays" to the investors $[E(R_M - R_f)]$; this premium can be estimated based upon past market returns, is relatively stable in the medium term, and is crucial to value any risky financial asset. The ratio between this premium and the market portfolio volatility (σ_M) determines the cost per unit of risk, also known as the market's "Sharpe index".

The product of these two elements – which can be interpreted as the amount and price of systematic risk, respectively – is the premium demanded by an investor, on top of the risk-free rate of return, to hold the i-th security.

The CAPM is a relatively simple method to determine the return demanded on a risky investment, based upon the latter's risk, the market risk, and the tendency of the two risks to "strike together". Indeed, the beta expression (5A.1) can be rewritten as:

$$\beta_i = \rho_{i,M} \frac{\sigma_i}{\sigma_M} \tag{5A.3}$$

It follows that this does not rise only with σ_i (the security's volatility), measured in relation to the average market risk as a whole (σ_M), but also with $\rho_{i,M}$, the correlation coefficient between the market's and individual asset returns. In fact, if a security were negatively correlated with the average market return, its beta would be negative, and the return demanded by investors to hold this security (a sort or "parachute share", whose return is higher when the set of investments available on the market experiences reduced or negative returns) would correctly be *lower* than the risk-free rate.

It is finally important to note that the CAPM is a single-factor model, in the sense that the covariance of the returns of risky assets is explained based upon the common dependence of the relevant returns on a single systematic factor (the market portfolio return). Other later models, such as the arbitrage pricing theory (APT), conversely, are grounded on the assumption that there are multiple systematic factors (for instance, interest rates, inflation, exchange rate, etc.) on which the returns of risky assets depend, and are therefore referred to as multi-factor models.

5A.3 ESTIMATION OF A STOCK'S BETA

A stock's beta is generally estimated by having recourse to a simple linear regression of the security's return on the market return. More in detail, estimation is based upon the following equation:

$$R_{i,t} - R_{f,t} = a_i + b_i(R_{M,t} - R_{f,t}) + \varepsilon_{i,t} \tag{5A.4}$$

Where:

- $R_{i,t}$ and $R_{m,t}$ indicate the returns of the individual i-th security and an index which is representative of the stock market for the period t;
- $R_{f,t}$ indicates the risk-free rate of return in the period t, generally approximated by the rate of return of short-term government securities;
- a_i and b_i are the two regression coefficients. While the value of a_i, tends, in the long run, to take values of zero, coefficient b_i represents the estimated beta of the stock.

Monthly return data relating to five-year periods are generally used for the estimation of equation (5A.4). This allows to have a sufficiently large number of observations (60) without necessarily using data which are too distant in time, with the risk of obtaining "obsolete" estimates.

Note that, in moving from the theoretical analysis which is typical of the CAPM to concrete estimation of a stock's beta, two simplifying hypotheses are introduced:

√ the market portfolio, which in the CAPM is the combination of all risky assets that are present in the economic system, is identified as the portfolio comprising all stocks listed on a given market;

√ the return of the risk-free asset is approximated by the return of short-term government securities.

Appendix 5B
Option Sensitivity Coefficients: "Greeks"

5B.1 INTRODUCTION

Among the various types of derivative instruments, option contracts are those characterized by the greatest degree of versatility and flexibility. Besides this positive feature, however, option contracts have a higher and more complex degree of risk than other derivative instruments. This is mainly due to the fact that an option's market value is sensitive to different variables, such as the underlying asset price, its volatility, short-term interest rates, and even the simple passing of time. More precisely, an option's value is influenced by the following variables:

✓ the strike price (X);
✓ the underlying asset market price (S);
✓ the residual maturity of the option contract, expressed as a fraction of a year (T);
✓ the short-term risk-free interest rate (i);
✓ the volatility (standard deviation) of the underlying asset price (σ).

These variables are the same as are found in the Black & Scholes pricing formulas for a call (C) and put (P) option on a non dividend paying stock:

$$C = S \cdot N(d_1) - Xe^{-iT} N(d_2) \tag{5B.1}$$

$$P = Xe^{-iT} N(d_2) - S \cdot N(-d_1) \tag{5B.2}$$

where $d_1 = \dfrac{\ln(S/X) + (r + \sigma^2/2)T}{\sigma\sqrt{T}}$ and $d_2 = d_1 - \sigma\sqrt{T}$.

So, every option has a market value which turns out to be a function of four market factors (we exclude the first variable (strike price), which is fixed upon stipulation of the contract). The effect of these four factors on an option's value can be estimated using option coefficients, or "greeks"; the main ones are shown in Table 5B.1.

Table 5B.1 Options' Greeks

Coefficient	Derivative	With respect to
Delta (δ)	First	Underlying asset's price (S)
Gamma (γ)	Second	
Vega (λ)	First	Volatility (σ)
Theta (θ)	First	Residual maturity (T)
Rho (ρ)	No	Interest rate (r)

5B.2   THE DELTA COEFFICIENT

An option's delta is the first derivative of the option's price function with respect to the underlying asset price, and expresses the sensitivity of the former to changes in the latter's market price. This parameter is different according to the type of option: a call option delta is positive, as upward changes in the underlying asset's price increase its value; a put option's delta is negative, as increases in the underlying asset price generate a decrease in the option's value. Analytically:

$$\delta_C = \frac{\partial C}{\partial S} = N(d_1) > 0 \qquad (5B.3)$$

$$\delta_P = \frac{\partial P}{\partial S} = N(d_1) - 1 < 0 \qquad (5B.4)$$

where δ_C and δ_P indicate the deltas of a call and put option, and $\partial C/\partial S$ and $\partial C/\partial S$ the first derivative of the function linking the values of a call and put option to the underlying asset market price, respectively.

An option's delta is positively correlated to its probability of exercise, and can also be interpreted as the hedge ratio, i.e., as the amount of the underlying asset required to hedge the option position. The delta coefficient is not constant over time, but varies according to the changes in the underlying asset price. For instance, the delta is high (in absolute value for put options) for in-the-money (ITM) options,[42] and low for out-of-the-money (OTM) options.[43] This is because the value of ITM options – which is mainly composed of their intrinsic value – is strongly influenced by changes in the underlying asset price. For deep-in-the-money options, the delta tends to one (minus one for put options), in the sense that changes in the underlying asset price get reflected in almost equivalent changes in the value of options. Vice versa, the value of OTM options, which is mainly represented by time value, is less sensitive to changes in the underlying asset's price. For deep-out-of-the-money options, the delta tends to zero, in the sense that changes in the underlying asset's price have almost no effect on the value of these options. Finally, the delta of at-the-money (ATM) options[44] is 0.5.

The delta coefficient measures the slope of the relation between an option's value and the underlying asset price, a curvilinear function. For this reason, if it is used to estimate the change in an option's value resulting from a change in the underlying asset price, the delta is a linear approximation of this function.[45] This is because the delta coefficient itself varies as the price of the asset underlying the individual option contract changes.[46] More

---

[42] In-the-money options are characterized by a positive intrinsic value. In the case of call options, this occurs when the strike price is lower than the underlying asset market price. Vice versa, in the case of a put option, this occurs when the strike price is higher than the market price.

[43] In the case of call options, out-of-the-money options are those whose strike price is higher than the underlying asset market price. Vice versa, in the case of put options, they are those whose strike price is lower than the market price.

[44] At-the-money options are those whose strike price is equal to the underlying asset's market price.

[45] The smaller the price change considered, the more accurate this approximation, in the sense that the "convexity" of the function of the options' value has a smaller effect if this change is limited. Vice versa, in the case of significant changes in the underlying asset's price, the delta provides an inaccurate indication of the change in the option's value.

[46] This is the reason why a price risk hedging policy based upon simple delta hedging must have recourse to continuous purchases/sales of the underlying asset to make it possible to maintain a delta-neutral position (rebalancing).

specifically, in the case of call options, the delta overestimates the decrease in the option's value connected with decreases in the underlying asset price, whereas it underestimates the increase in the option's value in case of an increase in the underlying asset's price (the opposite is true for put options).

5B.3   THE GAMMA COEFFICIENT

The deficiencies of the delta coefficient are mitigated by a second parameter, which is capable of providing a more accurate indication of options' sensitivity to changes in the underlying asset price. This coefficient, known as gamma (γ), measures the degree of convexity of the function linking an option's value to the underlying asset price, just as a bond's convexity.

More precisely, gamma is the second derivative of the function linking the option's value to the underlying asset price, or rather the first derivative of the delta:

$$\gamma_C = \frac{\partial^2 C}{\partial S^2} = \frac{N'(d_1)}{S\sigma\sqrt{T}} > 0 \qquad (5B.5)$$

$$\gamma_P = \frac{\partial^2 C}{\partial S^2} = \frac{N'(d_1)}{S\sigma\sqrt{T}} > 0 \qquad (5B.6)$$

Both call options and put options always have a positive gamma.[47] Gamma is high for ATM options and low for ITM and OTM options. This is because the delta of ATM options is more sensitive to changes in the underlying asset price. An option's gamma is also inversely correlated to the option's residual maturity, in the sense that – other things equal – options having a longer residual maturity have a lower gamma; this is because a longer residual maturity implies a higher time value and, consequently, a smaller convexity of the option's value function.

Just like convexity for a bond, an option's gamma is a favorable factor for option buyers, in the sense that a high value of this parameter amplifies the increases in the position's value connected with favourable price changes, but decreases the position's depreciations connected with unfavorable price changes.

As formula (5.30) shows, the gamma coefficient can be used to obtain a more accurate estimate of the change in an option's value resulting from a change in the underlying asset's price.

5B.4   THE THETA COEFFICIENT AND TIME DECAY
OF AN OPTION

A second variable affecting an option's value, regardless of the trend of market conditions, is the simple passing of time. As the residual maturity of an option decreases, the option value decreases as a result of the decrease in its time value. This depreciation effect is called time decay of an option.

---

[47] There is a "gamma negative" position only in case of *sale* of options.

The derivative of the change in value with respect to residual maturity is known as theta (θ) coefficient:

$$\theta_C = \frac{\partial C}{\partial T} = -\frac{SN'(d_1)\sigma}{2\sqrt{T}} - iXe^{-iT}N(d_2) < 0 \tag{5B.7}$$

$$\theta_P = \frac{\partial P}{\partial T} = -\frac{SN'(d_1)\sigma}{2\sqrt{T}} - iXe^{-iT}N(d_2) < 0 \tag{5B.8}$$

Theta is negative for both call options and put options. Moreover, there is a negative time bias for long option positions, and a positive time bias for short positions (sale of options).[48]

Other conditions being equal, theta is higher for ATM options, as these options have a higher time value. Moreover, theta is negatively correlated with an option's residual maturity, in the sense that – other conditions being equal – a longer residual maturity involves a lower theta, i.e., a lower sensitivity of the option's value to the change in residual maturity. This implies that, as residual maturity decreases, the option depreciates more rapidly as a result of the passing of time.

5B.5 THE VEGA COEFFICIENT

The vega coefficient,[49] which is generally indicated by the Greek letter lambda (λ), expresses the derivative of an option's value with respect to volatility:

$$\lambda_C = \frac{\partial C}{\partial \sigma} = S\sqrt{T}N'(d_1) > 0 \tag{5B.9}$$

$$\lambda_P = \frac{\partial P}{\partial \sigma} = S\sqrt{T}N'(d_1) > 0 \tag{5B.10}$$

Vega is positive for both call options and put options, in the sense that increases in the volatility expected by the market generate increases in the value of both types of options. The vega risk, i.e., the risk of increased (decreased) volatility for short (long) option positions, cannot be hedged by purchasing/selling the underlying asset, but only by purchasing/selling other options. Finally, it should be highlighted that this risk is not determined by the actual price volatility, but rather by the market expectation of the latter. Indeed, vega measures the sensitivity of an option's value to changes in implied volatility, i.e., in the volatility expected by market participants.

5B.6 THE RHO COEFFICIENT

The last variable affecting an option's market value is the short-term risk-free interest rate. More in detail, the zero-coupon yield to maturity which is equal to the residual maturity of the option under consideration.[50]

---

[48] Theta and gamma are therefore inversely correlated, in the sense that a long option position involves taking a gamma-positive, but theta-negative position, and vice versa. The ratio between an option's gamma and theta indicates the amount of gamma which is obtained by purchasing a unit of theta. For long option positions, the objective is generally to maximize the gamma/theta ratio. Vice versa, for short option positions, the attempt is to minimise this ratio.

[49] This coefficient is sometimes also referred to as lambda or sigma.

[50] See Appendix 3A for a review of the economic meaning and estimation criteria of zero-coupon rates.

The derivative of an option's value with respect to the interest rate is the *rho* (ρ) coefficient. From a logical point of view, the relation between these two quantities is dual. On the one hand, a higher interest rate decreases the present value of the option's expected final value (payoff at maturity): this means that a higher interest rate has a negative effect on the value of any option. On the other hand, a higher interest rate implies a higher forward price of the underlying asset,[51] so a higher value for call options and a lower value for put options. The two effects therefore act in the same direction in the case of put options (making the total effect negative), while they act in a conflicting way in the case of call options, for which, in any case, the first effect usually predominates.

So, in brief:

$$\rho_C = \frac{\partial C}{\partial i} = XTe^{-iT}N(d_2) < 0 \qquad (5B.11)$$

$$\rho_P = \frac{\partial P}{\partial i} = XTe^{-iT}N(d_2) < 0 \qquad (5B.12)$$

Other conditions being equal, the rho coefficient is higher for at-the-money options and lower for in-the-money and out-of-the-money options. This is because ATM options are characterized by a higher time value, and are therefore more sensitive to changes in the financial time value, which is measured precisely by the interest rate.

5B.7   SOME PROBLEMS WITH OPTION SENSITIVITY COEFFICIENTS

While delta, gamma, vega and rho coefficients prove to be empirically effective in esti-mating changes in an option's market value in the presence of changes in any of the relevant market variables, the *joint* use of these same coefficients produces less effective results in the presence of *joint* shocks of multiple market variables. The reason for this ineffectiveness is related to the fact that estimation of the change in the option's market value is based upon the initial value which these coefficients take before the shocks. The same value is however modified by changes in market variables. So, for instance, in the presence of a joint price and volatility change, the estimation of the effect of a changed volatility disregards the fact that the vega coefficient varies as a result of the different underlying asset price.

The latter limitation becomes particularly important if we consider that significant changes in the underlying asset price are often accompanied by changes in price volatili-ty. This is one of the main reasons why measurement of the risk connected with option trading is generally based not only upon an analysis of the sensitivity coefficients analyzed briefly in this appendix, but also on simulation models. The latter overcome the limitations connected with greeks by recalculating the whole market value of option portfolios based upon the estimated changes in market factors – through appropriate pricing formulae.

---

[51] The most widespread pricing models for bond options, such as the Black model, use the forward price as a variable explaining the option's value.

6
Volatility Estimation Models

6.1 INTRODUCTION

The variance-covariance approach presented in the previous chapter is based upon the assumption that market factor return volatilities and correlation coefficients can be estimated correctly. This is a complex issue, which, however, has been extensively addressed in the past, both from a theoretical and empirical point of view: indeed, its relevance is not limited to risk management, but extends to issues such as efficient portfolios and option pricing.[1]

The methods which can be used for this purpose can be grouped into two main categories. The first one includes models using historical volatility and correlation data to predict future volatility and correlations. The simplest ones among these models consider volatility and correlations as constant parameters, or, in other words, assume the relevant market factor returns to be characterized by a stable distribution over time. This assumption is clearly in contrast with the empirical evidence, which shows that volatility and correlations vary over time.

For this reason, models enabling volatility and correlations to change over time and trying to model this change process in different ways – while still using historical data – have been developed. In this case, past volatility and correlation estimates are used to construct predictions, but do not coincide with them. This class of models include algorithms based upon (simple or exponential) moving averages, as well as models from the GARCH (generalized autoregressive conditional heteroskedasticity) family.

A second method is the one based on volatility estimates implied in option prices. In this case historical values are only used indirectly, as implied volatility is itself a product of historical volatility. However, an option's implied volatility concerns a time horizon that is equal to the option's life, which does not necessarily coincide with the VaR model's time horizon.

Sections 6.2 to 6.4 will present historical data models in detail; section 6.5 will probe into the concept of implied volatility; section 6.6 will generalize previous results, extending them to covariance and correlation estimation.

6.2 VOLATILITY ESTIMATION BASED UPON HISTORICAL DATA: SIMPLE MOVING AVERAGES

The most widespread method to obtain a prediction of the return volatility of a given market factor (share price, exchange rate, interest rate, etc.) for a certain future period is based upon estimation of past volatility.[2] Indeed, this is the most widely used criterion both to

---

[1] The volatility estimate required to construct a VaR model, however, has different purposes to that connected with option pricing or efficient portfolios. As a matter of fact, this estimation is performed not so much in order to determine a market factor's average variability, but rather to determine the maximum potential change in the same market factor return – given a certain confidence level and a certain time horizon.

[2] In this case, we talk about estimated past volatility because of the simple fact that the latter cannot be observed directly, but simply "estimated". As a matter of fact, as will be noted below, for the same past period, numerous and different "estimates" of a market factor return volatility can be obtained, depending on the estimation criterion adopted.

value option contracts, and to determine an asset allocation policy based upon the mean-variance criterion, and, finally, to measure market risks according to a value-at-risk logic. Although apparently simple, this criterion may be based upon specific theoretical assumptions, which will be discussed below, and may follow very diverse calculation methods.

If x indicates the variable whose degree of volatility is to be measured, volatility (standard deviation) can be estimated as the square root of variance, using a sample of n historical observations. More in detail, volatility at time t can be estimated using the n observations from time $t - n$ to time $t - 1$, as shown in the following formula:

$$\sigma_t = \sqrt{\frac{\sum_{i=t-n}^{t-1} (x_i - \bar{x}_t)^2}{n - 1}} \tag{6.1}$$

where $\bar{x}_t$ is the sample mean calculated at time t (still using n observations from time $t - n$ to time $t - 1$). [3]

In the following period $(t + 1)$, volatility will be estimated based upon the data from $(t - n + 1)$ to t, moving the sample's time window forward by one period: this approach is referred to as "moving average method". So, a moving average is but an average relating to a fixed number of data which "drift" in time: the passing of time ensures that the most distant piece of data will be replaced by the most recent one, thus leaving the sample size unchanged.

If, instead of a generic variable x, we have a market factor return R_t, (6.1) will become:

$$\sigma_t = \sqrt{\frac{\sum_{i=t-n}^{t-1} (R_i - \bar{R}_t)^2}{n - 1}} \tag{6.2}$$

and if the time horizon from $t - n$ to $t - 1$ is short enough to make it possible to assume a mean return of zero, the estimated volatility will be given by:

$$\sigma_t = \sqrt{\frac{\sum_{i=t-n}^{t-1} R_i^2}{n - 1}} \tag{6.3}$$

The first part of Figure 6.1 shows the volatility pattern of the daily log return of the S&P 500 stock exchange index, estimated using moving averages calculated by applying (6.3) to monthly windows (n equal to 23 working days) in the period from 6 February through 28 December 2001. Conversely, the second part of the figure shows the volatility pattern of the daily logarithmic changes in the USD/EUR exchange rate (dollar price of the Euro),

---

[3] Depending on the frequency with which sample data are selected, different volatility data will be obtained: so, if daily data are used, a daily volatility measure will be obtained.

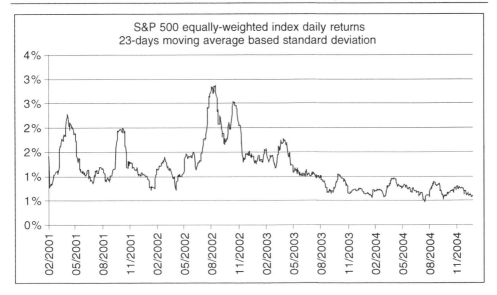

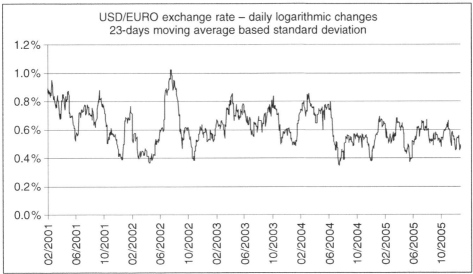

Figure 6.1   Two Examples of Volatility Estimated Using Simple Moving Averages

estimated by using (6.3) with n equal to 23, in the period from 5 February 2001 through 30 December 2005.

Using the simple moving average criterion to estimate historical volatility, which, in turn, is functional to predicting volatility with a view to risk management, involves two major problems.

The first one concerns selection of the past period of time over which volatility should be measured. Other conditions being equal, a larger number of observations (n) will result in more stable estimated volatility, because any shocks in the market factor will affect estimated volatility to a proportionally lesser degree. Moreover, a longer period of time will offer high information content, as the sample used to estimate volatility will be larger. At the same time, however, a very broad historical period will produce a volatility estimate which is slow to respond to sudden changes in market conditions, and therefore is not very "up-to-date". For instance, in the presence of a considerable sudden increase in market factor volatility, using historical volatility calculated based upon data for a long past period will in fact lead to assign a very small marginal weight to more recent conditions, which should better reflect future conditions.[4] It follows that, if historical volatility estimation is functional to predicting future volatility, the use of a large number of past observations may lead to less reliable results. This is the reason why the majority of financial institutions using VaR models tend to select relatively limited time intervals, generally ranging from 20 to 50 daily data, to estimate the daily volatility used in trading risk measurement. The effects of a different number of observations on the responsiveness of estimated volatility are exemplified in Figure 6.2, where the volatility of the S&P 500 index illustrated in Figure 6.1 was recalculated by setting, alternatively, n = 23, n = 50 and n = 90.

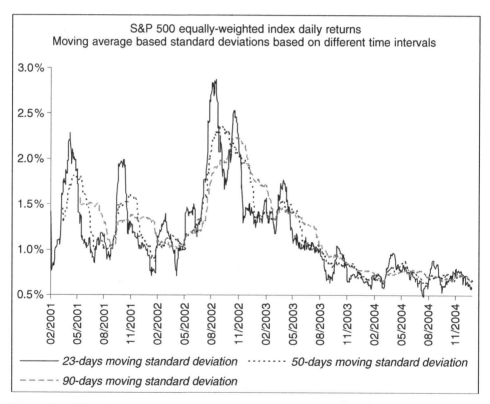

Figure 6.2   Effect of a Different Number of Observations on Estimated Volatility Responsiveness

---

[4] This is due to the fact that, when estimating historical volatility, equal weights are attributed to individual mean-square deviations. As will be seen shortly, there is an alternative solution based upon variable weights.

The second problem is generally referred to as "echo effect"[5] or "ghost features".[6] It consists in the fact that estimated volatility experiences a change (the fewer the observations in the sample, the more marked the change) not only when the market factor experiences a marked change, but also when the piece of data relating to this shock leaves the sample and is replaced by a more recent piece of data. While the first change in estimated volatility is fully justified, the second one (which always has an opposite sign to the first one) is not, because of the simple fact that when the data relating to the shock leaves the sample, no significant novelty is likely to have affected the market.

Figure 6.3 shows an example concerning the behaviour of the S&P 500 index volatility in September and October 2001. This volatility shows an upswing in mid-September, as a result of the well-known terrorist events (which caused some days of strongly negative returns – highlighted by the black bars in the bottom part of the figure); it is also equally dramatically reduced around mid-October, although in the presence of absolutely "normal" daily returns, and this happens solely because mid-September observations are leaving the sample used to calculate the standard deviation.

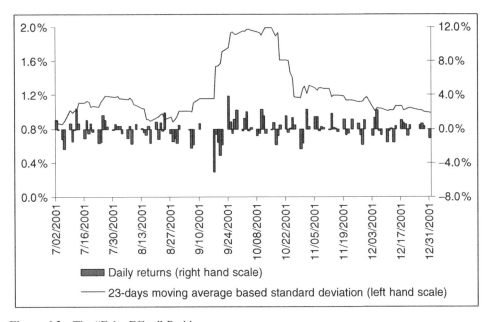

Figure 6.3   The "Echo Effect" Problem

6.3   VOLATILITY ESTIMATION BASED UPON HISTORICAL DATA: EXPONENTIAL MOVING AVERAGES

So, two problems need to be overcome: the trade-off between information content and responsiveness to more recent conditions (related to selection of optimal n), and the echo effect. For this reason, a second historical volatility estimation method, based upon the

---

[5] Cf. Figlewsky (1994), p 11.
[6] Cf. Alexander (1996), pp. 235–237.

use of an *exponential* moving average, has been developed. It differs from the simple moving average because, when calculating the mean of square deviations from the mean return, it attributes them non-equal weights.

The underlying logic is relatively simple: by using a large number of past observations, but assigning more recent ones greater weight, a volatility estimate which has high information content and, at the same time, is more sensitive to recent shocks will be obtained. Two major benefits are achieved this way: on the one hand, the estimate will respond to market factor shocks more rapidly; on the other hand, a marked market factor shock will "leave" the volatility estimate gradually, avoiding an echo effect.

An exponential average is a particular type of weighted mean in which the weights associated with the different observations are different powers of the same constant λ. For a generic variable x observed from $t - n$ to $t-1$, this average is calculated as:

$$\frac{\lambda^0 x_{t-1} + \lambda x_{t-2} + \lambda^2 x_{t-3} + \lambda^3 x_{t-4} + \cdots + \lambda^{n-1} x_{t-n}}{1 + \lambda + \lambda^2 + \lambda^3 + \cdots + \lambda^{n-1}} \quad \text{with} \quad 0 < \lambda < 1 \qquad (6.4)$$

Note that, as in any weighted mean, the sum of the weighted observations is divided by the sum of weights.

The constant λ is referred to as "decay factor", and indicates the "degree of persistence" of past sample observations. As a matter of fact, if λ is closer to one, its successive powers (λ^2, λ^3, λ^4) – which represent the weights associated to past observations – will approach zero very slowly; it follows that the average will less rapidly adapt to more recent conditions. Conversely, if λ is smaller, then its successive powers will tend to zero more rapidly, and past observations will more rapidly "leave" the estimate of σ. For this reason, $(1-\lambda)$ is referred to as the past observation "decay rate".

If we set $\lambda = 1$, the weighting would be the same for all past observations, and the exponential weighted average would coincide with the simple mean. So, for values of λ which are very close to 1, the exponential average tends to the simple mean, i.e., attributes high weights to time-distant observations, as well. Vice versa, for values of λ which are more distant from 1, the exponential average differs more markedly from the simple mean, attributing considerably different weights to observations relating to different points in time.

If we replace x with the squares of log returns R_i of a market factor with a zero mean, we will obtain an estimate of the variance based upon exponential moving averages.

$$\hat{\sigma}_t^2 = \frac{R_{t-1}^2 + \lambda R_{t-2}^2 + \lambda^2 R_{t-3}^2 + \cdots + \lambda^{n-1} R_{t-n}^2}{1 + \lambda + \lambda^2 + \cdots + \lambda^{n-1}} = \frac{\sum_{i=0}^{n-1} \lambda^i R_{t-1-i}^2}{\sum_{i=0}^{n-1} \lambda^i} = \frac{1 - \lambda}{1 - \lambda^n} \sum_{i=0}^{n-1} \lambda^i R_{t-1-i}^2$$

$$(6.5)$$

Note that, in (6.5), the summation $\sum_{i=0}^{n-1} \lambda^i$ at the denominator was developed in the following way:

$$\sum_{i=0}^{n-1} \lambda^i = 1 + \lambda + \lambda^2 + \cdots + \lambda^{n-1} \cdot \frac{1 - \lambda}{1 - \lambda} = \frac{1 - \lambda^n}{1 - \lambda}$$

The estimated volatility (standard deviation) therefore becomes:

$$\hat{\sigma}_t = \sqrt{\frac{1-\lambda}{1-\lambda^n} \sum_{i=0}^{n-1} \lambda^i R_{t-1-i}^2} \qquad (6.6)$$

If λ is sufficiently small and/or n sufficiently large, then $\lambda^n \cong 0$, and (6.6) can be approximated using a simpler expression:

$$\hat{\sigma}_t \cong \sqrt{(1-\lambda) \sum_{i=0}^{n-1} \lambda^i R_{t-1-i}^2} \qquad (6.7)$$

Moreover, again if λ is sufficiently small and/or n sufficiently large, (6.5) lends itself to being approximated as follows:

$$\hat{\sigma}_t^2 \cong (1-\lambda) \sum_{i=0}^{\infty} \lambda^i R_{t-1-i}^2 = (1-\lambda) \left[R_{t-1}^2 + \sum_{i=1}^{\infty} \lambda^i R_{t-1-i}^2 \right] =$$

$$= (1-\lambda) R_{t-1}^2 + \lambda(1-\lambda) \sum_{i=1}^{\infty} \lambda^{i-1} R_{t-1-i}^2 = (1-\lambda) R_{t-1}^2 + \lambda \hat{\sigma}_{t-1}^2 \qquad (6.8)$$

(6.8) shows the "adaptive" mechanism by which variance is estimated: in practice, it is recalculated every day by taking the estimate for the previous day and adjusting it (for a small portion, $1-\lambda$, which is equal to the "decay rate") with the square of the return recorded on the previous day.

Figure 6.4 shows the S&P index volatility which has already been presented in Figure 6.3 (standard deviation based upon a 23-day simple moving average – equation 6.3) again, and supplements it with the estimate obtained using the exponential moving average method (equation 6.6, with λ arbitrarily set at 0.94). Note the 11 September shock generates an immediate significant increase in estimated volatility; however, unlike what happens with simple moving averages, using the exponential moving averages no abrupt decrease in volatility occurs when the shock data gets out of the sample (23 days later), because its weight had already been progressively reduced as days passed, generating a more gradual decline in estimated volatility.

So, volatility estimation based upon the exponential moving average method makes it possible to achieve some advantages over the simple average method. However, it poses some practical problems, as well, and mainly:

√ the selection of the decay factor λ;
√ the selection of the number of past observations.

With regard to the first problem, λ should depend on the rate at which market factor return volatility is thought to vary over time. In this respect, if the "true" market factor volatility is thought to change slowly in time, it would be more correct to select a λ close to 1, so as to give a high weight to more distant observations, as well. Vice versa, if the market factor volatility is thought to vary often, even abruptly, it would be more

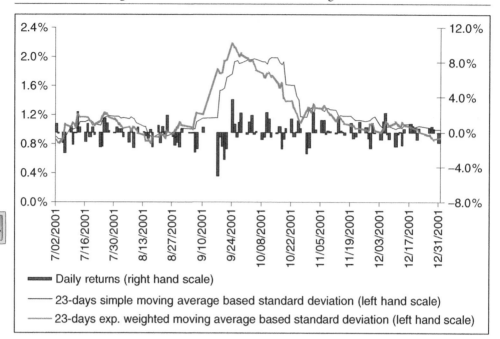

Figure 6.4   An Example of Volatility Estimation Based Upon an Exponential Moving Average

correct to use a smaller λ. With a view to risk measurement, and therefore to potential loss measurement, λ should also depend on the position's holding period. As a matter of fact – other conditions being equal – the shorter this period, the greater is the need for the estimated volatility, and therefore for the estimated potential loss, to more rapidly adapt to new market conditions, and so the lower should λ be.

Figure 6.5 shows that, if a higher value of λ (0.99) is used, a more stable estimated volatility, which is therefore less responsive to more recent market conditions, will be obtained. Vice versa, if a smaller value of λ (0.9) is used, the estimate will, in turn, become more volatile, as new observations receive a proportionally higher weight.[7] It must furthermore be noted that the quite common choice of a single λ factor – determined as the optimal decay factor based upon a more or less large historical data sample and used for different risk factors over longer or shorter time intervals – poses some problems :

√ first of all, using a single parameter for different variables or financial assets conflicts with the empirical evidence that, on some markets, increased volatility tends to persist for many days, whereas, on other markets, an increase usually appears as a simple temporary shock;

√ in the second place, it is frequently the case that the optimal decay factor of the same variable changes significantly over time; it is therefore preferable – at least theoretically – to frequently update this factor, by letting market data determine its optimal

---

[7] The values of λ used by the RiskMetrics™ database are 0.94 for daily volatility estimates (trading portfolio), and 0.97 for monthly volatility estimates (investment portfolio).

value[8] rather that imposing it from the outside and keeping it unchanged for long periods of time.

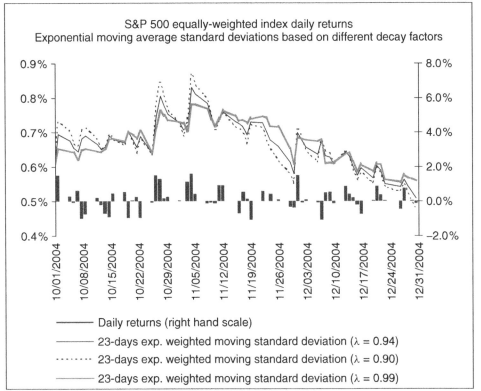

Figure 6.5   An Example of Historical Volatility Estimation Based Upon Different Decay Factors

The second problem – i.e., the choice of the number of past observations – must be evaluated considering different elements. On the one hand, a broader historical series will make it possible to minimize sampling noise and to obtain more reliable estimates; on the other hand, it might be advisable to focus on a shorter historical series in order for data to more accurately reflect recent market conditions, or simply because no broader series is available.

However, the ability of data to reflect current market conditions also depends on how frequently historical volatility estimates are updated. If estimates are updated frequently (for instance, every day), broader historical series can be used, so as to maximize the information content and therefore minimize sampling noise, because the high updating frequency (combined with the use of decreasing weights for more remote observations)

---

[8] This process to determine the optimal value of lambda is generally based on minimization of the root-mean-square error (RMSE) connected with volatility prediction. In practice, the optimal lambda value is the one minimising this prediction error. Of course, the optimal value closely depends on the selected data sample, and must therefore be periodically updated.

will make it possible to reduce the problem of poor consistency with recent market conditions.

The absence of sufficiently broad historical series is a likely problem when working with returns for relatively broad time intervals. Indeed, while in the case of daily returns, a few months of data may be enough to obtain a highly numerous sample and to estimate volatility with adequate accuracy, when working with monthly or annual returns, data for a longer, even multi-year period would be needed in order to obtain an identical number of observations. These are not always available: just think of the case of financial instruments which were introduced onto the market relatively recently. This may cause one to content oneself with a more limited number of observations.

6.4   VOLATILITY PREDICTION: GARCH MODELS

The figures above all clearly showed – to a greater or lesser degree – that volatility is not constant over time, nor can be considered as a constant to which a simple sampling noise is added. Indeed, volatility experiences significant fluctuations. This phenomenon, which is often referred to as volatility clustering, indicates that market factors often experience periods of greater volatility, which may even persist for long periods of time. This problem is addressed explicitly by GARCH (generalized autoregressive conditional heteroskedasticity) models.

Heteroskedasticity means time-changing variance, and is in contrast to the constant variance hypothesis. A historical series showing heteroskedasticity is characterized by high-volatility periods interrupted by relatively quiet periods (i.e., by the already mentioned volatility clustering); this phenomenon is particularly evident in historical series of a financial nature, especially if they are recorded at close time intervals, i.e., very frequently (on a daily or weekly basis). *Conditional* indicates that the predictions obtained are based upon the information available in the previous period: in practice, conditional volatility estimates reflect the current level of uncertainty generated by past shocks. While historical volatility is an *ex-post* return variability measure, and, in this sense, summarizes the price shocks which occurred in the estimation period, conditional volatility tends to capture the rate of "persistence" of these shocks, and thus summarises the effect of past volatility on the current level of uncertainty about future events. Conversely, *autoregressive* refers to the method used to model conditional heteroskedasticity, which is based on variance "self" -regression. In practice, this means that past volatility levels influence future levels. Finally, *generalized* refers to a particular type of model, which was introduced by Tim Bollersev in 1986, and was a generalization of the first autoregressive conditional variance (ARCH) model devised by Robert Engle in 1982. Bollersev's formulation has been very successful because it is general enough to adequately adapt to different types of financial variables. In the following years, additional alternative versions were also developed.

Autoregressive conditional heteroskedasticity models therefore allow to predict future volatility by using a regression based upon the past values of this same volatility, generating a time-varying volatility estimate.

The logic underlying GARCH models and their use for volatility prediction purposes are analyzed briefly below.

First of all, the difference between an unconditional and a conditional estimate needs to be clarified. The former is typically obtained using a more or less large historical data sample: for instance, the unconditional mean of a data set y_t (with $t = 1, 2, \ldots, T$) can be estimated by the sample mean:

$$\bar{y}_t = \sum_{t=1}^{T} \frac{y_t}{T} \tag{6.9}$$

Vice versa, if the variable depends on one or more other variables, a conditional mean can be estimated by having recourse, for instance, to a least squares regression. So, if y depended linearly – unless there was a noise factor – on the value of a certain x, we could estimate conditional mean[9] as:

$$\bar{y}_t|_{x=\bar{x}_t} = \alpha + \beta \bar{x}_t \tag{6.10}$$

If, conversely, y turned out to linearly depend on its past value, the conditional mean estimation model would become

$$\bar{y}_t|_{y_{t-1}} = \alpha + \beta y_{t-1} \tag{6.11}$$

i.e., a first-order autoregressive model, usually referred to as AR(1).

The key difference between unconditional mean and conditional mean is therefore related to the fact that the former is a constant, while the latter needs a specification model – to be estimated by a regression technique – and results in a time-varying estimate.[10]

The same logic is applied in the case of unconditional variance and conditional variance. The former is a constant estimated as sample variance. Conversely, the latter is time-varying, and is estimated based upon a given model. In this sense, the different versions of GARCH models represent different specifications of the model "explaining" conditional variance.[11]

To start with, let us consider the original version of the ARCH model proposed by Engle. It considers variance as a function of the prediction errors ε made in p past periods. In symbols

$$\sigma_t^2 = \alpha_0 + \alpha_1 \varepsilon_{t-1}^2 + \cdots + \alpha_p \varepsilon_{t-p}^2 \quad \text{with} \quad \alpha_0 > 0 \ \alpha_1, \ldots, \alpha_p \geqslant 0^{[12]} \tag{6.12}$$

So, the model estimates variance as a moving average of p squared past prediction errors;[13] for this reason, it is referred to as "p delay model", or simply ARCH(p).

---

[9] When estimating parameters α and β of the model, the common hypotheses relating to errors ε_t (zero mean, serial independence, identical distribution) are usually introduced.

[10] The majority of historical series econometric models are aimed at predicting the mean of a certain variable by using an equation to be estimated as (6.10). On the contrary, the primary purpose of GARCH models is to model and predict the variance of a random variable.

[11] The construction of an autoregressive conditional heteroskedasticity model would, in fact, involve two distinct specifications: one for the mean, and one for variance. In financial applications, however, the mean is often set equal to zero or to a constant. Consider that, while a possible variance specification error will not significantly harm predictions of the mean, in the case of incorrect mean specification, predictions of variance will also be affected, and therefore biased. See Figlewski (1994), p. 20.

[12] In order for the model's stability to be ensured (i.e., in order to prevent estimated variance from "exploding" towards greater and greater values), the sum of error coefficients also needs to be less than one.

[13] As will be seen better below, if the variable considered is given (as in our case) by market factor returns which are assumed to have a zero mean, then the error ε_t will coincide with R_t.

In practice, if a sudden shock of the variable occurs, this will cause a prediction error, which, in turn, if its coefficient α is positive, will generate an increase in the predicted volatility for p future periods (the fact that squared prediction errors are considered results in the increase occurring regardless of the error's sign). So, a first marked change in the variable is thought to be likely to be followed by others; this is consistent with the empirical evidence that a significant price change tends to be followed by just as many significant changes. In this sense, the ARCH model explicitly recognizes the difference between unconditional volatility and conditional volatility, acknowledging that the latter varies in time in relation to past prediction errors; it also adequately models the fact that a marked change in a certain market factor tends to persist in time, generating a volatility clustering phenomenon as described above.

The main limitation of the ARCH model is that its empirical applications often required a large number of delays, making the model not very flexible and burdensome. The generalization introduced by Bollersev (GARCH), conversely, has made it more flexible and capable of obtaining the same degree of accuracy using fewer delays. Its analytical formulation is as follows:

$$\sigma_t^2 = \alpha_0 + \alpha_1 \varepsilon_{t-1}^2 + \cdots + \alpha_p \varepsilon_{t-p}^2 + \beta_1 \sigma_{t-1}^2 + \beta_2 \sigma_{t-2}^2 + \cdots + \beta_q \sigma_{t-q}^2$$

$$\text{with:} \quad \alpha_0 > 0 \alpha_1, \ldots, \alpha_p, \beta_1, \ldots, \beta_q \geqslant 0 \qquad (6.13)$$

In (6.13), conditional variance is modelled by inserting not only p prediction error delays, but also q delays relating to past values of variance, hence the name $GARCH(p,q)$. The former are aimed at capturing the short/very short-term effects related to the trend of the variable considered, the latter, conversely, are aimed at capturing long-term effects; conditional variance therefore depends on its historical values, as well.

The majority of applications of the GARCH model are based upon the $GARCH(1,1)$ version, which considers only one prediction error (the last one), and the value of variance in the previous period. Analytically:

$$\sigma_t^2 = \alpha_0 + \alpha_1 \varepsilon_{t-1}^2 + \beta_1 \sigma_{t-1}^2 \qquad (6.14)$$

So, (6.14) specifies conditional variance at time t as a function of three factors: (i) a constant (α_0), (ii) the variance prediction made in the previous period (σ_{t-1}^2), and (iii) the prediction error (ε_{t-1}^2), i.e., what was learnt about the trend of the variable.

An estimate of the unconditional expected value (i.e., the "theoretical", long-term value of variance) is also implied in the model; if such a value σ^2 exists, it will represent the unconditional expected value σ_t^2, of σ_{t-1}^2 and also of ε_{t-1}^2 (as it represents the mean-square deviation); if the three quantities in (6.13) are replaced with σ^2 and the latter is calculated, the following will be obtained:

$$\sigma^2 = \frac{\alpha_0}{1 - \alpha_1 - \beta_1}. \qquad (6.15)$$

(note that, in order for long-term variance to take a positive and finite value, the sum of α_1 and β_1 needs to be lower than 1).

The model can therefore be rewritten as:

$$\sigma_t^2 = (1 - \alpha_1 - \beta_1)\sigma^2 + \alpha_1\varepsilon_{t-1}^2 + \beta_1\sigma_{t-1}^2 \tag{6.16}$$

The GARCH(1,1) model is therefore based upon a quite intuitive prediction strategy: the conditional variance estimate in a certain period is a weighted mean of long-term variance, the expected variance for the previous period, and a shock for the last period. The last component reflects the belief – which is typical of GARCH models – that volatility, besides varying in time, is characterized by a non-predictable component.

If the variable considered is given (as in our case) by market factor returns which are assumed to have a zero mean, then the error ε_t coincides with R_t. The model (6.14) to be estimated therefore becomes:

$$\sigma_t^2 = \alpha_0 + \alpha_1 R_{t-1}^2 + \beta_1\sigma_{t-1}^2 \tag{6.17}$$

In applications to financial markets, the delayed variance coefficient (β_1) generally takes values above 0.7; vice versa, the prediction error coefficient (α_1) takes smaller values. The former indicates the "rate of persistence" of a volatility shock: high delay coefficients indicate that a change in volatility tends to persist for a long time. Vice versa, the latter indicates the rapidity with which volatility adapts to new market shocks, i.e., new information: higher coefficients result in predictions which are more sensitive to recent conditions, and therefore more erratic. In this sense, the GARCH model is close to the exponential moving average criterion presented above, in the sense that it acknowledges the existence of a volatility "decay factor". However, it significantly differs from it because, instead of arbitrarily determining this factor, it lets it be determined by the market data.

Indeed, the coefficients in equation (6.17) must be statistically estimated, so as to select the values which are most consistent with past historical data; this can be done, for instance, by an estimation algorithm based upon the maximum likelihood criterion.

This algorithm was used to estimate a *GARCH*(1,1) model on the daily returns of the Standard & Poor's index which were considered in the first part of Figure 6.1. The estimated parameters are 0.000002 (α_0), 0.085 (α_1) and 0.905 (β_1); in Figure 6.6, the volatility estimates obtained using these parameters are compared with those obtained previously using the exponential moving average method (using a decay factor λ of 0.94).

It is important to note that, although it relies on one delay only, the *GARCH(1,1)* model is actually characterized by an "infinite memory". As a matter of fact, since (6.14) is true for any t (including $t-1$), it can be rewritten as:

$$\sigma_t^2 = \alpha_0 + \alpha_1\varepsilon_{t-1}^2 + \beta_1(\alpha_0 + \alpha_1\varepsilon_{t-2}^2 + \beta_1\sigma_{t-2}^2) \tag{6.18}$$

σ_{t-2}^2 can also be replaced by an expression derived from (6.14), obtaining:

$$\sigma_t^2 = \alpha_0 + \alpha_1\varepsilon_{t-1}^2 + \beta_1[\alpha_0 + \alpha_1\varepsilon_{t-2}^2 + \beta_1(\alpha_0 + \alpha_1\varepsilon_{t-2}^2 + \beta_1\sigma_{t-3}^2)] \tag{6.19}$$

Similarly, if the term σ_{t-i}^2 is recursively replaced, the following will be obtained:

$$\sigma_t^2 = \alpha_0 \sum_{i=1}^{\infty} \beta_1 + \alpha_1 \sum_{i=1}^{\infty} \beta_1^{i-1}\varepsilon_{t-i}^2 = \frac{\alpha_0}{(1 - \beta_1)} + \alpha_1 \sum_{i=1}^{\infty} \beta_1^{i-1}\varepsilon_{t-i}^2 \tag{6.20}$$

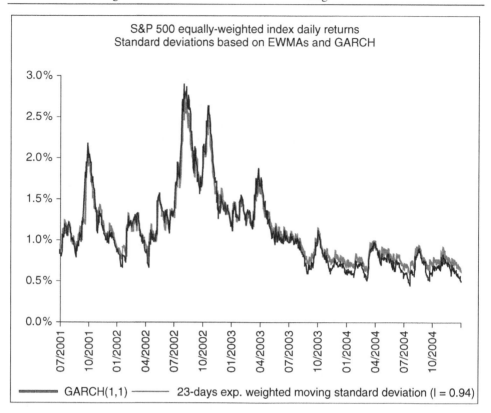

Figure 6.6   Estimates Based Upon GARCH(1,1) and Exponential Moving Averages

(6.19) shows that a GARCH(1,1) model is equivalent to an ARCH model with infinite delays, whose coefficients β_i are bound to decrease in geometric progression as more time-distant shocks are considered.

The GARCH model briefly illustrated herein has several merits:

√ it explicitly acknowledges the existence of a serial correlation phenomenon and expresses it through an autoregressive model;
√ it attaches adequate importance to the new information incorporated into market shocks;
√ it lets the volatility decay factor be determined by market data.

Next to these advantages, however, Bollersev's model has some limitations.

First of all, it may be more complex and burdensome than simply using a moving average – whether simple or exponential – especially if more than one delay per variable is used.

Second, the GARCH model retains the normality hypothesis, although, in this case, this hypothesis refers to prediction error distribution. It follows that, in the presence of a skewed distribution or greater kurtosis than normal, the GARCH model may not offer adequate results.

Finally, the GARCH model, in its original version proposed by Bollersev, considers the impact of a market shock on volatility prediction to be independent of its sign. In other words, as errors are squared, their effect on prediction turns out to be independent of whether they were excess or deficit errors. This is in contrast with the considerable empirical evidence, especially for stock markets, showing that implied volatility generally increases following a market slump, whereas it may even remain unchanged following an increase in prices. This phenomenon, which is referred to as "leverage effect", is generally explained by having recourse to the effects connected with the financial structure of the companies issuing shares and their financial risk. The rationale is as follows: when a share price decreases, the market value of equity also decreases, and therefore the company's financial structure also changes; the company registers an increase in its financial leverage, and therefore its financial risk, as well. On the contrary, when the stock price increases, the financial risk decreases, and so does expected shareholder return volatility.

In an attempt to overcome some limitations of the GARCH model, numerous alternative versions of the original generalization proposed by Bollersev have been suggested. The most popular ones are Exponential GARCH (EGARCH), Asymmetric GARCH (AGARCH), and Integrated GARCH (IGARCH).[14]

The first two are both attempts to overcome the last problem described, i.e., non-consideration of the sign of prediction errors. In practice, EGARCH does nothing but model the natural logarithm of variance instead of variance, so that the right-hand part of the equation may also become negative without causing any problems. In this way, prediction errors need not be squared, but are considered twice: in absolute value or with their sign: the different response of market participants to "good" versus "bad news" is thus adequately considered. The equation for the EGARCH model is as follows:

$$\log \sigma_t^2 = \alpha_0 + \alpha_1 \frac{|\varepsilon_{t-1}|}{\sigma_{t-1}} + \beta_1 \sigma_{t-1}^2 + \gamma \frac{\varepsilon_{t-1}}{\sigma_{t-1}} \qquad (6.21)$$

The AGARCH version mainly aims at considering the skew response of volatility to sudden upward or downward shocks. Its conditional variance specification equation is as follows:

$$\sigma_t^2 = \alpha_0 + \alpha_1 (\varepsilon_{t-1} - \xi)^2 + \beta_1 \sigma_{t-1}^2 \qquad (6.22)$$

In this case, the skewness issue is addressed by introducing an additional parameter (ξ) which, as it is positive by definition, amplifies the effect of negative shocks and mitigates the effect of upward shocks on volatility prediction. Moreover, the AGARCH model generally uses a Student's t-distribution rather than a normal distribution of prediction errors, thus offering greater flexibility also in terms of kurtosis.

The third alternative version, IGARCH, is derived from the GARCH(1,1) model by requiring the sum of coefficients α_1 and β_1 to be one.[15] So, (6.14) becomes:

$$\sigma_t^2 = \alpha_0 + (1 - \beta_1) \varepsilon_{t-1}^2 + \beta_1 \sigma_{t-1}^2 \qquad (6.23)$$

---

[14] We just consider these versions, mainly because they are the only versions which are concretely used to predict the volatility of financial variables for risk management purposes.
[15] Please note that, in this case, unconditional variance, i.e., long-term variance, takes an infinite value, or, better, turns out to be indefinite. Hence the name of variance-integrated model.

The model therefore introduces a necessary trade-off between variance persistence (coefficient β_i) and effect of more recent surprises (term α_1, replaced here by $1 - \beta$).

IGARCH is also interesting because, as it assumes a value of α_0 of zero, an exponential average model with infinite delays is obtained. Indeed, if we rewrite the equation of a generic GARCH model using (6.20), we cancel α_0 and replace β_1 with the symbol λ (and therefore replace α_1 with $1 - \lambda$), we will obtain the following:

$$\sigma_t^2 = (1 - \lambda) \sum_{i=1}^{\infty} \lambda^{i-1} \varepsilon_{t-i}^2 \qquad (6.24)$$

which is equivalent to the exponential moving average model presented above (equation 6.8).

GARCH models have been used predominantly used in the literature to *explain* the behavior of the variance of financial variables, rather than to *predict* its trend. In fact, their application for prediction purposes poses three main problems.

First of all, they need a large number of data in order for estimation of the coefficients resulting from the use of the maximum likelihood criterion to be statistically "robust".

Second, as for any econometric model, their ability to correctly describe a given data sample is in direct proportion to their complexity, and therefore to the number of parameters used. However, a more complex model (with higher p and q) tends to become more easily "obsolete" when it is used for out of sample prediction purposes. More in general, in order for a model to be useful for predictions, it needs to be as stable in time as possible, i.e., its coefficients must not require continuous updates. This is particularly true if it is used for risk management purposes, where the coefficients estimated based upon a certain historical sample are typically maintained unchanged to predict volatility over a future period, which (depending on the holding period of positions) may also not be short. Just as the decay factor of an exponential moving average is liable to become quickly obsolete if the rate of persistence of volatility changes over time, the coefficients of a GARCH model are liable to "aging", as well; both estimates should theoretically be continuously updated in order for them to be representative of recent conditions.

Finally, GARCH models work relatively well if one wants to predict only the volatility for the immediately following period; conversely, they become less and less informative if one tries to make predictions regarding more distant periods of time.

To understand why, let us imagine using a GARCH(1,1) model not to estimate today's volatility, but to predict volatility at time $t+1$. (6.14) would become

$$\sigma_{t+1}^2 = \alpha_0 + \alpha_1 \varepsilon_t^2 + \beta_1 \sigma_t^2 \qquad (6.25)$$

and would require us to know the prediction error at time t, which we do not know yet. Of course, we could replace ε_t^2 with its expected value, i.e., σ_t^2, and obtain a prediction of σ_{t+1}^2 as

$$\sigma_{t+1}^2 = \alpha_0 + \alpha_1 \sigma_t^2 + \beta_1 \sigma_t^2 = \alpha_0 + (\alpha_1 + \beta_1) \sigma_t^2 \qquad (6.26)$$

Similarly, if we were interested in predicting volatility at a future instant $t + k$, we could use the following expression:

$$\sigma_{t+k}^2 = \alpha_0 \sum_{i=1}^{k-1} (\alpha_1 + \beta_1)^i + (\alpha_1 + \beta_1)^k \sigma_t^2 \qquad (6.27)$$

However, it is evident that such predictions contain no new information compared to today (in particular, they do not take account of errors $\varepsilon_{t+1}, \ldots, \varepsilon_{t+k-1}$ which will occur from today to $t + k$). The prediction will then end up converging towards long-term variance (cf. equation 6.15), at a rate that will depend on the value of $(\alpha_1 + \beta_1)$.[16]

This limitation is particularly serious within the framework of risk management, if we think that volatility predictions – based upon which the values at risk of individual positions or portfolios are estimated – cannot be updated day by day, but are usually kept constant for longer time intervals.

In general, the greater complexity connected with the use of conditional heteroskedasticity models may not always be fully justified. As a matter of fact, GARCH models may show a better ability to explain a given historical series of returns but do not always guarantee a better performance than standard exponential smoothing techniques, when used for "out-of-sample" analyses.

6.5   VOLATILITY PREDICTION: IMPLIED VOLATILITY

A second method to predict the volatility of financial variables is based upon option prices. An option's price – whatever the adopted pricing model – is a function of five variables: the strike price (X), the underlying asset market price (S), the option's residual maturity (T), the risk-free interest rate (r), and the underlying asset volatility (σ). By entering these five variables into the selected pricing model, the option's value can be derived. However, if the option's market price is known, as all variables but volatility are known, the pricing model can be used to calculate the volatility which is implied in the option price.

As option pricing formulas such as Black & Scholes' cannot be inverted analytically, the calculation of implied volatility is generally based upon an iterative process; the most commonly used algorithms include, for instance, the Newton-Raphson, or tangent, method. This process, which is similar to the one followed to calculate a bond's actual yield to maturity, consists of four steps:

(1) first of all, the option's theoretical price is calculated by entering an arbitrarily selected volatility value $(\hat{\sigma})$ into the selected pricing model;
(2) once the option's theoretical value, $O(\hat{\sigma})$, has been obtained, this value is compared with the market price O_M; if the market price is higher (lower), the input volatility is increased (decreased) by a value equal to $\dfrac{|O(\hat{\sigma}) - O_M|}{\Lambda}$, where Λ (lambda or vega) represents the partial derivative of the option price function with respect to volatility.
(3) the resulting new volatility data are entered into the pricing model in such a way as to repeat the step above until convergence between $O(\hat{\sigma})$ and O_M is reached.[17]

This process may lead to different implied volatility measures depending on the option contract used. Indeed, at-the-money (ATM) options generate lower implied volatility values than are obtained using in-the-money (ITM) or out-of-the-money (OTM) options.

---

[16] In this connection, see Figlewski (1994), p. 24.
[17] If the reference pricing model is Black & Scholes, convergence is always ensured if the value $\hat{\sigma} = \left| \ln\left(\dfrac{S}{X}\right) + rt \right| \cdot \dfrac{2}{t}$ is used as the initial volatility input.

This phenomenon, which is known as "volatility smile" (because the implied volatility chart of options having different strike prices looks like a smile), is generally explained based upon the greater sensitivity of ATM options to changes in volatility (higher vega).[18] This greater sensitivity would make it possible to obtain the same profit or risk premium with a lower volatility spread than for ITM and OTM options. This phenomenon makes it more cost-effective to estimate implied volatility using ATM options, which are generally characterized by a more liquid and efficient market.

Once the problems connected with calculation of implied volatility have been clarified, we can discuss the adequacy of this information as a tool to predict future volatility. First of all, it should be made clear that implied volatility radically differs, from a logical standpoint, from the volatility estimates described in the sections above. As a matter of fact, the latter – however they are calculated – are all measures obtained through more or less complex historical data processing; they are therefore backward-looking measures, which are based upon the assumption that the past, in a more or less articulate manner, is a good tool to predict the future. On the contrary, implied volatility, as it is derived from a present price, is the result of market expectations about the future trend of volatility, and is therefore entirely forward-looking. In this sense, it could appear as a better prediction tool, because it is a market price, and therefore summarizes the expectations of market participants "trading volatility" on the market. This apparent advantage, however, is subject to two important conditions:

√ first, the pricing model adopted needs to be reliable and, most of all, to be adopted by market participants; as a matter of fact, implied volatility derived from a pricing model other than the one used by market participants would otherwise not be representative of the latter's expectations;

√ second, the market on which the option contract is traded must be a liquid and efficient one, free from any structural flaws; indeed, these flaws would give rise to non-equilibrium prices, which would therefore not adequately reflect market expectations about the future trend of volatility.

It must finally be noted that, notwithstanding the advantage of being a forward-looking measure, implied volatility has two main disadvantages as a tool to predict volatility for risk management purposes. In the first place, its use is clearly subordinated to the existence of an option contract whose underlying asset is the one whose return volatility one intends to predict; this option must also be traded on a liquid, efficient, and, most of all, organized market, from which information concerning traded prices can be derived continuously. In the second place, in order for the volatility measure to be consistent with the desired time horizon, the option's residual maturity needs to coincide with the time horizon selected for the risk management system.

The above-mentioned conditions mean that implied volatility does not really represent a reliable method to predict the volatility of financial variables for risk management purposes. It may supplement the predictions offered by a different method, and point out any deviations from these predictions – for variables for which there is an efficient and

---

[18] The volatility smile phenomenon is also alternatively explained as the consequence of a correction made by the market on account of the fact that, as the return distribution is characterised by fatter tails than implied in a normal distribution, Black & Scholes' model involves an incorrect valuation of in- and out-of-the-money options. See Hull (1996), p. 379.

liquid option market. Such deviations would indicate that market predictions significantly deviate from those implied in the past history of prices, and could prompt a financial institution to revise its estimates.

6.6   COVARIANCE AND CORRELATION ESTIMATION

In the sections above, we have examined in detail how variance (and its square root, i.e., volatility) can be estimated from historical data or from expectations which are implied in option prices.

However, as the reader may remember from the previous chapter, in order to be able to estimate a portfolio's value at risk using the parametric method, variances are not sufficient; one also needs to estimate of covariances, or correlations,[19] among the different market factor returns.

In general, both historical data methods and methods based upon the parameters implied in option prices can be used to estimate covariances, as well as volatility.

If R_t and Q_t are the returns of two risk factors (for instance, the S&P 500 Wall Street index and the FTSE100 London Stock Exchange index), and we want to estimate their covariance through exponential moving averages, we could change equation (6.5), which has already been used for variance of a risk factor's return, as follows:[20]

$$\hat{\sigma}^2_{R,Q;t} = \frac{1-\lambda}{1-\lambda^n} \sum_{i=0}^{n-1} \lambda^i R_{t-1-i} Q_{t-1-i} \tag{6.28}$$

In this case, too, as was already the case for volatility estimation, the value of λ and the sample size will need to be selected more or less arbitrarily, remembering that a value of λ which is closer to zero will make covariance estimate more responsive to recent shocks (in particular when faced with data pointing out a considerable and simultaneous surge in R and Q).

Similarly, the covariance between R and Q can be estimated through a GARCH(1,1) model. The model will take the following form:

$$\sigma^2_{R,Q;t} = \alpha_0 + \alpha_1 R_{t-1} Q_{t-1} + \beta_1 \sigma^2_{R,Q;t-1} \tag{6.29}$$

and can be estimated – through the maximum likelihood method – from the past data of R and Q.

Finally, not only volatilities, but also implied *correlation* estimates can theoretically be derived from option prices. However, this requires complex methods and market data which are often not available.

One method, for instance, involves using option prices for three related prices: X, Y and (X-Y). For example, if one has the volatilities implied in the prices of options on two Euro exchange rates, USD and YEN, and, at the same time, an estimate of implied volatility on the YEN/USD cross-rate – which can be expressed in log terms as the difference between the two Euro exchange rates (EUR/USD-EUR/YEN) – an estimate

---

[19] The following relation links covariance (σ^2_{xy}) and correlation coefficient (ρ): $\sigma^2_{xy} = \rho \sigma_x \sigma_y$. If estimates of σ_x and σ_y are known, then the knowledge of ρ implies knowledge of σ^2_{xy}, and vice versa.

[20] Similar to equation (6.8) seen above, one can easily show that the value for covariance in t depends on covariance in t-1 based on the following law:

$$\hat{\sigma}^2_{R,Q;t} = (1-\lambda) R_{t-1} Q_{t-1} + \lambda \hat{\sigma}^2_{R,Q;t-1}$$

of the implied correlation of the two Euro exchange rates (USD and YEN) can be obtained using the following formula:

$$\rho_{USD,YEN} = \frac{\sigma_{USD}^2 + \sigma_{YEN}^2 - \sigma_{USD-YEN}^2}{2\sigma_{USD}\sigma_{YEN}}$$

A second method to estimate implied correlations involves the use of quanto options prices, i.e., options whose underlying asset is both an exchange rate and a share price/stock exchange index.[21]

Once all variances and covariances have been estimated, their overall consistency needs to be tested. Indeed, if the New York index is positively correlated to the London index, and the latter is negatively correlated to the Tokyo one, it would be surprising (and unacceptable) to obtain a positive or nil correlation coefficient between the Japanese stock exchange and Wall Street.

More precisely, it needs to be tested that the variance and covariance matrix (a matrix which has variances on its main diagonal and covariances among the different variables in the remaining positions) is defined as positive.[22] Otherwise, variance and covariance estimates need to be adjusted until this condition is met.

SELECTED QUESTIONS AND EXERCISES

1. A stock, after being stable for some time, records a sudden, sharp decrease in price. Which of the following techniques for volatility estimation leads, all other things being equal, to the largest increase in daily VaR?

   (A) Historical volatility based on a 100-day sample, estimated through an exponentially-weighted moving average, with a λ of 0.94.
   (B) Historical volatility based on a 250-day sample, estimated through a simple moving average.
   (C) Historical volatility based on a 100-day sample, estimated through an exponentially-weighted moving average, with a λ of 0.97.
   (D) Historical volatility based on a 250-day sample, estimated through an exponentially-weighted moving average, with a λ of 0.94.

2. Consider the different techniques that can be used to estimate the volatility of market factor returns. Which of the following problems represents the so-called "ghost features" or "echo effect" phenomenon?

   (A) A volatility estimate having low informational content.
   (B) The fact that volatility cannot be estimated if markets are illiquid.
   (C) Sharp changes in the estimated volatility when the returns of the market factor have just experienced a strong change.
   (D) Sharp changes in the estimated volatility when the returns of the market factor have not experienced any remarkable change.

---

[21] In this connection, see Alexander (1996), p. 254.
[22] A matrix is defined as positive if, by pre- and postmultiplying it by any vector, no negative result can be obtained. In symbols, $\mathbf{V}$ is defined as positive if $\mathbf{x'Vx} \geq 0 \; \forall \mathbf{x}$.

3. Here are some statements against the use of implied volatility to estimate the volatility of market factor returns within a VaR model. Which one is *not* correct?

   (A) option prices may include a liquidity premium, when traded on an illiquid market.
   (B) prices for options traded over the counter may include a premium for counterparty risk, which cannot be easily isolated.
   (C) the volatility implied by option prices is the volatility in price of the option, not the volatility in the price of the underlying asset.
   (D) the pricing model used to compute σ can differ from the one adopted by market participants to price the option.

4. Assuming market volatility has lately been decreasing, which of the following represents a correct ranking – from the largest to the lowest – of volatility estimates?

   (A) Equally weighted moving average, exponentially weighted moving average with $\lambda = 0.94$, exponentially weighted moving average with $\lambda = 0.97$.
   (B) Equally weighted moving average, exponentially weighted moving average with $\lambda = 0.97$, exponentially weighted moving average with $\lambda = 0.94$.
   (C) Exponentially weighted moving average with $\lambda = 0.94$, exponentially weighted moving average with $\lambda = 0.97$, equally weighted moving average.
   (D) Exponentially weighted moving average with $\lambda = 0.94$, equally weighted moving average, exponentially weighted moving average with $\lambda = 0.97$.

5. A bank is using exponentially-weighted moving averages, based on a decay factor of 0.94 and a very large number of observations. As of yesterday evening, the volatility of daily percentage changes in prices used to be 13 % for stock Alpha, 8 % for stock Beta. Today, price changes for Alpha and Beta have been 3 % and 10 % respectively. Assuming that average returns are zero, update the volatility estimates for Alpha and Beta. Finally, suppose the correlation coefficient between the two stocks used to be 50 % as of yesterday evenings: can you update this value, too?

7

Simulation Models

7.1 INTRODUCTION

The attempt to overcome the problems connected with the variance-covariance approach has led to the development of simulation models. These models owe their name to the fact that, rather than just deriving VaR from a few synthetic risk factor distribution parameters (namely: variances and covariances), a large number of possible "scenarios" concerning the future market evolution (increase in interest rates, exchange rate depreciation, slump in the stock exchange index, etc.) are simulated. The simulation approaches are therefore more time-consuming and computationally-intensive, but, as we will see, they are also more flexible and, often, more accurate.

As a general rule, simulation models share three main features: recourse to full valuation, recourse to the percentile logic, greater freedom in modelling market factor changes. However, they include several approaches – mainly the historical simulation and Monte Carlo simulation approaches – which differ in how risk factor "scenarios" are generated. Let us start by explaining the three features which are common to all simulation models.

(a) Full valuation. We have seen that the variance-covariance approach estimates a portfolio *value change* (resulting from an extreme change in one or more market factors) through a system of usually[1] linear sensitivity coefficients (for instance, a bond's duration or an option's delta). Simulation models, conversely, are based upon a full valuation logic. In other words, the market value of the portfolio whose VaR is to be estimated is fully recalculated, by appropriate pricing formulae, on the basis of new (simulated) market factor values. So, for instance, rather than estimating the change in a bond's market value corresponding to a given increase in interest rates based upon the bond's modified duration, the new price of the bond is calculated using the new interest rate level, and the change in the bond's value is computed as the difference between the two prices (pre and post-shock). In order to be able to calculate the new value of the bond, the formula to calculate its price (which, in the case of a bond, is simply the present value – under the new interest-rate conditions – of the future cash flows associated with the security) needs to be known and applied. This means that simulation approaches require us to know the appropriate pricing formula for each of the financial instruments included in the portfolio whose VaR we want to estimate. If the pricing formulae being used are correct, simulation models will not give approximate, but exact portfolio value changes. The more the price-market factor relation deviates from a linear one, the more desirable this feature; for this reason, simulation models are generally considered to be more accurate to estimate VaR for portfolios containing a large amount of options or other financial instruments with "non-linear" payoff. Full valuation is therefore a more accurate answer to the problem of non-linear payoffs than the delta-gamma method described in Chapter 5.

While full valuation is generally used by most simulation models, one could apply the simulation logic (i.e., generating a large number of scenarios concerning the possible changes in risk factors) and, at the same time, calculating the possible portfolio

---

[1] The delta/gamma approach which was examined in Chapter 5 considers not only the linear term, but also a second-degree term. In any case, it is still based upon an approximation of the portfolio value change, obtained through a system of sensitivity coefficients.

value changes using the (linear or quadratic) sensitivity coefficient technique. In other words, the simulation approach and full valuation approach, although they are usually applied together, are two distinct mechanisms, aimed at solving different problems (see Figure 7.1). The simulation approach is used to generate the possible future values of risk factors, whereas full valuation is used to translate these values into the corresponding future value of the bank's portfolio.

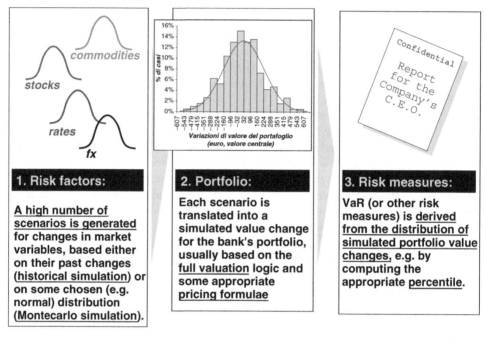

Figure 7.1   Main features of the simulation approaches

(b) Percentile logic. A second feature shared by all simulation models concerns the method to determine the VaR corresponding to the selected confidence level. In the variance/covariance approach, this problem is solved assuming that – given a normal distribution of market factor returns and a linear relation between the latter and the portfolio value changes – the percentiles of future loss distribution can be estimated from the standard deviation and a multiplying constant α. Conversely, in simulation models, once the probability distribution of N possible future portfolio values (corresponding to N simulated scenarios for risk factors) has been generated, VaR is estimated by cutting this empirical distribution at the percentile associated with the desired confidence level. For instance, given 10,000 market factor simulations generating 10,000 portfolio values, VaR at the 95 % confidence level is calculated by taking the 5th percentile (i.e., the 501st observation, starting from the worst one), and computing the difference between this value and the current portfolio value; if, for instance, the current portfolio value is 100 and the 5th percentile is 43, VaR will be 57.

Just as full valuation solves the problem of non-linear pricing relations, using a simulated probability distribution of portfolio values solves the problem of non-normal future loss distribution. Indeed, a simulated distribution is not bound to be normal, but can take any form; in particular, it will tend to deviate from the normal distribution when:

- the distribution of risk factor returns is not normal (for instance, because it is skew, or leptokurtic);
- the risk factor return-portfolio value relation is not linear (therefore, even if starting distributions are normal, the distribution which is obtained takes a different form).[2]

In these cases, the variance/covariance method would be highly inaccurate, as it requires the distribution to be normal, and uses percentiles from the standard normal to determine VaR. The simulation approach, conversely, proves to be more flexible, and can approximate possible future losses more accurately.

The empirical probability distribution "cut-off" technique can also overcome the problems related to the non-monotonic market factor-portfolio value relation (see the straddle example in Chapter 5). Indeed, possible portfolio values are ranked from the best to the worst one, regardless of the market factor movement which generated them. A significant loss based upon the selected confidence level (for instance, a result belonging to the worst 5 %), but generated by a non-extreme market factor movement will be disregarded in parametric models, but considered correctly in simulation models.

(c) Greater flexibility in modelling market factor changes. In Chapter 5, we have seen that parametric models are based on the assumption of a normal distribution of asset price changes (asset-normal distribution) or market factor changes (delta-normal distribution). The normal distribution hypothesis was closely functional to the possibility of estimating VaR using a scaling factor α of the standard deviation. However, we also mentioned that numerous empirical studies showed that the distribution of price and market factor returns is actually characterised by fat tails and by a higher level of kurtosis than the one of a normal distribution.

It would therefore be desirable to adopt hypotheses other than normality. However, this would make parametric VaR calculation more complex; in particular, while a combination of normal random variables is also a normal (which makes it possible to estimate the VaR of a portfolio exposed to multiple risk factors as a simple multiple of the standard deviation), this is not true if a different distribution, such as Student's t, is adopted.

On these grounds, numerous studies focusing on parametric models, although they acknowledge that market returns are not normal, then disregard the problem for analytical treatability reasons. At most, in some models, the selected multiple of the standard deviation is arbitrarily increased,[3] in order to take the problem of fat "tails" of the empirical probability distribution of market returns into consideration in some way.

Simulation models overcome this problem because they do not use a normal distribution to model market factor changes. More specifically, two procedures are possible:

---

[2] An example of a non-linear relation is the case – which was considered in Chapter 5 – of a non-monotonic relation between the change in the value of a straddle option trading strategy and the value of the underlying asset value change.

[3] A similar approach is also implicitly followed by the Basel Committee, which, in determining the capital requirements for market risks based upon the use of internal models, demands that the requirement arising from application of the latter should be multiplied by 3 (see Chapter 19). The multiplier indicated by the Committee has the function of protecting from model risk, i.e. the risk of using an unrealistic model (for instance, because it assumes normal distributions of returns, while the latter are actually fat-tailed).

– historical simulations generate risk factor scenarios from the empirical distribution arising from the historical series of past market factor changes;[4]
– Monte Carlo models, conversely, require that a distribution – on the basis of which simulations will be generated – should be defined. Theoretically, this distribution can be selected freely, but, in order for it to be of practical use, it must meet two key requirements: (i) reflect the empirical characteristics of market factor change distributions in the best possible way, and (ii) lend itself to generating random simulations. For this reason, in practice, a normal distribution is often used (whereby a possible advantage of the simulation approach is given up), as this makes it possible to rapidly generate a large number of scenarios. In other words, while Monte Carlo simulations have the advantages mentioned under (a) and (b) above (full valuation and percentile approach) over the parametric approach, if they use a normal distribution, they will not take advantage of the possibility of more realistically reflecting the distribution of market factor changes.

There is then a third approach (stress testing), which is complementary to the first two; rather than generating a large number of scenarios, so as to reasonably approximate the entire distribution of possible events, this focuses on few particularly unfavourable scenarios.

Table 7.1 Problems and solutions in VaR simulation models

				Features of the simulation approach		
		a) Full valuation	b) Percentile approach	c) Simulation approach (normal and other distributions)		
				Historical simulation	Monte Carlo simulation	
					With non-normal distributions	With normal distributions
Problems	Non-linear payoffs	✓	✓	×	×	×
	Non-normal market returns	×	✓	✓	✓	×
Legend: ✓ = solves the problem; × = does not solve the problem						

Table 7.1 summarizes the three features of the simulation approaches and the problems of parametric models which they remedy. The next two sections will provide a detailed explanation of both historical and Monte Carlo simulations. The following one will focus on stress testing.

---

[4] With reference to historical simulations, the simulation approach is also called "non-parametric" approach, because – as it does not advance any hypothesis about the functional form of distribution of market factor returns – it does not require that the parameters of this distribution should be estimated. This definition is obviously not suitable for Monte Carlo simulations.

7.2 HISTORICAL SIMULATIONS

In a historical simulation model, potential market factor changes are assumed to be properly represented by their historical empirical distribution, i.e., by the changes recorded over a past period. In other words, the distribution of risk factor changes is assumed to be stable over time, so that their past behaviour (for instance, the frequency of occurrence of extreme returns) is a reliable guidance to predict their possible future movements.

The risk factor changes recorded in the past are transformed into possible future values of the bank's portfolio through full valuation (thus eliminating any bias connected with linear or quadratic approximations of true pricing relations). After the portfolio value changes corresponding to each of the historical market factor changes have been calculated, these are ranked from the lowest to the highest one (from maximum loss to maximum profit). This way, an empirical probability distribution of portfolio value changes is obtained. The latter is "cut off" at the percentile corresponding to the required confidence level. The corresponding portfolio value change is equal to the desired VaR. The process is summarized in Table 7.2.

Table 7.2 Main steps of a historical simulation

Step	Activity
1	Selecting a sample of (for instance, daily) returns of the relevant market factor(s), relating to a given historical period (for instance, 250 days).
2	Revaluing the individual position or the portfolio at each of the historical market factor return values.
3	Reconstructing the empirical frequency distribution of the resulting position/portfolio values.
4	Cutting the distribution at the percentile corresponding to the desired confidence level.
5	Computing VaR as the difference between the above percentile and the current position/portfolio value

7.2.1 A first example: the VaR of a single position

Consider a bank which, as at 28 December 2004, held a call option, with a strike price of 1,300 dollars and a residual maturity of three months, on the S&P500 US stock exchange index (which, on that day, was quoted at 1,213.54 dollars). Given the value of market factors, the option's value is approximately 2.30 dollars.[5]

In order to simulate the possible evolution of the option's market value, the two years period from 1 January 2003 to 28 December 2004 is chosen as the historical reference sample. This historical sample comprises 500 daily returns.

Table 7.3 shows – in the first three columns – the evolution of the S&P500 index during the two years sample period, and the relevant daily log returns. For the sake of simplicity, only the first and last 20 data, chronologically, are reported.

---

[5] When determining the option's market value, the Black & Scholes model was used, assuming a risk-free rate of 10 % and an annual S&P500 index return volatility of 7.1 %.

Table 7.3 Example of historical simulation for a call option position

Data in chronological order			Data ranked based on daily log returns				
Date	S&P500	Daily log returns of the S&P500	Rank	Daily log returns of the S&P500	Simulated value of the S&P500	Simulated value of the call	Change in the value of the call
03/01/2003	908.6	0.0%	1	−3.6%	1170.8	0.18	−2.11
06/01/2003	929.0	2.2%	2	−3.0%	1178.1	0.30	−2.00
07/01/2003	922.9	−0.7%	3	−2.6%	1182.2	0.39	−1.90
08/01/2003	909.9	−1.4%	4	−2.5%	1183.3	0.42	−1.88
09/01/2003	927.6	1.9%	5	−2.3%	1185.8	0.49	−1.80
10/01/2003	927.6	0.0%	**6**	**−1.9%**	**1190.4**	**0.65**	**−1.65**
13/01/2003	926.3	−0.1%	7	−1.9%	1191.2	0.68	−1.61
14/01/2003	931.7	0.6%	8	−1.8%	1192.0	0.72	−1.58
15/01/2003	918.2	−1.5%	9	−1.8%	1192.1	0.72	−1.58
16/01/2003	914.6	−0.4%	10	−1.6%	1193.7	0.79	−1.50
17/01/2003	901.8	−1.4%	**11**	**−1.6%**	**1193.9**	**0.80**	**−1.50**
21/01/2003	887.6	−1.6%	12	−1.6%	1194.5	0.83	−1.47
22/01/2003	878.4	−1.0%	13	−1.6%	1194.7	0.84	−1.46
23/01/2003	887.3	1.0%	14	−1.6%	1194.8	0.84	−1.46
24/01/2003	861.4	−3.0%	15	−1.5%	1194.9	0.85	−1.45
27/01/2003	847.5	−1.6%	16	−1.5%	1195.1	0.85	−1.44
28/01/2003	858.5	1.3%	17	−1.5%	1195.1	0.86	−1.44
29/01/2003	864.4	0.7%	18	−1.5%	1195.4	0.87	−1.43
30/01/2003	844.6	−2.3%	19	−1.5%	1195.8	0.89	−1.41
31/01/2003	855.7	1.3%	20	−1.5%	1195.8	0.89	−1.40
...	...	...	...	...	...	...	...
30/11/2004	1173.8	−0.4%	481	1.6%	1233.1	5.44	3.15
01/12/2004	1191.4	1.5%	482	1.6%	1233.1	5.46	3.16

(continued overleaf)

Table 7.3 (*continued*)

Data in chronological order			Data ranked based on daily log returns				
Date	S&P500	Daily log returns of the S&P500	Rank	Daily log returns of the S&P500	Simulated value of the S&P500	Simulated value of the call	Change in the value of the call
02/12/2004	1190.3	−0.1 %	483	1.6 %	1233.2	5.48	3.18
03/12/2004	1191.2	0.1 %	484	1.6 %	1233.4	5.51	3.22
06/12/2004	1190.3	−0.1 %	485	1.7 %	1234.7	5.80	3.50
07/12/2004	1177.1	−1.1 %	486	1.8 %	1235.2	5.92	3.63
08/12/2004	1182.8	0.5 %	487	1.9 %	1236.6	6.26	3.96
09/12/2004	1189.2	0.5 %	488	1.9 %	1237.1	6.38	4.08
10/12/2004	1188.0	−0.1 %	489	1.9 %	1237.2	6.41	4.11
13/12/2004	1198.7	0.9 %	**490**	**1.9 %**	**1237.2**	**6.41**	**4.12**
14/12/2004	1203.4	0.4 %	491	1.9 %	1237.3	6.43	4.14
15/12/2004	1205.7	0.2 %	492	2.1 %	1239.6	7.02	4.72
16/12/2004	1203.2	−0.2 %	493	2.1 %	1239.9	7.11	4.81
17/12/2004	1194.2	−0.8 %	494	2.2 %	1240.7	7.32	5.02
20/12/2004	1194.7	0.0 %	**495**	**2.2 %**	**1240.7**	**7.33**	**5.03**
21/12/2004	1205.5	0.9 %	496	2.2 %	1240.8	7.36	5.06
22/12/2004	1209.6	0.3 %	497	2.3 %	1241.4	7.53	5.23
23/12/2004	1210.1	0.0 %	498	2.6 %	1245.2	8.66	6.36
27/12/2004	1204.9	−0.4 %	499	3.4 %	1255.4	12.23	9.93
28/12/2004	1213.5	0.7 %	500	3.5 %	1256.5	12.70	10.40

Conversely, the following two columns report the returns in order of size, starting from the worst ones. Once again, only the first and last twenty data are shown.

The sixth column shows the values which the S&P500 index could take the following day if, starting from the current value (1,213.54 dollars), it experienced a logarithmic change equal to the one shown in the previous column.[6] The seventh column shows what the option's market value would be, given this new value of the underlying asset;[7] the

---

[6] In practice, values are obtained as $1,213.54e^r$, where r is the daily log return.
[7] To generate these option values, recourse was also had to the Black & Scholes model, leaving the risk-free return and volatility hypotheses unchanged.

last column rewrites these values as differences from the option's current value (2.30 dollars).

As can be noted, extreme market factor return values correspond to extreme option values; this is because the relation between a call's value and the value of its underlying asset, although not linear, is monotonic (see Figure 7.2).

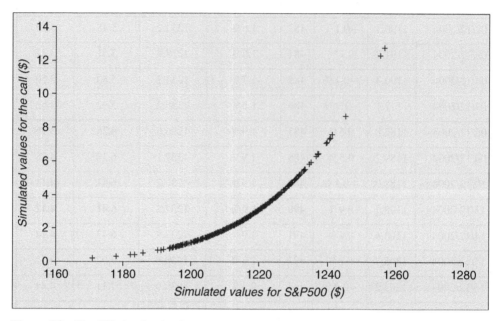

Figure 7.2   The 500 simulated values

At this point, assume we want to determine the VaR corresponding to a 99 % confidence level. This is equal to 1.65 dollars. This value corresponds to the sixth most significant negative change in the option's market value. As the sample under consideration comprises 500 daily data, this means that the loss suffered by the bank would be larger than the identified one only in 5 out of the 500 calculated changes, i.e., only in 1 % of the cases. Likewise, the VaR corresponding to a 98 per cent confidence level is 1.5 dollars, i.e., the eleventh highest loss.

If, on the contrary, the bank had sold the option, i.e., had a short position with respect to the option's price, the VaR corresponding to the different confidence levels should be calculated using the data related to the positive changes in the option's market value. So, for instance, the VaR corresponding to 99 % confidence would be 5.03 dollars. Similarly, the VaR corresponding to 98 % confidence would be 4.12.

As can be noted, VaRs for a long position on the option under consideration are on average lower than those for a short position – the confidence level being equal. This indicates that the distribution of market value changes is skewed, and has a more marked left tail. This result is graphically highlighted in Figure 7.3, which shows the frequency distribution of the option's market value changes. Note that the value −1.65, i.e., VaR at 99 %, was highlighted; it is easy to see that this value "outdistances" 1 % of worst cases on its left.

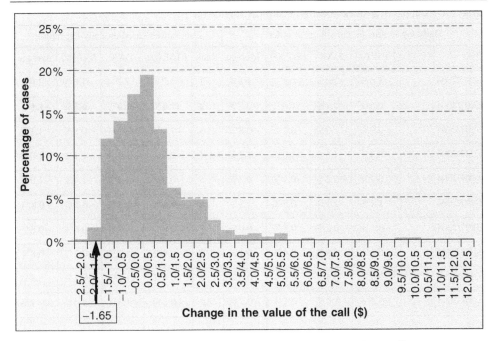

Figure 7.3 Frequency distribution of simulated changes in the value of the call

7.2.2   Estimation of a portfolio's VaR

Let's now consider a second example, relating to a portfolio which is sensitive to the joint evolution of multiple market factors. In particular, let us assume a bank which, as at 9 December 2004, had a stock portfolio equally consisting of shares from the British (FTSE 100), German (DAX), and US (S&P500) stock exchange indexes.

Table 7.4 shows the daily returns[8] for the three indexes for the 100-day period from 22 July to 8 December 2004. The return which would have been obtained on a portfolio like the bank's – consisting equally of shares from the three domestic markets – on each of those days is also shown (in practice, this is the simple mean of the three returns). Note that these are not the returns which were actually experienced by the bank's portfolio (whose composition probably did not remain constant over time) on those days, but the returns which the bank's *current* portfolio (which includes equally-weighted British, German, US shares) would experience if, on the following day, similar market factor movements to those highlighted by past history were to occur.

As above, the first columns are in chronological order, while the right-hand part of the Table is ranked with reference to the mean return of the three indexes (i.e., the changes in the bank's portfolio). Note that the ascending order of returns is respected for the portfolio, but not for the individual markets: the worst return of the portfolio does not necessarily correspond to the worst return of the individual stock exchange indexes.

In this case, too, the VaR corresponding to the different confidence levels can be determined following the percentile logic, i.e., by cutting the historical empirical distribution

---

[8] For the sake of simplicity, only the first ten and last ten data are shown.

Table 7.4 Example of a stock portfolio historical simulation

| Daily log returns in chronological order | | | | | Data ranked based on daily log returns | | | | |
Date	FTSE100	DAX	S&P500	Average	Rank	FTSE100	DAX	S&P500	Average
22/07/2004	−1.6%	−2.0%	0.3%	−1.1%	1	−1.7%	−2.7%	−1.6%	−2.0%
23/07/2004	0.5%	−0.1%	−1.0%	−0.2%	**2**	**−1.6%**	**−2.0%**	**0.3%**	**−1.1%**
26/07/2004	−0.9%	−1.2%	−0.2%	−0.8%	3	−1.1%	−2.1%	−0.1%	−1.1%
27/07/2004	0.9%	1.6%	1.0%	1.2%	4	−0.9%	−1.1%	−1.1%	−1.0%
28/07/2004	0.7%	−0.2%	0.1%	0.2%	5	−0.3%	−1.2%	−1.4%	−1.0%
29/07/2004	1.4%	2.1%	0.5%	1.3%	**6**	**−0.8%**	**−1.5%**	**−0.2%**	**−0.8%**
30/07/2004	−0.1%	0.2%	0.1%	0.0%	7	−0.8%	−0.9%	−0.6%	−0.8%
02/08/2004	0.1%	−0.8%	0.4%	−0.1%	8	−0.9%	−1.1%	−0.3%	−0.8%
03/08/2004	0.3%	0.4%	−0.6%	0.0%	9	−0.9%	−1.2%	−0.2%	−0.8%
04/08/2004	−0.5%	−1.4%	−0.1%	−0.7%	10	−0.8%	−1.3%	0.0%	−0.7%
...	...	...	...	...	...	...	...	...	...
25/11/2004	0.7%	0.8%	0.0%	0.5%	91	1.1%	1.3%	0.0%	0.8%
26/11/2004	−0.3%	−0.1%	0.1%	−0.1%	92	0.5%	1.6%	0.6%	0.9%
29/11/2004	0.2%	−0.2%	−0.3%	−0.1%	93	0.9%	1.0%	0.9%	0.9%
30/11/2004	−1.0%	−0.5%	−0.4%	−0.6%	94	0.8%	0.8%	1.3%	1.0%
01/12/2004	0.7%	1.4%	1.5%	1.2%	**95**	**0.9%**	**1.6%**	**1.0%**	**1.2%**
02/12/2004	0.3%	0.7%	−0.1%	0.3%	96	0.7%	1.4%	1.5%	1.2%
03/12/2004	−0.1%	−0.2%	0.1%	−0.1%	97	1.1%	1.4%	1.4%	1.3%
06/12/2004	−0.5%	−0.4%	−0.1%	−0.3%	98	1.0%	1.7%	1.3%	1.3%
07/12/2004	0.1%	0.4%	−1.1%	−0.2%	**99**	**1.4%**	**2.1%**	**0.5%**	**1.3%**
08/12/2004	−0.5%	−0.3%	0.5%	−0.1%	100	1.9%	2.6%	1.5%	2.0%

at the percentile corresponding to the desired confidence level. So, for instance, the 99%
confidence level VaR is equal to a 1.1% decrease in the portfolio's market value. This is
the second-largest negative change in the portfolio, i.e., the one which would be exceeded
(in absolute value) only in one out of 100 cases. Similarly, VaR at a 95% confidence
level would be equal to a −0.8% negative change in the portfolio's market value.

  If the bank had taken a short position on its portfolio – for instance, by selling future
contracts on the stock exchange indexes under consideration – the corresponding VaRs
would be 1.2% (95% confidence) and 1.3% (99% confidence), respectively.

7.2.3   A comparison between historical simulations and the variance-covariance approach

The historical simulation model is an example of a non-parametric technique, because – as it does not assume any specific functional form of the distribution of market factor changes *ex ante* – it does not require to estimate the parameters of market factors returns distribution.

Based upon the same 100 data of past equity returns, we could alternatively have assumed the probability distribution of market factor returns (and, therefore, of portfolio value changes, as well) to be normal, and we could have applied the parametric variance-covariance approach. For this purpose, it would have been sufficient to estimate the historical standard deviation of the simulated portfolio's constant-weight returns, which is 0.65 %, and to apply the scaling factor corresponding to the desired confidence level[9] to this value.

Table 7.5 Compared approaches

	Variances/ Covariances	Historical simulation
VaR at 95 % - long position	1.03 %	0.85 %
VaR at 99 % - long position	1.46 %	1.12 %
VaR at 95 % - short position	1.03 %	1.2 %
VaR at 99 % - short position	1.46 %	1.3 %
Mean	0.00 %	0.08 %
Standard Deviation	0.63 %	0.63 %
Skewness	0.000	−0.013
(Excess) kurtosis	0.000	0.868

Table 7.5 and Figure 7.4 show the results of this comparison. As can be noted, the values obtained with the historical simulation approach are different from those derived using the variance-covariance approach. In general, those who are in favor of historical simulations usually argue their preference for this VaR estimation methodology on the basis of its ability to capture "fat tails" of the empirical distributions of market factor returns. So, they believe that historical simulations generate more conservative and, therefore, on average higher VaR estimates than those arising from the variance-covariance approach. The example illustrated here shows that this is not necessarily true.

However, when looking at the comparison between the historical frequency distribution of returns and the normal distribution with a mean of zero and a standard deviation of 0.63 % (Figure 7.3), we realize that – for sufficiently broad confidence intervals – the

---

[9] For the sake of simplicity, let us imagine to calculate the standard deviation by attributing equal weights to all past observations (therefore, without applying the exponentially weighted moving averages and GARCH models examined in Chapter 6). Note that we estimated the standard deviation by using the 100 observations concerning the mean returns of the three market factors directly; alternatively, we could have estimated the standard deviations of the three indexes and the relevant covariances separately, and we could then have constructed the standard deviation of the equally-weighted portfolio using formula (5.17) from Chapter 5.

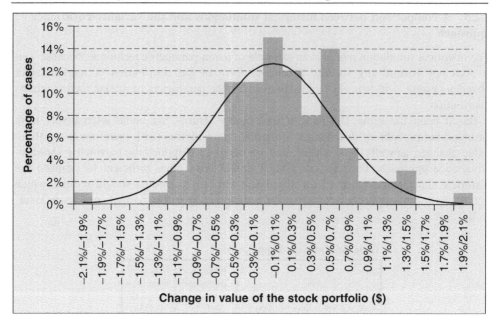

Figure 7.4   Historical distribution and normal distribution

distribution actually takes fatter tails. In particular, value changes in the order of (plus or minus) 2 % are to be considered as virtually impossible if the normal distribution is adopted, but they actually occurred in the past, although in a very modest proportion of cases.

The historical distribution's "fat tails" are confirmed by the historical distribution's kurtosis index (also referred to as excess kurtosis), which takes a positive value, showing that the centre of the distribution and the tails are more likely to occur than a normal distribution would suggest.

In general, whether a methodology is more or less conservative than another one depends on the functional form of the historical distribution of market factor returns. Note that, in this case, the values obtained by applying the two methods are not that different. This is due to two main reasons. First, the portfolio return distribution is not that different from a normal one – as, on the other hand, can also be seen from the parameters of the skewness index – because it is obtained, in turn, as the sum of the distribution of the returns of three different market factors. Second, the position under consideration is characterized by a linear sensitivity to the changes in the relevant market factors.

7.2.4   Merits and limitations of the historical simulation method

After the technical characteristics and background rationale underlying the historical simulation method have been discussed, the main advantages and disadvantages connected therewith can be highlighted briefly. The historical simulation model has mainly five merits:

(1) First of all, historical simulations are a solution to the risk measurement problem whose underlying logic is **easily understandable and communicable** among a bank's

various units, as well as to the top management. The result reached by this methodo-logy is the loss which would be obtained if past conditions – in terms of joint market factor changes – were to occur again in the future. The insight underlying this logic is easily understandable also to those who are not aware of the nature of the underlying individual position, or the techniques used to obtain this result.

(2) A second advantage of historical simulations is connected with the fact that they **do not require any particular hypothesis concerning the functional form of the distribution of market factor returns**. Actually, they require the (implied) hypo-thesis that the distribution of future returns is correctly approximated by the historical distribution. It follows that, if market factor returns are not normally distributed, but have a probabilistic behaviour which is stable over time (for instance, because their skewness or leptokurtosis, if any, remain constant), the historical simulation model provides more accurate indications than parametric models.

(3) In the third place, historical simulations **do not require the variance-covariance matrix** of the market factors which can affect the value of the portfolio considered **to be estimated**. The risk connected with portfolios whose value is affected by multiple market variables is calculated based upon the joint changes in these variables which occurred over the selected historical period. It follows that historical simulations cap-ture the correlation structure reflected in joint market factor changes,[10] and implicitly assume that it will remain constant in the future, as well.

(4) As has already been stated, historical simulations **allow to capture the risk of port-folios whose sensitivity to market factor changes is non-linear or non-monotonic**, because they are based upon full valuation.

(5) Finally, historical simulations tend to generate very stable VaR measures, which are not very responsive to changes in market conditions, especially if the confidence level is high. This is due to the fact that VaR will not change until a higher return (in absolute value) than the one corresponding to the selected percentile occurs on the market, or until the latter leaves the historical estimation sample.

Notwithstanding these advantages, historical simulations suffer from three main limita-tions:

(1) First of all, revaluing the entire portfolio of a financial institution's positions according to past market conditions is particularly **computationally-intensive**, and can therefore take too long a time with respect to the risk quantification requirements of a bank's trading activity. In general, the more numerous and complex the instruments in the portfolio and the larger the number of market factors to which the portfolio is sensitive, the higher its computing intensiveness. This limitation, which is common to the Monte Carlo simulation model, however, has lost in importance as a result of the continuous progress in computing power.

(2) In the second place, as has already been mentioned, historical simulations **implicitly assume the probability distribution of market factor changes to be stable (sta-tionary) over time**. In other words, although the historical simulation model does not advance any hypothesis about the nature of the probability distribution of market factor changes, it implicitly assumes that the future distribution will be the same as the

---

[10] This aspect is evident from the stock portfolio example shown in Table 7.3.

past one, i.e., that historical returns will come from probability distributions which are valid in the different points in time (today, one month ago, next month), independent and identically distributed (i.i.d.). If, on the contrary, the (non-observable) distribution of market factor returns changes over time, in particular if it is heteroskedastic, then the empirical probability distribution used as an input of the model will be a hybrid of realisations of differently distributed variables, and, as such, will have little either conceptual or operational significance. In other words, if the underlying return distribution is not constant over time, the empirical historical distribution cannot be considered as a representation of it.

(3) The third and last limitation of the historical simulation method – which is probably the most serious one from the point of view of its application – concerns the fact that the **available time series are limited**, especially if the selected time horizon for VaR calculation is longer than one day. The limited number of available historical observations typically results in a poor definition of the empirical probability distribution tails. Indeed, the only market factor changes which the model considers to be possible are those which occurred in the past, in the time horizon which was taken as a reference. Extreme events, as such, may be heavily over- or underrepresented in the selected historical sample compared to their very long-term theoretical frequency: for instance, if a 10 % reduction in the S&P500 index were possible, on average, once every 100 days, in the last 500 days it might have occurred only three, or as many as seven times. On the other hand, increasing the length of the reference time series as much as possible may be counterproductive, because it will become more likely that the distribution stability hypothesis may be violated. In other words, if we go too far back in time, we are liable to base our estimate of the future return distribution on data extracted from a now "obsolete" distribution. A trade-off relation with regard to the optimum length of the historical reference series therefore exists: considerations relating to the stability of the distribution of market factor changes would suggest that it should be short while requirements of an adequate representation of extreme phenomena would demand it to be long.[11]

7.2.5   The hybrid approach

One way to ease this trade-off was suggested by Boudoukh, Richardson and Whitelaw (1998), who tried to combine the merits of the two models illustrated so far – the variance-covariance and historical simulation models – into a single approach, referred to as "hybrid approach". In particular, the purpose of the hybrid approach is to combine the advantage connected with the use of exponentially decreasing weights with the typical

---

[11] As was noted by Maspero (1997), the problem becomes more serious if VaR calculation is required for longer holding periods than one day. In this case, given the number of available daily observations, the historical sample is reduced in proportion to the holding period. For instance, 1,000 historical observations will result in only 100 independent observations if a decadal holding period is considered. Sometimes, to solve the problem, it was suggested that overlapping periods should be considered. In this case, the 1,000 daily observations from the previous example could result in 990 decadal data corresponding to intervals: $[(t_1 \ldots t_{11}); (t_2 \ldots t_{12}); \ldots . (t_{990} \ldots t_{1,000})]$. This procedure has precise statistical limitation: indeed, observations will become serially correlated. A generic n-th piece of data, for instance, will share 9/10 of the time period with data n-1 and n+1, 8/10 with data n-2 and n+2, and so on. One may therefore legitimately expect that the historical series of the resulting 990 observations will be less volatile than a series of 990 independent observations. The overlapping observation technique may result in strongly misleading data, and only provides an illusory answer to the problem of the lack of data.

advantage of historical simulations. i.e., not advancing any hypothesis about the functional form of the distribution of market factor returns. The idea is therefore to use a relatively long historical reference series, but, at the same time, to assign a relatively higher weight to those returns extracted from the historical distribution which are closer in time.

For this purpose, the hybrid approach involves introducing an additional phase – consisting in assigning each past observation a weight – into the historical simulation method: the more recent the observation, the greater the weight. This can be done by using a similar logic to the one which is typical of the exponential weighted moving averages used in the variance-covariance approach for historical volatility estimation. In other words, given n historical observations, from $t-1$ to $t-n$, each of them is attributed a weight W_{t-i} equal to:

$$W_{t-i} = \frac{\lambda^i}{\sum_{i=1}^{n} \lambda^i} \quad \text{with} \quad 0 < \lambda < 1 \tag{7.1}$$

In this way, the more recent the past observations, the greater the weight they receive. Moreover, the lower the lambda value, the greater the speed at which the weight assigned to past data decreases.

Now, the VaR associated with the desired confidence level is obtained by cutting the empirical distribution no longer at the relevant percentile, but rather at the value where the cumulative weight reaches the desired confidence level. In this way, the individual returns extracted from the historical distribution will not contribute to determine VaR solely as a function of their relative intensity, but also on the basis of their relative weight, i.e., of their relative distance/closeness in time to the moment of valuation.

To clarify how VaR is estimated in the hybrid approach, consider the stock portfolio example shown in Table 7.4. For this purpose, the values of the portfolio's returns – both in chronological order (first four columns), and ranked in ascending order (last five columns) – are shown again in Table 7.6. A weight which decreases exponentially as data move farther from the valuation date (hypothetically, 9 December 2004) is also associated with each historical return data. To construct these weights, a λ value of 0.94 was used. Finally, the last column shows the cumulative weight corresponding to each return data, i.e., the sum of the weights associated with it and with all lower returns.

The different confidence levels VaRs can now be estimated based upon the data shown in the last three columns of the table. So, for instance, VaR at a 99 % confidence level is given by the historical return at which the cumulative weight – obtained from the lowest return – is 1 %. As can be seen from the table, the cumulative weight experiences a "leap" from 0.87 % to 3.56 % at the switch from the ninth to the tenth largest negative return (in absolute value), i.e. from -1.09 % to -1.04 %. Following a conservative criterion, 99 % confidence level VaR will therefore be 1.09 %. Alternatively, a linear interpolation could be used. In this case, 99 % VaR could be determined as:

$$VaR_{99\%} = 1.09\% \cdot \frac{(3.56\% - 1\%)}{(3.56\% - 0.87\%)} + 1.04\% \cdot \frac{(1\% - 0.87\%)}{(3.56\% - 0.87\%)} \cong 1.087\%$$

Table 7.7 shows the VaR measures obtained with the historical simulation method and hybrid approach, respectively. Note that, in this case, the hybrid approach – for a long position – results in slightly smaller risk measures. This is mainly due to the fact that most marked reductions in the market factors affecting the stock portfolio occurred in the

Table 7.6 Example of a simulation based upon the hybrid method

	Daily log returns in chronological order				Data ranked based on daily log returns				
Date	$t - i$	Simulated portfolio returns	Weights W_i $(\lambda^i/\Sigma\lambda^i)$		Date	$t - i$	Simulated portfolio returns	Weights W_i $(\lambda^i/\Sigma\lambda^i)$	Cumulated weights (ΣW_i)
22/07/2004	$t - 100$	−1.12%	0.01 %		06/08/2004	$t - 89$	−1.99%	0.03 %	0.03 %
23/07/2004	$t - 99$	−0.20%	0.01 %		22/07/2004	$t - 100$	−1.12%	0.01 %	0.04 %
26/07/2004	$t - 98$	−0.76%	0.01 %		25/10/2004	$t - 33$	−1.09%	0.83 %	0.87 %
27/07/2004	$t - 97$	1.16 %	0.02 %		19/11/2004	$t - 14$	−1.04%	2.69 %	3.56 %
28/07/2004	$t - 96$	0.20 %	0.02 %		22/09/2004	$t - 56$	−0.99%	0.20 %	3.76 %
29/07/2004	$t - 95$	1.34 %	0.02 %		12/10/2004	$t - 42$	−0.85%	0.48 %	4.23 %
30/07/2004	$t - 94$	0.05 %	0.02 %		27/09/2004	$t - 53$	−0.78%	0.24 %	4.48 %
02/08/2004	$t - 93$	−0.12%	0.02 %		11/08/2004	$t - 86$	−0.77%	0.03 %	4.51 %
03/08/2004	$t - 92$	0.02 %	0.02 %		26/07/2004	$t - 98$	−0.76%	0.01 %	4.52 %
04/08/2004	$t - 91$	−0.66%	0.02 %		20/10/2004	$t - 36$	−0.70%	0.69 %	5.21 %
05/08/2004	$t - 90$	−0.46%	0.02 %		04/08/2004	$t - 91$	−0.66%	0.02 %	5.23 %
...	...	...	...		...	...	...	...	...
25/11/2004	$t - 10$	0.52 %	3.45 %		01/11/2004	$t - 28$	0.80 %	1.13 %	90.01 %
26/11/2004	$t - 9$	−0.11%	3.66 %		17/11/2004	$t - 16$	0.89 %	2.38 %	92.38 %
29/11/2004	$t - 8$	−0.12%	3.90 %		11/11/2004	$t - 20$	0.94 %	1.86 %	94.24 %
30/11/2004	$t - 7$	−0.63%	4.15 %		10/08/2004	$t - 87$	0.98 %	0.03 %	94.27 %
01/12/2004	$t - 6$	1.21 %	4.41 %		27/07/2004	$t - 97$	1.16 %	0.02 %	94.28 %
02/12/2004	$t - 5$	0.32 %	4.69 %		01/12/2004	$t - 6$	1.21 %	4.41 %	98.70 %
03/12/2004	$t - 4$	−0.06%	4.99 %		16/08/2004	$t - 83$	1.30 %	0.04 %	98.73 %
06/12/2004	$t - 3$	−0.32%	5.31 %		27/10/2004	$t - 31$	1.34 %	0.94 %	99.67 %
07/12/2004	$t - 2$	−0.18%	5.65 %		29/07/2004	$t - 95$	1.34 %	0.02 %	99.69 %
08/12/2004	$t - 1$	−0.10%	6.01 %		01/10/2004	$t - 49$	2.01 %	0.31 %	100.00 %

initial part of the sample $(t - 89, t - 100)$. It follows that, in the hybrid approach, they are attributed relatively smaller weights.

In general, the hybrid approach combines the merits of historical simulations (no explicit hypothesis about the functional form of the distribution of market factor returns, full valuation, preservation of the correlation structure) with the typical advantages of the

Table 7.7 VaR measures: historical simulations and hybrid approach compared

	Historical simulation	*Hybrid simulation*
VaR at 95 % - long position	0.85 %	0.72 %
VaR at 99 % - long position	1.12 %	1.087 %
VaR at 95 % - short position	1.16 %	1.17 %
VaR at 99 % - short position	1.34 %	−1.31%

exponential moving average technique examined in Chapter 6 (high information content connected with the use of a large historical sample and greater responsiveness to recent data, thanks to the decreasing weight technique). This approach therefore provides a first answer to two major problems of historical simulations which were highlighted above: on the one hand, the problem connected with the hypothesis of stability ("i.i.d.-ness") of the distribution of risk factor returns (considering that, even if the distribution changes over time, more weight will be attributed to closer observations, i.e., to those coming from distributions which are more similar to the current one); on the other hand, the problem of the optimal length of the historical series (as a matter of fact, precisely because it reduces the biases related to violation of the i.i.d.-ness hypothesis, it makes it possible to use more data, thus ensuring a better definition of the distribution tails).

7.2.6 Bootstrapping and path generation

So far, we have assumed the time horizon over which VaR is calculated to be similar to the frequency with which historical sample data were collected. Of course, it will not necessarily be so. For instance, a bank might have a historical series of daily returns available, but be interested in VaR over a one-week risk horizon.

In this case (see footnote 11), the bank could use the same historical series to generate returns on a weekly basis; this, however, would lead to a reduction in the number of available observations. For instance, given 701 daily observations, the bank would no longer have 700 daily returns, but 100 weekly returns.

An alternative approach to the problem comes from the bootstrapping and path generation method.

Bootstrapping, in practice, means that, rather than using each past return included in the historical returns sample once and only once, a large number N of values will be extracted from the sample (and the extracted value will be reintroduced into the sample every time, so that the same return can be extracted twice or more[12]).

Let us refer to the first of these N returns as $R_{1,t+1}$. Let us imagine that it is a daily return, and that the bank is interested in estimating VaR over a one-week time period.

We will first use this return to determine the value taken by the risk factor (for instance, a stock exchange index S) on which the portfolio value depends[13] on the following day.

---

[12] By applying bootstrapping as described, residuals are implicitly assumed to have an identical probability of being extracted (uniform distribution). A higher sensitivity to the current trend can be obtained by attributing recent observations greater weights and having the latter decrease exponentially as observations "grow old".

[13] The described procedure also applies if there is more than one risk factor.

We will obtain the following:

$$S_{1,t+1} = S_t e^{R_{1,t+1}}$$

(note that, since R is a logarithmic return, continuous compounding was used).

At this point, a new daily return $R_{1,t+2}$ expressing the possible risk factor return *on the second day* of this first scenario can be extracted from the past return sample by using bootstrapping again. By applying it to S_{t+1}, we can generate a hypothetical value for the risk factor at time t+2:

$$S_{1,t+2} = S_t e^{R_{1,t+1} + R_{1,t+2}}$$

This procedure can be repeated for the third and following days, until a vector of seven returns $(R_{1,t+1}, \ldots, R_{1,t+7})$ is obtained, which allows to estimate the possible value of the risk factor in one week's time:

$$S_{1,t+7} = S_t e^{\sum_{i=1}^{7} R_{1,t+i}}$$

Based upon this value, the full valuation logic can be applied to obtain the value of the bank's portfolio in this first scenario.

Obviously, the vector generated so far is only *one* possible path which the risk factor (and portfolio) value could follow in the next seven days. $N-1$ more paths need to be generated in order to be able to construct a distribution of N possible values of the bank's portfolio in one week time. Figure 7.5 – using the 100 daily returns of the portfolio in Table 7.4 as the historical sample – shows a single path for the portfolio value over seven successive days (first panel), five paths (second panel), and finally one hundred paths (third panel) whose frequency distribution is represented by a bar chart. From this distribution, it will be possible to identify the desired percentile (for instance, the first one) and the relevant VaR (in this example, VaR at 99 %).

As is clearly shown by the Figure, path generation by bootstrapping simulates not only the total change in market variables throughout the period considered, but also the evolutionary path leading them to their final value. It therefore offers the advantage of making it possible to also analyze the risk connected with particular option categories, such as some exotic options, whose payoff depends not only on the value that the relevant market variables will take upon maturity, but also on the evolutionary path that these same variables followed during the period which was the subject of the simulation.[14]

7.2.7 Filtered historical simulations

Path generation by the bootstrap method leads to correct results if daily returns are identically and independently distributed (i. i. d.). Indeed, if this were not the case, a path based upon daily returns all extracted from the same distribution (and without a return value being influenced in any way by the value of the previous ones) would lead to an unrealistic representation of the probability distribution of the possible portfolio values at the end of the risk horizon.

We have seen that the hybrid approach is a possible tool to make the hypothesis of stable distribution of risk factor returns more realistic (as it attributes greater weights to

---

[14] In this case, reference is made to such instruments as Asian options. See Hull (1993), pp. 414–431, for a review of these instruments.

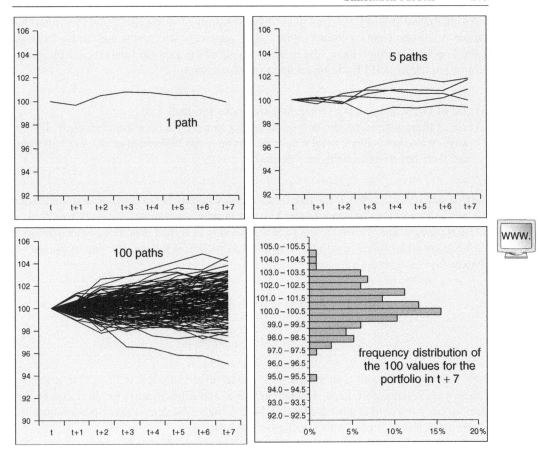

Figure 7.5   Generation of weekly paths through bootstrapping

more recent returns, and therefore to the volatility levels shown by the market in the latest period). However, this is just a partial and approximate answer;[15] this arouses an interest in further solutions to the problem.

The first proposal came from Hull and White (1998), who suggested that historical data should be adjusted based upon current (or predicted) risk factor volatility conditions. This approach, referred to as "volatility weighted", allows to obtain VaR estimates other than those implied in the historical reference sample which are more sensitive to current market conditions.

In practice, in the presence of increased volatility, historical returns are adjusted upwards, thus leading to higher VaR estimates than those implied in the historical distribution. Hull and White's work stopped at the insight that market factor heteroskedasticity can be incorporated into the historical simulation logic by rescaling time series for conditional volatility based upon the information available at the time of VaR estimation; however, it left room for flexibility with regard to how this can be done.

---

[15] Pritsker (2001) shows that both historical simulations and the hybrid approach respond slowly and in a skewed manner to changes in the degree of risk, as reflected in the risk factor volatility.

An alternative strategy, referred to as "filtered historical simulations", was proposed by Barone-Adesi and Giannopoulos (1996).[16] This approach, which was used to control risk at the London Clearing House, the clearing house of the London International Financial Futures Exchange (LIFFE), is based upon two basic ideas:

(i) use of GARCH models to filter data and make residuals i.i.d.;
(ii) use of these filtered residuals to generate scenarios by a bootstrap technique. In this way, an attempt is made to take both the non-normal distribution of risk factor returns and their heteroskedasticity into account.

The first step considers that, if the risk factor return volatility is not constant, but stochastic, it is necessary to model it accordingly. For this purpose, it assumes volatility to follow a GARCH process, and it estimates its parameters using historical data. For instance, returns can be assumed to follow a simple GARCH(1,1) model, similar to the one examined in Chapter 6:

$$R_t = \varepsilon_t \tag{7.2}$$

$$\sigma_t^2 = \alpha_0 + \alpha_1 \varepsilon_{t-1}^2 + \beta_1 \sigma_{t-1}^2 \tag{7.3}$$

Even if returns followed a more complex model than indicated in (7.2) (for instance, if they were serially correlated, so that each one would be affected by the value of the previous one), it would in any case be possible to remove the deterministic portion through a regression, and to focus on the stochastic residuals.

After the coefficients of the above equations have been estimated, it becomes possible to standardize ("filter") historical returns by dividing them by the estimate of conditional volatility for the corresponding period.

$$e_t = \varepsilon_t / \sigma_t \tag{7.4}$$

If the model is correct, these standardized returns are i.i.d., and can therefore be used for historical simulation.

The second step introduces the filtered bootstrap technique to generate random data from a historical sample. Bootstrapping is used to randomly extract (and reintroduce) a large number N of values; the starting sample, however, is not the historical return sample, but the filtered return sample.

Each of the e_i (with $i = 1, \ldots, N$) generated through random extractions is then multiplied by the estimated conditional volatility for the period $t+1$ for which VaR is to be estimated (for instance, the following day). In this way, an entire distribution of risk factor returns which is consistent with the past history, but also with the current volatility, is simulated.

---

[16] See also Barone-Adesi, Borgoin and Giannopoulos (1998), and Barone-Adesi, Giannopoulos and Vosper (1998).

Thus, if the first extracted residual is defined as e_1, the first shock being simulated for time $t+1$ will be obtained by calculating the following:

$$\varepsilon_1 = e_1 \cdot \hat{\sigma}_{t+1} \tag{7.5}$$

where $\hat{\sigma}_{t+1}$ is the conditional volatility prediction obtained based upon the GARCH model.

Similarly, $\varepsilon_2, \varepsilon_3, \ldots \varepsilon_N$ values are generated. From each of them, the bank's portfolio is revalued, so as to obtain a distribution of N possible future values. VaR is finally obtained by cutting this distribution at the desired percentile, and computing the difference between this percentile and the current portfolio value.

If the risk horizon is greater than the frequency of calculation of returns, a filtered version of the path generation method examined in the section above can be applied. Let us refer to the first daily return generated previously (which we referred to so far simply as ε_1) as $\varepsilon_{1,t+1}$. Note that this is not the "filtered" return, but the one which has already been "weighted" for current volatility. As above, the value taken by the risk factor S on the following day in the first scenario can be determined from this return:

$$S_{1,t+1} = S_t e^{\varepsilon_{1,t+1}}$$

Moreover, an estimate $\hat{\sigma}_{t+2}$ of the volatility level in two days' time can be obtained from the simulated return by applying (7.3).

$$\hat{\sigma}_{t+2}^2 = \alpha_0 + \alpha_1 {\varepsilon_{t+1}}^2 + \beta_1 {\sigma_{t+1}}^2$$

At this point, a new random value $e_{1,t+2}$ expressing the possible filtered return on the second day of this first scenario can be extracted from the filtered return sample by using bootstrapping again. By multiplying this value by the volatility estimate, a simulated return consistent with the volatility predicted for the second day is generated.

$$\varepsilon_{1,t+2} = e_{2,t+2} \cdot \hat{\sigma}_{t+2}$$

As above, this procedure can be repeated for the third and next days, until a vector of seven returns $(\varepsilon_{1,t+1}, \ldots, \varepsilon_{1,t+7})$ – each of which is adjusted for the relevant estimated volatility – is obtained. This vector allows to estimate the possible value of the risk factor (and therefore also of the bank's portfolio) in this first scenario in one week's time.

$$S_{1,t+7} = S_t e^{\sum_{i=1}^{7} \varepsilon_{1,t+i}}$$

$N-1$ more paths will then need to be generated by the same procedure, in order to be able to construct a distribution of N possible values of the bank's portfolio in one week's time which is similar to the one in Figure 7.5. From this distribution, the desired percentile and VaR can be identified.

7.3 MONTE CARLO SIMULATIONS

We have seen that, in the bootstrap approach, the historical sample is used as a "warehouse" from which data are drawn by randomly extracting values. Monte Carlo simulations[18] are also based upon the generation of random data, but through a more complex

---

[18] The origin of the term Monte Carlo dates back to the forties, when this term designated a simulation plan developed during the testing of the first atomic bomb. The working team involved in the plan included, among

mechanism. They involve the estimation of the parameters of a particular probability distribution (for instance a normal, a Student t-distribution, etc.) from the historical sample, and then the extraction of N simulated values for the risk factor(s) from this probability distribution. In this way, this technique allows to generate a number of values which may even be larger than the number of observations in the historical sample. On the other hand, it requires an act of faith on the "right" risk factor probability distribution: it is therefore a parametric technique.

Monte Carlo simulations were originally used in finance as a pricing tool for complex products, such as some exotic options, for which no analytical solution could be obtained. In practice, if some hypotheses often used in pricing models are valid (market completeness, no arbitrage opportunities, no transaction costs, divisibility of assets and the possibility of short sales), then the price of a derivative instrument will be given by the expected value (calculated using a risk-neutral probability distribution) of its future payoff discounted back at the risk-free rate. This expected value can be calculated by simulating a large number of possible evolutions of market conditions and calculating the mean of the values which the payoff would take at each of the simulated scenarios. If the number of simulations is sufficiently large, this mean value will be a non-biased estimator of the "true" expected value of the payoff.

If we consider an asset V whose price depends upon a single market variable x, this method would involve extracting a large number of values for this variable from the theoretical distribution,[19] while recalculating the position's market price at each of the simulated scenarios. In the case of an asset V whose market value depends on multiple market factors $x_1, x_2, \ldots x_m$, the Monte Carlo method requires each individual variable to be simulated by extracting it from an appropriate joint probability distribution and recalculating the position's market value at each of the simulated scenarios. In this case, the non-arbitrage constraints connected with the joint evolution of the different variables need to be complied with (in other words, the values taken by the different market variables in each individual scenario must be consistent with one another, and therefore "arbitrage free"). In both cases, once the distribution of future values has been obtained, it will be possible to calculate its mean. So, in general, in the case of derivative products, the Monte Carlo method is used to estimate the expected value of a function of one or more random variables; in analytical terms, this amounts to approximately estimating the probability-weighted integral of a function $V(x_1, x_2, \ldots x_m)$ in a space whose size is m (greater than or equal to one), equal to the number of relevant market factors.

Conversely, the application of Monte Carlo simulations to risk management issues is more recent, and dates back to the 80's. The logic is the same as the one used in pricing: from an appropriately parameterized theoretical distribution, the evolution of a market variable will be simulated a large number of times, and the market value of the individual risk position at each of the resulting scenarios will be calculated. Once the probability distribution of the changes in the market value of the position has been obtained, VaR will be estimated following the percentile logic which has already been illustrated with reference to historical simulations. So, the purpose is not to estimate the *expected value* of the portfolio – as in pricing applications – but to rearrange observations, cut them off at the desired percentile, and identify the relevant VaR.

---

others, Von Neumann, Ulam and Fermi, i.e., some of the most eminent physicists and mathematicians of the past century. Recourse to simulations became necessary because the problems addressed by physicists had reached a level of substantial analytical untreatability.

[19] Generally, approximately 10,000 "simulation paths" are used.

7.3.1   Estimating the VaR of a single position

Estimating the VaR of a position whose value is sensitive to the returns x of a single market factor consists of five steps:

(a) Selecting the probability density function $f(x)$ which best approximates the distribution of the returns of the market factor.
(b) Estimating the parameters (mean, standard deviation, etc.) of distribution f.
(c) Simulating N market factor scenarios from distribution f.
(d) Calculating the change in the position's market value at each of the simulated scenarios.
(e) Cutting off the resulting probability distribution at the percentile corresponding to the desired confidence level.

Note that steps (d) and (e) are similar to historical simulations. Vice versa, steps (a) – (c) are the peculiar feature of Monte Carlo simulations.

Step (a) is probably the most critical one: if the selected distribution does not correctly represent the possible future risk factor evolution, the scenarios generated for this factor and for the position, as well as VaR, will also be unrealistic. From a practical point of view, however, step (c) is also particularly challenging; this requires having recourse to a random number generator[20] through which N values will be extracted from the risk factor probability distribution. The most frequently used method is based upon two "ingredients": the inverse of the distribution function associated with f, which we will refer to as $F^{-1}(p)$,[21] and a set of N random extractions from a uniform distribution with values ranging from zero to one.[22] In this case, step c) can, in turn, be broken down into the two following steps (to be repeated N times):

(c1) extracting a number p from the uniform distribution.
(c2) calculating the value x so that $x = F^{-1}(p)$.

This procedure will become clearer through an example. Consider a bank which purchased an at-the-money call option with one-year maturity on the CAC40 index. Today, the index is quoted at 100 Euros, and the option's market value (assuming a risk-free rate of 3 % and an annual stock market return volatility of 20 %) is 9.413 Euros.

After analysing the historical series of returns of the index, the bank's risk manager concludes that the distribution $f(x)$ which best approximates the actual return distribution is a normal distribution with a mean μ of 0.15 % and a standard deviation σ of 1.5 %.[23]

---

[20] Very often, "pseudorandom" numbers rather than actual random numbers are used. The latter are aimed at more uniformly "filling" the reference domain, thus avoiding concentrations in some sub-areas which often accompany the use of random numbers. See, e.g. Jorion (2001) for more details.
[21] If f(x) is the probability density function of x, the associated distribution function, $F(x) = \int_{-\infty}^{x} f(t)dt$, will express the probability p of occurrence of values lower than or equal to x. The inverse of the distribution function, $F^{-1}(p)$, will express a value x such that the associated distribution function will be worth p, i.e., a value x such that the probability of occurrence of values lower than or equal to x will be exactly p.
[22] The uniform distribution has a density function defined as: $f_U(u) = \begin{cases} 1 & 0 \le u \le 1 \\ 0 & otherwise \end{cases}$. In practice, all values included in the [0,1] range, including extremes, are considered to be equally probable.
[23] Although Monte Carlo simulations prove to be particularly advantageous precisely when market factor return distribution is other than the normal, for the sake of simplicity, the example shown is based upon this distribution.

The risk manager will therefore extract N values ranging from zero to one, by means of a random number generator based upon a [0.1] uniform distribution (see first column in Table 7.8). He/she will associate the corresponding value $x = F^{-1}(p)$ with each of these values p, using the inverse of the distribution function of a normal distribution with a mean of 0.15 % and a standard deviation of 1.5 %.

To be precise, since software routines exist for computers, calculating the inverse of the distribution function of a standard normal distribution (which we will refer to here as $\Phi^{-1}(p)$), the value of $F^{-1}(p)$ can simply be obtained as:

$$F^{-1}(p) = \Phi^{-1}(p) \cdot \sigma + \mu$$

i.e., by first generating a value v distributed according to a standard normal (see the second column in the table), and then converting[24] it into a value x (third column) from a normal distribution with a mean of 0.15 % and a standard deviation of 1.5 %:

$$x = v \cdot \sigma + \mu \tag{7.6}$$

This procedure is represented in Figure 7.6 (panels I-III). As can be seen, first, a number p, ranging from 0 to 1, selected in such a way that all the values in the range are equally probable, is generated. Then, this value is interpreted as the cumulative probability generated by a standard normal distribution function (the area under the curve of panel II), and the value v of the standard normal random variable which would have determined such a cumulative probability is identified. Finally, the value is "adjusted" to make it consistent with the parameters μ and σ estimated from the historical data of the changes in the CAC40 stock exchange index on which the call is written. At this point, it can be interpreted as a possible change x in the stock exchange index.[25]

Going back to Table 7.8, we can see how the different values of x generated by this technique are used for VaR calculation. Indeed, the fourth column shows the value of the index itself (whose starting value at t was – as the reader will remember – 100) at time $t+1$ for each rate of change x in the CAC40 index. Based upon this value, the fifth column in the table shows the corresponding value of the call option at $t+1$, and the sixth one shows the difference between this value and the call's current market value (9.413). This procedure is summarised in panel IV of Figure 7.6.

For the sake of simplicity, Table 7.8 only reports the first 10 out of 1,000 simulated values. Based on all 1,000 values, the VaRs corresponding to the different confidence levels can be estimated by cutting the distribution at the percentile corresponding to the desired confidence level. So, for instance, using simulated values to generate Table 7.8, the 95 % confidence level VaR was 1.25 Euros, while the 99 % VaR was 1.77 Euros. Of course, if 1,000 more values were generated, the results might be slightly different; however, if more scenarios (for instance, $N = 20,000$ or $N = 100,000$) were used, they would become much more stable, and therefore much more reliable.

---

[24] (7.6) is derived simply by remembering that a standard normal variable v can be obtained from a variable x distributed according to a generic normal distribution with mean μ and standard deviation σ, as: $v = \dfrac{x - \mu}{\sigma}$.

[25] The technique which has just been illustrated allows to sample from any distribution f, provided that the inverse of the distribution function $F_X^{-1}(p)$ can be calculated. For some distributions, the inverse of the distribution function cannot be expressed in an analytical form; in this case, recourse is had to numeric approximations or other techniques. See Maspero (1997) for more details on this aspect.

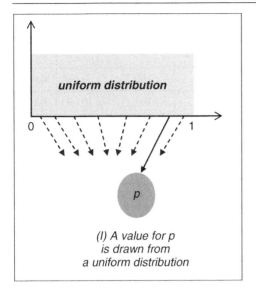

(I) A value for p
is drawn from
a uniform distribution

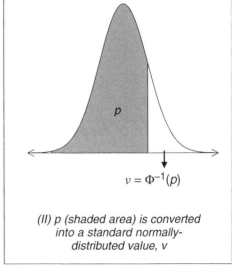

$v = \Phi^{-1}(p)$

(II) p (shaded area) is converted
into a standard normally-
distributed value, v

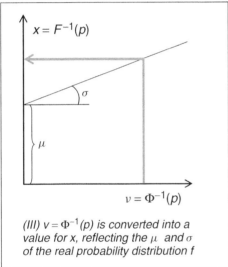

(III) $v = \Phi^{-1}(p)$ is converted into a
value for x, reflecting the μ and σ
of the real probability distribution f

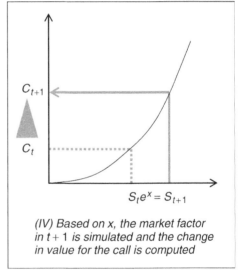

(IV) Based on x, the market factor
in $t + 1$ is simulated and the change
in value for the call is computed

Figure 7.6   Generation of normally distributed values and revaluation of the position

7.3.2   Estimating portfolio VaR

When we move from a position whose market value is a function of a single market factor to a position or portfolio which is sensitive to the evolution of m market factors, VaR estimation requires considering the structure of correlations among these factors' returns. Indeed, the Monte Carlo method, unlike the historical simulation model (which reproduces the joint changes which occurred in the past) cannot capture these correlations "automatically".

If we just simulated N scenarios for each market factor in an independent manner, the result might be unrealistic: risk factors would be uncorrelated, whereas, in reality, their

Table 7.8 An Example of VaR estimation through a Monte Carlo simulation

Scenario #	p (uniformly distributed)	$v = \Phi^{-1}(p)$	$x = F^{-1}(p) = v \cdot \sigma + \mu$	$S_t + 1 = S_t \cdot e^x$	c	Δc
1	0.663	0.420	0.008	100.78	9.888	0.475
2	0.739	0.639	0.011	101.11	10.093	0.679
3	0.465	−0.087	0.000	100.02	9.425	0.012
4	0.301	−0.521	−0.006	99.37	9.040	−0.373
5	0.363	−0.349	−0.004	99.63	9.191	−0.222
6	0.286	−0.564	−0.007	99.31	9.003	−0.411
7	0.397	−0.260	−0.002	99.76	9.270	−0.143
8	0.686	0.484	0.009	100.88	9.947	0.534
9	0.434	−0.167	−0.001	99.90	9.353	−0.060
10	0.600	0.254	0.005	100.53	9.735	0.321
...	...	...	...	...	...	...
991	0.317	−0.477	−0.006	99.44	9.079	−0.334
992	0.598	0.248	0.005	100.52	9.730	0.316
993	0.606	0.268	0.006	100.55	9.748	0.334
994	0.264	−0.632	−0.008	99.21	8.944	−0.470
995	0.690	0.495	0.009	100.90	9.958	0.545
996	0.375	−0.318	−0.003	99.67	9.219	−0.194
997	0.945	1.598	0.025	102.58	11.021	1.608
998	0.712	0.559	0.010	100.99	10.018	0.605
999	0.444	−0.142	−0.001	99.94	9.376	−0.038
1000	0.657	0.406	0.008	100.76	9.875	0.461

realizations might occur more or less interdependently.

So, in the case of a portfolio, Monte Carlo simulations must be enriched – compared to what was illustrated in the previous section – to make sure that simulated scenarios take account of the correlation among factors.

The five steps which were considered in the above paragraph shall therefore be changed as follows:

(a) Selecting the *joint* probability density function $f(x_1, \ldots, x_m)$ which best approximates the distribution of the returns of the m market factors.
(b) Estimating the parameters (means, *variances and covariances*, etc.) of distribution f.
(c) Simulating N scenarios for m market factors from distribution f.

(d) Calculating the change in the position's market value at each of the simulated scenarios.

(e) Cutting the resulting probability distribution at the percentile relating to the desired confidence level.

Note that, while steps (d) and (e) remain unchanged, the first two steps now require specifying and parameterizing a *joint* probability distribution which can describe the possible simultaneous changes in all m market factors. Among the parameters, an important role is played by the variance-covariance matrix (referred to using the capital letter Σ): this is a symmetrical matrix similar to the correlation matrix C which was examined in Chapter 5, that accommodates, on its main diagonal, the variances of the *m* market factors, and, in the remaining positions, the covariances among different market factors.

This matrix (estimated using the techniques examined in Chapter 6), will be crucial in the procedure to generate the future changes in the *m* risk factors. To this end, it shall first be decomposed into two triangular matrices A and A^T (which are mutual transposes), constructed in such a way that, if they are multiplied, matrix Σ will be obtained again.[26] In general, the two matrices A e A^T can always be obtained from a correct variance-covariance matrix; a widely used procedure to identify A and A^T is the so-called "*Cholesky decomposition.*[27]"

Before we see how matrix A and its transpose are used, let us ask ourselves what would happen if we just applied the procedure examined in Figure 7.6 *m* times to generate a scenario relating to *m* factors:

- the first step would generate *m* random values $(p_1, p_2, \ldots p_m)$ ranging from 0 to 1;
- the second step would translate them into as many values (v_1, v_2, v_3) from a standard normal;
- the third step would adjust them using equation (7.6), generating $x_1, x_2, \ldots, x_m$, in such a way as to reflect their true mean and variance values. The *covariance* among the different x_i values would however be intrinsically nil, because they would have been generated parallelly, but independently.

---

[26] A matrix is called triangular if all the elements above or below its main diagonal are equal to zero. Matrix A^T, which is the transpose of matrix A, is a matrix whose rows are the columns of A. The product of two matrices is an operation, obtained according to a particular algebra, whose result is another matrix; it can be done in Excel using the function =MATR.PRODUCT (Matrix1;Matrix2).

[27] Take as an example the case of two variables only, A and B. The covariance matrix can be decomposed as follows:

$$\Sigma = \begin{bmatrix} \sigma_A^2 & \sigma_{A,B}^2 \\ \sigma_B^2 & \sigma_B^2 \end{bmatrix} = \begin{bmatrix} \sigma_A & 0 \\ \dfrac{\sigma_{A,B}^2}{\sigma_A} & \sqrt{\sigma_B^2 - \left(\dfrac{\sigma_{A,B}^2}{\sigma_A}\right)^2} \end{bmatrix} \begin{bmatrix} \sigma_A & \dfrac{\sigma_{A,B}^2}{\sigma_A} \\ 0 & \sqrt{\sigma_B^2 - \left(\dfrac{\sigma_{A,B}^2}{\sigma_A}\right)^2} \end{bmatrix} = AA'$$

Similarly, the correlation matrix can be decomposed as follows:

$$\Sigma = \begin{vmatrix} 1 & \rho \\ \rho & 1 \end{vmatrix} = \begin{vmatrix} 1 & 0 \\ \rho & (1-\rho^2)^{1/2} \end{vmatrix} \begin{vmatrix} 1 & \rho \\ 0 & (1-\rho^2)^{1/2} \end{vmatrix}$$

Conversely, if we want to "inject correlation" into these values, the third step will need to be changed as follows. Instead of acting on each individual value v_i, i.e., multiplying it by the relevant standard deviation and adding the relevant mean, we will combine all m values into a vector, which we will call $\mathbf{v}$; from this, we will derive vector $\mathbf{x}$ (which will contain the changes in m market factors) by applying the following formula, which, in practice, is the "multivariate" version of (7.6):

$$\mathbf{x} = \mathbf{v} \cdot \mathbf{A} + \boldsymbol{\mu} \qquad (7.7)$$

Where $\boldsymbol{\mu}$ is the vector of m mean market factor returns, and $\mathbf{A}$ is the matrix which was obtained previously by decomposing $\boldsymbol{\Sigma}$.

The resulting vector $\mathbf{x}$ (from which the values of m market variables at $t+1$ can be calculated, and the portfolio can be revalued according to the full valuation logic) will only be one of the N scenarios required to construct the distribution of future portfolio values. We can therefore call it $\mathbf{x}_1$, and use the procedure described above to generate a new vector $\mathbf{p}$, a new $\mathbf{v}$ and – through (7.7) – a second scenario $\mathbf{x}_2$. We will then continue by generating $\mathbf{x}_3$, $\mathbf{x}_4$, and all other scenarios until $\mathbf{x}_N$, each of which will be associated – through full valuation – with the corresponding future portfolio value. Once the entire distribution of possible future portfolio values (and the relevant changes from the current value) has been constructed, it will be possible to identify the desired percentile to calculate VaR.

To understand this procedure, we will introduce an example. In particular, we will add a short position on an at-the-money call option, still with 1-year maturity, on the DAX German stock exchange index to the call on the CAC40 index which was considered in the previous section. We will then assume that the distribution of daily DAX returns can be represented by a normal with a mean of 0.18 % and a standard deviation of 1.24 %. We will finally assume that the correlation coefficient between the returns of the two stock exchange indexes is 0.75. Note that the portfolio consists of a long position on the MIB 30 index and a short position on the DAX index. It follows that a positive correlation between the returns of the two indexes implies a natural hedging, i.e., risk diversification, effect.

Table 7.9 reports the simulated values which would be obtained by applying (7.6) to separately generate the returns of the two stock exchange indexes. These values would be highly unrealistic, in the sense that they would be implicitly based upon the hypothesis of independence of the returns of the two stock exchange indexes. In other words, the evolution of the two indexes is simulated separately and independently, without considering their positive correlation.

Figure 7.7 graphically shows the data from Table 7.9: note that the independence hypothesis generates a cloud of relatively uniformly scattered points in the four quadrants of the diagram.

As, in reality, the CAC40 and DAX returns are characterized by a correlation of 0.75, the generation of future scenarios requires that this correlation should be taken into adequate consideration. For this purpose, we will build the variance-covariance matrix.

$$\boldsymbol{\Sigma} = \begin{bmatrix} \sigma_{CAC}^2 & \sigma_{CAC,DAX}^2 \\ \sigma_{CAC,DAX}^2 & \sigma_{DAX}^2 \end{bmatrix} = \begin{bmatrix} \sigma_{CAC}^2 & \rho_{CAC,DAX}\sigma_{CAC}\sigma_{DAX} \\ \rho_{CAC,DAX}\sigma_{CAC}\sigma_{DAX} & \sigma_{DAX}^2 \end{bmatrix}$$

$$\cong \begin{bmatrix} 0,023\,\% & 0,014\,\% \\ 0,014\,\% & 0,015\,\% \end{bmatrix}$$

Table 7.9 An Example of Monte Carlo simulation with independent returns

Scenario #	Call on the CAC40 index			Call on the DAX index		
	p_1 (uniformly distributed)	$v_1 = \Phi^{-1}(p_1)$	$x_1 = F^{-1}(p) = \Phi^{-1}(p)\cdot\sigma + \mu_1$	p_2 (uniformly distributed)	$v_2 = \Phi^{-1}(p_2)$	$x_2 = F^{-1}p = \Phi^{-1}(p)\cdot\sigma_2 + \mu_2$
1	0.848	1.029	0.017	0.464	−0.091	0.000
2	0.678	0.463	0.008	0.112	−1.214	−0.017
3	0.165	−0.975	−0.013	0.227	−0.748	−0.010
4	0.674	0.451	0.008	0.159	−0.997	−0.013
5	0.967	1.834	0.029	0.616	0.296	0.006
6	0.597	0.245	0.005	0.263	−0.633	−0.008
7	0.816	0.900	0.015	0.595	0.240	0.005
8	0.253	−0.664	−0.008	0.199	−0.845	−0.011
9	0.057	−1.582	−0.022	0.210	−0.806	−0.011
10	0.384	−0.294	−0.003	0.158	−1.004	−0.014
...	...	...	...	...	...	...
990	0.592	0.232	0.005	0.657	0.403	0.008
991	0.954	1.682	0.027	0.515	0.039	0.002
992	0.690	0.497	0.009	0.903	1.298	0.021
993	0.628	0.327	0.006	0.808	0.870	0.015
994	0.237	−0.718	−0.009	0.690	0.495	0.009
995	0.520	0.049	0.002	0.172	−0.946	−0.013
996	0.491	−0.023	0.001	0.683	0.476	0.009
997	0.949	1.634	0.026	0.965	1.814	0.029
998	0.754	0.688	0.012	0.683	0.476	0.009
999	0.709	0.551	0.010	0.987	2.227	0.035
1000	0.696	0.512	0.009	0.397	−0.260	−0.002

This matrix can be decomposed into the following product using the Cholesky's method (see footnote 27):

$$\Sigma \cong \begin{bmatrix} 0,023\,\% & 0,014\,\% \\ 0,014\,\% & 0,015\,\% \end{bmatrix} \cong \begin{bmatrix} 1,500\,\% & 0,000\,\% \\ 0,930\,\% & 0,820\,\% \end{bmatrix} \cdot \begin{bmatrix} 1,500\,\% & 0,930\,\% \\ 0,000\,\% & 0,820\,\% \end{bmatrix} = \mathbf{AA}'$$

Remembering that the vector of means is given by

$$\mu = \begin{bmatrix} 0,15\,\% \\ 0,18\,\% \end{bmatrix}$$

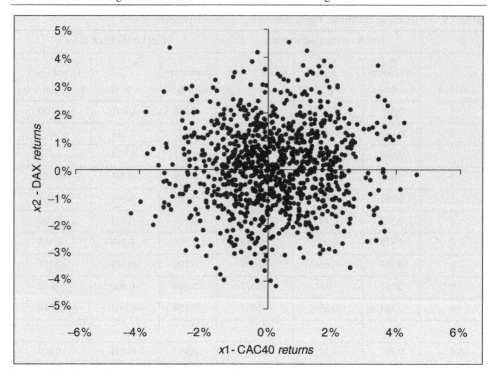

Figure 7.7 Example of a joint simulation with independent returns

it now becomes possible to apply (7.7) and generate correlated scenarios for the two risk factors. The results are shown in Table 7.10.

Figure 7.8 graphically shows the results of the joint simulation of the two market factor returns. Note that the positive correlation between the two stock exchange indexes is now fully captured by the data.

Table 7.10 also shows the changes in the two options' market values (columns 10 and 13), and the consequent change in the portfolio's market value. Since the portfolio consists of a long position (call on the CAC40) and a short position (call on the DAX), the positive correlation seen in Figure 7.8 translates into a negative correlation between the profits and losses of the two positions.

This effect is highlighted by Table 7.11, which shows the VaR measures corresponding to two different confidence levels that are obtained by simulating the joint evolution of the two stock exchange indexes, assuming independence (Table 7.9) and positive correlation (Table 7.10). Note that the VaR measures for the second case are smaller.

7.3.3 Merits and limitations of Monte Carlo simulations

There are several advantages connected with the use of Monte Carlo simulations:

(1) A first advantage is common to all simulation methods having recourse to full valuation: by simulating the market factor evolutions and recalculating the market values of the positions comprising the entire portfolio, the issue of non-linear and/or non-monotonic position payoffs is overcome.

Table 7.10 An Example of Monte Carlo simulation with correlated returns

j	Vector $\mathbf{p}_j$ p_1	p_2	Vector $\mathbf{v}_j$ (uncorrelated) $v_1 = \Phi^{-1}(p_1)$	$v_2 = \Phi^{-1}(p_2)$	Vector $\mathbf{x}_j = \mathbf{v}A+\mu$ (correlated) $x_1 = v_1.\sigma_1 + \mu_1$	$x_2 = v_2.\sigma_2 + \mu_2$	Market factor 1 (CAC40) $S_{1,t+1} = S_{1,t}.e^{x1}$	c_1	Δc_1	Market factor 2 (DAX) $S_{2,t+1} = S_{2,t}.e^{x2}$	c_2	Δc_2	Portfolio $P = c_1 - c_2$	$\Delta P = \Delta c_1 - \Delta c_2$
1	0.426	0.683	−0.187	0.475	0.003	0.006	100.31	9.602	0.188	100.57	7.837	0.352	1.765	0.540
2	0.254	0.368	−0.662	−0.337	−0.012	−0.001	98.85	8.738	−0.676	99.90	7.426	−0.059	1.311	−0.734
3	0.651	0.732	0.388	0.619	0.013	0.007	101.32	10.218	0.805	100.69	7.911	0.426	2.307	1.230
4	0.785	0.245	0.789	−0.691	0.007	−0.004	100.69	9.833	0.420	99.61	7.252	−0.233	2.581	0.187
5	0.446	0.354	−0.135	−0.375	−0.004	−0.001	99.60	9.175	−0.238	99.87	7.408	−0.077	1.767	−0.316
6	0.883	0.074	1.190	−1.446	0.006	−0.010	100.59	9.772	0.358	99.00	6.889	−0.596	2.883	−0.238
7	0.917	0.076	1.387	−1.430	0.009	−0.010	100.91	9.963	0.550	99.01	6.897	−0.588	3.067	−0.039
8	0.615	0.469	0.293	−0.079	0.005	0.001	100.52	9.726	0.313	100.12	7.556	0.071	2.171	0.384
9	0.882	0.452	1.187	−0.122	0.018	0.001	101.83	10.543	1.130	100.08	7.534	0.049	3.009	1.179
10	0.109	0.672	−1.232	0.446	−0.013	0.005	98.72	8.666	−0.748	100.55	7.822	0.337	0.844	−0.411
⋮	⋮	⋮	⋮	⋮	⋮	⋮	⋮	⋮	⋮	⋮	⋮	⋮	⋮	⋮
990	0.053	0.687	−1.614	0.487	−0.018	0.006	98.20	8.367	−1.047	100.58	7.843	0.358	0.524	−0.689

(continued overleaf)

Table 7.10 (*continued*)

j	Vector $\mathbf{p}_j$		Vector $\mathbf{v}_j$ (uncorrelated)		Vector $\mathbf{x}_j = \mathbf{v}A+\mu$ (correlated)		Market factor 1 (CAC40)			Market factor 2 (DAX)			Portfolio	
	p_1	p_2	$v_1 = \Phi^{-1}(p_1)$	$v_2 = \Phi^{-1}(p_2)$	$x_1 = v_1 \cdot \sigma_1 + \mu_1$	$x_2 = v_2 \cdot \sigma_2 + \mu_2$	$S_{1,t+1} = S_{1,t} \cdot e^{x1}$	c_1	Δc_1	$S_{2,t+1} = S_{2,t} \cdot e^{x2}$	c_2	Δc_2	$P = c_1 - c_2$	$\Delta P = \Delta c_1 - \Delta c_2$
991	0.372	0.035	−0.326	−1.808	−0.020	−0.013	98.00	8.255	−1.159	98.71	6.719	−0.766	1.536	−1.924
992	0.573	0.787	0.184	0.797	0.012	0.008	101.17	10.129	0.716	100.84	8.003	0.518	2.126	1.234
993	0.735	0.385	0.627	−0.292	0.008	−0.001	100.82	9.912	0.499	99.94	7.449	−0.036	2.463	0.462
994	0.982	0.385	2.096	−0.291	0.030	−0.001	103.07	11.339	1.926	99.94	7.449	−0.036	3.90	1.890
995	0.497	0.745	−0.007	0.660	0.008	0.007	100.76	9.872	0.458	100.72	7.932	0.447	1.940	0.905
996	0.238	0.124	−0.714	−1.153	−0.020	−0.008	98.03	8.270	−1.144	99.24	7.028	−0.457	1.242	−1.600
997	0.913	0.534	1.357	0.084	0.023	0.002	102.29	10.834	1.421	100.25	7.638	0.153	3.197	1.574
998	0.669	0.069	0.438	−1.481	−0.006	−0.010	99.43	9.076	−0.337	98.97	6.873	−0.612	2.204	−0.949
999	0.686	0.744	0.485	0.655	0.015	0.007	101.50	10.332	0.918	100.72	7.930	0.445	2.402	1.363
1000	0.941	0.894	1.566	1.251	0.037	0.012	103.73	11.777	2.363	101.21	8.242	0.757	3.535	3.120

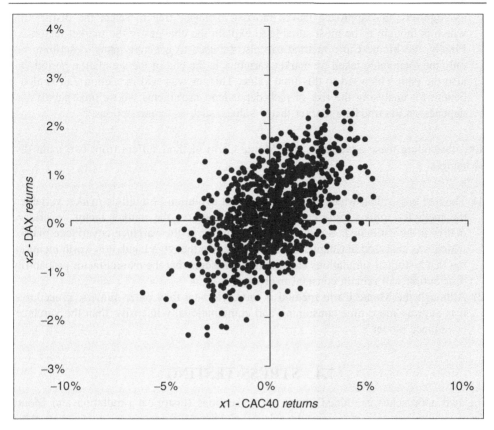

Figure 7.8 Example of a Joint Simulation with Correlated Returns ($\rho = 0.75$)

Table 7.11 Example of VaR of a portfolio consisting of two positions

	Independent	75 %-correlated
VaR at 99 %	−3.280	−2.915
VaR at 95 %	−2.172	−1.959

(2) A second advantage of Monte Carlo simulations – which is significant in the case of portfolios whose market value is a function of several market variables – is connected with their computing efficiency, in the sense that the time taken to make the required simulations increases linearly with the increase in the number of variables considered – unlike other numeric procedures, for which the time required increases exponentially with the increase in the number of variables considered.[28]

(3) A third merit of the Monte Carlo method consists in the fact that it lends itself to being used with any probability distribution of market factor returns. In other terms, unlike the variance-covariance approach, which is based on the normal distribution

---

[28] Reference is made to such numeric procedures as binomial trees or the finite difference method.

assumptions, this approach leaves the risk manager free to select the distribution which is thought to be most suitable to explain the changes in the market factors.

(4) Finally, the Monte Carlo method can also be used to generate paths, describing not only the final value taken by market variables at the end of the simulation period, but also the path which led to this final value. This, as was said in section 2.6, is also a benefit for analysing the risk of path dependent instruments whose final payoff also depends on intermediate market factor values, such as exotic options.[29]

Notwithstanding these advantages, the Monte Carlo method suffers from two main disadvantages.

(1) The first one is that, when simulating the joint evolution of multiple market variables, the method – unlike historical simulations – requires the market factor covariance matrix to be estimated. So, the issue of stability of the variance-covariance matrix, which was analyzed in Chapter 5, arises again. On the other hand, it is worth mentioning that historical simulations also implicitly assume that the market factor probability distribution will remain constant over time.

(2) Although the Monte Carlo method is more efficient than other numeric procedures, it is anyway more time-consuming and computationally-intensive than the variance-covariance model.

7.4   STRESS TESTING

The two approaches examined in the above sections (historical simulation and Monte Carlo simulation) aim at generating a large number of scenarios, so as to reasonably approximate the entire distribution of possible events.

An alternative solution is based upon estimation of the effects – in terms of potential losses – connected with extreme events, i.e., upon market evolution hypotheses which, although unlikely, are thought to be possible. In practice, the portfolio's market value is revalued under the market conditions which are typical of extremely pessimistic scenarios, determining the loss by difference from the current value. These *stress tests* share the logic of simulation models, as they also rely on revaluing the portfolio under simulated conditions. However, rather than replicating realistically the possible market factor changes, they simulate them in a predominantly arbitrary and subjective manner.

Stress tests are a tool aimed at identifying and managing situations which can cause extraordinary losses. The construction of the extreme scenarios upon which stress tests rely can be based upon the following:

(1) replication of the strongest market shocks which occurred in the past;[30]

(2) statistical measures, i.e., large multiples of historical volatility (for instance, a fall in a stock exchange index by 10 times the historical standard deviation of the relevant return)

---

[29] In this case, reference is made to such instruments as Asian options. See Hull (1993), pp. 414–431, for a review of these instruments.

[30] In this connection, see Jackson (1995), pp. 177–184.

(3) totally subjective assumptions, such as a generalized 10 % stock market slump, a 1 % parallel upward shift in the yield curve, a widening of corporate bond yield spreads by one percentage point.

The first criterion, which is typically the most widespread one within the framework of stress testing methodologies, is based upon revaluing the portfolio by simulating shocks of similar proportions to those which occurred in the past. Shocks which are frequently used for this purpose are the stock market crashes in October 1987 and April 2000, the foreign-exchange market crash in September 1992, the bond market crash in April 1994, the Asian currency crisis in the summer of 1997, and the Russian debt crisis in August 1998.

The second approach is typical of the so-called "factor push analysis (FPA)" techniques, which suggest "pushing" the individual market factors in a more unfavorable direction by a certain number of times the relevant standard deviation, and thus calculating the combined effect of all adverse changes on the portfolio's market value. FPA has the advantage of being relatively easy to implement; moreover, like all simulation techniques based upon full valuation, it does not require the payoff linearity hypothesis; finally, it allows one to identify a portfolio's worst possible result, which can be very useful to identify its vulnerabilities. Notwithstanding these advantages, however, FPA has some major disadvantages: first of all, it is not sure that the most substantial losses will be associated with the most marked market factor changes (as was noted in Chapter 5, in the presence of positions characterized by non-monotonic sensitivity, the most marked losses may be associated with smaller changes in the relevant market factors); moreover, it generally does not consider the correlations among the different market factors; finally, the potential loss results derived from FPA – because of the way they were constructed – cannot be associated with any specific probability of occurrence.

The third criterion was adopted, for instance, by the Derivatives Policy Group, which, in 1995, published some examples of subjective hypotheses which should guide stress tests and help the individual financial institutions identify particular vulnerabilities to significant changes in one or more market factors. These are particularly high shocks, such as:

√ one hundred basis point upward or downward shifts in the yield curve;
√ a more or less 25 basis point change in the slope of the yield curve;
√ ten percentage point upward or downward changes in stock exchange indexes;
√ more or less 6 percentage point changes in exchange rates;
√ more or less 20 percentage point changes in volatility.

The stress tests proposed by the DPG are clearly unidimensional, in the sense that market factors are "stressed" individually, and the portfolio is revalued at the simulated change in each of them. In this way, however, correlations among the different market factors are completely disregarded.

An alternative stress testing method is grounded upon "multidimensional" stress tests. The latter are based upon joint simulation of marked changes in multiple market factors at the same time. Once again, these may rely upon subjective judgements[31] or, alternatively,

---

[31] Take the example of Factor Push Analysis, which, by "stressing" all risk factors jointly, assumes implicitly that they are perfectly correlated.

historical experience. So, for instance, during the collapse of the European monetary system's foreign exchange agreements in 1992, the sudden depreciation of the Italian lira and pound sterling was accompanied by a significant reduction in these two currencies' interest rates and a concurrent uptrend on the relevant bond markets. Similarly, the October 1987 stock market slump had considerable effects on bond and foreign-exchange markets, as well.

Multidimensional scenarios, in turn, can be implemented according to two different operational logics: *simple or predictive* scenarios.

In simple scenarios, a certain number of risk factors are "stressed" – i.e., their values are changed towards extreme levels – while the remaining factors are left unchanged. For instance, a simple scenario could involve a 50 % depreciation of the Euro versus the dollar and a 40 % depreciation versus the pound sterling, a three percentage point reduction in the Euro money market rates, and a 30 % recovery of the main European stock exchange indexes, and, at the same time, leave all other market variables (Euro-yen exchange rate, bond yield, etc.) unchanged. This type of procedure – although appreciable for its transparency and simplicity – is arbitrary and unrealistic.

In predictive scenarios, on the contrary, besides advancing arbitrary hypotheses on the possible evolution of a certain subset of market variables, the remaining risk factors are also adjusted based upon their correlation with the former. So, for instance, in the scenario described in the previous subsection, the Euro-yen exchange rate would not remain constant, but would be changed based upon its past correlation with the Euro/dollar exchange rate, the Euro/pound sterling exchange rate, the Euro monetary market rates, and the main European stock exchange indexes.[32]

At this point, it is important to note that stress tests – unlike the methodologies illustrated in the previous sections – are not of way of estimating a portfolio's VaR. Indeed, since they are based upon quite discretionary and subjective hypotheses about the size of the different market factor shocks, they do not make it possible to associate a probabilistic dimension, or better a confidence level, with the corresponding loss. This is the reason why stress tests should complement, rather than replace, a VaR model to measure a financial institution's trading portfolio's market risks. The main reason why it is important for a VaR model to be complemented by stress tests relates to the fact that VaR models are usually based upon relatively recent historical data. They therefore typically do not capture those extreme events occurring with a limited frequency, which are rarely included in the dataset used for VaR estimation.

On the other hand, this "complementary" use is recommended by supervisory authorities: stress tests are explicitly required by the Basel Committee for those banks wishing to use their own internal risk management models to determine their mandatory capital requirement.[33]

Notwithstanding the fact that scenarios are built arbitrarily and cannot be associated with any probability of occurrence, stress tests have the following merits:

---

[32] More formally, if we divide the risk factor vector x into two vectors x_1 and x_2, of which only the first one is the subject of explicit hypotheses about the possible shock suffered by factors, the shocks for the factors included in the second vector will be determined as means which are conditional upon the values taken by x_1. The formula to calculate these conditional means is, *de facto*, the one which is typically used to estimate a multiple linear regression of each element of x_2 on all market variables included in x_1. For details, see Mina and Xiao (2001).

[33] See Chapters 19 and 20.

√ They are simple to implement, and their results can be easily communicated to the top management.

√ They allow one to overcome the restrictive hypotheses characterizing VaR models, such as those connected with the form and stationarity of the distribution of market factor returns.

√ They allow one to simulate liquidity crisis episodes like the ones which occurred at the end of 1998, when the secondary market of numerous bond market segments experienced slumps due to a lack of liquidity.

√ They allow one to jointly simulate extreme scenarios for multiple market factors, and therefore to simulate any crisis episodes during which significant increases in correlations among the different market factors will occur.

√ Finally, the possibly most important aspect is that stress tests can be tailor-made for each specific trading portfolio depending on its size, composition by instruments and relevant sensitivity. As a matter of fact, each portfolio has specific characteristics which make it more or less vulnerable to changes in some market factors than in others. Stress tests can therefore be particularly effective in highlighting these vulnerabilities.

Finally, as was noted by Jorion (2000), it is important for stress tests not to be considered as simple theoretical exercises which are an end in themselves; on the contrary, they must necessarily be followed by practical actions. There is conversely the risk that, once a strong vulnerability to a particular scenario (which would generate significant losses) has been identified, the bank's management may decide not to do anything, in the belief that such a scenario is very unlikely. Such an attitude would make the development of stress tests totally useless. The identification of an area of vulnerability must be followed by measures ranging from buying hedges to changing the portfolio's composition, from restructuring the business towards a greater degree of diversification to arranging a contingency plan aimed at coping with particular evolutionary market scenarios.

SELECTED QUESTIONS AND EXERCISES

1. Which of the following statements concerning Monte Carlo simulations is correct?

   (A) Monte Carlo simulations, unlike the parametric approach, have the advantage of preserving the structure of the correlations among market factor returns.
   (B) Monte Carlo simulations have the advantage of not requiring any assumption on the shape of the of the probability distributions of market factor returns.
   (C) Monte Carlo simulations allow to estimate the VaR of a portfolio, with the desired confidence level, using the percentile technique.
   (D) Monte Carlo simulations allow to estimate the VaR of a portfolio, with the desired confidence level, using a multiple of the standard deviation of the market factor returns.

2. A European bank computes the VaR associated to its overall position in US dollars, based on parametric VaR and historical simulations. The two results are different (€100,000 and €102,000, respectively) regardless of the fact that they are based on the same data series and the same confidence level. Consider the following statements:

   (I) The distribution of the percent changes in the euro/dollar exchange rate is not normal.

(II) The distribution of the percent changes in the euro/dollar exchange rate is asymmetrical.

(III) The distribution of the percent changes in the euro/dollar exchange rates has a greater kurtosis than the normal distribution.

What statements are certainly true:

(A) Only I;
(B) I, II and III;
(C) Only I and II;
(D) Only I and III.

3. Read the following statements on Monte Carlo simulations:

(I) Monte Carlo simulations are more accurate than the parametric approach when the value of the bank's portfolio is a linear function of the risk factors, and the risk factor returns are normally distributed.

(II) Monte Carlo simulations are quicker than the parametric approach.

(III) Monte Carlo simulations can be made more precise through the delta/gamma approach.

(IV) Monte Carlo simulations require the assumption that risk factor returns are uncorrelated with each other, since otherwise the Cholesky decomposition could not be computed.

Which one(s) would you agree with?

(A) Only II;
(B) Only III;
(C) I and IV;
(D) None of them.

4. Consider the following statements: "historical simulations...

(i) ...are totally distribution-free, meaning that users to not have to make hypotheses on the shape of the probability distribution of market factor returns";

(ii) ...are stationary, meaning that the variance of market factor returns is supposed to be constant";

(iii) ...are equivalent to parametric models (including models where volatilities are exponentially-weighted) if the probability of past factor returns is close to normal";

(iv) ...are extremely demanding in terms of past data, especially if VaR is based on a long holding period".

Which ones would you agree with?

(A) all;
(B) ii and iv;
(C) i and iii;
(D) only iv.

5. Following a brief period of sharp changes in market prices, a bank using historical simulations to estimate VaR decides to switch to a model based on hybrid simulations, adopting a decay factor λ of 0.95. Which of the following is true?

(A) The new model is likely to lead to an increase in VaR, which can be mitigated by setting λ at 0.98.

(B) The new model is likely to lead to a decrease in VaR, which can be mitigated by setting λ at 0.98.

(C) The new model is likely to lead to an increase in VaR, which can be mitigated by setting λ at 0.90.

(D) The new model is likely to lead to a decrease in VaR, which can be mitigated by setting λ at 0.90.

8

Evaluating VaR Models

8.1 INTRODUCTION

The spread of VaR models as key market risk measurement tools has increasingly called for the development of techniques to evaluate the quality of these models. The academic world and financial community have thus started to wonder as to the quality of the risk measures generated by VaR models and their ability to correctly predict trading portfolio losses.

Such questions are of great interest for regulatory authorities, as well: as we will see in Chapter 19, as from 1996, the Basel Committee requires that a VaR model should be regularly backtested to determine its relevant predictive ability as a pre-condition for using that same model to determine the market risk capital requirement.

This backtesting is based upon a comparison between the model's indications and trading results – more precisely, upon a comparison between daily estimated VaR and the actual losses for the following day. The underlying logic is relatively simple: if the model is correct, actual losses should exceed VaR with a frequency that is consistent with the one defined by the confidence level. For instance, if daily VaR is 100 and the model's confidence level is 99 %, we are likely to expect losses in excess of 100 only in 1 % of cases, i.e., on 2.5 out of 250 annual trading days. If the number of days on which losses exceed 100 is lower than, equal to or slightly higher than 2.5, the model is likely to be adequate. Vice versa, if the number of days on which losses exceed 100 is significantly different from the confidence level's predictions, the model is likely to be inadequate.

However apparently simple, backtesting a VaR model poses numerous problems, and can follow different logics. During the last 10 years, numerous alternative models have been proposed to evaluate the accuracy of a VaR model. The purpose of this chapter is to address these problems and to analyze the alternative solutions which were offered to them. After illustrating the results generated by alternative VaR models on a simplified stock portfolio, this chapter will focus on some VaR model backtesting techniques, briefly illustrating their logic, merits and limitations. At the end of the chapter, we will briefly analyse the choices made by the Basel Committee concerning VaR models backtesting.

8.2 AN EXAMPLE OF BACKTESTING: A STOCK PORTFOLIO VAR

Before focusing on a review of the problems connected with backtesting a VaR model, take the example of an equally-weighted portfolio consisting of investments in two stock exchange indexes – FTSE100 and Dow Jones Industrial Average – over a 1-year period (257 daily data) ranging from 26 July 2005 to 22 July 2006. Figure 8.1 shows the evolution of the portfolio value over the period. Overall, the portfolio started at a value of approximately 6,000 Euros, and closed the period at a value of 6,817, with a return of approximately 13.6 %.

Figure 8.2 shows the evolution of daily portfolio return and daily VaR estimated using the variance-covariance approach at a 95 % confidence level over the period. In this case, the volatility and correlation between the two indexes are estimated using the simple

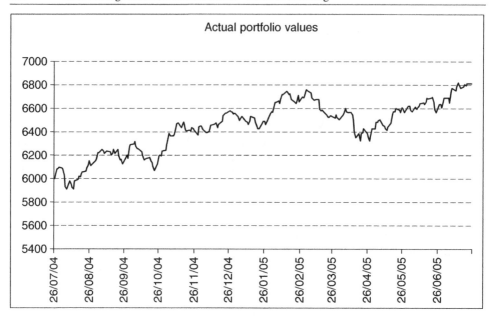

Figure 8.1 Evolution of a Diversified Stock Portfolio Value

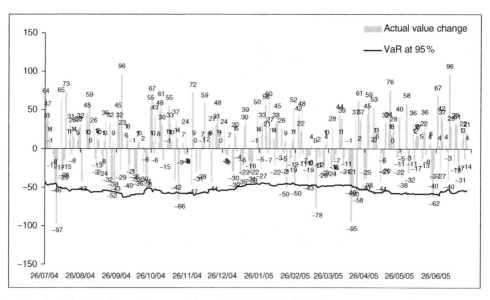

Figure 8.2 Backtesting of a Parametric Simple Volatility Model

average criterion. To estimate volatility and consequently VaR, the data from the previous three months are used.

Note that the portfolio's daily loss exceeds VaR only on 10 out of the 257 days considered, i.e., in 3.9 % of cases. This result appears to be fairly consistent with the desired confidence level. However, it must be pointed out that – notwithstanding a frequency of "exceptions" which is consistent with the 95 % confidence level – the value of estimation errors connected with these exceptions reaches significant amounts in some cases, and sometimes (on 5 August 2004 and 14 April 2005) exceeds 100 % of the estimated VaR.[1]

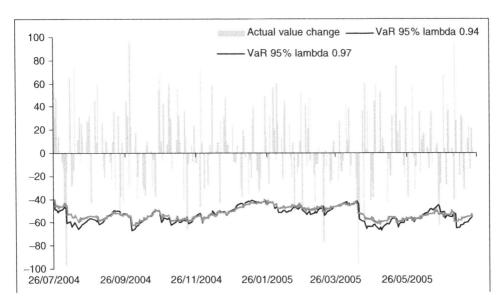

Figure 8.3   Backtesting of a Parametric Exponential Volatility Model

Figure 8.3 shows the evolution of daily VaR estimated using the variance-covariance approach with volatility estimated through the exponential average criterion with two different decay factors: 0.94 and 0.97. Note that a lower lambda generates a VaR estimate which is more responsive to recent conditions, and therefore, in turn, more volatile. This means that VaR will increase more rapidly in the presence of strongly negative or positive recent returns, and, on the other hand, will decrease more quickly when daily price changes take small values. It follows that the ability to estimate the portfolio risk will be better when large losses are preceded by other large losses, whereas it will be worse (compared to a more modest decay factor) when large losses follow on relatively calm periods. In the specific case represented in Figure 8.3, VaR with a decay factor of 0.94 performs slightly better (9 exceptions out of 257 days) than VaR with a decay factor of 0.97 (10 exceptions), even if the two models' error rates are substantially similar (3.5 % vs. 3.9 %). It is however to be mentioned that a smaller decay factor may be more complex to use when one wishes to use it as a risk limit for traders and as a tool to measure their performance, because it generates more volatile VaRs.[2]

Figure 8.4 shows the evolution of daily VaR estimated using the historical simulation model. In this case, the fifth percentile of a sample consisting of the value changes that the

---

[1] As will be better clarified below, although this may be a considerable problem from a risk management point of view, it cannot be used as a parameter to evaluate a VaR model. Indeed, these models just express the probability that a given threshold will be exceeded, but do not say anything about the size of excess losses.
[2] The excessive volatility of VaR measures may make it difficult to introduce an effective risk limits system. Indeed, a trader who is aware of this volatility would tend to underuse the risk capacity assigned to him/her for fear of a sudden increase in his/her positions' VaR.

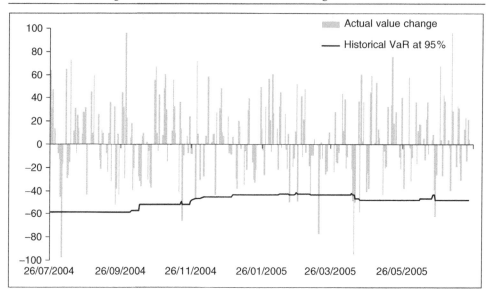

Figure 8.4   Backtesting of a Historical Simulation Model

portfolio would have recorded – given its current composition – based upon the prices in the prior 6 months was selected for each day. Note that VaR obtained using the historical simulation method shows a peculiar trend over time, which is characterized by a certain stability interrupted by sudden "leaps". This is due to the fact that VaR is based upon the value of the loss for the percentile corresponding to the selected confidence level. This loss will remain constant until: (i) a higher loss replacing the previous one occurs, or (ii) this same loss "leaves" the estimation sample. The figure shows a number of exceptions of 11, with a maximum error (on 14 April 2005) of 119% of VaR. So, the result which is obtained by applying this approach turns out to be fairly similar to the one connected with the variance-covariance approach based upon simple averages.

The consistency between these two results is justified by the nature of the distribution of portfolio returns, which – as highlighted in Figure 8.5 – looks reasonably like a normal. As a consequence, in a portfolio like the one being analysed - which, on the other hand, is also characterized by a linear payoff – the typical advantages of historical simulations (full valuation and return distribution not tied to any known random variable) will be reduced.

Finally, Figure 8.6 jointly shows the evolution of daily VaR measured using 3 of the criteria illustrated above: variance-covariance with simple moving average, variance-covariance with exponential moving average and a lambda of 0.94, and historical simulation. Note that the second approach shows much more marked VaR variability.

Table 8.1 reports some performance measures relating to the three approaches.

The examples we have just seen referred to a simplified portfolio and a limited time horizon. If we want to generalize, reference can be made to a major empirical study conducted by Darryl Hendricks (1996).

The author compared 4 historical VaR models (with time horizons of 125, 250, 500 and 1,250 days, respectively) with 8 variance/covariance VaR models of the simple average (calculated over 50, 125, 250, 500 and 1,250 days) and exponential average type

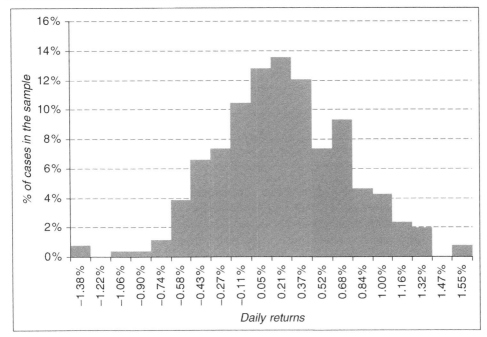

Figure 8.5   Empirical Distribution of Stock Portfolio Returns

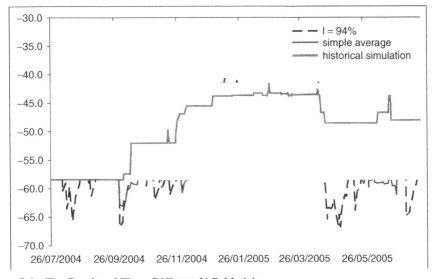

Figure 8.6   The Results of Three Different VaR Models

(with λ of 0.94, 0.97 and 0.99). A thousand different currency portfolios, each consisting of 8 randomly weighted different currencies, were generated. The daily VaR of each of these 1,000 portfolios was calculated using each of the 12 different models for approximately 12 years (3,000 daily observations, from January 1993 to December 1995), with two different confidence intervals (95 % and 99 %). *De facto*, 72,000,000 individual VaR estimates were generated.

Table 8.1 Performance of different VaR estimation approaches

	Number of exceptions	Maximum error as a percentage of estimated VaR
Parametric (simple average)	11	109 %
Parametric ($\lambda = 94\,\%$)	9	115 %
Parametric ($\lambda = 97\,\%$)	10	110 %
Historical	11	119 %

Table 8.2 shows the results of this study. In particular, the percentage of non-excess losses and the mean actual loss/VaR ratio in those cases in which the former exceeds the latter are shown. With reference to this second ratio, the last row in the table shows the theoretical value which it should take if the distribution of market factor returns were normal and VaR were correct.

Table 8.2 Empirical results of Hendricks's study (1996)

	Number of non exceptions/ total days % ratio		Excess loss/VaR mean ratio	
Confidence level	*95 %*	*99 %*	*95 %*	*99 %*
Methodology				
simple average 50 days	94.8	98.3	1.41	1.46
simple average 125 days	95.1	98.4	1.38	1.44
simple average 250 days	95.3	98.4	1.37	1.44
simple average 500 days	95.4	98.4	1.38	1.46
simple average 1,250 days	95.4	98.5	1.36	1.44
exponential average ($\lambda = 0.94$)	94.7	98.2	1.41	1.44
exponential average ($\lambda = 0.97$)	95.0	98.4	1.38	1.42
exponential average ($\lambda = 0.99$)	95.4	98.5	1.35	1.40
Historical simulation 125 days	94.4	98.3	1.48	1.48
Historical simulation 250 days	94.9	98.7	1.43	1.37
Historical simulation 500 days	94.8	98.8	1.44	1.37
Historical simulation 1,250 days	95.1	99.0	1.41	1.30
Normal distr. reference value			1.254	1.145

Source: Hendricks (1996).

As far as the first ratio is concerned, the models perform altogether well, as they considerably approach the theoretical value indicated by the confidence level. However, a review of the second ratio shows that excess losses are on average much higher than the loss expected assuming normality (for the 99 % confidence level, even two or three times as high). This implies that the difference between the normal distribution and the actual data distribution is particularly sensitive "beyond VaR", i.e., in the extreme tails of the distribution.

The examples illustrated so far have highlighted that a correct evaluation of the quality of a VaR model should be based upon two different aspects:

√ the consistency between the number of exceptions, i.e., the number of days on which losses exceed estimated VaR, and the confidence level adopted for VaR estimation.
√ the "size" of the exceptions, i.e., the value of the loss in excess of the VaR measure.

As will be noted in Chapter 19, the backtesting methodology proposed by the Basel Committee to evaluate the quality of a VaR model is based solely upon the first of these two criteria. From this point of view, the illustrated example showed that – the number of exceptions being equal – the performance of alternative models can differ considerably depending on the size of the loss.

When presenting our backtesting examples, for the sake of simplicity, we did not linger over how to construct the daily profit and loss measure with which the VaR estimated on the previous day should be compared. For this purpose, there are three alternative solutions:

(1) the P&L (capital gain or loss) coming from the actual acquisitions and sale of the portfolio positions which were *actually traded by the bank*;
(2) the P&L which is obtained by *revaluing* the portfolio held by the bank at the end of the day *under the new market conditions* at that time;
(3) the P&L which is obtained by revaluing the portfolio held by the bank *at the end of the previous day* under the new market conditions at the end of the day.

The first solution is clearly inadequate. Basing a valuation only on actually realized P&L (and not also on the one implied in the new market values of portfolio positions) would be against the same mark-to-market logic on which the whole trading activity is based. The second solution would be "sullied" by the changes in the composition of the bank's portfolio which occurred during the day and which could obviously not have been predicted by the VaR model on the previous evening. The third solution, referred to as "static P&L", is the most appropriate one, because it compares VaR with a more homogeneous P&L result. As a matter of fact, a portfolio's VaR is generally estimated at the end of a trading day based upon the portfolio's composition at that time: in this sense, it does not incorporate the trading activity which will be performed on the following day. The potential loss for the following day is estimated assuming that the portfolio's composition will remain unchanged. The quality of this estimate (i.e., its ability to predict the impact that changes in market conditions will have on the portfolio) must therefore be evaluated "with constant composition".[3]

---

[3] Although the third solution is theoretically preferable for evaluating the quality of a VaR model, the most relevant losses from a management perspective are obviously those used by the second solution, which also considers intraday trading, and therefore the changes experienced by the composition of the portfolio during the day.

8.3   ALTERNATIVE VaR MODEL BACKTESTING TECHNIQUES

In the example in Figures 8.1 to 8.6, it was approximately concluded that a number of daily exceptions of 9, 10 or 11 over a year consisting of 257 trading days is relatively satisfactory, because it is consistent with the 95 % confidence level. This conclusion, however, was not supported by any statistical significance measure.

The problem can be expressed in these terms:

(i) what is the maximum percentage of exceptions which is consistent with the model's confidence level?
(ii) What is the minimum percentage of exceptions beyond which it must be concluded that the model is not good (and, in particular, that the bank is exposed to higher risks than indicated by VaR)?

The answers to these questions also depend on the number of available observations. Consider the case of a VaR model with a 99 % confidence level: if this model is tested on 100 observations, and 2 exceptions (2 %) are obtained, it can hardly be concluded with any certainty that it is incorrect. On the one hand, the percentage of exceptions is twice as high as expected (2 % instead of 1 %), on the other hand, the error is small, as it is due to a single observation. The situation would be very different – and it would be possible to state with greater certainty that the model is incorrect – if 200 exceptions out of 10,000 observations had been recorded.

To answer the above-mentioned questions, numerous statistical tests were proposed during the second half of the nineties. In that period, evaluating the quality of a VaR model through backtesting gained in importance, for two reasons:

√ the growing spread of VaR models as market risk management and measurement tools;
√ the possibility granted by the Basel Committee to banks of using their models to determine the market risk capital requirement, and the related need for supervisory authorities to "validate" these models.

Tests can be divided into three main categories:

(i) tests based upon the frequency of exceptions (see sections 8.3.1–8.3.2);
(ii) tests based upon a loss function (see section 8.3.3);
(iii) tests based upon the entire profit and loss distribution (see section 8.3.4).

The first type of tests (some examples of which will be presented in sections 8.3.1–8.3.2) are based upon the same logic as was adopted in the previous section, i.e., a comparison between the number of days on which the loss exceeded VaR and the relevant confidence level. The second type (of which an example will be given in section 8.3.3), conversely, consider not only the frequency, but also the size of losses, in the belief that there is an interest – for both the bank and the supervisory authorities – to minimize these "excess losses". The third type, rather than focusing on excess loss values only, makes a comparison between the entire distribution of the value changes predicted by the VaR model and the actual trading profits and losses.

If the tested hypothesis ("null hypothesis") is rejected, the losses experienced by the bank will not be consistent with the VaR model hypotheses, and, consequently, the latter must be considered as inaccurate. If, on the contrary, the null hypothesis cannot be rejected, then the model will be acceptably accurate.

For these evaluation methods, as in any hypothesis test, there are two types of errors: type I (rejecting the null hypothesis when it is correct), and type II (accepting the null hypothesis when it is false). When we select a test for risk management purposes, we are strongly interested in its ability to reject the null hypothesis when this is incorrect, i.e., in its ability to minimise the type II error ("power" of the test); this is because we want to avoid classifying an inaccurate model as accurate. As we will see, since there is a trade-off between the two errors (when the first one is minimized, the second one will increase, and vice versa), we will be ready to accept a fairly high margin of type I error, unlike what happens in many classical statistical tests.

8.3.1 The unconditional coverage test

Among the first ones to propose formal statistical tests to analyze the quality of a VaR model was Paul Kupiec (1995). His test – also referred to as "proportion of failures test" – is based upon reviewing how frequently portfolio losses exceed VaR. In practice, the hypothesis to be empirically tested ("null hypothesis") is that the frequency of empirical exceptions, π, is consistent with the desired "theoretical" one, α, i.e., that the exception rate implied in the values observed upon backtesting is actually α (in brief, that π is "covered" by α). This test is not conditional upon any further hypotheses (for instance, about the sequence of occurrence of errors over time), and is therefore called "unconditional coverage".[4] The alternative hypothesis to the null hypothesis is that the exception rate implied in the values observed upon backtesting will be *higher* than α (i.e., that the model is underestimating the risk of extreme losses).[5]

If the null hypothesis is correct (i.e., if the probability of observing an exception is actually α), then the probability of observing x exceptions (number of days on which the loss exceeds VaR) in a sample of N observations (with an exception rate equal to $\pi \equiv x/N$) will be given by a binomial distribution, and will be:

$$prob(x|\alpha, N) = \binom{N}{x} \alpha^x (1 - \alpha)^{N-x} \qquad (8.1)$$

where $\binom{N}{x} = \dfrac{N!}{(N - x)!x!}$

and, as usual, $a!$ refers to the factorial of the integer a.

Considering, for instance, a sample of 250 daily observations relating to a VaR model with a 99 % confidence level, the probability of obtaining x exceptions will be given by:

$$prob(x; |1\,\%, 250) = \binom{250}{x} 0.01^x \cdot 0.99^{250-x} \qquad (8.1.b)$$

---

[4] As will be seen in more detail below, other methods allow to test more sophisticated hypotheses, and, for this reason, are known as conditional coverage tests.
[5] For an empirical analysis based upon unconditional coverage, see Saita and Sironi (2002), who reviewed some alternative VaR models applied to international stock portfolios.

So, for instance, the probability of obtaining 4 exceptions will be given by:

$$prob(4|1\%, 250) = \frac{250 \cdot 249 \cdot 248 \cdot 247}{4 \cdot 3 \cdot 2 \cdot 1} \cdot 0.01^4 \cdot 0.99^{246} = 0.134 = 13.4\%$$

while the probability of obtaining 2 exceptions will be:

$$prob(2|1\%, 250) = \frac{250 \cdot 249}{2 \cdot 1} \cdot 0.01^2 \cdot 0.99^{248} = 0.257 = 25.7\%$$

In this way, the probability associated with any number of exceptions can be calculated: Table 8.3 (column 1) and Figure 8.7 show these probabilities together with the corresponding probabilities of making type I errors by rejecting the model as incorrect. We remind the reader that these distributions are valid if the null hypothesis is true, i.e., if the probability of observing an excess loss is actually equal to α (and, therefore, the VaR model is accurate).

Table 8.3 Probabilities associated with exception and type I errors

x	(1) prob(x)	(2) $\Sigma[prob(x)]$	(3) 1-$\Sigma[prob(x)]$
0	8.1%	8.1%	91.9%
1	20.5%	28.6%	71.4%
2	25.7%	54.3%	45.7%
3	21.5%	75.8%	24.2%
4	13.4%	89.2%	10.8%
5	6.7%	95.9%	4.1%
6	2.7%	98.6%	1.4%
7	1.0%	99.6%	0.4%
8	0.3%	99.9%	0.1%
9	0.1%	100.0%	0.0%
10	0.0%	100.0%	0.0%

So, if the model is correct, the probability of occurrence of a number of exceptions equal to or lower than 4 is 89.2% (see column 2 in the Table and lighter area in the Figure). It follows that the probability of having more than 4 exceptions is 10.8% (column 3 in the Table and shaded area in the Figure, which corresponds to the probabilities highlighted in the shaded cells of the Table).

So, if we followed the rule of rejecting the null hypothesis (and therefore considering the model as incorrect) whenever more than four exceptions occur, we would run into a possible type I error (by rejecting a correct model) in 10.8% of cases. If, conversely, a more "tolerant" rule were adopted, and the model were only rejected if there are more

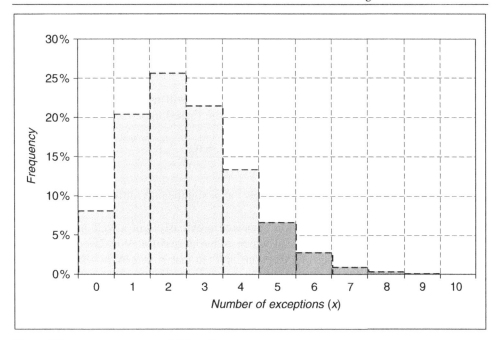

Figure 8.7   Example of Binomial Distribution

than six exceptions, at that point, the risk of rejecting a correct model would be virtually zero (to be precise, equal to 1.4 % of cases, as is shown in the third column in the Table).

Since the error we are most worried about is not so much to reject a correct model, but rather to trust an incorrect model (type II error), and since there is a trade-off between the two types of error (as one decreases, the other one will increase), we prefer a rule exposing us to a considerable type I error. Of the two above-mentioned thresholds, the one providing for a maximum of 4 exceptions will therefore be preferable (because it is more "virtuous") to the one accepting 6.

The rules provided for by the Basel Committee are inspired by such a logic. In particular, (as is explained in the Appendix to this chapter), up to 4 exceptions, the model is considered to be of good quality (a "green area" indicating that the thresholds which are considered to be virtuous and reassuring are met); up to 9 exceptions, the model is considered to be only partially adequate ("yellow area"); 10 and more exceptions, the model is considered to be inaccurate ("red area").

Let us now turn to a proper inferential test. The consistency between the actual exception rate recorded by backtesting ($\pi \equiv x/N$) and the theoretical exception rate if the model is correct (α) can be estimated through a classical likelihood ratio test.

This type of test is based upon the ratio between two likelihood functions. One of them is of a non-constrained one: the probability of obtaining an error is simply set equal to the error rate observed in the sample (which, since it was observed directly, represents the most likely value in the light of backtesting results):

$$L(x|\pi) = \pi^x(1 - \pi)^{N-x} \qquad (8.2)$$

The other likelihood function, conversely, is tied to compliance with the null hypothesis. Regardless of the observed value π, the probability of an exception is therefore set equal to α:

$$L(x|\pi = \alpha) = \alpha^x (1 - \alpha)^{N-x} \tag{8.3}$$

If π is not significantly different from α, this function will take very similar values to the former. As a consequence, the following statistic (based upon the logarithm of their ratio):

$$LR_{uc}(\alpha) = -2\ln\left[\frac{\alpha^x (1 - \alpha)^{N-x}}{\pi^x (1 - \pi)^{N-x}}\right] \tag{8.4}$$

will take values close to zero.[6] If, conversely, π is significantly different from α, (8.4) will take high positive values.

Let us consider the case – which was reviewed previously – of a VaR model with a 99 per cent confidence level ($\alpha = 1\%$) which is backtested for $N = 250$ days. Let us assume that the detected number of exceptions is 4 (so that $\pi \equiv x/N = 4/250 \cong 1.6\%$). In this case, (8.4) will take a value higher than zero, and equal to

$$LR_{uc} = -2\ln\left[\frac{1\%^4 (1 - 1\%)^{250-4}}{1.6\%^4 (.)^{250-4}}\right] \cong 0.77$$

To understand whether this value should be considered too far from zero, it is useful to know that, if the null hypothesis ($\pi = \alpha$) is correct, the LR_{uc} statistic will be distributed according to a chi-square distribution with 1 degree of freedom:

$$LR_{uc} \approx \chi_1^2 \quad \text{if} \quad \pi = \alpha$$

So, it is possible to:

- determine a threshold value which will result in a sufficiently high type I error (a small type I error would result in a high type II error); for instance, a value of 2.7055 could be selected as the threshold, since a chi-square with one degree of freedom can generate values above 2.7055 (see Figure 8.8) only in 10% of the cases.
- reject the null hypothesis (declaring the model to be inadequate) only if LR_{uc} is above the threshold (if the null hypothesis is correct, this will only occur in 10% of the cases, which is as if to say that the type I error is 10%).

In the example we have just seen, since 0.77 does not exceed 2.7055, we will be induced not to reject the null hypothesis, and therefore to consider the backtested VaR model as a good one. If, conversely, the value of the LR_{uc} statistic were higher than 2.7055, then the model could be "rejected". If we were ready to accept a higher type I error (which, in general, corresponds to a more modest type II error), we would set the threshold at lower levels: for instance, a threshold of 0.4549 would generate a type I error in 50% of the cases (see Figure 8.8 again) and – given an LR_{uc} value of 0.77 – would lead to reject the VaR model. If the threshold were set exactly at 0.77, the type I error would be 38%: we can therefore conclude that, in the presence of an LR_{uc} value of 0.77, the

---

[6] The LR_{uc} statistic (where uc stands for "unconditional coverage") represents the Kupiec's test.

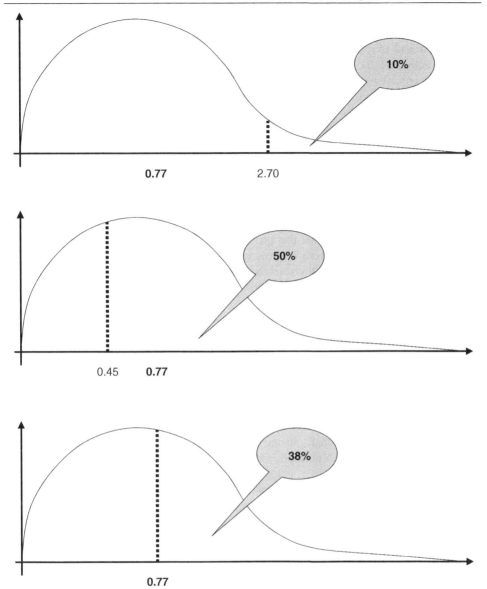

Figure 8.8 Interpretation of the LR_{uc} Value and its p-Value

choice of considering the model as inadequate would involve a (far from modest) risk of error of 38 %.

This value is referred to as the test's p-value; we can define it as the probability – in case the null hypothesis is correct – of obtaining higher LR_{uc} values than the observed one. In more formal terms:

$$p \equiv 1 - \Phi_{\chi_1^2}(LR_{uc}) \qquad (8.5)$$

where $\Phi_{\chi_1^2}(.)$ indicates the cumulative density function of a chi-square with one degree of freedom. In practice, the lower the p-value, the less reliable the model; for instance, if a bank thought it could accept the null hypothesis provided that the type I error were at least 15%, a p-value of 16% would lead to "save" the VaR model, while a p-value of 11% would lead to reject it.

The selection of the threshold value, i.e., the test's statistical significance level, is therefore a crucial point within the framework of backtesting. This selection depends upon the cost associated with the two types of errors (type I and II) which can be made when evaluating the quality of a VaR model. In the case of VaR models, type II errors (considering an incorrect model to be correct) can be considered to be the more costly ones. For this reason, relatively high statistical significance levels – not lower than 10% – are often used in risk management.

It can be demonstrated that the statistical power of the Kupiec's test (defined as the complement to one of the type II error) is fairly low; in other words, there is always a high probability of accepting the null hypothesis when it is false. The greater the decrease in the value α of the null hypothesis, i.e., the higher the model's confidence level, and the smaller the sample size, the higher this probability. This is mainly due to the fact that, for high confidence levels, exceptions become rarer events – the sample size being equal. In general, the Kupiec's test is believed to require a sample consisting of a large number of data (approximately 10 years of daily data) in order to be able to generate truly reliable results.

8.3.2   The conditional coverage test

A limitation of the Kupiec's test is that it focuses only on the number of exceptions generated by a VaR model, without considering the time distribution of these exceptions. In this sense, a model alternating periods in which VaR is underestimated (and therefore the number of exceptions is high) with periods in which VaR is overestimated (and therefore the number of exceptions is low) could also be acceptable if this statistical test were used. The test is "unconditional", in the sense that the quality of a model is evaluated independently of its ability to promptly respond to new market conditions.

To better clarify this difference, consider a VaR model with a 99% confidence level generating 10 exceptions in a sample of 1,000 observations. Whether exceptions are concentrated over ten successive days during which a market shock period occurs or, conversely, are scattered over 10 days far from one another represents an important difference. In the former case, the model – however characterized by a number of exceptions which is consistent with the confidence level – will be inadequate from a "conditional" viewpoint, because it will be unable to respond properly to the new information available.

If a model can promptly react to new information, then the probability of occurrence of an exception on day t should be independent of any exceptions recorded on the previous day $(t-1)$, whether or not an exception occurred. If, conversely, exceptions are clustered, then we are likely to expect that, if an exception occurred on day $t-1$, the (conditional) probability of having another exception on day t will be higher than average. Such a behavior, however, is not desirable: in such a case, on the day after an exception, the risk manager should increase VaR to levels above the normal one, so that the conditional probability of an exception remains in line with the desired value α.

A test aimed at evaluating the conditional coverage of a VaR model was proposed by Christoffersen (1998), who extended the LR_{uc} statistic to test that exceptions are serially independent. In other words, he tested that the probability of observing an exception on a given day is independent of whether or not an exception was recorded on the previous day.

For this purpose, Christoffersen defined:

✓ $\pi_{1,1}$ as the probability that an exception at $t-1$ would be followed by another exception at t;

✓ $\pi_{1,0}$ as the probability that an exception at $t-1$ would be followed by a non-exception at t;

✓ $\pi_{0,1}$ as the probability that an exception would occur at t without this having occurred on the previous day;

✓ $\pi_{0,0}$ the probability that there would be no exceptions either at $t-1$ or at t.

At this point, testing the serial independence of exceptions *de facto* means testing the following condition:

$$\pi_{1,1} = \pi_{0,1} = \pi \tag{8.6}$$

i.e., that:

$$\pi_{0,0} = \pi_{1,0} = 1 - \pi \tag{8.7}$$

Both equations actually indicate the same thing, i.e., that the probability of having or not an exception at t is independent of whether or not an exception occurred at $t-1$. If this hypothesis were to be rejected, we should conclude that the probability of an exception depends on the presence of exceptions on the previous day (i.e., that there is a first-order dependency between exceptions).

At this point, consider a sample of N observations and define:

– $N_{1,1}$ as the number of exceptions which were preceded by another exception;
– $N_{0,1}$ as the number of exceptions which were not preceded by another exception (note that, by definition, we will have $N_{0,1} + N_{1,1} \equiv x$);
– $N_{1,0}$ as the number of exceptions which were not followed by another exception.
– $N_{0,0}$ as the number of non-exceptions preceded by other non-exceptions.

Based upon these values, conditional probabilities can be estimated through the relevant sample frequencies:

$$\hat{\pi}_{0,1} = \frac{N_{0,1}}{N_{0,0} + N_{0,1}} \tag{8.8}$$

$$\hat{\pi}_{1,1} = \frac{N_{1,1}}{N_{1,0} + N_{1,1}} \tag{8.9}$$

$$\hat{\pi}_{0,0} = \frac{N_{0,0}}{N_{0,0} + N_{1,0}} = 1 - \hat{\pi}_{0,1} \tag{8.10}$$

$$\hat{\pi}_{1,0} = \frac{N_{1,0}}{N_{1,0} + N_{0,0}} = 1 - \hat{\pi}_{1,1} \tag{8.11}$$

Using these values, the likelihood function of the N observations in the sample will in general be:

$$L(x|\pi_{0,0}, \pi_{1,0}, \pi_{0,1}, \pi_{1,1}) = (1 - \pi_{0,1})^{N_{0,0}} \pi_{0,1}^{N_{0,1}} (1 - \pi_{1,1})^{N_{1,0}} \pi_{1,1}^{N_{1,1}} \tag{8.12}$$

If, conversely, we admit that there is serial independence (imposing the constraints shown in (8.6) and (8.7)), the constrained likelihood function will be given by:

$$L(x|\pi) = (1-\pi)^{N_{0,0}+N_{1,0}}\pi^{N_{0,1}+N_{1,1}} = (1-\pi)^{N-x}\pi^x \tag{8.13}$$

To test whether imposing the constraint[7] significantly reduces likelihood, we can construct the following likelihood ratio:

$$LR_{ind} = -2\ln\left[\frac{L(x|\pi)}{L(x|\pi_{0,0}, \pi_{1,0}, \pi_{0,1}, \pi_{1,1})}\right] \tag{8.14}$$

where the term at the numerator represents the probability of obtaining x exceptions (likelihood) under the hypothesis that exceptions are serially independent. Conversely, the term at the denominator indicates the maximum probability for the observed data.

The LR_{ind} statistic is asymptotically distributed as a chi-square with one degree of freedom. The null hypothesis of serial independence is therefore to be rejected when LR_{ind} is higher than the threshold value determined based upon the significance level desired for the test.

At this point, it is important to note that the test of conditions (8.6) and (8.7) does not give us any information about the correctness of parameter α (which, in fact, does not appear in the LR_{ind} equation, either). This implies that, by using this statistic, only the independence of exceptions, and not the overall correctness of the model (i.e., the fact that $\pi = \alpha$), can be tested.

In order to obtain a complete conditional coverage test, the two unconditional coverage (8.4) and independence (8.14) tests must be combined. We will thus obtain a test ("conditional coverage test") aimed at jointly testing the hypothesis that the average number of exceptions is correct, and the hypothesis that they are serially independent. This test is given by:

$$LR_{cc} = -2\ln\left[\frac{L(x|\pi = \alpha)}{L(\pi_{0,0}, \pi_{1,0}, \pi_{0,1}, \pi_{1,1})}\right] \tag{8.15}$$

In practice, the denominator still represents the unconstrained likelihood function used in (8.14), whereas the numerator (equation (8.3) is derived from (8.12) imposing the double constraint that

$$\pi_{01} = \pi_{11} = \alpha$$

Since there are two constraints, LR_{cc} is distributed asymptotically as a chi-square with two degrees of freedom.[8]

---

[7] Note that, as the sum $\pi_{0,0} + \pi_{0,1} + \pi_{1,0} + \pi_{1,1}$ must in any case be 1, (8.6) necessarily implies (8.7), and vice versa. We are therefore imposing *one constraint only*, and this explains why the LR_{ind} test is distributed as a chi-square with *one degree of freedom*.

[8] See Saita and Sironi (2002) for an empirical analysis of the conditional coverage of alternative VaR models applied to different international stock portfolios based upon (8.16).

The properties of the logarithm, however, imply that the statistic corresponding to conditional coverage will be given by the sum of the two previous likelihood ratios:[9]

$$LR_{cc} = LR_{uc} + LR_{ind} \qquad (8.16)$$

In general, the backtesting methodology proposed by Christoffersen is more comprehensive and efficient than the previously analysed one. It is more comprehensive because it takes into account the issue of independence among exceptions that is not taken into consideration by the unconditional coverage test. It is more efficient because the decomposition of the conditional coverage test into its independence and unconditional coverage components enables to more clearly highlight the causes which can lead one to reject a particular VaR model.

8.3.3   The Lopez test based upon a loss function

The backtesting models based upon the number of exceptions as described in the previous sections pose two main problems. The first one relates to their low statistical power. The second one relates to the fact that they completely disregard the size of losses. In other words, the fact that an exception was caused by a loss which exceeded VaR by 10% or rather by a loss equal to three times VaR is quite insignificant. What matters is the number of exceptions (and, as was seen, their independence).

An alternative to evaluating a VaR model through statistical tests was proposed by Lopez (1999). This alternative is based upon minimization of a loss function constructed in such a way as to consider the risk manager's or supervisory authority's interests. The loss function can be constructed by the user based upon his/her own interests and objectives. In general terms, the loss (cost) associated with day $t+1$ will take the following form:

$$C_{t+1} = \begin{cases} f(\varepsilon_{t+1}, VaR_t) & \text{if} \quad \varepsilon_{t+1} < VaR_t \\ g(\varepsilon_{t+1}, VaR_t) & \text{if} \quad \varepsilon_{t+1} \geq VaR_t \end{cases} \quad \text{with } f(x, y) \geq g(x, y) \forall x, y \qquad (8.17)$$

In (8.17), ε_{t+1} is the portfolio return observed at $t+1$, and VaR_t is the estimated VaR developed in period t and referring to period $t+1$, in percentage terms (absolute VaR divided by the portfolio's market value on the evening of day t).

Once C_{t+1} values for the N days (or, more in general, the N sub-periods) comprising the backtesting sample have been obtained, the total loss can be calculated:

$$C_M = \sum_{i=1}^{N} C_{t+i} \qquad (8.18)$$

---

[9] As a matter of fact, the following is derived from (8.15)

$$LR_{cc} = -2 \ln \left[\frac{L(x|\pi = \alpha)}{L(x|\pi_{0,0}, \pi_{1,0}, \pi_{0,1}, \pi_{1,1})} \right] = -2 \ln \left[\frac{L(x|\pi = \alpha)}{L(x|\pi)} \cdot \frac{L(x|\pi)}{L(x|\pi_{0,0}, \pi_{1,0}, \pi_{0,1}, \pi_{1,1})} \right]$$

$$= -2 \ln \left[\frac{L(x|\pi = \alpha)}{L(x|\pi)} \right] - 2 \ln \left[\frac{L(x|\pi)}{L(x|\pi_{0,0}, \pi_{1,0}, \pi_{0,1}, \pi_{1,1})} \right] = LR_{uc} + LR_{ind}$$

Lopez suggested using this total loss to compare models for different institutions, or for the same institution in different periods. A formally more elegant solution involves constructing a reference benchmark, referred to as C*, by which the quality of a model can be judged (it will be judged inadequate whenever $C_M \geq C^*$). For this purpose, Lopez suggested using an "optimum" VaR model – i.e., one constructed assuming that the true stochastic process driving market factor returns is known – to generate C*.[10]

The author described three alternative loss functions: a binary function, which takes a value of 1 when an exception occurs and 0 otherwise; a "zone" loss function, which reflects the current backtesting pattern proposed by the Basel Committee (see Appendix 8A); and a loss function increasing with the error (difference between the observed loss and VaR). In the first case, the following ratio is obtained:

$$C_{t+1} = \begin{cases} 1 & \text{if} \quad \varepsilon_{t+1} < VaR_t \\ 0 & \text{if} \quad \varepsilon_{t+1} \geq VaR_t \end{cases} \tag{8.19}$$

Note that, by cumulating the losses for multiple successive periods, the total cost measure obtained is *de facto* equivalent to the number of exceptions (and therefore close to the logic of the LR tests which were examined in the previous sections). However, Lopez made a different use of it: he waived statistical inference tools and obtained a relative performance measure which can be employed in a comparison between different time periods, different institutions, or for a specially calculated reference value. From this point of view, if, on the one hand, Kupiec's and Christoffersen's theoretical patterns enable to more formally deal with the problem and require no elements for comparison, on the other hand, Lopez's loss function is easier to understand and simpler to use.

The loss function approach becomes particularly interesting when the third functional form indicated above – i.e., the one assigning each exception a growing cost as the error increases – is used. In particular, the function proposed by Lopez is as follows:

$$C_{t+1} = \begin{cases} 1 + (\varepsilon_{t+1} - VaR_t)^2 & se \quad \varepsilon_{t+1} < VaR_t \\ 0 & se \quad \varepsilon_{t+1} \geq VaR_t \end{cases} \tag{8.20}$$

As can be noted, this function assigns higher scores to larger exceptions; the decision to square errors makes the loss function particularly sensitive to large deviations.

Lopez's approach is appreciable, because it does not just count the number of exceptions, but also evaluates their size. However, such an approach tends to evaluate the quality of a VaR model based upon a feature which is unrelated to the logic of these models. Indeed, a position's VaR is defined as the loss L which – given a certain time period – can only be exceeded in a percentage of cases equal to α:

$$\Pr(L > VaR) = \alpha \tag{8.21}$$

From (8.21), we understand that VaR models are constructed without paying any attention to the size of losses, but by making reference solely to the frequency of excess losses.

---

[10] Lopez proposed generating a series of "optimum" estimates and the corresponding series of profits and losses, to obtain a C_M value over the selected backtesting period (e.g., 250 days as in the case of Basel). By repeating this procedure many times, a probability distribution of C_M for an optimum model would be obtained. At this point, a given percentile (for instance, the 80th) can be selected as C* value, i.e., as the benchmark to evaluate models.

Given this approach, the correctness of a VaR model should be evaluated only based upon the frequency of "excess losses", and not based upon their size, as well. However, the amount of extreme losses is certainly a very interesting variable for banks, investors and regulatory authorities; this justifies the approach followed by Lopez, and makes it interesting.

8.3.4   Tests based upon the entire distribution

The backtesting methods illustrated so far are based upon exceptions – i.e., the cases in which losses are in excess of VaR. So, they focus their attention solely on one tail of the profit and loss distribution, and not on the entire distribution. This causes the backtesting procedure to be based upon events (excess losses) that are rare by definition, and therefore to use only a small portion of the available sample to construct statistical tests. For instance, a VaR model with a 99 % confidence level should only have three or four daily exceptions over one year: so, a test based upon the number and size of exceptions only uses three or four data out of a total of 250 sample observations.

For this reason, a different approach, referred to as "distribution forecast method", was proposed by Crnkovic and Drachman (1996), and then drawn on – although in a different way – by Diebold, Gunther and Tay (1998) and Berkowitz (2001). It assumes that, in reality, a risk manager implicitly tries to predict the *entire probability distribution* of profits and losses, and could therefore evaluate the quality of his/her predictions by relying upon the entire distribution, rather than just one tail.

The approach proposed by these authors involves considering the probability distribution used at the end of day t to calculate VaR for each day included in the backtesting period, and finding – within this distribution – the percentile p_t corresponding to the return ε_{t+1} which was actually observed on the following day. The idea is that, if the distributions observed in order to derive VaR and the empirical return distribution are consistent, the value p_t derived for the N days in the backtesting period should follow a uniform distribution and be serially uncorrelated. Different null-hypothesis testing techniques actually co-exist within this framework, which is only briefly described here.[11]

Crnkovic and Drachman proposed an indicator (Kupier's test) based upon the distance between the predicted probability distribution of portfolio returns and their actual distribution: this statistical test measures the distance between two cumulative probability density functions, and is considered to be more reliable because it is equally sensitive to all distribution values (whereas other tests, such as the Kolmogorov-Smirnov test, tend to overestimate the importance of observations close to the median).

Diebold et al. (1998) underlined that inferential tests, although they are formally elegant, are often of poor practical use, because they can lead to rejection of the null hypothesis without, however, giving any indications about the "true" data distribution. So, they privilege a graphical analysis of the percentile distribution associated with observed returns, calculated with reference to the probability density function of the model which is used for VaR calculation. If the bars all take a roughly identical height, then the percentile distribution is uniform, and the model can be considered as accurate. Otherwise, the form of the bars helps understand where the inaccuracy of the model stems from: for instance,

---

[11] See Christoffersen (2003), pp. 191–193, for more details on this approach.

if the central and extreme bars are higher than the mean, the "true" distribution of returns is likely to be leptokurtic – for instance, a Student's t-distribution.

Finally, Berwovitz (2001) introduced an innovation based upon such a data transformation as to obtain a new normally distributed random variable and to then be able to have recourse to the classical statistical tests associated with the Gaussian.

SELECTED QUESTIONS AND EXERCISES

1. The backtesting of a daily VaR measure involves comparing...

    (A) ... actual daily losses with the VaRs estimated by the model the day before.

    (B) ... static daily losses (that is, losses computed assuming that the composition of the portfolio remains unchanged throughout the trading day) with the average VaR for the whole backtesting period.

    (C) ... static daily losses with the VaRs estimated by the model the day before.

    (D) ... actual daily losses with static daily losses, only when the latter exceed the daily VaR.

2. A bank is backtesting its VaR model on a sample of 400 past daily returns. On 12 days out of 400, losses have exceeded the 99 % VaR. Using a binomial distribution, compute the probability associated with such an outcome, if the VaR model is correct. Also, compute the unconditional coverage test (using equation 8.4 in the Chapter) and (using the simplified Table below or the function CHIDIST in MS Excel) estimate the Type I error (p-value). What is the practical meaning of this error value?

Cumulative probability function of x according to a chi-square distribution with m degrees of freedom									
x	0.25	0.5	1	2.5	5	10	20	40	80	160
M										
1	38.29 %	52.05 %	68.27 %	88.62 %	97.47 %	99.84 %	100.00 %	100.00 %	100.00 %	100.00 %
12	0.00 %	0.00 %	0.00 %	0.18 %	4.20 %	38.40 %	93.29 %	99.99 %	100.00 %	100.00 %
100	0.00 %	0.00 %	0.00 %	0.00 %	0.00 %	0.00 %	0.00 %	0.00 %	7.03 %	99.99 %

3. Which of the following statements are true?

    "Stress testing a VaR model for market risk may imply the need to ...

    (I) ...compute the VaR associated to different scenarios which correspond to extreme shocks of market factors returns which already occurred in the past."

    (II) ... compute the VaR associated to different scenarios which correspond to extreme shocks of market factors returns which never occurred in the past."

    (III) ... compute the VaR associated to different scenarios which correspond to the average changes of market factors' returns which already occurred in the past."

    (IV) ... compute the VaR associated to different scenarios which correspond to the average expected future changes of market factors' returns."

(A) II only.
(B) I and II.
(C) I and III.
(D) II and IV.

4. A bank has backtested its VaR model on a set of 500 observations, finding 7 consecutive exceptions (that is, values that exceed VaR). Compute the unconditional coverage test, the serial independence test and the conditional coverage test. Using the function CHIDIST in MS Excel or the Table below, compute the p-values of the three tests. Comment the results.

Cumulative probability function of x according to a chi-square distribution with m degrees of freedom									
x	0.2	0.5	0.7	5	6.2	6.9	7.5	10	15	20
m										
1	34.53 %	52.05 %	59.72 %	97.47 %	98.72 %	99.14 %	99.38 %	99.84 %	99.99 %	100.00 %
2	9.52 %	22.12 %	29.53 %	91.79 %	95.50 %	96.83 %	97.65 %	99.33 %	99.94 %	100.00 %
7	0.00 %	0.06 %	0.17 %	34.00 %	48.34 %	56.06 %	62.13 %	81.14 %	96.40 %	99.44 %

5. Which of the following criteria is used by the Basel Committee to measure the quality of an internal market risk measurement model (see Appendix 8A to answer this question)?

(A) Comparing the size of the losses exceeding VaR with the ones implied in a chi-squared distribution.
(B) Comparing the frequency of the losses exceeding VaR with the ones implied in a chi-squared distribution.
(C) Comparing the frequency of the losses exceeding VaR with the ones implied in the model's confidence level.
(D) Comparing the size of the losses exceeding VaR with the ones implied in the model's confidence level.

Appendix 8A
VaR Model Backtesting According to the Basel Committee

The Basel Committee has allowed more sophisticated banks to use their own internal models – in lieu of the standard rules applying to all credit institutions – to determine minimum market risk capital requirements. These standard rules, as well as the (qualitative and quantitative) conditions imposed upon those banks wishing to use their own internal models, will be presented in detail in Chapter 19.

What matters here is that these conditions include the obligation to regularly backtest the model on a quarterly basis, based upon the last 250 daily trading results. If backtesting outcomes are not fully reassuring, the minimum capital requirement generated by the model (equal to the mean of decadal VaRs for the last 60 days multiplied by a factor of 3) will be increased; more precisely, the multiplying factor will be increased from 3 to 4; the worse the model's performance, the greater the increase.

Let us consider, for instance, a model calculating daily VaR at a 99 % confidence level. In this case, we are likely to expect excess losses only in 1 % of the cases, i.e., on 2.5 out of 250 annual trading days. If the "number of exceptions", i.e., the number of days on which losses are in excess of VaR, is lower than, equal to, or slightly higher than 2.5, we are likely to assume that the model being used has a satisfactory quality level. Vice versa, if the number of exceptions is significantly higher than predicted by the adopted confidence level, we are likely to assume that the model being used poses some problems.

Based upon this logic, the multiplying factor ranges from 3 (if the number of exceptions is equal to a maximum of 4) to 4 (if the number of exceptions is 10 or more). Table 8A.1 shows the multiplying factor values, and highlights the division into three different areas (green, yellow, and red) which was adopted by the Basel Committee. Note that, if the internal model falls within the red area, the multiplying factor of 3 will be raised to 4.

If backtesting results are in the yellow area, then the multiplying factor will take values ranging from 3 to 4.

The increase may not be fully applied by the Authorities. In particular, it should always be applied if exceptions are due to *model integrity* issues (risk positions were reported incorrectly) or *model accuracy* issues (the model does not measure risk with sufficient accuracy). If, conversely, exceptions are due to *intraday trading* (risk positions changed during the trading day), the authority should "seriously consider" applying the increase, which, however, would not be mandatory. The Committee finally acknowledges that exceptions could occur simply because of the *market trend* (i.e., because markets were particularly volatile, or because correlations changed rapidly); in this case, it is not clear whether the increase should be applied (the Committee just states that this type of exceptions are "expected to occur at least some of the time").

The determination of the multiplying factor as implied in Table 8A.1 is based upon the logic set forth in section 8.3.1. More specifically, the Committee assumes that the probability of observing a certain number x of exceptions is given by equation (8.1) (since backtesting is conducted on 250 observations, by equation 8.1b), and uses the binomial distribution which has already been seen in Table 8.3 to set multiplying factors,

Table 8A.1 Basel Committee Internal Models Multiplying Factor

Area	Number of exceptions	Increase	Multiplying factor
Green	0	0.00	3.00
	1	0.00	3.00
	2	0.00	3.00
	3	0.00	3.00
	4	0.00	3.00
Yellow	5	0.40	3.40
	6	0.50	3.50
	7	0.65	3.65
	8	0.75	3.75
	9	0.85	3.85
Red	≥ 10	1.00	4.00

Source: Basel Committee (1996).

with the intent to minimize both type I errors (rejection of a good model) and type II errors (acceptance of a bad model).

These error probabilities are shown in Table 8A.2, which was drawn up by the Committee and is an extension of Table 8.3. The first part of the Table (columns 2–3) considers type I error, and is therefore drawn up in the assumption that the model is correct (α is actually 1 %, as it should be if the confidence level is 99 %). Column (2) shows the probabilities of obtaining a certain number of exceptions, in the case of a sample of 250 daily data (for instance, a 13.4 % probability of obtaining 4 exceptions). Column (3) shows the probability that, by rejecting the model as inaccurate when at least x exceptions are obtained, an error of rejecting a correct model is made.

Conversely, the next columns (4–6) assume that the model is not correct, and, in particular, that the "true" probability of obtaining excess losses is 3 %. Column (4) calculates the probability of obtaining a certain number of exceptions based upon a binomial with $\alpha = 3$ %; in a 250 data sample, the highest probability will be recorded at a number of exceptions of 7 and 8 (since 3 % of 250 is approximately 7.5). Conversely, column (5) shows the probability of making a type II error in the presence of x exceptions: for instance, if we decide to consider a model generating up to 8 exceptions as correct, the risk that it will actually have an α of 3 % would be 52.4 % (i.e., the sum of the probabilities associated with a number of exceptions from zero to 8, as shown in column 4). Finally, the last column in the table shows the *power* of the test, which, by definition, is equal to the complement to one of the probability of making a type II error.

Table 8A.2 Probability of Obtaining Exceptions (T = 250)

Area	Number of exceptions (x) (1)	Null hypothesis: the model is correct ($\alpha = 1\%$)		Alternative hypothesis: the model is incorrect ($\alpha = 3\%$)		
		Probability prob(x) (2)	Cumulative probability = probability of a type I error (rejection of a correct model) (3)	Probability $P(X = N)$ (4)	Cumulative probability = probability of a type II error (acceptance of an incorrect model) (5)	Power of the test (Model rejection) $P(X \geq N)$ (6)
Green	0	8.1%	100%	0.0%	0.0%	100.0%
	1	20.5%	91.9%	0.4%	0.0%	100.0%
	2	25.7%	71.4%	1.5%	0.4%	99.6%
	3	21.5%	45.7%	3.8%	1.9%	98.1%
	4	13.4%	24.2%	7.2%	5.7%	94.3%
Yellow	5	6.7%	10.8%	10.9%	12.8%	87.2%
	6	2.7%	4.1%	13.8%	23.7%	76.3%

Table 8A.2 (*continued*)

Area	Number of exceptions x (1)	Null hypothesis: the model is correct ($\alpha = 1\%$)		Alternative hypothesis: the model is incorrect ($\alpha = 3\%$)		
		Probability prob(x) (2)	Cumulative probability = probability of a type I error (rejection of a correct model) (3)	Probability $P(X = N)$ (4)	Cumulative probability = probability of a type II error (acceptance of an incorrect model) (5)	Power of the test (Model rejection) $P(X \geq N)$ (6)
	7	1.0%	1.4%	14.9%	37.5%	62.5%
	8	0.3%	0.4%	14.0%	52.4%	47.6%
	9	0.1%	0.1%	11.6%	66.3%	33.7%
Red	10	0.0%	0.0%	8.6%	77.9%	21.1%
	11	0.0%	0.0%	5.8%	86.6%	13.4%

Source: Basel Committee (1996).

As can be noted, with a number of exceptions of 5 or more, the probability of making a type I error (rejecting a correct model) is 10.8 %. This means that, based upon the rules adopted by the Committee, one out of ten banks is penalised (by an increased multiplying factor) even though it has a correct model. Symmetrically, however, if we go so far as to accept a number of exceptions of up to 5, the probability of making a type II error (accepting an incorrect model) will be 12.8 %.

9

VaR Models:
Summary, Applications and Limitations

9.1 INTRODUCTION

The market risk measurement models illustrated in the previous chapters are used by financial institutions for a variety of purposes, the most important of which include comparing and integrating different risks; imposing restrictions on the operational autonomy of the trading units in charge of different financial instruments and markets; and constructing risk-adjusted performance measures.

These models have been subject to several criticisms by academics, practitioners, and representatives of supervisory authorities. In some respects, during the nineties, a sort of ideological battle arose between advocates and opponents of VaR models.[1]

As will be noted, many of these criticisms – however formally correct – stem from a misunderstanding of the purposes of VaR models, i.e., a somewhat naïve overestimation of their real potential. Other criticisms, conversely, underline real and even marked defects of VaR models, which need to be known in order for these models to be used in a wise and sensible manner.

After a brief comparative analysis of the alternative approaches illustrated in the previous chapters (variance-covariance, historical simulations, hybrid approach, Monte Carlo simulations), this chapter will linger over some important applications of VaR models, which enable highlighting their merits: the possibility of expressing risks according to a common language, which makes the risks connected with different instruments comparable and aggregatable; the introduction of a risk limits system; and the measurement of risk-adjusted returns.

Then, attention will be focused on the limitations of VaR models. After reviewing some "false defects" of these models, whose poor consistency will be highlighted, the analysis will linger over two major real issues of VaR measures, and over an alternative risk measure – expected shortfall – which makes it possible to overcome these limitations.

9.2 A SUMMARY OVERVIEW OF THE DIFFERENT MODELS

In this section, we will summarize the different methodologies which can be used to estimate a portfolio VaR, comparing their advantages and disadvantages.

In the previous chapters, we have already lingered in detail over the individual models' features. Here, we will just refer to them synoptically. For this purpose, Table 9.1 reports schematically the main assumptions adopted and criteria followed by the different models, as well as their merits and limitations.

None of the models described in the Table is a "better" solution than the other ones in absolute terms: each of them is more or less adequate depending on the purposes which are to be pursued.

---

[1] See Jorion (1997) and Taleb (1997).

Table 9.1 A comparison among alternative VaR models

Model	Variance-covariance	Historical simulations	Hybrid	Monte Carlo Simulations
Distribution of market factor returns	Normal multivariate, adjusted for recent volatility	Stationary (historical)	Historical, adjusted for recent volatility	Completely flexible
Confidence level determination	As a multiple of the standard deviation	As a percentile of the distribution of portfolio value changes	As a percentile of the weighted distribution of portfolio value changes	As a percentile of the simulated distribution of portfolio value changes
Change in the positions' market values	Approximated by either linear functions (e.g., options' "greeks") or quadratic functions (delta-gamma method)	Calculated from the new market conditions ("full valuation"), even though linear approximations can also be used		
Interaction among multiple market factors	Through a correlation matrix	Implied in the historical distribution	Implied in the historical distribution	Through a correlation matrix and Cholesky's decomposition
Merits	√ Fast computing √ It does not require a pricing model for each position	√ It does not require explicit hypotheses about risk factor distribution √ It does not require explicit volatility and correlation estimates (it preserves past ones)		√ It can be used for complex portfolios √ Totally flexible distribution of market factors
Limitations	√ It assumes normal distributions √ It requires an explicit volatility and correlation estimate √ Linear payoff hp.	√ It requires a large historical sample √ It requires a pricing model for each position		√ Computationally intensive √ It requires a pricing model for each position

So, for instance, if the purpose is to measure the risk-adjusted return of the bank's individual trading units (both *ex ante* – based upon earnings estimates – and *ex post* – based upon actually achieved results), the variance-covariance model is likely to be the best option. Indeed, its limitations (in particular, the assumption of a normal distribution of market factor returns) are relatively unimportant if the purpose is to measure the individual units' risks on a daily basis, impose restrictions upon their autonomy, and calculate their risk-adjusted return. If, on the one hand, it is true that the normality assumption may lead to disregard "extreme" events related to the presence of "fat tails" in the return distribution (going as far as to potentially underestimate the capital required by the bank to cope with such scenarios), the variance/covariance approach nevertheless has the merit of being simple, rapidly computable, and responsive to possible increases in risk factor volatility.

Likewise, if a bank has a high amount of positions characterized by non-linear payoffs (such as options) in its portfolio, full valuation (historical or Monte Carlo simulation) models are likely to be more adequate.

Again, if the purpose is to measure the bank's aggregate risk to test whether the available economic capital is sufficient, the construction of stress scenarios is likely to be more adequate, as "extreme" events have inevitably to be considered for this purpose.

In no case will it be possible to maintain that any approach is more *accurate* than others. We may have models characterized by hypotheses which are more or less consistent with the current market situation or the bank's specific situation; or, again, methods which are more or less correct from the point of view of the analytical procedure. As, in any case, these are always *prediction* models, none of them can be defined as most accurate *a priori*.

9.3   APPLICATIONS OF VAR MODELS

9.3.1   Comparison among different risks

A first use of VaR models is to make different risks comparable, facilitating the use of a common "language" among the banks' different business units.

Assume, for example, that we want to measure the risk of three different positions: bonds, foreign exchange options, and stocks. If the individual traders who created these positions were asked to illustrate their risk profiles, the answers given would probably not be comparable in any way. The first trader would most likely report the duration and convexity (or basis point value) of her bonds; the second one would describe the delta, gamma, vega, theta and rho coefficient of her options; the third one, conversely, would provide indications about the traded stocks' volatility and beta.

These are different and mutually incompatible languages. What is a 6-year duration equivalent to, in terms of a stock's beta? How does a position in treasury bond options with a delta of 0.7 compare with a forward position in a foreign currency?

It therefore becomes impossible – for the bank's top management wishing to evaluate the individual positions' risk/return profiles and to impose risk limits upon traders – to compare the three risks. Besides referring to market factors characterized by a different degree of volatility, the measures provided are built based upon different methodologies. Thus, it is not possible to understand which position is generating more risk for the bank.

If the three traders had just reported the simple *nominal values* of their respective portfolios, the situation would have been even more confused. As a matter of fact, it would not have been possible to make any comparison, or to realize the actual riskiness of the three positions.

On the contrary, VaR enables proceeding from an individual position's degree of risk – expressed by different measures for the various types of risk (duration and convexity, "greeks" for options, beta for stocks, etc.) – and constructing homogeneous risk measures (in terms of confidence level, holding period, etc.), taking into account the different market factors' degrees of volatility. In other words, risk is rewritten in such a way that it can be compared and aggregated across different positions.

Assume we want to compare the risk connected with a long position in 10-year Treasury bonds (quoted at par) with the one connected with the sale of an at-the-money call option with 1-year maturity on the dollar. The features, in terms of sensitivity and volatility coefficients of the relevant market factors, are shown in Table 9.2.

Table 9.2 The risk profiles of two positions

Treasury Bonds		Call Option on USD	
Price	100	EUR/USD spot	1
Nominal amount	EUR 100,000	Notional amount	USD 100,000
Maturity	10 years	Market value	EUR 7,740
Coupon	6%	Maturity	1 year
Modified Duration	7.36	Strike	1
Modified Convexity	65.79	Implied volatility	10%
Yield to Maturity	6%	Delta	0.5

The features illustrated in the Table help us clarify the nature of the two positions and their relevant degree of exposure to possible changes in the relevant market factors (yield to maturity for the 10-year bond, EUR/USD exchange rate and relevant volatility for the call option); however, they do not allow us to compare the risks of the two positions, and therefore to bring it back to a common measurement unit. As a matter of fact, it is not possible to answer the very simple question: "which of the two positions is riskier?".

To find the answer, we need information about daily market factor volatility. Let us assume that it is 25 basis points for the 10-year yield to maturity, 1.5% for the EUR/USD exchange rate, and 0.2% for the option's implied volatility. For the sake of simplicity, let us also assume that the last two risk factors (dollar exchange rate and its volatility) are perfectly correlated. At this point, by adopting a given confidence level (for instance, 99%), the VaR connected with the two positions can be estimated.

More precisely, to calculate Treasury bonds position VaR, let us adopt a variance-covariance approach and delta/gamma approximation. As was seen in Chapter 5 (equation 5.29), the changes in the position's market value can be calculated as:

$$\Delta MV \cong \delta \cdot \Delta r + \frac{\gamma}{2} \cdot (\Delta r)^2$$

In our case, the coefficient δ (which depends on the first derivative of the bond's value with respect to changes in its yield to maturity) is given by modified duration (7.36 years) multiplied by the value of the exposure (100,000 euros); the coefficient γ (which captures the second-order effect) is given by modified convexity (65.79) changed in sign and multiplied by the value of the exposure.

To obtain the 99% confidence level VaR, we must enter into the formula the change in the market factor ΔR corresponding to the 99th percentile of the distribution of the

possible changes in yield to maturity; under a normality hypothesis, this percentile will
be 2.33 times the standard deviation.

VaR will therefore be estimated as:

$$VaR_{T-Bond} = 7.36 \cdot 100,000 \cdot 2.33 \cdot 0.25\% - \frac{65.79}{2} \cdot 100,000 \cdot (2.33 \cdot 0.25\%)^2$$

$$= 4,169$$

To calculate the VaR of the option position, we could also use a delta/gamma approach
(which, however, would require us to know the gamma coefficient of the call, which
is not shown in the Table). Conversely, for this exercise, let us use a full valuation
approach. In particular, let us adopt the Black and Scholes formula as the pricing function,
and recalculate the "fair" value of the call at a value corresponding to the "worst case
scenario" (99th percentile) for the two risk factors (EUR/USD exchange rate and its
volatility). As the bank has a short position on the call, it will experience a loss when
the option increases in value: we must therefore simulate the effects of an increase in the
price of the underlying asset (EUR/USD exchange rate) and an increase in volatility. As
we have assumed that these two market factors are 100 % correlated, we can just select
the 99th percentile separately for each of them.[2]

If we assume that their percentage changes are normally distributed, this percentile
will simply be 2.33 times the standard deviation: so, we will obtain a change of 3.5 %
(2.33·1.5 %) for the exchange rate (which will bring the spot exchange rate to the level
of 1.035 euros per US dollar) and 0.47 % (2.33·0.2 %) for volatility (which will therefore
rise from 10 % to 10.47 %). VaR will then be obtained as the difference between the value
of the call in the presence of these "extreme" market conditions and its current value.

$$VaR_{call} = c(1.035; 10.47\%) - c(1; 10\%) = 9.601 - 6.805 = 2.797$$

The details of the calculation are shown in Table 9.3 (note that a 5 % value was used for
the one-year risk-free interest rate).

We can therefore conclude that, if the hypotheses and methodologies we used reasonably
approximate reality, the position in Treasury bonds is generating more risk than the call
option, although the nominal values of the two positions are similar. Indeed, the maximum
daily loss which might be incurred by the bank in 99 % of the cases is almost twice as
high (4,169 euros versus 2,797 euros) in the case of government bonds.

The example we have just seen shows two major advantages of VaR:

√ VaR facilitates "horizontal" communication, i.e., communication among traders working
at different desks (and therefore taking positions in different financial instruments and
markets), because it allows them to compare the risk of their positions using a uniform
logic;

---

[2] The fact that the correlation is 100 % means that when the change in the exchange rate is positioned on a
given percentile (for instance, the 99th), the change in volatility will also be positioned on the same percentile.
If the correlation between the two risk factors had not been perfect, we should have used a different approach,
based upon generation of scenarios (e.g., a Monte Carlo simulation) or, as has already been mentioned in the
text, on the delta/gamma approach.

Table 9.3 Calculation of a call's VaR using full valuation

		Stressed market conditions	Current market conditions
Spot rate	S	1.034895	1
Strike rate	X	1	1
Interest rate	r	5 %	5 %
Volatility	σ	10.47 %	10 %
Time to maturity	T	1	1
Components of the Black/Scholes formula	d_1	0.858	0.55
	d_2	0.753	0.45
	$N(d_1)$	0.805	0.709
	$N(d_2)$	0.774	0.674
Value of the call (based on the Black/Scholes formula)	$1	0.096016	0.06805
Difference	VaR	2796.68	
	$100,000	9601.64	6804.95

√ VaR facilitates "vertical" communication to the financial institution's senior management; if they are informed and aware of the hypotheses and limitations underlying VaR calculation, they can assess the risks of the two positions and request updated information without coming up against different terminologies (modified duration, convexity, basis point value, beta, delta, gamma, vega, etc.) for each individual trading unit.

A further advantage, which is not illustrated in this example, but has already been presented in the previous chapters, is the fact that VaR enables aggregating the risks connected with different positions, thus facilitating calculation of the risk of portfolios consisting of numerous exposures. In order to proceed to this aggregation, the degree of correlation among the risk factors affecting the values of the different positions[3] will need to be estimated. This in turn can be done in many different ways, depending on the model adopted: for instance, through a market factor correlation matrix in the case of the variance-covariance approach, or past data relating to joint changes in market factors in the case of a historical simulation model.

---

[3] So, for instance, to calculate the daily VaRs at 99 % of the two positions illustrated in Table 9.2, the correlation between the risk factors underlying the value of Government securities (yield to maturity) and the value of the call (spot exchange and its volatility) would also need to be known.

9.3.2 Determination of risk taking limits

A second important application of VaR relates to the introduction of risk limits to the individual trading units. An example may be useful to understand how this is possible, and what advantages can be derived.

Let us assume that the aggregate value at risk limit (for instance, decadal VaR at 97.5 %) allocated to a risk-taking unit – for the sake of simplicity, the one taking positions on the euro interest rate curve – is 500,000 euros; in other words, the bank established that the trading of euro interest rate sensitive positions must at any time be such as not to cause any loss in excess of half a million euros in the ten following days (except for 1 % of extreme events, which can cause worse losses). The head of this trading unit is free to allocate this VaR limit (which corresponds to an equivalent amount of economic capital raised by the bank from its shareholders) among the different risky positions. Let us assume that the available capital is allocated among the individual desks as shown in Table 9.4. From these values (second column in the Table), each individual trader will be able to determine the maximum exposure which is compatible with his/her VaR (third column), based upon the individual position's degree of sensitivity to the relevant market factors (interest rate, exchange rate, etc.) and volatility level.[4]

Table 9.4 Example of capital allocation in the euro interest rate risk taking unit

Desk	VaR limit	Exposure limit (rounded off)
Treasury bonds	160,000 euros	32,650,000 euros
Treasury bills	70,000 euros	70,000,000 euros
Forward-rate agreements	120,000 euros	100,000,000 euros
5-year Interest Rate Swaps	150,000 euros	80,000,000 euros
Total	500,000 euros	

So, for instance, a VaR limit of 160,000 euros is imposed upon the desk trading in long-term government securities (Treasury bonds). For the sake of simplicity, let us assume that this value was derived using the parametric approach through a linear approximation based upon modified duration; in this case, from equation (5.7) in Chapter 5:

$$(1) VaR = MV \cdot MD \cdot \alpha \cdot \sigma \tag{9.1}$$

we can derive:

$$(2)\ MV = \frac{VaR}{MD \cdot \alpha \cdot \sigma} \tag{9.2}$$

---

[4] The Table just adds the VaRs of the different desks to obtain the trading unit total VaR. This procedure is correct only if the risk factors underlying the different subportfolios are perfectly correlated. Otherwise, the total VaR should be lower than the sum of the individual VaRs, to take into account the benefits of diversification: this phenomenon was illustrated in the previous Chapters. However, as will be seen below in this chapter, there are cases in which VaR does not ensure this risk "subadditivity", and is therefore the butt of harsh criticism.

Assuming a volatility of decadal changes in long-term interest rates (σ) of 4 basis points (0.04%), a 97.5% confidence level (α equal to approx. 1.96), and a modified duration of 6.25 years, a VaR of 160,000 euros corresponds to a market value of approximately 32.7 million euros (to be precise, 32,653,661 euros).

Note that any changes in market conditions (changes in σ) or in the portfolio's composition (changes in MD) will generate an "automatic" adjustment of the exposure which is compatible with a given VaR. In particular, (9.2) shows that, if the market becomes more volatile, and/or if the manager increases the average portfolio duration, then the size of the portfolio (market value) will need to be reduced in order for it to remain within the assigned VaR limit. This will encourage, *inter alia*, reallocation of the Treasury's aggregate portfolio towards markets characterized by temporarily less strained conditions.

The VaR limit can also be converted into risk measures other than the portfolio market value, with which bond traders might be more familiar.

A first example is the basis point value, or *DV01*, (the change generated in a bond portfolio value by a change in the interest rate of one basis point, i.e., 0.01%). To this end, it is sufficient to proceed from equation (9.1); rather than considering a change in long-term rates of $\alpha \cdot \sigma$ (corresponding to the 97.5 percentile of a normal distribution), let us assume that it is equal to one basis point:

$$DV01 = MV \cdot MD \cdot 0.01\% = VaR \frac{0.01\%}{\alpha \cdot \sigma} \qquad (9.3)$$

If volatility (σ) is equal to 0.04%, the 97.5% confidence level VaR (α equal to approximately 1.96) corresponds to a basis point value of 20,409 euros.[5]

A second example is the nominal (rather than market) value of the exposure. Assuming that the bank's long-term bond portfolio comprises only one Treasury Bond whose market price P is 110 cents per euro of face value, the nominal value corresponding to a MV of 32,653,661 euros will be 29,685,147 euros (MV/P).

If VaR limits can be "translated" into other measures, how should they be expressed? The answer depends on the aim pursued and on how they are used. For a trader, it is certainly convenient to have an immediate, real-time translation in terms of market value and DV01 (or beta, in the case of stock portfolios), which can be combined with his/her interest rate expectations. Vice versa, for the head of the trading room or, at an even higher level, for the director of the finance area, continuous monitoring of the evolution of the aggregate value at risk becomes more important. Again, for reporting to the regulatory authorities, it is often necessary to think in terms of nominal value of positions.

9.3.3 The construction of risk-adjusted performance (RAP) measures

A third major application of VaR models relates to the calculation of the risk-adjusted return of individual positions or individual desks. As a matter of fact, since value at risk is a quantitative measure of the risk associated with a given position (and therefore of the economic capital required to "support" it), it can be used to "risk-adjust" that position's return.

---

[5] Similarly, based upon the relations between portfolio beta and VaR which were examined in Chapter 5, the VaR of a stock portfolio of a given size could be converted into a beta limit (or again, for a given beta, into a position limit).

Although they take on different names at different institutions,[6] risk-adjusted return measures are all generally computed as a simple profit/risk ratio, which we can call RAROC (risk-adjusted return on capital).

Risk-adjusted return can be estimated *ex ante,* as the ratio between expected profit and value at risk, and calculated *ex post,* as the ratio between actually achieved profit and absorbed capital.

In the former case, we have:

$$RAROC_{ex\text{-}ante} = \frac{E(P)}{VaR_{ex\text{-}ante}} \qquad (9.4)$$

where $E(P)$ indicates the expected profit generated by a certain position or a certain risk taking unit, and $VaR_{ex\text{-}ante}$ indicates the risk limit assigned to it (also referred to as *allocated* capital at risk, or CaR).

Conversely, in the latter case, we have:

$$RAROC_{ex\text{-}post} = \frac{P}{VaR_{ex\text{-}post}} \qquad (9.5)$$

where P is the actual profit, and $VaR_{ex\text{-}post}$ indicates the (maximum or mean) VaR achieved in the period (also referred to as *absorbed* capital at risk, or *CaR*), i.e., the risk which was actually taken.

These performance measures can be used by the management for different purposes:[7]

√ to help traders make more efficient decisions by comparing the risk-adjusted return profiles of different positions *ex ante*;

√ to build an incentive system based not only upon profit, but also upon the risk connected with the achievement of a given profit;

√ to compare the performance of different risk taking units *ex post* in order to determine which of them is making best use of the capital allocated to it by the bank, and is therefore worthy of receiving more.

On the basis of its own ex ante RAROC, every risk-taking unit can compete with the other ones to obtain more capital, and therefore to increase its own operational capability in the following months. However, this virtuous internal competition mechanism cannot an analysis of the return which was actually achieved in the past, that is measured by *ex post* RAROC.

As will be illustrated more in detail in Chapter 22, risk-adjusted performance measures have applications at a variety of levels (individual risk positions, business units, or entire business areas), and, in all these cases, enable testing whether there is any value creation for the bank as a whole. Indeed, assuming that the cost of risk capital (r_e) – i.e., the return demanded by the bank's shareholders – is known, there will be value creation when the RAROC of the unit or portfolio considered is higher than that cost.

---

[6] Ranging from the more traditional RAROC (Risk-Adjusted Return on Capital) originally introduced by Bankers Trust to the more recent RORAC (Return on Risk-Adjusted Capital) and RARORAC (Risk-Adjusted Return on Risk-Adjusted Capital).

[7] See Chapter 21 of this book for a more thorough analysis of the issues connected with the construction and use or RAP measures.

Many banks express RAROC directly as the difference between the profitability ratio in (9.4) or (9.5) and the cost of capital r_e. This way, a positive (negative) RAROC can immediately be associated with value creation (destruction)[8].

9.4   SIX "FALSE SHORTCOMINGS" OF VAR

Since their introduction, VaR models have often been subject to more or less explicit criticisms by practitioners, academics, and representatives of supervisory authorities. These criticisms, although not groundless, are often only the consequence of a poor understanding of the purposes of VaR models and the reasons underlying their development.

These models are just *tools* facilitating risk management, but must not be considered as a panacea that can simply and mechanically solve the problem. For instance, introducing a risk management system based upon the VaR logic requires – prior to some software which can measure each individual position's or portfolio's value at risk – hard work to construct an adequate data base (the so-called data warehouse, which collects and represents a financial institution's risk positions). Those who invest huge resources to buy a software package based upon a VaR logic without first constructing an adequate data warehouse (and without adequately considering the software tool's capability to interface with this data system) will run inevitably into mistakes and disappointments. These mistakes, however, cannot be attributed to the VaR logic, but rather to how it was actually implemented.

The six major criticisms of VaR will be analyzed below in this section. In our opinion, these criticisms stem from a misinterpretation of the purposes of the models, and we will try to respond to them.

9.4.1   VaR models disregard exceptional events

The first criticism claims that, since VaR models define risk as the potential loss (over a certain time period) *associated with a certain confidence level*, they are unable to cover the entire range of the possible events that a financial institution must be able to cope with. In other words, if risk is defined, for instance, as the maximum loss in 99 % of cases, 1 % of future scenarios will be disregarded.

Although formally correct, this criticism neglects three key aspects. In the first place, the purpose of VaR models is not to make a bank "not liable to bankruptcy", but rather to indicate the amount of capital required to limit the risk of bankruptcy to an acceptable percentage of cases. From this point of view, the losses associated with "extreme" events that are not included in the confidence interval are not noteworthy, because they will not concern the shareholders in the bank (whose capital, which is hypothetically equal to VaR, will have already been completely "exhausted" by losses), but rather the liquidator or the regulatory authorities in charge of managing the bank's bankruptcy. So, as extreme events do not "absorb" capital, they will not become part of current risk management (based upon which transactions are priced, the different business units' risk-adjusted returns are measured, and limits to their operations are defined); thus, they shall not be considered by shareholders, but, if anything, by public authorities, who are interested in predicting the costs of a possible "bailout", or by the bank's creditors or deposit insurers, who are interested in estimating possible losses in case of default.

---

[8] Examples where RAROCs is computed this way will be presented, e.g., in Chapters 15 and 16 of this book.

In the second place, the confidence level used in calculating VaR may be increased at will, if needed, so as to capture a higher percentage of events, if this is considered to be appropriate in order to have a more comprehensive picture of the possible future scenarios. If a bank increases its VaR model's confidence level, and adjusts its capital endowment accordingly, its creditors will feel more protected, and the cost of debt capital will be lower; however, it will be necessary to generate a higher income, so as to leave the return on capital provided by shareholders unchanged.

Finally, it should be noted that a total protection level, i.e., a 100 % confidence level VaR, would be neither theoretically desirable, nor practically achievable: a financial institution wishing such a level of protection (and therefore wishing to eliminate any form of risk for third parties) should be entirely financed with equity capital, and would thus betray its primary role, i.e., measuring, pricing and managing risks.

9.4.2   VaR models disregard customer relations

A second criticism of VaR is that its mechanical application might lead a bank to abruptly terminate all positions whose risk-adjusted return is inadequate. Thus, the value of long term customer relations will not be properly taken into account, and the bank will act with a short term view ("short-termism").

In reality VaR models, just like any other management technique, represent a simple tool which is naturally and necessarily to be complemented by subjective evaluations by the bank's management. As a consequence, if a given transaction's risk-adjusted return calculated based upon the relevant VaR were insufficient to adequately remunerate the economic capital, and therefore pointed to value destruction, the bank's management could in any case keep the investment in the portfolio based upon a subjective evaluation of the long-term relation with the counterparty. In any case, the indication of the risk-adjusted return estimated based upon VaR would be a useful tool, and would force the management to express the rationale which suggest making the investment, or keeping the asset in the bank's portfolio.

9.4.3   VaR models are based upon unrealistic assumptions

A third criticism concerns the assumptions underlying the different criteria to calculate value at risk. Some institutions may find these assumptions as unrealistic and therefore refuse to adopt a VaR model as a tool for risk measurement, risk control, risk-adjusted return measurement, and capital allocation among the different business units.

In reply to this criticism, we would argue that, whether one likes it or not, each financial institution chooses to hold a certain level of capital, and to implicitly allocate it to the different risk taking business units (often based upon a non-transparent perception of their risk levels). The difference lies in the fact that those who adopt a VaR model are aware of their capital sizing and allocation logics, as well as the (sometimes questionable) hypotheses upon which these measures are based; those who do not have a model, proceed in a considerably more opaque manner.

However, since the assumption underlying a VaR model have been fully expressed and understood, they can be appropriately changed in the presence of particular market conditions, or specific subjective evaluations by the management. In conclusion, awareness of the models and their limitations is certainly preferable to ignorance, even when the latter uses precisely the existence of limitations in available models as a shield.

9.4.4   VaR models generate diverging results

VaR models have been criticized implicitly by some researchers who found considerable discrepancies[9] when empirically comparing the results generated by the different
approaches presented in the previous chapters. Although these discrepancies are not
an explicit and direct demonstration of the unreliability of the VaR methodology, they
allegedly suggest that the results of these models should be used with caution.

This criticism also disguises poor understanding of the purposes of VaR models. Indeed,
it is true that the results of these models strongly depend on the approach used (as well as
on the specific hypotheses adopted, the historical sample size, the reference time horizon,
the number of identified risk factors, how positions are mapped to these factors, and much
more). So, they should not be considered as a univocal (and almost "magical") measure
of the capital required to support risks.

However, if results are used to consistently and homogeneously introduce risk limits
and risk-adjusted performance measures into all of a financial institution's business units,
what is key is not so much that VaR is univocally determined, but rather that homogeneous criteria are used for all of the bank's risk taking units. In this way, even if the
risk – meaning the maximum potential loss – should, *ex post,* turn out to be over- or
underestimated, this over- or under-estimation will have uniformly concerned all business units, and will therefore not have generated any bias in strategic capital allocation
decisions.

9.4.5   VaR models amplify market instability

If all financial institutions trading in the financial markets adopt a VaR model, in conjunction with any market shock and consequent increase in volatility, the traders from these
institutions will be likely to all receive the same operational signal. Take the example
illustrated in section 9.3, relating to the VaR limit on a government securities portfolio:
when σ increases, the maximum exposure (expressed in terms of market value) which
is compatible with the limit will shrink, requiring the unwinding, or at least a reduction,
of the position. If all banks behave in the same way, generalized sales will heighten the
market downtrend, turning a slump into an actual crash.

In reality, this criticism, which is often raised by the specialized financial press, suffers
from two main limitations. First of all, this argument is based on the assumption that
VaR models are all the same, while we know that they differ in many respects (market
factor identification, volatility and correlation estimation criteria, hypotheses concerning
the distribution of market return factors, confidence level, etc), and therefore generate
different risk measures.

In any case, it is true that, in the presence of market crises, traders from the different
financial institutions tend to adopt uniform behaviors (which, in turn, amplify crises). This
trend, however, does not stem from the development and use of VaR models, but rather
from human nature and from how financial markets work.

---

[9] See Beder (1995), Drudi, Generale and Majnoni (1996), Marshall and Siegel (1996), and Jordan and Mackay
(1996). As was noted by Beder, "...VAR calculations differ significantly for the same portfolio. VARs are
extremely dependent on parameters, data, assumptions and methodology...Variances in the VAR statistic ranged
as much as 14 times for the same portfolio, depending on the type of VAR calculation and the time horizon".
On the other hand, the same discrepancy of results was noticed by the Basel Committee during an experiment
in which some of the major international banks provided their results – in terms of capital at risk – for the
same virtual portfolio.

9.4.6   VaR measures "come too late, when damage has already been done"

One last criticism towards VaR measures concerns the delay with which they reflect any market shocks, and their consequent ineffectiveness in preventing losses. This criticism, however technically correct, is also affected by a misunderstanding of the real purposes of a VaR measure, and can be rejected based upon multiple arguments.

First of all, it should be understood that the "delay" mainly comes from the fact that VaR models are based upon estimated historical volatility to predict future volatility: from this point of view, if VaR models were fed with more sophisticated predictions (for instance, based upon the volatility implied in option prices), risk measures capable of anticipating any market crisis phenomena could be obtained. However, this result would depend on the quality of the prediction used, and would not be guaranteed in any way.

Also, there are estimation techniques based upon historical data which are nevertheless sufficiently responsive to more recent market conditions (take the example of exponentially weighted moving averages, when lambda is set at a sufficiently low value), and therefore capable of promptly reflecting market shocks.

Moreover, regardless of the ability of VaR models to reflect and rapidly "incorporate" any crisis episodes, we should consider two aspects. First, the inability to anticipate extreme market changes is a limitation which is inherent in any prediction technique. Second, as has already been highlighted above, the ultimate purpose of a VaR model is not to anticipate possible crashes by incorporating extreme events, but rather to uniformly and consistently generate risk measures based upon "normal" conditions of the different security markets for a bank's different business units.

9.5   TWO REAL PROBLEMS OF VAR MODELS

If the criticisms illustrated above are mostly the consequence of a misunderstanding of the real objectives of VaR models, it is also true that these models suffer from some considerable limitations, which have encouraged the development of alternative risk measures. Below, we are presenting the two main ones (which are closely connected with each other, as will be explained below).

9.5.1   The Size of Losses

As was illustrated in the previous chapters, VaR is a risk measure whose purpose is to answer this question:

What is the maximum loss which could be incurred within a given time horizon, except for a small percentage, for instance 1%, of worst cases?

A position's or portfolio's VaR is therefore a probabilistic measure which takes different values at different confidence levels. If the confidence level is defined as c and the loss is defined as L, we will have:

$$Pr(L > VaR) = 1 - c \qquad (9.6)$$

What really matters is therefore the *probability* that the actual loss will be in excess of VaR. If this happens, the model will provide no information about the size of this excess loss.

This deficiency may be very significant. Take the example of two stock portfolios, H and K, characterized by the same market value (1 million euros) and the same daily VaR at a 99 % confidence level (50,000 euros). Assume that VaR was estimated by means of a (historical or Monte Carlo) simulation approach using a (historical or simulated) sample of 500 observations.

Table 9.5 reports the ten most significant losses recorded by the two portfolios – ranked from the highest to the lowest one. It can be noted that – VaR being equal – the two portfolios actually show significant differences in terms of risk. Indeed, the largest loss for portfolio H is 150,000 euros, exceeding VaR by 200 %. Conversely, the maximum loss for portfolio K is 60,000 euros, exceeding VaR only by 20 %. Likewise, the expected value of the excess losses is 100,000 euros for portfolio H: this mean that the expected loss in excess of VaR ("expected excess loss") is 50,000, i.e., equal to VaR itself; vice versa, the expected excess loss is 5,000 euros (55, 000−50, 000), i.e., 10 % of VaR, for portfolio K.

Table 9.5 Example of losses relating to two stock portfolios

Losses (ranked starting from the worst one)		Portfolio H	Portfolio K
1		150,000	60,000
2		120,000	56,000
3		100,000	55,000
4		70,000	53,000
5		60,000	51,000
6		50,000	50,000
7		48,000	45,000
8		45,000	40,000
9		42,000	35,000
10		40,000	30,000
VaR(99 %)	$VaR_{99\%}$	50,000	50,000
Maximum Loss	L_{max}	150,000	60,000
Maximum Excess Loss	$L_{max} - VaR_{99\%}$	100,000	10,000
Maximum Excess Loss/VaR		200 %	20 %
Expected Excess Loss	$E\ (L\text{-}VaR_{99\%}\ |L > VaR_{99\%})$	50,000	5,000
Expected Excess Loss/VaR		100 %	10 %

9.5.2   Non-subadditivity

A second major limitation of VaR measures is non-compliance with one of the essential properties of a consistent risk measure,[10] i.e., subadditivity.

This term refers to the fact that the risk of a portfolio consisting of multiple positions must not be higher than the sum of the risks of the individual positions.

For instance, if a portfolio consisting of two positions, X and Y, is considered, a risk measure $F(.)$ is subadditive if the following condition is always met:

$$F(X + Y) \leq F(X) + F(Y) \tag{9.7}$$

This property depends on the fact that any portfolio benefits, to a greater or lesser degree, from a diversification effect related to the fact that there is an imperfect correlation among the different market factors.

This property must be true not only when multiple positions are "assembled", but also when the joint effect of multiple market factors upon a certain asset in the portfolio is considered. So, for instance, the risk relating to a foreign currency denominated bond can be "mapped" into an equivalent portfolio consisting of two components: a foreign currency deposit and an exchange rate risk-free foreign bond; if the two factors (exchange rate and foreign interest rate curve) are not perfectly correlated, the total risk will be lower than the sum of the risks of the individual components.

In the previous chapters, we encountered several examples in which application of VaR gave rise to results in compliance with the subadditivity principle. However, it is possible to construct examples showing that this property, however intuitive, may not be guaranteed by VaR. In other words, it may be that:

$$VaR(X + Y) > VaR(X) + VaR(Y) \tag{9.8}$$

This happens typically when the joint distribution of market factors is characterized by fat tails, and is therefore different from the multivariate normal.[11] Indeed, this phenomenon occurs more frequently in the case of credit risk than in the case of market risks.

Take the example of two securities, A and B, whose future value probability distribution is represented in Table 9.6, panel (a). For both, the value in one year's time could be 100 euros in 95 % of cases, 90 euros in 4 % of cases, 70 euros in 1 % of cases. There follows an expected value (probability weighted average) of 99.3 euros. For the sake of simplicity, let us assume that, today, the current value of these securities (panel b) is exactly 99.3 euros (the example would remain valid anyway, even if the current value were different). Based upon the difference between the possible future values and the current value, panel (c) shows the distribution of possible future value changes. In panel

---

[10] Here, consistent risk measure means a risk measure complying with some essential axioms. These axioms are translation invariance (adding an amount of cash to the portfolio will reduce the risk by the same amount), positive homogeneity of degree one (if the size of each position is doubled, the portfolio risk will also be doubled), monotonicity (if the losses on portfolio A are greater than those on portfolio B in every possible future scenario, then the risk of portfolio A must be greater than that of portfolio B), and subadditivity. For more details, see Artzner et al. (1993).

[11] See Artzner, Delbaen, Eber and Heath (1999).

Table 9.6 Distribution of the future values of two securities

	Security A	Security B
(a) Distribution of future values		
Probability	MV	MV
1 %	70	70
4 %	90	90
95 %	100	100
E(MV)	99.3	99.3
(b) Current value		
	V	V
Value	99.3	99.3
(c) Future value changes		
Probability	ΔV	ΔV
1 %	−29.3	−29.3
4 %	−9.3	−9.3
95 %	0.7	0.7
(d) Synthetic measures		
E(ΔV)	0.0	0.0
VaR at 99 %	9.3	9.3

(d), the mean and VaR at 99 % (the value "isolating" one per cent of worst cases) of this distribution are displayed. The latter value is 9.3 euros for each of the two securities.

Now, let us assume that the two securities are held by the same investor within a single portfolio. Let us also assume that they are independent, i.e., that the possible future values of A are uncorrelated to those of B. This lack of correlation must result in a risk diversification effect: in other words, a consistent (and, in particular, subadditive) risk measure must lead to a lower value for the portfolio than the sum of the risks of the two securities taken separately. We would therefore expect the VaR of the portfolio comprising A and B to be lower than 18.6 (9.3 plus 9.3) euros.

Table 9.7 provides the joint probability distribution of the value changes in A and B (first row and first column) and in the sum portfolio containing them both – under an independence hypothesis. For instance, as both securities could experience a decrease in value of 29.3 euros in 1 % of cases, the Table shows that the sum portfolio would experience a decrease in value of 58.6 (29.3 plus 29.3) in 0.01 % (1 % by 1 %) of cases.

Table 9.7 Distribution of the future values of the portfolio comprising the two securities: double-entry table

		Security B		
		−29.3	−9.3	0.7
		1%	4%	95%
Security A	−29.3	−58.6	−38.6	−28.6
	1%	0.01%	0.04%	0.95%
	−9.3	−38.6	−18.6	−8.6
	4%	0.04%	0.16%	3.80%
	0.7	−28.6	−8.6	1.4
	95%	0.95%	3.80%	90.25%

Table 9.8 Distribution of the future values of the portfolio comprising the two securities: re-ranked table

Probability	Cumulative probability	Value
0.01%	0.01%	−58.6
0.08%	0.09%	−38.6
1.90%	1.99%	−28.6
0.16%	2.15%	−18.6
7.60%	9.75%	−8.6
90.25%	100.00%	1.4
VaR at 99%		28.6

Table 9.8 re-ranks the nine values of the possible changes in the sum portfolio, starting from the worst one (note that events characterized by the same portfolio market value were aggregated on a single row).

The row in grey highlights the first percentile, i.e., the value leaving (at least) 1% of worst cases behind it. This value is VaR at 99%, and is equal to a loss of 28.6 euros, which is considerably higher than the sum of the individual positions' VaRs for an equal confidence level. It was therefore shown that:

$$VaR(A + B) > VaR(A) + VaR(B)$$

This result is mainly due to the fact that the individual positions' VaRs underestimate their risk by totally disregarding the size of excess losses.

So, it is possible that VaR may not meet the subadditivity requirement. However, this problem never occurs if VaR is calculated according to the parametric approach, assuming that portfolio value changes are described by a normal distribution. As a matter of fact, in this case, VaR is simply a multiple α (a function of the desired confidence level) of the standard deviation. From the formula to calculate the variance of a two-security portfolio

$$\sigma_{A+B}^2 = \sigma_A^2 + 2\rho\sigma_A\sigma_B + \sigma_B^2$$

(with $\rho \leq 1$), it therefore follows that:

$$\sigma_{A+B} \leq \sigma_A + \sigma_B$$
$$\alpha\sigma_{A+B} \leq \alpha\sigma_A + \alpha\sigma_B$$
$$VaR_{A+B} \leq VaR_A + VaR_B$$

which ensures subadditivity.

However, when the empirical distribution of value changes takes a form which is clearly dissimilar to the normal (as in the example in Table 9.6), it is not possible to adopt the parametric approach just because it would ensure subadditivity. On the contrary, different distributions (for instance, historical distribution) need to be used, which results in VaR being exposed to a risk of non-subadditivity.

9.6   AN ALTERNATIVE RISK MEASURE: EXPECTED SHORTFALL (ES)

The two problems of VaR as described above (non-consideration of the size of excess losses and violation of subadditivity) can be overcome by having recourse to an alternative risk measure, referred to as expected shortfall (ES).[12] ES can be defined as the *expected value of all losses in excess of VaR*.

Hence:

$$ES = E[-(\Delta MV - E(\Delta MV))|-(\Delta MV - E(\Delta MV)) > VaR] \qquad (9.9)$$

where "|", as usual, means "such that", and market value changes (ΔMV) were changed in sign because they are losses (negative values), and we are interested in their absolute value.

This is a conditional average which does not consider all possible values of ΔMV, but only those whose distance from the mean exceeds VaR.

ES can also be written as a function of future values (MV), rather than of their changes ΔMV:[13]

$$ES = E[-(MV - E(MV))|-(MV - E(MV)) > VaR] \qquad (9.10)$$

Alternatively, if we assume (as we generally did in the previous chapters) that the expected value of market value changes ($E(\Delta MV)$) is zero, then ES will be simplified, and can be written as

$$ES = E[-\Delta MV|-\Delta MV > VaR] \qquad (9.11)$$

---

[12] Other names of this same measures are average shortfall (AS), conditional VaR (CVaR), or extreme value at risk (EVaR).

[13] In practice, it is sufficient to add and subtract the current portfolio value within the two round brackets.

Note that this measure, like VaR, is characterized by a given confidence level and a given time horizon.

To understand the meaning and construction logic of Expected Shortfall, it is useful to go back to Table 9.5. As the reader may remember, for each of the two portfolios represented therein, there were five possible scenarios (the first five rows in the Table) in which the loss was in excess of VaR. Expected Shortfall is but the mean of these five losses (value changes ΔVM changed in sign). It will therefore be 100,000 euros for portfolio H, and 55,000 euros for portfolio K. This is a one-year ES, with a 99 % confidence level, as the probability distribution of value changes in Table 9.5 refers to a one-year time horizon, and the VaR used as the "threshold" to select the scenarios on which the conditional average was to be calculated adopted exactly a 99 % confidence level.

If, conversely, we take the two securities A and B in Table 9.6, we can immediately see that, for each of them, one-year ES at a 99 % confidence level is 29.3 euros. Indeed, there is only one excess loss value, which therefore coincides with the conditional average. Note that, for the sum portfolio comprising A and B, the value of ES is 40.8 euros: this is the (probability weighted) average of the loss values (58.6 and 38.6) as shown in the first two rows in Table 9.8 i.e., of all and only the portfolio's excess losses (28.6). In detail:

$$ES_{99\%} = 58.6 \cdot \frac{0.01\%}{0.09\%} + 38.6 \cdot \frac{0.08\%}{0.09\%} \cong 40.8$$

Unlike the portfolio VaR (which is higher than the sum of the VaRs for the two individual securities), the portfolio *ES* meets the subadditivity condition. It can be demonstrated that this is not by accident, but that Expected Shortfall ensures compliance with this property, and is a consistent risk measure.

For this reason, in more recent years, numerous researchers and several financial institutions have paid more attention to ES as a risk indicator.

From an economic point of view, while VaR represents the economic capital which needs to be paid into a bank to limit its probability of bankruptcy to 1-c (where c is the VaR's confidence level), some interesting economic meanings can be attached also to ES. More specifically, the *difference* between ES and VaR can be seen as:

- the expected cost that the regulatory authorities should incur to bail out a bank if its capital (set equal to VaR) were not enough;
- the expected payment that a risk neutral insurer would have to face, if the bank had insured itself against the risk of excess losses.

SELECTED QUESTIONS AND EXERCISES

1. A bank holds two positions, in stocks and T-bonds respectively. The stock portfolio is currently worth 80,000 euros and has an average beta of 95 %; the T-bonds have a market value of 100,000 euros and a modified duration of 7 years. The volatility of percent changes in the stock-market index is estimated at 15 %; the volatility of absolute changes in the yield to maturity of 7-year Treasury bonds is estimated at 2 %. Based on a 99 % VaR, which of the two portfolios is currently riskier? By how much? How would the result change if the bank were to adopt a 95 % VaR? And what would happen if, given a 99 % VaR, the equity portfolio volatility were to change from 15 %

to 25%? [To solve this exercise, recall that $N^{-1}(99\%) \cong 2.33$ and $N^{-1}(95\%) \cong 1.64$, where $N^{-1}(.)$ is the inverse of the normal cumulative density function]

2. The fixed-income desk of Bank Alpha has been assigned a VaR limit (computed at a 99% confidence level) of 10 million euros. Currently, the market value and modified duration of the portfolio are 100 million euros and 3 years. The yield curve is assumed to be flat and the volatility of absolute shifts in rates is 1.1%. First, check if the desk is exceeding the VaR limit, and if so by how much. Then, outline two alternative strategies to align the actual VaR with the VaR limit (either increasing or decreasing risk), involving: (i) a sale/purchase of bonds; (ii) a bond trade to change duration, while leaving the portfolio market value unchanged. Finally, suppose markets experience a shock, and volatility increases to 3%: how could the bank's portfolio be recalibrated to comply with the VaR limit?

3. The VaR of a portfolio made of two positions is 50 million euros. In which of the following cases would parametric VaR increase because one of the two positions has been sold?

(A) If the two positions have opposite signs (short and long) and are exposed to negatively-correlated market factors.
(B) If the two market factors, to which the two positions are exposed, are totally independent.
(C) If the two positions have the same sign (both long or short) and are exposed to negatively-correlated market factors.
(D) Parametric VaR never increases, because it guarantees subadditivity.

4. Which of the following statements are true?

"From an economic perspective, expected shortfall can be interpreted as ..."

(I.) "..VaR, plus the expected cost that the regulatory authorities would have to sustain in order to save the bank (paying for its losses) if its capital were not enough to cover them".
(II.) "...the dividend the bank would have to pay to its shareholders in order to make it attractive for them to pay in a capital equal to VaR.";
(III.) "...VaR, plus the (risk neutral) cost a bank would face if it wanted to insure itself against losses larger than VaR.";
(IV.) "...VaR with a 100% confidence level".

(A) I and IV;
(B) II and IV;
(C) I only;
(D) I, III and IV.

5. Based on the following probability distribution of portfolio losses, and using a confidence level of 95%, compute VaR (defined as the maximum loss L, such that the probability of experiencing losses greater than L is 5%) and expected shortfall.

Probability	Losses, ordered from the worst (euro mln)
0.50 %	1000
0.30 %	100
1 %	80
1.60 %	70
0.80 %	65
0.80 %	60
1 %	50
1.30 %	30
0.40 %	20
92.30 %	0

Also, highlight how the VaR and expected shortfall (still with a 95 % confidence) would change if the maximum loss, rather than 1 billion euros (as stated in the Table) were 500 million euros.

Appendix 9A
Extreme Value Theory

In the previous Chapters, the main portfolio VaR estimation approaches were analyzed. However, an approach which has become fairly popular over the past few years, especially in the academic literature, was neglected: the Extreme Value Theory (EVT) approach, which was developed in the nineties by such authors as Longin, Embrechts, Danielsson and de Vries.[14] It assumes that a risk manager's interest is focused on the extreme values of the distribution of future values, and, in particular, on heavy losses. Therefore, the utmost care needs to be used in order to accurately estimate the form of the distribution tails; to this end, the statistical extreme value theory can provide a valuable methodological support.

Of course, the distribution of extreme tails is not known *a priori*. However, EVT states that, in the case of a very large sample, it converges towards a limit distribution characterized by a peculiar functional form: in particular, a relatively simple distribution, known as generalized Pareto distribution. It is therefore possible to "lean on" this distribution to analytically find a reasonable approximation of the VaR associated with the desired confidence level.

As a rule, EVT is based upon the hypothesis that risk factor returns are *i.i.d.*, i.e., independent and identically distributed. This hypothesis – as was noted in Chapter 6 – is often violated in the short term, since variance tends to vary over time. However, it is precisely with reference to short time horizons that EVT is particularly useful, because the problem of "fat tails" and of the consequent non-normality of return distribution is particularly critical. To get out of this deadlock, and to be able to adopt the hypothesis of *i.i.d.* returns, EVT considers standardised returns, z_t, which are obtained by dividing returns r_t by their estimated volatility:

$$(A.1) z_t = \frac{r_t}{\sigma_t} \sim i.i.d \qquad (9A.1)$$

For standardised returns, the constant and independent distribution hypothesis is much more reasonable than for "raw" returns. It is therefore possible to apply the extreme value theory to standardised returns, and then combine EVT with the variance estimation models analysed in Chapter 6 to obtain VaR measures.

As stated above, EVT focuses on an analysis of the tails. Assuming that the standardised return distribution is as shown in Figure 9.A.1, EVT will therefore analyse a specific part of it, for instance the grey tail associated with standardised return values higher than a certain threshold u.[15]

The cumulative probability density function $F_u(.)$ associated with the tail (which expresses the probability of observing a value of z equal to or lower than a certain level $u + x$, that is conditional upon the fact that observed values z are in any case higher

---

[14] The major papers to which this approach can be traced back are Longin (1994), Embrechts, Kluppelberg and Milkosch (1997), and Danielsson and de Vries (1996, 1997).
[15] Similarly, we could analyse lower values than a certain threshold – u, corresponding to the left tail. In Figure 9A.1 we chose to focus on the right tail because this makes notation simpler.

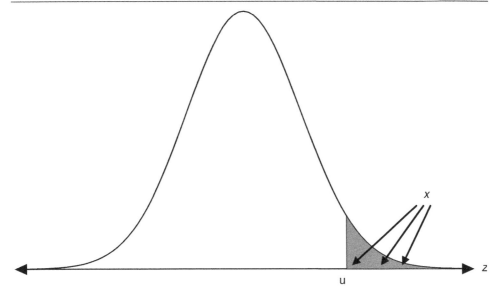

Figure 9A.1   Example of Standardised Return Distribution

than u) can be written as:

$$F_u(x) = \Pr\{z \leq u + x | z > u\}$$ (9A.2)

which, in practice, is equivalent to

$$F_u(x) = \frac{F(x + u) - F(u)}{1 - F(u)}$$ (9A.3)

where F(.) is the cumulative probability density function of standardized returns z.

The form of $F_u(x)$ will crucially depend upon the selected threshold value u. The key result of EVT states that, as the threshold value u increases, for almost all known distributions, $F_u(x)$ will converge to the generalized Pareto distribution, $G(x; \xi, \beta)$, where:

$$G(x; \xi, \beta) = \begin{cases} 1 - (1 + \xi x / \beta) & if \quad \xi \neq 0 \\ 1 - e^{-x/\beta} & if \quad \xi = 0 \end{cases}$$ (9A.4)

with $\beta > 0$ and $\begin{cases} x \geq 0 & if \quad \xi \geq 0 \\ 0 \leq x \leq -\beta/\xi & if \quad \xi < 0 \end{cases}$

ξ represents the key parameter defining the tail and taking a positive value for distributions characterized by fat tails, i.e., for those which are more interesting for risk management purposes. Conversely, it takes a value of zero in the case of a normal distribution.

The generalized Pareto distribution can therefore be used to estimate the cumulative density function for observations beyond the threshold u, i.e., for extreme (positive, but also negative) returns in a distribution's right or left tail. On the other hand, these estimates can be achieved in a closed form, i.e., without having recourse to numerical optimization procedures, and are therefore relatively simple to calculate.

EVT therefore allows one to focus the attention on the tails. Moreover, note that it enables analyzing each of the two tails separately, without necessarily having recourse to the symmetry hypothesis, which is often unrealistic in finance.

Notwithstanding these advantages, EVT also has a major limitation, i.e., the selection of the threshold u. The latter must be made considering a trade-off between the validity of the EVT itself and the uncertainty (variance) of estimates. Indeed, in order for the tail distribution to be approximated by a generalised Pareto distribution, u must be sufficiently high (if, conversely, u is set at too low a level, there is a risk that the key result of the EVT will no longer hold). However, if the value of u is too high, only few empirical observations will be located in the extreme tail, and this will make the estimation of parameter ξ extremely complex (random). For samples of approximately 1,000 daily observations (approximately 4–5 years of data), a general rule is to set the threshold at such a value as to retain some 5 % of observations, i.e., approximately 50 data which can be used to estimate ξ, on the tail. The threshold u will therefore be the 95th percentile of sample data.

Part III
Credit Risk

INTRODUCTION TO PART III

In the last decade of the 20th century, nearly all the major international banks invested heavily in human and technological resources in order to reorganize their methods of assessing and managing credit risk. This revolutionary process was by no means limited to a mere technical innovation associated with risk measurement methods, but affected one of the most traditional, established areas of banking, namely credit. It involved aspects such as counterparty selection and loan pricing; the degree of independence granted to the bank's risk-taking units; the criteria used to set business objectives and performance targets; methods of measuring results and establishing incentives; and the logic behind the composition of credit portfolios.

This reorganization process was based on the development of credit risk measurement models that appropriately quantify the degree of risk associated with different credit exposures, and enable banks to use their overall risk-taking capacity more efficiently. These models, which operate according to the same logic as market-risk VaR models seen in Part II of this book, are designed to estimate the riskiness of a specific credit exposure (such as a loan, bond or OTC derivative) or of a whole exposure portfolio, and consequently the amount of economic capital it absorbs.

After a brief explanation of what is meant by "credit risk", this introduction will illustrate the main components of this type of risk, in order to clarify the logic used in the later chapters, to deal with them individually.

OUR DEFINITION OF CREDIT RISK

The term "credit risk" refers to *the possibility that an unexpected change in a counterparty's creditworthiness may generate a corresponding unexpected change in the market value of the associated credit exposure.*

This simple definition incorporates three concepts, which are by no means obvious or universally accepted, and need to be explained in some detail.

1. *Default risk and migration risk* – First of all, credit risk is not limited to the possibility of the counterparty's default: even a mere deterioration in its creditworthiness constitutes a manifestation of credit risk. Consider a fixed-interest loan, for example: if the borrower's creditworthiness deteriorates, the market value of the loan, determined by the present value of the associated cash flows, will obviously be reduced. The reason is that the present value of future flows should be determined using a discount rate which, in addition to the risk-free rate for the corresponding maturity, also incorporates a spread (risk premium) that reflects the likelihood of the borrower's default. A deterioration in creditworthiness increases that probability, and thus generates automatically a corresponding increase in the spread and a reduction in present value. This would also apply to a variable-rate loan in which the spread paid by the borrower over the market rate, is set in advance and not modifiable. In general, the greater the variation in spread and the greater the residual life of the debt, the greater the reduction in the value of a credit exposure resulting from a deterioration in the borrower's credit rating.

To sum up, credit risk therefore comprises two different cases: the risk of default and the risk of migration. The first represents the risk of loss resulting from the borrower's actual insolvency (whereby payments are interrupted), while the second represents the risk of loss resulting from a mere deterioration in its credit rating.

According to this logic, credit risk measurement and management should be based not on a simple binomial distribution of the possible events ("default" versus "non-default"), but rather on a discrete or continuous distribution, in which default merely represents the extreme event, next to other events in which the borrower remains solvent, but the probability of a future default gradually increases. This is the only way to define both risk categories adequately.[1]

2. *Risk as an unexpected event* – A second concept implicit in the original definition is that in order to be considered as a risk, the variation in the counterparty's credit rating must be unexpected. If a bank has issued a loan knowing that the counterparty will suffer a future deterioration in quality (profitability, solvency, liquidity, etc.), that deterioration will have been suitably evaluated and factored into the decision to grant the loan and the pricing process (that is, the choice of the interest rate applied). In fact, expected developments in the borrower's economic/financial status are always taken into due consideration when the probability of default and the associated interest rate are determined. The *real risk* is represented by the possibility that those evaluations could later prove incorrect, that is, that a deterioration in the counterparty *unforeseen* by the lender occurs. In this respect, proper risk only relates to events which, though foreseeable, are unexpected.

3. *Credit exposure* – A third point to be considered relates to the concept of credit exposure. Credit risk is by no means limited to the "classic" forms of credit granted by a bank (on-balance-sheet loans and securities), but also includes off-balance-sheet operations[2] such as guarantees, derivative contracts traded over the counter (for which substitution risk or pre-settlement risk is incurred[3]), and transactions in securities, foreign currencies or derivatives pending final settlement (settlement risk).[4]

Finally, it should be noted that our initial definition refers to the market value of credit exposures. This poses two problems.

First of all, many credit exposures are recorded into financial institution's books at historical value, not at market value. However, correct measurement of credit risk and its effects would require valuations to be based on the economic value of the exposure, namely on the price that an arms-length purchaser (or a secondary market, if available) would attribute to the exposure if it were sold by the bank.

---

[1] Some banks still decide whether or not to grant a loan based on a binomial distribution: if the counterparty is considered reliable, the probability of future default is not quantified and the loan is issued; if it is considered unreliable, the loan is simply not granted. Reliable counterparties are all considered equal, and "not liable to become insolvent" in the period corresponding to the maturity of the loan. The probability of default is not explicitly quantified, although it is often evaluated implicitly, and this explains why different spreads are applied to different customers.

[2] The supervisory authorities require both on- and off-balance-sheet exposures to be covered by capital when the capital requirements relating to credit risk are computed (see Part V).

[3] OTC derivatives actually entail two forms of credit risk: pre-settlement risk (the risk that a counterparty will default prior to the derivative instrument's final settlement on expiry, while the value of the derivative is be positive); settlement risk (arising when the final settlement of the contract entails a time gap between the two parties' settlements, so that one of the two may not fulfil its obligations). As indicated in the text, the latter also applies to any securities/currency transaction for which the final settlement has not yet been completed. Further details are provided in Chapter 16.

[4] Credit risk also includes the risk of changes in bond prices, which the Basel Committee on Banking Supervision (see Part V) classifies as "specific risk" within market risks (see Chapter 19). However, if movements in bond prices arise from factors specific to individual issuers, which are affecting their creditworthiness, the associated risk should rather be classified as a credit risk.

Secondly, the majority of the credit exposures of a financial institution consist of illiquid assets, for which no developed secondary market exists; the market value can therefore only be estimated on the basis of an internal asset-pricing model.

EXPECTED AND UNEXPECTED LOSS

In the case of credit risk, it is useful to make a distinction between expected and unexpected loss. They will be discussed separately in the following sections.

(a) Expected loss (EL)

This is the mean value of the probability distribution of future losses. Many credit risk management studies in the past have focused mainly on this component however, being expected, it does not strictly represent a risk. In practice, the expected loss is estimated *ex ante* by the lender, which hedges its risk by adding a suitable spread to the interest rate charged on the loan: thus if the borrower defaults should take place exactly as expected, the lender would obtain exactly the net return anticipated at issuance.

Estimating the expected loss on a credit exposure requires three parameters to be estimated:

  (i) the expected value of the exposure in the event of default (*EAD – exposure at default*), a random variable represented by the current exposure plus the possible variation in the size of the loan which may take from now to the date of possible default;
 (ii) the probability that the borrower will default (*PD*);
(iii) the expected loss rate in the event of default (*LGD – loss given default*), namely the percentage of exposure that the bank forecasts that it will be unable to recover (e.g. by seizing collateral, calling in guarantees or proving the debt in bankruptcy); it is equal to one minus the expected recovery rate (*RR*) on the exposure.

To sum up:

$$EL = \overline{EAD} \cdot PD \cdot \overline{LGD} \tag{1}$$

The last two components, PD and LGD, will be analyzed in the next few chapters. As regards exposure at default (EAD), it is sufficient to observe that it represents a stochastic variable whose volatility depends on the type of facility granted to the borrower. In the case of a credit line, for example, the bank undertakes to lend a certain amount of funds to the customer, which chooses which portion to use and when. This means that the true size of the actual loan may vary over time due to decisions external to the bank. Similarly, in the case of a derivative traded on an over-the-counter market (OTC) where the bank is exposed to the risk of default by the counterparty, the value of the contract is uncertain, and depends on the shifts in one or more market factors.[5]

However, the EAD is often deterministic and easily quantifiable. For example, many bank loans entail a non-stochastic exposure, following a pre-determined repayment plan of the capital and interest (so that the customer has no discretion as to the amount of the

---

[5] The subject of credit exposure associated with a position in OTC derivatives is dealt with in Chapter 15.

loan that he/she will be using in the future). The same applies to bonds, where cash flows are wholly defined at the time of issue.

Therefore, the credit exposure may have a certain or uncertain value. If it is uncertain, the borrower benefits from an option which enables it to vary the size of the loan (although within certain limits). As companies having financial difficulties tend to use their loan facilities up to the maximum amount, there is a risk that the exposure will increase close to the default. This creates an "exposure risk", namely the risk that exposure at default will be greater than the amount originally expected.[6]

In general, estimating the *EAD* requires to measure the drawn portion (DP) and the undrawn portion (UP) of the loan. A credit conversion factor (CCF) must also be estimated, which represents the percentage of the undrawn portion that could be used by the borrower close to the time of default.[7] Analytically:

$$EAD = DP + UP \cdot CCF \tag{2}$$

Let us assume, for example, that a 1 million euro credit line has been granted, with a drawn portion (DP) of € 600,000 and a CCF of 60 %. In this case:

$$EAD = 600.000 + 400.000 \cdot 60\% = 840.000$$

The fact that part of the undrawn portion is included in the EAD will inevitably lead the lender to estimate a greater expected loss, and require a higher price for the loan. However, this price increase (which compensates for the risk implicit in the undrawn portion) need not necessarily be transferred entirely to the spread applied to the drawn portion of the loan. Such a practice would cause the bank to price itself out of the market, because it would be applying very high spreads, especially on loans to the best companies, which (as documented by Asarnow & Marker, 1995) often only use a modest portion of the total loan (and therefore present a high ratio between UP and DP).

In practice, the higher expected loss connected with the undrawn portion is usually covered by a commission proportional to the UP. This commission, usually known as the "back-end fee" or "commitment fee", is very common in the UK and US markets. This allows a more rational pricing of the expected loss, since the costs of the expected loss are correctly allocated to the drawn portion (through the spread in the interest rate) and to the undrawn portion (through the commission on the bank's "commitment to lend", which represents the value of the implied option enjoyed by the borrower). In some countries, however, especially in continental Europe, the commitment fee is little used, and banks prefer to minimise their exposure risk by issuing revokable loans (which can be called in by the bank without notice).

(b) Unexpected loss (UL)

The true credit risk (ie. the risk that the loss will prove greater than originally estimated) is associated with unexpected loss. In general terms, this can be defined as the variability of the loss around its mean value, i.e. around the EL.

---

[6] As we shall see, many credit risk measurement models devote relatively little attention to exposure risk, focusing mainly on default risk and recovery risk.

[7] An empirical analysis of the US market shows that the CCF data fall within a range of approx. 40 % to 75 % See Asarnow and Marker (1995).

As will be seen in later Chapters, the distinction between expected and unexpected loss is important when dealing with a diversified portfolio of exposures. The expected loss on such a portfolio is simply equal to the sum of the expected losses on the individual loans in it, whereas the volatility of the total portfolio loss is generally lower than the sum of the volatilities of the losses on individual loans, and much more so if the correlation between individual loans is low. In other words, while expected loss cannot be reduced by diversifying the portfolio (e.g. across industries or geographical areas), unexpected loss (i.e. the volatility of losses around the mean) can be reduced through a suitable portfolio strategy, distributing the risk across industries, countries, etc. This means that an effective loan portfolio diversification policy, while leaving total expected returns unchanged, can significantly reduce total credit risk.

The distinction between expected and unexpected loss is also particularly significant from an economic standpoint. On the one hand, the expected loss on a loan portfolio should give rise to provisions, recorded as a cost in the profit and loss account and generating a reserve in the bank's balance sheet.[8] On the other hand, the unexpected loss should be covered by the bank's capital because, as the shareholders benefit from any results above expectations (when actual losses are lower than anticipated), they also must cover higher than expected losses with their own funds.

THE MAIN TYPES OF CREDIT RISK

Credit risk comprises the following main risks:

- *default risk*: this is the risk connected with a default by the counterparty, which declares bankruptcy, goes into liquidation or otherwise defaults on the loan; such a risk leads to a loss equal to the product of the exposure at default (EAD) and loss given default (LGD);
- *migration risk*: as seen above, this is the risk connected with a deterioration in the counterparty's creditworthiness; it is also known as the "downgrading risk" when the borrower has a public credit rating and might be downgraded by the organisation (e.g. rating agency) that issued it;
- *spread risk*: this is the risk associated with a rise in the spreads required of borrowers (e.g. bond issuers) by the market; in the event of increased risk aversion by investors, the spread associated with a given probability of default (and therefore a given rating class) may increase[9]; in such a case the market value of the securities declines, without any reduction in the issuer's credit rating;
- *recovery risk*: indicates the risk that the recovery rate actually recorded after the liquidation of the insolvent counterparty's assets will be less than the amount originally estimated, because the liquidation value was lower than estimated or simply because the recovery process took longer than expected;

---

[8] However, such reasoning, which is correct from the economic standpoint, is unfortunately not fully supported by the international accounting standards. The IFRS (International Financial Reporting Standards) state that loan loss reserves can only be created to cover specific obligations deriving from past events, and not to cover "generic" future losses.

[9] In particular, if the market is "frightened" by political events, Acts of God or major financial crashes, the spread differential between the best-quality and worst-quality bonds may increase. This phenomenon is known as "flight to quality".

– *pre-settlement or substitution risk*: indicates the risk that the bank's counterparty in an OTC (over-the-counter) derivative will become insolvent before the maturity of the contract, thus forcing the bank to "replace" it at new (and potentially less favourable) market conditions;

– *country risk*: indicates the risk that a non-resident counterparty will be unable to meet its obligations due to events of a political or legislative nature, such as the introduction of foreign exchange constraints, which prevent it from repaying its debt.[10]

This classification based on the drivers underlying the risk (default, deterioration in credit-worthiness, increased risk aversion, reduced recovery rate), and the nature of the exposure (OTC derivatives, non-resident counterparties), will serve as a guideline throughout the next Chapters of this book (see Figure 1).

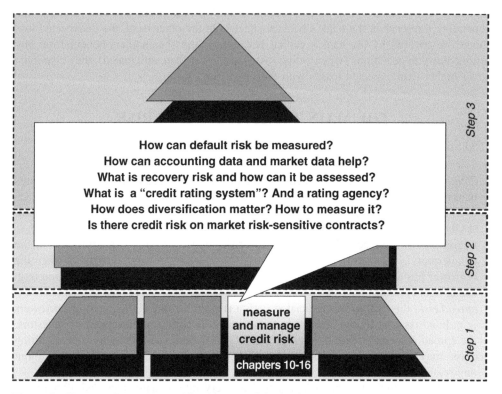

How can default risk be measured?
How can accounting data and market data help?
What is recovery risk and how can it be assessed?
What is a "credit rating system"? And a rating agency?
How does diversification matter? How to measure it?
Is there credit risk on market risk-sensitive contracts?

measure and manage credit risk

chapters 10-16

Step 3

Step 2

Step 1

Figure 1   Key questions addressed by this part of the book

Chapter 10 is devoted to "credit scoring" models designed to estimate the probability of default of a borrower, and will discuss their benefits and limitation, as well as their main technical characteristics. It deals with models which are mainly based on accounting data and comprise linear discriminant analysis, logit and probit models, as well as some more

---

[10] Although it is similar to default risk, this risk is normally considered as a separate category because of the special features associated with its valuation (which requires the analysis of aspects such as the currency reserves of the foreign country, its balance of payments, etc.).

recent techniques (neural networks and genetic algorithms). Models like discriminant analysis, probit and logit are based on a deductive approach designed to identify the economic causes driving default; neural networks and genetic algorithms, instead, follow a purely empirical inductive approach.

Chapter 11 is devoted to models based on capital market data. Unlike credit-scoring models, which are based on accounting data, these models use price, return and volatility data, which can be obtained from the stock and bond markets. The logic of the models, as well as their advantages and limitations, are illustrated with several examples. The first group of models uses the spreads between rates on corporate bonds and risk-free rates; the second group uses share prices (and estimates credit risk through option pricing models like the one originally developed by Black, Merton and Scholes) and includes the model by Robert Merton (1974) and the one developed by KMV Corporation.

Chapter 12 is devoted to the estimation of recovery relates in the event of default. This is becoming increasingly important, especially since the approval of the new Basel Accord on banks' capital (known as "Basel II", see Chapter 20), and has attracted work from many banks and academics. Theoretical schemes are complemented by a survey of the empirical studies produced during the last few years. The chapter ends with an analysis of recovery risk and its possible link with default risk.

Chapter 13 deals with internal rating systems, a subject to which whole books have been devoted. We will just illustrate the main input variables and criteria underlying the rating assignment process, the problems connected with the quantification of the default rates associated with different rating classes (rating quantification), and the methods of evaluating the quality of a rating system (rating validation).

Chapter 14 is devoted to measurement of the unexpected loss on a credit portfolio. This is equivalent to estimating the amount of capital to be held against the portfolio, also referred to as the economic capital associate with it (or absorbed by the credit portfolio). After a short presentation of two preliminary issues (the choice of the most suitable time horizon and confidence level), we will cover the technical characteristics, advantages and limitations of the main models proposed by large international banks, as well as a quick comparison of their strengths and weaknesses. The Chapter ends with a glance at some problems still to be solved by such credit portfolio models.

Chapter 15 examines the applications of credit risk measurement models. In particular, using real-life examples, it shows how credit risk estimates can be used to introduce a risk-adjusted pricing system, to set up risk-adjusted performance measures, to develop a system of limits on the operating units originating loans, based on the actual risk of individual exposures, and finally to optimize the bank's overall portfolio mix.

The last Chapter of this part of the book analyses the problem of estimating the exposure at default of derivative contracts traded on OTC markets. After a brief description of some methods proposed by supervisors, we look at alternative criteria for measuring current and potential exposure, and present some tools used to reduce this component of risk.

Principles for the Assessment of Banks' Management of Credit Risk

A. Establishing an appropriate credit risk environment

1: The board of directors should have responsibility for approving and periodically (at least annually) reviewing the credit risk strategy and significant credit risk policies of the bank. The strategy should reflect the bank's tolerance for risk and the level of profitability the bank expects to achieve for incurring various credit risks.

2: Senior management should have responsibility for implementing the credit risk strategy approved by the board of directors and for developing policies and procedures for identifying, measuring, monitoring and controlling credit risk. Such policies and procedures should address credit risk in all of the bank's activities and at both the individual credit and portfolio levels.

3: Banks should identify and manage credit risk inherent in all products and activities. Banks should ensure that the risks of products and activities new to them are subject to adequate risk management procedures and controls before being introduced or undertaken, and approved in advance by the board of directors or its appropriate committee.

B. Operating under a sound credit granting process

4: Banks must operate within sound, well-defined credit-granting criteria. These criteria should include a clear indication of the bank's target market and a thorough understanding of the borrower or counterparty, as well as the purpose and structure of the credit, and its source of repayment.

5: Banks should establish overall credit limits at the level of individual borrowers and counterparties, and groups of connected counterparties that aggregate in a comparable and meaningful manner different types of exposures, both in the banking and trading book and on and off the balance sheet.

6: Banks should have a clearly-established process in place for approving new credits as well as the amendment, renewal and re-financing of existing credits.

7: All extensions of credit must be made on an arm's-length basis. In particular, credits to related companies and individuals must be authorised on an exception basis, monitored with particular care and other appropriate steps taken to control or mitigate the risks of non-arm's length lending.

C. Maintaining an appropriate credit administration, measurement and monitoring process

8: Banks should have in place a system for the ongoing administration of their various credit risk-bearing portfolios.

9: Banks must have in place a system for monitoring the condition of individual credits, including determining the adequacy of provisions and reserves.

10: Banks are encouraged to develop and utilize an internal risk rating system in managing credit risk. The rating system should be consistent with the nature, size and complexity of a bank's activities.

11: Banks must have information systems and analytical techniques that enable management to measure the credit risk inherent in all on- and off-balance sheet activities.

The management information system should provide adequate information on the composition of the credit portfolio, including identification of any concentrations of risk.

12: Banks must have in place a system for monitoring the overall composition and quality of the credit portfolio.

13: Banks should take into consideration potential future changes in economic conditions when assessing individual credits and their credit portfolios, and should assess their credit risk exposures under stressful conditions.

D. Ensuring adequate controls over credit risk

14: Banks must establish a system of independent, ongoing assessment of the bank's credit risk management processes and the results of such reviews should be communicated directly to the board of directors and senior management.

15: Banks must ensure that the credit-granting function is being managed properly and that credit exposures are within levels consistent with prudential standards and internal limits. Banks should establish and enforce internal controls and other practices to ensure that exceptions to policies, procedures and limits are reported in a timely manner to the appropriate level of management for action.

16: Banks must have a system in place for early remedial action on deteriorating credits, managing problem credits and similar workout situations.

E. The role of supervisors

17: Supervisors should require that banks have an effective system in place to identify, measure, monitor and control credit risk as part of an overall approach to risk management. Supervisors should conduct an independent evaluation of a bank's strategies, policies, procedures and practices related to the granting of credit and the ongoing management of the portfolio. Supervisors should consider setting prudential limits to restrict bank exposures to single borrowers or groups of connected counterparties.

Source: Basel Committee (2000b).

10
Credit-Scoring Models

10.1 INTRODUCTION

Among the most widely used models to forecast a company's default, is a class of statistical models, generally known as "credit-scoring models". These are multivariate models which use the main economic and financial indicators of a company as input, attributing a weight to each of them, that reflects its relative importance in forecasting default. The result is an index of creditworthiness expressed as a numerical score, which indirectly measures the borrower's probability of default.

Although the techniques underlying credit-scoring models were devised in the 1930s by authors such as Fisher (1936) and Durand (1941), the decisive boost to the development and spread of these models came in the 1960s, with studies by Beaver (1967), Altman (1968) and others.

Three categories of credit-scoring models[1] will be presented in this chapter[2]: i) linear discriminant analysis[3]; (ii) regression models (linear, logit and probit); (iii) some recent heuristic inductive models such as neural networks and genetic algorithms. The first two categories are based on a deductive approach designed to explain the economic causes of default, while the third one, as will be seen later, follows a purely empirical inductive approach.

The chapter ends with an examination of the two main methods of using credit-scoring models, and the main limitations and problems which these models have in common.

10.2 LINEAR DISCRIMINANT ANALYSIS

Linear discriminant analysis, which was studied by Fisher as early as 1936, is based on the identification of the variables (typically economic and financial ratios taken from financial statements) which make it possible to "discriminate" better between healthy companies and "abnormal" ones (which can be defined in a variety of ways, e.g., companies which have gone into liquidation or undergone financial restructuring processes, or rather companies whose debt has been classified as doubtful by the banking system).

10.2.1 The discriminant function

Basically, discriminant analysis is a classification technique which uses data obtained from a sample of companies to draw a boundary that separates the group of reliable ones from the group of insolvent ones. This separation is based on a *discriminant function*. Figure 10.1 shows the Fisher model in the (simplified) case in which reliable (A) and

---

[1] Other models used to forecast default are "classification trees" and "trait recognition" analysis. For further details see, for example, Breimann et al. (1983) or Kolari et al. (1996).
[2] For a general introduction to credit-scoring models and their limitations, see also Altman et al. (1981).
[3] The application of discriminant analysis to default forecasting was pioneered by Edward Altman, whose studies in the 70s represent an impressive body of research on which many subsequent results draw.

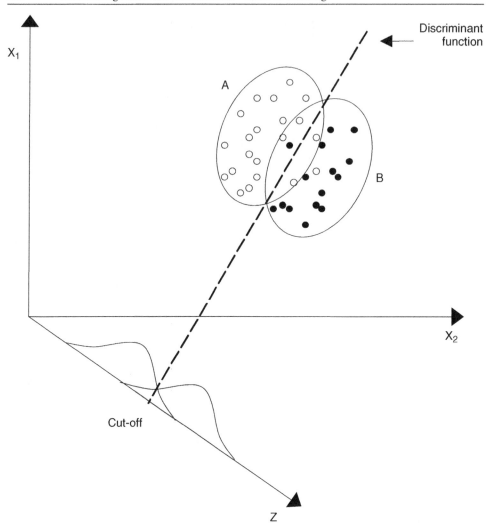

Figure 10.1 Graphic representation of linear discriminant analysis

insolvent companies (B) are described by only two variables, x_1 and x_2. The score generated by combining the two original variables is shown on the z axis. The mechanism used to construct this score will now be discussed in detail.

Discriminant analysis, in its simplest version (linear discriminant analysis), constructs the score z as a linear combination of the independent variables. In the case shown in Figure 10.1, these variables are x_1 and x_2. In more general terms, given n independent variables, the score will be computed as

$$z = \sum_{j=1}^{n} \gamma_j x_j \tag{10.1}$$

For the generic, ith company, the score will therefore be calculated as follows:

$$z_i = \sum_{j=1}^{n} \gamma_j x_{i,j} \qquad\qquad 10.2$$

The coefficients γ_j of this linear combination are chosen so as to obtain a score z which discriminates as clearly as possible between abnormal and healthy companies. In other words, the z_i values obtained must be such as to maximize the distance between the means (z_A and z_B) of the two groups of healthy and abnormal companies. These means are called *centroids*.

In practice, one wants the z_i values of "healthy" (bad) companies to be as similar as possible to one another and as different as possible from those of the "bad" (healthy) ones. It can be shown (see Appendix 10.A) that this condition is satisfied if the vector of the gamma coefficients is calculated as follows:

$$\gamma = \Sigma^{-1}(\mathbf{x_1} - \mathbf{x_2}) \qquad\qquad (10.3)$$

where $\mathbf{x_A}$ and $\mathbf{x_B}$ are vectors containing the mean values of the n independent variables for the group of healthy companies and the group of abnormal ones, and Σ is the matrix of variances and covariances between the n independent variables.

An example will clarify the process. Table 10.1 shows a sample of 24 healthy and 14 abnormal companies[4]; for the sake of simplicity, only two independent variables have been recorded, namely the ratio between unauthorized overdrafts and the total loan issued by the bank, and the ratio between financial expenses and turnover. The same data are shown in graphic form in Figure 10.2.

Note that, for abnormal companies, the data were not recorded when the financial crisis was already apparent, but some months earlier (e.g. one year earlier). In fact our model is not designed to spot manifestly-insolvent companies (a task for which no special skill is indeed necessary!) but rather to identify companies that could become insolvent in the near future.

As can be seen from the graph, in the case of abnormal companies both variables (and especially x_1) tend to take higher values than for healthy companies. This impression is reinforced by the mean values shown in Table 10.2, that is by the following vectors:

$$\mathbf{x_A} = \begin{bmatrix} 0.29 \\ 0.11 \end{bmatrix}; \mathbf{x_B} = \begin{bmatrix} 0.67 \\ 0.31 \end{bmatrix}$$

We will now summarize the two "natural" variables (x_1 and x_2) into an "artificial" variable (the score z) built in such a way as to maximize the distance between healthy and abnormal companies. In order to calculate this z, we compute coefficients γ_j by applying (10.3). To do this, we first need to estimate Σ (the matrix of variances/covariances between the two natural variables) according to the following procedure.

---

[4] The example is deliberately simplified. In practice, far more observations are needed to obtain robust results. Moreover, although it is not necessary for the number of abnormal companies to be equal to the number of healthy ones, it is advisable that it be high enough to grant an adequate significance to the estimated model. Paradoxically, when estimating a model of this kind, a bank which has suffered many defaults in the past is at an advantage, since it is easier for it to gather an adequate sample.

Table 10.1 A simplified example

"Good" companies:	x_1: interest expenses over turnover	x_2: unauthorized overdrafts over total credit exposure	"Bad" companies:	x_1: interest expenses over turnover	x_2: unauthorized overdrafts over total credit exposure
Company 1	0 %	0 %	Company 25	74 %	36 %
Company 2	72 %	40 %	Company 26	85 %	10 %
Company 3	75 %	31 %	Company 27	67 %	42 %
Company 4	7 %	2 %	Company 28	71 %	38 %
Company 5	2 %	0 %	Company 29	70 %	43 %
Company 6	1 %	2 %	Company 30	72 %	64 %
Company 7	27 %	5 %	Company 31	52 %	37 %
Company 8	42 %	3 %	Company 32	81 %	32 %
Company 9	36 %	12 %	Company 33	60 %	51 %
Company 10	12 %	9 %	Company 34	72 %	0 %
Company 11	65 %	25 %	Company 35	58 %	6 %
Company 12	16 %	9 %	Company 36	64 %	11 %
Company 13	45 %	5 %	Company 37	55 %	21 %
Company 14	0 %	0 %	Company 38	65 %	47 %
Company 15	65 %	0 %			
Company 16	16 %	2 %			
Company 17	70 %	33 %			
Company 18	29 %	15 %			
Company 19	0 %	32 %			
Company 20	0 %	0 %			
Company 21	54 %	19 %			
Company 22	9 %	0 %			
Company 23	0 %	4 %			
Company 24	57 %	24 %			
Mean values:	29.1 %	11.3 %		67.4 %	31.2 %

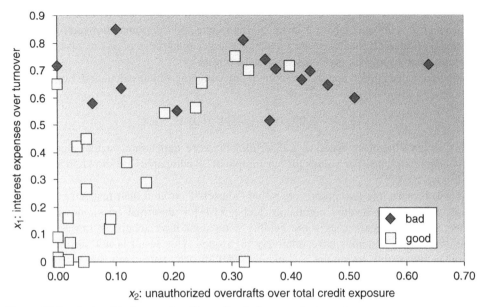

Figure 10.2   A simplified example of how discriminant analysis works

The first step is to calculate one matrix of variances and covariances for each group of companies: healthy (Σ_A) and abnormal (Σ_B):

$$\Sigma_A = \begin{bmatrix} 0.076 & 0.023 \\ 0.023 & 0.016 \end{bmatrix}; \Sigma_B = \begin{bmatrix} 0.000 & -0.001 \\ -0.001 & 0.036 \end{bmatrix}$$

The "average" Σ, valid for both groups, is then obtained from these two matrices by computing the mean, weighted by the number of companies (n_A, n_B) present in each group[5]:

$$\Sigma = \frac{n_A - 1}{n_A + n_B - 2}\Sigma_A + \frac{n_B - 1}{n_A + n_B - 2}\Sigma_B = \frac{23}{36}\Sigma_A + \frac{13}{36}\Sigma_B = \begin{bmatrix} 0.052 & 0.014 \\ 0.014 & 0.023 \end{bmatrix}$$

This Σ will then be inverted according to the normal rules of matrix algebra, to obtain

$$\Sigma^{-1} = \begin{bmatrix} 23.4 & -14.3 \\ -14.3 & 51.9 \end{bmatrix}$$

It is now possible to apply (10.3) and find the values of the γ coefficients:

$$\gamma \equiv \Sigma^{-1}(\mathbf{x}_A - \mathbf{x}_B) = \begin{bmatrix} 23.4 & -14.3 \\ -14.3 & 51.9 \end{bmatrix} \cdot \begin{bmatrix} 0.29 - 0.67 \\ 0.11 - 0.31 \end{bmatrix} =$$

$$= \begin{bmatrix} 23.4 \cdot (-0.38) - 14.3 \cdot (-0.20) \\ -14.3 \cdot (-0.38) + 51.9 \cdot (-0.20) \end{bmatrix} = \begin{bmatrix} -6.09 \\ -4.84 \end{bmatrix}$$

Based on these values, the score z_i of the generic company i will be calculated as follows:

$$z_i = \gamma'\mathbf{x}_i = -6.09 \cdot x_{1,i} - 4.84 \cdot x_{2,i}$$

---

[5] The formula includes $n_A - 1$ and $n_B - 1$ because when variances and covariances are computed, it is usual to divide by the number of observations in the sample *minus one*.

Note that a negative weights has been assigned to both variables (high financial charges on turnover reduce the company's score, and the same applies to unauthorized overdrafts), and that x_1 (although its values are on average larger than those of x_2) receives a higher weighting, confirming its greater discriminant power.

Using the values found above, the score of any company can be calculated. For example, for company 2 this is:

$$z_2 = -6.09 \cdot 0.27 - 4.84 \cdot 0.05 \cong -1.85$$

Each company therefore receives a discriminant score depending on its values for the independent variables. The values for our sample of 38 companies are shown in Table 10.2 and Figure 10.3.

As will be seen, the two groups are rather "clustered" around their respective centroids (equal to -2.32 for healthy companies and -5.61 for abnormal ones); however, they are not perfectly separate, as some healthy companies have relatively low scores, and some abnormal companies have relatively high ones. This result is not surprising: it is obviously impossible to predict a company's default very effectively by just using two simple financial indicators! However, the procedure followed (construction of the vectors of the means, construction and inversion of the matrix of variances and covariances, and calculation of the γ_j with equation 10.3) would remain unchanged and could easily be applied also when considering $m > 2$ independent variables.

If we want to set a cut-off point below which a company is rejected (the bank refuses to grant a loan) because it is too risky, we could use the point halfway between the two centroids, namely:

$$\alpha \equiv \frac{1}{2}\gamma'(\mathbf{x}_A + \mathbf{x}_B) \cong -3.97 \tag{10.4}$$

The comparison between this cut-off point and the values in Table 10.2 (especially those in italics), demonstrates that this threshold would cause the bank to refuse loans to no less than six healthy companies, and to grant a loan to one abnormal company (company 35). This confirms that the discriminant power of the model is rather limited.

10.2.2 Wilks' Lambda

A widely used index to measure the success rate of a model (that is, its actual discriminant capacity) is Wilks' Lambda.[6] It is given by the ratio between the sum of the deviances of the scores within the two groups of healthy and abnormal companies (the so-called "within" deviances) and the total deviance in the sample:

$$\Lambda = \frac{\displaystyle\sum_{i \in A}(z_i - z_A)^2 + \sum_{i \in B}(z_i - z_B)^2}{\displaystyle\sum_{i=1}^{n}(z_i - \bar{z})^2} \tag{10.5}$$

Where $\bar{z}$ represents the mean of z_i in the entire sample of healthy and abnormal companies.

---

[6] Other measurements of the success of a discriminant model are the "hit rate" (the percentage of cases correctly classified) or measures such as the ROC curve and the Accuracy Ratio, presented in Chapter 13 (see also Sobehart Keenan, 2001).

Table 10.2 A simplified example (continued): values for scores and default probabilities

"Good" companies:	z_i	PD	"Bad" companies:	z_i	PD
Company 1	0.000	1.1%	Company 25	−6.237	85.0%
Company 2	−6.295	85.7%	Company 26	−5.657	76.0%
Company 3	−6.065	82.6%	Company 27	−6.085	82.9%
Company 4	−0.526	1.8%	Company 28	−6.106	83.2%
Company 5	−0.097	1.2%	Company 29	−6.349	86.3%
Company 6	−0.131	1.2%	Company 30	−7.481	95.2%
Company 7	−1.850	6.6%	Company 31	−4.920	60.2%
Company 8	−2.733	14.5%	Company 32	−6.479	87.8%
Company 9	−2.784	15.2%	Company 33	−6.130	83.6%
Company 10	−1.167	3.4%	Company 34	−4.352	46.2%
Company 11	−5.186	66.4%	Company 35	−3.809	33.3%
Company 12	−1.397	4.3%	Company 36	−4.403	47.5%
Company 13	−2.975	17.8%	Company 37	−4.362	46.4%
Company 14	0.000	1.1%	Company 38	−6.189	84.3%
Company 15	−3.957	36.6%			
Company 16	−1.067	3.1%			
Company 17	−5.847	79.3%			
Company 18	−2.498	11.9%			
Company 19	−1.549	4.9%			
Company 20	−0.005	1.1%			
Company 21	−4.195	42.3%			
Company 22	−0.548	1.9%			
Company 23	−0.213	1.3%			
Company 24	−4.591	52.2%			
Mean values:	−2.32	22.4%		−5.61	71.3%

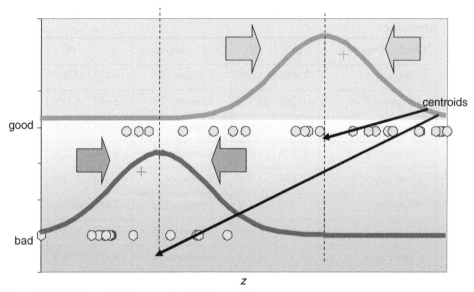

Figure 10.3 Values of z for our simplified example

If a model is very effective, and the scores for the individual healthy (or abnormal) companies are very similar to one another, the two deviances in the numerator will be close to zero, as will the entire Wilks' Lambda. However, if the discriminant capacity is low and the two centroids are very similar to one another, the sum of the within deviances will be close to the total deviance, and the ratio will be close to 1.

In our simplified example, the value of Wilks' Lambda is approximately 55%, indicating that its discriminant capacity is by no means perfect.

10.2.3 Altman's Z-score

The best-known discriminant score applied to credit risk is probably the one developed by Edward Altman in 1968 for listed US companies. It is a function of five independent variables, and is formulated as follows:[7]

$$z_i = 1.2 \cdot x_{i,1} + 1.4 \cdot x_{i,2} + 3.3 \cdot x_{i,3} + 0.6 \cdot x_{i,4} + 1.0 \cdot x_{i,5} \qquad (10.6)$$

where:

x_1 = working capital/total assets
x_2 = retained profits/total assets
x_3 = earnings before interest and tax/total assets
x_4 = market value of equity/book value of total liabilities
x_5 = turnover/total assets

The greater the z score of a company, the better its quality (because its probability of default is lower). Altman sets the cut-off point between "sufficiently reliable" companies and excessively risky ones at a value of 1.81. This cut-off value was obtained as the average between the mean value of z for a sample of healthy companies and the mean value of z for a sample of companies which have subsequently become insolvent.

---

[7] This is the Z-score for manufacturers. A Z'-score for non-manufacturer industrials (the so-called Z''-score) was also developed by Altman.

If we assume, for example, that company Delta presents the following financial indicators: $x_1 = 0.25; x_2 = 0; x_3 = -0.10; x_4 = 0.20; x_5 = 1.6$, the corresponding z value is:

$$z_{Delta} = 1.2 \cdot 0.25 + 1.4 \cdot 0 - 3.3 \cdot 0.10 + 0.6 \cdot 0.20 + 1.0 \cdot 1.6 = 1.69$$

Company Delta would therefore be classified as too risky on the basis of Altman's model.[8]

10.2.4 From the score to the probability of default

Discriminant analysis is sometimes used to produce a direct estimate of the probability of default associated with the individual companies analyzed. It can be shown[9] that if the independent variables are distributed according to a multivariate normal distribution, the probability that a company is abnormal (i.e. in practice, that it will default in the coming months) is given by:

$$PD = p(B|\mathbf{x}_i) = \cfrac{1}{1 + \cfrac{1 - \pi_B}{\pi_B} e^{z_i - \alpha}} \qquad (10.7)$$

where z_i and α are the quantities defined in (10.2) and (10.4), while π_B represents the "prior probability of default", a measure of the "average" quality of the bank's loan portfolio, which does not depend on the characteristics of the individual customer but on the general characteristics of the market.[10]

Equation (10.7) can be applied to the simplified example shown in Table 10.1; lacking more accurate information, we will simply use the proportion of abnormal companies in our sample ($14/38 \cong 37\%$) as π_B. The result is shown in Table 10.2: as will be seen, the lower the score, the greater the probability of default.

As already mentioned, the results of the model are by no means perfect. There are a number of healthy companies for which a high probability of default is forecast, whereas for company 35, which is to go into liquidation a few months later, the estimated PD is 33%, a value much lower than 100%.

If the value of π_B were to be reduced, equation (10.7) would give lower probabilities of default. Conversely, if it were raised, all the PDs of the individual customers would be higher. The reason is that, when assessing a customer's risk of default, (10.7) does not only take account of the customer's economic/financial indicators (independent variables x_j), but also of the average quality of the portfolio. The formula can therefore be made more optimistic or conservative, having regard to general market conditions.

---

[8] Two cut-off values are often used in practice instead of just one. A company with a score below the lower cut-off point is considered too risky, whereas a company with a score above the upper cut-off point is considered reliable; finally, a company with a score between the two cut-off values is classified in a "grey area" where the model is unable to provide sufficiently reliable results, and different techniques need to be used. Figure 10.3 also shows that score levels exist for which definite indications cannot be given.

[9] see Altman et al. (1981).

[10] For example, if the bank knows that historically, one customer in a hundred defaults, it could set π_B at 1%. The value of π_B can also be modified over time to account for particularly favourable or unfavourable phases of the credit cycle, provided that these phases are not already reflected in changes of the financial indicators x_j on which the score is based.

The cut-off point indicated in (10.4) can also be modified to take account of the PDs and the average portfolio quality expressed by π_B. In particular, we may decide to refuse a loan to a customer only if its PD (estimated through equation 10.7) exceeds 50 %, i.e. if:

$$PD = \frac{1}{1 + \dfrac{1 - \pi_B}{\pi_B}e^{z_i-\alpha}} > 0.5$$

Some trivial algebra leads to re-writing this condition as:

$$z_i < \alpha + \ln \frac{\pi_B}{1 - \pi_B} \equiv \alpha' \tag{10.8}$$

In practice, a customer is considered too risky whenever its score falls below a new cut-off point, α', given by the "old" α and an extra term increasing with π_B. This means that if the average quality of the portfolio is poor, and therefore π_B is high, our cut-off point is raised, and the customer is therefore more likely to be refused a loan. Note that if π_B were exactly 50 %, the new α' would be equal to α, because the prior probability would not add any new information to the model.

In our example, as $\pi_B \cong 37\%$ (lower than 50 %), the cut-off point calculated with (10.8) is lower than α, and therefore relatively more "optimistic" than the one previously calculated with (10.4). Thus:

$$\alpha' = -3.97 + \ln \frac{0.37}{1 - 0.37} \cong -4.5$$

Consequently, applicants like company 21 (previously rejected) would be considered acceptable, as their PD is below 50 %, and (the two things are algebraically equivalent) their score is above the new cut-off point α'.

10.2.5 The cost of errors

In the previous section we chose to classify a borrower as acceptable if its PD is below 50 %. However, it is obvious that no bank will choose to lend money to companies with a PD of 30 % or 40 %, although these values are below 50 % (and the survival probability is therefore greater than the probability of default). Banks tend to lend only to companies with PD values reasonably close to zero, such as 0.5 %, 1 % or 2 %.

This is not a matter of prudence, but a reasoning that takes account of the different costs of the two errors a bank can make:

 (i) classifying an insolvent company as healthy (type I error);
 (ii) classifying a healthy company as insolvent (type II error).

A type I error generally produces a cost (which we will indicate as $C(A|B)$, i.e. "the cost of assigning a Group B (abnormal) customer to Group A, containing healthy companies"), corresponding to the interest and capital lost as a result of the default of the company incorrectly classified as "healthy" (and assigned a loan).

A type II error produces a lower cost $C(B|A)$, corresponding to the foregone profit in fees and net interest income which would have been earned from the rejected "healthy" customer.

Based on these simple considerations, the cut-off point can be calibrated (namely, increased) as to account for the different costs associated with the two types of error. In particular, a bank could decide to refuse a loan to a customer whenever the *expected cost* of a type I error (cost of error weighted for the probability that it will occur) exceeds the *expected cost* of a type II error. That is, whenever:

$$C(A|B) \cdot PD > C(B|A) \cdot (1 - PD)$$

By replacing PD by the expression in (10.7) and applying some trivial algebra, the condition can be rewritten as:[11]

$$z_i < \alpha + \log \frac{\pi_B C(A|B)}{(1 - \pi_B) \cdot C(B|A)} = \alpha' + \log \frac{C(A|B)}{C(B|A)} \equiv \alpha'' \qquad (10.9)$$

In practice, a customer is considered too risky whenever its score is lower than a new cut-off point, α'', given by the "old" α plus a term which increases with π_B, and with the ratio between the cost of a type I error and a type II error.

Going back to our example, assume that type I error leads to the loss of 70 % of the principal (that is, that 30 % can be recovered, e.g. by seizing a collateral), and that type II error leads to missed earnings equal to 2 % of the principal. The cut-off point will be modified as follows:

$$\alpha'' = -3.97 + \ln \frac{0.37 \cdot 70 \%}{(1 - 0.37) \cdot 2 \%} \cong -0.95$$

and all companies with z_i values below the new cut-off will be refused a loan.

Table 10.3, which shows the decisions generated by the model on the basis of our three different cut-off points, demonstrates that the change from α' to α'' makes it much more selective (a loan is now granted to only 8 companies out of 38). The reason is easy to see: we have "taught" our model that granting a loan to an undeserving company is a much more serious mistake than an unjustified rejection. We have therefore made it more prudent. Of course, if customers were to provide more collateral, the cost of a type II error would fall (e.g. from 70 % to 30 %), as would α''. This would allow more loans to be granted. The cut-off point α'' therefore depends partly on the loan's LGD (which can be estimated as explained in Chapter 12).

10.2.6 The selection of discriminant variables

In our example, we assumed that the two independent variables on which the score were based were already known. In practice, identifying the indicators which will be used to estimate the model is an extremely delicate, laborious task. In general, the selection of discriminant variables can follow two main procedures: (i) the simultaneous or direct method; (ii) the stepwise method.

In the first case, the model is constructed on an *a priori* basis. In other words, the variables are selected on the basis of theoretical reasoning, and the corresponding discriminant coefficients are estimated jointly. In the second case, the variables are selected from a long list of "candidates", on the basis of the discriminating capacity demonstrated by each one on the data in the estimation sample.

---

[11] This procedure for the adjustment of the optimal credit score cutoff was first suggested by Altman et al. (1977), where they tried to quantify the type I and II errors.

Table 10.3 Decisions prompted by the model based on different cut-off points

"Good"	Cut-off point			"Bad"	Cut-off point		
companies	α	α'	α''	companies	α	α'	α''
Company 1	✓	✓	✓	Company 25	☒	☒	☒
Company 2	☒	☒	☒	Company 26	☒	☒	☒
Company 3	☒	☒	☒	Company 27	☒	☒	☒
Company 4	✓	✓	✓	Company 28	☒	☒	☒
Company 5	✓	✓	✓	Company 29	☒	☒	☒
Company 6	✓	✓	✓	Company 30	☒	☒	☒
Company 7	✓	✓	☒	Company 31	☒	☒	☒
Company 8	✓	✓	☒	Company 32	☒	☒	☒
Company 9	✓	✓	☒	Company 33	☒	☒	☒
Company 10	✓	✓	☒	Company 34	☒	✓	☒
Company 11	☒	☒	☒	Company 35	✓	✓	☒
Company 12	✓	✓	☒	Company 36	☒	✓	☒
Company 13	✓	✓	☒	Company 37	☒	✓	☒
Company 14	✓	✓	✓	Company 38	☒	☒	☒
Company 15	✓	✓	☒				
Company 16	✓	✓	☒				
Company 17	☒	☒	☒				
Company 18	✓	✓	☒				
Company 19	✓	✓	☒				
Company 20	✓	✓	✓				
Company 21	☒	✓	☒				
Company 22	✓	✓	✓				
Company 23	✓	✓	✓				
Company 24	☒	☒	☒				

Legend: ✓ = grant the loan; ☒ = reject the application

This can be done by initially including all the variables and subsequently removing those with lower discriminating power ("backward elimination"), or by including a single variable and progressively adding those which most improve the discriminating power of the model ("forward selection"). Hybrid stepwise selection procedures which combine both of these methods can also be used; in this case, variables will be both added and removed (in particular, those which become basically redundant after the introduction of other indicators will be removed).

Although stepwise methods are very powerful, they can be counterproductive when they lead to the inclusion of variables whose economic significance is unclear, or whose coefficient γ_j has the opposite sign from what was reasonably expected from an economic standpoint (e.g. the case in which a *higher* profitability index *reduces* the score). For this reason, such methods should always be used under the supervision of an expert who helps to select the variables, understand their economic meaning, and eliminate counter-intuitive indicators.

10.2.7   Some hypotheses underlying discriminant analysis

Linear discriminant analysis models, such as the one proposed by Altman, are based on the hypothesis that the variance and covariance matrices of the independent variables (x_j) are equal for the two groups of companies. In practice, empirical data often seem to suggest the opposite (and in fact this was also true for the data of the simplified example shown in the previous sections).

When such a problem of heteroscedasticity between groups arises, more sophisticated versions of the model can be used (*heteroscedastic* or *quadratic* discriminant analysis); however, these versions involve estimating a larger number of parameters (as two matrices Σ need to be estimated). If there are too few data points in the sample, the estimates will be imprecise, and this may entirely offset the advantages associated with a more sophisticated theoretical model. Moreover, functions based on quadratic discriminant analysis are less readable and hence less useful in practical terms; this has certainly limited their use for real-life applications in banks.

Furthermore, as mentioned above, formulae like (10.7), which convert the score to a probability of default, assume that the independent variables follow a multivariate normal distribution; however, empirical analysis often demonstrates that this hypothesis is unrealistic. In fact, as many economic/financial indicators are structurally limited between 0 and 100 % (e.g. the ratio of stocks to assets), a distribution taking unlimited values (between minus and plus infinity), such as the normal distribution, is intuitively incorrect. For these reasons, many banks prefer to calculate the PDs associated with different levels of score z with methods other than (10.7), e.g. by observing over time the actual default rates associated with given score ranges.[12]

10.3   REGRESSION MODELS

10.3.1   The linear probabilistic model

In this model, the variables that lead to the default of a company, and their weights, are identified with a simple linear regression. The model comprises four stages.

---

[12] See Chapter 13 for more details on this "rating quantification" procedure.

(1) *Sample selection.* A sample formed by a sufficiently large number of companies is selected. As in the case of discriminant analysis, they are divided into two groups, identified by a binary state variable (dummy variable) y, which only takes value 0 or 1. In particular, $y_i = 1$ if company i is abnormal, while $y_i = 0$ if the company is healthy.

(2) *Selection of independent variables.* For each company i, m significant variables (x_{i1}, $x_i, \ldots x_{ij}, \ldots x_{im}$) are recorded. As in the case of discriminant analysis, these are usually economic/financial indicators (financial leverage, profitability, liquidity and turnover rate of investments, etc.), measured prior to default (e.g. a year earlier).

(3) *Estimating coefficients.* The following model is estimated, usually based on ordinary least squares:

$$y_i = \alpha + \sum_{j=1}^{m} \beta_j x_{i,j} + \varepsilon_i \qquad (10.10)$$

where the β_j represent the regression coefficients.

(4) *Estimated probability of default.* The model is consequently used to estimate the probability of default of new companies applying for bank loans.

For example, let us assume that a bank has estimated the following linear function based on a sample of healthy and abnormal companies:

$$y_i = 0.03 + 0.25 \cdot x_{i,1} - 5 \cdot x_{i,2} + 0.7 \cdot x_{i,3} \qquad (10.11)$$

where:

$x_1 =$ debt to equity ratio (an indicator of financial leverage);
$x_2 =$ ratio between gross operating profit and total assets
   (an indicator of operational profitability);
$x_3 =$ ratio between financial charges and gross operating profit
   (an indicator of debt sustainability).

Now let us assume that a new company applies for a loan, for which those three indicators have the following values: $x_1 = 5; x_2 = 0.3; x_3 = 0.4$. Based on (10.11), the probability of default of the company will be estimated as:

$$z = 0.03 + 0.25 \cdot 5 - 5 \cdot 0.3 + 0.7 \cdot 0.4 \cong 6\%$$

However simple and apparently effective the model may seem, it has a major drawback: y (the probability of default) make take on values outside the 0–100 % range. Let us assume, for example, that a second company presents the following values for the independent variables: $x_1 = 4; x_2 = 0.3; x_3 = 0.5$. Its probability of default will be estimated as:

$$z = 0.03 + 0.25 \cdot 4 - 5 \cdot 0.3 + 0.7 \cdot 0.5 \cong -12\%$$

which is obviously absurd. For this reason, if the value y generated by the model (based on the customer's $x_{i,j}$s) is above 100 % or below 0 %, it is usually truncated at those limits.

However, further problems still remain. In particular, the variance of the residuals of the model linear is not constant, but suffers from heteroscedasticity. This, in turn, causes coefficient estimates to be imprecise and distorted. This, too, explains why the linear form is never used in practice, and non-linear functions are preferred, as in the probit and logit models.

10.3.2 The logit and probit models

In the logit model, the linear relationship (10.10) is adjusted through an exponential transformation, called the logistic transformation:

$$y_i = f(w_i) = \frac{1}{1 + e^{-w_i}} \tag{10.12}$$

where the independent variable w_i is given by the linear function of the financial indicators x_{ij} already seen in (10.10):

$$w_i = \alpha + \sum_{j=1}^{m} \beta_j x_{i,j} \tag{10.13}$$

By combining (10.12) and (10.13), and adding the usual random disturbance term, we obtain the logit model:

$$y_i = \frac{1}{1 + e^{-\alpha - \sum_j \beta_j x_j}} + \varepsilon_i \tag{10.14}$$

The range of values generated by the logistic function (the function's "codomain") is now limited to the interval (0,1). This guarantees that the dependent variable y_i is always between 0 and 100 %, and can therefore be correctly interpreted as a probability of default.

Also, transformations alternative to the logistic one can be used, provided that their codomain is always between 0 and 1. Thus, for example, a normal cumulative density function could be used instead of (10.12); in that case, the final model is called "normit", or more commonly "probit". The main difference between the two models lies in the fact that the logistic function has "fatter" tails; in practice, this does not produce any significant differences between the two models unless the sample includes numerous observations with extreme values of w_i.

10.4 INDUCTIVE MODELS

10.4.1 Neural networks[13]

The credit-scoring models examined so far have a common denominator: the attempt to identify the fundamental relationships which explain the economic/financial balance of a company, and can therefore be used to forecast default. In other words, these models are based on the *structural* characteristics that explain the state of health of a company, and the choice of relevant variables, though calibrated with statistical techniques, always reflects some *a priori* choice based on economic reasoning. Thus, for example, these models include financial leverage or the ratio between financial charges and operating profit, because it is assumed that an excessive recourse to borrowing or a weakening of

---

[13] This section is based on Gabbi (1999).

the operational profitability will increase the risk of default.[14] In this respect, these models follow a "structural" approach: they start with assumptions made by an analyst (e.g. "a company that makes excessive use of borrowing will not be able to repay all its debts") and seek confirmation for these assumptions in an empirical data sample.

Neural networks, however, use a purely inductive process: if, starting from a data sample, a certain empirical regularity is found (e.g. that many abnormal companies present values in variable x_j above some cut-off point k), this regularity is used, in a substantially uncritical, "agnostic" way, to forecast future defaults by other companies. Hence, instead of relying on deductively determined rules, a purely empirical approach is used.

Structural models are transparent and based on solid, proven algorithms which use inferential tests to verify the real significance of the estimated coefficients (net of the random effects due to sampling). By contrast, inductive models are often "black boxes", which can be used to generate results rapidly, but whose logic may not be fully understood.

However, an inductive approach, even a "black-box" one, may prove useful, typically when it is complex or impossible to devise deductive rules governing a certain phenomenon (in our case, a company's default).

Moreover, in the case of credit risk, structural models can be "learned" with time and neutralised by the companies requesting loans. In other words companies, including those at high risk of default, may reconstruct the logic followed by the structural model and adopt suitable accounting policies to influence the result (thus enabling them to obtain loans from banks using the model). This means that a structural model, even if well constructed, may lose effectiveness with time. In this respect, what is generally considered a drawback of the black-box approach, namely its failure to express the structure of the relationship between corporate financial data and default (and in general the lack of a sufficiently simple and recognisable structure), becomes an advantage.

Neural networks are based on a black-box, inductive approach. They attempt to mimic the learning mechanism of human knowledge and memory, capturing some aspects that cannot incorporated in a simple calculation algorithm.

In general, a neural network consists of a large number of elements, called "neurons", which are connected to one another by elementary relations called "synapses". The neurons are arranged in "layers"; each neuron in the outermost layer of the network receives an input of n variables (which, in the case of models used to forecast default, can be the usual economic/financial indicators described in sections 10.2 and 10.3) and processes them with a linear or, more often, non-linear function, the result of which is passed on to the neurons in the next layer. These neurons also process the input received with a further function, and transmit a new output to the next layer in the network. After one or more "hidden layers", the network generates a final result. In the case of default forecasting, the result may be, for example, a numerical score which must have a value as close as possible to 1 for abnormal companies and as close as possible to 0 for healthy companies. Figure 10.4 shows a simple example of a neural network.

The coefficients of the individual elementary functions that make up the network are estimated (or "learned" by the network) by means of an iterative mechanism. In practice, the values of the coefficients are gradually modified to obtain results as similar as possible to the desired ones (e.g., one for defaulted companies, zero for healthy ones). The learning process of a network is therefore a gradual attempt to identify the correct weights to be

---

[14] These variables are only accepted if the corresponding coefficients are not only statistically significant, but also have the expected mathematical sign.

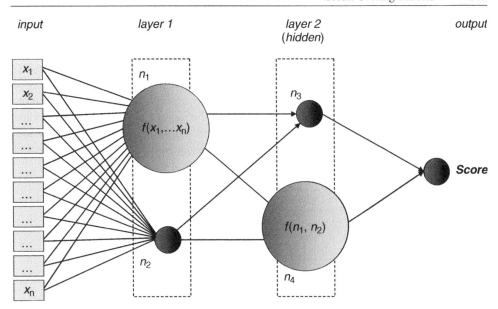

Figure 10.4 Example of the structure of a neural network

Table 10.4 Dataset for identification of rules

Observations	x_1	x_2	y
A	6	4	10
B	5	3	8
C	7	6	13
D	8	5	13
E	6	8	14
F	3	9	12

attributed to the input variables and the synapses of the hidden layers, so as to obtain a
result similar to that of the (unknown) function to be approximated.

Consider the example in Table 10.4[15]: starting from the values of variables x_1 and
x_2, imagine you want to reconstruct the value of y. Of course, anyone familiar with
elementary algebraic functions will notice at first sight that y is simply the sum of x_1
and x_2. Obviously, if that relationship were already known, it would be useless to look
for it, but it would be much more convenient to use a simple spreadsheet to perform the
calculations rapidly. However, the knowledge of the function often does represent the
obstacle arising in the case of credit risk (and in many other financial problems): if the
relationships between the variables that generate the default (be they corporate financial
data or macroeconomic, environmental factors) could have been identified, a structural

---

[15] This example is taken from Gabbi (1999).

model could have been estimated; if this has not been possible, we must seek to estimate the relationship inductively.

The neural network, through a lattice of elementary functions similar to the one shown in Figure 10.4, can approximate the functional form that links the variables. Initially, starting with a wholly random set of coefficients, the network will produce values of y which are very far away from the correct ones. However, by making repeated attempts (called "epochs"), and modifying the coefficients of the elementary functions every time so as to approach the desired values, the network will gradually reduce the error made. Table 10.5 compares the real values of y with those which could be generated by a neural network[16] after a sufficiently large number of "epochs".

Table 10.5 Neural network solutions

Observation	x_1	x_2	*real* y	y generated by network	Error
A	6	4	10	10.60	−0.60
B	5	3	8	9.41	−1.41
C	7	6	13	12.56	0.44
D	8	5	13	12.52	0.48
E	6	8	14	13.31	0.69
F	3	9	12	12.04	−0.04

The results of the network are imprecise, and clearly unacceptable for the problem posed. However, this kind of approximation is useful for problems (such as default forecasting) for which a function generating an exact solution is not known.

10.4.2   Genetic algorithms[17]

Developed by John Holland in the 60s and 70s,[18] genetic algorithms, like neural networks, are inspired by the behavior of biological organisms: their operation is based on a transposition of Darwin's principles of natural selection and "survival of the fittest". In order to understand the structure of genetic algorithms, a short digression on the process of natural development described by Charles Darwin in "The Origin of Species" is therefore required.

Individuals belonging to an animal species compete with one another for essential resources, such as food and shelter; they also continually compete to attract a mate. Given a certain population, only the individuals with good characteristics to interact with the external environment (that is, with a high level of "fitness") have a high probability to survive, and consequently to reproduce. This evolution process therefore leads to a continuous improvement of the species, because only the best individuals transfer their genetic assets to future generations.

[16] In practice, in such a simple case, a good neural network would be able to reduce the error to nil.
[17] This section is based on Pomante (1999)
[18] The book "*Adaptation in Natural and Artificial Systems*", published by Holland in 1975, is the fundamental text on genetic algorithms.

Two other mechanisms, apart from natural selection, are involved in the development and improvement of the species. Firstly, when two individuals mate, genetic recombination ("crossover") can lead to offspring with better characteristics ("superfit") than those of each individual in past generations; this greater genetic quality then spreads among the members of the population by means of further reproduction. Secondly, the genetic heritage contained in the chromosomes of the individuals may change as a result of sudden, albeit rare random mutations of individual genes.

Genetic algorithms simulate the process of evolution just described. The "individuals" required to evolve are obviously not living beings, but *possible solutions to a problem*.

In particular, suppose we want to generate a function based on a set of balance sheet indicators $(x_1, x_2, \ldots, x_n)$, constructed in such a way as to assign high values to healthy companies and low values to abnormal ones.

If, for the sake of simplicity, we consider a linear function:

$$z = \alpha_0 + \alpha_1 x_1 + \alpha_2 x_2 + \ldots \ldots + \alpha_m x_m$$

each individual is represented by a vector $\alpha = [\alpha_0 \ldots \alpha_m]'$ which indicates the algebraic sign and weight with which the various balance sheet indicators are included in the construction of z. Nil values of one or more α_j indicate that the corresponding economic/financial indicators are not used by this individual/solution.

To select and refine the best solutions, genetic algorithms operate as follows:

(a) a first population (or "generation") of s individuals/solutions is randomly generated;
(b) the *fitness* of the s individuals, namely their ability to represent a good solution to the problem, is calculated with an evaluation function. In the case of default forecasting, a check is made, for example, to ensure that a low score is assigned to abnormal companies and a high score to healthy ones, and the fitness value of each solution measures the extent to which it approaches this ideal situation;
(c) a *selection* algorithm (called the "genetic operator") is applied which, taking due account of the individual fitnesses of the solutions, identifies the individuals bound to survive and those bound to die (in other words, a higher probability of survival is attributed to the best solutions, namely those which correctly classified the highest percentage of companies in the sample);
(d) the application of a second "genetic operator", called the "*crossover*" or "*recombination*" operator, enables the surviving individuals to reproduce; in this way a second generation of s solutions is generated, the genetic assets of which are inherited from the *parents* (the new solutions present vectors α obtained by combining solutions from the previous generation[19]);
(e) the application of the genetic operator of *mutation* introduces (with a very low probability) the possibility of a random small modification in one or more of the new-generation solutions (in practice, solutions obtained by recombination can undergo a random change in the value of one of the coefficients α_j);

---

[19] The genetic recombination that takes place between a pair of solutions with a high level of fitness does not systematically lead to the best individuals; application of the crossover operator can also lead to the destruction of the parents' good genetic characteristics. However, the fact that the genetic algorithm does not focus on a single solution, but extends its analysis to an entire population of individuals, ensures an effective process of exploring the search space of solutions.

(f) the fitness of each individual belonging to this new generation of solutions ("children" of the first generation, and in some cases further transformed by genetic mutation) is measured. If none of them is wholly satisfactory, the process is further replicated (from point "c" to point "e")[20] until a solution is found that is considered attractive (in our case, a solution that correctly classifies all companies) or until the improvement in fitness from one generation to another is substantially nil.

Figure 10.5 shows a graphic representation of the structure of genetic algorithms.

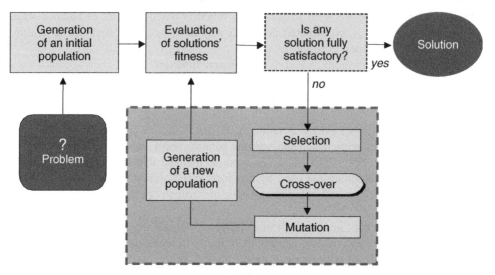

Figure 10.5   The structure of a genetic algorithm
Source: Pomante (1999).

Given an initial population of solutions, genetic algorithms, by repeatedly applying pre-defined rules, produce solutions with an increasing level of fitness. However, the process of improvement in the quality of the results is not destined to last for ever: when the optimum solutions have been produced, having a high level of fitness and being very much similar to one another, they generate (by recombination) a new generation of solutions that will be quite similar to their "parents"; thus a process of convergence is triggered which causes the new individuals to become increasingly similar, and often actually identical. The process whereby genetic algorithms explore the search space of solutions has a partly random nature, as the initial population is generated randomly.[21] However, this process does not evolve at random: the use of the fitness function and the genetic operators of selection and recombination allows the space of the solutions to be explored in an effective way, thank to the information set obtained from the previous steps of the exploration. Genetic algorithms thus perform a kind of "adaptive search"; they move in space, guided by the memory of past attempts, and exploration takes place exploiting the information obtained during past research. The principle that enables this process to produce useful solutions is the *competition* among solutions.

---

[20] Some applications require the creation of thousands of generations in series.
[21] The genetic operator of *mutation* introduces a further random element.

Genetic algorithms do not guarantee to identify the "ideal" solution to the problem for which they are used, but they do allow good solutions to be obtained very quickly. The simplicity, effectiveness and generality of this family of "adaptive search techniques" is such that they have been applied to very different fields.[22] Genetic algorithms have proved particularly effective in areas where other research methods had been producing poor results due to the presence of a solution space which is not only large, but also little-known or "noisy".[23] The proven ability of genetic algorithms to perform well even in this kind of situations is due to their ability to work without any previous knowledge of the solution space; however, they always require that a valuation function can be specified, through which fitness values can be computed.

10.5   USES, LIMITATIONS AND PROBLEMS OF CREDIT-SCORING MODELS

Credit-scoring models can be used for two distinct purposes:

(i) simple default forecasting, performed by separating substantially reliable from excessively risky loans;
(ii) estimating the borrower's risk level, namely the probability of default, by assigning a different PD to each borrower or by aggregating borrowers into a finite number of discrete grades, each with its own PD.

As seen in the example relating to discriminant analysis, the first use requires a cut-off point to be established,[24] below which the loan application will be rejected (use for new applications) or a loan already issued will be reported to the managers for checks to be made (use as an early-warning system). According to this logic, all debts which exceed the minimum cut-off point of the score are considered equally reliable.

The second use, which is now widely employed in many banks, requires the risk of individual borrowers, including those considered reliable to be measured analytically. In particular, a PD is assigned to each borrower on the basis of the score obtained, and can be used, for example, to estimate the expected loss on its debt exposure, as indicated in the introduction to this part of the book. The PD can be estimated at individual borrower level with formulae such as (10.7) and (10.14). However, these formulas are often based on fairly unrealistic starting hypotheses (the normality of the balance-sheet indicators for 10.7, the existence of a logistic relationship between balance-sheet indicators and PD for 10.14); thus, as mentioned above, many banks prefer not to estimate a specific PD for each customer, but to follow a different, two-step procedure. First, customers with similar scores (e.g. from -10 to -5, from -5 to 0, etc.) are grouped into a finite number of grades; in the following years, the bank observes the percentage of defaults which actually take

---

[22] A particularly unusual application is the one that uses genetic algorithms as tools for witnesses to identify criminals. In order to reconstruct the features of a suspect, an initial population of faces is created. The witness carefully analyzes each figure, and attributes a rating to each one on the basis of its similarity to the suspect. This rating is used as the fitness of the individual solutions. The application of genetic operators of *selection*, *crossover* (recombination of the facial characteristics of the solutions is performed at this stage) and *mutation* then leads to a second population. The process is then replicated until a face which strongly resembles that of the suspect is obtained.

[23] Even when another method proves more effective than genetic algorithms in the search for the solution to a problem, they can still represent a useful tool to refine the solution obtained with the other method.

[24] Or two cut-off points, separated by a grey area (see foot note 7).

place within each grade, and this percentage (empirical default rate) is used as a PD estimate for all customers belonging to a given class.[25]

When credit-scoring models are used, attention must be paid to some problems. This is especially true if the models are used not only to decide which companies to lend to, but also to estimate their PD. Those problems are illustrated briefly below.

- A first important problem relates to the definition of an "abnormal" or "insolvent" company. Different "degrees of insolvency" exist, ranging from a simple delay in payment of interest to the compulsory liquidation of the company, with many intermediate stages. The definition used to break down the estimation sample obviously affects the results of the model, even when it is applied to a new company. Thus, for example, if a very broad definition of insolvency is used (e.g., a simple delay in the payment of interest), a model will be obtained which classifies a large number of companies as insolvent and assigns higher PDs.
- A second problem is associated with the fact that the meaningfulness of the independent variables used by the scoring model may vary over time, due to the effect of the economic cycle, financial market variables and other factors; there is no economic reason why the weight of the individual economic/financial indicators used to explain default should remain unchanged.
- A third problem is due to the fact that credit-scoring models ignore numerous qualitative factors, which can be highly significant in determining the insolvency of a company[26]. They include the company's reputation (which influences its ability to access alternative sources of credit), the stage of the economic cycle, the quality of management and the outlook for the industry to which the company belongs.
- A fourth problem is due to the fact that the companies in the estimation sample should belong, as far as possible, to the same industry. There are two reasons for this: (i) because the individual economic/financial indicators take very different mean values from industry to industry; and (ii) because the same indicator may have a different importance in determining default in the various industries. In practice, however, the difficulty of obtaining data from a large number of insolvent companies often forces banks to work with samples that include companies in different industries.
- Precisely because complete data often exists only for a few defaulting companies (whereas it is advisable to work with large samples in order to estimate the models with sufficient accuracy), there is often a risk that the estimation samples will be "unbalanced", and include an excessively high percentage of healthy companies. Paradoxically, from this standpoint, a bank with poor historical portfolio quality is in a better position than a bank which has suffered few defaults in the past (and therefore is forced to work with estimate samples which are either too small or significantly unbalanced).

---

[25] See Chapter 13 for further details.

[26] Also, a number of subjective passages are present in credit-scoring models: the choice of the sample of companies used to generate the scoring function, the definition of insolvency used to distinguish *a priori* between the two sub-samples, the choice of the starting independent variables, together with more technical, statistical choices (e.g., whether or not to perform an initial transformation of the input variables based on principal component analysis so as to eliminate the problem of correlation between independent variables). However, these subjective decisions are only involved in the construction of the model. Once constructed, the model is applied objectively to all companies.

SELECTED QUESTIONS AND EXERCISES

1. A bank has analysed the financial statements of "good" and "bad" (i.e., defaulted) customers and found that:
   - the ratio of equity to total assets was on average 50 % for "goods" and 20 % for "bads";

   - the ratio of liquid assets to short-term liabilities was on average 2 for "goods" and 0.4 for "bads".
   - the variance/covariance matrix between the two ratios is the following:

$$\Sigma = \begin{bmatrix} 0.04 & 0.07 \\ 0.07 & 0.51 \end{bmatrix}$$

   - its inverse is

$$\Sigma^{-1} = \begin{bmatrix} 32.9 & -4.52 \\ -4.52 & 2.58 \end{bmatrix}$$

The bank wants to use this information in a discriminant analysis model.
   Compute:
   - the coefficients of the discriminant function;
   - the centroids;
   - the threshold to be used to separate good and bad customers, if the ex ante probability (prior) of having a bad customer is 10 % and error costs are not available;
   - the threshold (based on the same priors as above) for a customer with error costs of 20,000 euros (loan granted to a customer that will default) and 1,800 euros (loan refused to a good customer).

2. In a discriminant analysis model, if a borrower offers collateral that reduces the expected LGD...

   (A) ...his/her score remains the same, while his/her PD gets reduced;
   (B) ...his/her PD remains constant, while the cut-off point decreases as the costs associated to a wrong classification change;
   (C) ...his/her score remains constant, while the cut-off point increases as the costs associated to a wrong classification decrease;
   (D) ...his/her score, PD and cut-off point remain all unchanged.

3. A customer has applied for a loan of 500,000 euros, providing a cash collateral of 100,000 (so that, in the event of default, the loss to the bank would be equal to 80 % of the loan). The rate applied would be 12 %; the cost of funds and all other operating expenses for the bank would amount to 10 %, leaving a net profit margin of 2 %.
   The customer's score, based on a discriminant analysis model, is 6.1. This is below the minimum threshold for a loan to be issued, which (based on the error costs shown above and on a prior "bad" probability of 10 %) would be 7.
   How much more cash collateral should the customer provide, leaving the 12 % rate unchanged, for his loan request to be approved?
   Based on the information in this exercise, could you also estimate the customer's PD?

4. Consider the following statements on linear probability models and logit models:

    (i) Linear probability models need to be truncated between 0 and 1, for their results to be equal to those of a logit model;

    (ii) Linear probability models need to be truncated between 0 and 1, for their output ranges to be equal to those of a logit model;

    (iii) Linear probability models and logit models have the same coefficients, but the estimated PDs are different because logit models involve a non-linear filter;

    (iv) Linear probability models, unlike logits, generate biased estimates.

Which ones would you agree with?

(A) ii) and iii);
(B) iv) only;
(C) ii) and iv);
(D) all of them.

5. A scoring model has been modified by adding a new input, which is 95 % correlated with an input that already was in the model and that was considered highly significant by the bank's experts. Which of the following changes in the model's performance would you expect?

    (A) A strong improvement in the model, since the new input will also be highly significant;

    (B) A strong decrease in performance, because we are duplicating information;

    (C) This cannot be told in advance, as it depends on the specific data sample;

    (D) Almost no change in performance.

Appendix 10A
The Estimation of the Gamma Coefficients in Linear Discriminant Analysis

Equation (10.3):

$$\gamma = \Sigma^{-1}(x_1 - x_2)$$

was used in this chapter to compute the γ coefficients of the linear discriminant analysis model. We now demonstrate how this formula was obtained.

We wish to construct our discriminant function

$$z = \sum_{j=1}^{n} \gamma_j x_j = \gamma' x$$

by choosing γ in such a way as to maximise the (standardised) distance between the centroids, namely

$$\underset{\gamma}{Max} \; \frac{|z_A - z_B|}{\sigma_z} = \frac{|\gamma' x_A - \gamma' x_B|}{\sigma_z} \tag{10A.1}$$

To avoid working with the absolute value (a non-differentiable function), we can work on the square q of the expression in [10A.1] and rewrite our problem as follows:

$$\underset{\gamma}{Max} \; \frac{(\gamma' x_A - \gamma' x_B)^2}{\sigma_z^2} = \frac{(\gamma' x_A - \gamma' x_B)^2}{\gamma' \Sigma \gamma} \equiv q(\gamma) \tag{10A.2}$$

Before proceeding, note that function $q(.)$ is homogeneous of degree zero in γ. In other words: $q(k\gamma) = q(\gamma)$ for any real scalar k. In fact:

$$q(k\gamma) = \frac{(k\gamma' x_A - k\gamma' x_B)^2}{k\gamma' \Sigma k\gamma} = \frac{k^2(\gamma' x_A - \gamma' x_B)^2}{k^2 \gamma' \Sigma \gamma} = q(\gamma)$$

This remark will be useful very soon.

Next, to identify γ which maximizes q, we will calculate the gradient of q and require it to be equal to zero:

$$\frac{\partial q}{\partial \gamma} = \frac{2(\gamma' x_A - \gamma' x_B)(x_A - x_B)\gamma' \Sigma \gamma - 2\Sigma \gamma (\gamma' x_A - \gamma' x_B)^2}{(\gamma' \Sigma \gamma)^2} = 0 \tag{10A.3}$$

i.e. require its numerator–ignoring the scalar $2(\gamma' x_B - \gamma' x_B)$- to be nil:

$$(x_A - x_A)\gamma' \Sigma \gamma - \Sigma \gamma (\gamma' x_B - \gamma' x_B) = 0 \tag{10A.4}$$

$$\gamma = \Sigma^{-1}(x_A - x_B) \frac{\gamma' \Sigma \gamma}{(\gamma' x_A - \gamma' x_B)} \tag{10A.5}$$

Now, consider the quantity $\dfrac{\gamma'\Sigma\gamma}{(\gamma'\mathbf{x}_A - \gamma'\mathbf{x}_B)}$ in (10A.5) it is a scalar. As $q(\gamma)$ is homogeneous of grade 0, this scalar can be eliminated from the solution without altering the value of $q(.)$. Thus, (10A.5) simply becomes

$$\gamma = \Sigma^{-1}(\mathbf{x}_1 - \mathbf{x}_2)$$

that is, equation (10.3) in the body of the chapter.

11

Capital Market Models

11.1 INTRODUCTION

In recent decades, the development of international capital markets (both stocks and bonds) has been accompanied by development in the mathematical asset pricing models being used. In many areas of finance, this has led to securities prices – which summarize all available information, as well as of the expectations of investors – being used as input in estimating the value of other market variables. Take, for example, the use of spot rates in order to get to the forward rates, or the use of options prices in order to estimate the volatility of the underlying asset.

This would also include models that use the price of stocks and bonds as an input, in order to estimate the likelihood of default by the issuing company (i.e. capital market approaches). In this chapter, we will look at the characteristics of these models, their basic assumptions, and their potential applications.

In section 11.2, we present a number of examples of models based on bond prices or, to be more precise, on the term structure of spreads between corporate bonds (which include an element of default risk), and risk-free government bonds. Section 11.3, then, analyzes structural models based on the contingent claims approach, which was originally developed by Nobel Prize winner Robert Merton in the early 70's, and shows how these models can be applied using stock prices as an input.

11.2 THE APPROACH BASED ON CORPORATE BOND SPREADS

The starting point for the approach based on the term structure of bond spreads is relatively simple and intuitive. The higher yields demanded by investors for "risky" bonds (as compared with securities of the same maturity that are free from default risk) reflect market expectations as to the likelihood of issuer default. These spreads, therefore, represent a summary of all available information on the factors (both specific and systemic) that influence the probability of default (PD).

Specifically, the data needed as input for these models is as follows:

- the curve of the spreads between the yields of the zero-coupon corporate bonds of a given company and the zero-coupon yields of risk-free securities (essentially, Treasury bonds);
- an estimate of the expected recovery rate on corporate bonds in the event of default.

Based on this data, we can then calculate the data related to expected default rates for each future period. In particular, we have two ways in which we can estimate PD over a time horizon of more than one year, and these ways will be analyzed in sequence below. We may, in fact, use either the spreads on long-term bonds or the spreads implied by forward rates.

11.2.1   Foreword: continuously compounded interest rates

In this chapter, interest rates (r) will be expressed as continuously compounded rates. Practically speaking, the value (V) of a debt at year-end will be equal to the initial capital (C) multiplied by an exponential function as follows:

$$V = Ce^r$$

rather than using the standard equation for simple or compound interest:

$$V = C(1 + r)$$

The reason for this will become clear later in this section. For now, it is sufficient to note that it is always possible to switch from a simple or compound rate (r_s) to the corresponding continuously compounded rate (r_c) by simply imposing that both lead to the same final value, given the same initial capital. From:

$$Ce^{r_c} = V = C(1 + r_s)$$

we get:

$$r_s = e^{r_c} - 1; \quad r_c = \ln(1 + r_s)$$

For example, a continuously compounded rate of 4% equals a simple (or annually compounded) rate of approximately 3.92%.

11.2.2   Estimating the one-year probability of default

Let us assume that the PD of a company that has issued a bond is equal to p. Let us further assume that, in the event of default, investors will lose all of their capital (LGD = 100%), i.e. they will be unable to recover anything. Finally, let r be the one-year risk-free rate (given by the yield on one-year treasury bills), and let $r^* = r + d$ be the yield on risky one-year corporate bond (where d represents the spread between the risk-free security and the corporate bond).

A risk-neutral investor[1] should be indifferent to the two investment alternatives (i.e. the risky bond and the risk-free government bond) when the value of one euro invested in the risk-free security is equal to the value of one euro invested in the corporate bond, weighted by the probability that the bond will be redeemed as scheduled:

$$e^r = (1 - p)e^{r+d} \tag{11.1}$$

from which we get:

$$p = 1 - e^{-d} \tag{11.2}$$

---

[1] We will return to the effects of assuming risk-neutrality later in this chapter. This assumption requires that an investor be indifferent to either a risk-free investment or a risky one, as long as the expected final value of both are the same. For example, such an investor would be indifferent to a certain future payment of one million euros or a lottery that has a 1% chance of paying 100 million euros and a 99% probability of paying nothing.

From (11.2), we see that p is an increasing function of d: the greater the spread (d) required by the market, the greater the probability of default. We also see that the PD implied in bond rates does *not* depend on the level of the rates (i.e. on r and r^*), but solely on the spread between them.[2]

Let us assume that r^* is equal to 5% and that r is equal to 4%. The spread d would then be 1% and we would have:

$$p = 1 - e^{-0,01} = 0,995\%$$

This, therefore, is the value of PD that leads investors to demand a one percent risk premium (5%–4%) over the risk-free rate.

At this point, let us assume that, more realistically, in case of default creditors are able to recover a portion k of the capital invested, plus related interest at the rate r^*, by participating in the liquidation of the business after the default.

In this case, a risk-neutral investor would be indifferent to the two investments (the risk-free security and the corporate bond) if:

$$e^r = [(1 - p) + pk]e^{r+d} = [1 - p(1 - k)]e^{r+d} \tag{11.3}$$

from which we get:

$$p = \frac{1 - e^{-d}}{1 - k} \tag{11.4}$$

Note that $1 - k$ represents the expected loss given default (LGD) on the bond, expressed as a percentage of the initial capital.

If the spread d is still equal to 1% and the recovery rate k is 50%, from (11.4) we get:

$$p = \frac{1 - e^{-0,01}}{1 - 0,5} = 1,99\%$$

This is twice as much as the probability of default obtained above (assuming a zero recovery rate). This is quite logical: if investors continue to demand the same risk premium ($d = 1\%$) despite an expected recovery in the event of default of 50%, this means that they are estimating a PD that is significantly higher than in our previous example based on the assumption of a zero recovery.

11.2.3 Probabilities of default beyond one year

Thus far, we have limited ourselves to the simpler case of interest rates for one year and, using the spread, we have calculated the implied probability of default for the issuer.

We must now extend our analysis to the more complex, and realistic, case of longer maturities. As we will see, using the spreads for various maturities, we are able to estimate the PDs for various time horizons.

Let us take the curve of zero-coupon risk-free rates at various maturities, as well as the curve for zero-coupon rates on the corporate bonds of a given issuer and the related

---

[2] This simplification is made possible by the use of continuously compounded rates. If we were to rewrite (11.1) and (11.2) using traditional simple or compound rates, we would see that it is not possible to write p as a function of the spread alone, but the absolute level of interest rates must be specified, as well.

Table 11.1 Continuously compounded *zero-coupon* rates

Maturity (years)	Return on risk-free bonds (r_T)	Return on risky corporate bonds (r_T^*)	Spread (d_T)	p_T	p_T' conditional on no prior default
1	4.00 %	5.00 %	1.00 %	2.49 %	2.49 %
2	4.10 %	5.20 %	1.10 %	5.44 %	3.03 %
3	4.20 %	5.50 %	1.30 %	9.56 %	4.36 %
4	4.30 %	5.80 %	1.50 %	14.56 %	5.52 %
5	4.50 %	6.20 %	1.70 %	20.37 %	6.80 %

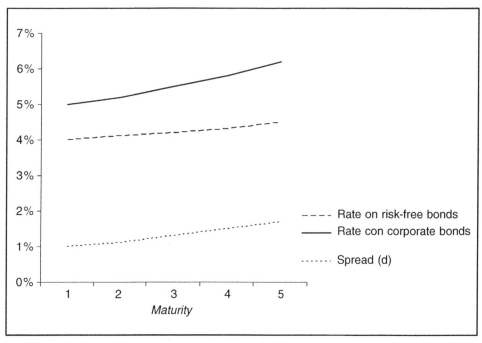

Figure 11.1 Zero-coupon rates on corporate bonds and risk-free bonds

spreads (see the first four columns of Table 11.1 and Figure 11.1 below). In this example, we can see that the spread increases as the maturity increases.

We will now use p_T to indicate the *cumulative* probability of default for a period of T years, i.e. the probability that the issuer will default *between today and the end of the* T^{th} *year*.

If investors in T-year corporate bonds are risk neutral, they will expect the final value of one euro invested in the corporate bond (redemption of the principal weighted for the probability that the bond will be redeemed as scheduled, plus the recovery value k weighted by the probability of default) to be equal to the value of one euro invested in the risk-free security. Generalizing equation (11.3) above, we therefore impose that:

$$e^{r_T T} = [1 - p_T + p_T k]e^{(r_T + d_T)T} = [1 - p_T(1 - k)]e^{(r_T + d_T)T} \qquad (11.5)$$

from which we get:

$$p_T = \frac{1 - e^{-d_T T}}{1 - k} \qquad (11.6)$$

Applying (11.6), we get the cumulative probabilities of default associated with the various maturities.[3] An example is shown in column five of Table 11.1, where we have assumed a value for k of 60%: we can see that, as the time horizon increases, cumulative PDs also increase, since each one incorporates the risk of the previous periods plus the risk of default in year T.

Let us indicate by $s_T \equiv 1 - p_T$ the probability that the debtor survives (i.e. does not default) between now and the end of year T. Also, let us use s'_T to indicate the *marginal* survival probability during year T, i.e. the probability (conditional on no default through the end of year $T - 1$) that the debtor will not default during year T. Accordingly, for any T, we have:

$$s_T = s_{T-1} \cdot s'_T \qquad 11.7$$

In other words, the probability of survival from 0 to T is given by the product of the probability of survival from 0 to $T - 1$ and the (marginal) probability of survival for year T. It follows, then, that the marginal probability of survival can be expressed as follows:

$$s'_T = \frac{s_T}{s_{T-1}} \qquad (11.8)$$

The marginal probability *of default* during year T (p'_T) will then be one minus the related marginal probabilities of survival:

$$p'_T = 1 - s'_T = 1 - \frac{s_T}{s_{T-1}} = 1 - \frac{1 - p_T}{1 - p_{T-1}} \qquad (11.9)$$

Applying (11.9), we can use cumulative probabilities of default in order to estimate the marginal default probabilities associated with the spreads in Table 11.1. For example, the marginal probability of default for year two (again assuming that k is equal to 60%) would be equal to:

$$p'_2 = 1 - \frac{1 - p_2}{1 - p_1} = 1 - \frac{1 - 5.44\%}{1 - 2.49\%} \cong 3.03\%$$

This value and those for the subsequent years are shown in the last column of Table 1.

---

[3] As noted by Hull (2005), this formula provides precise results only if the recovery rate k refers to the bond's no-default value. In practice, this may not be true, and in such cases, the formula is only an approximation.

11.2.4 An alternative approach

An alternative approach[4] to computing marginal PDs uses the zero-coupon forward rates,[5] i.e. the forward rates implied by the curves shown in the table above.[6] Based on the theory of expectations,[7] these rates represent the rates expected by the market on investments starting in the future.

Given the spot rates at years T and $T - 1$, the forward rate for a one-year transaction starting on $T - 1$ can be expressed as follows:

$$_{T-1}r_1 = r_T T - r_{T-1}(T - 1) \qquad (11.10)$$

Based on this relationship, Table 11.2 shows the one-year forward rates for investments starting from years 0, 1, 2, 3 and 4 (with the first, actually being spot rates). As before, these are continuously compounded rates.

Table 11.2 One-year forward rates

Starting date	Maturity (years)	Forward rate on risk-free bonds $(_{T-1}r_1)$	Forward rate on risky corporate bonds $(_{T-1}r^*_1)$	Forward spread $(_{T-1}d_1)$	p'_T conditional on no prior default	p_T
0	1	4.00 %	5.00 %	1.00 %	2.49 %	2.49 %
1	2	4.20 %	5.40 %	1.20 %	2.98 %	5.40 %
2	3	4.40 %	6.10 %	1.70 %	4.21 %	9.38 %
3	4	4.60 %	6.70 %	2.10 %	5.20 %	14.09 %
4	5	5.30 %	7.80 %	2.50 %	6.17 %	19.39 %

It is interesting to note that the spreads between the spot rates for risky and risk-free securities happen to be lower than the spreads between the corresponding forward rates. This is due to the fact that the curve of the spot spreads is positively sloping and, therefore, assumes that spreads are expected to increase in the future. From such expectations it follows, then, that the curve of forward spreads is higher than the curve of spot spreads (Figure 11.2).

Now that we have the spreads for subsequent years, we can estimate the probability of default for years beyond the first using the same criteria used to calculate the probability of default for year one.

In particular, given that p'_T represents the probability of default during the Tth year, assuming that the debtor survives through the end of year $T - 1$, we can rewrite equation (11.3) as follows:

$$e^{T-1r_1} = [(1 - p'_{T-1}) + p'_{T-1}k]e^{T-1r_1 + T-1d_1} = [1 - p'_{T-1}(1 - k)]e^{T-1r_1 + T-1d_1} \qquad (11.11)$$

where the left-hand side is the final amount of a risk-free forward investment and the right-hand side denotes the expected final amount of a forward investment in the corporate

---

[4] The relationship between PDs and forward rates is used by Elton, et al. (2001), for example.
[5] See Appendix 3A of Chapter 3.
[6] For the economic significance and the calculation criteria of forward rates, see Appendix 1B .
[7] See Appendix 1A of Chapter 1.

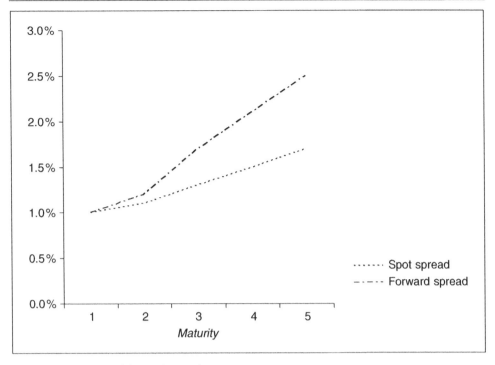

Figure 11.2 Spot and forward spreads

bond. From this relationship, we then get the probability of default after T years, along the same lines as equation (11.4) above:

$$p'_T = \frac{1 - e^{-T-1d_1}}{1 - k} \tag{11.12}$$

Thus, taking year two as an example and applying (11.12) with an assumed recovery rate k of 60%, we get the following probability of default:

$$p'_2 = \frac{1 - e^{-1,20\%}}{1 - 60\%} \cong 2.98\%$$

This value and those of the subsequent years are shown in the fifth column of Table 11.2. By rewriting as follows the relationship between marginal and cumulative PDs in (11.9):

$$p_T = 1 - (1 - p'_T)(1 - p_{T-1}) \tag{11.3}$$

we can find the cumulative PDs associated with these marginal PDs. For example, the cumulative 2-year PD would be:

$$p_2 = 1 - (1 - p'_2)(1 - p_1) = 1 - (1 - 2.98\%)(1 - 2.49\%) \cong 5.40\%$$

Alternatively, given that the cumulative probability of survival can be seen as the product of all marginal probabilities of survival for all years from 1 to T:

$$s_T = \prod_{t=1}^{T} s_t' = \prod_{t=1}^{T} (1 - p_t') \tag{11.14}$$

we can calculate the cumulative PDs directly as

$$p_T \equiv 1 - s_T = \prod_{t=1}^{T} (1 - p_t') \tag{11.15}$$

i.e. as a function of just the marginal PDs. For example, p_3, the probability of default from now until the end of year 3, can be calculated as

$$p_3 = \prod_{t=1}^{3} (1 - p_t') = (1 - p_1')(1 - p_2')(1 - p_3') =$$
$$= (1 - 2.49\%)(1 - 2.98\%)(1 - 4.21\%) \cong 9.38\%$$

The result of the application of (11.15) to all the data of our example is shown in the last column of Table 11.2. It is interesting to note that this alternative method based on forward rates provides results that are, on the whole, similar to the first method (see Table 11.1).

11.2.5 Benefits and limitations of the approach based on corporate bond spreads

The method described here has two main benefits:

- it uses market data that is, by nature, objective and, therefore, exogenous to the subjective assessments of the individual financial institution;
- it is a forward-looking model in that it is able to estimate the default rates that the market is expecting for the future and not those that occurred in the past. This makes it superior, for example, to the approaches adopted by ratings agencies, which take the percentage of defaulted bonds in the various ratings classes and use them as an estimate of future PDs for the given classes.[8]

However, the approach based on the term structure of spreads also has a number of limitations.

The first and foremost is the assumption that the entire difference between the risk-adjusted and risk-free rate can be attributed to credit risk, whereas often a portion of the corporate bond spread simply reflects the fact that corporate bonds are less liquid. Take, in particular, the second variant that uses forward rates: we used the forward rates as if they were an unbiased estimate of future spot rates, assuming that expectations theory was valid. However, this theory is difficult to support, especially for longer maturities

---

[8] See Chapter 13.

where increasing liquidity premiums are found that are clearly not directly related to default risk.

A second assumption underlying these models is risk neutrality. In equation (11.3), we assumed that the buyer of a bond was indifferent to receiving the (certain) amount for a treasury bond or the (risky) amount for a corporate bond, as long as the expected value for the two was the same. In reality, however, in order to trade a risk-free investment for a risky one, investors demand a premium, i.e. they demand that the expected future amount for the risky security be equal to that of the risk-free security plus a premium R. Equation (11.3) therefore becomes

$$e^r + R = [1 - p^*(1 - k)]e^{r+d} \qquad (11.16)$$

Comparing the two equations, it becomes clear that the value of p that solves (3) is higher than that value p^* that solves (11.16). Given that (11.16) reflects an investor's true mindset,[9] i.e. risk-averse, we must conclude that equation (11.3) and subsequent equations *overestimate* PD values. These PDs based on risk neutrality are therefore known as risk-neutral PDs and may be used in a number of asset-pricing models (e.g. to estimate the fair value of a credit default swap); however, they are not directly comparable with real-life PDs (nor with annual bond default rates, which are the empirical manifestation of real PDs).

Along with these theoretical limitations, the approach described above also suffers from some clear operational limitations. First of all, it cannot be applied to companies that do not issue listed bonds, and even to companies with a range of listed debt instruments, that does not provide a complete range of zero-coupon rates for all relevant maturities. Zero-coupon rates can be calculated indirectly based on coupon-bearing securities through a bootstrapping procedure (see Appendix 3A); however, the company in question still needs to have issued securities in a variety of maturities, in order for the entire spread curve to be estimated.

In conclusion, we should note that the relationship between spreads and PDs can also be used in a different manner. It is possible, for example, for a bank to have an estimated PD for a customer, which they then use to determine the "fair" rate for a loan. Relationships such as that of equation (11.3) can therefore be used to set the spread d as a function of the customer's (risk-free) PD. This topic is discussed further in Appendix 11A and in Chapter 15.

11.3   STRUCTURAL MODELS BASED ON STOCK PRICES

11.3.1   An introduction to structural models

A second approach based on information gathered from capital markets owes its origins to the options pricing model originally developed by Black and Scholes (1973). This approach, based on contingent claims analysis, was first applied to default risk by Robert Merton in 1974.

---

[9] The risk-neutrality assumption, by stating that investors only demand to be compensated for the expected loss and not also for the potential volatility of losses, implicitly ignores the significance of the unexpected losses, i.e. it ignores what, strictly speaking, is the essence of credit risk (see the introduction to this section of the book).

Merton's model uses stock prices as input and seeks to determine the equilibrium bond spread, in addition to estimating PD. It has been subsequently enhanced a number of times in order to attempt to eliminate certain unrealistic assumptions and to make it easier to apply in practice.

The model is based on one very simple intuition: a company defaults when the value of its assets becomes lower than the value of its liabilities. In fact, when the investments made by a company using funds lent by banks and bondholders are unable to generate the cash flows that were originally expected, shareholders suffer a loss on the risk capital they invested in the company. If the value of capital reaches zero (i.e. if the value of assets is less than the liabilities to third parties), shareholders have already lost everything they could lose, and the principle of limited liability states that they are not required to invest any further capital in the company in order to pay the company's debts. As a result, when the first payment to the creditors is due, the shareholders will be better off by declaring bankruptcy and leaving the company (the net value of which is now negative) in the hands of the creditors.

In other words, it can be said that shareholders have the option of defaulting and giving the company to the creditors, rather than repaying the debt, when the value of liabilities is greater than the value of the company's assets.

Merton's model and the variants discussed below are generally referred to as *structural models*. As we will see, this term comes from the fact that these models focus on the structural traits of a company that determine its PD, i.e. the value of assets, the value of debt (and, consequently, the degree of leverage), and the volatility of asset values. As such, they measure both financial risk (connected with financial leverage) and business risk (due to the actual volatility of the assets).

Conversely, models based on bond spreads, such as those described in section 11.2 above, are referred to as *reduced models* because they ignore the causes driving default, but simply acknowledge the fact that default is possible and reduce the problem to estimating its likelihood using bond spreads.

11.3.2 Merton's model: general structure

The model Merton originally devised in 1974 describes the financial structure of the borrowing firm in a simplified manner. It assumes that a company has just one single liability, i.e. a zero-coupon debt (either a bank loan or a bond) that calls for repayment of the principal in a lump sum upon maturity. More specifically, this liability calls for the repayment of an amount F at time T and has a market value of B. The company's assets, also evaluated at market value and not at book value, are equal to V. The difference between V and B represents the value of risk capital E. We will use B_0, V_0 and E_0 to indicate the current value (today) of these three amounts.

The market value of the company's assets fluctuates from moment to moment in a partially unpredictable manner. More specifically, Merton assumed that instantaneous percent changes in V (dV/V) could be described by the following geometric Brownian motion:

$$\frac{dV}{V} = \mu dt + \sigma_v dz = \mu dt + \sigma_v \varepsilon \sqrt{dt} \tag{11.17}$$

where μ is the expected instantaneous yield on the assets and dz (equal to the product of a standard normally-distributed term ε and the square root of time) is a random disturbance, the effects of which are either reduced or amplified by the coefficient σ_V (which represents the rate of variability of the geometric Brownian motion).

Practically speaking, the percent changes in assets ("asset returns") evolve stochastically, and the uncertainty as to their future path increases with the time horizon. This phenomenon is shown in Figure 11.3.

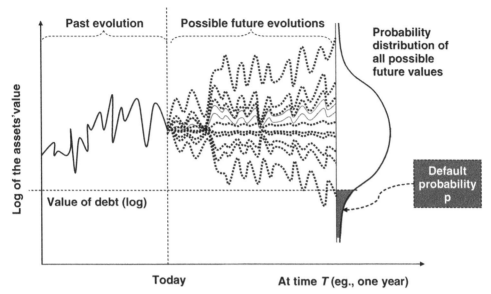

Figure 11.3 The logic behind Merton's model

Credit risk concerns the possibility that the value of the company's assets, V_{rmT}, will be less than the repayment value of the loan, F, as of the maturity of the debt (T). This possibility increases as the following increase:

- the ratio B_0/V_0, i.e. the company's leverage at $T = 0$;
- the volatility of the company's asset yield, measured as the standard deviation of the asset yield σ_V;
- the debt's maturity.

A company's probability of default can be expressed as the probability that $V_T < F$. Visually, this probability is equal to an area under the normal distribution (see the highlighted tail in Figure 11.3), which represents all negative asset yields that are large enough to lead from V_0 to a V_T that is lower than the repayment value (F) of the debt.

All other things being equal, this area increases as:

(i)   the beginning market value of assets (V_0) decreases;
(ii) the nominal value of debt (F) increases;
(iii) the volatility of the market value of assets increases (with a higher σ_V, the distribution becomes more "squashed" and the tails therefore thicken);
(iv) the debt's maturity increases.

In particular, given a certain value for T, the first three variables represent all relevant information needed to determine a company's probability of default:

(i) the outlook for the company, its industry, and the economy, which affects the company's expected future cash flows, the present value of which represents the current market value of its assets (V_0);

(ii) the company's financial risk, which is summarized by the ratio of assets to liabilities, i.e. by the leverage;

(iii) the level of business risk, which is implicit in the volatility of the asset returns.

11.3.3   Merton's model: the role of contingent claims analysis

As we have seen, shareholders have the option of handing over their company to creditors rather than repaying the company's debt. In short, they can trade V_T for F when the former is lower than the latter.

This can be considered as a put option (i.e. the option to sell at an agreed upon price) that the company's lenders (e.g. a bank) have granted the shareholders. Specifically, it is a put option on the value of the company's assets, where the strike price is equal to the face value of the debt (F) at maturity T.

Figure 11.4 shows this concept in the form of a graph. For values of V_T that are higher than the face value of the debt (F), such as V_2, the asset value is enough to pay the debtholder (e.g., the bank) the entire principal and related accrued interest. The difference ($V_2 - F$) remains with the company's shareholders. Conversely, for values of V that are less than the value of the debt, such as V_1, the company is insolvent and the bank only receives a portion of the amount due. This, as we can see in Figure 11.4, is quite similar to the payoff profile of a short put option.

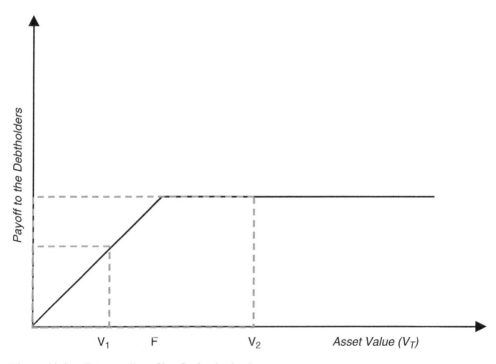

Figure 11.4   The payoff profile of a lender bank

It can be easily shown that, in order to hedge the credit risk of the loan, the bank could, in turn, acquire a long put option on the value of the company's assets (V) with the same maturity as the loan (T) and a strike price equal to the debt repayment (F). The combination of the loan and the put option would provide a risk-free payoff (independent of the asset value at maturity) of F, as shown in Table 11.3 (where P_0 indicates the premium paid at time 0 for the put option).

Table 11.3 Payoff at time 0 and T on a loan and a long put option

	Payoff at time 0	Payoff at T	
		if $V_T < F$	if $V_T > F$
Loan	$-B_0$	V_T	F
Put option	$-P_0$	$F - V_T$	0
Total	$-(B_0 + P_0)$	F	F

The last row of the table shows that the bank, by adding up the loan and a long put option on the value of the company's assets, could eliminate credit risk, thereby transforming their risky position into a risk-free one.

If such a combination is free from risk, then its equilibrium value ($B_0 + P_0$) must be equal to the present value of a risk-free security paying F on maturity. In short:

$$P_0 + B_0 = Fe^{-rT} \qquad (11.17)$$

Furthermore, the value of the put option, P_0, can be calculated using an options pricing model. Merton uses the model originally developed by Black and Scholes (1973),[10] thereby obtaining the following result:

$$P_0 = Fe^{-rT} N(-d_2) - N(-d_1) V_0 \qquad (11.18)$$

---

[10] The Black & Scholes formulas for the value of a call option (C) and a put option (P) are the following:

$$C = S \cdot N(d_1) - Xe^{-rT} N(d_2)$$
$$P = Xe^{-iT} N(-d_2) - S \cdot N(-d_1)$$

where:
$$d_1 = \frac{\ln(S/X) + (r + \sigma^2/2)T}{\sigma\sqrt{T}}$$
$$d_2 = d_1 - \sigma\sqrt{T}$$

S, X, T, r and σ indicate the market price of the underlying assets, the strike price of the option, the maturity of the option, the risk-free rate, and the standard deviation of returns on the underlying assets, respectively.

where $N(.)$ is the standard normal cumulative density function[11], while d_1 and d_2 are defined as follows:

$$d_1 = \frac{\ln(V_0/F) + (r + 1/2\sigma_V^2)T}{\sigma_V\sqrt{T}} = \frac{\ln(V_0/Fe^{-rT}) + 1/2\sigma_V^2 T}{\sigma_V\sqrt{T}}$$

$$= \frac{1/2\sigma_V^2 T - \ln(L)}{\sigma_V\sqrt{T}} \tag{11.18a}$$

$$d_2 = -\frac{1/2\sigma_V^2 T + \ln(L)}{\sigma_V\sqrt{T}} = d_1 - \sigma_V\sqrt{T} \tag{11.18b}$$

where $L = \dfrac{Fe^{-rT}}{V}$ represent a measure of the debtor firm's leverage.

From (11.17)–(11.18), we obtain three important results:

(i) the current market value, B_0, of the loan;
(ii) the lending rate that should be required by the bank and the related premium over the risk-free rate;
(iii) the (risk-neutral) probability of default for the debtor.

11.3.4 Merton's model: loan value and equilibrium spread

The market value of the loan, B_0, can be determined by substituting the value of P_0 in (11.18) into (11.17). That is:

$$B_0 = Fe^{-rT}[1 - N(-d_2)] + N(-d_1)V_0 = Fe^{-rT}\left[N(d_2) + \frac{1}{L}N(-d_1)\right] \tag{11.19}$$

Equation (11.19) shows that the value of the loan increases as the debtor's leverage and the loan's maturity decrease.

The loan's equilibrium yield is the discount rate r^* that makes the present value of the final repayment F equal to the current market value of the loan, B_0. Formally:

$$Fe^{-r^*T} = B_0 \tag{11.20}$$

from which we get:

$$r^* = -\frac{\ln\dfrac{B_0}{F}}{T} = -\frac{\ln\dfrac{Fe^{-rT} - P_0}{F}}{T} \tag{11.21}$$

Substituting (11.18) into (11.21), we can then calculate r^*, as well as the equilibrium spread $d \equiv r^* - r$. This can be easily shown to be the following:

$$d \equiv r^* - r = -\frac{1}{T}\ln\left[N(d_2) + \frac{V_0}{Fe^{-rT}}N(-d_1)\right] \tag{11.22}$$

---

[11] $N(d)$ indicates the probability, as shown in the statistical tables for the standard normal distribution, associated with a value less than or equal to d.

where $\dfrac{V_0}{Fe^{-rT}} = \dfrac{1}{L}$ is the inverse of the leverage index L used above.

In order to fully understand the implications of (11.22), consider the following example. Take a company with a current market value of its assets (V_0) of 100,000 euros, a volatility (σ_V) of 10 % and a debt face value (F) of 90,000 euros. Assume that the debt's maturity (T) is one year and that the risk-free rate (r) is 5 %.

The leverage L of the company is equal to the ratio between (Fe^{-rT}) and V_0, or 85.61 %. Using this value and the other data provided above, we can estimate the market value of the debt, B_0, and the equilibrium risk premium (d). We first compute:

$$d_1 = \frac{1/2\sigma_V^2 T - \ln(L)}{\sigma_V \sqrt{T}} = 1,603605$$

$$d_2 = d_1 - \sigma_V \sqrt{T} = 1,503605$$

$$N(-d_1) = 0,054401$$

$$N(d_2) = 0,933658$$

from which we get:

$$B_0 = Fe^{-rT}\left[N(d_2) + \frac{1}{L}N(-d_1) \right] = 85.371$$

$$d = -\frac{1}{T} \ln\left[N(d_2) + \frac{1}{L}N(-d_1) \right] = 0,280\,\%$$

The company should then be granted an interest rate of 5.28 %, i.e. the risk-free rate plus the premium d.

Table 11.4 generalizes our example by calculating the various values of the equilibrium spread (in the case of a one-year loan and a risk-free rate of 5 %) for various levels of leverage and various volatilities of the asset returns.

Table 11.4 Risk premiums at various levels of leverage and asset yield volatility (T=1; r=5 %)

σ_A	5 %	10 %	15 %	20 %	25 %	30 %
L						
50 %	0.000 %	0.000 %	0.000 %	0.002 %	0.029 %	0.149 %
60 %	0.000 %	0.000 %	0.002 %	0.044 %	0.243 %	0.700 %
70 %	0.000 %	0.001 %	0.052 %	0.355 %	1.032 %	2.063 %
80 %	0.000 %	0.050 %	0.506 %	1.494 %	2.873 %	4.519 %
90 %	0.033 %	0.795 %	2.272 %	4.070 %	6.036 %	8.112 %
100 %	2.015 %	4.069 %	6.165 %	8.301 %	10.478 %	12.696 %

As we can see, the risk premium (or spread) increases as the degree of leverage (i.e. the company's financial risk) and asset volatility (i.e. the company's business risk) increase, all else remaining equal.

11.3.5 Merton's model: probability of default

The third result that can be derived from Merton's model is the company's probability of default, which can be expressed as the probability that the market value of the company's assets will be less than the repayment value of the loan at maturity. Specifically:

$$p = \Pr(V_T < F) \tag{11.23}$$

As we have seen, this is the probability of exercising the loan's implicit put option. Using the Black and Scholes model, it can be shown that the probability of exercising a put option may be expressed as follows:

$$1 - N(d_2) = N(-d_2)$$

It is then possible to calculate the PD as

$$PD = p = \Pr(V_T < F) = N(-d_2) = 1 - N(d_2) \tag{11.24}$$

In the example above, where $V_0 = 100,000$, $F = 90.000$ (so $L = 85.61\,\%$), $\sigma_v = 10\,\%$, $r = 5\,\%$, and $T = 1$, the company's PD is equal to:

$$p = \Pr(V_T < F) = 1 - N(d_2) = N(-d_2) = 6{,}63\,\%$$

Before we continue, it is important to underscore that PDs obtained through (11.24) represent (as in the models discussed in section 11.2 above) *risk-neutral* probabilities of default. This is because, in deriving equation (11.24), the expected return on assets (μ in equation 11.17) has been replaced, for the sake of convenience, by the risk-free rate r.

We are therefore assuming that someone who invests in the risky assets of a company does so without demanding a premium over the yield on risk-free securities. Thus, as seen in section 11.2 above, we are assuming a risk-neutral investor; this, for reasons similar to those laid out in section 11.2.5, leads to overestimate the PD[12]

11.3.6 The term structure of credit spreads and default probabilities

One interesting result from Merton's model is the fact that the spread curve rises for companies with a relatively low PD, while it declines for companies with higher PDs.

The example shown in Table 11.5 assumes a risk-free rate of 5 % and estimates the cumulative probabilities of default (equation 11.24) and the corresponding spreads on annual continuously compounded rates (equation 11.22) for two companies with different leverage and different asset variability. The same results are also shown in Figure 11.5.

As we can see in this example, all else being equal, longer maturities lead to *declining* risk premiums when the probability of default is high. Although somewhat counterintuitive, this is due to the fact that, for companies with a very high probability of default, there is a significant risk that they will not "survive" the first year. However, if they do get past the first year, the probability of becoming insolvent in subsequent years declines significantly, given that many of them will actually *improve* their credit rating. In fact,

---

[12] For further details, see Appendix 11B.

Table 11.5 Probability of default (p) and risk premium (d) by maturity

Maturity (years)	$L = 90\%$; Sigma (σ_V) $= 20\%$		$L = 75\%$; Sigma (σ_V) $= 10\%$	
	p (cumulative PD)	d (spread)	p (cumulative PD)	d (spread)
1	33.48 %	4.07 %	0.24 %	0.01 %
2	40.86 %	3.69 %	2.48 %	0.06 %
3	44.79 %	3.37 %	5.77 %	0.13 %
4	47.47 %	3.12 %	9.04 %	0.19 %
5	49.52 %	2.93 %	12.00 %	0.24 %
6	51.19 %	2.77 %	14.64 %	0.28 %
7	52.61 %	2.64 %	16.98 %	0.31 %
8	53.85 %	2.53 %	19.06 %	0.33 %
9	54.95 %	2.44 %	20.93 %	0.35 %
10	55.95 %	2.36 %	22.61 %	0.36 %

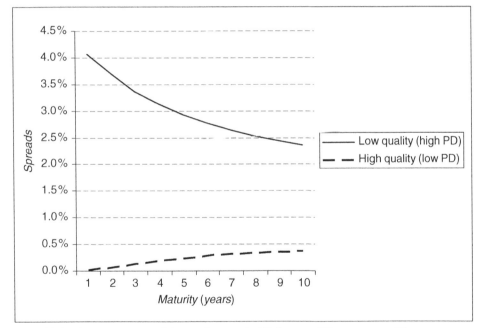

Figure 11.5   Term structures of the credit spreads (d) for two different types of borrower

while a high asset volatility does cause a great many companies to default during the first year, it also leads an equally significant number of borrowers to considerably reduce their leverage, which, in turn, reduces the probability of default in the coming years. As a result, the longer the time horizon, the more the curve of marginal PDs declines. Those declining PDs justify the decreasing term structure of the spreads shown in Figure 11.6.

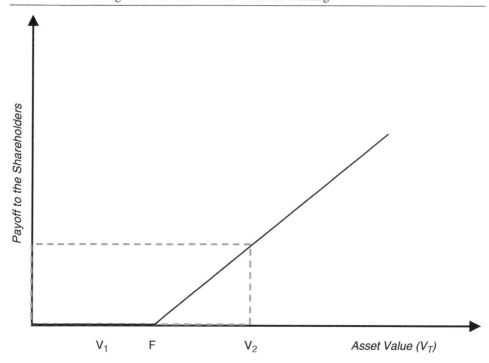

Figure 11.6   Shareholder payoff profile

11.3.7 Strengths and limitations of Merton's model

There are two important benefits to Merton's model. First of all, it is effective in showing what variables drive a company's PD (and, therefore, the credit spreads required on its debt). Those are: (i) the ratio of debt to assets (leverage), which represents financial risk and (ii) the volatility of asset value returns, which depends on the variability in the expected operating cash flows generated by the company, and therefore represents the level of business risk.

Secondly, using these inputs Merton's model enables us to calculate PDs and spreads in an objective, clear, and formally elegant way.

The model does, however, have a number of limitations, which are particularly significant when shifting from pure theory to the actual use the model for empirical estimates of PDs or spreads. These problems fall into several categories:

- The first group is connected with the simplistic assumption of a single zero-coupon liability where principal and interest are repaid in a lump sum upon maturity. In real life, of course, companies have complex financial structures with liabilities that have a variety of maturities and periodic interest payments, as well as a number of different levels of seniority and security. Furthermore, companies can default at any time, regardless of the maturity of their liabilities, e.g. when they miss the payment of a bond coupon (or do not pay interest on bank loans). For this reason, Merton's model has been subject to a number of enhancements aimed at making the company's debt structure more complex and realistic.[13]

- A second problem of Merton's model is that it assumes that the distribution of asset asset returns is a standard normal; such an assumption may not realistic.
- A third problem, and the most significant in terms of the model's application, is the fact that a number of the model's inputs, particularly the market value of assets (V_0) and the volatility of asset returns (σ_V), are not observable directly on the market. In fact, the market value of assets is the sum of the value of capital and debt (i.e. $V = E + B$). The value of the former may be observed if the company is listed publicly, but the value of the latter could only be observed only if all of the company's liabilities were bonds that are actively traded on the secondary market (which is clearly not very likely). Under these conditions, the asset value could be estimated as the sum of these two components, and it would be possible to measure its present value and its past volatility. However, this is clearly not realistic, given that most companies also finance themselves through unlisted bonds, bank loans, trade payables, and other forms of financing that have no liquid secondary market.
- A fourth limit of Merton's model arises from the assumption of constant risk-free interest rates. This assumption, which fails to allow for an analysis of the relationship between interest-rate risk and equity risk, has been removed by various authors, such as Kim, Ramaswamy and Sundaresan (1993), who have proposed an *à la Merton* model with stochastic interest rates and bankruptcy costs.
- Another problem is related to the arbitrage-free nature of models like the one by Black and Scholes, which was used by Merton. This type of models assume that arbitrages can constantly be carried out on the assets underlying an option (in our case, the company's assets). This, too, looks unrealistic, given that a the assets of a company (unlike its equity) are not normally traded on financial markets.
- A final problem of Merton's model is the fact that it focuses solely on default risk, without considering migration risk, i.e. the risk of a deterioration in the issuer's credit

---

[13] This type of problem has been dealt with by several authors. Geske (1977) introduced the possibility that a company should default prior to the debt's maturity, due to liabilities that pay interest or covenants. In Geske's model, namely, default may occur in conjunction with the payment date of an outflow of interest expense, even when the value of assets is greater than that of the debt, if that payment brought the value of equity to such a level that it would be inconvenient for shareholders to make the payment. Black and Cox (1976) considered the possibility that default could occur at any time when the value of assets falls below a certain threshold K, which is linked to the minimum equity value imposed by a bond covenant. Based on the empirical fact that companies often continue to operate even when the asset value falls below the total value of liabilities, because of long-term debt that does not need to be paid immediately, Vasicek (1984) introduced a distinction between short-term and long-term debt. His model treats default as an event that occurs when the value of assets falls below a certain threshold, to be set between the value of short-term debt and that of total debt. Perhaps the best known extension to Merton's model is the one proposed by Longstaff and Schwartz in 1995: this differs from Merton's original framework in three key ways. First, default occurs simultaneously for all liabilities when the value of assets falls below a predefined threshold K, as in Black and Cox (1976). Secondly, rather than deriving the payoff at default for each debt category *endogenously* (based on assumptions regarding the ratio of assets to debt and the different seniority of the various debt categories), Longstaff and Schwarz consider the recovery rate to be an exogenous constant, set through negotiations that are to take place after the default. Finally, the risk-free interest rate is stochastic. The model produces results that are consistent with empirical observations, and for this reason has been used by several financial institutions, particularly for pricing purposes. In particular, the model produces probabilities of default that increase with maturities, spreads that increase with the correlation between interest rates and the asset values, and decrease as yields on government bonds rise.

rating.[14] In other words, Merton's model provides no indication as to the likelihood that the company's credit rating should decline, despite remaining solvent[15].

11.3.8   The KMV model for calculating V_0 and σ_V

The first three problems listed above (simplistic debt structure, normally-distributed asset returns, and difficulties in estimating V_0 and σ_V) are expressly dealt with by the model developed by KMV,[16] a California-based firm that was recently acquired by Moody's Investor Services. In this section, we will be focusing on the last of these (the empirical calculation of V_0 and σ_V), while the first two will be discussed in the following section.

This model starts from the intuition (which is implied in Merton's model[17]) that the value of equity (E) is equal to the value of a call option on the market value of the company's assets, with a maturity equal to the residual life of its debt (T) and a strike price equal to the nominal repayment value of the debt (F). Table 11.6 shows how the two positions produce the same result at maturity (T); this is also shown graphically in Figure 11.6.

Table 11.6 Matrix of payoffs as a shareholder or for the purchase of a call option on asset value with a strike price of F

	Payoff at time 0	Payoff at T	
		if $V_T < F$	if $V_T > F$
Shareholder	$-E_0$	0	$(V_T - F)$
Purchase of a call option	$-C_0$	0	$(V_T - F)$

As we can see, for values of V_T below the face value of debt, the company is insolvent and the remaining assets are entirely used to repay the debt. As a result, shareholders lose the entire value of their initial investment (E_0) and receive nothing. Conversely, if the asset value is greater than the face value of debt, the difference $V_T - F$ represents shareholder wealth (with unlimited potential gains). This is exactly the payoff of a long call option.

If the two positions (shareholder and buyer of a call option on the asset value with a strike price of F and a maturity of T) are equivalent in terms of payoff upon maturity, it

---

[14] As we will see below, this limitation can be overcome by considering multiple thresholds, rather than a single threshold for the level of assets at which default occurs. In other words, we would need to set thresholds, assuming a discrete distribution of market values for assets, at which the company is either upgraded or downgraded. This is what the *CreditMetrics*™ model described in Chapter 14 does.

[15] See Chapter 14 for a generalized version of the Merton's model, providing for migration risk.

[16] The acronym KMV comes from the last names of the three founding partners, Steven Kealhofer, John Andrew McQuown, and Oldrich Vasicek. Kealhofer and Vasicek were professors at the University of California, Berkeley.

[17] We know that, by definition, $V_0 = E_0 + B_0$. Furthermore, according to Merton's model, $B_0 = Fe^{-rT} - P_0$, where P_0 is the value of a put option. It follows, then, that $V_0 = E_0 + Fe^{-rT} - P_0$, i.e. $V_0 + P_0 = E_0 + Fe^{-rT}$. Now, one simply needs to recall that, according to the so called "put/call parity" between European options, $S + p = c + Xe^{-rT}$ (where the symbols maintain the meanings specified in footnote 10): it follows that E_0 coincides with the value c of a call option on V, with a maturity of T and a strike price of F.

follows that the related initial cost must also be the same. The market value of equity can therefore be expressed using a pricing formula for call options. If we adopt the formula by Black and Scholes (as was done for Merton's model[18]), we have:

$$E_0 = V_0 \cdot N(d_1) - Fe^{-rT}N(d_2) \tag{11.25}$$

If we are analyzing a listed company, E_0 is known and is equal to the company's market capitalization. We could then look for a value of V_0 that is consistent with this empirical value of E_0, and in this way we could determine V_0 (which, as mentioned above, is not directly observable on the market).

However, V_0 is not the only unknown in equation (11.25). As the reader may recall, d_1 and d_2 (as well as V_0) depend on asset volatility σ_V: this, too, is an unknown variable (since it cannot be observed on the market). Therefore, there can be infinite pairs of values for V_0 and σ_V that are consistent with the observed value of E_0, and one cannot tell which of these is the right one.

In order to find a unique solution, we need to find a second equation that connects V_0 and σ_V, so as to create a system of two equations with two unknowns. This second equation can be obtained by applying a theorem of stochastic calculus known as Ito's lemma, and can be shown to be the following:[19]

$$\sigma_E = \frac{V_0}{E_0}N(d_1)\sigma_V \tag{11.26}$$

The left-hand side member is the volatility of the market value of equity (σ_E), which, in the case of a publicly listed firm, can be estimated empirically (e.g. as the standard deviation of the stock's past returns) and can therefore be considered a known variable. The right-hand side again includes our two unknowns, V_0 and σ_V (both explicitly and "hidden" in the term d_1). As such, we can unite (25) and (26) into the following system

$$\begin{cases} E_0 = V_0 N(d_1) - Fe^{-rT}N(d_2) \\ \sigma_E = \dfrac{V_0}{E_0}N(d_1)\sigma_V \end{cases}$$

and solve it for values of V_0 and σ_V that are consistent with the observed values of E_0 and σ_E.

The solution cannot be derived directly, isolating the unknowns V_0 and σ_V, because these unknowns appear multiple times in both equations (given that d_1 and d_2 are non-linear functions of both V_0 and σ_V). Therefore, the system must be solved iteratively: we choose two initial estimates of the unknowns and iteratively change both V_0 and σ_V until (11.25)–(11.26) generate the values of E_0 and σ_E that have been observed empirically on the stock market.

---

[18] See footnote 10.

[19] Intuitively, the greater the leverage of the company, the more equation (11.26) expresses the volatility of equity yields as a function of asset volatility. This can be explained by the fact that business risk first affects shareholders, and only later (when the market value of assets becomes less than the value of liabilities to third parties) does it affect bondholders. As a result, the greater the percentage of assets that are financed with debt, the greater the variability of assets amplifies the volatility of equity.

Take, for example, a publicly listed company with a market capitalization (E_0) of €10 million and an annual standard deviation of stock yields (σ_E) of 50 %. Assume that the company has a sole liability maturing in $T = 1$ years with a nominal value (F) of €90 million. Finally, assume a risk-free rate (r) of 5 %.

Let us now have a look at the iterative process necessary in order to find the current market value of assets (V_0) and the volatility of the asset returns (σ_V). We start by assigning two random (but realistic) values to these two unknowns. For the market value of assets we could use, for example, the sum of the face value of debt and the market value of equity (90+10 = €100 million), while for asset return volatility we could use a value that is less than equity volatility (e.g. 10 % instead of 50 %).

Substituting these values into our system, we get

$$\begin{cases} E_0 = 14{,}63 \\ \sigma_E = 65\,\% \end{cases}$$

These values for V_0 and σ_V seem to be too high, given that they generate values of E_0 and σ_E that are higher than those observed empirically. We could then try lower values, such as $V_0 = 90$ and $\sigma_V = 2\%$. The new values from the system would then be

$$\begin{cases} E_0 = 4{,}39 \\ \sigma_E = 41\,\% \end{cases}$$

This time, our solutions are too low, so we can now try values that are slightly higher and keep trying. In reality, it would be better to automate this process using some ad-hoc software[20] to change V_0 and σ_V until we get the values of E_0 and σ_E that fit with our two empirical values. The data for this problem and an example of the possible computer output are shown in Table 11.7. As we can see, the values that are consistent with $E_0 = $ €10 million and $\sigma_E = 50\%$ are $V_0 = $ €95,576,493 and $\sigma_V = 5.33\%$.

With these values of V_0 and σ_V, we can then use Merton's equations in order to calculate the values of PD and the loan's equilibrium spread (equations 11.24 and 11.22). The results are shown in the third section of Table 11.8 above.

Somewhat paradoxically, however, after calculating V_0 and σ_V, the KMV model *does not use them in the formulas recommended by Merton*, but rather follows a different procedure. This procedure (which is discussed in detail in the next section) makes it possible to remove the assumption that asset returns are normally–distributed, and to calculate real-life PDs, rather than risk-neutral ones.

11.3.9 The KMV approach and the calculation of PD

Rather than calculating a company's probability of default directly, using equation (11.24) and the values of V_0 and σ_V, KMV takes a two-step approach:

(1) first, a risk index is computed called the "distance to default" (DD): although this index is related to PD (better companies are assigned a higher DD value), it cannot be directly interpreted as a probability;

---

[20] This can also be done using the "Solver" tool in Excel.

Table 11.7 Calculation of market value as asset volatility

Input	
Market value of equity (E)	10,000,000
Standard deviation of equity yields (σ_E)	50 %
Nominal value of debt repayment (F)	90,000,000
Risk-free interest rate (r)	5 %
Debt maturity (T)	1
Output	
Market value of assets (V_0)	95,576,493
Standard deviation of annual asset yields (σ_V)	5.33 %
Additional output of the Merton model	
Market value of debt (B_0), equation	85,576,495
Equilibrium spread d	0.04 %
Equilibrium rate ($r^* = r + d$)	5.04 %
Risk-neutral probability of default (p)	2.07 %

(2) DD is then converted into a probability of default based on an empirical law which is based to past evidence.

We will now look at these two phases in greater detail.[21] We must first, however, introduce the concept of default point (*DP*), which is another innovation of KMV over Merton's model.

As we have seen, in Merton's model default occurs when the value of assets falls below the face value of debt: a limitation of this model is that it assumes that debt is comprised of single liability with a maturity of *T* years. The KMV model, on the other hand, acknowledges that real companies finance their activities with a combination of both short-term and long-term debt. While it is important that the value of assets remain higher than the value of short-term debt (which is to be repaid in the near future), it is possible that assets fall below the level of total debt without the company becoming insolvent,[22] given that the long-term portion of debt need only be repaid in the more distant future.

---

[21] The process is similar to the one many banks follow in order to associate PDs with their scoring models, as described in the previous chapter (whereby each debtor is first assigned a score–which cannot be directly interpreted as a PD–and then this score is translated into a PD based on past default rates). Equation (11.24) of Merton's model "compacts" these two phases into a single step in much the same way that discriminant analysis computes a company's PD directly, starting from its financial data. The KMV model separates the two, making PD calculation more accessible and flexible.

[22] This intuition of KMV is based on empirical data. In fact, by observing hundreds of defaulted U.S. firms, KMV noticed that default occurred when the value of assets reached a threshold that was usually between short-term liabilities and total liabilities.

As a result, rather than considering the critical default threshold to be the total value of debt F, the KMV model uses a value, which it calls the default point (DP), equal to all short-term debt (STD) plus 50 % of long-term debt (LTD). Hence,

$$DP = STD + \frac{1}{2}LTD \tag{11.27}$$

In this manner, it is possible to acknowledge the different maturities of a company's debt in a more realistic manner than in the Merton's model.

Now that we have understood the concept of default point, let us turn to a formal definition of distance to default (DD). Distance to default is equal to the difference between asset value[23] and the default point, expressed as a multiple of the standard deviation of assets. That is:

$$DD = \frac{V_0 - DP}{V_0 \cdot \sigma_V} \tag{11.28}$$

Let us take, for example, a company with € 6 million in short-term debt and € 2 million in long-term debt. Let us further assume that, based on (11.25) and (11.26), we have estimated an asset value of € 10 million with a volatility σ_V of 10 %.

The default point will then be

$$DP = 6 + \frac{1}{2}2 = 7 \text{ million}$$

and the distance to default will be

$$DD = \frac{10 - 7}{10 \cdot 10\%} = 3$$

Notice that the distance between the asset value and the default point has been weighted by asset volatility. In fact, a € 3 million cushion between asset value and default point would be considered more or less significant based on the past variability of the company's assets. If, for example, the company operates in a highly volatile industry, and its value in past years has undergone sharp fluctuations, then even a gap of € 3 million could be eaten up rather quickly, so € 3 million would, in such a case, imply a low "default protection". Equation (11.28) takes this into account. If, for example, our company's σ_V were 30 %, rather than just 10 %, then its DD would fall to just 1.

The second phase in KMV's PD calculation procedure is based on the empirical link between DD and actual past rates of default. To that end, the model's authors calculated DD on past data from a vast sample of companies, some of which ended in default. For various DD ranges, they then computed the percentage of companies that actually defaulted. An example of this type of empirical evidence is shown in both Table 11.8 and Figure 11.7.

As we can see, the data suggest a fairly precise empirical correlation between DD and past default frequencies. Once a company's DD is known, this correlation can be used to calculate the associated PD (which the authors of the KMV model refer to as *expected*

---

[23] For the sake of simplicity, we use the current value of assets, V_0. Alternative versions of DD may use the expected value of assets upon maturity.

Table 11.8 Example of the DD/PD relationship

DD (approximate value)	(a) # of companies	(b) # of defaulted companies	(c) = (b) / (a) Default frequency
1	9000	720	8 %
2	15000	450	3 %
3	20000	200	1 %
4	35000	150	0,4 %
5	40000	28	0,07 %
6	42000	17	0,04 %

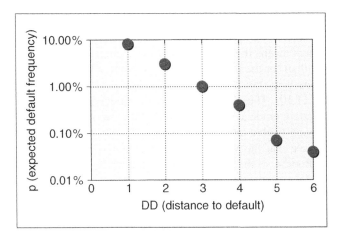

Figure 11.7   The link between DDs and PDs (expected default frequencies)

default frequency, or EDF). Accordingly, the example company seen above (with V_0 of € 10 million, default point of € 7 million, and σ_V of 10 %), having a DD of 3, could be assigned a PD of about 1 %.

11.3.10   Benefits and limitations of the KMV model

The model developed by KMV gained a great deal of popularity and is currently used by many international banks in the U.S., Europe, and Asia. Its popularity comes from its three advantages over other means of estimating PDs (and in particular over the approach followed by rating agencies such as Moody's and Standard & Poor's).

- The first of these advantages is the speed with which the EDFs adapt to the changing financial conditions of the companies being evaluated. Empirical evidence has, in fact, shown that the KVM's EDFs increase quickly, following a worsening in a company's creditworthiness, as opposed to agency ratings, which tend to react with a significant delay.[24] This benefit is primarily due to the fact that EDFs are based on market data (E_0 and σ_E), which is reactive and highly forward-looking.

- A second important benefit is that the EDFs do not swing significantly as economic cycles change, as opposed to the empirical default rates associated with agency ratings. In general, these default rates tend to increase during recessionary phases and to decrease during periods of expansion. This is due to the fact that agencies assign ratings in a somewhat "rigid" way (in part because the agencies change their assessments slowly and in part because they adopt a so-called through-the-cycle approach[25] based on long-term assessments, rather than on short-term PDs). If the composition of the ratings grades remains stable, when the health of obligors assigned to these grades worsens (improves), default rates of the individual grades tend to increase (decrease). Conversely, the EDFs for the individual KMV rating grades (based on DD values) do not change much throughout economic cycles. This is due to the fact that, during a recession, the worsening of a company's creditworthiness translates into an immediate decline in its DD and a consequent shift into a lower DD grade (based on a so- called a point-in-time approach). It follows, then, that the risk characteristics (and the empirical default rates) of a given DD grade remain unchanged because the companies whose creditworthiness worsens (improves) "migrate" to worse (better) classes. This approach to assigning ratings means that rating changes (or "migrations") are more frequent for the KMV model than for the traditional rating agencies. This difference can be seen by comparing the one-year transition matrices for Standard & Poor's and for KMV, (see Tables 11.9 and 11.10). These matrices show the frequency with which the companies belonging to a certain grade at the start of the year (rows) migrate towards other grades during the following twelve months or (along the diagonal) remain in the same grades. One can clearly see that the values along the diagonal are, on average, much higher for Standard & Poor's, so the likelihood of migrating to other ratings grades is much higher in the KMV system.
- A third benefit is that, while all companies assigned by an agency to a given grade share the same estimate of PD (based on the historical default rate for that grade), the KMV model allows each company to be assigned a specific EDF value, which is obtained through the empirical function linking DD and EDF (see Figure 11.7). This is a potentially significant benefit since empirical analyze have shown that, within a given traditional rating grade (e.g. AA), there is a significant variability in the PDs from the best companies to the worst. The rating agencies themselves acknowledge this difference by adding qualifiers to their ratings (e.g. AA+, AA and AA-) in order to distinguish between the various notches within a given class.

These models do, however, have two main limitations:

- They cannot be used to compute the probability of default of unlisted companies, given that the market value and volatility of equity are unavailable. This is clearly very important for banks lending primarily to small and medium-sized businesses that have no direct access to the capital markets. Over the years, KMV has sought to solve this problem in a variety of ways. One solution (the "private-firm model") is based on the use of market data for listed companies that are similar (e.g. by industry, level of leverage, and size) to the company being assessed. The underlying assumption here

---

[24] Generally speaking, changes in EDF tend to anticipate a ratings downgrade by the agencies by approximately one year.

[25] See Chapter 13 for further details.

Table 11.9 One-year transition matrix – Standard & Poor's

Initial rating	Rating at year-end (%)							
	AAA	AA	A	BBB	BB	B	CCC	Default
AAA	90.81	8.33	0.68	0.06	0.12	0.00	0.00	0.00
AA	0.70	90.65	7.79	0.64	0.06	0.14	0.02	0.00
A	0.09	2.27	91.05	5.52	0.74	0.26	0.01	0.06
BBB	0.02	0.33	5.95	86.93	5.30	1.17	1.12	0.18
BB	0.03	0.14	0.67	7.73	80.53	8.84	1.00	1.06
B	0.00	0.11	0.24	0.43	6.48	83.46	4.07	5.20
CCC	0.22	0.00	0.22	1.30	2.38	11.24	64.86	19.79

Source: Standard & Poor's CreditWeek (1996).

Table 11.10 One-year transition matrix – KMV

Initial rating	Rating at year-end (%)							
	AAA	AA	A	BBB	BB	B	CCC	Default
AAA	66.26	22.22	7.37	2.45	0.86	0.67	0.14	0.02
AA	21.66	43.04	25.83	6.56	1.99	0.68	0.20	0.04
A	2.76	20.34	44.19	22.94	7.42	1.97	0.28	0.10
BBB	0.30	2.80	22.63	42.54	23.52	6.95	1.00	0.26
BB	0.08	0.24	3.69	22.93	44.41	24.53	3.41	0.71
B	0.01	0.05	0.39	3.48	20.47	53.00	20.58	2.01
CCC	0.00	0.01	0.09	0.26	1.79	17.77	69.94	10.13

Source: Crohuy, Galai, Mark, 2001 – Note: The rating grades associated with different DD values have been calibrated on intervals similar to those of Standard & Poor's for the purposes of comparison with Table 11.9.

is that the asset returns of the unlisted company – which cannot be observed – are highly correlated to those of its peer group of publicly listed firms.[26] A second solution ("RiskCalc v3.1"), which was adopted after KMV joined the Moody's group, is to

---

[26] In order to estimate the two unknowns that are, in turn, needed to calculate DD (i.e. the market value and volatility of assets), the private firm model uses data from comparable publicly-listed firms. Specifically, the market value of assets is estimated based on the book value of assets, assuming that the relationship between the ratios of market asset value to book asset value of the unlisted company and of its comparable publicly-listed companies (e.g. from the same industry) is the same as the relationship between the ratio of EBITDA to book asset value (in practice, assuming that companies with higher returns on book asset value also have a higher ratio of market asset value to book asset value). Similarly, asset volatility for the unlisted firm is calculated by assuming a stable relationship between size and asset volatility. In practice, the underlying assumption is that the asset volatility of the unlisted company is similar to that of publicly-listed companies of similar size.

calculate a score for the unlisted company based primarily on its financials and not unlike those presented in Chapter 10, but including in the input variables also the average distance to default for a peer group of listed companies that are similar to the company being analyzed. The use of an average DD, together with backward-looking indicators such the company's financial ratios, makes the model's forecasts more reactive and forward looking by taking into account the sentiment of the capital markets regarding the outlook for the industry in which the company belongs.

- Models based on the contingent claims approach are based on the assumption that equity markets are informationally-efficient. As such, the market price and the volatility of equity returns are used as inputs in order to calculate the market value and volatility of the company's assets. Clearly, if capital markets are inefficient, illiquid or simply unable to adequately reflect all available information, such data becomes fairly unreliable. Also, in inefficient equity markets, stock prices tend to be particularly volatile; accordingly, PD estimates based on such data tend to be unstable, as well. Therefore, there is a risk that the ratings assigned to the companies will be highly variable.

SELECTED QUESTIONS AND EXERCISES

1. The following Table reports the (continuously compounded) returns on single A rated corporate bonds and Government bonds (risk free rate) with residual maturity of 1 and 2 years. Calculate the 1 and 2 years expected loss rates for the risky securities and highlight the main limit/assumption underlying this method.

Maturity Security	1 year	2 years
Treasury (Risk Free)	4.50 %	4.70 %
Rating A	4.75 %	5.00 %

2. Company Alfa pays – on one-year zero coupon bonds – a 2 % spread over the yield of Treasury bonds with the same structure and maturity. On the 2-year zero-coupon bond, the difference with respect to the equivalent maturity Treasury securities is 2.5 %. Knowing investors expect, in case of Alfa's default, a recovery rate of one third of the final face value, calculate the (risk-neutral) probability of default that the market is implicitly assigning to Alfa for the second year only.

3. The Merton model proves that a loan to a risky company corresponds to a portfolio composed of a risk-free loan plus ...:
   (A) a long position on a call option;
   (B) a short position on a put option;
   (C) a long position on a put option;
   (D) a short position on a call option;

4. A company, having assets worth 100 million euros, with a volatility of 15 %, is replacing all its debts with just one large loan, with a face value of 85 million euros and a maturity of two years. Risk-free rates are currently at 6 % (continuously compounded). Using Merton's model, check whether the "fair" rate to be applied to the loan could be less than 6.5 %. Also, suppose the company is willing to raise 20 million euros of new equity, to be invested in such a way that asset volatility would stay unchanged.

Do you think the "fair" loan rate would decrease, after such a capital injection? Do you think it could be less than 6.1%?

5. Which of the following information is not necessary to estimate the expected default frequency of a listed company using the KMV model?
   (A) The volatility of equity returns
   (B) The market value of the company's assets
   (C) The company's rating
   (D) The accounting value of the company's debt

6. In the KMV model, the "distance to default" is expressed:
   (A) in the same unit measure as the one of the company's assets;
   (B) as a pure number;
   (C) in the same unit measure as the one of the company's assets' standard deviation;
   (D) in the same unit measure as the one of the company's assets' log.

Appendix 11A
Calculating the Fair Spread on a Loan

In section 11.2, we assumed that we knew the spread of a given bond and that we wanted to calculate the issuer's PD. However, equations such as (11.3) can also be used the other way round, i.e. to calculate the premium that a bank should apply for a given company when the PD and expected recovery rate are known.

To that aim, we can easily rewrite equation (11.3) as follows:

$$s = -\ln[1 - p(1-k)] = -\ln(1 - PD \cdot LGD) \tag{11A.1}$$

If, for example, the PD is equal to 1.5 % and the recovery rate k is 0 % (LGD 100 %), we get:

$$s = -\ln(1 - 1{,}5\% \cdot 100\%) \cong 1{,}51\%$$

If, on the other hand, the bank were able to obtain collateral that limits the expected LGD to 40 %, the spread would fall to

$$s = -\ln(1 - 1{,}5\% \cdot 40\%) \cong 0{,}60\%$$

Equation (11A.1) uses the spread between *continuously compounded* rates (as we have done throughout the chapter); however, the rates on bank loans are often set as simple or annually compounded rates. As such, it may be useful to rewrite (11.3) using simple or annually compounded interest rates (indicated with the subscript "s"):

$$1 + r_s = [1 - p(1-k)](1 + r_s^*) = [1 - p(1-k)](1 + r_s + s_s) \tag{11A.2}$$

and calculate the spread (between simple or annually compounded rates) as

$$s_s = \frac{1 + r_s}{1 - p(1-k)} - 1 - r_s = \frac{p(1-k)(1+r_s)}{1 - p(1-k)} = \frac{PD \cdot LGD}{1 - PD \cdot LGD}(1 + r_s) \tag{11A.3}$$

Therefore, if PD $= 1{,}5\%$, LGD $= 40\%$, and $r_s = 6\%$, we will get the following spread to be added to the risk-free rate (either simple or annually compounded):

$$s_s = \frac{PD \cdot LGD}{1 - PD \cdot LGD}(1 + r_s) = \frac{1{,}5\% \cdot 40\%}{1 - 1{,}5\% \cdot 40\%}(1 + 6\%) \cong 0{,}64\%$$

In other words, the rate for this risky loan ($r_s^* \equiv r_s + s_s$) will be equal to 6.64 %.

We can see, then, that the spread between simple or annually compounded rates is:

- different from that of continuously compounded rates (0.60 %, given the same PD and LGD);
- a function not only of the borrower's PD and LGD, but also of the risk-free rate. We can easily see, in fact, that if r_s were 8 % rather than 6 %, equation (A.3) would give us a spread of 0.65 %.

Appendix 11B
Real and Risk-Neutral Probabilities of Default

A company's probability of default can be calculated, based on an *à la Merton* model, by considering the probability that the asset value upon debt maturity (V_T) will be less than the repayment value (F) of the debt. As indicated by equation (11.17), Merton's model assumes that asset values follow a geometric Brownian motion. From (11.17), we can also obtain the equation for the asset value upon maturity, V_T:

$$V_T = V_0 \cdot e^{\left(\mu - \frac{\sigma_V^2}{2}\right)T + \sigma_V \sqrt{T} \cdot Z} \tag{11B.1}$$

As shown in this chapter, the probability of default is:

$$p = \Pr(V_T < F) \tag{11B.2}$$

Substituting B.1 into B.2 we then get:

$$p^* = \Pr\left(V_0 \cdot e^{\left(\mu - \frac{\sigma_V^2}{2}\right)T + \sigma_V \sqrt{T} \cdot Z} < F\right)$$

$$= \Pr\left[\left(\mu - \frac{\sigma_V^2}{2}\right)T + \sigma_V \sqrt{T} \cdot Z < \ln\left(\frac{F}{V_0}\right)\right] =$$

$$= \Pr\left[Z < \frac{\ln\left(\frac{F}{V_0}\right) - \left(\mu - \frac{\sigma_V^2}{2}\right)T}{\sigma_V \sqrt{T}}\right] = \Pr\left[Z < \frac{\ln\left(\frac{Fe^{-\mu T}}{V_0}\right) + \frac{\sigma_V^2}{2}T}{\sigma_V \sqrt{T}}\right] \tag{11B.3}$$

Considering that Z is a normal standard deviation, B.3 can be rewritten as follows:

$$p^* = N\left(\frac{\ln\left(\frac{Fe^{-\mu T}}{V_0}\right) + \frac{\sigma_V^2}{2}T}{\sigma_V \sqrt{T}}\right) = N(-d_2^*) \tag{11B.4}$$

We can then see that (B.4) is similar to equation (11.24) used in this chapter in order to calculate PD, but with *one important difference*. In place of our usual d_2 (computed according to 11.18b), we have a modified version, indicated as d^*_2, which is calculated using the real rate of return μ, rather than the risk-free rate r.

Thus, equation (11.24) is just a simplified version of the real equation for PD (i.e. B.4) obtained by substituting the true expected return on assets μ with the risk-free rate

r. As a result, (11.24) generates a risk-neutral probability of default, which is only valid in a risk-neutral world in which $\mu = r$ (i.e. a world in which an investor in the assets of a risky company settles for an expected rate of return r that is in line with that of a risk-free investment). In the real world, however, investors demand that $\mu > r$, so the real PD provided by B.4 will be different than that of equation (11.24). Specifically, we will have $d_2^* < d_2$; therefore, $N\ (-d_2^*)\ > N(-d_2)$ and $p > p^*$. Accordingly Merton's model, just like the models based on bond spreads presented in section 11.2, generates risk-neutral probabilities that overstate real-world probabilities.

12
LGD and Recovery Risk

12.1 INTRODUCTION

The loss rate given default – or simply loss given default (LGD[1]) – is the loss rate experienced by a lender on a credit exposure if the borrower defaults. It is given by one minus the recovery rate (RR) and can take any value between 0 % and 100 %. Formally:

$$LGD = 1 - RR \qquad (12.1)$$

The LGD is never known when a new loan is issued, nor it is perfectly known even when the default occurs, at least if there is no secondary market for the defaulted exposure. If, on the opposite, the exposure can be traded on a liquid secondary market, than the LGD and the RR can be estimated based on the market price after the default. Generally speaking, however, the LGD can be known with certainty only when the whole recovery (workout) process is over.

In the late 90's, a survey by a Task Force appointed by the Basel Committee, concerning the rating systems of the major world banks, highlighted that only few of them carried out separate estimates for the LGDs of the exposures and the PDs of the borrowers. Many, in fact, used to estimate directly the expected loss rate (EL rate), given by the product of the two. Also, the major rating agencies like Moody's, Standard & Poor's and Fitchratings did not, as a rule, produce separate evaluations for the PD and LGD of corporate bonds.[2]

In 1999, the Task Force prompted the banks to adopt separate estimation models for PDs and recovery rates, as those two parameters mostly depend on different mechanisms and risk factors. Such an invitation was reiterated in 2004 by the new Basel accord on minimum bank capital, which required banks to adopt ad hoc rating systems for the LGD.

Latterly, most banks have followed such suggestions. We therefore wish to cover separately, in this Chapter, the techniques used to estimate LGD and the recovery rate.[3]

We will first show what factors affect the expected recovery rate on a credit exposure, and what criteria can be followed in its estimation. Subsequently, we will cover the meaning and characteristics of recovery risk in a narrow sense, that is, of the risk that the final, ex post recovery rate on a defaulted exposure be different from what had been expected ex ante. A final section will be devoted to the link between default risk (PD) and recovery risk (LGD).

---

[1] In principle one should indicate the loss rate given default as LGDR (LGD rate) and use LGD for the absolute loss given default (in euros or dollars). However, "LGD" is used by most practitioners (and by the new Basel accord on bank capital, see Chapter 20) to indicate the loss rate, while the absolute loss is usually indicated as LGD·EAD.

[2] Usually rating agencies assign *issue ratings* to bonds, which embed an assessment of both the LGD of the exposure and the PD of the borrower. Such issue ratings are often the same as the borrower's issuer rating (describing PD alone), unless the bond is subordinated. When this is the case, the issue rating is lower than the issuer's rating by one notch (if the latter is investment-grade, that is, with a rating between AAA and BBB−) or two (when the issuer has a *speculative grade* rating, between BB+ and CCC).

[3] See Altman et al. (2005) for a more complete presentation.

12.2   WHAT FACTORS DRIVE RECOVERY RATES?

Factors affecting LGD can be grouped in four main categories: the characteristics of the credit exposure, those of the borrower, the peculiarities of the bank managing the recovery process and, finally, some external factors.

(I) The characteristics of the exposure include: the presence of any collateral (be it represented by financial assets of other goods, such as plants, real estate, inventories) and its degree of effectiveness (that is, how easily it can be seized and liquidated); the priority level of the exposure, which can be senior or subordinated to other exposures; any guarantees provided by third parties (like banks, holding companies of public sector entities);

(II) The characteristics of the borrower include: the industry in which the company operates (which may affect the liquidation process, that is, the ease with which the companies' assets can be sold and turned into cash for the creditors;[4] the country in which the obligor operates, which may affect the speed and effectiveness of the bankruptcy procedures; some financial ratios, like the leverage (namely, the ratio between total assets and liabilities, which shows how many euros of assets

Table 12.1 The drivers of recovery rates

Factor types	Factors	Component affected
Characteristics of the exposure	Collateral	Amount recovered
	Seniority	
	Guarantees (holding company, banks government, etc.)	
Characteristics of the borrower	Industry	Likelihood to find a buyer for the defaulted company and price at which it can be sold
	Country	Duration of the recovery procedures
	Financial ratios	Amount recovered
Bank's internal factors	Speed and effectiveness of recovery procedures	Amount recovered and duration of the process
	Sales of non-performing loans and use of out-of-Court settlements	Amount recovered and duration of the process
External, "macroeconomic" factors	State of the economic cycle	Amount recovered
	Interest rates	Present value of the recoveries

---

[4] An empirical analysis of the role of industries in shaping recovery rates can be found in Altman and Kishore (1996), Acharya et al. (2003) and Hu and Perraudin (2002).

are reported in the balance sheet for each euro of debt to be paid back) and the
ratio of EBITDA (earnings before interest taxes depreciation and amortization) to
total turnover (which indicates whether the defaulted company is still capable of
generating an acceptable level of cash flow);

(III) Some *characteristics of the bank*, such as the efficiency levels of the department
which takes care of the recovery process (workout department) or the frequency with
which out-of-Court settlements are reached with the borrowers, or non-performing
loans are spun-off and sold to third parties.[5]

(IV) *External factors,* such as the state of the economic cycle (if the economy is in
recession, the value at which the companies assets can be liquidated is likely to
be lower) and the level of the interest rates (higher rates reduce the present value
of recoveries); actually, the economic cycle, while driving the liquidation value of
assets and LGD, is also likely to affect the default probability of the borrowers. A
problem may therefore arise, due to the correlation between default risk and recovery
risk; we will return to that in the last part of the Chapter.

Table 12.1 summarizes the above. The first two columns indicate the different types of
factors affecting LGD, while the third one shows what component(s) of the LGD is more
likely to be affected; more details on the impact of some of these factors (like seniority
or the industry of the borrower) will be provided in section 12.4.

12.3   THE ESTIMATION OF RECOVERY RATES

12.3.1   Market LGD and Default LGD

Recovery rates on defaulted exposures can be computed based on different approaches[6]:

– *Market LGD* – The first approach (*market LGD*) uses prices of defaulted exposures
as an estimate of the recovery rate. In practice, if a defaulted bond trades at 30 cents
a euro, one can infer that the market is estimating a 30 % recovery rate (hence, a
70 % LGD). This approach can be used only for those exposures (indeed, not the
majority of a traditional bank's loan book) for which a secondary market exists. A
variation of this approach estimates the recovery rate based on the market value of the
new financial instruments (usually, shares or very long-term bonds) that are offered
to lenders in exchange for their defaulted bonds. Such instruments are usually issued
(and their market price becomes known) only when the restructuring process is over
and the company emerges from default; their value must then be discounted back in
time to the moment when the default took place, using an adequate discount rate. This
is called the *emergence LGD*. A third method for computing market LGD is based on
the use of spreads on performing (not-defaulted) bonds as a source of information; in
fact, as shown in Chapter 11, spreads on corporate bonds also depend on the expected
recovery rate. Assuming the bank can separately estimate other factors affecting spreads

---

[5] Sales of non performing loans and out-of-Court settlements, while reducing the face value of the recovery
(compared to what could be obtained by the bank based on a formal bankruptcy procedure), also reduce
significantly the duration of the recovery process. The financial effect of this shorter recovery time often offsets
the lower recovered amount.

[6] Cfr. Schuermann (2005).

(namely, the PD of the borrower), the *LGD* implied by market spreads can then be worked out; this approach is called *implicit market LGD*.
- *Workout LGD* – Market data surely are a very objective and up-to-date source of information for LGD estimation. However, they are available only for corporate bonds issued by large or very large companies. Most traditional banking loans are not traded, hence no market price can be observed. One must therefore turn to a different approach, based on the measurement of the actual recoveries experienced by the banks in the months (or years) after a default took place. This approach (workout LGD) requires that an historical database be compiled, where all defaulted exposures are filed and, for each of them, all information on recovered amounts, recovery lags and recovery procedures are recorded. Such data will then be segmented based on the type of exposure, on different types of borrowers, on the recovery procedure used, so that a finite number of clusters can be identified, made up of similar cases leading to similar LGDs. Such clusters will then be used as guideline to estimate the expected LGD on future defaults.

When comparing the results obtained with the market LGD and the workout LGD approach, one must bear in mind that the definition of default, as well as the duration and effectiveness of the recovery process, may be quite different for bonds and for bank loans. Values derived from one approach must be carefully evaluated, before they can be compared with estimates based on the other one.

Also, two banks may come up with totally different estimates of LGD even if both are using the workout approach. In Chapter 10 we saw how a wider or narrower definition of default may affect the estimated PDs: the same occurs also with recovery rates. A wider definition of default (including, e.g., any delay on due payments) will not only lead to higher default rates, but also to higher recoveries, since most "defaulted" borrowers will be in a better shape than if the bank had adopted a narrower, and more severe definition of default (e.g. a definition including only formal bankruptcies), and will therefore reimburse a higher share of the defaulted exposure. Conversely, a narrower definition of default, including only companies that really are in bad health, will necessarily imply lower recovery rates.

It is therefore advisable that banks adopt a homogeneous definition of default, in order to be able to pool and compare their estimates; moreover, the definition of default must be the same both in the estimation of PDs and LGDs, or the estimates of the bank's overall credit risk will turn out to be inconsistent and biased.

12.3.2   Computing workout LGDs

Workout LGD must be analyzed according to an "economic" perspective, rather than based on mere accounting data: that is, all relevant factors that may reduce the final economic value of the recovered part of the exposure must be taken into account. This includes the discount effect associated to the time span between the emergence of the default and the actual recovery, but also the various direct and indirect administrative costs associated with collecting information on the exposure.

Such an approach leads to computing workout LGD based on formulas like the following:

$$RR = \frac{DNR}{EAD} = \frac{FR}{EAD} \cdot \frac{FR - AC}{FR} \cdot (1 + r)^{-T} \tag{12.2}$$

Where:

RR is the actual recovery rate on a defaulted exposure;

DNR is the discounted net value of the recovery, that is, the present value at the time of default of all recovered amounts, net of all costs;

EAD is the exposure at default;

FR is the face value of the recovered amount, as recorded in the bank's accounting data;

AC are the administrative costs connected with the workout procedure on the defaulted exposure;

r is a discount rate

T is the duration of the recovery process.

Suppose, for example, that an exposure at default of 100 million euros has lead to a recovery of 60 million euros after six months. Also, assume costs of 1 million euros have been faced during the workout process, and that a discount rate of 10 % is deemed reasonable. This will lead to a recovery rate of

$$RR = \frac{60}{100} \cdot \frac{60 - 1}{60} \cdot (1 + 10\%)^{-0.5} = 56.3\%$$

and to a LGD of 43.7 %.

To apply equation (12.2) to real-life, more complex examples, some of its components of require some further discussion.

First, the face value of the recovery must comprise any fees collected from the defaulted borrower, including fees from late payment. However, such fees – together with any unpaid late fees included in the bank's income statement – must be added also to the original exposure at default.

Administrative costs should encompass all direct and indirect expenses faced by the bank to collect any payments on the defaulted loan (including the cost of external legal advisors). Note that the factor $(FR - AC)/FR$ describes the incidence of administrative costs per recovered euro, while the analysis of past data can provide some precious insight on it. The estimation of LGDs on future defaults might also be based on the market price of the recovery services provided by some specialised provider. Since most large banking groups tend to use a dedicated unit (the so-called "bad bank") for the workout of their distressed loans, the internal transfer prices charged by this unit might be used as a guideline to estimate the future impact of administrative costs. For example, if the recovery fees were expressed as a constant share of the recovered amount (i.e., if $AC = k\ FR$), then $(FR - AC)/FR$ would simplify to $(1 - k)$.

The discount rate *r*, to be used in the computation of the present value of FR at the time of default, might be based on historical values, that is, on average market rates observed between the default and the end of the workout process. However, this would clearly lead to a backward-looking measure, which would not account for the present (and future) market conditions. When estimating LGDs on future bad loans, a bank is concerned with the interest rates that might prevail on the market after a new default has surfaced. Since a bank's PDs usually imply a one-year risk horizon, estimated LGDs actually refer to defaults that might emerge one year later. If these considerations are correct, then the use of past interest rates would clearly be irrational and unjustified. Instead, in computing the present value of the recoveries on future defaults, one-year forward interest rates should be used as a quick forecast of the future spot rates. For example, if the expected duration of the recovery process is T years, a T-year forward rate for investments starting one year later ($_1r_T$) should be used.

Finally, the duration of the workout process, T, should be computed in a financial sense, accounting for the existence of any intermediate flows. In the case of distressed bank loans, in fact, recoveries might take place only gradually, and different amounts of money might be cashed in at different moments in time. The same might happen with exposures, if the original exposure at default is subsequently adjusted because of late payment fees, or because some further amount has to be loaded onto the borrower's account (e.g., some unpaid discounted receivables). In such cases, the total exposure at default – on which the recovery rate must be computed – will be given by the sum of all partial loadings.

Figure 12.1 shows an example of multiple loadings and recoveries. The obligor originally defaulted for 100 dollars, but some further 10 dollars were debited on his/her account two months later. The bank managed to recover 35 dollars at the end of the first year, and another 35 dollars at the end of year two. So 110 represents the total EAD, and 70 is the face value of the recovery (FR), according to the bank's accounting books. Although the recovery process seemingly took two years, this would clearly overstate its financial duration.

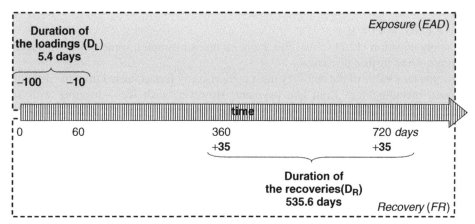

Figure 12.1 The financial duration of the workout process when multiple loadings and multiple recoveries are present

Since not all loadings (x^-) took place at the beginning of the workout period, the default must not be situated at time zero, but at some intermediate date between 0 and 60 days. Using a flat yield curve and an interest rate r of 5% for all maturities, one can compute the Macaulay duration of the loadings (D_L):

$$D_L = \frac{\sum_{t=0}^{T} tx_t^- (1+i)^{-t}}{\sum_{t=0}^{T} x_t^- (1+i)^{-t}} = \frac{0 \cdot 100(1+5\%)^{-0/360} + 60 \cdot 10(1+5\%)^{-10/360}}{100(1+5\%)^{-0/360} + 10(1+5\%)^{-10/360}} \cong 5.4 \text{ days}$$

Similarly, the financial duration D_R associated with the total recovery (FR) is not two years; rather, it must be computed as a weighted mean of the maturities associated with the two inflows (x^+). Using Macaulay's formula we obtain:

$$D_R = \frac{\sum_{t=0}^{T} t x_t^+ (1+i)^{-t}}{\sum_{t=0}^{T} x_t^+ (1+i)^{-t}}$$

$$= \frac{360 \cdot 35(1+5\%)^{-360/360} + 720 \cdot 35(1+5\%)^{-720/360}}{35(1+5\%)^{-360/360} + 35(1+5\%)^{-720/360}} \cong 535.6 \text{ days}$$

The financial duration of the workout process, T, to be used in equation (12.2), is then given by

$$T = D_L - D_C = 535.6 - 5.4 = 530.2 \text{ days.}^7$$

12.4 FROM PAST DATA TO LGD ESTIMATES

Suppose a database of LGDs has been compiled according to the methodology above, based on past data and on some assumptions on future interest rates. The empirical frequency distribution of those values must then be described and summarized by means of some key indicators that will be used to estimate LGDs on potential future defaults.

In principle, one might compute the mean of such a distribution and use it as a rough-and-dirty appraisal of future LGDs. However, risk managers usually should not be interested in mean values since only the *deviations from the expected value* represent risk in a strict sense.[8] Furthermore, in the case of recovery rates and LGDs the mean happens to be a very poor indicator, as most values tend to cluster near 0 and 1.

This happens because some exposures (like leasing or mortgages on residential real estate) tend to have high recovery rates (close to 100 %), while unsecured overdrafts tend to have recovery rates close to 0, especially if the defaulted company was a new customer to the bank.

Such a situation is shown in Figure 12.2 which is based on the actual data of a medium-sized European bank. In such a U-shaped distribution, the probability of observing values which are close to the mean is dramatically low.

One way to deal with this problem is to use conditional means rather than just one overall average value. The bank should break down the database of past LGDs by identifying some clusters that share similar characteristics and for which the "within" variance in

---

[7] Note that the recovery rate based on an exposure (EAD) of 110, a nominal recovery (FR) of 70 and a duration (T) of 530.2 days is very similar to the recovery rate computed by discounting the single cash flows

in Figure 12.1, that is: $RR = \dfrac{\sum_{t=0}^{T} x_t^+ (1+i)^{-t}}{\sum_{t=0}^{T} x_t^- (1+i)^{-t}} = \dfrac{35(1+5\%)^{-360/360} + 35(1+5\%)^{-720/360}}{100(1+5\%)^{-0/360} + 10(1+5\%)^{-60/360}} = \dfrac{65}{109} \cong 59.2\%.$

However, the use of total cash flows and duration is more compact and flexible than this analytical computation of individual discounted cash flows.

[8] This aspect (recovery risk in a narrow sense) will be dealt with in section 12.5.

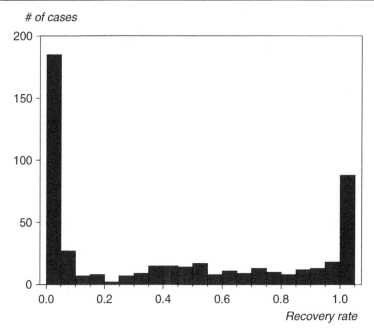

Figure 12.2   Empirical distribution of bank recovery rates

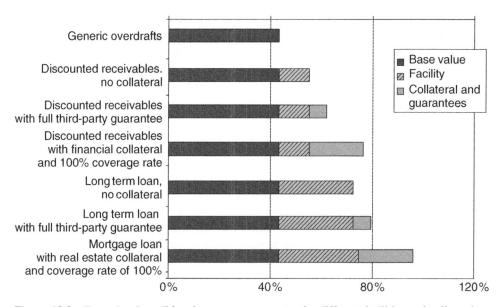

Figure 12.3   Example of conditional mean recovery rates for different facilities and collaterals

empirical recovery rates is relatively low. Cluster means would then offer a more reliable approximation of the expected loss rates on different loans.

Such conditional means – $\mu(\mathbf{x})$ – can be estimated through linear or non-linear least squares, based on a vector $\mathbf{x}$ describing the most significant features of each facility in the

LGD database. Those features should include the facility type (e.g., overdrafts, discounted receivables, long-term loans), the type of collateral (e.g., financial instruments, real estate, physical capital) and its coverage rate, the presence of any guarantees (e.g., a guarantee from the borrower's parent company, which might induce him/her to pay back a significant share of the defaulted exposure), and all other factors that are statistically significant in explaining empirical differences among past recovery rates (see Table 12.1).

The $\mu(\mathbf{x})$ can be expressed as a linear function of the x_is. In this case, the effects on LGD of different factors (e.g., of a given facility type and a full collateralisation through Treasury bonds) will be additive, and the conditional average LGD will simply be the sum of the unconditional value plus a set of adjustments (see Figure 12.3 for an example). The contributions of the different loan characteristics to the expected recovery rate will then be transparent and easy to assess. However, since a linear function can take any value between minus and plus infinity, conditional means might happen to suggest a loss rate greater than 100%, or even a negative LGD. This clearly counterintuitive behaviour can be avoided if a non-linear function, bounded between 0 and 1 (like the logistic function, or the normal cumulative density function), is used to represent the link between the loan features and $\mu(\mathbf{x})$.

12.5   RESULTS FROM SELECTED EMPIRICAL STUDIES

Empirical evidence on recovery rates for corporate bonds is generally based on market LGDs. While the number of empirical studies on recovery rates has increased since the second half of the 1990s, they are still rather limited. Robust estimates of recovery rates can only be obtained if a large number of defaults occur. Given the relatively rare occurrence of default events, this also means that the estimates of recovery rates tend to be based on relatively small empirical samples. In addition to this, since most of the default events involved speculative grade bonds, estimates of recovery rates for investment grade bonds tend to be rare.

Table 12.2 reports the results in terms of mean recovery rates – by seniority and security – obtained by four of the main empirical studies based on corporate bond defaults data. All empirical studies confirm that the recovery rate increases with the security of the defaulted bond and decreases with its degree of subordination. Results also tend to be rather similar in terms of average recovery rates.

Table 12.2 Comparison of mean recovery rates from different empirical studies

Study	Senior Secured	Senior Unsecured	Senior Subordinated	Subordinated
Fons (1994)	65%	48%	40%	30%
Altman & Kishore (1996)	58%	48%	34%	31%
Van de Castle & Keisman (1999)	66%	49%	37%	26%
Hu & Perraudin (2002)	53%	50%	38%	33%

Despite these similar results, which would appear encouraging when one wants to estimate the recovery rate of a bond exposure, two important problems must be highlighted. First, a

Table 12.3 Recovery rates on defaulted bonds (% values)

	Carty & Lieberman			Altman & Kishore		
Seniority class	Number	Mean	Std. dev.	Number	Mean	Std. dev.
Senior Secured	115	53.80%	26.80%	85	57.89%	22.99%
Senior Unsecured	278	51.13%	25.45%	221	47.65%	26.71%
Senior Subordinated	196	38.52%	23.81%	177	34.38%	25.08%
Subordinated	226	32.74%	20.18%	214	31.34%	22.42%
Junior Subordinated	9	17.09%	10.90%	–	–	–

Source: Carty L.V. e Lieberman D. (1996a); Altman E. e Kishore, V.M. (1996).

significant cross-section variability of recovery rates is typically reported by the empirical studies. Table 12.3 reports more details on two of the above studies, the one by Altman and Kishore, and shows the high standard deviation that characterizes recovery rates of bonds with different seniority and subordination. This is indeed always higher than 20%.[9]

Second, recovery rates tend to be unstable over time. Figure 12.4 shows the evolution, over time, of the average recovery rates on *senior secured* bonds and subordinated bonds. One can see that RRs fluctuate over time, so that ex post results may differ significantly

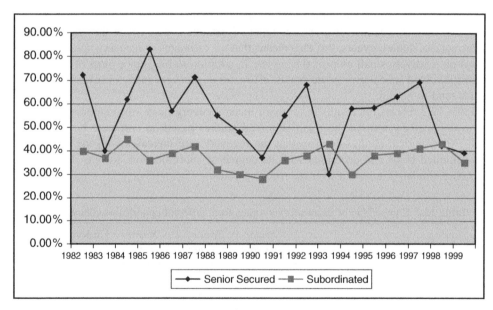

Figure 12.4   Recovery rates for different seniorities: 1982–1999
Source: Moody's.

---

[9] Note that, in case the recovery rate probability distribution were a uniform (rectangular) one, meaning that all values from 0% to 100% of the recovery rate have the same probability to occur, its standard deviation would be approximately equal to 29%. The reported standard deviation results therefore imply a high degree of uncertainty concerning the expected recovery rate.

from ex ante estimates (giving rise to a recovery risk that will be further discussed in section 12.5). Also, one year can be found (1993) in which the "classic" relationship between RRs on senior and subordinated exposures is not supported by the data. This suggests that LGD clusters based on variables like those surveyed in this paragraph, although they may help banks to produce an acceptable estimate of individual LGDs on different loans, are far from error-free.

Finally, it must be stressed that bonds' recovery rates might be industry specific. Indeed, the business activity of a company dictates the nature of its assets. Other things being equal, firms with more tangible and liquid assets should allow higher recovery rates to their creditors in case of default. Table 12.4, based on Moody's data, reports average recovery rates by industry of the issuer. Note that these values tend to be significantly different between industries.

Table 12.4 Average Recovery Rates by Issuer Industry

Industry	Average	Volatility	Number of defaults
Transportation	38.6 %	27.4 %	72
Industrial	40.5 %	24.4 %	728
Insurance	39.8 %	21.4 %	12
Banking	22.6 %	16.6 %	25
Public Utility	69.6 %	21.8 %	57
Finance	45.6 %	31.2 %	11
Thrifts	25.6 %	26.3 %	20
Securities	15.4 %	2.0 %	2
Real Estate	25.7 %	17.2 %	8
Other non-bank	24.8 %	15.4 %	15
Sovereign	56.8 %	27.4 %	8

Source: Hu and Perraudin (2002).

As far as bank loans are concerned, an important study on recovery rates was published by Carty and Lieberman (1996) comparing results based on market LGDs (prices recorded on the market for large syndicated loans soon after default) and workout LGDs (estimates based on the discounted cash flows associated with recoveries occurred after default). The former approach leads to an average recovery rate (on a sample of 58 loans) of 71 % and a median of 77 %. In the latter, the mean is close to 79 %, while the median value is 92 %.

The study was subsequently updated by Carty (1998) where secured and unsecured loans are treated separately. For the former, estimates based on actual recoveries (AR) are contrasted with market prices (MP). The main results are summarized in Table 12.5.

Based on market prices one month after the default, Gupton et al. (2000) find mean recovery rates of 69.5 % for secured loans, 52.1 % for unsecured ones. The same methodology is used by Hamilton et al. (2002) on a sample of secured bank loans, finding an average recovery of 71.3 %.

Table 12.5 Recovery estimates on bank loans

Type of loans	N.	Mean	Median	Min.	Max.	Std. Dev.
Secured (AR)	178	86.7 %	100.0 %	7.4 %	128.7 %	22.8 %
Unsecured (AR)	19	79.4 %	90.0 %	23.6 %	100.4 %	26.6 %
Secured (MP)	72	72.8 %	79.75 %	15.00 %	98.00 %	20.97 %

Source: Carty (1998).

Van De Castle and Keisman (1999) reports the results of a study based on about 1,200 defaulted exposures, of which 258 are bank loans. Recovery rate estimates are based on secondary market prices, adjusted to account for debt/equity and other debt/asset swaps. The average RR is 84.5 %. The authors also develop a simple regression model to test the effect on recoveries of different collateral types and of the seniority levels.

12.6   RECOVERY RISK

By "recovery risk" we mean the risk that the actual recovery rate achieved by the bank when the workout process is over may differ from the one initially estimated (e.g., based on the dataset including past recoveries).

Equation (12.2) helps us understand why such a recovery risk exists. In fact, it includes four variables, for which it is impossible to specify a value with certainty:

√ The amount to be recovered (FR);
√ The workout administrative expenses (AC);
√ The discount rate (r);
√ The duration (T) of the recovery process.

Those four stochastic variables are the sources of recovery risk.[10]

Many empirical data suggest that recovery risk may be quite sizeable: going back to Table 12.2 e.g., we see that, even when different degrees of subordination are accounted for, recovery rates on individual bonds may significantly differ from one another; also, Figure 12.4 has shown that even mean recovery rates (which of course are less volatile than the recovery rates on individual bonds) may dramatically fluctuate over time.[11]

The recovery rate is bounded between 0 % and 100 %: suppose we do not have any information on it and assume that all values in this bracket are equally likely. In other words, suppose they follow a uniform distribution. Such distribution would have a mean of 0.5 (50 %); also, its standard deviation would be given by $\sqrt{\dfrac{100\% - 0\%}{12}}$ that is about 29 %. The standard deviations in Table 12.2, all above 20 %, are rather close to this 29 %, and therefore show how volatile and dispersed recovery rates tend to be.

---

[10] Of course, (12.2) also includes another stochastic amount, that is the EAD. As seen in the introduction to this part of the book, however, the volatility of the EAD is usually dealt with as a separate type of risk, exposure risk, which is separately measured (and separately managed) from recovery risk.

[11] This volatility can be seen also in Figure 12.5, where the average recovery rate in the 1978–2001 fluctuates between a minimum of 12 % and a maximum of 76 %.

Also, it must be noticed that the values in Table 12.2 come from studies where the market LGD approach was used. Accordingly, recovery rates were computed based on bond prices after the issuer's default. Such values tend to cluster around the central values of the 0%–100% interval: in fact, if an investor were to believe that some bond will be reimbursed in full with a probability of 50%, and that no reimbursement will be obtained in the remaining 0% of cases, he/she is likely to price such a bond at about 50 cents a euro.

However, when LGDs are computer based on the workout approach, the probability distribution of recovery rates is likely to cluster on the extreme values, that is, on 0% and 100%. In fact (see again Figure 12.2), many bank exposures either are 100%-recovered or remain totally unpaid. Accordingly, the volatility of the recovery rates is significantly higher than those shown in Table 12.2, and usually exceeds the values typical of a uniform distribution (29%).[12]

This must be borne in mind when choosing a theoretical probability distribution to be used in the estimation of recovery risk. Clearly, normal distributions are unfit to correctly represent distributions like the one in Figure 12.2. Instead, beta distributions are often used:[13] they are quite flexible, can be bounded between 0% and 100% and their parameters can be chosen in such a way to have one or two modes. Also, they can be quickly estimated based on the generalized method of moments, simply using the sample mean and variance of recovery rates.[14]

The volatility of recovery rates (that is, the recovery risk) increases the overall credit risk of an exposure. To see why, let us consider a one-euro loan and compute a very simple risk measure: the standard deviation of future losses. For the sake of simplicity, we adopt a binary approach, where the only event generating losses is the default of the borrower. Under this hypothesis, only two events may occur: default (with a loss of 1-RR) and no default (with a loss of zero). Those are shown in Table 12.6.

The expected loss will then be given by:

$$EL = PD \cdot LGD \tag{12.3}$$

Table 12.6 A simple, binomial approach

Event	Loss	Probability
Default	LGD	PD
No default	0	1-PD

---

[12] E.g., in 2001 the Bank of Italy estimated that the standard deviation of the banks' recovery rates was of about 37%.

[13] As an alternative to beta distributions, non-parametric beta kernel methods have also been suggested (Renault & Scaillet, 2003; Hagmann et al., 2005) to estimate the probability distribution without imposing too much structure on the data.

[14] See, e.g. Finger et al. (1997); Crouhy et al. (2001). The beta probability density function is: $f_{a,b}(x) = \frac{1}{\beta(a,b)} x^{a-1}(1-x)^{b-1} 1_{[0,1]}(x)$ where $\beta(a,b)$ is the beta function, a, b are two parameters to be specified by the user. $1_{[0,1]}$ is an indicator function taking value 1 if $x \in [0, 1]$ and 0 otherwise. This ensures that the values of x are bounded between 0 and 1. The parameters a and b are usually chosen in such a way that the mean and the variance of the distribution equate the mean and variance of sample data. This is done by setting: $\hat{b} = \frac{\hat{m}(\hat{m} - 1^2)}{\hat{v}} + \hat{m} - 1; \hat{a} = \frac{\hat{b} - \hat{m}}{\hat{m} - 1}$, where $\hat{m}$ and $\hat{v}$ are the sample mean and variance of the recovery rates.

If the LGD is non-stochastic (that is, if no recovery risk is present) the volatility of the losses will be:

$$\sigma_L = LGD \cdot \sqrt{PD \cdot (1 - PD)} \qquad (12.4)$$

where $PD \cdot (1 - PD)$ is the variance of the indicator (bernoulli) variable representing default, and taking a value of 1 in the case of default, zero otherwise.

Assuming, e.g., a PD of 0.5 % and a LGD of 50 %, equation (12.4) leads to the following standard deviation:

$$\sigma_L = 0.5 \cdot \sqrt{0.005 \cdot 0.995} = 3.53\,\%$$

If, instead, we assume that LGD is stochastic, with an expected value of $\overline{LGD}$ and a standard deviation of σ_{LGD} (that is, if we inject recovery risk in the model), then (12.4) becomes:[15]

$$\sigma_L = \sqrt{PD \cdot (1 - PD)(\overline{LGD})^2 + PD^2 \cdot \sigma_{LGD}^2 + PD \cdot (1 - PD) \cdot \sigma_{LGD}^2} \qquad (12.5)$$

which simplifies into:[16]

$$UL = \sqrt{PD \cdot (1 - PD) \cdot \overline{LGD}^2 + PD \cdot \sigma_{LGD}^2} \qquad (12.6)$$

In the example above, if 50 % were the expected LGD $(\overline{LGD})$, around which a volatility σ_{LGD} of 20 % is present, then the standard deviation of future losses would be

$$UL = \sqrt{0.005 \cdot 0.995 \cdot 0.25 + 0.005 \cdot 0.22} \cong 3.80\,\%$$

This value is higher that the one computer before (assuming a constant recovery rate).

Comparing (12.5) and (12.6) it is interesting to note that the impact of σ_{LGD} is stronger when the PD is higher, that is, for low-quality customers.

12.7   THE LINK BETWEEN DEFAULT RISK AND RECOVERY RISK

Current credit risk models treat PD and LGD as two independent stochastic variables.[17] This is equivalent to considering them as functions of different factors. Indeed, default

---

[15] To get (12.5) we use the formula for the standard deviation of the product of two independent stochastic variables. Given x and y, stochastic and independent, and $z = xy$, we have:

$$\sigma_z^2 = \mu_x^2 \cdot \sigma_y^2 + \mu_y^2 \cdot \sigma_x^2 + \sigma_x^2 \sigma_y^2$$

If x is a Bernoulli variable representing default (and therefore the PD can be seen as its mean) and y is LGD, this formula leads to (12.5). Note that, for the sake of simplicity, we are assuming that default and recovery are independent.

[16] From (12.5) we get (12.6) by computing the last product in the square root, that is:
$$\sigma_L = \sqrt{PD \cdot (1 - PD)\overline{LGD}^2 + PD^2 \cdot \sigma_{LGD}^2 + PD \cdot \sigma_{LGD}^2 - PD^2 \cdot \sigma_{LGD}^2}.$$

[17] See Altman et al. (2003, 2005) for a detailed analysis of the way alternative credit risk models treat the relationship between PD and LGD.

rates mainly depend on the economic and financial conditions of the issuer/borrower, which in turn are a function of firm specific factors (e.g. management, leverage, profitability, liquidity, etc.), industry specific factors (earnings prospects, competition, regulation, barriers to entry, etc.) and general economic cycle conditions. On the other side, recovery rates are well documented to be mainly a function of specific factors such as seniority and security in debt instruments (see Table 12.4 above).

However, common systematic factors affecting both default rates and recovery rates may exist. These factors can be macroeconomic ones (e.g. business failure rates, actual foreign exchange rate, stock market activity, and the economic cycle in general) and firm's asset value expectations. Indeed, several reasons behind a negative correlation between default and recovery rates can be identified.

(1) *Chain effects*: if default rates increase due to an economic downturn and part of the assets of the defaulting companies are represented by claims/credits to other companies, then a decrease in recovery rates would also follow.
(2) *Financial assets and interest rates*: if the collateral for some specific debt instruments is based on financial assets (e.g., fixed income securities) and default rates increase following a rise in interest rates, then a corresponding decrease in recovery rates could occur.
(3) *Real estate and interest rates*: if the collateral for debt instruments is based on real estate asset, then an increase in default rates caused by a recession could be accompanied by a decrease in real estate prices and in recovery rates.
(4) *Industry specific effects*: if default rates increases in specific industries are caused by decreases in sales/turnover due to product substitution (as it happens, e. g., in high tech or pharmaceutical companies, etc.), then a decrease in the value of inventories could also follow. This would in turn lead to a decrease in recovery rates.

These are just a few of the possible theoretical reasons justifying a negative correlation between default rates and recovery rates. The Merton model (see Chapter 11) also suggest that PD and RR may be correlated, since the borrower's leverage clearly affects both the default probability and the amount of company assets per unit of debt; this intuition is further developed in Appendix 12.A.

Moving from theoretical aspects to empirical evidence, US junk bond data indeed do indicate (see Table 12.7) that recovery rates for defaulted bonds are correlated with macroeconomic conditions and the aggregate risk of default.

In fact, the data in the Table show that, since 1980, recovery rates have decreased at the beginning of business cycle contractions, as in 1981 and 1990, and increased during economic expansions, as in the mid-80s and mid-90s. Even more significant are the data concerning the last four years, from 1999 to 2002, when bond default rates increased and recovery rates significantly decreased.

Following this kind of empirical evidence, new approaches explicitly modelling and empirically investigating the relationship between PD and RR have been developed during the last few years.

Frye (2000a and 2000b) proposed a model where a single systematic factor – the state of the economy – may cause default to rise and RRs to decline. The intuition is relatively simple: if a borrower defaults on a loan, a bank's recovery may depend on the value of the loan collateral. The value of the collateral, like the value of other assets, depends on economic conditions. If the economy experiences a recession, RRs may decrease

Table 12.7 Default Rates, Recovery Rates and Losses

Year	Par Value Outstanding (a) ($ MMs)	Par Value of Defaults (b) ($ MMs)	Default rate	Weighted Price after Default (Recovery Rate)	Weighted Coupon	Default Loss (c)
2001	$ 649,000	$ 63,609	9.80 %	25.5	9.18 %	7.76 %
2000	$ 597,200	$ 30,295	5.07 %	26.4	8.54 %	3.95 %
1999	$ 567,400	$ 23,532	4.15 %	27.9	10.55 %	3.21 %
1998	$ 465,500	$ 7,464	1.60 %	35.9	9.46 %	1.10 %
1997	$ 335,400	$ 4,200	1.25 %	54.2	11.87 %	0.65 %
1996	$ 271,000	$ 3,336	1.23 %	51.9	8.92 %	0.65 %
1995	$ 240,000	$ 4,551	1.90 %	40.6	11.83 %	1.24 %
1994	$ 235,000	$ 3,418	1.45 %	39.4	10.25 %	0.96 %
1993	$ 206,907	$ 2,287	1.11 %	56.6	12.98 %	0.56 %
1992	$ 163,000	$ 5,545	3.40 %	50.1	12.32 %	1.91 %
1991	$ 183,600	$ 18,862	10.27 %	36.0	11.59 %	7.16 %
1990	$ 181,000	$ 18,354	10.14 %	23.4	12.94 %	8.42 %
1989	$ 189,258	$ 8,110	4.29 %	38.3	13.40 %	2.93 %
1988	$ 148,187	$ 3,944	2.66 %	43.6	11.91 %	1.66 %
1987	$ 129,557	$ 1,736	1.34 %	62.0	12.07 %	0.59 %
1986	$ 90,243	$ 3,156	3.50 %	34.5	10.61 %	2.48 %
1985	$ 58,088	$ 992	1.71 %	45.9	13.69 %	1.04 %
1984	$ 40,939	$ 344	0.84 %	48.6	12.23 %	0.48 %
1983	$ 27,492	$ 301	1.09 %	55.7	10.11 %	0.54 %
1982	$ 18,109	$ 577	3.19 %	38.6	9.61 %	2.11 %
Weighted Average			4.19 %	37.2	10.60 %	3.16 %

Notes: (a) measured at mid-year, excludes defaulted issues; (b) does not include Texaco's bankruptcy in 1987; (c) includes lost coupon as well as principal loss.
Source: Altman, Brady, Resti, Sironi (2005).

just as default rates tend to increase. Based on this model, Frye performs an empirical analysis (2000b and 2000c) and concludes that in a severe economic downturn, bond recoveries might decline 20–25 percentage points from their normal-year average. Loan recoveries may decline by a similar amount, but from a higher level.

Using Moody's historical bond market data, Hu and Perraudin (2002) examined the dependence between recovery rates and default rates. They first standardized the quarterly recovery data in order to filter out the volatility of recovery rates given by the variation over time in the pool of borrowers rated by Moody's. They found that correlations between quarterly recovery rates and default rates for bonds issued by US-domiciled obligors were 22 % for post 1982 data (1983–2000) and 19 % for the 1971–2000 period.

Altman, Brady, Resti and Sironi (2005) investigated empirically the determinants of bonds' recovery rates and found a negative correlation between default rates and RRs (see Figure 12.5 and again Table 12.6). However, they found that a single systematic risk factor – i.e. the performance of the economy – is less predictive than the above-mentioned theoretical models would suggest. They rather emphasised the role played by supply and demand of defaulted bonds in determining aggregate recovery rates. Their econometric models assign a key role to the supply of defaulted bonds and show that this variable, together with variables that proxy the size of the high yield bond market, explains a substantial proportion of the variance in bond recovery rates aggregated across all seniority and collateral levels.

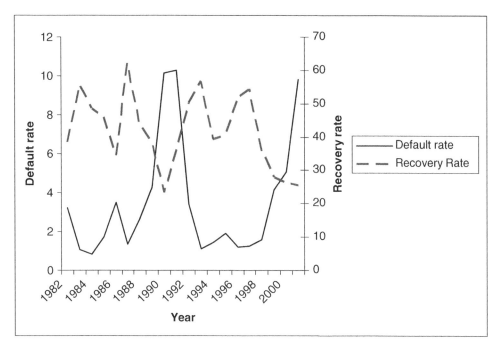

Figure 12.5   The relationship between default rates and recovery rates on corporate bonds
Source: Altman et al. (2005).

The most widely used credit pricing and VAR models are based on the assumption of independence between PD and LGD, and treat RR either as a constant parameter or as a stochastic variable independent from PD. In the latter case, RR volatility is assumed to represent an idiosyncratic risk which can be eliminated through adequate portfolio diversification. If, instead, recoveries were treated as correlated with defaults, then their variability would represent a systematic risk factor and should attract a risk premium.

A negative correlation between PD and LGD would have significant effects on both expected and unexpected losses.

These were estimated, through a simulation exercise, by Altman et al. (2001). This study estimated EL, UL and Value at Risk (VAR) of a credit portfolio according to three alternative assumptions:

(a) deterministic (fixed) recovery rates;
(b) recovery rates that are stochastic, yet uncorrelated with the probability of default;
(c) stochastic RRs, negatively correlated with default probabilities.

Introducing this third hypothesis prompts a significant increase (30%) both in risk measures (unexpected losses) and in the expected cost of defaults (see Table 12.8). The latter result looks especially important since expected losses on a 1-euro exposure are generally thought to be computed correctly by multiplying the (long term) average PD by the expected LGD (based on the same logic used in the introduction to this part of the book); yet, such a straightforward practice is found to be incorrect, and may seriously understate the actual loss, when default and recovery risk are correlated.

Table 12.8 The simulation exercise

Main results of the LGD simulation				
	LGD modelled according to approach			
	(a)	*(b)*	*(c)*	*% error**
Expected Loss	46.26	45.81	59.85	29.4%
Standard Error	98.17	97.84	127.16	29.5%
95% VAR	189.91	187.96	244.86	28.9%
99% VAR	435.41	437.08	564.46	29.6%
99.5% VAR	549.05	545.83	710.15	29.3%
99.9% VAR	809.22	814.52	1053.13	30.1%
				* computed as $[(c) - (a)]/(a)$

Source: Altman, Resti and Sironi (2001).

SELECTED QUESTIONS AND EXERCISES

1. A customer defaults on a 20 million euro loan. Over the following 4 years, the bank manages to recover 18 million euros, 20% of which have been absorbed by legal and administrative expenses. The duration of the recovery process (taking into account intermediate recoveries) has been 2.5 years. The average discount rate over the recovery period can be set at 8%, annually compounded. Compute the recovery rate on the defaulted loan.

2. On 1 January, 2003, a customer's default on a credit line worth 10 million euros. On 1 April 2003, the customer's bank has to pay 3 more million euros, on a guarantee. On 1 June 2004, the bank manages to liquidate a collateral, with net proceedings of 4 million euros. Further recoveries are recorded on 1 October 2004 (500,000 euros)

and finally on 1 May 2005 (2 million euros). Assuming a 360-day year and a flat rate curve at 10 %:

(i) compute total EAD, total recovery and the ratio (R) of the two; (ii) compute the ratio of the present value (at default) of total EAD and total recovery, by discounting individual cash flows and compare it to R: why do you think it is lower? (iii) Compute the duration of the recovery process. Multiply R by a discount factor based on this duration: compare the result to the one obtained by discounting individual cash flows.

3. Consider the following statements regarding recovery risk:

(i) senior bonds usually have lower LGDs that junior bonds and preference shares;
(ii) loans to utilities tend to have higher recovery rates because the defaulted firm may still be able to generate a considerable cash flow, making it easier for the bank to find a buyer for the firm, undertaking to pay a share of the defaulted debt;
(iii) the ratio between assets and liabilities of the defaulted firm tends to be negatively correlated to LGD;
(iv) the country of incorporation of the defaulted borrower may affect LGD, through the speed and effectiveness of bankruptcy procedures.

Which ones would you agree on?

(A) All but (iii);
(B) All but (i);
(C) All of them;
(D) All but (ii).

4. By "recovery risk" we mean the fact that, usually,:

(A) LGD is larger than zero;
(B) LGD and the recovery rate may, in total, be lower than one;
(C) the volatility of LGD is different from the one of the recovery rate;
(D) the volatility of LGD is different from zero.

5. Using a binomial (default-mode) model, calculate the loss volatility for a one euro loan with the following features: (i) a 0.8 % PD, (ii) a 40 % expected LGD, (iii) a 6 % LGD standard deviation assuming that PD and LGD are independent variables.

Appendix 12A

The Relationship between PD and RR in the Merton model

Merton-like default models provide us with a framework for deriving the expected recovery rate on a defaulted firm, as well as its default probability. While the latter was given much attention by subsequent research (see, e.g. Crosbie, 1999), the former has been somewhat overlooked.

As shown in Chapter 11, in Merton's model, the asset value of the firm follows a geometric Brownian motion:

$$dV = \mu V dt + \sigma_V V dz \tag{12A.1}$$

where μ and σ_V are the firm's asset value drift and the volatility rate and dz is a Wiener process. This implies that the log of the asset value at a given future date T

$$\ln V_T = \ln V_0 + \left(\mu - \frac{\sigma_V^2}{2} \right) T + \sigma_V \sqrt{T} \varepsilon \tag{12A.2}$$

follows a normal distribution with mean $\ln V_0 + \left(\mu - \frac{\sigma_V^2}{2} \right) T$ and variance $\sigma_V^2 T$. In turn, the asset value at time T will follow a lognormal distribution with mean $V_0 e^{\mu T}$ and variance $V_0^2 e^{2\mu T} (e^{\sigma_V^2 t} - 1)$.

As stated in Chapter 11, default happens if, at time T, the value of the firm's assets, V_T, is lower than its debt[18] F. That means that the firm's *probability of default, PD*, equals:

$$PD = p[V_T < F] = N \left(-\frac{\log \frac{V_0}{F} + \left(\mu + \frac{\sigma_V^2}{2} \right) T}{\sigma_V \sqrt{T}} \right) = N(-d_2^*) \tag{12A.3}$$

where $N(.)$ is the normal c.d.f.[19]

Now, assuming that no liquidation costs exist, when default occurs the recovery rate RR will be given by the ratio of the asset value to the debt, V_T/F. The expected recovery rate therefore is $E(V_T/F)$, that is $E(V_T)/F$. However, this is true only if $V_F < F$, otherwise no default happens and no recovery can be observed. More formally, *the expected recovery rate, RR,* can then be defined as:

$$E \left(\frac{V_T}{F} | V_T < F \right) = \frac{1}{F} E(V_T | V_T < F) \tag{12A.4}$$

---

[18] Short-term debt due at time t can be used instead, since the inability to repay long-term debt does not, by itself, trigger insolvency.

[19] Note that, as in Appendix 11B to Chapter 11, we are computing the real-world PD, based on the risk-adjusted return μ on corporate assets. Results for risk-neutral PDs and recovery rates would be similar.

that is, as $1/F$ times the mean of a truncated lognormal variable. This, in turn, is given by:

$$E(V_F|V_T < F) = e^{\mu_* + \frac{\sigma_*^2}{2}} \frac{\Phi\left(\dfrac{\ln F - \mu_*}{\sigma_*} - \sigma_*\right)}{\Phi\left(\dfrac{\log F - \mu_*}{\sigma_*}\right)} \tag{12A.5}$$

(see Liu et al. [1997], for a formal proof), where $\mu_* = \log V_0 + \left(\mu - \dfrac{\sigma_V^2}{2}\right) T$ and $\sigma_*^2 = \sigma_V^2 T$ are the mean and variance of $\ln V_T$.

Plugging these two quantities into (12A.4) holds:

$$E(V_T|V_T < F) = e^{\log V_0 + \mu T} \frac{\Phi\left(-\dfrac{\log \dfrac{V_0}{F} + \left(\mu + \dfrac{\sigma_V^2}{2}\right) T}{\sigma_V \sqrt{T}}\right)}{\Phi\left(-\dfrac{\log \dfrac{V_0}{F} + \left(\mu - \dfrac{\sigma_V^2}{2}\right) T}{\sigma_V \sqrt{T}}\right)}$$

$$= V_0 e^{\mu T} \frac{\Phi(-d_1^*)}{\Phi(-d_2^*)} = E(V_T) \frac{\Phi(-d_1^*)}{\Phi(-d_2^*)}$$

The expected recovery rate therefore is:

$$RR = E\left(\frac{V_T}{F}|V_T < F\right) = \frac{V0}{F} e^{\mu T} \frac{\Phi(-d_1^*)}{\Phi(-d_2^*)} = E\left(\frac{V_T}{F}\right) \frac{\Phi(-d_1^*)}{\Phi(-d_2^*)}$$

Figure 12A.1 shows PD and RR. The left panel shows the normal distribution for $\ln V_T$, with PD given by the grey area on the left; the right panel shows the lognormal distribution for V_T/F, the expected RR being the average of the values below 1, i.e., the mean of the values in the grey tail.

Given the expressions for PD and RR derived above, we can make sensitivity analyses on the link between those two variables. Figures 12A.2–4 consider the case of a firm with debt (F) worth 80, total assets (V_0) of 100, an annual asset volatility of 20 % and an expected return on assets of 5 %. This base case will be indicated by dotted vertical lines in the graphs; each time, one of the three main variables (F, V_T and σ_V) will be shocked (both halved and doubled) to see how PD and RR change.

First, in Figure 12A.2, we see that an increase in debt makes default more likely, while reducing the recovery rate on the defaulted loan (this could happen when a firm has to face an unexpected liability, e.g. because of legal claims due to polluting factories, oil leaks and so on); the opposite happens in Figure 12A.3, when the initial value of the firm's assets is revised upwards (e.g., for a pharmaceutical concern announcing a new treatment for some lethal disease), the PD shrinks and the RR grows higher.

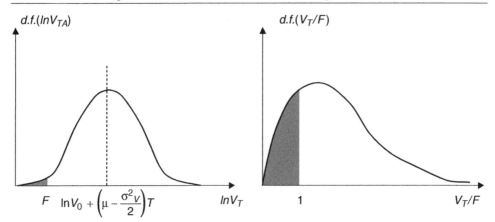

Figure A12.1   PD and RR

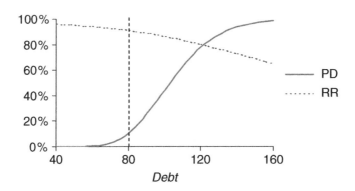

Figure 12A.2   The effect of debt value on PD and RR

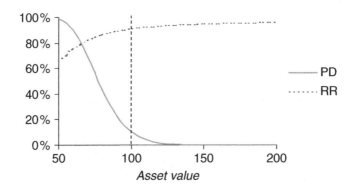

Figure 12A.3   The effect of asset value on PD and RR

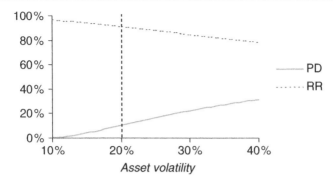

Figure 12A.4 Effect of asset volatility on PD and RR

Finally, in Figure 12A.4, we see what happens when asset volatility increases. This could be the case of the telecommunications industry in 2000: as the demand for e-commerce and Internet services has slowed down, the value of the investments made in broadband lines and 3G charters has become more uncertain. From Figure 12A.4 we see that, in such instances, an increase in asset volatility – even leaving leverage unchanged – brings about higher default probabilities and lower recovery rates.

13

Rating Systems

13.1 INTRODUCTION

In earlier chapters we considered the mathematical/statistical methods used to estimate the PD and, more generally, to evaluate the creditworthiness of a borrower and a credit exposure. Next to these approaches, more qualitative methods can be found, like those used by international credit rating agencies such as Moody's, Standard & Poor's and FitchRatings: these are based on non-automatic evaluations carried out by human experts analyzing company data and "soft" information that cannot be rigidly structured.

In recent decades, banks developing rating systems have generally used both the above-mentioned approaches. Thus, for example, rating systems for the assessment of medium-sized companies may comprise both qualitative analyses carried out by experts and a quantitative model, such as discriminant analysis or logit, helping to summarize the most relevant features of the company's financial indicators. Moreover, quantitative elements (such as the analysis of financial ratios, cash flows, and the mean industry ratios) are also included in the rating assignment process followed by agencies, although these do not use automatic models like those described in Chapters 10 and 11.

In the last 20 years, rating systems have acquired increasing importance on the credit and financial markets. Rating agencies now play a crucial role in determining the return on bonds, and therefore the cost for issuers;[1] similarly, banks' internal ratings are one of the main determinants of the interest rate charged to customers. The new capital adequacy scheme introduced by the Basel Committee in 2004 has definitely contributed to this trend.[2]

Generally speaking, a credit rating represents a concise evaluation of creditworthiness. Issuer ratings (also known as PD ratings) focus on the ability of a borrower to honour its obligations promptly and in full; issue ratings ("facility ratings"), instead, jointly analyze the borrower's PD and the possible recovery rate in the event of default (RR) on a specific exposure. PD ratings are based on the borrower's economic/financial data and on qualitative aspects such as the competitive position, product portfolio and management quality, the economic outlook of the industry in which the borrower operates, and possible legislative changes affecting corporate profits.

This chapter describes the construction and management of a rating system. First, we will discuss the criteria underlying the *rating assignment* step, presenting briefly the procedures followed by the main rating agencies and by the internal systems developed by banks. Next, we will consider the *rating quantification* step, i.e. the estimate of a PD measurement associated with the different rating grades. Finally, we will focus on the methods used to evaluate the quality of a rating system, that is, on the *rating validation* step.

---

[1] Gabbi and Sironi (2004) showed that over 75% of the cross-section variability of primary market spreads corporate eurobonds is explained by rating differences.
[2] See Chapter 20.

13.2   RATING ASSIGNMENT

13.2.1   Internal ratings and agency ratings: how do they differ?

Rating assignment criteria, like those presented in this section, may differ considerably depending on whether they refer to "external" ratings (assigned by agencies to bond issuers) or internal ratings (assigned by banks to their own customers). These differences arise from three main factors: (i) the borrowers being evaluated, (ii) the available information, and (iii) the rater's system of targets and incentives. They are briefly discussed below.

(i) Rating agencies perform a "delegated monitoring", on behalf of investors participating in the bond market. Namely, they help to reduce the information asymmetry between the issuer of a financial instrument and investors, regarding the former's ability to pay back its debt. Hence their assessments focus on entities issuing bonds on the capital markets, like sovereign agencies, multilateral development banks or large financial and non-financial companies. These are large organizations, which have often been in the market for very long time, running business in many geographical areas and often in many industries. Banks, conversely, rate a more wide-ranging array of borrowers, including large corporate customers, small firms and individual retail customers. Bond issuers rated by agencies are large enough to justify the costs associated with accurate, lengthy, structured analyses;[3] in the case of small companies applying for bank loans, the costs of the rating process must be kept under control, and this may include resorting to automatic evaluation models.

(ii) The second difference relates to the information available. Information which is routinely obtained for large companies evaluated by agencies (share prices, bond spreads, audited accounts, etc.) is often unavailable for smaller bank borrowers. Also, even for the same borrower, agencies and banks have access to different types of information. In fact, while at the initial stage both parties can access a large amount of (sometimes confidential) information,[4] at later stages the bank enjoys a valuable source of additional information which is not available to agencies: the borrower's bank account turnover and the way it uses the loan. For example, if the borrower constantly uses its credit line up to the maximum allowed amount, or even makes unauthorized overdrafts, this sometimes represents an early signal (unavailable to rating agencies) of a deterioration in its liquidity. This kind of analysis (sometimes referred to as "trend analysis") is often used as an input by banks for periodic reviews of their customers' ratings.

(iii) Finally, the activity of agencies and banks is guided by different incentive systems. Rating agencies aim to offer an independent credit opinion to investors, based on a set of objective and precise criteria. Although they earn fees from the rated companies they must protect their reputation, i.e. the credibility of their opinions, to stay in business. It is necessary to avoid that a deterioration in the issuer's creditworthiness "contradicts" the evaluations previously issued by the agency, forcing it to downgrade

---

[3] In the case of rating agencies in particular, the costs of rating activities are borne by the issuer, which pays the agency a fee.

[4] Both banks and agencies enjoy a considerable bargaining power: the borrower is willing to provide information because it wishes to obtain credit from the bank, or because it is aware that the rate paid on its bonds depends crucially on the agencies' ratings.

the rating. For this reason, rating agencies tend to produce ratings that are as robust and stable as possible, by evaluating companies based on their expected performance in the medium/long-term. This means that if the economy is going through a phase of expansion, but the issuer is considered vulnerable in the event of a recession, a lower rating will be assigned, which somewhat anticipates the adverse effects of a possible worsening of the economic cycle. Conversely, banks producing internal ratings are both the issuer and receiver of their evaluations, and are more interested in protecting their loans than their reputation as a "flawless" analyst. Hence, ratings must be as reactive as possible, i.e. able to quickly reflect any changes in economic/financial conditions. What matters, here, is not so much the *stability* of the rating (and its ability to anticipate medium/long-term evaluations), but rather its ability to correctly reflect current conditions, promptly detecting any deterioration. This difference in the objectives of banks and agencies, leads to a major difference in their rating assignment criteria. As noticed by Carey and Treacy (2000), rating agencies adopt a *"through-the-cycle"* perspective (i.e. they evaluate a company's ability to repay its debt throughout the whole economic cycle, including recessions, even if the current economic trend is favourable); conversely, banks base their ratings on the *"point-in-time"* approach, which evaluates the creditworthiness of a borrower based only on current conditions and on those expected for the immediate future. The future period covered by a "point-in-time" forecast will usually be proportional to the maturity of the loan: as many banks grant a considerable amount of demand or short-term loans, the evaluation horizon of the "point-in-time" approach tends to be fairly short.[5]

These differences relate to the "issuer rating" or PD rating. However, we know that the possible loss on a loan depends not only on the probability of default, but also on the loss given default (LGD).[6] When this component, too, is assessed, this gives rise to the "issue rating" or "facility rating" of a specific exposure (note that different exposures to the same borrower might enjoy different issue ratings, based on their characteristics). Here again, the methods used by rating agencies and banks may differ.

In the case of agencies, passing from issuer to issue rating may involve a reduction in the rating ("notching down"), according to the degree of subordination of the exposure. In the case of senior secured issues, the issue rating generally coincides with the issuer rating; in the case of subordinated bonds, the issue rating is reduced by one notch if the issuer has an investment grade rating (for example, using the Standard & Poor's scale, it is reduced from an A- issuer rating to a BBB+ issue rating) or two notches if the issuer has a speculative grade rating (e.g. from B+ to B-). This rating reduction is due to the fact that subordinated issues enjoy a lower recovery rate in the event of default. Conversely, the issue rating may be in line with the issuer rating or even above ("notching up") given the presence of collateral (secured bonds), guarantees or covenants.

For a long time, recovery rates on credit exposures have not been separately and explicitly rated by agencies, although their evaluations could be worked out indirectly, by comparing issuer and issue rating. In recent years, however, the expected recovery rates

---

[5] The use of "point-in-time" evaluations may be reduced by the new Basel Capital Accord, which requires banks to assign the rating with a medium-term time horizon, taking account of the effects of possible adverse macroeconomic conditions ("Although the time horizon used in PD estimation is one year, banks are expected to use a longer time horizon in assigning ratings. The bank must assess of the borrower's ability to perform despite adverse economic conditions or the occurrence of unexpected events").

[6] For an analysis of this component, see the previous chapter.

have become the subject of ad hoc rating procedures: for example, since 2003 Standard & Poor's has been publishing "recovery ratings", which measure recovery prospects on a number of rated loans. A similar service is supplied by Fitchratings.[7]

In the case of banks' internal ratings, the estimate of the LGD is not necessarily incorporated into an exposure-specific rating (that is, into a facility rating). Rather, the two dimensions leading to the estimation of expected losses on an exposure are often measured separately: next to a PD rating system (measuring borrower risk) LGDs are estimated explicitly on individual loans; these two quantities can then be combined to estimate the expected loss on different exposures.

13.2.2   The assignment of agency ratings

Rating agencies were created in the early years of the last century, in the USA. In the second half of the 1800's the US financial markets had witnessed a considerable spread of bonds issued by railway companies; in the last few years of the century, however, a formidable wave of bankruptcies, which also involved bonds issued by local authorities, thoroughly shook the public's confidence in companies issuing debt instruments. In this context, in 1909, John Moody published his first assessment of a bond. Gradually, over the following years, as the agency gained a favourable reputation with the public, companies interested in raising new funds discovered the usefulness of accessing the markets with a rating. In the next 100 years or so, Moody's agency kept expanding, and is now present in 17 countries with some 800 analysts.

Standard Statistics assigned its first rating to a corporate bond in 1916; a merger with the specialized publisher Poor's Publishing led to the creation of Standard & Poor's in 1941. John Fitch's publishing company released its first rating in 1924, and through a series of takeovers, the company became what today's Fitchratings.[8]

Ratings have gained increasing acceptance over the last 100 years; however, their spread in the main advanced economies is still uneven. According to Estrella (2000), out of every 100 industrial companies with sales of at least 500 million dollars, 50 are rated in the US (by Moody's, Standard & Poor's or both), 12%–13% in Holland and the UK, around 5% in France, and only around 1–2% in countries like Germany and Italy.

In the past, agencies used to publish their own ratings without seeking a fee, and funded themselves through the sale of publications and analytical material. This business model was jeopardized by the development of photocopying machines, and the practice of asking the rated company for a commission then became widespread.[9] Agencies may get paid on a per-issue basis, or by means of a fixed periodic fee. Further sources of income may include training activities and services supplied to banks and other financial intermediaries that wish to develop their own internal rating processes.

Agency ratings (especially issuer ratings and ratings of long-term issues) are accompanied by an indication of the future outlook, which may be positive, negative, or stable.

---

[7] See Chew and Kerr (2005).

[8] Apart from the three firms mentioned in the text, which enjoy a considerable presence on the entire global market, the rating industry includes another hundred or so agencies working at national or local levels, which often use quantitative models to produce low-cost assessments for a large number of issuers and issues. See Estrella (2000).

[9] This practice underwent a sharp acceleration in the 1970s when, after the Penn Central Railroad collapse, savers deserted the market of short-term corporate liabilities (commercial papers). Being unable to tap the market with new issues, other companies experienced liquidity crises and collapsed, which increased investors' fears; to reassure investors, many issuers then decided to pay for the services of a rating agency.

This indicates that the agency may decide to review its assessment for better or worse in the next one to two-year period, but in no way represents a guarantee or announcement that the rating will be changed. A "creditwatch" status (positive or negative) indicates that new events have affected the issuer (e.g. the company has suddenly announced a takeover that could weaken its creditworthiness), about which the agency is collecting information; and that it may update its assessment on the basis of such information, usually within six months.[10]

The first assignment of a rating may take several weeks or months. This time is necessary to obtain all relevant information from the company, and to transform this huge mass of data (often qualitative and therefore difficult to assess in an automated, objective manner) into a concise judgement by means of a standardized procedure that must remain the same across time and across issuers.

At major agencies, the issuer is first analyzed by a team that carries out research and analysis. This involves both business risk and financial risk analysis.

Business risk analysis involves the study of the market and industry in which the issuer operates, in order to assess its competitive position and prospects and verify whether sales and profit margins are likely to come under pressure. Future management strategies, as disclosed by the company, are also considered, as well as the management skills demonstrated in the past, and the soundness of its governance schemes.

Financial risk analysis starts from the company's financial data (including financial statements, any future budgets disclosed by the company, and the agencies' own simulations of expected cash flows and their adequacy to repay the debt). Financial ratios are computed to assess the financial soundness of the company (e.g. the ratio between total net debt and operating income), and are often compared with the "typical" values of companies to which the agency has already assigned a certain rating (known as "median values"), in order to ensure consistency with the ratings issued in the past. An example is shown in Table 13.1: unsurprisingly, higher ratings are associated with higher profitability and capitalisation.

This comparison with median values is not automatic or mandatory; however, it represents a useful means to make ratings more uniform (over time and for different issuers). Comparisons between the issuer's ratios and median ratios may be adjusted on the basis of the company's business risk: e.g. higher indebtedness may be considered acceptable, and lead to a comparatively higher rating, if the company has a stable market share in a counter-cyclical industry, and its cash flows are considered highly stable. Examples of this interaction are shown in Tables 13.2 and 13.3; note that lower cash flows (Table 13.2) and higher leverages (Table 13.3) are deemed compatible with a given rating, provided that the company's business risk is perceived to be low. However, this flexibility is not unlimited: e.g. a firm with a cash flow below 80 % of its debt will not be given an AAA rating, however low its business risk is.

The "quantitative" data taken from the financial statement therefore represent only one component of a more complex process.[11] The approach followed by large rating agencies

---

[10] To sum up: while *outlook* indicates that the agency has information not yet fully incorporated into the rating, which is insufficient to alter it but suggests a possible future upgrade or downgrade, *creditwatch* indicates that the agency is awaiting a more precise picture of one or more significant events.

[11] The information analyzed is taken from publicly-available sources and private materials supplied by the issuer's management; these latter materials cannot normally be used in the agency's press releases and reports unless the issuer has disclosed them to the market in the meantime. The agency expressly relies on the accuracy

Table 13.1 Median financial ratios for different rating classes (3-year means: 1998–2000) – US Corporates

	AAA	AA	A	BBB	BB	B	CCC
EBIT interest coverage	21.4	10.1	6.1	3.7	2.1	0.8	0.1
EBITDA interest coverage	26.5	12.9	9.1	5.3	3.4	1.8	1.3
Free operating cash flow/total debt (%)	84.2	25.2	15.0	8.5	2.6	(3.2)	(12.9)
Funds from operations/total debt (%)	128.8	55.4	43.2	30.8	18.8	7.8	1.6
Return on capital (%)	34.9	21.7	19.4	13.6	11.6	6.6	1.0
Operating income/sales (%)	27.0	22.1	18.6	15.4	15.9	11.9	11.9
Long-term debt/capital (%)	13.3	28.2	33.9	42.5	57.2	69.7	68.8
Total debt/capital (%)	22.9	37.7	42.5	48.2	62.6	74.8	87.7
Number of companies	8	29	136	218	273	281	22

Source: Standard & Poor's, quoted in De Servigny, Renault (2004), p. 27.

Table 13.2 Minimum "cash flow coverage" ratio (Free cash flow/Debt) for different rating classes (%)

Business risk rating	*Final rating*				
	AAA	AA	A	BBB	BB
Excellent (AAA/AA)	80	60	40	25	10
Above average (A)	150	80	50	30	15
Average (BBB)	–	105	60	35	20
Below average (BB)	–	–	85	40	25
Well below average (B)	–	–	–	65	45

Source: Standard & Poor's (2003).

is based on *interaction* between financial risk and business risk, just like the Merton model described in Chapter 11.

Table 13.4 summarizes the main stages in this process.[12] After the two risk profiles (business risk and financial risk) have been analyzed, projections are usually drawn up regarding the company's future ability to generate operational cash flows. The company's

---

and completeness of the data received from the company, its advisers and management, although its analysts may try to clarify and resolve inconsistencies in such data, primarily in the financial statements.

[12] Appendix 13A to this chapter contains more detailed information about the rating assignment process used by rating agencies.

Table 13.3 Maximum leverage (Debt/Capital)for different rating classes (%)

Business risk rating	Final rating				
	AAA	AA	A	BBB	BB
Excellent (AAA/AA)	30	40	50	60	70
Above average (A)	20	25	40	50	60
Average (BBB)	–	15	30	40	55
Below average (BB)	–	–	25	35	45
Well below average (B)	–	–	–	25	35

Source: Standard & Poor's (2003).

debt capacity can be evaluated on the basis of these projections. This evaluation is accompanied by a sensitivity analysis designed to assess how the company's debt capacity would react under some worst-case scenarios, such as reduced demand, a decrease in efficiency, higher interest rates, or other adverse events.

Table 13.4 The process of analysis underlying an agency's rating assignment

Industry analysis: current situation and future prospects	Competitive position analysis	Economic/financial situation analysis
	Economic/financial projections	
Debt capacity analysis		
Sensitivity analysis toward critical risk factors		

The results of these analyses are discussed by a rating committee, which considers the adequacy of the information received, the consistency between financial risk and business risk, and expected future developments in the company's strategies, income flows and financial balance. The rating committee agrees on a rating, which is usually communicated to the issuer before being disclosed to the market. If the company does not agree with the agency's opinion, it may request an appeal by asking the committee to consider new information not yet analysed. The rating may be reconsidered on the basis of this new information. If the issuer does not object to the final rating,[13] this is made public through the main financial information channels and a press release. Ratings are also published on the agencies' websites, where additional reports and communications, describing the company's strategic and financial profile in greater detail, are also made available to subscribers.

Rating agencies do not specify the exact PDs associated with individual issuers, but simply assign them to rating grades, indicated by letters (like AAA, AA, A, BBB, etc.) or alphanumeric strings (like AAA, AA1, AA2, AA3, etc.)

Table 13.5 shows the rating classes used by the three major agencies, Moody's, Fitch and Standard & Poor's, with brief definitions of the associated risk profile.[14] The definitions of the rating classes are not quantitative: the rating is a discrete ordinal qualitative variable (which measures the credit risk of one company relative to others). Ratings are divided into investment-grade ones (featuring high reliability) and speculative-grade ones (investments involving a higher risk, but also higher interest rates).

The assignment of an issuer to a given rating grade represents an indirect estimate of its PD. In fact, PDs can be derived from studies regarding the percentage of companies that have defaulted in the past within each rating grade; such statistics are periodically made public by the agencies, and customarily used by investors and other market participants. We will return to this in section 13.3 (rating quantification).

13.2.3   Rating assessment in bank internal rating systems

We saw in section 13.2 how the PD ratings estimated internally by banks differ from those of rating agencies in several respects (different type of companies rated, different data sources available, and different incentive systems, which lead to a different evaluation horizon). However, bank ratings are similar to agency ratings in that they also represent a concise opinion of a company's ability to meet its commitments, based on an assessment of financial risk and business risk. Accordingly, the main factors reviewed remain unchanged: profitability, financial leverage, liquidity, industry, management quality, competitive position, etc.

Generally speaking, each bank follows different procedures and practices, but there are some common traits, to which this section will be devoted: choosing the number of rating classes, selecting the relevant information, defining default, moving from PD ratings to the evaluation of individual credit exposures, setting the timing and scope of rating reviews.

As regards the number of classes (that is, the "granularity" of the rating system), some surveys conducted in the USA and at international level (Basel Committee, 2000b, Carey & Treacy, 2000, English & Nelson, 1998) show considerable variability between banks. The number of "pass" classes (classes including "reliable" customers and "non-impaired loans" also known as "non-problem grades") is around ten on average, but can range from two to over twenty. The number of classes devoted to "problematic" customers (whose

---

[13] In many countries, if the issuer does not agree with the agency's opinion, it may request the agency to treat the rating as confidential. This is justified by the fact that the rating is primarily a service purchased by the issuer to reassure potential investors.

[14] It should be borne in mind that the rating assigned to a company cannot normally be better than that of the country in which it operates. The very few exceptions to this rule include Toyota, to which S&P has attributed an AAA rating; this rating is higher than that of Japan (AA−) in view of the company's low level of dependence on the country's economy, partly due to the geographical diversification of its business.

Table 13.5 Rating classes: definition and meaning

Moody's	S&P and Fitch	Definitions		Description
Aaa	AAA	Investment grade	High investment grade	Good-quality assets, wide diversification and established size, excellent market positioning, distinctive managerial skills, and very high debt-coverage capacity
Aa1	AA+			Good quality and liquidity of assets, well
Aa2	AA			established on the market with diversified
Aa3	AA−			outlets, good-quality management, and sound debt-coverage capacity
A1	A+		Lower investment grade	Satisfactory quality and liquidity of assets,
A2	A			average market positioning and quality of
A3	A−			management, normal credit standards, average debt-coverage capacity
Baa1	BBB+			Acceptable quality and liquidity of assets,
Baa2	BBB			though with an appreciable degree of risk,
Baa3	BBB−			weaker debt-coverage capacity
Ba1	BB+	Non-investment grade	Below investment grade	Acceptable quality and liquidity of assets,
Ba2	BB			though with a significant degree of risk, low
Ba3	BB−			diversification of business, limited liquidity, and limited debt-coverage margins
B1	B+		Speculative grade	Credit under review, quality of assets
B2	B			acceptable, though with temporary liquidity
B3	B−			difficulties, high financial leverage, some weaknesses in management, positioning and market positioning
Caa	CCC	High risk	High risk	As above, but with evident difficulties, and
Ca	CC			debt management sometimes tense and hectic. Uncertainty regarding the payment of interest, but not yet of the capital.

Source: Maino and Masera (2003).

loans should in principle be revoked) is three on average, but can range from nil to six. In general, granularity increases with the age of the rating system, and is usually higher for banks having better and more deeply-rooted credit risk management skills.

A higher granularity may be preferable for two reasons: on the one hand, it helps to prevent excessive concentration of borrowers in one or a few classes, on the other hand it allows more accurate loan pricing,[15] thus helping the bank to better compete on the market. In fact, as the interest rate on a loan depends on its PD,[16] combining a number of borrowers in a single rating class (which corresponds to a single PD) is equivalent (other conditions being equal) to charging all these borrowers the same interest rate. This rate will be too high for the best borrowers (which will be able to find cheaper rates elsewhere and consequently leave the bank), and too low for the worst ones (whose demand for credit will increase). Conversely, dividing borrowers into a larger number of classes produces more precise PD estimates and allows rates to be more directly connected with the actual risk content of individual borrowers.[17]

As regards the information used, banks' rating systems differ considerably, depending on the market segment (large conglomerates, corporations, small firms, individuals or families), for which they are developed. In the case of companies, the main inputs could include the following:

– economic/financial indicators obtained from the financial statements, which can be analyzed directly by an expert or, in some cases, may be processed automatically by a scoring system (like those presented in Chapter 10);
– qualitative variables (which typically cannot be processed with a scoring model) such as management quality, competitive positioning and the quality and degree of innovation of the company's products;
– an analysis of the state and outlook of the industry in which the company operates, usually performed by a specialist analyst;
– for companies which are already with the bank, a "trend analysis" of the way the company is running its payments and using its current credit lines (e.g., unauthorized overdrafts and payment delays, unpaid bills and other receivables, etc.);
– data from the Central Credit Registry or Credit Bureaus, if available. These are inter-bank consortiums (managed by the supervisory authorities or private companies) which collect information about the loans granted by each bank and return it in aggregated form to all the banks participating in the data-gathering scheme. Through these registries, data can be obtained about the relationship between the company and the entire banking system, checking, e.g. whether it has recently requested loans from other banks, or increased the used portion of its credit lines.[18]

In the case of small loans to individuals and families (known as the "retail" sector), the available inputs would of course be quite different, and include information like payrolls or tax statements. Also, the available information could be processed in a fully-automated way, by weighting each variable with a coefficient estimated through a statistical model. In these cases, qualitative variables (usually collected by asking the borrower to fill in a questionnaire) would be converted into a dummy variable, and then entered in statistical

---

[15] See Chapter 15.
[16] See Appendix 11A.
[17] This ability to differentiate rates offered to customers is especially important in the "large corporate" segment, where banks compete more aggressively and customers are more "mobile".
[18] While central credit registries exist, e.g., in Spain, France and Italy, they are not very common in the English-speaking countries. For further details, see Trucharte Artigas (2004).

models. Their contribution to early default detection could be evaluated through statistical tests, based on the characteristics of loans defaulted in the past (as we did for financial ratios in Chapter 10).

Automatic scoring systems may also be used for small-medium enterprises, although scores are reviewed and changed based on the the analysts' subjective evaluations. In the case of larger counterparties, credit analysts play a central role: the outputs of scoring systems, where available, are just used as an input to the analysts' work, and can be overridden if their results are considered unreliable (e.g. on the basis of qualitative information known to the analyst, which scoring models typically do not process).[19]

These different mixes of automated and human-based resources are mainly due to two factors: on the one hand, the earnings generated by loans to individuals and small companies are often too low to absorb the costs of a highly customized analysis and monitoring process, and therefore may require standardised, low-cost rating procedures; on the other hand, since the number of large counterparties is generally limited, they cannot be analyzed by means of a statistical model simply because it would be impossible to obtain a sample large enough to make statistical estimates significant.

The assignment of a bank's PD rating sometimes involves several stages, implying the production of "partial" ratings, i.e. opinions that only incorporate some aspects of the analysis. Thus, for example, there might be a first-level rating based solely on a financial statement analysis (possibly carried out by a scoring model) a second-level rating adding qualitative information about the company, and a third-level rating that also takes account of industry and country prospects.

The rating of individual facilities implies the estimation of their expected loss rate, based on the borrower's PD rating and the facility's estimated LGD (see Chapter 12). As mentioned in section 13.2.1, most banks keep those two risk dimensions separate, considering default risk and recovery risk separately. Some financial institutions, however, prefer to evaluate individual exposures directly, assigning them to classes with similar expected loss (EL) rates. This one-dimensional approach requires the rating to be attributed directly to the loan ("facility rating"), and is sometimes used for retail exposures such as home loans and credit cards.

13.3 RATING QUANTIFICATION

13.3.1 The possible approaches

After a borrower has been assigned a rating, the latter must be converted into a PD before it can be used for risk measurement purposes. There are three possible approaches to this problem:

- *the statistical approach*, whereby an individual PD is calculated for each borrower based on the score obtained with a credit-scoring model. Although this approach is quick and enables a specific PD to be assigned to each customer, it presents two drawbacks. Firstly, it only works when the customer is evaluated through a statistical model (whereas in the case of a qualitative valuation performed by an expert no such statistical shortcuts exist for generating default probabilities). Secondly, it may be based on

---

[19] For a more detailed analysis, see the Basel Committee survey of rating systems (2000b), which expressly states that "...statistically-based approaches have a more prominent role in small corporate lending than for middle market or large corporates...".

unrealistic assumptions: in Chapter 10, e.g., we saw that PDs obtained from discriminant analysis scores assume that the distribution of the input variables is normal. Due to these two drawbacks, the statistical approach is used seldom and with caution.

– *the actuarial approach* based on actual default frequencies. This approach requires that past default rates recorded in the various rating classes be used as an estimate of the future PD of borrowers in each class. Thus, for example, if the past data show that 1 % of the customers assigned to class BB tend to default within one year, a PD of 1 % will be assigned to all the borrowers now present in that class. This approach is generally followed by rating agencies, which periodically publish statistics on the defaults recorded in earlier years and decades. Many banks also use the same approach, although their results are not made public. The actuarial approach will be covered in detail in the next two sections of this paragraph.

– *the mapping approach*. Precisely because public data for the default rates of agency-rated companies exist, many banks find it useful to establish a link ("mapping") between their internal ratings and those by Moody's or Standard & Poor's (e.g. by establishing, on the basis of a subjective judgement, that an internal rating of "10" is equivalent to Standard & Poor's "AAA"). After bank ratings are mapped to the external ones, the default rates published by the agencies are used to estimate the PDs associated with the former. This approach requires great caution, as the link between internal and agency ratings may entail several flaws. For example, we saw that agencies use a "through-the-cycle" approach, while banks rate "point-in-time": this difference alone could make the mapping unstable and unreliable.

13.3.2   The actuarial approach: marginal, cumulative and annualized default rates

The major international rating agencies began to publish default rate (or "mortality") data for rated companies in the 1990s. Data relating to "rating migrations", i.e. the frequency with which the companies in the various rating classes "migrate" towards other classes (migration rates), are also published periodically; these data are organised in matrices called *transition matrices*.

The following procedure is used to estimate this data:

– at the beginning of each year, issuers (or issues) are grouped by rating grade (each year is called a "cohort" or pool);
– each pool is monitored in the following years, and the (one-year and *n*-year) default rates for each rating grade are recorded;
– the one-year and n-year default rates for different pools can be averaged to obtain more stable results.

This procedure involves the computation of marginal and cumulative default rates (*d*). The *marginal default rate for year t* is given by

$$d'_t = \frac{D_t}{N_t} \qquad (13.1)$$

where D_t indicates the number of defaults recorded in year t, and N_t the number of issuers (or bonds) present *at the start* of year t. Note that, equivalently,

$$s_t' = \frac{N_t - D_t}{N_t} = 1 - d_t' \qquad (13.2)$$

can also be used to indicate the *marginal survival rate* in year t.

The marginal default rates computed on a sample of bond issues can be used as an estimate of the probability that an issue will become insolvent within t years of its launch. Table 13.6 shows an example based on Moody's ratings.

Table 13.6 Marginal default rates (d_t') on a sample of bonds rated by Moody's

t	1	2	3	4	5	6	7	8	9	10
Rating										
Aaa	0.01%	0.02%	0.03%	0.03%	0.07%	0.07%	0.11%	0.12%	0.14%	0.15%
Aa1	0.02%	0.05%	0.07%	0.08%	0.10%	0.10%	0.11%	0.12%	0.13%	0.15%
Aa2	0.02%	0.08%	0.12%	0.12%	0.14%	0.12%	0.11%	0.11%	0.13%	0.15%
Aa3	0.03%	0.08%	0.13%	0.14%	0.17%	0.15%	0.12%	0.16%	0.19%	0.22%
A1	0.05%	0.09%	0.14%	0.16%	0.21%	0.18%	0.14%	0.20%	0.24%	0.28%
A2	0.06%	0.09%	0.15%	0.18%	0.24%	0.20%	0.15%	0.24%	0.30%	0.35%
A3	0.09%	0.18%	0.23%	0.30%	0.33%	0.30%	0.31%	0.38%	0.42%	0.42%
Baa1	0.13%	0.27%	0.31%	0.43%	0.42%	0.40%	0.47%	0.51%	0.53%	0.50%
Baa2	0.16%	0.36%	0.40%	0.55%	0.51%	0.49%	0.63%	0.64%	0.65%	0.57%
Baa3	0.70%	1.11%	1.11%	1.19%	1.15%	0.98%	0.93%	0.91%	0.90%	0.84%
Ba1	1.25%	1.85%	1.82%	1.84%	1.80%	1.47%	1.22%	1.17%	1.15%	1.11%
Ba2	1.79%	2.59%	2.53%	2.48%	2.44%	1.96%	1.51%	1.44%	1.40%	1.39%
Ba3	3.96%	3.90%	3.53%	3.12%	2.71%	2.60%	1.81%	1.75%	1.50%	1.47%
B1	6.14%	5.21%	4.54%	3.75%	2.98%	3.25%	2.11%	2.05%	1.60%	1.55%
B2	8.31%	6.52%	5.54%	4.39%	3.24%	3.90%	2.41%	2.35%	1.70%	1.64%
B3	15.08%	6.82%	5.21%	3.80%	3.14%	4.43%	2.58%	1.69%	2.54%	2.01%

Source: *Moody's* (1996).

Note that

√ The worst rating grades tend to have the highest p_t' values; hence, agency ratings seem to perform well, in that they correctly identify the riskiness of the issuers;

√ The marginal default rates increase with t for the best rating classes, while the reverse applies to the worst ones. This is also shown in Figure 13.1 (which for the sake of simplicity only contains the data for classes A1 and B1) and looks consistent with the results of the Merton model (see Chapter 11).[20] Such a behaviour is explained by the so-called *"rating drift"* effect: in the years following a bond issue, highly-rated companies (that do not default) happen to migrate to worse rating classes (having higher default rates); conversely, low-rated companies (unless they default) may improve their ratings and therefore reduce their marginal default rate over the years.

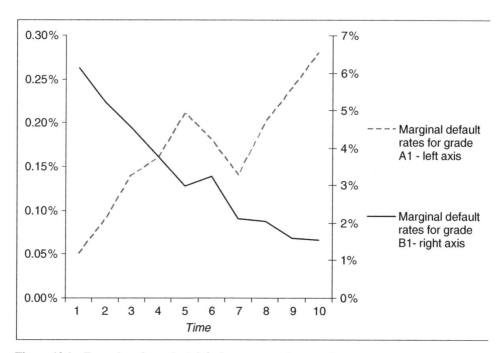

Figure 13.1   Examples of marginal default rate curves by maturity

We now define the *cumulative default rate* for the period between 0 and T, d_T, as:

$$d_T = \frac{\sum_{t=1}^{T} D_t}{N_1} \tag{13.3}$$

Note that this is given by all the defaults occurring between 0 and T, divided by the initial size of the pool. Similarly, the relative cumulative survival rate between 0 and T is given by:

$$s_T = 1 - p_T = \frac{N_1 - \sum_{t=1}^{T} D_t}{N_1} \tag{13.4}$$

---

[20] This phenomenon explains the different slope of the spread curves for investment grade and speculative grade securities, also illustrated in Chapter 11.

As, by definition, $N_{t+1} = N_t - D_t$, then s_t can be rewritten as

$$s_T = \prod_{t=1}^{T} s_t' \tag{13.5}$$

and hence

$$d_T = 1 - s_T = 1 - \prod_{t=1}^{T} (1 - d_t') \tag{13.6}$$

Cumulative default rates can then be obtained from marginal default rates, using (13.6). Cumulative default rates represent a proxy for the probability of default from the moment a bond is launched until a given number of years after the issue.

Table 13.7 Example of marginal and cumulative default rates

Year	d_T'	s_T'	d_T
1	0.0 %	100.0 %	0.0 %
2	0.91 %	99.09 %	0.91 %
3	3.66 %	96.34 %	4.54 %
4	1.93 %	98.07 %	6.38 %
5	2.78 %	97.22 %	8.98 %

Consider, for example, the marginal default (and survival) rates shown in Table 13.7. The cumulative default rate for the fifth year will be:

$$d_5 = 1 - (0.9909 \cdot 0.9634 \cdot 0.9807 \cdot 0.9722) = 1 - 0.9103 = 8.98\,\%$$

Other values for various years are indicated in the fourth column of the Table.

Table 13.8 shows an example of cumulative default rates recorded by Standard & Poor's.[21] Once again, notice the high correlation between rating classes and mean default rates. Unlike marginal default rates shown in Table 13.6, cumulative default rates obviously grow with T.

Starting from a cumulative default rate d_T, it is also possible to compute the corresponding *average annual default rate* $\bar{d}_T$, i.e. the value which, when substituted for the various marginal default rates, would produce d_T. In symbols, recalling (13.6):

$$\bar{d}_T = d^* \left| 1 - \prod_{t=1}^{T} (1 - d^*) = 1 - (1 - d^*)^T = d_T \right.$$

---

[21] The cumulative default rates shown in Table 13.8 are obtained from different pools from those used to estimate the marginal default rates in Table 13.6, and it is therefore impossible to derive one from the other with (13.6). As an exercise, readers should calculate the cumulative rates implicit in Table 13.6 and the marginal rates implicit in Table 13.8.

Table 13.8 Cumulative default rates (d_T) by rating class – % values

YEAR	1	2	3	4	5	6	7	8	9	10
CLASS										
AAA	0.00	0.00	0.06	0.12	0.19	0.35	0.52	0.82	0.93	1.06
AA	0.00	0.02	0.10	0.20	0.35	0.53	0.70	0.84	0.91	1.00
A	0.05	0.14	0.24	0.39	0.58	0.77	0.97	1.22	1.49	1.76
BBB	0.18	0.42	0.67	1.21	1.68	2.18	2.66	3.07	3.38	3.71
BB	0.91	2.95	5.15	7.32	9.25	11.22	12.29	13.40	14.33	15.07
B	4.74	9.91	14.29	17.42	19.70	21.26	22.56	23.75	24.71	25.55
CCC	18.90	26.01	30.99	35.10	39.02	39.88	40.87	41.17	41.86	42.72
INV. GRADE	0.07	0.18	0.31	0.54	0.78	1.05	1.31	1.58	1.79	2.02
SPEC. GRADE	3.75	7.60	11.03	13.79	16.03	17.72	18.90	20.00	20.93	21.73

Source: Standard & Poor's (1998).

Hence:

$$\overline{d}_T = 1 - \sqrt[T]{1 - d_T} \qquad (13.7)$$

Mean annual default rates can prove useful in setting the spread required to cover the expected loss on a loan. This spread (see Chapter 15) is a function of the PD and the expected recovery rate. However, for multi-annual loans, the cumulative default rate covering all years between the issue and the maturity of the loan would overstate the average "per annum" risk of the exposure. Using it to calculate the interest rate spread (which by definition is always expressed on an annual basis) would eventually generate a much higher premium than actually required. Consequently, average annual default rates like those generated by (13.7) will prove more suitable for this kind of applications.

Using the data from Table 13.7, Table 13.9 shows an example of annual default rates. The annual rates are significantly lower than the cumulative default rates.

Table 13.9 Marginal, cumulative and average default rates for BB-rated exposures

Year	MDR	CDR	ADR
1	0.0 %	0.0 %	0.00 %
2	0.91 %	0.91 %	0.46 %
3	3.66 %	4.54 %	1.54 %
4	1.93 %	6.38 %	1.63 %
5	2.78 %	8.98 %	1.86 %

Estimating d'_t, d_T and $\overline{d}_T$ is seemingly simple. In practice, however, some technical issues need to be taken into account, which can lead to slightly different approaches. These issues relate in particular to: (i) the definition of default, (ii) the nature of the data, and (iii) the nature of the sample used.

The definition of default, as we have seen for credit-scoring models (Chapter 10), can vary significantly in the analyses lead by different authors. Thus, for example, *Standard & Poor's* defines it as failure to meet any financial obligation (the default consequently arises on the first due date when the issuer fails to make a due interest payment or to repay capital).[22] Conversely, *Moody's* adopts a broader definition, which includes any non-payment or late payment of interest and/or capital, bankruptcy, compulsory liquidation and debt restructuring.[23]

The *data* can relate to the value of the bonds, the number of bonds or the number of issuers. In the first case, the default rate for a given rating class is calculated as the ratio between the value of the defaulted bonds in period t and the total value outstanding at the start of the same period. In the second case, the default rate for a given rating class is calculated as the ratio between the number of defaulted issues in t and the number of issues at the start of t (without taking account of the different amounts issued). In the third case, the relevant variable is the number of issuers: companies present in the sample with several securities are therefore counted only once. The first criterion was followed, for example, by Altman (1989), while the other two are followed by *Moody's* and *Standard & Poor's*.[24] The choice to assign greater weight to defaults on larger issues is correct if the aim is to estimate the expected "cost" of defaults; however, if the aim is to estimate the probability of default by a company belonging to a given rating class, there is no reason why larger issues should be given a larger weight.

Finally, the third issue concerns the nature of the sample. The cohort formed at time zero, on which default rates will be computed for the following years, can be formed only by newly-issued bonds or by all bonds outstanding at that time (including bonds issued in earlier periods). The first approach is followed by Altman and Kao, for example, while the second one (which Altman et al., 1998, describe as the "static pool approach") is generally used by rating agencies.[25]

These two approaches can produce slightly different results. The reason is that in the case of newly-issued bonds, the default rate in the first year is generally much lower; thus if issues made in earlier years are included in the cohort at time zero, the mean default

---

[22] "A default occurs upon the first occurrence of a payment default on any financial obligation, rated or unrated, other than a financial obligation subject to a bona fide commercial dispute; an exception occurs when an interest payment missed on the due date is made within the grace period". See Standard & Poor's (1998), p. 4.

[23] "Moody's defines default as any missed or delayed disbursement of interest and/or principal, bankruptcy, receivership, or distressed exchange where: (i) the issuer offered bondholders a new security or package of securities that amount to a diminished financial obligation (such as preferred or common stock, or debt with a lower coupon or par amount); or (ii) the exchange had the apparent purpose of helping the borrower avoid default". See Carty and Lieberman (1996b).

[24] As noticed by Carty and Lieberman (1996b) of Moody's, "To calculate default rates, which are estimates of the default probability component of ratings, we use the issuer as the unit of study rather than individual debt instruments or outstanding dollar amounts of debt. Because Moody's intends its ratings to support credit decisions, which do not vary with either the size or the number of bonds that a firm has outstanding, we believe this methodology produces more meaningful estimates of the probability of default. Because the likelihood of default is essentially the same for all of a firm's public debt issues, irrespective of size, weighting our statistics by the number of bond issues or their par amounts would simply bias our results towards the characteristics of large issuers".

[25] See Standard & Poor's (1998), p. 5.

rate will probably be higher. This difference, referred to as the "aging effect", is explained by the fact that a company which has just issued a bond has just received a significant injection of cash; as a result, it will almost certainly be able to meet its commitments to creditors (interest payments, and possibly the repayment of earlier debts).

The approach used by Altman (whereby only newly-issued bonds are included in the pool) is also known as the "mortality rate" approach.[26] This is because this approach resembles the one used in the insurance industry to set the premiums payable on life insurance policies, where a mortality rate is associated with the insured's age, measured from birth.

It should be noticed that the actuarial approach discussed in this section is based on two demanding hypotheses: first, the PD is assumed to be identical for all companies in the same rating class (a variable which is continuous by nature, such as PD, is therefore approximated with a system of discrete values); second, the PD associated with a certain rating class is assumed to remain stationary over time (so that future PDs will be equal to the past ones, which have produced the observed empirical default rates).

Altman (1989) has shown that the first of these two hypotheses is often not supported by empirical evidence. His analysis shows that there are significant differences between the default rates of specific sub-groups of companies belonging to the same rating class (to the extent that some sub-groups of a rating class can have higher default rates than other sub-groups of companies belonging to worse rating classes).[27] As regards the second hypothesis, Altman's study indicates that the default rates experienced over a given period may significantly differ from the mean historical default rates recorded in previous years.

13.3.3   The actuarial approach: migration rates

As well as for estimating PDs, the actuarial approach can be used to estimate the frequency with which the companies in a given rating class "migrate" towards other rating classes. As in the case of default rates, a number of statistics on this phenomenon are periodically published by Standard & Poor's, Fitch and Moody's. Tables 13.10 and 13.11 contain two examples.

The two tables show several facts. Firstly, the best rating classes are the most stable: for example, the *Standard & Poor's* data show that an AAA-rated company has an 88.77 % probability of being in the same class a year later. This falls to 53.15 % for a company which was initially rated CCC.

Secondly, it is interesting to note that the best rating classes (AAA and Aaa) have a practically nil default rate (see the second last columns in the two tables, which confirm the data in Tables 13.6 and 13.8). Thus if we were to focus on default published (ignoring migration risk[28]), this type of exposure would be considered virtually risk-free. Note, however, that investors buying in an AAA-rated bond have an 8 % probability of seeing it downgraded, i.e. to suffer a reduction in value associated with a deterioration in creditworthiness.

Migration rates based on agency ratings are not easily comparable with those related to a bank's internal system. This follows from the different rating approaches used (through-the-cycle versus point-in-time, as seen in section 13.2). In the *through-the-cycle* approach,

---

[26] See Altman (1989).
[27] According to Altman, this is explained by the delay with which rating agencies (which rate issuers "through the cycle") decide to upgrade or downgrade a company.
[28] See the introduction to this part of the book.

Table 13.10 1-year transition matrix – Standard & Poor's

Initial rating	Year-end rating (%)								
	AAA	AA	A	BBB	BB	B	CCC	Default	N.R.
AAA	88.77	7.80	0.68	0.05	0.10	0.00	0.00	0.00	2.60
AA	0.68	88.28	7.42	0.55	0.05	0.15	0.02	0.00	3.03
A	0.07	2.25	87.88	4.88	0.61	0.25	0.01	0.05	4.01
BBB	0.03	0.28	5.33	83.01	4.44	0.99	0.10	0.18	5.63
BB	0.02	0.10	0.53	7.07	74.44	7.27	0.79	0.91	8.87
B	0.00	0.08	0.25	0.41	6.12	73.03	3.32	4.74	12.06
CCC	0.16	0.00	0.32	0.97	2.26	9.86	53.15	18.90	14.38

"N.R." indicates companies which are no longer rated at the end of the year, and have therefore been excluded from the sample. Source: Standard & Poor's (1998).

Table 13.11 1-year transition matrix – *Moody's*

Initial rating	Year-end rating (%)								
	Aaa	Aa	A	Baa	Ba	B	Caa	Default	WR
Aaa	88.32	6.15	0.99	0.23	0.02	0.00	0.00	0.00	4.29
Aa	1.21	86.76	5.76	0.66	0.16	0.02	0.00	0.06	5.36
A	0.07	2.30	86.09	4.67	0.63	0.10	0.02	0.12	5.99
Baa	0.03	0.24	3.87	82.52	4.68	0.61	0.06	0.28	7.71
Ba	0.01	0.08	0.39	4.61	79.03	4.96	0.41	1.11	9.39
B	0.00	0.04	0.13	0.060	5.79	76.30	3.08	3.49	10.53
Caa	0.00	0.02	0.04	0.34	1.26	5.29	71.87	12.41	8.78

WR indicates companies for which the rating has been withdrawn. Source: Carty (1998).

possible future changes in the economic cycle are factored into the rating from the outset; the economic trend in the following years consequently has a relatively modest effect on the rating, so migrations towards other rating classes are comparatively limited. However, precisely because the companies assigned to a given rating class remain largely the same, the default rates recorded in that class may be relatively unstable over time: lower values are recorded when macroeconomic conditions are good, higher rates are experienced as the economic cycle worsens.

If the rating is assigned on a point-in-time basis, then companies will be moved to different rating classes as soon as they show signs of improvement or worsening. This will lead to higher migration rates. However, as the companies assigned to a given rating class will always be consistent with a given level of short-term risk, one-year default rates will tend to be more stable over time (Table 13.12).

Table 13.12 Comparison of rating assignment processes

	POINT IN TIME	THROUGH THE CYCLE
Migration rates	Higher	Lower
Default rates	Stable	Unstable

13.4 RATING VALIDATION

A rating system should be checked periodically to assess its effectiveness. In other words, it is necessary to establish whether the ratings issued by the system are consistent with the ex post behaviour of the companies rated. This assessment process has become especially significant with the new Basel Accord on bank capital adequacy (see Chapter 20): the Accord states that banks wishing to use internal ratings to compute mandatory capital requirements must subject their systems to the "validation" by the supervisory authorities.[29]

In general, the validation should cover the quality of the inputs fed into the system, and the reliability of the methods used to process them. These two aspects will be reflected by the performance of the system, which can be validated according to several criteria.[30]

In this section, after briefly mentioning some commonsense rules for the evaluation of a rating system (section 13.4.1), we will focus on some simple quantitative criteria (contingency tables, ROC and CAP curves) to assess the performance of the bank's rating assignment process (section 13.4.2). We will finally turn to the issue of validating the rating quantification step, i.e. of verifying the consistency between the PDs assigned ex ante to the bank's rating grades and the actual ex post default rates.

13.4.1 Some qualitative criteria

Here are some simple rules-of-thumb which can be used as a first step to assess the adequacy of a rating system:

- default rates should increase monotonically as ratings worsen;
- the default rates on each rating class should be stable over time, especially in the case of ratings assigned according to the "point-in-time" approach;
- the percentage of exposures that remain in the same rating class from one year to the next should be sufficiently high;
- migration rates toward nearby rating classes should be higher than those toward more distant classes;
- most defaulting borrowers should have been classified in a low (i.e., bad) rating class for some years before the default took place.

---

[29] Although it is not yet entirely clear how this validation will work in practice, the Basel Committee has already drawn up some guidelines regarding the characteristics required of an internal rating system (number of classes, definition of default, rating assignment process, and entities involved in the process).
[30] See Basel Committee on Banking Supervision (2005).

13.4.2   Quantitative criteria for validating rating assignments

In addition to these simple rules, some more sophisticated methods have been proposed to verify the appropriateness of the rating assignment process.

A first method is based on contingency tables. It can be used for very basic rating systems, where the bank's potential customers are classified in a purely binary manner (by separating "healthy" companies from "too risky" ones). A contingency table is a matrix (see Table 13.13) comparing the forecasts of a model with the events that actually took place later (e.g. one year after the model produced its rating). Its four quadrants indicate:

- the number N_1 of companies correctly rated as "healthy" by the model;
- the number N_2 of companies incorrectly rated as healthy, corresponding to the number of Type I errors;
- the number N_3 of companies incorrectly rated as being too risky, corresponding to the number of Type II errors;
- the number N_4 of companies correctly rated as high-risk.

Table 13.13 Example of a Contingency Table

		Performing	Defaulting
Rating by model	Low-risk ("pass")	Correct valuation (N_1 cases)	Type I errors (N_2 cases)
	High-risk ("fail")	Type II errors (N_3 cases)	Correct evaluations (N_4 cases)

Several performance indicators can be calculated using the values in the contingency table. The main ones are:

- *sensitivity* (the percentage of correctly-identified defaulting companies), given by $\dfrac{N_4}{N_2 + N_4}$;
- *specificity* (the percentage of correctly-identified healthy companies): $\dfrac{N_1}{N_1 + N_3}$;
- the *"alpha" error rate* (E_α, the percentage of defaulting companies incorrectly classified as healthy): $\dfrac{N_2}{N_2 + N_4}$;
- the *"beta" error rate* (E_β, the percentage of healthy companies incorrectly classified as insolvent): $\dfrac{N_3}{N_1 + N_3}$.
- the *hit rate* (the percentage of correctly-classified companies: $\dfrac{N_1 + N_4}{N_1 + N_2 + N_3 + N_4}$
  $= \dfrac{N_1 + N_4}{N}$

The quality of the credit-scoring or rating model should be evaluated by jointly analysing the values of E_α and E_β, also in the light of the different costs of the two types of error. Note that, as seen in Chapter 10, the level of E_α and E_β depends to a crucial extent on the cut-off value used to discriminate between healthy and insolvent companies (i.e. to distinguish between the "pass" and "fail" rating classes): a more conservative cut-off value tends to produce more type II and fewer type I errors. An accurate model evaluation therefore requires to investigate how its performance responds when the cut-off point is changed.

Based on this intuition, another method for model validation has been developed: the ROC (Receiver Operating Characteristic) curve. This is a graph analyzing the error levels associated with *all possible values of the cut-off point* that separates "pass" from "fail" borrowers. Namely, for each possible cut-off point k, the graph shows:

- on the x-axis, the corresponding value of the type II error (E_β), also indicated as F_k (where F stands for "false alarm", as these are healthy companies classified as "fails");
- on the y-axis, the corresponding sensitivity value, indicated as H_k.[31]

The lower the first indicator (F_k) and the higher the second (H_k), the better the rating system. In particular, when k is increased, a good model will be able to isolate all abnormal companies effectively (with a rapid increase in sensitivity H_k), without classifying a significant portion of healthy companies as abnormal (i.e. keeping the type II error, F_k, at low values).

Figure 13.2 shows an example of ROC curve (indicated as the "real model"). The steeper the slope of the initial stretch of the curve, the fewer "false alarms" there will be compared with companies correctly identified as high-risk, and the better the performance of the model.

As observed by De Servigny and Renault (2004), the ROC curve expresses the trade-off between Type I errors ($1 - H_k$) and Type II errors (F_k).

This figure shows two theoretical ROC curves as benchmarks:

- The first one is the curve of a "perfect model", for which a value of k exists that allows 100% (H_k) of abnormal companies to be classified correctly, without making even one mistake ($F_k = 0$). As the maximum value for both F_k and H_k is 100%, the area to the South-East of the ROC curve ("*area under ROC curve*", or AUROC) for a perfect model is exactly 1 (see Figure 13.3, left-hand panel).
- The second curve is that of a wholly "naive" model, which lacks any real ability to separate healthy from abnormal companies. In this model, when the cut-off point varies, the percentage of healthy companies classified as abnormal (F_k) and the share of correctly-classified defaulted companies (H_k) remain constant. The ROC curve is therefore given by the diagonal of the graph, and the AUROC is 0.5 (Figure 13.3, right-hand panel).

The AUROC is often used to summarize the performance of a model with a single figure and is also known as the "*coefficient of concordance*" (CoC). It can be shown that the AUROC can be interpreted as the probability of correctly classifying, given any two

---

[31] The letter H stands for "hit rate" (i.e. the success rate). However, sensitivity is a success rate limited to abnormal companies, and is therefore different from the true overall hit rate, defined above.

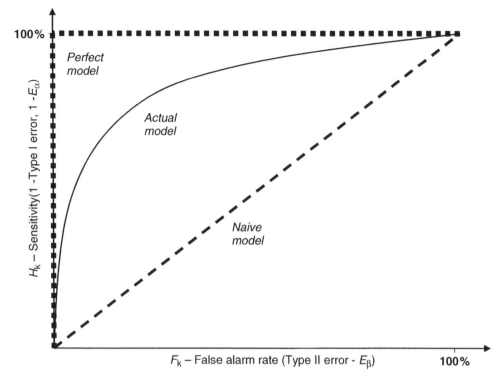

Figure 13.2 Examples of ROC curves

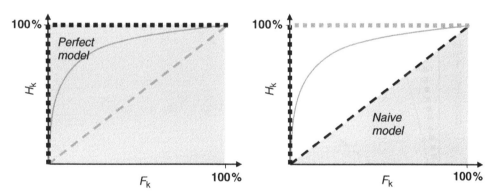

Figure 13.3 Different areas under the ROC curve (AUROC)

companies, the healthy and abnormal one: for the perfect model, this is 100%, for the naïve one (which is equivalent to tossing a coin) this is obviously 50%. It is also possible to construct confidence intervals for AUROC, which help to understand its "true" value, by quantifying the possible bias associated with the random noise in the data sample.[32]

---

[32] Engelmann et al. (2002, 2003).

A further performance measure is the Gini curve, or "*cumulative accuracy profile*" (CAP). Imagine that we have a sample of N companies, all rated by a model, and that we take an increasing portion of them (each time taking $S = 1, 2, 3,\ldots, N-1, N$ companies), starting with the worst scores; we report S (number of companies considered) on the horizontal axis of a graph. Within each of these sub-samples, we count the companies which actually did default, and report this quantity ($D(S)$, which clearly cannot exceed S) on the vertical axis.

Figure 13.4 reports three examples of CAP curves. First, consider an "ideal model": as it has a perfect forecasting capacity, all the sub-samples containing $S \le N_2 + N_4$ companies will consist of abnormal companies only (in other words, $D(S) = S$ for any $S \le N_2 + N_4$). For $S \le N_2 + N_4$, D(S) will remain constant and equal to $N_2 + N_4$ (as there are no more abnormal companies, even a perfect model obviously cannot find them!).

Now, consider a naïve model which has zero forecasting capacity. The abnormal companies will always be a constant percentage p (given by $(N_2 + N_4)/N$) of the number of companies S considered: in other words, $D(S) = p \cdot S$ for any S.

Finally, consider a real-life model: its curve will lay between these two extreme cases. The closer it is to the ideal model, the more effective the actual model will be.

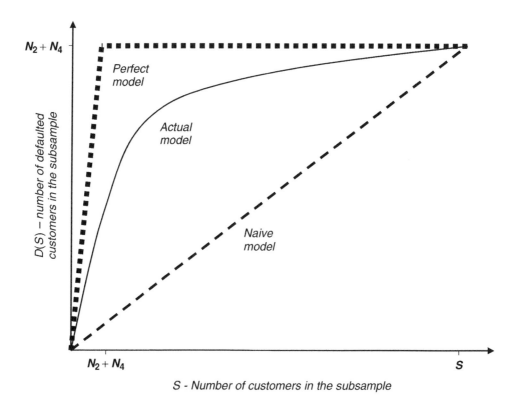

S - Number of customers in the subsample

Figure 13.4   Curves measuring the accuracy of different models

To make the results more readable, the CAP curve is usually based not on the absolute values, but rather on the *percentage* of customers in the various sub-samples (the horizontal axis therefore shows S/N, not S) and the corresponding percentage of abnormal customers (the horizontal axis will therefore show $D(S)/D(N)$, where $D(N) = N_2 + N_4$ is the number of abnormal customers in the entire sample). A typical CAP curve is therefore the one in Figure 13.5.

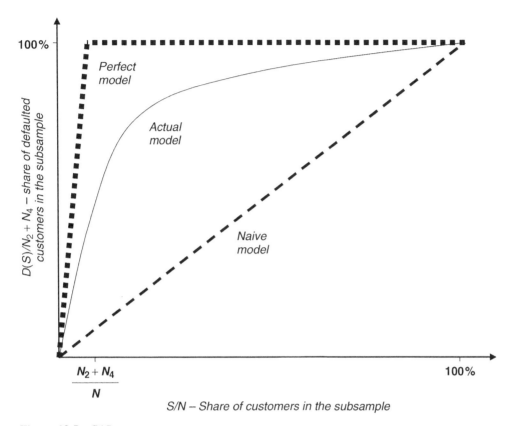

Figure 13.5 CAP curves

A possible performance indicator of a rating system, called the Gini ratio or *Accuracy Ratio* (AR), is given by a ratio of two areas. The numerator is the area between the CAP curve of the real rating system and that of the naïve model (area B in Figure 13.6); the denominator is the area between the CAP curve of a perfect model and, again, that of the naïve one (area A+B in the Figure):

$$G = \frac{B}{A + B} \tag{13.8}$$

The Gini ratio may take values between 0 and 1. The higher the ratio, the better the performance of the rating system.

Methods like the CAP curve (or the ROC curve) can be applied not only to credit-scoring models producing continuous scores, but also to rating systems based on the classification of borrowers into a number of discrete classes. Consider, for example, the 10-class system shown in Table 13.14. The Table shows the number C_j of companies assigned to each class (ranked from the worst to the best); for the sake of simplicity,

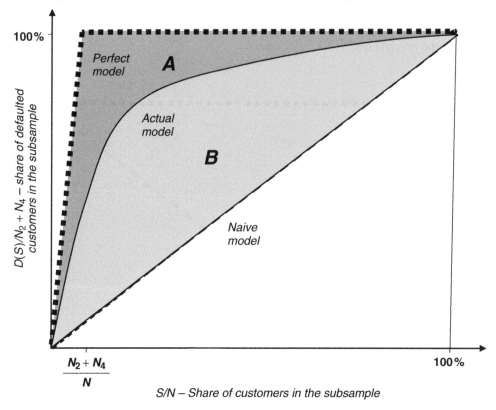

Figure 13.6   Areas used to compute the Accuracy Ratio

this will be 100 for all classes. For each class the Table also shows the number D_j of defaulted companies.

The data in the Table can be used to draw the CAP curve of the rating system (Figure 13.7). Based on it, one can then measure:

- the area between the CAP curves of the rating system and that of a naïve model (area B), amounting to 0.29;
- the area between the CAP curves of a perfect system and that of a naïve model (area A+B), amounting to 0.45;
- the ratio between the two (accuracy ratio), namely 64%.

The ROC and CAP curves represent two different ways of presenting the same information, namely the level of accuracy of a rating system. Indeed, it can be shown that AR (based on the CAP curve) and AUROC (derived from the ROC curve) are linked by the following relationship:[33]

$$AR = 2 \cdot AUROC - 1 \tag{13.9}$$

---

[33] Engelmann et al. (2002).

Table 13.14 CAP curve: example for a system of 10 rating classes

Rating class j	Customers, C_j	Defaulted customers, D_j	Subsample $S = \sum_{i \le j} C_i$	Defaults in S $D(S) = \sum_{i \le j} D_i$	S/N	$D/D(N)$
			Absolute values		Percent values	
10	100	24	100	24	10 %	2 %
9	100	12	200	36	20 %	4 %
8	100	8	300	44	30 %	4 %
7	100	6	400	50	40 %	5 %
6	100	4	500	54	50 %	5 %
5	100	3	600	57	60 %	6 %
4	100	2	700	59	70 %	6 %
3	100	1	800	60	80 %	6 %
2	100	0	900	60	90 %	6 %
1	100	0	1000	60	100 %	6 %
Total	1000	60				

In this way, it is always possible to move from one indicator to the other. Also, confidence intervals derived for the AUROC can easily be extended to the accuracy ratio and vice versa.

It is important to note that the results obtained with the ROC and CAP curves, and therefore the values of AUROC and AR, depend crucially on the sample used. In other words, equally effective rating systems may present very different performance indicators, depending on the size and characteristics of the sample. Sobeheart and Keenan (2004) demonstrate this with an effective example: "suppose we have two default prediction models A and B capable of sorting riskiness with perfect accuracy in any sample. We apply model A to sample S_A, where 5 % of the observations are defaults, and model B to sample S_B, where 10 % of the observations are defaults. Then we sort the samples and select a cut-off level – say the worst 5 % of scored companies. Since the models are ideal, the performance of model A on sample S_A at a 5 % cut-off is 100 %, while for sample S_B the performance of model B is only 50 % at the same cut-off. Clearly, suggesting that model A is better than model B because of the higher capture rate is wrong. The problem is that the selected cut-off has a different meaning in terms of sample rejection for any two samples with different numbers of defaults".

This "sample dependency" has two major consequences. The first is that it is impossible to define a priori a minimum cut-off point for the accuracy ratio above which a rating system can be considered "good" or "acceptable". The second is that a comparison of the efficacy of two rating systems should generally be performed on the basis of the same sample of observations, or similar samples.

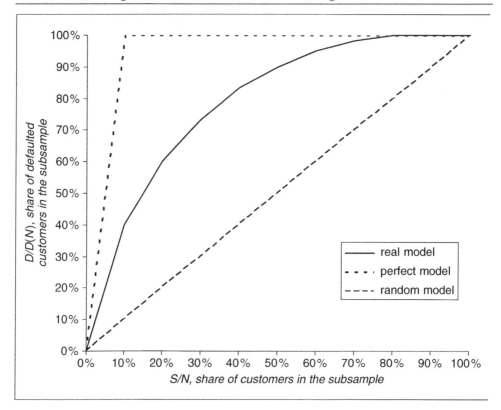

Figure 13.7   Example of CAP curve for a system of 10 rating classes

13.4.3   The validation of the rating quantification step

The methods examined above (contingency tables, ROC, AUROC, CAP, AR) can be used to validate the rating assignment step, that is, the process through which the rating system classifies borrowers into rating grades or assigns them a score.

Recently, the attention of researchers has also focused on the rating quantification step, where rating classes or scores are converted to PDs.

The models proposed are based on a comparison between the ex ante PD of the customers in a given rating class (as estimated by the bank) and the ex post default rates for that class. Namely, they seek to derive, for each rating class, a confidence interval within which the values of the empirical default rates can be considered acceptable.

A first approach, based on the use of binomial distribution, is similar to the Kupiec test described in Chapter 8. If the number of customers in a bucket is high enough, the binomial distribution converges to a normal distribution, and the extremes of the interval, based on a confidence level α, are given by

$$\left(\hat{p} - N^{-1}(\alpha)\sqrt{\frac{\hat{p}(1-\hat{p})}{N}}; \hat{p} + N^{-1}(\alpha)\sqrt{\frac{\hat{p}(1-\hat{p})}{N}} \right) \qquad (13.10)$$

where $\hat{p}$ represents the PD estimated by the bank, and N the number of customers in the rating class. Thus, for example, if a bank has estimated a PD of 1 % for a rating class containing N = 1000 customers, the 95 % confidence interval will be given by

$$\left(0,01 - N^{-1}(95\,\%)\sqrt{\frac{0.01 \cdot 0.99}{1,000}}; 0,01 + N^{-1}(95\,\%)\sqrt{\frac{0.01 \cdot 0.99}{1,000}}\right) = (0.0048; 0.0152)$$

The maximum acceptable default rate would therefore be 1.52 %. As there are 1000 customers, this means that for a PD of 1 % to be considered credible, the maximum acceptable number of defaults is 15. If 16 or more defaults take place in this rating class, the ex ante PD should be questioned.

This kind of confidence intervals may prove too narrow in practice. The reason is that, by using a binomial distribution, they implicitly assume that individual defaults are not uncorrelated. In practice, however, bank borrowers and bond issuers tend to default "in clusters", following the economic cycle: defaults are more frequent during phases of recession, and become rarer during economic expansions. This means that defaults are not perfectly independent but come in "waves". Due to such waves, the actual default rate on a rating class may swing around its expected value (the ex ante PD), sometimes considerably, without implying that the ex ante PD is wrong.

Table 13.15 The effect of default correlation on the upper extreme of the confidence interval ($\hat{p} = 1\,\%, N = 1000$)

No correlation (binomial approach, equation 13.9)	15
Asset correlation (ρ) of 5 %	
Method 1: Gordy (2003)	24
Method 2: Beta distribution	25
Asset correlation (ρ) of 20 %	
Method 1: Gordy (2003)	39
Method 2: Beta distribution	42

Source: Tasche, 2003.

Tasche (2003) proposes two methods for deriving confidence intervals when defaults are correlated. The first uses the Gordy model (2003) for a portfolio of correlated defaults, and completes it with the adjustment factor proposed by Martin and Wilde (2002); the second models empirical default rates with a beta distribution, estimated with the method of moments. In both cases, the "correlated" confidence intervals are wider than those obtained with a simple binomial distribution. Table 13.15 (Tasche, 2005) shows how the upper extreme (maximum acceptable number of defaults) of the confidence interval in our example can change, when correlation between individual defaults is introduced. Parameter ρ ("asset correlation") is a measurement of the dependence between different defaults, to be explained in detail in Chapter 14: the stronger this correlation, the greater the maximum number of defaults compatible with the hypothesis that a PD of 1 % is correct.

SELECTED QUESTIONS AND EXERCISES

1. Based on similar information and a similar rating scale, Bank Alpha and Bank Beta have assigned different ratings to the same company. In fact, the rating issued by Alpha, AA, is considerably better than the one issued by Beta (BBB). Which of the following may explain the difference?

    (A) Beta rates "through the cycle" while Alpha rates "point in time", and the economy is now in a recession;
    (B) Alpha rates "through the cycle" while Beta rates "point in time", and the economy is now in a recession;
    (C) Beta rates "through the cycle" while Alpha rates "point in time", and the economy is now booming;
    (D) Alpha rates "through the cycle" while Beta rates "point in time", and the economy is now booming.

2. The marginal default rates in the first three years after issuance for a given class of bonds are 0.5 %, 0.8 % and 1.2 % respectively. Compute the cumulated default rate and the average annual default rate for the three-year period.

3. Using the one-year transition matrix in Table 13.10 and assuming that one-year transitions are serially uncorrelated (so that the same transition matrix can be used twice in a row), compute the probability that a BBB-rated bond

    (i) is still BBB-rated at the end of year one and defaults by the end of year two;
    (ii) has been upgraded to class AA at the end of year one and defaults by the end of year two;
    (iii) has been downgraded to class B at the end of year one and defaults by the end of year two;
    (iv) has migrated to any other rating class (excluding those mentioned under i-iii) at the end of year one and defaults by the end of year two;
    (v) has already defaulted by the end of year one.
    Can you now estimate the two-year probability of default of BBB-rated bond?

4. A bank has been using a scoring model to evaluate 15 borrowers, 4 of which have then defaulted. The Table below shows their scores (high scores mean low risk) and highlights the defaulted ones. Using the data and a squared sheet of paper, draw the CAP curve. Then, add the CAP curve for the perfect model and the one for a random model (in computing the number of defaulted customers spotted by the random model, take care to round it at the closest integer). Finally, suppose customer 5 had been given a score of 3 and customer 13 had been given a score of 3.5: how would the Gini ratio change? Should this be interpreted as an improvement or a worsening in model performance?

Customer	Score	Default?
1	0.4	0
2	0.7	1
3	1.2	1
4	1.5	1
5	2.6	0
6	3.2	0
7	3.3	0
8	4	0
9	4.3	0
10	4.3	0
11	5	0
12	5.7	0
13	6	1
14	8	0
15	8.5	0

5. Based on the data from the previous example, try setting the threshold dividing "bad" and "good" firms at 0, 0.5, 1, and keep increasing by 0.5 units until you reach 9. For each threshold, compute the false alarm rate and the sensitivity ratio, and report those values in a Table. Based on the Table, draw the ROC curve of the model. Complete the graph by drawing the ROC curve of a "perfect" model. Now, compare your graph to the one drawn in exercise 4: how do they differ?

14
Portfolio Models

14.1 INTRODUCTION

Following the logic illustrated in the introduction to this part of the book, the possible losses on a credit exposure can be broken down into two components: expected loss and unexpected loss, with the latter reflecting the possibility that actual losses may be greater *a posteriori* than originally expected by the bank.

There are various ways to quantify unexpected loss. The simplest one is the standard deviation (volatility) of the probability distribution of future losses. As an alternative, a percentile of the distribution of future losses can be used, determined according to a certain confidence level. This second approach leads to a measurement of value at risk similar to those seen for market risk in the second part of this volume.

The distinction between expected and unexpected loss is not simply a theoretical abstraction: it reflects a precise operational requirement. In fact, expected loss must be covered by an adequate amount of reserves and "loaded" directly on the interest rate charged to the borrower. Unexpected loss (and particularly value at risk), on the other hand, must be reflected into an adequate amount of equity, and for this reason is also referred to as the "economic capital" absorbed by a credit exposure (or by a portfolio of credits).

The previous chapters illustrated models and techniques for estimating the probability of default (PD) and the recovery rate in the event of default (RR or LGD) of credit exposures. These parameters, along with an estimate of the EAD (exposure at default) are necessary and usually sufficient for estimating expected loss. On the other hand, estimating unexpected loss (that is, economic capital) requires additional parameters and computation models, to which this chapter is devoted.

Two preliminary choices are examined first: the time horizon ("risk horizon") and the confidence level for VaR computations. This is followed by an illustration of the characteristics, merits and limitations of the main models to estimate unexpected loss on a portfolio of credit exposures, that were developed during the second half of the Nineties. Following a logic similar to that of the VaR models for market risks, they seek to determine the maximum loss a credit portfolio can face during a predetermined time horizon with a certain confidence level (that is, the so-called "maximum probable loss").

In particular, the analysis dwells on four models[1]:

√ *CreditMetrics*™, a model originally proposed by the U.S. bank *J.P. Morgan*, based on the data for migration rates, default rates and *spreads* (versus government bond yields) of obligors belonging to the various rating categories;
√ *CreditPortfolioView*™, a model developed by the consulting firm *McKinsey*, based on econometric analysis of the relationship between default/migration rates and the state of the macroeconomic cycle;

---

[1] One model not explicitly considered here is the one recently proposed by Standard & Poor's, known as the "Portfolio Risk Tracker". For an examination of the characteristics of this model, see Servigny et al. (2003). As observed in the final section of this chapter, this model is of a more "advanced" generation than the models analyzed in this chapter and attempts to overcome a few of the principal problems of first-generation models.

√ *CreditRisk+*™, a model proposed by *Credit Suisse Financial Products* (CSFP), a London-based subsidiary of the Swiss banking group Credit Suisse, based on the "actuarial" mathematical models used in the insurance industry;

√ *PortfolioManager*™, a model developed by the California-based company *KMV*, based on the Merton model and the approaches to estimating default probability illustrated in Chapter 11.

The chapter closes with a comparison of these four models and an analysis of the problems that still affect this family of techniques and will likely be confronted with the next generation of models.

14.2 SELECTING TIME HORIZON AND CONFIDENCE LEVEL

The models presented in this chapter must deal with two common problems: the choice of a reference time horizon and the choice of a confidence level. Before analyzing the individual models, it is therefore advisable to dwell briefly on these two problems.

14.2.1 The choice of the risk horizon

The VaR on a portfolio of credits depends on the distribution of possible future losses. We must therefore specify to what future time interval we wish to make reference. The distribution of losses for the next three years will obviously be more uncertain than that for the next three days. A reference time horizon ("risk horizon") must therefore be chosen and kept constant in all construction phases of a model to estimate losses on a loan portfolio.

Theoretically, following the pattern used for market risks[2], the choice of this time horizon should be based on two factors:

– the first, and most important, is objective in nature (and thus does not depend on the subjective preferences of the bank). It is represented by the degree of liquidity of the market in which the existing credit exposures can be sold. If, in fact, the exposures in a portfolio can be reasonably sold in the space of n days, there is no reason why the bank should be concerned by the possible losses over a broader interval of time, considering that after the nth day the risk positions will have already been sold or, as they say, "closed".
– the second, instead, is more subjective, in the sense that it depends on the preferences of the investor (in particular, the bank) that holds the credit portfolio. This is based on the holding period of the bank, that is, the period of time for which the bank intends to retain the portfolio.

Both these factors are of little use, however, in the case of credit risk: in fact, because many bank loans are illiquid, no secondary market normally exists for them. Therefore, even if the bank had a brief holding period (i.e. wished to retain the loans in its portfolio for only a short time), the absence of a market is which to sell the credits (and the limited availability of risk transfer instruments, such as credit derivatives[3]) would not permit the bank to "close" its positions within the desired term.

---

[2] See the second part of this book.
[3] Credit derivatives enable creditors to transfer risk while retaining their relationship with the client. For an analysis of the market and technical characteristics these products, see Appendix 15A.

It would therefore seem inevitable to take the final maturity of each loan as its risk horizon, considering that all the losses, from now until that date, are bound to impact the bank.

However, this solution would involve some major problems. First, using differentiated risk horizons referring to the maturity of the individual credits, the bank would have to make estimates of PD, LGD and EAD over different time horizons, and this would make the estimation of those parameters even more complex and uncertain.

Secondly, it would be practically impossible to "combine" the losses on the individual credits to determine a probability distribution of total losses: it would make no sense, in fact, to sum the possible losses in the next three months on a short-term loan with the possible losses at ten years on a mortgage.

Thirdly, many credit exposures have no contractual maturity. In particular, current account overdrafts are authorized "at sight", i.e. are freely revocable at any time. In reality, since they are reviewed on an annual basis, and the bank cannot check the health of the obligor every day, they are often equivalent to one-year short-term loans[4] but their actual maturity is not easy to determine.

For these reasons, the time horizon of credit risk models is often set conventionally at one year. This is the solution generally adopted by the models presented in this chapter.

There are several good reasons that justify this choice:

(1) All the parameters estimated by the rating system of a bank (and in particular PD, LGD, EAD and sometimes migration probabilities) usually refer to a one-year time horizon. These parameters, besides being used to estimate expected loss (see the introduction to this part of the volume) are also used to measure unexpected loss, based on the portfolio models that will be described in the following sections. If those models adopted a time horizon other than one year, the parameters estimated by the bank rating system would have to be adapted to this different risk horizon. This could lead to errors and confusion.

(2) Many banks use the economic capital estimated with the models presented in this chapter as an input to their annual budgets. In particular (as we shall see in the sixth part of this book), in the different phases of the budgeting and reporting process, the various operating units of the bank are required to provide a profits flow that is adequate to reward the capital needed to cover the risks they generate. The time horizon for computing economic capital must therefore be consistent with the time framework of the budgeting and reporting process, usually equal to one year.

(3) A one-year horizon is usually sufficient for the bank to organize a capital increase sufficient to restore equity to its optimal level after it has been eroded by unexpected losses. In this sense, it is true that a long-term loan which cannot be sold in a secondary market can cause the bank a flow of losses greater than that projected on a one-year time horizon; however, a year's time should suffice to raise new capital and provide for these additional losses.

(4) If risk measurement is carried out to enable the bank to perform a more correct pricing of loans (that is, to fix lending rates which adequately incorporate both the cost of the expected loss and the cost of the capital needed to cover unexpected losses), then

---

[4] We also observe that a sudden demand for repayment of sight loans could generate adverse selection phenomena, in the sense that only the best credits would likely be repaid (while the less reliable debtors would be unable to repay their loans immediately). The result would be a deterioration in the quality of the bank's loan portfolio.

such risk measurement must not be calibrated on the final maturity of the loan but on its repricing period. A risk horizon of one year should therefore be adequate for long-term loans for which the bank has the right to revise the rate every 12 months.

(5) Another reason sometimes invoked in favour of selecting a one-year horizon is that it coincides, for many banks, with the average portfolio turnover period. In other terms, in the span of one year, on the average, the bank revises or renews all its loans (multi-year loans, in fact, are offset by short-term facilities that can be revised several times a year). One year therefore corresponds to the time needed, on average, to implement a corrective action on the loan portfolio.[5]

Lastly, the decision to set the risk horizon at one year, although arbitrary, becomes acceptable when the bank uses a VaR model based on a multinomial type, such as Creditmetrics. In this type of model, in fact, part of the risks due to a time horizon going beyond one year are indirectly accounted for by capturing the fact that exposures may migrate to a lower rating class by the end of the year. This mechanism is described in detail in section 14.3.

To conclude, Table 14.1 summarizes the main reasons cited in this paragraph for choosing the risk horizon.

Table 14.1 The choice of the risk horizon

Objective	Key factors	Ideal horizon
Risk measurement and control	Effective liquidity of positions and holding period of the bank	Residual life of exposures
Simplification	Consistency with the time horizon used in estimating PD and other risk parameters	1 year
Measurement of the risk-adjusted performance (RAP) of the various bank units	Frequency of the budgeting process Frequency of the reporting process Capital allocation	1 year 1 year 1 year
Consistency between risk and capital	Time necessary to collect new capital	1 year
Implementing corrective actions on the portfolio	Average portfolio turnover period	1 year
Pricing	Maturity of exposures Frequency of rate revisions	Residual life of exposures 1 year

---

[5] This last reason is not really convincing, especially if we consider the credit risk of individual exposures rather than that the "average" risk on the entire portfolio. In fact, if an exposure has a life to maturity greater than one year, the rollover of other loans in the portfolio has no impact on the risks it generates: lacking a secondary market in which the position can be sold, it remains in the portfolio until its natural maturity.

14.2.2   The choice of the confidence level

Selecting a confidence level for computing the VaR is a more delicate step, in the case of credit risk, for example, than it is when market risk are estimated following the parametric approach.

In the parametric approach to market risks, in fact, the VaR is simply a multiple of the standard deviation: it is therefore enough to multiply this value by a different scalar factor to obtain measures of VaR associated with various levels of confidence. In the case of the credit risks, the situation is quite different: the VaR must, in fact, be derived by determining analytically the appropriate percentile of the distribution of future losses. The change to a different confidence level can therefore result in a significantly different VaR.

In the case of credit losses, instead, the use of zero-mean normal distributions (on which the parametric approach to market risk is based) must necessarily be discarded, for at least two reasons:

- the mean of the distribution of losses is greater than zero. In fact, it is the sum of the expected losses on the individual credits in the portfolio, whose value (see the introduction to third part of this volume) can be estimated as the product of the respective PD, LGD and EAD.[6] This quantity is obviously greater than zero.[7]
- the distribution of losses or of the unit loss rates [8] is strongly asymmetrical. Empirical data show, in fact, that a credit portfolio is quite likely to face limited losses while highly significant losses are much more seldom recorded (e.g. during periods of heavy economic recession).[9] This phenomenon is illustrated in Figure 14.1.

Probability distributions other than the normal must therefore be used, as well as simulation-based approaches, (using the percentiles of the simulated frequency distribution, as already illustrated for historical or Monte Carlo simulations regarding market risks). This, as mentioned above, makes the model less flexible and can cause the VaR to change in unpredictable ways, if the selected confidence level is changed.

A bank estimating credit risk VaR, must therefore commit itself to adopt, from the outset, a confidence level that is as credible and acceptable as possible to its management, to the supervisory authorities, the shareholders and the rating agencies.

Also, the confidence level used should be uniform across all the bank's business areas and therefore for all types of risk. In this sense, this parameter should be selected by the top management and should be taken as given by the Credit Department and the Risk Management Department.

---

[6] The product PD·LGD·EAD leads to correct results when the three risk factors (default, recovery and exposure risk) are uncorrelated. In the case where PD and LGD are correlated, see Chapter 12.

[7] Of course, the mean of the distribution of profits and losses of a portfolio exposed to market risks is also generally not zero. However, as shown in Chapter 5, if a very short risk horizon is used (as is the case for many portfolios of readily-liquidable securities), the expected return can be assumed to be zero.

[8] The unit loss rate is given by the absolute loss divided by the initial value of the credit portfolio. E.g., a loss of 5 on a portfolio initially worth 200, would lead to a unit loss rate of 2.5 %.

[9] The asymmetry in the distribution of the loss rates is also due to the fact that they cannot take negative values, whereas they can reach extremely high positive levels, much larger than the expected loss rate. Thus, for example, on a portfolio with expected loss rate of 1 %, loss rates are likely to exceed 2 % (mean + 1 %), while it is clearly impossible to observe loss rates below 0 % (mean − 1 %).

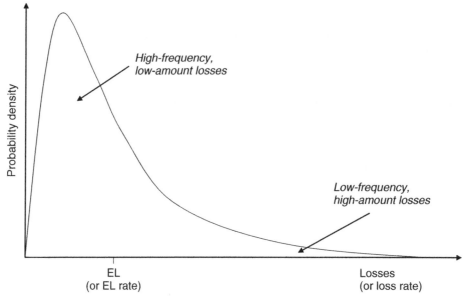

Figure 14.1   The distribution of loss probabilities on credits

14.3   THE MIGRATION APPROACH: *CREDITMETRICS*™

One well-known model for estimating credit risk on a portfolio of exposures (loans or bonds) is *CreditMetrics*™ (Gupton et al., 1997), originally introduced by the US bank *J.P. Morgan*. Its name is reminiscent of the better-known *RiskMetrics*™, developed by J.P. Morgan for market risks; however, as we shall see, it uses a different approach and solutions.

CreditMetrics™ is a method for estimating the distribution of changes in the market value of a portfolio of credit exposures, that may occur within a given risk horizon (generally one year). That distribution can be used to find the expected loss (EL) and various measurements of unexpected loss (UL) such as the standard deviation of losses, the percentiles and the VaR associated.

CreditMetrics™ is a multinomial model, so it considers both the losses due to a default and those linked to migration of the obligor to a different rating class (in fact, some authors use the term "migration approach"[10]).

Although it relies partly of the conceptual tools developed by Merton (see Chapter 11), it is a reduced-form model[11]. Unlike the structural models, in fact, *CreditMetrics*™ does not derive the probability of default (or migration) based on the characteristics of the company (market value and volatility of assets, value of debt), but simply uses as input historical data on default and migration rates by rating class.[12] From this viewpoint, it can therefore be termed an "agnostic" model.

---

[10] See Crouhy, Galai and Mark (2000), pp. 315–355.

[11] Other examples of reduced-form models are Jarrow and Turnbull (1995), Jarrow, Lando and Turnbull (1997), Lando (1998), Duffie and Singleton (1999), and Duffie (1998). For a survey of the general characteristics of these models, see Altman, Resti and Sironi (2004).

[12] Along with reduced and structural models, another class of models of a macroeconomic nature explains the evolution of default and migration rates on the basis of the economic cycle. One example is CreditPortfolioView (see section 5).

14.3.1   Estimating risk on a single credit exposure

CreditMetrics™ assumes that each exposure in a bank's portfolio has been assigned a rating (either by the bank itself or by an external rating agency). It further assumes that in the past the bank has recorded the one-year default and migration rates associated with the various rating grades, and that those rates (we provide an example in Table 14.2) are indicative of the default and migration probabilities for the future (that is, for the subsequent year).

Table 14.2 One-year transition matrix

INITIAL RATING	RATING AT YEAR-END (%)							
	AAA	AA	A	BBB	BB	B	CCC	Default
AAA	90.81	8.33	0.68	0.06	0.12	0.00	0.00	0.00
AA	0.70	90.65	7.79	0.64	0.06	0.14	0.02	0.00
A	0.09	2.27	91.05	5.52	0.74	0.26	0.01	0.06
BBB	0.02	0.33	5.95	86.93	5.30	1.17	0.12	0.18
BB	0.03	0.14	0.67	7.73	80.53	8.84	1.00	1.06
B	0.00	0.11	0.24	0.43	6.48	83.46	4.07	5.20
CCC	0.22	0.00	0.22	1.30	2.38	11.24	64.86	19.79

Source: S&P CreditWeek (15 April 1996).

The data in the table indicate, for example, that the probability that a BB-rated company will retain its initial rating in the subsequent year is 80.53 %. The probability of migrating toward the adjacent grades is relatively high: 7.73 % for an upgrade to class BBB, 8.83 % for a downgrade to class B. The probability of migrating toward the more distant grades is lower, the probability of ending the year in default is 1.06 %. We note that default is only one of the possible "credit events", i.e. events that can affect the value of a credit. This is an "absorbing" status in the sense that, once a company defaults, it can no longer return to a healthy ("performing") state.

The data in Table 14.2 show that a credit assigned today to grade BBB could be found one year later in any of the seven rating classes. So, since the value of an exposure depends on its creditworthiness, it could assume seven different values. Let us now derive these possible *credit values in one year's time.*

The value of the credit in one year, just like the value of any other investment, will simply be the present value of the expected future cash flows (interest plus repayment of the principal[13]), *computed a year from now,* using a discount rate adequate to the future rating of the obligor.

---

[13] For the sake of simplicity, let us imagine we know without uncertainty the cash flows expected from the credit. Incidentally, notice that this may be not true: in the case of a loan commitment, for example, the credit drawn could vary unpredictably over time; also, the value of an over-the-counter derivative (for which the bank has a counterparty risk) will depend on the future behaviour of the underlying market factors (see Chapter 16).

Let us consider, for example, a security[14] that involves the payment of a coupon equal to € 6 million for the first four years and a final coupon to be paid at the end of year 5 along with repayment of the principal (for a total of € 106 million). Let us imagine we wish to know its present value not today, but one year from now. This means (see Figure 14.2) that the first cash flow should *not* be discounted, since it will be collected right when the present value is computed (a year from now); the second would be discounted over a one-year period (distance between time 2 and time 1) and so forth.

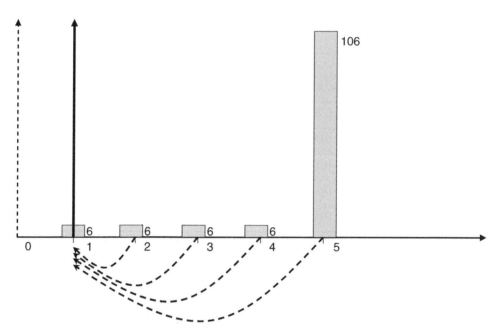

Figure 14.2   An example of discounted cash flows in one year's time

The discount must not be based on current rates, of course, but reflecting the possible values of market (spot) rates in one year's time. If we are willing to accept the expectations theory presented in Chapter 1 (or if we consider the error margins implicit in that theory as acceptable), we can use the forward rates for transactions starting in one year. More precisely, since in one year the credit could find itself in any of the seven rating classes, the computation of the present value will have to be repeated seven times, using seven different forward rate curves.

Table 14.3, taken from Gupton et al. (1997), provides an example of one-year forward zero-coupon rate curves for the various rating classes. The data are also shown in graphic form in Figure 14.3[15].

---

[14] This example is taken from Gupton et al. (1997).
[15] As you will note, the curves are positively skewed, with the sole exception of the worse class, CCC. The data are therefore consistent with the projections of the Merton model (Chapter 11) and with the curve of the marginal default rates (Chapter 13).

Table 14.3 Example of a one-year forward zero coupon rate curve (%)

Maturity Rating class	1 year	2 years	3 years	4 years
AAA	3.60	4.17	4.73	5.12
AA	3.65	4.22	4.78	5.17
A	3.72	4.32	4.93	5.32
BBB	4.10	4.67	5.25	5.63
BB	5.55	6.02	6.78	7.27
B	6.05	7.02	8.03	8.52
CCC	15.05	15.02	14.03	13.52

Data refer to the S&P *rating* classes. Source: Gupton, Finger and Bhatia (1997).

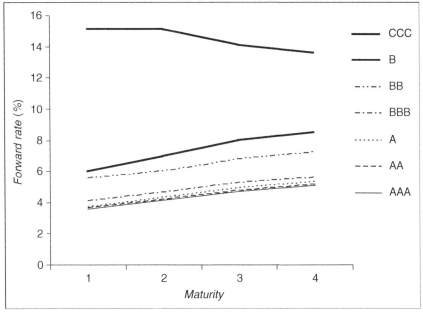

Figure 14.3 Example of forward zero-coupon curves

Let us now consider the bond in Figure 14.2 and imagine that at the end of the first year it is still in class BBB. Its *present value in a year's time* (FV, *future value* or *forward value*) would be:

$$FV_{1.BBB} = 6 + \frac{6}{(1 + 4.10\%)} + \frac{6}{(1 + 4.67\%)^2} + \frac{6}{(1 + 5.25\%)^3}$$
$$+ \frac{106}{(1 + 5.63\%)^4} = 107.53$$

If, however, the issuer were downgraded to class BB, the value would be:

$$FV_{1,BB} = 6 + \frac{6}{(1 + 5.55\,\%)} + \frac{6}{(1 + 6.02\,\%)^2} + \frac{6}{(1 + 6.78\,\%)^3}$$
$$+ \frac{106}{(1 + 7.27\,\%)^4} = 102.01$$

As expected, a downgrade would therefore cause a reduction in value of € 5.52 million (107.53-102.01).

In the same way, using other forward curves in Table 14.3, we can find the market value of the bond at year-end for all possible rating classes; the results are shown in Table 14.4. Note that each value is associated with its probability, derived from the transition matrix (Table 14.2).

If the issuer defaulted, the market value of the credit would become its recovery value (*EAD·RR*). The bank could estimate this with its own internal model (see Chapter 12) or based on the studies published by rating agencies, which estimate various expected recovery rates according to the degree of seniority of the bond and the security provided. Table 14.4 shows an example of these data.

Table 14.4 Estimated recovery rates – %

Category	Senior Secured	Senior Unsecured	Senior Subordinated	Subordinated	Junior Subordinated
Mean	53.80	51.13	38.52	32.74	17.09
Std. dev. (%)	26.86	25.45	23.81	20.18	10.90

Source: Gupton, Finger and Bhatia (1997).

Assume that the bond in Figure 14.2 was of the "senior secured" type: based on the estimates in Table 14.5, the bank thus assigns it a value of € 53.80 million in case of default.[16] This value is then added to Table 14.4, assigning it a probability equal to the PD of a BBB-rated obligor (see again Table 14.2).

Based on the data in Table 14.5, we can compute the expected value of the credit in a year's time, that is € 107.07 million, by simply averaging the eight values computed earlier, each weighted by its own probability. The possible future values of the credit can therefore be re-expressed (see the last column of Table 14.5) as changes (ΔV_j) from the expected value.

Note that the expected value (107.07 million) is different from the value in the case where the obligor remains in the initial rating class ($FV_{1,BBB} = 107.53$); the difference between the two values ($107.53 - 107.07 = 0.46$) can be regarded as a measure of the *expected loss* (EL) on the bond.

---

[16] For the sake of simplicity, we are assuming that the EAD is the same as the par value of principal (100 million) and that the bank's estimate is so certain and reliable that we can overlook recovery risk (see Chapter 12).

Table 14.5 Distribution of one-year market values of a BBB bond

State at year-end (j)	Present value in a year's time (FV $_j$)	Probability, p_j (%)	$\Delta V_j = FV_j - E(FV)$
AAA	109.35	0.02	2.28
AA	109.17	0.33	2.10
A	108.64	5.95	1.57
BBB	107.53	86.93	0.46
BB	102.01	5.3	-5.07
B	98.09	1.17	-8.99
CCC	83.63	0.12	-23.45
Default	53.80	0.18	-53.27
Mean, $E(FV) = \Sigma p_j FV_j$	107.07		

The probability distribution in Table 14.5 can also provide the standard deviation of the future values of the credit, computed as usual as:

$$\sigma_{FV} = \sigma_{\Delta V} = \sqrt{\sum_j [FV_j - E(FV)]^2 p_j} = \sqrt{\sum_j \Delta V_j^2 p_j} \cong 2.9$$

We can also compute the value at risk associated with a certain confidence level, by "cutting" the distribution of value changes at the desired percentile. To that end, it may be useful to re-write the ΔV_j next to their probabilities and cumulative probabilities, computed starting with the worst losses (see Table 14.6).

Table 14.6 Values and cumulative probabilities

ΔV_j	Probability, p_j (%)	Cumulative probability (%) $c_i = \sum_{V_j \leq V_i} p_j$
-53.27	0.18	0.18
-23.45	0.12	0.30
-8.99	1.17	1.47
-5.07	5.30	6.77
0.46	86.93	93.70
1.57	5.95	99.65
2.1	0.33	99.98
2.28	0.02	100

Thus, for example, the VaR at 99 % confidence can be found by cutting the distribution at a loss value (8.99) that isolates at least 1 % of the worst cases.[17] The VaR at 95 % is found in a similar way, by isolating at least 5 % of the worst cases, and is equal to 5.07.

If, instead of computing VaR by the percentile method, we had used the parametric approach based on the normal distribution, we would have found quite different values, over- or underestimated with respect to the real ones:

$$VaR_{99\%} = N^{-1}(0.99) \cdot \sigma_{\Delta V} \cong 2.32 \cdot 2.9 \cong 6.75$$

$$VaR_{95\%} = N^{-1}(0.95) \cdot \sigma_{\Delta V} \cong 1.64 \cdot 2.9 \cong 4.77$$

The reason is that the distribution of future values of the credit (from which the distribution of value changes derives) is heavily skewed (see Figure 14.4) and cannot be approximated with a normal distribution. Confirming what we saw in section 14.2, in fact, strong negative changes in value are relatively unlikely, while small changes are rather more frequent. Note that, since this is the distribution of future values (and not that of future losses), the tail of the distribution is skewed to the left (lower values) rather than to the right (greater losses) as in Figure 14.4.

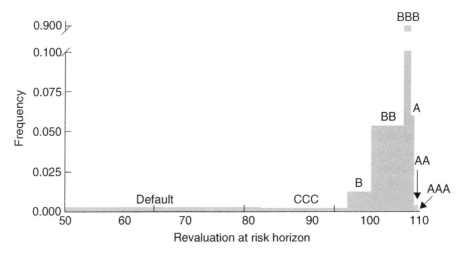

Figure 14.4   The distribution of forward values (FV$_j$)
Source: Gupton et al., 1997

14.3.2   Estimating the risk of a two-exposure portfolio

Let us now move on from the case of a single exposure to that of a portfolio. For the sake of simplicity, let us initially consider just two exposures, a BB-rated bond and an A-rated one.

---

[17] Due to the discrete and non-continuous nature of the probability distribution, in reality the value −8.99 is exceeded in only 0.3 % of the cases (0.12 %+0.18%). However, if we consider the value −5.07, it would be exceeded in 1.47 % of the cases (0.12 %+0.18%+1.17%), greater than the 1 % we are seeking. Note that this is consistent with the general definition provided by footnote 13 in the Introduction to Part II.

If the defaults and migrations of the two issuers were independent, the joint probability distribution could be immediately computed. So, for example, the probability that both remain in their initial classes would be the product of the two respective probabilities. Using the data shown in Table 14.2, we would have: 80.53 % × 91.05 % = 73.32 %; similarly, the probability that both default would be: 0.06 % × 1.06 %≅0.00 %. Table 14.7 shows these joint probabilities, computed assuming independence.

Table 14.7 Probability of joint migration of two issuers with ratings A and BB, assuming independence of the relative migration rates

		Issuer A							
		AAA	AA	A	BBB	BB	B	CCC	Default
Issuer BB		0.09	2.27	91.05	5.52	0.74	0.26	0.01	0.06
AAA	0.03	0.00	0.00	0.03	0.00	0.00	0.00	0.00	0.00
AA	0.14	0.00	0.00	0.13	0.01	0.00	0.00	0.00	0.00
A	0.67	0.00	0.02	0.61	0.40	0.00	0.00	0.00	0.00
BBB	7.73	0.01	0.18	7.04	0.43	0.06	0.02	0.00	0.00
BB	80.53	0.07	1.83	73.32	4.45	0.60	0.20	0.01	0.05
B	8.84	0.01	0.20	8.05	0.49	0.07	0.02	0.00	0.00
CCC	1.00	0.00	0.02	0.91	0.06	0.01	0.00	0.00	0.00
Default	1.06	0.00	0.02	0.97	0.06	0.01	0.00	0.00	0.00

The assumption of independence, however, is not realistic. It is a known fact that rating changes and defaults of companies are partly the result of common factors, such as the economic cycle, shifts in interest rates, changes in commodity prices, and so forth.

The joint probabilities must therefore be estimated assuming that a certain correlation exists between the two obligors. To that end, *CreditMetrics™*:

(a) uses a modified version of the Merton model, where not only defaults but also migrations toward different ratings depend on changes in the value of corporate assets (that is on asset value returns, AVR);
(b) estimates the correlation between the asset value returns of the two obligors;
(c) based on that correlation, derives a distribution of joint probabilities that, unlike Table 14.7, does not imply independence.

Let us therefore begin by seeing how the Merton model, based originally on a binomial approach (survival/default), can be extended to the multinomial case that includes defaults and migrations between different ratings.

Figure 14.5 represents the standardized probability distribution of the AVRs (which we shall indicate as r_{BB}) of a BB-rated company. As we saw with the Merton model, it is assumed to be normal.

If, next year, an r_{BB} occurred such as to drastically reduce the asset values, the firm would default (as suggested by the original version of the Merton model). Let us use Z_{def} to represent the threshold[18] below which the AVRs result in company default. With AVRs above that threshold, the company would remain in business; this is not to say, however, that its rating would remain unchanged. We can imagine that a second threshold exists, Z_{CCC}, such that if r_{BB} is between Z_{def} and Z_{CCC} the sharp decline in asset value causes the bank's analysts to downgrade the company to a CCC rating. At the opposite extreme will be a threshold Z_{AA} such that, if the r_{BB} goes beyond it, the analysts will assign the company an AAA rating. We can further imagine that two thresholds exist, Z_{BB} and Z_{BBB}, such that if the AVR is between them, the value of company assets does not change enough to justify a rating change, and the firm remains in class BBB. A complete system of such thresholds (known as *asset value return thresholds*, or AVRT) is represented in Figure 14.5.

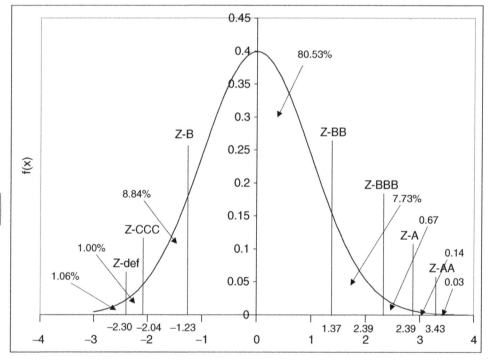

Figure 14.5   A "multinomial" Merton model with default and migrations

---

[18] In the Merton model, this threshold was equal to the face value of the debt, F. As we shall see, in Creditmetrics it is derived indirectly from the transition matrix.

In Merton's structural model, the estimate of Z_{def} involves an analysis of corporate debt, the current value of corporate assets and its volatility. In Creditmetrics, which is a reduced-form model, all the AVRTs are derived indirectly from the probabilities shown in the transition matrix. For example, Z_{def} is selected such that the default probability (area under the curve left of the value Z_{def}) is precisely the PD indicated in the last column of the transition matrix (1.06 %) in the case of a BB bond. That is:

$$\int_{-\infty}^{Z_{def}} f(r_{BB})dr_{BB} = F(Z_{def}) = PD = 1.06\%$$

Since the probability density function of the AVRs is normal, the condition becomes $N(Z_{def}) = 1.06\%$, hence $Z_{def} = N^{-1}(1.06\%) \cong -2.3$.

Similarly, Z_{CCC} will be selected such that the area included between Z_{def} and Z_{CCC} is equal to the probability of migration from BB to CCC ($p_{BB \to CCC}$) indicated in Table 14.2 (1 %), i.e. that:

$$\int_{Z_{def}}^{Z_{CCC}} f(r_{BB})dr_{BB} = N(Z_{CCC}) - N(Z_{def}) = p_{BB \to CCC} = 1\%$$

Hence: $Z_{CCC} = N^{-1}(1\% + 1.06\%) \cong -2.04$. Following the same line of reasoning, all other AVRTs can be derived (see Table 14.8).

Table 14.8 Probability of migration and associated AVR thresholds for a BB company

State at year end (j)	Transition probability ($p_{BB \to j}$)	Cumulative probability	AVRT (Z_j)
Default	1.06 %	1.06 %	−2.3
CCC	1.00 %	2.06 %	−2.04
B	8.84 %	10.90 %	−1.23
BB	80.53 %	91.43 %	1.37
BBB	7.73 %	99.16 %	2.39
A	0.67 %	99.83 %	2.93
AA	0.14 %	99.97 %	3.43
AAA	0.03 %	100.00 %	

We have considered a company with a BB rating, because this is the rating of the first bond included in the bank portfolio. The same logic can be followed for the AVRs, r_A,

Table 14.9 Migration probabilities and relative thresholds for a A company

State at end-year (j)	Transition probability ($p_{A \to j}$)	Cumulative probability	AVRT (Z_j)
Default	0.06 %	0.06 %	−3.24
CCC	0.01 %	0.07 %	−3.19
B	0.26 %	0.33 %	−2.72
BB	0.74 %	1.07 %	−2.30
BBB	5.52 %	6.59 %	−1.51
A	91.05 %	97.64 %	1.98
AA	2.27 %	99.91 %	3.12
AAA	0.09 %	100.00 %	

of a company with an A rating (like the issuer of the second bond in our portfolio): the associated AVRTs are indicated in Table 14.9.

Furthermore, if the standardized AVRs of each of the two companies are described by a standard normal distribution, then the joint AVR distribution of the two companies is described by a standardized bivariate normal.

This distribution, in the generic case of two random variables x and y, has the following probability density function:

$$f(x; y; \rho) = \frac{1}{2\pi \sqrt{1 - \rho^2}} e^{-\frac{x^2 - 2\rho xy + y^2}{2(1 - \rho^2)}}$$

while its cumulative density function (probability that x is less than X and, at the same time, y is less than Y) is given by the following double integral, which can be easily computed (or better, approximated) with many ready-made software routines:

$$\Pr(x < X; y < Y) = \int_{-\infty}^{Y} \int_{-\infty}^{X} \frac{1}{2\pi \sqrt{1 - \rho^2}} e^{-\frac{x^2 - 2\rho xy + y^2}{2(1 - \rho^2)}} \, dx \, dy = N(X; Y; \rho) \qquad (14.1)$$

As we see, both functions depend on the parameter ρ, which indicates the correlation between the asset value returns of the first and second obligor (in short: asset correlation). Let us imagine, for now, that we have already estimated this parameter (which will be examined in detail below) and that the percent changes in asset values of the two obligors are characterized by a correlation coefficient of 20 %.[19]

At this point, we can use (14.1), the value of ρ and the values of the AVRTs shown in Tables 14.7 and 14.8 to estimate the joint default and migration probabilities of the two

---

[19] Note that this correlation is the correlation between asset returns or "asset correlation". It differs, therefore, from correlation between defaults, or "default correlation". More details on the difference between the two are provided in Appendix 14A to the present chapter.

obligors. To begin with, the joint default probability will be found as:

$$\Pr(r_{BB} < -2.3; r_A < -3.24) = N(-2.3; -3.24; 0.2) \cong 0.000054 \qquad (14.1a)$$

while the probability that both companies retain their initial ratings can be found as:

$$\Pr(-1.23 < r_{BB} < 1.37; -1.51 < r_A < 1.98) =$$

$$= \int_{-1.51}^{1.98} \int_{-1.23}^{1.37} \frac{1}{2\pi \sqrt{1 - 0.2^2}} e^{-\frac{r_{BB}^2 - 0.4 r_{BB} r_A + r_A^2}{2(1 - 0.2^2)}} dr_{BB} dr_{AA} =$$

$$= N(1.37; 1.98; 0.2) - N(1.37; -1.51; 0.2) +$$

$$- N(-1, 23; 1.98; 0.2) + N(1.23; -1.51; 0.2) \cong 0.7365$$

that is, 73.65 %.

Following this logic, we can compute all joint probabilities and thus obtain the probability matrix shown in Table 14.10 which, unlike Table 14.7, assumes correlation between the obligors.

Table 14.10 Joint probabilities of two obligors (with A and BB ratings) assuming correlation between asset value returns of 20 % – Values %

Issuer BB	Issuer A								Total
	AAA	AA	A	BBB	BB	B	CCC	Default	
AAA	0.00	0.00	0.03	0.00	0.00	0.00	0.00	0.00	0.03
AA	0.00	0.01	0.13	0.00	0.00	0.00	0.00	0.00	0.14
A	0.00	0.04	0.61	0.01	0.00	0.00	0.00	0.00	0.67
BBB	0.02	0.35	7.10	0.20	0.02	0.01	0.00	0.00	7.69
BB	0.07	1.79	73.65	4.24	0.56	0.18	0.01	0.04	80.53
B	0.00	0.08	7.80	0.79	0.13	0.05	0.00	0.01	8.87
CCC	0.00	0.01	0.85	0.11	0.02	0.01	0.00	0.00	1.00
Default	0.00	0.01	0.90	0.13	0.02	0.01	0.00	0.00	1.07
Total	0.09	2.29	91.06	5.48	0.75	0.26	0.01	0.06	100.00

Source: Gupton, Finger and Bhatia (1997).

Note that the values differ from those in Table 14.7. The probability, for example, that both obligors remain in their initial rating grades is 73.65 % rather than 73.32 %; the probability that both move up one grade is 0.35 % rather than 0.18 %; the probability that both move down one grade is 0.79 % rather than 0.49 %. In general, the probability that both will experience similar changes is enhanced, while it is less likely that rating changes will occur in opposite directions. The positive asset correlation (equal to 20 %) with which the values in Table 14.10 were computed thus means that the two obligors tend to evolve in a similar manner.

For each of the 64 states described in Table 14.10, it is possible to compute the value of our portfolio. This is simply the sum of the future values for the two bonds, each of which obtained by discounting the associated cash flows (in one year) with a forward rate in line with their supposed new rating (following a procedure similar to that followed to generate the values in Table 14.5). E.g., the value of the portfolio when the first credit retains a BB rating and the second one moves to a rating of CCC, is given by the sum of the forward value of the former, computing by discounting its cash flow with the forward rates for grade BB, plus the forward value of the latter, based on the forward curve for grade CCC. In this way, each of the probabilities in Table 14.10 can be associated to a value for the portfolio.

This leads us to the probability distribution for the 64 possible future portfolio values. We can compute its mean and re-express the 64 values as differences (ΔV) from the mean. Sorting these 64 values in increasing order and finding the desired percentile, we can derive VaR estimates at various confidence levels, as seen in section 14.3.1.

14.3.3   Estimating asset correlation

In the previous section, we assumed we knew the correlation between the asset returns of the two obligors. Indeed, if both had been listed, we could have derived a historical series of their respective asset values from the historical series of their share prices (adopting the KMV methodology seen in Chapter 11) and then computed the correlation of the returns.

The bank's obligors, however, are often unlisted companies. Furthermore, a real portfolio includes a large number of obligors, so deriving all asset correlations one by one would be overly complex and time-consuming.[20]

CreditMetrics™ therefore adopts a simplified approach, based on two devices:

(a) it assumes that the asset returns of each company are determined by a set of systematic risk factors and one idiosyncratic factor. The idiosyncratic factor is specific to the individual company and has no correlation with any other factor.[21] The correlations between systematic factors must be estimated;
(b) to do this, *CreditMetrics* uses the correlations between the returns of the stock indices of various countries and industries; the correlation between the asset returns is therefore approximated through the correlation between equity returns.

More precisely, CreditMetrics assumes that the asset value return of a company j is given by a linear combination of one or more systematic factors I_k (linked, for example, to the performance of the chemical or automotive industry, and to that of the British or French economy) and a specific term ε. In detail:

$$r_j = \beta_{1,j} I_1 + \beta_{2,j} I_2 + \cdots + \beta_{n,j} I_n + \delta_j \varepsilon_j \qquad (14.2)$$

where β_{kj} indicates the weight of factor I_k in explaining the asset return of company j, while δ_j indicates the weight of the idiosyncratic component.

---

[20] In general, in a portfolio with n counterparties, one would need to estimate $n(n-1)/2$ correlations. For n equal to 100, 1,000, 2,000, the respective number of correlations would be 4,950, 499,500, 1,999,000.
[21] Thus, the variability associated with specific factors can be got rid of by diversifying the portfolio, but the variability caused by common factors cannot be eliminated.

For each obligor, the bank must specify this system of weights.[22] The weights, as we shall see, must also be standardized.

Regarding systematic factors, weights can be estimated by breaking down the revenues, assets and/or operating profits of the company by country and by industry. Regarding the idiosyncratic factor, larger values will usually be assigned to smaller companies; in fact, while the success or failure of a small company depends to a considerable extent on specific elements, the value of large industrial groups is more directly related to the general performance of the industry and national economy where they belong.

Table 14.11 shows an example involving two companies, A and B. Company A is a US banking-insurance group, while company B is an Italian manufacturing group, with interests in the financial sector and a stake in a French electric power company.

Table 14.11 Systematic and idiosyncratic factors of two companies A and B

	Non-standardized weights		Standardized weights	
Company (j)	A	B		
Systematic factors (partial list)	$w_{k,A}$	$w_{k,B}$	$\beta_{k,A}$	$\beta_{k,B}$
I_1 - U.S. banking industry	50 %		0.77	
I_2 - U.S. insurance industry	40 %	–	0.62	
I_3 - Italian automotive industry	–	40 %		0.75
I_4 - Italian financial industry	–	25 %		0.47
I_5 - French energy industry	–	20 %		0.37
factors specific	ε_A	ε_B	ε_A	ε_B
Specific Risk	10 %	15 %	0.15	0.28

The last two columns of the Table show the standardized weights. In fact, gross weights w must be scaled in such a way that the sum of their squares is equal to one; this is necessary for equation (14.2) to produce standardized AVRs (that is, AVRs having a standard deviation of one), like those used to generate Table 14.2.

Starting with standardized weights, we can express the standardized AVRs of the two companies as:

$$r_A = \beta_{1,A} I_1 + \beta_{2,A} I_2 + \delta_A \varepsilon_A$$

$$r_B = \beta_{3,B} I_3 + \beta_{4,B} I_4 + \beta_{5,B} I_5 + \delta_B \varepsilon_B$$

---

[22] For details, see Gupton et al. (1997).

Consequently, the correlation between the asset returns of company A and company B can be written as:

$$\rho_{A,B} = \beta_{1,A}\beta_{3,B}\rho_{1,3} + \beta_{2,A}\beta_{3,B}\rho_{2,3} + \beta_{1,A}\beta_{4,B}\rho_{1,4} + \beta_{2,A}\beta_{4,B}\rho_{2,4} +$$

$$+ \beta_{1,A}\beta_{5,B}\rho_{1,5} + \beta_{2,A}\beta_{5,B}\rho_{2,5} \qquad (14.3)$$

Where the ρs indicate correlations between systematic factors (all correlations with idiosyncratic factors are, by definition, zero).

Table 14.12 Example of correlations between systematic factors

	I_1	I_2	I_3	I_4	I_5
I_1 –US banking industry	100 %	70 %	10 %	30 %	10 %
I_2 –US insurance industry	70 %	100 %	20 %	20 %	15 %
I_3 –Italian automotive industry	10 %	20 %	100 %	45 %	20 %
I_4 –Italian financial industry	30 %	20 %	45 %	100 %	25 %
I_5 –French energy industry	10 %	15 %	20 %	25 %	100 %

Imagine that, based on the past behaviour of the stock indices of the various industries and countries in Table 14.10, the bank has estimated the correlations shown in Table 14.12. Applying (14.3) we find that the asset correlation between the two companies is equal to:

$$\rho_{A,B} = 0.77 \cdot 0.75 \cdot 0.10 + 0.62 \cdot 0.47 \cdot 0.20 + 0.77 \cdot 0.37 \cdot 0.30$$

$$+ 0.62 \cdot 0.75 \cdot 0.20 + 0.77 \cdot 0.47 \cdot 0.10 + 0.62 \cdot 0.37 \cdot 0.15 \cong 0.38$$

i.e. to 38 %.

14.3.4   Application to a portfolio of N positions

When the number N of obligors is greater than two, the number of countries for which a joint probability distribution must be computed grows very rapidly. In general, if the rating system includes g classes plus default, the joint probability distribution includes $(g+1)^N$ values. For example, given our system of seven rating classes and given 20 obligors, we would need to estimate 8^{20}, i.e. over a billion, different probabilities. Furthermore, the bivariate normal distribution (equation 14.1) would have to be replaced with an N-degree multivariate normal distribution, and this would greatly complicate the computations.

For this reason, it is better to estimate the distribution of future portfolio values (and of the differences ΔV from the expected value) by using Monte Carlo simulations, just like those presented in Chapter 7.

More precisely, the process of estimating the distribution of future portfolio values consists of the following steps:

(a) find the AVRTs corresponding to the various rating classes;
(b) estimate the asset correlations among N debtors, gathered in a matrix $\mathbf{C}$ of order $N \times N$;
(c) compute a matrix $\mathbf{T}$ – for example, through Cholesky factorization – such that $\mathbf{T'T=C}$;
(d) generate a vector $\mathbf{x}$ containing N random draws from N independent standard normal distributions. Transform it into a vector $\mathbf{r=Tx}$ containing a possible scenario for the N (correlated) asset value returns of the obligors;
(e) compare each value r_j of vector $\mathbf{r}$ with the AVRT of the associated obligor; based on this comparison, determine whether the obligor remains in the initial rating class, migrates to a different class, or defaults;
(f) compute the future value of each exposure in the portfolio as a function of the rating class so found in step (e) and the appropriate curve of forward rates (or as a recovery value, in case the obligor defaults);
(g) determine the future portfolio value in this scenario by summing the values of all N positions;
(h) return to point d) for a significant number of times, until you generate a distribution of simulated future portfolio values FV sufficiently numerous to approximate the theoretical one closely;
(i) calculate the mean of this distribution, rewrite portfolio values as differences from the mean, compute the standard deviation and the VaR associated with the desired confidence level. Also, compare the mean portfolio value with the value associated with the case when all credits remain in their initial classes: the difference between the two can be used as a measure of expected loss, similar to what we saw in section 14.3.1.

The Monte Carlo simulation method may require rather long computation times, but it generates fairly accurate results. It also offers two important advantages.

First, it offers a way to introduce recovery risk, which had been overlooked until now, into the Creditmetrics model. Recall that, in computing the distribution of future values in section 14.3.1, we assumed we knew "for sure" the recovery value in case of default (e.g., 53.8 million in the example of Table 14.5) and did consider the risk associated to a poor estimate. Now, in Monte Carlo simulations, we can enhance our model as follows: when the AVR of an obligor is less than his Z_{def} (so that a default occurs), rather than assigning the credit a fixed, predetermined recovery value, we can generate a random value drawn from an appropriate probability distribution. E.g., the beta distribution can be used, as it generates recovery rates between 0% and 100%, choosing its parameters in such a way that its mean and volatility be consistent with the mean recovery rate and volatility estimated by the bank (see, for example, the means and standard deviations in Table 14.4, based on historical values).[23]

Secondly, Monte Carlo simulations let us obtain not only the portfolio VaR but also the *marginal VaR* of an individual exposure or group of exposures. This is computed as the difference between the total portfolio VaR and a new, modified VaR recomputed

---

[23] In this way we account for the randomness of the recovery rate, which adds to the overall VaR of the portfolio. Note, however, that in this way the recovery risk of the individual debtors is purely idiosyncratic in nature (the model does not contemplate correlations between the recoveries on different exposures) and therefore fully diversifiable.

after excluding the exposure (or group of exposures) in question. E.g., suppose that the portfolio VaR is 100 million euros and that it decreases to 80 million euros if recomputed after excluding all Japanese customers from the portfolio: the marginal VaR of Japanese customers would then be 20 million. Marginal VaR indicates to what extent an exposure (or group of exposures) contributes to increasing portfolio risk when it is added to a group of pre-existing ones. If the new exposure is correlated weakly to the previous ones, i.e. the portfolio is getting well diversified, its marginal VaR will probably be quite limited. If, on the other hand, it refers to industries or geographical areas toward which the bank is already heavily exposed, than its marginal VaR will be greater. Through the marginal VaR it is therefore possible to quantify the costs of failure to diversify, expressed in terms of additional economic capital absorbed by the new exposures.

14.3.5 Merits and limitations of the CreditMetrics™ model

CreditMetrics offers numerous advantages, some evident immediately:

– It uses market data that are both objective and forward looking (forward rates, correlations between stock indices).
– It uses a "market value" approach based on which the value of credits is not found the historical book value, but rather the present value of future cash flows, discounted at an adequate rate (adjusted for counterparty risk).
– It considers not only default risk but also migration risk.
– It recognizes the asymmetrical nature of the distribution of future values of a credit portfolio (and thus of the relative losses).
– It makes it possible to compute of marginal risk measures, such as marginal VaR.

Against these advantages, *CreditMetrics*™ presents some evident problems.

– First of all, many of the inputs needed by the model can be readily obtained only if the bank possesses reliable estimates of its transition matrices, and if there is a liquid market from which to draw information on the forward rates requested on differently-rated credits.
– The model also assumes implicitly that the bank is operating in the credit market as a price-taker, that is, that the spreads paid by various rating classes are independent of the bank's lending policies.
– Another limitation regards the use of historical transition matrices. In fact, historical frequencies do not always reflect future probabilities adequately, nor is the transition matrix necessarily stable over time. Furthermore, it seems rather unrealistic to assume that these probabilities are equal for all companies belonging to a given rating class.
– This last aspect (default and migration rates equal for all obligors with a given rating) depends on the fact, mentioned earlier, that CreditMetrics is a reduced model that does not take into account the peculiarities of the individual companies (their leverage, the current value of their assets and its volatility) but only uses their "average" past behaviour patterns.
– The use of correlations between stock indices to measure the correlations between corporate assets also seems open to criticism. This assumption is like assuming that the assets of the companies are financed entirely through equity capital: only in this case, in fact, do equity returns coincide with asset returns. In the case of companies with

high financial leverage, on the other hand, equity returns are much more volatile than asset returns. The model also estimates the correlations between annual AVRs through correlations between equity returns, which usually have shorter horizons. This may introduce distortions, since the correlation coefficients change with as the time horizon over which they are estimated.

– Lastly, the choice of the β_{jk}s that link the AVRs of a company to the systematic factors (and of the weight associated with the idiosyncratic factor) is strongly discretionary, not to say arbitrary, and unsupported by an economically and financially sound methodology.

14.4 THE STRUCTURAL APPROACH: *PORTFOLIOMANAGER*™

Some problems met in the *CreditMetrics*™ model are solved by PortfolioManager, a model developed by the California-based company KMV.[24] This model is based on a structural methodology, similar to that seen in Chapter 11 for estimating the PD of a single obligor. The defaults are therefore explained through an economic model (based on the market value and volatility of company assets) and not only through past empirical data.

Apart from this fundamental difference, however, the model shares several characteristics with the previous one. As in *CreditMetrics*™, in fact, in *PortfolioManager*™ the correlation between the asset returns of the obligors is derived from correlations between the equity returns. More specifically, the AVR of an individual company is mapped to a multi-factor model in three distinct phases (see Figure 14.6):

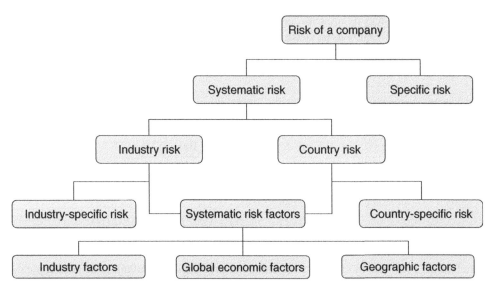

Figure 14.6   The mapping of a credit exposure in the PortfolioManager™ model

(i) systematic and specific components are separated;
(ii) the systematic component is linked to several factors associated with various industries and countries;

---

[24] See Bohn and Kealhofer (2001).

(iii) the return of each factor associated with an industry/country is broken down, in turn, into a specific risk component (*industry-specific risk* and *country-specific risk*) and a systematic risk component (which depends, for example, on the exposure of the country/industry to global economic performance).

Similar to what occurs in *CreditMetrics*™, therefore, the AVRs of a company are described by a combination of systematic factors and a specific factor. The correlation between pairs of companies can therefore still be derived as in the example of the previous section (on the basis of the βs linking the company to the factors and the pairwise correlations across systematic factors).

As in *CreditMetrics*™, a Monte Carlo simulation can therefore be performed: starting with the returns of the various risk factors (systematic factors as well as idiosyncratic risk components) a high number of scenarios is generated so that the distribution of future credit portfolio values can be approximated empirically. The analysis offers two possible variants.

The first is based on a risk-neutrality assumption and can be explained briefly with an example. Consider a risky one-year zero-coupon bond with a face value of 100, probability of default *PD* and loss given default equal to *LGD*.

The expected payoff p of the bond upon maturity is the following:

$$p = PD \cdot 100 \cdot (1 - LGD) + (1 - PD) \cdot 100 \tag{14.4}$$

It may be rewritten as the sum of a risk-free component p^*, equal to $100(1-LGD)$, which the creditor will collect in any case, and an uncertain component, $\tilde{p}$, equal to zero in case of default and to $\cdot(1 \ LGD)$ in the case of normal repayment of the loan:

$$p = 100 \cdot (1 - LGD) + (1 - PD) \cdot 100 \cdot LGD = p^* + \tilde{p} \tag{14.5}$$

A risk-neutral investor would assign the uncertain component $\tilde{p}$ a present value $PV_{\tilde{p}}$ equal to its expected future value discounted at the risk-free rate, i.e.:

$$PV_{\tilde{p}} = \frac{\tilde{p}}{1 + r} = \frac{(1 - PD^*) \cdot 100 \cdot LGD}{1 + r} \tag{14.6}$$

Then the present value of the bond (risky payoff plus risk-free payoff) would be

$$PV_p = \frac{p}{1 + r} = \frac{100 \cdot (1 - LGD) + (1 - PD^*) \cdot 100 \cdot LGD}{1 + r} \tag{14.7}$$

Note that in (14.6) and in (14.7) we are using the probability of default (PD*) corresponding to the expectations of a risk-neutral investor (risk neutral PD), which is generally greater than the real PD (as shown in Chapter 11). We know that this type of probability can be estimated using an *à la* Merton model whose inputs are the same as those used in the KMV model: market value and volatility of assets and default point. Supposing it has been estimated, we can now find the market value of the position, through equation (14.6).

Note two differences with respect to CreditMetrics. First, the distribution of possible events in one year's time is not multinomial but binomial; it is therefore impossible to estimate the losses from downgrading, but we must focus on the losses related to default.

Second, we need not know the spread the market requires of the obligor. In effect, if we wished, this spread (which we shall indicate with d) could be readily determined by recalling that the market value of the credit must be the same for both risk-neutral investors (who compute it using (14.6)) and for risk-averse investors (who compute it by discounting the par value, 100, at a rate r plus spread d). From the equation:

$$\frac{100 \cdot (1 - LGD) + (1 - PD^*) \cdot 100 \cdot LGD}{1 + r} = \frac{100}{1 + r + d}, \tag{14.8}$$

it follows that

$$d = \frac{(1 + r)LGD \cdot PD^*}{1 - PD^* \cdot LGD}. \tag{14.9}$$

This relationship is useful for the second variant offered, in CreditMonitor, for marking the portfolio to market. It involves constructing a certain number of discrete classes that group all the obligors with an expected default frequency (EDF) within a certain interval (e.g., between 0 % and 0.5 %, between 0.5 % and 1.5 % and so forth). A migration matrix must then be constructed for these "EDF classes", like the one in Table 14.13. Each class must also be associated with a credit spread, based on its mean risk-neutral PD. At this point, knowing the curves of the spreads, the distribution of future portfolio values can be reconstructed with a methodology similar to the one already presented for *CreditMetrics™*.

Table 14.13 Transition matrix at 1 year based on EDF classes (data in %)

		\multicolumn{8}{c}{Rating a year-end}
		AAA	AA	A	BBB	BB	B	CCC	Default
	AAA	66.26	22.22	7.37	2.45	0.86	0.67	0.14	0.02
	AA	21.66	43.04	25.83	6.56	1.99	0.68	0.20	0.04
Rating	A	2.76	20.34	44.19	22.94	7.42	1.97	0.28	0.10
at start	BBB	0.30	2.80	22.63	42.54	23.52	6.95	1.00	0.26
of year	BB	0.08	0.24	3.69	22.93	44.41	24.53	3.41	0.71
	B	0.01	0.05	0.39	3.48	20.47	53.00	20.58	2.01
	CCC	0.00	0.01	0.09	0.26	1.79	17.77	69.94	10.13

Source: Kealhofer, Kwok and Weng (1998).

It is important to observe that although these "EDF classes" seem similar to the rating classes used by *CreditMetrics™*, they are significantly different. First, they are based on the EDFs dictated by a model and not on the opinion of a team of analysts. Second, they are based on a point-in-time rating assignment approach (see Chapter 13) that generates higher migration rates (to appreciate this, compare Table 14.13 with Table 14.2 above).

14.5   THE MACROECONOMIC APPROACH: *CREDITPORTFOLIOVIEW*™

CreditPortfolioView™ is a model developed in 1997 by Tom Wilson, then a partner in consulting firm McKinsey (McKinsey, 1997). It is based on the observation that credit cycles depend on the economic cycle. Therefore, during phases of economic growth the migrations toward higher rating classes (upgrades) tend to be more frequent, while migration rates toward lower classes (downgrades) and defaults decline. The opposite occurs during recessions. Thus the transition matrices used in CreditMetrics should be adjusted, depending on the current phase of the cycle. *CreditPortfolioView*™ therefore proposes to link the probabilities of migration and default to macroeconomic variables such as interest rate levels, the employment rate, real GDP growth and the savings rate, thus "conditioning them" to the state of the economic cycle.

14.5.1   Estimating conditional default probabilities

Let us consider the probability of default p_{jt} at time t of a group or segment j of companies that react uniformly to changes in the economic cycle (generally companies in the same industry and same geographical area). *CreditPortfolioView*™ assumes that this probability varies with the economic cycle; operationally, it is modelled according to a logit function (see Chapter 10):

$$p_{jt} = \frac{1}{1 + e^{-y_{j,t}}} \qquad (14.10)$$

where $y_{j,t}$ represents the value at time t of a "health index" of the segment j based on macroeconomic factors. As index values rise, the default probability declines (in all cases, in a logit model, between zero and one).

In turn, the index $y_{j,t}$ is a linear combination of several macroeconomic variables $x_{j1}, x_{j2}, \dots x_{jn}$ (the rate of real GDP growth, the employment rate, the level of long-term interest rates, the level of public spending, etc.[25]):

$$y_{jt} = \beta_{j,0} + \beta_{j,1}x_{j,1,t} + \beta_{j,2}x_{j,2,t} + \beta_{j,3}x_{j,3,t} + \upsilon_{j,t} \qquad (14.11)$$

The value of coefficients $\beta_{j1}, \beta_{j2}, \dots \beta_{jn}$ is estimated based on historical experience, analysing the data on past default frequencies by segment; the last term, $\upsilon_{j,t}$, represents random error.[26] While the terms linked to macroeconomic factors represent a systematic risk component (affecting several segments that can share the same macroeconomic factors), the random term identifies the specific risk component associated with segment j.

Of course, in order to use (14.10) and (14.11) as forecasting tools, we must produce an estimate of the future values of macroeconomic factors. To this end, for each factor

---

[25] The variables used can differ for different j.
[26] The errors for each period t are assumed to be independent from $x_{j,t}$ and characterized by a normal distribution with mean zero and volatility σ_υ.

CreditPortfolioView™ uses a second-order auto-regressive model[27] – AR(2) – like the following:

$$x_{j,i,t} = \gamma_{i,0} + \gamma_{i,1} x_{j,i,t-1} + \gamma_{i,2} x_{j,i,t-2} + \varepsilon_{j,i,t} \tag{14.12}$$

where coefficients $\gamma_{i,j}$ must be estimated empirically and $\varepsilon_{j,i,t}$ represents a normally-distributed error term with mean zero.

14.5.2   Estimating the conditional transition matrix

The model is not limited to generating (with equations 14.10–14.12) a projection of the conditional default probabilities of the various segments, but also uses them to condition the entire transition probability matrix. In *CreditPortfolioView*™, in fact, the mean long-term transition matrix (unconditional) is adjusted to reflect the expected default probabilities for the subsequent year.

In particular, the model requires that the conditional PDs generated for segments including "speculative grade"[28] companies be compared to their long-term mean values. The decision to concentrate only on this type of issuers derives from the fact that their PDs are more sensitive to fluctuations in the economic cycle.

Table 14.14 CreditPortolioView: economic cycle and transition matrix

Relationship	Economic cycle phase	Default probability	Downgrade probability	Upgrade probability
$\dfrac{SDP_t}{\mu_{SDP}} > 1$	Recession	Increase	Increase	Decrease
$\dfrac{SDP_t}{\mu_{SDP}} < 1$	Expansion	Decrease	Decrease	Increase

If the value of these probabilities (speculative default probabilities) in year t is greater than their historical average (μ_{SDP}), this means that the phase of the economic cycle is unfavourable. In this case (see Table 14.14), the transition matrix is modified by increasing the default and downgrade probabilities and reducing the upgrade possibilities. If, on the other hand, the ratio SDP_t/μ_{SDP} is less than one, this means that the economic cycle phase is favourable. In this case, the transition matrix is modified by reducing the default and downgrade probabilities and increasing the upgrade probabilities.

The adjustment is greater for the lowest rating classes (precisely because they are more sensitive to the economic cycle) compared to the investment-grade ones.

Table 14.15 summarizes the five phases of the process for estimating the conditional transition matrix in *CreditPortfolioView*™.

Based on the above mechanism, *CreditPortfolioView*™ can also simulate multiyear transition processes, where the matrices for successive years are conditioned by the performance of the economy. This implies that depending on the sign (mainly positive or negative) of the coefficients $\gamma_{i,j}$ expressing the serial correlation of the macroeconomic variables, the

---

[27] In practice, the value of the dependent variable for period t is estimated based on a regression in which the independent variables are represented by the values assumed by the same dependent variable in the two previous periods (t-1 and t-2).

[28] Speculative grade or "non-investment grade" rating classes are those below BBB-/Baa3.

Table 14.15 The five phases of the CreditPortfolioView™ model

	Phase	Relevant equation
1	Estimate the macro variables for period t	$x_{j,i,t} = \gamma_{i,0} + \gamma_{i,1}x_{j,i,t-1} + \gamma_{i,2}x_{j,i,t-2} + \varepsilon_{j,i,t}$
2	Estimate the "health index" of individual segment j at time t	$y_{jt} = \beta_{j,0} + \beta_{j,1}x_{j,1,t} + \beta_{j,2}x_{j,2,t} + \beta_{j,3}x_{j,3,t} + \upsilon_{j,t}$
3	Estimate the conditional default probability of segment j at time t	$p_{jt} = \dfrac{1}{1 + e^{-y_{j,t}}}$
4	Estimate the relationship between "*speculative default probabilities*" simulated for period t and mean default probabilities	$\dfrac{SDP_t}{\mu_{SDP}}$
5	Adjust the transition matrix	

multiyear transitions can show a gradual worsening ($\gamma_{i,j}$ positive) or the return towards long-term average conditions ($\gamma_{i,j}$ negative).

14.5.3   Merits and limitations of CreditPortfolioView™

The main merit of *CreditPortfolioView™* is its attempt to identify the relationship between macroeconomic variables and portfolio credit risk. In this model, in fact, the worsening of economic conditions results in a worsening of the economic outlook of the obligors, as well as in an increase in default correlations.[29]

Nevertheless, the model suffers from two main limitations. First, the estimation of the coefficients β requires a broad base of historical data on the default rates of the individual segments. Second, the criterion followed for conditioning the transition matrix to the economic cycle, based on the simulated default probabilities of speculative-grade rating classes, seems rather arbitrary. Thus it does not necessarily produce better results than those obtainable by bank analysts simply correcting the matrix subjectively (based on their experience and the macroeconomic projections of industry and area specialists).

14.6   THE ACTUARIAL APPROACH: *CREDITRISK+*™ MODEL

CreditRisk+™, developed by *Credit Suisse Financial Products* in 1997 (CSFP, 1997) adopts an approach derived from the insurance business; more specifically, it applies to credit risk some instruments typical of the mathematics of insurance (actuarial mathematics).

The losses of an insurance company derive from two fundamental variables: (i) the frequency with which a certain type of event occurs (event frequency) and (ii) the amount the company must pay out when the event occurs (loss severity). It is easy to spot the

---

[29] For a given asset correlation ρ, in fact, the correlation between the defaults of two obligors is an increasing function of their PDs (see Appendix 14A). An increase in conditional PDs, all other things being equal, therefore produces an increase in the correlation between defaults.

analogy with credit risk, where the losses depend on the frequency of default events and the rate of loss given default; based on this analogy, it then becomes possible to use insurance-derived models for estimating credit losses.

These models (as one might guess from the analogy with insurance losses) can focus only on default risk; migration risk is not considered. Moreover, as we shall see, exposures at default (EAD) and recovery rates will be treated as deterministic: therefore neither exposure risk nor recovery risk can be estimated.

Despite these limitations, *Creditrisk+* ™ is highly effective in estimating the risk of portfolios with a large number of positions. It has therefore be applied extensively in the management of some traditional banking portfolios, such as loans to small and medium enterprises, consumer loans, and mortgages.

It should also be noted that this model (unlike structural models) does not seek to explain the process that leads a company to default, and does not produce PD estimates. On the contrary, it assumes that the default probabilities of the obligors and the recovery rates on their loans have already been estimated by other tools (such as the bank's internal rating system or the studies produced by the rating agencies). Another input needed by the model is, as we shall see, the volatility of the PD estimates, which can be approximated through the past volatility of default rates.

14.6.1 Estimating the probability distribution of defaults

Creditrisk+™ describes the probability distribution of the number of future defaults over a given risk horizon (e.g. in the next year) through a typical tool of actuarial mathematics: the *Poisson* distribution. Analytically, the probability $p(n)$ that n defaults occur within one year is computed as:

$$p(n) = \frac{e^{-\mu}\mu^n}{n!} \tag{14.13}$$

where μ ("expected number of defaults") represents the sum of all the PDs of the customers in the portfolio. For example, for a bank with 400 clients, each with a PD of 1%, the value of μ will be 4.

The probability that no defaults occur can then be found by:

$$p(0) = \frac{e^{-4}4^0}{0!} = 1.83\%$$

while the probability that a number of defaults equal to the expected value (4 out of 100) occurs can be found by:

$$p(4) = \frac{e^{-4}4^4}{4!} = 19.54\%$$

Figure 14.7 shows these and other values, computed with (14.13) for n between 0 and 10. Note that the probability distribution thus obtained (which displays a peak at μ) is quite different from normal and is skewed to the right. For high values of n, the probability gradually drops almost to zero; the probability that no default occurs (minimum value of n), on the other hand, is much greater than zero.

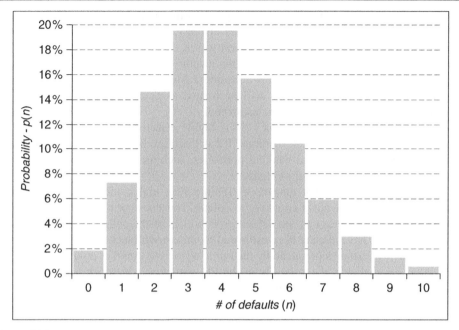

Figure 14.7   An example of Poisson distribution

The Poisson distribution has mean μ and standard deviation $\sqrt{\mu}$. It is a very "handy" distribution, since the only parameter necessary to estimate all the $p(n)$ is μ[30]. However, the Poisson distribution can only be used if two conditions are met:

(1) the individual PDs must be relatively small; otherwise, the Poisson provides a less and less satisfactory approximation of the real probability distribution. To understand this, note that the Poisson produces the same value for p(n) for a portfolio of 400 clients with PD of 1 % as for 100 clients with PD of 4 % (in both the cases, in fact, μ is equal to 4); in the second case, however, the quality of the approximation will be worse.
(2) The defaults of the individual obligors are all mutually independent. This second assumption is clearly unacceptable, since credit risk arises precisely from the fact that the obligors of a bank tend to default "in clusters" (due to recessions or regional/industry crises). It will therefore have to be removed later in this paragraph (see section 14.6.4).

14.6.2   The probability distribution of losses

To move from the distribution of the number of defaults to that of losses, we must consider the values of exposures and the associated expected recovery rates. If an obligor defaults, in fact, the bank suffers a loss equal to the value of the exposure less the amount recovered. In other words, the absolute loss given default of the ith obligor is equal to:

$$L_i = LGD_i \cdot EAD_i = (1 - RR_i) \cdot EAD_i \qquad (14.14)$$

---

[30] Let us suppose for now that μ is known with certainty; we shall remove this assumption later.

where, as usual, *EAD* represents the exposure at default and *RR* the recovery rate.

CreditRisk+™ assumes that the bank can estimate EAD and RR without error and associates to each obligor, without uncertainty, the value of L_i provided by (14.14).

If, for example, for a certain obligor we assume an exposure at default of € 100,000 and a recovery rate of 50 %, a loss *L* of 50,000 euros will be associated with it; the same will occur for an obligor with EAD of 200,000 euros and RR of 75 %.

CreditRisk+™ also adopts an artifice, aggregating all the exposures with similar L_i. This aggregation is called "*banding*", because all the L_i are aggregated into "bands" of roughly equivalent amount. More precisely, the L_i are divided by a constant quantity, *L*, and rounded to the nearest integer: all the clients with an equal post-rounding value are then assigned to the same band.

Consider, for example, a bank that has issued loans to 10 companies, each with its own L_i. Make *L* equal to 10,000 euros. Table 14.16 shows the loans and the relative band assignments.

Table 14.16 Example of banding

Company	Net exposure (L_i)	Net exposure L_i /L, with L=10,000	Rounded exposure	Band(j)
1	240,000	24	24	24
2	36,000	3.6	4	4
3	38,000	3.8	4	4
4	430,000	43	43	43
5	63,000	6.3	6	6
6	780,000	78	78	78
7	72,000	7.2	7	7
8	13,000	1.3	1	1
9	81,000	8.1	8	8
10	540,000	54	54	54

As we see, each exposure is assigned to a specific band *j* as a function of the amount L_i divided by *L* and rounded. Note that the second and third exposures both flow into band 4.

Each band represents a portfolio of loans, all characterized by approximately equivalent losses given default, equal to around *j·L*. This means that, within a given band, the losses are directly proportional to the number of defaults. The Poisson distribution discussed in the previous section (equation 14.13) can therefore also be used to represent the probability distribution of losses; instead of μ (number of defaults expected for the entire bank), we will now use a different μ_j for each band, equal to the number of expected defaults in that specific band.

Also, it can be shown that, to minimize the possible biases implicit in the banding process (which involves, as we have seen, a rounding to the nearest multiple of *L*), it is advisable to compute the μ_j as[31]

$$\mu_j = \sum_{i \in j} \frac{p_i L_i}{jL} \tag{14.15}$$

rather that simply as

$$\mu_j = \sum_{i \in j} p_i$$

Replacing this μ_j in (14.13) gives

$$p(n) = \frac{e^{-\mu_j} \mu_j^n}{n!} \tag{14.16}$$

which represents the probability associated with the occurrence, in band j, of n losses, each amounting to $j \cdot L$.

Alternatively, (14.16) can also be written as

$$p(nj) = \frac{e^{-\mu_j} \mu_j^n}{n!} \tag{14.17}$$

i.e. as the probability of observing $n \cdot j$ losses, each amounting to L.

Let us consider, for example, band 5 (which groups obligors with losses given default of around $5 \cdot L$ euros, i.e. 50,000 euros), and let us imagine we have computed with (14.15) an μ_j equal to 4. We can now estimate, with (14.16) or (14.17), the probabilities associated with the various levels of loss, shown in Table 14.17.

14.6.3 The distribution of losses of the entire portfolio

Now we must "reunite" the loss probability distributions *within each individual band* into a single loss probability distribution *for the entire bank*, which represents the final output of the model (from which we can derive the expected loss and measures of unexpected loss, such as the standard deviation and the VaR).

To that end, we must "merge" the Poisson distributions that describe the individual bands. A loss of 20,000 euros could, in fact, be generated by either two defaults in band 1 or one default in band 2; a loss of 120,000 could be obtained from an even greater number of bands. To achieve this integration, CreditRisk+ adopts a three-step approach.

(1) For each Poisson distribution associated with the individual bands, the corresponding *probability generating function* (p.g.f.) is derived. In statistics, the p.g.f. is a function of an auxiliary variable z that "summarizes" a probability distribution (including Poisson) and enjoys some special properties (to be used in the next step). In our case, it can be shown that the p.g.f. for the Poisson distribution of each band j, which we shall call $G_j(z)$, is given by:

$$G_j(z) = e^{-\mu_j + \mu_j z^j} \tag{14.18}$$

---

[31] In fact, if the exposures of a certain band had been rounded down on the average (i.e. if on the average $L_i > jL$), (14.15) would correct this error by producing a μ_j greater than the summation of all p_is in the band.

Table 14.17 The distribution of the losses relative to band
5 ($L_i \cong$ € 50,000)

Number of defaults (n)	Value of the loss njL	Probability (%)
0	0	1.83
1	50,000	7.33
2	100,000	14.65
3	150,000	19.54
4	200,000	19.54
5	250,000	15.63
6	300,000	10.42
7	350,000	5.95
8	400,000	2.98
9	450,000	1.32
10	500,000	0.53
11	550,000	0.19
12	600,000	0.06
13	650,000	0.02
14	700,000	0.01

(2) The second step involves deriving the p.g.f. of the entire portfolio by aggregating the p.g.f.s of the individual bands. More precisely, if the individual defaults are independent (and therefore the number of defaults in the various bands as well), the p.g.f. of the portfolio is simply the product of the p.g.f.s of the individual bands:

$$G(z) = \prod_j e^{-\mu_j + \mu_j z^j} = e^{-\mu + \sum_j \mu_j z^j} \qquad (14.19)$$

where $\mu = \sum_j \mu_j$.

(3) In the third step the portfolio p.g.f. in (14.19) is transformed back into a probability distribution. Given a p.g.f., in fact, it is always possible to find the various probabilities (in our case, the probabilities of a loss equal to nL for different values of n) by repeated differentiations. More precisely, the following relationship can be shown to hold:

$$p(nL) = \frac{1}{n!} \frac{d^n G(z)}{dz^n} \bigg|_{z=0} \qquad (14.20)$$

Equation (14.20) allows us to compute the probability associated with all possible levels of losses ($L, 2L, 3L$, etc.). Once this distribution of future loss probabilities has been obtained (no longer on a single band but on the entire portfolio), we can derive its mean (expected loss), as well as the chosen percentile and VaR (at 99 %, for example). This is shown graphically in Figure 8.

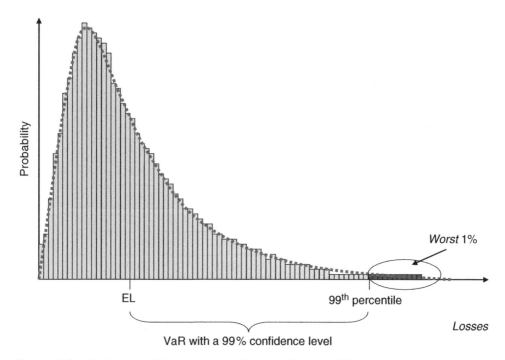

Figure 14.8 Distribution of future losses on the whole bank portfolio

14.6.4 Uncertainty about the average default rate and correlations

Until now, we have assumed that the number of defaults on a portfolio can be described with a *Poisson* distribution (with average μ and standard deviation $\sqrt{\mu}$).

If, however, we observe the statistics available on the number of actual defaults over time on portfolios with constant quality (μ), the standard deviation of the number of defaults is greater than $\sqrt{\mu}$. Table 14.18 shows an example: based on the data measured by Moody's in the period 1970–1995 for its rating classes, it shows the average number of defaults on a portfolio of 100 obligors (μ) and the standard deviation of the 26 annual data points used to compile it. The average number of defaults for 100 class B obligors, for example, is equal to 7.62. If this is μ, we would expect a volatility on the order of $\sqrt{7.62} = 2.76$. In reality, the standard deviation of the 26 annual values is much higher, equal to 5.1. The results would be similar for other rating classes.

The reason why the volatility of the real data is greater than the theoretical one implied by the Poisson distribution is that the latter assumes that the defaults of the individual clients are independent. In the real world, however, obligors tend to default in "clusters" or in "waves", since they are all affected, to a varying extent, by the economic cycle.

Indeed, given a portfolio of clients for which we wish to estimate the distribution of possible losses, the number of defaults expected in the successive year (μ) is not a fixed

Table 14.18 Number of annual defaults and their volatility – 1970–1995

	Annual defaults for 100 obligors	
Rating class	Average −μ	Standard deviation
Aaa	0.00	0.0
Aa	0.03	0.1
A	0.01	0.0
Baa	0.13	0.3
Ba	1.42	1.3
B	7.62	5.1

Source: Carty and Lieberman (1996b).

parameter known with certainty. In fact, it may exceed the average long-period value (if the economic cycle worsens) or drop below it (in the opposite case).

The authors of Creditrisk+ have thus modified the models presented in the preceding sections, considering μ not a constant but a random variable.[32] In this way, the model obtains a greater volatility of the number of defaults, consistent with empirical values like those in Table 14.18. Furthermore, even more importantly, treating μ as stochastic is one way to indirectly remove the assumption that defaults are independent, *adding to the model the assumption of default correlation*.

This last statement is not trivial and deserves a more precise explanation. We are saying that by varying μ we can use a probability distribution where the defaults, for a given μ, are *independent* (Poisson) to describe the real world, where the defaults are *correlated*. How is it possible?

Let us explain this through an example (Table 14.19). Imagine, for the sake of simplicity, a portfolio of just two obligors (Alpha Inc. and Beta Ltd.) whose PDs vary according to the economic cycle. In particular, if the economy is expanding, Alpha has a PD of 4%, Beta 2%. If, on the other hand, the economy is in recession, Alpha has a PD of 10%, Beta 6%. Note that in the first case we have $\mu = 0.06$, while in the second $\mu = 0.16$. The expected number of defaults is therefore a stochastic variable (which, in this simplified example, follows a Bernoulli distribution). For the sake of simplicity, we shall assign the same probability (50%) to an expansion and a recession.

Within each of these two scenarios (expansion or recession), we treat the defaults of the two obligors as independent. Consequently, we compute the joint probabilities simply as

---

[32] In particular, *CreditRisk+*™ assumes that the number of expected defaults, μ, follows a Gamma distribution with average μ_X and standard deviation σ_X. In that case, it can be demonstrated that the distribution of the number of defaults of the bank follows a negative binomial distribution. The probability of registering n cases of default is therefore equal to

$$p(n) = (1 - p_k)^{\alpha_k} \binom{n + \alpha_k - 1}{n} p_k^n, \text{ where}: \alpha = \left(\frac{\mu_X}{\sigma_X}\right)^2; \beta = \frac{\sigma_X^2}{\mu_X}, \text{ and } p_k = \frac{\beta_k}{1 + \beta_k}$$

This produces a distribution that, for a given average default rate, is characterized by a stronger skewness and by a thicker right tail: consequently, the probability associated with the occurrence of extreme losses increases.

the product of the individual probabilities. The probability that both borrowers default will therefore be equal to $4\% \cdot 2\% = 0.08\%$ in case of expansion and to $10\% \cdot 6\% = 0.60\%$ in case of recession. The other joint probabilities are indicated in the first two panels of Table 14.19.

Table 14.19 An example of correlated probabilities generated through uncorrelated scenarios

State I: Economic expansion				
		Alpha Inc.		
		Default	Survival	Total
Beta Ltd.	Default	0.08 %	1.92 %	2.00 %
	Survival	3.92 %	94.08 %	98.00 %
	Total	4.00 %	96.00 %	100.00 %

State II: Recession				
		Alpha Inc.		
		Default	Survival	Total
Beta Ltd.	Default	0.60 %	5.40 %	6.00 %
	Survival	9.40 %	84.60 %	94.00 %
	Total	10.00 %	90.00 %	100.00 %

Unconditional distribution (50 % x State I + 50 % x State II)				
		Alpha Inc.		
		Default	Survival	Total
Beta Ltd.	Default	0.34 %	3.66 %	4.00 %
	Survival	6.66 %	89.34 %	96.00 %
	Total	7.00 %	93.00 %	100.00 %

Starting with these two conditional probability distributions (expansion and recession) we now compute the unconditional probability distribution, valid when μ is not known with certainty. It is the average (with weights of 50 % and 50 %) of the probabilities valid in case of expansion or recession. Thus, for example, the PD of Alpha will be equal to the average of 4 % and 10 %, i.e. 7 %, while the joint default probability will be equal to the average of 0.08 % and 0.60 %, i.e. 0.34 %. All the values are indicated in the third panel of Table 14.19.

The combination of the two conditional distributions, each found by assuming independence, gives rise to a distribution that assumes correlation: to see it, we need only note that the joint default probability (0.34 %) is greater than the simple product of the PD of the two obligors (7 %·4 % = 0.28%).

Creditrisk+ works in the same way. For each possible value of μ, it uses a Poisson distribution, assuming independence. However, since μ is stochastic, the unconditional probability distribution (computed by integrating on all the possible values of μ) assumes correlation between the defaults. In other words, Creditrisk+ overcomes the assumption of independence between the obligors by making μ random.

More precisely, the model assumes that μ is a random variable function of n background factors, each representing a certain component of the economic cycle. We can think of those factors as variables that drive the cycle (inflation, level of the interest rates, foreign exchange rates, etc.) or directly as variables that capture the "degree of health" of a certain industry; for example, each factor X_k could be given from the number of insolvencies in industry k. Creditrisk+ assumes that each X_k follows a gamma distribution and the different X_k are mutually independent.

The average expected PD of a company is a linear function of one or more X_k. In fact, a company, let us say company A, may also be active in more than one industry. In that case, its loss given default L_A can be broken down, from the logical standpoint, into portions $(\theta_{A1}, \theta_{A2...} \theta_{An})$, each associated with the performance of a different industry. The bank's portfolio can therefore be viewed as a set of industry sub-portfolios, each consisting of the L_j (or, when multiple sectors are involved, of the θ_j) associated with a certain industry.

Starting from this breakdown, we can determine, analytically, the distribution of loss probabilities for the entire portfolio. An example is shown in Figure 14.9. The Figure (by comparison with the curve in Figure 14.6) shows how the distribution of the number of defaults is modified when μ is stochastic. As can be seen, it becomes more skewed and more "squeezed", i.e. more volatile. In other words, the probabilities associated with losses close to the average are reduced, while extreme losses become more likely. This is due to the fact that, while in the constant μ version (Figure 14.8), the uncertainty concerned only what individual obligors would actually default, but not their PDs, now the PDs are also to some extent unpredictable.[33]

Finally, notice that, based on the model just described, two companies will be correlated only if their respective exposures fall (wholly, L, or only partially, θ) in the same industry portfolio. In particular, it can be shown that the correlation between the default[34] of two companies A and B is given by:

$$\rho_{A,B} = \sqrt{p_A p_B} \sum_{k=1}^{n} \theta_{Ak}\theta_{Bk} \left(\frac{\sigma_k}{\mu_k}\right)^2 \tag{14.21}$$

where p_A, p_B represent the expected default probabilities of A and B and μ_k, σ_k represent the mean and volatility of the default rate of each of the n sectors. This formula shows

[33] Think of how the uncertainty facing a person flipping a coin ten times increases if he/she is not certain that the coin has been properly minted and hence not only ignores how many heads or tails may occur, but also whether the probability of obtaining a head or a tail is truly equal to 50 %.
[34] Note that this correlation between defaults (default correlation) is different from the correlation on asset returns (asset correlation) used by CreditMetrics™ (see Appendix 14A). It takes significantly lower values than asset correlation and its verification based on empirical data is made complex (especially for counterparties with higher creditworthiness) by the fact that, while default by an obligor is a rare phenomenon, the joint default of more than one counterparty is even rarer.

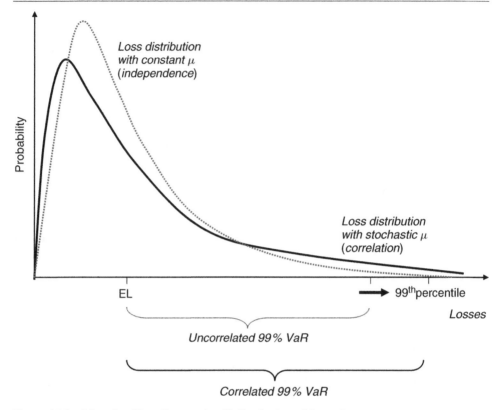

Figure 14.9 "Correlated" vs. "uncorrelated" distribution of future losses

that the correlation is equal to zero in two cases: if the expected number of defaults, as in sections 14.6.1–14.6.3, remains constant (and therefore σ_k is equal to zero) or if the two companies have no sector in common ($\theta_{Ak} \cdot \theta_{Bk} = 0 \forall k$).

14.6.5 Merits and limitations of CreditRisk+™

The *CreditRisk+™* model offers two important advantages. The first regards the relatively small amount of input required. The main data needed, in fact, are the PDs of the individual obligors, as well as the EADs and LGDs (to compute, with (14.14), the value of the absolute loss L_j given default). It is also necessary to know the "sensitivity" of the individual companies to the various background factors (i.e. the θ_{jk} seen in the previous section, which are known as *factor loadings*). However, no inputs like transition matrices or forward rate curves are required.

The second advantage concerns the possibility of deriving the probability distribution of future losses analytically, without resorting to Monte Carlo simulations. This makes *CreditRisk+™* particularly advantageous from the computational standpoint.

Nevertheless, *CreditRisk+™* also has some limitations. The definition of background factors and estimation of factor loadings are delicate, potentially arbitrary steps. Furthermore, since the model requires that the background factors be mutually independent, it is not possible to use variables with an immediate economic meaning (that is, financial variables like interest and exchange rates, or indices of real economy in the various country/sectors): instead, they must be "filtered" and made incorrelated through appropriate statistical procedures.

A second limitation is that the model focuses only on default risk and overlooks migration risk. This limitation is particularly important for exposures with maturities longer than a year. Let us consider, in fact, a long-term loan that does not default within 12 months but suffers an unforeseen reduction (even a severe one) in rating; this suggests that possible losses in the subsequent years may be considerably greater than originally anticipated by the bank. In a multinomial model, this longer-term risk is reflected in a lower value of the credit, even if the risk horizon is set at one year. In a binomial model, it is not recorded and therefore escapes the risk management "radars".

A third limitation of the model relates to the fact that recovery risk is overlooked (the model assumes that the expected recovery rates are estimated without error) and so is exposure risk (EADs of the obligors are assumed to be known with certainty).

14.7 A BRIEF COMPARISON OF THE MAIN MODELS

We can now carry out a brief comparative analysis of the models, whose main characteristics are shown in Table 14.20.

To be concise, we can classify the models based on five principal aspects:

– binomial models *(default mode)* versus multinomial models;
– future value models versus loss rate models;
– conditional models versus unconditional models;
– models based on a simulation approach versus models based on an analytical approach;
– models based on asset correlations versus models based on default correlations.

Default-mode versus multinomial models – The default-mode or binomial models consider only two possible states: default or survival. Losses occur only in case of default. Multinomial (also called multi-state) models, on the other hand, also consider the possibility of migrations to other rating classes. So even a simple downgrade results in a decrease in the market value of the credit and thus a loss.

The multinomial models are often called mark-to-market models, since they recalculate the value of the exposure "at market prices". In reality, it would be more correct to call them mark-to-model: in fact, it is often impossible to derive the values of the exposures from the market (think of all credit exposures without a liquid, efficient secondary market), so this must be estimated with an asset-pricing model (like the one based on the present value of future cash flows). Except *CreditRisk+.*™, which is a default mode model, all the other models illustrated in this chapter are multinomial models.

Future values versus loss rate – A second distinction concerns the fact that the model output is given by a distribution of future portfolio values or loss rates (i.e. losses divided by the present value of the portfolio). This distinction may seem irrelevant at first glance: in the first case, the loss corresponding to the desired confidence level is estimated indirectly as the difference between the forward value (value of the portfolio if all the credits

Table 14.20 A brief comparison of the models analyzed

Model	CreditMetrics™	PortfolioManager™	CreditRisk+™	CreditPortfolioView™
Risks covered	Migration, default and recovery	Migration, default and recovery	Default	Migration, default and recovery
Risk definition	Change in future (market) values	Losses from migrations and defaults	Losses from defaults	Change in future (market) values
Factors determining migration probability	Rating grade	Distance from *default point*	None (migration risk not considered)	*Rating*, but also economic cycle (differently for different industries or geographical areas)
Transition matrices	Constant and based on past experience	Determined by a microeconomic structure model	Non present	Determined by the macroeconomic cycle
Factors determining correlation at the portfolio level	*Asset correlation* estimated on the basis of the correlation between stock indices (multifactor model)	*Asset correlation* estimated on the basis of the correlation between stock indices (multifactor model)	*Factor loadings* (with independent background factors)	Macroeconomic factors
Sensitivity of estimates to the economic cycle	Yes, as far as obligors are up/downgraded (works well if the bank assigns the rating "point in time")	Yes, if the EDFs derived from the stock prices adjust according to the economic cycle	No. The *default* rate is volatile but independent of the cycle	Yes, by adjusting the transition matrices (and possibly also by up/downgrading borrowers)
Recovery rate	Fixed or random (beta distribution)	Random (beta distribution)	Deterministic	Random (empirical distribution)
Approach adopted	Simulations	Simulations	Analytical	Simulations

retain their original ratings) and any given future market value; in the second case, it is estimated directly. Indeed, the difference is subtler and concerns the causal factors underlying the loss. Future-value models, in fact, use as input the spread curve by maturity (related to the various rating grades) computed over risk-free rates (typically, on government securities). Hence, the spread represents an input of these models. On the contrary, in the loss-rate models, no prior knowledge of the spreads is needed, which in fact may become an output of the model. As will be shown in Chapter 15, in fact, "fair" spreads can be obtained based on the expected loss rate, the VaR and the unit cost (that is, the rate of return required by the bank shareholders[35]) of the capital the bank must hold to cover credit risk.

CreditMetrics™ is a typical market value model. *CreditRisk+™*, on the other hand, is a loss rate model. CreditPortfolioView and CreditManager can be used in both modes.

Conditional versus unconditional – In conditional models, such as *CreditPortfolioView™*, the estimates of default probability and migration based on historical frequencies are "conditioned" by the phase of the economic cycle, i.e. modified to reflect expansion or recession. In expansions, the historical default and downgrading rates are adjusted downward, while upgrade frequencies are increased. In recessions, of course, the opposite occurs. This "conditioning" is based on empirical evidence showing how default and migration rates react to the macroeconomic cycle. The unconditional models, on the contrary, make no such correction and always use long-term average data.

Though apparently incorrect and contrary to the empirical evidence, the unconditional approach has its own logic, if used along with a point-in-time rating system (such as those of many banks). In this case, in fact, the analysts assign a company to a certain rating class also based on the current state (and immediate future outlook) of the industries in which it operates, and more generally on overall macroeconomic conditions. Consequently, changes in the economic cycle are promptly echoed in a rating change. Thus if default and migration rates were to be conditioned to the cycle, this would result in the effect of the economic cycle being considered twice. If the rating system works "through-the-cycle", however, and more stable ratings are generated (that hardly react to the macroeconomic cycle), then the use of conditional transition matrices seems appropriate. However, even if the rating system is based, in principle, on a "through the cycle approach" it is unclear to what point an analyst, in formulating his/her opinion, can actually abstract from the current phase of the economic cycle.

Monte Carlo simulation versus analytical solution – Unlike the VaR models for market risks, which are often based on normal distributions, credit risk models must use different distributions that reflect the skewed nature of credit losses.

To achieve this result, one may proceed in two ways. First, one can formulate no explicit assumption on shape of the loss probability distribution, and simply generate it through a Monte Carlo simulation. Alternatively ("analytical solution") one can assume a probability density function which differs from the normal and is characterized by the desired degree of skew (e.g. a beta or a gamma distribution[36]). In practice, the analytical

---

[35] For details, see Chapter 15.
[36] Both these distributions are not just skewed, but also show a degree of skewness that decreases as the mean increases. Since the mean expresses the expected loss rate on the portfolio, this implies that the degree of skewness of the distribution decreases as the average rating of the obligors in the portfolio declines. This is

models replace the (arbitrary) assumption of a normal distribution with other assumptions, equally arbitrary but more consistent with the empirical evidence on credit risk. It thus becomes possible to derive the VaR and other measures of risk without resorting to simulation procedures.

Asset correlation versus default correlation – The correlation between obligors depends on the fact that their creditworthiness is a function not only of specific factors of the individual companies but also of common or "systematic" factors. It is therefore necessary, on the one hand, to establish what these systematic factor are and, on the other, to link those factors to the risk of a each credit exposure.

The models for measuring credit risk, from this viewpoint, follow a *bottom-up* approach, similar to that used to measure market risks on a portfolio of securities. In the case of market risks, the portfolio is "associated" with elementary risk factors (interest rates, foreign exchange rates, stock indices, etc.) by means of a suitable "mapping" of individual positions.[37] Likewise, the credit risk models associate the "health" of the individual obligors to several elementary systematic risk factors (e.g. industries or geographical areas), plus a specific or idiosyncratic risk component (which can be eliminated through portfolio diversification).[38]

In this context, the measurement of portfolio risk can be based on two different measures of correlation. The first is the correlation between default rates (*default correlation*), the second is the correlation between asset value returns of each pair of obligors (in turn, built starting with the correlations between national or industry stock indices).[39] While *CreditMetrics™* and *PortfolioManager™* use asset correlations, *Creditrisk+™* makes it possible to estimate a measure of default correlation, using (14.21). The difference is less substantive than it might seem: it is possible, in fact, under appropriate assumptions, to "translate" the asset correlations into default correlations and vice versa (see Appendix 14A).

14.8 SOME LIMITATIONS OF THE CREDIT RISK MODELS

The analysis of the models in this chapter shows that the banking and financial industry, supported by consultants and economists, have paid an enormous effort to improve their systems for measuring and managing credit risk. This effort has led to a level of sophistication unthinkable until a few years ago. The lending and credit management activity, the most traditional and sometimes the most antiquated of the various banking businesses, has undergone a sort of revolution. The measurement and management of credit risk at

---

consistent with the empirical fact that losses on a portfolio of investment grade obligors are more skewed than those on a portfolio of *junk bonds*.

[37] See Chapter 5.

[38] A more refined approach contemplates the breakdown of the "first level" systematic factors (industries, countries, geographical regions) based on their sensitivity to the changes in some "second level" systematic factors (macroeconomic variables such as interest rate levels, real GDP growth, foreign exchange rates, employment rates, etc.). Thus, for example, the textile industry might be particularly sensitive to changes in foreign exchange rates (if a large portion of production is exported) and less sensitive to interest rates (if the companies finance themselves primarily with equity). In this way, the changes in creditworthiness of each obligor are associated with changes in the "second level" factors, including an estimate of correlations (for example, the correlation between interest rates and foreign exchange rates or between inflation and GDP growth).

[39] The differences between these two definitions of correlation are further explained in Appendix 14A.

most of the major international banks benefit from young personnel with strong quantitative training, drawn by the prospect of working in a sector with interesting prospects for professional growth.

In spite of this progress, the models examined in the previous sections still present several limitations, which are briefly illustrated in the rest of this section. For this reason, we can think of them as "first-generation models",[40] to be replaced by more sophisticated schemes.

14.8.1   The treatment of recovery risk

Except for *CreditRisk+*™ (which considers LGD known with certainty), all the other models examined allow to treat recovery rate as random, and thus to consider recovery risk. They suffer from two limitations, however, partly interconnected.

First, recovery risk is usually treated as entirely idiosyncratic, i.e. independent of systematic risk factors and totally associated with the specific characteristics of the individual obligors and loans. If fluctuations in recovery rates on different exposures are mutually independent, then recovery risk is totally diversifiable. In other words, its impact can be reduced to zero by simply lending to a sufficiently large number of obligors. In reality, however, recovery risk (and not only default risk) may be partly systematic in nature; if this is the case, its impact on the credit risk of a portfolio becomes significant. A model that overlooks this fact could therefore underestimate total credit risk.

Secondly, changes in recovery rates are treated as independent from changes in default rates. On the contrary, PD and LGD may be driven by common factors and may therefore be positively correlated. As we saw in Chapter 12, this eventuality is supported by considerable empirical evidence, as well as by various theoretical reasons. Of course, a positive correlation between PD and LGD leads to greater losses (both expected and unexpected), since the two distinct drivers of credit risk tend to "strike together".

14.8.2   The assumption of independence between exposure risk and default risk

A second limitation of the models seen in this chapter is the fact that EAD is usually treated as known. Even if it were made stochastic (e.g., through a Monte Carlo simulation that generates various scenarios with values higher or lower than the expected EAD), it would be treated basically as independent of default probabilities (PD). In reality, these two risk factors might be correlated.

One example are the exposures related to OTC-traded derivatives. As illustrated in Chapter 16, they depend on the market factors affecting the current value of the derivative (interest rates, foreign exchange rates, etc.): if, for example, we consider an interest rate swap, the value of the position (and thus the exposure to credit risk, also known as loan equivalent exposure) would increase along with an increase in market rates. However, this increase in rates might also result in an increase in the default probability of the counterparty (particularly if it were heavily indebted short-term and had to renegotiate new debt at higher rates). This would result in a positive correlation between *EAD* and *PD*. In this case, the true VaR for credit risk would be greater than that found assuming the two variables to be independent. The models analyzed in this chapter thus underestimate VaR if there is a positive correlation between default risk and exposure risk.

---

[40] See Crouhy, Galai and Mark (2000), pp. 426–427.

14.8.3   The assumption of independence between credit risk and market risk

A third limitation concerns the assumption that credit risk and market risk are independent. The models examined assume, in fact, that the level of interest rates is known with certainty; in the same way, the models for market risks seen in the second part of this volume do not consider credit risk. In reality, the two risks may be correlated, as the following example illustrates.

Consider a corporate bond in euros issued by a company with a BBB rating. The bond is characterized by both credit risk (possibility that the issuer may default or be downgraded to a lower rating, or that the estimate of recovery rate is optimistic) and market risk (possible upward shift in the curve of zero-coupon rates in euros). In both cases, the price of the security would suffer a decrease. The models we have presented treat the two risk components separately.[41]

This criticism has led, in the late Nineties, to the development of some reduced-form models, mainly due to Duffie, Jarrow, Lando, Singleton and Turnbull. In these models, the level of interest rates is generally a random variable, and the default and migration probabilities are linked to systematic risk factors, including the level of interest rates. Credit risk and market risk are therefore considered jointly, and in an interconnected way. These models, however, have typically be applied to limited portfolios (e.g., traded corporate bonds); it seems difficult, however, to generalize them all the credits (including loans) of a bank.[42]

Another response to this criticism comes from a "second generation" model recently developed by Standard & Poor's ("*Portfolio Risk Tracker*", see Servigny et al., 2003). This model, in fact, assumes both stochastic interest rates[43] and stochastic spreads, treating market risk and credit risk (or, more properly, "spread risk") together. It also expressly manages the correlation between PD and LGD.

14.8.4   The impossibility of backtesting

One final problem relates to the impossibility of verifying the validity of the risk measurement generated by these models through statistically-reliable backtesting procedures. This is due to the fact that the time horizon adopted by the models (usually one year) is much longer than that used for market risk (typically one day). This implies that the historical data necessary to perform backtesting should cover an overly broad time horizon. The market risk models are often *backtested* by comparing the daily VaR for the past 250 days with the corresponding actual economic results (see Chapter 8): for credit risk, a similar comparison would require the use of data relative to the past 250 years!

Partly for this reason, the Basel Committee, which in 1996 had allowed the use of internal VaR models for market risk for regulatory purposes, when reforming the capital requirements in 2004, decided not to permit banks to use their own VaR models for credit risk to compute mandatory minimum capital.

---

[41] To this critique, one could object that the management of the two risks is typically carried out in a separate way within financial institutions. The unit required to measure/manage market risks is generally independent of the unit concerned with measuring and managing credit risk.

[42] Some of these models are used for pricing credit derivatives.

[43] The model thus allows analysts to treat floating-rate instruments without utilizing "*loan equivalent*" exposures (see Chapter 16).

Box 14.1: The opinion of The Economist

Model Behaviour

Banks' credit-risk models are mind-boggingly complex. But the question they try to answer is actually quite simple: how much of a bank's lending might plausibly turn bad? Armed with the answer, banks can set aside enough capital to make sure they stay solvent should the worst happen.

No model, of course, can take account of every possibility. Credit risk models try to put a value on how much a bank should realistically expect to lose in the 99.9 % or so of the time that passes for normality. This requires estimating three different things: the likelihood that any given borrower will default; the amount that might be recoverable if that happened; and the likelihood that the borrower will default at the same time others are doing so.

This last factor is crucial. In effect, it will decide whether some unforeseen event is likely to wreck the bank. Broadly speaking, the less likely it is that many loans will go bad at the same time – that is, the lower the correlation of the individual risks – the lower the risk will be of a big loss from bad loans.

None of this is easy to do. Many of the banking industry's brightest rocket scientists have given over the task. Credit Suisse Financial Products has launched "CreditRisk+", which attempts to provide an actuarial model of the likelihood that a loan will turn bad, much as an insurance firm would produce a forecast of likely claims. McKinsey, a consultancy, has a model that links default probabilities to macroeconomic variables, such as interest rates and growth in GDP. J.P. Morgan's "CreditMetrics™" applies a theoretical model developed by KMV, a Californian firm, which calculates the risk that a firm will default by looking at changes in the price of its shares.

With the help of Taylor-series expansions, range integrals, negative binomial distributions and so forth (we'll spare you the details), the models go from calculating the probability that any borrower will default, to estimating the chances that Wal-Mart, say, will default at the same time as Woolworth or that loans to French property developers will go bad at the same time as loans to Air France. This leads to a series of loss probabilities for the bank's entire portfolio of loans. This will indicate the maximum loss that the bank needs to prepare for by setting aside capital.

Credit-risk models have evolved from "value-at-risk" models, which were developed to estimate how much of a bank's trading portfolio – foreign exchange, cash, securities and derivatives – it could lose in a single day because of adverse movements in financial prices. These models have been criticised for assuming that past correlations in the prices of different assets will hold in future and for making simplistic assumptions about the range of possible price changes. They also fail when prices for the underlying assets become unavailable – when a stock market suspends trading, for example. These criticisms apply just as well to credit-risk models.

Value-at-risk models have one big advantage over credit-risk models, however. They generally deal with assets that are publicly traded, so there is a vast amount of data for the models to crunch. It is far harder to come up with data on the market value of loans or on how much of the value of bad loans banks eventually recover. That leaves it uncertain whether the results cranked out by credit-risk models are statistically valid. The models are clever, all right. But how much relation they bear to reality may not be clear until after the next recession.

Source: The Economist, February 28, 1998, p. 80. © The Economist Newspaper Limited, London

SELECTED QUESTIONS AND EXERCISES

1. Which of the following is used by the CreditMetrics model to estimate default correlations?

   (A) CreditMetrics does not use correlations and implicitly assumes they are zero, i.e. independence.
   (B) The equity returns correlations.
   (C) The correlations between corporate bond spreads with respect to Treasury returns.
   (D) The correlations between historical default rates.

2. A bank, using the Creditmetrics model, has issued a loan to a company classified as "Rating 3" by its internal rating system. The loan will pay a coupon of 5 million euros after exactly one year, another coupon of 5 million euros after exactly two years and a final flow (coupon + principal) of 105 million euros after exactly three years. The one-year transition matrix of the bank is the following:

		Final status					
		Rating 1	Rating 2	Rating 3	Rating 4	Rating 5	Default
Initial status	Rating 1	90.0%	5.0%	3.0%	1.0%	0.5%	0.5%
	Rating 2	4.0%	88.0%	4.0%	2.0%	1.0%	1.0%
	Rating 3	2.0%	4.5%	85.0%	5.0%	2.0%	1.5%
	Rating 4	1.0%	4.0%	9.0%	80.0%	3.5%	2.5%
	Rating 5	0.5%	3.5%	6.0%	10.0%	75.0%	5.0%

Assume that the zero-coupon curve is flat at 4% (yearly compounded), and that issuers falling into different rating classes pay the following premia, which are constant for all maturities:

Rating 1	Rating 2	Rating 3	Rating 4	Rating 5
0.26%	0.51%	0.76%	1.26%	2.52%

Based on the above and assuming that the loan as a recovery value (in the event of default) of 70 million euros, compute:

   (a) the probability distribution of the future values of the loan after one year;
   (b) the expected value of the loan (after one year);
   (c) the VaR, with a confidence level of 95%, of the loan (after one year).

3. Which of the following statements is true?

(A) Creditrisk+ does not take into account migration risk and is based on the assumption of independence between the different bank's borrowers.

(B) CreditRisk+ takes into account migration risk and allows to indirectly model the correlations between the bank's different borrowers.

(C) While not taking into account migration risk, CreditRisk+ allows to indirectly model the correlations between the bank's different borrowers.

(D) CreditRisk+ does take into account migration risk and allows to indirectly model the correlations between the bank's different borrowers.

4. The probability of obtaining a given number of defaults on a loan portfolio can be well proxied by a Poisson distribution only if:

(A) individual default probabilities are low and defaults are correlated;
(B) individual default probabilities are high and defaults are not correlated;
(C) individual default probabilities are low and defaults are not correlated;
(D) individual default probabilities are low, the number of loans is sufficiently large, and defaults are not correlated.

5. Default correlation is incorporated into the CreditRisk+ model...

(A) ... by making the expected number of defaults a stochastic variable;
(B) ... by making the expected number of customers in the portfolio a stochastic variable;
(C) ... by estimating the correlation coefficient between the value changes of the assets of the different clients' couples;
(D) ... by "banding" loans into a number of subportfolios where all exposures are approximately equal.

6. In case of a recession, the default probability of company Alpha is equal to 2 % while the one of company Beta is 4 %. In case of an economic expansion, both probabilities are halved. Based on a given economic scenario (recession or expansion), the defaults of the two companies can be considered independent. The analysts estimate that a recession has a 40 % probability to occur while an expansion has a 60 % probability to occur.

(1) Calculate the non conditional default probability of Alpha and Beta;
(2) Calculate the joint default probability of company Alpha and Beta conditional to the two scenarios;
(3) Calculate the joint default probability not conditional to any economic scenario, and indicate whether it signals a positive correlation between the two defaults.

7. A bank using the Creditmetrics model has estimated the following transition matrix and spot interest rates (zero coupon).

Transition Matrix

	A	B	C	D	E	default
A	98.0%	1.0%	0.3%	0.1%	0.1%	0.5%
B	0.8%	95.0%	1.5%	1.0%	0.7%	1.0%
C	0.2%	1.0%	93.0%	2.3%	2.0%	1.5%
D	0.1%	1.9%	3.0%	90.0%	3.0%	2.0%
E	0.0%	1.0%	3.0%	4.5%	87.5%	4.0%

Zero-coupon spot curves

	1 year	2 years	3 years	4 years	5 years	6 years
A	3.0%	3.5%	3.7%	4.0%	4.2%	4.6%
B	3.5%	4.0%	4.2%	4.5%	4.7%	5.1%
C	4.0%	4.5%	4.7%	5.0%	5.2%	5.6%
D	4.5%	5.0%	5.2%	5.5%	5.7%	6.1%
E	5.0%	5.5%	5.7%	6.0%	6.2%	6.6%

Assume the bank holds only one loan, granted to a C rated company; this loan has only one final cash flow (interest expenses plus principal repayment), equal to 1,000 euro, maturing in exactly two years. The estimated value of the loan in the event of a default is 400 euro. Using Creditmetrics, compute:

- the current value of the loan;
- its expected value;
- its 98% confidence level VaR over a one year horizon.

Appendix 14A
Asset correlation versus default correlation

The correlation between the returns on assets ("asset correlation") is a different concept from that of correlation between defaults ("default correlation"). The former takes values typically higher than the latter.

In presenting CreditMetrics (see equations 14.1 and 14.1a) we showed that, if the AVRs of two companies A and B are normally distributed, their joint default probability ($p_{A,B}$) can be written as:

$$p_{A,B} = \Pr(r_A < z_{def,A}; r_b < z_{def,B}) = N(z_{def,A}, z_{def,B}; \rho_{A,B}) \qquad (14A.1)$$

Where $\rho_{A,B}$ (or simply ρ) is the asset correlation, r_A and r_B are the AVRs of the two companies and $z_{def,A}, z_{def,B}$ are the respective default points. Recalling that the default point of a company j is that value of the AVRs that corresponds to a cumulative probability equal to the PD, p_j, of the obligor:

$$z_{def,j} = N^{-1}(p_j) \qquad (14A.2)$$

(14A.1) can be rewritten as

$$p_{A,B} = N(N^{-1}(p_A), N^{-1}(p_B); \rho_{A,B}) \qquad (14A.3)$$

Also, recalling that the coefficient of correlation between two random Bernoulli (i.e. dichotomous, i.e. binary) variables x and y is given by:

$$\rho_{x,y} = \frac{p_{x=1 \wedge y=1} - p_{x=1} p_{y=1}}{\sqrt{p_{x=1}(1 - p_{x=1}) p_{y=1}(1 - p_{y=1})}} \qquad (14A.4)$$

the coefficient of correlation $\delta_{A,B}$ between the defaults of A and B (both being binary variables) can be simply written as

$$\delta_{A,B} = \frac{p_{A,B} - p_A p_B}{\sqrt{p_A(1 - p_A)p_B(1 - p_B)}} = \frac{N(N^{-1}(p_A), N^{-1}(p_B); \rho_{A,B}) - p_A p_B}{\sqrt{p_A(1 - p_A)p_B(1 - p_B)}} \qquad (14A.5)$$

Note that 14A.5 creates a relationship between asset correlation ($\rho_{A,B}$) and default correlation ($\delta_{-A,B}$) in the case where the AVRs are normally distributed. Also note that this relationship is not fixed but depends on the PDs of the two obligors.

Let us consider, for example, the two companies seen in section 14.3.2, with initial ratings of A and BB. Their PDs were 0.06 % and 1.06 %, respectively. The joint default probability estimated on the basis of asset correlation of 20 % was equal to 0.0054 %.
(14A.5) tells us that the default correlation is equal to

$$\delta_{BB,A} = \frac{0.0054\,\% - (1.06\,\% \cdot 0.06\,\%)}{\sqrt{1.06\,\%(1 - 1.06\,\%)0.06\,\%(1 - 0.06\,\%)}} = 1.90\,\%$$

Note that it is around one-tenth the correlation between asset returns (20 %).

Some Applications of
Credit Risk Measurement Models

15.1 INTRODUCTION

While the previous chapters have focused on the various facets of credit risk measurement, in this chapter we will shown how the results derived there can be used to improve the effectiveness of a bank's actual operations.

This does not imply that the models presented above are totally reliable and free from defects. Indeed, the desire to translate them into real applications comes, in part, right from the awareness that further refinements are needed, and that only through the practical usage of these models in day-to-day bank operations will it be possible to bring out their deficiencies and to improve them.

The focus of this chapter will mainly be on two applications: loan pricing and risk-adjusted performance (RAP) measurement. We will also mention other applications, including establishing limits to the autonomy of the risk-taking units and optimizing portfolio composition.

In section 15.2 we will analyze each of the cost components that impact on the price of a loan and, in particular, costs related to expected and unexpected losses (which imply a certain consumption of economic capital); their impact will be demonstrated through an example.

In section 15.3, we will take a look at risk-adjusted performance. This issue becomes particularly important when a financial institution is operating as a price taker in a highly elastic market and is not, therefore, able to set the price for its products on its own.

Section 15.4 illustrates briefly how a system of limits can be imposed, based on expected loss and credit VaR measurements, on the autonomy of a bank's business units. In fact, the loss measures seen in the previous chapters allow significant improvements over traditional limit systems based on the nominal value of loan exposure.

Finally, section 15.5 will briefly mention one more class of applications that seek to optimize the overall composition of a loan portfolio.

15.2 LOAN PRICING

In 1999, a task force created by the Basel Committee to analyze the internal rating systems of the world's leading banks came to the conclusion that more than 80 % of banks with an in-house rating system used it to set interest rates in line with the risk content of their loans.

In other words, one of the most important and widespread uses of a credit risk measurement system is risk-adjusted pricing.

In fact, for quite some time, many banks had been setting lending rates in a manner that only partially accounted for the actual risk of the loans. On the one hand, this was made possible by the fact that the markets for bank loans were not fully competitive, and allowed for extra-profits to be reaped. On the other hand, this was due to the fact that in periods of economic expansion, banks tended to underestimate credit risk and apply rates that were too low, thereby destroying value for their shareholders. More generally, the rates applied to different customers were not sufficiently differentiated based on risk: this resulted in a cross-subsidization phenomenon, by which some groups of customers paid higher rates than required, thereby implicitly subsidizing other customer groups, paying interest rates below the level demanded by their actual risk level.

Such widespread mispricings were due to the very special time profile followed by the costs of a loan. In fact, only a portion of these costs becomes apparent at the time the loan is issued, whereas losses due to defaults can be assessed only at a later date. For this reason, in order to set prices in a rational manner, we also need to estimate the potential expected and unexpected losses based on techniques, like those surveyed in the previous chapters, that became available only in recent times.

A price-setting bank should set the price of a loan in such a way that it covers at least its production costs, either immediate or deferred. For the sake of simplicity, in the sections that follow, we will be setting prices at this minimum level;[1] obviously enough, if a bank is working as a monopolist or somehow benefits from its particular market position, it will be able to apply a rate that is above this minimum.

Also, we will not be giving any special consideration to direct and indirect operating costs, as this is kind of direct costing issues has already been tackled by most banks and refers to concepts that are quite different from the risk management and value creation issues discussed in this book. We will therefore be focusing on the "deferred cost" components linked to possible credit losses.

Before moving on, it is worth noticing that a bank is only free to set the prices of its loans (i.e. to act as a *price setter*) when it operates in a sufficiently inelastic market, where it enjoys an adequate market power. If, instead, a bank operates as a price taker, forced to accept the prices imposed upon it by the market, credit risk measurement models are still useful in that they enable a bank to identify (and refuse) loans for which the market rate is too low. Also, as shown in section 15.3, these models make it possible to compute the risk-adjusted performance of a loan, given its price, which can then be compared with the bank shareholders' profitability targets.

15.2.1 The cost of the expected loss

The first cost component is the expected loss. In order to cover the expected loss on a loan, the bank needs to apply a rate, equal to the risk-free rate r plus a spread d_{EL}, that makes the expected return on the loan (given its probability of default PD and the loss given default LGD[2]) equal to that of a risk-free investment of the same amount.[3]

$$(1 + r + d_{EL})[(1 - PD) + (1 - LGD) \cdot PD] = (1 + r) \qquad (15.1)$$

from which we get:

$$(1 + r + d_{EL}) = \frac{1 + r}{1 - PD \cdot LGD} - 1 \qquad (15.2)$$

---

[1] According to classical economic theory, under perfect competition, a company sets prices in order to *exactly* cover production costs. Of course, this does not mean that the company makes no profit (and is moved by pure philanthropy...). Cost components leading to the final prices also include the rate of return on capital, a "normal" or "physiological" rate of return demanded by shareholders on the capital provided to the firm (based on the returns provided by other investments and on the risk level of the company).
[2] Notice that in (15.1) the rate of recovery (1-LGD) refers to the final amount, $1 + r + d_1$, not to the initial principal.
[3] See also Appendix 11A.

or:

$$r + d_{EL} = \frac{r + PD \cdot LGD}{1 - PD \cdot LGD} = \frac{r + ELR}{1 - ELR} \qquad (15.3)$$

where ELR, the product of PD and LGD, is the expected loss rate.[4]
    The spread d_{EL} represents the cost of the expected loss:

$$d_{EL} = \frac{ELR \cdot (1 + r)}{1 - ELR} \qquad (15.4)$$

Consider a bank ("Bank A") that needs to price a loan. Its risk-free rate, r, will be the internal transfer rate (ITR)[5] consistent with the maturity of the loan, since this is the rate at which funds can be invested or raised. Let us assume, then, that the bank's ITR is 4%. Let us further assume that the probability of default (PD) of a given customer is 1% and the related loss given default (LGD) is 50%.
    In this case, the price of a loan with a residual life of one year will be:

$$TIT + d_{EL} = \frac{4\% + 0.5\%}{1 - 0.5\%} = 4.522\%$$

while from equation (15.4) we get:

$$d_{EL} = \frac{0.5\% \cdot (1 + 4\%)}{1 - 0.5\%} = 0.522\%$$

15.2.2 The cost of economic capital absorbed by unexpected losses

The price calculated above would be adequate for a risk-neutral bank, which would be indifferent to receiving a given amount M with certainty or an uncertain amount having an expected value of M.
    This, of course, is not very realistic. Banks, in particular, are risk averse because, if lending provides lower than expected returns (i.e. losses), they could go out of business. This would not be appreciated by their shareholders, and even less by their supervisors.
    In order to limit the risk of bankruptcy, banks must hold an amount of capital that is large enough to cover potential unexpected losses. This is why, as seen in Chapter 14, the VaR on a credit portfolio is also called the risk capital or economic capital associated with it. Therefore, in order to incorporate risk aversion into our pricing model, we need to ensure that the rate also covers the cost of economic capital held against unexpected losses.
    To that aim, suppose that, using the models described in the previous chapters, we have calculated the VaR for the bank's loan portfolio. Let us further imagine that we have allocated this VaR to the various individual credit exposures, associating each with

---

[4] Here we have assumed that exposure at default (EAD) be equal to the current exposure, i.e. that no exposure risk is present. If EAD were greater than the current exposure, we would need to adjust (3) to consider exposure risk, as well. As noted by Resti (2003), this could be done by using an adjusted LGD to account for the effect of exposure risk. However, as explained in the introduction to Part III, exposure risk due to the unused portion of a credit commitment should be priced through a commitment fee, rather than being included in the lending rate.

[5] See Chapter 4.

its own consumption of economic capital. That is, we have estimated the quantity of risk associated with each loan, which must be covered by the capital of the bank's shareholders. The cost of capital depends on the shareholders' return target, i.e. the cost of equity, r_e, that the bank has either explicitly or implicitly agreed to provide its owners. Taking this cost into consideration, equation (15.1) can be updated as follows:

$$(1 + r + d_{EL} + d_{UL})[(1 - PD) + (1 - LGD) \cdot PD] = (1 + r) + VaR(r_e - r) \quad (15.5)$$

where *VaR* indicates the amount of economic capital per euro of loan that is needed to cover the unexpected losses on the exposure (e.g. 7 cents per euro).

In practice, equation (15.5) requires the price given to the customer (which includes a spread both for the expected loss, d_{EL}, and for the unexpected loss, d_{UL}) to generate an expected amount equal to that of a risk-free investment *plus* a premium to be paid to shareholders $(r_e - r)$ on the capital provided to cover the risks of the loan.

The right-hand side of (15.5) can be interpreted as the cost of the funds needed to finance the loan. In this case, notice that VaR (i.e. economic capital) has only been charged the net risk premium $r_e - r$, because the loan is already entirely financed by debt, at a cost of $r\%$, and absorbs capital only "virtually". In other words, economic capital is not physically used to finance the loans, but is only "virtually absorbed" by the loans based on their riskiness.[6]

In order to see the second member of the equation as the cost of financing the loan, we can rewrite it as follows:

$$(1 + r) + VaR(r_e - r) = (1 + r)(1 - VaR) + (1 + r_e)VaR \quad (15.6)$$

For example, if VaR is 7 cents, equation (15.6) implies that, for each euro of loan, 93 cents must be financed with debt at the rate r, and 7 cents with capital, which needs to earn a rate $r_e > r$.

From (15.5), we have

$$r + d_{EL} + d_{UL} = \frac{r + ELR + VaR(r_e - r)}{1 - ELR} \quad (15.7)$$

and

$$d_{EL} + d_{UL} = \frac{(1 + r)ELR + VaR(r_e - r)}{1 - ELR} \quad (15.8)$$

Comparing (15.4) and (15.8), we then get

$$d_{UL} = \frac{VaR(r_e - r)}{1 - ELR} \quad (15.9)$$

which is the spread required to cover the cost of the unexpected loss.

Let us go back to the example in the previous section (PD = 1 %; LGD = 50 %; and a risk-free rate, ITR, of 4 %). Suppose that we have estimated that the capital absorbed by

---

[6] This step has significant repercussions on the calculation of the cost of capital for the various units of a bank (see Chapter 24). In fact, given that capital is not physically delivered to the various risk-taking units, the return on capital that these units must achieve will be solely a function of the risk premium and not of the risk-free rate (which may be obtained simply by investing the bank's capital on the interbank market).

the loan (*VaR*) is equal to 8 %, i.e. 8 cents for each euro lent and, finally, that the bank's cost of equity (r_e) is 12 %.

The price of the loan using equation (15.7) will be:

$$TIT + d_{EL} + d_{UL} = \frac{4\% + 0.5\% + 8\% \cdot (12\% - 4\%)}{1 - 0.5\%} \cong 5.166\%$$

and the cost of the unexpected loss (equation 15.9) will be:

$$d_{UL} = \frac{8\%(12\% - 4\%)}{1 - 0.5\%} \cong 0.643\%$$

The results of this example are summarised in Table 15.1 (second column). The sum of d_{EL} and d_{UL} represents the spread that the bank should add to the internal transfer rate in order to set the lending rate.

Table 15.1 Computation examples for lending rates

	Bank A (lower diversification benefits)	Bank B (stronger diversification benefits)
(a) VaR	8.000 %	6.000 %
(b) ITR	4.000 %	4.000 %
(c) d_{EL}	0.523 %	0.523 %
(d) d_{UL}	0.643 %	0.482 %
(e) Lending rate ($b + c + d$)	5.166 %	5.005 %

One of the most delicate steps when using this kind of formulae is the estimation of the VaR to be allocated to the loan. Indeed, given that the VaR calculation for an entire loan portfolio is already a difficult, delicate task (and one for which we need complex models, such as those discussed in Chapter 14), the allocation of this VaR to the various individual loans within the portfolio is a particularly challenging step.

On the one hand, we cannot calculate the VaR for each individual loan as if it were the bank's only asset (the so-called "stand-alone VaR") because this would lead us to ignore the risk diversification benefits resulting from holding more than one loan. In fact, the sum of the various standalone VaRs would be significantly higher than the VaR for the bank's portfolio.

On the other hand, it is not even advisable to turn to measures such as marginal VaR (see Chapter 14), because these would assign to each individual loan all the diversification benefits arising from its interaction with all of the bank's other loans. As a result, the sum of the marginal VaRs tends to be less than the VaR of the bank's portfolio, because the same diversification benefit is counted multiple times. Furthermore, if one or more of the remaining loans should be revoked or reach maturity, the benefits of loan diversification would decrease, and the marginal VaR originally applied on the loan would turn out to be underestimated, as would the loan's price.

Generally speaking, the portfolio VaR (economic capital) needs to be divided among the various loans in such a way that it:

– ensures that the sum of economic capital allocated to the individual loans coincides with the bank's capital;
– "rewards", with a comparatively lower "burden" of economic capital, those loans that better diversify risk as compared with the bank's portfolio as a whole. Therefore if, for example, a bank has considerable exposure in the oil industry, then loans to companies in this industry must be assigned a higher VaR than loans, say to fisheries or farms (having the same PDs, EADs and LGDs).

The latter point explains why two banks with similar rating systems (that is, that assign the same PDs, LGDs, and EADs to the same loan issued to the same client), paying the same ITR and the same cost of capital, but which have different portfolio mixes in place, could ask different rates on the same loan. The same position could, in fact, be priced differently by the two banks, as they could, based on their current portfolio compositions in terms of industries and countries, assign different VaRs to the loan, because the contribution it makes to overall portfolio risk is different.

Let us go back once more to our example above, and imagine that a second bank ("Bank B"), despite having calculated the same PD and the LGD, feels it needs to allocate only 6 cents per euro (rather than 8 cents) of economic capital to a loan because the borrower operates in an industry that is less correlated with those in which the bank already has a strong presence.

The second bank's price for the loan will then be:

$$TIT + d_{EL} + d_{UL} = \frac{4\% + 0.5\% + 6\% \cdot (12\% - 4\%)}{1 - 0.5\%} \cong 5.005\%$$

where:

$$d_{EL} = \frac{0.5\% \cdot (1 + 4\%)}{1 - 0.5\%} \cong 0.523\%$$

$$d_{UL} = \frac{8\%(12\% - 4\%)}{1 - 0.5\%} \cong 0.643\%$$

These results are also shown in Table 15.1 above (third column). It is interesting to note that the expected loss spread is the same for the two banks, given that it depends solely on the risk of the new loan (which we have assumed to be the same for the two banks) and not also on the composition of the bank's existing portfolio. Conversely, the unexpected loss spread is portfolio-dependent and is affected by the characteristics of the other loans already issued by the two banks.

From equation (15.7), we can see that the price is a function of five factors:[7]

(1) the probability of default by the borrower (PD);
(2) the loss given default (LGD);
(3) the economic capital (VaR) absorbed by the loan;

---

[7] As mentioned in the text, for the sake of simplicity we have ignored the bank's operating costs. However, the rate should obviously cover at least the variable costs directly attributable to the loan.

(4) the internal transfer rate for exposures of the same maturity (ITR);

(5) the banks' cost of equity (r_e).

The first factor (PD) is summarised in the counterparty's rating. The second (LGD) is a function of the type of loan and, in particular, of any collateral provided (see Chapter 12). The third factor is based on the interaction between the new loan and the overall credit portfolio of the bank. The last two are independent from the characteristics of the borrower/loan, and depend on more general factors, such as the level of interest rates, the state of the capital markets, and the bank's overall risk profile.

For the sake of simplicity, the examples seen in this section involved one-year loans. However, the same logic would apply to transactions with longer maturities. This makes it possible to set up "price lists" that show the minimum rates to be applied for various maturities, ratings classes, types of collateral, etc.

Table 15.2 shows an example, achieved by keeping LGD constant and varying the loan's maturity and borrower rating (each rating corresponds to a different PD used for pricing).

Of course, if we change the collateral and the loan's seniority, this would alter the expected LGD, and it would be necessary to update the values of this Table. The same would occur if we changed other initial parameters, such as the term structure of ITRs or the risk premium on shareholders' capital.

Price-lists like Table 15.2 can be used to help a branch to negotiate prices that are in line with the loan's risk level, thereby avoiding issuing loans at rates that are too low to pay the cost of the various types of loss (thereby destroying value for the bank's shareholders). This shows how important the pricing formulas discussed above can be are an important tool in managing credit risk.

15.3   RISK-ADJUSTED PERFORMANCE MEASUREMENT

In the previous section, we assumed that the bank was, to some extent, free to set the price of a loan. However, things could be quite different and the bank could be operating as a price taker in a highly elastic market. For example, the bank could be assessing the rate that a customer has been offered by another bank, in order to decide whether to make a similar or better offer.

In this case, it would be necessary to follow the opposite perspective to the one seen above. Starting with the interest rate, we would need to assess the economic viability of the loan, i.e. its impact on the bank's return on economic capital.

To do this, we set the exogenously fixed lending rate at $\bar{r}$ and substitute this into the first member of equation (15.7): we then can calculate the risk premium on shareholders' capital ($r_e^* - r$) implicit in this loan rate. From:

$$\bar{r} = \frac{r + ELR + VaR(r_e^* - r)}{1 - ELR}$$

it follows that:

$$r_e^* - r = Raroc = \frac{\bar{r} \cdot (1 - ELR) - r - ELR}{VaR} \tag{15.10}$$

Table 15.2 Prices by rating and maturity for a loan with LGD = 50%

Ratings class Maturity (years)	A	B	C	D	E	F	G	H	I	L	Note: ITR
1	4.10 %	4.25 %	4.45 %	4.70 %	5.00 %	5.40 %	5.80 %	6.25 %	6.60 %	7.00 %	4.00 %
2	4.35 %	4.52 %	4.85 %	5.10 %	5.40 %	5.78 %	6.15 %	6.50 %	6.83 %	7.18 %	4.20 %
3	4.62 %	4.78 %	5.20 %	5.55 %	5.78 %	6.14 %	6.47 %	6.75 %	7.05 %	7.35 %	4.40 %
4	4.83 %	5.00 %	5.47 %	5.85 %	6.11 %	6.43 %	6.71 %	6.95 %	7.21 %	7.45 %	4.55 %
5	5.05 %	5.25 %	5.72 %	6.15 %	6.42 %	6.72 %	6.94 %	7.13 %	7.36 %	7.54 %	4.70 %
6	5.25 %	5.48 %	5.91 %	6.40 %	6.67 %	6.95 %	7.10 %	7.26 %	7.45 %	7.56 %	4.80 %
7	5.45 %	5.70 %	6.08 %	6.63 %	7.00 %	7.16 %	7.26 %	7.38 %	7.54 %	7.60 %	4.90 %
8	5.65 %	5.90 %	6.20 %	6.85 %	7.17 %	7.29 %	7.35 %	7.45 %	7.57 %	7.60 %	4.95 %
9	5.85 %	6.12 %	6.30 %	7.00 %	7.30 %	7.40 %	7.45 %	7.52 %	7.60 %	7.62 %	5.00 %
10	6.00 %	6.25 %	6.35 %	7.10 %	7.36 %	7.45 %	7.50 %	7.52 %	7.56 %	7.60 %	5.00 %

Notice that r_e^* now indicates the return actually earned by shareholders, given $\bar{r}$, and no more stands for the "optimal" target rate (r_e). The premium over the risk-free rate associated with this r_e^* is a way of expressing the bank's risk-adjusted return on capital (RAROC).[8] This is the return (here expressed as the premium over the risk-free rate) on the capital absorbed by the risks (unexpected losses) associated with the loan.

Suppose that Bank B is about to issue the loan in our example (PD = 1 %, LGD = 50 %, VaR = 6 %, r = ITR = 4 %) at a fixed rate $\bar{r}$ = 4.8 % and wishes to assess the convenience of doing so. From equation (15.10) we get:

$$Raroc = \frac{4.8\% \cdot 0.995 - 4\% - 0.5\%}{6\%} = 4.6\%$$

This RAROC must then be compared with the shareholders' return target (also expressed as a spread over the risk-free rate r). If RAROC is greater than this target (i.e. *RAROC* > $r_e - r$), the loan would increase the market value of the bank's economic capital and would, therefore, create value for the shareholders. Conversely, if the risk-adjusted performance is less than the shareholder's target (i.e. *RAROC* < $r_e - r$), the loan would destroy value for the bank and therefore should not be issued.

In the previous section, we set the shareholders' performance target (r_e) at 12 %, leading to a spread over the risk-free rate of 8 %. This value is higher than the RAROC computed with equation (15.10). Therefore, a loan at a rate of 4.8 % would erode value and should not be issued.

In reality, however, the bank could still grant the loan based on other considerations, such as the potential for cross-selling (bundling the loan with other services that earn more, like payment services earning high fees, risk-hedging derivative contracts, etc.). The loan could also be issued in order to gain a new customer or to maintain a customer relationship that, on the whole, creates value for the bank. Even so, comparing RAROC with the shareholders' return target would still be very useful because it would require the manager that wants the loan to be approved to explain and quantify the side benefits that could be earned and which lead him/her to think that the transaction is desirable.

15.4 SETTING LIMITS ON RISK-TAKING UNITS

A third important application of credit risk measurement models involves setting limits on the autonomy of the bank's various risk-taking units (e.g. branches that issue loans).

Once a system for measuring credit risk has been introduced and developed, it is possible to grant each unit a level of autonomy that is no longer based on the face value of the loans, but rather is expressed in terms of overall risk (or, better, of expected and unexpected losses).[9] This makes it possible to acknowledge the different levels of risk associated with loans to parties with different ratings, different maturities, or backed by different collateral. It is also possible (although not easy) to account for different unexpected losses on loans that show a different correlation (e.g., based on industries or geographic areas) with the existing portfolio.

---

[8] This is sometimes called the risk-adjusted return on risk-adjusted capital (RARORAC) to stress the fact that the numerator is also adjusted for the expected loss. However, given that expected loss does not represent risk in a narrow sense (right because it is expected), we prefer RAROC.

[9] Note that only the unexpected loss can be considered a risk in the true meaning of the term.

A given risk-taking unit could, given a certain limit of expected loss or VaR, grant a greater volume of loans to companies with better ratings or limit volumes but increase margins through loans to borrowers with lower ratings. In order to increase its portfolio without exceeding assigned limits, the branch could also require better collateral in order to reduce expected LGD or even (if the limit is set in terms of VaR) take full advantage of the benefits of diversification by lending to companies that operate in industries in which the bank has more limited exposure.

Let us imagine, for example, that the branches of a bank are given a simple limit of expected loss of one billion euros. Since expected loss is the product of EAD, LGD and PD, we can see that an infinite array of portfolios could be compatible with this objective. Table 15.3 shows a number of examples of such portfolios. As we can see, the maximum (face[10]) value of the permitted loans become quite different based on borrower ratings and collaterals (LGDs). A branch could, for example, issue 800 billion in secured loans (with an estimated LGD of 25 %) to A-rated borrowers or less than 20 billion in junior loans (estimated LGD of 75 %) to G-rated borrowers, and so on.

Table 15.3 Example of EAD limits (in millions of euros) associated with an EL of €1bn

Rating class (PD value in italics)	Average LGD				
	10 %	25 %	50 %	75 %	100 %
A 0.5 %	2,000,000	800,000	400,000	266,667	200,000
B 1.0 %	1,000,000	400,000	200,000	133,333	100,000
C 1.5 %	666,667	266,667	133,333	88,889	66,667
D 2.0 %	500,000	200,000	100,000	66,667	50,000
E 3.0 %	333,333	133,333	66,667	44,444	33,333
F 4.5 %	222,222	88,889	44,444	29,630	22,222
G 7.0 %	142,857	57,143	28,571	19,048	14,286

The transition from the simple limits based on the loan face value, to more sophisticated credit risk limits based on the use of EL and UL does imply a number of organizational issues. The bank needs to determine how the units are aggregated (branches? groups of branches? bank divisions?), the frequency with which limits are revised, and how the system of VaR limits and the bank's global budgeting process are integrated. Additionally, risk measures that used to look robust when analyzed in the "laboratory" of the risk

---

[10] The face value is expressed in terms of EAD, i.e. the current exposure adjusted for the CCF presented in the introduction to this part of the book.

management department, often prove to have defects and weaknesses (and require further fine-tuning) when exposed to use by the areas of the bank that are more closely involved in actual operations.

15.5   OPTIMIZING THE COMPOSITION OF THE LOAN PORTFOLIO

A fourth, and final, application is connected with the active management of the bank's global loan portfolio. Credit risk VaR models can in fact be used to create efficient portfolios that minimize the risks related to concentration and correlation across borrowers and that take full advantage of the diversification potential provided by the market.

Clearly, optimizing a bank's loan portfolio is much different from optimizing a portfolio of securities that are freely tradable on the market. On the one hand, we need to consider the limited liquidity and transparency of the market for bank loans, which cannot be traded as easily as securities; on the other, the geographic and industry concentration of a bank's loan portfolio is often the result of a particular market position and the customer relationships established over time, both of which are an asset to the bank and must not be destroyed.

As a result, a loan portfolio can only be optimized gradually and in a limited manner. Essentially, the tools available in order to alter the composition of a portfolio and its characteristics in terms of concentration and correlation are the following:

– natural portfolio turnover, i.e. the ability to replace certain loans upon maturity with loans issued to different industries or geographic areas. In order to work, such a mechanism of portfolio optimization must be highly integrated into the bank's budgeting process. That is to say, each year, the various operating units of the bank must receive not only a set of volume and margin targets, but also indications as to which segments and regions to increase or reduce;
– the use of credit derivatives, securitizations, and the secondary loan sales market, three channels that enable the bank to transfer the risks of certain positions without ruining the relationship with the customer. Such channels make it possible to separate the functions of origination and credit risk management within the bank. Loan origination is primarily a commercial function seeking out, in an essentially independent manner, market opportunities in order to issue new loans and develop customer relationships. However, these new loans, once "packaged" (i.e. structured in terms of pricing conditions, guarantees, covenants, contract clauses, etc.) do not necessarily have to remain in the bank's loan portfolio until maturity, but can be sold on the market (which may include buying protection through a credit derivative, as well as creating a special-purpose vehicle to hand over risks to private investors), thereby improving the risk/return profile of the bank's portfolio.

These credit risk transfer tools (credit derivatives, securitization, loan sales) are discussed in greater detail in the Appendix to this chapter. The ability to truly use credit risk management models in order to optimize the risk/return profile of a bank's loan portfolio will depend, in the coming years, on the development and actual widespread use of these tools.

SELECTED QUESTIONS AND EXERCISES

1. Compute the interest rate to be charged on a loan to a corporate customer knowing that: (i) the PD is equal to 0.5 %, (ii) the recovery rate is equal to 40 % of the final loan value, (iii) the 99 % confidence level VaR is equal to 5 cents for each euro, (iv) the cost of funding (r) for the bank is equal to 4 % and (v) the cost of the bank's equity capital (r_e) is equal to 10 %.

2. A bank is issuing a one-year loan to a customer with a PD of 1 % and a LGD of 30 %. The internal transfer rate is 6 % and the capital at risk (VaR) absorbed by the loan is estimated at 13 cents per euro. Compute the rate on the loan that allows the bank to pay a 12 % return on equity (cost of equity) to its shareholders. Alternatively, assume the bank has to issue the loan at a pre-determined interest rate of 7 % and compute the Raroc of the loan (expressed as a net premium, over the ITR).

3. Both Bank Hollywood and Bank IronSteel are about to issue a loan to Company ABC, a media and entertainment group. Bank Hollywood operates mainly with TV stations and film producers, while most loans of Bank IronSteel have been issued to steel manufacturers and coke mines. Both banks assign the same PD to company ABC; however, Bank IronSteel, being less familiar with movie and song royalties has estimated a conservative 90 % LGD on the loan, while bank Hollywood expects a 40 % recovery rate. Based on the data above, what bank is more likely to offer the lower rate?

   (A) Bank Hollywood, because recovery expectations are better and firms like ABC already represent a significant share of its loan portfolio;
   (B) Bank IronSteel, because diversification benefits are higher;
   (C) The two banks will offer exactly the same rate, because the stand-alone VaR of a loan to ABC is the same regardless of the issuer;
   (D) Recovery expectations and diversification benefits work in two opposite ways, so more information would be needed to tell which bank is going to offer the lower rate.

4. A branch manager must be authorized by the head office before issuing a loan that involves an expected loss above 100,000 euros. The manager is about to issue a loan to a customer with PD = 1.4 % and an expected LGD of 40 %. What is the maximum amount that can be issued by the branch, without waiting for the head office?

5. Potomac Financial Holdings has sold a credit default swap on Riverside Inc.. Consider the following events (see Appendix 15A to answer this question):

   (i) Riverside Inc. is downgraded by Moody's and Standard & Poor's.
   (ii) Potomac Financial Holdings is downgraded by Moody's and Standard & Poor's.
   (iii) Potomac Financial Holdings and Riverside Inc. merge.
   (iv) Moody's changes the outlook for Riverside Inc. from stable to positive.

Which one(s) could reduce the value of the credit default swap?

(A) (ii) and (iii);
(B) all but (i);
(C) all of them;
(D) (ii) and (iv).

Appendix 15A
Credit Risk Transfer Tools

The need to manage credit risk more flexibly and more efficiently has led to the development of a set of tools for transferring this type of risk.

Credit derivatives, securitizations and loan sales make it possible to transform bank loans from illiquid assets – bound to the accounts of the originating intermediary until maturity – to tradable ones. In this Appendix, we will describe the key characteristics of these techniques.

15A.1 CREDIT DERIVATIVES

Beginning in the early 90's, forward contracts, swaps, and options involving credit risk gained popularity and came to be known as "credit derivatives". These instruments are highly customized, traded on the over-the-counter (OTC) market, and come in fairly significant sizes (roughly between 25 and 100 million dollars). The counterparties are primarily banks, institutional investors and, to a lesser extent, large non-financial companies. Trades are closed through an intermediary (usually a large investment bank), which can act as a broker (simply bringing the two counterparties together) or as a dealer (thereby becoming a counterparty in the transaction in their own right).

Terminology – There are certain elements and technical concepts that are common to all credit derivatives, and must be understood before we present the various contract types. A significant contribution toward the development of a unified, unambiguous terminology has been provided by the official definitions set by the International Swaps and Derivatives Dealers Association (ISDA), which has been acting to standardize the contracts of these instruments.[11]

The first element to be aware of is the so-called "underlying asset". Unlike for financial derivatives, this is not a stock price, an interest rate, or an exchange rate, but a "name", i.e. a party – a company, a public entity, or a sovereign state – involved in a loan for which the credit risk is being transferred using the derivative contract. This party is known as the "reference entity". It is important to note that the reference entity has nothing to do with the two counterparties stipulating the credit derivative and, in many cases, even ignores that the contract exists.

The payoff of a credit derivative is connected with the occurrence of a "credit event", i.e. an event associated with a clear worsening of the reference entity's creditworthiness. The ISDA has defined eight distinct credit events:

– *Bankruptcy*: including actual business closure or any form of insolvency proceedings concerning the reference entity;
– *Failure to pay* on an obligation (usually, subject to a materiality limit, so that failures to pay below a certain minimum amount are deemed negligible);
– *Downgrade*: any decrease in credit rating below a predefined level;

---

[11] The efforts of ISDA are particularly directed to creating uniform terminology by defining precisely the most common technical terms, as well as to standardizing a series of clauses and mechanisms that can be combined in a variety of ways by the parties in order to define the desired contract structure.

- *Repudiation*: the disaffirming or disclaiming of obligations of the reference entity;
- *Restructuring*: moratoriums, deferments or renegotiations of debts to an extent that it reduces the value for the creditor;
- *Cross acceleration*: breaches of contract which, although not resulting in a failure to pay, lead to the obligation being immediately due, and not reimbursed by the reference entity;
- *Cross default*: breaches of contract which, although not resulting in a failure to pay, lead to the obligation being immediately due;
- *Credit event upon merger*: mergers that result in the substantial worsening of the credit risk.

A credit derivative may cover one or more of these events. If the event occurs, one party (the "protection seller") pays the other (the "protection buyer"). It is not necessary for the protection buyer to have a credit exposure to the reference entity. The buyer may, in fact, simply wish to speculate, or "bet", on the occurrence of the given credit event.

The protection seller is the party to whom the credit risk is transferred. In return, the seller receives a premium upon signing the contract ("upfront") or a series of payments at regular dates.

In many contracts, there is also a "reference obligation", which is a particular debt issued by the reference entity. The purpose of the reference obligation (see below) may vary based on the type of contract. Generally speaking, the payments called for in a credit derivative depend on movements in the price of the reference obligation and are calculated by a "calculation agent", which may be one of the two counterparties or a third party.

If the reference obligation is a bond traded on an efficient and liquid secondary market, the calculation agent's job is limited to noting the price and calculating the payment in accordance with the procedures defined by contract. In other cases, the reference obligation may have a "thin" (or fairly insignificant) secondary market, so the calculation becomes more delicate,[12] also because the occurrence of a credit event further reduces (usually, drastically) the security's liquidity. In such cases, the calculation agent may compute the price by consulting several dealers.[13] In other cases, the reference obligation may be a non-tradable debt, such as a bank loan, so the calculation agent will need to determine its value independently. In these cases, in order to limit informational asymmetries, it would be best for the calculation agent to be the bank that issued the loan; however, if the bank is also a party in the credit derivative, this would clearly result in a conflict of interests, as the calculation agent would be able to set the derivative's cash flows at their advantage.

Nonetheless, contracts exist (although no precise data are available on the scope of the phenomenon) in which the calculation agent is one of the two counterparties in the derivative. In these cases, the calculation agent must have an undisputed reputation in the credit derivatives market, such that the risk of damaging this reputation is a sufficient motivation not to take undue advantage of their position. In many cases, it is also likely that the calculation agent is one of the two parties in the contract simply because the reference

---

[12] If a credit derivative were to always require a highly tradable reference obligation, the potential for market development would be drastically reduced. Even in broad-based, highly developed bond markets such as the US, a great many bond issues have a fairly illiquid secondary market.

[13] This procedure requires that prices be requested from a certain number of sources, established in advance by the contract, that act as brokers for the obligation to be valued. The calculation agent then sets the price as the average of the prices quoted by these sources.

obligation is very easy to value, the possibility for abuse is essentially inexistent, and it isn't worth the trouble to turn to a third party.

The main types of credit derivatives – In the same way as for financial derivatives (on interest rates, exchange rates, stock indexes, etc.), credit derivatives, too, can be divided into three main categories: forward contracts, swaps, and options. The most common types of contracts are credit spread forwards, total rate of return (TROR) swaps, credit default swaps, credit spread options, and credit default notes.

We can further distinguish between credit-default products and replication products. The former only transfer credit risk and, therefore, only result in a payoff when a credit event affects one or more parties. Among these, the most common are credit default swaps. Replication products, on the other hand, make it possible to create a synthetic asset that is sensitive to credit risk. In certain cases, these products transfer both credit risk and market risk. Their payoff depends on the cash flows and the market price of the reference obligation, and not just on a credit event. The most common ones are total return swaps.

Credit spread forwards are the simplest form of credit derivative.[14] A credit spread forward is a forward contract that calls for a payment upon maturity calculated on the difference between a predefined spread and the current spread of a corporate bond (generally over the yield on government bonds). The buyer of such an instrument undertakes to pay the seller the following amount p upon the expiration of the contract at time T:

$$p = (s_f - s_T) \cdot MD \cdot FV \qquad \qquad ((15A.1)$$

where s_f is the spread set by the parties when the forward contract was stipulated, s_T is the spread actually paid by the bond at T, MD is the modified duration of the bond, and FV is the face value of the bond.

If the credit rating of the bond issuer worsens, the price falls and the yield to maturity increases. For a given government bond yield, this leads to an increase in s_T above the contract spread s_f. The value of p in equation A.1 is then negative, so it is the seller who will have to pay a sum to the buyer of the credit spread forward, and thereby takes on the credit risk connected with the bond.

For example, a US bank that has Mexican treasury bonds in its portfolio can protect itself from an increase in the spread with US treasury bonds (increase that would lead to a reduction in the value of the securities) by buying a credit spread forward. The bank would then receive a payment equal to the difference between the agreed upon spread and the market one, multiplied by the average modified duration of the securities and by their face value.

Alternatively, a credit spread forward may also call for a payment based on the difference between an initially agreed upon price and the market price of a security at time T, rather than on the difference between two spreads.

Credit spread options are a variant of the credit spread forward, whereby the buyer has the right, but not the duty, to swap the current spread s_T and the predefined spread s_f. In exchange for this option, the buyer pays a premium either in advance or through periodic payments.

---

[14] Although contractually simpler, credit spread forwards were not the first credit derivatives to be developed. Initially, credit swaps and credit options were more common.

A *total rate of return (TROR) swap* is a contract in which the counterparties swap two periodic cash flows, both at variable rates. The first payment is indexed to a market parameter, such as Libor, while the other corresponds to the cash flows generated by a reference obligation (either a security or a bank loan).

Let us assume, for example, that Bank A has a loan in its portfolio and wishes to transfer the risk. With a TROR swap, Bank A agrees to pay Bank B a series of payments equal to the cash flows generated by the loan. In this way, Bank A effectively transfers the "total rate of return" of the loan: interest, fees, and capital gains (i.e. the difference between the initial price and the final price).

Bank B, in turn, undertakes to pay Bank A, on the same date, a flow of payments indexed to a market parameter (generally Libor) plus a given spread agreed upon by the parties (which, of course, depends on the credit rating of the loan being transferred).

Because the loans involved in a TROR swap normally bear interest at a variable rate, both legs of the swap vary with market rates. As such, there is no market risk to hedge, even if the contract can lead to a basis risk (e.g. if it calls for Libor-indexed payments, while the loan is indexed to the prime rate).

Upon maturity, Bank A pays Bank B a sum equal to the final repayment of the loan and receives a sum equal to the nominal value of the loan plus the last interest payment. Hence, if the loan is not paid in full, the consequences fall upon Bank B.

If, on the other hand, the borrower defaults prior to the swap's maturity, the swap is terminated and Bank B undertakes to pay Bank A the difference between the face value of the loan and its market value (which is generally determined by dealers). If, however, Bank B is not satisfied with the market value assigned to the loan, it could buy the loan from Bank A at its face value.[15]

TRORs are the second most common form of credit derivative after credit default swaps.

A *credit default swap* (CDS) is a contract in which in exchange for a periodic premium, the protection seller undertakes to make a payment to the protection buyer, upon occurrence of a credit event. For example, if Bank A wishes to protect itself against default risk for a company (the reference entity), it may pay a periodic (e.g. quarterly) premium to Bank B by which it acquires the right to receive a payment in the event of default by the reference entity.

Of course, the credit event must be defined based on objective and verifiable criteria (such as those defined by the ISDA). There are also "materiality thresholds" below which the protection seller is not required to make payment. For example, the breach must result in a total loss above a given percentage of the value of the reference obligation.

Although referred to as swaps, these contracts are actually options (with periodic, rather than upfront, payment of the premium). For this reason, they are also called credit default options. They can also be seen as letters of credit and, more generally, as loan guarantees or a form of credit insurance.

A *credit default note* is a monetary market instrument, similar to commercial paper, by which an investor takes over the risk of default of one or more reference obligations (or, more generally, of a portfolio of loans) in exchange for a higher return. Credit default

---

[15] As with credit spread forwards, TROR swaps can call for payments based solely on spreads. In such cases, the party transferring the loan risk would receive the difference between the value of the spread upon maturity of the swap and the spread initially set.

notes are normally issued by a special-purpose entity, the assets of which are entirely comprised of a certain portfolio of loans (usually sold by a bank) or, more often, of low-risk securities (e.g. government bonds) and a series of credit derivatives in which the special-purpose entity acts as the protection seller. The investors financing the special-purpose entity are, therefore, exposed to the risk that the notes are only partially redeemed if the assets of the entity post loan losses, or if the reference obligations of the credit derivatives are defaulted on.

The uses of credit derivatives – Credit derivatives enable a bank to reduce its exposure to credit risk for certain counterparties (by acting as protection buyer) without having to sell the related loans, or to earn fees (as protection seller) in exchange for exposure to credit risk for parties with which it does not have a direct customer relationship (due to geographic, size or specialization reasons). This enables the bank to somewhat increase the liquidity of its loans, as well as to optimize its loan portfolio and improve its risk/return efficiency.

Take the case of a German bank which has a high level of exposure to its domestic market. This bank is clearly in an advantageous position for carrying out loan origination to a German clientele, in that it can select its customers, set prices that are suited to the risks of the loan, and monitor the loan's development. However, it could reduce its portfolio risk through greater diversification by separating origination and risk taking, e.g. with a TROR swap. Such a contract would enable a non-German bank in, say, Japan to take on a position in Germany, while leaving the management of customer relations with the local bank. Generally speaking, a bank should buy protection in industry segments and geographic areas in which it has high levels of concentration and sell protection on companies operating in industries or areas that are correlated lowly with its core business.

The transfer of risk through credit derivatives is particularly useful for banks with portfolios that are highly concentrated in specific parties or industries. This is the case, for example, for banks that trade in OTC derivatives and often work with a limited number of large counterparties, to which they end up having significant levels of exposure. Of course, being OTC derivatives themselves, credit derivatives include a certain amount of counterparty risk related to possible default by the protection seller.

Another use of credit derivatives is connected with the creation of *synthetic financial assets*. Let us take, for example, a US pension fund that wishes to buy long-term (e.g. ten-year) Mexican treasury bills in order to take advantage of future improvements in Mexico's credit rating. Let us further imagine that the law or the pension fund's charter prohibit the purchase of foreign bonds with maturities beyond five years. The pension fund could, at this point, "park" its funds in US treasury bills and recreate the profits and risks of a long-term investment in Mexican bills by using a credit derivative.[16]

Credit derivatives have also been used to carry out "regulatory arbitrage", i.e. transactions that take advantage of differences between the risks of two positions and their regulatory treatment, e.g. in terms of minimum capital requirements. An example of regulatory arbitrage is when a party buys protection on loans to low-risk banks, thereby transferring the credit risk and "freeing up" the associated regulatory capital, and then sells protection (acquiring risk and, therefore, calling for more regulatory capital) on loans to more risky banks. In the past, regulations in certain countries required the quantity of

---

[16] This example also entails a form of regulatory arbitrage (see below). By rights, legislation or fund charters that prohibit the direct purchase of long-term Mexican securities should also prohibit credit derivatives that have this type of investment as the reference obligation.

regulatory capital freed-up and absorbed by the two derivatives to be the same, as long as all of the banks were located in OECD nations. In was possible, therefore, to be exposed to greater risks and earn higher margins while maintaining the same minimum capital requirement. Such forms of arbitrage have been made much more difficult by the new Basel Accord (known as Basel II – see Chapter 20), which has made capital requirements much more sensitive to a contract's risk content.

A further advantage of credit derivatives is their potential to overcome problems related to the *differentials in funding costs* of banks with different credit ratings. In order to better understand this point, take the case of an A-rated bank that can raise funds on the interbank market at the Libor rate. This bank would could not issue loans to companies with a rating of AAA, as such companies could get funded directly from the market at rates lower than Libor. However, if the bank wanted to add an exposure to such companies to its loan portfolio (in order to take advantage of greater diversification), it could become a protection seller in a credit derivative having the AAA-rated company as the reference entity. In the same way, financial institutions that benefit from lower funding costs could use this benefit to finance companies with a high credit rating and then buy credit risk protection using a credit swap.

Finally, credit derivatives can be extremely useful in *calculating the probability of default* of the reference entities by using models similar to those seen in Chapter 11 for bond spreads.

15A.2   SECURITIZATION SCHEMES

Banks wishing to spin off the risk of a pool of loans without using credit derivatives may resort to a technique known as securitization. This involves the creation of an ad-hoc company (usually called a *special-purpose vehicle*, SPV, or special-purpose entity) which buys a pool of assets (usually loans) from the bank. The SPV is bankruptcy-remote from the bank; that is, its default does not trigger the default of the bank and vice versa. Since the bank has originated the loans sold to the SPV, it is usually called the *originator*.

The SPV raises funds by issuing bonds with different levels of seniority. Senior bonds, usually rated by one or more rating agencies, are usually underwritten by institutional investors; junior bonds (also known as "junior securitization tranches", "first-loss tranches" or "equity tranches") are often underwritten by the bank itself, to reassure the market about the quality of the securitized assets (see Figure 15A.1).

The size of the first-loss tranche retained by the originator depends on the quality of the securitized assets, as well as on the rating that the SPV wishes to get on its senior bonds. In order to get high ratings on senior bonds backed by a pool of low-quality assets, the bank will have to underwrite a higher amount of junior bonds.

If, at redemption, the value of the SPV's assets has fallen below the value of its liabilities, losses up to the value of the equity tranche will be borne by the bank itself. Accordingly, securitizations can be seen as a way of transferring extreme risks, rather than as a plain risk-transfer technique like credit derivatives or loan sales. Also, securitizations are used as a funding channel which provides the bank with new scope for further loans (since spun-off assets can be replaced by new exposures).

Bonds issued by SPVs under a securitization scheme are also known as "asset-backed securities" (ABS). The assets sold to the SPV are often large pools of small exposures (such as mortgage loans or credit cards receivables or consumer loans) for which it

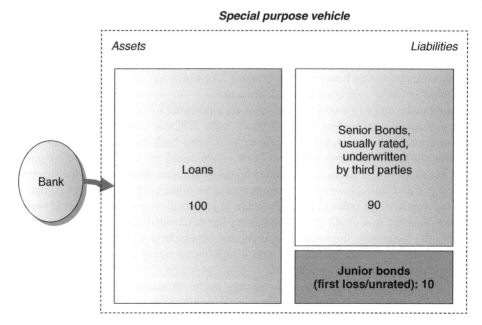

Figure 15A.1   A simple securitization scheme

would be impossible (or at least very impractical) to set up a high number of credit derivatives. Even royalty payments on David Bowie's songs have been reported to be used as securitized assets.

In *synthetic securitizations*, the SPV does not buy assets from the bank, but rather sells protection to the bank on some of the latter's assets, e.g. by means of a credit default swap. Funds raised from investors underwriting the SPV's bonds are then invested in low-risk securities, which can be seen as a cash collateral for the obligations undertaken by the SPV through the credit default swaps.

15A.3   LOAN SALES

Beginning in the late 70's, in the US, it gradually became standard practice to sell a bank loan, either in whole or in part, or a pool of loans directly (i.e. without issuing securities or using a special-purpose vehicle, as is done in securitizations). As such, a secondary loan sales market was slowly created, which has grown significantly over the last few decades.

The main forms of loan sales are participation, assignment and novation. A participation is not an actual loan sale, as the loan remains on the books of the selling bank. Instead, it calls for the "buyer" of the loan to establish a deposit with the "selling" bank in an amount equal to the value of the loan, and the bank undertakes to remunerate the deposit based on the amounts received on the loan that has been "sold". As such, it could be seen as a TROR that is entirely guaranteed by cash. In the event the borrower should default, the buyer of the loan has the right to any amounts that the bank may manage to recover. Assignment, on the other hand, involves the actual transfer of the loan from seller to buyer. Normally, however, this does not transfer the seller's obligations towards the borrower. Novation, then, is when the original loan is extinguished and replaced with an identical loan owned by the new lender.

In the US, the loan sales market is an over-the-counter market in which many types of loans are traded. It includes, for example, loans issued to emerging countries, leveraged commercial and industrial (C&I) loans, term loans, and revolving facilities.

Market participants, both buyers and sellers, include large-scale banks and non-bank financial institutions (mutual funds, hedge funds, vulture funds, insurance companies), as well as federal agencies. In addition to these, smaller local banks and foreign intermediaries access the market in order to increase the diversification of their own portfolios. Loan sellers also include banks that wish to restructure their loan portfolios, the so-called "bad banks" created in order to facilitate the liquidation of failing intermediaries, and the Federal Deposit Insurance Corporation (FDIC), which sells loans, both performing and non-performing, that it has acquired from failing banks.

Trading is facilitated by online brokers that match up buyers and sellers based on a set of predetermined criteria, in exchange for a fee. Note that this is a slower, less transparent market than ordinary financial markets, also because of the low level of standardization of the contracts being traded.

16

Counterparty Risk
on OTC Derivatives

16.1 INTRODUCTION

During the last twenty years, the sustained growth experienced by derivatives[1] traded
in OTC (over the counter) markets has prompted a need for an adequate measurement
of the credit risk associated with such contracts. In fact, OTC markets (unlike regulated
markets) do not benefit from risk-mitigation devices such as central clearing houses and
risk-based margins.[2]

Such a need has been increasingly felt, not only by financial institutions but also by
regulators. Accordingly, the latter have imposed, in the 1988 Basel Accord on bank capital
adequacy, that derivatives on interest rates and foreign exchange be included among the
off-balance sheet items affecting the volume of a bank's risk-weighted assets.

After 1988, regulators have issued some recommendations and general principles for
measuring and managing the credit risks associated with OTC derivatives,[3] which could
cause chain effects and jeopardize the stability of the financial system as a whole.

This chapter analyzes counterparty risk associated with the trading of OTC derivatives.
Various approaches are presented, aimed at making OTC exposures comparable to credit
exposures originated by traditional bank loans. This involves computing the *loan equivalent exposure* (LEE) of OTC derivatives (a measure of credit risk exposure that will be
carefully explained in the remainder of this chapter). To measure loan equivalents correctly, OTC positions must be marked to market; also, working hypotheses and statistical
tools must be used, that are quite close to those presented in the second part of this book
for market risk.

The next section discusses the nature of counterparty risk on OTC derivatives, giving
special emphasis to the so-called "pre-settlement risk". This will be further analyzed in the
following sections. Section 16.3 shows different approaches to assessing pre-settlement
risk, and shows in detail how loan equivalent exposures can be estimated; special care is
given to interest rate swaps (OTC contracts having long maturities, and therefore giving
rise to considerable counterparty risks). Section 16.4 shows how the LEE can be used to
estimate the Raroc of an OTC contract. Section 16.5 shows how counterparty risk, besides
being measured, can also be reduced through a number of useful tools: netting agreements,
margins, recouponing, guarantees, credit triggers and early redemption options.

---

[1] E.g.: forward rate agreements and currency forwards; interest rate swaps and currency swaps; options on
interest rates, currencies, bonds and stocks.

[2] Margins are a cash deposit, updated daily based on the contract's market value, so that all parties always hold
a positive balance on their account with the central clearing house. The clearinghouse acts as legal counterparty
to each trader buying or selling a contract; this means that, if bank A and bank B trade a derivative, each
of them will enter a separate contract with the clearinghouse and hence will have a legal right to see the
contract executed by the clearinghouse, regardless of the creditworthiness of the other bank. The effectiveness
of margins and clearinghouses has been highlighted, during recent years, by the fact that regulated futures
markets have virtually never defaulted, notwithstanding periods of high volatility and the default of some big
dealers. This effectiveness has been acknowledged also by the regulators, who have decided not to impose
capital requirements on derivatives traded in regulated markets.

[3] See Group of Thirty (1993) and Basel Committee (1993).

16.2   SETTLEMENT AND PRE-SETTLEMENT RISK

A financial instrument entailing one or more cash flows to be paid at a later date (as is the case with forward contracts) gives rise to two types of credit risk. The first one is pre-settlement risk, that is, the risk that the counterparty may default before the contract's final maturity. Such a risk produces a loss if, when the counterparty defaults, the market value of the contract is greater than zero. In this case, the bank will have to face a cost when substituting the defaulted contract with a similar one; this is why pre-settlement risk is also called *substitution risk*. If, on the other hand, the evolution of market factors (such as interest rates, exchange rates, etc.) had been such that the value of the contract was negative, then the default of the counterparty will not cause any loss.

The second type of risk is settlement risk, that is, the risk of the counterparty defaulting at the contract's final maturity (more specifically, when it is settled). The clearing of derivative contracts, in fact, may involve non-simultaneous payments: especially when the two parties operate in different time zones, there might be a slight delay between the traded cash flows. Hence, the party settling its obligations first will be exposed, for a short time span, to the risk that the other party may not perform as expected. This is also called "Herstatt risk", following the well-known bankruptcy of a German bank called Herstatt. German supervisors decided to shut down the bank in the early afternoon, that is, before the opening of the New York exchange; as a consequence, the bank did not settle some currency trades with US banks.

The difference between those two risks may be better appreciated with an example. Consider Bank A making a forward purchase of dollars from Bank B, on 30 July, at a price of 1.1 euros per dollar (to be delivered six months later).

For Bank A, pre-settlement risk involves the risk that, between July and December, B may default while forward dollars (for delivery on 31 December) trade at a price of more than 1.1 euros. E.g., if on 30 September B should go bankrupt and, that day, the price of forward dollars were 1.2 euros, then A would stand a loss of 0.1 euros per dollar (since, to receive dollars at the end of the year, it should enter into a new forward contract, at a higher price than originally planned).

Settlement risk, instead, refers to the possibility that, on 31 December, bank B may cash the euros without delivering the dollars. In this case, the potential loss for A would include the whole value of the transaction, that is, the value (in euros) of the undelivered dollars.

Settlement risk lasts for a very short time interval (never more than a few hours); pre-settlement risk, instead, has to be borne throughout the entire life of the contract. Moreover, settlement risk can be reduced using centralized clearing and settlement networks (like Euroclear, Cedel and others), which have become more and more customary during the latest years.

Let us then focus on the most complex and dangerous risk, pre-settlement risk, and present some alternative approaches to its measurement.

16.3   ESTIMATING PRE-SETTLEMENT RISK

Estimating pre-settlement risk is not a straightforward task. In fact, the future substitution cost of a contract does not only depend on its current value, but also on the further value increase that may occur between now and the counterparty's default. In other words, besides the *current exposure* one has to take into account the *future potential exposure*. Taken together, the current exposure (CE) and the future potential exposure

(FPE) represent the *loan equivalent exposure* (LEE) of an OTC derivative, that is, the value that can be assigned, in a "reasonably conservative" way, at the exposure in the event of a default.[4] Once the LEE of an OTC derivative has been estimated, we will assume that the credit risk of the contract is the same as the risk on a traditional loan, issued to the same counterparty, of a (non-stochastic) amount equal to the loan equivalent.

We therefore have that:

$$LEE = CE + FPE \qquad (16.1)$$

The CE is simply the current market value (if positive) of the derivative, and depends on the difference between the forward price (rate) set in the contract and the current market price (rate). The FPE, due to the possible increase in the value of the position, will depend on the contract's sensitivity to changes in the market price (rate), as well as on the volatility of the latter; hence, pre-settlement risk will be especially high in periods of sustained market volatility. LEE is then the sum of a known component (CE) and of a probabilistic component that must be carefully estimated.

Two simple ways to estimate the LEE were proposed in 1988, for regulatory purposes, by the Basel Committee on Banking Supervision. We will cover them in the next section, and then turn to a more sophisticated (and effective) approach, that has been devised originally for internal risk management objectives.[5]

16.3.1   Two approaches suggested by the Basel Committee (1988)

The Basel Committee, in the 1988 Accord on bank capital requirements and in an amendment released in 1995, dictates two methods for computing the LEE associated with derivative contracts on interest rates and currencies.

The first, and simpler, approach is the *original exposure method*. According to this method, CE and FPE are not assessed separately, but the LEE is computed directly as a fixed percentage (see Table 16.1) of the notional value of the contract.

As an example consider a European bank buying one million dollars at a forward exchange rate of 1.1 euros per dollar; the overall exposure to pre-settlement risk would be equal to the notional capital of the contract (1,100,000 euros) multiplied by 2% (as indicated in the Table), that is, 22,000 euros.

Table 16.1 The original exposure method–coefficients % to be applied to the notional value

LIFE TO MATURITY	UNDERLYING ASSET	INTEREST RATES	EXCHANGE RATES AND GOLD
Less than one year		0.5%	2.0%
Between one and two years		1.0%	5.0%
Increase for every additional year		1.0%	3.0%

Source: Basel Committee (1995).

---

[4] Summing the LEEs of all the contracts with a given counterparty, one can get the overall exposure to the risk of a default by that counterparty.

[5] Since 2004, as explained later in this chapter, this more sophisticated approach has been accepted also for regulatory purposes, provided that banks can prove that is applied carefully and uniformly, based on well-documented procedures and data.

There are mainly two shortcomings in this approach :

(1) The estimated exposure to counterparty risk is independent of the market value of the position. Accordingly, if in the example above the forward exchange rate would increase to 1.5 euros (making the value of contract significantly greater than zero), the LEE computed with the original exposure method would stay unchanged. The same would happen if the forward rate were to fall to 0.7 euros a dollar, so that the value of the contract would become significantly negative and would probably stay below zero until maturity, virtually wiping out any credit risk.

(2) The exposure to credit risk does not depend on the volatility, per unit of time, of the underlying asset.[6] In fact, Table 16.1 dictates equal coefficients for all interest rate derivatives and for all currency derivatives; yet, we know that, in the real world, forward contracts on British pounds will probably entail a lower risk than contracts on Japanese yen having the same notional and maturity. This is because market data show that the euro/pound exchange rate tends to be consistently less volatile than the euro/yen one: hence, forward contracts on pounds are less likely to take high market values, and to expose the bank to a significant counterparty risk.

The Basel Committee acknowledges that this method may be overly simplistic, and therefore accepts that it may be used by banks only if allowed by national supervisors. Moreover, to overcome (at least partially) its limitations, the Committee suggests another method, the so-called *current exposure* or *mark-to-market* method.

According to this approach, the CE is given by the current market value (MV) of the OTC contract, that is, by the cost the bank would face to replace the contract ("substitution cost") with an identical one, if the counterparty were to default. If the market value is negative, then there is no current exposure to credit risk, and CE is set to zero. To this CE, an estimate of FPE must be added, given by a fixed percentage (p) of the notional (N). The value of p, also called the "add-on" factor, depends on the underlying asset and increases with the maturity of the contract.

To sum up:

$$LEE = CE + FPE = \max(0, MV) + p \cdot N \qquad (16.2)$$

Table 16.2 shows the values of p to be used for different types of contracts.

The mark-to-market approach, being based on a formula that includes the current value of the contract, assigns higher LEEs to contract with higher market values; in this sense, it overcomes the first shortcoming discussed above. However, the second limitation of the original exposure method (which did not take into account the volatility of the underlying currency or rate) is not solved. In fact, Table 16.2 assigns the same coefficients to all contracts on a given class of financial assets (e.g., to all contract on currencies); the fact that different exchange rates (or interest rates) may show different volatilities (which furthermore tend to change over time) is therefore ignored.

---

[6] However, the coefficients in the Table increase with the life to maturity of the contracts. The Committee therefore acknowledges that, given the annual volatility of the underlying market factor, its value may be more and more different from the current one as the duration of the OTC contract increases.

[7] If the underlying asset of the OTC derivative is not indicated in the Table, then the coefficients for "other commodities" should be used. No add-on is required on basis swaps (whereby two different floating rates are traded): in this case, the capital requirement is therefore based only on the swap's current market value.

Table 16.2 Computing FPE with the add-on approach[7]

UNDERLYING ASSET / LIFE TO MATURITY	INTEREST RATES	EXCHANGE RATES AND GOLD	STOCKS AND STOCK INDICES	PRECIOUS METALS, EXCLUDING GOLD	OTHER COMMODITIES
<1 year	0.0 %	1.0 %	6.0 %	7.0 %	10.0 %
1–5 years	0.5 %	5.0 %	8.0 %	7.0 %	12.0 %
>5 years	1.5 %	7.5 %	10.0 %	8.0 %	15.0 %

Source: Basel Committee (1995).

16.3.2 A more sophisticated approach

Due to the shortcomings outlined above, banks have developed internal models which are more complete and sophisticated than the ones originally dictated by supervisors. The goal of those internal models, however, is the same as in the previous section: to develop an estimate of an OTC contract's loan equivalent exposure (LEE), given by the sum of current exposure (CE) and future potential exposure (FPE).

The CE is obviously given (as in the mark-to-market method) by the market value MV of the contract. However, unlike in the Basel Accord, negative MVs are usually accepted. A negative MV means that the present value of the inflows due to the contract were less than the present value of the outflows;[8] in this case, the bank's counterparty is the one facing a credit risk, due to the possible default of the bank itself.

The future potential exposure (FPE) can be computed based on a parametric approach similar to the one used for computing VaR on market risks (see Chapter 5). In fact, when estimating FPE, we wish to assess the maximum change in value, with a given confidence interval, that the contract might experience due to a favourable movement in market prices (rates). This of course depends on the sensitivity of the exposure to changes in the market prices (rates), as well as on the volatility of the latter.

Similar to what we saw for VaR, the potential exposure can then be computed as:

$$PFE = \delta \cdot \alpha \cdot \sigma \tag{16.3}$$

where δ is the sensitivity of the contract's market value to unit changes in the relevant market factor (exchange rate, interest rate, etc.), α is a multiple of volatility corresponding to the desired confidence interval and σ is the volatility or the movements in the market factor.

Based on this approach, the LEE will be:

$$LEE = MV + \delta \cdot \alpha \cdot \sigma \tag{16.4}$$

To see how equation (16.4) works, let us consider the following example. On 1 January, 2005, a Belgian bank holds a forward contract, with a life to maturity of six months, which

---

[8] In the case of a swap (see section 16.3.3), one should consider the present value of the certain net cash flows obtained by offsetting the swap with a new one, traded at current market conditions.

entails the purchase of one million dollars at 1.2 euros each. The forward exchange rate, that day, is 1.25 euros per dollar. To find the LEE, the following three steps are required:

(1) The current value of the position, based on present market conditions must be evaluated (marked-to-market). This will lead to a positive market value since, thank to the forward contract, the bank can buy at 1.2 euros a "good" (dollars with delivery in six months) that today is worth 1.25. Since the notional of the contract is one million dollars, the current exposure (total market value) will be:[9]

$$CE = MV = (1.25 - 1.2) \cdot 1,000,000 = 50,000$$

(2) Now, to assess the potential future exposure, we need to estimate the sensitivity factor δ, the volatility of the market factor σ, as well as to choose a confidence interval.

Regarding δ, note that if the forward exchange rate were to move from 1.25 to 1.25· $(1 + r)$, the new market value of the contract would be:

$$MV^* = [1.25 \cdot (1 + r) - 1.2] \cdot 1,000,000 = MV + r \cdot 1,250,000$$

Thus, the coefficient δ, linking changes in the contract's value to the returns, r, of the market factor, is equal to 1,250,000 (that is, to the current forward rate times the notional).

Suppose now that the standard deviation of the returns on the forward euro/dollar exchange rate (over a six-month period) is 5%,[10] and that the bank adopts a 97.5% confidence interval. Assuming normality of the market factor returns, this leads to the following future potential exposure:

$$FPE = \delta \cdot \alpha \cdot \sigma = 1,250,000 \cdot N^{-1}(97.5\%) \cdot 5\% \cong 122,498$$

(3) Finally, the loan equivalent can be computed, simply as the sum of the two components found above:

$$LEE = 50,000 + 122,498 = 172,498$$

Note how this procedure entails two advantages, compared to the approaches followed by the Basel Committee:

– unlike the original exposure method, it takes into account the link between market value and credit risk exposure;
– unlike the mark-to-market model, it accounts for the fact that, if the current value of the exposure (CE) is negative, then the future potential exposure must be very high, for the

---

[9] Note that the result should be multiplied by a six-month discount factor (which was omitted for the sake of simplicity).
[10] Percent changes in the price, in euros, of a dollar to be delivered six months later. Note that in Chapter 5 it was shown that forward exchange rates are not to be included among the risk factors used by a bank, since forward exchange contracts can always be "mapped" to three financially equivalent positions (a long spot position in the foreign currency, a long position on domestic interest rates and a short position on foreign interest rates). The relevant risk factors therefore are the spot exchange rate and the interest rates; it is not necessary, therefore, to explicitly estimate and monitor the volatility in the forward exchange rate.

exposure at default to be greater than zero. Accordingly, while in the mark-to-market approach we have:

$$LEE = \max(0, MV) + FPE$$

the internal methods discussed in this paragraph require that the LEE be the sum of MV and FPE, where the former may also take negative values. However, the loan equivalent as a whole, being a measure of credit risk, is not allowed to be less than zero (unless special "netting agreements" exist between the parties, to be presented later in the chapter). This leads to computing LEE as:

$$LEE = \max(0, MV + FPE)$$

Accordingly, if in the example above the current exposure had been negative (say, −25, 000 euros) the total LEE would have been 97,498 euros; if the CE had been equal to -200,000 euros, the total LEE would have been set to zero.
- Unlike both methods dictated by the Basel Committee, the approach presented in this section acknowledges the link between credit risk and the volatility of market factors, and therefore allows to update the LEE estimate when the markets become more or less volatile.

Thank to this sensitivity to current prices and volatilities, the method discussed above enables a bank to take into consideration the fact that credit risk may change even if no new contracts are traded, simply due to movements in market conditions. In fact, the exposure to counterparty risk may increase just because of a rise in the volatility (and/or of a change in the price) of the asset underlying the derivative. This leads to a sort of "passive exposure", independent of the will and of the operational choices of the financial institution holding the OTC contact. Because of this, it is advisable that derivative contracts (and, more generally, all credit exposures with stochastic EADs) be not allowed to use up the entire credit line assigned to a counterparty. In fact, if this should happen, then the overall credit limit could be exceeded "unintentionally", simply because of changes in market conditions.

The LEE, estimated according to the approach seen above, can be used to:

- compare the exposure associated with an OTC derivative to that due to a normal loan (e.g., by summing the two to verify that the counterparty's overall credit limit is complied with);
- assess the return on the economic capital absorbed by a given position in OTC derivatives, just like we did in Chapter 15 for "plain vanilla" loans;
- estimate the safety margins to be required from a given counterparty, to mitigate insolvency risk.

16.3.3   Estimating the loan equivalent exposure of an interest rate swap

We now apply the method seen above to a more complex and realistic example: an interest rate swap (IRS). Consider an IRS with a notional capital (N) of 50 million euros and a residual life of two years, which makes the holder receive a fixed rate r_s of 5 % per annum, compounded bi-annually (see Table 16.3), while paying a benchmark floating rate.

Assume that the current market rate (r_m) for a new IRS with duration equal to the time-to-maturity of the original swap (2 years) is 3 % per annum, compounded bi-annually

Table 16.3 Example of an Interest Rate Swap (IRS)

Sign of the position	Receives fixed, pays floating
Notional capital (N)	50,000,000
Frequency of payments	Bi-annual
Fixed rate (r_s)	5%
Life to maturity	2 years
Floating rate	Euribor

(that is, 2% less than the r_s). This means that the current value of the contract is positive. To lock in this profit, the bank holding the IRS may underwrite (at zero cost) an opposite swap (where it pays r_m and receives the floating rate), having the same maturity and notional.[11] The market value of the original swap would then be equal to the present value of the net cash flows originated (without uncertainty) by the two swaps. Having assumed bi-annual payments, the net face value of each cash net flow (x_t) would be:

$$x_t = \left(\frac{r_s}{2} - \frac{r_m}{2}\right) \cdot N = 1\% \cdot 50,000,000 = 500,000$$

The market value of the swap is given by the present value of all flows x_t expected in the following two years (that is, at the end of each of the four half-years), computed at the current market rate:[12].

$$MV_s = \sum_{t=1}^{4} \frac{x_t}{(1+r_m)^{\frac{t}{2}}} = \sum_{t=1}^{4} \frac{500,000}{(1+3.02\%)^{\frac{t}{2}}} \cong 1,927,192$$

Such a market value expresses the current exposure, that is, as mentioned above, the substitution cost (loss) that the bank would experience if the counterparty were to default today.

The future potential exposure depends on the sensitivity δ of the swap's market value to changes in r_m, as well as on the volatility of the latter.

To find the sensitivity, recall that a swap is financially equivalent to a portfolio of two positions (both with the same life to maturity as the swap): a long position on a fixed-rate bond paying r_s, plus a short position on a floating-rate bond indexed to the benchmark rate of the swap (e.g., to Euribor, as indicated in Table 16.3). In short:

$$MV_s = MV_F - MV_V \tag{16.5}$$

and therefore:

$$\Delta MV_s = \Delta MV_F - \Delta MV_V \tag{16.6}$$

---

[11] This way, the bank would both pay and receive the floating rate; furthermore, it would cash 5% fixed, while paying 3%.
[12] Note that the market rate r_m on new swaps is 3% *bi-annually compounded*. This would be equivalent to an actual annually-compounded rate of $(1+3\%/2)^2 - 1 \cong 3.02\%$

Table 16.4 Computing the *duration* of an *interest rate swap*

(I) Market value and duration of a fixed-rate security

Time, t (years)	Cash flows of the fixed-rate leg f_t	Present value of f_t, $PV(f_t)$	Total (MV_F)	$T \cdot PV(f_t)$	Total (a)	Duration $(b = a/MV_F)$	Modified duration $(c = b/(1 + r_m))$
0.5	1,250,000	1,231,527		615,764			
1	1,250,000	1,213,327		1,213,327			
1.5	1,250,000	1,195,396		1,793,094			
2	51,250,000	48,286,942		96,573,884			
			51,927,192		100,196,069	1.93	1.87

(continued overleaf)

Table 16.4 (*continued*)

(II) Market value of a floating-rate security

Time, t (years)	Cash flows of the variable-rate leg v_t	Present value of v_t, $PV(v_t)$	Total (MV_V)	Duration (d)	Modified duration ($e = d/(1 + r_m)$)
0.5	750,000	738,916			
1	750,000	727,996			
1.5	750,000	717,238			
2	50,750,000	47,815,850			
			50,000,000	0.50	0.49

Note: discount rates[13] as indicated in footnote 12.

---

[13]In the Table we assumed, for the sake of simplicity, that the zero coupon curve is flat at a level equal to the two-year swap rate (about 3.02 % annually compounded).

where MV_F and MV_V are the market values of the fixed-rate and variable-rate bonds, respectively. The sensitivity of the swap's market value to changes in interest rates can then be measured as the difference between the sensitivity of the long bond (leg) and that of the short position (leg).

As far as MV_F is concerned, recall that (see Chapter 2):

$$\Delta MV_F = -MV_F \cdot MD_F \cdot \Delta r_m$$

Where MD_F is the modified duration of the fixed-rate bond. In our case (see Table 16.4, upper part), this is:

$$\Delta MV_F = -51{,}927{,}192 \cdot 1.87_F \cdot \Delta r_m$$

Similarly, for the floating-rate bond we have:

$$\Delta MV_F = -MV_V \cdot MD_V \cdot \Delta r_e \cong -50{,}000{,}000 \cdot 0.49 \cdot \Delta r_e$$

where r_e denotes the floating rate (in our case, Euribor) and the duration has been set to 0.5 years (leading to a MD of 0.49) because we are assuming that the floating rate be fixed at the start of each half-year and paid six months later.[14]

Note that the difference between the market value of the fixed-rate bond and that of the floating rate bond is exactly the market value of the swap that we had computed above (1,927,192 euros).

If, for simplicity, we assume that the yield curve may only experience parallel shifts (so that $\Delta r_m = \Delta r_e = \Delta r$), then (16.6) implies that

$$\Delta MV_s = \Delta MV_F - \Delta MV_V = -(MV_F MD_F - MV_V MD_V)\Delta r \qquad (16.7)$$

Note that, since the modified duration of a swap may be written (like for any other portfolio) as the average of the modified durations of the two virtual bonds comprised in the swap (each one weighted by its market value):

$$MD_s = \frac{(MD_F \cdot MV_F - MD_V \cdot MV_V)}{MV_s} \qquad (16.8)$$

The quantity in parentheses in (16.7) can then be written as $MV_s \cdot MD_s$ and (16.7) becomes:

$$\Delta MV_s = -MV_s MD_s \Delta r \qquad (16.7a)$$

In our case, we have

$$MD_s = \frac{(51{,}927{,}192 \cdot 1.87 - 50{,}000{,}00 \cdot 0.49)}{1{,}927{,}182} = 37.87$$

and

$$MD_s MV_s = 37.87 \cdot 1{,}927{,}182 \cong 72{,}989{,}948 \cong -\frac{\Delta MV_s}{\Delta r}$$

---

[14] This is a standard result for the duration of a floating-rate bond on the dates when coupons are paid.

This is the δ coefficient linking movements in market rates to changes in the market value of the swap. It can now be plugged back into equation (16.3) to find the potential future exposure:

$$FPE_s = (MV_s \cdot MD_s) \cdot \alpha \cdot \sigma_{\Delta r} \tag{16.9}$$

Suppose, for example, that the volatility of absolute changes in rates (Δr) is 0.50%[15] and that the bank is using an α of 2 (implying a 97.7% confidence interval%). This would give:

$$FPE_s = (37.87 \cdot 1{,}927{,}182) \cdot 2 \cdot 0.50\% \cong 729{,}899$$

The loan equivalent exposure is therefore equal to:

$$LEE_s = CE_s + FPE_s = 1{,}927{,}192 + 729{,}899 \cong 2{,}652{,}091 \tag{16.10}$$

16.3.4 Amortization and diffusion effect

For the sake of simplicity, in the previous section we did not specify to *what moment in time* our FPE measure was relating. Indeed, between now (time 0) and the final maturity of the swap (time T) there exist infinitely many future moments τ: for each of them (see Figure 16.1), one may want to compute a different future potential exposure, and this would be perfectly legitimate.

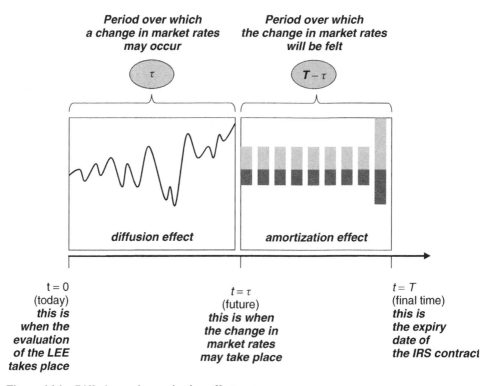

Figure 16.1   Diffusion and amortization effect

---

[15] Obviously, the actual volatility also depends on the time horizon over which the FPE is computed. For the sake of simplicity, this aspect is discussed separately in the next section.

In section 16.3.3 we saw, as an example, the case of a swap having a life to maturity of two years ($T = 2$): obviously, the effect of a change in rates on its value would also depend on when (that is, on what moment $\tau < T$) such a change may occur.

Namely, if we consider a rate change near the beginning of our two-year period ($\tau \cong 0$, e.g. in a week), that change is very likely to be small: in fact, it is very unlikely that, within just one week, rates may move to levels that are significantly far from the present ones. Nevertheless, the modified duration of the swap will be rather large: recall that, at time 0, it was equal to about 37.9; since the duration goes to zero only gradually, during the whole life of the swap, its value after just one week will still be considerable.

On the other hand, if we consider rate changes that may occur towards the end of two year period (at $\tau \cong 2$, e.g. one week before the final maturity T), those could be very significant: it would not be unsurprising if, during two years, rates were to move far away from the value recorded at time 0. Yet, the duration of the swap will, by that time, be very close to zero. Hence, the overall effect, on the value of the swap, of a (potentially large) change in rates could be very small.

This suggests that, in order to understand how life to maturity affects the LEE, we have to take into account two separate effects, working in opposite directions:

- the first one (a direct relationship between τ and the possible width of the change in rates) is called diffusion effect. It depends on the fact that potential changes in market rates become bigger and bigger as τ (the moment the new value of the swap will supposedly be computed) moves forward in time, and the life to maturity of the contract ($T - \tau$) shrinks. This is due to the fact that, under pretty general assumptions, the volatility of rate changes increases with the square root of time (see Chapter 5);
- The second one (an inverse relationship between τ and the sensitivity of the swap value to a change in rates) is called *amortization effect*. As seen above, it follows from the fact that the modified duration of the swap (weighted average of the modified durations of the two virtual bonds into which a swap can be decomposed) decreases with the contract's life to maturity, and therefore decreases as τ moves forward in time.

Figure 16.2 and Table 16.5 show how the diffusion effect works. Note that, given the annual volatility of interest rate changes, the potential variation grows wider as we increase the time interval over which it may be observed, that is, as we increase τ.

The graph is based on the following relationship:

$$\sigma_\tau = \sigma_1 \cdot \sqrt{\tau} \tag{16.11}$$

which in turn assumes that rate changes are serially incorrelated (as discussed in Chapter 5). In the Figure, spanning a time horizon of 10 years, we assumed that the annual volatility of the shifts in the yield curve (σ_1) be equal to 50 basis points (0.5%). This means that if, e.g., τ is set at four years, then we have:

$$\sigma_\tau = \sigma_1 \cdot \sqrt{\tau} = 0.5\% \cdot \sqrt{4} = 1\% \tag{16.12}$$

as indicated by the continuous curve. The dashed curve shows rate changes associated with a given confidence interval (97.5%) and is obtained by multiplying σ_t by a multiple α of $N^{-1}(97,5\%)$ (that is, of about 2). Accordingly, for example, the maximum rate

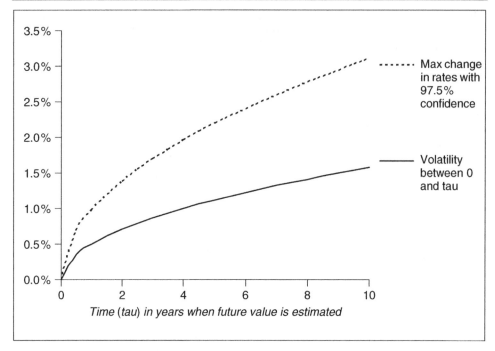

Figure 16.2   The relationship between τ and the diffusion effect

change over a 4-year time horizon, assuming a confidence level of 97.5 %, is found to be approximately 2 %.

Let us now consider an example of amortization effect. In the following, we evaluate the sensitivity to market rate changes of three different swaps, all with a notional of 100 million euros, life to maturity of 10 years and bi-annual coupon:

– a "par swap" with fixed rate $r_s = 8\%$, which we assume to be equal to the current market rate for new swaps, r_m;
– an "in the money" swap, with $r_s = 10\%$ (that is, above the market rate $r_m = 8\%$);
– an "out of the money" swap with $r_s = 6\%$ (that is, below $r_m = 8\%$).

From equation (16.7) we recall that the sensitivity to market rate changes of a swap is given by:

$$\delta = MV_F MD_F - MV_V MD_V \qquad (16.13)$$

As concerns the variable-rate bond, its value (evaluated immediately after a bi-annual coupon has been paid) will always be equal to the notional ($MV_V = 100$ million euros), while its duration (assuming coupon rates are set every six months, and coupons are settled six months later) will be 0.5 years. Giving a bi-annual compounded rate r_m of 8 %,[16] this leads to a modified duration MD_V of 0.462.

---
[16] This leads to a r_m of 8.16 % annually compounded.

Table 16.5 The relationship between τ and the diffusion effect

Evaluation time (τ), in years	Volatility between 0 and $\tau(\sigma_\tau)$	Max change in rates with 97.5% confidence ($\alpha \cdot \sigma_\tau$)
0	0.0%	0.0%
0.5	0.4%	0.7%
1	0.5%	1.0%
1.5	0.6%	1.2%
2	0.7%	1.4%
2.5	0.8%	1.5%
3	0.9%	1.7%
3.5	0.9%	1.8%
4	1.0%	2.0%
4.5	1.1%	2.1%
5	1.1%	2.2%
5.5	1.2%	2.3%
6	1.2%	2.4%
6.5	1.3%	2.5%
7	1.3%	2.6%
7.5	1.4%	2.7%
8	1.4%	2.8%
8.5	1.5%	2.9%
9	1.5%	2.9%
9.5	1.5%	3.0%
10	1.6%	3.1%

Let us now compute MV_F, MD_F and δ based on the formulae seen in the previous section. We repeat those computations now, in six months and for any possible τ between 0 and 10 years.[17] The results, for the three swaps, are reported in Table 16.6 and Figure 16.3.

The Figure clearly shows that, all other things equal, the sensitivity to rate changes is larger for the in-the-money swap; in fact, although its duration is smaller (because coupons weigh more), the market value of the virtual fixed-rate bond associated with this swap (and therefore, the value of the swap as a whole) is larger.

---

[17] More precisely, we are assuming that the duration is computed soon after the bi-annual payment due on the swap.

Table 16.6 The relationship between τ and the diffusion effect

Evaluation time (τ), in years	At par swap			In the money swap			Out of the money swap		
	MV_F	MD_F	δ_τ	MV_F	MD_F	δ_τ	MV_F	MD_F	δ_τ
0	100.0	6.5	607.2	113.6	6.3	665.0	86.4	6.9	549.3
0.5	100.0	6.3	585.2	113.1	6.1	638.8	86.9	6.7	531.6
1	100.0	6.1	562.4	112.7	5.8	611.9	87.3	6.4	512.9
1.5	100.0	5.8	538.7	112.2	5.6	584.0	87.8	6.1	493.3
2	100.0	5.6	514.0	111.7	5.4	555.3	88.3	5.9	472.7
2.5	100.0	5.3	488.3	111.1	5.1	525.7	88.9	5.6	450.9
3	100.0	5.1	461.6	110.6	4.9	495.1	89.4	5.3	428.1
3.5	100.0	4.8	433.9	110.0	4.6	463.6	90.0	5.0	404.1
4	100.0	4.5	405.0	109.4	4.4	431.2	90.6	4.7	378.8
4.5	100.0	4.2	374.9	108.8	4.1	397.7	91.2	4.4	352.2
5	100.0	3.9	343.7	108.1	3.8	363.1	91.9	4.0	324.3
5.5	100.0	3.6	311.2	107.4	3.5	327.5	92.6	3.7	295.0
6	100.0	3.2	277.5	106.7	3.2	290.8	93.3	3.3	264.1
6.5	100.0	2.9	242.3	106.0	2.8	253.0	94.0	3.0	231.7
7	100.0	2.5	205.8	105.2	2.5	214.0	94.8	2.6	197.6
7.5	100.0	2.1	167.8	104.5	2.1	173.8	95.5	2.2	161.8
8	100.0	1.7	128.3	103.6	1.7	132.4	96.4	1.8	124.2
8.5	100.0	1.3	87.2	102.8	1.3	89.7	97.2	1.3	84.7
9	100.0	0.9	44.4	101.9	0.9	45.7	98.1	0.9	43.2
9.5	100.0	0.5	0.0	101.0	0.5	0.4	99.0	0.5	−0.4
10	0.0	0.0	0.0	0.0	0.0	0.0	0.0	0.0	0.0

We now combine together the diffusion and the amortisation effect. In doing so, we compute the FPE of the swap for each τ between now and T. This is done using the data in Tables 16.5 and 16.6, and the FPE at time τ is computed as:

$$FPE_\tau = \delta_\tau \cdot \alpha \cdot \sigma_\tau \qquad (16.14)$$

The results are shown in Figure 16.4.

As can be seen, in the first years the quick increase in the volatility (σ_τ) prevails over the moderate reduction in the sensitivity δ. FPE therefore experience a rise, as τ moves forward in time. Yet, in the last part of the swap's life, the increase in volatility

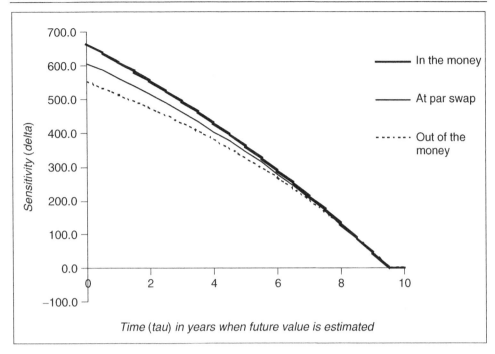

Figure 16.3   The relationship between τ and the amortization effect

(diffusion effect) is more limited, while the reduction in δ (amortization effect) is sharper: as a consequence, the potential exposure of the swap decreases, and finally becomes zero close to the final maturity of the contract.[18]

16.3.5   Peak exposure (PE) and average expected exposure (AEE)

As the FPE changes, according to the moment in time τ to which it refers, one has to choose the most appropriate time horizon (selecting the "best" τ for estimating counter-party risk measurement), or to find a way of summarizing different measures of exposure risk (relating to different τs) into just one figure. In other words: which, among the future exposures shown in Figure 16.4, should we pick up? And how can different values be combined into a single measure?

Several solutions have been proposed. The simplest one ("peak exposure criterion") is to use the maximum FPE_{τ} value. This way, counterparty risk will not be underestimated. However, one risks overestimating the effects of a default, if it were to occur close to the contract's start or end.

A second criterion, proposed by Zangari (1997b), is based on the "*average expected exposure*". This concept has been derived as follows. If the parametric approach holds,[19]

---

[18] More precisely, if the floating-rate coupon is fixed at the beginning of each six-month period and paid at the end, than the FPE goes to zero six months before the contract's final maturity, when the duration and the value of the fixed-rate leg are equal to the duration and value of the floating-rate one.

[19] That is, if the risk factors are normally-distributed and if the link between them and the value of the derivative is linear.

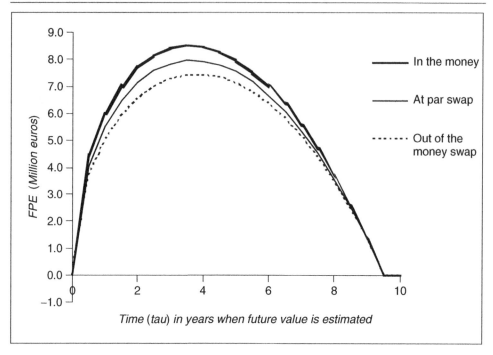

Figure 16.4   The relationship between τ and the FPE of a swap

then for every moment τ, the probability distribution of the market value v_τ of an OTC derivative is normally distributed (see Figure 16.5), with mean equal to the current market value of the position (which we indicate as $\mu_{v,\tau}$) and standard deviation equal to $\sigma_{v,\tau}$.

The latter is a function of the volatility of the market factor(s) and of the coefficient(s) linking market factor(s) to the market value of the OTC derivative.[20] For the swap seen in the previous sections, e.g., we had $\sigma_{v,\tau} = \delta_\tau \cdot \sigma_1 \sqrt{\tau}$, where σ_1 was the one-year volatility of the changes (Δr) in the market rate r_m. Based on the data in Tables 16.5 and 16.6, and considering, as an example, the "par swap" described above, we would have, for instance, $\sigma_{v,\tau} = 1.6$ million for $\tau = 3$ years, or $\sigma_{v,\tau} = 1.5$ million for $\tau = 5$ years.

Moreover, as the credit risk due to the possible default of a counterparty can never be negative, the credit risk exposure at time τ (E_τ) will be equal to v_τ when the latter is positive, and to zero if v_τ is negative:

$$E_\tau = \begin{cases} v_\tau & if \quad v_\tau \geq 0 \\ 0 & if \quad v_\tau < 0 \end{cases} \tag{16.15}$$

Hence, if v_τ is normally distributed, the probability distribution for E_τ is a positive truncated normal (see grey areas in Figure 16.5), which (according to a well-known result in statistics) has a mean of:

$$E(E_\tau) = \sigma_v \cdot f\left(\frac{\mu_{v,\tau}}{\sigma_{v,\tau}}\right) + \mu_\tau \cdot N\left(\frac{\mu_{v,\tau}}{\sigma_{v,\tau}}\right) \tag{16.16}$$

---

[20] In the example seen in the previous sections, we have assumed a flat rate curve, so that we could use just one risk factor (r_m) and one sensitivity measure (δ).

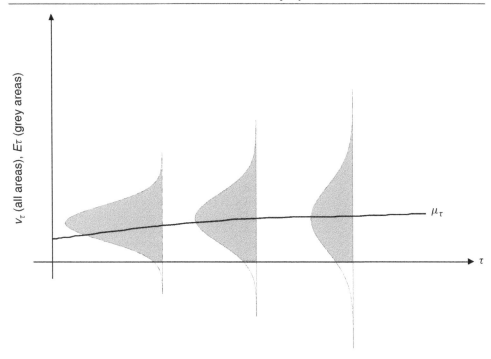

Figure 16.5   An example of how exposure to credit risk (E_τ) evolves over time

where $f(.)$ and $N(.)$ denote, respectively, the density function and the cumulated density function of a standard normal.

Consider again the par swap seen in the previous section; provided no change occurs in market rates, the current value of that contract is always zero ($\mu_\tau = 0$ for any τ). Table 16.7 shows how σ_τ and the expected exposure $E(E_\tau)$ change, based on different values of τ.

Note that the values in Table 16.7 are smaller than the FEPτ reported, for the same par swap, in Table 16.6. In fact, we are now considering a set of average values, while Table 16.6 focused on extreme values (associated with a confidence interval of 97.5 %). Figure 16.6 highlights this difference.

From an economic point of view, the reason for choosing the expected exposure ($E(E_\tau)$), rather than percentile-based measures like FEP$_\tau$, is that banks tend to have a high number of different contracts in place with the same counterparty. Hence, it is quite unlikely that the market value of all contracts agreed with a defaulted counterparty is significantly above the mean, when the default takes place.

Following Zangari we have now computed a measure of expected exposure $E(E_\tau)$ which is different from the "extreme" FEPs seen before. We have also shown that this value changes based on the τ used. Yet, we are still left with our original problem: if different levels of τ lead to different exposures, can we combine them together into just one figure?

Zangari (1997b) suggests to compute a weighted average of expected exposures for different τs, using a system of weights proportional to the discount factors associated with different maturities (so that the most remote ones will be given less importance).

Table 16.7 Expected loan equivalent exposure at time τ

Evaluation time (τ), in years	σ_v	$E(E_\tau)$	$(1 + r_\tau)^\tau$	w_τ
0.5	2.1	0.8	1.0	0.07
1	2.8	1.1	0.9	0.07
1.5	3.3	1.3	0.9	0.07
2	3.6	1.4	0.9	0.06
2.5	3.9	1.5	0.8	0.06
3	4.0	1.6	0.8	0.06
3.5	4.1	1.6	0.8	0.06
4	4.0	1.6	0.7	0.05
4.5	4.0	1.6	0.7	0.05
5	3.8	1.5	0.7	0.05
5.5	3.6	1.5	0.6	0.05
6	3.4	1.4	0.6	0.05
6.5	3.1	1.2	0.6	0.04
7	2.7	1.1	0.6	0.04
7.5	2.3	0.9	0.6	0.04
8	1.8	0.7	0.5	0.04
8.5	1.3	0.5	0.5	0.04
9	0.7	0.3	0.5	0.04
9.5	0.0	0.0	0.5	0.03
10	0.0	0.0	0.5	0.03
$AEE = \Sigma w_\tau \cdot E(E_\tau)$			1.16	

Such an average is called *Average Expected Exposure* (*AEE*):

$$AEE = \sum_\tau w_i \cdot E(E_\tau) \qquad (16.17)$$

where

$$w_i = \frac{(1 + r_\tau)^{-\tau}}{\sum_\tau (1 + r_\tau)^{-\tau}}$$

Going back to our "par swap" we can apply (16.17) and get an AEE of about 1.16 million euros (see again Table 16.7 for further details).

In 2004, the New Basel Accord on bank capital adequacy has decreed that methods based on formulae like equation (16.17) may be used by banks not only for internal risk-management purposes, but also for computing exposures on which regulatory capital requirements are applied.

This means that a further approach is now available (next to the current exposure method and, sometimes, the original exposure method[21]), called the "internal model method". This approach entails the computation of the Average Expected Exposure (which, in the Committee's jargon has been called EPE, that is, Expected Positive Exposure) and the use, for regulatory purposes, of a slightly adjusted (and more conservative) version of

---

[21] The original exposure method is no more part of the international capital regulation; however, as stated above, it may be used if allowed by national supervisors. In the European Union, e.g., the capital adequacy directives still allow for this method to be used.

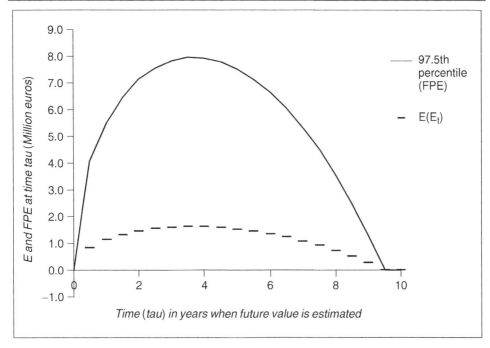

Figure 16.6 FPE_τ and $E(E_\tau)$ for the "at par" swap

it, called "effective EPE". More details can be found in Basel Committee on Banking Supervision (2005).

Finally, for banks that are not yet sophisticated enough to adopt the internal model method, the Committee has also devised one more approach, the so-called "standardized approach". This approach, while being less demanding than the one based on internal models, is more flexible than the original and current exposure methods and allows for the computation of the risk-reduction effects of bilateral netting agreements (see section 16.5.1).

16.3.6 Further approaches to LEE computation

In sections 16.3.3–16.3.5 we showed how the loan equivalent exposure of a derivative contract can be computed, based on a parametric approach where percentiles can be expressed as multiples of the market factors' historical volatility. However, just like we saw for market risk VaR in the second part of this book, the estimate of LEE can also be based on different approaches. Namely, two alternative methods are based on option pricing models and on historical simulations.

The first approach was developed in the second half of the 80's, and draws on the fact that the loan equivalent should be equal to the future loss (that is, to the value of the OTC contract, if positive) in the event of a default of the counterparty. In practice, as seen in the previous section, this means that:

$$E\tau = \max(0, v\tau) \tag{16.18}$$

Equation (16.18) is equivalent to the payoff of an European call option with maturity equal to τ and a strike price of zero. Option pricing models can therefore be used to compute its expected value.

Namely, we know that the value of an IRS paying fixed and receiving floating is equal to the market value of a fixed-rate bond with equal maturity and notional, and a coupon rate of r_s (the swap rate fixed in the contract), less the value of a floating rate bond with equal duration and notional. If, for the sake of simplicity, we assume that the floating rate be set immediately before the coupon payments, then the floating rate bond will always trade at par, and the value of the swap will simply be the difference between the market value of the fixed-rate bond (MV_F) and the notional (N). Equation (16.18) then becomes:

$$E\tau = \max(0, MV_{F,\tau} - N) \qquad (16.18a)$$

which indicates the value of a call written on a fixed-rate bond, with a strike price equal to the notional value of the swap. The expected value of such a call can easily be computed, if an estimate of the underlying asset's value and volatility is available.

In the historical simulation approach, instead, a high number of values for v_τ and E_τ are simulated using an appropriate random numbers generator, that produces many possible evolutionary paths for market factors. The maximum value for E_τ within a given confidence interval is then selected.[22] This approach, proposed jointly by the *Bank of England* and the *Federal Reserve* in 1986, is usually based on Monte Carlo simulation, and does not require LEE to be decomposed into CE and FPE, since it is computed directly from the simulation results.

16.3.7 Loan equivalent and Value at Risk: analogies and differences

The concepts of loan equivalent exposure and of market-risk VaR (discussed in the second part of this book) are to some extent similar, since both estimate the risk associated with a position based on the volatility of the underlying risk factors. Yet, some important differences between the two must be noticed:

- the LEE is measured on a single-contract (or single-counterparty) basis, while market-risk VaR is measured on a portfolio basis, that is, pooling together all assets in the bank's trading book;
- the LEE includes two components, related both to current exposure and to possible future exposure; conversely, VaR is computed as a value change relative to the current market value of the portfolio (assessed by means of a mark-to-market process) and therefore refers only to future exposure;
- as far as LEE is concerned, changes in the risk factors produce only an increase (or decrease) in credit risk exposure; in the case of VaR, they generate straight profits or losses;
- the risk horizon of VaR depends on the position's holding period and liquidity; the risk horizon of the LEE encompasses the whole life to maturity of the exposure;
- as far as market-risk VaR is concerned, risk can be reduced through hedging strategies (involving, e.g., the use of derivatives on stock indices, currencies or interest rates); the

---

[22] See Simons (1989) for an empirical analysis of this kind.

LEE for counterparty risk may only be reduced through bilateral netting agreements allowing for debts and credits, due to different contracts with the same counterparty, to offset each other;[23]
- the LEE of an off-balance sheet item does not represent its VaR. In fact, to transform the LEE into a VaR, one has to estimate the counterparty PD, the loss rate in the event of default (LGD) and the unexpected loss. Therefore, LEEs may not be directly used to price the credit risk in a derivative contract or to allocate risk-based capital.

16.4 RISK-ADJUSTED PERFORMANCE MEASUREMENT

Among the possible uses of LEE, one of the most important ones is the measurement of risk-adjusted performances.

Consider the following example: a customer buys forward from the bank one million US dollars, with delivery in one year. The market forward price x_m for the same maturity is now one euro per dollar; the bank adds to this a spread of 0.002 (2/1000) euros, setting the final forward price at 1.002 euros per dollar.

Also, suppose that the annual volatility of the changes, Δx, in the forward euro/dollar rate is 5%, and that the bank computes the LEE based on a 97.7% confidence interval (implying an α of about 2).

The loan equivalent of this contract would be given by:[24]

$$LEE = CE + FPE = (x_f - x_m) \cdot 1,000,000 + \delta \cdot \alpha \cdot \sigma_{\Delta x} =$$
$$= 2,000 + 1,000,000 \cdot 2 \cdot 5\% = 102,000 \qquad (16.19)$$

As mentioned above, the concept of "loan equivalent" implies that – as far counterparty risk is concerned – this forward sale of dollars is equivalent to issuing a plain-vanilla loan, of 102,000 euros, to the same customer.

Thus, the LEE is not yet a VaR estimate, indicating the amount of economic capital put at risk by the contract. To get the VaR we need to combine LEE with further risk parameters, like the PD and LGD of the exposure, as well as its correlation with other loans in the bank's portfolio. For the sake of simplicity, assume that this kind of analyses has lead to a VaR equal to 8% of the exposure. The capital at risk (economic capital) would then be:

$$CaR = 102,000 \cdot 8\% = 8,160$$

while the expected profit would be given by the spread (2/1000 euros for each dollar) times the notional, that is 2,000 dollars.

The risk-adjusted rate of return would then be equal to:

$$\frac{2,000}{8,160} \cong 24.5\%$$

Now, suppose the bank has agreed with its shareholders a return on capital absorbed (r_e) of 12%. The bank's Raroc, expressed as a premium above this cost of capital, would be:

$$Raroc = 24.5\% - 12\% = 12.5\%$$

---

[23] See. section 16.5.1
[24] Note that the spread $(x_f - x_m) \cdot 1,000,000$ will be cashed by the bank only in one year. Hence it should be discounted to get its present value. This has been skipped for the sake of simplicity.

The contract would then be generating an expected return greater than the shareholders' target-return. It would therefore create value for the bank.

More generally, we have:

$$Raroc = \frac{(x_f - x_m)N}{VaR[(x_f - x_m) \cdot N + N \cdot \alpha \cdot \sigma_{\Delta x}]} - r_e = \frac{x_f - x_m}{VaR[(x_f - x_m) + \alpha \cdot \sigma_{\Delta x}]} - r_e$$
(16.20)

where N is the notional of the contract and VaR indicates the unit economic capital (for a LEE of one euro), as estimated by the bank's credit VaR model. Note that, since our example involves a currency forward, the sensitivity of the contract to changes in the exchange rate is given by the notional, N.

Equation (16.20) could alternatively be used to find, based on the target-return required by shareholders (that is, on the bank's cost of capital), the minimum spread to be applied to the customer, to avoid destroying value (that is, to get a non-negative Raroc). Imposing that Raroc ≥ 0, equation (16.20) implies the following:

$$x_f - x_m \geq \frac{r_e \cdot VaR \cdot \alpha \cdot \sigma_{\Delta x}}{1 - r_e \cdot VaR}$$
(16.21)

Accordingly, in our example, the spread to the customer should be at least of

$$\frac{12\% \cdot 8\% \cdot 2 \cdot 5\%}{1 - 12\% \cdot 8\%} \cong 0.097\%$$

Generally speaking, the unit spread will increase with:

– the volatility of the underlying market factor;
– the credit VaR of the exposure (which, as we know, is affected by the counterparty's PD, the LGD and the correlations);
– the cost of capital of the bank.

16.5 RISK-MITIGATION TOOLS FOR PRE-SETTLEMENT RISK

There are several ways to reduce the LEE of an OTC deal, that is, its pre-settlement risk. In the following we cover the three main ones: (i) netting agreements; (ii) safety margins; (iii) recouponing and guarantees; (iv) credit triggers and early redemption options..

16.5.1 Bilateral netting agreements

Netting agreements (also known as "close out netting agreements") allow to net all positions towards a defaulting counterparty, so that those with negative market value may offset the ones having a positive current exposure.[25] In other words, the counterparty is not allowed to default on some contracts, while claiming the payments due on some other ones.

---

[25] In other words, all the positions with a given counterparty are marked-to-market, and the net balance is settled through a single payment.

Table 16.8 An example of bilateral/multilateral netting

	Current market value (MV) of the positions held by bank…					
	A		B		C	
Towards bank…	$MV > 0$	$MV < 0$	$MV > 0$	$MV < 0$	$MV > 0$	$MV < 0$
A	0	0	50	100	50	80
B	100	50	0	0	90	60
C	80	50	60	90	0	0

The effects of bilateral (and multilateral) netting agreements can be shown by means of a simple example.[26] Consider the three banks in Table 16.8.

Now, suppose bank C defaults and consider the position of bank A: if no netting agreement were available, bank A would incur a loss of 80. In fact, on one hand it would be forced to abide by the contracts where it is a debtor (50), on the other hand it would be missing the profits on positions where it is a creditor (80). However, if a bilateral netting agreement has been signed between A and C, the two positions would be offset against each other, and bank A would only lose the difference (30).

The position of bank A would further improve if all three banks were bound by a *multilateral* netting agreement. In this case, the exposures of both bank A and bank B towards bank C (the defaulted one) could be offset against each other. Accordingly, the net credit of A towards C (30, that is 80–50) could be netted with the net debit of B (−30, that is, 60–90). A net payment of 30 from B to A would then take place, and none of the two non-defaulted banks would incur losses.

Netting agreements were first accepted by regulators as a risk mitigation tool in the 1988 Basel Accord. However, only bilateral netting by *novation* for exposures of *identical maturity and currency* was considered acceptable. "Novation" means that two offset contracts had to be cancelled and replaced by a new, unique one.[27] As can be easily understood, only a very limited number of deals satisfied the requirements imposed by this kind of netting.

In November 1990, the Bank of International Settlements released a study (known as the "Lamfalussy Report") on interbank netting schemes. The report recognized the effectiveness of netting agreements in reducing credit and liquidity risks, provided that a number of requirements were complied with, relative to the legal enforceability of the agreements.

In the following years, the Basel Committee elaborated on the conclusions of the Lamfalussy Report, acknowledging the need to extend, beyond novation, the criteria for the regulatory recognition of netting agreements. In fact, a different type of netting agreements had significantly spread across banks, called "close out" agreements (also known as *in futurum* netting). The close-out clause states that, if a given event (usually default) occurs, all outstanding positions between two counterparties are immediately

---

[26] See Hendricks (1994) for further details.

[27] Netting by novation may only involve positions that already exist when the netting agreement is underwritten, and does not extend to new positions that may arise in the future.

closed, and the net present value is computed, offsetting contracts with positive and negative market value.

In April 1995, the Basel Committee amended the 1988 Accord, significantly enhancing the kind of bilateral netting agreements that were considered acceptable. In practice, any agreement could be accepted if, according to the bank's national supervisors, it made impossible, for the liquidator of the defaulted counterparty, to unbundle favourable and unfavourable contracts, claiming the settlement of the former while leaving the latter unpaid.[28]

The Basel Committee, instead, decided not to accept, for regulatory purposes, the so-called "walkaway clauses". Those are clauses that entitle the performing party to interrupt, partially or totally, payments to the non-performing (i.e., defaulted) one, even if the latter's credits were greater than its debts.

The effect of bilateral netting agreements was first limited only to the current exposure: CEs of contracts with positive and negative value could therefore be netted. On the other hand, the future potential exposures (FPEs) had to be aggregated regardless of the present sign of the exposure: more precisely, the notionals of all contracts (each one multiplied by the add-on coefficient shown in Table 16.2 above) had to be added together regardless of the fact that two contracts could, in fact, offset each other.

Such an approach could lead to a serious overestimation of risk. So, for example, if bank A entered into two swap contracts with bank B, having the same maturity, periodicity of payments, benchmark rates and notionals, but having opposite sign, the current exposure would be equal to the net market value of the two (that is, zero), but the future potential exposure would be computed by adding up the notionals of the two swaps, each one multiplied by its own add-on coefficient. Nevertheless, given a bilateral netting agreement between bank A and B, counterparty would always be zero for both banks, since the market value of the two opposite positions would always be identical.[29]

To overcome this excess of caution, the *International Swap and Derivatives Association* (ISDA) proposed a correction based on the so-called *Net-Gross Ratio* (NGR). This is given by the ratio between the *net replacement value* (NRV) of all positions outstanding with a given counterparty (computed as the summation of their market values, or simply as zero if such summation were negative) and their *gross replacement value* (GRV), obtained as the summation of all exposures having positive market value:

$$NGR = \frac{NRV}{GRV} = \frac{Max\left(\sum_i MV_i, 0\right)}{\sum_i Max(MV_i, 0)} \tag{16.22}$$

Based on the ISDA proposal, the FPE computed as suggested by the Basel Committee (that is, summing all notionals, each one multiplied by the add-on coefficient in Table 16.2) should have been scaled down by multiplying it by the *NGR* coefficient.

---

[28] Basel Committee (1995).

[29] The problem may turn out to be very important when assessing the additional risk due to further contracts with a given counterparty. When a netting agreement exist, a new deal may in fact decrease, rather than increase, total pre-settlement risk. Yet, even if this were the case, the approach proposed by the Basel Committee may lead to an increase in the FPE exceeding the decrease in the CE, hence to an increase in the total LEE.

Table 16.9 An example LEE computation for netted exposures, based on the original Basel Committee approach and the ISDA proposal

Contract	Notional (euro million) (a)	CE (market value, MV, euro million)	Life to maturity (years)	Add-on coefficient (see Table 16.2) (b)	FPE (euro million) (a × b)
IRS	20	1	5	0.5 %	0.1
Currency swap	10	−0.5	3	5 %	0.5

An example will prove useful in understanding how the tow approaches differ. Consider an IRS and a currency swap, both with the same counterparty (Table 16.9).

Based on the Committee's original approach, the LEE would have been given by the net market value $(1 - 0.5 = 0.5$ million euros) plus the sum of all FPEs on individual contracts $(0.1+0.5 = 0.6$ million euros), totalling 1.1 million euros.

To apply the ISDA approach we must first compute the NGR ratio: the numerator is the market value of the two contracts (0.5 million), while the denominator consists of the total value of all contracts having a positive current exposure (1 million). The NGR ratio is therefore equal to 50 %.

LEE is then given by the net current exposure (0.5 million), plus the sum of FPEs on individual contracts (0.6 million), weighted by the NGR ratio. In practice: $0.5 + 0.6 \cdot 50\%$ = 0.8 million euros.

The ISDA proposal was partially accepted by the Basel Committee in 1995. Yet, the Committee chose not to use the NGR ratio, but rather a modified version, given by:

$$NGR^* = 0.4 + 0.6 \cdot NGR$$

In the example above, NGR^* would be given by $0.4 + 0.6 \cdot 50\%$, that is, 70 %. The LEE of the counterparty would therefore amount to $0.5 + 0.6 \cdot 70\% = 0.92$ million euros.

The choice to replace NGR with NGR* is due to the fact that the Committee did not want the LEE to become zero when the net market value of the positions included in a bilateral netting agreement is not positive.

Finally, it must be noticed that, since 2004, the New Basel Accord (see Chapter 20) has entitled banks using the "internal model method", to compute counterparty risk by summing all *effective EPEs* (see section 16.3.5) related to the exposures of a single counterparty with which a valid netting agreement exists.

In 2004, one more method for taking into account the benefits of netting agreements was proposed by the Basel Committee. This is the so-called "standardised approach". According to this method, all long and short positions with a counterparty (with whom a valid netting agreement exists) have to be grouped into "hedging sets", that is, groups of contracts that depend on the same risk factor.[30] An example of a hedging set could be derivatives on long-term fixed-rate British Government bonds, as their value depends on the evolution of long-term British pound yields.

---

[30] Contracts involving more than one risk factor (e.g., currency forwards) have to be mapped into multiple virtual cash flows (see Chapter 5), each one associated with a different hedging set.

Within each hedging set, a net risk position must be computed, offsetting risk positions associated with long and short contracts (the "risk position" of a contract is usually its notional[31]). The net risk position of each set must then be multiplied by a coefficient ("credit conversion factor") reflecting the volatility of the risk factor (e.g., 0.2% for interest rates, 2.5% for exchange rates, 7.0% for equity). For each counterparty subject to a netting agreement, the sum of the net risk positions for all hedging sets, each one multiplied by its own credit conversion factor, is finally compared with the net current market value of all contracts. The LEE is given by the larger of these two quantities. Note that, this way, when the current net value of all contracts with a counterparty is zero or negative, the LEE is still positive, and depends on the net positions within each hedging set, weighted by an appropriate volatility factor. This captures the fact that, if the bank is exposed to one or more risk factors, the net value of the contracts could become positive in the future.

16.5.2 Safety margins

A further tool to reduce pre-settlement risk entails the use of safety margins based on the LEE. Margins applied to OTC derivatives are similar to those required by central clearinghouses on futures. Two counterparties entering a futures contract, in fact, have to provide an initial margin when the contract is agreed upon; the margin will then be increased or decreased based on the daily changes in the market value of the contract. This mechanism, together with a number of guarantees and mutual-support agreements among the institutional investors participating in the market, has prevented futures exchanges from recording any significant default in the past years, even in periods of high price volatility.

Therefore, it has been sometimes argued that swap exchanges should be created, adopting the same margin systems and clearinghouses as futures exchanges and settling profits and losses on a daily basis.[32] However, as such proposals have never been translated into actual projects, many institutions have started using margins on a bilateral basis, without a central clearinghouse.

For example, if a customer enters in an IRS with the bank, with a notional of 10 million euros and a LEE of 500,000 euros, the bank may require him/her to pay a deposit equal to the LEE, or a fraction thereof. Such a margin would reduce credit risk for the bank and could be provided in cash, as well as through interest-bearing, low-risk securities (e.g., Treasury bills), thereby reducing the opportunity cost for the customer.

The most common solution involves requiring a margin (through cash or low-risk securities) when the current exposure exceeds a given threshold. On the other hand, no initial margin is required when the contract is started, as its initial value is usually zero. A system of margins is usually characterised by three key elements: the level of the threshold, the update frequency, the kind of financial assets accepted as a deposit.

- the threshold is usually the same for both parties, although asymmetric thresholds may be agreed to reflect their different creditworthiness (rating). In this case, the party with

---

[31] For non-linear derivatives, the delta-equivalent (value of the underlying asset times the option's delta) must be used. For derivatives on bonds, the risk position will be the notional multiplied by the modified duration.

[32] This need is very much felt for long-term contracts (including both IRS and currency swaps). On one hand, a long maturity may involve wide swings in the market factors; on the other hand, it increases the counterparty's probability of default.

a lower rating will be assigned a lower threshold, that is, it may be called to provide a margin even following a smaller change in the initial value of the contract;
- setting the update frequency involves a trade-off between operational complexity and risk mitigation. The lower the frequency, the higher the potential change in the value of the contract and the risk that the counterparty may default in the meantime. Nevertheless, a recent survey, lead by ISDA (2003) among fifteen large OTC derivatives dealers, has shown that banks tend to use high (mostly daily) frequencies.
- The assets accepted as a deposit can be either cash or securities. For the latter, adjustment factors ("haircuts") are sometimes adopted (so that one euro of securities is equivalent to x cents of cash), accounting for their credit risk and liquidity. Adjustment factors are lower for riskier securities, such as long-term Government bonds and corporate bonds.

To be really effective, margins should be adopted by all institutions operating on the OTC market. In fact, if an institution does not require margins, it may attract customers and make it more difficult, for the remaining banks and dealers, to subject their counterparties to a system of safety deposits.

16.5.3 Recouponing and guarantees[33]

As an alternative to safety margins, *recouponing* has been devised, that is, the periodic settlement of the market value of the OTC contract (current exposure), to be replaced by a new one in line with current market conditions (that is, implying a current exposure of zero).

Recouponing may prove useful if, for instance, there are doubts on the actual enforceability of the collateral; it also can be indicated for those intermediaries which do not want (or are not allowed to) provide safety margins. In 1995, the Basel Committee has accepted implicitly recouponing (without using this word) as a risk mitigant, by suggesting that the add-on coefficients in Table 16.2 be reduced when this kind of agreements exist.

Another risk mitigation technique involves the provision of guarantees by a third party having a better credit rating than the original counterparty. Guarantees do not affect the value of the LEE, but decrease the credit risk associated with a given loan equivalent (e.g., because the PD of the original counterparty can be substituted with that of the guarantor, usually lower). The improvement in credit risk following a guarantee does not depend only on the better credit rating enjoyed by the guarantor, but also on the fact that the bank will face a loss only if both the guarantor and the original counterparty default jointly. The probability of a joint default could be very low if the two companies are not significantly correlated. On the other hand, when correlation is substantial (e.g., when a subsidiary gets a guarantee from its holding company), joint defaults may be rather likely: in this case, only the first risk-mitigating effect mentioned above (rating substitution, or PD substitution) will hold, while the "joint default effect" will be negligible.

16.5.4 Credit triggers and early redemption options

These are clauses providing for the early termination of the contract if a given event occurs ("credit triggers"), usually a rating downgrade for one of the two parties, or simply at

---

[33] This section and the next one are based on Maspero (1998).

the mere discretion of one counterparty ("early redemption clauses" or "early redemption options").

A credit trigger gives one party the right, but not the duty, to terminate the contract, asking for the settlement of its current value. Note that a party may also decide not to use a credit trigger, e.g. if the downgrade of its counterparty is considered temporary, or not enough strong to affect its ability and willingness to perform its future obligations.

As shown in Chapter 13, marginal default probabilities for an investment-grade issuer are usually increasing with time: while in the first twelve months after a new issue the one-year default probability is almost negligible, nevertheless it grows more and more considerable in the following years. This, among other things, depends on the fact that the issuer may have migrated into a worse rating class before defaulting. Such a phenomenon is widely documented by the "transition matrices" disclosed by Moody's and Standard & Poor's (see Chapter 13), which indicate the probabilities associated with transitions to different rating classes.

Credit triggers help mitigating credit risk, because they ensure that the OTC contract will remain valid only as long as the counterparty holds a good rating. If, instead, it should migrate into a worse rating class, then the trigger will allow from the prompt termination of the contract.

Based on marginal default probabilities and on n-year transition matrices, one can even estimate the "value" of a credit trigger. An example is provided in Table 16.10.

Table 16.10 The value of a credit trigger for an AA-rated counterparty and the effect of different trigger thresholds

Years	1	3	5	10	15	20	25
Rating class							
AA	0.00 %	0.06 %	0.19 %	0.81 %	1.73 %	2.77 %	3.80 %
AA/A	0.00 %	0.00 %	0.00 %	0.00 %	0.00 %	0.00 %	0.00 %
% reduction	0.00 %	100.0 %	100.0 %	100.0 %	100.0 %	100.0 %	100.0 %
AA/BBB	0.00 %	0.01 %	0.04 %	0.12 %	0.21 %	0.27 %	0.32 %
% reduction	0.00 %	76.47 %	79.23 %	84.67 %	88.06 %	90.15 %	91.48 %
AA/BB	0.00 %	0.02 %	0.06 %	0.23 %	0.42 %	0.60 %	0.75 %
% reduction	0.00 %	66.27 %	67.68 %	72.16 %	75.84 %	78.43 %	80.21 %

Source: Maspero (1998).

The columns of the Table report the maturity of a hypothetical OTC contract for which the credit trigger has been designed. The first row shows how the cumulative default rates for an AA-rated counterparty evolves, starting from the moment when the OTC derivative is created: they show that, e.g, the 10-year default probability of the counterparty is expected to be 0.81 %.

The second row ("AA/A") shows the probability that the contract may default if a credit trigger is present, providing for contract termination if the counterparty's rating is downgraded to A or below. As can be seen, such a trigger should totally wipe out any default risk. This is because, transition matrices show that all defaults by AA-rated borrowers have first implied a transition into a worse rating class.

The rows labelled "AA/BBB" and "AA/BB" show the contract's probability of default if the trigger threshold is set, respectively at BBB or BB. In this case, we see that probabilities do not go to zero, but nevertheless decrease considerably. E.g., the 10-year expected default probability (0.81 % if no trigger were present) falls to 0.12 % or 0.23 % respectively, denoting a significant reduction in credit risk.

However, data in Table 16.10 require two caveats:

- rating agency data used as a starting point in this kind of exercises are based on a given historical sample (usually, US rated issuers observed in the latest 20–25 years). The rating standards used by agencies should remain the same across time and countries; nevertheless, the effectiveness of their assessments could depend on the country where, and the period when, they are issued (e.g., because of different accounting standards, of the different opaqueness of corporate policies).
- Results like those in Table 16.10 are based on n-year transition matrices, which are often estimated by combining shorter-term transition matrices (e.g., one-year) based on an assumption of *markovianity* of the stochastic process driving ratings. This means that the migration probabilities are assumed to depend only on the present rating, regardless of the past rating history. Such a working hypothesis, although quite convenient, is often contradicted by empirical evidence. According to Moody's, e.g., the probability of a Baa-rated company to experience a downgrade in the following year changes from 6.3 % to 3.2 % if the company has just been upgraded from a worse class; on the other hand, it jumps to 11.5 % if the company has just experienced a downgrading. Such a trend effect calls for caution when analysing results like those presented in Table 16.10.

Early redemption clauses, or options, allow both parties to terminate the contract at a given future date, simply by settling its current value (based on a set of criteria indicated in detail by the clause).

In principle, the probability of such options to be exercised should increase as a counterparty's creditworthiness grows worse. However, if a downgrade takes place but the current value of the exposure is negative, the early redemption clause may not be used, since it would involve a payment, not a cash inflow. The clause is more likely to be used if the current exposure is positive; even so, however, the following two aspects must be taken into consideration:

- sometimes, it is not possible to use early redemption options selectively, that is, only on a single contract or group of contracts. Actually, the clause may involve termination of *all* contracts outstanding with a given counterparty, including those having a negative current value;
- even if selective termination is provided for (and contracts having positive value can be "cherry-picked"), using the clause may trigger liquidity problems for the counterparty,

that may eventually lead to a default (whereas, if no early termination had been required, the counterparty would have overcome a temporary crisis and stayed performing on its obligations).

SELECTED QUESTIONS AND EXERCISES

1. A Dutch bank holds a long OTC currency forward, whereby 100,000 British pounds can be bought at 1.5 euros a pound. The current forward rate for the same maturity (14 months) is 1.7 euros; the current spot exchange rate is 1.65 euros. Compute the LEE of the contract using both the original exposure method and the current exposure method (and the coefficients reported in Tables 16.1 and 16.2 in this Chapter). What would happen to those two LEEs if the current spot rate would move to 1.6 euros? Would both of them change? By how much?

2. A bank holds a short forward on oil, with a notional of 2,000 barrels and a forward price (in six months) of 80 euros a barrel. Assume that the current six-month forward price is 75 euros a barrel and that the monthly volatility of forward price changes for oil is 3%. Compute the CE, FPE and LEE of the exposure. In computing the CE, use a 95% confidence level and assume that the six-month interest rate is 5% per annum, continuously compounded.

3. A bank holds a three-year IRS paying variable and receiving a fixed rate of 5%, bi-annually compounded; the current swap rate for the same maturity is 4% and the yield curve is flat. Assuming an annual volatility of absolute changes in yields of 4% and based on a 99% confidence interval, compute the CE of the swap today and the FPE in six months.

4. Consider again the swap in exercise 3 and find:

   (i) the FPE_τ in 6, 12, 18, 24, 30 and 36 months;
   (ii) the peak exposure associated with the maximum FPE_τ;
   (iii) the expected value of the swap, μ_τ in 6, 12, 18, 24, 30 and 36 months;
   (iv) the average expected exposure.

5. Bank Alpha has a number of OTC contracts in place with Bank Beta, as indicated by the Table below. Bank Alpha computes the LEE on OTC derivatives with the current exposure method and the two banks are bound by a valid netting agreement. Assuming you are Bank Alpha and using the "add-on" factors in Table 16.2, compute the total LEE associated with Bank Beta using the ISDA approach (based on the NGR ratio) and the Basel Committee approach (based on NGR*).

Contract	Current value (euros)	Notional in euros	Maturity
Forward purchase of gold	−1000	50000	9 months
FRA	1200	200000	6 months
Short call on the stock index	−2000	40000	8 months
Forward sale of oil	4000	30000	15 months

Part IV
Operational Risk

INTRODUCTION TO PART IV

During the second half of the 90's and the early 2000's, operational risk (OR) has become more and more significant for the financial industry. The reasons behind this growing importance are mainly the following:

√ The financial industry is one of the economic sectors where investments in information systems and technology have been more significant. These investments inevitably expose banks and other financial institutions to the risk of system failures, as well as to the risk of human errors in the programming and use of these systems. A price wrongly input into the system by a trader may, for example, be enough to cause huge losses.

√ The growth of electronic dealing exposes banks to the risk of external frauds and to other risks linked to system security.

√ The increasing wave of mergers and acquisitions in the financial industry may lead (and sometimes has led) to problems and risks due to the integration of information systems.

√ New, sophisticated financial instruments have been developed, which are traded on ad-hoc OTC markets and require very specialized technical skills. This has created the risk that a small group of disloyal traders (thanks to ill-designed reporting procedures and escalation policies) may cause significant losses to the bank, by creating risk positions whose value and risk implications are not fully understood by the bank's senior management.

√ A significant impetus to the development of measurement and management systems for operational risk came from the New Basel Capital Accord, which in 2004 introduced an ad-hoc capital requirement for this type of risk (see Chapter 21).

Despite this increasing importance, OR is still lagging behind other types of risks analyzed in this book as far as measurement systems and management models are concerned. Indeed, as of the early 2000s many large financial institutions had not yet developed either a precise measurement methodology, or a clear management policy, not to mention an effective capital allocation system for this type of risk. This delay is partly related to the difficulties experienced in achieving a correct and universally-shared definition of OR: even the standard definition used by banks for regulatory purposes only dates back to 2004.

However, such a delay may also represent a significant opportunity, for banks and scholars investing in OR management techniques. Indeed, some analysts believe that OR represents the risk category for which the investments in technological and human resources will be most significant in the following years. While this may represent an extreme view, it is certainly true that significant investments will be made by banks and other financial institutions in this particular type of risk management area. Hopefully the results, in terms of methodological rigour and risk measures accuracy, will be similar to the ones achieved by the market and credit risk models analysed in Parts I–III of this book.

Indeed, over the last few years an impressive range of instruments have been developed by software houses and consultancy firms for OR reporting and data collection. Think, e.g., of *OpRisk*, a software launched in 2001 by Algorithmics which has been subsequently integrated by *OpCapital*,[1] as well as of *Horizon*, a software for OR management and reporting developed by the consultancy firm Pricewaterhouse.

In addition to that, a number of applications have been developed for the construction of common databases which are based on joint efforts. An example of this type of cooperative efforts is represented by *Morexchange* (*Multinational Operational Risk Exchange*), a database originally introduced in November 2000 by major financial institutions such as JP Morgan, CIBC and Royal Bank of Canada. This database, which is managed by the software company *NetRisk* in New York, collects all the operational risk loss data of the member banks, analyze them, standardize them in order to make them comparable across banks of different sizes, and gives them back on an aggregate basis to all member banks. This allows them to obtain a much larger database than the one they would be able to obtain based on their own internal data only. It is also agreed that *Morexchange* will be merged with ORX (*Operational Risk Exchange*), another collective database, therefore leading to a larger number of member banks.[2]

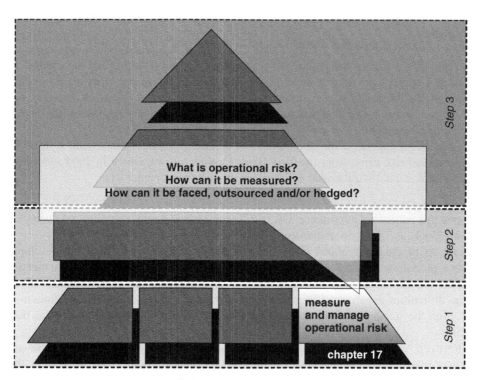

Figure 1   Key questions addressed by this Part of the Book

---

[1] OpCapital is a software module which allows to identify the distributions that best proxy the ones from which the banks' internal OR loss data have been generated and uses these distributions to estimate operational-risk VaR.

[2] Similar initiatives have been promoted by national bank associations, giving rise to consortia through which banks share their OR loss data (e.g. in 2001, the Italian Banking Association). Private vendors, collecting operational risk loss data, also exist. Two examples are represented by OpRisk Analytics and OpVantage, a division of Fitch Risk Management. Both vendors gather information on operational losses exceeding $ 1 million and collect data from public sources such as news reports, court filings, and regulatory authorities filings. As well as classifying losses by business line and causal type, these databases also include descriptive information concerning each loss.

This part of the book (see Figure 1) deals with the definition, measurement and management of OR. More specifically, after a survey of the peculiarities of OR and of the problems related to its measurement, we analyze a model that adopts the same kind of logic used for market and credit risks and allows to estimate the VaR associated to this type of risk. We then look at how Extreme Value Theory (see Chapter 9) can help in OR measurement. This part of the book also looks at the problems related to OR management, the recent trends concerning OR transfer, and the main objectives that a financial institution should pursue in managing OR.

17

Operational Risk: Definition, Measurement and Management

17.1 INTRODUCTION

In the previous chapters we analyzed how to measure financial risks such as interest rate risk, market risks and credit risk. These risks are related to the evolution of both market factors (such as interest rates, exchange rates and stock prices) and a bank's counterparties creditworthiness. In this chapter we focus our attention on a different type of risk: operational risk (OR).

As reported by a recent study of the Federal Reserve Bank of Boston,[1] financial institutions have experienced more than 100 operational loss events exceeding $100 million over the past decade. Examples include the $691 million rogue trading loss at Allfirst Financial, the $484 million settlement due to misleading sale practices at Household Finance, and the estimated $140 million loss stemming from the 9/11 attack at the Bank of New York.

The first issue to be addressed, when dealing with the measurement of this new type of risk, is its definition. Indeed, although in 2004 a common definition of operational risk was agreed for regulatory purposes (see Chapter 21), no clear consensus still exists among practitioners and researchers. The following are just a few of the definitions used by some major international banks, as reported in their financial accounts:

- √ "The potential of any activity to damage the organization, including physical, financial, legal risks and risks to business relationships".
- √ "The risk that deficiencies in information systems or internal controls will result in financial loss, failure to meet regulatory requirements or an adverse impact on the bank's reputation".
- √ "The risk of loss through inadequate systems, controls and procedures, human error or management failure".
- √ "All risks which are not banking (i.e. it excludes credit, market, and trading risks, and those arising from business decisions etc.)".

As we can see, OR is defined in rather different ways, and can be related to potential losses arising from information systems failures, human errors, inadequate procedures and controls, sometimes even including reputational, regulatory and legal risks. In one of the above definitions, OR is even defined in a residual way, by relating it to all risks which differ from the financial ones typically faced by a bank (interest rate risk, market risks and credit risk).

The problem of appropriately defining OR is also made more crucial by the fact that in some specific circumstances the losses associated with this type of risk may, at first sight, appear to be related to other risk types. Take as an example the collapse of UK-based Barings Bank back in 1995: it became insolvent following the losses accumulated by an

---

[1] See de Fontnouvelle et al. (2003).

individual trader, Nick Leeson, in its trading activity on the Nikkei stock index derivatives. Even if these losses could apparently be related to market risks – the Nikkei stock index continued to decrease causing significant losses on the outstanding long futures positions and on the short put options positions accumulated by the bank – they should in reality be associated to OR. Indeed, these losses could be attributed to three main factors: (i) inadequate controls and procedures, as the internal risk limits concerning individual positions were not respected, (ii) fraud, as the trader hided its losses for a relatively long period of time through the creation of special internal accounts, and finally (iii) management incompetence, as the senior managers did not react in any way to the accumulation of losses and proved ineffective in preventing the build up of risky positions that were significantly larger than the ones allowed by the internal risk control system.

This chapter is devoted to the definition, measurement and management of OR. The second section deals with the problem of correctly defining OR and surveys some peculiarities of this type of risk. In the third paragraph, we focus on the methodologies that can be used to measure OR. Finally, section 17.4 analyzes the problems related to the management of OR, highlighting some of the risk transfer instruments – such as insurance contracts – that have been developed for OR by the insurance industry and financial markets in general in the last few years.

17.2   OR: HOW CAN WE DEFINE IT?

In the original version of the capital adequacy framework reform proposals, published in January 2001 (Basel Committee, 2001a), the Basel Committee on Banking Supervision adopted a rather precise, although quite wide, definition of OR: "The risk that deficiencies in information systems or internal controls will result in unexpected loss. The risk is associated with human error, system failures and inadequate procedures and controls". In a following document published in September of the same year (Basel Committee, 2001b) dedicated specifically to OR, the Risk Management Group (RMG) of the Basel Committee developed a standardized definition of operational risk: "the risk of loss resulting from inadequate or failed internal processes, people and systems or from external events". This definition, which was then confirmed by the Committee in the final accord of 2004, has been adopted by industry representatives and can now be considered the standard definition of OR. It includes legal risk but, as indicated by the Basel Committee, excludes reputation risk, and strategic risks.

The main difference between the two definitions above stems from the fact that the latter explicitly includes external events among the risk factors driving OR losses. The Basel Committee therefore associates to OR the unexpected losses deriving from four main types of risk factors: (i) human errors, (ii) information system failures, (iii) inadequate procedures and controls, (iv) external events.

17.2.1   OR risk factors

In this chapter, we follow the logic proposed by the Basel Committee and share the definition based on four types of risk factors.

People. The first factor refers to losses coming from events such as human errors, frauds, violations of internal rules and procedures (unauthorized trading, insider dealing) and, more generally, problems of incompetence and negligence of the financial institution human resources. There are many examples of significant losses suffered by major financial institutions which can be related to this factor:

- In May 2001, a Lehman Brothers dealer in London wrongly input a 300 USD million value for a stock market trade rather than USD 3 million, causing a 120 points reduction in the FTSE 100 stock market index;
- In December 2001 UBS Warburg suffered a USD 50 million loss in its Japanese equity portfolio due to a data entry error regarding the number of shares of a stock trade;
- At the beginning of 2002 *Allied Irish Bank* suffered a USD 750 million loss on a significant trading position built by a trader of its US subsidiary who clearly violated the internal rules of the bank (see Box 17.1).

Box 17.1: An example of operational risk

"Oops"

Allied Irish Banks can survive a rogue trader: its independence may not

It was only last month that Susan Keating, chief executive of Allfirst, one of America's 50 biggest banks, joined the executive committee of its parent company, Allied Irish Banks (AIB). It was, Ms Keating said, an affirmation of AIB's commitment to its American subsidiary. AIB may now be reconsidering that commitment, after the astonishing news that a foreign-exchange trader at Allfirst's Baltimore headquarters managed to lose $750m in unauthorised trading. The trader, John Rusnak, is now being grilled by the Federal Bureau of Investigation. Another Barings? Allied Irish has been swift to assure investors that the loss poses no threat to the bank's survival.

That is probably right, but its independence is nevertheless in doubt. News of the alleged fraud, which appeared to have been concealed using fictitious option trades, was enough to send Allied's shares down by a fifth at the start of the trading, though they later recovered a bit. The write-off raises questions about a management that was once highly rated. Rumours have resurfaced that Royal Bank of Scotland, one of Britain's biggest banks since its acquisition of NatWest in 2000, is keen to add AIB to the stable.

Allied Irish Banks and its rival, Bank of Ireland, together dominate Ireland's banking market, with more than three-quarters of all deposits between them. They earn fat returns in their home market, but both have expanded overseas, partly because they that home will not be so cosy forever. AIB always had the reputation of being the more innovative and better managed of the two banks. Now AIB managers have the unenviable task of working out how on earth Allfirst's controls proved so inadequate. That might be the opportunity the Scots have been waiting for.

Source: The Economist, 9 February, 2002. © *The Economist Newspaper Limited, London*

Systems. This factor includes the events related to information systems and technology in general. They include hardware and/or software failures, computer hacking or viruses, and telecommunications failures. The growing reliance of the financial industry on information systems and, more generally, on technological resources, has significantly increased the importance of this type of risk. A number of examples of significant losses suffered by financial institutions are also extensively documented, regarding this type of risk factor. They typically include losses originated by events such as unauthorized access to information and systems security, excessive risk taking due to software failures, loss of data due to information system failures, and utility outages.

Processes. This factor includes the losses that originate from inadequacies in the internal processes and procedures. Examples include events such as the violation of the information system security due to insufficient controls (security risk), errors in the execution and/or settlement of securities and foreign currency transactions (transaction and settlement errors), inadequate record-keeping, accounting and taxation errors, mispricing and errors in risk measurement due to problems in the internal models and methodologies (model risk), and breaches of mandate.

External events. This final factor includes all the losses a bank may suffer as a consequence of a wide range of external events which typically are not under the control of the bank's management. These include events such as changes in the political, regulatory and legal environment that negatively affect the bank's profitability, operational failures at suppliers or outsourced operations, criminal acts such as theft, vandalism, robbery, or terrorism, and natural events such as fire, earthquake and other natural disasters. This type of OR losses are significantly different from the ones related to people, systems and processes. Indeed, while the latter can be minimized, both in their frequency and their impacts, through the development of adequate internal procedures (e.g., clearly defining individual responsibilities, and adequate internal control policies), the occurrence of external events does not depend on the banks' internal investments, policies and efforts, although the bank management plays a role in trying to minimize their impact on the P&L account, e.g. through adequate contingency plans.

External factors might also cause reputational losses (although these do not fall into operational risk, as defined by the Basel Committee). Think, e.g., of a bank financing a company which is subsequently found guilty of selling weapons to a rogue state supporting terrorism: if the bank's brand and the company's name are repeatedly mentioned together in the press, the bank is likely to suffer a damage, e.g., because customers may want to move their accounts.[2]

Table 17.1 reports the above classification of OR main factors.

17.2.2 Some peculiarities of OR

Before moving to the analysis of the alternative criteria to measure OR, it is important to take a look at some peculiarities of this type of risk.

---

[2] At the beginning of 2002, a medium-sized US bank was threatened (and its senior management actually attacked) by an environmentalist action group, because of financing a company operating in biotechnologies and genetically-modified food.

Table 17.1 Operational risk and its main factors

PEOPLE	SYSTEMS	PROCESSES	EXTERNAL EVENTS
Fraud, collusion and other criminal activities	IT problems (hardware or software failures, computer hacking or viruses, etc.)	Execution, registration, settlement and documentation errors (*transaction risk*)	Criminal activities (theft, terrorism or vandalism)
Violation of internal or external rules (unauthorized trading, insider dealing, etc.)	Unauthorised access to information and systems security	Errors in models, methodologies and mark to market (*model risk*)	Political and military events (wars or international sanctions)
Errors related to management incompetence or negligence	Unavailability and questionable integrity of data	Accounting and taxation errors	Changes in the political, legal, regulatory and tax environment (*strategic risk*)
Loss of important employees (illness, injury, problems in retaining staff, etc.)	Telecommunications failures	Inadequate formalization of internal procedures. Compliance issues.	Natural events (fire, earthquake, flood, etc.)
Violations of systems security	Utility outages	Breach of mandate	Operational failure at suppliers or outsourced operations
		Inadequate definition and attribution of responsibilities	

The most relevant one is related to the fact that OR, contrary to market and credit risks, is not taken on a voluntary basis but is simply a natural consequence of the different activities performed by a financial institution.

Indeed, a bank can avoid a specific type of market risk by closing (or avoiding) trading positions which are sensitive to that market specific factor; alternatively, it could hedge that specific exposure by trading a derivative instrument. Assume a bank is expecting the French stock exchange to perform badly: it could simply avoid taking a long position on the French equity market or hedge any pre-existing position by selling stock index futures on the CAC 40 index. In the same way, a bank can avoid a specific credit risk by simply refusing to grant a loan or by buying protection through an OTC credit derivative.

This line of reasoning does not apply to OR. Indeed, the only way to avoid OR is to close down any banking business. As shown by the examples above, OR is intrinsically connected to all banking activities, from lending to securities trading and underwriting, from payment services to investment banking. This simply means that a bank cannot avoid this type of risk. Furthermore, despite the recent development of a number of risk transfer instruments,[3] OR hedging is hampered by the lack of a liquid secondary market, like those available for interest, market and credit risks.

A second important feature of OR, which makes it different from other risk types such as interest or market risks, relates to its nature of "pure risk" as opposed to "speculative risks". By this, we mean that while for interest or market risks, risk originates from the volatility of returns, which in turn may lead to either positive results (profits) or negative

---

[3] See section 17.4.

ones (losses), OR (like casualty risks covered by insurance policies) does not give rise to return variability but simply to the possibility of losses.[4] Indeed, it would quite difficult to imagine a human error or an IT failure generating unexpected profits!

A third important peculiarity of OR (linked to the previous one) is that it does not involve an increasing relationship between risk and expected returns. In fact, while in the case of financial risks (such as interest rate, market or credit risks) higher risks are typically associated to higher expected returns, this is not the case for OR. Indeed, if we exclude the cost savings which may result from lower investments in effective internal processes, procedures and controls, there is no reason to expect a higher OR to be associated to a higher profitability for the bank. Lending money at a high interest rate to a high leverage company or investing in the equity capital of a small biotech company both represent high risk investments, with possibilities of significant losses. However, they are also associated to a relatively high expected return. Assume a bank operating in the securities settlement business does not enforce adequate internal controls and procedures and is therefore exposed to a significant risk of human and information system errors. While this too does represent a risky activity, there is no reason to expect it to generate higher profits for the bank.

A fourth peculiarity of OR is related to its complexity, as far as identification and understanding of risks are involved. This is clearly reflected by the different definitions of OR that can be found in the financial industry, and is most likely the consequence of the wide heterogeneity of the factors that generate OR losses. Such a complexity becomes fully apparent when OR is to be measured: indeed, as we shall see in the next section, measuring OR also requires to overcome significant problems related to data availability, extreme and rare events, etc.

Finally, it is worth stressing that, as mentioned above, OR is different from other banking risks because of the lack of hedging instruments. Indeed, while in recent years a

Table 17.2 OR peculiarities

FINANCIAL RISKS (INTEREST RATE, MARKET, CREDIT)	OPERATIONAL RISK
Consciously and willingly faced	Unavoidable
"Speculative" risks, implying losses or profits	Pure risks, implying losses only
Consistent with an increasing relationship between risk and expected return	Not consistent with an increasing relationship between risk and expected return
Easy to identify and understand	Difficult to identify and understand
Comparatively easy to measure and quantify	Difficult to measure and quantify
Large availability of hedging instruments	Lack of effective hedging instruments
Comparatively easy to price and transfer	Difficult to price and transfer

---

[4] An exception to this rule is represented by external events. Indeed, events such as changes in the regulatory, fiscal or political context in which a bank operates may give rise both to unexpected losses and to unexpected profits if these changes affect the bank's profitability favourably.

number of financial institutions and insurance companies have started to offer risk transfer instruments which allow to hedge losses arising from some specific (and mainly external) events, a liquid secondary market for the OR hedging does not yet exist.[5]

The peculiarities of OR and its main differences with respect to financial risks are summarized in Table 17.2.

17.3 MEASURING OR

This section describes a step-by-step approach to the measurement of OR. Such an approach is aimed at highlighting the implications of an effective OR measurement system for the organizational structure of the bank; indeed, as we shall see, the different profiles of operational risk will have to be defined through the active participation of the senior and middle management running the various business lines of the bank. Since the main aim of this paragraph is to help the reader understand the managerial implications of setting up an OR measurement system, the techniques used, by way of example, for the assessment and quantification of expected and unexpected losses will deliberately be kept very simple. Appendix 17A will describe a more sophisticated, statistical approach based on EVT (extreme value theory, see Chapter 9).

Before we enter into the details of the various phases of an OR measurement system, let us first briefly discuss the main criteria and objectives of an OR measurement system.

First, measuring OR requires an appropriate mapping process of the bank's – and eventually of other banks – historical losses to the relevant risk factors. This allows one to build an adequate database, which can then be used to measure OR accurately. Second, measuring OR requires to distinguish between an expected loss component, which should be covered by adequate provisions, and an unexpected loss component, which should be covered by the bank's equity capital. Finally, an appropriate OR measurement system should be aimed at estimating the amount of economic capital absorbed by this type of risk. This implies that the measurement system should be consistent with the criteria (time horizon, confidence level, etc.) used by the bank for the measurement of the other types of risks.

Let us now look at the problems which are typically faced by a bank trying to measure OR.

√ The first problem comes from the fact that some of the events related to OR tend to produce losses which are difficult to quantify. Take the example of a bank whose franchise has been negatively affected by a regulatory change. Quantifying the loss requires an estimate of the negative impact of such change on the bank's future earnings, which could be quite difficult.

√ A second problem is related to the fact that some of the OR events are quite rare. This means that an individual bank has a limited direct experience of such losses. This in turns makes it quite difficult to estimate the probability distribution of these events in a statistically significant way. A bank may then decide to turn to pooled data, like those recorded in publicly available databases: however, this is likely to pose several challenges. First, and most significant, not all losses are reported publicly. Also, as larger

---

[5] In the case of credit risk we do not only refer to *credit derivatives* but also to all the transactions such as *loan sales* and *securitization* which allow to transfer risk. A typical example is represented by the CBO (*collateralized bond obligations*) and CLO (*collateralized loan obligations*) markets.

losses are more likely to have been reported, a positive relationship may exist between the loss amount and the probability that it is included in public data sources. If such a relationship exists, then the data are not a random sample from the population of all operational losses, but rather a biased sample containing a disproportionate number of very large losses. Statistical inference based on such samples can yield biased parameter estimates: namely, the presence of too many large losses is likely to lead to an upward-biased estimate of the bank's exposure to OR. To avoid such a problem, banks may decide to pool together their internal databases on operational losses, subject to a mutual confidentiality commitment (see the introduction to this part of the book).

√ A third problem relates to the low reliability of past historical data for the estimate of both the probability and the loss size of future OR events. Take, e.g., losses originated by errors in the IT systems for interbank payments or international securities settlement. These kind of loss events have become less and less frequent over time thanks to technological and organizational progress. Their historical frequency is therefore a bad proxy for their future probability; conversely, past data may underestimate the threat posed by new classes of operational risks, like those related to hackers and computer crime.

√ Finally, OR measurement is negatively affected by the fact that it has become "fashionable" only in rather recent times. Indeed, banks all over the world started to seriously analyse this type of risk and collect relevant data only in the late 90's. OR measurement therefore suffers from a relative lack of statistically significant time series of loss data, which are needed to estimate expected and unexpected losses. Indeed, the lack of reliable internal operational loss data has often prevented banks from improving the statistical techniques used for OR measurement. Due to the unavailability of adequate databases, many banks are still to achieve proper risk quantification models covering operational risk.

Having stated the main objectives and characteristics of an OR management system, let us introduce our simplified approach. As indicated by Figure 17.1, the next sections will discuss a number of different phases that will build up a complete OR measurement process.

17.3.1 Identifying the risk factors

The first phase in OR measurement requires to estimate the relevant risk factors. This means defining a list of the events which the bank would consider as part of OR. This phase is particularly important as it should also allow to build a common language across the different business units of the bank. Table 17.1 reports an example of the possible outcome of this first phase.

17.3.2 Mapping business units and estimating risk exposure

The second phase requires to map, to the factors identified in the first phase, the various business lines and activities carried out by individual business units. This means that one needs to identify all relevant OR events for each business unit. For example, it is quite likely that "internal fraud" events play a major role for the trading unit, while being almost irrelevant for the securities placement business.

---

1. Identification of the risk factors

⇩

2. Estimating exposures to the risk factors – *Exposure Indicator* (EI)
(*mapping* business processes)

⇩

3. Estimating probability of occurrence of the risky events – *Probability of Event* (PE)

⇩

4. Estimating loss in case of events (*severity*) – *Loss Given Event* (LGE and LGER)

⇩

5. Estimating expected loss – *Expected Loss* (EL = EI x PE x LGER)

⇩

6. Estimating unexpected loss – *Unexpected Loss* (UL)

⇩

7. Estimating OR capital at risk (CaR)

Figure 17.1   The different phases of the OR measurement process

This phase is similar to the "risk factor mapping" process that banks have to carry out regarding financial risks (see, e.g., Chapters 3 and 5). More specifically, one needs to identify (see Table 17.3):

 (i) for each business unit, the relevant risk factors;
(ii) for each business line with in a business unit, one or more exposure indicators (EI) representing its vulnerability to different risk factors. These EIs could be P&L variables, such as gross operating income, or balance sheet aggregates, like total asset under management.[6]

17.3.3   Estimating the probability of the risky events

The third phase of the measurement process requires to estimate a probability of occurrence for each risk factor/business unit combination. This estimate may be based on different techniques and data sources depending on whether loss events are frequent, so that internal bank data are likely to be enough to allow a statistically significant estimate, or events, in which case other data sources need to be identified (like pooled databases

---

[6] This exposure indicator may not be needed in case a monetary definition of the average loss for each OR event is adopted rather than a percentage of the exposure one (see next section).

Table 17.3 Mapping business units to risk factors

				Risk factors			
				People	Technology	Processes	External events
Business Unit	*Business Line*	Activity	Exposure indicator (EI)				
Investment Banking	Corporate Finance	Merchant Banking, Advisory Services, Securities u/w & placement	TR	X		X	X
	Securities u/w & placement		GI		X	X	X
	Trading & Sales	Proprietary Trading, Sales, Mkt Making	GI	X	X	X	
Banking	Retail Banking	Retail Banking, Cards, Private Banking	GI		X	X	X
	Corporate Banking	Corporate Lending, Project Finance	GI	X			X
	Payment and Settlement	Payment and Settlement	GI		X	X	
	Agency services	Corporate Agency, Custody	TR		X	X	
Other	Asset Management	Unit trusts, segregated accounts	AM		X	X	X
	Insurance	Life & Casualty Insurance	TP				
	Retail Brokerage	Retail Brokerage	GI	X		X	

Legend: TR = total revenues, GI = gross operating income, AM = assets under management, TP = total premiums.

run by interbank consortia,[7] as well as data provided by professional data vendors[8]). The former events typically tend to generate relatively low losses: hence, they are generally labelled as *"high frequency low impact (HFLI) events"*. Conversely, less frequent events are often associated with more significant losses and therefore are called *"low frequency high impact (LFHI) events"*. As a result, probability distribution for OR losses tend to be

---

[7] An example of such cooperative efforts is *Morexchange* (*Multinational Operational Risk Exchange*), a database originally introduced in November 2000 by major financial institutions such as JP Morgan, CIBC and Royal Bank of Canada. This database, managed by the a New York-based software company called *NetRisk*, collects all operational loss data from the member banks, which are analysed and standardised in order to make them comparable across banks of different sizes, and finally returned on an aggregate basis to all member banks.
[8] Two examples are represented by OpRisk Analytics and OpVantage, a division of Fitch Risk Management. Both vendors gather information on operational losses exceeding $1 million and collect data from public sources such as news reports, court filings, and regulatory authorities filings.

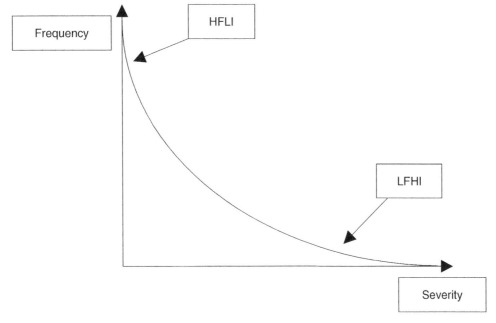

Figure 17.2   High frequency – low impact versus low frequency – high impact events

highly skewed to the right (see Figure 17.2);[9] furthermore, due to the special relevance of extreme losses, the right tail of the distribution is often modelled though ad hoc estimation techniques, like Extreme Value Theory (see Chapter 9).

The probability of each different type of OR event (that is, of each business unit/risk factor combination) can be estimated subjectively by the bank's management, based either on qualitative judgement or a formal rating system. Such ratings capture the relevance of a given specific risk factor for the individual business unit, business line or activity, i.e., their vulnerability to the risk factor. Such a rating system can then be used, just as for credit ratings, to quantify the probability of occurrence associated with different rating classes. Table 17.4 reports a simplified example for a bank's trading unit: this is based on a 1 to 10 scale, where each value is associated to probability range covering a one-year risk horizon.

The synthetic judgements or ratings assigned to each business unit should reflect both the intrinsic risk of the BU and the level and quality of the controls in place. Indeed, the introduction of a more effective system of internal controls should, other things equal, lead to a better rating and therefore a lower risk.

The main shortcoming of this "risk quantification" phase is that it is mostly based on the managers' subjective appraisal of risks. This can be mitigated in two ways:

- the exposure indicators and the risk levels assigned to each business unit should reflect a consensus within the banking industry; in other words, while each bank may have a

---

[9] Figure 17.1 only looks at the two most common types of events. However, combinations represented by high frequency-high impact (HFHI) events and low frequency-low impact (LFLI) events, while less common, can also be identified.

Table 17.4 Example of OR exposure for a bank's trading unit

Risk factor	Qualitative judgement	Rating (1 = low risk; 10 = high risk)	Probability range
1. Human resources			
– fraud	Average/Low	3	0.3%–0.5%
– negligence	Average	5	1.0%–2.0%
– violation of internal rules	High	9	7.0%–10.0%
2. Technology			
– systems failures	Average	4	0.5%–1.0%
– software errors	Average/High	8	5.0%–7.0%
– telecommunication	Low	2	0.1%–0.3%
3. Processes			
– model risk	High	10	>10.0%
– transaction risk	Average	6	2.0%–3.0%
– documentation risk	Average/Low	3	0.3%–0.5%
4. External events			
– political risk	Low	1	0.0%–0.1%
– regulatory/fiscal risk	Average/High	8	5.0%–7.0%
– natural events	Low	2	0.1%–0.3%

    different risk profile as compared to the industry average, industry data should always be used as a benchmark to assess the credibility of the valuation process;
- the valuation of each business unit risk profile should be performed by an independent unit, such as the internal audit department, based on rigorous, objective and well-defined criteria, which have to be consistent with the best market practices and applied in a uniform way to all the bank's business units; these criteria should be made explicit and periodically updated.

Finally, it is important to highlight that, while based on subjective judgement and discretionary valuations, the approach described above is relatively flexible and can be easily tailored to the organizational complexity of the bank, taking account of its risk profile and the quality of the controls in place.

17.3.4 Estimating the losses

The distinction between HFLI and LFHI events is also relevant for the fourth phase of the OR measurement process, i.e. when one wants to estimate the average loss associated to each type of risky event. Indeed, once the probability of each event ("*probability of event*" – PE) has been estimated, a measure of the loss in the case of an event ("*loss given event*" – LGE) is needed to quantify the expected loss.

The loss given event can be expressed as either a monetary amount – average dollar loss – or a percentage of the exposure indicator. In the latter case it is called loss given event *rate* (LGER).

Table 17.5 reports some information sources that can be used to estimate PE and LGE.

Table 17.5 Information sources for the measurement of OR

Probability of event (PE)	Loss given event (LGE)
√ Internal audit reports √ Internal historical events data √ Management reports √ Experts' opinions (Delphi techniques[10]) √ Vendors' estimates √ Budgets √ Business plans	√ Management interviews √ Internal historical loss data √ Historical loss data from other banks or consortium data series √ Industry benchmark √ External estimates (consultants, dataproviders, vendors, etc.)

Source: adapted from Crouhy, Galai, Mark (2000).

Table 17.6 reports some examples of information sources that can be used for some specific OR events.

Table 17.6 OR risk factors: example of cause, effect and information source

Risk factor	Cause	Effect	Information source
People	Loss of key human resources acquired by competitors	Variance in revenues and profits (recruiting & training expenses, negative impact on the existing HR)	√ Delphi technique
Process	Productivity decrease due to an unexpected increase in the business volume	Variance in process costs with respect to the expected levels	√ Historical series √ External estimates
Technology	Costs related to the updating of information systems	Variance in technological resources management and maintenance costs	√ Historical series √ External estimates √ Industry benchmarks

The estimate of LGE can also be based on a subjective valuation performed by the bank's management;[11] however, estimates based on actual historical data look preferable.

---

[10] Delphi are iterative techniques aimed at developing consensus among different people which can be used to obtain a group estimate of the probability of future events.

[11] An example is given by the bottom-up approach adopted by the Italian Banking Association for its common database of OR losses, where the indicator can take four different values:

Tables 17.7 and 17.8 are taken from an international survey published by the Basel Committee based on the data of 89 international banks from 19 countries in Europe, North and South America, Asia, and Australasia. Here banks were asked to provide data on all individual OR losses exceeding € 10,000 in 2001, categorized into eight standardised business lines and seven event types (producing a total of 56 business line/event type combinations).

The 89 participating banks in the survey reported 47,269 individual losses above the € 10,000 threshold (an average of 528 losses per bank). Table 17.7 shows the loss events reported in each business line/event type combination, while Table 17.8 reports the associated loss amounts.

As shown by Table 17.7, loss events cluster in four out of eight business lines, the highest concentration being in Retail Banking. This business line accounts for 61 % of observations, followed by Trading & Sales (11 %), Commercial Banking and Retail Brokerage (7 % each): altogether, these four business lines account for 86 % of loss events. A similar clustering is found for event types: indeed, 42 % of the loss events are due to External Fraud and another 35 % to Execution, Delivery & Process Management. Employment Practices & Workplace Safety and Clients, Products & Business Practices followed with 9 % and 7 % respectively. Altogether, these four event types accounted for 93 % of the loss events.

There is also evidence of considerable clustering for business line/event type combinations. One single cell – External Fraud in Retail Banking–accounts for over 36 % of the loss events.

Loss amounts (Table 17.8) are more evenly distributed across business lines and event types than the number of loss events. However, Retail Banking accounts for the largest share (slightly above 29 %); this is much less than the 42 % share reported in Table 17.7 and reflects the prevalence of smaller-than-average losses. Commercial Banking accounts for slightly less than 29 % of the losses amounts; this is much more than the share of the number of losses incurred by this business line (7 %) and is due to large operational losses due to Damage to Physical Assets and, to a lesser extent, to Execution, Delivery & Process Management events. As regards event types, loss amounts were concentrated in four categories: Execution, Delivery & Process Management (29 %); Damage to Physical Assets (24 %), External Fraud (16 %) and Clients, Products & Business Practices (13 %). Finally, looking at individual cells, two cases – Damage to Physical Assets in Commercial Banking and Retail Brokerage – account for 20 % of gross losses.

17.3.5 Estimating expected loss

The fifth phase of the measurement process builds on the data obtained in the previous three phases and is aimed at estimating the expected loss (EL). This is given by the product of three variables: (i) the exposure indicator (EI), the probability of the event (PE), and (iii) the expected loss given event rate (LGER):

$$EL = EI \cdot PE \cdot \overline{LGER} \tag{17.1}$$

√ 1 = minimum (very low impact on the P&L);
√ 2 = significant (significant impact on the P&L);
√ 3 = critical (very important impact on the P&L);
√ 4 = catastrophic (impossible to guarantee business continuity).

Table 17.7 Number of individual loss events per business line and event type Sample 1: All Bank and all losses 89 banks reporting

	Internal Fraud	External Fraud	Employment Practices & Workplace Safety	Clients Products & Business Practices	Damage to Physical Assets	Business Disruption & System Failures	Execution, Delivery & Process Management	No Event Type Information	Total
Corporate Finance	17	20	73	73	16	8	214	2	423
	0.04 %	0.04 %	0.15 %	0.15 %	0.03 %	0.02 %	0.45 %	0.00 %	0.89 %
Trading & Sales	47	95	101	108	33	137	4.603	8	5.132
	0.10 %	0.20 %	0.21 %	0.23 %	0.07 %	0.29 %	9.74 %	0.02 %	10.86 %
Retail Banking	1.268	17.107	2.063	2.125	520	163	5.289	347	28.882
	2.68 %	36.19 %	4.36 %	4.50 %	1.10 %	0.34 %	11.19 %	0.73 %	61.10 %
Commercial Banking	84	1.799	82	308	50	47	1.012	32	3.414
	0.18 %	3.81 %	0.17 %	0.65 %	0.11 %	0.10 %	2.14 %	0.07 %	7.22 %
Payment & Settlement	23	322	54	25	9	82	1.334	3	1.852
	0.05 %	0.68 %	0.11 %	0.05 %	0.02 %	0.17 %	2.82 %	0.01 %	3.92 %
Agency Services	3	15	19	27	8	32	1.381	5	1.490
	0.01 %	0.03 %	0.04 %	0.06 %	0.02 %	0.07 %	2.92 %	0.01 %	3.15 %
Asset Management	28	44	39	131	6	16	837	8	1.109
	0.06 %	0.09 %	0.08 %	0.28 %	0.01 %	0.03 %	1.77 %	0.02 %	2.35 %
Retail Brokerage	59	20	794	539	7	50	1.773	26	3.268
	0.12 %	0.04 %	1.68 %	1.14 %	0.01 %	0.11 %	3.75 %	0.06 %	6.91 %
No Business Line information	35	617	803	54	13	6	135	36	1.699
	0.07 %	1.31 %	1.70 %	0.11 %	0.03 %	0.01 %	0.29 %	0.08 %	3.59 %
Total	1.564	20.039	4.028	3.390	662	541	16.578	467	47.269
	3.31 %	42.39 %	8.52 %	7.17 %	1.40 %	1.14 %	35.07 %	0.99 %	100.00 %
Legend	Greater than 20 %	10 % through 20 %		5 % through 10 %		2.5 % through 5 %			

Table 17.8 Total gross loss amounts by business line and event type sample 1: All Bank and all losses millions of euros 89 banks reporting

	Internal Fraud	External Fraud	Employment Practices & Workplace safety	Clients Products & Business Practices	Damage to Physical Assets	Business Disruption & System Failures	Execution Delivery & Process Management	No Event Type Information	Total
Corporate Finance	49.4 0.63%	5.0 0.06%	2.5 0.03%	157.9 2.03%	8.0 0.10%	0.5 0.01%	49.6 0.64%	0.6 0.01%	273.5 3.51%
Trading & Sales	59.5 0.76%	40.4 0.52%	64.8 0.83%	193.4 2.48%	87.9 1.13%	17.6 0.23%	698.4 8.96%	1.1 0.1%	1,163.1 14.92%
Retail Banking	331.9 4.26%	787.1 10.10%	340.0 4.36%	254.1 3.26%	87.5 1.12%	26.5 0.34%	424.5 5.45%	37.4 0.48%	2,289.0 29.36%
Commercial Banking	21.2 0.27%	324.9 4.17%	20.4 0.26%	156.4 2.01%	1,072.9 13.76%	18.2 0.23%	619.4 7.95%	23.2 0.30%	2,258.8 28.95%
Payment & Settlement	23.0 0.29%	21.0 0.27%	11.6 0.15%	10.5 0.13%	15.0 0.19%	78.6 1.01%	93.5 1.20%	0.3 0.00%	253.4 3.25%
Agency Services	0.2 0.00%	3.9 0.05%	7.6 0.10%	5.0 0.06%	100.0 1.28%	40.1 0.51%	174.1 2.23%	0.8 0.01%	331.6 4.25%
Asset Management	6.4 0.08%	4.6 0.06%	10.2 0.13%	77.0 0.99%	2.3 0.03%	2.3 0.03%	113.2 1.45%	0.05 0.01%	216.5 2.78%
Retail Brokerage	61.5 0.79%	1.2 0.02%	50.7 0.65%	158.6 2.03%	513.2 6.68%	28.0 0.36%	97.1 1.25%	3.4 0.04%	913.7 11.72%
No Business Line information	10.5 0.13%	23.4 0.30%	18.7 0.24%	11.5 0.15%	6.7 0.09%	0.7 0.01%	22.7 0.29%	3.8 0.05%	97.9 1.26%
Total	563.5 7.23%	1,211.3 15.54%	526.6 6.76%	1024.5 13.14%	1,893.4 24.29%	212.5 2.73%	2,292.6 29.41%	71.1 0.91%	7,795.5 100.00%
Legend	Greater than 10%			5% through 10%		10%		2.5% through 5%	

Source: Basel Committee, 2003, "The 2002 Loss Data Collection Exercise for Operational Risk: Summary of the Data Collected", March, Basel.

The choice of the appropriate exposure indicator must be consistent with that of the loss given event rate. Indeed, $\overline{LGER}$ should represent the percentage of EI which would get lost – on average – in case the risky event occurs.

Also, it is important to highlight that equation (17.1) is based on the assumption of a linear relationship between LGER and EI. For some types of OR events, this relationship could not be linear. Take the example of internal frauds: the LGER – measured as a percentage of gross operating income (GOI), could be a decreasing function of the same GOI. In this case the value of LGER should be periodically re-estimated as market conditions and bank characteristics change over time.

A simple way to address this problem is to use a LGE variable which is directly expressed as a monetary amount rather than as a percentage of an EI. In other words, the expected loss would be estimated as the product of two variables:

$$EL = PE \cdot \overline{LGE} \tag{17.2}$$

Similarly to what we saw for credit risk, the expected component of operational losses component must be covered by reserves, with provisions and uses recorded in the profit and loss account. On the other side, the unexpected loss component must be covered by the bank's economic capital.

17.3.6 Estimating unexpected loss

The sixth phase of the measurement process requires to estimate the OR unexpected loss. This, just as for market and credit risk, depends on the volatility of OR losses. Two business units may be characterized by a similar OR expected loss but present a different degree of uncertainty, i.e. different unexpected losses. Consider, as an example, the data reported in Table 17.9.

Table 17.9 The estimate of expected loss for two different business units

Business Unit	A	B
Average probability of occurrence of risky events (PE) – %	0.2 %	10 %
Avg. loss in case of occurrence of the events $(\overline{LGE})$ – Euro mln	100	2
Expected loss (EL) – Euro mln	0.2	0.2

Unit A is exposed to low-probability events which would generate a significant average loss (LFHI events), while unit B is exposed to high-probability events associated with a low average loss (HFLI events). As HFLI are likely to be imperfectly correlated (and therefore imply some risk diversification benefits) unit B's losses are more stable and less volatile than unit A's, i.e. that unit B has lower unexpected losses.

UL can be estimated: (i) for the bank as a whole, based on internal historical data series, (ii) separately for each business unit, based once again on internal data, (iii) separately for each risk factor using external data time series coming from pooled databases or from external providers, (iv) separately for each business unit and for each risk factor, using a combination of internal and external historical data.

Approaches (i) and (ii) are more likely to be adopted for HFLI events, while approaches (iii) and (iv) generally represent the only available option a bank can resort to for the measurement of LFHI events. External data are generally rescaled based on the bank's exposure indicators and further adjusted to account for the effectiveness of its risk control systems.

When no historical loss data are available, an alternative simplified approach assumes that losses are binomially distributed, that is, that only two possible outcomes exist at the end of the risk horizon: either the loss event occurs or not. In the former case, the bank's loss is equal to $\overline{LGE}$, in the latter, the loss is nihil (see Table 17.10). A simplified measure of unexpected loss can then be obtained as the standard deviation of this binomial distribution.

Table 17.10 The binomial approach for the estimation of unexpected loss

Event	Loss	Probability
Occurrence of the risky event	$\overline{LGE}$	PE
No occurrence of the risky event	0	1-PE

In fact, the first two moments of the loss distribution are simply

$$\mu = EL = PE \cdot LGE + (1 - PE) \cdot 0 = PE \cdot LGE \tag{17.2}$$

$$\sigma = LGE \cdot \sqrt{PE \cdot (1 - PE)} \tag{17.3}$$

E.g., assuming an average probability of event of 1% and a loss given event of 50,000 euros, we have:

$$\sigma = 50,000 \cdot \sqrt{0.01 \cdot 0.99} = 4,975$$

This approach looks appealing, because of its simplicity and minimal data requirements. Also, it provides estimates of UL which are consistent with our intuition: going back to Table 17.9, the standard deviation of unit A, the one exposed to LFHI events, would be equal to 223,383 euros, while unit B, the one exposed to HFLI events, would have a σ of 43,589 euros.

More generally, for a given level of expected loss, the standard deviation computed with (17.3) increases for lower PEs (and larger LGEs). This is shown in Figure 17.3, where EL is kept constant at 500,000 euros: σ is clearly higher for LFHI events than for HFLI ones.

Equation (17.3) treats LGE as constant, ruling out any uncertainty on the loss given event. This is clearly unrealistic. If LGE is thought to be stochastic, with variance σ_{LGE}^2, then the standard deviation of losses:

$$\sigma = \sqrt{PE \cdot (1 - PE)(LGE)^2 + PE^2 \cdot \sigma_{LGE}^2 + PE \cdot (1 - PE) \cdot \sigma_{LGE}^2} \tag{17.4}$$

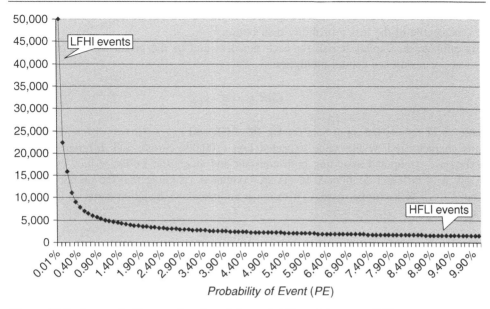

Figure 17.3   Loss volatility as a function of the probability of the event (PE)

that is:[12]

$$\sigma = \sqrt{PE \cdot (1 - PE)(LGE)^2 + PE \cdot \sigma_{LGE}^2} \qquad (17.5)$$

Let's assume that the volatility of LGE is 100,000 and keep all other data unchanged from the previous example (PE = 1 %, LGE = 50, 000 euros). The loss volatility would then be equal to 11,169 euros, significantly higher than the one obtained assuming a constant LGE (4,975 euro).

17.3.7   Estimating Capital at Risk against OR

The seventh and last phase of the OR measurement process involves the estimation of capital at risk. Indeed, while σ represents the volatility of OR losses, capital at risk measures the amount of capital absorbed by operational risks, that is, the maximum potential loss due to OR, within a given confidence level and a given time horizon (usually one year).

Different approaches can be followed to estimate such measure. A first simplified approach is based on the following steps:

(i) assume a specific functional form for the probability distribution of OR losses and keep it unchanged for all business units;

---

[12] Equation (17.5) can be obtained from equation (17.4) in the following way:

$$\sigma = \sqrt{PE \cdot (1 - PE)(LGE)^2 + PE^2 \cdot \sigma_{LGE}^2 + PE \cdot \sigma_{LGE}^2 - PE^2 \cdot \sigma_{LGE}^2}$$

(ii) from this distribution, obtain a capital multiplier k to be used to get the desired x-th percentile of the loss probability distribution;[13]

(iii) estimate the capital at risk for each business unit as the product of its σ and the above-mentioned capital multiplier:

$$CaR_{x\%} = \sigma \cdot k_{x\%} \qquad (17.6)$$

Table 17.11 reports the input data for EI, PE, LGE and σ_{LGE} for two different business units characterized by the same expected loss (100,000 euros), and different standard deviations – computed assuming both constant and stochastic LGEs. Values for capital at risk with different confidence levels are computed assuming that the probability distribution of OR losses be normal (with mean and standard deviation equal to EL and σ respectively).

Table 17.11 Unexpected loss and capital at risk for two business units

		Unit A	Unit B
		Input	
EI		1,000,000	1,000,000
PE		0.20 %	5.00 %
LGER		5.00 %	0.20 %
Sigma LGER		10.00 %	0.50 %
		Output	
EL		100	100
UL with constant LGER		2,234	436
UL with stochastic LGER		4,999	1,200
CaR with confidence level:	95.0 %	8,223	1,974
	97.5 %	9,798	2,352
	99.0 %	11,829	2,792
	99.5 %	12,877	3,091
	99.9 %	15,448	3,708

A more sophisticated approach for calculating OR capital at risk assumes that the shape of the probability distribution for OR losses faced by different business units will be different, leading to different capital multipliers. This second approach, while theoretically more precise, clearly requires a higher volume of data which may not be readily available, as

---

[13] E.g., if one assumes that the probability distribution of OR losses is normal, then $k_{99\%}$ would be equal to 2.33. Due to the considerable skewness and kurtosis of real-life OR loss distributions, however, a higher capital multiplier would be needed.

loss events are clearly less frequent when the analysis is carried out separately for each business unit.

A third approach requires that, as in the case of market and credit risks, OR capital at risk be estimated using simulation approaches. The relative lack of historical data makes it advisable to use Monte Carlo simulations, which typically require less data than historical simulations. Once a functional form of the OR loss distribution has been estimated or assumed, it is possible to simulate future losses associated with different scenarios and to build a simulated distribution on which the appropriate percentile can be read.

The probability distribution of OR losses can also been obtained by using two different distributions for the probability (PE) and the severity (LGE) of the loss events. For example, following an actuarial approach, the probability could be modelled through a Poisson distribution,[14] while severity could be depicted through a log-normal or beta distribution.[15] The probability distribution for OR losses – on which an appropriate percentile can be chosen to measure OR capital at risk – can then be obtained as the convolution of the two different distributions of frequency and severity. Convolution can in turn be based on different techniques, one of which is tabulation. As a simplified example, assume that the PE and LGE of a business line have the probability distributions reported in Table 17.12.

Table 17.12 Distribution of Frequency and Severity

Frequency		Severity	
Probability	Number of risky events	Probability	Amount
0.6	0	0.5	1,000
0.3	1	0.3	10,000
0.1	2	0.2	100,000

Based on the above data and assuming independence between PE and LGE, it is possible to calculate the probabilities associated to different loss amounts, i.e. the loss distribution, as reported in Table 17.13, using a tabulation technique. The probability associated to a zero loss is given by the probability of having zero risky events, i.e. 0.6. The probability of having just one loss of 1,000 euro is equal to $0.3*0.5 = 0.15$, i.e. 15 %. The probability of having two losses of 1,000 and 100,000 euro respectively (and viceversa), for a total loss of 101,000 euro, is equal to: $0.1*0.5*0.2 = 0.01$.

Table 17.14 reports the loss distribution of this business line by aggregating the losses of equivalent amount.

Once the OR loss distribution is known, one can estimate the business unit CaR at different confidence levels. Based on a 98 % confidence level, e.g., VaR would be equal to the corresponding percentile (101,000 euro) minus the expected loss (11,750 euro), i.e. 89,250 euro. Indeed, the probability of suffering a larger loss would be equal to 1.6 % (1.2 % + 0.4 %).

This concludes our discussion of the different phases of an OR risk measurement system. Again, it is important to stress that the actual statistical assumptions that were used by the way of example were deliberately simplified, as the emphasis was laid on the various organizational and managerial implications of OR measurement. A short discussion of more sophisticated techniques can be found in Appendix 17A.

---

[14] See section 14.6.1.
[15] See section 14.7.3.

Table 17.13 Probability distribution of losses

Number of losses	Loss 1	Loss 2	Total loss	Probability
0	–	–	–	0.600
1	1,000	–	1,000	0.150
1	10,000	–	10,000	0.090
1	100,000	–	100,000	0.060
2	1,000	1,000	2,000	0.025
2	1,000	10,000	11,000	0.015
2	1,000	100,000	101,000	0.010
2	10,000	1,000	11,000	0.015
2	10,000	10,000	20,000	0.009
2	10,000	100,000	110,000	0.006
2	100,000	1,000	101,000	0.010
2	100,000	10,000	110,000	0.006
2	100,000	100,000	200,000	0.004
			Total	1.000

Table 17.14 Probability distribution of losses

Loss	Probability	Cumulative probability
0	0.600	0.600
1,000	0.150	0.750
2,000	0.025	0.775
10,000	0.090	0.865
11,000	0.030	0.895
20,000	0.009	0.904
100,000	0.060	0.964
101,000	0.020	0.984
110,000	0.012	0.996
200,000	0.004	1.000
Total	1.000	

17.4 TOWARDS AN OR MANAGEMENT SYSTEM

Before looking at the problems related to OR management, it is important to highlight which are the main objectives that such a management system should be pursuing.

First of all, an OR management system should not be aimed, as is the case for other banking risks, at the optimization of the risk-return profile, but rather at the minimization of the sources of this type of risk. Indeed, while an increase of the other types of risk is usually associated to an increase in expected profits, this is not necessarily the case for OR. However, a significant reduction in OR, while it might prove a very ambitious objective in practice, would require significant investments in risk prevention and control systems: hence, a policy aimed at minimizing OR is generally constrained by the amount of costs a bank would incur. Therefore, one needs to identify an optimal level of OR, below which the increase in costs would overcomes the benefits of risk reduction. In a way, one could argue that in the case of OR the risk-expected return trade-off typical of financial risks gets substituted by a risk-cost trade-off.

A second important objective of an OR management system should be to promote a virtuous incentive to risk reduction. For such an incentive to work, it is necessary to assess the amount of economic capital absorbed by each business unit due to OR: this amount of capital, together with those due to other risks, should in turn be used to estimate the business unit risk-adjusted performance, by including the OR capital in the denominator of each unit's Raroc. This would lead to a decentralized system of incentives for OR reduction and, at the same time, promote the introduction of adequate risk control policies which rely both on the bank's central services, such as the internal audit, and the individual business units activities.

Indeed, the relationship between OR and internal controls is twofold: on one side, the actual degree of OR is a function of the current control mechanisms; on the other side, the OR measurement system should promote new investments in control procedures, based on a strict cost/benefit analysis.

Having clarified the main objectives that should guide an OR management system, we now focus on the actual available options for OR risk management policies. For each type of OR risk (see Figure 17.4), the bank may decide to:

√ *Keep it*: this means that the risk profile is considered to be consistent with the risk-taking capacity of the bank, that is, with its risk appetite and the equity capital available. This option may be chosen also because of the costs that would be incurred if the bank were to further reduce OR or to transfer it. This is typically the case of high frequency low impact events (HFLI) and low frequency low impact events (LFLI). Indeed, the expected loss related to this type of events can be covered through adequate provisions. On the other side, given the low LGE the unexpected loss can be covered by the bank's economic capital.

√ *Insure*: the possibility to buy insurance coverage for these types of risks is relatively recent and is related to product innovations introduced by some major insurance and reinsurance companies. Such insurance contracts are viewed as a form of "outsourcing". This process is similar to what is occurring in the management of information systems, procurement, and real estate assets, which are increasingly being delegated to outside companies to which banks pay a fee or a rent. Similarly, the coverage of certain operational risks which are considered to be outside of the bank's "core business" (i.e. management of financial risks) is being "outsourced" and entrusted to specialized companies (insurance firms). Insurance policies have been stipulated, for example, on losses deriving from the dishonesty/incompetence of personnel (known as bankers' blanket bonds[16]) such as the unauthorized trading of securities; policies against claims for compensation advanced by customers; and insurance against the damage deriving to the bank or to third parties from the malfunctioning of IT and e-commerce systems. Insurance policies are typically used for low frequency and high impact events (LFHI), generally due to external factors, such as natural (earthquakes, floods, etc.), or political and regulatory ones (foreign exchange controls, regulatory changes, etc.).[17] Note that these are risky events which are typically out of the bank's control, as only in this case it is possible to avoid the moral hazard problems (see below in this section) which would make it impossible to obtain an insurance coverage. These low-frequency events are not usually captured by VaR models, as the latter are based on confidence levels which are generally too low to capture such low probability events. The transfer of this type of risks through insurance policies therefore represents a correct policy, also in light of the capacity of the insurance industry to diversify these kind of risks adequately. The economic rationale underlying the trend toward risk transfer is based on two main advantages of an insurance contract (see also Chapter 21): *risk-pooling* and *cash flow smoothing*. Risk diversification allows the *pooling,* through a unique "tank" of economic capital, of different risks which are imperfectly correlated. On the other hand, by transferring the OR losses to an external entity, a financial institution is able to achieve a higher stability of its cash flows, thereby improving earnings quality and reducing the cost of its capital. This in turn increases the market value of the bank's capital and its price/book ratio, creating shareholders' value. These benefits of *"risk pooling"* and *"cash flow smoothing"* are to some extent offset by some typical limitations of insurance contracts. First, while equity capital paid in by the shareholders is readily available, the "insurance capital" only represents a commitment to pay, the value of which depends on the creditworthiness of the insurance company; in a sense, then, operational risks are not really eliminated, but rather transformed into credit risks. This explains the importance usually attached to the credit rating of the insurance company.[18] Second, we have *adverse selection* and *moral hazard* problems. The former refer to the fact that the demand for insurance coverage typically comes from the most risky counterparties (the ones for which an insurance coverage is most valuable); however, insurance companies often are not in a position to estimate the actual risk of each counterparty and therefore charge a uniform premium to all counterparties with similar risk characteristics, prompting the best counterparties to leave. Moral hazard

---

[16] *Fidelity bonds* or *bankers' blanket bonds* protect the insured against losses due to theft/misappropriation or other dishonest behaviour on the part of employees. The term "blanket" refers to the fact that the group of persons covered by the policy is not expressly identified by name. Blanket bonds represent a form of risk coverage mandatory for some types of US banking institutions.

[17] An example of the role of OR insurance coverage is represented by the September 2001 twin towers terrorist attack. Indeed, the World Trade Center collapse represented the largest OR loss in history, with losses for the insurance industry amounting to a total of more than USD 70 bn. This huge loss has been shared adequately among many different US and European insurance companies. According to Standard & Poor's, the 20 insurance groups which took on the largest losses had a total equity capital of approximately USD 300 bn, which was therefore significantly larger than the suffered loss.

[18] The Basel Committee only allows insurance coverage to reduce a bank's OR capital requirement if and only if the insurance company has a rating of single A or better (see Chapter 21).

means that, once an insurance contract is stipulated, the customer is no longer interested in keeping risk under control, as any loss will be borne by the insurer. This explains why insurance companies usually require the customer to bear part of the insured losses. Also, as mentioned above, moral hazard explains why the risks covered through insurance are usually those far from the core business of a financial institution, and therefore less likely to be affected by its management policies.

√ *Hedge*: this kind of management policy is typically used for those risks which are seen as incompatible with the risk-taking capacity of the bank. Due to the lack of a complete market of derivative instruments, hedging is usually achieved through risk reduction policies based on significant investments in human resources, control processes, and IT systems. This option is used generally for high frequency high impact events (HFHI) due to bank-specific causes, not to external factors. Indeed, for this type of events insurance coverage would be made more difficult to achieve, more expensive, and less effective by the above mentioned moral hazard problems.

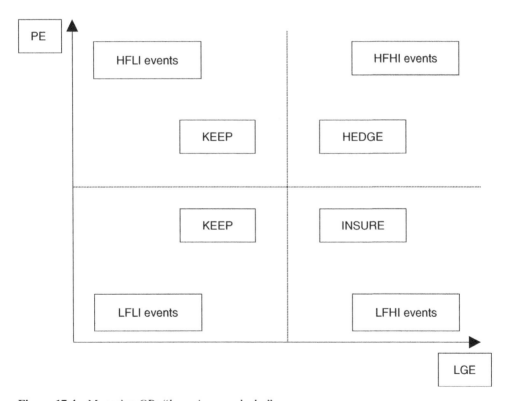

Figure 17.4   Managing OR: *"keep, insure o hedge"*

17.5   FINAL REMARKS

Despite its increasing importance during the last few years, OR still represents a risk type for which measurement and control systems are at an embryonic stage, compared to the other risk types analysed in the previous sections of this book. Many financial institutions worldwide have not yet developed a precise OR measurement methodology, a clear management policy, nor an effective system to allocate capital to the different risk-taking units.

Major international banks have started to systematically collect data on OR losses only in the late 90's. Over time, these data series will allow to develop adequate risk measurement systems. This lack of data, as well as the complexities related to OR definition, has played a major role in the delay experienced in the development of OR measurement models. A significant acceleration, however, has occurred with the introduction of the new capital requirements in 2004.[19]

Some analysts believe that in the coming years OR represents the risk type which will command the largest investments in human and technological resources in the banking industry. While this may represent an extreme view, it is certainly true that significant investments will be made. These will most likely lead to similar results, both in terms of methodological advances and data availability, as the ones already achieved by the banking industry in the area of market and credit risks.

Box 17.2: The ten Basel Committee principles for the management of operational risk

Developing an Appropriate Risk Management Environment

Principle 1: The board of directors should be aware of the major aspects of the bank's operational risks as a distinct risk category that should be managed, and it should approve and periodically review the bank's operational risk management framework. The framework should provide a firm-wide definition of operational risk and lay down the principles of how operational risk is to be identified, assessed, monitored, and controlled/mitigated.

Principle 2: The board of directors should ensure that the bank's operational risk management framework is subject to effective and comprehensive internal audit by operationally independent, appropriately trained and competent staff. The internal audit function should not be directly responsible for operational risk management.

Principle 3: Senior management should have responsibility for implementing the operational risk management framework approved by the board of directors. The framework should be consistently implemented throughout the whole banking organisation, and all levels of staff should understand their responsibilities with respect to operational risk management. Senior management should also have responsibility for developing policies, processes and procedures for managing operational risk in all of the bank's material products, activities, processes and systems.

Risk Management: Identification, Assessment, Monitoring, and Mitigation/Control

Principle 4: Banks should identify and assess the operational risk inherent in all material products, activities, processes and systems. Banks should also ensure that

---

[19] See Chapter 21.

before new products, activities, processes and systems are introduced or undertaken, the operational risk inherent in them is subject to adequate assessment procedures.

Principle 5: Banks should implement a process to regularly monitor operational risk profiles and material exposures to losses. There should be regular reporting of pertinent information to senior management and the board of directors that supports the proactive management of operational risk.

Principle 6: Banks should have policies, processes and procedures to control and/or mitigate material operational risks. Banks should periodically review their risk limitation and control strategies and should adjust their operational risk profile accordingly using appropriate strategies, in light of their overall risk appetite and profile.

Principle 7: Banks should have in place contingency and business continuity plans to ensure their ability to operate on an ongoing basis and limit losses in the event of severe business disruption.

Role of Supervisors

Principle 8: Banking supervisors should require that all banks, regardless of size, have an effective framework in place to identify, assess, monitor and control/mitigate material operational risks as part of an overall approach to risk management.

Principle 9: Supervisors should conduct, directly or indirectly, regular independent evaluation of a bank's policies, procedures and practices related to operational risks. Supervisors should ensure that there are appropriate mechanisms in place which allow them to remain apprised of developments at banks.

Role of Disclosure

Principle 10: Banks should make sufficient public disclosure to allow market participants to assess their approach to operational risk management.

SELECTED QUESTIONS AND EXERCISES

1. Consider the following statements: operational Risk is different from "financial risks" (like market or credit risk) because...

   (I) ...it cannot be avoided;
  (II) ...it affects insurance companies, not banks;
 (III) ...an increase in risk does not necessarily bring about higher expected returns;
 (IV) ...it cannot be covered through capital.

Which one(s) would you agree with?

  (A) Only IV;
  (B) Only I;
  (C) I and III;
  (D) I and II.

2. For each of the following loss events, indicate the risk factor(s) (people, systems, processes or external events) to which it can be ascribed:

   – the tax rate on the bank's bestselling certificates of deposit is raised from 10 % to 30 %, causing a drop in demand;
   – some customer files are missing/incomplete and the backup data cannot be reconciled with the original ones;
   – an expense item was improperly treated as tax-deductible, leading to underestimating taxable profits and to evading taxes, so that the bank now has to pay a fine;
   – the bank's chief treasury officer illegally had some FX profits moved to his personal account in Monte Carlo.

3. What is an exposure indicator (EI), when it comes to operational risk?

   (A) A measure of loss experienced by the bank in the past.
   (B) A measure of loss expected by the bank in the future.
   (C) A scale variable, indicating how severe an operational loss could be, if it were to happen in a given business line and/or because of a certain type of risk factor.
   (D) A parameter measuring the correlation among two different business lines and/or risk factors.

4. A typical probability distribution for operational losses tends to be...

   (A) ...symmetric, because high-frequency, low-impact events are totally balanced by low-frequency, high-impact events;
   (B) ...skewed to the right, as it shows both high-frequency, low-impact events and low-frequency, high-impact events.
   (C) ...skewed to the left, as it shows both high-frequency, low-impact events and low-frequency, high-impact events.
   (D) ...uniform, since you have both high and low impact events, and they all tend to happen with both high and low the same frequencies.

5. Consider two business lines, both of which face an equal volume of expected losses (e.g., 100,000 euros) due to operational risk. The former estimates a probability of event (PE) of 1 %, while the latter has a PE of 5 %. The estimated volatility of Loss Given Event (LGE) is 500 euros for both business lines. Based on equation (17.5), compute and compare the volatilities of the operational losses for the two business lines. What does this example teach us, regarding LFHI and HFLI events?

Appendix 17A

OR measurement and EVT

In this Appendix, based on a research paper by Moscadelli (2004), we show how Extreme Value Theory (EVT) can be used as a tool for Operational Risk quantification.

As shown in Chapter 9, EVT is a mathematical tool increasingly used by risk managers to model the extreme tails of probability distributions (namely, loss distributions). More specifically, given a random variable z, the cumulative probability function for excesses $x = z - u$ beyond a given extreme threshold u, that is

$$F_u(x) = \Pr\{z \le u + x | z > u\} \tag{17A.1}$$

can be described, under pretty general conditions, by means of a Generalised Pareto Distribution:

$$G(x; \xi, \beta) = \begin{cases} 1 - (1 + \xi x / \beta) & \text{if} \quad \xi \ne 0 \\ 1 - e^{-x/\beta} & \text{if} \quad \xi = 0 \end{cases} \tag{17A.2}$$

with $\beta > 0$ and having $\begin{cases} x \ge 0 & \text{if} \quad \xi \ge 0 \\ 0 \le x \le -\beta/\xi & \text{if} \quad \xi < 0 \end{cases}$

where ξ is the key parameter taking a positive value for distributions characterised by fat tails.

This approach proves especially useful for operational loss data, like those collected in 2002 by the Basel Committee and reported in Tables 17.7 and 17.8.

Indeed, if one were to try and model such data by means of standard distributions, the results (although quite acceptable in the central part of the distribution) would be totally inadequate to represent tail losses, that is, those extreme cases on which the actual focus of OR management lies. An example is provided in Figure 17A.1. Here, the 2002 data concerning a specific business line (Corporate Finance) have been fitted by means of a standard probability distribution (lognormal) as well as through a more sophisticated function (the Gumbel distribution, a special case of the Generalized Extreme Value distribution): the graph shows actual and fitted cumulative probabilities focusing on the right tail of the loss distribution. As can be seen, the likelihood of extreme losses is dramatically underestimated; this can lead to unsatisfactory results, as far as risk measurement and management are concerned.

Let us then resort to EVT; after setting u at a value large enough for equation 17A.2 to hold (e.g., 400,000 euros), σ and ξ can be estimated by maximum likelihood, thereby identifying a GPD function correctly fitting the tail of the loss distribution. Figure 17A.2 reports the results in the case of the same business line presented in Figure 17A.1 (Corporate Finance); note that the values on the x axis are expressed as excess losses beyond the 400,000 euro threshold.

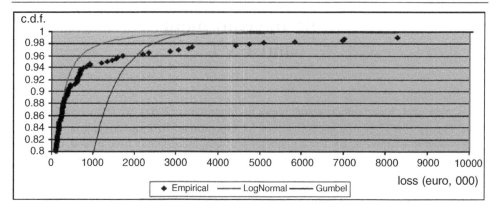

Figure 17A.1 Actual losses versus Gumbel and lognormal distributions – the case of Corporate Finance
Source: Moscadelli (2004)

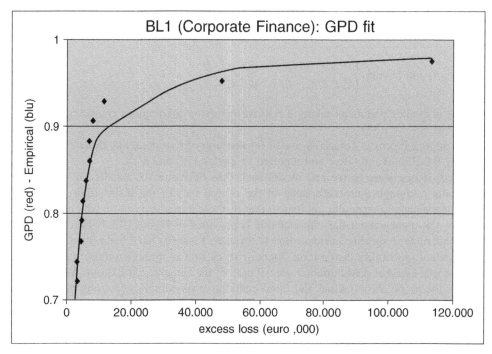

Figure 17A.2 Actual excess losses versus a GPD function
Source: Moscadelli, 2004

Having achieved a better representation of extreme cases, various measures of unexpected loss can now be derived. In his research paper, Moscadelli suggests "median shortfall", that is, the median of the observations lying beyond the u threshold; this indicator looks appealing because, unlike expected shortfall, it can be computed also when the variance of the tail distribution is infinite.

Distributions like the one portrayed in Figure 17A.2 represent losses, thereby combining two different risk profiles, relating to the frequency (PE) and the severity (LGE) of operational risks. However, if one is interested in disentangling those two components, it can be shown (see, e.g. Smith, 1989) that the probability distribution of the number of losses exceeding the threshold u can be modelled as a Poisson process, while the corresponding excess losses are independent and follow a GPD distribution.

Part V
Regulatory Capital Requirements

INTRODUCTION TO PART V

When a bank develops its own risk management system with the aim of measuring the amount of capital taken up by its risky assets, it must also take into account the constraints posed by the applicable regulations.

More specifically, the key regulatory constraint today stems from the mandatory capital requirements proposed by the Basel Committee in 1988 and later implemented by the supervisory authorities of over 150 countries, including the European Union.

These capital requirements were originally focused on credit risk only, but were then extended to market risks (in 1996) and operational risks (in 2004). The changes introduced in 1996 and 2004 are particularly significant as they allow banks to use their own internal models for regulatory purposes, i.e. for the calculation of the mandatory capital requirements.

In 2004, in addition to extending the scope of application of capital requirements to include also operational risks, the Basel Committee also completely redefined the 1988 Accord on credit risk. Also in this instance, internal rating systems were identified as suitable tools for measuring capital adequacy for regulatory purposes.[1]

Furthermore, the 2004 reform of credit risk requirements was an attempt at making it harder to perform "regulatory arbitrage"[2] operations, that is, transactions that several banks had performed in order to sidestep (e.g., through financial innovations such as credit derivatives, asset securitizations and loan sales) the 1988 regulations.

Another goal of the 2004 reform was to align the regulation to the progress made by credit risk measurement and management models in the 16 years following the 1988 Accord.

Finally, the 2004 reform did not focus only on mandatory capital requirements, but also tried to give a broader and more significant role to the monitoring activities put in place by national supervisors, as well as to the discipline applied by the market to the banks raising funds from professional investors.

As this Part of the book will show, the capital requirements that were originally imposed by the Basel Committee in 1988 played a key role in defining the management policies of each individual bank (microeconomic effects) and in terms of strengthening the stability of the international banking system as a whole (macroeconomic effects).

At a microeconomic level, the capital requirements had a major effect on the development paths chosen by banks in the past 15 years and fostered the emergence of new management and organizational models.

---

[1] According to the US Federal Reserve, "internal risk models, and in particular credit risk models, present significant challenges as well as important opportunities for supervisors. Ongoing financial innovations, such as securitization, are rendering the formal risk based capital standards increasingly less relevant to the largest banks by providing ever more cost-effective means for undertaking regulatory capital arbitrage. As credit exposures have become more complex and opaque, banks have invested heavily to improve the quality of their internal risk measurement systems. It would seem that supervisors, too, must adapt their methods for assessing credit risk and capital adequacy to the changing realities of the marketplace, or face a steady erosion in the effectiveness of capital based regulatory/supervisory policies". Federal Reserve Board (1998), pp. 33–34.

[2] The most common forms of regulatory arbitrage include asset securitization, whereby an asset posted in the balance sheet is converted into an off-balance asset which is subject to less stringent capital standards, and the replacement of assets characterized by high capital requirements, compared with their actual risk rate (e.g. loans to private companies with AAA ratings), with assets featuring a low capital charge compared to their actual risk rate (e.g. loans to a sovereign entity or an OECD bank with a low rating). Note that the latter example will become clearer after reading Chapter 18.

At a macroeconomic level, the 1988 Accord made the capitalization levels of the individual national banking systems more homogeneous, aligning them within a range that is sustainable on the medium term. A larger capitalization has strengthened the stability of the banking systems, which thus managed to survive relatively undamaged to some major international crises such as the recession of the early 1990's, the 1994 Mexican crisis, the 1997–1998 Asian-Russian crisis, the 1998 failure of the *Long Term Capital Management* fund, and, more recently, the collapse of the securities markets following the "technological" bubble of the late 1990's, as well as the uncertainties that emerged after 11 September 2001. The Basel Committee itself has recently defined the banks' capitalization level as "satisfactory", stating that the Committee does not deem necessary to provide for an overall increase in the capital held by intermediaries.

Figure 1 shows the main questions addressed in this part of the book.

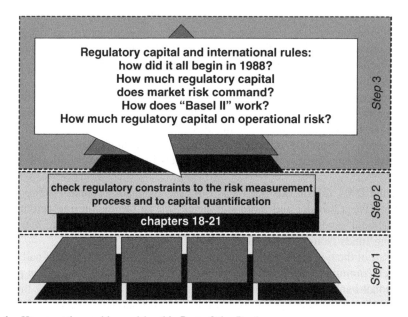

Figure 1   Key questions addressed by this Part of the Book

Chapter 18 provides a brief overview of the characteristics of the first Capital Accord that was reached by the Basel Committee in 1988, dwelling also on its limitations and the reasons that prompted its revision in the following years. Chapter 19 shows how capital requirements were extended to market risks by an ad hoc amendment to the Accord introduced in January 1996, after a public consultation round begun in 1993. Chapter 20 is devoted to the revised Accord released in 2004 after a 5-year consultation process involving authorities, scholars, and major banks. It shows how such proposals are based on similar rationales as those adopted in the models for measuring capital at risk discussed in the first four Parts of this book. Finally, Chapter 21 explores the capital requirements concerning operational risks.

18

The 1988 Capital Accord

18.1 INTRODUCTION

Regulatory requirements based on capital ratios were first proposed by the Basel Committee[1] in December 1987[2] and then ratified in the Capital Accord of July 1988. The Accord was later adopted, with slight changes, by the European Union[3] and the national banking regulators of more than 100 countries. Originally it only applied to banks that operated on an international scale, but many national authorities (including the European Union) decided to make it binding for all banks, including those with domestic operations only.

The Committee had already been working for several years on the introduction of uniform international capital requirements. A proposal similar to the 1987 plan had been presented by the governors of the G10 central banks in September 1986, in a report[4] discussed subsequently at the Fourth Conference on International Supervision in Amsterdam. Also, in January 1987, an initial agreement on a common framework for the measurement of bank capital adequacy had been reached by the US and UK authorities.[5]

There were three main reasons why regulators aimed to establish uniform capital requirements on an international scale:

- it would help prevent bank crises, by discouraging excessive risk taking;
- by having the requirements apply to consolidated accounts, it would foster the soundness of institutions controlled by foreign banking groups, promoting greater stability in the international financial markets;
- it would eliminate the competitive distortions produced by differences in national regulations, by helping create an international level playing field (uniform competitive conditions no matter what country a bank is in).[6] To achieve this third objective, the Committee recommended that the Accord be adopted even in countries it did not represent.

The first two objectives come into focus if we consider how the main banking systems have historically moved toward a gradual decrease in capitalization (Figure 18.1). The ratio of capital to total assets was once quite high (in the late 1800s the most advanced

---

[1] The Basel Committee is an advisory body comprised of the supervisory authorities of the Group of 10 countries (which actually number 11: Belgium, Canada, France, Germany, Italy, Japan, the Netherlands, Sweden, Switzerland, the United Kingdom and the United States), plus Luxembourg and Spain. For a summary of the role and characteristics of the Basel Committee, see Appendix 18A to this chapter.

[2] See Basel Committee (1987).

[3] See EU (1989).

[4] See Basel Committee (1986).

[5] See Bank of England and Federal Reserve Board (1987).

[6] As the Committee expressly affirms: "Two fundamental objectives lie at the heart of the Committee's work on regulatory convergence. These are, firstly, that the new framework should serve to strengthen the soundness and stability of the international banking system; and secondly that the framework should be fair and have a high degree of consistency in its application to banks in different countries with a view to diminishing an existing source of competitive inequality among international banks".

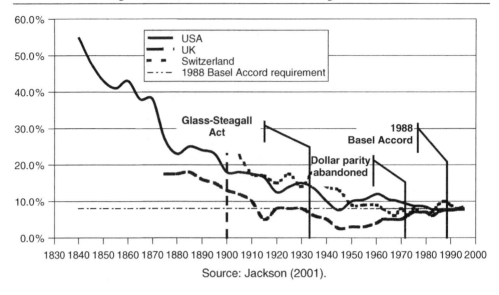

Source: Jackson (2001).

Figure 18.1 Trend in capital-to-assets ratio in various banking systems

banking systems had a ratio of 15–20%), but then it dwindled progressively, reaching a low in the 1970's.

As for the third objective (preventing competitive distortions among banks in different countries), an unspoken aim of the Accord was to reduce the advantage of Japanese banks, which according to British and US banks operated with a much lower capital-to-assets ratio than their main competitors in the G-10 countries.[7] As the British and Americans saw it, this smaller capital ratio meant a lower average weighted cost of funds, which during the course of the 1980s had allowed Japanese banks to gain an undue share of the international bank loans market.[8]

To achieve these objectives, the Accord required banks to comply with a minimum ratio of 8% (the "capital ratio", also known as the "risk asset ratio" or RAR) between capital and risk-weighted assets. In the next sections, we shall explain how the ratio is calculated, and describe the shortcomings that led to the reform of 2004.

---

[7] Pettway et al. (1991) give an example of the favourable treatment Japanese banks received from the Finance Ministry in terms of financial and capital ratios in comparison with American banks. Wagster's (1996) analysis of a sample of large banks shows that before the Basel Accord, the average capital-to-assets ratio in Japan was 2.11%, versus 3.32% for Germany, 4.90% for the United States, 5.05% for Canada, 5.41% for the United Kingdom and 6.29% for Switzerland. Including undisclosed reserves, however, Japan's ratio would go up to 12.35%. In fact, recent estimates by De Nederlandsche Bank reported by the Basel Committee on Banking Supervision (1999a) show that in 1988, Japanese banks had the highest average ratio of capital to risk-weighted assets, at nearly 12%. This is because that ratio allows the inclusion of part of the undisclosed reserves contributing to Tier 2 capital.

[8] According to Zimmer and McCauley (1991), Japanese banks almost tripled their share of the market for loans to US manufacturing and commercial companies from 1984 to 1989. Wagster (1996) reports that by the end of the decade, Japanese banks accounted for 38% of international loans, including 12% of the US market and 23% of the British market.

18.2   THE CAPITAL RATIO

The 1988 Accord requires banks to have "regulatory capital" amounting to at least 8%[9] of total risk-weighted assets:

$$CR = \frac{RC}{\sum_i A_i \cdot w_i} \geq 8\% \tag{18.1}$$

where:

CR = capital ratio;
RC = regulatory capital;
A_i = i-th asset
w_i = risk weight of the i-th asset

Let's take a closer look at the three elements included in (18.1): regulatory capital, assets, and risk weights.

18.2.1   Regulatory capital (RC)

As shown in Table 18.1, capital is split into two categories: *Tier 1 capital* and *Tier 2/3 (supplementary)* capital. Tier 1 capital is comprised of the "weightier," more "valuable" components, those with a strong ability to protect third parties from the effects of any losses suffered by the bank. Supplementary capital is made up of instruments more comparable to debt.

18.2.1.1   Tier 1 capital

Tier 1 capital is comprised mainly of paid-up share capital, disclosed reserves (share premium account, legal reserve, retained earnings, etc.), and certain general provisions and innovative capital instruments.

Specifically, general reserves – such as the reserve for general banking risks required in many countries of the European Union – only contribute to Tier 1 capital if:

– the provisions are post-tax, or are in any case adjusted for all potential tax liabilities;
– their size, distributions and provisions are shown separately in the bank's financial statements;
– they are immediately and unconditionally available for the coverage of losses (which must transit through the profit and loss account).

The opportunity to create general provisions has also been limited, within the EU, by the adoption of International Financial Reporting Standard (IFRS) No. 39, also known as IAS39. This standard allows contingency reserves to be created only against certain, identified future liabilities, not against general business risks.

---

[9] The ratio must be at least 8% at the consolidated level, while the minimum for individual banks within a group is 7%.

Table 18.1 Components of regulatory capital in the Basel Capital Accord

Component	Conditions for inclusion	Limits and restrictions
UPPER TIER 1		
Paid-up share capital/ordinary (common) shares		At least 4 % of risk-weighted assets
Disclosed reserves (e.g. share premium reserves or retained earnings)	General provisions are accepted only if they derive from post-tax earnings or are adjusted for tax liabilities, if they are shown separately in the bank's financial statements, and if they are immediately available for the coverage of losses (transiting through the profit and loss account).	
LOWER TIER 1		
Innovative capital instruments	Capital securities, preferred securities, preference shares	No more than 15 % of Tier 1
UPPER TIER 2		
Undisclosed reserves	Allowed only if they transit through the profit and loss account, if they are free from charges or other known liabilities, if they are free and immediately available to cover unexpected future losses, and if they have been accepted by the supervisory authorities.	No more than 100 % of Tier 1
Revaluation reserves	For hidden reserves, there is a prudential deduction of 55 % of the difference between market value and recognized cost.	
General loan loss provisions	These are allowed only if created to cover unidentified losses, and may not exceed 1.25 %/0.6 % of risk-weighted assets.	
Hybrid capital instruments	Unsecured, subordinated and fully subscribed; not redeemable at the holder's initiative or without consent of the supervisory authorities; can be used to cover losses without the need to liquidate the bank; can be deferred if the bank's profits do not allow payment.	

Lower Tier 2		
Subordinated term debt	Original term to maturity of at least 5 years. Amortized at 20 % per year if maturing in less than 5 years.	No more than 50 % of Tier 1
Tier 3 (For Market Risks Only)		
Short-term subordinated loans	Original term to maturity of at least 2 years. Deferrable if the bank cannot meet the minimum capital ratio.	No more than 250 % of Tier 1 for market risk.
Deductions		
Goodwill		Deducted from Tier 1
Investments in non-consolidated banks and financial institutions		Deducted from total capital

Source: Basel Committee on Banking Supervision (1988) (as amended).

"Innovative capital instruments" were admitted by the Basel Committee in October 1998[10] and must also meet some conditions:

- they must be unsecured and exempt from any restrictions allowing investors to redeem them before maturity;
- they must be permanent;
- they must be callable at the initiative of the issuer only after a minimum of five years from the date of issue, subject to prior approval by the supervisory authorities, who may require that the instruments be replaced by others of the same or better capital quality;
- there must be a clause stating that if the remuneration is not paid within a certain period, the right of remuneration is not deferred but entirely forfeited;
- they must be able to absorb losses by the bank on a going-concern basis;
- they must be junior to all other general creditors and subordinated debt.

In addition, innovative capital instruments cannot make up more than 15 % of Tier 1 capital (any extra can be counted toward Tier 2). This is why they are known as "lower Tier 1", as opposed to "upper Tier 1" for the other components.

Finally, to determine the amount of Tier 1 capital, goodwill and any other items so noted by the national banking regulators must be subtracted from the sum of the elements mentioned above.

18.2.1.2 Supplementary capital (Tier 2 and Tier 3)

The second category refers to *supplementary capital*, which is further split into *Tier 2* and *Tier 3*.

Tier 2 is made up of undisclosed reserves, revaluation reserves, general provisions, hybrid capital instruments and subordinated term debt.

Undisclosed reserves, allowed by some countries and not by others, are special reserves created through retained after-tax earnings that are not shown in the financial statements. That aspect aside, they must be as solid as ordinary "disclosed" reserves, which means they cannot be encumbered by charges or other known liabilities but must be free and immediately available to cover unexpected future losses.

Revaluation reserves are those stemming from the revaluation of assets reported originally at their historical cost. They can be disclosed in the financial statements or else hidden or latent, i.e. associated with potential gains that have not been realized yet. Hidden reserves are allowed in the computation of supplementary capital up to 45 % of their value (hence, of the value of the unrealized gain). The 55 % disallowance takes account of the possible decline in the market prices of these assets (which would reduce the gains in question), and of the taxes that would apply to the gains when realized. Hidden reserves were especially significant for Japanese and German banks, which have large stock portfolios that are carried in the balance sheet at cost.

General provisions and *general loan loss reserves* are liability items created against unidentified losses (if they are ascribed to specific assets and represent a reduction in the assets' value, they cannot be counted as supplementary capital). The Basel Accord allows these to count toward Tier 2 up to a maximum of 1.25 % of risk-weighted assets.[11] For

---

[10] Basel Committee on Banking Supervision (1998).

[11] The 2004 Accord changed that limit to 0.6 % of credit-risk-weighted assets for banks that use their own internal rating system for regulatory purposes (see Chapter 20).

European banks, these reserves also conflict somewhat with the new accounting standards (see Chapter 20), which limit the possibility to create general provisions against losses that are merely potential.

Hybrid capital instruments combine features of shareholders' equity and forms of debt. They differ from country to country, as defined by each regulator. They must, however, meet the following minimum requirements:

- they must be fully paid up, unsecured, and subordinate to the bank's entire remaining debt;
- they cannot be redeemed at the creditor's initiative, or without prior authorization from the supervisory authorities;
- they must be available to participate in losses without triggering liquidation of the bank (this is the main difference with respect to conventional subordinated debt);
- if they entitle holders to periodic remuneration that cannot be waived or reduced, it must be possible to defer this if the bank's profits do not allow payment.

Subordinated term debt is unsecured debt with an original term of at least five years, whose redemption, if the bank defaults, is subordinate to the full satisfaction of other creditors. During the last five years before maturity, the amount which can be computed as Tier 2 capital is reduced to 20 % per year. This correction – known as regulatory amortization – reflects the debt's decreasing value as a form of capital as it approaches maturity.

Unlike hybrid instruments, subordinated term debt cannot participate in losses without putting the bank in liquidation. For that reason, it cannot exceed 50 % of Tier 1 Capital and is known as "Lower Tier 2" (versus "Upper Tier 2," the remaining elements of supplementary capital).

Tier 3, introduced in 1996, is comprised of short-term subordinated debt and counts toward regulatory capital only as coverage of market risk; in other words, the requirements for credit risk and operational risk must be met through Tier 1 and Tier 2. The subordinated debt included in Tier 3 must meet the following conditions:

- it must be fully paid up, unsecured, and subordinate to the bank's entire remaining debt;
- it must have an original minimum term of at least two years (if the term is indefinite, at least two years' notice must be required for redemption);
- it cannot be redeemed in advance, unless approved by the supervisory authorities;
- there has to be a "lock-in" clause by which the bank will defer principal and/or interest payments if it falls below the minimum capital ratio plus 20 %.[12]

In any case, *Tier 3 capital cannot exceed* 250 % of the Tier 1 Capital used for the coverage of market risks.[13]

Supplementary capital is then reduced by loan loss forecasts and losses from securities trading. It may not exceed Tier 1 capital and can therefore be no more than 50 % of a bank's total regulatory capital.

---

[12] The additional 20%, provided for by the Basel Committee, does not apply in EU regulations whereby the lock-in clause is triggered only if the bank falls below the regulatory minimum.

[13] Using C_1 to indicate the amount of Tier 1 capital used for market risk capital requirements and C_3 to indicate Tier 3, this means that $C_3 < 2.5 \cdot C_1$, so $C_1 > 0.286 \cdot (C_1 + C_3)$. Market risk capital requirements must therefore be covered at least 28.6 % by Tier 1. The European Union regulations are somewhat stricter ($C_3 < 1.5 \cdot C_1$, therefore $C_1 > 0.4 \cdot [C_1 + C_3]$).

Finally, total capital is curtailed by the value of equity investments in other financial institutions,[14] to prevent what is known as "double gearing".[15]

18.2.2   Risk weights (w$_i$)

Table 18.2 summarizes the weights assigned to the main assets. As we can see, assets which are considered to be riskier are given a higher weight (suggesting the need for greater amounts of capital). More specifically, assets are divided into four categories: no risk (0 %), low (20 %), medium (50 %) and full (100 %). Assets are assigned to one of these categories on the basis of three criteria: *liquidity* (highest for cash, lower for securities, even lower for loans and real estate), *debtor type* (governments and central banks, supranational institutions, public entities, banks, corporates), and the debtor's *country of residence* (OECD or non-OECD).

Table 18.2 Risk weights for on-balance sheet assets

$w_i = 0\,\%$	$w_i = 20\,\%$	$w_i = 50\,\%$	$w_i = 100\,\%$
Cash and cash equivalents	Claims on multilateral development banks	Loans secured by mortgage on residential property	Claims on the private sector
Claims on central banks and central governments of OECD countries	Claims on banks in OECD countries		Equity investments in private companies
Government bonds issued by OECD countries	Claims on public entities in OECD countries		Claims on banks and central governments outside the OECD
	Claims on banks in OECD countries with a maturity of less than one year		Plant and other fixed assets

Source: Basel Committee (1988).

We thus arrive at the following weights[16] (w_i):

- 0 % for cash and for claims on central governments, central banks and the European Union;
- 20 % for claims on banks and the public sector;
- 50 % for secured mortgage loans for the purchase of residential real estate;

---

[14] These investments (which include holdings in insurance companies) are deducted 50 % from Tier 1 capital and 50 % from supplementary capital.

[15] An example will clarify the logic behind this rule. Let's take two banks, A and B, which carry out a capital increase of the same amount. Bank A uses its own funds to subscribe to the full capital increase of Bank B, and vice versa. If equity investments did not have to be deducted from capital, both A and B would have increased their own capitalization, but for the banking system as a whole there would have been no injection of fresh funds nor any improvement in overall stability.

[16] The 1988 Accord also reduced the weights of assets secured by collateral (in particular, loans collateralized by cash or government securities were considered to be risk-free) or third-party guarantees (in which case the guarantor's risk weight could be used if it were lower than the principal debtor's). Similar allowances were extended and refined in the 2004 Accord (see Chapter 20).

- 100 % for claims on the private sector, equity investments, and investments in subordinated loans and hybrid capital instruments not deducted from regulatory capital.

18.2.3   Assets included in the capital ratio (A_i)

The assets captured by the denominator of equation (18.1) are not just "on-balance sheet" items, but also "off-balance sheet" assets such as endorsement credits, forward contracts and other over-the-counter (OTC) derivatives. These last are included in (18.1) for the amount of their "loan equivalent exposure." The rules for calculating loan equivalent exposure for OTC derivatives are explained in Chapter 16. For off balance sheet items like guarantees and loan commitments, the loan equivalent exposure is obtained by multiplying the nominal value by a credit conversion factor (see Table 18.3), which increases with the likelihood of actual credit exposure.

Table 18.3 Credit conversion factors for off-balance sheet assets

Conversion factor	Type of off-balance sheet exposure
0 %	Commitments that can be unconditionally cancelled at any time.[17]
20 %	Commitments with an original maturity of up to one year. Self-liquidating short-term commitments associated with business transactions (e.g. documentary credits on merchandise that serves as a warranty).
50 %	Commitments with an original maturity of more than one year. Commitments associated with non-financial transactions (performance bonds, bid bonds, warranties and stand-by letters of credit related to specific transactions). Documentary credits granted and confirmed. Note issuance facilities (NIFs) and revolving underwriting facilities (RUFs). Other lending commitments (unutilized credit lines) with an original maturity of over one year.
100 %	Direct credit substitutes (sureties, acceptances, irrevocable standby letters of credit). Asset sales with recourse, in which the bank bears the credit risk.

Source: Basel Committee (1988).

18.3   SHORTCOMINGS OF THE CAPITAL ADEQUACY FRAMEWORK

The approach recommended in 1988 had several limitations. The most important ones are discussed below.

---

[17] The 1988 Accord also admitted, on principle, a zero risk-weight for short-term commitments as long as the total amount was negligible ("on a *de minimis* ground").

18.3.1 Focus on credit risk only

Aside from the liquidity factor, the framework described above and the risk-weights shown in Table 18.2 concentrate on credit risk only. Other kinds of risk are ignored, particularly interest rate and market risks. Regarding OTC derivatives, for example, the link between market factors and the asset's value is limited to an estimate of the losses that would be incurred in the event of counterparty default, which is again a measure of credit risk. No account is taken of the risks arising from currency or maturity mismatch.

Since 1974, however, a string of banking crises have shown how much danger is brought about by speculation in foreign currencies (in which many banks engaged after the abandonment of the fixed exchange rate system established at the Bretton Woods Conference in 1944) or in interest rates through maturity transformation (a policy followed by numerous Savings & Loans in the United States).

To remedy this problem, in 1996 the Basel Committee issued an amendment that extended capital requirements to market risks (see Chapter 19).

18.3.2 Poor differentiation of risk

Table 18.2 treats all loans to private commercial and industrial companies as a single risk category (weighted at 100%). This implies that all private firms are considered to be equally risky, and loans to companies with different ratings are all subject to the same capital requirement.

Likewise, all exposures to non-OECD countries are considered riskier than the exposures to those in the OECD. Paradoxically, then, China – a non-OECD country rated A2 by Moody's – is treated as riskier than Turkey, an OECD country with a rating of Ba3 (see Table 18.4).

18.3.3 Limited recognition of the link between maturity and credit risk

A loan is more or less risky depending on its residual life. All other conditions being equal, loans with a longer residual duration are riskier (because by the end of the risk horizon, they may have migrated to a worse rating class even if they are not in default), and require a greater amount of economic capital.

The 1988 Accord almost completely ignored the link between maturity and credit risk, affording a few minor benefits (in the form of a lower capital requirement) to just a handful of short-term items such as off-balance sheet items and interbank loans.

18.3.4 Disregard for portfolio diversification

An obvious flaw in the 1998 scheme is the failure to consider the benefits of diversifying risk. For a proper assessment of a bank's loan portfolio, it is not enough to measure the risk of individual exposures, since their correlation is also important. If the rules do not recognize this effect, and portfolios with a high number of well diversified loans require the same amount of capital as portfolios concentrated heavily on a few borrowers (or countries or industries), then there is no incentive to diversify credit risk.

Table 18.4 Moody's rating of major countries (sovereign ratings)

	Long term ratings on government bonds	
	Foreign currency	Domestic currency
Argentina	B3	B3
Australia	Aaa	Aaa
Austria	Aaa	Aaa
Belgium	Aa1	Aa1
Brazil	Ba3	Ba3
Canada	Aaa	Aaa
Chile	A2	A1
China	A2	–
Colombia	Ba2	Baa3
Czech Republic	A1	A1
Denmark	Aaa	Aaa
Ecuador	Caa1	B3
Egypt	Ba1	Baa3*
France	Aaa*	Aaa
Germany	Aaa	Aaa
Greece	A1	A1
Hong Kong	A1	Aa3
Hungary	A1	A1
India	Baa3*	Ba2
Indonesia	B1	B1
Ireland	Aaa	Aaa
Israel	A2	A2
Italy	Aa2	Aa2
Japan	Aaa*	A2

(continued overleaf)

Table 18.4 (*continued*)

	Long term ratings on government bonds	
	Foreign currency	Domestic currency
Korea	A3	A3
Kuwait	A2*	A2*
Malaysia	A3	A3
Mexico	Baa1	Baa1
Netherlands	Aaa*	Aaa
New Zealand	Aaa	Aaa
Norway	Aaa*	Aaa
Portugal	Aa2	Aa2
Romania	Ba1	Ba1
Russia	Baa2	Baa2
Saudi Arabia	A3*	A3
Singapore	Aaa*	Aaa
South Africa	Baa1	A2
Spain	Aaa	Aaa
Sweden	Aaa	Aaa
Switzerland	Aaa*	Aaa
Taiwan	Aa3*	Aa3
Turkey	Ba3	Ba3
United Kingdom	Aaa*	Aaa
United States of America	Aaa*	Aaa
Uruguay	B3	B3
Venezuela	B2	B1
* Issuer rating		

Source: *www.moodys.com, July 2006.*

18.3.5 Limited recognition of risk mitigation tools

A further limitation, which became especially flagrant in the latter half of the 1990s, is that the Accord gave very little recognition[18] to the risk-mitigating benefits of guarantees and credit derivatives. Thus, banks had insufficient incentives to use these tools.

18.3.6 "Regulatory arbitrage"

Because of the shortcomings mentioned above, risks measured on the basis of the 1998 Accord were very different from those estimated according to internal rating and VaR models, such as those discussed in the third part of this book. Similar discrepancies encouraged banks to engage in "regulatory arbitrage," which let them:

√ increase forms of credit exposure for which the capital requirements were less stringent than the absorbed capital measured by internal models (e.g. mortgage loans for residential real estate, weighted 50%, and loans to high-risk OECD countries);
√ transfer to third parties, for example through securitization or loan sales, the less risky forms of credit exposures whose capital requirements were higher than the actual degree of risk (e.g., loans to highly rated private companies).

Such moves wound up worsening the quality of loan portfolios, and were therefore in sharp contrast with the aims of a regulatory policy like the 1998 Accord: to make the banking system more stable. Banks, in effect, were led to replace loans of good quality – but whose capital requirements were comparatively high and which were therefore "expensive" from a capital standpoint – with those of lesser quality, which could bring in greater spreads and would absorb a relatively modest amount of capital.

18.4 CONCLUSIONS

Despite these limitations, the 1998 Accord did manage to reverse the gradual decline in the capitalization of large banks. As shown in Figure 18.2, in the years after 1988 the average capital ratio of major banks increased in all major economically developed countries, except Germany and Japan. The main international banking groups continued to keep their capitalization above the 8% minimum in the late 1990s, as shown in Figure 18.3.

What's more, the Basel Committee did not sit idle after 1988, but worked to enrich and complete the original design of the Accord. In 1996 it approved an amendment on market risks, and in 1999 it began an in-depth reform of credit risk requirements and addressed the issue of operational risk, leading to a new Accord in 2004. These are the subjects of the next three Chapters.

SELECTED QUESTIONS AND EXERCISES

1. A bank, having a Tier 1 capital of 10 million euros, issues 22 million euros of subordinated debt with a maturity of 7 years, paying a fixed and not-deferrable coupon,

---

[18] See footnote 16.

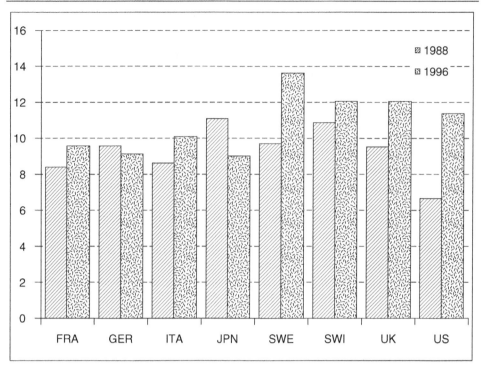

Source: Bank for International Settlements (1998).

Figure 18.2   Average capital ratio (%) of the main international banks

which represent all of its Tier 2 capital. How much is the total regulatory capital of the bank?

(A) 15 million euros;
(B) 20 million euros;
(C) 10 million euros;
(D) 22 million euros.

2. A bank issues a 4-year performance bond of euro 5 million, in the interest of a non-financial firm headquartered in a OECD country. How much are the risk-weighted assets associated with the performance bond?

(A) 5 million euros;
(B) 2.5 million euros;
(C) 1.25 million euros;
(D) 0 euros, as performance bonds are always unconditionally cancellable.

3. Which of the following represents a "regulatory arbitrage"?

(A) A bank operates in such a way as to increase its regulatory capital without a corresponding increase in risk.
(B) A bank operates in such a way as to cut down its capital without a corresponding decrease in risk.

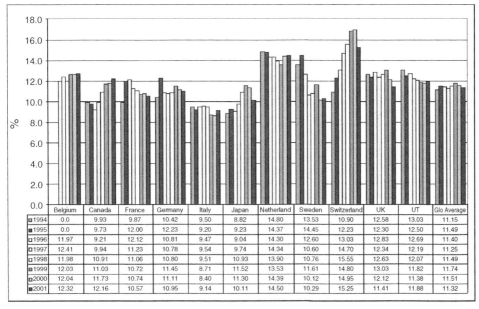

	Belgium	Canada	France	Germany	Italy	Japan	Netherland	Sweden	Switzerland	UK	UT	Glo Average
1994	0.0	9.93	9.87	10.42	9.50	8.82	14.80	13.53	10.90	12.58	13.03	11.15
1995	0.0	9.73	12.00	12.23	9.20	9.23	14.37	14.45	12.23	12.30	12.50	11.49
1996	11.97	9.21	12.12	10.81	9.47	9.04	14.30	12.60	13.03	12.83	12.69	11.40
1997	12.41	9.94	11.23	10.78	9.54	9.74	14.34	10.60	14.70	12.34	12.19	11.25
1998	11.98	10.91	11.06	10.80	9.51	10.93	13.90	10.76	15.55	12.63	12.07	11.49
1999	12.03	11.03	10.72	11.45	8.71	11.52	13.53	11.61	14.80	13.03	11.82	11.74
2000	12.04	11.73	10.74	11.11	8.40	11.30	14.39	10.12	14.95	12.12	11.38	11.51
2001	12.32	12.16	10.57	10.95	9.14	10.11	14.50	10.29	15.25	11.41	11.88	11.32

Source: Ferrari (2002).

Figure 18.3 Average capital ratio of the main international banks: 1994–2001

(C) A bank operates in such a way as to alter the composition of its regulatory capital in order to reduce its funding costs.

(D) A bank operates in such a way as to sell or securitize risky assets that commanded a zero capital requirement.

4. Consider the data for Acme Bank in the following Table and compute its regulatory capital

Capital items	*Amount*
Shareholders' Equity	50
Reserves due to retained earnings	18
Preference shares	20
Revaluation reserves	20
Perpetual subordinated loans with deferrable coupon	20
10-year subordinated debt – residual life of 6 years	60

5. Consider the data for Acme Bank in the following Table and compute its risk-weighted assets. Using the results of exercise 4, also compute the bank's Tier 1 and total capital ratios.

Assets	Amount
Loans to non-financial companies	500
Residential mortgage loans to retail customers	200
Mortgage loans secured by commercial real estate	100
Loans to UK banks	400
Loans to non-OECD banks	200
UK Treasury Gilts	100
Listed equity portfolio	50
Cash	50
Buildings and other fixed assets	150
Off-balance sheet items	*Amount*
Unconditionally-cancellable credit lines to non-financial companies	400
6-month documentary credits to non-financial companies	100

Appendix 18A
The Basel Committee

The Basel Committee on Banking Supervision was established in late 1974 by the governors of the central banks of the G10 countries, in the aftermath of a wave of international financial crises that culminated in the default of Germany's Herstatt Bank.

The Committee members come from thirteen countries: Belgium, Canada, France, Germany, Japan, the United Kingdom, Italy, Luxembourg, the Netherlands, Spain,[19] the United States, Sweden and Switzerland. Each country is represented by its central bank and by any other authority responsible for supervising the banking system.

The Committee serves as a forum for discussion and cooperation on matters of international banking supervision. At first, it focused on branches and subsidiaries of foreign banks and on how to allocate responsibilities (supervision and the function of lender of last resort) between the authorities of the host country and those of the bank's home country. Thus, the Committee's proposals and recommendations concerned only international banking activities conducted through foreign branches and subsidiaries, and were guided by two principles: to make sure no banking establishment would escape supervision by an authority (national or foreign), and to guarantee that supervision was adequate. The proposals and recommendations were formalized in the 1975 "Concordat," which was revised in 1983.

Since the late 1980s, the Committee's tasks have gradually extended to all means of making bank supervision more effective. It pursues this goal in three ways: (i) by exchanging information on the regulatory policies of individual countries, (ii) by improving supervisory techniques for international banking activities, and (iii) by setting minimum regulatory standards. The Committee has dedicated special attention to capital adequacy, which is aimed at ensuring the solvency of individual banks (and thus the stability of the entire international banking system), and on making sure internationally active banks based in different countries work under uniform competitive conditions.

The Committee has no legislative power or supranational authority, and its recommendations do not have legal force. Its scope is to define guidelines and recommendations that can then be adopted by individual political and regulatory authorities (e.g. by the EU Commission and Parliament).

The Basel Committee reports to the central bank governors of the G10 countries, who meet periodically at the Bank for International Settlements.

In the mid-1990s, the Basel Committee began to work frequently with the International Organization of Securities Commissions (IOSCO), a worldwide assembly of market and security regulators. Since 1995 the two bodies have published 10 joint reports on derivatives trading by banks and investment firms. The Basel Committee has also partnered recently with securities commissions and insurance supervisors, establishing in 1996 the Joint Forum on Financial Conglomerates, which fosters cooperation and information sharing among supervisory authorities.

---

[19] Spain has only been a member since February 2001.

The Capital Requirements for Market Risks

19.1 INTRODUCTION

Several financial institutions have contributed to the development of models for measuring market risks, as they have often had the merit of making their internal methodologies public. A significant impulse, however, has also come from the supervisory authorities, in at least three ways:

– when capital requirements were extended to market risks, the authorities adopted a methodology similar to VaR models, imposing mark-to-market for positions and a minimum amount of capital capable of covering "a significant portion of the losses that would have been registered during any two-week holding period over the past five years";
– the authorities used moral suasion to persuade those financial institutions with a significant trading activity to develop rigorous market risk measurement systems and and provide for an adequate organizational structure;
– the authorities permitted the more advanced banks to adopt their own internal models to determine the capital requirement related to their trading portfolios. This was indeed a revolutionary step: the supervisory authorities did not impose any directive concerning the actual content of the models, but rather limited their action to verifying their robustness and effectiveness. In this way, they agreed to limit their regulatory powers to enable banks to use a single risk measurement model for both regulatory and internal management purposes.

In this way the authorities have often provided the decisive impulse for introducing a risk-management system: indeed, their requirements have forced banks to develop a data warehouse based on the market values of their positions; the availability of these data have then acted as an incentive for developing internal models.

This chapter examines in detail the evolution of supervisory regulations on market risks. After a brief presentation of the origin and general characteristics of the capital ratios related to market risks, the focus will shift to the requirements for the different types of positions (bonds, stocks and currencies) contemplated by the so-called standardized approach. We then discuss the internal models approach, dwelling on the conditions (qualitative and quantitative) imposed on banks that wish to adopt it. The chapter closes with an examination of the advantages and limitations of the internal model approach.

19.2 ORIGINS AND CHARACTERISTICS OF CAPITAL REQUIREMENTS

19.2.1 Origins of the requirements

As already discussed in Chapter 18, the content of the 1988 Basel Agreement was limited to credit risk and did not regard market risks such as foreign exchange and interest rate risk. This limitation has assumed growing importance because of several factors: the growth in trading activity, particularly in derivatives, on the part of many large banks; the increased volatility of the financial markets; and the securitization of financial assets, which has led many banks to increase their presence in the capital markets.

To overcome this limitation, the Basel Committee formulated some proposals, presented in April 1993 and revised two years later. In 1993 the European Union also intervened with a directive of its own (93/6/EU) that replaced Directive 89/647 on the solvency of credit institutions.[1]

The 1993 directive – recently reviewed and amended by directive 2006/49–presents a few differences with respect to the Committee documents. First of all, it has the force of law and is not simply a proposal. Furthermore, it imposes capital requirements on market risks not only for banks[2] but also for securities firms, for which, given their activity, these requirements represent the main instruments of supervisory regulation. Lastly, along with the requirements on market risks, it establishes capital requirements on concentration risk, counterparty risk, and settlement risk.[3]

19.2.2 Logic and scope of application

In presenting the structure of the capital requirements on market risks, we shall take the proposals presented by the Basel Committee as a reference. As we shall see, the provisions of Directive 93/6 differ only minimally from the Committee's scheme.

Market risk is defined as the risk of losses in on- and off-balance sheet positions as a result of adverse changes in market factors. These factors include interest rates, stock prices, foreign exchange rates and commodities' prices.

A capital requirement is associated with each of these four risk categories, corresponding ideally to the coverage "of a significant portion of the losses that would have been incurred during any holding period of two weeks on a representative portfolio over the previous five years". A similar criterion underlies various assumptions that recall the VaR models described in the second part of this volume:

– the risk horizon (holding period) of the positions is equal to two weeks;
– the sample of historical data for estimation of market factors return volatility is equal to five years;
– capital must cover a significant portion, but not 100 %, of the possible losses.

Regarding positions in equities, debt securities and commodities, the capital requirements for market risks are limited to the positions included in the trading portfolio. This is defined as the "bank's proprietary positions in financial instruments which are intentionally held for short-term resale and/or which are taken on by the bank with the intention of benefiting

---

[1] The criteria for measuring market risks were discussed, in the late 80's and early 90's, in three different supranational venues: the Basel Committee, the European Union and the International Organization of Securities Commissions (IOSCO), the international organization formed in 1987 that includes the main capital markets supervisory authorities. While the activity of the first two institutions (which have strong links since seven of the EU member states participate in the Committee activities) gave rise to the documents mentioned in the text, the activity of IOSCO has not yet achieved significant results due to divergences within the organization.
[2] Banks whose trading portfolio does not exceed €15 million and 5 % of total outstanding positions are exempted.
[3] In this regard, see Appendix 19A to this chapter.

in the short-term from actual and/or expected differences between their buying and selling prices, or from other price or interest-rate changes, and positions in financial instruments arising from matched principal brokering and market making, or positions taken in order to hedge other elements of the trading book".

The trading book therefore includes positions which taken with a short term horizon and for speculative purposes (or trading with customers). The counterpart of the trading portfolio is the "banking book", which includes the positions that, though resting on the same market variables (and thus creating similar risks), are taken for different purposes (especially for medium/long-term investment).

19.2.3 The "building blocks" approach

The standardized approach to the computation of capital requirements is based on a *"building block"* approach. In other words, the total requirement is the sum of some elements, stacked one on the other like the building blocks children play with.

In particular (see Figure 19.1), the requirement is the sum of the requirements on:

– debt securities;
– equities;
– currencies;
– commodities;

and the risk on debt and equity securities is divided, in turn, into two components:

– *generic risk*, i.e. the risk of losses caused by a generally adverse change in the market factors (particularly rising interest rates for bonds and declining stock market indices for equities);
– *specific risk*, i.e. the risk of losses on specific securities, caused by an adverse change in the factors related to an individual issuer (bankruptcy, business crisis, etc.).

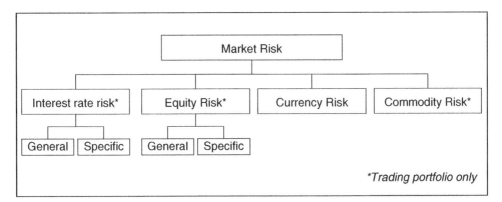

Figure 19.1   Structure of the capital requirements related to market risks

The capital requirements for positions in debt and equity securities *replace* the existing requirements based on credit risk. The relative positions are therefore not included in the assets taken as a reference in computing the capital ratio presented in Chapters 18 and 20.

It is impossible to conclude *a priori* whether this substitution produces a greater or lesser capital burden.

On the other side, the capital requirements for foreign exchange and commodity risks are *incremental* with respect to the credit risk one and thus represent an additional burden.

With the introduction of capital requirements for market risks, the minimum regulatory capital therefore became equal to the sum of the following three components:

(1) credit risk capital requirement (only for the banking book);
(2) market risks capital requirements (only for the trading book), which also includes the specific component linked to credit risk of individual issuers;
(3) foreign exchange risk capital requirement on the entire balance sheet (both trading and banking portfolios).

To these the 2004 Basel II reform added a capital requirement for operational risk (see Chapter 21).

Banks in the European Union, as mentioned earlier, must also add the capital requirements related to settlement risk, counterparty risk and concentration risk (see Appendix 19A to this chapter).

19.2.4   Tier 3 Capital

As already mentioned in Chapter 18, the capital requirements covering market risk can be satisfied not only with Tier 1 and Tier 2 capital but also with a special form of supplementary capital (consisting of subordinated loans with maturity of two to five years) known as Tier 3.

The inclusion of this item, with relatively short maturity, in the regulatory capital that qualifies to cover market risks is justified by the short term horizon of such risks. We refer to Chapter 18 for further details on Tier 3 capital.

19.3   THE CAPITAL REQUIREMENT ON DEBT SECURITIES

The requirement applies to fixed- and floating-rate bonds, derivatives on interest rates (futures, options, swaps and forward rate agreements) and on credit risk (credit derivatives), and to other instruments whose market values behave like those of debt securities, such as fixed-dividend non-convertible preferred stock.

19.3.1   The requirement for specific risk

The capital requirement associated with specific risk, for each bond issue, is equal to a certain percentage of the net amount[4] held by the bank. This percentage (see Table 19.1) depends on the type of issuer, its rating, and in some cases the residual life of the security. "Qualifying issues" are bonds issued by public entities other than the state and by multilateral development banks, as well as bonds that have received an "investment grade" rating from at least two rating agencies recognized by the authorities (or from only one, provided that no other recognized agency has issued a non-investment grade

---

[4] Offsetting long and short positions is permitted only if the issue is exactly the same in both cases.

Table 19.1 Capital requirement for specific risk on debt securities

	Life to maturity		
	0–6 months	6–24 months	over 2 years
Government bonds with rating AAA to AA−	0%		
Government bonds with rating A+ to BBB− and "qualifying bonds"	0.25%	1%	1.60%
Any bonds, with rating BB+ to BB−	8.00%		
Any bonds, with rating below BB−	12.00%		
Any unrated bonds	8.00%		

rating) or issued by listed companies that the bank deems of comparable quality. The rating-based weightings were introduced in 2004 and are uniform with those cited in the new Basel Accord (see Chapter 20) for credit risk on the banking book.

Derivative instruments on interest rates (forward rate agreements, interest rate futures, interest rate swaps, options on futures, caps, floors and collars) are included in the computation of the requirement for debt securities limited to generic risk. In the case of futures and options on specific debt securities or baskets of securities, however, the same band of specific risk for the issuer(s) is applied.

19.3.2 The requirement for generic risk

The capital requirement to cover generic risk is based on a cash-flow mapping procedure similar to that presented in Chapter 3. It is based on 13 maturity buckets, grouped into three zones (time zones) and is structured as follows:

(I) For each bond i in the portfolio, the net position NP_i is computed as the difference between the long and short positions held by the bank, including off-balance sheet items.[5]

(II) The net positions are then slotted into the 13 time bands (see Table 19.2). Those bands are based on maturities (or renegotiation dates) as well as on the effect of coupons on the duration. For example, items with high coupons and a life-to-maturity between 5 and 7 years are grouped together with positions with low (or zero) coupons and a life-to-maturity between 4.3 and 5.7 years (in both cases, a modified duration of 4.65 years is assumed).

(III) Each net position is then multiplied by a band-specific risk weight (see last column of Table 19.2) obtained by the Basel Committee as the product between the band's estimated average modified duration (MD_i) and a "reasonable" movement in its yield, Δr (see again Table 19.2: note that, based on the empirical behavior of the yield curve, long-term yields are assumed to be less volatile than short-term ones).

---

[5] In addition to bonds, this operation is also performed for derivatives on interest rates, following procedures described later in this section.

Table 19.2 Factors for calculating the Basel Committee Indicator

Zone	Band	Life to maturity		Average modified duration (MD)	Change in Yield (Δr)	Risk weight ($w = MD \cdot \Delta r$)
		If coupon $< 3\%$	If coupon $\geq 3\%$			
1	1	Up to 1 month	Up to 1 month	0.00	1.00 %	0.00 %
	2	1–3 months	1–3 months	0.20	1.00 %	0.20 %
	3	3–6 months	3–6 months	0.40	1.00 %	0.40 %
	4	6–12 months	6–12 months	0.70	1.00 %	0.70 %
2	5	1.0–1.9 years	1–2 years	1.40	0.90 %	1.25 %
	6	1.9–2.8 years	2–3 years	2.20	0.80 %	1.75 %
	7	2.8–3.6 years	3–4 years	3.00	0.75 %	2.25 %
3	8	3.6–4.3 years	4–5 years	3.65	0.75 %	2.75 %
	9	4.3–5.7 years	5–7 years	4.65	0.70 %	3.25 %
	10	5.7–7.3 years	7–10 years	5.80	0.65 %	3.75 %
	11	7.3–9.3 years	10–15 years	7.50	0.60 %	4.50 %
	12	9.3–10.6 years	15–20 years	8.75	0.60 %	5.25 %
	13	10.6–12 years	Over 20 years	1000	0.60 %	6.00 %
	14	12–20 years	–	13.50	0.60 %	8.00 %
	15	Over 20 years	–	21.00	0.60 %	12.50 %

As shown in Chapter 3, the weighted net position (WNP_i), which is the product $NP_i \cdot MD_i \cdot \Delta r_i$, estimates the expected change in the value of the net position following a change in market yields.[6]

(IV) Within each time band j, the sum of all the weighted net long positions (WNP_i^+) is then netted against the sum of to the weighted net short positions (WNP_i^-), producing the overall net position for band j, NP_j:

$$NP_j = \sum_{i \in j} WNP_i^+ - \sum_{i \in j} WNP_i^- \tag{19.1}$$

However, since bonds within a band do not have exactly the same duration (different maturities and coupons may exist within the band), the netting is not full, and a 10 % capital charge k_j (called "vertical disallowance") is applied to the offset amount.

$$k_j = 10\% \cdot \min \left(\sum_{i \in j} WNP_i^+, \sum_{i \in j} WNP_i^- \right) \tag{19.2}$$

---

[6] More precisely, the change ΔNP_i is given by *minus* $NP_i \cdot MD_i \cdot \Delta r_i$.

Consider for example time band 2 in Table 19.3: the sum of the weighted long positions is 110 million euros and the sum of the weighted short positions is 90 million. Hence the overall net position (NP_2) will be 20 million, while the capital charge k_2 due to the vertical disallowance will be 10%·90 million (that is, 9 million).

(V) The overall net positions of time bands are then offset against each other. More precisely, bands are gathered into three zones (see Table 19.2); within each zone, l, the sum of all long NP_js (NP_j^+) and of all short NP_js (NP_j^-) are computed. The overall net position for zone k is then found as

$$NP_l = \sum_{j \in l} NP_j^+ - \sum_{j \in l} NP_j^- \tag{19.3}$$

To account for the fact that the yields to maturity of different time bands within a zone may fluctuate independently of each other (so that a full netting may be overly optimistic) a capital charge k_j (called "horizontal disallowance") is applied to the smaller of the offsetting positions:

$$k_l = c \cdot \min \left(\sum_{j \in l} NP_j^+, \sum_{j \in l} NP_j^- \right) \tag{19.4}$$

The coefficient c is equal to 40% for zone 1 and to 30% for zones 2 and 3; this difference is due to the fact that medium- and long-term yields are thought to be more correlated among themselves than short-term yields (up to one year).

Consider, e.g., zone 1 in Table 19.4 (which is based on the results of Table 19.3). The sum of the net long band positions is 30 million, while the sum of the short ones is 10. The overall net position for zone 1 therefore is 20 million The offset portion (10 million) is subject to a 40% capital requirement (4 million);.

(VII) Finally, the net positions (NP_l) of the three zones (NP_1, NP_2 and NP_3) are netted. If opposite positions in adjacent zones are offset, the disallowance factor is 40%; the disallowance factor between zone 1 and zone 3 is 100% (in practice, no netting is allowed between those two zones).

Table 19.5 shows an example (based on the results of Tables 19.3 and 19.4). First, balances are offset between zone 1 and 2, and a capital charge k is computed on the offset amount (20), multiplied by the 40% disallowance factor (for adjacent zones). A negative balance of 100 remains, in zone 2, that can be offset against the net long position in zone 3: again, this is subject to a 40% disallowance factor (that is, to a capital charge of 40). The overall net position of the bank ($NP_1 + NP_2 + NP_3$) is 100 million; this, too, must be covered by a capital charge.

Summing up, the total capital charge on general market risk will be given by:

(a) the vertical disallowances (10%) computed within each time band (48 million in our example, see Table 19.3);
(b) the horizontal disallowances (40% for zone 1, 30% for zones 2 and 3) computed across bands, but within zones (19 million, see Table 19.4);
(c) the horizontal disallowances (40% if adjacent, 100% otherwise) across zones (48 million, see Table 19.5);
(d) the net weighted position across zones (100 million, see again Table 19.5).

Table 19.3 An example of time bands, vertical disallowances and netted positions

Time band j	ΣWNP_i^+	ΣWNP_i^-	$min(\Sigma WNPi^+, \Sigma WNP_i^+)$	k_j	$NP_j = \Sigma WNPi^+ - \Sigma WNP_i^+$
1	0	0	0	0	0
2	110	90	90	9	20
3	90	100	90	9	-10
4	60	50	50	5	10
5	20	80	20	2	-60
6	60	30	30	3	30
7	10	100	10	1	-90
8	50	40	40	4	10
9	35	40	35	3.5	-5
10	20	25	20	2	-5
11	30	40	30	3	-10
12	60	20	20	2	40
13	70	10	10	1	60
14	100	30	30	3	70
15	45	5	5	0.5	40
Σk				48	

Thus, in our example, the capital charge due to general market risk will be 215 million euros.

If the trading portfolio includes securities in several different currencies, the computation just seen is performed separately for each currency. This takes into account the fact that the yield curves for different currencies vary independently; therefore, long and short positions in different currencies cannot be offset.

In computing the requirement for generic risk, the derivative instruments on interest rates (forward rate agreements, interest rate futures, interest rate swaps, options on futures, on debt securities and on swaps, caps, floors and collars) must be considered, as well as bonds. To be associated with the 13 time bands of Table 19.2, each position in derivatives must first be broken down (or "mapped", see Chapter 5) into two virtual positions in government securities.

Thus, for example, a long (short) position in futures is mapped into a short (long) position in a government security with maturity equal to the settlement date of the futures and a long (shot) position in a government security with maturity equal to the maturity of the underlying of the futures contract. Similarly, a long (buy) position in an FRA(3,6) is broken down into a long position in a virtual government security with three-month maturity

Table 19.4 Netting within zones and horizontal allowances

Zone l	Time band j	NP_l^+	NP_l^-	$min(\Sigma NP_j^+, \Sigma NP_j^+)$	k_l	$NP_l = \Sigma NPj^+ - \Sigma NP_j^+$
1	1					
	2	20				
	3		10			
	4	10				
	Total	*30*	*10*	*10*	*4*	*20*
2	5		60			
	6	30				
	7		90			
	Total	*30*	*150*	*30*	*9*	*−120*
3	8	10				
	9		5			
	10		5			
	11		10			
	12	40				
	13	60				
	14	70				
	15	40				
	Total	*220*	*20*	*20*	*6*	*200*
Σk					19	

Table 19.5 Netting across zones

		K
NP_1	20	
NP_2	−120	
$Min(|NP_1|, |NP_2|)$	20	8
$\Delta = NP_1 + NP_2$	−100	
NP_3	200	
$Min(|\Delta|, |NP_3|)$	100	40
$NP_1 + NP_2 + NP_3$	100	100
Σk		148

and a six-month short position.[7] In the same way, an interest rate swap is "mapped" into two virtual positions in government securities, both maturing on the expiration of the swap contract, one long (short) with fixed rate and one short (long) with floating rate (depending on whether the swap contract calls for payment of floating or fixed rate).[8]

The treatment of options is more complex. Indeed, the value of an option depends on a number of market variables: the price of the underlying asset, its volatility, residual life and interest rate.[9] A position in options is therefore equivalent to a number of risk positions, in the sense that several market variables can generate losses.

To reflect both price changes in the underlying and changes in its volatility, two alternative methods can be used.[10] A first method envisaged by the Basel Committee and the European directive is called "delta plus" and mainly considers the risk associated with the price of the underlying asset. This approach requires converting interest rate options into corresponding long or short positions on interest rates (termed "delta-equivalent positions") by multiplying the value of the underlying by the option's delta coefficient. There are also additional requirements related to the gamma coefficient (to reflect the fact that the ratio between the value of an option and the price of the underlying is not linear) and the vega coefficient, which measures the sensitivity of an option to changes in volatility.

A second method is called "scenario matrix analysis" and is based on a simulation procedure. The bank must select all the options dependent on a certain risk factor (the six-month rate, for example) and construct a grid of scenarios corresponding to the different values of this factor and its volatility. In the case of options related to the six-month rate, for example, the effects of a 1 % reduction/increase in the current value, a 25 % reduction/increase in its volatility and a series of intermediate cases are necessary. For each of these scenarios, the value of the options linked to the selected risk factor must be recomputed according to a full-valuation approach. The capital requirement will be equal to the loss associated with the least favourable scenario. If the purpose of the options is hedging (e.g. a cap associated with a floating-rate loan), the simulation can be applied to a portfolio including both the options and the financial instruments hedged.

Positions in derivative instruments can be offset only if the following conditions are met:

- for futures and forward contracts, if the positions are of opposite signs of equal notional value and denominated in the same currency;
- for FRAs and swaps, if the market rate used as a benchmark is the same and if the difference between contractual interest rates is no greater than 0.15 % (15 b.p.);
- for FRAs, swaps and forward contracts, if the expiration dates of the two positions to be offset (or the subsequent date for revising the rate, for floating-rate positions) are exactly the same day (if less than one month) or are no more than seven days apart (if between one month and one year) or are no more than 30 days apart (if greater than one year).

---

[7] The purchase of an FRA(3,6), in fact, is equivalent (see Appendix 4A, Chapter 4) to blocking a funding rate for the future period that goes from "three months" to "six months".

[8] On the mapping of interest rate swaps, see Chapter 5.

[9] See Appendix 5C to Chapter 5.

[10] There is also a simplified methodology for banks that use options exclusively as buyers (and whose primary purpose is therefore to hedge rather than speculate).

We would also point out that, for computing the requirement for generic market risk, the Basel Committee proposed a method alternative to the one illustrated in this section (and based on Table 19.2). This approach adopts as a measure of rate change sensitivity the actual modified duration *of the individual positions* in securities (rather than the average modified duration of the respective time band). It is therefore more precise, and for this reason the disallowance factor within the time bands ("vertical disallowance") is reduced to 5%. Apart from these differences, the method based on the actual duration is similar to the one presented in this section.

19.4 POSITIONS IN EQUITY SECURITIES: SPECIFIC AND GENERIC REQUIREMENTS

The capital requirement related to equity securities has been the object of several divergences within the Basel Committee, due in part to an attempt, partially failed, to reach common solutions with the supervisory authorities of securities firms (IOSCO). The proposals of the Committee are therefore more generic than those related to debt securities and leave greater discretion to the national supervisory authorities. Greater precision can be found, however, in the European Union directive.

The instruments covered by this requirement include common stocks, whether voting or non-voting, convertible securities that behave like equities, commitments to buy or sell equity securities and derivative instruments (futures on stock market indices, options on indices or on individual securities).

The requirement for specific risk, according to the Basel Committee, is equal to 8% of the *gross general position*, i.e. the sum of all long and all short positions in equities and similar securities (only the long and short positions on the same security can be offset). It drops to 4% in the case of liquid and well-diversified portfolios.[11] This coefficient was reduced (to 4%, and to 2% for liquid, well-diversified portfolios) in the European Union directive.

The capital requirement for generic risk is equal to 8% of the net overall position (NOP), computed as the absolute value of the difference between the sum of the long positions and the sum of the short positions.

Note that the net position must be computed separately for each individual national market (long and short positions related to different markets cannot be offset). In the presence of N national markets, the requirement on generic risk will therefore be given by:

$$k_g = 8\% \cdot \sum_{i=1}^{N} NOP_i \qquad (19.5)$$

where NOP_i indicates the net overall position related to the i-th market:

To compute the capital requirement on equities, the positions in derivative instruments are converted into positions in the underlying equity securities, as we saw for debt securities. More specifically, futures and forward contracts on individual equity securities or

---

[11] Liquid and well-diversified portfolios are those containing no stocks in companies whose debt securities are considered "non-qualifying" (see section 19.3), containing securities regarded as highly liquid by the competent authorities based on objective criteria objectives, and where no individual position represents more than 5% of the total value of the securities portfolio.

on market indices are registered based on the market value of the individual securities or indices. Futures on an index can also be broken down into a number of positions relative to the number of securities included in the index. Positions in options, on the other hand, are converted into positions on the underlying equities based on their delta coefficient.

19.5 THE REQUIREMENT FOR POSITIONS IN FOREIGN CURRENCIES

The standardized approach to computing the capital requirement on foreign exchange risk[12] is divided into three phases. The first phase is to compute, for each foreign currency position j, the bank's *net position* NP_j, given by the sum of:[13]

– the net spot position (i.e., all asset items less all liability items, including accrued interest, denominated in the relevant currency);
– the net forward position (i.e., all amounts to be received less all amounts to be paid under forward foreign exchange transactions, including currency futures and the principal on currency swaps not included in the spot position);
– guarantees (and similar instruments) that are certain to be called and are likely to be irrecoverable;
– net future income/expenses not yet accrued but already fully hedged (at the discretion of the reporting bank);
– depending on particular accounting conventions in different countries, any other item representing a profit or loss in foreign currencies;
– the net delta-based equivalent of the total book of foreign currency options.

The second phase involves summing the net positive (long) positions (NP_j^+) and the net negative (short) positions (NP_j^-) on the different currencies, the latter taken in absolute value. The larger of these two sums is called the "net open foreign exchange position". The capital requirement is then set equal to 8% of this net open position:

$$k_{FX} = 8\% \cdot Max\left(\sum_j NP_j^+, \left|\sum_j NP_j^-\right|\right) \qquad (19.6)$$

Let us consider the example in Table 19.6

Table 19.6 Example of net foreign currency positions

Currency	US dollar	British pound	Japanese yen	Swiss franc	Australian dollar	Canadian dollar	Total
NP_j (€ mns)	30	−15	25	−30	5	−3	12
NP_j^+	30		25		5		60
$\|NP_j^-\|$		15		30		3	48

---

[12] The Basel Committee asks that the net position in gold be included among the foreign exchange positions.
[13] The positions in basket-currencies can be considered either as positions in independent currencies or spread among the individual currencies in the basket.

The sum of the long positions is equal to 60 million euros, while the sum of the short positions is 48 million euros. The result is:

$$k_{FX} = 8\% \cdot Max\,(60,\,48) = 4.8$$

It is interesting to note that this simplified approach represents a sort of compromise between two extreme approaches, one hardly prudent, the other highly conservative.

The first approach assumes a perfect correlation (100 %) between exchange rate changes of the different currencies. In other words, it assumes that when the euro appreciates/depreciates, it does so to the same extent against all the foreign currencies. If this is true, it is right to offset the long and short positions not only within the individual currencies but also among the various currencies, computing the capital ratio as:

$$k_{FX}^{min} = 8\% \cdot \left| \sum_j NP_j \right| = 8\% \cdot \left| \sum_j NP_j^+ + \sum_j NP_j^- \right| \tag{19.7}$$

which in our example would give $8\% \cdot 12 = 0.96$.

The second approach assumes a perfectly negative correlation (-100%) between the exchange rates for the long and short positions. In other words, if the euro depreciates against currencies where the bank is "long", it simultaneously appreciates against the currencies where the bank is "short". In this case, both the net positive and net negative positions are considered in determining losses, and the capital ratio must be computed as

$$k_{FX}^{Max} = 8\% \cdot \left(\sum_j NP_j^+ + \left| \sum_j NP_j^- \right| \right) \tag{19.8}$$

which in our example would take the capital requirement to $8\% \cdot 108 = 8.64$.

These are obviously two extreme hypotheses: in reality, the correlation will be neither perfectly positive nor perfectly negative. It will therefore be reasonable to set the capital requirement by selecting a value midway between k^{min} and k^{Max}; this value coincides precisely with the k_{FX} seen earlier. In fact:

$$\frac{k_{FX}^{min} + k_{FX}^{Max}}{2} = 8\% \frac{\sum_j NP_j^+ + \left| \sum_j NP_j^- \right| + \left| \sum_j NP_j^+ + \sum_j NP_j^- \right|}{2} =$$

$$= 8\% \left[\frac{\max\left(\sum_j NP_j^+, \left| \sum_j NP_j^- \right| \right) + \min\left(\sum_j NP_j^+, \left| \sum_j NP_j^- \right| \right)}{2} + \right.$$

$$\left. + \frac{\max\left(\sum_j NP_j^+, \left| \sum_j NP_j^- \right| \right) - \min\left(\sum_j NP_j^+, \left| \sum_j NP_j^- \right| \right)}{2} \right] =$$

$$= 8\% \cdot \max\left(\sum_j NP_j^+, \left| \sum_j NP_j^- \right| \right) = k_{FX}$$

Indeed, in our case, $k_{FX} = 4.8 = (0.96 + 8.64)/2$.

Lastly, we note that both the Basel Committee and the European Union directive provide that banks whose assets in foreign currencies are negligible with respect to their total assets can be exempted from the capital requirement on foreign exchange risk.

19.6   THE REQUIREMENT FOR COMMODITY POSITIONS

Financial intermediaries that invest in commodities such as oil, copper or silver, directly or more often through derivative instruments,[14] are exposed to a series of risks. The most obvious is directional risk, linked to changes in the spot prices of commodities. Forward positions and positions in derivative instruments also involve basis risk (possible misalignments between the prices of two commodities that in the past had always had similar price movements), interest rate risk (forward prices of commodities also depend on interest rates) and so-called "forward gap risk", i.e. the risk that forward prices may diverge from their expected levels for reasons unrelated either to spot prices or interest rates.

The Basel Committee has established that the capital requirement on commodities can be computed in two ways. Both require that, for each commodity (or group of commodities with strongly correlated prices), the banks identify their long and short positions (spot and forward positions, positions in derivative instruments), expressed in standard units of measurement (barrels, gallons, grams, etc.) and valued in domestic currency at the current spot price.

According to the simplified method, the capital requirement for each commodity is given by 15 % of the net position (long less short positions) plus 3 % of the gross position (long plus short positions).

According to the "maturity ladder" method, the positions assumed in each commodity must be broken down among seven maturity bands like those seen (Table 19.2) for the capital requirement on generic interest rate risk. Long and short positions can be offset within each band by applying a capital requirement of 1.5 % to the offset portion. Offsetting is also possible between different bands, subject to a requirement of 0.6 %. Lastly, the residual net balance (not offset) is subject to a capital requirement of 15 %.

Both these methods are rather rudimentary and do not permit an accurate measurement of the risk associated with investments in commodities. Suffice it to say, in this regard, that all commodities, regardless of their actual volatility, are subject to the same capital ratio. For this reason, banks that operate heavily in commodities are encouraged to adopt the internal model approach, which will be discussed in the next section.

19.7   THE USE OF INTERNAL MODELS

19.7.1   Criticism of the Basel Committee proposals

From its proposal in 1993, the standardized approach to measuring market risks was the object of heavy criticism, especially by large banks who already developed sophisticated models for measuring this type of risk. This criticism focused both on a few technical features of the proposals and on the logic underlying the general framework adopted by the Committee.

The criticism concerning the proposals' technical features included some directed at mechanisms regarded as overly onerous and inconsistent with the general criterion set

---

[14] The price of gold is less volatile than that of other commodities. For this reason, positions in gold are not treated as commodities but, as observed earlier, as foreign currency positions.

forth by the Committee (imposition of a capital requirement that would cover potential losses over a time period of ten days with a 95 % confidence level). In particular, the following were regarded as excessive:

- the vertical disallowance (non-offsetting factor) of 10 % within the time bands in computing generic risk on debt securities;
- the requirement of 8 % (4 % in the case of liquid and well-diversified portfolios) for generic risk on equity securities, which in effect was subsequently halved in the EU directive;
- the impossibility to offset positions in different equity markets, a decision in contrast with the fact that, though not perfectly correlated, the stock markets of different countries often tend to experience similar movements.

Also, the "delta equivalent" mechanism was regarded as rather imprudent, considering that linear approximations prove inadequate to capture real changes in value on options, especially when there are significant price changes.

As far as the general framework of the proposals is concerned, the main points of criticism were the following:

- the "building blocks" approach, which required the summing of the capital requirements computed separately for four different risk categories (debt securities, equity securities, commodities, and foreign currencies), overestimated the risk because it failed to reflect the imperfect correlation among the different market factors;[15]
- this approach also requires breaking down the risk by type of financial instrument (equity securities, debt securities, positions in foreign currencies and commodities) rather than by type of underlying risk;
- the standardized approach assigned little value to the internal models developed by banks and would have forced them to compute two different measures of risk: for risk management purposes, estimated by internal models, and for regulatory purposes, estimated by the standardized approach.

Another more general criticism regarded the rather artificial distinction between trading book and banking book. In fact, this distinction prevents a bank from considering its entire interest rate risk exposure, which does not emerge only from the bonds held for trading purposes but also from those held for investment purposes and, more generally, from the complex of assets and liabilities in the banking book (as shown in the first part of this volume). Consequently, a long position on interest rates in the trading portfolio might be more than offset by a short position in the investment portfolio or by a positive duration gap. This distinction also discouraged banks from measuring and managing financial risks in a truly integrated manner.

19.7.2 The 1995 revised draft

Some of this criticism persuaded the Basel Committee to review its 1993 proposal and publish a new draft in April 1995. The most significant changes included the possibility

---

[15] Given two stochastic variables x and y, let us recall that $\sigma_{x+y} = \sigma_x + \sigma_y$ is true if and only if their correlation is 100 %. Otherwise, $\sigma_{x+y} < \sigma_x + \sigma_y$.

for banks to choose between the above described standardized system and *an internal model* for risk measurement. To be accepted for regulatory purposes, however, the internal models had to conform to a few minimum requirements.

This need for uniformity became relevant after a simulation exercise conducted by the Committee: 15 banks from different countries were asked to assess the risk of a virtual portfolio of 350 positions, providing the total VaR and that related to interest rate, foreign exchange and equity risks (given a holding period of ten days and a 99 % confidence level). Some of the banks provided diverging results, due primarily to differences:

- in the historical sample used to estimate volatility;
- in the risk factors used, particularly for interest rate risk (yield curves with a different number of nodes, possibility of non-parallel shifts of the yield curve, possibility of changes in the spreads between different curves, etc.);
- in the criterion for aggregating the different types of risk;
- in the criteria for measuring the risk of option portfolios.

This empirical evidence persuaded the Committee to require that a few minimum criteria be followed so that internal models could be used in lieu of the standardized approach. In particular, it established the following *quantitative* requirements, still in force:

- VaR must be estimated daily;
- the confidence level must be at least 99 %;
- the holding period must be at least ten working days;
- the historical sample for estimating volatility must be at least one year;
- the data on volatility and correlations must be updated at least quarterly;
- total VaR must be obtained by summing the VaRs for the different market factors (thus assuming perfect correlation);
- the models must adequately reflect the different risk profiles (delta, gamma and vega) of option contracts.

The quantitative requirements were accompanied by, and are still accompanied by, the following qualitative criteria:

- banks must have an independent risk management unit, responsible for designing and implementing the risk management system. This unit must perform periodic back-testing, i.e. *ex post* comparisons, between the estimated risk measures and the actual changes in portfolio value;
- the risk measurement model must be supplemented by regular stress tests, aimed at simulating potential losses in extreme market situations;
- the adequacy and functioning of the risk measurement model must be verified and controlled regularly;
- top management must be actively involved in the risk control process and consider that control as an essential aspect of operations, allocating sufficient resources to it;
- the internal risk measurement model must be closely integrated into the daily risk management process and used in conjunction with the internal limits on trading and exposure;
- the model must in any case be explicitly approved by the supervisory authorities, which verify that it is conceptually correct, applied with integrity and historically

accurate in forecasting losses, and that the bank has sufficient specialized personnel to manage it.

If the internal model complies with these criteria, it can be used to determine the minimum regulatory capital against market risks. In particular, each day the capital requirement will be given by the average of the the previous 60 days VaRs multiplied by a safety factor F established by the authorities, or by the VaR of the previous day, if greater.

If, as often occurs, the internal model estimates the generic market risks only, and does not properly address the specific risks related to the individual securities and issuers, then capital must be supplemented by the specific risk requirement (k_{SR}) computed by the standardized approach. In summary, the capital requirement on market risks will be given by:

$$k_{MKT} = \max \left[VaR_{t-1}, F \cdot \frac{\sum_{i=1}^{60} VaR_{t-i}}{60} \right] + k_{SR} \qquad (19.9)$$

where VaR_{t-1} indicates the ten-day VaR for day $t-1$, with a 99 % confidence level, and F represents the multiplying factor. This factor is established by the national supervisory authorities but can in no case be less than 3. More precisely, it varies from 3 to 4 according to the quality of the internal model. It is therefore increased in inverse proportion to the past performance of the model, measured through backtesting.[16] This provides an incentive to improve the quality of the internal models.

19.7.3 The final amendment of January 1996

As expected, the draft of April 1995 was heavily criticized. Four objections seem particularly significant:

(1) The safety factor F, equal to at least 3, was judged arbitrary and so high as to eliminate any form of incentive for banks to adopt the internal models' approach;
(2) the fact that total VaR is determined as the sum of the VaRs on the individual risks is equivalent to ignoring the benefits of diversification among positions which are sensitive to different market factors (foreign exchange rates, interest rates, equity prices), thus overestimating overall risk and discouraging banks from adopting portfolio diversification policies.
(3) the indication that F could be increased to above 3 was extremely vague. It was established to be inversely proportional to the quality of the model (i.e. its ability to forecast losses correctly), but no transparent criteria were established for measuring this quality and thus for determining the extent of the increase.
(4) Lastly, there was criticism of a failure to recognize internal models for estimating specific risk, due to the fact that they were regarded as concentrating solely on generic risk.

---

[16] See Chapter 8.

These objections were satisfied in the final text of the reform, approved in January 1996 (Basel Committee, 1996) in the form of an amendment to the 1988 Capital Accord. In particular:

(1) the amendment confirmed that the safety factor F is equal to 3. This decision was motivated by the fact that the average of daily VaRs "must be converted into a capital requirement that offers a sufficient cushion for cumulative losses deriving from adverse market conditions for an extended period of time". The theoretical limits of the internal models (normality and stability of the distributions, linearity of the payoffs, etc.) and the fact that they overlook the intra-day risks (because they are based on closing prices) and cannot forecast the effects of extreme shocks or liquidity crises were cited in favor of a high safety factor.

(2) More objective, transparent criteria were established for determining whether to increase F to over 3. It was clarified that this depends on the results of specific backtesting to be performed quarterly, based on a comparison of actual losses to indications from internal models (the Basel Committee backtesting criteria and the ones for determining F were presented in Chapter 8).

(3) The criticism regarding the failure to recognize the benefits of diversification was also partially satisfied. In fact, the Committee introduced the possibility of using "empirical correlations not only within broad risk categories but also between different risk categories, provided that the supervisory authority is satisfied that the bank's system for measuring correlations is sound and implemented with integrity". The Committee took the opportunity to approve another amendment to make the use of internal models more flexible and permitted the estimation of 10-day VaR using data on daily volatility multiplied by the square root of 10.[17]

(4) Lastly, the amendment confirmed the inability of internal models to grasp specific risk adequately. The Committee did not forbid their use for estimating this risk component; however, it also imposed a lower limit on the capital requirement estimated with internal models, which cannot be less than 50% of the requirement computed by the standardized approach.

Lastly, the amendment indicated the conditions to be followed when a bank possesses an internal model acceptable to the authorities but is not yet able to apply it to the entire range of market risks or outstanding positions, so this model is used in conjunction with the standardized approach:

- each broad class of risks must be assessed on the basis of a single approach;
- banks cannot modify the combination of the two approaches without valid reasons;
- banks that use an internal model for a certain risk category must, in time, extend it to include all their positions;
- banks that use internal models are not permitted to return to the standardized approach.

19.7.4 Advantages and limitations of the internal model approach

The internal model approach represents a sort of revolution in supervisory policy: for the first time, in fact, financial institutions were allowed to determine their own capital

---

[17] See Chapter 5.

requirements based on risk measurements produced in-house (although subject to numerous conditions and to an explicit process of validation by the supervisory authorities).

It therefore represented a move from a detached relationship between the supervisory authority and supervised banks towards a closer relationship based on trust, collaboration, and the exchange of competences and information. It represented a recognition that supervisory authorities and banks, though their objectives are different, share a common interest in the stability of the individual intermediaries and of the financial system as a whole.

However, this kind of evolution also gives rise to the risk of "regulatory capture": the supervisory authorities, after analyzing the banks' models, may impose changes and finally approve them. This means that they become less free in the future to point out limitations and errors in instruments that they themselves helped design. In this respect, their independence might be partially "captured" by the banks, and any problems of inadequacy in the banks' risk management system might not be pointed out or pointed out late.

Another limitation of the internal model approach is associated with the existence of the safety factor F equal to at least 3. This multiplying factor, as we saw, was criticized back in 1995 as excessive. It is clear that if the internal model approach leads to capital requirements which are higher than those contemplated by the standardized approach, the banks would have no incentive to adopt it.

In this regard, it is interesting to mention the results of an empirical study by Saita and Sironi (2002). Using daily yield data on seven different equity markets,[18] they compared the capital requirement computed with the standard approach and with different types of internal models (parametric model with volatility estimated by exponential moving averages, parametric model with volatility estimated by a GARCH model, or historical simulations) for seven different typical portfolios valued in dollars.[19] Table 19.7 reports the results: in particular, it shows the percentage of days, in the period 1985–1999, in which the use of an internal model would have produced a *lower* capital requirement than the standardized approach.

As the Table shows, the latter generally requires less capital; however, internal models become more advantageous as the portfolio becomes more internationally diversified. In fact, they permit more frequent savings of capital (38.6% of days) in the case of an equally weighted portfolio in the seven equity markets and less frequent for a portfolio heavily concentrated in the US market. Since the standardized approach fails to recognize diversification among several equity markets, it is comparatively more penalizing for well-diversified portfolios. Indeed, by adding the capital requirement on generic risk of equity securities to the requirement on foreign exchange risk, the standardized approach is simply more penalizing the larger the fraction of the portfolio denominated in foreign currencies.

The internal models approach is more advantageous the more a bank's trading portfolio is diversified internationally. It is therefore clear why the internal models method has thus far been adopted primarily by large international banks, with heavily diversified trading portfolios and with branches and subsidiaries in the world's main financial markets.

19.7.5 The pre-commitment approach

As observed by the Basel Committee, a safety factor of three is also justified by the numerous limitations of internal models: the use of historical volatilities, the assumption

---

[18] France, Germany, Japan, Italy, Switzerland, UK, USA.
[19] The analysis only considers equity positions (and not even derivatives or short positions).

Table 19.7 Comparison of capital requirements – standardized approach and internal models

Portfolio	% of days in which the internal model approach requires less capital than the standardized approach			
	Parametric with EWMA	Parametric with GARCH	Historical simulations	Average
Equally Weighted	44.1 %	31.7 %	40.1 %	38.6 %
25 % USA, 75 % EW	41.2 %	33.9 %	44.2 %	39.7 %
25 % USA, 75 % MSCI	37.5 %	31.2 %	35.7 %	34.8 %
50 % USA, 50 % EW	30.0 %	28.1 %	35.2 %	31.1 %
MSCI	24.6 %	19.0 %	20.0 %	21.2 %
75 % USA, 25 % EW	5.9 %	1.3 %	1.3 %	2.8 %
75 % USA, 25 % MSCI	7.5 %	1.3 %	0.0 %	3.0 %
Average	27.3 %	20.9 %	25.2 %	24.5 %

Key EW = equally weighted. MSCI = weights assigned in conformity with the Morgan Stanley Capital International index. Source: Saita-Sironi (2002).

of a linear relationship between changes in risk factors and changes in the value of financial assets, the lack of attention to the risk of liquidity crises, and the assumption of a normal distribution for market factor returns.

In this regard, Table 19.8 shows the frequency with which weekly changes in the yields on British, US and German 10-year treasury notes exceeded certain extreme thresholds, expressed as volatility multiples, in the period 1989–1993. These frequencies are compared with the probabilities implicit in a normal distribution: as the table shows, the actual frequencies are significantly higher.

Table 19.8 Weekly changes in the yields on 10-year instruments

Change (expressed as a multiple of the standard deviation)	Actual frequency (period 1989–93)			Probability assigned by a normal distribution
	UK	US	Germany	
3	2.3 %	2.8 %	1.5 %	0.3 %
4	0.6 %	0.4 %	0.2 %	0.006 %
5	0.2 %	0.4 %	0.0 %	0.0 %
6	0.2 %	0.1 %	0.0 %	0.0 %
Maximum multiple of the standard deviation	6.4	7.6	4.1	

Source: Chew (1994).

The use of a normal distribution thus makes it difficult to employ internal models to estimate the losses associated with "extreme" events, since that distribution depicts exceptionally marked changes in market factors as almost impossible (to the point that stress testing must be used to project the impact of highly pessimistic scenarios, to which the model would otherwise assign too low a probability).

The problem of "fat tails" can also be understood by simply noting that over the past 20 years banks have had to cope with numerous abnormal events in the equity markets (October 1987, April 2000, September 2001), foreign exchange markets (autumn 1992), and bond markets (January–February 1994), probably more than a normal distribution would have suggested. It is precisely the need to narrow this gap between empirical data and normal distribution that justifies the safety factor imposed by the Basel Committee.

Paul Kupiec and James O'Brien, two economists of the *Federal Reserve Board* of the United States, suggested a possible alternative solution to the problem. According to this proposal (called the "pre-commitment approach"), each bank would be required to "declare" in advance each quarter the capital put at risk by its trading activity.[20] This amount, decided autonomously by each bank based on its internal models and certified by the supervisory authority, would represent the capital requirement for market risks. However, the individual banks would be subject to a penalty each time their trading losses during the quarter exceed the amount of capital initially declared. The possible penalties would be: (i) a fine, (ii) the imposition of a capital requirement, for the following period, greater than that declared by the bank, (iii) the imposition of a capital increase or a reduction of dividends.

The pre-commitment approach offers four main advantages:

- it recognizes the role of banks' internal risk management;
- it shifts the focus from ten-day VaR to potential losses over a longer time horizon of three months;
- it provides banks with an incentive to limit their risk taking activity to their initial declarations;
- it stimulates the supervisory authorities to monitor the losses actually incurred by the individual banks (expressed in market values).

Along with these advantages, however, the proposal also presents some significant drawbacks that make its adoption quite problematic. First of all, it would allow banks to reduce their capital requirement on market risks independently when they have difficulty complying with it (as after they have suffered losses). Secondly, it would force banks to increase capital (or pay a fine) precisely when their capital has been reduced by losses greater than expected. Lastly, since the results would only be audited, and penalties levied, every three months (or in any case at discrete time intervals), this would enable the individual banks to accumulate new risk positions without any immediate impact on their capital requirement.

SELECTED QUESTIONS AND EXERCISES

1. Which of the following quantitative requirements is not necessary for a bank's internal model on market risk to get validated by the Basel Committee for capital computation purposes?

---

[20] Kupiec, O'Brien (1995).

(A) 10-day time horizon;
(B) 3-month minimum update frequency for volatility and correlation estimates;
(C) Measurement of VaR at least once a fortnight;
(D) Minimum confidence level of 99 %.

2. A bank holds the following equity portfolio (L and S denote long and short positions, respectively):

Position	Market	Type of shares	Amount (euro m)
L	New York Stock Exchange	Liquid and well diversified portfolio	100
S	New York Stock Exchange	Liquid and well diversified portfolio, made of different stocks than the previous one	60
L	Frankfurt Stock Exchange	Shares of one single company (Alpha GMBH)	40
S	Frankfurt Stock Exchange	Liquid and well diversified portfolio, including 3 m of stocks by Alpha GMBH	70

Compute the capital requirements for the bank, against generic and specific risk.

3. A bank holds 1 million euros in a BB-rated bond and is contemplating to replace it with a bond of the same amount, but issued by an unrated company. Based on the standardized approach, its capital requirement against market risk is going to:

(A) increase, as the creditworthiness of the unrated bond might be below BB;
(B) decrease, as the creditworthiness of the unrated bond might be above BB;
(C) stay unchanged;
(D) this depends on whether the bond is a "qualifying issue" or not.

4. Consider a bank with the following simplified structure of assets and liabilities:

Assets	Amount (euro m)	Liabilities	Amount (euro m)
Short-term T-Bills, coupon 6 %, T-bond, 6 % coupon, with a life to maturity of 15 days	100	Fixed rate bonds, coupon 4 %, life to maturity 5.2 years	300
Medium term notes, fixed rate, coupon 2 %, life to maturity 3 years	400	Zero coupon bonds, life to maturity 8 years	200

Compute the capital requirement against generic risk on debt securities. Also, state how much of it is due to "vertical disallowance" factors.

5. The capital requirement for currency positions is computed against the larger of the total long and the total short position across all currencies. This implies that:

(A) The correlation between the change in value of a long position and that of a short position in the same currency is thought to be close to -100%;

(B) The correlation between the exchange rates of the currencies in which the bank is long and those of the currencies on which the bank is short is thought to be close to 100%;

(C) The correlation between the exchange rates of the currencies in which the bank is long and those of the currencies on which the bank is short is thought to be close to -100%;

(D) The correlation between the exchange rates of the currencies in which the bank is long and those of the currencies on which the bank is short is thought to be at some unspecified level between -100% and 100%.

Appendix 19A

Capital Requirements Related to Settlement, Counterparty and Concentration Risks

In addition to capital requirements for market risks, the June 1993 European directive also contemplated requirements associated with other trading-related risks (settlement, counterparty and concentration risks). These requirements, partially revised by the European Parliament and by the European Commission in 2005, are designed to reflect the interdependence between market risks and counterparty risk.

SETTLEMENT RISK[21]

This is the risk that a counterparty may default during the settlement of a securities transaction. It concerns transactions on equity and debt securities, executed but not yet settled, which present a difference between the contract price (P_n) and the current market price (P_m) favourable to the bank. This risk can be quantified, in the case of publicly traded securities, based on the difference between the agreed contract price and current market price.

The capital requirement k_S is determined as a percentage a of the difference between contract price and market price:[22]

$$k_s = (P_m - P_n) \cdot a \qquad (19A.1)$$

The percentages are indicated in table A.1 (the longer the period of time since contract termination, the higher the percentage).

Table 19A.1 Capital requirement relative to settlement risk

Number of days following expiration	a (%)
5–15	8
16–30	50
31–45	75
46 or more	100

---

[21] In the European directive, the expression "settlement risk" has a different meaning than in Chapter 16 of this volume. In that context, settlement risk concerns the possibility that, when a financial transaction is settled, only one of the two legs of the transaction is regularly paid, due to the default of one of two parties. In this case, however, the risk is that neither of the two flows advantageous to the bank are exchanged. In this sense, the risk is similar to pre-settlement risk, with the peculiarity that it concerns a contract which has already been executed

[22] An alternative method, based only on the contract price, was abolished in 2005.

COUNTERPARTY RISK

Counterparty risk concerns transactions left incomplete, i.e. when the bank has paid but has not yet received the securities or has delivered securities but has not received any payment. In the case of international transactions, the capital requirement is applied only if more than one day has already passed since the payment/delivery date. It is equal to the normal requirement on credit risk computed (on the base of the mechanisms to be described in Chapter 20) on the expected amount not yet received (payment or market value of the securities). If more than five working days pass and payment has not yet been received, it is deducted directly from the bank's equity capital, as if it were a loss.

CONCENTRATION RISK

The banks of the European Union are subject to a concentration limit, set forth in Directive 92/121/EC (dedicated to the "monitoring and control of large exposures"). Its purpose is to limit the concentration of risky assets in the banking portfolio. In brief, the directive states that no loan to a single obligor or group can exceed 25 % of the bank's equity. If, however, a bank exceeds these limits due to positions in securities included in the trading portfolio, a capital requirement is imposed on it proportional to the excess exposure (computed as the difference between the value of the total exposure to the customer and 25 % of the regulatory capital). The requirement is twice the normal requirement on the specific risk of the securities (be they debt or equity). If the excess persists for more than ten days, then the requirement is equal to a multiple of the normal requirement on specific risk, and the higher the total exposure to the customer the higher the multiple. Example: the multiple is two if the exposure does not exceed 40 % of the bank's equity, rises to five if the exposure is between 80 % and 90 % of equity, and is nine for exposures greater than 250 % of equity.

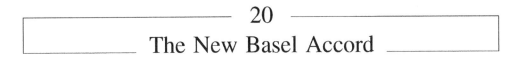

20.1 INTRODUCTION

The limitations inherent in the framework designed by the Basel Committee in 1988 and the biases originating from regulatory arbitrage operations led the supervisory authorities to start a review of such framework in 1999.

While in 1988 the supervisors chose to require that banks adopt an easy, homogeneous mechanism which, however, was far too simple to allow a real risk assessment, when reforming the old Accord they tried to give a more relevant role to the credit risk measurement models developed by banks, though testing their reliability and integrity.

This choice was also caused by the increasing complexity of the financial portfolios traded by the largest banks, which makes it increasingly difficult to define a single prudential framework based on simple coefficients, suitable for all banks based on a "one-size-fits-all" rationale.

This chapter offers an analysis of the contents, benefits, and limitations of the New Basel Capital Accord. More specifically, section 20.2 gives a brief overview of the goals and general features of the reform put forward by the Basel Committee, while section 20.3 starts examining the new capital requirements outlined in "pillar one" of the new Accord, illustrating the new "standard approach" to credit risk measurement. Section 20.4 provides a detailed insight into one of the most revolutionary aspects of the revised Accord, i.e. the internal ratings-based approach. Section 20.5 is devoted to the new role played by national supervisors, which, in compliance with "pillar two" of the New Accord, are required to strengthen their supervisory process. Section 20.6 is focused on the so-called "market discipline" envisaged in pillar three of the Accord. Section 20.7 examines the benefits and limitations of the reform, whereas section 20.8 analyzes the potential impact of the revised framework and the issue of "procyclicality" of the new capital requirements.

20.2 GOALS AND CONTENTS OF THE REFORM

The 2004 reform is the result of a long and careful process. After an initial consultative document published in June 1999 (Basel Committee, 1999b), which merely outlined the general guidelines of the reform project, the Committee started an intensive consultation process which, in combination with quantitative simulations on the likely impact of such reform, resulted into the 2001 and 2003 drafts, and then into the final version of June 2004.

The document drafted in June 1999 already made it clear that the reform would not only affect the capital requirement calculation rules, but would also rely on three mutually reinforcing pillars, i.e.:

(1) The new rules for calculating capital requirements;
(2) The supervision of banks by national supervisory authorities aimed at ensuring that they adopt suitable systems for measuring and controlling their risks and capital adequacy;
(3) A strengthening of the discipline exercised by capital markets, which might "punish" excessively risky banks by increasing their funding costs or even by refusing to

finance them. In order for this monitoring – which adds on to the supervisory activity carried out by supervisors – to be effective, the market must be duly informed on the banks' risk and capitalization conditions. Thus, "pillar three" requires banks to meet specific disclosure obligations vis-à-vis the market.

In general, the scope of the reform is so broad that it is commonly known as "Basel II", underlining that it is not a mere add-on but a fully-fledged re-writing of the 1988 Accord.

As was illustrated in Chapter 18, such Accord stated two goals, i.e. ensuring solvency of the banking system, and promoting consistent competitive conditions (*"leveling the international playing field"*) for banks of different countries. The reform sets a new goal, i.e. promoting a set of capital requirements that are more sensitive to the degree of actual risks to which bank portfolios are exposed,[1] narrowing the gap between economic capital – as measured by banks' internal models – and the regulatory capital required by the Basel Committee.[2] To this purpose, the reform requires that the minimum regulatory capital cover a broader range of risks (credit and market risks as well as, for the first time ever, operational risks); it redefines the capital calculation rules in order for them to better reflect the portfolios' actual risk; it recognizes the crucial role of the supervisory process implemented by supervisory authorities; and it helps the capital markets discipline banks' behaviour.

As was the case with the July 1988 Accord, Basel II applies at a consolidated level to banks and banking groups operating internationally. However, some national supervisory authorities chose to apply it also to domestic banks: this is the approach followed by the EU Directives 2006/48 and 2006/49, whereby "Basel II" was introduced in the EU legislation. Conversely, other supervisory authorities may decide to allow banks to implement only some of the alternative regulatory capital calculation methods set forth in the new Accord. The US supervisory authorities seem to opt for the latter option in that they invited their banks with significant international operations to implement only the "advanced internal rating" method (see section 20.3 below).

The revised Accord came into force at the end of 2006. However, a further year was granted for more advanced approaches in order to carry out impact studies. During such period, the new system shall be implemented in parallel to the 1988 framework. Therefore, the more advanced approaches shall come into full force by the end of 2007.

A further three-year period is also established during which the capital requirement of each bank cannot drop below a predefined percentage of the minimum capital as calculated in compliance with the 1988 requirements. Such "floor" amounts to 95 %, 90 %, and 80 % for 2007, 2008, and 2009 respectively.

The Committee also reserved the right to change (or better "calibrate") the requirements after their coming into force. More specifically, the capital requirements as calculated according to the internal ratings approach may be changed by multiplying them by a scaling factor (presently equal to 1.06[3]) if they appear to be too low.

---

[1] As was pointed out by the Committee, " The objective of greater risk sensitivity has received near-universal approval. The 1988 Accord, which does not adequately reflect changes in risk, creates incentives for banks to make high-risk investments that may contribute to cyclicality over the business cycle. In so doing, the Accord may understate the risks and hence overstate the capital adequacy of banks".

[2] See Chapter 22 for a thorough discussion of the differences between regulatory and economic capital.

[3] In short, the capital requirement would be 6 % higher than the amount calculated by referring to internal ratings.

20.3 PILLAR ONE: THE STANDARD APPROACH TO CREDIT RISK

We saw that, according to the new Accord, bank supervision will be based on three mutually-reinforcing components (the so-called "pillars" of the Accord), i.e. minimum capital requirements, supervisory review process and market discipline. Although all of them are equally meaningful in the supervisors' eyes, the banks' attention has been drawn mostly by pillar one, since it contains the new quantitative rules for computing minimum capital requirements.

As mentioned above, the new capital requirements will not be limited to credit risk. Capital charges on market risk (see Chapter 19) were almost untouched by the 2004 reform and still are computed according to the guidelines set in 1996; furthermore, a new requirement was introduced on operational risk, which is likely to absorb a non-trivial amount of capital and will be covered separately in Chapter 21.

As concerns credit risk, pillar one marks a break with the past, since loans issued to similar counterparts (e.g., private firms, or sovereigns) will require different capital coverage depending on their intrinsic riskiness, as evaluated by some external rating agency ("standard approach") or by the bank itself ("internal ratings-based", or IRB, approach). In this section, we present in detail the so-called standard approach (also called "new standard approach", as it innovates over the 1988 rules); the IRB approach will be covered in section 20.4.

20.3.1 Risk Weighting

Under the standard approach, the amount of required capital for a loan of one euro granted to private parties, with no valid collateral or guarantees (which now amounts to eights cents), might drop to 1.6 cents or increase to 12 cents, depending on the rating granted to the borrower by one or more external credit assessment institutions (hereinafter referred to as "ECAI"). Such institutions may be rating agencies, as are already known today, or other institutions recognized by the national supervisory authorities (for instance, export credit agencies). In order to be admitted as qualified ECAI agencies, they must meet a set of minimum requirements (specifically in terms of independence, transparency, and consistency of rating criteria[4]). A bank might use ratings from multiple ECAIs, though always within a set of rules aimed at preventing "cherry-picking" phenomena whose goal is to deliberately reduce the total capital requirements: in short, selecting the agency offering the most favorable rating for each client is not allowed.

Better ratings are associated with lower weights in the calculation of risk-weighted assets. Furthermore, as in the 1988 Accord, different categories of counterparts (e.g. non-financial companies, States, banks) shall be given different weighting scales. Table 20.1 offers an overview of these two sets of criteria (rating classes and categories of counter-parts), using the classes developed by Standard and Poor's and Fitch as an example of rating scale.

Although the Table might appear a bit complex at a first glance, its meaning is rather intuitive: rows show the different classes of borrowers identified by Basel II (corporates,

---

[4] Six requirements are to be met: (i) objectivity (rigorous, systematic method for granting judgments, subject to validation based on historical experience), (ii) independence, (iii) availability of public data supporting the validation, (iv) transparency of the method, (v) adequacy of resources, and (vi) credibility of assessments.

Table 20.1 Risk Weights in the standard approach

	AAA	AAA−	AA+	AA	AA−	A+	A	A−	BBB+	BBB	BBB−	BB+	BB	BB−	B+	B	B−	Below B−	Unrated	Past-due
Corporates	20%					50%			100%						150%				100%	150%
Sovereign entities	0%					20%			50%			100%						150%	100%	
Banks	20%					50%						100%						150%	50%	
Banks, depending on the country of incorporation	20%					50%			100%									150%	100%	
Retail											75%									
Residential real estate mortganges											35%									100%
Non-residential real estate mortgages					From 100% to 50%, upon discretion of the national supervisory authorities															150%

sovereign entities, banks, small enterprises, and private parties grouped in the "retail portfolios" category) plus some specific types of loans; columns show the different ratings that might be assigned to a counterpart. By combining rows and columns, for instance, a loan of € 100 to a non-financial company with a AAA rating translates into € 20 of risk-weighted assets, thus leading to a capital requirement of $20 \times 8\% = €1.6$ (or, in other words, 1.6 % of the non-weighted exposure). Similarly, a loan of € 100 to a sovereign State with a rating lower than B- produces a non-weighted exposure of € 150, thus leading to a capital requirement of $150 \times 8\% = €12$ (12 % of the nominal value).[5]

The last two columns need some brief clarifications. First, exposures to unrated companies (i.e. where no rating has been assigned by a qualified ECAI) are subject to a 100 % weight (as in the 1988 Accord). This is likely to be the case also with a high percentage of European non-financial companies (although many of them, as illustrated below, have access to a favorable treatment within the category of the retail portfolio). Secondly, past-due loans (i.e. loans whose interest or principal repayment is overdue by over 90 days) are subject to a 150 % risk weight (as is the case with the worst rating buckets), since the delay in repayment is likely to stem from difficulties on the part of the borrower.[6]

A few comments on some of the Table rows are also appropriate. First, exposures to banks might be weighted in two different ways:[7] They may be classified based on the rating assigned to the borrowing bank, or based on the rating of the country where the bank is headquartered. In the latter case, all credit institutions having their registered office in the same State are given the same weight (for instance, 20 % if they are based in a State with a rating of at least AA−). Credit with banks may also be subject to more favorable terms[8] in case of loans with a maximum initial maturity of three months.

Secondly, retail loans (which, for simplicity, may be defined as loans of no more than Euro 1 million granted to individuals and small enterprises[9]) fall into a separate category other than loans to corporates. Such loans almost invariably have no rating, but, because they are highly fractioned (and thus guarantee a good risk diversification), are nonetheless subject to a reduced weighting coefficient of 75 %. Also, as in the 1988 Accord, loans backed by a mortgage on the borrower's home are given a reduced risk weight (down from today's 50 % to 35 %), while for mortgages on other types of real estates the supervisors of each individual country has the option of reducing the weight down to 50 %, provided that the assets involved are subject to a small price-fluctuation risk.

Finally, the standard approach also offers a specific weighting system (not showed in Table 20.1) for securitization transactions (see Chapter 15). This system imposes considerable capital requirements onto banks investing in junior or equity tranches (which are often subscribed by the originating bank in order to facilitate placement of the remaining

---

[5] With reference to sovereign States, note that being an OECD country is no longer one of the criteria for calculating risk-weights.
[6] Weights below 150 % might still be used for mortgages (see Table 20.1) or loans that are covered sufficiently by analytical write-offs.
[7] National supervisors will select one of the two available options and their choice will be implemented consistently to all regulated entities.
[8] The risk weight associated with the next higher rating class is assigned, still subject to the minimum requirement of 20 %.
[9] Specifically, the retail portfolio might include exposures to individuals or small enterprises for no more than Euro 1 million, represented by specific types of products (revolving credits, such as credit cards and bank overdrafts, personal loans and leases, credit facilities and credit lines to small enterprises, specifically excluding securities) and sufficiently fractioned (for instance, supervisory authorities might require that no exposure to a single counterparty exceeds 0.2 % of the total retail portfolio).

securities of the special purpose vehicle), and is aimed at avoiding an uncontrolled development of a high-risk junk loan market.

20.3.2 Collateral and Guarantees

Except for the last two rows, the capital coefficients set forth in Table 20.1 refer to unsecured loans. As a matter of fact, the standard approach offers the option of reducing the capital requirement by obtaining suitable collaterals. Two approaches, with an increasing degree of complexity, are suggested:

(1) The "simple approach", which applies to a specific list of financial collaterals (cash, gold, debt securities, some types of listed stocks and units of mutual funds investing only in the above-listed assets), and
(2) The "comprehensive approach", which also applies to all other listed stocks.

With the simple approach, the exposure portion covered with a valid collateral is weighted by the coefficient established for the collateral (for instance, the applicable coefficient for sovereign States if the collateral is made of government bonds) instead of using the debtor's coefficient (although, as a general rule, a minimum weight of 20 % is required).

Table 20.2 Haircuts established for different types of collaterals

Collateral	Rating	Maturity	Haircut
Cash (in the same currency)			0.0 %
Government bonds	From AAA to AA−	Within 1 year	0.5 %
		From 1 to 5 years	2.0 %
		Over 5 years	4.0 %
	From A+ to BBB−	Within 1 year	1.0 %
		From 1 to 5 years	3.0 %
		Over 5 years	6.0 %
	From BB+ to BB−	Any	15.0 %
Non-government bonds	From AAA to AA−	Within 1 year	1.0 %
		From 1 to 5 years	4.0 %
		Over 5 years	8.0 %
	From A+ to BBB− and bank bonds with no rating	Within 1 year	2.0 %
		From 1 to 5 years	6.0 %
		Over 5 years	12.0 %
Stocks included in the major indexes and gold			15.0 %
Other listed stocks			25.0 %

With the comprehensive method, no capital requirement is applied on the exposure portion backed by a valid collateral. However, in the calculation of such portion, the value of the collateral must be reduced by a haircut reflecting the risk that the market value of the financial instrument provided by the debtor may fall during the loan term.

Therefore, haircuts reflect the collaterals' market risk and have been assessed by the Committee by using VaR models similar to those illustrated in the second part of this book. So, they are obviously stricter for securities such as stocks or bonds with a long duration (see Table 20.2), as they are more exposed to the effects of volatility in market factors. They are also increased as the number of days that the bank needs to recalculate the collateral's market value or to request the debtor to provide for an addition increases. Such an increase reflects the principles illustrated in Chapter 6 and equals the square root of the number of days.

Among risk-mitigating instruments, the Accord also includes guarantees and credit derivatives (provided that they are issued by States or other public authorities, banks and other financial institutions subject to supervision, non-financial companies with a rating of at least A−). With such guarantees, the debtor's risk weight is replaced by the guarantor's one, which usually implies a lower capital requirement. Incidentally, a similar solution (the so called "guaranteed by guarantor replacement") represents a simplified and prudential approach: indeed, with a loan backed by a guarantee the bank only risks losses if the guarantor's default occurs *together with the main debtor's default* (an event that, as such, is more rare than a default of the guarantor only). So, the weighting associated with the loan should somehow take into account the low risk associated with the event of a joint default. However, the possibility to take this effect ("double default effect") into account is offered only to those banks that use the internal ratings method.

20.4 THE INTERNAL RATINGS-BASED APPROACH

20.4.1 Risk Factors

Banks applying for the internal ratings approach (whose risk measurement systems must be approved by the national supervisory authorities) are fully or partly responsible for assessing the degree of risk associated with each individual loan and to the credit portfolio as a whole.

In this respect, the 2004 Accord – explicitly or implicitly – identifies six major "risk drivers" that are likely to define the extent of possible future losses on a credit exposure. In short (see also Table 20.3), such risk drivers are:

(1) Default risk, measured through the one-year *probability of default* (PD) as captured by the bank's rating system (see Chapter 13);
(2) Recovery risk, measured though the *loss given default* or LGD. Such loss must include the costs incurred in the recovery process and the financial value of the time between default and (partial) recovery;
(3) Exposure risk, due to the fact that the *exposure at default* (EAD) might differ (also largely) from the current one.
(4) The three profiles mentioned above refer to losses incurred into by a bank in case of the debtor's default. As shown in Chapter 14, another factor needs to be taken into account. Indeed, loans with longer maturities are also subject to a downgrading

risk.[10] Such a downgrading risk increases with the *maturity* (M) of a loan[11]; hence, maturity is the fourth risk profile to be measured.

(5) Moving from the analysis of a stand-alone exposure to the assessment of risk at a portfolio level, two further factors come into play. The former is the *granularity* of the exposures (i.e. the tendency to grant few large credit lines versus a high number of loans for smaller amounts). The formulas for calculating the minimum capital requirement set forth in the Accord are based on the assumption – to be analyzed in detail later in this chapter – that the portfolio has an infinite granularity, i.e. a null concentration[12] (in other words, it is made up of an extremely large number of small exposures).

(6) The second relevant parameter at a credit portfolio level is the *correlation* among borrowers. It is higher if the bank grants loans to borrowers that are concentrated in few geographical areas or industries, i.e. borrowers exposed to common risk factors, while it is lower if the bank's portfolio is highly diversified to borrowers whose conditions appear to be relatively independent. The Committee opted for a simplified framework, specifying the values for correlation among borrowers through a system based on a few large, standard categories. Therefore, banks are not required to check the actual degree of diversification of their portfolios

Factors from 1 to 4 (PD, LGD, EAD, and maturity) are the fundamental parameters to be adequately measured by a rating system.

Depending on the degree of sophistication of their models and on their historical data, banks might be allowed to use two different approaches:[13]

- A *foundation approach*, allowing to estimate only the debtors' PD using their own internal methods, while requiring to refer to pre-established values set by the Authorities for LGD, EAD, and maturity;
- An *advanced approach* that allows to measure all four risk profiles with the banks' internal methodologies (whose effectiveness and robustness, however, is to be demonstrated clearly).[14]

---

[10] Let us take a 10-year loan as an example. The borrower creditworthiness is assessed with a specific rating reflecting its PD in the following 12 months. After one year, the debtor does not default, but has badly worsened so that its rating is downgraded to a much higher risk level. If the bank were free to renegotiate the loan terms, it would now require a larger rate spread in order to compensate for the higher risk level. However, it cannot do so because the loan was granted for 10 years upon pre-defined terms. Hence, the economic value of the loan has decreased and, in fact, this lower value is a loss (even if it is not recorded on any secondary market). The longer the loan maturity, i.e. the number of years in which the transaction will continue to operate with an inadequate spread, the larger the loss.

[11] Furthermore, the risk is higher for high-rating loans since those with a medium-low rating, in addition to being downgraded, may also be upgraded.

[12] This is obviously an unrealistic assumption. The individual national Supervisors may require corrections, under the provisions of pillar two (see section 20.5).

[13] Following a so-called "evolutionary" approach, banks will first be prompted to adopt the foundation approach: only as they grow more confident about their internal estimates (and can show the regulators the databases on which those estimates are based) will they be allowed to move to the advanced approach.

[14] Considering the highly diversified and heterogeneous characteristics of retail loans granted by individual banks, which cannot be summarized in a unique set of parameters defined by the Authorities, the foundation approach cannot be adopted for this portfolio. In other words, all banks wishing to apply an internal ratings system will directly use the advanced approach, thus internally estimating not only PD, but also LGD and EAD (indeed, no adjustment for maturity is envisaged for the retail portfolio). However, such parameters do not need to be estimated for each loan or each counterpart (it would be too time-consuming, considering the

Table 20.3 Risk factors included in the Revised Accord

Factor	Meaning	Features	Notes	Entity qualified for assessment
PD	Probability that the counterpart becomes insolvent	Calculated on a time horizon of 12 months, but keeping into account any possible economic downturn	A default occurs when the debtor is "unable or unwilling to pay in full" and in any case after a delay of over 90/180 days	The bank, provided that it has an internal ratings system validated by the Supervisors.
LGD	Loss unit rate in case of insolvency	Calculated considering loan recovery costs and the financial value of time	Affected by the technical form and by the provision of collaterals	The Supervisors or the bank, provided that the latter has an *advanced* rating system validated by the Supervisors
EAD	Bank's exposure at the time of default	Calculated considering the available margins on credit lines by cash and by signature	Constant for technical forms with a pre-established sinking plan	
Maturity (M)	Loan maturity	Calculated as a duration, i.e. considering repayments expected before the final expiry date		
Granularity	Tendency to grant few, large loans or several small loans	Pre-established and not calculated (it is assumed to be infinite)	Possible correction within the framework of "pillar two"	The Supervisors
Correlation	Tendency of different debtors to "default simultaneously"	Pre-established and not calculated (different values for different types of clients)		

As mentioned above, banks are in no case allowed to measure the granularity and correlation of their loan portfolio as they are fixed at "standard" levels by the Authorities and identical for all banks subject to the Accord.

This means that banks, despite their ability to estimate the inputs in the credit risk assessment model, are not authorized to replace the model designed by the Authorities

---

large number of positions included in the retail portfolio) and banks will simply group retail loans in pools having homogeneous quality and technical form, and measure their characteristics (past default rate, unit loss rate, degree of utilization of available margins, etc.) at the level of the entire pool and not of each individual loan. This approach based on large categories should make it easier (and more cost effective) to manage the rating system for retail customers.

(see section 20.4.3) with their own internal ones. Indeed, the Committee considered the latter models to be too "young" to be fully reliable. Specifically, the Committee justified its rejection of internal credit risk models with two main arguments:

– Lack and poor reliability of input data necessary for such models and in particular of data on correlations among borrowers;
– Inability to validate the output of the model on an *ex post* basis, by means of statistically significant back tests, due to the long time horizon – usually one year – adopted by the credit risk models.[15]

20.4.2 Minimum Requirements of the Internal Ratings System

If a bank wants to be authorized to use its own internal ratings system for calculating the minimum capital requirement, it must comply with a set of minimum requirements. The general principle underlying such requirements is that the risk estimate procedures must be able to correctly differentiate among different risk levels, providing a correct, accurate, and consistent assessment in line with the bank's past experience.

The first requirement is that the risk measurement for a client be kept rigorously separate from the risk measurements of the individual loans granted to such client.[16] Indeed, the former can be measured in terms of a specific probability of default (PD), while, in the case of individual loans, different and further issues are at stake, such as the expected recovery rate (which depends on LGD) and the exposure risk (EAD, which increases with the available undrawn margins). Consequently, a bank would be wrong to upgrade the customer's rating if such customer provides collaterals on the loans. In fact, such collaterals would not change the default probability of the counterpart, but only the consequences that any default would cause on the actual amount of losses.

As to the customers' PD, banks are required to document in writing the key characteristics of the adopted measurement systems. It is therefore necessary to specify the definitions given to the different "creditworthiness grade" (seven as a minimum) of the rating scale, and especially the "plausible and intuitive" criteria used for granting a specific creditworthiness grade to a given counterpart. Such specifications must be detailed so as to allow the bank's analysts (even if they are based in different areas or facilities) to work homogeneously and consistently, and to allow any internal auditors (in addition to the Supervisory Authority) to easily understand its structure and logics.

The New Accord does not elaborate on how the PD rating system of a bank should be built; so it does not identify which indicators (for instance which balance-sheet ratios) should be used for granting a rating, nor does it oblige banks to adopt automatic systems, based on statistical scoring techniques.[17] In this respect, although the Accord provides for the use of statistical algorithms, it only accepts them as a primary or partial basis for rating

---

[15] Backtesting of market risk models (see Chapter 8) is carried out by comparing the daily VaR for the past 250 days with the corresponding economic results (P&L) of the trading activity (see the previous chapter). Given the time horizon of credit risk portfolio models – typically one year – , a similar comparison would require using past data relating to 250 years!
[16] However, an exception to this principle is envisaged for retail loans whose evaluation is carried out within large homogeneous categories (and not for each individual counterpart or loan) and can be done directly by referring to the "expected loss unit rate", which includes the effects of PD, LGD, and EAD.
[17] See Chapter 10. See also Resti (2002a) for an introduction to the differences between scoring algorithms and the approach followed by rating agencies.

assignments, a sort of preliminary tool subject to the supervision of human experts, aimed at ensuring that all relevant information are taken into account (including information that do not fall within the scope of the algorithm). The Accord actually states that, in assigning ratings, banks should take into account all relevant available information, making sure that it is sufficiently up-to-date.[18]

The Committee gave a definition of default to be referred to for estimating PD. A debtor is insolvent if one of the following two conditions occurs:

- a *subjective* condition: the bank deems unlikely that the borrower fulfills its obligations in full. This evaluation may result from the bank having partly written off the original exposures, set up specific provisions, or granted a credit restructuring (waiving or deferring part of the scheduled payments), or from the borrower having filed for bankruptcy or for a procedure aimed at protection from creditors;
- an *objective* condition: the counterpart is more than 90 days late in fulfilling at least one of its obligations. This term can be extended to 180 days for loans to private parties and families (retail portfolio) or public administrations, since these types of debtors are often late in paying, without this implying necessarily their unwillingness or inability to fulfill their obligations.

As to the measurement of LGD, EAD and maturity a distinction should be made, as mentioned above, between banks that are authorized to use the foundation or the advanced approach. For the former, LGD, EAD and maturity are measured based on the criteria required by the Regulators.

Foundation approach – LGD is fixed at 45 % for all unsubordinated and unsecured exposures. Such value is increased to 75 % for subordinated loans subscribed by the bank, but can be reduced for loans assisted by adequate collateral. If, for instance, collateral represented by financial instruments similar to those admitted in the standard approach (see section 20.3.2) is provided, LGD can be reduced down to 0 %, depending on the security value as corrected by the haircuts set forth in Table 20.2. Three other types of non-financial securities are also accepted: trade receivables, real estate properties (both residential and commercial), and other collaterals (including equipment or machinery, but excluding any asset acquired by the bank following the debtor's default). If such securities are provided, LGD may drop to 40 % (35 % for trade receivables and real estate properties).

On the other hand, EAD is equal to 100 % of the current exposure, plus 75 % of any available margin on credit lines that are not immediately and unconditionally revocable. Off-balance sheet exposures are transformed into loan equivalents based on the credit conversion factors illustrated in Chapter 18. By convention, maturity is 2.5 years for all credits.

Advanced approach – Banks are authorized to use their internal estimates for LGD and EAD, provided that they satisfy the Regulators that such models are conceptually sound and consistent with the past experience. Estimates must represent a long-term default-weighted average, and be based on data relating to similar exposures and counterparts.

---

[18] Such information may include ratings granted by external agencies, provided that they appear consistent with the other information available to the bank. The Accord specifically states that different categories of counterparts (for instance, large corporations, SMEs, private parties, banks) might require different algorithms and rating processes.

Banks are required to use historical data concerning an entire economic cycle and in any case no less than seven years[19] (five years for retail loans).

As described in Chapter 12, LGD has to be measured in an economic and not merely in an accounting manner, correcting the face value of recoveries by the effect of all factors that are likely to reduce its present value (specifically the discounting effect due to the time necessary for recovery, as well as administrative, direct and indirect, costs associated with recovery). The Basel Committee also provided that, in estimating LGD, banks should take into account the state of the economic cycle. This allows to account for the correlation between LGD and PD that resulted from some empirical studies (see Chapter 12), due to the fact that recovery rates tend to decrease in recession phases, when default rates increase.

Finally, maturity must be estimated taking into account the impact of any intermediate payments during the loan life (more specifically, the duration formula set forth in Chapter 2 shall be used, taking zero as the interest rate). The value thus calculated should be truncated, if necessary, to five years, while maturities of less than one year are authorized only in few specific cases.

Next to the above-mentioned requirements, which relate to the technical characteristics of the rating *system*, there are others – just as important – concerning the way the instruments described above must be transferred into the operational reality of the bank, i.e. the interaction between the rating system and the *process* for assessing, granting and managing loans.

The revised Accord expressly provides that a rating system featuring all the above-listed requirements is not acceptable – for the purpose of capital requirements – unless it plays "an essential role in authorizing credit lines, in risk management, internal capital allocation, and corporate governance functions".

The goal thus is for the rating system, notwithstanding the necessary exceptions, to gradually become the decision-making infrastructure to be placed at the core of the loan granting decisions, the calculation of provisions against future losses, the estimation of the economic capital allocated to the individual business areas relating to the bank's credit portfolio, and finally (although this is not expressly required by the Accord), the definition of fair lending rates covering expected and unexpected losses.[20]

This obligation to make effective and large use of the rating system looks as an appropriate and far-sighted requirement, as the gradual fine-tuning of a risk assessment model can only be achieved through its daily implementation, i.e. through a comparison between its results and the operational and commercial know-how of those in charge of customer relationships.

As to the corporate functions affected by the rating process, the Accord provides that banks set up independent credit risk control units responsible for designing or selecting, implementing, reviewing rating systems, and overlooking their ex post performance. In order to avoid any "conflict of interests", such units must be functionally independent of the staff that, in any respect, is responsible for the origination of loans. Furthermore, the assignment of ratings to individual clients and their periodic review are to be carried out and/or approved by entities that do not directly benefit from credit granting. This seems to draw a rather sharp distinction between customer relationship managers (who "sell"

---

[19] Pursuant to Directive 2006/49, EU banks may be granted up to three years' discount when the New Accord is implemented for the first time.
[20] See Chapter 15.

loans to the clients and meet their own budgets based on the results of such sales) and risk managers (who assess the creditworthiness of borrowers and loans).

The Accord further provides that the internal auditing function or another independent entity review the bank's rating system and its operation once a year. Finally, all material aspects of the rating process shall be approved by the Board of Directors (or its executive committee) and by the management of the bank. Such bodies must have a general knowledge of the system and an in-depth knowledge of the reports to be submitted to the management.

20.4.3   From the Rating System to the Minimum Capital Requirements

With the standard approach, the minimum capital associated with an exposure is simply 8% of risk-weighted assets, where weighting is to be carried out subject to the system described in Table 20.1 (subject to adjustments due to any securities as described in section 20.3). The IRB approach, on the other hand, relies on a more complex mechanism for transforming the characteristics of a loan (PD, LGD, EAD, maturity) and of its portfolio (granularity and correlation) into a capital requirement..

Such a mechanism is based on a simple credit risk model, whose structure[21] and parameters shall be analyzed in this section. Also, some adjustments to the basic model will be illustrated, introduced in order to account for the distinction between expected and unexpected losses, and for the effect that a longer maturity has on credit risk.

The reference model – Consider a credit portfolio made up of a large number of small loans (i.e. an "infinitely granular" portfolio). Suppose, in line with Merton's model,[22] that every borrower defaults if and only if the value of its assets drops below a specific threshold (e.g. the value of debt) at the end of a given time horizon. Let us also assume that the percentage change that shall occur next year in the asset value of the i-th borrower (asset value return, AVR, see Chapter 14) can be expressed as:

$$Z_i = w \cdot Z + \sqrt{1 - w^2} \cdot \varepsilon_i \tag{20.1}$$

i.e. as a linear combination[23] of two components: factor Z, which is correlated to the macroeconomic cycle (and thus impacts on all borrowers in the same way), and factor ε_i, which only depends on the individual (idiosyncratic) risk of the borrower.

Depending on the weights used in the formula, a borrower may be more or less exposed to the cycle: as w increases, all borrowers tend to be more and more correlated to one another, while a decrease in w means that the idiosyncratic characteristics prevail and that the individual borrowers are more independent.

Note that this representation of the effect of the macroeconomic variables on a company's asset value is a simplification of the multifactor models (e.g. CreditMetrics, Creditrisk+) described in Chapter 14, where two or more random variables represent different industries, geographical areas, or macroeconomic factors. However, such models would

---

[21] For a short introduction see Finger (2001), while for a more detailed and rigorous description of the model see Gordy (2001).

[22] See Chapter 11.

[23] Note that, since Z and ε_i have a unit variance, and the variance of the sum of two random independent values, $\mathrm{var}(\alpha x_1 + \beta x_2)$, is always equal to $\alpha^2 \mathrm{var}(x_1) + \beta^2 \mathrm{var}(x_2)$, in order for Z_i to follow a standard normal distribution we have to impose that $\alpha^2 + \beta^2 = 1$. In our case, this was done by making the second weight equal to the square root of $1 - w^2$, where w is the first weight.

hardly be "manageable" for regulatory purposes.[24] For this reason, the Basel Committee decided to adopt a framework based on a single factor such as the model presented in this section.

If we assume that Z and ε_i follow a standard normal distribution, then equation (20.1) implies that Z_i also is standard-normally distributed. For each pair of i and j borrowers, the correlation between asset value returns ("asset correlation", see Chapter 14) is given by:

$$\rho(Z_i, Z_j) = w^2 \qquad (20.2)$$

Quite logically, the higher the dependence (w) of each company's assets on the macroeconomic cycle, the higher the correlation (ρ) between the asset returns of the two companies.

We know that borrower i becomes insolvent if and only if $Z_i < \alpha$, where α represents its default point. If $p_i = PD$ is the unconditional probability of default (independent of the value of factor Z) of such borrower, then $N(\alpha) = p_i$ (see Figure 20.1), where $N(.)$ indicates the standard normal cumulative probability distribution.

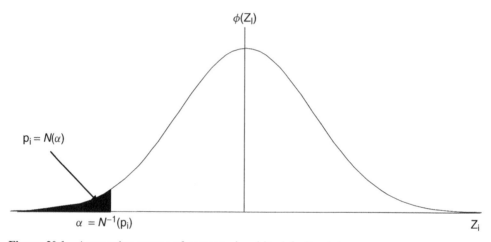

Figure 20.1   Asset value returns of company i and its default point α

Let us now assume that we know the trend of the macroeconomic variable in the next year (obviously, this is an unrealistic assumption, which will be removed later on). This is like assuming we know the specific value (let us say Z^*) that macroeconomic factor Z shall take. Then,

$$Z_i = w \cdot Z^* + \sqrt{1 - w^2} \cdot \varepsilon_i \qquad (20.3)$$

and company i shall become insolvent if and only if

$$Z_i = w \cdot Z^* + \sqrt{1 - w^2} \cdot \varepsilon_i < \alpha \qquad (20.4)$$

i.e. if

$$\varepsilon_i < \frac{\alpha - w \cdot Z^*}{\sqrt{1 - w^2}} = \frac{N^{-1}(p_i) - w \cdot Z^*}{\sqrt{1 - w^2}} \qquad (20.5)$$

---

[24] A multifactor model would make calculations more complex and, above all, would make the capital requirements on a new loan dependent on the portfolio composition of each bank.

As ε_i follows a normal standard distribution, the probability of default for borrower i, *subject to* $Z = Z^*$, simplifies to

$$p_i|_{Z=Z*} = N\left[\frac{N^{-1}(p_i) - w \cdot Z^*}{\sqrt{1-w^2}}\right] = f(Z^*; p_i, w) \qquad (20.6)$$

Therefore, the conditional probability is a function $f(.)$ of Z^*, of unconditional PD and of parameter w.

Note that, since the portfolio is infinitely granular, the actual default rate experienced when $Z = Z^*$ shall be exactly equal to this conditional probability of default. In other words, with a very large number of loans (similarly to what happens in Monte carlo simulations when the number of scenarios increases), the casual (idiosyncratic) error fades away and the observed distribution tends to overlap the theoretical distribution. The conditional probability showed in equation (20.6) can thus be considered as the actual default rate or (assuming an exposure of 1 Euro and an *LGD* of 100 %) as *the loss that the loan portfolio will actually incur into if the macroeconomic factor takes a value of Z*.*

However, we do not know what value factor Z will take: infinite values of Z^* can generate infinite values of our future losses. But, since we know that Z follows a standard normal distribution, where the x-th percentile is given by

$$Z_x|N(Z_i) = x \qquad (20.7)$$

we can use equation (20.6) to identify a loss value L, which shall only be exceeded in $x\%$ of cases. Such value is

$$L = f(Z_x; p_i, w) = p_i|_{Z=Z^*} = N\left[\frac{N^{-1}(p_i) - w \cdot N^{-1}(x)}{\sqrt{1-w^2}}\right] = g(x, p_i, w) \qquad (20.8)$$

This equation provides the amount of capital and reserves necessary to cover $1 - x\%$ of all possible losses. Assuming, for instance,[25] that $x = 0.1\%$ and $\rho = w^2 = 15\%$, the resulting capital requirement would now only depend on the borrower's unconditional *PD*:

$$L = g(X, PD, w) = \Phi\left[\frac{\Phi^{-1}(PD) - \sqrt{15\%} \cdot \Phi^{-1}(0.1\%)}{\sqrt{1-15\%}}\right]$$

$$= \Phi\left[\frac{\Phi^{-1}(PD) + \sqrt{15\%} \cdot \Phi^{-1}(99.9\%)}{\sqrt{1-15\%}}\right] \qquad (20.9)$$

In order to consider the default rate as a unit loss (on a Euro-denominated loan), we forced an LGD of 100 %. This assumption can be easily removed by scaling the result

---

[25] The parameterization selected for the example under (20.9) is not casual. Indeed, it is the core of a weighting function that is actually included in the 2004 Accord and specifically the one indicated by the Basel Committee for retail portfolios secured by mortgage on residential real estate (see Basel Committee, 2006, §328). Note that, in order to transform equation (20.9) into a form that would be – also from a visual standpoint – more similar to the one included in the Accord, we assumed that $N(x) \equiv -N(1-x)$.

of (20.8) by the LGD (and assuming that a loan of 2 Euro with an *LGD* of 50 % can be treated as a loan of 1 Euro with an LGD of 100 %[26]):

$$L = LGD \cdot g(x, PD, w) = LGD \cdot N \left[\frac{N^{-1}(PD) - w \cdot N^{-1}(x)}{\sqrt{1 - w^2}} \right] \qquad (20.10)$$

Choosing parameters – Given the structure of equation (20.10), parameters x and w play a crucial role in establishing the capital requirement for the given level of *PD*. Indeed, the smaller the value of x (i.e. the percentage of cases regulators decide to leave "uncovered" because the value of losses is not matched by an adequate amount of capital and reserves), the "stricter" the model, which leads to higher capital requirements. The Basel Committee opted for a value of x equal to 0.1 %, thus accepting that the capital and reserves required by pillar one may not be enough in one case out of one thousand.

As far as w (and its square value $\rho = w^2$) is concerned, it can be shown that increasing this parameter, while leaving PD and LGD unchanged, produces a higher capital requirement.[27] This depends on the fact that the more the loans of a portfolio are sensitive to the macroeconomic factor Z, the more they tend to default simultaneously, thus making extreme risks more likely.

Of course, not all exposures in a bank's loan portfolio are equally sensitive to macroeconomic risks. Quite conversely, it is likely that:

- smaller loans (especially loans to private individuals) are relatively more exposed to risks of individual nature (linked to the ε component, i.e. honesty and ability of the individual borrower);
- less reliable borrowers, i.e. those with a higher PD, are such because of idiosyncratic risks, i.e. diversifiable risks (also linked to ε).

Therefore, these two classes of borrowers might receive a lower *asset correlation*. For this reason, the Basel Committee has decided not to select a single ρ value applicable to all exposures, but rather different ρs for several "families" (subportfolios) of similar loans. Table 20.4 shows the main subportfolios[28] into which banks using the internal ratings approach have to sort their loans, and the ρ values selected by the Committee for each of them.

The ρs grow as one moves from exposures to smaller entities (specifically the retail portfolio, which – as was the case with the standard approach – includes individuals and small enterprises) to loans granted to large counterparts (corporates, States, banks, project financing transactions, or the financing of highly volatile commercial real estate). In addition to this general criterion, the values reflect the following:

(1) Within retail loans, a distinction is made between generic exposures, loans secured with residential real estates, and qualifying revolving exposures. Residential real estate

---

[26] Note that LGDs are considered to be deterministic. In other words, once a bank estimates the LGD of a loan, this forecast shall always be correct, with no risk for the actual LGDs to be higher than expected. As was illustrated in Chapter 12, this choice implies ignoring the recovery risk.

[27] This appears clearly from the structure of equation (20.10), as $N(.)$ is a strictly growing function and considering that, being $x = 0.1$, $N^{-1}(x)$ produces a negative quantity.

[28] For the sake of brevity, this chapter shall skip some specific portfolios, such as investments in venture capital, in assets deriving from securitization transactions, in "packages" of commercial credits purchased in bulk. For such topics, reference should be made directly to the Basel Committee (2006).

loans are assigned a higher correlation than the remaining retail exposures, as the asset value (thus the borrower's wealth and ability to pay back the loan) depends on the general evolution of the real estate market, and this increases the likelihood of multiple defaults occurring at the same time. Qualifying rotating loans (small exposures to individuals, such as credit card balances, characterized by a high stability of past loss rates), are assigned a particularly low ρ value because they allow a significant portfolio diversification.

(2) Some subportfolios, instead of a single ρ value, are subject to a range of values (for example, 12%–24% for loans to enterprises). The specific value selected for each exposure is inversely related to the borrower's PD (see Figure 20.2). In other words, clients with higher PD values are assigned lower ρ values, based on the assumption that their risk is mostly idiosyncratic (i.e. is linked to specific shortages of each individual borrower more than to possible "systemic" crises). The opposite applies to high-quality customers, whose potential default appears to be mainly due to possible macroeconomic shocks, i.e. more "contagious" phenomena.

(3) Finally, a class of "medium-sized" enterprises is introduced. These are too large to be included in the retail portfolio, but have a consolidated turnover of less than Euro 50 million. They benefit from a reduction in ρ of 4% if their turnover does not exceed Euro 5 million. Such reduction decreases as the turnover gets closer to the maximum threshold of Euro 50 million (for instance, for a turnover lying exactly in the middle between Euro 5 and 50, i.e. Euro 27.5 million, the reduction of the ρ value would be 2%).

Table 20.4 and Figure 20.2 represent the endpoint of an extremely complex debate that has involved scholars, banks, and authorities for a few years. As a matter of fact, the first proposal put forward by the Committee was based on much simpler assumptions and envisaged an asset correlation of 20% for corporations, banks, and sovereign States, and of 8% for the retail portfolio. The selection of 20% for corporations was the result of analyses carried out at the major international banks and on data regarding listed companies.[29] It was particularly criticized by banks in continental Europe. with reference to companies of smaller size. German, Japanese, and Italian banks, also through the commitment shown by their supervisors, managed to persuade the Committee to adopt the more articulated version set forth in Table 20.4. Such solution accounts for the fact that small and medium enterprises, where the vast majority of exposures of European banks is concentrated, are, as mentioned above, less correlated to the economic cycle than large corporations (that are more influenced by common macroeconomic factors such as interest rates, growth in aggregate demand, employment rate, etc.).

For each loan, equation (20.10) can be used to obtain the unit capital requirement a bank has to set aside in order to tackle 99.9% of potential future cases by simply replacing the loan's PD and LGD, and the ρ value of the relevant portfolio (taken from Table 20.4 and, if necessary, from Figure 20.2). However, this is not yet the complete formula for calculating the capital requirement: two additional steps have to be taken into consideration. The first has to do with the distinction between expected and unexpected losses, while the second deals with the effect of maturity.

Expected and unexpected losses – The capital quantified with equation (20.10) covers every possible future loss up to a certain level of confidence (specifically, up to

[29] See Lopez (2000).

Table 20.4 Subportfolios and ρ values

Subportfolio	Description/remarks	Asset correlation (ρ)
Qualifying revolving retail exposures	Exposures to individuals for no more than €100,000 (with an actual balance fluctuating depending on withdrawals and repayments), with no collateral or guarantees backing them and showing a low volatility in past loss rates.	4%
Retail loans secured by a mortgage on residential real estates	Mortgage loans on residential real estates granted to the owner/tenant.	15%
General retail exposures, including small enterprises	Exposures to individuals; loans to small enterprises managed as retail loans, if the total exposure of the banking group to the small enterprise (on a consolidated basis) is lower than €1 million.	3%–16% depending on PD (see Figure 20.2).
Exposure to corporates, sovereign entities and banks	It includes specialized lending transactions (e.g. project financing) and excludes lending for high-volatility commercial real estates (for banks that can evaluate them with their own internal ratings system).	12–24% depending on PD (see Figure 20.2)
Exposure to medium-sized enterprises	Companies belonging to a group whose consolidated turnover does not exceed Euro 50 million, but do not satisfy the requirements for inclusion in the retail portfolio.	As in the previous cases, but with a "discount" that may be as high as 4% if the consolidated turnover does not exceed Euro 5 million (see Figure 2 for an example).
Lending to high-volatility commercial real estates	Only for banks that can evaluate them with their own internal ratings system (the others can adopt a simplified solution).	12%–30% depending on PD (see Figure 2).

99.9% of cases). Figure 20.3 shows this concept: the capital requirement suggested by equation (20.10) is sufficient to cover all possible losses except for 0.1% of worst situations (the small dark area on the far right-hand side). This means that such coverage includes both expected losses and some percentage of unexpected losses, which would only occur in specific extreme scenarios:

$$L = EL + UL \tag{20.11}$$

It is known that EL, being an expected value, should be considered as a production cost rather than a risk. Therefore, it should be expensed in the bank's profit and loss account

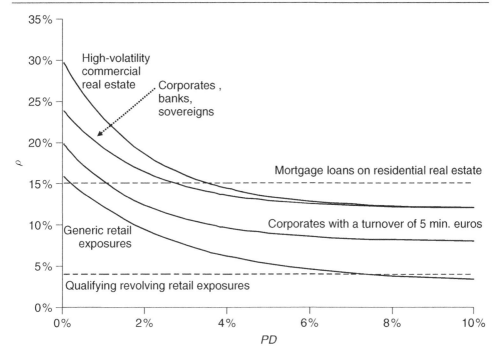

Figure 20.2 ρ values for different subportfolios and PDs

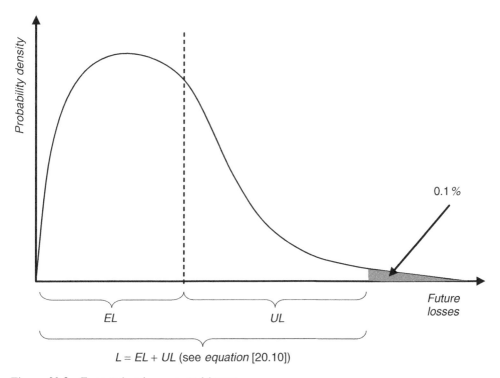

Figure 20.3   Expected and unexpected losses

and set aside as a reserve. On the other hand, *UL* has to be covered with shareholders' capital so as to avoid default if actual losses were to exceed the expected value in a given year.

It is thus useful to make a distinction between the two components used in equation (20.10): the expected loss, to be covered with reserves, and the unexpected loss, to be covered with capital. Incidentally, it is relatively easy to quantify these two factors, as the expected loss on a loan for one Euro is generally[30] obtained as the product *PD·LGD*. Given equation (20.10), and since x = 0.1 %, then:

$$EL = PD \cdot LGD \tag{20.12}$$

$$UL = LGD \cdot N \left[\frac{N^{-1}(PD) - w \cdot N^{-1}(0.1\,\%)}{\sqrt{1 - w^2}} \right] - PD \cdot LGD \tag{20.13}$$

The 2004 Accord requires banks adopting the IRB method to separately quantify expected and unexpected losses and establishes that

- The expected loss (calculated for every position by multiplying unit *EL* by *EAD*) may be covered through provisioning by the bank (for instance, specific provisions, partial depreciations, general provisions at the level of specific portfolios – such as those applicable for country risk – and general provisions as such); should such provisions be insufficient, the uncovered *EL* share can be covered with capital;
- The absolute unexpected loss (calculated for each position by multiplying unit *UL* by *EAD*) should be covered with capital (thus, *UL* can be considered as a *capital requirement in a narrow sense*, while *EL* represents a requirement that can be fulfilled also with provisioning).[31]

Clearly, the correspondence between *EL* and reserves on the one hand, and *UL* and capital on the other hand, is not rigid and absolute. In essence, what the 2004 Accord dictates is that *EL may* (but does not necessarily have to) be covered with provisions, while *UL has to be* covered mainly[32] with capital.

The distinction between EL and UL was introduced by the Committee only in 2004, in the final version of the Accord. Before such date, the Accord only posed a general capital requirement that was calibrated so as to cover both types of losses. This was a major discrepancy with the logics followed by the banks' internal models, which quite clearly separate(see Chapter 14) expected from unexpected losses.

The effect of maturity and the "scaling factor" – Equation (20.13) does not yet represent the final version of the formula that was approved in 2004 for the calculation of unexpected losses (thus, the capital requirement strictly speaking). Indeed, we still have to factor in the impact of the effect that the loan maturity plays on risk.

---

[30] Particularly under the assumption that PD and/or LGD are known with certainty, or that PD and LGD are two independent random variables whose mean value is used.

[31] A limited percentage (up to 7.5 %) of total *UL* (i.e. the value obtained by adding the *UL* of all individual loans) can also be covered with provisions, provided that the latter are higher than the total *EL* (obtained by adding all *EL* values of the individual loans). Half of such provisions shall be considered as capital in the strictest sense ("Tier 1 capital") and half as supplementary capital ("Tier 2 capital").

[32] See footnote 31.

The reason why maturity must also be considered is that equations (20.10) and (20.13) derive from a *binomial* model, where losses are incurred on a loan only if the related borrower is in default. However, as explained in Chapter 14 and in section 20.4.1, long-term loans may undergo a reduction in their fair value even when no proper *default* occurred, simply because the borrower's rating was downgraded. The longer the maturity of the loan, the stronger this effect.

In order to account for this downgrading risk,[33] equation (20.13) must be adjusted based on the loan maturity (i.e. M).[34] Thus, the Basel Committee requires to recalculate UL by multiplying it by the following *maturity adjustment factor*:

$$b = \frac{1 + (M - 2.5)(\alpha - \beta \ln PD)^2}{1 - 1.5 \cdot (\alpha - \beta \ln PD)^2} \qquad (20.14)$$

where $\ln PD$ indicates the natural logarithm of PD, while α and β are two parameters equal to 11.852 % and 5.478 % respectively.[35]

Note that this factor is equal to one (and thus it does not change UL) when the loan maturity M is one year. Longer maturities imply an increase in UL and in the capital requirement. The higher the quality of the borrowers (PD close to zero), the higher this increase tends to be, because such borrowers are more exposed to the risk of being downgraded.

If we assume that the maturity of a given loan to a borrower with a PD of 1 % is three years, equation (20.14) becomes:

$$b = \frac{1 + (3 - 2.5)(11.852\% - 5.478\% \ln 1\%)^2}{1 - 1.5 \cdot (11.852\% - 5.478\% \ln 1\%)^2} \cong 1.346$$

UL must then be adjusted by increasing it by approximately 35 %. More generally, taking equation (20.14) into consideration, the capital requirement ($UL^* = b \cdot UL$) becomes:[36]

$$UL^* = b \cdot \left\{ LGD \cdot N \left[\frac{N^{-1}(PD) - w \cdot N^{-1}(0, 1\%)}{\sqrt{1 - w^2}} \right] - PD \cdot LGD \right\} \qquad (20.15)$$

Finally, in order to avoid that a shift to the internal ratings method may cause an excessive decrease in the banks' capital, the Basel Committee reserves the right to include in the calculation of the final capital requirement (herein referred to as UL^{**}) a scaling factor σ to be agreed upon at an international level (see section 20.2). This factor is presently and temporarily established at 1.06. The complete formula for calculating UL^{**} on a loan

---

[33] See the introduction to Part III of this book.

[34] Note that, by definition, all changes in ratings are unexpected (if it were possible to foresee them, the borrower would be assigned a different creditworthiness grade right from the beginning). Therefore, only the calculation of UL (20.12) has to be corrected by the downgrading risk factor, while the formula for expected loss ([11]) remains unchanged.

[35] The text of the Accord (Basel Committee, 2006, §272) defines as *maturity adjustment* only $(\alpha - \beta \ln PD)^2$, while it is clear that only by considering the entire equation (20.14) one can obtain a proper expression of a maturity adjustment factor.

[36] Note that, due to a decision of the Basel Committee, no maturity adjustment takes place for retail exposures. In this case, by convention we may assume $b \equiv 1$.

for one Euro, including both the maturity adjustment and the scaling factor, is then the following

$$UL^{**} = \sigma \cdot b \cdot \left\{ LGD \cdot N \left[\frac{N^{-1}(PD) - w \cdot N^{-1}(0, 1\%)}{\sqrt{1 - w^2}} \right] - PD \cdot LGD \right\} \qquad (20.16)$$

By multiplying equation (20.16) and (20.12) by EAD, one can calculate, respectively, the quantity of capital and reserves required for each loan. To conclude this section, a short summary is included below, in order to recap how these rules work.

*A **summary example** –* Consider a three-year loan with EAD of 100,000 euros, issued to a company with PD 1 % and a turnover of 5 million euros, with an estimated LGD of 45 %. The absolute expected loss shall simply be equal to

$$EL \cdot EAD = PD \cdot LGD \cdot EAD = 1\% \cdot 45\% \cdot 100,000 = 450 \text{ euros}$$

The absolute unexpected loss shall be:

$$UL^{**} \cdot EAD = \sigma \cdot b \cdot \left\{ LGD \cdot \Phi \left[\frac{\Phi^{-1}(PD) - w \cdot \Phi^{-1}(0.1\%)}{\sqrt{1 - w^2}} \right] - PD \cdot LGD \right\} \cdot EAD$$

In this case, $\rho = w^2$ is approximately 15.3 % (in fact, we are using the third curve from the top of those illustrated in Figure 20.2, reading the ρ value matching a PD of 1 %); therefore, w is approximately 39.1 %. Furthermore, as the example in the previous section showed, the b factor is close to 1.346. Assuming that the scaling factor is actually equal to 1.06, the result would be:

$$UL^{**} \cdot EAD = 1.06 \cdot 1.346$$

$$\cdot \left\{ 45\% \cdot N \left[\frac{N^{-1}(1\%) - 39.1\% \cdot N^{-1}(0,1\%)}{\sqrt{1 - 15.3\%}} \right] - 1\% \cdot 45\% \right\} \cdot 100,000$$

$$= 6561.1 \text{ euros}$$

This absolute unexpected loss must be covered with capital. Therefore, in per-euro terms (taking as reference *EAD* as measure of exposure), the capital requirement is approximately 6.6 %. This value becomes approximately 7 % if one considers also the expected loss (which can be covered either through capital or reserves). In both cases, the result is lower than the 8 % established in the old 1988 Accord; this is mainly due to the relatively low *PD* of the borrower.[37]

20.5   PILLAR TWO: A NEW ROLE FOR SUPERVISORY AUTHORITIES

Even in its most sophisticated version based on the internal ratings approach, pillar one fails to model with sufficient flexibility some crucial aspects of credit risk, such as credit concentration and correlation. Furthermore, the first pillar does not cover some types of

---

[37] A PD of 1 % broadly corresponds to a rating of BB/BB+ (the best among those of speculative grade) on Standard & Poor's scale.

risk (for instance, the interest rate risk on the banking book analyzed in the first part of this book) which, though important, are difficult to measure through a universally-valid framework. Also, the effectiveness of the models set by pillar one largely depends on the organizational solutions put in place by the individual banks and on the degree of involvement of the corporate top management in the risk control and measurement policies.

In order to tackle these aspects properly, it is important that supervisory authorities perform a review of the risk measurement process carried out by the individual banks, testing the soundness of the quantitative and organizational models adopted and requiring, where necessary, a further capital buffer in addition to that calculated with the rules described so far.

Pillar two of the Accord is devoted to such supervisory review, with a view to complementing the quantitative rules illustrated above. This involves an interaction between the national supervisory authorities and the banks, so as to account for the specific risk profiles of the individual banking institutions. Namely, the prudential control process established by pillar two is based on four principles:

(1) Banks must set up a system of processes and techniques aimed at establishing the overall capital adequacy as a function of their own risk profile, as well as a strategy aimed at maintaining adequate levels of capitalization.
(2) The supervisory authorities must evaluate these processes, techniques, and strategies, as well as the ability of banks to ensure compliance with mandatory capital requirements. Should they find that such aspects are not satisfactory, supervisors should take prudential actions such as those prescribed below, under Principles (3) and (4).
(3) Supervisory authorities expect banks to operate with an amount of capital in excess of the minimum requirements and may request banks to hold a higher amount of capital than the minimum requirement. This is due to the fact that it may be expensive for banks to collect additional capital if this has to be done quickly or under unfavorable market conditions. The capital in excess of the minimum requirement should depend on the experience and results reached by the bank in risk management and control, on the kind of markets on which it operates, and on the volatility of its revenues.
(4) Supervisory authorities should promptly intervene in order to avoid that the capital drops below the minimum requirement and should demand that remedies are promptly put in place if the capital is not maintained/brought back to a level above the minimum regulatory requirement.

Within the framework of pillar two, supervisors should check the following:

- compliance with the requirements (for instance, in terms of depth of historical series, number of rating buckets, etc.) established in pillar one;
- control of risks covered by pillar one but quantified in a too simplified manner (for instance, concentration risk);
- other risk profiles which are not included in pillar one (e.g. the already mentioned interest rate risk on the "banking book");
- the effect played by some bank-external factors (such as the economic cycle or technological progress) on risks.

As far as the interest rate risk on the "banking book" is concerned, supervisory authorities should concentrate mainly on "anomalous" banks (defined as those banks where a 2%

change in market rates would cause a value reduction of at least 20 % in the regulatory capital), and have the power to impose a mandatory minimum capital requirement on a national scale.

As to the effect of the economic cycle on risk, all banks adopting the internal ratings approach should share with the supervisors the results of their stress-testing exercises aimed at simulating the effects of a moderate recession (e.g. two consecutive months of zero growth) on PD, LGD, and EAD, and thus on the minimum capital requirement.

More generally, pillar two recognizes that the risk a bank is exposed to depends not only on numeric and objective parameters but also on qualitative issues such as the organizational layout of the bank, the quality of the monitoring processes, and the management quality.

20.6   PILLAR THREE: MARKET DISCIPLINE

20.6.1   The Rationale Underlying Market Discipline

One of the reasons why minimum capital requirements are necessary for banks is the fact that banks are "special" enterprises. Indeed, they

- show a high degree of "opacity" which makes it difficult to correctly evaluate the risk of their investments;
- are financed by individuals (depositors) that are unable to properly evaluate risk and to suitably price it by demanding higher rates to riskier banks;
- play a major role in the economic system – as channels for the transmission of monetary policy and managers of a large part of the payment system – and thus are entitled to use instruments such as special funding from the Central Bank and deposit insurance, which together create a safety net that discourages creditors to assess the bank's soundness.

Therefore, banks' creditors would hardly be efficient at performing this disciplinary function that banks themselves perform with enterprises (monitoring the degree of risk, imposing interest rate conditions consistent with such degree of risk, and even denying loans when risks are too high). An industrial or commercial company increasing its risk profile (for instance, by adopting a higher financial leverage) would most likely suffer an increase in the loan cost. A similar "market discipline" effect (meaning that the financial markets "penalize" risky companies by financing them less and at higher rates) is much weaker if the borrower is a bank.

Pillar three is aimed at removing those factors that make it hard to apply market discipline onto banks. Specifically, it requires that banks comply with strict disclosure criteria, requiring that they provide investors with a prompt and detailed information report on risks and capital. This way, banks' creditors should be in a position to more correctly and timely evaluate their actual levels of risk.

20.6.2   The Reporting Obligations

Back in September 1998,[38] the Basel Committee already recommended that banks provide the market with information on six key areas: (i) their economic and financial results, (ii)

---

[38] Basel Committee (1998), "Enhancing Bank Transparency", September.

their financial structure (capitalization and liquidity), (iii) their strategies and procedures for risk management, (iv) their exposures to the different risk categories, (v) accounting policies, (vi) management and corporate governance.

The June 2004 Accord follows the same approach. In order to avoid overloading banks with complex and unnecessary tasks, and to avoid "flooding" the market with non-essential data, the Accord specifies that financial institutions shall only report information defined as "relevant" (i.e. data that, if omitted or misrepresented, might alter or affect the judgment of an investor). A list of key data to be made available to the public is also provided:

√ size and composition of capital and risky assets;
√ distribution of credit exposures among the different PD groups and the default rate recorded on each rating bucket;
√ risk measurement and control systems in place;
√ accounting practices in use;
√ capital allocation criteria within the bank.

As a rule, such information should be disseminated every six months (or once a year for qualitative data concerning the bank's credit policies, its management systems and reporting, or every three months for capital coefficients and related aggregates). However, these transparency requirements shall not apply to information that, if known by the bank's competitors, might reduce the bank's value, thus reducing its competitive advantages.

20.6.3   Other Necessary Conditions for Market Discipline

Pillar three tackles only one of the issues that hinder market discipline versus banks, i.e. poor transparency on risk conditions. Indeed, there are other necessary conditions to be met in order for market discipline to operate correctly. In addition to transparency, it is necessary that:

(1) there exist creditors who are "not protected" by a public guarantee (be it mandatory deposit insurance, or the fact that the bank is owned by the State);
(2) there are no conjectural guarantees, such as those connected to a supervisory policy of "*too big to fail*" (TBTF);
(3) the management pursues the interests of its shareholders and thus promptly responds to the signals coming from the capital markets.

The first point led several observers to back up the reform proposals aimed at obliging banks to issue subordinated debts.[39] Indeed, subordinated creditors are paid back after the bank's other bond holders and on a residual basis. At the same time, unlike shareholders, they do not benefit from any extreme "bets" made by the bank (as their remuneration is fixed and is not affected by extraordinary corporate profits). Thus, they have a very similar payoff as supervisory authorities and depositors' insurance funds. This should motivate them strongly to perform a careful risk monitoring activity.

However, subordinated creditors might also be poorly sensitive to risk (and thus hardly incentivized to carry out an efficient monitoring and disciplinary action) if the bank is

---

[39] See Flannery (1998).

protected by explicit or implicit guarantees.[40] Therefore, creditors who are not secured by banks – not only subordinated creditors but also bond holders and other banks – should not expect any help from the authorities in case the issuer falls into a financial crisis. From this viewpoint, the experience of several European Countries, where the costs of banking crises are often borne by the national government, seems to point to the need for a reform.

The third point underlines the need for the bank's management to pursue the goal of maximization of their shareholders' value and thus to act so as to avoid an increase in the cost of liabilities due to any increase in the assets risk level. If, on the other hand, the management pursues its own "private" interests (for example, aggressive growth policies through acquisitions), it might decide to bear the higher cost of funding, regardless of the damage that this would cause to the shareholders. In order for the market discipline to work, it is thus necessary that the banks' governance forces managers to care for the interests of the shareholders.

20.7   PROS AND CONS OF BASEL II

The 2004 reform features a few major pros. First of all, it increases the flexibility and risk sensitiveness of the capital ratios for credit risk. This is clearly demonstrated by Figure 20.4, which compares the capital requirements introduced by the 1988 Accord and those introduced by the reform for loans granted to companies (with a turnover of more than Euro 50 million) belonging to different rating buckets (which, for the sake of simplicity, are showed with the scale designed by Standard & Poor's). Compared to the old "flat" requirement of 8 %, now the increase in flexibility is highest when the internal ratings approach is applied. Figure 20.4 only shows the foundation approach, assuming that maturity, EAD, and LGD are fixed and equal to 2.5 years, one Euro, and 45 %, respectively. With the advanced approach, where the bank is free to internally estimate also these three risk parameters, flexibility would be even higher.

Secondly, the reform recognizes the advantages, in terms of risk diversification, of retail portfolios with exposures to individual, families, and small enterprises. Figure 20.5 compares the old 1988 requirement with the new minimum capital requirements. The new standard approach clearly causes the regulatory capital to decrease by one fourth (from 8 % to 6 %). On the other hand, the internal ratings approach allows to calibrate the capital requirement according to the customer's risk level, reaching the point where much riskier counterparts than the average (PD close to 6 %) are subject to a higher capital requirement than the "old" 8 %.

Another, more general, advantage is that the Accord not only reforms the capital requirements (pillar one), but it also extends the role and tasks of the supervisory authorities and of the market. More specifically, the 2004 Accord not only disciplines the banks' behaviour, but it also redefines the tasks, responsibilities, and professional resources required from the supervisory authorities themselves. It is therefore important to consider the three pillars as equally important and as strictly related to one another, i.e. as parts of an overall regulatory framework that cannot be assessed separately.

---

[40] For example, Sironi (2003) shows that the German Landesbanks, enjoying an explicit guarantee by their Lander (State), may get funding through subordinated bonds at rates that on average are 50 basis points (0.5 %) lower than the ones that subordinated investors would require for the same risk level if no such guarantee were granted.

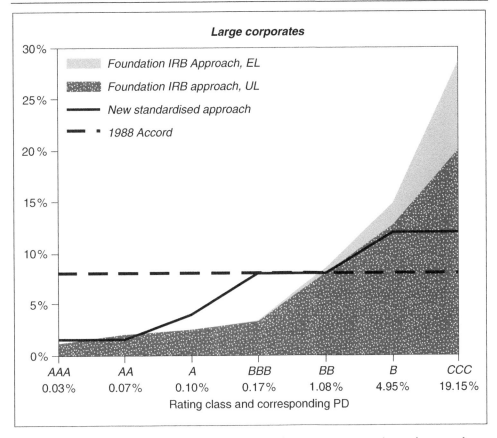

Figure 20.4 Capital requirements for exposures to large corporates under various regulatory regimes

A further positive aspect is the evolutionary approach followed in the area of credit risk (and operational risk, see Chapter 21). Indeed, it starts with an exogenous capitalization requirement that is fully independent of the internal risk management system put in place by the banks, and goes as far as partly recognizing the risk parameters estimated with such systems (PD in the foundation approach, and LGD, EAD, and maturity in the advanced approach). Banks are invited and enticed to move from simpler to more sophisticated approaches as their internal resources and skills allow them to adopt more complex methodologies. Over a few years, this very rationale may lead to recognizing internal models for measuring credit risk on a portfolio basis, thus overcoming the simplifications that are inherent in the model presented in section 20.4.

The emphasis placed on organizational and operational issues also appears to be particularly appropriate. For instance, as mentioned above, in order for internal ratings systems to be recognized and validated by the supervisory authorities, the reform explicitly requires an actual use of the system for management purposes. Thus, a rating system shall not be acceptable for calculating capital requirements unless it plays "an essential role in granting credit lines, risk management, internal capital allocation, and in the corporate governance functions." Furthermore, in several points the reform provides for a direct responsibility of

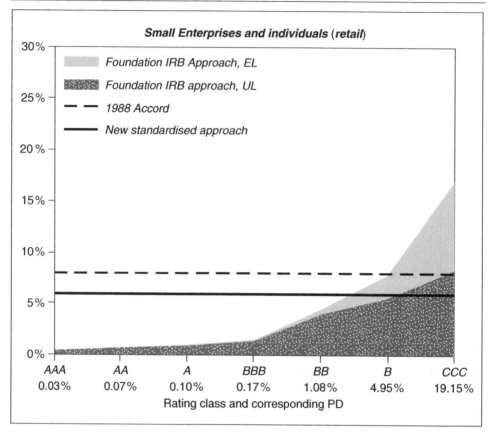

Figure 20.5 Capital requirements for retail exposures under various regulatory regimes (exposures other than mortgages and qualifying revolving exposures)

corporate functions other than risk management (such as internal audit, and the very Top Management), which are called upon understanding the basic mechanisms of the system, supervise over its integrity, and use the estimates as part of the corporate strategies and management practices.

Finally, several sections of the revised Accord are to be appreciated as they help banks to develop their own ratings systems in line with the international best practice, thus protecting them against possible mistakes and naivety. Such provisions represent a sort of "operational guide" for banks committed to building an internal ratings system and, although they may appear oversimplistic, they could certainly not be taken for granted before the introduction of "Basel II". Such provisions include the requirement that the ratings system be two-dimensional, i.e. to separately evaluate the borrower's probability of default and the loss in case of loan default; the introduction of an adjustment for residual maturity in order to account for the risk of downgrading; an attempt at reducing the possibility to resort to regulatory arbitrage by an extremely accurate treatment of securitization transactions, credit mitigation techniques and credit derivatives.

Next to these pros, there are also cons and open issues. One of the first drawbacks of the Basel Committee proposals has to do with the risk weights established for the different rating buckets in the standard approach. As a matter of fact, they are relatively undifferentiated compared to what emerges from data on historical default rates and spreads of corporate bonds, as demonstrated by some recent empirical studies.[41] For instance, the historical data provided by *Moody's* on default rates at one year for class B3 are approximately 100 times higher (15.03 % versus 0.13 %) than the rates for class Baa1. However, class B3 is subject to a risk weight of 150 %, while class Baa1 is subject to a risk weight of 100 %. From a 1:100 ratio between default rates, a 2:3 ratio is reached for risk weights.

However, this limited risk sensitivity of the new risk weights must be understood and accepted, since it was dictated by political reasons: the Basel Committee, in fact, feared that a migration from a "flat" regime (where all loans to a given category of borrowers were subject to the same capital requirement) to a more risk-sensitive one could bring about unwanted effects (e.g. a severe credit rationing for riskier firms, leading to an economic recession) and therefore took care to prevent any disruptive change.

A second limitation relates to the totally rigid and unrealistic way in which the internal ratings system measures the concentration and correlations among borrowers. As to the former, in 2001 the Committee had provided for the calculation of a "granularity" measure of the loan portfolio based on the Herfindahl index. However, such proposal was abandoned during the negotiations for the drafting of the final Accord, and the application of any correction was left to the national authorities within the framework of pillar two. As far as correlation is concerned, the approach based on the subportfolios set forth in section 20.5, while on the one hand exempting banks from measuring the actual degree of diversification of their portfolios, on the other hand operates so that the capital "consumption" linked to a new loan becomes independent of the composition of the pre-existing portfolio. This clashes with the notion of marginal capital (or marginal VaR) set forth in Chapter 14.

A third limitation – as illustrated earlier – is connected with pillar three and specifically with the possibility to make market discipline on banks truly effective. The reform does tackle the issue of disclosure, but it does not face the problems linked to incentives for bank creditors to perform an efficient risk monitoring activity.

Another – often quoted – limitation of the revised Basel Accord is its complexity. Indeed, in its full version (Basel Committee on Banking Supervision, 2006) the Accord is a 333 page volume illustrating in detail issues and mechanisms that are not simple, often offering several alternative solutions. Actually, we believe that what appears to be complex is the subject of the Accord (risk management) and not the Accord in itself. Length and complexity are therefore unavoidable, when tackling this subject in an exhaustive and in-depth manner.

A further problem raised by the Accord – procyclicality – shall be dealt with in the final part of this chapter.

20.8   THE IMPACT OF BASEL II

20.8.1   The Impact on First Implementation

The new capital requirements were subject to several quantitative impact studies (or QIS) aimed at testing the potential consequences of the new legislation which were coordinated

---

[41] See Altman and Saunders (2001) and Resti and Sironi (2007).

by the Basel Committee itself. Such studies were based on simulations performed by a broad sample of banks based in different countries, which were asked to calculate the capital requirement based on the new regulations and to compare it with the capital requirement based on the 1988 rules.

A particularly challenging study called QIS5 was carried out in 2005–2006 on a sample of 382 banks in 32 countries. Such banks were divided into two groups:

– "Group 1": large, highly diversified banks characterized by a tier 1 capital of over three billion Euros and by strong international operations;
– "Group 2": regional or specialized banks, with a tier 1 capital of less than three billion Euros, whose business is mainly concentrated in one country or in specific business areas.

Table 20.5 reports the key results of this study. They are to be taken very cautiously because the exercise required to estimate parameters, such as PD, LGD, or EAD, before many of the banks involved had sufficiently tested their credit risk measurement systems.

Table 20.5 QIS 5 results – % change in capital requirement

	Standardized approach	FIRB approach	AIRB approach	Most likely approach
G10* Group 1	1.7	−1.3	−7.1	−6.8
G10 Group 2	−1.3	−12.3	−26.7	−11.3
CEBS** Group 1	−0.9	−3.2	−8.3	−7.7
CEBS Group 2	−3.0	−16.6	−26.6	−15.4
Other** non-G10 Group 1	1.8	−16.2	−29.0	−20.7
Other non-G10 Group 2	38.2	11.4	−1.0	19.5

*Includes the 13 member countries of the Basel Committee (see Appendix 18A to Chapter 18). **Countries participating in the works of the Committee of European Banking Supervisors; in addition to the European G10 countries, the group includes Bulgaria, Cyprus, Czech Republic, Finland, Greece, Hungary, Ireland, Malta, Norway, Poland, and Portugal ***Australia, Bahrain, Brazil, Chile, India, Indonesia, Peru, and Singapore.
Source: Basel Committee (2006b).

Four key results emerge:

– In general, a decrease in the capital requirement is found, which is particularly remarkable with the IRB approach (especially in the advanced version). However, it is worth pointing out that the QIS5 results do not take into account the floors mentioned in section 20.2 and therefore might overestimate the possible reduction in the minimum regulatory capital. A small increase is recorded for G10 banks if the standard approach is implemented. Much higher increases are recorded by banks in non-G10 countries and non-CEBS countries (Australia, Bahrain, Brazil, Chile, India, Indonesia, Peru, and Singapore). More specifically, among Group 2 banks an increase of approximately 20 % is observed, also based on the data of the last column, where the capital of each

bank in the sample was calculated with the approach (standardized, IRB foundation, or IRB advanced) which it is likely to be adopted as from 2007/2008;
- The impact of Basel II varies largely for each individual banks, as demonstrated by the large discrepancy among the individual data reported in Figure 20.6. The higher risk sensitivity of the new requirements causes different banks to be subject to more diversified capital requirements;
- On average, smaller banks (Group 2) appear to be more favored;
- European banks appear to be slightly more favored over the average G10 banks.

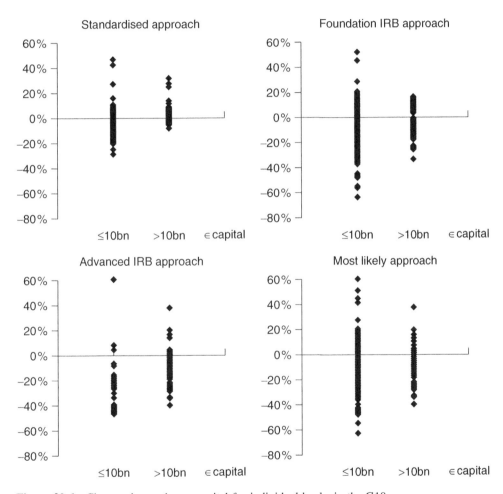

Figure 20.6   Changes in regulatory capital for individual banks in the G10
Source: Basel Committee on Banking Supervision, 2006b

Table 20.6 shows the contribution of the individual segments to the overall change in the regulatory capital. With the standardized approach, the total change is exactly the one showed in Table 20.5; for the internal ratings approach, the two columns in Table 20.5 (foundation and advanced) were merged into one, selecting for each bank the approach

Table 20.6 QIS 5 results – Contribution of regulatory capital to the % change

	Standardized Approach				Most likely IRB Approach			
	G10	G10	CEBS	CEBS	G10	G10	CEBS	CEBS
	Group 1	**Group 2**	**Group 1**	**Group 2**	**Group 1**	**Group 2**	**Group 1**	**Group 2**
Wholesale; of which:	2.5	−0.9	1.9	−1.2	−3.3	−3.9	−3.2	−3.1
– Corporate	0.9	−1	−0.3	−0.6	−5	−4.5	−4	−3.6
– Bank	1.5	0.2	1.8	−0.7	0.4	0.1	−0.2	0
– Sovereign	0.2	−0.1	0.4	0.1	1.3	0.6	0.9	0.5
SME corporate	−0.2	−0.1	−0.4	0.2	−1.3	−2.2	−1.3	−2.4
Retail; of which:	−7.1	−9	−9	−10.6	−8.1	−17.3	−8.9	−20
– Mortgage	−6.3	−6.2	−7.8	−7.2	−7.6	−12.6	−8.9	−14.4
– Revolving	−0.1	−0.3	−0.2	−0.3	0.3	−0.2	0.8	−0.4
– Other	−0.7	−2.5	−1	−3.1	−0.9	−4.5	−0.8	−5.2
SME retail	−0.4	−1.2	−0.9	−1.7	−1.4	−3.3	−2	−4
Market risk	0	0	0	0	0	0	−0.1	0
Operational risk	5.6	8.3	5.5	9	6.1	7.5	5.8	7.7
Other	1	1.4	2	1.1	3.2	5	2	3.8
Total	1.7	−1.3	−0.9	−3	−4.5	−14.1	−7.5	−18

Source: Basel Committee (2006b).

that it is most likely to adopt as from 2007/2008. An analysis of these more detailed data allows to better understand the results emerging from the previous table:

– The increase in the overall regulatory capital associated with the standard approach is mainly caused by the new requirement on operational risk (Chapter 21). Indeed, without it the impact of Basel II on minimum capital requirements would remain negative. However, for Group 1 banks a tightening of capital requirements is recorded also in the wholesale area due to the higher capital consumption associated with interbank loans and loans to sovereign States;
– The IRB approach leads to capital savings in almost all of the segments of the loan portfolio. Loans to sovereign States are penalized in terms of capital absorption, while lendings to customers – especially to private (retail) individuals and small enterprises (SMEs) – benefit from a major reduction. The benefit is particularly high for smaller banks (Group 2), where these customer segments account for a high share of their credit portfolios. This explains one of the results emerging from the previous table.

20.8.2 The Dynamic Impact: Procyclicality

The previous section illustrated the likely impact of the Revised Accord in static terms, i.e. during its first implementation. However, the criticisms raised by several observers mainly focused on its dynamic impact, i.e. on how the new capital requirements may evolve over time.

More specifically, the capital requirements designed by Basel II – being based on ratings – may strengthen the fluctuations of the economic cycle (i.e. evolve in a procyclical manner) and have negative effects on the stability of the banking system.

Indeed, if the capital ratios depend on the (external or internal) ratings of the counterparts, a recession, leading to higher default rates and more frequent downgradings, would lead to an increase in the minimum required capital. As it would be difficult to collect new capital during a recession, in order to maintain the ratio between capital and risk weighted assets, banks would end up granting less credit to the economy, and this would expose companies to further financial distress, thus strengthening the recession. Similarly, at a time of strong economic growth associated with a general upgrading of the creditworthiness of counterparts, the capital ratios would decrease, thus allowing banks to provide more credit to the economy.

In general, any capital adequacy system, be it based on ratings or not, tends to be procyclical. Indeed, during recessions default rates increase, which in turn requires larger provisions and writeoffs, thus reducing the banks' capital endowment and possibly leading to a credit crunch. The novelty introduced by Basel II is that procyclicality stems not only from the evolution of defaults, but also from changes in the borrowers' ratings. The consequence is a stronger procyclical effect, due to the evolution of both default rates and migration rates (upgradings and downgradings).

However, procyclicality does not depend merely on the way in which capital requirements are technically designed. Two more factors are also important: the provisioning policies implemented by banks and the operation of their internal ratings systems. These three aspects are analyzed below.

Procyclicality and design of capital requirements – A system of capital ratios based on ratings tends to be more procyclical than a system based on fixed weights such as the one dictated in 1988. However, this higher procyclicality depends on two factors.

The first is the strength of the correlation between ratings and risk weights. Under the standard approach, as shown in section 20.3, this is based on the risk weights showed in Table 20.1. This weighting system is very "cautious" in increasing capital requirements as the rating worsens (indeed, a 1:100 ratio between default rates corresponds to a 2:3 ratio between the related risk weights). This choice, although somehow unsatisfactory (because it represents the relationship between rating and risk in a very unrealistic way), appears to be advisable if the goal is to reduce procyclicality: indeed, the weights in Table 20.1 imply that the increase in the capital requirement, due to a downgrading, turns out to be generally small.

Under the internal ratings approach, the capital requirement is given by equations (20.12) and (20.16), i.e. by the regulatory functions connecting PD with the minimum capital requirement. A key parameter in defining the form of such functions is asset correlation ρ: The higher the value of ρ, the smaller the benefit deriving from a diversification and therefore, for a given PD, the higher the capital requirement. As seen in section 20.5, the value of ρ proposed in 2001 for companies (a fixed 20 % irrespective of PD) was replaced (during the third quantitative impact study – or QIS3 – carried out in 2003) by a system of variable ρ values starting from 24 % and decreasing to 12 % for companies with a higher PD.[42] Consequently, as PD increases, the benefits from diversification also increase: the 2003 regulatory function thus produces a less remarkable increase in capital requirements as PD increases (i.e. when the borrower is placed in a worse rating bucket).

Figure 20.7 shows the regulatory function for companies in three versions: (i) the one in force in January 2001 ("*CP2 corporate*"), (ii) the 2003 version for large corporations (*QIS3 corporate*); (iii) the 2003 version for companies with a turnover of no more than Euro 5 million (*QIS 3 SME*). The picture shows that, compared to the first version of January 2001, the curve slope is much flatter, thus significantly reducing the level and reactivity to rating of the capital requirements.

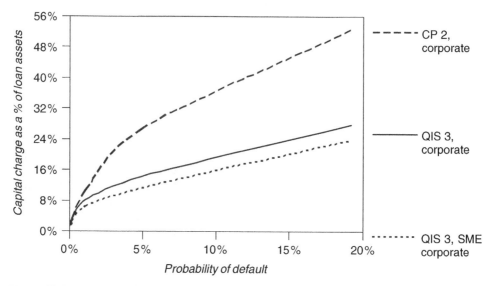

Figure 20.7   Capital ratio as a function of PD

This lower steepness of the curve implies a major decline in the system's degree of procyclicality. With a deterioration of the economic cycle, and consequently an increase in the counterparts' PD, the increase in the risk weight becomes less severe. Therefore, the final version of the Accord (whose parameters reflect those of CP3) is less procyclical than the draft of January 2001.[43]

---

[42] The range varies from 20 % to 8 % for companies with a turnover of no more than Euro 5 million (see Table 20.4).

[43] To understand the extent of the evolution of the Basel Committee's proposals in terms of minimum capital requirement, take, for example, a loan of Euro 100 to a company with a PD of 2 %, an LGD of 50 %, and a maturity of 3 years. A similar loan would imply a capital requirement of Euro 8 in 1988 and of Euro 15 pursuant to the 2001 draft. With the changes approved in 2003 (which are basically confirmed in the final version of the Accord), the capital requirement becomes Euro 10.1, which drops to approximately Euro 8.9 if the company has a turnover of Euro 25 million (and to approximately Euro 5 if the company's turnover is Euro 5 million). For a small enterprise falling within the retail portfolio, the capital "consumption" would be even smaller, dropping to Euro 5.5.

A second characteristic that affects the procyclicality of capital requirements is linked to whether they take as reference only the unexpected loss (*UL*) component or also the expected loss (*EL + UL*). Indeed, in the first case, against a procyclical capital ratio, banks may adopt "anti-cyclical" provisioning policies, increasing their provisioning during times of strong economic growth (when profit margins allow it) and using reserves during recession periods, when loan losses increase. A similar approach would be consistent with a correct economic rationale: reserves are set aside when credits – that will give rise to future losses – are originated, i.e. during the phases of highest growth in lending. Thus, a procyclical capital requirement, relating to UL only, might be compensated with anti-cyclical provisioning policies.

If, on the other hand, capital requirements include both UL and EL, procyclicality tends to extend also to reserves. Then, it becomes hard, or at least less profitable, for banks to adopt anti-cyclical provisioning policies.

Also from this viewpoint, the final text of the Accord has made an important – though partial – progress. As was previously illustrated, in the final version of the Accord the capital requirement based on internal ratings is calibrated only on the unexpected loss (equation 20.16), while the expected loss (EL) component can be covered by means of credit adjustments.

This is a major innovation, not only because it addresses several criticisms raised by academics and bankers in the past years, but also because it lays the ground for a dynamic provisioning policy, based on expected losses rather than on actual losses. However, it should be noted that, although the 2004 Accord follows a correct pattern, it is too weak in this respect. Indeed, expected losses *may* (rather than *must*) be covered with reserves. It is therefore possible to cover them with shareholders' equity capital.

Provisioning policies and accounting standards – As illustrated in the previous point, the provisioning policies adopted by banks can make a given regulatory capital adequacy framework more or less procyclical. Dynamic policies would increase provisions during periods of strong growth and high profits, thus allowing one to reduce charges in the profit and loss account during recession phases, and decreasing procyclicality of capital requirements. On the other hand, policies that tend to expense only actual losses in the profit and loss account are more procyclical due to the simple fact that losses are higher during recession periods.

One of the possible solutions to the issue of procyclicality is offered by a system of statistical provisions, also known as dynamic provisioning, such as the one that has been recently adopted by the Spanish regulatory authorities. Such system allows to set aside provisions, ever since a loan is granted, in proportion to the long-term average expected loss for the different types of borrowers. These provisions may be used during periods of unfavorable economic cycle, characterized by high percentages of bad debts.

The system was introduced in 2000, following a strong growth in bank lending recorded in the 1990's. It requires banks to calculate statistic provisions based on internal models or based on a standard method (which assigns coefficients ranging from 0 % to 1.5 % to the different loan categories, based on their risk rate). The total credit thus weighted measures the so-called latent losses (LL), which are then compared with provisions made for specific deteriorated credits (actual losses or AL). If the former is higher (see Figure 20.8, left-hand side), the statistical reserve (SR) has to be increased up to three times the latent risk. Conversely, if the latent risk is lower than the specific provisions (Figure 20.8, right-hand side), the statistical reserve can be reduced. This way, the statistical provisions (LL) mitigate the impact of actual losses (AL) on the profit and loss account ("P&L" in

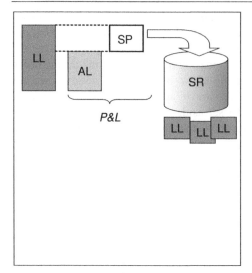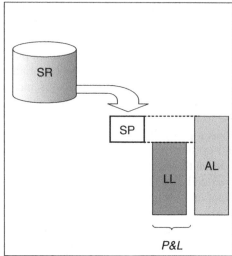

Figure 20.8 How statistical provisioning works

Figure 20.8), and, since they evolve in the opposite direction to the latter versus the cycle trend, they reduce the procyclicality of the overall provisions.

Accounting standards play a crucial role in establishing the possibility/profitability of similar dynamic provisioning schemes. Unlike the regulatory capital legislation, the accounting standards often vary from country to country.

Furthermore, within each country, the accounting, regulatory, and fiscal regulations are often different because they pursue different goals.

The supervisory authorities, interested in ensuring stability of the banking system, tend to consider provisions as a buffer against future losses and therefore are in favour of a provisioning system based on expected losses. The accounting rules, aimed at ensuring accuracy of financial statements, are more inclined to support provisioning policies based on actual losses incurred that can be proved on an objective basis. Finally, fiscal provisions, focused on the amount and distribution of tax revenues, tend to oppose profit-smoothing accounting policies that would use provisions in order to differ the fiscal drag in time.

As a general rule, provisions may fall into three categories:

– General provisions, made on the basis of assessments of entire portfolios and aimed at covering a risk even if it is only a likely risk;
– Adjustments made on a lump-sum basis on homogeneous subsets of credits (for instance, loans to residents in a given foreign country in crisis, or loans to private parties in poor areas, etc.);
– Adjustments made on an analytical basis on individual loans.

The possibility to actually make these three types of adjustments is established, in the European Union, by the International Accounting Standards (IAS) or International Financial Reporting Standards (IFRS).

Standard IFRS/IAS No. 39 (that was first drawn up in 1999 by the International Accounting Standards Committee, which then became the international Accounting

Standards Board or IASB, and adopted as from 2005[44]) is particularly important as it provides that balance sheets in the banking industry use the concept of fair value more extensively, at least for financial instruments held for trading purposes. The fair value is defined as the price that can be obtained if an asset were transferred to the market under normal conditions and under normal business operation (i.e. not because of mandatory winding-up). The principle of fair value requires that an asset posted in the balance sheet be written up or written down based on changes in its fair value, to be estimated at market prices or at the price of the income flows generated by the asset itself.

For bank loans, the fair value principle was "softened" by the "amortized cost" principle, whereby the value of a loan is calculated as the present value of the expected cash flows, which decrease if the borrower runs into such difficulties as to possibly need loan restructuring.

More specifically, IFRS 39 provides that credits be posted at the nominal amount established based on their depreciation plan (i.e. the above-mentioned "amortized cost"), unless there is objective evidence of their deterioration. As was previously mentioned, in such case the loan has to be posted at an amount equal to the actual value of the new expected future cash flows, while the related difference compared to the nominal value is to be posted in the profit and loss account. The text of IAS 39 also includes several examples of events that would be considered as "objective evidence" of deterioration, thus giving rise to value adjustments.

The nominal cash flows of each loan are discounted at different rates based on the borrower's rating. Specifically, for each loan, its original internal rate of return (or yield to maturity) is used as discount rate. However, if the borrower is downgraded, the rate should remain unchanged. Therefore, also the loan value remains unchanged, unless the bank estimates a decrease in future cash flows. From this viewpoint, IFRS 39 is quite far from the rationale of the multinomial models for credit risk management (see, for instance, CreditMetrics in Chapter 14), which associate a downgrading to an increase in the discount rate and a decrease in the loan value for a given cash flow plan.

As far as loan adjustments are concerned, IFRS 39 refers to the concept of incurred loss. Indeed, adjustments are admitted only for incurred losses (or estimated losses but always based on a new evidence, one that has *already occurred* and was not there at the time the loan was granted). Therefore, it is not admissible to make provisions based on future expected losses, even if they are estimated on the basis of statistical criteria, such as those used in the rating systems implemented by banks.

Using the principles of fair value and amortised cost will most probably lead to a higher degree of transparency, due to a more accurate identification of risks. However, this may

---

[44] In December 2000, the Joint Working Group of Standard Setters (JWG), a group including the IASB and the national bodies in charge of defining accounting standards, suggested to extend the use of fair value to all financial instruments, including loans and bank deposits. This proposal was greeted with scepticism by the banking community and the supervisory authorities because of the difficulties in correctly evaluating financial instruments that are not traded on a secondary liquid market, and because of the impact that such practice would have on profit volatility. In August 2001, the IASB started reviewing IAS 39, and in 2002 drew up a draft that, among other things, provides for the possibility for companies to adopt (irrevocable option) the fair value criteria for every financial instrument. Following to several criticisms raised by the financial community, the IASB prepared a new version of IAS's 39 and 32. In Europe, the European Parliament and the European Council adopted a regulation (1606/2002) whereby listed companies are obliged to apply the IAS standard in preparing the financial statements for every financial year starting from January 2005. The new international accounting standards have thus become part of the EU legislation (EU Commission's Regulation No. 1725 of 2003, Regulations No. 2086 and 2236–2238 of 2004).

increase volatility of banks' profits and the procyclicality of their credit policies, since it makes it harder to set up "statistical" reserves for expected losses.

The ratings assignment process – A third element affecting the degree of procyclicality of capital requirements is the process followed by banks to assign a rating to their clients.

More specifically, procyclicality depends on whether the bank implements a point-in-time approach or a through-the-cycle approach (see Chapter 13). In the first case, the judgment would reflect the current (or short-term) conditions of the economic cycle and thus it is most likely to change as the economic situation changes. In the second case, the judgment would be more stable as the cycle changes.

Several banks adopt point-in-time rating systems. This is due to the fact that adopting a through-the-cycle approach would lead to excessively strict assessments, especially for short-term loans, and thus to an excessively high pricing that would make the bank poorly competitive compared to its competitors. Point-in-time rating systems are more procyclical than through-the-cycle systems. Indeed, they produce more frequent migrations among rating buckets.

The 2004 final version of the Accord tackled this issue by requiring banks to – at least partly – modify their rating approach. Namely, it requires banks to assign the rating with a medium-term time horizon, taking account of the effects of possible adverse macroeconomic conditions. In the Committee's words: "Although the time horizon used in PD estimation is one year, banks are expected to use a longer time horizon in assigning ratings. The bank must assess of the borrower's ability to perform despite adverse economic conditions or the occurrence of unexpected events".

Although, on the one hand, this provision is dictated by praiseworthy intentions (i.e. reducing the degree of procyclicality of capital requirements), on the other hand it appears far too general and ambiguous (one wonders, for instance, how a bank could foresee events that are defined as "unexpected"...). Furthermore, it risks discouraging banks (especially those with a short-maturity loan portfolio) from following the rating assignment process that best suits their management needs, thus creating a gap between "regulatory" ratings, granted in writing and documented, and "management" ratings, which analysts have in mind when authorizing the provision of a given short-maturity loan.

Box 20.1 The Good Tailors of Basel

Regulators are still struggling with their monster regime for banks

The Basel committee of rich-country bank supervisors has learned not to make rash promises about its timetable for setting a new capital regime for banks. Originally planned for 2004, the regime, called Basel 2, was knocked back a year last June and has now slipped even further. Without an official announcement, members of the committee talk about a starting date of 2006.

Basel 2 will revolutionize the supervision of leading banks, adjusting the capital required by the regulators to the banks' own measures of the risks they run. It is intended to replace the crude workings of Basel 1, in force since 1988, with greater detail–far too much, indeed. At the same time, the capital rules are also being designed to suit all the other banks in industrialized countries, and eventually worldwide. A version must be applied at the same time to all banks and investment firms in the European Union, under an EU directive yet to be written.

The exercise was never expected to be easy. Critics, including The Economist, suggested that it could be done more simply by starting with a small group of the world's biggest banks. Now it seems that the Basel rule makers are beyond the point of no return: they are determined to have a workable version of Basel 2 agreed by the end of the year. Before then they will ask banks to road-test a newly calibrated set of rules, probably in June, so that they can produce a final consultation paper in the last quarter of the year. This is the third test, or quantitative impact study, designed to ensure that the rules will not reduce overall capital in the banking system, or distort financial markets. The biggest challenge is to persuade banks to progress towards a more advanced measurement of risk, using their own credit ratings rather than those of external agencies such as Moody's and Standard GBP Poor's. They need to be encouraged by a potential capital saving, but not one that gives them too great a competitive advantage over less sophisticated banks. Previous calibrations have failed to get this right. The first proposals gave little advantage to banks using advanced methods of measuring; later drafts gave too much.

A handful of other knotty issues need to be unravelled before June, mostly in the quantitative part of the regime, known as "pillar one". There, the treatment of loans to small and medium-sized companies raises concern, especially in Germany; too heavy a charge might starve these companies of credit. The Basel experts think that they have fixed this issue by acknowledging a diversification effect in lending to smaller firms: for banks that spread their lending among small businesses, risk charges can be lowered.

A related task is to modify – even reverse – the incentive given to short-term rather than long-term lending. The Germans, again, worry that Basel 2 will erode the kind of long-term bank lending that is the backbone of corporate Germany. It could also reduce developing countries' access to long-term capital, making them more crisis-prone.

The Basel experts fear that banks will be tempted to arbitrage the difference between the risk-weighting demanded by regulators for a portfolio of loans sold as securities and the risk suggested by their own credit-risk models. Regulators have made such models taboo since they examined them in 1998 and found them wanting – they need huge amounts of data which have not yet been collected. Banks' own models have not been considered for Basel 2, but a regulator says they may be discussed in four or five years' time.

Finally, there is the issue of procyclicality, a concern that a risk-sensitive regime will require banks to raise more capital, and cut back lending, at the toughest part of an economic cycle, so needlessly exacerbating a downturn. Basel experts think this danger can be overcome by asking banks to stress-test their portfolios during good times, for worst-case outcomes, and then build up capital accordingly. Surely a simpler answer is to require an extra buffer of capital – which most well-managed banks have anyway. Yet that would hardly be in the spirit of a risk-based regime.

There is no doubt that the Basel 2 exercise has heightened awareness of risk among banks. It has prompted them to overhaul their credit-scoring methods and to tighten up their operations. It has also forced them to get to grips with a hitherto unregulated area of risk: Basel 2 requires capital as a buffer for operational risk–losses from events such as business interruptions, bomb attacks and rogue trading. The argument continues, though, over whether this risk is measurable and can be solved by carrying more capital. Is capital a better buffer against a rogue trader than the assurance of better controls?

Supervisors are encouraging a shift from capital charges based on hard ratios to charges that reward good risk management. A second part of the Basel 2 regime, called "pillar two", relies on continuous review by supervisors of a bank's risk management, and of its handling of exposures that cannot be assessed in merely quantitative terms. The last part, "pillar three", encourages more public disclosure by banks of their structure, performance and risk positions.

The endeavour to build a comprehensive regime, however, threatens daily to add complexity rather than to shed it. The Basel committee touchingly notes that it will seek to balance the need for sensitivity towards risk with the need to be "sufficiently clear and flexible". One committee member confesses that the opposite tends to be true. "As soon as you develop an approach, it's not too long before you hear from the banks complaining about something. So you adjust at the cost of a more complex calculation for everybody." Another committee member refers to the "great monster" of Basel 2.

A man went to his tailor for the final fitting of a suit and found one sleeve and one leg too short. "Hunch yourself like this, and bend your leg like that", said the tailor ",and you'll find it fits". And so it did. The man paid his tailor and hobbled into the street. "Look at that poor fellow, all doubled up", said a passer-by. "Well," said his companion, "at least he has a good tailor".

The tailors of Basel 2 may yet produce a similar suit.

Source: The Economist, 22–28 February 2002. © The Economist Newspaper Limited, London

SELECTED QUESTIONS AND EXERCISES

1. Which is the regulatory capital charge for a loan to an industrial company with a AA rating in the 1988 capital adequacy framework and in the standardised approach of the Basel II Accord?

   (A) 100 % and 20 % respectively;
   (B) 8 % and 1.6 % respectively;
   (C) 50 % and 20 % respectively;
   (D) 8 % and 4 % respectively.

2. A loan of euro 20 million, to an unrated, non-financial company is secured by an equal amount of 2-year, unrated bonds issued by a bank. What is the capital requirement against the loan according to the standardised approach of the Basel II Accord? How would it change if the collateral were to be replaced by a cash deposit of euro 5 million? What if the two collaterals were pledged together?

3. In order for the bank to have a proper internal rating system, the Head of the Credit Department sets up a new Credit Risk Control Unit, which is entrusted with the task of creating and managing the bank's rating models, and will report directly to the Head of the Credit Department. Will such a rating system qualify for use under the IRB approach?

(A) Definitely yes.
(B) This depends on a set of requirements, like the number of rating grades and the amount of historical data on which the system has been developed and tested.
(C) No.
(D) Yes, but only if the Credit Risk Control Unit does not directly benefit from the loans originated by the bank.

4. Consider a ten-year mortgage loan secured by residential real estate, with an EAD of Euro 250,000 and an estimated LGD of 10%. Supposing the customer's PD is 2% and using a 1.06 scale factor, compute the capital requirement against EL and UL on the loan (hint: before you try to solve this exercise, carefully review the footnotes in section 20.4).

5. Consider the following statements: the Credit VaR model used by the Basel Committee to derive the regulatory function in the IRB approach assumes that:

(I) all exposures are infinitely small;
(II) correlations stay the same regardless of the country/industry in which the borrower operates;
(III) recovery rates can be foretold with certainty;
(IV) the bank knows the state of the macroeconomic cycle in the following 12 months.

Which of them would you agree with?

(A) Only I;
(B) All of them;
(C) All but IV;
(D) I and IV.

21

Capital Requirements
on Operational Risk

21.1 INTRODUCTION

The 2004 New Basel Capital Accord also introduced capital requirements to cover operational risk (OR). The purpose of this extension was to make mandatory capital requirements more sensitive to the actual risk profile of banks, bringing them closer to the risk measurement criteria they adopt internally.

The 1988 agreement recognized explicitly that the capital requirement of 8 % of risk weighted assets, though related to credit risk, was also intended to cover indirectly the other kinds of risk. This coverage was not only indirect but also imprecise, since a bank exposed to credit risk is not necessarily more vulnerable to market risk or operational risk.

To make the correlation between risks and capital more precise, capital requirements on market risks (Chapter 19) were first introduced in 1996. Then, in 2004, as the requirement on credit risk became increasingly precise, an ad-hoc capital requirement for operational risk needed to be developed.

This chapter analyzes this capital requirement, pointing out its advantages and limitations, and dwells on its implications for banks.

21.2 THE CAPITAL REQUIREMENT ON OPERATIONAL RISK

An important premise concerns the definition of operational risk. As observed in Chapter 17, the Basel Committee adopted a definition based on four categories of causal factors: internal processes, human resources, systems, and external events. Operational risk, in fact, is defined as "...*the risk of loss resulting from inadequate or failed internal processes, people and systems or from external events*". As explicitly clarified by the Committee, this definition includes legal risk but excludes strategic and reputational risk.

It is important to point out that the capital requirement for OR was designed by the Basel Committee so as to provide coverage for both expected and unexpected losses. While acknowledging that capital should provide coverage only for the latter, the Committee felt that accounting differences and the general absence (or inadequacy) of explicit reserves intended to cover OR expected losses made it necessary to impose a minimum capital based on both components.[1]

The Committee also stressed that the capital requirement must be intended to cover both direct and indirect losses. The latter are associated with any additional costs or payments to third parties that a bank must sustain to mend the consequences of problems arising from OR events. The capital requirement for OR became effective at the end of 2006.

The system for measuring the OR capital requirement proposed by the Basel Committee is based on three alternative approaches of increasing complexity and precision:

---

[1] As we shall see, the only exception to this rule is reserved to banks that adopt the "advanced" approach, provided they demonstrate that the expected loss component is already reflected in their pricing policies and provisions.

(i) the *Basic Indicator Approach*, (ii) the *Standardized Approach* and (iii) the *Advanced Measurement Approaches*.

The Committee hopes that banks will move from the simplest approach toward the more advanced one as their OR measurement and management systems become more sophisticated. Once a bank has adopted a more advanced approach, it will no longer be authorized to revert to a simpler one. It will be permitted, however, to adopt different approaches for different business lines, as long as it follows the path of increasing sophistication. A bank could therefore adopt the basic indicator or standardized approaches for retail banking and at the same time the advanced measurement approach for trading.

21.2.1 The Basic Indicator Approach

Under the first and simplest approach, the b*asic indicator approach*, the capital requirement is based on the bank's gross operating income (GOI), equal to the sum of net interest income and net non-interest income (derived primarily from service fees and trading gains[2]). The gross operating income of a bank measures its gross operating revenues and is roughly equivalent to the turnover of industrial companies. It is therefore a measure of "pure" size, which provides no indications about the "quality" of the company revenues (and therefore nothing about the risk level of the operational processes carried out to generate those revenues).

The gross operating income is multiplied by a risk factor – known as α – which has been set by the Basel Committee at 15 %. This figure is based on the data provided to the Committee by a small number of banks that in 2000 already had operational risk measurement systems in place.[3] More precisely, the α factor of 15 % is applied to the average value of gross operating income for the previous three years (any negative values are excluded from the computation of the average) to obtain the capital requirement k_{OR} for OR:

$$k_{OR} = \alpha \cdot \frac{\sum_{i=1}^{3} \max(0, GOI_{t-i})}{N} = 15\% \cdot \frac{\sum_{i=1}^{3} \max(0, GOI_{t-i})}{N} \qquad (21.1)$$

where k_{OR} represents the capital requirement for *OR*, *GOI* the gross operating income of the bank and N the number of years, among the last three, in which GOI was positive.

This first approach is extremely simplified and imprecise, since the different levels of exposure to operational risk of the bank's various businesses, are not taken into consideration. Indeed, the Basel Committee considers it suitable only for small, relatively unsophisticated banks and affirms that "internationally active banks and banks with significant operational risk exposures (for example, specialized processing banks) are expected

---

[2] GOI must be gross of the operating costs and charge-offs (due, for example, to the legal interest accrued on delinquent loans). Also, it excludes any gains or losses on the sale of securities belonging to the "banking book" and extraordinary items.

[3] The first *quantitative impact study* (QIS) relative to OR, to which 14 banks in various countries contributed, indicated that on average banks were allocating 15 % of their economic capital (12 % of their regulatory capital) to OR. The Committee felt that a similar result might be achieved by requiring that the capital for operational risk be equal to 15 % of gross operating income, and consequently fixed the value of alpha. It is interesting to recall that initially (2001) the Committee intended to impose a heavier requirement (30 % of gross operating income, i.e. around 20 % of the total capital requirement), and then changed its mind based on the results of the QIS.

to use an approach that is more sophisticated than the Basic Indicator Approach and that is appropriate for the risk profile of the institution".

21.2.2 The Standardized Approach

Under the *standardized approach*, the capital requirement is measured separately for the main business lines by multiplying their gross operating income by a specific risk factor, β_i, different for each business line. This approach thus captures, at least in part, the different levels of risk of the various business areas in which a bank operates. Consequently, it produces a larger capital requirement for banks that operate in intrinsically riskier sectors.

The Committee requires that all the operating income of a bank be associated with one and only one business line among the eight indicated in the third column of Table 21.1: the mapping of the bank's various activities to the different businesses must follow the scheme of the table and must also be clearly documented, subject to independent review, approved by the board of directors under the responsibility of senior management. The system for "mapping" income must also take into account any internal transfers across business lines through "shadow pricing" mechanisms such as the internal transfer rates seen in Chapter 4 of this book.

The values of the β_I factors, again, must be multiplied by the gross operating income referring to the average for the last three years. The gross operating income of one or more business lines may be negative, but the total at the bank level must be positive (otherwise, the capital requirement for that year would be zero).

As we mentioned already, for each business line the capital requirement is computed by multiplying the three-year average gross operating income by a specific beta factor. The Basel Committee fixed the beta factors associated with the eight business lines (see Table 21.2), as they did for the α factor of the previous section. Those values reflect the historical ratios between the losses recorded in the past by the banking industry in the various business lines and their GOIs.

Thus, for example, the capital requirement for retail banking is equal to 12 % of the average gross operating income recorded in the last three years by the retail banking business. The overall capital requirement of the bank is equal to the sum of the requirements for the eight business lines.

As mentioned above, the gross operating income of a business line can be negative in one or more years, provided that the overall bank result is positive. Otherwise, in estimating the three-year average, it is forced to zero.

Summing up, the capital requirement for OR under the standardized approach is equal to:

$$k_{OR} = \sum_{i=1}^{3} \frac{Max\left(\sum_{j=1}^{8} \beta_j \cdot GOI_{j,t-i}, 0\right)}{3} \tag{21.2}$$

where $GOI_{j,t-i}$ indicates the gross operating income of the j-th business line in the year $t - i$, while the β_j are the factors indicated in Table 21.2.

Note that the choice of computing the bank's capital requirement as the sum of those for individual business lines implicitly assumes a perfect correlation among the various types of loss events. In practice, it is assumed that the losses connected to the OR of

Table 21.1 The process of mapping of the activity to the business lines

Activity Groups	Businesses	Business Lines	Business Units
Mergers and acquisitions, underwriting, privatizations, securitization, research, debt (government, high yield), equity, syndications, IPOs, secondary private placements	Corporate Finance	Corporate Finance	Investment Banking
	Municipal/Government Finance		
	Merchant Banking		
	Advisory Services		
Fixed income, equity, foreign exchange, commodities, credit, funding, own position securities, lending and repos, brokerage, debt, prime brokerage	Sales	Trading & Sales	
	Market Making		
	Proprietary Positions		
	Treasury		
Retail lending and deposits, banking services, trust and estates	Retail Banking	Retail Banking	Banking
Private lending and deposits, banking services, trust and estates, investment advice	Private Banking		
Merchant/commercial/corporate cards, private labels and retail	Card Services		
Project finance, real estate, export finance, trade finance, factoring, leasing, lending, guarantees, bills of exchange	Commercial Banking	Commercial Banking	
Payments and collections, funds transfer, clearing and settlement	External Clients	Payment and Settlement	
Escrow, depository receipts, securities lending (customers), corporate actions	Custody	Agency Services	
Issuer and paying agents	Corporate Agency		
	Corporate Trust		
Pooled, segregated, retail, institutional, closed, open, private equity	Discretionary Fund Management	Asset Management	Others
Pooled, segregated, retail, institutional, closed, open	Non-Discretionary Fund Management		
Execution and full service	Retail Brokerage	Retail Brokerage	

Source: Basel Committee (2006).

Table 21.2 Business lines and beta factors in the standardized approach

j	Business line	Beta Factor (β_j)
1	Corporate finance	18 %
2	Trading and sales	18 %
3	Retail banking	12 %
4	Commercial banking	15 %
5	Payments and settlements	18 %
6	Agency services	15 %
7	Asset management	12 %
8	Retail brokerage	12 %

Source: Basel Committee (2006).

the various business lines do not tend to offset each other over time but instead tend to occur simultaneously. The bank is therefore required to have sufficient capital to cover all losses deriving from events that might reasonably occur jointly.

Comparing the standardized and basic approaches, we note that the β factors may be greater or smaller than α: the latter, in fact, is equal to 15 %, while the values shown in Table 21.2 range between 12 % (activity with low operational risk) and 18 % (activity with high operating risk). A bank that moves from the basic to the standardized approach might therefore find that its capital requirement is lower or higher, depending on its portfolio of activities.[4]

In both the basic and standard approaches, the basis for computing the capital requirement is gross operating income. This measure, as we mentioned already, is gross of any loan-loss charge-offs or provisions, so it tends to assume higher values for banks that lend to riskier customers at higher interest rates (thus with higher net interest income) but on the other hand have larger loan losses. For these banks, formulas like (21.2) would result in a higher k_{OR} not because their operational risk is larger but because the quality of their credit portfolio is lower. This would not be correct, since the risks related to lower loan quality are already considered, for capital adequacy purposes, through the mechanisms described in Chapters 18 and 20 and should not affect the estimate of operational risk.

For this reason, the Basel Committee provided that the individual national supervisory authorities could also allow for an "Alternative Standard Approach" (ASA). In this approach, the actual GOI of the two business lines which are particularly vulnerable to the kind of biases just mentioned (retail banking and commercial banking) can be replaced by a "conventional" GOI equal to 3.5 % of the outstanding loans in the past three years (not risk-weighted and gross of loan-loss provisions). Retail banking should include retail loans, loans to small and midsize enterprises (SMEs) included in the retail portfolio, and

---

[4] The standard approach, on the other hand, seems more favourable to banks that have experienced negative GOI in one or more of the past three years. In fact, while (21.1) requires that any negative GOIs be eliminated from the computation of average gross operating income, (21.2) permits them to be replaced by a zero value, which reduces the computation of the requirement k_{OR}.

retail purchased receivables; commercial banking should encompass, loans to companies belonging to the "corporate" portfolio (including the small and midsize enterprises in this portfolio and purchased receivables), to sovereign entities and to banks.

21.2.3 The requirements for adopting the standardized approach

While the first approach, the basic indicator, can be adopted by any bank, provided it complies with the principles shown in Appendix 17A to Chapter 17, the adoption of the standardised approach is subject to compliance with some specific conditions.

In order to adopt the standardized approach, a bank must demonstrate that its Board of Directors and top management are actively involved in the supervision of the operational risk management methodologies. These methodologies must also be conceptually sound and solidly implemented, also through the deployment of adequate resources. Furthermore, as mentioned earlier, the criteria for "mapping" income and assets to the various business lines must be documented adequately.

If a bank adopting the standardized approach is significantly active on an international scale,[5] it must in any case invest adequately in internal systems for measuring operational risk. In other words, for this category of banks, the standardized approach must not represent an "alibi" for not investing in models and methodologies for controlling operational risk.

Banks are therefore required to have a system for managing operational risks, and its design and implementation must be assigned to an ad hoc organizational unit. This system must be integrated into the bank's risk management framework and must be revised and validated periodically by external auditors and/or the supervisory authorities. Furthermore, the exposure to operational risk must be reported periodically, also to top management, and a system of incentives must exist that induces the bank to reduce its operational risks. Lastly, the losses actually incurred because of OR must be filed on a single business line basis.

21.2.4 Advanced measurement approaches

The third approach actually consists of a variety of possible methodologies for which the Basel Accord only sets some minimum requirements. These "advanced measurement approaches" are basically the internal models developed by individual banks: in other words, a bank that has developed a model for measuring OR that enables it to determine its economic capital, can use it also to determine its minimum capital requirement, subject to some qualitative and quantitative conditions.

The Basel Committee thus recognizes the possibility that banks use their internal estimates of future OR losses to quantify their capital requirement, as it already occurs for market risks. In so doing, the Committee leaves each bank, wishing to adopt an advanced approach, free to choose its own methodology and imposes no particular model.

It is nevertheless interesting to recall that, in a 2001 working paper drafted in preparation for the 2004 Accord,[6] the Basel Committee mentioned three possible approaches to

---

[5] It is important to remember that the Basel Accord, from its inception in 1988, focused primarily on banks with strong international activity. It is therefore no surprise that it contains some provisions designed expressly for this category of intermediaries.

[6] Basel Committee on Banking Supervision (2001f).

estimating operational risk, on which banks could base their internal models: the *internal measurement approach*, the *loss distribution approach*, and the *scorecard approach*. They were not included in the final version of the agreement but still provide a good example of what the supervisory authorities expect from banks.

The *internal measurement approach* required that the activities of the bank be segmented into predefined business lines and a range of possible risky events be identified. For each business line/event category intersection, the supervisory authority would identify a risk exposure indicator (EI) that reflected the size of the bank's activity, while the bank would estimate the risk parameters (PE, probability of event, and LGE, loss given event). The product of the three parameters (EI, PE and LGE) would represent the expected loss (see Chapter 17), while the unexpected loss would be estimated as the product of expected loss times a factor ("gamma") defined for each business line/event category intersection, based on the skew and kurtosis of the relative distribution of losses.[7]

The loss distribution approach required banks to estimate the entire loss probability distribution for each business line and "cut" it at the desired percentile. More precisely, for each business line they had to estimate the distributions of the number of losses and the "loss given event" (using, for example, a Poisson distribution[8] and a beta distribution, respectively[9]), or using Monte Carlo simulations. The total capital requirement could be less than the sum of the capital requirements on the individual business lines, if the bank was able to demonstrate the imperfect correlation among the various loss classes.

The scorecard approach required each bank to determine the total capital allocated to OR and then assign it to the individual business lines based on their relative risk profile. This profile was determined by means of "scorecards" reporting a number of indicators, to be as objective as possible, of the "intrinsic" riskiness of each business line, and the effectiveness of the control systems in place for each of them.

21.2.5 The requirements for adopting advanced approaches

A bank wishing to adopt its own internal model for computing OR capital requirements must comply with a few general conditions:

- its board of directors and senior management, as appropriate, must be actively involved in the oversight of the operational risk management framework;
- the risk management system must be conceptually sound and implemented with integrity;
- the resources must be sufficient in the use of the approach in the major business lines as well as the control and audit area.

Then there are other conditions of a more "technical" nature, both qualitative and quantitative. Of the former, the most important are:

- the bank must have an independent unit for controlling and monitoring OR;

---

[7] In particular, the more skewed and leptokurtic the loss distribution, the larger the gamma factor. Evidently, the most delicate aspect of this approach was precisely the estimate of the gamma factors, considering the limited knowledge on the real form of the OR losses distribution for the various types of businesses and events.

[8] See Chapter 14.

[9] See section 14.7.3.

- the system for measuring OR must be closely integrated into the day-to-day risk management processes of the bank. In this sense, the bank must have a system for allocating operational risk capital to major business lines so as to create incentives to reduce risk;
- OR exposures and actual losses must be regularly reported to business unit management, senior management, and to the board of directors;
- internal and external auditors must perform regular reviews of the OR management processes and measurement systems. The external auditors, along with the supervisory authorities, must ensure that the internal audits are conducted adequately and that the data flows and process associated with the risk measurement system are transparent and readily accessible.

The quantitative requirements are primarily the following:

- The bank must be able to demonstrate that its internal model adequately captures extreme events, i.e. the 'tail-loss' events. More specifically, the measure of risk must be consistent with the parameters established for the internal ratings-based approach for credit risk: a confidence level of 99.9 % and a holding period of one year.[10]
- The OR measurement system must be consistent with the categorisation of events shown in Table 21.3. As can be seen, this represents a detailed classification of the events included in the general definition provided at the start of this chapter, similar to that presented in Chapter 17 and intended to limit their scope more precisely and prevent possible omissions when designing the system.

Table 21.3 Main categories of operational risk events

Event-Type Category (Level 1)	Definition	Categories (Level 2)	Activity Examples (Level 3)
Internal fraud	Losses due to acts of a type intended to defraud, misappropriate property or circumvent regulations, the law or company policy, excluding diversity/discrimination events, which involves at least one internal party	Unauthorized Activity	Transactions not reported (intentional) Transaction type unauthorized (w/monetary loss) Mismarking of position (intentional)
			Fraud/credit fraud/worthless deposits Theft/extortion/embezzlement/robbery

---

[10] Note that the Basel Committee, though unifying the confidence level and holding period required for credit and operational risk, continues to require different parameters regarding market risk (a 99 % confidence level and a holding period of at least ten working days). While the different holding period can be justified by the different "liquidity" of the exposures, the choice of different confidence levels seems less convincing. We must bear in mind, however, that the safety factor F equal to three (or more if the model's backtesting is not satisfactory), imposed on banks for regulatory purposes (see Chapter 19) is equivalent to "shifting" the actual level of VaR coverage on market risks toward a percentile higher than 99 %.

Table 21.3 (*continued*)

Event-Type Category (Level 1)	Definition	Categories (Level 2)	Activity Examples (Level 3)
		Theft and Fraud	Misappropriation of assets
			Malicious destruction of assets
			Forgery
			Check kiting
			Smuggling
			Account take-over/impersonation/etc.
			Tax non-compliance/evasion (willful)
			Bribes/kickbacks
			Insider trading (not on firm's account)
External fraud	Losses due to acts of a type intended to defraud, misappropriate property or circumvent the law, by a third party	Theft and Fraud	Theft/Robbery Forgery Check kiting
		Systems Security	Hacking damage
			Theft of information (w/monetary loss)
Employment Practices and Workplace Safety	Losses arising from acts inconsistent with employment, health or safety laws or agreements, from payment of personal injury claims, or from diversity/ discrimination events	Employee Relations	Compensation, benefit, termination issues
			Organized labour activity
		Safe Environment	General liability (slip and fall, etc.)
			Employee health & safety rules events
			Workers compensation
		Diversity & Discrimination	All discrimination types

(*continued overleaf*)

Table 21.3 (*continued*)

Event-Type Category (Level 1)	Definition	Categories (Level 2)	Activity Examples (Level 3)
Clients, Products & Business Practices	Losses arising from an unintentional or negligent failure to meet a professional obligation to specific clients (including fiduciary and suitability requirements), or from the nature or design of a product.	Suitability, Disclosure & Fiduciary	Fiduciary breaches/guideline violations Suitability/disclosure issues (KYC, etc.) Retail customer disclosure violations Breach of privacy Aggressive sales Account churning Misuse of confidential information Lender liability
		Improper Business or Market Practices	Antitrust Improper trade/market practices Market manipulation Insider trading (on firm's account) Unlicensed activity Money laundering
		Product Flaws	Product defects (unauthorized, etc.) Model errors
		Selection, Sponsorship & Exposure	Failure to investigate client per guidelines Exceeding client exposure limits
		Advisory Activities	Disputes over performance of advisory activities
Damage to Physical Assets	Losses arising from loss or damage to physical assets from natural disaster or other events.	Disasters and other events	Natural disaster losses Human losses from external sources (terrorism, vandalism)
Business disruption and system failures	Losses arising from disruption of business or system failures	Systems	Hardware Software Telecommunications Utility outage/disruptions

- The capital requirement must cover both expected and unexpected losses. A bank can limit itself to covering just unexpected loss only if it demonstrates that the expected loss is already adequately covered with provisions or with appropriate pricing policies (i.e. covered by past income or by expected future income).
- Generally speaking, the total OR capital requirement should be the sum of the requirements for the individual business lines. If, however, the bank feels that some risk diversification occurs among the various business lines, then the total requirement may be less than the sum of the individual requirements. To that end, the bank must be capable of producing estimates of the correlations among business lines, based on a sound, robust methodology that reflects the uncertainty that typically characterizes these estimates in periods of stress. The estimates must therefore derive from empirical data collected over a sufficiently long time-window, that includes periods of stress.
- Some conditions refer to the data (internal and external) used by the bank in constructing its models. The internal data are considered an essential requisite for developing a credible OR measurement system and must cover at least five years (a period of only three years is acceptable when advanced models are first adopted). If the bank has modified its operating procedures after some historical data have been recorded, it is permitted to re-scale or modify them to make them more significant. The internal data must be associated to the business lines defined in Table 20.2 and the event categories indicated in Table 20.3; however, for the purpose of its operational risk measurement and management procedures, the bank is free to adopt a different classification. The internal data must include all significant loss events, excluding losses below a minimum materiality threshold (e.g. € 10,000). Each loss must be associated with the date on which it occurred, the factor that caused it, and any amount recovered. External data (provided by interbank consortia or specialized data vendors) must be utilized if the bank feels exposed to significant but highly infrequent losses for which internal data might not provide adequate support. The bank must document the cases in which the external data are used and the way in which they are incorporated into its models.
- the estimates of OR exposure must also be based on scenario analyses based on opinions by experts. These opinions may concern, for example, the parameters of the OR losses distribution or the correlation among the losses suffered by different business lines;
- in addition to the data (internal and external) and the scenario analyses, the risk assessment process must also consider the external environment and the bank's internal control system. Changes in these factors must be reflected in the model OR estimation, which cannot therefore be limited to mechanically processing historical data, but must be "forward looking".

Lastly, a few rules concern banking groups operating, through own subsidiaries, in foreign countries. If these groups can produce reliable and accurate estimates of the correlation among business lines, they can take into account the benefits of diversification both at the group level and at the level of the individual subsidiaries. However, if required by the host supervisors (that is, the supervisors of the countries where the subsidiary, or group of subsidiaries, is located), they cannot consider the diversification benefits due to the imperfect correlation with other units of the group located in different countries, but only those present internally.

21.2.6   The role of the second and third pillars

As observed in Chapter 20, the new capital adequacy framework proposed by the Basel Committee is based on three pillars. The first establishes rules for the computation of capital requirements. The second concerns the supervision of the risk management systems and capital adequacy policies of banks by the national supervisory authorities. The third intends to enhance the market discipline effect that investors exercise (or should exercise) over the risk and capital policies of banks.

Briefly, the second pillar (see Chapter 20) requires the supervisory authorities to ascertain that each bank has developed an effective system for measuring and controlling risks and set up adequate strategies to ensure its capital adequacy on an ongoing basis. If this is not the case, the authorities impose corrective actions on the bank, which may include an increase in the total capital requirement beyond the level dictated by the first pillar. With reference to OR, the Basel Committee issued a few cardinal principles for its management (see Appendix 17A) that should guide the action taken by the national supervisory authorities in applying the second pillar.

Regarding the third pillar, the Basel Committee has stated a set of minimum information that each bank is required to disclose to the market, so that the market will be able to correctly assess the risk profile of the bank and price its debt accordingly. With reference to OR, each bank must disclose the following information:

– the type of approach adopted in determining its capital requirement;
– the strategies and processes underlying the OR management system;
– the structure and organization of the risk management function;
– the management strategies, as well as he coverage and mitigation policies, adopted for OR;
– a description of the advanced approaches adopted, if any.

21.2.7   The role of insurance coverage

As observed in Chapter 17, the purchase of insurance coverage for OR-related losses is relatively recent and was made possible by some product innovations introduced by major insurance and reinsurance groups.

Insurance policies have been stipulated, for example, on losses deriving from the dishonesty/incompetence of personnel (known as *bankers' blanket bonds*[11]) such as the unauthorized trading of securities; also, the market has witnessed the stipulation of policies against claims for compensation advanced by customers as well as of insurance contracts against the damage deriving to the bank or to third parties from the malfunctioning of IT and e-commerce systems.

As mentioned in Chapter 17, such insurance contracts are viewed as a form of "outsourcing". This process is similar to what is occurring in the management of information systems, procurement, and real estate assets, which are increasingly being delegated to outside companies to which banks pay a fee or a rent. Similarly, the coverage of certain operational risks which are considered to be outside of the bank's "core business"

---

[11] Fidelity bonds or bankers' blanket bonds protect the insured against losses due to theft/misappropriation or other dishonest behaviour on the part of employees. The term "blanket" refers to the fact that the group of persons covered by the policy is not expressly identified by name. Blanket bonds represent a form of risk coverage mandatory for some types of US banking institutions.

(i.e. management of financial risks) is being "outsourced" and entrusted to specialized companies (insurance firms).

Back in November 2001, the Basel Committee recommended the use of these risk transfer instruments.[12] However, amid protests from banks and insurance companies, it initially decided that they would not trigger any reduction in the capital requirements. In the 2004 agreement, it was therefore decided to allow banks with adequate insurance coverage to reduce the OR capital requirement. This reduction, however, only applies to banks that adopt the advanced models approach, and cannot exceed 20 % of the total gross (that is, in absence of coverage) requirement. This recognition of coverage is also subject to compliance with a few requirements: briefly, the insurance company must have a high rating (at least single A or equivalent), the coverage must have a minimum duration of one year and provide for a minimum notice of 90 days for cancellation.

The decision to allow capital reduction for insurance coverage only to banks that adopt advanced approaches was due to the fact that the basic and standardized approaches do not provide a sufficiently precise picture of the origin and extent of a bank's existing risks, and thus are not even sufficient to understand in what way the insurance policies may actually reduce such risks.

21.3   WEAKNESSES OF THE 2004 ACCORD

The regulations on capital requirements for OR were subject to heavy criticism from the international financial community. A first criticism was based on the idea that OR, unlike market and credit risks, is a typically "idiosyncratic", not "systemic", risk. Consider market risk: a general decline in the equity or bond markets can result in significant losses for a large number of financial institutions, jeopardizing the stability of the entire system. Likewise, for credit risk, an increase in the default rates of companies associated with a deterioration in the economic cycle affects the entire banking industry, making it increasingly unstable. In the case of OR, on the other hand, losses are generally the result of specific factors affecting individual banks (employee dishonesty/errors, legal liability toward third parties, etc.) and no "contagion" effect occurs to the other banks. Consequently, OR jeopardizes the survival of *individual* intermediaries, but not the overall stability of the system. Since this stability is the "public good" that the supervisory authorities are interested in protecting, it is not clear why it was necessary to extend capital requirements to operational risk.

A second criticism, leveled in particular by the *International Swap and Derivatives Association* (ISDA), is based on the difficulty of measuring this risk category adequately and objectively. As already observed in Chapter 17, the state of progress on OR measurement models is still well behind that of other risk types (to the point that in 2004 the Basel Committee was unable to indicate the content of an advanced model and had to limit itself to prescribing a series of rather generic minimum requirements). Consequently, the capital requirement associated with this risk may be rather imprecise and ineffective.

A third criticism concerns the possible negative consequences of a capital requirement on OR. Indeed, if the management of a bank feels that this risk is already covered, through

---

[12] As stated in the November 2001 document: "Insurance is an effective tool for mitigating operational risks by reducing the economic impact of operational losses, and therefore should have explicit recognition within the capital framework of the new Basel Capital Accord to appropriately reflect the risk profile of institutions and encourage prudent and sound risk management."

a specified portion of minimum regulatory capital, it might devote less attention to process innovations designed to mitigate it and make it less threatening.

A fourth criticism concerns the basic indicator and standardized approaches, which make a bank's capital coverage proportional to its gross operating income. Such a scale variable is extremely imprecise: there is no reason why a bank with a large gross income must also face a higher amount of OR. On the contrary, a bank may be more profitable because it has more efficient, accountable operating procedures in place, that generate fewer operational risks. Paradoxically, the basic indicator and standardized approaches will charge such a bank with a *higher* capital requirement. Furthermore, the decision to make capital requirement proportional to the size of the bank seems to have no empirical support. A study by Shi, Samad-Khan and Medapa (2000), in fact, shows that the variability of losses related to OR is only explained to a minimal extent by size variables such as total assets, total revenues, or the number of employees.

As a result of choosing gross operating income as a scale variable, the capital requirements for OR, unlike those for credit and market risks, give banks no incentive to reduce the existing risk. A bank that wishes to "save" capital can, for example, decrease its capital requirement on credit risk by lending to customers with lower PD or requiring better collateral. Similarly, a bank can reduce its regulatory capital on market risks, for example, by reducing the duration of the bonds in its portfolio. In the case of the basic indicator and standardized approaches, on the other hand, the only way to reduce the capital requirement on operational risk is to reduce the gross operating income of the bank, i.e. be less productive and profitable. This really does not appear to be a particularly "instructive" mechanism in terms of risk reduction.

More generally, the basic indicator and standardized approaches have been criticized, especially by banking associations, for their top-down logic, which computes the capital requirement by starting with the gross operating income of the entire bank or an entire business line. This approach is viewed as unsatisfactory because: (i) it gives banks no incentive to improve their internal control systems, (ii) it does not provide any indication about the causes of OR and thus does not support risk reduction actions, and (iii) it does not support the banks in formulating policies to transfer to third parties the risk inherent in certain business processes.

In addition to the criticism explicitly formulated by the financial community, other critical aspects of the regulations on operational risk need to be highlighted. First, the 99.9 % confidence level prescribed in the advanced approaches seems rather high: it corresponds to a default probability of one per thousand, and one might ask whether any company has ever survived for 1,000 years! One might object that such a confidence level is also required for credit risk; however, two important differences make the case of operational risk different:

- as mentioned earlier, credit risk is systemic in nature, while operational risk is primarily idiosyncratic. Thus, while in the case of credit risk a high confidence level reflects the need to avoid general contagion and disarray, in the case of operational risk a lower confidence level might be acceptable and compatible with the overall stability of the banking system;
- adopting a 99.9 % confidence level in the case of operational risks means including natural catastrophes among the events that must be covered with shareholders' capital; the probability of such events is extremely low and their consequences, in terms of losses and thus the capital required to cover them, are particularly high (low frequency-high

impact events–LFHI). Indeed, it is unlikely a bank could "cover" this type of events through its equity capital, while some kind of insurance coverage would seem more appropriate (not to say inevitable). Catastrophic risks, in fact, are highly diversifiable and thus particularly attractive for insurance companies.

Secondly, the fact that the total capital requirement must be computed as the sum of the capital requirements for each of the business lines lends itself to criticism. Indeed, this rule (which applies to the standardized approach and, in the absence of rigorous, reliable estimates, also to the advanced approaches) eliminates any incentive to diversification. In the absence of correlation estimates, it would probably be more proper to compute the total capital requirement assuming that the various business lines are independent, rather than perfectly correlated.

21.4   FINAL REMARKS

The introduction of a capital requirement on OR represented an important, and in many respects appreciable, innovation. In fact, it marked a welcome effort, to make the range of risks covered by regulatory capital broader in scope and more precise, by narrowing the gap between banks' internal risk measures and those used by the authorities to calibrate the minimum capital requirements.

We have seen, however, that the solutions adopted in 2004 lend themselves to numerous criticisms and probably represent only a first step on the road to correct measurement of operational risks. It is therefore important that the capital requirements dictated by the Basel Committee, and particularly the simplified solutions offered by the basic indicator and standardized approaches, do not hamper the fine-tuning and calibration of adequate internal models for measuring and managing OR. From this standpoint, the fact that the 2004 agreement favors the advanced methods is particular valuable. The Basel Committee, in fact, has asked banks to gradually shift toward this methodology and has established that it will not be possible for authorized banks that adopt the advanced approaches to revert to the simpler ones. Furthermore, precisely to favor the adoption of the advanced approaches, the 2004 Accord established that they could also be adopted for just one or more business lines.

In fact, only through an internal model can operational risk be measured and managed in a "virtuous" manner. One key goal of any OR management system, in fact, should be to measure the actual capital absorption related to each individual business unit (including also capital absorbed by OR) and to estimate the actual risk-adjusted profitability of those units (i.e. their Raroc). This mechanism would provide an incentive to the managers responsible for the individual business units to reduce the OR they generate and to develop an adequate control policy, by actively supporting the work of the central offices (such as internal audit). Generally speaking, controls would not represent a sunk cost but an investment, capable of increasing the risk-adjusted profitability of a business unit whenever the cost of those controls is lower than the opportunity-cost of the capital freed up by the reduction in operational risk.

SELECTED QUESTIONS AND EXERCISES

1. During the latest three years, a bank has recorded a gross operating income of 13, −10, 10 million euros respectively (where -10 denotes a loss of 10 million euros).

According to the basic indicator approach and assuming alpha is 15%, the capital requirement against operational risk will amount to:

(A) 1,500,000 euros;
(B) 650,000 euros;
(C) 1,150,000 euros;
(D) 1,725,000 euros.

2. The Table below reports the last three figures for the gross operating income (GOI) of banks Alpha and Beta, expressed in million euros.

	Beta	Alpha
$t-3$	10	15
$t-2$	10	10
$t-1$	10	5

   Both banks are using the basic indicator approach for the computation of the capital requirement against operational risk. Do you think that the capital charge for bank Alpha should be:

(A) ... higher than for bank Beta, since the GOI is more volatile;
(B) ... lower than for bank Beta, since the GOI is decreasing over the years;
(C) ... equal to that of bank Beta, since the three-year average of GOI is the same;
(D) ... lower than for bank Beta, because the GOI for last year is lower.

3. The table below reports the gross operating income in million euros, for all the business lines of a bank, over the last three years. Compute the bank's capital charge against operational risk under both the basic indicator and the standardised approach. Carefully explain all the causes underlying the difference between the two results.

	Gross Operating Income		
Business line	$t-3$	$t-2$	$t-1$
Corporate finance	40	30	40
Trading and sales	100	-120	60
Retail banking	40	40	40
Payments and settlements	20	25	30
Asset management	30	5	20
Bank	230	-20	190

4. Bank Soandso, a medium-sized institution operating mainly in the corporate finance, trading and settlement businesses, is contemplating ways of reducing its capital requirement for operational risk, which is currently being computed according to the basic indicator approach. Consider the following alternatives:

   I. cut business and reduce gross operating income;
  II. switch to the standardised approach;
 III. switch to advanced approaches;
  IV. cut the trading and settlement business and increase retail banking and asset management services, while leaving total GOI unchanged.

   Which alternatives, if any, will surely NOT help Bank Soandso to reduce its capital charge?

   (A) None of them;
   (B) All of them;
   (C) II and IV;
   (D) I and III.

5. Capital requirements against operational risk have been fiercely criticized because:

   (A) they cover only the systematic part of operational risk, while it is mainly idiosyncratic in nature;
   (B) they cover a risk, operational risk, which is mainly idiosyncratic in nature and hence poses no threat to the system's stability;
   (C) they do not help prevent systemic operational risks, such as the spread of fraud across multiple banks due to "contagion effects";
   (D) they do not cover typical systemic risks, like strategic and reputational risk, hence leaving the financial system exposed to possible systemic crises.

Part VI

Capital Management and Value Creation

INTRODUCTION TO PART VI

In the previous chapters we described how financial intermediaries face a number of risks (interest rate, market, credit, and operational risks, just to mention the most important ones). Such risk taking activity, when carefully measured and managed, generates profits. On the other hand, in order to perform such activity, several production factors are necessary: human resources, investments, technology, and above all an adequate capital endowment, allowing the bank to absorb any possible loss.

In a way, the capital provided by a bank's shareholders is the core element in this architecture: on the one hand, it allows to take risks, and on the other hand, it requires that such risks produce an appropriate remuneration.

Capital is an expensive (because it requires a risk premium above the cost of borrowing) and often scarce resource (because the shareholders' financial resources are limited). It is thus necessary that capital be managed efficiently and allocated in an objective and transparent manner among the different business units of the bank, so as to be able to measure and maximize the profit flow generated against a given amount of risk. In other words, because a financial institution has a limited risk-taking capacity, it must carefully size its capital endowment and thus select the business areas that are most likely to generate the highest remuneration.

It is therefore necessary to link capital management to value creation, while accurately and promptly monitoring costs (in terms of capital absorbed by potential losses) and benefits (in terms of net profit) generated by the different types of risk.

To this end, the management should establish the amount and type of risks that the bank is willing to take, collect enough capital resources to cover such risks, agree with the shareholders on a capital remuneration target in line with the risk borne by the bank, and allocate capital to the business units that are in a position to produce the desired profit flow. This process does not occur once and for all, but requires a continuous adjustment. More specifically, the business areas that cannot reach the profitability target agreed upon with the shareholders should be analyzed, restructured, and eventually abandoned.

A similar risk quantification, capital management and allocation, and performance measurement process cannot be simply considered as a numeric exercise to be entrusted to risk management experts. It is rather the core element of a bank's entrepreneurial strategy.

The theory of contestable markets suggests that only companies enjoying a "comparative advantage" can – over time – earn higher returns than those consistent with the degree of risk they undertake. Thus, capital management and allocation call for an identification of those business areas in which the bank has a competitive advantage and can therefore generate higher returns than those produced by its competitors as a whole.

The capital management process implies making strategic, operational, and financial decisions. For instance, if the bank were to identify an amount of capital in excess back of the existing risks (thus finding that the capital provided by the shareholders is higher than the one required by its activities), it might expand the most profitable business units or, if the supervisory authorities and the rating agencies so allow, "return" the capital in excess to the shareholders by paying extraordinary dividends or buying back some company's shares, thus changing its financial structure.

Moreover, given the amount of capital that is necessary to tackle risks (economic capital) and to comply with the supervisors' requirements (regulatory capital), the goal of value creation can be pursued also by optimizing the composition of the capital collected by the bank so as to minimize its average unit cost. To this purpose, in addition to the "core" shareholders' capital, all the types of innovative and hybrid capital instruments are to be used (e.g. preferred shares, perpetual subordinated loans, contingent capital) that are available in the financial markets.

The above-mentioned capital management process, although simple and attractive from a conceptual viewpoint, is very complex in terms of implementation. Indeed, in order for it to work, it is necessary to set up data, processes and instruments allowing to answer the following questions:

1. *Risk measurement and capital sizing*: "How much capital is necessary to bear the overall risk taken by a financial institution?" – "How does regulation affect the capital sizing process?"
2. *Optimization of the capital structure*: "How should the different types of capital instruments be combined in order to obtain an efficient and not too expensive capital endowment?"
3. *Capital allocation*: "How should the capital estimated as provided under point 1 and collected as provided under point 2 be allocated among the various divisions/businesses of a financial institution? How should consistent methodological criteria be established so that they apply to the different types of risks undertaken and to the various divisions/companies of a banking group?"
4. *Compliance with exogenous constraints*: "How should the capital management and allocation process be matched with the minimum capital requirements imposed by supervisory authorities?"
5. *Negotiation and communication with the market*: "Which profitability target should be agreed upon with the shareholders? How can a bank persuade the market and analysts that its value creation policy is a reliable one, thus avoiding dangerous discrepancies between the value created by the bank and the value perceived by investors?"

In order to find a solution to similar issues, different corporate responsibility centers should be involved – in a delicate balance – in the process of capital management and shareholders' value creation (see Figure 1).

The bank's *risk management* function measures the extent, type, and sources of the risks that are presently borne by the bank, producing timely and updated reports for the management of the different business units and for the top management. It also suggests risk optimization and diversification policies based, for instance, on the use of long and short positions on derivative contracts, or on the sale or purchase of credit exposures.

The *top management*, depending on the market opportunities (for instance, possible acquisitions, launch of new product companies, etc.) and on the risk levels that are deemed to be sustainable, designs an overall strategy aimed at maximizing the financial institution's capital profitability. To do this, it analyzes expectations concerning the growth rates of the individual businesses (commercial banking, investment banking, asset management, etc.), of the various customer segments (retail, corporate, institutional, etc.), and of the different geographical areas where the group operates. It also takes into account any available capital in excess and the propensity of the majority shareholders and of the market to allow for possible capital increases (endogenous constraints), as well as the requirements (exogenous constraints) posed by supervisory authorities.

The treasury department plans the funding necessary to pursue the growth targets, optimizing the bank's financial structure with a view to minimizing the cost of capital. As will be described later on, while for non-financial companies optimizing the capital structure mainly involves selecting the appropriate leverage, for a bank the issue involves optimizing the composition of its equity capital and of the regulatory capital required by supervisory authorities. A bank's capital needs can also be reduced by resorting to financial and credit derivatives, securitizations, loan sales (see Chapter 15) and contingent capital (see Chapter 22).

The planning department defines budgets for each individual business unit in line with the targets established by the senior management. In doing this, it also takes into account the amount of risks taken by the individual units and how such risks might be affected by the policies designed by the top management. To this purpose and with the support of the risk management function, it allocates the capital collected by the treasury department to the different business units, taking into consideration – if necessary – the contribution of the individual business areas to risk diversification, and calculates their risk-adjusted performance.

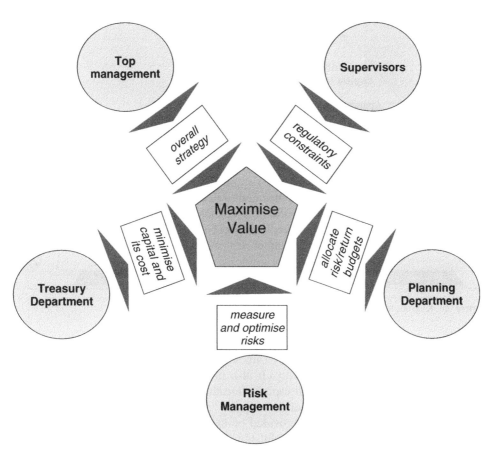

Figure 1   How different subjects interact in the value-creation process

This final section of the book (see Figure 2) is devoted to analyzing the above-mentioned activities and issues. It is worth pointing out that these are relatively recent issues that still lack a single, generally accepted conceptual framework and for which the individual financial institutions around the world are implementing different solutions. Therefore, while the risk measurement and management methods illustrated in the previous chapters are relatively consolidated and generally independent of the individual characteristics of each bank, the concepts and methodologies used in the capital management and allocation process are largely affected by institutional, market, and organizational factors.

After a brief introduction on the various definitions of capital, Chapter 22 dwells on the issues relating to the calculation of the total amount of capital required by a bank and to the definition of its optimal composition.

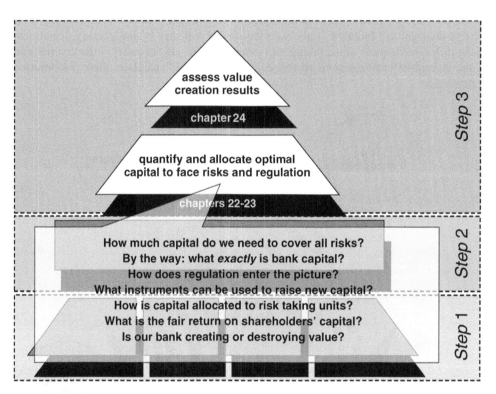

Figure 2   Key questions addressed in this Part of the book

Chapter 23 is devoted to the capital allocation process. It specifically deals with the criteria that should guide capital allocation among individual business units and the assessment of their risk-adjusted profitability. It also investigates some organizational issues relating to the risk management and capital allocation process in general.

Chapter 24 focuses on the issue of defining the "right" capital profitability target for a bank, that is the cost of the capital provided by the shareholders. Once this target return is defined, it plays a crucial role in establishing the ability of a bank to create value for its shareholders. Indeed, various value-creation metrics can be implemented, like EVA o or the Raroc measures already mentioned in Chapter 15, through which risk-adjusted profitability can be assessed under both a short-term and a long-term perspective.

22
Capital Management

22.1 INTRODUCTION

The management of a financial institution's capital has two primary purposes:

(i) to ensure that the available capital base is in line with the overall level of risk being undertaken, as well as with the exogenous constraints imposed by capital requirements, by the rating that the institution wishes to achieve, and by its development plans; and

(ii) to optimize the composition of capital by selecting the combination of financial instruments that minimize, subject to the limits set by the supervisory authorities, the cost of capital.

Generally speaking, the two functions discussed above are carried out by the bank's chief financial officer or treasurer.[1] These functions imply the planning and implementation of extraordinary financing transactions (capital increases, issues of hybrid securities, etc.) and therefore require sufficient familiarity with the capital markets and a constant focus on their current conditions.

They are activities that take place prior to the process of allocating capital to a bank's various units (see Chapter 23), by which the bank's overall risk taking capacity is "virtually" allocated to the various business units in order to maximize profitability.

In other words, while capital allocation (next chapter) concerns the "ideal" management of capital, i.e. its figurative allocation to the various business units, favoring those that are able to provide a higher risk-adjusted profitability, capital management (this chapter) involves the actual "physical" management of a bank's capital base.

In section 22.2, we will first take a brief look at the alternative definitions of capital before turning to a more detailed discussion of how to determine the "optimal" amount of capital, which in turn determines the bank's risk-taking capacity. A special emphasis will be placed on the effect of the exogenous limits imposed by capital regulation, as well as on how these limits impact on the interest rates charged by the bank and on the risk-adjusted performance of its loans. We will then turn to capital quality, i.e. its composition. More specifically, in section 22.3, we will analyze the problem of determining the optimal capital mix by illustrating the technical features of the main financial instruments that can be computed as regulatory capital and their use by the leading international banks. In section 22.4, we will then focus on innovative forms of capital, such as *insurance capital* and *contingent capital*, which are not allowed (except to a very limited extent) among the instruments considered for regulatory capital, but which are, nonetheless, able to meet a portion of a bank's capital need and do not require any funding.

---

[1] In certain companies, some of these tasks are given to the Asset & Liability Committee (ALCO) or to special-purpose units responsible for capital management and for optimizing regulatory capital.

22.2 DEFINING AND MEASURING CAPITAL

22.2.1 The definition of capital

The determination of a bank's optimal capital has been the subject of many studies and remains today an issue on which academics, bankers, and regulators have differing views. Before looking at the factors that determine the "optimal" capital of a given bank, we must first clarify what we mean by "capital". Indeed, a variety of definitions can be found. These include:

- *Regulatory capital (RC)*: i.e. the set of capital instruments that can be computed for regulatory purposes. It is composed primarily of two categories (see Chapter 18): *Tier 1 capital* (T1), also known as *core capital*, which is composed primarily of share capital, retained earnings, general risk reserves, other explicit reserves, and certain innovative instruments such as preference shares; and *supplementary capital*, which is, in turn, composed of *Tier 2 capital* (T2) – revaluation reserves, medium and long-term subordinated debt, and other hybrid instruments – and *Tier 3 capital* (T3), i.e. short-term subordinated debt considered solely for the purposes of market risk capital requirements. Below, we will be using RC, T1, T2 and T3 to indicate a bank's actual regulatory capital levels, while RC* and T1* will be used to indicate the minimum levels (of total capital and tier 1, respectively) that a bank is required to maintain given its risk weighted assets.[2]
- *Book-value capital (BVC)*: this is based on the accounting standards used for financial reporting purposes and is equivalent to the difference between the bank's assets and liabilities as they appear on the balance sheet. To some extent, this is similar to Tier 1 capital for regulatory purposes. Indeed, it does not include items such as subordinated debt, which are a part of Tier 2 and Tier 3 capital as they imply fixed interest payments and/or redemption upon maturity.
- *Fair-value capital (FVC)*: i.e. the fair value of the bank's assets minus the fair value of its liabilities. This differs from book-value capital in that the assets and liabilities are not taken at the value at which they were entered into the bank's books (which may be the historic cost and therefore represent an outdated, meaningless value), but at a value in line with current market conditions. Book-value capital and fair-value capital would only be the same if the banks accounts were kept on a fair-value basis (see Chapter 2). The fair value of assets and liabilities is equal to the present value of the cash flows that they will generate in the future. As such, it includes intangible assets, such as trademarks, patents, and goodwill, which, despite being intangible, have the capacity for generating greater future revenues.[3] This, then, represents a further difference from book-value capital, which normally only includes goodwill if it has been recognized on the balance sheet as a result of extraordinary transactions (typically acquisitions).
- *Market capitalization (MC)*: i.e. the market value of an individual stock multiplied by the number of shares outstanding (including any preference shares and the like). It can only be calculated for banks that are publicly listed. It corresponds to the present

---

[2] Core capital (see Chapter 18) must account for at least 50 % of the total capital. Conversely, there is no minimum requirement for supplementary capital.

[3] For example, the present value of fees to be received on advisory or asset management services that the bank will be able to sell thanks to its reputation or to customer loyalty.

value of the cash flows that shareholders will receive in the future (dividends and any value received upon divestment), discounted at an appropriate risk-adjusted rate. If the market is efficient, the information available is complete, and investors are rational, this value will coincide with fair-market capital. However, it is not uncommon for the market not to have all information needed in order to value a bank's assets, liabilities and net worth; furthermore, investors' valuations are often affected by overall upward and downward trends in the market as a whole (e.g. buying at a high price on the belief that the stock will rise even further). For this reason, market capitalization does not normally coincide with fair-value capital, but rather with the *perceived* fair value as seen by equity investors in a given market context.

– *Economic capital (EC)*: i.e. the amount of capital needed to "reasonably" cover the risks being faced by a bank. As we have seen in previous Parts of this book, this is also known as capital at risk (CaR), and can be measured using the concept of value at risk (VaR),[4] i.e. as the maximum loss to be expected, within a sufficiently wide confidence interval, over a given period of time. In previous chapters, we have looked at methods (parametric models, simulation models, etc) of calculating the capital at risk associated with individual portfolios of activities (e.g. a trading portfolio) or individual risk factors (e.g. credit risk). Here, we will use economic capital and capital at risk to mean the capital needed to face *all* risks that, as a whole, impact upon the entire bank.[5] Notice that, while the other definitions of capital surveyed above provide a snapshot, from various angles, of the amount of capital actually *available* to a bank (i.e. available capital, or AC), economic capital measures the capital *needed* or *desirable* given the current risks.

These various definitions of capital serve a variety of purposes: to protect a bank's creditors (particularly private investors), thereby ensuring stability for the financial system as a whole (RC); to express the financial value of the bank as a business in a sufficiently accurate, but also prudent and objective, manner (BVC); to measure the fair value of the investment made by shareholders (FVC); to calculate the value that the market assigns to the bank based on market estimates of future earnings (MC); and to assess the overall risk being faced (EC).

There are also a number of relationships among the various definitions of capital, that a bank must, or at least should, respect (see Figure 22.1). First of all, the available regulatory

---

[4] VaR is here considered as a synonymous with capital at risk or economic capital. However, there are other methods for calculating capital at risk, such as the one proposed by Merton & Perold, who define it as "the smallest amount that can be invested to insure the value of the firm's net assets against a loss in value relative to the risk-free investment of those net assets". This is the cost of a put option which depends on the spread paid on the various classes of liabilities; in other words, "risk capital is implicitly or explicitly used to purchase insurance from a variety of potential providers. [...] The economic cost of risk capital to the firm is thus the spread it pays in the purchase of this insurance" (Merton & Perold, 1993). As interesting as this is from a theoretical point of view, the method proposed presents a number of problems in its actual application. First, it implies the existence of efficient markets for the various sources of funds of a financial intermediary, given that it assumes that the pricing of the various liabilities adequately reflects the bank's level of risk, i.e. the volatility of the cash flows associated with its operations. Second, even if we assume that the market players were rational and informed, it would be difficult to calculate the spread of the various classes of liabilities in a sufficiently timely manner, given that many of these liabilities lack an appropriate liquid secondary market (take, for example, certificates of deposit for private customers) and are, therefore, unable to reflect the changes in the bank's risk profile – and in its risk capital – in a timely manner (both of which are altered continuously by the bank's trading activities, its lending activities, and so on).

[5] See also section 2.3 below.

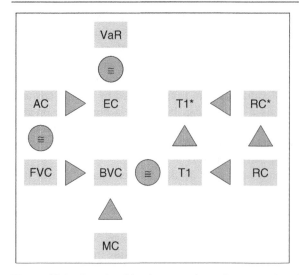
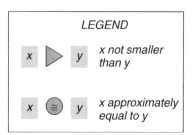

Figure 22.1   Relationships between the main types of capital

capital (RC and T1) must be greater than the minimum set by regulators (RC* and T1*):

$$RC \geq RC^* \tag{22.1}$$

$$T1 \geq T1^* \tag{22.2}$$

Secondly, economic capital (EC) should be covered in its entirety by the bank's available capital (AC):

$$AC \geq EC \tag{22.3}$$

We will be returning to this relationship below, but first we must have a clear understanding as to which measure of available capital of those presented above is the most appropriate: RC, BVC, FVC, or MC?

Regulatory capital (RC) would appear to be relatively inadequate, given that it also includes debt securities (i.e. subordinated debt, which takes a lower priority than other liabilities and therefore, as with shareholders' equity, is a sort of cushion at the expense of which repayment to the bank's other creditors is guaranteed). As such, it does not measure the true net worth of the bank.

Book-value capital (BVC) is clearly an inadequate measure of the net worth of the shareholders' investment (and, therefore, of the bank's risk taking capacity), given that it is based on outdated information (particularly when assets are reported at their historical cost). This explains why financial institutions that go bankrupt or are placed under receivership often show positive book-value capital until shortly prior to going bankrupt (the most striking example being perhaps the infamous savings and loan crisis in the US).

Market capitalization (MC) presents a number of defects. First of all, it can only truly be used when the financial institution is publicly listed. Secondly, it can be biased (either upwards or downwards) in connection with the movements of the market as a whole. On the other hand, it is an objective value that encapsulates the views of a multitude of committed investors (in that they risk their own capital when they trade in the bank's stock) that are sufficiently informed (in particular, large-scale investors, the investments of which influence the market price, normally act in response to analyses conducted by expert analysts).

For a variety of reasons, fair-value capital (FVC) is an ideal metric because it expresses the true economic value of the shareholders' investment. However, it is not without its own defects. Firstly, precisely because it is an "ideal" metric, it may be hard to turn it into practice: when a fair value must be attributed to each and every asset and liability, this requires a number of estimates and assumptions that are, at least in part, fairly arbitrary. Secondly, being a present value, it should be constantly recalculated, or at least recalculated each time that the bank's portfolio of assets and liabilities undergoes a significant change. Thirdly, it represents the value of the bank as a going concern. The liquidation value of the bank, which is available to cover losses in the event the bank should cease operations, may actually be lower, given that certain assets (e.g. certain components of goodwill, such as reputation and customer relationships) may not be easily and fully transferable to others. Despite these defects, it would appear that fair-value capital is, at least theoretically, the most appropriate measure of AC. Relationship (22.3) therefore becomes:

$$FVC \geq EC \qquad (22.3b)$$

It is also reasonable for the fair-value capital of a sound financial institution to be greater than book-value capital, given that its assets will have appreciated over time more than the accounting figures show, so:

$$FVC > BVC \qquad (22.4)$$

In the case of a publicly listed bank, this means that market value (or MC) will normally be larger than book value. In other words, the price-to-book ratio will be greater than 1:

$$MC > BVC \qquad (22.5)$$

However, it is more difficult to establish a relationship between a bank's fair value (FVC) and the value perceived by the stock market (MC). In periods of rapid growth in stock prices, it is possible to have $MC > FVC$, i.e. that investors will tend to attribute a higher value to the bank than its actual intrinsic value. The opposite may be true in phases of falling prices or market panic, when the fear of further price drops may lead investors to sell a bank's shares at a price that is lower than the security's fair value, because they believe that it will then be possible to buy them back at a lower price.

22.2.2   The relationship between economic capital and available capital

Equation (22.3) shows the relationship between the risk-taking capacity and the actual risk being faced. Note that, in real life, three possible situations may occur:

– AC > EC: in this case, available capital is not fully used. There are two alternative ways to address such an unbalance : (i) take on additional risks by increasing the bank's portfolio of assets; in this case the new assets must be selected in such a way as to remunerate the economic capital absorbed by the new risks at a rate that is consistent with the target return agreed upon with the bank's shareholders; or (ii) return the excess

capital to the bank's shareholders in the form of extraordinary dividends or through shares buy-back.
- AC < EC: when the risks taken on are greater than the available capital. There, it is necessary to raise new capital or reduce risk (e.g. through credit derivatives or by selling assets), and in doing so it would be best to eliminate those positions that provide the lowest return on the absorbed capital.
- AC = EC: this is the "best-case" scenario, where a financial institution's risk-taking capacity is fully used. However, such a "perfect balance" may make the bank too inflexible in taking on new risk (given that it would be necessary to increase available capital at the same time). Therefore, it may be acceptable to maintain a stable excess of available capital over economic capital (AC − EC > 0), so as to make the bank's operations more fluid.

Comparing available and economic capital is certainly attractive, both theoretically and in practice, due to its simplicity. However, it does present two problems. First, the estimate of economic capital produced by the bank could be inaccurate. In previous chapters, when discussing market risk, credit risk, and operational risk, we have met many problems that affect the estimates of VaR (e.g. unrealistic assumptions, such as the normal distribution of market factors' returns or the stability of the variance-covariance matrix; difficulties in estimating parameters such as asset and default correlations; a lack of data on infrequent, high-impact operational risk losses; and so on), and we have also seen how various working assumptions can lead to different values for VaR. Such issues become particularly significant when we attempt to integrate a variety of risks and to produce a measure of risk which, rather than being limited to specific portfolios, encompasses the entire range of activities being performed by a financial group (which may operate in different markets, such as lending and insurance or Europe and the US).[6]

A second problem is connected with exogenous factors that affect the bank. Indeed, equations (22.3) and (22.3b) ignore the existence of a minimum level of regulatory capital (see Figure 22.1). Can we really quantify capital (and allocate it to the various business units) if we ignore this constraint and focus solely on capital at risk as measured by internal models? Of course we cannot. Although one may recognize the limitations of the current schemes for computing capital requirements, or even question the appropriateness of using such schemes, there can be no doubt that they represent an unavoidable factor to be taken into account when determining a bank's optimal level of capital. Failure to observe minimum capital requirements can expose the bank to heavy sanctions by the supervisory authorities, and severely affect the bank's reputation in the marketplace. Therefore, a bank's capital must be adequate not only from an economic point of view, but also from a regulatory one.[7]

---

[6] Moreover, generally speaking, VaR models used to compute economic capital are usually calibrated under "normal" market conditions. Under abnormal market conditions, i.e. given particularly accentuated crises, the underlying assumptions of these models and the calculation of the parameters used to feed them could be unrealistic. Nonetheless, it is precisely these circumstances that must be taken into account when assessing a bank's overall level of capital.

[7] A second external constraint, for rated banks, comes in the form of ratings, as the agencies only assign an investment-grade rating to banks with a certain minimum level of tier 1 capital. A rating downgrade could result in an increase in the cost of debt and a loss of reputation in the capital markets. Therefore, it may also be appropriate to calibrate the available capital so that it meets the standards adopted by these agencies.

The two problems mentioned above (the complexity of economic capital computation and the role of regulatory constraints) will now be discussed thoroughly in the following two sections.

22.2.3   Calculating a bank's economic capital

As we have seen, banks normally have partial measures of risk for the various types of risk that characterize their assets. In order to calculate a bank's total economic capital, these partial measures must be:

- completed, in order to ensure that all of the main risk factors and all of the most important business units (even those that are set up as autonomous companies) are included in, or "mapped" by, the risk measurement system;
- rescaled, so that the partial VaRs become compatible, particularly in terms of the confidence level and time horizon;
- aggregated, taking account of any potential benefits of diversification connected with the imperfect correlation among the various risks.

With regard to the first issue, some banks have risk measurement systems that only cover certain types of risk and only for a limited portion of their portfolios. Indeed, while market risk on trading portfolios and credit risk on securities and loans have, for years, been the target of high levels of investment, which have led to models that are now fairly extensive and reliable, other risk factors (e.g. operational risk, interest rate risk on the banking book, and liquidity risk) have long been overlooked. Therefore, it may be necessary to use simplified, unsophisticated risk measures based more on common sense than on objective data. Furthermore, it is possible that certain companies within a financial group do not have sufficiently formalized models of risk management and measurement. This is particularly true for financial institutions that have been involved in mergers or acquisitions: in these cases, it is necessary to "export" and adapt the risk management systems of the parent company, while taking care to integrate the particular characteristics of the market in which the individual subsidiaries operate. This calibration process may be difficult and, to some extent, arbitrary when there is a lack of data for the purposes of robust risk estimates.

Also, rescaling the confidence level and the time horizons of the various models is no easy task. Take, for example, the case of VaR on market risk, which is normally computed over a time horizon of 10 business days with a 99 % confidence level (for banks that follow the Basel Committee's recommendations), and imagine having to align this VaR with that of credit risk, which is measured over a one-year time horizon with a 99.9 % confidence level. This is only relatively easy (see Table 22.1) when VaR is estimated using a parametric approach (see Chapter 5). In this case:

- the confidence level may be changed by simply multiplying the 99 % VaR by a scaling factor equal to the ratio, $\alpha_{99.9\%}/\alpha_{99\%}$, of two percentiles of the standard normal distribution. Specifically, given that $\alpha_{99\%} \simeq 2.33$ and $\alpha_{99.9\%} \simeq 3.09$, the 99.9 % VaR will be roughly 1.3 times that of the 99 % confidence level.
- the time horizon may be calibrated by multiplying VaR by a factor equal to the square root of time (see section 2.3 of Chapter 5). In our example, if we assume that one year is made up of 250 business days, and therefore 25 ten-day periods, this factor will be

5. Note, however, that this only works if the changes of the risk factors are serially independent. If movements in the market factors were somehow "persistent", such that the result of one 10-day period influences that of the following period, this rule would underestimate the VaR.

Table 22.1 Example of VaR rescaling for a 10-day, 99 %-confidence VaR of 100 euros.

		Time horizon	
		10 days	250 days
Confidence	99 % (2.33)	100.0	500.0
level and α	99.90 % (3.09)	132.8	664.2

If, on the other hand, VaR is not based on a parametric approach, rescaling the time horizon and confidence level becomes more complicated, and may require that changes be made to the risk-measurement models. More specifically, the shift to a longer time horizon may require additional data, which may not always be available. For this reason, some financial institutions use the "square root of time" rule, even when the conditions for its use are not entirely met, and then adjust the result upward in a subjective, arbitrary manner in order to compensate for any errors.

The third issue mentioned above (i.e. the aggregation of different business units and risk measures) is the most complex one. First, there is no one-to-one relationship between business units and risk types (i.e. "one risk, one owner"), as a given unit (whether it be a company division or a standalone firm) normally faces multiple types of risk (see Figure 22.2). It is therefore necessary to decide whether to first aggregate business units and then risks (i.e. "by rows") or the other way around (i.e. "by columns"). The latter is the most transparent approach, in the sense that it provides a picture of the vulnerability of the various risk factors for the entire financial group; however, it requires the information

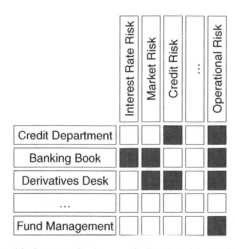

Figure 22.2   The relationship between business units/legal entities and risk types

systems of the various units to be able to feed a common database for each type of risk (e.g. a central file of all loan positions or all positions denominated in yen), and this may be difficult if the business units are separate legal entities potentially located in different countries.

Furthermore, in order to aggregate different types of risk, a sufficient knowledge must be gained of the structure of the various correlations. If risks are highly correlated (e.g. if higher losses from market risk tend to arise when the bank is suffering the greatest credit losses), then the bank must be prepared to face extreme losses connected with these different risks *jointly*. This means that total economic capital will simply be the sum of the economic capital related to each individual risk. Note that a similar approach, although it may look too extreme or simplistic, was basically adopted by the 2004 Basel Accord (see Chapter 20), which calls for the capital for each of the various risks to simply be summed (see Figure 22.3).

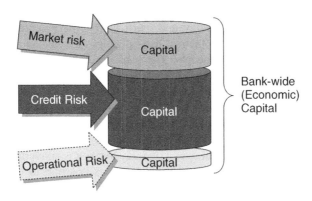

Figure 22.3   Risk aggregation according to the Basel Accord

However, the correlation between the various risk types is likely not to be perfect, and it is reasonable to assume that a certain diversification effect exists. Quantifying this effect can be very difficult: according to a study of the Joint Forum established under the aegis of the Basel Committee,[8] many banks handle the matter by simply assuming that the economic capital for the various risks is proportionate to the respective standard deviations (which can be adjusted to take account of leptokurtosis[9]) and hence using, for economic capital, the formula for the standard deviation of the sum of multiple random variables:

$$EC = \sqrt{\sum_{i=1}^{n}\sum_{j=1}^{n} \rho_{ij} EC_i EC_j} \tag{22.6}$$

where EC_i is the economic capital related to a certain type of risk, n is the number of types of risk considered, and ρ_{ij} indicates the correlation between the ith and j^{th} risk ($\rho = 1$ if $i = j$).

The results generated by (22.6) are clearly deeply affected by the values of the ρs. Their estimation is, therefore, crucial to the results of this standard statistical approach.

---

[8] Basel Committee on Banking Supervision 2003c.
[9] See Oliver, Wyman and Co. (2001), Appendix B in particular.

Such estimation may be based on historical data related to the losses associated with different types of risk (this requires the availability of detailed information over a long period of time); alternatively, it is possible to associate each type of risk to a proxy variable (e.g. a stock market index in the case of market risk or historical default rates in the case of credit risk) and then determine the correlations between risk factors based on the correlations between these proxies. Also, it is not uncommon for correlations to be established arbitrarily based on the experience of senior management and of the risk management unit.

A simplified hypothetical example of calculating economic capital, taken from the aforementioned Joint Forum study, is provided in Box 22.1. This example demonstrates the practical use of the rules for adjusting the time horizon and confidence level, as well as for aggregating capital for the various types of risk, presented in this section.

Box 22.1: A hypothetical example

To illustrate the general methodology and, particularly, the potential diversification benefits, let us assume that a hypothetical bank decides to create an economic capital model based on the following concepts. The bank separately estimates its economic capital requirements for its market, credit and operational risks. Because it wishes to earn a "AA" rating from the external credit rating agencies, the bank chooses a common one-year time horizon and the 99.97 percent level of confidence.

The firm calculates its VaR for market risk every business day. Its trading department uses an analytical model to estimate VaR over a one-day horizon at a 99 % confidence level. The amount of capital needed over a one-day horizon is converted to that needed over a full year by using a multiplicative factor. It is possible to convert the 99 % confidence level to 99.97 % by using another multiplicative factor. Using these factors introduces assumptions that may or may not correspond to actual experience. For example, use of the time conversion factor, with no adjustments, implies that no account will be taken of any optionality effects. Also, the selection of a 99.97 % confidence level means that a loss greater than the estimated amount would occur 0.03 % of the time, or once in 3,333 years. The reliability of the resulting estimate would obviously be difficult to verify empirically. For simplicity, let us assume that the bank's estimate of economic capital for market risk incorporates all interest rate or asset/liability risk. Moreover, as this estimate is derived from a VaR framework, it will implicitly take into account diversification effects across all of the major types of market risk factors, including interest rates, foreign exchange rates, equity prices, etc. Assume that the net result is a market risk economic capital estimate of $ 1 billion.

Next, assume that the bank has developed a statistical model for credit risk. This model is built around internal ratings of the bank's borrowers that provide estimates of the likelihood that the borrowers will default, how much the bank can recover in the event of default, and the likelihood that lines of credit will be drawn down in the event of default. Further, the model incorporates assumptions on the inter-relationships between variables. For example, the model calculates the correlation between default rates for loans to various commercial sectors. The bank is likely to have one methodology for its larger commercial loans and a different methodology for its retail credits. In general, a bank may have any number of methodologies for numerous loan segments. If lending areas are modelled separately, then the amount of economic capital estimated for each area need to be combined. In making the combination, the bank either implicitly or explicitly incorporates various correlation assumptions. Assume that the bank's total estimate of economic capital for credit risk is $3 billion.

Finally, assume that the bank has developed an estimate of economic capital for operational risk by considering the frequency of large losses for firms active in similar businesses, with some allowance for differences in management controls and procedures. This estimate of economic capital for operational risk is $2 billion.

Now that the bank has estimated the economic capital needed for each of market, credit and operational risks, the separate requirements must be combined into a total figure. The hypothetical bank uses the standard statistical approach to aggregating these figures on the basis of correlation assumptions. We now consider the effect of various correlation assumptions.

In one scenario, the bank assumes conservatively that its market, credit and operational risks are perfectly correlated. If it needs $1 billion in economic capital for market risk, $3 billion for credit risk, and $2 billion for operational risk, then its total economic capital requirement is the sum of these, or $6 billion. Alternatively, the bank might assume that the three risks are completely uncorrelated, so that the correlations between each pair of risks are zero. Under this assumption, the aggregate economic capital estimate is only $3.74 billion. This represents a decline of nearly 40% relative to the $6 billion estimate under the perfect correlation assumption. In a third scenario, the bank estimates a 0.8 correlation between market and credit risk, a 0.4 correlation between market and operational risk, and a 0.4 correlation between credit and operational risk. Under these assumptions, the bank estimates its total economic capital requirement as $5.02 billion. Thus, even with these higher correlation assumptions, the recognition of diversification benefits would result in a 16% capital saving – a significant sum. The example serves to illustrate the practical significance of the cross-risk correlation assumptions. This point is further reinforced by considering the differences in the calculated return on economic capital that would result from these different assumptions.

Source: Basel Committee on Banking Supervision, 2003c

22.2.4 The relationship between economic capital and regulatory capital

Let us return now to the second problem mentioned in section 22.2.2, namely the external constraint imposed by regulatory capital. Far from being merely theoretical, this constraint is often significant from a practical point of view. Many studies[10] have, in fact, shown that it is not uncommon for the capital amount required by the supervisory authorities, given a certain pool of risky assets, to be much higher than the economic capital derived by internal models.

This gap can be explained by the fact that internal models could use a lower confidence level than the one adopted (either explicitly or implicitly) by the supervisory authorities. Regulators are, in fact, interested in imposing sufficient capital to cover even extreme losses resulting from stress scenarios that could lead to systemic crises.

---

[10] See Arak (1992), pp. 25–36, Gumerlock (1993), pp. 86–91, Heldring (1995).

Internal models, on the other hand, seek to achieve a different goal, i.e. that of measuring potential losses (and, therefore, also the proper return for the risks of the bank and of its individual business units) under normal conditions. The differing perspectives of banks and regulators can also be explained by looking at the difference between "risk" and "uncertainty" as proposed in 1921 by Frank H. Knight.[11] According to Knight, risk is measurable in that statistical methods enable us to associate a probability to certain events. Uncertainty, on the other hand, is, by its very nature, something that cannot be measured. Banks focus on the former, while regulators need to take both into consideration. Therefore, minimum regulatory capital may be considered a measure of the capital needed to face even "extreme" market conditions that are not considered in the calculation of capital at risk.

Furthermore, it represents the minimum capital needed for a bank to do business, without incurring extensive costs both in terms of reputation (loss or credibility, increase in the cost of funds on wholesale markets, reduction in placing power on financial markets) and legal issues (sanctions, appointment of a special manager by the supervisors, and in principle even the loss of the bank's charter). In this sense, the cost of Tier 1 capital[12] "imposed" by regulators in excess of economic capital (i.e. the cost of T1* – EC) may be considered the "price to pay" in order for a bank to keep its charter and remain in business.

We must therefore consider regulatory capital as a floor below which, under normal conditions, a bank should not fall. As such, our analysis must be based on three different aggregates:

- the bank's Tier 1 capital (T1);
- the related minimum requirement (T1*);
- economic capital (EC), which represents the actual risk taken on by the bank.

A bank that wishes to minimize the risk of operating with capital levels that are below the minimum requirements must have Tier 1 capital equal to the minimum (T1*) plus the amount that could reasonably be lost given the existing risks:

$$T1 = T1^* + EC \qquad (22.7)$$

In this case, even if there should be a loss in the amount of EC, with a consequent reduction in capital, the amount of core capital available would remain sufficient to cover the minimum requirement T1*.

While capital levels such as the ones required by equation (22.7), which would be significantly higher than economic capital, would be well received by regulators, they would also be less than optimal for the bank's shareholders. Indeed, equation (22.7) requires the bank to hold capital in excess of the actual risks; in other words, it would force the bank to park in risk-free assets a portion of the capital provided by its shareholders.

---

[11] See Knight (1986), pp. 61–65.
[12] Supplementary capital is ignored, given that, despite being suited to the objectives of regulators (i.e. protecting depositors), it is primarily made up of debt capital and, as such, it cannot be considered to be an expression of a bank's risk-taking capacity.

Also, it is reasonable to assume that, in the event of exceptionally high losses, the bank could temporarily operate at a level of T1 that was below T1*, on the condition that its shareholders assure regulators that the balance between capital and risks will quickly be restored.[13] Therefore, a bank may decide to hold an amount of core capital equal to the minimum requirement plus a percentage q (less than 100 %) of economic capital:

$$T1 = T1^* + q \cdot EC \qquad (22.8)$$

The value of q will actually depend on the (more or less rigid) position taken by regulators and on the preferences of the bank's shareholders. If shareholders are willing to provide the bank with higher levels of capital (thereby accepting a reduction in leverage and in per-unit performance) in order to avoid the costs of an unexpected capital increase,[14] then q will be close to 100 % and equation (22.8) will tend towards equation (22.7). If, on the other hand, shareholders and regulators are willing to face the risks of having to unexpectedly turn to the equity markets to restore capital adequacy, then q can take on a lower value.

Note that, given equation (22.8), if the value of q is low enough and if EC is greater than T1*, then the actual level of Tier 1 capital (T1) could be less than capital at risk. One may then wonder whether this goes against equation (22.3), which requires available capital (AC) to be greater than economic capital. However, such a conflict is merely apparent. As we have seen, the best approximation of AC is fair-value capital, which is normally higher (see Figure 22.1), and sometimes much higher, than T1 capital.[15] Therefore, the stockmarket and equity analysts might accept a value of T1 that is less than EC if they feel that Tier 1 capital fails to represent the true value of the bank, which is deemed to be sufficient to respect equation (3b).[16]

An indirect proof of the validity of equation (22.8) can be seen in the empirical data regarding the capitalization of the world's leading banks. Figure 22.3 shows that, in all G10 countries, the level of capitalization of the leading banks is much higher than the minimum requirements of the 1988 Basel Accord (4 %), with the average Tier 1 ratio in the various countries – with the sole exception of Japan in 1995 and 1996 – remaining systematically above 5 %.

Figures on the individual banks provide similar indications. Figure 22.5 below shows the ratio of total regulatory capital (RC) to risk-weighted assets for a number of leading European banking groups. With a few exceptions, the majority of these groups have ratios that are significantly higher than the minimum requirement (i.e. RC*) of 8 %.

---

[13] By rapidly raising new capital, accepting a merger with a better capitalized bank, or selling some of its risky assets (loans, branches, equity investments, etc.). The path of disposals is often the one followed by banks experiencing a crisis as an alternative or in addition to raising new capital in order to restore its capital ratios. However, it is clear that selling assets during an emergency is not the way to obtain the best price and often results in further economic losses due to the difference between the true value of the assets being sold and the price actually obtained. Such losses are not recognized when accounting for assets at historical cost and are, therefore, often deemed acceptable by the management of banks in trouble.

[14] And the other costs specified in footnote 13 above.

[15] Note, too, that core capital is calculated based on accounting figures, which are, in turn, normally based on the historical cost of non-current assets (even in the event of revaluations, the related reserves are included among tier 2). Furthermore, it is, by definition, net of goodwill.

[16] If, on the other hand, the bank should feel it necessary, in order to reassure analysts and regulators, to fully cover economic capital with core capital, then equation (22.8) should be rewritten as $T1 = \max(EC, T1^* + q \cdot EC)$.

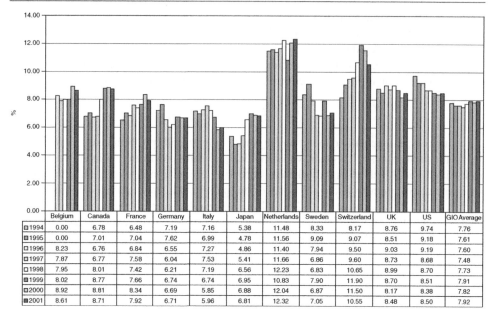

	Belgium	Canada	France	Germany	Italy	Japan	Netherlands	Sweden	Switzerland	UK	US	G10 Average
1994	0.00	6.78	6.48	7.19	7.16	5.38	11.48	8.33	8.17	8.76	9.74	7.76
1995	0.00	7.01	7.04	7.62	6.99	4.78	11.56	9.09	9.07	8.51	9.18	7.61
1996	8.23	6.76	6.84	6.55	7.27	4.86	11.40	7.94	9.50	9.03	9.19	7.60
1997	7.87	6.77	7.58	6.04	7.53	5.41	11.66	6.86	9.60	8.73	8.68	7.48
1998	7.95	8.01	7.42	6.21	7.19	6.56	12.23	6.83	10.65	8.99	8.70	7.73
1999	8.02	8.77	7.66	6.74	6.74	6.95	10.83	7.90	11.90	8.70	8.51	7.91
2000	8.92	8.81	8.34	6.69	5.85	6.88	12.04	6.87	11.50	8.17	8.38	7.82
2001	8.61	8.71	7.92	6.71	5.96	6.81	12.32	7.05	10.55	8.48	8.50	7.92

Figure 22.4   Tier 1 ratios of the G10's largest banks
Source: Ferrari (2002).

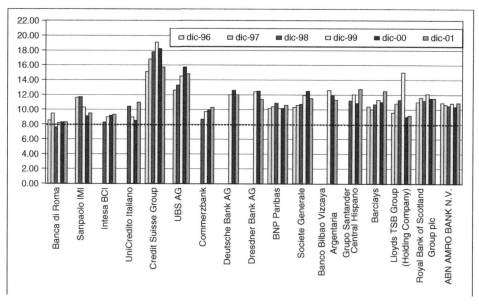

Figure 22.5   Capital ratios of a number of leading European banking groups
Source: Maino & Masera (2002).

22.2.5 The constraints imposed by regulatory capital: implications on pricing and performance measurement

Equations (22.7) and (22.8) have important implications on pricing and the performance of a bank's risky assets. Among assets, loans are likely to be the most important case.

In Chapter 15, loan pricing for a price-maker bank was described with the following equation:

$$r + d_{EL} + d_{UL} = \frac{r + ELR + VaR(r_e - r)}{1 - ELR} \tag{22.9}$$

where r was the risk-free rate, d_{EL} the expected loss spread, d_{UL} the unexpected loss spread, $r + d_{EL} + d_{UL}$ the rate on the loan, ELR the expected loss rate on the loan (equal to PD times LGD), VaR the value at risk for each euro lent, and r_e the cost of equity capital "agreed upon" by management and shareholders.

In that same chapter, Raroc for a loan granted at fixed rate $\bar{r}$ by a price-taker bank (expressed as a premium over the risk-free rate) was described with the following equation:

$$r_e^* - r = Raroc = \frac{\bar{r} \cdot (1 - ELR) - r - ELR}{VaR} \tag{22.10}$$

where r_e^* represents the return on capital as it was actually received by the shareholders.

Now we are able to make these two equations more realistic by taking into account the constraint placed on the bank by regulators. This constraint can be expressed in two ways:

– the first has been discussed at length in the previous section and is summarized in equations (22.7) and (22.8): the capital committed by the bank to cover the risks implicit in a loan is not given simply by VaR, or economic capital. Indeed, equations (22.7) and (22.8) demonstrate that the amount of tier 1 capital (i.e. share capital, reserves, and the like) that the bank must require from its shareholders to fund a loan is a function of both economic capital and the minimum level of regulatory capital. In the examples of this section, we will be using equation (22.8); to get equation (22.7) all we need to do is set $q = 1$;
– the second constraint concerns the cost of supplementary capital. Indeed, it is not necessary for a bank to cover all of its capital needs with core capital, in other words to impose that T1 = RC*. A portion of the total requirement (up to 50%) may be covered by supplementary capital. Specifically, given that tier 3 capital may only be used for the purposes of market risk, in the case of a loan, the difference between RC* and T1 may be covered by Tier 2 capital (T2); therefore, we have $T2 = RC^* - T1$ or, using equation (22.8), $T2 = RC^* - T1^* - q \cdot EC$. Tier 2 capital, given that is it made up primarily of subordinated debt,[17] has a higher cost than the senior debt of a bank. We can indicate this cost with r_j (the cost of junior debt), while using r_s (the cost of senior debt) to indicate the cost of normal financing raised by the bank on the wholesale market. While r_s for a highly rated bank can be approximated, as we have seen in Chapter 15, using the risk-free rate, the value of r_j will always be higher.

---

[17] We shall assume, for the sake of simplicity, that new tier 2 capital for the loan is made up entirely of subordinated (junior) debt and that its cost can therefore be approximated at the cost of this form of debt.

It will therefore be necessary to take this higher cost of funding into account when pricing the loan or determining its Raroc.

Based on these two observations, equation (22.9) should be rewritten as follows:

$$r + d_{EL} + d_{UL} = \frac{[r_s + (r_j - r_s)(\widehat{RC}^* - \widehat{T1}^* - q\widehat{EC})] + ELR + (\widehat{T1}^* + q\widehat{EC})(r_e - r_s)}{1 - ELR}$$

$$(22.11)$$

where $\widehat{RC}^*$ and $\widehat{T1}^*$ indicate the loan's total capital requirement and the core capital requirement, respectively (based on the rules presented in Chapters 18 and 20), while $\widehat{EC}$ represents the portion of the bank's economic capital allocated (based on the criteria that we have seen in Chapter 15 and which will be discussed further in Chapter 23) to the loan itself. The circumflex ("hat") indicates that all of these variables are expressed on a per-unit basis, i.e. per euro lent.

Compared with equation (22.9), equation (22.11) contains two important changes:

- the Tier 1 capital held for the loan is no longer simply equal to VaR or EC, but, as indicated in equation (22.8), to the minimum requirement T1* plus a percentage q (potentially even 100 %) of economic capital;
- the risk-free rate appears only in the first member as a basis for calculating the spreads. In the second member, it has been replaced by the bank's actual funding costs, assuming that the bank pays a rate r_s on its senior debt plus a premium $r_j - r_s$ on the portion $(\widehat{RC}^* - \widehat{T1}^* + q\widehat{EC})$ funded by subordinated debt, or a premium $r_e - r_s$ on the portion $(\widehat{T1}^* + q\widehat{EC})$ covered by equity capital.

We can better understand how equation (22.11) works by way of an example (see Table 22.2). Let us assume that a bank calculates the capital requirement for credit risk using the standardized approach (see Chapter 20) and grants a 1 million euros loan to a private company that is risk-weighted at 100 %. The regulatory capital required for this loan (RC*) will be 80,000 euros, of which € 40,000 (T1*) core capital. We then have $\widehat{RC}^* = 8\%$ and $\widehat{T1}^* = 4\%$.

The bank estimates the company has a PD of 2 % and a LGD of 50 %, leading to an expected loss rate (ELR) of 1 %. Using its internal model, the bank also calculates that the economic capital allocated to the loan (considering the benefits of diversification) is equal to 36,000 euros ($\widehat{EC} = 3.6\%$).

The bank operates with a relatively high q (75 %), which could be due to the moral suasion exercised by regulators or to the desire to minimize the cost of unexpected capital deficiencies. The risk-free rate is 4 %; the cost of new senior debt raised on the interbank market is 4.1 %, and the cost of the bank's subordinated debt is 4.8 %. The cost of equity capital, finally, is 8.8 %, which is equal to a 4.8 % premium over the risk-free rate and of 4.7 % over the cost of the bank's senior debt.

Applying equation (22.11), we get a loan price of 5.48 %, which corresponds to a premium over the risk-free rate of 1.48 %. It is also interesting to note that by applying equation (22.9), i.e. the equation taken from Chapter 15, the price would have been 5.23 %; however, by issuing a loan at this rate, the bank would essentially have "forgotten" to charge to the customer the cost of its bank charter and would have applied a price that was insufficient to cover all of its operating costs. Finally, note that if management,

Table 22.2 An example of calculating a loan's price and Raroc

		Totals		Per-unit amounts
Loan amount		1,000,000		1
Minimum regulatory capital required	RC*	80,000	$\widehat{RC}^*$	8%
Minimum core capital required	T1*	40,000	$\widehat{T1}^*$	4%
Economic capital allocated to the loan	EC	36,000	$\widehat{EC}$	3.6%
Percentage of EC covered by tier 1 capital			q	75%
Probability of Default			PD	2%
Loss Given Default			LGD	50%
Risk-free interest rate			R	4.0%
Cost of senior debt			r_s	4.1%
Cost of subordinated (junior) debt			r_j	4.8%
Price-maker bank: cost of capital			r_e	8.8%
Price-taker bank: loan price			$\bar{r}$	5.3%

supported by shareholders who are prepared to pay in additional capital when necessary and by a less severe position taken by regulators, were able to reduce q to 25%, the loan could have been granted at a lower price (i.e. at a rate of 5.41%). However, it is quite likely that a lower level of tier 1 capital would increase perceived risk as seen by the bank's lenders, so we would need to increase our estimates of r_s and r_j.

If the bank acts as a price taker and the price that can be applied to the loan is set a level of $\bar{r}$, we can use a modified version of equation (22.10)[18] in order to calculate Raroc.

$$Raroc = r_e^* - r = \frac{\bar{r}(1 - ELR) - [r_s + (r_j - r_s)(\widehat{RC}^* - \widehat{T1}^* - q\widehat{EC})] - ELR}{\widehat{T1}^* + q\widehat{EC}} + (r_s - r)$$

(22.12)

We see here that equation (22.12), unlike equation (22.10), takes into account the actual level of the bank's tier 1 capital and the actual costs of funding. Furthermore, because Raroc is expressed as a premium over the risk-free rate and not based on the rate at which the bank receives funding, the final outcome is adjusted for the difference between r_s and r.

Let us return to our example in Table 22.2 and imagine that the rate of the loan ($\bar{r}$) is set at 5.3% because, for example, the customer is able to obtain financing at this rate from another lender. Therefore, our bank is operating as a price-taker and wishes to calculate the loan's Raroc.

Applying equation (22.12), we get a Raroc, expressed as a premium over the risk-free rate, of 2.16%. This premium is lower than the premium (4.8%) implicit in the cost of

---

[18] Equation (22.12) is derived from (22.10) by setting $r + d_{EL} + d_{UL} = \bar{r}$ and setting the actual return on capital r_e^* as the unknown.

capital in Table 22.2 (8.8 % with a risk free rate of 4 %); therefore, issuing this loan at a rate of 5.3 % destroys value and would not be advisable (unless the customer produces other revenues that may lead the bank to issue the loan anyway, even "at a loss").

It is interesting to note that equation (22.10) would have given us a Raroc (again expressed as a premium over the risk-free rate) of 6.86 %, which is greater than the 4.8 %, thereby giving the impression that a lending rate of 5.3 % would be enough to sufficiently remunerate the shareholders.

22.2.6 The determinants of capitalization

Equation (22.8) would appear to indicate that there are essentially three main factors determining the actual level of a bank's Tier 1 capital, namely: the level of risk (EC), the capital requirement set by regulators ($T1^*$), and the margins of flexibility deemed to be acceptable in restoring regulatory capital in the event of significant losses (q).

In reality, a bank's capital serves not only the purpose of providing a cushion to potential risks and losses, but has other functions, as well. Primarily:

– capital is a form of funding that is particularly suited to those activities that provide income gradually over time, such as fixed assets, equity investments, goodwill paid on company acquisitions, and, generally, all illiquid investments that cannot be sold without the risk of heavy losses. A level of equity capital that more than covers fixed assets and non-current financial assets enables the bank to operate with adequate free capital margins without its strategies being compromised by the creditors' appetite for short-term returns;
– capital represents an option on future restructurings; as such, it goes beyond merely absorbing losses and enables the bank to carry out any necessary strategies of corporate growth or business restructuring, for example by participating in mergers with other companies in the industry or by investing in the technology needed to reposition the company's offering in response to an evolving marketplace. In particular, as mentioned in relation to equation (22.8), an appropriate level of capital means that the bank will not be forced to raise funds on the market during unfavorable conditions of the economic cycle (i.e. when there is a limited availability of risk capital and it is more expensive to issue new capital) and will be able to develop its growth plans without being conditioned by any unfavourable external circumstances;
– capital also helps to establish a bank's reputation, which makes it easier for the bank to extend its network of relationships with customers, suppliers, and human resources. This is because the availability of sufficient equity capital represents a source of reassurance for the other agents that provide additional funds, assets, services, and professional skills.

Taking these important functions into account, the main factors that affect a bank's optimal level of capital can be summarized as follows (see Figure 22.6):

(1) the capital requirements set by regulators, whether such rules be explicit or implicit (e.g. the value of "q" in equation 22.8). In that regard, it is well known that some supervisory authorities informally "recommend" a Tier 1 ratio of 6 %, i.e. higher than the minimum 4 %, which leads banks to maintain an amount of T1 that is significantly higher than T1*;

(2) corporate development plans and related levels of risk: although not explicit in equation (22.8), it is clear that these plans indirectly affect the value of economic capital (EC) over time;

(3) the potential for mergers with other banks and for acquisitions of smaller banks, which could make it appropriate to maintain a higher level of free capital for new investments;

(4) the condition of the capital markets, which can make it more or less simple (and convenient) to raise new capital;

(5) the rating that a bank seeks to achieve, which can be seen as an external constraint (i.e. as a minimum level of Tier 1 capital, say T1**, to be added to the T1* set by regulators) or as a variable indirectly included in equation (22.8) through EC.[19]

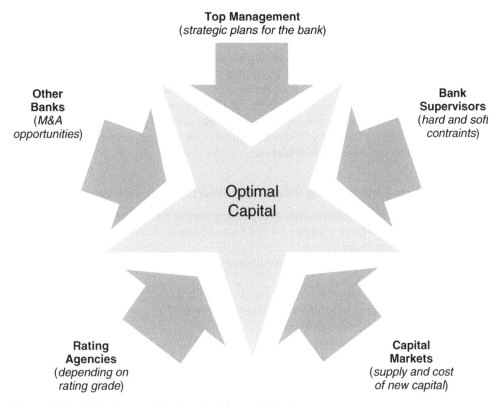

Figure 22.6 Main factors affecting a bank's capitalization

22.3 OPTIMIZING REGULATORY CAPITAL

We have seen how regulation can be a significant external constraint on a bank's ability to determine its optimal level of capital. More specifically, equation (22.8) relates available core capital to the minimum Tier 1 requirement. This relationship, together with

---

[19] A better rating implies that the bank has a lower probability of default; therefore, the VaR models used to calculate economic capital (EC) must be calibrated to a higher confidence level. For more information, see Chapter 5.

equation (22.1), implies that the portion of compulsory capital not covered by core capital needs to be covered by Tier 2 and (where applicable – see Chapter 18) Tier 3 capital:

$$T2 + T3 \geq RC^* - T1^* - q \cdot EC \tag{22.13}$$

Equations (22.8) and (22.13) indicate the amount of regulatory capital (Tiers 1 through 3) that the bank decides to maintain. We can see that a lower value for q, all else remaining equal, would result in a shift in regulatory capital from Tier 1 to Tier 2. Furthermore, within core and supplementary capital, a bank can make use of a variety of instruments with differing costs.

A crucial phase in managing a bank's capital and its cost is the selection of the *optimal composition* of regulatory capital (between the various classes of capital – i.e. Tier 1, Tier 2 and tier 3 – and within each class) based on a rational use of the various financial instruments that can be included within this aggregate. From this point of view, the challenge that a bank faces is different from that of a non-financial company for which the optimization of financial structure primarily means selecting the best use of leverage (i.e. the ratio of debt to equity). A bank is not free to establish its own degree of leverage, as this is determined by the capital ratios set by regulators (in addition to strategic factors such as capital needs connected with plans for future growth); however, it does have control over the composition of its capital, as the rules set by the supervisory authorities leave room for a certain flexibility in selecting the mix of core and supplementary capital, as well as the individual capital instruments.

22.3.1 Technical features of the different regulatory capital instruments

A full classification of the components of regulatory capital has already been provided in Chapter 18. Here we will be focusing on the financial instruments that a bank is able to issue on the capital markets.

These capital instruments include both ordinary shares and the following (see Table 22.3):

– instruments with characteristics similar to equity (*lower Tier 1*);
– hybrid capital instruments (*upper Tier 2*);
– subordinated medium and long-term debt (*lower Tier 2*);
– short-term subordinated loans issued to cover market risks (*Tier 3*).

These instruments come with a variety of benefits, such as:

– reducing the cost of capital;
– broadening, at least from a regulatory point of view, the bank's capital base (with positive implications also in terms of credit rating and credit standing on the capital markets) without diluting the voting rights of the existing shareholders;
– providing greater flexibility to the bank's capital structure;
– diversifying the sources of funding by issuing capital instruments in a variety of currencies, in part to hedge assets denominated in a foreign currency.

The possibility to include an instrument in core or supplementary capital depends on its characteristics. More specifically, in the ideal continuum ranging from ordinary shares to

Table 22.3 Financial instruments that can be included in regulatory capital

Component	*Conditions for inclusion*	**Limits and restrictions**
UPPER TIER 1		
Common equity	None	At least 4 % of risk-weighted assets
LOWER TIER 1		
Innovative capital instruments	Capital securities, preferred securities, preference shares, instruments with any explicit feature – other than a pure call option – which might lead to the instrument being redeemed.	No more than 15 % of Tier 1
UPPER TIER 2		
Hybrid capital instruments	Unsecured, subordinated and fully subscribed; not redeemable at the holder's initiative or without consent of the supervisory authorities; can be used to cover losses without the need to liquidate the bank; can be deferred if the bank's profits do not allow payment.	
LOWER TIER 2		
Subordinated term debt	Original term to maturity of at least 5 years. Amortized at 20 % per year if maturing in less than 5 years.	No more than 50 % of Tier 1
TIER 3 (FOR MARKET RISKS ONLY)		
Short-term subordinated loans	Original term to maturity of at least 2 years. Deferrable if the bank cannot meet the minimum capital ratio.	No more than 250 % of Tier 1 for market risk.

Source: Basel Committee (1998b, 2006).

debt, the higher the equity content of an instrument (i.e. its capacity to absorb a bank's losses without needing to resort to extraordinary measures), the closer it will be to Tier 1.

To that end, we must consider the following aspects (see Table 22.4):

– *maturity*: a long-term, or even perpetual, instrument provides a more stable source of funding than a medium or short-term instrument. Beyond the formal maturity of the instrument, one also has to check for any clauses that enable the issuing bank to redeem the securities in advance, thereby effectively sidestepping the originally established maturity;
– the *ability to absorb losses*: each of the various instruments provides the issuer with a different capacity to use it to cover losses. More specifically, failure to redeem the funds received and their use to cover losses may require that the bank first be liquidated

Table 22.4 A comparison of the characteristics of the various capital instruments

Characteristic	Innovative capital	Hybrid capital	"Ordinary" subordinated loans	Subordinated loans to cover market risk
	(Lower tier 1)	(Upper tier 2)	(Lower tier 2)	(tier 3)
Maturity	Redemption cannot be initiated by the investor or without the authorization of the supervisory body and no earlier than 5 years from the date of issue	Redemption cannot be initiated by the investor or without supervisory body authorization	Greater than or equal to 5 years	Greater than or equal to 2 years. However, a lock-in clause must require that remuneration and redemption be suspended in the event the bank's capital falls below minimum regulatory requirements.
Absorption of losses	Must be able to absorb the losses of the bank on a going-concern basis	Must be able to absorb the losses of the bank on a going-concern basis	Cannot be used to cover a bank's current losses unless the bank has been formally liquidated	
Degree of subordination	Absolute: subordinate, in the event of liquidation, to all subordinate, ordinary, and privileged creditors	Subordinate, in the event of liquidation, to ordinary and privileged creditors		
Type of remuneration	Variable (connected with earnings, as for ordinary shares) or fixed, as for debt securities	Predetermined, as with debt securities		
Cumulation of remuneration	Not possible	Possible	The ability to suspend the payment of interest is not required	Possible, given the aforementioned lock-in clause

Source: Basel Committee (1998b and 2006), Ferrari (2002).

(as in the case of debt securities) or simply that the directors or shareholders decide to do so (as with share capital);
- the *degree of subordination in the event of crises*: an instrument that, in the event of a crisis, is only redeemed after other creditors have been repaid is, evidently, a more suitable cushion for losses and is, therefore, more similar to equity;
- *remuneration* and *cumulation*: the remuneration of certain instruments depends on the bank's earnings (as is the case with ordinary shares), whereas other receive a preset coupon (as with bonds). Still other have intermediate mechanisms of remuneration which, for example, provide the option of deferring (or "cumulating", i.e. the coupon for one year is put off until the following year) or canceling the coupon in the event of losses.

With regard to *maturity*, the innovative capital instruments included within lower Tier 1, given that they are similar to equity, must be of a permanent nature. Nonetheless, just as a bank may decide to buy back its own shares, it may also decide to redeem lower Tier 1 instruments. In such cases, however, it is necessary for redemption to be decided by the issuer (and not by the investor) with the approval of the supervisory authority; furthermore, it cannot take place within five years of issue. In the case of hybrid instruments, there is no constraint on minimum maturity; however, here too, early redemption cannot be initiated by the investor and must be approved by regulators. For subordinated debt, minimum maturities of five (Tier 2) and two (Tier 3) years are established. Tier 3 sub debt also requires a lock-in clause which explicitly suspends redemption and payment of interest if the bank's capital falls below the minimum regulatory requirements.

As for capacity to *absorb losses*, both lower Tier 1 and upper Tier 2 capital must be able to absorb losses without interrupting the normal operations of the bank (i.e. without undergoing liquidation or similar procedures). In the case of ordinary subordinated loans, the coverage of losses takes place only after liquidation, since in this case subordinated loans can be reimbursed only after the other creditors have been repaid.

With regard to *subordination*, in the event of liquidation, innovative capital instruments take priority only over equity as far as redemption is concerned and are subordinate to all instruments included within Tiers 2 and 3. However, there is no precise hierarchy of redemption between hybrid instruments and subordinated loans, with such decision being left to the discretion of the issuer. Remember, however, that the former can be used to cover losses even if the bank is not being liquidated: this indirectly results in a natural "hierarchy" that leads to consider upper Tier 2 securities as riskier, for investors, than those included in lower Tier 2.

Remuneration of the innovative instruments within lower Tier 1 can either be fixed or linked to the bank's earnings. Tier 2 and Tier 3 capital instruments, on the other hand, can only receive fixed remuneration.

The unpaid periodic remuneration of innovative capital instruments (lower Tier 1) cannot be cumulated (but is cancelled and not deferred). For hybrid instruments, however, remuneration can be cumulated. For ordinary subordinated loans, cumulation is not an issue, as the payment of interest cannot be suspended. In the case of Tier 3, the lock-in clause can provide for unpaid amounts to be cumulated.

22.3.2   The actual use of the various instruments included within regulatory capital

In this section, we will show how some of the world's leading banks have made increasing use, during the late 90's, of the ability to diversify the composition of regulatory capital, thereby optimizing costs.

Our first example concerns the use of Tier 2 capital. Figure 22.7 shows how the use of this type of capital by the leading publicly listed banks of the G10 countries has varied significantly throughout the latter part of the 90's. Whereas countries such as Sweden, the Netherlands, and France have reduced their levels of Tier 2 capital, banks in Japan, Switzerland, and Italy have made an increasing use of this form of capital, thanks in part to significant issues of subordinated debt and, more recently, of hybrid capital.

Subordinated loans – We can see the role played by subordinated loans in Table 22.5, which shows the data for 50 major European banks. During the twelve year period from 1988 to 2000, many banks completed dozens of issues either directly or through subsidiaries.

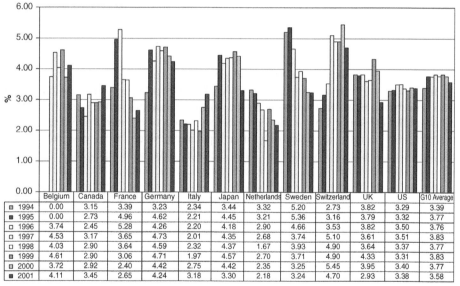

	Belgium	Canada	France	Germany	Italy	Japan	Netherlands	Sweden	Switzerland	UK	US	G10 Average
☐ 1994	0.00	3.15	3.39	3.23	2.34	3.44	3.32	5.20	2.73	3.82	3.29	3.39
■ 1995	0.00	2.73	4.96	4.62	2.21	4.45	3.21	5.36	3.16	3.79	3.32	3.77
☐ 1996	3.74	2.45	5.28	4.26	2.20	4.18	2.90	4.66	3.53	3.82	3.50	3.76
☐ 1997	4.53	3.17	3.65	4.73	2.01	4.35	2.68	3.74	5.10	3.61	3.51	3.83
☐ 1998	4.03	2.90	3.64	4.59	2.32	4.37	1.67	3.93	4.90	3.64	3.37	3.77
■ 1999	4.61	2.90	3.06	4.71	1.97	4.57	2.70	3.71	4.90	4.33	3.31	3.83
☐ 2000	3.72	2.92	2.40	4.42	2.75	4.42	2.35	3.25	5.45	3.95	3.40	3.77
■ 2001	4.11	3.45	2.65	4.24	3.18	3.30	2.18	3.24	4.70	2.93	3.38	3.58

Source: Ferrari (2002).

Figure 22.7   Tier 2 ratios of the G10's largest banks
Source: Ferrari (2002).

Subordinated debt has a cost that is generally 40–100 basis points greater than treasury bonds (depending on the issuer's rating and the security's maturity, as shown in Table 22.6). Assuming a government bond yield of 3 %, the cost would therefore be between 3.4 % and 4 %. This compares with a cost of Tier 1 capital for banks which averages between 6 % and 9 % (see Chapter 24). Furthermore, the interest paid on subordinated loans is generally tax deductible (as for any debt). It follows, then, that a greater use of subordinated debt can significantly reduce the average cost of a bank's regulatory capital.

Table 22.5 European Banks: Top 50 issuers of SNDs (1988–2000)

Rank	Issuer	No. of issues Total	Amount (USD m) Total	Avg. issue	Issuing bank (USD m) Total assets	Total SD	SD/TA
1	ABN AMRO Bank NV	38	11,567	304	504,122	11,039	2.19%
2	National Westminster Bank	26	11,067	426	285,979	12,153	4.25%
3	Lloyds TSB Group	30	10,540	351	240,957	5,156	2.14%
4	Banco Santander C.H.A.	39	10,145	260	255,549	8,117	3.18%
5	Credit Suisse Group (*)	62	9,517	153	475,018	12,031	2.53%
6	Union Bank of Switzerland	45	9,455	210	610,365	8,982	1.47%
7	HSBC Holdings Plc	29	9,202	317	599,777	12,188	2.03%
8	Banca Intesa (**)	50	8,585	172	312,170	8,832	2.83%
9	Abbey National plc	22	8,082	367	263,183	5,294	2.01%
10	Societe Generale	52	7,514	145	407,478	6,479	1.59%
11	Bayerische HypoVereinsbank	49	7,134	146	483,981	9,401	1.94%
12	Royal Bank of Scotland Group	25	7,130	285	143,898	3,311	2.30%
13	Dresdner Bank AG	35	6,271	179	397,026	8,049	2.03%
14	Barclays Bank plc	22	6,141	279	397,660	4,590	1.15%
15	Banco Bilbao Vizcaya Arg. (**)	23	5,839	254	236,256	3,312	1.40%
16	Commerzbank AG	51	5,176	101	370,279	5,871	1.59%
17	Halifax plc	17	5,134	302	222,148	3,876	1.74%
18	Deutsche Bank AG	22	4,686	213	807,339	11,053	1.37%
19	ING Groep	21	4,611	220	495,092	7,974	1.61%
20	BNP Paribas (**)	41	4,299	105	701,787	10,005	1.43%
21	MeritaNordbanken Group	40	3,901	98	104,457	3,064	2.93%
22	Almanij Kredietbank Group (*)	46	3,827	83	198,213	5,327	2.69%
23	Bank of Scotland	15	3,772	251	143,898	3,248	2.26%
24	Fortis Banque S.A.(*)	49	3,359	69	323,538	7,142	1.43%

(*continued overleaf*)

Table 22.5 (*continued*)

Rank	Issuer	No. of issues	Amount (USD m)		Issuing bank (USD m)		
		Total	Total	Avg. issue	Total assets	Total SD	SD/TA
25	Credit Agricole (*)	49	3,236	66	440,506	4,626	1.05 %
26	Bayerische Landesbank GZ	21	3,049	145	263,290	3,965	1.51 %
27	Westdeutsche Landesb.GZ (*)	16	2,898	181	403,890	4,371	1.08 %
28	Groupe Banques Pop. (*)	36	2,858	79	92,189	3,084	3.35 %
29	San Paolo IMI (*)	22	2,812	128	140,467	1,512	1.08 %
30	Skandinaviska Enskilda Bank	23	2,278	99	86,301	914	1.06 %
31	Credit Lyonnais SA	26	2,201	85	173,342	4,005	2.31 %
32	Den Danske Bank A/S	10	2,104	210	98,958	3,021	3.05 %
33	Bankgesellschaft Berlin AG (*)	14	2,048	146	217,785	2,477	1.14 %
34	Swedbank	22	2,043	93	101,285	3,080	3.04 %
35	Dexia Group	41	2,014	49	245,082	3,121	1.27 %
36	Bank of Ireland	6	1,888	315	54,507	874	1.60 %
37	Bank Austria	21	1,812	86	140,267	3,632	2.59 %
38	Allied Irish Banks plc	8	1,660	208	65,396	1,989	3.04 %
39	Woolwich Plc	9	1,598	178	53,332	1,361	2.55 %
40	Landesbank Baden-Wurt. (*)	6	1,427	238	250,317	3,794	1.52 %
41	Norddeutsche Landesb. GZ (*)	21	1,275	61	169,109	1,829	1.08 %
42	Credit Mut. Centre Est Eur. (*)	23	1,199	52	168,059	2,636	1.57 %
43	Banque Generale du Lux. (*)	21	1,019	49	35,685	630	1.77 %
44	Credit National (***)	8	978	122	55,080	1,435	2.60 %
45	Unicredito Italiano	6	874	146	169,708	1,412	0.83 %
46	Landesbank Hessen-Thur. GZ	7	847	121	113,678	897	0.79 %

Table 22.5 (*continued*)

Rank	Issuer	No. of issues Total	Amount (USD m) Total	Avg. issue	Issuing bank (USD m) Total assets	Total SD	SD/TA
47	DG Bank Deutsche Genos. (*)	11	782	71	256,926	2,531	0.99 %
48	IKB Deutsche Industriebank (*)	10	743	74	29,667	507	1.71 %
49	Credit Commercial de France	16	646	40	69,452	697	1.00 %
50	Landesb. Schleswig-Hol.GZ (*)	13	616	47	113,919	1,317	2.15 %
	Totale	**1315**	**211,860**	**161**	**12,988,369**	**236,213**	**1.82 %**

(*)Terminal year 1998; (**)Pro-forma statements after merger. Source: based on FitchIBCA and Capital Data BondWare data.

Table 22.6 Subordinated debt spreads over corresponding Treasury yields for US and EU banks

Rating	US Banks Number of issues	Average spread (basis points)	EU Banks Number of issues	Average spread (basis points)
AAA/Aaa	0	–	17	43.6
AA+/Aa1	0	–	40	43.7
AA/Aa2	5	12.4	45	63.8
AA-/Aa3	12	73.4	73	82.0
A+/A1	52	80.5	43	82.6
A/A2	146	81.9	34	94.9
A-/A3	104	90.5	34	96.0
BBB+/Baa1	35	102.6	4	76.3
BBB/Baa2	27	124.1	0	–
BBB-/Baa3	18	123.3	0	–
BB+/Ba1	0	–	0	–
BB/Ba2	3	177.2	0	–
Totale	402	90	290	74.8

Source: Sironi (2002).

However, this benefit is kept in check by both regulators and the financial nature of subordinated debt. On the one hand, lower Tier 2 capital cannot exceed 50% of Tier 1 capital (see Table 22.3), so there is a threshold on how much this type of debt can be used as a component of regulatory capital. On the other one, although regulators allow it to be used as capital due to its ability to protect the bank's senior creditors, subordinated debt is not true capital, given that it must be periodically remunerated and the principal must be repaid upon maturity. Therefore, an excessive use of this type of debt ends up compromising the bank's financial management by depriving it of the flexibility it needs to invest in long-term projects.

Hybrid capital – The growth in Tier 2 capital can also be explained, particularly in recent years, by the issue of hybrid instruments. This includes, for example, Canadian long-term preference shares, *titres participatifs* and *titres subordonnés à durée indéterminée* in France, German Genußscheine, perpetual subordinated debt and preference shares in the UK, and mandatory convertible debt instruments in the US.

Preferred shares are particularly common. This type of stock pays a fixed dividend and guarantees the holder a privileged (as compared with the other shareholders) right to the redemption of capital in the event the company should be liquidated. However, the fixed dividend for preferred stock, which is in some ways similar to a bond's coupon, may be suspended, particularly in the event of unfavorable trends in the company's profits (its distribution retains priority over any dividends to be paid to ordinary shareholders). This greater protection of capital is normally offset by a lack of voting rights, which makes preferred shares essentially irrelevant in terms of corporate governance. Finally, such securities often include the option to be converted into ordinary shares based on predefined conditions.

Beginning in the second half of the 90's, we have seen an increasing use of this type of capital instrument by the world's leading banks. On the whole, in the six-year period 1995–2000, banks of the G10 nations made 1,173 issues of innovative capital instruments in essentially increasing amounts over time and totaling more than USD 215 billion (see Table 22.7).

Table 22.7 Issues of hybrid instruments by the leading banks of the G10 nations

	Amount (in millions of $)	%	Number of issues	Average in millions of $
1995	25,565.525	11.85	201	127.192
1996	25,935.753	12.02	158	164.150
1997	34,940.793	16.19	201	173.835
1998	20,804.708	9.64	120	173.373
1999	50,894.390	23.59	239	212.947
2000	57,643.322	26.71	254	226.942
Total	215,784.491	100.00	1173	183.959

Source: Capital Data Bondware.

22.4   OTHER INSTRUMENTS NOT INCLUDED WITHIN REGULATORY CAPITAL

Given the importance of regulatory constraints in determining a bank's optimal level of capital, the instruments that can be included in regulatory capital play a crucial role in selecting the best mix of capital resources.

Nonetheless, capital management does not limit itself to regulatory capital and relations with regulators. As indicated in equations (22.3) and (22.3b), a bank must also reassure analysts, creditors, and shareholders as to the balance between risk and the level of capital resources actually available to absorb any losses (AC), which can be approximated with fair-value capital (FVC). The importance of this "dialogue" with investors is certainly going to increase in the years to come, given that the rules surrounding pillar three of Basel II (see Chapter 20) will place greater emphasis on the market's ability to penalize banks that are deemed to have insufficient capital, in part through measurements of available capital that go beyond mere regulatory capital.

We can therefore look to a broader range of instruments than those that can be included among regulatory capital. More specifically, in recent years a number of banks have begun to experiment with the use of forms of insurance capital or contingent capital, which will be discussed in this section.

We may not expect to see these highly innovative instruments of capital management to be accepted into regulatory capital any time soon. The atypical nature of such contracts, the many discretionary aspects they contain, the lack of proven practices and legal support, and the existence of potential credit risk are just the main factors that make such inclusion unlikely for the time being. However, we should not forget that the Basel Accord of 2004 has, for the first time, included forms of insurance capital in regulatory capital which were previously excluded. The same sort of thing could, over time, happen with some of other innovative instruments presented below.

22.4.1   Insurance capital

The concept behind insurance capital – Insurance contracts are, at times, referred to as "insurance capital", given that, just like capital, they cover potential losses and prevent the rights of creditors from being compromised. However, unlike actual capital, their ability to absorb losses is not universal, but selective, i.e. limited to losses that result from the events specified in the policy.

Examples of insurance policies that are already widespread among banks include: theft insurance; fixed asset damage insurance (e.g. fire, earthquake, flood); insurance against losses resulting from employee fraud or incompetence (i.e. bankers blanket bonds[20]), such as unauthorized securities trading; policies against claims for damages filed by customers; insurance against damage to the bank or to third parties resulting from the malfunctioning of electronic commerce and other information systems.

As already mentioned in Chapter 17, this trend in transferring risk is justified by two key benefits inherent in an insurance contract: risk pooling (or diversification) and cash

---

[20] Fidelity bonds, or bankers blanket bonds, protect the insured from losses due to theft/embezzlement or other such conduct by disloyal employees. The term "blanket" refers to the fact that the people covered by the policy are not expressly specified by name. Blanket bonds are a mandatory form of risk coverage for certain types of US banks.

flow smoothing. With risk pooling, the charges taken on by an insurance company are less than those that would have been faced by the individual insured parties due to the imperfect correlation between the risks of the insurance company's various customers. The ability to transfer losses through insurance also helps to smooth out the cash flows of the insured party, thereby reducing the volatility of profits and improving earnings quality, hence reducing the cost of traditional equity capital.[21]

However, these benefits come with certain limitations of insurance contracts, which tend to limit their use. Firstly, while a bank's capital is, by definition, available, given that it has been paid in by shareholders and invested in the company, "insurance capital" is only a commitment to pay, the value of which depends on the credit standing of the insurance company. The second aspect concerns the phenomena of adverse selection and moral hazard. In other words, there is the risk that, in order to limit costs, banks may request insurance coverage without providing the insurance company with sufficient information on their true level of risk, and there is also the risk that, once insurance coverage has been obtained, the bank may be less careful in managing risk, knowing that the related losses are now the responsibility of the insurance company. A third limitation is related to the difficulty in defining the types of loss covered by an insurance policy in a sufficiently objective and measurable manner. The attempt to find objective parameters may result in a fundamental risk of incomplete coverage. For example, a policy may protect a bank against fire damage as estimated by regulators, but the real damage could be greater.[22]

Integrated risk insurance – As mentioned above, one of the key differences between traditional cash capital and insurance capital lies in the type of loss coverage, with equity capital providing universal coverage and insurance capital providing selective coverage (related to a specific event). However, in recent years, a number of forms of *integrated risk insurance*, i.e. contracts that cover a basket of risks jointly, have become increasingly popular. We can now distinguish between types of integrated insurance depending on *how* the risks are integrated and *which risks* are aggregated.

As far as the first type of distinction is concerned, we can distinguish between blended, or basket, products (or multi-line/multi-year products), and double-trigger products.

Blended products are policies that cover multiple lines of risk within a single coverage limit. Normally, the coverage limit is less than the sum of the coverage limits that would have been set for multiple independent insurance policies (because it is unlikely that all of the insured events will occur at the same time); therefore, the premium paid on the policy is also lower. Such contracts are also often multi-year policies because, in this way, they take advantage of the serial independence of the loss events, as well as of the imperfect correlation between the various risks, thereby further reducing cost.[23] Surprisingly, basket policies tend to aggregate "families" of similar risks (e.g. risks related to fraud, computer

---

[21] Indeed, a lower cost of capital – considering, too, the impact of insurance premiums on future earnings – can increase a bank's market value and its price-to-book ratio, thereby creating value for shareholders.

[22] These limitations create a sort of wedge between the value of the coverage for the buyer (which is reduced as a result of credit and basis risks) and the cost for the insurance company (which incurs into screening and monitoring costs needed to limit adverse selection and moral hazard). As a result, the transfer, or "outsourcing", of risk through insurance capital is only beneficial when the value creation related to risk pooling and cash flow smoothing is particularly high and cannot be achieved by other means.

[23] The coverage limit is valid for the entire insured period, although it can be "restored", if necessary, by paying an additional premium.

crime, employee infidelity, etc.), with the result that the reduction in cost resulting from diversification is less than it would be if the various risks were completely different. The reason for this is, in part, due to the products' history, as different risks are typically insured by different companies.

With double-trigger products, insurance coverage only takes place when two different types of event occur at the same time, for example a fire (first trigger) that results in a loss in revenues for the insured of at least 5 % (second trigger). It is fairly common for one of the insured events to be of a "macro" nature (and therefore objective), with the second being of a "micro" nature, i.e. connected with day to day business. One benefit of this is that it tends to limit the moral hazard while keeping the basis risk within acceptable limits.

As for the *types of risk* integrated, we can distinguish between pure insurance risks, financial insurance risks, and business risk.

"Insurance" risks are those that are typically covered by an insurance contract, such as property risk, fidelity (or blanket) bonds, professional negligence, suits filed by customers and former employees, and so on. These insurance risks are then joined by financial risks (or "liquid risks", which capital markets can also give a value to), such as currency risk, interest rate risk, or commodity risk.[24] The double-trigger policies discussed above often integrate disaster and market risks, such as put options on market indexes that are only exercisable following a natural disaster.

The joint coverage of traditional and financial risks can even be extended to include most risk factors that are likely to impact upon a company's profits. More specifically, alongside the potential sources of loss, the reduced earnings due, for example, to declining demand during a recession or to a forced suspension of operations can also be insured. In this way, the object of the contract becomes the entire "business risk" of the company insured. This type of product includes the "earnings per share protection programmes" by which an insurance company undertakes to cover, within a given coverage limit, any operational risk that cannot be controlled by the insured (plant downtime, infrastructure damage, the loss of large clients, etc.).[25] Integrated business risk insurance demonstrates how much the traditional differences between equity capital and insurance capital (used to cover a wide range of generic risks) can be reduced.

Integrated risk insurance policies are still not particularly widespread and are especially difficult to define in contractual terms; however, they demonstrate to what point capital paid in by shareholders can be replaced by the "outsourcing" of risks to specialists such as insurance companies.

22.4.2 Contingent capital

Technical characteristics – A contingent capital contract (see Figure 22.8) calls for an *institutional* investor (which may be a reinsurer or other company with a high credit standing) to *undertake* to buy the newly issued shares of a company (e.g. a bank) given predetermined conditions as defined by the contract. The company, in turn, pays the

---

[24] In the past, for example, the US insurance company AIG developed a multi-year product known as Commodity-Embedded Insurance (COIN), which integrates "traditional" coverage (such as third-party and environmental liability) and financial coverage (such as cost increases for the purchase of precious commodities). See Aon Risk Services (1999).

[25] See Aon Risk Services (1999). In past years, earnings protection policies have been purchased by large-scale manufacturing firms such as British Aerospace and Honeywell (see Clow, 1999), but they are also suited to covering operational and business risk for banks.

1) Upon origination of the contract

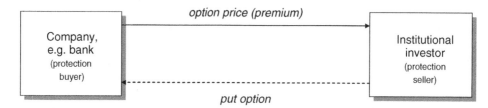

2) Upon exercise of the option

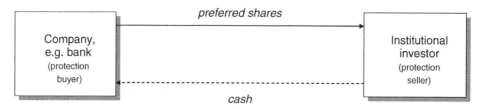

Figure 22.8   Typical flows of a contingent capital (equity put) contract

investor for this commitment, which is normally of multi-year duration, in the form of an annual premium.

Note that:

– the commitment is asymmetrical, i.e. it only concerns the investor and not the issuing company; the latter only buys a put option on the new risk capital and has the right, but not the obligation, of increasing its capital;
– the terms and conditions for the purchase of the new equity are set forth in the contract, which thereby insures not only the availability of new capital, but also its issue at conditions that do not excessively penalize the company's existing shareholders;
– given the over-the-counter and long-term nature of the contract, the protection seller cannot sell the contract to third parties;
– the value of the contract depends upon the protection seller's ability and willingness to honour the commitment. The first aspect (i.e. ability) can be certified by a high credit rating, while the second (i.e. willingness) is reasonably certain if contingent capital is purchased by an institutional investor, as this investor will prefer to honor the contract, even if this involves a loss, in order not to jeopardize the reputation it needs in order to enter into other such transactions in the future;
– the issuer's exercise of the put option is not unconditional, but is subordinate to a trigger event or is otherwise not directly controllable by the issuing company. Typical examples of trigger events are natural disasters that can be "objectively" measured by the relevant authorities;[26] however, it is also possible to specify other detrimental events as trigger events, such as a collapse in demand (as indicated by a decline in GDP below a given threshold) or a sharp drop in credit quality (marked by an increase in the number of bankruptcies for every 100,000 companies in operation).

---

[26] In such cases, a contingent capital contract is referred to as a catastrophic equity put (or CatEPut).

In this type of contract, the investor does not normally undertake to buy ordinary shares, but rather hybrid forms of capital that are recognized as regulatory capital by supervisors (see section 22.3 of this chapter). In this way, the protection seller is better protected from business risk than "normal" shareholders, while shareholders do not risk having to dilute their controlling rights.

In the event that the issuer is a publicly listed company, there is sometimes also an exercise window (see Figure 22.9), i.e. a range of values with an upper and lower limit within which the price of the ordinary shares must fall in order for the put option to actually be exercisable. This window provides a second condition, in addition to the trigger event mentioned above, which is necessary for the protection seller to take on the newly issued capital.

The upper limit may be of limited significance, given that when the stock rises above a certain maximum the put option will be of limited or no value. It should be seen as a sort of "deductible" within which the issuer will receive no assistance from the contingent capital. The lower limit, however, is of greater importance, because below this level the contingent capital contract becomes null and void precisely when its usefulness for the issuer would be greatest. The purpose of this constraint is to prevent the issuer from pursuing excessively risky strategies in the belief that it can, nonetheless, count on the "safety net" of contingent capital. In this way, it protects the protection seller from moral hazard and contributes to reducing the cost of the option.

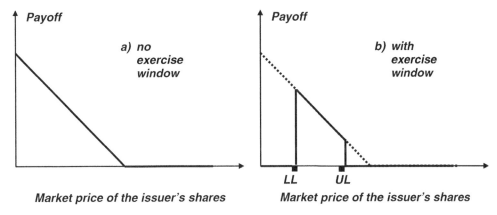

Figure 22.9 Effects of the upper (UL) and lower (LL) limit on an equity put's payoff
Source: based on data from Doherty (1997).

A particular type of contingent capital contract is reverse convertible debt, which enables the issuer to convert bonds into stock at a preset conversion rate upon the occurrence of a given trigger event. Payment of the new shares by institutional investors that have sold the put option does not take place in cash, but in bonds. Given that, when a certain event detrimental to the issuer should occur, the value of the bonds held by the investor will decline, this conversion option is less costly for the protection seller than a simple equity put, because the protection seller is able to pay for the shares with a "currency" (the bonds of the issuing company) that has been devalued. For the protection buyer, on the other hand, forced conversion eliminates the credit risk underlying the option (i.e. the risk that the protection seller will fail to meet its obligations). For this reason, reverse convertible debt can be freely sold to third parties.

A *reverse* convertible contract could, for example, call for the conversion of a sub-ordinated loan into preferred shares, thereby enabling the issuing bank to "transform" Tier 2 capital into Tier 1 upon occurrence of some serious loss event. Such a contract, if approved by regulators, could make it possible to keep q in equation (22.8) to relatively low levels, while providing the possibility of restoring its Tier 1 capital in the event of significant losses.

Strengths and weaknesses – Compared to other forms of risk coverage (e.g. traditional equity capital and insurance capital), contingent capital offers the following benefits:

- it makes it possible to pool various risks that are only partially correlated into a single portfolio (i.e. that of the protection seller, who sells multiple equity puts to various companies);
- unlike insurance capital, it doesn't require that the protection seller take on a loss with-out receiving something in return, because the protection seller becomes a shareholder of the issuing company, thereby sharing in the potential for recovery following the loss;[27]
- it is also an interesting means of optimizing leverage, which makes it possible to give capital back to the shareholders and to increase the return on their investment. Indeed, while the coverage provided by contingent capital costs less than shareholders capital (and is also tax deductible), the replacement of equity capital with a combination of debt and put options on new capital may have particularly positive effects in terms of value creation;
- it is not just a means of ex ante optimization of capital, but also, and above all, allows for better management of the company's recovery following significant losses, by help-ing companies that have been through a period of crisis to raise the capital needed to reorganize and to continue their operations without incurring excessive costs.[28] Particu-larly for banks, contingent capital can enable them to rapidly restore minimum capital requirements following significant losses in order to maintain their charter (without having to find new investors or sell a portion of their assets at unfavorable conditions);
- it makes it possible to mitigate the procyclical aspects inherent in mandatory capital requirements (see Chapter 20). Indeed, if a bank obtains the ability to expand its capital base through the purchase of an equity put, it will be easier to restore its capital to risk-weighted assets ratio, even if such assets increase due to a recession;
- finally, it is likely to be well received by rating agencies because it indicates a capacity to keep leverage under control even in times of difficulty. Leverage is indeed one of the key variables on which rating agencies base their judgements, as it is symptomatic

---

[27] For this reason, coverage using contingent capital is significantly less costly than traditional policies. It is estimated, for example, that in the case of RLI Corporation (one of the first companies to use contingent capital instruments in 1996) the premium paid (roughly 195 basis points per year) was somewhere in the range of 20–25 % of the margin required by a normal insurance policy.
[28] When a bank sustains large losses, its capital is seriously compromised; however, the value of its brand and its market position can remain significantly positive. This value risks to be eroded if the lack of liquidity compromises operations. Instead, the ability to access capital markets at predefined conditions enables the bank to raise the necessary resources at conditions that are not excessively "dilutive", thereby protecting the investment of its existing shareholders.

of a company's ability to absorb any operating losses internally without compromising its creditors. As a result, if a bank can ensure that its capital will not decline in the future, its rating should be noticeably higher; this is also a consequence of the "through-the-cycle" approach used by rating agencies (see Chapter 13).

Contingent capital instruments are not without their limitations. The most significant is the highly fiduciary nature of the contract, which – as with insurance capital – is typically based on a long-term commitment. As a result, counterparty risk is high, which makes it virtually impossible to create a secondary market for equity put contracts unless they are bundled with other investment instruments.[29] In addition, the difficulty in defining the trigger events precisely means that we cannot exclude the possibility of legal risks due to imperfections in the contract. Finally, there can be moral hazard on the part of the protection buyer, particularly when the trigger event is dependent upon or in some way affected by the conduct of the issuing company (e.g. when an equity put is contingent upon the level of profits or reserves of the company itself). Because of these limitations, one can understand why regulators have so far been cautious when it comes to contingent capital instruments.

SELECTED QUESTIONS AND EXERCISES

1. Consider the following statements. In a well-managed bank...

   (I) ... available capital should always significantly exceed fair value capital;
   (II) ... economic capital should always be covered through available capital;
   (III) ... book value capital, and namely those components in it that qualify as tier 1 capital, should always exceed the minimum requirements imposed on regulatory capital;
   (IV) ... market capitalisation should usually be above book value capital.

   Which of them would you consider correct?

   (A) All of them;
   (B) Only III;
   (C) Only I;
   (D) Only II and IV

2. A bank has computed the following estimates, regarding its economic capital:
   – the 10-day VaR for market risk at a 99 % confidence level is 100 million euros; a normal distribution is deemed appropriate, and 10-day returns are thought to be serially independent; this also includes interest rate risk on the banking book;
   – the one-year (250 working days) economic capital against credit risk, measured at a 99.9 % confidence level, is 400 million euros;
   – the one-year (250 working days) economic capital against operational risk, measured at a 99.9 % confidence level, is 50 million euros.

---

[29] For example, reverse convertible debt, or a portfolio of short equity puts backed by government bonds in an amount equal to the strike price of the puts. A "synthetic" product such as this would enable the final investor to receive a premium over the risk-free rate (equal to the premium received annually on the puts) by taking on the risk of a "forced" conversion into shares.

Using equation (22.6), compute the bank's overall economic capital on a one-year risk horizon, with 99.9 % confidence. Assume market, credit and operational risks are independent. Then check how the result would change if a 20 % correlation were assumed between market and credit risk.

3. Consider a bank issuing a 1 million euro loan to a private company having a capital requirement of 4 % (of which, as usual, at least 50 % must be tier 1 capital). The borrower has a PD of 1 % and a LGD of 70 %; the diversified economic capital allocated to the loan is 4.5 cents per euro.

   The bank wants its Tier 1 capital to cover both the minimum regulatory requirement and 50 % of economic capital. The risk-free rate is 5 %, the cost of new senior debt raised on the interbank market is 5.05 % and the cost of new subordinated loans is 5.80 %. The bank's shareholders expect to get a 5 % premium over the risk-free rate. Using equation (22.11), and ignoring operating costs for the sake of simplicity, compute the minimum lending rate which is compatible with the shareholder's target return.

4. Contingent capital is based on derivative contracts that enable a bank to:

   (A) raise new capital in the future, from a pre-committed party, at market prices;
   (B) issue new shares, in the future, to a pre-determined investor, at a price to be agreed;
   (C) unconditionally raise new capital from a pre-committed party, at pre-determined prices;
   (D) issue new shares, in the future, to a pre-determined investor and at a pre-determined price, if one or more events beyond its control happen.

5. A reverse convertible debt, embedding a contingent equity put, involves ...

   (A) ... a commitment to underwrite new capital, and therefore crucially depend on the underwriter's standing;
   (B) ... a commitment which is funded in cash, and therefore can be subsequently traded on a secondary market;
   (C) ... a commitment to accept lower coupon rates if one or more "trigger events" materialize;
   (D) ... a commitment, from the bank, to swap the debt with newly-issued shares, at a predetermined conversion rate.

23

Capital Allocation

23.1 INTRODUCTION

Now that we have shown the criteria guiding the "physical" management of capital, i.e. the choice of its optimal size and composition, we may move on to discuss its "ideal" management, i.e. its allocation to the bank's different risk-taking units.

Allocating capital means assigning a notional amount of capital to each business unit, requiring that they remunerate this capital adequately so as to meet the expectations of shareholders. This lays the groundwork for an effective system of risk-adjusted performance measurement, which makes it possible to determine which of a bank's business units are creating shareholders' value and which are absorbing resources that could be used more efficiently. This capital allocation process may concern a limited number of large business units (i.e. loans to large corporates, retail loans, asset management, securities trading, etc.) or might be pushed to a more detailed level (even as far as, for example, allocating a portion of capital to each of a bank's individual branches). Such a process is subject to constant revision: indeed, as we shall see in this chapter, it is quite normal for the capital allocated to a certain business unit not to coincide, in the following months, with the amount of capital actually absorbed by its risk-taking activities.

This shift from risk measurement to bank-wide capital allocation comes with a great many complex challenges, which, as we shall see, concern both technical aspects, connected with the creation and standardization of the risk metrics of the various areas of business, as well as managerial aspects related to the company's culture and organization.

Capital allocation policies should take into account a number of important considerations, including the following:

- capital allocation must be able to translate the final objective of shareholders' value creation into a set of clear, transparent, and accepted criteria supporting the strategic and operating decisions of the entire bank's management, at all levels;
- there must be a set of rules and incentives aimed at generating a healthy competition among the different units/divisions of the bank or financial group;
- however, this competition must not hinder an appropriate level of collaboration between those same units. Indeed, there is the risk that the fear of "being measured" and compared to others could create a climate of conflict. In such cases, it becomes difficult to share information and get the cooperation needed to create an effective system of capital allocation that embraces all the key business areas. For this reason, it is important for the process to be introduced gradually in order to ensure that the criteria the system is based upon are fully accepted by the various units whose results are being measured.
- Capital allocation must not be based on rigid rules and automated processes. The measurement of the risks taken on by the various business units (and of the amount of capital needed to cover them), while being based on models and criteria defined by the bank's risk management unit, must always be performed within a broader framework, one which takes account, for example, of the long-term profitability outlook of the various units/divisions. It is therefore essential to avoid that capital allocation becomes

a sort of "private affair" of the risk management unit, as well as to ensure that senior management is actively involved and that the planning department is also lending its support. Otherwise, the risk is that the "mechanic" may replace the driver: in other words, that by laying too much emphasis on technical aspects, one may lose sight of the true objectives of the capital allocation process.

– An efficient capital allocation process requires the active involvement of the senior management, both in defining the "rules of the game" and in the use of capital allocation results for strategic and operational purposes. With regard to the rules, in order to allocate capital one must first define the bank's degree of risk aversion (and, therefore, its optimal amount of capital and the cost of this capital), its plans for future development, and the profitability outlooks expected from each of the various business units. These parameters can be set in a credible way only when the top managerial levels of the bank are involved. As for the results, the calculations of return on capital for the various risk-taking units, based on their capital allocation, must not prove a mere theoretical exercise, but rather affect the way in which the range of businesses in which the bank is involved is recalibrated and redesigned. For this to happen, senior management must fully comprehend the importance and significance of the process, as well as the rules that guide the process and the main steps necessary to its implementation.

– Hence the capital allocation process, no matter how finely-tuned it is, must not (and actually cannot) replace the skills of an effective team of senior managers: a clear, shared strategy; strategies to control costs while placing a keen focus on employee motivation; the ability to identify the businesses and segments with the greatest growth and profit potentials; and precise, but not rigid, organizational architectures.

In this chapter, we will describe the main steps of the capital allocation process. In section 23.2, we will discuss the various approaches that can be taken in order to allocate the proper amount of capital to each business unit. Section 23.3 describes how one can (and must) adjust these measures in order to make them consistent with the bank's total level of capital, estimated as discussed in Chapter 22. In section 23.4, we will focus on the difference between the capital allocated (ex ante) to the various business units and the capital absorbed (ex post) by them, while showing how to create a logical bridge between the two concepts. In section 23.5, we will see how allocated capital and absorbed capital can be used to estimate risk-adjusted performance (i.e. Raroc) for each individual business unit. In section 23.6, we will discuss the issue of efficient capital allocation, while in section 23.7, we will focus on the organizational aspects of the capital allocation process.

23.2 MEASURING CAPITAL FOR THE INDIVIDUAL BUSINESS UNITS

Whether they are aware of it or not, all financial institutions are always allocating capital to their different businesses. In other words, a financial institution's risk-taking capacity, i.e. its capital, is implicitly absorbed by its various business units, based on their respective levels of risk. In order to assess the efficiency of this (implicit) capital allocation process, so as to change and optimize it, it is therefore necessary to make it explicit, by measuring the amount of capital absorbed by the risks faced by each business unit.

This is a bottom-up process, in the sense that we need to start with data regarding the individual business units in order to understand the amount of capital they currently absorb. Once we know the current capital allocation, the overall level of capital, and the target allocation that the top management would like to achieve, we can then establish a top-down process that periodically reallocates capital.

In this section, we will look at the various approaches to estimating the amount of capital needed to cover the risks of the various business areas within a bank. Three such methods will be discussed: the "benchmark capital" approach; the model-based approach; and the earnings-at-risk (EaR) approach. These approaches are not mutually exclusive, but rather can complement each other based on the characteristics of the various business areas and the data available.

23.2.1   The "benchmark capital" approach

As noted by Saita (2004), one solution to capital allocation is the benchmark capital approach. This involves creating a sample of single-business enterprises, i.e. enterprises whose sole, or prevalent, activity is that of the business unit for which we want to estimate capital. It is then necessary to compute the average capitalization of the sample companies (e.g. as a ratio to sales) and to use this benchmark capital figure to calculate the capital allocated to the business unit.

Assume, for example, that a bank has a private banking unit producing investment and banking services for high net worth individuals. In order to calculate the amount of capital absorbed, we would select a sample of independent private banks and look at their actual capital levels (expressed, for example, as a percentage of gross operating income). By computing the average of this ratio (capital/GOI) for the sample of single-business companies, and multiplying it by the gross operating income of the private banking unit, one would then get an estimate of its level of capital.

This solution is attractive for its simplicity; however, it presents a number of problems: the difficulties experienced in gathering a sufficient sample of single-business companies; the possibility that, despite conducting an apparently similar business, these companies could have different risk profiles; the need to approximate economic capital using publicly available data, whether it be book-value capital or market capitalization (see Chapter 22).[1]

23.2.2   The model-based approach

VaR models like those presented in the first parts of this book have experienced a dramatic development over the last 15 years, and are now being used by virtually all of the leading banks. Hence, one may estimate the economic capital of the individual business units by applying to them the same risk-measurement models that are normally used for the bank as a whole.

This approach presents three main problems, namely:

(1) it requires risk-aggregation procedures that are different from those normally used by banks in calculating their overall capital levels;
(2) because the various VaR models are built upon different assumptions and criteria, they generate risk measures that often need to be rescaled before they can be integrated;

---

[1] Furthermore, even if measured correctly, the capital of mono-business firms could overestimate the capital needed by the business unit of the bank. The reason for this is that, unlike a mono-business firm, the business unit benefits from a risk-diversification effect due to the imperfect correlation between its activities and those of the bank's other units. This issue, which is also common to the approaches presented in the following two paragraphs, will be discussed in section 23.3.

(3) finally, the VaR models available to most banks are not yet equipped to consider all existing risks, so that there are certain types of risk that essentially fall "off the radar" of these VaR models.

Let us now briefly discuss these three issues in more detail.

1. Risk-aggregation criteria – The first issue concerns the manner in which the various types of risk (interest-rate risk, market risk, credit risk, etc.) of the bank's different business units are aggregated. As we have seen in Chapter 22, risk aggregation is normally carried out by risk type (see Figure 23.1, left panel): e.g. the F/X risk of all foreign currency-denominated portfolios (including loans, securities, off-balance sheet items, etc.) are usually stored in a single database. The same is done for operational risk, for credit risk, and for all different types of risk, that are aggregated following the criteria described in the previous chapter.

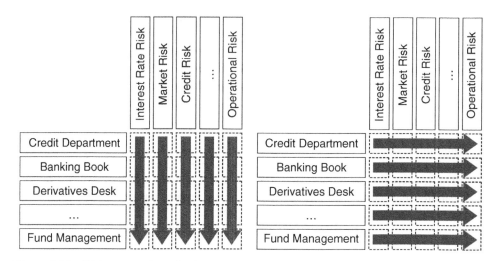

Figure 23.1   Risk-aggregation criteria across business units and risk types

However, in order to quantify the amount of capital associated with the risks faced by different business units/areas, the various types of risk must be measured and aggregated on a business unit basis (see Figure 23.1, right panel). This brings an additional level of complexity to the bank's risk measurement system, as the models for credit, market, operational and other risks must be applied separately to the individual business units as if they were totally independent enterprises.[2]

2. Model harmonization – As discussed in Chapter 22, the harmonization problem essentially concerns two aspects: the time horizon and the confidence level.

---

[2] In order to simplify the process, we can seek to centralize certain types of risk within a single business unit through notional transactions such as those that are discussed in Chapter 4. Therefore, the "credit" business unit could transfer the interest-rate risk on its fixed-rate loans to treasury by entering into an interest rate swap. In the same way, the foreign currency desk, which uses over-the-counter currency swaps, could transfer default risk to the credit unit by purchasing a credit derivative from this unit. However, it may be difficult to establish an objective price for this type of "virtual" transaction, which would impact on the costs and revenues of the various business units.

As concerns the time horizon, harmonization is generally achieved by re-scaling all risk measures to a common one-year time horizon. This is done for a number of reasons. The most important one being that allocated capital is normally used for budget and reporting purposes, two tasks which are carried out over a twelve-month period.[3] As seen in Chapters 5 and 22, if the returns of the different risk factors are serially independent, VaR can be scaled to a different time horizon simply by multiplying it by the square root of the time.

Confidence levels can also be harmonized simply by rescaling VaR when this is estimated using the parametric models for market risks seen in Chapter 5, which assume a normal distribution of risk factor returns (for an example, see also Chapter 22). Extending this solution to other types of models runs the risk of introducing significant inaccuracies, particularly if the risk factors are highly skewed, as in the case of credit risk. This approach, as observed by Hall (2002), could lead to a significant bias in the estimated amount of capital absorbed by the different risks. In such cases, it is necessary to modify the model used and to recalculate VaR at the new confidence level by running, for example, Monte Carlo simulations.

3. Risks not covered by the models – The third issue concerns the fact that certain business areas involve risks that go beyond the traditional financial risks (i.e. interest-rate, market, and credit risk) usually covered by a bank's internal models. Indeed, a number of businesses do not involve a traditional intermediation process (based on the bank jointly holding financial assets and liabilities), but still generate revenues and, therefore, earnings. Think, e.g., of asset management, advisory services, and payment services.

If we were to measure the capital at risk for these business areas using a classic VaR approach, we would get no result. With asset management, for example, the risk of a drop in stock prices or the default risk of corporate bond issuers are borne by the customers and not by the bank, so credit and market risk for the bank is zero.

However, this does not mean that this business is risk-free: in fact, the profits generated by business areas like asset management are volatile and unpredictable over time. If profits decrease, then the bank's economic value (i.e. the present value of all its future profits) also decreases. Therefore, these business areas present risks that, although they are different from standard financial risks, could lead to losses for the bank's shareholders.

Profit volatility can partly be explained by operational risk.[4] However, other factors, as well, contribute to the volatility of earnings, e.g. unexpected changes in demand or incorrect management decisions made by the bank. The term "business risk" is normally used to indicate all factors that can lead to an unexpected change in business volumes and, therefore, in profits.

In order to measure the capital absorbed by business risk, we can take an approach that is different from traditional VaR models, as described in the following section.

23.2.3 The Earnings-at-Risk (EaR) approach

Rather than using the volatility of the market value of assets, one can estimate capital at risk based on the volatility of earnings.[5] As with VaR models, one can use a parametric

---

[3] Other factors in favour of choosing a one-year risk time horizon are discussed in Chapter 14 with regard to VaR models for credit risk.
[4] See Chapter 17.
[5] I.e. earnings less any accounting distortions. Alternatively, cash flows can be used directly.

approach, as well as an approach based on historical data or simulations. In this section, we present a brief example of the parametric approach and the one based on historical data.[6]

Table 23.1 and Figure 23.2 below show the earnings generated by a bank's asset management unit. As mentioned above, this business is not typically exposed to interest-rate and market risks, given that any losses are incurred by its customers. The figures show profits constantly on the rise, given that the business unit has continued to grow over time, as we can see from the number of employees. However, profits per employee have varied widely around the expected value (€ 10,628 per employee) due to cyclical changes in the volume and type of asset management services requested by the public.

Table 23.1 Historical profits of the Asset Management unit

Year	Profits (euro millions)	Size (# of employees)	Profits per employee (euros)
1996	3.23	350	9,233
1997	3.70	381	9,708
1998	4.67	421	11,087
1999	4.86	483	10,059
2000	4.77	543	8,782
2001	6.05	598	10,107
2002	7.41	662	11,197
2003	7.50	758	9,893
2004	8.13	867	9,369
2005	8.28	937	8,843
2006	10.97	1.032	10,628
Average			9,901
Standard deviation			825.95

The erratic nature of these per-unit profits results in a level of business risk which we now wish to measure. One approach is to use the historical data. We take past historical per-unit profits, sort them in increasing order, re-write them as differences from the mean (see Table 23.2 and Figure 23.3), and finally isolate a percentile of this distribution (e.g. a confidence level of 99 %, which can be obtained by linear interpolation of the worst and second-worst profit figures), which comes to −1,112.8 euros, that is, to a decrease in profits of 1,112.8 euros per employee. Assuming, now, that the business unit currently has 800 employees, then earnings at risk (EaR) can be estimated as 1,112.8·800 ≅ 0.89 million euros.

As an alternative, one may use a parametric approach. Assume that the distribution of profits around the mean is known and given, for example, by a normal distribution.

---

[6] For an example of this type of approach, see Yoshifuji (1997) among others.

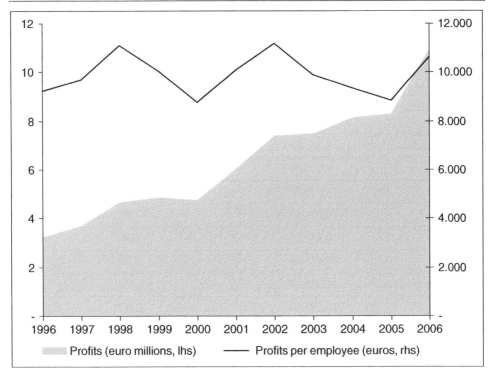

Figure 23.2   Historical data for the Asset Management unit

In this case, the 99th percentile can be obtained by multiplying the standard deviation by the desired percentile ($\alpha_{99\%} \cong 2.32$) of the standard normal distribution. In our case, because the standard deviation of profits per employee (and therefore also that of the differences from the mean) is approximately 826 euros, the percentile will be: $2.32 \cdot 826 \cong$ € 1921. Multiplied by our 800 employees, this results in an estimate of earnings at risk of approximately 1.54 million euros. As we can see, this is significantly different from the figure obtained using historical data. Given the limited data available (our sample has just 11 observations), we cannot say with certainty which of the two values is more reliable. However, we have obtained an estimate of the order of magnitude (say in the area of 1.2 million euros) of the EaR associated with this business unit.

To transform EaR into capital at risk (VaR) one must define the nature, either temporary or permanent, of the potential drop in profits. If this reduction is just temporary, then it can be absorbed by an identical amount of capital, so that VaR = EaR.

However, assume that the decline is permanent (and therefore also applies to all subsequent years). In this case, the potential loss to be covered by capital at risk is equal to the reduction in the value of the bank resulting not only from the decline in current profits, but also from the enduring drop in all future earnings. This value decrease, which corresponds to economic capital, can be expressed as follows:

$$EC = CaR = VaR = \frac{EaR}{r_e} \qquad (23.1)$$

Table 23.2 Profits per employee in increasing order

Year	Profits (euros) per employee	Profits per employee – difference from the mean
2000	8,781.80	−1,119
2005	8,842.99	−1,056
1996	9,233.41	−667
2004	9,369.17	−532
1997	9,708.50	−192
2003	9,892.56	−8
1999	10,059.50	159
2001	10,106.58	206
2006	10,628.46	728
1998	11,087.27	1,187
2002	11,197.34	1,297
99 % percentile	11,186,33	−1,112.767

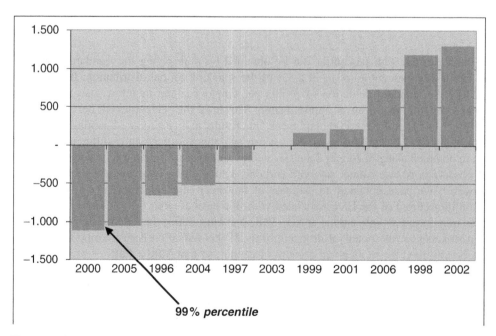

Figure 23.3   Unexpected profits ranked in increasing order

where r_e represents the bank's cost of capital,[7] to be further defined in Chapter 24. Equation (23.1) calculates EC as the present value of all the lower future annual profits, EaR, expected *every year in the future*.[8] In our case, for example, assuming a cost of capital of 8 %, the EaR of the asset management unit (1.2 million euros) would correspond to a VaR of 15 million euros.[9]

However, this assumption may be overly severe and unrealistic. Indeed, Figure 23.2 shows that the drops in profits are normally of a temporary nature. Therefore, it may be more appropriate to assume that the lower profits are gradually absorbed over a relatively short period, say three years. In this case, given an EaR of 1.2 million euros, a reasonable estimate of capital at risk could be as follows:[10]

$$EC = CaR = VaR = \frac{1,200,000}{1 + 8\%} + \frac{800,000}{(1 + 8\%)^2} + \frac{400,000}{(1 + 8\%)^3} \cong 2,114,515 \qquad (23.2)$$

As mentioned above, the EaR approach enables us to measure the risk of business areas that do not entail taking on financial risks. In practice, this method can also be used for activities that involve financial risks, and, indeed, such a solution has been adopted by certain US banks in the past.[11] The decision to focus on profit volatility (regardless of its nature, whether it be capital losses, lower fees, or lower interest income) has two fundamental benefits:

- once a time series is available, for the past profits of a business unit, it is not necessary to separate the different types of risk that it has been facing;
- it allows to account for risks that are difficult to measure, such as operational and business risk.

However, the earnings-at-risk method does also present a number of significant limitations:

- it underestimates the true risk of certain businesses, such as securities trading. In fact, a bank could have highly risky positions in securities and options in its portfolio and yet have experienced modest profit volatility in the past. This happens because the risk profile of a trading portfolio can be altered easily and quickly, which makes historical data fairly unreliable and requires that we use a method based on the sensitivity of the *current* positions to market factors and on their volatility;
- it can only be applied to business units or divisions that encompass a large number of individual activities, in order for the assumptions of stability (historical approach) or

---

[7] Saita (2000). A similar formula has been proposed by Matten (1996), but using the risk-free rate, r, in place of the cost of capital, r_e.

[8] I.e. the formula ($V = R/r$) for the present value V of a perpetuity with a payment of R valued at the rate of r.

[9] As observed by Saita (2007), as an alternative to the term $1/r_e$, we can also use the price-to-earnings ratio of a sample of mono-business firms that operate exclusively in the asset management industry (similar to the sample used in section 23.2.1 to calculate benchmark capital). Further, assuming that lower earnings translate into lower dividends (either entirely or based on the bank's average payout ratio), we can use dividend discount models, such as Gordon's model for calculating the impact of EaR on the value of the bank, i.e. on economic capital.

[10] Alternatively, we can also use more sophisticated models that calculate the persistence of lower profits through an econometric analysis of the series of historical profits, such as mean-reverting models.

[11] See Chew and Gumerlock (1993).

normality (parametric approach) of the profits distribution to hold. Therefore, it cannot be used to calculate the capital at risk related to individual customers or transactions, or, therefore, for pricing purposes;

– it requires the business units to have been active for a sufficient number of years and that there have not been changes to such an extent that the significance of past data has been compromised. For example, if the divisions of a bank have undergone reorganizations or mergers, historical data may not be sufficiently homogenous and reliable.

Despite these limitations, EaR measures can be highly valuable in calculating an approximate value for the capital at risk associated with activities for which other approaches are not available.

23.3 THE RELATIONSHIP BETWEEN ALLOCATED CAPITAL AND TOTAL CAPITAL

23.3.1 The concept of diversified capital

In the previous section, we discussed how a certain amount of economic capital can be allocated to each division or business unit. We will now see how these measures can be made consistent with the bank's total economic capital.[12]

Of course, this is not just a simple problem of addition. This is because, when we consider the different business areas as parts of the bank's total portfolio of businesses (and no longer as stand-alone entities), their capital"consumption" falls as a result of the benefits of diversification.

Take, for example, three business units (Figure 23.4), each with its own economic capital (calculated as described in section 23.2 above). Also, assume that we have calculated economic capital for the bank as a whole as described in Chapter 22: this will be less than the sum of the partial ECs because the volatility of the bank's total losses will be lessened by the imperfect correlation, e.g., between the market risks on investment banking and the operational risks on asset management. The difference between the sum of the standalone ECs and the EC for the bank is due to the effect of cross-unit diversification and can be "redistributed" to the individual business areas, thereby reducing their capital consumption. In this case, the EC of a business unit less the diversification effect is referred to as *diversified economic capital* (DEC).

Calculating diversified capital is a very delicate process and must meet a number of prerequisites:

– diversified capital must be *additive*; that is to say, the total of the capitals allocated to the various business units must coincide with the economic capital of the bank;
– diversified capital must be *incentive-compatible*; i.e. it must reward, with a greater discount over standalone capital, the units that contribute most to diversifying a bank's risks;

---

[12] In this chapter, we refer primarily to economic capital (EC) as the measure of the bank's total capital. This is because, on the one hand, economic capital, and not regulatory capital, expresses the amount of resources that shareholders must keep within the bank in the form of available capital (AC > EC) in order to absorb risks and "reassure" the market. On the other hand, even if the bank adjusts its level of capital in consideration of both economic capital and regulatory requirements (see equations 22.7 and 22.8), allocation of the latter to the various business units is not particularly difficult (as the process is guided by clear rules defined by regulators), so the most delicate and most important process is the allocation of economic capital.

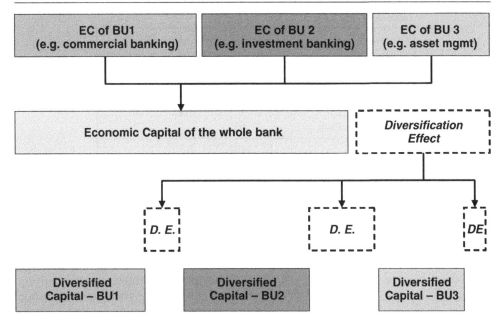

Figure 23.4 The diversification effect and diversified economic capital

– as it is going to play a key role in the strategic decisions of senior management, diversified capital must be computed in a clear and *transparent* way.

In the section below, we will look at the approaches that can be adopted in order to compute diversified economic capital.

23.3.2   Calculating diversified capital

The main methods for calculating diversified capital are the following:

– the proportional apportionment method;
– the marginal economic capital method;
– the correlation method.

The proportional apportionment method – This approach is very simple and easy to understand, but is intrinsically imprecise. It entails distributing the benefits of diversification among the various business units in a manner that is proportionate to their standalone economic capital.

   Take, for example, Table 23.3: the benefits of cross-unit diversification for the bank as a whole come to 80 million euros (i.e. the difference between the sum of the individual ECs and the total EC). If we distribute this among the various units in proportion with their standalone capital, we get the figures shown in the last column.

   This approach has two advantages: first, we do not have to calculate the correlation between the various divisions, which underlies the benefits of diversification; second, it enables us to isolate the EC of the individual divisions from the operations of the other

Table 23.3 The apportionment method

Division	EC (millions of euros)	DEC (millions of euros)
Commercial Banking	150	112.5
Investment Banking	120	90
Asset Management	50	37.5
Whole Bank	240	

areas of business, in the sense that any changes in the asset portfolio of one business unit have only a very modest impact on the economic capital absorbed by the others.

The main disadvantage, of course, is that the distribution of the diversification benefits ignores the actual contribution made by the individual divisions to the bank's overall level of risk. For example, investment banking could be a highly volatile business and, as such, could consume a high level of standalone EC, but could, nonetheless, be negatively correlated to the other business areas (and therefore generate significant diversification benefits). The apportionment method would not capture this fact and would cause the bank's senior management to underestimate the benefits, also in terms of Raroc,[13] of operating in the investment banking industry. Indeed, proportionate apportionment only partially satisfies the prerequisites listed above; i.e. it is additive and transparent, but not incentive-compatible.

The marginal EC method – A second method is based on the concept of marginal economic capital, also known (see Chapters 14 and 15) as marginal VaR. Marginal capital is defined as the increase in economic capital as a result of adding a given asset (in our case: a business unit) to a certain portfolio. As such, it is calculated by comparing two VaRs, computed by including business unit i for which we wish to calculate the marginal VaR (i.e. the bank's EC) or by leaving it out ($EC_{\neg i}$).

Making reference again to the data in Table 23.3, assume that we wish to recalculate the bank's total capital at risk after eliminating all exposures, securities, profits and losses related to the commercial banking business. EC (which is 240 million including commercial banking, as shown in Table 23.3) might fall, for example, to 110 million ($EC_{\neg 1}$). The marginal economic capital (EC_1') associated with commercial banking would, therefore, be 130 million. Table 23.4 shows the same process applied to all three divisions.

Note that, for all of the divisions, marginal capital is less than standalone EC. Indeed, it is logical for the risks of a given business unit, when added to a diversified portfolio of businesses, to be less than the risks it faces when considered on its own.[14] More specifically, the ratio between marginal and standalone capital is lower for the units that are less correlated with the bank's other businesses (such as asset management, where the ratio EC'/EC is 50%). Therefore, marginal capital is incentive compatible because

---

[13] See section 23.5
[14] Note that this property, which is always desirable from an economic point of view, may not actually be ensured by certain VaR measures, particularly the VaR measures that are not sub-additive as discussed in Chapter 9.

Table 23.4 The marginal economic capital method

Division	EC	Bank EC w/o this division $(EC_{\neg i})$	Marginal EC $(EC_i' = EC - EC_{\neg i})$	DEC
Commercial Banking	150	110	130	145.1
Investment Banking	120	180	60	67.0
Asset Management	50	215	25	27.9
Whole Bank	240			
Total			*215*	*240*

Note: figures in millions of euros.

it generates a larger "discount" over standalone capital for the units that are best at diversifying the risks of the entire bank.

However, we can easily see that marginal capital fails to meet the prerequisite of being additive (see Merton & Perold, 1993). Indeed, the sum of the three business units' EC's (215) is lower than the bank's total EC (240). This is because, when calculating the additional capital required by a business unit, marginal capital assumes that it is always added to the portfolio as the last one. Therefore, for example, the investment banking division generates a marginal capital of just 60 million because it benefits from the imperfect correlation with the commercial banking and asset management divisions. However, asset management also generates a modest marginal capital because it benefits from the correlation with investment banking (as well as commercial banking), so the same diversification effect is counted twice.

For this reason, marginal capital *EC'*, can be seen as an underestimation of the true capital consumption of a given business unit. It may only be appropriate if the bank were considering an acquisition of a new business unit, which would actually (and not just for the sake of calculation) be added to the existing business portfolio. In other words, the marginal capital method considers each individual division as if it were a new business being added to the bank's existing businesses, which is an appropriate assumption when considering the potential of a new, unexplored area of business, but is less suited to evaluating businesses that a bank has been operating in for some time.[15]

Note that the inability to comply with the additivity prerequisite is a very concrete and practical problem. Imagine that the bank has "promised" its shareholders a return on economic capital of 10 %, which equals profits of 24 million. Requiring that its business units generate a return of 10 % on their respective EC' (which total 215 million), the bank would achieve total profits of just 21.5 million, for a return of 8.96 % (i.e. less than shareholders' expectations) on its total economic capital.

---

[15] In the same way, this method could be interesting if we were measuring the capital consumption related to a new project, such as participating in a large syndicated loan. Nonetheless, in both cases, if the portfolio of existing businesses should change, particularly if there were a reduction in businesses that are less correlated with the new business unit or new project, marginal economic capital could be insufficient to take account of the true risks.

In order to meet this problem, we can calculate diversified capital by adjusting EC' using a constant equal to the ratio between total risk capital (240) and the sum of the marginal risk capital figures (215). Therefore, for the ith business unit we would have:

$$DEC_i = EC'_i \frac{EC}{\sum_i EC'_i} \qquad (23.3)$$

Applying this simplified approach, we get the DEC figures shown in the last column of Table 23.4.

Even though it can be made additive in this way, the marginal capital method still presents two limitations. The first is the excessive computational burden: the calculations that lead to the estimation of VaR with and without a certain business unit are rather complex and time-consuming, especially when based on simulations and when the number of business units is large. The second, which is a consequence of the first, is the limited transparency, given that a keen familiarity with all of the bank's risk management models is often necessary in order to understand the drivers of marginal VaR. The first problem can be mitigated by approximating marginal capital using a parametric approach, which will be described at the end of this paragraph.

The correlation method[16] – A bank's economic capital (EC) can be expressed as a multiple k of the standard deviation of the distribution of total losses:

$$EC = k\sigma \qquad (23.4)$$

In the same way, the standalone economic capital for the ith business unit can be expressed as

$$EC_i = k_i \sigma_i \qquad (23.5)$$

where the multiple k_i is generally different from k and depends on the form of the loss distribution for business unit i.

Furthermore, since the total losses of a bank are the sum of the losses of the individual business units, their standard deviation σ can always be expressed as

$$\sigma = \sqrt{\sum_i \sum_j \rho_{i,j} \sigma_i \sigma_j} \qquad (23.6)$$

(where the subscripts i and j indicate the individual business units) or, equivalently, as[17]

$$\sigma = \sum_i \rho_{i,T} \sigma_i \qquad (23.7)$$

---

[16] The correlation approach to calculating diversified capital (which is also referred to as component VaR, given its capacity to "compose" the bank's economic capital in a perfectly additive manner) has been dealt with by James (1996), Matten (1996) and Sironi (1996), among others.

[17] For details on how equations (23.7) and (23.8) were derived, see Appendix 23A at the end of this chapter.

where $\rho_{i,T}$ indicates the correlation between the losses of the ith business unit and those of the bank as a whole, which can be calculated as follows:

$$\rho_{i,T} = \frac{\sum_j \sigma_j \rho_{i,j}}{\sigma} \qquad (23.8)$$

Substituting equation (23.7) into (23.4) we get

$$EC = \sum_i \rho_{i,T} k \sigma_i = \sum_i \rho_{i,T} \frac{k}{k_i} EC_i = \sum_i DEC_i \qquad (23.9)$$

In other words, equation (23.9) states that we can calculate the diversified economic capital (DEC) of a business unit as

$$DEC_i = \rho_{i,T} \frac{k}{k_i} EC_i \qquad (23.10)$$

i.e. by adjusting standalone economic capital by the correlation between the losses of the ith business unit and those of the whole bank and by a factor, k/k_j, which takes account of the different form of the loss probability distribution.

Note that the diversified capital figure obtained with equation (23.10) is additive (as indicated in equation 23.9, the sum of the DECs of the various business units coincides with the bank's economic capital) and includes a greater discount over the standalone economic capital for business units showing a lower correlation with the bank as a whole.[18]

Let us now take a closer look at the factor k/k_j. Suppose that a given business unit has a k_j that is significantly greater than k (because, for example, its losses follow a highly skewed distribution and the percentile associated with economic capital is a large number of standard deviations away from the mean). In this case, our scaling factor is significantly lower than one, and the business unit receives a large discount in the transition from standalone capital to diversified capital. This (and hence the factorization process in equation 23.9) may not be correct, given that a highly positive skew indicates the potential for extremely high levels of risk. If a bank wishes to allocate economic capital in such a way that also accounts for the existence of extreme losses, it may prefer to avoid such discounts in the event of highly skewed distributions.

In this case, the factor k/k_j, which is different for each business unit, may be replaced by a constant factor chosen in such a way as to ensure that the results are additive. More specifically, using a fixed factor equal to $\dfrac{EC}{\sum_i \rho_{i,T} EC_i}$, the diversified capital of the business units can be calculated as

$$DEC_i = \frac{EC}{\sum_i \rho_{i,T} EC_i} \rho_{i,T} EC_i \qquad (23.10b)$$

---

[18] If the correlation is negative, economic capital may also be negative. This is an extreme case in which a business unit frees up capital, rather than absorbing it, because it reduces the volatility of the bank's total losses. As with securities that have a negative beta in the capital asset pricing model, such a business unit could also generate profits at less than the risk-free rate and still be a good investment for shareholders, precisely because of its ability to reduce the overall losses of the bank.

It can then be easily shown that the DEC_i values calculated with equation (23.10b) satisfy equation (23.9), i.e. that they are perfectly additive.

Finally, note that, if the values of k_i for the various business units are not too different from the k for the bank as a whole, then diversified capital can be calculated simply as:

$$DEC_i = \rho_{i,T} EC_i \qquad (23.10c)$$

and equation (23.9) will still be (at least approximately) satisfied:

$$EC \cong \sum_i \rho_{i,T} EC_i$$

In this case, correlations are all we need to move from standalone capital to diversified capital.[19]

In order to show how these formulae work, we shall turn again to the three business units of Tables 23.3 and 23.4. Their standalone ECs are shown again in Table 23.5 (second column), together with the economic capital for the entire bank.

The third column shows the correlation coefficients for the losses of each division and those of the bank as a whole; such correlations can either be estimated directly using, for example, a Monte Carlo simulation, or calculated from pairwise correlations between business units (see Table 23.6) by using equation (23.8). Note that the estimation of pairwise correlations like those in Table 23.6 will be discussed in the next section.

Table 23.5 The correlation approach

Division	EC	$\rho_{i,T}$	$\rho_{i,T} \cdot EC$	DEC	σ	$k = EC/\sigma$
Commercial Banking	150	86.9%	130.3	119.0	37	4.1
Investment Banking	120	85.6%	102.7	93.9	40	3.0
Asset Management	50	59.3%	29.7	27.1	8	6.3
Whole Bank	240				71.1	3.4
Total			262.7	240.0		

Table 23.6 The correlation coefficients between the business units

	CB	IB	AM
Commercial Banking (CB)	100%	50%	60%
Investment Banking (IB)	50%	100%	30%
Asset Management (AM)	60%	30%	100%

---

[19] According to the Basel Committee on Banking Supervision (2003c), this solution is common practice by a number of leading banks. It is simply a different way of expressing equation (22.6) of Chapter 22, which, in that context, was used to aggregate economic capital among the various types of risk, rather than to allocate economic capital to the different business units.

Using the correlations in the third column of Table 23.5, we now show how to calculate diversified capital. First of all, we use equation (23.10c) and obtain the results shown in column four of the Table. As we can see, the total of these values does *not* equal the economic capital for the bank as a whole. The reason for this is that the distributions of the losses of the three business units take different shapes, as indicated by the coefficients k_i shown in the last column of the Table.

We then calculate the scaling factor for equation (23.10b):

$$\frac{EC}{\sum_i \rho_{i,T} EC_i} \cong \frac{240}{262.7} \cong 0.914$$

and then use equation (23.10b) to calculate the diversified capital of the various business units (see column five).

Note that, as with the DECs based on marginal capital shown in Table 23.4, the DECs of Table 23.5 "reward" more (with a significant discount over standalone capital) the investment banking and asset management divisions. However, the discount on the capital allocated to the investment banking division is less significant than in Table 23.4. This is due to the fact that the two approaches (i.e. the marginal capital and correlation approaches) measure diversification from different angles. The marginal capital method analyzes the benefits of diversification when a business unit is the last to be added to the portfolio, while the correlation approach measures these benefits by looking at the overall composition of the existing portfolio.[20]

The correlation approach can also be used to streamline the calculation of marginal capital by using a parametric approach. As we have seen above, marginal capital is given by the equation

$$EC'_i = EC - EC_{\neg i}$$

where $EC_{\neg i}$ is the capital of the bank without business unit i. Applying equation (23.4), this can be rewritten as:

$$EC_{\neg i} = k_{\neg i} \sigma_{\neg i} \tag{23.11}$$

Furthermore, given equation (23.6), $\sigma_{\neg i}$ (the standard deviation of the bank's losses without business unit i) can be expressed as

$$\sigma_{\neg i} = \sqrt{\sum_{h \neq i} \sum_{j \neq i} \rho_{h,j} \sigma_h \sigma_j} \tag{23.12}$$

If we are willing to overlook the correction factor related to the different shape of the loss distribution (in other words, if we accept to assume that all of the k_i and $k_{\neg i}$ are

---

[20] Finally, we should note that, when using equation (23.10) to calculate DEC, the values of the DECs of the three units would have been 108, 116 and 16 million, respectively. Therefore, asset management would have had a significantly lower DEC. The reason for this is that, as indicated by a k_i of roughly double that of the bank, the distribution of the losses of this unit appears to have a pronounced right tail, i.e. a relatively modest number of cases in which losses are very high (which may, for example, be due to the high level of operational risk). The standalone economic capital of this business unit reaches 60 million as a result of this significant skewness, while equation (23.10) removes the effects by actually ignoring the existence of extreme loss scenarios.

not significantly different from k), then equations (23.11), (23.12) and (23.5) may be combined as follows:

$$EC_{\neg i} = \sqrt{\sum_{h \neq i} \sum_{j \neq i} \rho_{h,j} EC_h EC_j} \qquad (23.13)$$

and the marginal capital of business unit i can be reduced to:

$$EC_i' = EC - \sqrt{\sum_{h \neq i} \sum_{j \neq i} \rho_{h,j} EC_h EC_j} \qquad (23.14)$$

which can be calculated much more quickly, without having to resort to any special procedures like Monte Carlo simulations.

In the case of the first business unit, for example, equation (23.14) equals:

$$EC_1' = EC - \sqrt{\sum_{h=2,3} \sum_{j=2,3} \rho_{h,j} EC_h EC_j} = EC - \sqrt{EC_2^2 + 2\rho_{2,3} EC_2 EC_3 + EC_3^2}$$

$$= 240 - \sqrt{120^2 + 2 \cdot 0,3 \cdot 120 \cdot 50 + 50^2} \cong 96.8$$

The remaining results are shown in Table 23.7. As was the case also in Table 23.4, the sum of the marginal capitals is lower than the economic capital for the entire bank. It is therefore advisable to apply a scaling factor in order to make the DECs additive. Furthermore, the figures obtained in Table 23.7 are only partially similar to those of Table 23.4, as precision has been sacrificed for the sake of computational simplicity.[21]

Table 23.7 The marginal capital approach – calculation simplified by using correlations

Division	EC	EC'	DEC
Commercial Banking	150	96.8	147.0
Investment Banking	120	55.6	84.4
Asset Management	50	5.7	8.6
Whole Bank	240		
Total		158.1	

23.3.3 Calculating the correlations used in determining diversified capital

The formulae used to calculate DEC based on correlations (equations 23.10, 23.10b and 23.10c) require the knowledge of the correlation coefficients (ρ_{iT}) between the total losses for the bank and those of the individual business units.

---

[21] In particular, note how asset management receives significantly less capital than that of Table 23.3. The reason for this is that, assuming all k values are the same, equation (23.14) ignores the significant skewness of the distribution of losses for this business unit and ensures a large discount as compared with standalone capital, which takes this skewness into consideration. A similar result is also described in note 20.

As we have seen, these calculations can also be derived (equation 23.8) from the matrix of pairwise correlations between business units (see Table 23.6); the latter is also needed in the simplified calculation (equation 23.14) of DEC based on marginal capital.

In this section, we discuss three ways in which pairwise correlations can be estimated, namely:

- through subjective assumptions;
- based on historical data;
- using Monte Carlo simulations.

Subjective assumptions – This method requires that correlations be estimated by the bank's management or with the help of outside consultants. Although actually used by several financial institutions,[22] it clearly presents a number of problems. First, it should be the risk measurement tools that guide the views of management, and not the other way around. Second, this approach does not make (formal) use of the information inherent in the historical data on the profits of the individual business units, which are often kept on file for management control purposes. Finally, there is also the risk that the correlation between business units changes over time due to their evolving operating policies, without this change being promptly reflected in the management subjective estimates.

Historical data – In this case, the bank may use either outside information (equity returns for single-business financial institutions as in the benchmark capital approach) or in-house data (profits of the various divisions, which are kept on file for management control purposes).

The first option suffers from both a lack of publicly listed companies that are truly specialized in a given area of business, and even if such firms exist, their risk profiles are unlikely to be comparable to those of the bank's business units. As such, the second variant (as proposed by Matten, 1996, among others) is probably the most common approach.[23] The simplest version of this approach requires a time series of (usually quarterly) earnings for the bank's various business units, upon which correlations are computed. However, a number of problems may arise: the first (as statisticians are aware) is that the correlation coefficient could be affected by the frequency of the data, such that it would be inappropriate to apply a set of quarterly data to an annual risk time horizon (as is normally used for economic capital); a second limitation, as noted by Saita (2007), is that interim data can underestimate the correlation when we encounter cross-unit autocorrelation in the profits of the various business units.[24]

An alternative to calculating correlations directly is the multi-factor approach proposed by Alexander and Pezier (2003), which calculates the sensitivity of the profits of each business unit (π_i) to n predefined risk factors $(x_1, x_2, \ldots x_n,$ e.g. market variables or economic indicators). In other words, for each business unit the following equation must be estimated:

$$\pi_i = \alpha_i + \beta_{i,1}x_1 + \beta_2x_2 + \cdots + +\beta_{i,n}x_n + \varepsilon_i \qquad (23.15)$$

---

[22] See the Joint Forum (2003), pp. 24–25.

[23] Basel Committee on Banking Supervision (2003b).

[24] In other words, we can have situations in which the profits of period t for one unit are correlated with those of period $t+1$ or $t+2$ of another unit. For details, see Saita (2007).

where α_i and $\beta_1, \beta_2, \ldots \beta_n$ represent the coefficients to be estimated and ε_i is the unexplained portion of profits. Using these equations, Alexander and Pezier show how it is possible to calculate the correlations between the profits of the various business units. Also, they show how to calculate the variability of the bank's total profits given the variability of the risk factors. Although interesting from a theoretical point of view, this approach presents a number of problems in terms of its actual application, not least of which are the identification of the risk factors and the specification of their probability distributions.

Generally speaking, all of the approaches based on internal historical data are hindered by the fact that past data may not be adequately representative of the current level of risk. Furthermore, when we encounter cases of corporate restructuring (which are increasingly common in the banking industry), the apportionment of past data by business areas may be inconsistent with the way in which the bank's current business units are organized.

Monte Carlo simulations – This approach may be used when the models used to calculate the bank's total economic capital make use of Monte Carlo simulations (see Chapters 6 and 14), that is, on the simulation of a large number of scenarios. In this case, for each scenario, losses can be allocated to the different business units by creating an $s x u$ matrix in which the result of s scenarios is distributed across u business units. This matrix, which can also be used for other capital allocation purposes,[25] enables us to estimate the correlation coefficients between the profits of the different units (see Table 23.6) or between these profits and those of the bank ($\rho_{i,T}$).

This approach has the significant advantage that the correlations do not reflect the past exposure to risk of the different units, but their current exposure. However, it also requires that we have an integrated model to compute the bank's economic capital based on simulations, a conceptually complex tool which requires a great deal of computational effort and is not currently available to most banks. Therefore, this approach is most often used to distribute to the different business units *a specific type of risk* for which the bank has a simulation model, e.g. in order to allocate capital for credit risk to divisions that follow different customer segments (e.g. large corporate, corporate, small businesses, households) without considering the effect of any market, operational or business risks.

23.4 CAPITAL ALLOCATED AND CAPITAL ABSORBED

Tables 23.3 through 23.7 provide a number of alternative ways to calculate the capital allocated to the different business units (expressed in terms of both standalone EC and DEC), based on the amount of risk they are currently taking (and possibly on the expected growth rates for their businesses).

Through this type of calculations, senior management and the planning department determine the amount of capital to be assigned to the business units as part of their yearly budget, meaning that these units will have to generate sufficient earnings in order to remunerate the share of shareholders' capital that they have received.

However, notice that the capital initially allocated to a business unit based on its current risks and any expected increases (i.e. its *allocated* capital) does not necessarily match

---

[25] For example, if the bank uses expected shortfall as a measure of risk rather than VaR, this matrix enables us to allocate the expected shortfall to the various business units based on incremental expected shortfall measures, which go beyond the scope of this chapter.

the capital absorbed by the risks it actually takes on in the following months (i.e. its *absorbed* capital or *used* capital). For example, the division in charge of consumer credit could experience a greater-than-expected increase in its risk exposure due to a boom in the credit card market. In the same way, the derivatives trading desk could reduce its exposure to market risk due to a lack of adequate trading opportunities. In short, the ex post "consumption" of capital may be different than the ex ante allocation.

This risk is reinforced by the fact that the individual business units, when negotiating budget targets, often tend to get management to agree to the lowest level of capital possible (also taking advantage of the methodological uncertainty that surrounds calculations like those of Tables 23.3–23.7). A low amount of allocated capital means a lower level of profits that must be generated in order to ensure an adequate capital remuneration; any excess profits over this threshold will then be claimed by management as value creation. On the other hand if, during the financial year, the risks incurred by a business unit (as measured by the bank's risk measurement models) should point to a level (i.e. to an amount of absorbed capital) that is greater than the economic capital allocated in the budget, the business unit can always request an extra injection of capital.

It is therefore necessary to design a mechanism that limits such moral hazards and opportunistic behaviours and avoids the risk that the amount of capital allocated at the beginning of each year is systematically lower than the amount of capital absorbed throughout the year by the risks actually taken on.

One possible mechanism (Saita, 2007) would require that, for any capital supplements (i.e. the difference between absorbed capital and allocated capital), the business unit be asked to pay a penalty p in addition to the target return defined by shareholders, i.e. a "fine" for not having requested the right amount of capital at the right time.

Obviously, the value of p is crucial. If it is too low, there is the risk that it will not affect the behavior of the business units and that the problem of underestimating absorbed capital will remain. If it is too high, it could handicap the business units when faced with any unforeseen business opportunities, which would have to be passed up, even if they would be able to generate the level of profits required by shareholders, because they do not allow to cover the additional cost of the penalty p.

The value of p should also be high enough to generate payments from the business units to senior management that are sufficient to cover the cost of the extra capital (that is not being allocated to any business unit) that it needs to hold in order to face unexpected capital requests. Since this will cause the bank's available capital to be greater than economic capital (AC > EC) (see Chapter 22), then the penalty p must be high enough to adequately remunerate the difference between the two. When such a difference becomes too high, a higher value of p, besides helping to remunerate this difference, will motivate the business units to request a higher level of allocated capital, thereby closing the gap between AC and EC.

The value of p also depends on the mechanisms and relationships that govern the budget and the ex ante capital allocation process. If this is a bottom-up process in which the business units voluntarily tender to obtain a certain level of capital to sustain their risk taking activities, then p should be high enough to punish those who willfully request a level of capital that is too low. If, on the other hand, it is a top-down process in which each unit is "passively" given a certain amount of capital from above, then p could be lower because the business units are not entirely responsible for the capital received.

Finally, p can also depend on the type of activities conducted by a given business unit, so that more flexible businesses with more liquid secondary markets (enabling them to adjust their risk levels more quickly and easily) may be asked to pay a higher p than that of less flexible areas of business that lack adequate secondary markets.

The penalty coefficient p applies to cases in which absorbed capital exceeds allocated capital. In the opposite case, that is when a business unit uses an amount of capital that is *less* than the capital allocated in the budget, it simply must generate profits still based on its ex ante *allocated* capital. Indeed, this rule is an incentive towards the full use of allocated capital and prevents a "scarce" resource such as shareholder capital from being parked in a business unit that fails to take full advantage of its risk-taking capacity.

The link between allocated capital and absorbed capital is summarized in Figure 23.5. Note that we cannot say if a business unit will have to pay more, in terms of the minimum level of profits to be achieved, in the case of underestimating allocated capital (left side) or when overestimating it (right side).

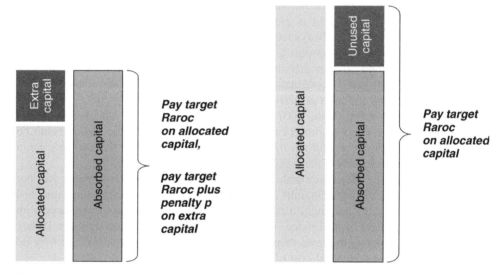

Figure 23.5   Managing the gap between allocated and absorbed capital

The difference between allocated capital and absorbed capital also affects the way in which a risk capital measurement needs to be rescaled, for example, from a 10-day to an annual time horizon.

If the goal is to allocate capital based on current risks, the best way (even with all due caution related to the assumption of serial independence of the risk factors' returns) is to multiply the current 10-day VaR by the square root of 25 (i.e. the number of 10-day periods in one year of 250 days).

However, if the goal is to measure the average amount of capital absorbed throughout the year, it would be better to calculate an average of the different 10-day VaRs (or of the daily VaRs). Nonetheless, this average could "hide" different levels of risk, especially if there have been peaks in risk exposure.

Take, for example, two trading desks, A and B, that have experienced an average 10-day VaR of 10 million during the year (25 periods), for an annualized VaR of 50 million.[26]

---

[26] Example taken from Saita (2007).

However, the first unit has held VaR perfectly constant (i.e. 25 periods with VaR at 10 million), while the second posted a zero VaR for 24 periods (e.g. due to derivatives contracts used as a hedge) and a VaR of 250 million for just one period. Clearly, we cannot conclude that their capital absorption has been the same, given that the second unit exposed the bank to very high levels of risk, even though this was for a short period of time.

One solution could be to take the maximum 10-day VaR for each unit (i.e. 10 for A and 250 for B) and multiply it by 5 (i.e. the square root of 25) in order to adjust it to an annual time horizon (so we would have 50 for A and 1250 for B).

A second, less extreme, solution (Saita, 2007) uses the square root of the sum of the squares of the VaRs recorded in each period. In the case of business unit A, this would result in:

$$\overline{VaR}_A = \sqrt{\sum_{t=1}^{25} VaR_{A,t}^2} = \sqrt{10^2 + 10^2 + \cdots + 10^2} = 50$$

while for B we would have:

$$\overline{VaR}_B = \sqrt{\sum_{t=1}^{25} VaR_{B,t}^2} = \sqrt{0^2 + 0^2 + \cdots + 0^2 + 250^2} = 250$$

This would enable us to take account of the greater volatility in unit B VaRs, as well as the fact that it did not risk a VaR of 250 for the whole year, but rather for just 10 days.

23.5 CALCULATING RISK-ADJUSTED PERFORMANCE

Once each business unit has been assigned a forecasted measure of risk (allocated capital) or an actual measure of risk (absorbed capital), the next step is to measure the return on that capital.

As already done in previous chapters,[27] we will use Raroc, which is the ratio of a measure of earnings to a measure of capital. For the sake of simplicity, we will be using absolute Raroc figures; however, the reader will remember that Raroc can also be expressed as the difference between the absolute return on capital and the risk-free rate in order to show the risk premium that the bank pays to its shareholders.

In this section, we will first focus on the so-called ex-ante Raroc (i.e. the ratio of expected earnings to allocated capital), based on which we can forecast the return on the capital assigned to the various business units. This indicator will then be compared with the *ex-post* Raroc (i.e. the ratio of actual earnings to the greater of allocated and absorbed capital, as indicated in section 23.4[28]).

When calculating Raroc, we will be referring solely to economic capital. In the real world, as we have seen in Chapter 22, a bank could determine its level of book-value

---

[27] See Chapters 15 and 22.
[28] In addition to the observations made in section 23.4, the use of allocated capital in ex-post Raroc is also justified by the discontinuous nature of the capital allocation process, which makes it difficult to immediately reallocate capital to other units in the event it should not be used. For more information, see Saita (2007).

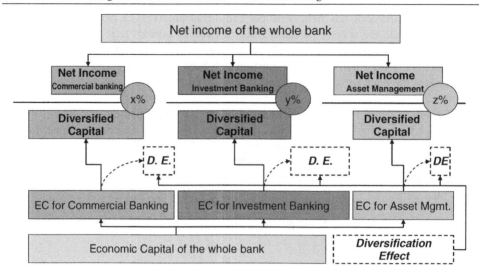

Figure 23.6 Return/risk allocation and the computation of diversified Raroc

capital (and *core capital* in particular) based on both economic capital and on minimum capital requirements. In this case (see Chapter 22), capital is determined as

$$T1 = T1^* + q \cdot EC \tag{23.16}$$

where the parameter q represents the level of "caution" imposed upon management by shareholders and by regulators.

However, it should also be noted that the investment actually "risked" by shareholders is not book-value capital, but rather the level of capital actually available, which also includes items (such as goodwill) that are not included in core capital. Available capital, *AC*, as we have seen in Chapter 22, is required to cover economic capital *EC*.

For this reason, despite the importance of regulatory constraints such as equation (23.16), economic capital is a natural point of reference in measuring shareholders' investment return. Therefore, we shall define Raroc as the ratio of net earnings to economic capital.

The numerator – The income of each business unit must be calculated by taking all of its cost components into account, including operating costs, costs of funding, and expected loss on risky assets. It must also consider any costs connected with supplementary capital (particularly the cost of subordinated debt), as well as, for the purposes of ex-post Raroc, the costs connected with the penalty *p* paid on any absorbed capital that exceeds allocated capital.

It will also be necessary to allocate to each business unit the indirect costs related to the services received from the support units (e.g. the costs of data processing services provided by EDP) and the costs/revenues related to services received from/provided to other business units (e.g. the hedging of interest-rate risk between the loans office and the treasury office).

Internal cost accounting schemes go beyond the scope of this book and are more closely related to management control than to risk management and value creation. Therefore, we shall assume that we already have all the data on the net income of the various business units. More specifically, for each of the business units listed in Tables 23.3–23.7, we will have a budget value for income and an actual income figure (see Table 23.8). We will also consider the profits for the bank, simply calculated as the sum of the profits of the individual business units (see also Figure 23.6).

Table 23.8 Profits by business unit

	Profits	
	Budget	Actual
Commercial Banking	12	13
Investment Banking	24	26
Asset Management	5	4
Bank	41	43

The denominator – The measure of economic capital that is most appropriate will depend on the point of view being taken. We will first consider the point of view of the top management, which assesses the various businesses with a top down approach, thereby taking all benefits of diversification into account. For this reason, each business unit will be assigned a diversified economic capital (DEC). As such, our Raroc will be a *diversified Raroc*. We will then see how this point of view must be altered when Raroc is designed to assess the performance of the managers who lead the different business units and to define bonuses and incentives.

Let us assume that our bank has adopted a system of DECs based on the correlation approach (Table 23.5). Table 23.9 shows these figures and the consequent (diversified, ex-ante) Rarocs for the various business units.

Table 23.9 DEC and diversified, ex-ante Raroc by business unit

	Diversified Allocated Economic Capital (Table 23.5)	Profits in the budget	Diversified, Ex-ante Raroc
Commercial Banking	119.0	12	10.1 %
Investment Banking	93.9	24	25.6 %
Asset Management	27.1	5	18.5 %
Bank	240	41	17.1 %
Bank (actual capital)	260	41	15.8 %

We shall further assume that the bank's cost of capital (see Chapter 24), i.e. the target return agreed with the shareholders, is 15 %. Such a target looks on the whole realistic, given that expected earnings lead to a return on economic capital of 17.1 %. Note, however, that the bank's economic capital may not coincide with available capital, i.e. with the shareholders' investment. As discussed previously, the bank may wish to have a cushion of available capital that is not absorbed by risks (AC – EC) in order to face risks that are greater than expected. For example, if actual available capital were 260 million, the excess over economic capital (20 million) would be allocated to senior management and would dilute the actual expected return on the capital invested by shareholders to 15.8 %.

Based on the DEC calculated with the correlation approach, the commercial banking unit would appear to be unable to achieve the target return of 15 %. The gap between the target return and the ex-ante Raroc may suggest that the commercial banking unit is not, at least according to budget data, an area of business that is able to create value for the shareholders and therefore deserving to be further developed.

Table 23.10 shows additional Raroc measures (again diversified and ex-ante) obtained using other measures of DEC that we have seen above. This is to demonstrate how an apparently "technical" step, such as the selection of a measure of diversified capital, can have a direct and significant impact on the measurement of expected risk-adjusted performance assigned to the different business units.

Table 23.10 Rarocs based on alternative DECs

	Diversified Allocated Economic Capital			Diversified, Ex-ante Raroc		
	Apportionment (Table 23.3)	Marginal Capital (Table 23.4)	Marginal Capital simplified (Table 23.7)	Apportionment	Marginal Capital	Marginal Capital simplified
Commercial Banking	112.5	145.1	147.0	10.7 %	8.3 %	8.2 %
Investment Banking	90	67.0	84.4	26.7 %	35.8 %	28.4 %
Asset Management	37.5	27.9	8.6	13.3 %	17.9 %	57.9 %
Bank	*240*	*240*	*240*	*17.1 %*	*17.1 %*	*17.1 %*

Note that the limited profitability of the commercial banking division is clear regardless of the DEC measure used. At the other end of the spectrum, the expectations for the investment banking division are high in all cases. However, the expected returns on capital allocated to the asset management unit vary significantly according to the DEC measure used.

The Rarocs of Table 23.9 are only expected values; as such, they are to be compared with the ex-post Rarocs (see Table 23.11) based on actual profits and absorbed capital. In Table 23.11, we see that the shortfall in the returns of the commercial banking division compared with the target of 15 % is confirmed, so senior management should consider restructuring this business unit in order to increase its earnings potential and to reduce its costs. We can also see that, during the year, the investment banking unit absorbed slightly more capital than the amount originally allocated by budget; however, despite paying the penalty p to senior management on the difference between allocated and absorbed capital (16.8 million[29]), it was still able to generate better-than-expected profits. Finally, the asset

---

[29] Such a penalty has been accounted for by the figure for "actual profits" in Table 23.11.

Table 23.11 Absorbed capital and diversified, ex-post Raroc

	Diversified Absorbed Capital	Actual Profits	Diversified, ex-post Raroc
Commercial Banking	119.0	13.0	10.9 %
Investment Banking	110.3	26.0	23.6 %
Asset Management	27.1	4.0	14.8 %
Bank	256.4	43	16.8 %
Bank (available capital, AC)	260	43	16.5 %

management unit performance that was slightly lower than expected, but was essentially in line with the minimum target approved by shareholders.

One might think that the management of the different units should be rewarded based on these Rarocs, namely based on the difference between the Rarocs achieved in Table 23.11 and the bank's cost of capital; in reality, in order to measure the value created or eroded by the management of the various business units, we need to use a *non*-diversified measure of economic capital (Figure 23.7).

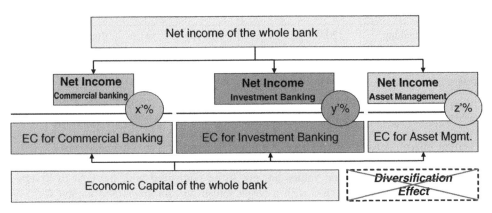

Figure 23.7   Return/risk allocation and the computation of stand-alone Rarocs

This is because the management of a business unit only controls diversification *within* its own area of business, and is basically unable to affect the degree of correlation between the profits of its own division and those of the other divisions of the bank. In order to avoid punishing or rewarding the management for a diversification effect that they do not control (that is, that does not depend on their management decisions), we must calculate a standalone Raroc, that is, a Raroc based on standalone capital.[30]

---

[30] In other words, it is only necessary to consider the diversification within each unit, thereby ignoring cross-unit diversification. For example, commercial banking might include a portfolio of retail customers and one of wholesale customers (large corporates, other banks, etc.). The benefits resulting from the imperfect correlation between these two activities (benefits that are managed and maximized by the management of the business unit) would clearly be a part of the standalone EC of this business unit and would, therefore, positively affect its standalone Raroc.

To summarize, if the goal is to allocate capital efficiently and to take advantage of diversification wherever possible, then we need to use diversified Raroc, as this is the only way to adequately measure the benefits that a given division can bring to the risk/return profile of the bank as a whole. If, however, our goal is to assess the performance of an individual division and its management (and to determine any extra compensation), then we need to use standalone Raroc, as both of the variables used in calculating this indicator (profits and standalone economic capital) can be controlled by the business unit's management.

Table 23.12 shows both the ex-ante and ex-post standalone Raroc figures. Notice that, as was the case for its diversified capital, the standalone capital absorbed by the investment banking unit has been greater than its standalone allocated capital. However, as noticed above, also the business unit's net profits were higher than expected (despite having to pay the penalty p connected with the greater absorption of capital).

Table 23.12 Standalone Raroc measures

	Ex-ante perspective			Ex-post perspective		
	Standalone Allocated Capital	Profits in the Budget	Standalone Ex-ante Raroc	Standalone Absorbed Capital	Actual Profits	Standalone Ex-post Raroc
Commercial Banking	150.0	12.0	8.0%	150.0	13.0	8.7%
Investment Banking	120.0	24.0	20.0%	141.0	26.0	18.4%
Asset Management	50.0	5.0	10.0%	50.0	4.0	8.0%
Total	320.0	41.0		341.0		
Target (15% on AC)			12.2%			11.4%

A correct interpretation of the figures in Table 23.12 requires two explanations:

- First, the standalone Raroc values are not to be compared with the cost of diversified capital (15%), but rather with a target return on *non-diversified* capital (EC) or on capital actually available (AC). This target return is chosen in such a way as to ensure that shareholders are properly remunerated. In our case, for example, a return of 15% on the risk capital invested by shareholders (260 million) means generating net profits of 36 million. This target, when compared with total non-diversified capital of 320 million (341 million in ex-post terms), translates into a target return of 12.2% and 11.4%, respectively.[31]
- However, these targets should not be the only figures used in evaluating ex-post performance. Take the commercial banking division as an example: this division generated a standalone ex-post Raroc of 8.7%, which is lower than both of the target returns specified above. As such, from a strategic point of view, this performance would appear to be inadequate. However, from a tactical point of view (i.e. considering the constraints

---

[31] For the sake of simplicity, when absorbed capital is greater than allocated capital, Table 23.12 adjusts the target return of all units downward. In reality, this adjustment might only concern the units that have absorbed a greater-than-expected volume of capital (in our case, investment banking).

and inflexibility that management has to face over the short term), the unit generated profits that exceeded their budget. This, too, must be taken into account when assessing performance and allocating incentives.

The examples of Tables 23.9–23.12 show how Raroc can be used in order to decide how to allocate shareholder resources efficiently (an issue we will discuss further in the following paragraph) and evaluate the performance of the individual business units and their management. In this effort, Raroc can act as a sort of "common language" for all the bank's business units, as well as a reference benchmark for the negotiations between the divisions and the bank's top management: a compass to guide the bank (and the behaviour of its components) on its quest towards the creation of value.

To conclude this section, a number of criticisms addressed to Raroc measures (some of which are partially justified) should be recalled briefly:

- As noted by Dowd (1998), Raroc tends towards infinity as its denominator, i.e. economic capital or VaR, tends to zero. According to Dowd, this implies that a risk-free position has an infinite Raroc and that it should be possible to maximize Raroc simply by investing in risk-free assets. In reality, one should remember that Raroc's numerator (net income) always comprises all costs of an asset, including funding costs. The buyer of a risk-free financial asset receives earnings at the risk-free rate r, but should also pay a certain rate, say r^*, on the funds raised to finance the purchase of that risk-free asset. If this asset were the buyer's only investment, the market would demand a rate of $r^* = r$, so the Raroc numerator and denominator would both be zero and the ratio would not tend towards infinity.[32]
- The maximization of Raroc could lead a bank to ignore areas of business that are, nonetheless, profitable. For example, a bank with an average Raroc of 25 % could decide to close a business unit with a (diversified) Raroc of 20 % because it contributes to a decrease in the bank's average Raroc. However, if the shareholders' target return were 15 %, this would mean abandoning a business that created shareholders' value. While this is a reasonable criticism, it is not a weakness of Raroc per se, but rather of an improper use of Raroc. One must remember that value creation cannot be achieved by simply maximizing Raroc, but rather implies (as explained in the next paragraph) a more complex process of capital allocation.
- Raroc is affected by all of the methodological uncertainties that surround the calculation of economic capital and diversified economic capital. As we have seen above, there are a number of alternative approaches to calculating these measures, and each of them requires certain assumptions or simplifications. Table 23.10 has clearly shown how a different measure of economic capital can alter the values of Raroc and the way senior management evaluates the various business areas. However, by using Raroc, we can, over time, achieve measures of economic capital that are more reliable. Only if management uses these measures as a common "paradigm" will it be willing to invest in models and databases that can improve the process of identifying and integrating risks, thereby improving the quality of techniques that measure EC, DEC and Raroc.

---

[32] One might object that a bank often has funding costs on the retail market that are less than r (e.g. deposits that are held at a rate of $r < r^*$). Nonetheless, business on the retail market has its own costs (e.g. the operating costs of a branch network) and its own risks (e.g. operational risks related to human error or fraud). Both of these factors will be reflected in the Raroc calculation, i.e. in the numerator and denominator, respectively. As such, it will not be possible to have an infinite Raroc.

23.6   OPTIMIZING THE ALLOCATION OF CAPITAL

In the paragraphs above, we have seen how to calculate the amount of capital absorbed by the different business units (section 23.2), how to make this figure consistent with the bank's total economic capital (section 23.3), and how to measure risk-adjusted returns (section 23.5). We will now see how this information can be used in order to allocate shareholder capital in the best possible way to the different business units.

23.6.1   A model for optimal capital allocation

The optimal allocation of capital among multiple assets or asset classes is a longstanding financial challenge. On this topic, a classic reference point is portfolio theory as originally introduced by Harry Markowitz (1952), which states that the optimal distribution of capital among multiple financial instruments depends on expected returns, volatilities, and correlations.

A typical allocation model requires that the portion of capital x_i allocated to the ith business unit, which generates a Raroc of r_i, be determined in a way that maximizes total Raroc:

$$\underset{x_i}{Max} \sum_{i=1}^{n} x_i r_i \qquad (23.17)$$

with the following four constraints:

(1) all allocation percentages must be positive: $x_i \geq 0$ for any given i;
(2) the sum of the percentages allocated to the n business units must equal 100%:

$$\sum_{i=1}^{n} x_i = 1;$$

(3) the optimal capital allocations, x_i, must not differ from the current capital allocation q_i more than a given quantity d (e.g. not more than 5%). Hence: $|x_i - q_i| \leq d$. The reason for this is that it is not possible for the operating structure of a bank to be altered radically in the short term, shifting resources from one area of business to another in a short period of time;
(4) a bank's economic capital must not exceed available capital.

If the optimal allocation cannot differ too much from the current allocation (i.e. if the value of d is low), we might also assume that the parameter k seen in section 23.2.3 (which expresses the bank's VaR as a number of standard deviations for the portfolio) remains essentially constant. If we accept this, rather significant, simplification, the third constraint may be rewritten as:

$$k \cdot \sum_{i=1}^{n} \sum_{j=1}^{n} \frac{x_i \, x_j}{q_i \, q_j} \rho_{i,j} \sigma_i \sigma_j \leqslant EC \qquad (23.18)$$

where $\rho_{i,j}$ indicates the correlation between the losses of units i and j (see Table 23.5). In other words, equation (23.18) states that the maximum probable loss on the "optimized" portfolio must not exceed the capital that the bank has currently committed to the coverage of risks.

Given these simplifications, the problem may be resolved with an algorithm of constrained optimization. Let us take our example of the previous sections. Table 23.13 shows the Rarocs calculated using the correlation approach, the shares of economic capital absorbed by current risks (based on the DECs calculated using the correlation approach), and the volatility of losses (σ_i) in absolute (euro million) terms. Setting d to 5%, the result of this optimization is as shown in column five of Table 23.13.

Table 23.13 An example of optimal capital reallocation ($d = 5\%$)

	Raroc (ri)	Actual shares of EC (q_i)	Volatility of losses (σ_i)	Optimal shares of EC (x_i)
Commercial Banking	10.1%	49.6%	37	44.6%
Investment Banking	25.6%	39.1%	40	41.5%
Asset Management	18.5%	11.3%	8	13.9%
Total	17.1%			

As we can see, this optimization favours a significant reduction in commercial banking, which fails to generate adequate returns, and an expansion in the areas of asset management and investment banking, which:

– generate higher levels of risk-adjusted returns;
– are less correlated with the bank's other areas of business and, therefore, have a high risk diversification capacity.

The value of Raroc for the bank as a whole following this optimization would reach 17.7%. This gives us a general idea as to the potential Raroc gains that would result from this restructuring.

Although theoretically simple and streamlined, a model for the optimal allocation of capital such as the one we have just seen is overly mechanical and, therefore, is of limited use in the real world. Indeed, such a model is based on a number of unrealistic assumptions:

– The Rarocs of the individual business units are taken as constants. This means that we are assuming, for example, that if the commercial banking unit is reduced to 20% (selling off branches, reducing loans to customers, etc.) it would still be able to generate the same return on absorbed capital. In reality, it is likely that, if a unit is forced to reduce its business volume, its Raroc would either improve (because the less profitable areas would be eliminated) or worsen (e.g. as a result of the greater impact of fixed costs).
– The same could be said for volatility and correlation. Indeed, if business units are reduced or expanded, it is likely that this would alter not only the amount of current risks, but also the "quality" of those risks. Therefore, the diversification ability of the different business units could either increase or be compromised.
– Finally, as we have mentioned above, equation (23.18) assumes that, as the share of capital allocated to the various units changes, the manner of distributing company losses (or, at least, the parameter k which links volatility to VaR) remains the same. On the whole, this assumption also seems rather unrealistic.

In conclusion, the model presented above may be seen as a useful point of reference in the optimal allocation of capital, but it is clearly not a turnkey solution to real-world problems surrounding the management of a bank's risk capital.

23.6.2 A more realistic model

The optimal allocation of capital must be based on a more complex process, which varies from bank to bank. Nonetheless, we can summarize a number of clear steps in terms of the objectives and organizational processes involved, thereby defining a generalized six-stage framework (see Figure 23.8):[33]

1. Analysis of internal and external constraints. In this stage, we calculate the minimum regulatory requirements, i.e. regulatory capital, of the various business units. We also calculate total available capital, in terms of both regulatory capital and fair-value capital.[34] Based on the bank's risk aversion, we then determine the share of economic capital that we want to cover with regulatory capital (equation 23.16) and the cushion of available capital (AC) not absorbed by economic capital (EC) that we wish to maintain in order to absorb any increases in the level of risk of existing activities.[35]

2. Analysis of risks. We first measure the risks connected with the individual business units, i.e. their standalone ECs, and consider the benefits of diversification in order to calculate DEC. We then verify that the bank's economic capital is in line with its risk aversion, as defined in the previous stage.

3. Target setting. Here, we define a target return on absorbed capital (i.e the cost of capital) that is compatible with the bank's level of risk and the expectations of shareholders. The feasibility of this target is then determined, given past performance. This objective is then published in a transparent, credible manner both to investors and analysts and to the various business units.

4. Capital allocation In this stage, we analyze the diversified, ex-ante Rarocs of the individual businesses. Based on the outcome, we then establish any (short-term) tactics and (long-term) strategies for optimizing the bank's overall portfolio of activities. The business units are then involved in defining any changes in their capital allocations and the implications these would have on their risk-taking capacity. For example, a reallocation of capital from commercial banking to asset management would imply that the commercial banking unit would have to reduce its loan volumes, and/or to favour customers with lower PDs and/or to require greater guarantees (so as to realign the volume of risks with the lower level of capital received), while asset management would have to develop new

---

[33] It is important to note that the six stages proposed here can be adopted both at the bank level and for the allocation of capital "received" by each business unit to its different activities or structures.
[34] See Chapter 22.
[35] As observed by Froot and Stein (1998), risk aversion and the availability of capital in a financial institution are closely linked. In other words, the capital needed does not depend solely on the bank's portfolio, but also on its risk aversion. From a more practical point of view, this means that a bank might decide not to allocate all of its available capital to its risk-taking units, but rather to keep a portion of capital in "reserve", which, to a certain extent, corresponds to the "strategic" level of risk aversion set as a target by the bank's senior management. In other words, a portion of the capital is used to reduce the bank's risk aversion.

customers and increase its assets under management in order to avoid diluting its return on allocated capital.

5. *Definition of incentive schemes.* Based on the standalone economic capital of the various business units, we establish a level of net profits necessary for each in order to provide an adequate return on the economic capital provided by the bank's shareholders. Based on the past performance of the various units, we then establish a second profit target (which may either by higher or lower than the previous one) to be used in determining monetary incentives.

6. *Analysis of results.* In this stage, at the end of the year we calculate the ex-post Rarocs (both diversified and standalone) of the various business units. Based on the standalone Rarocs, we then calculate the bonuses to be paid to the management of the different business units. Using the diversified Rarocs, we check the appropriateness of the capital allocation decisions made during stage 4, and we define any necessary adjustment. Based on the bank's overall Raroc, we then determine the incentives for senior management. In the following periods, these results influence how the bank sets profit targets (stage 3) and contribute to altering external constraints where necessary.

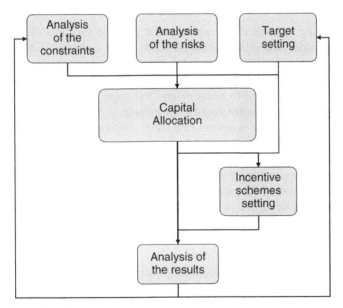

Figure 23.8   The capital allocation process

The process described above must be performed on a periodic basis (e.g. annually or quarterly); however, the allocation of capital should be seen as a dynamic, ongoing process, which sees the various business units competing in an internal "marketplace" for the allocation of a scarce resource (i.e. capital) with the aim of maximizing risk-adjusted returns and creating shareholders' value. This internal market should operate on the basis of rules that are not so different from those of a stock market, where companies compete on a daily basis, and not only through a discrete-time process, in order to attract the capital of investors.

23.7   THE ORGANIZATIONAL ASPECTS OF THE CAPITAL ALLOCATION PROCESS

In the paragraphs above, we have focused our attention on the methods and techniques of the capital allocation process, but this does not mean that organizational issues are of any less importance. Indeed, an adequate organizational structure is critical to the success of this process, as demonstrated by the significant reorganizations seen in recent years within leading international financial institutions.

Regulators, too, have repeatedly highlighted the importance of organizational issues. The Basel Committee has even linked the existence of an effective organizational structure to the ability to use internal models in calculating capital related to market risk, and organizational issues are an important part of "pillar II" of the new 2004 Basel Accord.[36]

However, it is difficult to make recommendations concerning these issues that could be universally applied to all banks. Indeed, an efficient capital allocation process cannot ignore the individual bank's existing organizational structure and the factors that define its corporate culture (the business units' autonomy in decision-making, the extent of knowledge centralization, transparency in communication, level of risk aversion, etc.). We can, however, provide a number of general guidelines.

First of all, a number of mistakes must be avoided:

- Some banks place the entire risk management function (not just the unit responsible for preparing proper risk-adjusted budgets based on the capital absorbed by the various units) within the management control department. This has made it more difficult for them to fully understand the risk models that are based on market data rather than on accounting data, as they are to some extent "estrange" to the managerial culture and background of the management control department.
- At the opposite end of the spectrum, we have situations in which the unit in charge of risk measurement and the one in charge of measuring the individual business units' profits and losses are not sufficiently coordinated, so that the system for risk-adjusted performance measurement is relatively inconsistent and methodologically fragile.
- The procedures for controlling the different types of risk are often adopted at different points in time and by different units, and hence risk becoming uncoordinated and inconsistent. Audits of procedures and models are also frequently not conducted in a systematic manner.
- In the same way, control of the different types of risk is often fragmented into different units, and the related responsibilities are not clearly defined. This can result in the same type of risk being monitored by different units or in certain types of risk not being monitored at all.
- There is often a lack of a clear distinction between who decides how much risk to take on and how to allocate it, who implements these decisions, and who controls the outcome (e.g. measuring risk, setting operating limits, measuring results).
- Information systems are often outdated and insufficient for the purposes of proper capital allocation.

At the same time, there are a number of guidelines that should be followed:

---

[36] See Chapter 20.

- Three functions should be kept separate: defining the overall risk-taking strategy; managing operations of the various risk-taking units; and measuring risk and risk-adjusted performances.
- Responsibility for the different types of risk should be assigned in an unambiguous manner based on the principle "one risk, one owner".
- Risk management should also be kept separate from management control, but both offices should be involved in the capital allocation process through the use of common models, policies and databases.
- Senior management should be actively involved in the process.
- The procedures for measuring risk and allocating capital should be transparent, universally accepted, and uniform. In particular, as we rise from individual business units through to senior management, the risk measures specific to the various business segments (e.g. the greeks for options, LGD for loans, etc.) should be summarized in a measure of allocated capital that is the same for all of the bank's units.
- The risks taken on and the changes in allocated capital should be reported quickly to senior management based on specific escalation policies.
- The systems of risk measurement and capital allocation should be verified regularly by an internal audit unit.
- The allocated capital of the various units should translate into constraints on their operations and should favour the measurement of their performance.

Without claiming to come up the "ideal" model for all banks, it is possible to define an organizational structure that is consistent with all of the above listed points. This structure is based primarily on two bodies: the Capital Allocation Committee and the Risk Management Committee.

The first is responsible for defining the strategic guidelines for the bank's risk-taking and capital allocation policies. This committee, which includes members of senior management, performs the following functions:

√ establishing capital at risk limits for the bank as a whole, based on the available capital and the constraints set by regulators;
√ determining shareholder profit targets (i.e. cost of capital);
√ defining procedures for allocating capital among the bank's different business units by establishing the rules of the "internal market" for capital or guiding the entire process from above;[37]
√ periodically reassessing strategy based on expected and actual Raroc figures.

The Risk Management Committee, in turn, is a sort of operating arm of the Capital Allocation Committee and performs the following functions of a more technical nature:[38]

√ providing technical advice to the Capital Allocation Committee in defining the guiding principles of the bank's risk management strategy;

---

[37] See Saita (2007).

[38] The Risk Management Committee may, at least in part, be seen as an evolution of the Asset & Liability Committee which can be found in many financial institutions. Indeed, while the latter committee is generally concerned with just two types of risk (i.e. interest-rate and liquidity risk), the Risk Management Committee extends its activities to the entire range of risks taken on by the bank.

✓ defining the procedures for measuring capital at risk for the bank's different business units and divisions (confidence levels, time horizons, estimates of volatilities and correlations, etc.) in line with the principles and objectives defined by the Capital Allocation Committee;

✓ controlling and verifying the capital at risk measurements and Raroc values provided by management control and the different business units;

✓ controlling the bank's internal mechanisms for transferring risk and the related notional prices/rates;

✓ allocating capital to the various divisions of the bank in line with the procedures defined by the Capital Allocation Committee.

The coordination of the two committees can be facilitated by having the head of the Risk Management Committee serving also on the Capital Allocation Committee.

SELECTED QUESTIONS AND EXERCISES

1. The economic capital for Bank Alpha, consisting of three business units (A, B and C) is 800 million euros. Based on the data reported in the following table, compute the diversified economic capital for each business unit according to the following three alternative criteria: (i) the proportional method, (ii) correlations (see equation 23.10b) iii) parametric marginal CaR, based on equation (23.13). Briefly discuss the advantages and disadvantages of the three alternative criteria.

	Correlations			σ	EC
Unit	A	B	C		
A	1	0	0.5	90	400
B	0	1	0.25	100	500
C	0.5	0.25	1	60	300
Whole Bank				159	800

2. The table below indicates the yearly profits of a private banking unit over the last eleven years. Note that the size of the unit has stayed almost unchanged over time, so euro profits (rather than profits per employee or the like), are used.

Year	Profits (euro m)	Year	Profits (euro m)
1996	8.12	2002	8.39
1997	6.96	2003	5.3
1998	5.69	2004	5.25
1999	6.76	2005	7.04
2000	5.06	2006	6.09
2001	8.32		

Based on such data compute the yearly EaR (Earnings at Risk) of the private banking unit at a 99 % confidence level, under both the historical and the parametric approach. Assuming that any profit drop can be linearly (i.e., gradually) recovered in five years, estimate the VaR (Value at Risk) associated with each of the two EaR figures.

3. A bank's fixed-income desk owns two zero-coupon bonds. The former has a maturity of one year and a market value of euro 50 million, the latter has a maturity of three years and a market value of euro 150 million. The monthly volatility of interest rates is equal to 0.5 %, while that of 3-year rates is equal to 0.3 %; the current level of both rates is equal to 5 %, and the correlation between the two rates is 50 %.
The equity desk of the same bank has three long positions in three different stocks, each one with a market value of euro 30 million and betas of 100 %, 70 % and 110 % respectively; the monthly volatility of the market index is 4 %.
The first desk (fixed income) has promised to the top management to deliver a monthly income of euro 1 million, while the second one (equity) has committed to a monthly income of euro 2 million. Using a 99 % confidence level ($\alpha = 2.326$) and a parametric VaR, compute the monthly ex ante stand-alone Raroc of the two desks.

4. At the beginning of the year, the business unit "Foreign Exchange Trading" had agreed with the bank's Budget Department and the Top Management an allocated capital of 100 million euros, undertaking to produce net profits of 20 million. During the year, it delivered an actual profit of euro 28 million; however, due to an unexpected increase in market volatility, it absorbed capital for euro 120 million.
Based on the bank's internal capital allocation rules, the penalty rate, p, to be paid on the difference between absorbed and allocated capital is 5 %. Compute the ex ante and ex post Raroc of the FX Trading unit; comment on the difference between the two figures.

5. Consider the following statements on Raroc.

(I) The strategic viability of a business should be evaluated based on its stand-alone Raroc, while the performance of its management should be evaluated in the light of its diversified Raroc.
(II) Both the strategic viability of a business and the performance of its management should be evaluated in the light of its diversified Raroc.
(III) The strategic viability of a business should be evaluated based on its diversified Raroc, while the performance of its management should be evaluated in the light of its stand-alone Raroc.
(IV) Stand alone and diversified Rarocs should be compared against two different hurdle rates.

Which one(s) would you agree on?

(A) Only IV;
(B) Only III;
(C) I and IV;
(D) III and IV.

Using l_j to indicate the losses of business unit j and $l = \Sigma l_j$ to indicate the total losses for the bank, one can show that the covariance between the two may be expressed as

$$\text{cov}(l_i, l) = E\left[(l_i - \bar{l}_i) \cdot \sum_j (l_j - \bar{l}_j) \right] = \sum_j [E(l_i - \bar{l}_i)(l_j - \bar{l}_j)] = \sum_j \text{cov}(l_i, l_j).$$

(23A.1)

where $E(.)$ indicates the expected value operator and $\bar{x}$ the average of the random variable x.

It follows, then, that the variance of the total losses may be expressed as

$$\sigma^2 = \sum_i \sum_j \text{cov}(l_i, l_j) = \sum_i cov(l_i, l) = \sum_i \rho_{i,T}\sigma_i\sigma$$

(23A.2)

Dividing both members by σ, we then get equation (23.7) in Chapter 23.

Rewriting (23A.1) as $\rho_{i,T}\sigma_i\sigma = \sum_j \rho_{i,j}\sigma_i\sigma_j$ and dividing both members by $\sigma_{i\sigma}$, we get equation (23.8) in Chapter 23.

Appendix 23B
The Virtual Nature of Capital Allocation

The capital allocation process described in this chapter is purely virtual. Indeed, capital is not physically delivered to the individual business units that take on risks, but rather "ideally allocated" to them (or absorbed by them[39]) based on their risks.[40] If, for instance, a capital amounting to 10 million euros is allocated to the unit that manages foreign exchange risk, this means that the risks it takes cannot exceed € 10 million, not that this unit physically receives a capital of € 10 million to manage.

As capital is not physically delivered to the individual risk-taking units, the performance that they have to achieve on allocated capital only depends on the risk premium, not on the risk-free rate. Indeed, the latter can be simply obtained by investing the capital in risk-free assets.

To understand this concept, consider an example: Bank Archimedes is characterized by an economic capital (EC) of 100 million euros, split into four key divisions (see Table 23B.1): Credit Department, Finance Department (in charge of market risk management), Leasing & Factoring and Asset Management.

Assume that the bank's cost of capital r_e (see Chapter 24) is equal to the risk-free rate plus 10 %. Since the risk-free rate is presently equal to 3 %, r_e equals 13 %.

One might assume that the various divisions to which the bank's capital is allocated are to achieve a return on capital of 13 %. In other words, that the profits they generate, net of all costs, should be equal to 13 % of the capital received.

As a matter of fact, such conclusion would be correct only if capital allocation implied a physical delivery of capital to the bank divisions. If allocation is a purely ideal process, a given capital endowment can be seen simply as a protection against unexpected losses, which is "parked" within the bank and may be invested in risk-free assets. Therefore, it already earns the risk-free rate, and the task of the business units is only to generate an additional return equal to the difference between the cost of capital after taxes (13 %) and the risk-free rate (3 %). In the case of Bank Archimedes, this difference is 10 %. Hence, the different business units have to generate an annual profit of at least 10 % of the allocated capital. This means, for example, that the Credit Department has to generate a profit, after funding costs, expected losses and any operating costs, equal to a minimum of € 6 million.

In the example showed in Table 23B.1, the overall profit generated by the various business units is indeed equal to € 10 million. The remaining three millions that are needed to reach the 13 % target return on capital come from investing capital in risk-free assets.

One may object that a bank does not necessarily wish to invest its shareholders' capital in risk-free assets. However, bear in mind that this investment may be only a virtual one, as illustrated by the following example.

---

[39] As is well known, the term "allocation" describes an ex ante perspective, while the term "absorption" is referred to an ex post prospective.

[40] As Merton and Perold (1993) observed, "Allocating the costs of risk capital to individual businesses or projects is a problem for organizations that operate in a more or less decentralized fashion ...there is no simple way to do so. Moreover, any allocation must necessarily be imputed, if only because highly risky principal transactions often require little or no up-front expenditure of cash".

Table 23B.1 Example of capital allocation across the units of Bank Archimedes

Bank business unit	Capital allocation (mln. of Euro)	Annual profit target (mln. of Euro)
Credit	60	6
Finance	25	2.5
Leasing & Factoring	10	1
Asset management	5	0.5
Total	100	10

Consider Bank Pythagoras, characterized by just two branches, A and B, and by a treasury in charge of managing the financial balances of the two branches, as well as the bank's interest rate risk (see Chapter 4). Table 23B.2 shows the balance sheets of the two branches (assuming that loans and certificates of deposit are recorded at their fair value).

Table 23B.2 Balance sheet of the two branches of Bank Pythagoras (in mln Euro)

Branch	Assets with customers (1-year loans)	Liabilities with customers (1-year certificates of deposit)	Net financial balance
A	50	60	10
B	50	30	−20
Total	100	90	−10

As a whole, Bank Pythagoras has total assets of 100 million euros and total liabilities of Euro 90 million euros. The balance between the two is funded with equity capital (Euro 10 million). Branch A is characterized by a funding excess, while branch B by an excess in loans. If they were two separate banks, the former would lend funds on the interbank market, while the latter would turn to the interbank market as a borrower. Since they belong to the same bank, the funds in excess from branch A are channeled to the treasury, which in turn provides branch B with the funds needed for its loan portfolio (20 million euros). All transfers occur at the 1-year internal transfer rate (ITR) which, for the sake of simplicity, is assumed to be equal to the risk-free rate (3 %).

Suppose that the bank's target for return on capital (10 million euros) is equal to 13 %. Also, suppose that, based on the credit risk faced by the two branches, an economic capital of 5 million euros has been allocated to each one of them, while no capital was allocated to the treasury.[41] Therefore, the two branches must generate profits, after funding costs, expected losses and operating costs, equal to 10 % of the allocated capital. That is, each branch must deliver 500,000 euros in profits, with a total of Euro 1 million for the bank as a whole.

To this amount, one must add the return required by the actual use of capital by branch B. Indeed, it received 20 million euros by the bank treasury: these include Euro 10 million provided by branch A, plus an extra 10 million euros consisting of the bank's capital, that is "physically" used by branch B.

---

[41] Please note that this implies that any possible interest rate risk has to be covered.

In practice, the bank's capital (10 million euros) had been virtually allocated to the two branches in equal amounts and physically used only by branch B. Both branches are therefore bound to generate a profit equal to the risk premium (10 %) on the allocated capital. Furthermore branch B is also required to also provide a return, at the risk-free rate (3 %), on the "physically" received capital.[42]

The example highlights two important points:

– The capital allocation process does not require that capital be invested in risk-free assets, but also allows to use it to fund risky assets;
– The ITR plays a crucial role in the capital allocation process: indeed, the possibility to meet the desired target return on capital (13 % in this example) depends on the way this parameter is set.[43]

To conclude, two aspects should be underlined.

The fund transfer process that takes place within the bank based on a system of internal transfer rates is logically distinct from the risk measurement and management activities: a purely "virtual" capital allocation allows to keep these two issues separate. In fact, since

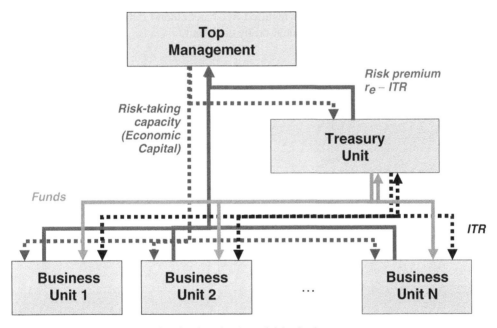

Figure 23B.1   The two transfer circuits of a financial institution

---

[42] A possible alternative interpretation is one that considers treasury as a unit in charge of "physically" managing capital. Having received an ideal capital allocation equal to zero, the treasury cannot take any risk and therefore has to generate a return on capital equal to the risk-free rate.

[43] Using an appropriate ITR, in addition to facilitating the measurement of profitability of the individual bank units and thus the pricing process of assets and liabilities, allows to separate the different risk categories, attributing them to the units that are in charge of managing them. As Koch (1992, p. 434) observed, "The principal advantage of internal funds transfer pricing is that it separates interest rate risk from credit risk in ALCO pricing decisions. Lending divisions can focus on asset quality, while fund management determines how much of a mismatch between asset and liability maturities or durations is appropriate". Therefore, ITR is crucial for an effective risk management and capital allocation process.

the risk of each individual unit is accounted for by the amount of capital it receives, then there is no need to differentiate internal transfer rates based on risk.

In practice, within a financial institution there exist two different parallel circuits. One is the *fund transfer* circuit, which is based on the internal transfer rate and is usually managed by the treasury. The other one is the *risk transfer* circuit, which is based on the difference between the cost of capital and the internal transfer rate (r_e – ITR) and is managed by the top management unit with the technical support of the risk management, planning, and capital management departments. Figure 23B.1 shows a schematic representation of these two circuits.

The second aspect relates to ITR calculation. Some banks use a weighted average of the marginal cost of debt (approximated by an interbank rate) and risk capital (expressing the return expected by shareholders). Such method, although consistent with some past theoretical literature[44] and aimed at accounting also for the risk premium required by equity capital, is basically affected by the following problem: the risk premium is applied to the amount of assets held by a business unit, not to the amount of risk it generates. On the other hand, if capital is allocated in a purely virtual manner (as we did in the examples shown in this Appendix), then it is possible (see again Figure 23B.1) to apply a pure cost of debt rate to the funding required by the business units, while applying a risk premium (namely, the risk premium required by shareholders) only to allocated capital, which reflects the amount of risks taken on by each unit.

---

[44] Watson (1977).

24

Cost of Capital and Value Creation

24.1 INTRODUCTION

Chapter 22 dealt with the "physical" management of capital (i.e. the selection of the optimal capital endowment and of its composition); on the other hand, Chapter 23 dealt with its "ideal" management (i.e. with the allocation of capital to risk-taking units) and further investigated a topic that was touched upon in other chapters of this book, i.e. the calculation of an indicator of risk-adjusted return on capital (Raroc).

To complete the picture, it is finally necessary to focus on the estimate of a bank's "fair" cost of capital. This will enable us to conclude our analysis of the techniques aimed at measuring value creation for the shareholders.

More specifically, the issues analyzed in this chapter can be summarized in the following questions:

- How is risk management connected with capital budgeting, i.e. with the assessment of a bank's individual risk-taking units?
- How can the cost of capital for a bank be estimated?
- Is it appropriate to compare the cost of capital for a bank with its accounting ROE (return on equity)?
- How should a bank's or its business units' Raroc be evaluated, taking also future prospects into account?
- What are the similarities and the differences between Raroc and other value creation measures such as EVA?

These are obviously far-reaching questions, on which academics, supervisory agencies, and operators have been focusing their attention, and which will not receive a comprehensive and conclusive answer from this book. However, an analysis of the key technical aspects of the value-creation assessment process, together with some practical examples relating to major European banks, may be useful to set the appropriate framework for such issues and suggest some possible solutions.

To that aim, section 24.2 provides a summary overview of the connections between risk management, capital budgeting, and the optimal financial structure of a bank. Section 24.3 analyzes the peculiarities of banks, which make it impossible to apply the typical capital budgeting principles used for non-financial enterprises. Section 24.4 focuses on the calculation of the cost of capital and illustrates three alternative methods, while section 24.5 shows some empirical examples. Section 24.6 demonstrates how to compare the cost of capital with Raroc in order to highlight the actual value creation margins of the bank. Finally, section 24.7 briefly illustrates the EVA (Economic Value Added) methodology and shows how it can be connected to Raroc-based measures.

24.2 THE LINK BETWEEN RISK MANAGEMENT AND CAPITAL BUDGETING

According to the classical approach which assumes frictionless financial markets (with perfect information, no taxes or bankruptcy costs and no conflicts between the shareholders and the management), risk management, capital management (that is, the optimization of the financial leverage and of the funding mix) and capital budgeting (the selection of the best investment projects) are basically unconnected to one another. This is due to two main reasons:

(i) in perfect markets all risks are liquid and can be offset with suitable hedging instruments;

(ii) the price of risk is the same for all market participants and does not depend in any way on the nature of the pre-existing asset portfolio of the individual enterprises.

The same conclusion may be reached based on the Modigliani-Miller theorem. In this case, the risk management activity is unconnected to capital-structure and capital-budgeting decisions. Adopting a different financial leverage based on risk or a different cost of capital based on risk would in any case lead to the same result in terms of investment choices (i.e. capital budgeting) and thus make risk measurement itself irrelevant.

As a matter of fact, the assumption that capital markets operate without frictions is clearly unrealistic. Indeed, the very existence of many financial intermediaries is justified by the presence of market imperfections and by the illiquid nature of many risks. If markets are not perfect, then risk management does affect financial structure optimization and capital budgeting activities.

In order to understand why, consider a liquid risk, such as the FX risk on a position denominated in foreign currency, and an illiquid risk, such as the credit risk on a loan to a small enterprise. In the first case, risk can be eliminated by means of a hedging derivative. Therefore, risk management and investment can be separated, i.e. one can select the investment first and then decide whether to keep its risk in the bank's portfolio. Conversely, in the second case the only way to reduce risk is to change the investment characteristics (e.g. requiring a collateral). Hence, in the real world, risk management (as described in the first three parts of this book) is strongly connected to decisions concerning the optimal financial structure and the investment selection.

The issues relating to the optimal financial structure and to capital allocation were dealt with in the two previous chapters; this chapter shall illustrate how to check the bank's ability to create value for the shareholders, once the bank's cost of capital is known.

24.3 CAPITAL BUDGETING IN BANKS AND IN NON-FINANCIAL ENTERPRISES

The cost of capital used by a company to fund its business or any new project is known as "weighted average cost of capital" (*WACC or w*):

$$w = \frac{D \cdot r_d + E \cdot r_e}{D + E} \tag{24.1}$$

As shown above, it represents an average of the rate paid on debt (r_d) and the cost of capital (r_e), weighted by the respective amounts (D and E).

Three working hypotheses are usually adopted in capital budgeting schemes for non-financial enterprises:

(i) The first is that WACC does not depend on the financial leverage (i.e. on the D/E ratio between debt and risk capital), but only depends on the assets' riskiness. In other words, because a change in the liabilities structure does not change the level and volatility of the cash flows expected from corporate assets, the weighted average cost of capital as a whole, required by shareholders and lenders together, must remain unchanged even if the financial structure changes.[1] If w does not depend on D/E, it may be useful to assume an unlevered financial structure where D equals zero and w equals r_e. This way, unlevered r_e becomes the only parameter to be estimated in order to know the cost of the capital invested in a project. Thus, the funding and investment decisions are totally separate and independent. Accordingly, the selection of the best projects is totally separate from any choice relating to capital sizing and composition.

(ii) The different degree of risk of each project translates into a different cost of funds gathered to implement it: an investment with a higher degree of variability in future cash flows is assessed (i.e. the related future cash flows are discounted) by assuming a higher discount rate (that is, a higher *unlevered* r_e).[2]

(iii) The cost of risk capital r_e is often estimated through the *Capital Asset Pricing Model*. According to such model (see Chapter 5, Appendix 5A), while the total risk of a project can be measured through the standard deviation of its returns only its systematic (not diversifiable) risk is relevant for its remuneration; systematic risk is generally captured through the project's beta which, in turn, can be inferred from the average beta of the industry or sector to which the project can be referred. Thus, a project that, on average, is riskier than the company's remaining assets, shall be funded with a higher cost of equity.

The three principles mentioned above change considerably for banks. Indeed, investment-related and capital management decisions cannot be separated so sharply. The different degree of risk taken by the individual business units of a banking institution translates into different amounts of capital absorbed. On the other hand, the cost of shareholders' equity remains unchanged for all the bank's business units, irrespective of the degree of risk.[3] Furthermore, the definition of risk that is adopted in this case does not rely on the standard deviation of the returns, but on VaR, i.e. the potential loss linked to a pre-established range of confidence.

These differences in the two approaches are due to three main factors:

- In a bank, it is impossible to apply the so-called "separation principle" (according to which investment decisions are separate from, and independent from, funding decisions). Based on this principle, a non-financial enterprise can establish the ideal

[1] This is true in an ideal world where all forms of funding are equally taxed. In reality, because interest expenses on debt are deductible from taxable income, there may be an optimal financial structure (i.e. an optimal ratio between D and E) that minimizes w. See Brealey and Myers (2000).

[2] In general, an investment creates value if the present value of its cash flows – after operating costs but before financial costs – discounted at the WACC, is higher than the cost of the investment itself, i.e. if its net present value is higher than zero. Though this principle was criticized by many authors (e.g. Stulz 1999), it still guides the capital budgeting activities of most non-financial enterprises.

[3] In fact, some banks use a different cost of capital in their budgets for different business areas. However, this differentiation does not depend on the degree of risk, but rather on expected profitability. For instance, the asset management unit may need a higher return on the allocated capital simply because this business, on average, is more profitable. Thus, the bank's top management, when allocating a minimum profitability target to the managers of each individual business unit, takes into account the different market situation of each individual business unit.

financial structure by minimizing its after-tax WACC,[4] and then keep such structure
unchanged for each and every investment project. However, in the case of banks, where
the business risk is strictly related to the financial risk, any changes in the asset mix
would bring about modifications in the liabilities and capital structure, so separation
would not work.

– The constraints posed by supervisory authorities provide that different capital requirements be applied based on the different type of assets held by banks, depending on
their riskiness. When translating a different asset riskiness into a different *amount* of
capital (rather than into a different *cost* of capital), banks simply replicate the logic
followed by regulatory requirements.

– It is difficult to get data on the degree of systematic risk of the different activities performed by a bank. As a matter of fact, many of the risks taken by a bank cannot simply
be traced to individual assets: for instance, interest rate risk and foreign exchange risk
both depend on a combination of existing assets and liabilities, while the counterparty
risk associated with over-the-counter derivatives depends on off-balance sheet items.

For these reasons, banks and non-financial enterprises resort to different value creation
measures.

In non-financial enterprises, the contribution of the different activities to the overall value creation of the firm is measured with capital budgeting techniques based on
the separation principle: first, the optimal financial structure is determined by minimizing
WACC, then the different projects and business units are evaluated by assuming a constant
financial structure and a variable (risk-dependent) cost of capital. Accordingly, the cost of
capital of an individual business unit not only depend on financial risk – i.e. on financial
leverage which is assumed to be the same across the whole enterprise – but also on the
business risk faced by each individual business, generally measured through its beta.

As mentioned above, banks have been following a different approach. Until the 1980's,
the management control department of banks did not allocate capital to the individual
business units and, when assessing their contribution to the overall corporate profitability,
simply quantified – by means of management accounting systems and internal transfer
rates/prices – the share of the bank's net profit generated by each of them. This allowed
one to measure the contribution of the individual units to profits, not their contribution to
risks. Furthermore, at a bank-wide level, net profits were usually referred to book-value
capital, thus obtaining a return on equity measure that was poorly correlated to the actual
amount of risks faced by the bank.

Later on, Raroc[5] and value-creation metrics became increasingly popular. Such measures are based on a uniform cost of capital and on a variable amount of allocated capital.
According to this paradigm in its simplest form[6] (see Chapter 23), a business area creates
value for the shareholders if and only if its current Raroc (diversified, and measured on
an *ex post* basis) is higher than the bank's cost of capital.

As was already mentioned, the same approach can be used in order to "price" individual
products and transactions so that they create value for the shareholders.[7] For instance,

---

[4] See footnote 1.

[5] Originally, the Raroc method was developed by Bankers Trust at the end of the 1990's. See Zaik, Walter,
Kelling and James (1996).

[6] We return to the comparison between Raroc and cost of capital in section 24.6

[7] As noted in other parts of this book (see Chapter 15), if operational costs are left out for the sake of simplicity,
then the bank's risk-adjusted return on capital matches the premium required by its shareholders if the lending
rate is set in such a way to cover the cost of funding, the expected loss rate, and the cost of risk.

with a loan (see Chapter 15) the minimum lending rate r^* compatible with a cost of capital equal to r_e is given by:[8]

$$r^* = \frac{r + ELR + VaR(r_e - r)}{1 - ELR} \qquad (24.2)$$

where r is the marginal cost of the bank's debt (i.e. its internal transfer rate or ITR), VaR is the diversified equity capital (DEC, see Chapter 23) associated with the loan, ELR is the expected loss rate of the loan, calculated by multiplying PD by LGD.

Note that the cost of capital (r_e) enters equation (24.2) with the same magnitude as Value at Risk (VaR). In other words, a mistake in estimating the cost of capital would produce the same effects – in terms of total error – as a biased estimate of the economic capital. If the cost of capital is underestimated, this leads to setting lower prices than necessary and to overestimating the bank's ability to generate value; if it is overestimated, the bank is overpricing its loans (thus missing good business opportunities) and may withdraw from business areas that are wrongly perceived as unprofitable.

It is thus necessary that this parameter be estimated correctly, in order to avoid that unrealistic values of r_e lead to wrong conclusions. The following section analyzes a few possible techniques for estimating the cost of capital.

24.4   ESTIMATING THE COST OF CAPITAL

Three main methods are used, both in academic literature and in professional practice, to calculate the "fair" or "adequate" cost of capital: one is based on the dividend valuation model, one on the price/earnings ratio, and one on the capital asset pricing model. Each model is presented in the following sections together with a discussion of its advantages, disadvantages, and actual applicability.

24.4.1   The method based on the dividend discount model

The value that a shareholder attaches to the bank's shares is a function of two factors, i.e. the dividends that the shareholder expects to collect, and the risk-adjusted return on capital that he/she considers to be "fair" based on the bank's risk features (i.e. the cost of capital).

One of the best known models for evaluating a company (including banks), the Dividend Valuation Model,[9] assumes that both the above-mentioned factors (dividends and cost of capital) are known, and derives the equilibrium value of the bank. More specifically, knowing the cost of capital r_e and the flow of expected dividends d_1, d_2, d_∞, the share value v can be calculated as follows:

$$v = \sum_{t=1}^{\infty} \frac{d_t}{(1 + r_e)^t} \qquad (24.3)$$

Equation (24.3) simply states that the share value, similarly to the value of any financial asset, is equal to the present value of its future cash flows, discounted at a risk-adjusted

---

[8] See Chapter 22 for details on how equation (24.2) should be modified when the optimal capital endowment is chosen on the basis of exogenous constraints (and namely of a minimum capital requirement).
[9] Gordon (1962).

rate. Since it is unrealistic to assume that a complete forecast of all future dividends is known, it is often assumed that such dividends grow at a constant rate g, starting from their current value[10] d_0. In this case, equation (24.3) becomes:

$$v = \frac{d_0 \cdot (1+g)}{(r_e - g)} \qquad (24.4)$$

Let us now assume that v is known. Indeed, in an efficient market the value of the bank's shares is simply equal to their current price p. If $v = p$ is known, then equation (24.4) can be used to calculate the equilibrium value of any other parameter. Specifically, we can calculate the value of r_e which is in line with the observed market price p, simply as

$$r_e = \frac{d_0 \cdot (1+g)}{p} + g \qquad (24.5)$$

Equation (24.5) indicates that the cost of capital is given by the dividend yield at time 1 (ratio between future dividend and price), plus the expected growth rate of dividends. For instance, if the share price is Euro 20, the dividend for last year is Euro 1 and the estimated growth rate of dividends is 5 %, equation (24.5) leads to estimate a cost of capital equal to:

$$r_e = \frac{1 \cdot (1+5\%)}{20} + 5\% = 10.25\%$$

The major drawback of the dividend discount model is that it requires to specify a forecast of all future dividends, or their growth rate g.

Incidentally, note that the latter can also be inferred from the bank's ROE (return on equity) using the following equation:

$$g = Roe \cdot (1 - \pi) \qquad (24.6)$$

where π is the bank's payout ratio, i.e. the share of profits paid out as dividends. In short, equation (24.6) indicates that the undistributed share of ROE, $(1 - \pi)$, becomes new capital invested in the bank. If the bank's profitability (that is, its ability to reward capital) stays unchanged over time, then an increase in available capital will produce an equal increase (g) in profits and dividends. In order to calculate g, one can therefore simply specify a value for the payout ratio expected by the bank (derived, for instance, by its past history) and a long-term "sustainable" value for the ROE (which is conceptually simple, but may prove rather difficult in practice).

Note that, however, the very hypothesis that the bank's dividends grow forever at a constant rate appears to be unfeasible. To make it somehow more realistic, equation (24.4) can be re-written assuming that one knows the values of dividends $d_1, d_2, \ldots d_n$ expected for the first n years and then using a constant growth rate g in the following years:

$$v = \sum_{t=1}^{n} \frac{d_t}{(1+r_e)^t} + \frac{1}{(1+r_e)^n} \frac{d_n \cdot (1+g)}{(r_e - g)} \qquad (24.7)$$

As before, this new expression for v can be equalled to the current share price p, and r_e can then be calculated, e.g. by means of an iterative procedure. Using (24.7), the

---

[10] Therefore, $d_1 = d_0(1 + g)$, $d_2 = d_0(1 + g)^2$, etc.. The value of g must be smaller than r_e, otherwise equation (24.4) would produce an infinite value.

consequences of a wrong estimate of g would be less severe than with (24.4) and (24.5). Note that the dividends for the first n periods can be calculated by applying a constant payout ratio π, derived from the expected profit forecasts made by financial analysts (*consensus forecasts*).[11]

Going back to the example of the bank with a share value p of Euro 20, let us assume that the profit per share expected for the next four years is respectively Euro 2, 2.2, 2.4, and 2.5, and that the bank usually pays out 40 % of its profits. Still using (but only from the fifth year on) a g of 5 % and applying equation (24.7), we would get:

$$20 = \frac{2 \cdot 40\,\%}{(1+r_e)^1} + \frac{2.2 \cdot 40\,\%}{(1+r_e)^2} + \frac{2.4 \cdot 40\,\%}{(1+r_e)^3} + \frac{2.5 \cdot 40\,\%}{(1+r_e)^4}$$
$$+ \frac{1}{(1+r_e)^4} \frac{2.5 \cdot 40\,\% \cdot (1+5\,\%)}{(r_e - 5\,\%)}$$

By means of iterations, one can found the value of r_e consistent with this equation, which is equal approximately to 9.3 %.

However, it should be pointed out that a bank's payout ratio may be all but constant. In fact, since banks tend to pay out dividends that stay rather constant over time, even when its profits are lower or higher than the average, their payout ratio may change considerably year after year.

24.4.2 The method based on the price/earnings ratio

Another criterion is based on the price/earnings (p/e) ratio of the bank's shares. This is given by the ratio between the price of a share and the net corporate profits divided by the number of shares (earnings per share[12]).

Thus, its reciprocal represents the ratio between net earnings gained by a share and the price to be paid in order to own it. For instance, a share may be entitled to earnings per share of 50 cents and cost Euro 5. In this case, if earnings per share are stable, investors purchasing such a share shall get a 10 % return. If they buy shares at that price, it means that 10 % is the "fair" return that they consider enough to reward their risks. In other words, 10 %, i.e. the reciprocal of the p/e ratio, represents the fair cost of capital:

$$r_e = \frac{1}{e/p} = \frac{e}{p} \tag{24.8}$$

This approach is affected by a number of problems. First of all, it should be pointed out that the two pieces of data used to calculate the price/earnings ratio refer to two different points in time: while price is a recent piece of information, earnings are often referred to the last complete financial year or quarter. The problem can be tackled by taking as price the average data for the whole financial period to which earnings refer. However, in so doing one is forced to use past data, which are not necessarily in line with the present conditions of the stock market. An alternative solution is to use the current price (for

---

[11] In fact, expected profit estimates should not be bank-internal estimates based on privileged information unavailable to the market, but rather "public" estimates in line with the profitability prospects that the market assigns to the bank when establishing its share price.
[12] Earnings are identified with a small e because in this chapter capital E is used to identify a company's equity endowment.

instance an average of prices in the past month) and an estimate of earnings that financial analysts expect for the current period.

A more severe limitation is that earnings per share (as measured based on the latest available financial statement or on the analysts' expectations) usually do not reflect the long-term profitability expectations of shareholders. As a matter of fact, a share price not only discounts the current earnings but also all future expected profits. Hence, assuming that the amount of current earnings is constant, companies with better future earning prospects appear to have a higher price/earnings ratio (and therefore, based on equation 24.9, an unduly low cost of capital).

A third limitation, which is partly connected to the previous one, is related to the cyclical nature of profits. Bank profitability is known to be strongly related to the evolution of interest rates and to the overall economic situation. If, because of the economic cycle, a bank experiences a significant decrease (increase) in earnings in a given year, the market is likely to anticipate a future rebound (decrease) in profitability, thus the share price is likely to decrease (increase) less markedly than the profits. In this case, equation (24.8) would underestimate (overestimate) the actual cost of capital.

In order to account for these limitations, equation (24.8) should be computed on the basis of a long-term "average" p/e ratio. Furthermore, for banks with strongly increasing earnings, it should be adjusted based on the expected earnings growth rate.

Finally, a further problem involves the different nature of data used to calculate the price/earnings ratio. While price is set by the market, earnings is an accounting value. This problem is usually tackled by correcting the book profits so as to make them more similar to a cash-flow measure (e.g., by adding back to profits amortization and depreciation items, other than those covering expected losses[13]). However, regardless of their accuracy, such corrections are often insufficient to bridge the gap between market data and accounting data, given the degree of discretionality that the management enjoys in drawing up financial accounts.

24.4.3 The method based on the Capital Asset Pricing Model (CAPM)

The third method is based on the Capital Asset Pricing Model[14]. As is well known, this model subdivides the risk of a share i into two components: diversifiable risk – connected with issuer-specific factors, which can be eliminated by appropriately diversifying the portfolio – and non-diversifiable or systematic risk – which depends on general market factors and thus cannot be eliminated. The latter component is measured by the beta coefficient, which measures the link between the performance of the share r_i and the performance r_m of the stock market as a whole. It can be computed as follows

$$\beta_i = \frac{cov(r_i, r_m)}{var(r_m)} \tag{24.9}$$

Since the diversifiable component can be eliminated, the performance requested by shareholders, $\bar{r}_i$, only depends on the systematic component. The company's cost of capital i is thus a function of its beta according to the following formula:

$$r_e = \bar{r}_i = r + \beta_i \cdot (\bar{r}_m - r) \tag{24.10}$$

where r represents the risk-free rate and $\bar{r}_m$ is the return expected by the market portfolio.

---

[13] For an analysis of this problem and its possible solutions, see Zimmer and McCauley (1991).
[14] See Chapter 5, Appendix 5A.

Using the CAPM, it is enough to estimate the bank's beta and formulate a hypothesis on the risk premium required, in equilibrium, by the stock market $(\bar{r}_m - r)$, in order to be able to produce an estimate of the bank's cost of capital. If, for example, the risk-free rate is 4 %, the bank has a beta of 90 %, and the market risk premium is 5.5 percentage points, equation (24.10) leads to estimate the following cost of capital:

$$r_e = 4\% + 90\% \cdot 5.5\% = 8.95\%$$

This approach, like the previous two, is affected by a number of limitations:

− The CAPM assumes the existence of perfect, highly liquid capital markets with no transaction costs, characterized by the presence of rational, well informed operators with homogeneous expectations.
− The CAPM requires an estimate of the bank's beta, which is usually calculated from past data. This estimate may become unstable over time and may fail to accurately represent the degree of systematic risk incurred by the bank's shareholders over the following years or months.
− The choice of a value for the market risk premium $(\bar{r}_m - r)$ is also a somewhat complex step. Empirical studies, often based on the US market, show results ranging from 4 % to 6 %. Also in this case, as for the beta, historical values are to be taken with caution since they are used to estimate a future variable.

Two further issues stem from the definition of risk adopted by the CAPM, which is different from the one usually adopted in models based on economic capital and Raroc. First of all, the CAPM measures risk through the volatility (standard deviation) of returns, while economic capital is based on a definition of risk as the highest potential loss associated with a given time horizon and a given confidence interval. Secondly, economic capital is usually a diversified measure (see Chapter 23) which accounts for the contribution of a certain business area to the bank's overall risk (not to the market portfolio); unlike the CAPM, it includes a non-systematic risk component.[15]

A solution to the first issue was offered by Kupiec (2000) and is based on an insurance-oriented definition of risk capital (similar to the one that was originally proposed by Merton and Perold, 1993). Here, the risk connected to a specific activity is defined as the value of the investment that is necessary to make it risk free or, in other words, to purchase an adequate insurance coverage to make its cash flows certain. Though interesting, this solution is quite radical: instead of suggesting adjustments or corrections to the Raroc or cost of capital, Kupiec suggests that a totally different risk definition be adopted (and hence a different definition of the threshold rate that is necessary to establish whether there is value creation). This would lead to totally abandon the VaR model and replace it with a different theoretical approach which, incidentally, does not seem to have become very popular among practitioners.

A possible solution to the second issue was offered by Crouhy, Turnbull and Wakeman (1999), suggesting to calculate a measure of "*adjusted Raroc*" $(Raroc_a)$ as:

$$Raroc_a = \frac{Raroc - r}{\beta_a} \qquad (24.11)$$

[15] Zaik, Walter, Kelling and James (1996), Froot and Stein (1998) and Kupiec (2000) recognize the potential problems connected to the fact that VaR measures, and thus economic capital measures, when measuring risk do not consider the joint variation of returns with market risk factors.

where β_a is the beta coefficient of the specific investment project, activity or business unit to be evaluated, *assuming that the bank performs no other activities*. This correction transforms the risk-adjusted return on capital into an excess return over the risk-free rate and weights such an excess return by its degree of systematic risk.[16] The adjusted Raroc should thus be compared to the market risk premium $(\bar{r}_m - r)$. Adjusted Raroc values that are higher (lower) than the market risk premium would indicate value creation (destruction). Though interesting, the solution offered by Crouhy, Turnbull and Wakeman does pose other problems, most notably difficulties in estimating the betas of the individual activities or investments.

Despite the above-mentioned limitations, the CAPM still is the most commonly used method and, among those analyzed here, the most solid from a theoretical standpoint. Its main advantage is that it takes into consideration the alternative investment opportunities available to the bank shareholders (risk-free investments, investments in the market index), and sets the bank's return on capital based on its systematic risk.

24.4.4 Caveats

In calculating the cost of capital, a few tricky aspects should be taken into account. One involves the definition of capital used in the three above-mentioned approaches. They all embrace the perspective of the investor who purchases bank shares at market prices, hence they measure capital based on market capitalization (see Chapter 22).

When the rate r_e estimated with these methods is applied to a different definition of capital, it should be suitably adjusted. Assume, for example, that the bank drew up a development plan where capital is expressed at book value and the value creation targets are expressed as ROE (return on capital). If there is a significant difference between market capitalization and book-value capital, i.e. a Price to Book (p/b) ratio that is significantly different from one, the bank might be unable to adequately reward its shareholders even if its ROE is greater than r_e. Suppose, for instance, that the estimated cost of capital equals 10 %, market capitalization is Euro 210 million, and book value capital is Euro 70 million (hence, the price/book ratio is 3). In this case, producing an ROE of 10 %, i.e. a net profit of 10 % of the book value capital (Euro 7 million), would imply a mere 3.3 % return to investors, which would fall largely below their expectations. In such a case, the ROE must in fact be compared with an "adjusted" (i.e. multiplied by the price/book ratio) cost of capital, $\check{r}_e$:

$$\check{r}_e = r_e \frac{p}{b} \qquad (24.12)$$

As a matter of fact, a value of $\check{r}_e$ of 30 %, applied to book value capital (70), shall produce a 10 % return for investors purchasing shares at market prices (210).

A second issue relates to the "net" nature of the cost of capital estimated by the three methods shown above. They refer to dividends, net profit, or to the return expected by rational investors: in all three cases, the return thus obtained is always after taxes. As such, it should always be compared with Raroc measures based on the bank's net profits. If gross profits are used (as is the case, for instance, in formulas such as (24.2) that equals the gross profit of a loan to its expected cost), then the cost of capital must be re-written

---

[16] In this sense, the adjusted Raroc shows a similar formulation to Treynor's index, which relates the excess return of a share over the risk-free rate to the beta of the share.

in gross terms ($\hat{r}_e$), simply as:

$$\hat{r}_e = \frac{r_e}{1 - \tau} \tag{24.13}$$

where τ is the marginal tax rate paid by the bank.

One third and last issue involves the need to keep r_e relatively stable. Indeed, the cost of capital cannot vary too frequently, and it should be updated only when significant or exceptional events occur.[17] In fact, since it is used to assess the economic viability of the different business units absorbing bank capital, it is a leading variable that plays a role in medium-long term strategic decisions. It is thus obvious that such a parameter cannot be affected by continuous updates following from changing market conditions.[18]

24.5 SOME EMPIRICAL EXAMPLES

Table 24.1 shows values for beta, p/b ratio, p/e ratio, and *payout ratio* (π) for a sample of European banks included in the Morgan Stanley Eurotop 300 index.

In the next three columns, the table shows the values of r_e estimated with the dividend discount model, the price/earnings ratio and the CAPM. In addition to the input data on the individual shares, a risk-free return rate (r) of 5%, a risk premium ($r_m - r_m$) of 5%, and a profit growth rate of 5% were used for all banks. The latter represents a nominal growth rate, which includes the effect of inflation. For instance, if the expected inflation rate is 2%, then the real profit growth rate is approximately 3%.[19] Please note that, for the sake of simplicity, we are assuming that the market assigns the same growth prospects to the entire banking sector.

In order to be able to use the input showed in the Table, the computation of r_e with the dividend discount model has been based the following variant of equation (24.5):

$$r_e = \frac{d_0 \cdot (1 + g)}{p} + g = \frac{e \cdot \pi \cdot (1 + g)}{p} + g = \frac{\pi \cdot (1 + g)}{p/e} + g \tag{24.5b}$$

Looking at the results in the Table, note how the smallest values are – in general – those deriving from the price/earnings ratio approach. This is due to the fact that this model – at least in its simplest version illustrated in equation (24.8) – does not take into account expectations on future growth.

The r_e values estimated with the techniques described in section 24.4 are based on the bank's market capitalization and must be compared with profitability measures also based on market capitalization (e.g., Raroc measures, if one assumes that market capitalization is a good proxy for economic capital). As was explained in the last part of the previous section, in order for them to be compared with measures based on book value capital – such as ROE – they have to be multiplied (see 24.12) by the p/b ratio. The

---

[17] For instance, major changes in real interest rates, the inflation rate, or the bank's beta (the latter being due to a major change in the bank's riskiness).

[18] As Uyemura and Van Deventer observed, "What is much more important than whether the hurdle rate on any given day is 14% or 18%, is that the bank avoid activities that have returns that are negative or substantially below the hurdle (e.g., below 10%).", Uyemura and Van Deventer (1993), p. 54.

[19] This value, although apparently small, is by itself optimistic. Indeed, a constant real growth rate of 3% may derive either from a real economic growth rate equal to 3% or from the assumption that, faced with lower real economic growth rates, the banking sector experiences a growth in its importance in the overall economic system.

Table 24.1 Computation examples for a group of European banks

Bank/Group Name	Beta β	Price to Book Value p/b	Price/ Earnings Ratio p/e	Dividend payout ratio π	r_e (based on market capitalization) Discounted Dividends (equation 5), using $g = 5\%$	r_e Price/ earnings (equation 8)	r_e Capm ($r = 5\%$, $r_m - r = 5\%$)	$\check{r}_e$ (based on book value) Discounted Dividends	$\check{r}_e$ Price/ earnings	$\check{r}_e$ Capm	2005 Roe
	(a)	(b)	(c)	(d)	(e) = (d)(1+5%) /(c)+5%	(f) = 1/(c)	(g) = 5% +(a)5%	(e)(b)	(f)(b)	(g)(b)	
Abn Amro Holding Nv	122 %	1.81	9	45.3 %	10.28 %	11.11 %	10.12 %	18.6 %	20.1 %	18.3 %	23.7 %
Alliance & Leics.Plc.	63 %	2.75	13.4	59.3 %	9.64 %	7.46 %	7.13 %	17.5 %	13.5 %	12.9 %	22.0 %
Allied Irish Banks Plc.	86 %	2.29	13.3	43.3 %	8.41 %	7.52 %	8.32 %	15.2 %	13.6 %	15.1 %	19.9 %
Alpha Bank Sa	123 %	3.57	18.7	47.7 %	7.68 %	5.35 %	10.13 %	13.9 %	9.7 %	18.3 %	23.9 %
Ang.Ir.Bk. Corp.Plc.	91 %	3.92	15.1	18.5 %	6.29 %	6.62 %	8.54 %	11.4 %	12.0 %	15.4 %	29.3 %
Bnp Paribas	101 %	1.54	9.6	37.4 %	9.09 %	10.42 %	9.06 %	16.5 %	18.9 %	16.4 %	15.9 %
Banca Intesa	163 %	1.9	12.1	43.5 %	8.77 %	8.26 %	12.16 %	15.9 %	15.0 %	22.0 %	18.7 %
Banca Monte Dei Paschi	116 %	1.94	16	50.0 %	8.28 %	6.25 %	9.78 %	15.0 %	11.3 %	17.7 %	10.9 %
Banche Popolari Unite	70 %	1.48	12.2	37.8 %	8.26 %	8.20 %	7.50 %	14.9 %	14.8 %	13.6 %	15.4 %
Bbv Argentaria Sa	154 %	3.33	13.7	47.4 %	8.63 %	7.30 %	11.71 %	15.6 %	13.2 %	21.2 %	25.9 %

Bnc.Comercial Portugues	148%	2.44	16.5	31.8%	7.02%	6.06%	11.38%	12.7%	11.0%	20.6%	25.3%
Banco De Sabadell Sa	48%	2.4	23.8	45.3%	7.00%	4.20%	6.39%	12.7%	7.6%	11.6%	13.6%
Bca. Verona Novara	67%	1.94	18.9	43.5%	7.42%	5.29%	7.36%	13.4%	9.6%	13.3%	15.4%
Banco Popular Espanol	52%	2.83	15.6	49.6%	8.34%	6.41%	6.60%	15.1%	11.6%	11.9%	20.0%
Bnc.Stdr.Ctl.Hisp.Sa	161%	1.79	15.9	41.7%	7.75%	6.29%	12.06%	14.0%	11.4%	21.8%	16.8%
Banesto	71%	2.8	16.8	0.0%	5.00%	5.95%	7.54%	9.1%	10.8%	13.6%	17.1%
Bank Of Ireland Plc.	90%	2.49	11.8	38.5%	8.42%	8.47%	8.48%	15.2%	15.3%	15.3%	26.9%
Barclays Plc.	119%	2.29	11.3	48.9%	9.54%	8.85%	9.97%	17.3%	16.0%	18.0%	20.7%
Bayer.Hypo-Und-Vbk.Ag	187%	1.61	11.2	29.1%	7.73%	8.93%	13.36%	14.0%	16.2%	24.2%	5.2%
Capitalia Spa	170%	1.83	14.8	48.8%	8.46%	6.76%	12.51%	15.3%	12.2%	22.6%	12.9%
Commerzbank Ag	194%	1.47	10.1	25.9%	7.69%	9.90%	13.68%	13.9%	17.9%	24.8%	10.4%
Credit Agricole Sa	100%	1.43	11.1	35.1%	8.32%	9.01%	9.01%	15.1%	16.3%	16.3%	13.7%
Credit Suisse Group	209%	1.83	11.7	38.6%	8.47%	8.55%	14.47%	15.3%	15.5%	26.2%	14.7%

(continued overleaf)

Table 24.1 (continued)

Bank/Group Name	Beta β	Price to Book Value p/b	Price/ Earnings Ratio p/e	Dividend payout ratio π	r_e (based on market capitalization)			$\breve{r}_e$ (based on book value)			2005 Roe
					Discounted Dividends (equation 5), using $g = 5\%$	Price/ earnings (equation 8)	Capm ($r = 5\%$, $r_m - r = 5\%$)	Discounted Dividends	Price/ earnings	Capm	
	(a)	(b)	(c)	(d)	$(e) = (d)(1+5\%)/(c)+5\%$	$(f) = 1/(c)$	$(g) = 5\% +(a)5\%$	(e)(b)	(f)(b)	(g)(b)	
Danske Bank A/S	60 %	1.87	11.3	49.0 %	9.55 %	8.85 %	6.98 %	17.3 %	16.0 %	12.6 %	18.2 %
Dexia	152 %	1.45	10.3	38.0 %	8.87 %	9.71 %	11.59 %	16.1 %	17.6 %	21.0 %	15.6 %
Dnb Nor Asa	89 %	1.8	10.2	46.1 %	9.75 %	9.80 %	8.44 %	17.6 %	17.7 %	15.3 %	19.1 %
Efg Eurobank Ergasias Sa	113 %	3.27	22.1	58.1 %	7.76 %	4.52 %	9.66 %	14.0 %	8.2 %	17.5 %	21.7 %
Erste Bank Ag	107 %	2.43	14.1	18.6 %	6.38 %	7.09 %	9.36 %	11.6 %	12.8 %	16.9 %	18.8 %
Fortis Nv	125 %	2.42	9.1	37.8 %	9.36 %	10.99 %	10.23 %	16.9 %	19.9 %	18.5 %	30.1 %
Fortis Nv	148 %	2.41	9.1	37.8 %	9.36 %	10.99 %	11.41 %	16.9 %	19.9 %	20.6 %	30.1 %
Hbos Plc.	95 %	2.08	10,9	43,9 %	9.23 %	9,17 %	8,76 %	16,7 %	16.6 %	15,9 %	18,7 %
Hsbc Holdings Plc.	101 %	2	12,7	54,8 %	9.53 %	7,87 %	9,05 %	17,2 %	14,3 %	16,4 %	16,9 %
Kbc Groupe Sa	110 %	1,93	11	40,0 %	8,82 %	9,09 %	9,49 %	16,0 %	16,5 %	17,2 %	16,1 %
Lloyds Tsb Group Plc.	114 %	2,92	11,9	76,7 %	11,77 %	8,40 %	9,68 %	21,3 %	15,2 %	17,5 %	23,5 %
Mediobanca	125 %	2,33	26,9	70,6 %	7,76 %	3,72 %	10,27 %	14,0 %	6,7 %	18,6 %	10,7 %

Natexis Banque Pop.	76 %	1,59	23.5	33.6 %	6.50 %	4.26 %	7,82 %	11,8 %	7,7 %	14,2 %	14.0 %
National Bk.Of Greece	155 %	3,56	29,4	48.1 %	6,72 %	3,40 %	11,77 %	12,2 %	6,2 %	21,3 %	24.9 %
Nordea Bank Ab	88 %	1,84	10.7	41,0 %	9,03 %	9,35 %	8,40 %	16,3 %	16,9 %	15,2 %	17,9 %
Northern Rock Plc.	86 %	2,71	13.5	41,5 %	8,23 %	7,41 %	8,28 %	14,9 %	13,4 %	15,0 %	22,7 %
Royal Bk.Of Sctl.Gp.Plc.	111 %	1,6	10.1	42.8 %	9,45 %	9,90 %	9,57 %	17,1 %	17,9 %	17,3 %	15.6 %
San Paolo Imi	171 %	2,27	12.8	53.8 %	9,41 %	7,81 %	12,57 %	17,0 %	14,1 %	22,7 %	15.4 %
Se Banken	81 %	2,02	13.6	37.8 %	7,92 %	7,35 %	8,04 %	14,3 %	13,3 %	14,6 %	15.5 %
Societe Generale	121 %	1,99	10.6	41.4 %	9,10 %	9,43 %	10,05 %	16,5 %	17,1 %	18,2 %	21.1 %
Std.Chartered Plc.	138 %	2,51	15.1	44.4 %	8,08 %	6,62 %	10,92 %	14,6 %	12,0 %	19,8 %	18.5 %
Svenska Handbkn. Ab	54 %	1,85	10.9	41.2 %	8,97 %	9,17 %	6,70 %	16,2 %	16,6 %	12,1 %	17.9 %
Swedbank Ab	64 %	1,82	8.2	32.4 %	9,15 %	12,20 %	7,22 %	16,6 %	22,1 %	13,1 %	24.3 %
Ubs Ag	118 %	2,98	12.5	32.7 %	7,75 %	8,00 %	9,90 %	14,0 %	14,5 %	17,9 %	35.9 %
Unicredito Italiano Spa	82 %	1,79	13.9	60.0 %	9,53 %	7,19 %	8,10 %	17,2 %	13,0 %	14,7 %	10.1 %
Average values	*112 %*	*223 %*	*1390 %*	*42 %*	*8.19 %*	*7.20 %*	*9.61 %*	*14.8 %*	*13.0 %*	*17.4 %*	*19.0 %*

Data as of June 30, 2006 – Source: Datastream.

next three columns of the Table show the values of $\breve{r}_e$ adjusted by p/b ratio. Please note how, with p/b ratios usually in excess of 100 %, the values of $\breve{r}_e$ are usually higher than the corresponding r_e values.

Based on such values, the banks' book-value ROEs (derived from their financial statements for 2005) appear to be mostly satisfactory. In fact, the average $\breve{r}_e$ values expected by the shareholders are usually in the 13 %–17% range, while the ROE values delivered by the management are around 19 %.

24.6   VALUE CREATION AND RAROC

The previous chapter discussed some possible methods for calculating the current Raroc of the bank and its business units; the previous section outlined some techniques for estimating the bank's cost of capital, i.e. the target return expected by its shareholders. This section shall illustrate how these two measures can be compared, to get an indication of the value creation achieved by the bank or its business units.

In its simplest version, the Raroc method can be applied on a single-period basis. In practice, the current Raroc – at a bank or business unit level – is compared with the cost of capital. A business creates value if

$$Raroc > r_e, \tag{24.14}$$

On the other hand, $Raroc < r_e$ indicates value destruction.

This rule is only apparently simple. As a matter of fact, this chapter and the previous two showed that the definition of the two measures to be compared in (24.14) is subject to several inaccuracies and approximations. Furthermore, different approaches are often available for estimating the same parameter, none of which is preferable on an a priori basis. In this respect, one may recall several difficult passages that have been discussed above, and namely:

(1) Obtaining an economic capital measure that really embraces all risks that a bank or a business unit is exposed to;
(2) Selecting a capital measure that truly mirrors the amount of resources delivered by the shareholders to the bank;
(3) Taking into account the impact of regulatory constraints on the optimal capital endowment;
(4) Calculating a set of diversified capital measures, which scale down the stand-alone economic capital of the individual business units to account for their contribution to bank-wide risk diversification;
(5) Taking into account, alternatively or jointly, both the ex-ante allocated capital and the ex post absorbed capital of the different business units;
(6) The fact that all these alternatives translate into different Raroc measures, which (as seen in Chapter 23) can considerably differ from one another;
(7) Estimating the bank's cost of capital, considering that different models may lead to remarkably different values.

In addition to these methodological caveats involving the estimations of Raroc and r_e, a more "philosophical" remark should be made, one that affects the very soundness of a method based on a mere comparison between cost of capital and current *Raroc*. Indeed, in evaluating the value creation margins of a specific business (or of the bank as a whole), one should not only consider current *Raroc* ($Raroc_1$), but also those that are reasonably expected for the future ($Raroc_2, Raroc_3, \ldots$).

It thus becomes necessary to adopt a multi-period approach and to draw a comparison between the dividend flows expected for all future years and the value that a shareholder might cash in by selling his/her share of the bank's economic capital[20] (EC_1).

According to this approach, there is value creation if

$$\pi Raroc_1 EC_1 (1+r_e)^{-1} + \pi Raroc_2 EC_2 (1+r_e)^{-2} + \cdots > EC_1 \qquad (24.15)$$

where π represents, as previously, the dividend payout ratio (which is assumed to be constant for the sake of simplicity).

Usually, detailed forecasts for expected Raroc values are only available for the first n years: for example, there may be a strategic plan setting out Raroc values "promised" to investors for the following three-year period. It is then reasonable to assume that Raroc shall remain unchanged for the following years.

In this case, equation (24.15) can be re-written as:

$$\pi \sum_{t=1}^{n} \frac{Raroc_t EC_t}{(1+r_e)^t} + \pi \frac{Raroc_n}{(1+r_e)^n} \sum_{t=1}^{\infty} \frac{EC_{n+t}}{(1+r_e)^t} > EC_1 \qquad (24.16)$$

Note that, given a volume of net profits (earnings) of e_i, then economic capital will increase over time because of retained earnings, that is:

$$EC_{t+1} = EC_t + (1-\pi)e_t \qquad (24.17)$$

Also, note that using the definition of Raroc:

$$Raroc_t = \frac{e_t}{EC_t} \qquad (24.18)$$

equation (24.17) can be re-written as

$$EC_{t+1} = EC_t + (1-\pi)Raroc_t EC_t = EC_t[1 + (1-\pi)Raroc_t] \qquad (24.19)$$

Based on (24.19), one can compute the first n values for the future economic capital. The following values (starting from $n+1$) can be obtained more easily, given the assumption that Raroc remains unchanged:

$$EC_{n+t} = EC_n[1 + (1-\pi)Raroc_n]^t \qquad (24.20)$$

Equation (24.15) can then be re-written as:

$$\pi \sum_{t=1}^{n} \frac{Raroc_t EC_t}{(1+r_e)^t} + \pi \frac{Raroc_n}{(1+r_e)^n} EC_n \sum_{t=1}^{\infty} \left[\frac{1 + (1-\pi)Raroc_n}{1+r_e} \right]^t > \frac{EC_1}{r_e} \qquad (24.21)$$

---

[20] We are implicitly assuming that $EC = AC$, i.e. that the bank uses all of its risk-taking capacity. Please note that EC_1 indicates the economic capital, available at time $t = 0$, that is necessary to cover the risks of period $t = 1$.

i.e. using the formula for the present value of a perpetual annuity, as:

$$\pi \sum_{t=1}^{n} \frac{Raroc_t EC_t}{(1+r_e)^t} + \pi \frac{Raroc_n}{(1+r_e)^n} \frac{EC_n}{k} > \frac{EC_1}{r_e} \qquad (24.22)$$

with[21]

$$k = \frac{1+r_e}{1+(1-\pi)Raroc_n} - 1$$

Let us assume, for instance, that the bank has a current Raroc ($Raroc_1$) of 5%, but has committed itself – via a credible strategic plan – to bringing such value to 7% and then to 10% in the following two years (and to keeping it unchanged in the years to follow). Its cost of capital r_e (estimated with one of the approaches illustrated in the first part of this chapter) is equal to 8.5%. In this case, $n = 3$ and equation (24.22) becomes:

$$\pi \sum_{t=1}^{3} \frac{Raroc_t EC_t}{(1+r_e)^t} + \pi \frac{Raroc_3}{(1+r_e)^3} \frac{EC_3}{k} > EC_1$$

Table 24.2 shows the calculation of the variables that appear in the formula. The final result is:

$$9.50 + 124.59 = 134.09 > 100$$

Hence, despite the low current Raroc value, the bank seems to have committed itself to an effective value creation path.

Table 24.2 Example of how multi-period Raroc can be used

T	$Raroc_t$	EC_t	$\dfrac{Raroc_t EC_t}{(1+r_e)^t}$
1	5%	100	4.61
2	7%	102.5	6.09
3	10%	106.1	8.31
Total			19.01
Payout ratio	π	50%	
Cost of capital	r_e	8.50%	
	k	3.33%	
Value			134.09

Please note that if all Raroc values were equal to the cost of capital, then the quantity in the left-hand side would be exactly equal to 100 (i.e. the value of the economic capital),

---

[21] Note that it is necessary that $Raroc_n < r_e/(1-\pi)$, otherwise the bank would produces "excessive" Raroc flows and its value would become infinite.

irrespective of the payout ratio adopted. If future Raroc values are, on average, higher than r_e, this quantity is greater than 100, irrespective of the value of current Raroc. In this case, value creation increases as the dividend payout π decreases: this is because, since the bank rewards risks above their "fair" market price, shareholders will be better off by leaving their profits with the company rather than cashing in dividends and trying to invest them elsewhere. If, on the other hand, Raroc values were lower than the cost of capital, then a low value of π would further worsen the results in terms of value creation.

Finally, note that EC_1, which we assumed to be equal to 100, simply represents a scale factor. Taking any other positive value as reference, the conclusions reached through equation (24.22) would be unaffected.

24.7 VALUE CREATION AND EVA

The Raroc, both in its single and multi-period version, is an effective way to add rigor and transparency to the assessment of the results, in terms of value creation, achieved by the bank and its different business units.

However, a different value creation metric – called "*Economic Value Added*" (EVA)[22] – has recently become popular with financial and non-financial enterprises.

EVA measures the value created by a company in a given period of time, net of the cost of invested capital (including equity capital and debt). In symbols:

$$EVA = \bar{e} - w \cdot (D + E) \tag{24.23}$$

where $\bar{e}$ stands for operating profits after taxes but gross of interest expenses on debt ("net operating profits after taxes").

A simple example may help to understand the logic of EVA. Consider a company (Figure 24.1) collecting 200 million euros as debt (D) and 100 million euros as equity (E), undertaking to pay a debt rate r_d of 8 % and a cost of capital r_e of 12 % (thus having an average weighted cost of capital, w, of 9.3 %). Operating profits (after taxes but before interests payable on debt) amount to 60 million euros. EVA is the difference between these profits and the cost of invested capital 28 million euros, i.e. 9.3 % of € 300 million), that is, the net value (32 million euros) created in excess of the amount that is necessary to pay out the funds used.

There is value creation if

$$EVA > 0 \tag{24.24}$$

On the other hand, a negative EVA indicates that the capital used was remunerated less than it should have been. From this viewpoint, EVA represents a similar signal to the differential between Raroc and r_e. Similarly to equation (24.14), EVA uses a one-period logic. However, instead of referring to percentage values, it measures the absolute amount (for instance, in millions of euros) of the value created by a company and for this reason it may be considered more "tangible".

Please note that, given the definition of w (WACC, weighted average cost of capital) stated in equation (24.1), EVA can be re-written as follows:

$$EVA = \bar{e} - r_d^* \cdot D - \breve{r}_e \cdot E \tag{24.25}$$

---

[22] For an in-dept overview, see Stern and Stewart (1991), Uyemura, Kantor and Pettit (1996),

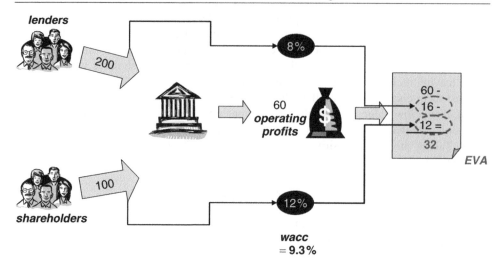

Figure 24.1   The logic behind economic value added

The rates used in equation (24.25) deserve some brief explanations (see Table 24.3):

– Since E is usually estimated based on book value capital,[23] $\check{r}_e$ should be used, i.e. the value (see equation 23.12) of the cost of capital adjusted by multiplying the value of r_e (estimated from market data) by the price/book ratio;
– On the other hand, r_e has not to be adjusted as indicated in equation (23.13), since it is compared with a measure of profit after taxes $(\overline{e}_t)$;
– For the same reason (since the comparison is made with a measure of net profit after taxes), the cost of debt r_d should be adjusted so as to account for the tax benefits linked to the deductibility of interests payable on loans. For this reason, in equation (24.22) it was indicated as r_d^* instead of r_d. The link between the two quantities is:

$$r_d^* = r_d(1 - \tau) \tag{24.26}$$

where τ is the bank's tax rate. So, for instance, the 8 % net cost (r_d^*) indicated in Figure 24.1 might be the result of a gross rate r_d of 10 % and a tax rate τ of 20 %.

Applying equation (24.25) to the previous example, one gets: $60 - 16 - 12 = 32$. Obviously, the value of EVA remains unchanged.

When computing EVA for non-financial enterprises, debt D only includes medium-long term items (bonds, long-term bank loans, etc.), whereas other forms of financing (short-term liquidity lines, accounts receivables, etc.) are not included in the invested capital because they are connected to the the the firm's operating management (hence, their cost is already accounted for when computing $\overline{e}_t$).

---

[23] According to the EVA method, book value capital has to undergo some adjustments (which entail, for instance, subtracting latent capital losses that have not yet been posted in the profit and loss account, or adding any cost items that did not cause any actual cash outflow). Nonetheless, the capital estimate used here is undoubtedly based on accounting data and not, for instance, on the stockmarket price or the amount of capital at risk.

In the case of a bank (see again Table 24.3), even the issuance of medium-long term debt securities can be considered as part of the operating management, especially if the bank, thanks to its branch network and to its placing power, can place bonds with private clients paying less than market rates. Therefore, the value of D for banks usually includes only bonds issued to professional investors and paying rate in line with market conditions, such as subordinated loans. Instead, the interests payable on the remaining financial liabilities (deposits, as well as bonds targeted to the retail market) are included in the calculation of operating profits $\bar{e}$.

Table 24.3 The components of the EVA formula

	Non-financial enterprises	Banks
$\bar{e}$	Operating profits after taxes but before the cost of D	Operating profits (including net interest income) after taxes but before the cost of D.
$\check{r}_e$	Cost of capital adjusted by the price to book ratio, but not adjusted by the tax rate	
r_d^*	Debt rate adjusted by tax savings	
E	Adjusted accounting capital	
D	Bonds and long-term bank loans (excluding short-term liquidity lines, accounts receivables, etc.)	Bonds issued at market rates, subordinated bonds (excluding deposits and bonds targeted at retail customers)

Considering equations (24.25) and (24.26), EVA shall be positive if and only if

$$\bar{e} - r_d^* \cdot D > \check{r}_e \cdot E \tag{24.27}$$

i.e., since the cost of debt is the main difference[24] between $\bar{e}$ and the bank's net profit e, if

$$e > \check{r}_e \cdot E = r_e \cdot \frac{p}{b} E = r_e \cdot MC \tag{24.28}$$

where MC is the market capitalization (see Chapter 22) of the bank.

If we assume that the capital available at the bank (AC) can be reasonably equaled to the market capitalization MC and that it is fully used to take risks (i.e. EC≅ AC ≅ MC), then equation (24.28) becomes

$$\frac{e}{MC} \cong \frac{e}{EC} = Raroc > r_e \tag{24.29}$$

Hence, if EC≅ AC ≅ MC, then Raroc (equation 24.14) and EVA (equation 24.24) lead to the same conclusions.

---

[24] The EVA method envisages several adjustments in moving from net profit e to $\bar{e}$, aimed at eliminating the impact of the non-recurrent or discretionally-quantified profit and loss components. However, the main difference between $\bar{e}$ and e is certainly attributable to the cost of debt.

Of course, the assumption that EC and MC are similar may be unrealistic. As showed in Chapters 22 and 23, available capital might be higher than economic capital, for instance because the bank wants to preserve a capital buffer to cover any unexpected risk increase, or because the applicable regulations require it to keep an amount of capital in excess of the risks it is currently facing. Furthermore, as pointed out by de Servigny and Renault (2004), economic capital depends on the amount of existing risks, while market capitalization depends on the value that investors attach to the bank and takes into account, for instance, the goodwill arising from future profits. Thus, Raroc and EVA lead to the same conclusions (i.e.: equation 24.28 may work as a connection between equations 24.14 and 24.24) only if: i) the bank constantly equals available capital (i.e. risk.-taking capacity) and economic capital (i.e. existing risks or risks budgeted for the following months); ii) the market correctly evaluates the bank's "fair value", without biases due to incorrect information or irrational panic/euphoria phenomena.

If this is not the case, EVA and Raroc do *not* necessarily lead to the same conclusions. Incidentally, it seems to us that Raroc is more transparent and effective in enabling the bank's management to focus on capital at risk (EC), hence on the connection between risk and shareholder value creation.

Similarly to Raroc, EVA lends itself to being applied not only at the bank level, but also for individual business units (or even individual transactions). This requires that book value capital and subordinated loans be allocated to the individual business units (or transactions) in the bank, taking into account any regulatory constraints and the amount of risk faced by different units.

However, since EVA is based on the book value capital (as opposed to economic capital), it may be less straightforward to apply it across business units using the capital allocation techniques analyzed in Chapter 23. Namely, since book-value capital is not affected by diversification effects, it may prove hard to assign a measure of diversified capital (DEC) to each business unit to try and account for its riskiness in the light of the diversification benefits that it provides to the bank.

24.8   CONCLUSIONS

Risk management plays a major role in banks, not only as a mere technical instrument for measuring and controlling the risks in place, but also and most importantly for its links with capital management (that is, financial structure optimization), as well as with capital budgeting (that is, the selection of businesses and projects that maximize value creation for the shareholders).

This chapter, after reviewing some peculiarities of financial institutions that make it impossible to apply the same capital budgeting principles and techniques used for non-financial enterprises, presented some techniques for the estimation of the cost of capital and the measurement of shareholder value creation in banks.

We finally discussed some concise measures, such as Raroc or EVA, which can send a brief and clear message to the top management concerning the value created/destroyed by the bank and by individual business units. Hopefully, the reader is now aware that such key indicators are, in fact, only the highest pinnacle of an extremely complex and fragile architecture, described in the 24 chapters of this book.

Risk measurement, as presented in the first four parts of this book, allows to estimate, in a reasonably effective way, the amount of capital required to cover the risks arising from the different businesses carried out by a financial institution. Furthermore, it allows to implement pricing schemes that ensure that the cost of risks be "collected" from risk-generating counterparties (such as debtors, securities issuers, derivatives buyers, etc.).

Regulation, which builds the focus of the fifth part of the book, inspires and supports the bank's risk measurement activities and affects – sometimes heavily – the management's decisions on the optimal amount of capital and its composition.

Finally, capital management, the allocation of capital to the bank's business units, as well as the estimation of its "fair" cost, enable managers to plan in good time – and to monitor over time – how much value is delivered to shareholders and how.

This is no magic formula, but rather a patient and in-depth work required to study optimal solutions and to look for feasible ones. It is not just a set of more or less sophisticated techniques, but rather a paradigm that must become a common and shared asset of the whole bank, starting with its Top Management, inspiring its strategies, tactics, and goals.

Finally, it is not a body of consolidated and established results, but rather an open challenge, calling for new developments and skills, both in terms of techniques and in terms of strategic vision.

SELECTED QUESTIONS AND EXERCISES

1. On Monday, Bank Gamma's shares traded at 7 euros each. The last dividend per share was 50 cents and the consensus, among equity analysts, was that dividends would increase by 3 % per annum. On Thursday, however, Bank Gamma announced a management shake-up and new, more ambitious targets, including a 4.5 % yearly increase in dividends: the share price jumped to 7.62 euros.

   Based on the dividend discount model, what was Bank Gamma's cost of equity before the announcement? How did it change? What are, in your opinion, the motivations behind such a change?

2. Bank Theta's price/earnings ratio, based on the current stock price and the latest past earnings figure, is 25. The long-term average for the ratio is 22. The consensus estimate for next year is 20. Based on these three figures, compute the bank's cost of capital. Compare the results and explain the differences.

3. The Table below reports some market data for Bank Sigma.

	Beta β	Price to Book Value p/b	Price/Earnings Ratio p/e	Dividend payout ratio π
Bank Sigma	90 %	2	10	40 %

   The long-term risk-free rate is 8 %; the market risk premium can be reasonably esti-mated at 6 %. The bank has just announced a Roe (return on equity) target, for the current year, of 18 %, and a dividend growth of 7 % for all the following years. In the light of the market data above, and based on all three methods used in the Chapter (dividend discount, price/earnings and CAPM), evaluate whether such a Roe target is adequate, from the shareholders' point of view. Accordingly, state if, in your opinion, the bank's market price is likely to increase or decrease in response to the Roe announcement?

4. Bank Delta has announced a Raroc, for the current year, of 8 %, while its cost of capital is 10 %. However, the bank feels confident that for the following three years its Raroc will be 9 %, while from the fourth year onwards the long term Raroc is expected to be 10.5 %.

   Assuming a dividend payout ratio of 35 %, assess the value creation process of Bank Delta both from a single-year and a multi-year standpoint.

5. Bank Soandso has a book-value capital of 200 million euros, on which it pays a cost of capital $\breve{r}_e$ of 20 %, and a debt amount, issued to professional investors and made up mainly of subordinated debt, of 180 million, on which it pays an average rate of 10 %. Last year, the bank produced a net operating income after tax (based on a tax rate of 33 %) of 90 million euros. Compute the bank's weighted average cost of capital (factoring in the "tax-shield" effect of debt) and its EVA. Comment on whether the bank is creating or destroying value for its shareholders.

Bibliography

Abken, P. A., (1994), "Over-the-Counter Financial Derivatives: Risky Business?", *Economic Review*, Federal Reserve Bank of Atlanta, March-April, 1–22.

Acerbi, C., Nordio, C. and Sirtori, C., (2001), "Expected Shortfall as a Tool for Financial Risk Management", AbaxBank, mimeo.

Acerbi, C. and Tasche, D., (2001), *On the Coherence of Expected Shortfall*, working paper.

Acharya, V. V., Bharath, S. T. and Srinivasan, A., (2003), "Understanding the Recovery Rates on Defaulted Securities", Working Paper, London Business School.

Aguais S. and Santomero, A. M., (1998), "Incorporating New Fixed Income Approaches Into Commercial Loan Valuation", *The Journal of Lending & Credit Risk Management*, February, 58–65.

Alexander, C. (edited by), (1996), *The Handbook of Risk Management and Analysis*, John Wiley & Sons, Chichester.

Alexander, C., (1994) "History debunked", *Risk*, 7, (12).

Alexander C., and Pezier, J., (2003), *On the Aggregation of Market and Credit Risks*, ISMA Centre Discussion Papers in Finance, 2003–13, University of Reading, October.

Altman, E. I., (1968), "Financial Ratios, Discriminant Analysis and the Prediction of Corporate Bankruptcy", *Journal of Finance*, September, 589–609.

Altman, E. I., (1989), "Measuring Corporate Bond Mortality and Performance", *Journal of Finance* 44, 909–922.

Altman E. I., (1993), "Valuation, Loss Reserves, and Pricing of Commercial Loans", *The Journal of Commercial Lending*, August, 8–25.

Altman E. I. and Haldeman, R., (1995), "Corporate Credit Scoring Models: Approaches and Tests for Successful Implementation", *The Journal of Commercial Lending*, May, 10–22.

Altman, E., R. Haldeman and P. Narayanan, 1977, "ZETA Analysis: A New Model to Identify Bankruptcy Risk of Corporations," *Journal of Banking & Finance*, Vol. 1, No. 1, July, 29–54.

Altman, E. I. and Kishore, V. M., (1996), "Almost Everything You Wanted to Know About Recoveries on Defaulted Bonds", *Financial Analysts Journal*, 52, November/December, 57–64.

Altman, E. I. and Suggit, H. J., (1997), *Default Rates in the Syndicated Bank Loan Market: a Mortality Analysis*, in New York University, Working Paper Series, S-97-39, 1–29.

Altman E. I. and Saunders, A., (1998), "Credit risk measurement: Developments over the last 20 years", *Journal of Banking & Finance*, n.21, 1721–1742.

Altman, E. I., Caouette, J. and Narayanan, P., (1998), *Managing Credit Risk: The Next Great Financial Challenge*, John Wiley & Sons Inc, New York.

Altman, E. I. and Saunders, A., (2001), "An analysis and critique of the BIS proposal on capital adequacy and ratings", *Journal of Banking and Finance*, vol. 25(1), 25–46.

Altman, E. I., Resti, A. and Sironi, A., (2001), *Analyzing and Explaining Default Recovery Rates*, a Report submitted to ISDA, London, January.

Altman, E. I., Resti, A. and Sironi, A., (2004), "Default Recovery Rates in Credit Risk Modeling: A Review of the Literature and Empirical Evidence", Economic Notes, 33(2), 183–208.

Altman, E. I., Brady, B., Resti A. and Sironi, A., (2005), "The Link Between Default and Recovery Rates: Theory, Empirical Evidence and Implications", *Journal of Business*, 78(6), 2203–2228.

Altman, E. I. and Fanjul, G., (2004), *"Defaults and Returns in the High Yield Bond Market: Analysis Through 2003 and Through Second Quarter 2004,"* NYU Salomon Center Special Reports, January and July.

Altman E. I., Avery R. B., Eisenbeis R. A., and Sinkey Jr. J. F., (1981) *Application of Classification Techniques in Business, Banking and Finance*, JAI Press, Greenwich (CT).

Altman E. I., Resti A., and Sironi A., (2005) *Recovery Risk – The Next Challenge in Credit Risk Management*, Risk Books, London.

Ando, A., Auerbach, A. J., (1990), "The Cost of Capital in Japan: Recent Evidence and Further Results", *Journal of the Japanese and International Economies*, 4, 323–350.

Aon Risk Services (1999) *"Enterprise Risk Management/part II"*, AON Insights, n. 4, Aon Corporation.

Arak, M., (1992), "The Effect of the New Risk-Based Capital Requirements on the Market for Swaps", *Journal of Financial Services Research*, 6(1), 25–36.

Arak, M., Goodman L. S. and Rones, A., (1987), "Defining Credit Exposures for Risk Management Products", *Review of Research in Banking and Finance*, n. 3, Winter.

Artzner, P., Delbaen, F. Eber, J. M. and Heath, D., (1999), "Definition of Coherent Measures of Risk", *Mathematical Finance*, 9, July, 203–228.

Asarnow E. and Marker, J., (1995), "Historical Performance of the U.S. Corporate Loan Market: 1988–1993", *Journal of Commercial Bank Lending*, Spring, 13–32.

Asarnow, E. and Edwards, D., (1995), "Measuring Loss on Defaulted Bank Loans: a 24 year Study", *Journal of Commercial Bank Lending*, 77 (7),11–23.

Bank for International Settlements, (2002), *The Central Bank Survey of Foreign Exchange Market Activity in April 2001*, March.

Bank of England and Federal Reserve Board, (1987), *Convergence of capital adequacy in the United Kingdom and the United States,* January.

Barone-Adesi, G., and Giannopoulos, K., (1996), "A Simplified Approach to the Conditional Estimation of Value at Risk", *Futures and Options World*, October, 68–72.

Barone-Adesi, G., Borgoin, F. and Giannopoulos, K., (1998), "Don't Look Back", *Risk*, 11, 100–104.

Barone-Adesi, G., Giannopoulos, K. and Vosper, L., (1998), "VaR Without Correlations for Non-Linear Portfolios", *Journal of Futures Markets*, 19, 583–602.

Basel Committee on Banking Supervision, (1986), *Report on International Developments in Banking Supervision,* n. 5, Bank for International Settlements, Basel, September.

Basel Committee on Banking Supervision, (1987), *Proposals for the International Convergence of Capital Measurement and Capital Standards*, Bank for International Settlements, Basel, December.

Basel Committee on Banking Supervision, (1988), *International Convergence of Capital Measurement and Capital Standards*, Bank for International Settlements, Basel, July.

Basel Committee on Banking Supervision, (1993a), *The Supervisory Recognition of Netting for Capital Adequacy Purposes*, Consultative Proposal, Bank for International Settlements, Basel, April.

Basel Committee on Banking Supervision, (1993b), *The prudential supervision of netting, market risks and interest rate risk*, Consultative proposal, Bank for International Settlements, Basel, April.

Basel Committee on Banking Supervision, (1995), *Basel Capital Accord: Treatment of Potential Exposure for Off-Balance Sheet Items*, Bank for International Settlements, Basel.

Basel Committee on Banking Supervision, (1996), *Amendment to the Capital Accord to incorporate market risks,* Bank for International Settlements, Basel, January.

Basel Committee on Banking Supervision, (1997), *Principles for the Management of Interest Rate Risk*, Consultative document, Bank for International Settlements, September.

Basel Committee on Banking Supervision, (1998a), *Amendment to the Basel Capital Accord of July 1988*, Bank for International Settlements, Basel.

Basel Committee on Banking Supervision, (1998b), *Instruments eligible for inclusion in Tier 1 capital*, press release, Bank for International Settlements, 27 October.

Basel Committee on Banking Supervision, (1999a), *Capital Requirements and Bank Behaviour: The Impact of the Basel Accord*, by a working group led by Patricia Jackson, Working Papers, N.1, Bank for International Settlements, April.

Basel Committee on Banking Supervision, (1999b), *A new capital adequacy framework*, Bank for International Settlements, Basel, June.

Basel Committee on Banking Supervision, (1999c), *Principles for the management of credit risk*, Bank for International Settlements, Basel, July.

Basel Committee on Banking Supervision, (1999d), *Credit Risk Modeling: Current Practices and Applications*, Bank for International Settlements, Basel, June.

Basel Committee on Banking Supervision, (2000a), *A New Capital Adequacy Framework: Pillar 3, Market Discipline,* Consultative Paper n. 65, Bank for International Settlements, Basel, January.

Basel Committee on Banking Supervision, (2000b), *Range of Practices in Banks' Internal Rating Systems,* Bank for International Settlements, Basel, January.

Basel Committee on Banking Supervision, (2000c), *Credit Rating and Complementary sources of credit quality information*, working paper n. 3, Bank for International Settlements, August.

Basel Committee on Banking Supervision, (2000d), *Principles for the Management of Credit Risk,* Bank for International Settlements, Basel, September.

Basel Committee on Banking Supervision, (2001a), *The New Basel Capital Accord,* Consultative Paper, Bank for International Settlements, Basel, January.

Basel Committee on Banking Supervision, (2001b), *The New Basel Capital Accord: an explanatory note*, Bank for International Settlements, Basel, January.

Basel Committee on Banking Supervision, (2001c), *The Internal Ratings-Based Approach*, Consultative Document, BIS, Basel, January.

Basel Committee on Banking Supervision, (2001d), *Potential Modifications to the Committee's Proposals*, Bank for International Settlements, Basel, November.

Basel Committee on Banking Supervision, (2001e), *Operational Risk, Consultative Document, support document to the New Basel Capital Accord*, January, Bank for International Settlements, Basel.

Basel Committee on Banking Supervision, (2001f), *Working Paper on the Regulatory Treatment of Operational Risk*, Bank for International Settlements, Basel, September.

Basel Committee on Banking Supervision, (2003a), *The New Basel Capital Accord, Consultative document*, Bank for International Settlements, Basel, April.

Basel Committee on Banking Supervision, (2003b), *Quantitative Impact Study 3*, Overview of Global Results, Bank for International Settlements, Basel, May.

Basel Committee on Banking Supervision, (2003c), *Trends in risk integration and aggregation*, Bank for International Settlements, Basel, August.

Basel Committee on Banking Supervision, (2004a), *International Convergence of Capital Measurement and Capital Standards: a Revised Framework*, Bank for International Settlements, Basel, June.

Basel Committee on Banking Supervision, (2004b), *Principles for the Management and Supervision of Interest Rate Risk*, Bank for International Settlements, Basel, July.

Basel Committee on Banking Supervision, (2005), *The Application of Basel II to Trading Activities and the Treatment of Double Default Effects*, Bank for International Settlements, Basel, July.

Basel Committee on Banking Supervision, (2006) *International Convergence of Capital Measurement and Capital Standards – A Revised Framework – Comprehensive Version*, Bank for International Settlements, Basel, June.

Basel Committee on Banking Supervision, *"Studies on the Validation of Internal Rating Systems"* Working Paper, 14, Bank for International Settlements, Basel (2005).

Beaver, W., (1967), "Financial ratios as predictors of failures", Empirical Research in Accounting: Selected Studies – 1966, supplement to *Journal of Accounting Research*, 4, 71–111.

Becketti, S., (1993), "Are Derivatives Too Risky for Banks?", *Economic Review*, Federal Reserve Bank of Kansas City, Third Quarter.

Beder, T. S., (1995), "VaR : Seductive but Dangerous", *Financial Analyst Journal*, September-October, 12–24.

Belkin B., Suchower, S. and Forest, L., (1998a), "The Effect of Systematic Credit Risk on Loan Portfolio Value-at-Risk and Loan Pricing", *CreditMetrics Monitor*, First Quarter, 17–28.

Bennet, P., (1984), "Applying portfolio theory to global bank lending", *Journal of Banking and Finance*, 8, (2), June, 153–170.

Benson P., and Zangari, P., (1997), "A General Approach to Calculating VaR without Volatilities and Correlations", *RiskMetrics™ Monitor*, J.P.Morgan-Reuters, Second Quarter, 19–23.

Berger A. N., Davies, S. M. and Flannery, M. J., (2000), "Comparing Market and Supervisory Assessments of Bank Performance: Who Knows What and When?", *Journal of Money, Credit and Banking*, 32, (3) 641–67, Part II, August.

Berger, A. N., Herring, R. and Szego, G. P. ,(1995), "The Role of Capital in Financial Institutions", *Journal of Banking and Finance*, 19, 393–430.

Berkowitz, J., (2001), "Testing Density Forecasts, Applications to Risk Management", *Journal of Business and Economic Statistics*, 19, 465–474.

Berkowitz, J. and O'Brien, J., (2002), "How Accurate are the Value-at-Risk Models at Commercial Banks?", *Journal of Finance*, 57, 1093–1112.

Bessis, J., (1994), "Asset/Liability Management, Regulations, and the Management of Performance in Banking Institutions", in C. S. Stone and A. Zissu, (eds), *Global Risk Based Capital Regulations*, Volume II, Irwin Inc., Chicago.da

Bessis, J., (1998), *Risk Management in Banking*, John Wiley & Sons, Chichester.

Bierwag, G. O., Kaufman, G. G. and Toevs, A. (1983), "Duration: Its Development and Use in Bond Portfolio Management", *Financial Analysts Journal*, 39, 15–35.

Black, F. and Scholes, M., (1973), "The pricing of options and corporate liabilities", *Journal of Political Economy*, 637–659.

Black, F. and Cox, J. C., (1976), "Valuing Corporate Securities: Some Effects of Bond Indenture Provisions", *Journal of Finance*, 31, 351–367.

Blattberg, R. and Gonedes, N., (1974), "A comparison of the stable and student as statistical models for stock prices", *Journal of Business*, April, 47(2), 244–80.

Bliss, R. R., "Market Discipline and Subordinated Debt: A Review of Some Salient Issues", *Federal Reserve Bank of Chicago Economic Review*, First Quarter, (2001), 24–45.

Board of Governors of the Federal Reserve System, (1998), *Sound Credit Risk Management and the use of internal credit risk ratings at large banking organization*, September.

Board of Governors of the Federal Reserve System, (1999), *"Using Subordinated Debt as an Instrument of Market Discipline"*, prepared by the Study Group on Subordinated Notes and Debentures of the Federal Reserve System, *Staff Study* 172.

Board of Governors of the Federal Reserve System and United States Department of Treasury, (2000), *"The Feasibility and Desirability of Mandatory Subordinated Debt"*, a Report by the Board of Governors of the Federal Reserve System and the Secretary of the U.S. Department of the Treasury, December.

Bock, J. T., (1996), "VAR Approaches to market-risk measurement", in *Financial Derivatives & Risk Management*, 6, June.

Bollersev, T., (1986), "Generalized Autoregressive Conditional Heteroskedasticity", *Journal of Econometrics*, 31, 307–327.

Bollerslev, T., Engle, R. F. and Wooldridge, J. M., (1986), "A capital asset pricing model with time-varying covariances", *Journal of Political Economics*, 96(1), 116–31.

Bohn, J. and S. Kealhofer, (2001), *"Portfolio Management of Default Risk"*, working paper, KMV.

Borio, C., Furfine, C. and Lowe, P., (2001), *"Procyclicality of the financial system and financial stability: issues and policy options"*, BIS papers No.1, March, Basel.

Boudoukh J., Richardson, M. and Whitelaw, R., (1998), "The Best of Both Worlds", *Risk*, May, 64–67.

Boyle, P., (1977), "Options: a Monte Carlo Approach", *Journal of Financial Economics*, 4, 323–338.

Boyle, P., Broadie, M. and Glasserman, P., (1997), "Monte Carlo Methods for Security Pricing, *Journal of Economic Dynamics and Control* 21, 1267–1321.

Brealey, R. A. and Myers, S. C., (2000), *Principles of Corporate Finance*, 6th edn, Irwin McGraw-Hill, New York.

Bralver, C. and Kuritzkes, A., (1993), "Risk Adjusted Performance Measurement in the Trading Room", *Journal of Applied Corporate Finance*, 6 (3), Fall, 104–108.

Breimann, L., Friedmann, J. H., Olshen, R. A. and Stone, C. J., (1983) *Classification and Regression Trees*. Wadsworth Publishers.

Brickell, M., (1994), "New Tools for New Rules", *Risk*, 7 (1), January.

Cantor, R., and Packer, F., (1994), "The Credit Rating Industry", *Federal Reserve Bank of New York Quarterly Review*, 2, Summer-Fall, 1–26.

Carey, Mark, (1999), *Implementation of credit risk models at major international banks*, Federal Reserve Board, October.

Carey, M. and William Treacy, F., (2000), "Credit Risk Ratings at Large US Banks", *Journal of Banking and Finance*, 24, 167–201.

Carey, M. and Hrycay, M., (2001), "Parameterizing Credit-Risk Models with Rating Data", *Journal of Banking and Finance*, 25 (1), 197–270.

Carty, L. V., (1998), Moody's Rating Migration and Credit Quality Correlation, 1920–1996, in S. Das (ed.), *Credit Derivatives: Trading & Management of Credit & Default Risk*, John Wiley & Sons, Inc, New York.

Carty, L. and Lieberman, D., (1996a), *Defaulted Bank Loan Recoveries*, Moody's Investors Service, November.

Carty, L. and Lieberman, D., (1996b), *Corporate Bond Defaults and Default Rates 1938–1995*, Global Credit Research, Moody's Investors Service.

Carty L. and Lieberman, D., (1998), *Historical Default Rates of Corporate Bond Issuers, 1920–1996*, in S. Das (ed.), *Credit Derivatives: Trading & Management of Credit & Default Risk*, John Wiley & Sons, Singapore, 317–348.

European Union, (1989), Council Directive 89/647/EEC on a solvency ratio for credit institutions, *Official Journal*, N. L386, 14–22.

European Union (1993), Council Directive 93/6/EEC on the capital adequacy of investment firms and credit institutions, *Official Journal*, N. L141/1.

Chew, L., (1994), "Shock Treatment", *Risk*, 7, (9), September.

Chew, W. H. and Kerr, S. S. "Recovery Ratings: A Fundamental Approach to Estimating Recovery Risk" in E. I. Altman, A. Resti, and A. Sironi (eds) *Recovery Risk – The Next Challenge in Credit Risk Management*, Risk Books, London.

Chew, L. and Gumerlock, R., (1993), "When the snoozing had to stop", *Risk*, 6, (9), September.

Christoffersen, P. F., (1998), "Evaluating Interval Forecasts", *International Economic Review*, November, 39, 841–862.

Christoffersen, P. F., (2003), *Elements of Financial Risk Management*, Academic Press, Elsevier Science.

Clow R., (1999) *"Who's afraid of Contingent capital? – The insurance industry doesn't mind braving hurricanes and typhoons. Equity options are another story"*, Institutional Investor Magazine, March.

Cohen, K. J. and Hammer, F. S., (1967), "Linear Programming and Optimal Bank Asset Management Decisions", *Journal of Finance*, May, 147–168.

Copeland, T. E., and Weston, J. F., (1988), *Financial Theory and Corporate Policy*, 3rd edn, Addison-Wesley Publishing Company.

Covitz, D. M., Hancock, D. and Kwast, M., (2000), "Mandatory Subordinated Debt: Would Banks Face More Market Discipline?", mimeo, Board of Governors of the Federal Reserve System.

Cox, J., Ingersoll, J. and Ross, S., (1985), "A Theory of the Term Structure of Interest Rates", *Econometrica*, 53, 385–407.

Credit Suisse Financial Products, (1997), *CreditRisk+. A Credit Risk Management Framework*, Technical Document.

Crnkovic, C. and Drachman, J., (1996), "Quality Control", *Risk*, September, 138–143.

Crosbie, P., (1999), *Modeling Default Risk*, KMV Corporation, San Francisco, reproduced in S. Das (a cura di), *Credit Derivatives. Trading and Management of Credit and Default Risk*, John Wiley and Sons, Ltd, Singapore, 299–315.

Crouhy M. and Galai, D., (1994), "The Interaction Between the Financial and Investment Decisions of the Firm: The Case of Issuing Warrants in a Levered Firm", *Journal of Banking and Finance*, 18, (5), October, 861–880.

Crouhy, M., Turnbull, S. and Wakeman, L., (1999), "Measuring Risk-Adjusted Performance", *The Journal of Risk*, 2, (1), 1–31.

Crouhy, M., Galai, D. and Mark, R., (2000), "A Comparative Analysis of Current Credit Risk Models", *Journal of Banking & Finance*, 24, 59–117.

Crouhy, M., Galai, D. and Mark, R., (2000), *Risk Management*, McGraw-Hill, New York.

Cooper, I. and Mella A., (1991), "The default risk of swaps", *Journal of Finance*, 46, 597–620.

Damodaran, A., (2001), *Investment Valuation*, John Wiley & Sons, New York.

Danielsson, J. and de Vries, C. G., (1997), *Multivariate stochastic volatility models: estimation and a comparison with VGARCH models*. Department of Economics, University of Iceland, mimeo.

Das, S. (ed.), (1998), *Credit Derivatives: Trading & Management of Credit & Default Risk*, John Wiley & Sons, Singapore.

de Fontnouvelle P., DeJesus-Rueff, V. Jordan, J. and Rosengren, E., (2003) *"Using Loss Data to Quantify Operational Risk"*, mimeo, Federal Reserve Bank of Boston (also available at http://ssrn.com/abstract=395083).

de Servigny, A. and Renault, O., (2004), *Measuring and Managing Credit Risk*, McGraw-Hill, New York.

de Servigny, A., Peretyatkin, V. Perraudin, W. and Renault, O., (2003), *"Portfolio Risk Tracker : Description of the Methodology"*, technical document, Standard & Poor's Risk Solutions, New York.

Diebold F. X., Hickman, A. Inoue, A. and Schuermann, T., (1997), *"Converting 1-Day Volatility to h-Day Volatility: Scaling by $\sqrt{h}$ Is Worse than You Think"*, Wharton School Working Paper Series, n.97–34.

Diebold, F. X., Gunther, T. and Tay, A., (1998), "Evaluating Density Forecasts, with Applications to Financial Risk Management", *International Economic Review*, 39, 863–883.

Dimson, E. and Marsh, P., (1995), "Capital Requirements for Securities Firms", *Journal of Finance* 50, 821–851.

Doherty N. A., (1997) "Financial Innovation in the Management of Catastrophe Risk", *Journal of Applied Corporate Finance*, 10(3), 84–95.

Dowd, K., (1998), *Beyond Value at Risk: The New Science of Risk Management*, John Wiley & Sons, Chichester.

Duffee G. R., (1996), "On Measuring credit risk of derivatives instruments", *Journal of Banking & Finance*, 20, 805–833.

Duffee, G. R., (1999), "Estimating the Price of Default Risk", *Review of Financial Studies*, Spring, 12(1), 197–225.

Duffie, D., (1998), "Defaultable Term Structure Models with Fractional Recovery of Par", Graduate School of Business, Stanford University.

Duffie, D. and Singleton, K. J., (1999), "Modeling the Term Structures of Defaultable Bonds", *Review of Financial Studies*, 12, 687–720.

Dupire, B., (2001), *Monte Carlo Methodologies and Applications for Pricing and Risk Management*, RiskBooks, London.

Durand, D., (1941), *"Risk elements in consumer instalments financing"*, working paper, NBER.

Elton E. and Gruber, M. J. Deepak Agrawal and Christopher Mann "Explaining the Rate Spread on Corporate Bonds", *The Journal of Finance*, LVI(1), 247–278.

Embrechts, P., Klupperlberg, C. and Mikosch, T., (1997), *Modelling Extreme Events for Insurance and Finance*, Springer, Berlin, Germany.

Embrechts P., McNeil, A. and Straumann, D., (1999), *Correlation and Dependence in Risk Management: Properties and Pitfalls*, Risk Lab Working Papers, Zurich, August.

Emery, K., Cantor, R. and Avner, R., (2004), "Recovery Rates on North American Syndicated Bank Loans, 1989–2003, Moody's Investors Service, New York, March.

Engelmann, B., Hayden, E. and Tasche, D. "Testing rating accuracy", *Risk*, January (2003), available on www.risk.net.

Engelmann, B., Hayden, E. and Tasche, D. Measuring the Discriminative Power of Rating Systems, mimeo, November (2002).

Engle, R. F., "Autoregressive conditional heteroschedasticity with estimates of the variance of United Kingdom inflation", *Econometrica*, 50, (4), 987–1008.

Engle, R. F., and Mezrich, J., (1995), "Grappling with GARCH", *Risk*, 8, (9), 112–117.

English W. B., and Nelson W. R., (1998), "Bank Risk Rating of Business Loans", *Finance and Economics Discussion Series*, Federal Reserve Board, Washington D.C.

Ervin, D. W. and Wilde, T., (2001), "Procyclicality in the new Basel Accord", *Risk*, October.

Estrella A., (1998), "Formulas or Supervision? Remarks on the Future of Regulatory Capital", *Economic Policy Review*, Federal Reserve Bank of New York.

Estrella, A., Hendricks, D. Kambhu, J. Shin S. and Walter, S., (1994), "The Price Risk of Options Positions: Measurement and Capital Requirements", in *Federal Reserve Bank of New York Quarterly Review*, Summer-Fall, 29–43.

European Central Bank, (2000), *Mergers and Acquisitions Involving the EU Banking Industry – Facts and Implications*, December.

Evanoff, D. D. and Wall, L. D., (2000), *Subordinated Debt and Bank Capital Reform*, Federal Reserve Bank of Chicago, WP 2000–07.

Evanoff, D. D. and Wall, L. D., (2001), "Sub-debt Yield Spreads as Bank Risk Measures", *Journal of Financial Services Research*, 19, (2/3), December, 121–45.

Fama, E., (1977), "Risk-Adjusted Discount Rates and Capital Budgeting Under Uncertainty", *Journal of Financial Economics*, 5, August, 3–24.

Fama, E. F. and French, K. R., (1993), "Common Risk Factors in the Returns on Stocks and Bonds", *Journal of Financial Economics* 33, 3–56.

Federal Reserve, (1998), *Credit Risk Models at Major U.S. Banking Institutions: Current State of the Art and Implications for Assessment of Capital Adequacy*, Federal Reserve System Task Force on Internal Credit Risk Models, May, 1–55.

Ferrari, Pierpaolo, (2002), "La gestione del capitale: un'analisi comparata della struttura del patrimonio delle principali banche internazionali", in A. Sironi and F. Saita (eds), *Gestione del capitale e creazione di valore nelle banche: profili teorici ed esperienze delle principali banche italiane*, Bancaria Editrice, Roma.

Figlewski, S., (1994), "Forecasting volatility using historical data", New York University Salomon Center, Leonard N.Stern School of Business, *Working Paper Series* n. S 94–13.

Finger, C., (1999), "Conditional Approaches for CreditMetrics® Portfolio Distributions", *CreditMetrics® Monitor*, April.

Fisher, R., (1936), "The use of multiple measurements in taxonomic problems", *Annals of Eugenics*, 7, 179–188.

Fisher, I., (1965), *The Theory of Interest*, August M.Kelley Publishers, New York, (reprinted from the 1930 edition).

Fitch, (1997), "Syndicated Bank Loan Recovery Study," by R. Grossman, M. Brennan and J. Vento, October.

Fitch, (2001), *"Bank Loan and Bond Recovery Study: 1997–2001,"* by S. O'Shea, S. Bonelli and R. Grossman, March.

Flannery, M. J., (1998), "Using Market Information in prudential Bank Supervision: a Review of the U.S. Empirical Evidence", *Journal of Money, Credit and Banking*, 30, 273–305.

Flannery M. J., (2001), "The Faces of Market Discipline", *Journal of Financial Services Research*, 19, (2/3), December, 107–19.

Fons, J., (1987), "The Default Premium and Corporate Bond Experience," *Journal of Finance*, 42, (1).

Fons, J. S., (1994), "Using Default Rates to Model the Term Structure of Credit Risk", *Financial Analyst Journal*, 50, September-October, 25–32.

Foss G., (1992), "Capital Allocation and Pricing Credit Risk", *The Journal of Commercial Lending*, October, 35–45.

Froot, K. A. and Stein, J. C., (1998), "Risk Management, capital budgeting, and capital structure policy for financial institutions: an integrated approach", *Journal of Financial Economics* 47, 55–82.

Frye, J., (2000a), "Collateral Damage", *Risk*, April, 91–94.

Frye, J., (2000b), "Collateral Damage Detected", Federal Reserve Bank of Chicago, Working Paper, *Emerging Issues Series*, October, 1–14.

Frye, J., (2000c), "Depressing Recoveries", *Risk*, November.

Gabbi, G. and Sironi, A., (2004), "Which Factors Affect Corporate Bonds Pricing? Empirical Evidence from Eurobonds' Primary Market Spreads", *The European Journal of Finance*, February (2005), 11 (1), 59–74.

Gabbi, G., (1999), "L'utilizzo delle reti neurali per la misurazione del rischio di credito", in A. Sironi and M. Marsella, *La misurazione e la gestione del rischio di credito. Modelli strumenti e politiche*, Bancaria Editrice, Roma.

Galai, D., (1978), "On the Boness and Black-Scholes Models for Valuation of Call Options", *Journal of Financial and Quantitative Analysis* 13, 15–27.

Geske, R., (1977), "The Valuation of Corporate Liabilities as Compound Options", *Journal of Financial and Quantitative Analysis*, 12, 541–552.

Gluck, J., (1996), "Measuring and Controlling the Credit Risk of Derivatives", in R. Klein, and J. Lederman, (eds.), *Derivatives Risk and Responsibility*, Irwin & Co., Chicago.

Gollinger, T. L. Morgan, J. B. ,(1993), *Calculation of an efficient frontier for commercial loan portfolio*, The Journal of Portfolio Management, Winter, 39–46.

Gordon, M., (1962), *The Investment, Financing and Valuation of the Corporation*, Irwin & Co., Chicago.

Gordy, M., (2000a), "A Comparative Anatomy of Credit Risk Models", *Journal of Banking and Finance*, January, 119–149.

Gordy, M. B., (2000b), "Credit VaR Models and Risk-Bucket Capital Rules: A Reconciliation", Working Paper, *Federal Reserve Board*, March.

Gordy, M. B., (2003), "A Risk-Factor Model Foundation for Ratings-Based Bank Capital Rules", *Journal of Financial Intermediation*, 12, 199–232.

Greene W., (2003) *Econometric Analysis*, Prentice-Hall, Upper Saddle River (NJ).

Grossman R. J., Brennan, and W. T. Vento, J., (1998), "Syndicated bank loan recovery study", in *CreditMetrics® Monitor*, First Quarter, 29–36.

Group of Thirty, (1993), *Derivatives: Practices and Principles*, Global Derivative Study Group, Washington DC, July.

Gumerlock, R., (1993), "Double Trouble", *Risk*, 6, (9), September, 80–91.

Gupton, G. M., Finger C. C. and Bhatia, M., (1997), *"CreditMetrics - Technical Document"*, J.P. Morgan, New York.

Gupton, G. M., Gates, D. and Carty, L. V., (2000), "Bank Loan Loss Given Default", Moody's Investors Service, Global Credit Research, November.

Hall, C., (2002), "Economic Capital: Towards and Integrated Risk Framework", *Risk*, October, 33–38.

Hammersley, J. M., and Handscomb, D. C., (1964), *Monte Carlo Methods*, Methuen, London.

Hamilton, D. T., Gupton, G. M. and Berthault, A., (2001), "Default and Recovery Rates of Corporate Bond Issuers: 2000", Moody's Investors Service, February.

Hamilton, D. T., Cantor, R. and Ou, S., (2002), "Default and Recovery Rates of Corporate Bond Issuers: a Statistical Review of Moody's Ratings Performance 1970–2001", Moody's Investors Service, Global Credit Research, February.

Hancock, D. and Kwast, M. L., (1999), *"Using Subordinated Debt as an Instrument of Market Discipline"*, Report of a Study Group on Subordinated Notes and Debentures, Board of Governors of the Federal Reserve System, *Staff Study* 172, December.

Hancock D. and Kwast, M., (2001), "Using Subordinated Debt to Monitor Bank Holding Companies: Is it Feasible?", *Journal of Financial Services Research*, 20, (2/3), October.

Heldring, O., (1995), "Alpha Plus", *Risk*, 8, (1), January, 17–19.

Hempel, G. H. and Simonson, D. G., (1991), *Bank Financial Management: Strategies and Techniques for a Changing Industry*, John Wiley & Sons, Inc., New York.

Hempel, G. H. and Yawitz, J. B., (1978), *Financial Management of Financial Institutions*, Prentice-Hall, New Jersey.

Hendricks, D., (1994), "Netting Agreements and the Credit Exposures of OTC Derivatives Portfolios", *Federal Reserve Bank of New York Quarterly Review*, Spring.

Hendricks D., (1996), "Evaluation of Value-at-Risk Models Using Historical Data", *Economic Policy Review*, Federal Reserve Bank of New York, 2, (1), April, 39–69.

Hendricks, D. and Barker, D., (1992), "Monte Carlo simulations for interest rate swaps", Working Paper, Federal Reserve Bank of New York, New York.

Hicks, J. R., Value and Capital, Oxford, Clarendon Press, (1946).

Hsieh D., (1988), "The Statistical Properties of Daily Exchange Rates: 1974–1983", *Journal of International Economics*, 13, 171–186.

Hu, Yen-Ting, and Perraudin, W., (2002), *"The Dependence of Recovery Rates and Defaults"*, BirkBeck College, mimeo, February.

Hull, J., (2005), *Options, Futures and Other Derivative Securities*, Prentice-Hall, Englewood Cliffs.

Hull, J., (1989), "Assessing Credit Risk in a Financial Institution's Off-Balance Sheet Commitments", *Journal of Financial and Quantitative Analysis*, 24, December, 489–501.

Hull, J. and White, A., (1995), "The Impact of Default Risk on the Prices of Options and Other Derivative Securities", *Journal of Banking and Finance*, 19, 299–322.

Hull, J. and White, A., (1998), "Incorporating Volatility Updating into the Historical Simulation Method for Value at Risk", *Journal of Risk*, 1, 5–19.

Hussain, H., (2002), *Managing Operational Risk in Financial Markets*, Butterworth Heinemann.

Irving R., (1997), "From the Makers of. . ." , *Risk*, 10(4), 22–25.

Iscoe I., Kreinin A. and Rosen D., (1999), *An Integrated Market and Credit Risk Portfolio Model,* Algo Research Quarterly, Sept., 2 (3), Toronto.

ISDA, (1998), *Credit Risk and Regulatory Capital*, International Swaps and Derivatives Association, March.

Jackson, P., (1995), "Risk measurement and capital requirements for banks", *Bank of England Quarterly Bulletin*, May 35(2), 177–184.

Jackson, P., (2001), "A Central Banker's Perspective on Basel II", Documentation to support the Speech at the 4th Conference on *Managing Capital for Financial Institutions*, Bank of England, London, 21/22 November.

Jamshidian, F. and Zhu, Y., (1997), "Scenario simulation: theory and methodology", *Finance and Stochastics*, 1, 43–67.

James, C., (1996), *RAROC Based Capital Budgeting and Performance Evaluation: A Case Study of Bank Capital Allocation*, Financial Institutions Center, The Wharton School, University of Pennsylvania, Working Paper 96–40.

Jarrow, R., (2000), "Estimating Recovery Rates and (Pseudo) Default Probabilities Implicit in Debt and Equity Prices," Working Paper, Cornell.

Jarrow, R. A. and Turnbull, S. M., (1995), "Pricing Derivatives on Financial Securities Subject to Credit Risk", *Journal of Finance* 50, 53–86.

Jarrow, R. A., Lando, D. and Turnbull, S. M., (1997), "A Markov Model for the Term Structure of Credit Risk Spreads", *Review of Financial Studies*, 10, 481–523.

Jokivuolle, E. and Peura, S., (2000), "A Model for Estimating Recovery Rates and Collateral Haircuts for Bank Loans", Bank of Finland Discussion Paper, February.

Joint Forum Working Group, (2003), *Trends in risk integration and aggregation*, Bank for International Settlements, Basel, August.

Jones D., and Mingo, J., (1998), "Industry Practices in Credit-Risk Modeling and Internal Capital Allocations", Federal Reserve Bank of New York, *Economic Policy Review* 4, (3): 53–60.

Jones D. and Mingo, J., (1999), "Credit-Risk Modeling and Internal Capital Allocation Processes: Implications for a Models-Based Regulatory Bank Capital Standard", *Journal of Economics and Business*, 51, (2): 79–108.

Jones, E., Mason, S. and Rosenfeld, E., (1984), "Contingent Claims Analysis of Corporate Capital Structures: An Empirical Investigation", *The Journal of Finance* 39, 611–625.

Jones D., (2000), "Emerging Problems with the Accord: Regulatory Capital Arbitrage and Related Issues", *Journal of Banking and Finance*, January.

Jonkhart M., (1979), "On the term structure of interest rates and the risk of default", *Journal of Banking and Finance*, 253–262.

Jordan, J. V. and Mackay, R. J., (1996), *Assessing Value at Risk for Equity Portfolios: Implementing Alternative Techniques*, in Beckstrom, Campbell and Fabozzi, (ed.), *Handbook of Firmwide Risk Management*.

Jorion, P., (1995), "Predicting Volatility in the Foreign Exchange Market", *Journal of Finance*, 50, 507–528.

Jorion P., (1996), "Risk2: Measuring the Risk in Value at Risk", *Financial Analyst Journal*, 52, 47–56.

Jorion, P., (1997), *In defense of VaR*, mimeo, University of California at Irvine (www.gsm.uci.edu/~jorion).

Jorion P., (1999), *"Risk Management Lessons from Long-Term Capital Management"*, mimeo, University of California at Irvine (www.gsm.uci.edu/~jorion).

Jorion, P., (2001), *Value at Risk: the New Benchmark for Managing Financial Risk*, McGraw-Hill, 2nd edn.

Kao, D. L., and Kallberg, J. G., (1994), "Strategies for Measuring and Managing Risk Concentrations in Loan Portfolios", *The Journal of Commercial Lending*, January.

Kealhofer S., Kwok, S. and Weng, W., (1998), "Uses and abuses of bond default rates", *CreditMetrics Monitor*, First Quarter, 37–54.

Kiesel R., Perraudin W., and Taylor, A., (1999), *The Structure of Credit Risk*, Birkbeck College, London.

Kim I. J., Ramaswamy, K. and Sundaresan, S., (1993), "Does Default Risk in Coupons Affect the Valuation of Corporate Bonds? A Contingent Claims Model", *Financial Management*, 22, (3), 117–131.

King, J. L., (2000), *Operational Risk, Measurement and Modelling*, John Wiley & Sons, Ltd, Chichester.

Knight, F. H., (1986), "Risk, Uncertainty and Profit", in AA.VV., *The Economic Nature of the Firm*, Cambridge University Press, Cambridge.

Koch, T. W., (1992), *Bank Management*, The Dryden Press, Harcourt Brace Jovanovich College Publishers, Orlando, Florida, Second Edition.

Kolari, J., Caputo, M. and Wagner, D. "Trait Recognition: An Alternative Approach to Early Warning Systems in Commercial Banking", *Journal of Business Finance and Accounting*, December (1996), 1415–34.

Koyluoglu H. U., and Hickman, A., (1998), *A Generalized Framework for Credit Risk Portfolio Models*, Working Paper, Oliver & Wyman Company, New York.

Kupiec, P. H., (1995), "Techniques for Verifying the Accuracy of Risk Measurement Models", *Journal of Derivatives*, Winter, 73–84.

Kupiec P. H. and O' Brien, J. M., (1995), "A Precommitment Approach to Capital Requirements for Market Risk", *Finance and Economic Discussion Series*, Federal Reserve Board of Governors, 95–36.

Kupiec P. H. and O' Brien, J. M., (1997), "The Precommitment Approach: Using Incentives to Set Market Risk Capital Requirements", *Finance and Economic Discussion Series*, Federal Reserve Board of Governors, 97–14.

Kupiec, P., (2000), *Estimating Credit Risk Capital: What's the Use?*, Working Paper, International Monetary Fund.

Kuritzkes A., Schuerman, T. and Weiner, S. M., (2002), *Risk Measurement, Risk Management and Capital Adequacy in Financial Conglomerates*, Wharton Financial Institutions Center, Working Papers Series, n. 03–02.

Lando, D., (1998), "On Cox Processes and Credit Risky Securities", *Review of Derivatives Research*, 2, 99–120.

Lawrence, C. and Robinson, G., (1995), "Liquid Measures", *Risk*, 8, (7), July.

Levich, R. M., (2001), *International Financial Markets: Prices and Policies*, 2nd edn, McGraw Hill, New York.

Lintner, J., (1965), "The Valuation of Risk Assets and the Selection of Risky Investments in Stock Portfolios and Capital Budgets", *Review of Economics and Statistics*, February.

Longin, F., (1994), *Optimal margin levels in futures markets: a parametric extreme-based method*, London Business School, Institute of Finance and Accounting, working paper, 192–194.

Longstaff, Fr. A., and Schwartz E. S., (1995), "A Simple Approach to Valuing Risky Fixed and Floating Rate Debt", *Journal of Finance*, 50, 789–819.

Lopez, J. A., (1997), "Regulatory Evaluation of Value-at-Risk Models", Federal Reserve Bank of New York, working paper.

Lopez, J. A., (1999), "Methods for Evaluating Value at Risk Estimates", *Federal Reserve Bank of San Francisco Economic Review*, n. 2.

Lopez J. A. and Saidenberg M. R., (2000), "Evaluating Credit Risk Models", *Journal of Banking and Finance*, January.

Lopez, J. A., (2002), "The Empirical Relationship Between Average Asset Correlation, Firm Probability of Default and Asset Size", Working Papers in Applied Economic Theory, n. 05, *Federal Reserve Bank of San Francisco*.

Maccario, A., Sironi, A. and Zazzara C., (2002), "Is Banks' Cost of Equity Capital Different Across Countries? Evidence from the G10 Countries' Major Banks", paper presented at the *European Financial Management Conference*, Copenhagen, June.

Maino, R. and Masera, R., (2003), "Sistema produttivo e industria bancaria in Italia: nuovi assetti competitivi nella prospettiva di Basilea 2", SanPaolo IMI, mimeo.

Markovitz, H., (1952), "Portfolio selection", *Journal of Finance*, 7, 77–91.

Marshall, C. and Siegel, M., (1997), "Value at Risk: Implementing a Risk Measurement Standard", *Journal of Derivatives* 4, 91–110.

Marshall, C. L., (2001), Measuring and Managing Operational Risk in Financial Institutions, John Wiley & Sons, Singapore.

Martin, R. and Wilde, T., (2002) Unsystematic Credit Risk. *Risk* 15(12), 123–128.

Mason, J. M., (1979), *Financial Management of Commercial Banks*, Warren, Gorham & Lamont, Boston and New York.

Maspero, D., (1997), "I modelli VaR basati sulle simulazioni", in A. Sironi and M. Marsella (eds), *La misurazione e la gestione dei rischi di mercato. Modelli, strumenti, politiche*, Il Mulino, Bologna.

Maspero, D., (1998), *Il rischio di credito nei derivati OTC*, in A. Sironi and M. Marsella (eds), *La misurazione e la gestione del rischio di credito. Modelli, strumenti e politiche*, Bancaria, Roma.

Matten, C., (1996), *Managing Bank Capital*, John Wiley & Sons, Ltd, Chichester.

Matten, Chris, (2000), *Managing Bank Capital*, John Wiley & Sons, Ltd, 2nd edition, Chichester.

McAllister P. H. and Mingo, J. J., (1994), "Commercial Loan Risk Management, Credit-Scoring, and Pricing: The Need for a New Shared Database", *The Journal of Commercial Lending*, May, 6–22.

McKinney, G. W., (1977), "A Perspective on the Use of Models in the Management of Bank Funds", *Journal of Bank Research*, Summer, 122–127.

McQuown, J. A., (1997), *Market versus Accounting-Based Measures of Default Risk*, in I. Nelken (edited by), *Option Embedded Bonds*, Irwin Professional Publishing, Chicago.

Merton, R. C., (1974), "On the Pricing of Corporate Debt: The Risk Structure of Interest Rates", *Journal of Finance*, 2, 449–471.

Merton, R. and Perold, A., (1993), "Theory of Risk Capital in Financial Firms", *Journal of Applied Corporate Finance*, Vol. 6, No. 3, 16–32.

Miller, M. H. and Modigliani, F., (1961), "Dividend Policy, growth and the valuation of shares", *Journal of Business* 34, 411–433.

Mina, J. and Xiao, J. Y. (2001). Return to RiskMetrics: the evolution of a standard, RiskMetrics Group, New York.

Mingo J. J., (2000), "Policy Implications of the Federal Reserve Study of Credit Risk Models at Major U.S. Banking Institutions", *Journal of Banking and Finance*, 24(1-2), 15–33.

Modigliani, F. and Miller, M., (1958), "The Cost of Capital, Corporation Finance and the Theory of Investment", *American Economic Review* 48, 261–297.

Modigliani, F. and Miller, M. H., (1963), "Corporate Income Taxes and the Cost of Capital: A Correction", *American Economic Review*, vol. 53(3), 433–43, June.

Mood, A. M., Graybill, F. A. and Boes, D. C. (1974) *Introduction to the Theory of Statistics*, McGraw-Hill, New York.

Moody's Investors Service, (1999), *Historical Default Rates of Corporate Bond Issuers*, 1920–1998, New York, January.

Moody's Investor Service, (2000), "RiskCalc private model: Moody's default model for private firms", May.

Moody's, (2001), "Default and Recovery Rates of Corporate Bond Issuers: 2000", by D. Hamilton, G. Gupta and A. Berthault, February.

Morgan, JP, (1995), *RiskMetrics^{TM}*. Technical Document, New York, May.

Morgan, JP, (1996), "An improved methodology for measuring VaR", *RiskMetrics^{TM} Monitor*, Second quarter, June, 7–25.

Moscadelli, M. (2004) "The modelling of operational risk: experience with the analysis of the data collected by the Basel Committee", Temi di Discussione, n. 517, Bank of Italy, Rome.

Mossin, J., (1966), "Equilibrium in a Capital Asset Market", *Econometrica*, October.

Nickell P., Perraudin W. and Varotto S., (2000), "The Stability of Rating Transitions", *Journal of Banking and Finance*, Special Issue, January.

Nickell P., Perraudin W. and Varotto S., (1999), "Ratings-Versus Equity-Based Credit Risk Models: An empirical investigation", *Bank of England working paper*.

Oliver, Wyman & Company, (2001) Study on the risk profile and capital adequacy of financial conglomerates–A Study Commissioned by: De Nederlandsche Bank, Pensioen- & Verzekeringskamer, Stichting Toezicht Effectenverkeer, Nederlandse Vereniging van Banken, Verbond van Verzekeraars, February.

Ong, M., (1999), *Internal Credit Risk Models: Capital Allocation and Performance Measurement*, Risk Books, London.

Oda N. and Muranaga, J., (1997), "A New Framework for Measuring the Credit Risk of a Portfolio – Ex VaR Model", Institute for Monetary and Economic Studies (IMES), Bank of Japan, *Discussion Paper* n. 97-E-1, 1–45.

Paul, C. R., (1995), "Netting: a means of limiting credit exposure", *Journal of International Banking Law*, 10, 93–98, March.

Perold, A. F., (1999), *Capital Allocation in Financial Firms*, working paper, Harvard University, Graduate School of Business Administration.

Pettway, R. H., Kanedo, T. and Young, M. T., (1991), "International bank capital standards and the costs of issuing capital securities by Japanese banks", *Journal of Banking & Finance* 15, 559–580.

Picoult, E., (1997), "Calculating Value at Risk with Monte Carlo Simulations", in *Risk Management for Financial Institutions*, Risk Publications, London, 73–92.

Pomante, U., (1999), "I modelli basati sugli algoritmi genetici", in A. Sironi and M. Marsella, *La misurazione e la gestione del rischio di credito. Modelli strumenti e politiche*, Bancaria Editrice, Roma.

Pringle, J. J., (1974), "The Capital Decision in Commercial Banks", *The Journal of Finance*, June.

Pritsker, M., (2001), "The Hidden Dangers of Historical Simulations", mimeo, The Federal Reserve Board, Washington.

Ramaswami M., (1996), "Why capital at risk is the recommended measure", *Financial Derivatives & Risk Management*, 6, June.

Rappaport, A., *Creating Shareholder Value*, Free Press, New York, (1986).

Resti, A., (2002a), *The New Basel Capital Accord: Structure, possible Changes, micro- and macroeconomic Effects*, Centre for European Policy Studies, Brussels.

Resti, A., (2002b), "Il capitale in banca: significato e funzione economica", in A. Sironi e F. Saita, (eds), 2002, *Gestione del capitale e creazione di valore nelle banche. Modelli, strumenti ed esperienze delle grandi banche italiane*, Bancaria, Roma.

Resti, A., (2002c), "The Risk/Return Effects of Loan Portfolio Diversification: an Empirical Test based on Italian Banks", *Research in Banking and Finance*, Volume 2.

Resti, A., (2002d), "Replicating Agency Ratings through Multinomial Scoring Models", in Ong M. (ed.), *Credit Ratings. Methodologies, Rationale and Default Risk*, RiskBooks, London.

Resti, A. and Sironi, A., (2004), "Loss Given Default and Recovery Risk: from Basel II Standards to Effective Risk Management Tools", in M. K.Ong,(ed.), *The Basel Handbook: a Guide for Financial Practitioners*, Risk Books, London.

Resti, A. and Sironi, A., (2007) "The risk-weights in the New Basel Capital Accord: Lessons from bond spreads based on a simple structural model", *Journal of Financial Intermediation*. 16(1), 64–90.

Rogalski, R. and Vinso, J., (1978), "Empirical properties of foreign exchange rates", *Journal of International Business Studies*, Fall.

Roll R., (1988), "R^2", *Journal of Finance*, XLIII, 2, 541–566.

Ross, S. A., (1976), "Arbitrage Theory of Capital Asset Pricing", *Journal of Economic Theory*, December.

Rubinstein, R. Y., (1981), *Simulation and the Monte Carlo Method*, John Wiley & Sons, Inc, New York.

Saita, F., (1999), "Allocation of Risk Capital in Financial Institutions", *Financial Management*, 28, (3), 95–111.

Saita, F., (2004), *Risk Capital Aggregation: the Risk manager's Perspective*, mimeo.

Saita F. (2007) *Value at Risk and Bank Capital Management*, Academic Press, Elsevier Science, San Diego.

Saita, F. and Sironi, A., (2002), "Banks' Market Risk Management and Capital Regulation: a Critical Assessment", in *Financial Services in he Evolving Global Marketplace*, E. O. Lyn and G. P. J. Papaioannou, (eds), Hofstra University, New York.

Saunders, A., (2000), *Financial Institutions Management: a modern perspective*, McGraw Hill, New York, 3rd edn.

Saunders, A., and Allen, L. (2002), *Credit Risk Measurement: New Approaches to Value at Risk and other Paradigms,* 2nd edn, John Wiley & Sons Inc, New York.

Schuermann, Til, (2005) "What do we know about Loss Given Default?", in Altman E. I., Resti A., Sironi A. (eds) *Recovery Risk –* The Next Challenge in Credit Risk Management, Risk Books, London.

Sharpe, W., (1963), "A Simplified Model of Portfolio Analysis", *Management Science*, January, 277–93.

Sharpe, W., (1964), "Capital Asset Prices: A Theory of Market Equilibrium Under Condition of Risk", *Journal of Finance*, 19, 425–442.

Shearer M. A. and Christensen, R., (1998), "Migration Analysis: Combining Approaches for Better Results", *The Journal of Lending & Credit Risk Management*, April, 52–56.

Shih, J., Samad-Khan, A., Medapa, P. (2000) "Is the Size of an Operational Loss Related to Firm Size?", *Operational Risk*, January.

Simons, K., (1989), "Measuring Credit Risk in Interest Rate Swaps", *New England Economics Review*, Nov./Dec., 29–38

Sironi, A., (2002), "Strengthening Banks' Market Discipline and Levelling the Playing Field: Are the Two Compatible?", *Journal of Banking and Finance*, 26/5, 1065–1092, May.

Sironi, A. and Zazzara, C., (2002), "The New Basel Accord: Implications for Italian Banks", *Review of Financial Economics*, 12/(1) 99–126.

Sironi, A., (2003), "Testing for Market Discipline in the European Banking Industry: Evidence from Subordinated Debt Issues", *Journal of Money, Credit and Banking*, 35, June, 443–472.

Smithson, C. and Smith, C., (1998), *Managing Financial Risk: A Guide to Derivatives Products, Financial Engineering and Value Maximization*, Mc Graw Hill, New York.

Sobehart, J. and Keenan, S., (2001), "Measuring Default Accurately", *Risk*, 11 (41), s31–s33.

Sobehart, J., and Keenan, S., (2004), "The score for credit" *Risk*, February, 17(2).

Standard & Poor's, (1998), *Ratings Performance 1997: Stability & Transition*, January.

Standard & Poor's, (2000), *Recoveries on Defaulted Bonds Tied to Seniority Ratings*, by L. Brand and R. Behar, *CreditWeek*, February.

Standard & Poor's, (2001), *Rating Performance 2000. Default, Transitions, Recovery and Spreads*, January.

Standard and Poor's (2003), *Corporate Ratings Criteria*, McGraw-Hill, New York, also available on www.standardandpoors.com.

Stern, J. and Stewart, G. B. III, (1991), *The Quest for Value: The EVA™ Management Guide*, Harper Collins, New York.

Stoughton, N., and Zechner, J., (1999), "Optimal Capital Allocation using RAROC and EVA", working paper, University of California, Irvine.

Stulz, R., (1999), "What's Wrong with Modern Capital Budgeting?", *Financial Practice and Education*, 9, (2), 7–11.

Stulz, R., (2000), *Financial Engineering and Risk Management*, Southwestern Publishing, New York.

Sundaresan, S., (1991), "Valuation of Swaps", in S. J. Khoury (ed.) *Recent Developments in International Banking and Finance*, cap XII, North Holland.

Taleb, N., (1997), *Against Value at Risk: Nassim Taleb replies to Philippe Jorion*, mimeo.

Tasche, D., (2003), A traffic lights approach to PD validation, mimeo, Deutsche Bundesbank.

Tavakoli J. M., (1998), *Credit Derivatives. A Guide to Instruments and Applications*, John Wiley & Sons, New York.

Taylor, S. J., (1986), *Modelling Financial Times Series*, John Wiley & Sons, Ltd, Chichester, UK.

Treacy, W. F., and Carey, M., (2000), "Credit risk rating systems at large US banks", *Journal of Banking & Finance*, Special Issue, 24, (1/2), 167–201.

Trucharte Artigas, C., (2004), *A review of Credit Registers and their use for Basel II*, mimeo, Financial Stability Institute, Bank for International Settlements, Basel.

Uyemura D. G. and Van Deventer, D. R., (1993), *Financial Risk Management in Banking*, Probus Publishing Company, Cambridge, England.

Uyemura, D. G., Kantor and C. and Pettit, J. M., (1996), "EVA for Banks: Value Creation, Risk Management and Profitability Measurement", *Journal of Applied Corporate Finance*, 9, (2), Summer, 94–113.

Van Den Brink, G., (2002), *Operational risk. The new challenge for banks*, Palgrave.

Van de Castle, K. and Keisman, D., (2000), "Suddenly Structure Mattered: Insights into Recoveries of Defaulted Loans", *Standard & Poor's Corporate Ratings*, May 24.

Van de Castle, K. and Keisman, D., (1999), "Recovering Your Money: Insights Into Losses from Defaults", Standard & Poor's Report.

Vasicek, O. A., (1984), *Credit Valuation*, KMV Corporation, March.

Vojta, G. J., (1973), "*Bank capital adequacy*", Citicorp, New York, 1973, reproduced in T. M. Havrilesky and J. T. Boorman, "*Current Perspectives in Banking*", A.H.M. Publishing Co., Arlington, (1980).

Wagster, J. D., (1996), "Impact of the 1988 Basel Accord on International Banks", *Journal of Finance* 51, 1321–1346.

Wall, L. D. and Peterson, P. P., (1998), "The Choice of Capital Instruments", *Economic Review, Federal Reserve Bank of Atlanta*, Second Quarter, 4–17.

Watson, R. D., (1977), "The Marginal Cost of Funds Concept in Banking", *Journal of Bank Research*, Autumn.

Watson, R. D., (1978), "Estimating the Cost of Your Bank's Funds", *Business Review*, May/June, 3–11.

Whittaker J. and Li, W., (1997), "An Introduction to Credit Derivatives", *Risk*, Credit Risk Supplement, July.

Williams, J. B., (1938), *The Theory of Investment Value*, Harvard University Press, Cambridge, Massachusetts.

Wilson, D., (1995), "Marriage of Ideals", *Risk*, 8, (7), July, 66–82.

Wilson, T. C., (1992), "RAROC Remodelled", *Risk*, 5, (6), September, 112–119.

Wilson, T. C., (1993), "Infinite Wisdom", *Risk*, 6, (6), June, 37–45.

Wilson, T. C., (1996), "*Calculating Risk Capital*", in *The Handbook of Risk Management and Analysis*, C. Alexander, (ed.) 193–232, John Wiley and Sons, Ltd, Chichester.

Wilson, T. C., (1997a), "Portfolio Credit Risk (I)", *Risk*, 10, (9), 111–117.

Wilson, T. C., (1997b), "Portfolio Credit Risk (II)", *Risk*, 10, (10), 56–61.

Wilson, T. C., (1998), "Portfolio Credit Risk", Federal Reserve Board of New York, *Economic Policy Review*, October, 71–82.

Yoshifuji S. (1997), "The EaR Model and the Expanded VaR Model: An Application to Bond Portfolios", *IMES Discussion Paper 97-E-9*, September.

Zaik, E., Walter, J., Kelling, G., and James, C., (1996), "RAROC at Bank of America", *Journal of Applied Corporate Finance*, 9, (2), Summer, 83–92.

Zangari, P., (1997a), "Streamlining the Market Risk Measurement Process", *RiskMetrics*™ *Monitor*, J. P. Morgan-Reuters, First Quarter, 29–35.

Zangari, P., (1997b), "On Measuring Credit Exposure", *RiskMetrics*™ *Monitor*, J.P.Morgan-Reuters, First Quarter, 3–22.

Zazzara, C., (2002), "Credit Risk in the Traditional Banking Book: a VaR Approach Under Correlated Defaults", *Research in Banking and Finance*, 1, February.

Zimmer, S. A. and McCauley, R. N., (1991), "Bank Cost of Capital and International Competition", *Federal Reserve Bank of New York Quarterly Review*, Winter, 33–59.

Index

risk-adjusted performance (RAP) measures
  258–60
  risk-adjusted return on capital (RAROC)
    259–60
risk analysis (business and financial) 373
  median financial ratios 373–4
risk horizon 402
risk management 654, 756
  integration in day-to-day bank management 5
  supervision by independent unit 5
risk management systems, and involvement of
    senior management 4–5
risk-mitigation tools for pre-settlement risk 496
  bilateral netting agreements 496–500
  credit triggers and early redemption options
    501–4
  recouponing and guarantees 501
  safety margins 500–1
risk-neutral probability of default 343–4
risk positions (mapping of)
  bonds 143
  foreign currency bonds 133–5
  forward currency positions 135–8
  forward rate agreements 139–40
  stock positions 140–3
RiskMetrics model 57, 110
  VaR model 67
  and variance-covariance approach 115
ROC (Receiver Operating Characteristic) curve
    390
  sample dependency 395
  see also AUROC ("area under ROC curve")
ROE (return on equity), use as a performance
    indicator 36

SA (rate-sensitive assets) 9
securitization process 106
securitization schemes 469–70,517, 559
senior management, and risk management systems
    4–5
serial independence of returns hypothesis 126–7
simple moving averages method (volatility
    estimation) 163–5
  problems 165–7
simulation techniques approach/simulation models
    185
  differences from variance-covariance approach
    112
  problems and solutions 188
  see also full valuation (shared feature of
    simulation models); historical simulations;
    market factor changes (modeling freedom
    in)/(shared feature of simulation models);
    Monte Carlo simulations; percentile logic
    (shared feature of simulation model); stress
    tests; value at risk (VaR) models
  shared features 185–8

simulated distribution deviation from normal
    conditions 187
SL (rate-sensitive liabilities) 9
special purpose vehicle (SPV) 469–79
spread risk, type of credit risk 281
standard approach to credit risk (Pillar One of New
    Basel Capital Accord) 593
  collateral and guarantees 596–7
  risk weighting 593–6
Standard & Poor's 372
  definition of default, 385
  "Portfolio Risk Tracker," 401
  use of qualitative methods for creditworthiness
    determination 369
"standard shock," 3
statistical approach to credit rating quantification
    379–80
stockmarket betas 154
  and CAPM 154–5
  estimation of a stock's beta 155–6
straddle example see non-monotonic portfolio
    example
stress tests 188, 218
  advantages 221
  extreme scenarios method 218–19
  factor push analysis (FPA) techniques 219
  guidelines from the Derivative Policy Group
    219
  "multidimensional" approaches/simple or
    predictive scenarios 219–20
  requirements for 220
  simulating shocks 219
strike rate, 98
structural models based on stock prices 321–2
  see also KMV model; Merton's model
Student's t-distribution 145–6
substitution risk 474
supervisory authorities/new role (Pillar Two of New
    Basel Capital Accord) 612–13, 612–14
  fundamental principles 613
supplementary capital see Tier 2 and 3 capital
swaption 88–9

tangent method 179
term structure 57
  bootstrapping 58
  objectives 57–8
  vertices (considerations for choosing) 58–9
theta coefficient 159–60
Tier 2 and 3 capital (supplementary) T2/T3, 549,
    552–4, 568, 658
Tier 1 capital (T1) 549, 549–52, 658
time horizon selection (VaR models) 124
  factors for consideration 124–5
  volatility estimations (techniques for) 125–6
trading book 4, 594, 567–8,579
trait recognition analysis 287

Printed and bound by CPI Group (UK) Ltd, Croydon, CR0 4YY

23/04/2025

14660948-0005